T0190012

Lecture Notes in Computer Science 4173

Commenced Publication in 1973
Founding and Former Series Editors:
Gerhard Goos, Juris Hartmanis, and Jan van Leeuwen

Editorial Board

Samira El Yacoubi   Bastien Chopard
Stefania Bandini (Eds.)

Cellular Automata

7th International Conference on Cellular Automata
for Research and Industry, ACRI 2006
Perpignan, France, September 20-23, 2006
Proceedings

Springer

Volume Editors

Samira El Yacoubi
Laboratoire de Théorie des Systèmes (LTS) - MEPS
Université de Perpignan
France
E-mail: yacoubi@univ-perp.fr

Bastien Chopard
Centre Universitaire d'Informatique (CU)
Université de Genève
Switzerland
E-mail: Bastien.Chopard@cui.unige.ch

Stefania Bandini
Dipartimento di Informatica, Sistemistica e Comunicazione
Università degli Studi di Milano-Bicocca
20126 Milano
Italy
E-mail: bandini@disco.unimib.it

Library of Congress Control Number: 2006932514

CR Subject Classification (1998): F.1.1, F.2.2, I.6, C.2

LNCS Sublibrary: SL 1 – Theoretical Computer Science and General Issues

ISSN   0302-9743
ISBN-10   3-540-40929-7 Springer Berlin Heidelberg New York
ISBN-13   978-3-540-40929-8 Springer Berlin Heidelberg New York

Springer is a part of Springer Science+Business Media

springer.com

© Springer-Verlag Berlin Heidelberg 2006

Typesetting: Camera-ready by author, data conversion by Scientific Publishing Services, Chennai, India
Printed on acid-free paper   SPIN: 11861201   06/3142   5 4 3 2 1 0

Preface

This volume constitutes the proceedings of the International Conference on Cellular Automata for Research and Industry, ACRI 2006, which took place in Perpignan, France, September 20–23, 2006. The conference, which was organized by the laboratory of Mathematics and Physics for Systems (MEPS), University of Perpignan, France, was the seventh in a series of conferences inaugurated in 1994 in Rende, Italy: ACRI 1996 in Milan, Italy, ACRI 1998 in Trieste, Italy, ACRI 2000 in Karlsruhe, Germany, ACRI 2002 in Geneva, Switzerland and ACRI 2004 in Amsterdam, The Netherlands.

The ACRI conference is traditionally focussed on challenging problems and new research in theoretical aspects including cellular automata tools and computational sciences. It is also concerned with applications and the solution of problems from the fields of physics, engineering and life sciences. Its primary goal is to discuss problems from various areas, to identify new issues and to enlarge the research field of CA. Since its inception, the ACRI conference has attracted an ever growing community and has raised knowledge and interest in the study of cellular automata for both new entrants into the field as well as researchers already working on particular aspects of cellular automata.

First invented by von Neumann, cellular automata models have been popularized and investigated in several areas during the last decades. They provide a mathematically rigorous framework for a class of discrete dynamical systems that allow complex, unpredictable behavior to emerge from the deterministic local interactions of many simple components acting in parallel.

ACRI 2006 brought together over 100 distinguished mathematicians, computer scientists and other researchers working in the field of CA theory and applications. A special interest was devoted to the general concepts, theories, methods and techniques associated with modelling, analysis and implementation in various systems (e.g., biological, physical, ecological, social). Cellular Automata are classically run on a regular lattice and with perfect synchronicity and homogeneity. ACRI 2006 encouraged recent trends which consider asynchronous, inhomogeneous and non–autonomous cellular automata with unstructured environments. In order to highlight the multidisciplinarity of the cellular automata research area, the First International Workshop on Crowds and Cellular Automata was organized within the scope of ACRI 2006 at the University of Perpignan, 19–20 September.

The volume contains 72 refereed papers addressing various important topics in cellular automata, covering theoretical results and highlighting potential applications. A total of 53 papers were presented as oral talks and 19 as posters during the conference by speakers coming from about 15 different countries. These papers were selected among 100 submitted contributions. Each paper was reviewed by at least two members of the scientific committee. We are extremely grateful to these referees, who accepted the difficult task of selecting papers. Their expertise and efficiency ensured the high quality of the conference. The volume also contains 11 extended abstracts dealing with crowds and cellular automata, which were presented during the C&CA workshop.

Five invited speakers of worldwide reputation presented the latest trends in the field in the context of standard cellular automata and beyond. We would like to take this opportunity to express our sincere thanks to Raffaello D'Andrea from Cornell University, Paolo De Los Rios from the Ecole Polytechnique Fédérale de Lausanne, Sergey Gavrilets from the University of Tennessee, Moshe Sipper from Ben–Gurion University, and Marco Tomassini from the Université de Lausanne, who kindly accepted our invitation to give plenary lectures at ACRI 2006. Moreover, we were very honored that Andrew Wuensche from the University of Sussex accepted to give a demo of Discrete Dynamics Lab and show his very recent work on 2D hexagonal cellular automata with computational abilities.

This volume is divided into two parts. The first part deals with theoretical aspects and computational analysis of CA and the second one with applications derived from physical, biological, environmental and other systems. Each part is partitioned into chapters containing a number of papers in alphabetical order.

It should be stressed that this conference would have been impossible without the help and continuous encouragement of a number of people, especially the members of steering committee, who strongly supported the organization of ACRI 2006 in Perpignan. First of all, we would like to thank the authors, who showed their interest in ACRI 2006 by submitting their papers for consideration. We wish to extend our gratitude to Stefania Bandini and Andrew Adamatzky, the organizers of the first workshop "Crowds and Cellular Automata" (C&CA), who helped to introduce the ACRI conference to other scientific communities.

It is a pleasure to express our sincere thanks to our colleagues of the Organizing Committee and to Paolo Mereghetti for the successful job he carried out in editing this volume. A special word of thanks goes to Yves Maurissen for the huge amount of work he did during the organization of this conference and the practical assistance he provided to the participants.

Finally, the organization of ACRI 2006 was made possible thanks to the financial or technical support of the board and several departments of the University of Perpignan (Centre de Ressources Informatiques – CRI, Service de la Communication, etc), the Scientific and Parallel Computing Group from the University of Geneva (Switzerland), the commune of Perpignan, the Academia of Science (Morocco) and other institutions and local authorities.

September 2006
Samira El Yacoubi
Bastien Chopard
Stefania Bandini

P. Rizzi (Italy)
R. Serra (Italy)
M.C. Simon (France)
M. Sipper (Israel)
G. Sirakoulis (Greece)
P. Sloot (The Netherlands)
G. Spezzano (Italy)
D. Talia (Italy)

G. Tempesti (Switzerland)
M. Tomassini (Switzerland)
L. Torenvliet (The Netherlands)
H. Umeo (Japan)
R. Vollmar (Germany)
T. Worsch (Germany)
A. Zomaya (Australia)

Sponsoring Institutions

Laboratoire de Mathématique et Physique pour les Systèmes (MEPS)
Département d'Informatique, CUI, Université de Genève
Université de Perpignan (BQR)
Pôle Universitaire Européen de Montpellier
Mairie de Perpignan
Région Languedoc Roussillon
Service Universitaire des Relations Internationales (SURI)
Service de la Communication de l'Université de Perpignan
Académie des Sciences et Techniques du Royaume du Maroc

Table of Contents

Computational Theory

PART 2: Applications
Population Dynamics

Physical Modeling

Urban, Environmental and Social Modeling

Traffic and Boolean Networks

Multi–agents and Robotics

Crypto and Security

Dynamical Systems

Crowds and Cellular Automata

Distributed Sensing, Actuation, Communication, and Control in Emerging Industrial Applications

R. D'Andrea

Cornell University, 101 Rhodes Hall Ithaca, NY 14853
rd28@cornell.edu

The continued development of inexpensive sensors, embedded computation, and communication networks has greatly increased the opportunity for designing, deploying, and controlling large interconnected systems. Applications range from "smart" structures embedded with sensors, actuators, and compute power, to multi–vehicle autonomous systems.

This talk will present our experiences with these types of systems, ranging from the very theoretical to the very applied.

S. El Yacoubi, B. Chopard, and S. Bandini (Eds.): ACRI 2006, LNCS 4173, p. 1, 2006.
© Springer-Verlag Berlin Heidelberg 2006

Models of Complex Networks and How Diseases Spread on Them

P. De Los Rios

Laboratoire de Biophysique Statistique – ITP – FSB, Ecole Polytechnique Fédérale de Lausanne (BSP),
1015 Lausanne Switzerland
Paolo.DeLosRios@epfl.ch

Complex heterogeneous networks have recently become one of the leading frameworks to describe a variety complex systems. After a review of the current evidence and of the corresponding models, I will address the spreading of epidemics on complex networks: current understanding, approximation methods and ways to systematically improve them.

S. El Yacoubi, B. Chopard, and S. Bandini (Eds.): ACRI 2006, LNCS 4173, p. 2, 2006.

CA Simulation of Biological Evolution in Genetic Hyperspace

Michael A. Saum[1] and Sergey Gavrilets[1,2]

[1] Department of Mathematics
University of Tennessee, Knoxville
Knoxville, TN
msaum@math.utk.edu
[2] Department of Ecology and Evolutionary Biology
University of Tennessee, Knoxville
Knoxville, TN
gavrila@tiem.utk.edu

Abstract. Realistic simulation of biological evolution by necessity requires simplification and reduction in the dimensionality of the corresponding dynamic system. Even when this is done, the dynamics remain complex. We utilize a Stochastic Cellular Automata model to gain a better understanding of the evolutionary dynamics involved in the origin of new species, specifically focusing on rapid speciation in an island metapopulation environment. The effects of reproductive isolation, mutation, migration, spatial structure, and extinction on the emergence of new species are all studied numerically within this context.

1 Introduction

From the fossil records and radioactive dating we know that life has existed on earth for more than 3 billion years [1]. Until the Cambrian explosion around 540 million years ago, life was restricted mainly to single-celled organisms. From the Cambrian explosion onward however, there has been a steady increase in biodiversity, punctuated by a number of large extinction events. These extinction events caused sharp but relatively brief dips in biodiversity and the fossil record supports these claims. In our attempt to understand some of the dynamics involved in this process, we decided to look at the speciation process and see if we could model it in a way that would provide insight into some of the factors which determine the dynamic behavior of what is an extremely complex process.

Speciation is the process by which new species are formed via evolutionary dynamics. Speciation can be controlled (or driven) by a number of factors including mutation, recombination and segregation, genetic drift, migration, natural and sexual selection [1,2,3]. Throughout this paper we say that two populations are of different species if they are reproductively isolated, i.e., no mating producing both viable and fertile offspring between the two populations occurs. That is, we will use the biological species concept [1,2]. In our model, we can identify reproductively isolated populations by measuring the differences in their genes;

S. El Yacoubi, B. Chopard, and S. Bandini (Eds.): ACRI 2006, LNCS 4173, pp. 3–12, 2006.

if their genes are sufficiently different, then there is a very low probability that they can mate to produce viable and fertile offspring.

Speciation processes are difficult to verify via experiments or observations. Primary of course is the fact that the time-scales involved in speciation typically are much longer than human life span. In addition, there does not exist a continuous fossil record documenting new species, i.e., there are many gaps in the fossil record. Moreover, existing data on genetic differences between extant species can be interpreted in a number of alternative ways.

We are thus led to different methods of investigating the speciation process by using mathematical models. By necessity, models limit the number of parameters associated with complex behavior. This implies that all factors may not be taken into account in the simulation of complex processes. However, computer models do provide a metaphor for the actual dynamics, assuming of course the model's algorithms accurately reflect in some sense the actual dynamics being modeled, i.e., the model is consistent.

Here, we describe a stochastic cellular automata explicit genetic model of speciation in an island metapopulation. Typically, cellular automata used in biological application are characterized by a rather small number of states: two or, very rarely, three, usually focusing on whether a patch is occupied or not [4,5,6,7,8,9,10,11,12]. However, even the simplest known biological organisms have hundreds of genes and hundreds of thousands of DNA base pairs [1,3]. This implies that the number of possible genetic states for an organism is astronomically large. For example, assuming that an organism has only 500 genes each coded by 1000 DNA base pairs, there can be potentially $4^{500000} \approx 9.9 \times 10^{301029}$ different genetic states. This enormous dimensionality requires one to develop new methods of modeling, analyzing, and visualizing the behavior of the corresponding cellular automata. Below we describe some of the approaches that we have developed within the context of studying speciation.

2   The CA Deme-Based Metapopulation Model

A common method for performing numerical studies of biological evolution and speciation is to use an individual-based model in which a finite collection of individuals are tracked through the birth-reproduction-death cycle as well as the migration-mutation-survival cycle. Unfortunately, individual-based models require an enormous amount of computational resources to obtain meaningful results and are currently not practical for studying large-scale biological diversification. Here, instead of an individual-based model we build a deme-based model [3,13,14] in which for each local population we explicitly describe only the genetic state of its most common genotype. This simplified approach is justified if mutation and migration are sufficiently rare and the local population size is sufficiently small so that only a negligible amount of genetic variation is maintained within each local population most of the time. We will ignore the dynamics of local population sizes. Following Hubbell [15], we disregard ecological differences between the species. Our main focus will be on genetic incompatibilities (i.e. reproductive isolation) between different populations.

Reproductive isolation will be defined by the threshold model [3,13] in which two genotypes are not reproductively isolated and, thus, belong to the same species if they differ in less than K_m genes. We will refer to parameter K_m as mating threshold. In some implementations of the model, we allow for multiple populations per patch. A simple heuristic approach for doing this is to introduce another threshold genetic distance, say K_c ($> K_m$), reaching which will allow for coexistence in a patch. We will refer to parameter K_c as coexistence threshold. If the genetic divergence between two populations is below K_c, the competition between them prevents their coexistence.

We consider here a large area divided into smaller connected areas called patches. Each patch can be empty or occupied by one or more populations. We model the habitat patches as nodes on a two dimensional grid. This is a spatially explicit metapopulation model (which is often also called a *lattice model* or *stepping-stone model*), in which migration is restricted to close or neighboring patches.

Our metapopulation model simulates evolution of bit strings in a two dimensional geometry. Each bit string can be considered to represent the DNA of a population. The length L of this binary DNA string is specified as input. Note that the number of possible genetic states is 2^L. We then simulate metapopulation dynamics within and between a given set of habitat niches (or patches).

What we are left with then after a time is a situation in which many genetically different populations exist in different habitat patches. Through a clustering process, we can then determine which populations are *close* to each other genetically by some measure. This process of grouping thus determines clusters of similar populations, or species.

Our model dynamics occur on a time generation basis. For each generation we determine stochastically whether each of the major events occurs in the following order:

1. Patch Extinction.
2. Single Population Extinction.
3. DNA Strand Mutation.
4. Population Migration.

Patch extinction is a situation where all populations in a specific patch go extinct. The exact details are not important, it could be due to depletion of a viable food supply in the habitat patch or due to some catastrophic extinction event which wipes out the populations such as a fatal disease epidemic.

Single population extinction can occur under similar circumstances, however rather than the whole patch (which can include many populations) going extinct, only a single population within the patch goes extinct.

Migration of individuals has two effects. First, migrants can found a new population in a patch previously not occupied by a species. Second, migrants coming into an occupied patch can bring genes that may spread in a local population (see below).

Bit strings change independently at each locus. The probability per generation that an allele at a locus changes to an alternative state is set to be

$$\mu_e = \mu + m\,\mathcal{N}, \tag{1}$$

where μ is the probability of mutation per locus, m is the probability of migration, and $\mathcal{N}$ is the number of neighboring populations of the same species that have the alternative allele fixed at the locus under consideration. Expression (1) utilizes the fact that the probability of fixation of an allele that does not affect fitness is equal to its frequency [16]. With migration, new alleles are brought in the patch both by mutation (at rate μ) and migration (at rate $m\mathcal{N}$). In this approximation, the only role of migration is to bring in new alleles that are quickly fixed or lost by random genetic drift. For example, if initially both the focal population and its four neighbors have allele 0 at the locus under consideration, then the probability that an alternative allele 1 is fixed in the focal population per generation is $\mu_e = \mu$. However, once this has happened, the probability of focal population switching back to allele 0 is $\mu_e = \mu + 4m$. If the migration rate m is much larger than the mutation rate per locus μ, switching back will happen much faster. As time increases, populations accumulate different mutations, diverge genetically and become reproductively isolated species.

3 Model Implementation

There are two main computer programs utilized to implement our model of the speciation process, Evolve and Cluster. As described above, *Evolve* simulates the evolution of bit strings in a two dimensional grid based geometry undergoing evolutionary dynamical processes. *Cluster* then determines which group of bit strings or populations are within a specified Hamming distance of each other. The clustering method is single linkage clustering [17] with an input parameter K. In most cases, we set parameter K to the mating threshold K_m. This procedure produces clusters of mutually compatible populations (i.e. biological species).

Since the clustering process is hierarchical in nature, output from Cluster can also be used to identify and group populations in a taxonomic manner, providing insight into the hierarchical structure of the simulated populations. For example, let us specify an increasing sequence of clustering thresholds $K_1 < K_2 < K_3 <$ .... Then, all populations at a genetic distance less than K_1 can be thought of as belonging to the same species, all populations at genetic distances that are larger or equal than K_1 but are smaller than K_2 can be thought of as belonging to different species within the same genus, all populations at genetic distances that are larger or equal than K_2 but are smaller than K_3 can be thought of as belonging to different species and genera within the same family, etc.

Evolve-Cluster accepts a wide variety of input and produces a wide variety of output. In order to provide focus on identifiable trends, we will concentrate in this paper on the following input to and output from the Evolve-Cluster simulations as shown in Table 1. (Note that there is no correlation between the input and output items, they are just lists).

Table 1. Evolve-Cluster Input/Output Parameters of Interest

Input Parameters	Output
Geometry (1D, 2D, size)	Number of Clusters (Species), N_S
Bitwise Mutation Probability, μ	Average Pairwise Distance, $\bar{d}$
Deme Extinction Probability, E_D	Average Distance from Founder, $\bar{d}_f$
Population Extinction Probability, E_p	Time to Speciation, T
DNA strand length, L	Duration of Radiation Event, τ
Population Migration Probability, m	Cluster Diameter
Patch Carrying Capacity	Cluster Range Distribution
Mating, Coexistence and Clustering Thresholds	Cluster Average Pairwise Distance

One can visualize our model as follows: Each population is a point in a genetic hyperspace; the clade (i.e., the whole system of populations) is a cloud of points which changes its size, structure, and location in the genetic hyperspace. The diameter of this cloud can be characterized by the average pairwise distance $\bar{d}$ between members of the clade measuring how diversified the clade is. The average distance to the founder $\bar{d}_f$ characterizes the extent of the overall change (see Figure 1). As time increases, populations get farther and farther away from each other while at the same time moving farther away from the founding population. Of course there is a limit as to how much $\bar{d}_f$ and $\bar{d}$ increase due to the finite number of loci under consideration. In fact it can be shown that $\bar{d}_f \to \frac{L}{2}$ and $\bar{d} \to \frac{L}{2+g(\mu)}$ as $t \to \infty$. [Here, $g(\mu) \to 0$ as $\mu \to \infty$ and $g(\mu) > 0$ for all $\mu > 0$. Essentially $g(\mu) \sim 1/\mu$.]

In addition, we can easily calculate how long it takes for speciation to occur, how many species emerge, and what parameters affect the rate of speciation and species diversity.

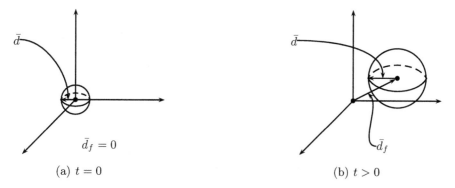

(a) $t = 0$ (b) $t > 0$

Fig. 1. The average pairwise distance $\bar{d}$ and the average distance to the founder $\bar{d}_f$ at two different time moments. The clades are represented by the spheres.

Figure 2 illustrates a *typical* speciation curve (i.e., the number of species or clusters vs. time). This figure also explains the meaning of two statistics: the

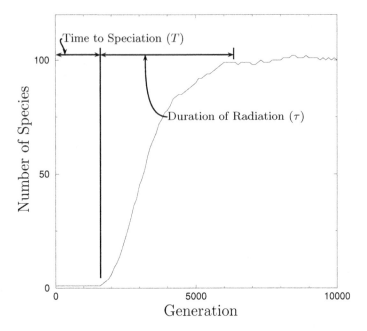

Fig. 2. A typical speciation curve

time to speciation T and the duration of radiation τ. Note that the number of species stays at 1 for a small amount of time, then rises relatively quickly to reach a stochastic equilibrium level.

All data and results reported in this paper are based on multiple runs of the same set of parameters, usually between 30 and 50 repeats.

Distance from the Founder, $\bar{d}_f$

One quick check that our model is working well is based on analysis of how certain dynamics match the theory. In [18, Eq. 4c], it was shown that the average Hamming distance from a single founding population changes according to equation

$$\bar{d}_f(t) = \frac{L}{2}[1 - \exp(-c(\mu)t)] \tag{2}$$

where $c(\mu)$ a function only of μ, the mutation rate. This is basically a solution to a random walk problem on the binary hypercube. Our model showed that the fit to Equation 2 over hundreds of runs with varying parameter sets truly is a function only of the mutation rate μ and time. This perhaps is the single best indication that our model is performing well with prediction and is internally consistent with the basic mathematical evolutionary theory concepts of mutation, migration, and extinction.

4   Parameter Studies

Since the Evolve-Cluster model seems to be modeling some aspects of the speciation process well when compared with other models, it now remains to identify other characteristics of our model. Specifically we will be analyzing the effect of changing input parameters to first see if the results make qualitative sense and then use our model to uncover *hidden* trends and quantitative results.

Geometry Size, Mating Threshold, and Clustering Threshold

Figure 3 contains summary graphs of nine different parameter sets. The graphs are ordered from top to bottom increasing in 2-D geometry size, 10×10, 14×14, and 20×20. The graphs are ordered from left to right increasing in mating threshold $K_m = 5, 10$, and 15. Each graph is the summary of fifty runs with $L = 256$, $m = 0.02$ and $\mu = 0.00004$. On each graph there are five curves. The three speciation curves are for the different clustering thresholds K, while the other two curves are the average pairwise distance $(\bar{d})$ between all populations and the average distance from the founder $(\bar{d}_f)$ as a function of time.

In our model, extensive diversification occurs relatively fast. The graphs in Figure 3 illustrate the fact that $\bar{d}$ dominates initially, while $\bar{d}_f$ eventually becomes larger than $\bar{d}$ and stays that way. In addition, the asymptotics are consistent with those discussed in the previous section. This trend can be understood by considering the metaphor introduced above; the ball changes diameter quicker than moving away from the origin initially, i.e., genetic changes go into producing diversity at a rate quicker than moving the clade as a whole genetically away from the founding population. After a short time, movement away from the founder dominates while at the same time genetic diversity between the populations also increases.

In our model, the probability of a genetic change μ_e (see equation 1) depends on the number of neighboring populations of the same species and, thus, on mating threshold K_m. With a higher K_m, there are more neighbors of the same species which effectively reduces the rate of change and dampens $\bar{d}$ expansion. This is evidenced by the fact that the higher the mating threshold K_m, the closer the curves $\bar{d}$ and $\bar{d}_f$ track each other. Since the number of loci L and mutation probability μ are the same in all of these cases, the $\bar{d}_f$ curve is the same in all graphs as expected. It also appears that the larger the size of the system, the greater the difference between $\bar{d}$ and $\bar{d}_f$, although the asymptotics still remain the same as described above. This can be explained by the fact that with a larger geometry, $\bar{d}$ increases unchecked by physical boundaries until boundary effects coupled with the finite number of loci L effectively dampens $\bar{d}$ expansion and the asymptotics take over.

As the clustering threshold K increases, the number of species decreases. This is as expected, since larger clusters (clusters containing more populations) implies there are less clusters. It is also clear that the number of species increases as geometry size increases. It appears here that boundary effects do play a role in speciation, effectively suppressing the speciation process to some extent.

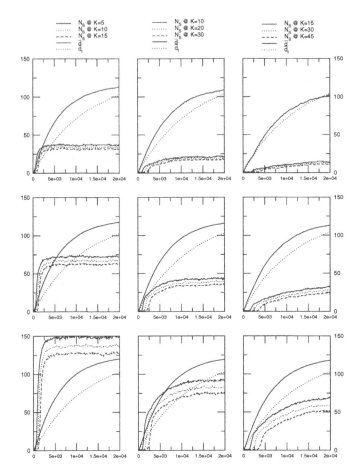

Fig. 3. The effects of geometry size, mating threshold K_m, and clustering threshold K on the number of species N_S, the average pairwise distance $\bar{d}$, and the average distance to the founder $\bar{d}_f$ as functions of time

The time to speciation T increases as K_m increases. This is due to the fact that it takes longer to accumulate enough genetic differences to separate populations into new species. The duration of radiation τ increases as K_m increases. This is due to the observation that radiation still occurs, but is not as rapid as at lower mating threshold values, more evidence of negative mutation pressure applied by the higher mating threshold.

There are other observations which can be made from the graphs shown in Figure 3, including

- T increases as geometry size increases,
- τ is approximately constant as geometry size increases,
- The difference between the number of species at different clustering levels remains constant in time,

- The difference between the number of species at different clustering levels is approximately constant as mating threshold increases,
- The difference between the number of species at different clustering levels increases as geometry size increases,
- τ appears to be much less that T in all cases.

Migration and Patch Carrying Capacity

One of the parameter studies undertaken was to increase the carrying capacity of each patch in the geometry so that multiple populations per patch could exist at any time. With multiple populations allowed, the evolutionary dynamics consist of a series of population splits followed by accumulation of additional genetic differences between emerging species which eventually allows for their coexistence in the same patch (when genetic distance is $> K_c$), which in turn leads to range expansions and increase in the number of populations per patch.

Figure 4 illustrates some results for a clustering threshold of $K = 2$ letting migration rate m vary. Part (a) shows the number of species in the system which we normalized by the patch carrying capacity (i.e., the number of populations per patch). Note that increasing the patch carrying capacity increases the number of species N_S in the system disproportionately. N_S is essentially constant with a slight decreasing trend as m increases. Part (b) shows that the average pairwise distance $\bar{d}$ increases with the patch carrying capacity; $\bar{d}$ does not appear to depend on the migration rate. Overall, allowing for multiple populations per patch stimulates population expansion into multiple ecological habitat niches allowing for rapid speciation to occur in parallel resulting in even more diversification, all in approximately the same time frame.

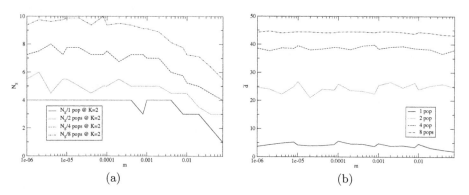

(a)   (b)

Fig. 4. The effects of migration rate m on the normalized number of species and on the average pairwise distance $\bar{d}$ in a model with 1, 2, 4 or 8 populations per patch

5   Conclusions

Our CA based metapopulation model allows us to investigate the dynamics of genetic diversification in a large dimensional state space. The adaptive radiation regime observed in the model is a rich source of data for helping one to better understand the speciation process.

References

1. Futuyma, D.J.: Evolutionary biology. Sinauer, Sunderlands, MA (1998)
2. Coyne, J.A., Orr, H.A.: Speciation. Sinauer Associates, Sunderland, MA (2004)
3. Gavrilets, S.: Fitness landscapes and the origin of species. Princeton University Press, Princeton, NJ (2004)
4. Wolfram, S.: Statistical mechanics of cellular automata. Reviews of Modern Physics **55** (1983) 601–644
5. Huberman, B.A., Glance, N.S.: Evolutionary games and computer simulations. Proceedings of the National Acedemy of Sciences USA **90** (1993) 7716–7718
6. Keymer, J.E., Marquet, P.A., Johnson, A.R.: Pattern formation in a patch occupancy metapopulation model: A cellular automata approach. Journal of Theoretical Biology **194** (1998) 79–90
7. Keymer, J.E., Marquet, P.A., Velasco-Hernández, J.X., Levin, S.A.: Extinction thresholds and metapopulation persistence in dynamic landscapes. American Naturalist **156** (2000) 478–494
8. Molofsky, J., Durrett, R., Dushoff, J., Griffeath, D., Levin, S.: Local frequency dependence and global coexistence. Theoretical Population Biology **55** (1999) 270–282
9. Molofsky, J., Bever, J.D., Antonovics, J.: Coexistence under positive frequency dependence. Proceedings of the Royal Society London Series B **268** (2001) 273–277
10. Durrett, R., Buttel, L., Harrison, R.: Spatial models for hybrid zones. Heredity **84** (2000) 9–19
11. Carrillo, C., Britton, N.F., Mogie, M.: Coexistence of sexual and asexual conspecifics: a cellular automaton model. Journal of Theoretical Biology **275-285** (2002) 217
12. Ganguly, N., Sikdar, B.K., Deutsch, A., Canright, G., Chaudhuri, P.P.: A survey on cellular automata. Technical Report Centre for High Performance Computing, Dresden University of Technology (December 2003)
13. Gavrilets, S., Acton, R., Gravner, J.: Dynamics of speciation and diversification in a metapopulation. Evolution **54** (2000) 1493–1501
14. Gavrilets, S.: Speciation in metapopulations. In Hanski, I., Gaggiotti, O., eds.: Ecology, genetics and evolution of metapopulations. Elsevier, Amsterdam (2004) 275–303
15. Hubbell, S.P.: The unified neutral theory of biodiversity and biogeography. Princeton University Press, Princeton (2001)
16. Kimura, M.: The neutral theory of molecular evolution. Cambridge University Press, New York (1983)
17. Everitt, B.S.: Cluster analysis. Arnold, London (1993)
18. Gavrilets, S.: Dynamics of clade diversification on the morphological hypercube. Proc. R. Soc. Lond. B **266** (1999) 817–824

Attaining Human–Competitive Game Playing with Genetic Programming

M. Sipper

Department of Computer Science, Ben–Gurion University, P.O. Box 653, Be'er Sheva, Israel
sipper@cs.bgu.ac.il

We have recently shown that genetically programming game players, after having imbued the evolutionary process with human intelligence, produces human–competitive strategies for three games: backgammon, chess endgames, and robocode (tank–fight simulation). Evolved game players are able to hold their own – and often win – against human or human–based competitors. This talk has a twofold objective: first, to review our recent results of applying genetic programming in the domain of games; second, to formulate the merits of genetic programming in acting as a tool for developing strategies in general, and to discuss the possible design of a strategizing machine.

S. El Yacoubi, B. Chopard, and S. Bandini (Eds.): ACRI 2006, LNCS 4173, p. 13, 2006.
© Springer-Verlag Berlin Heidelberg 2006

Generalized Automata Networks

Marco Tomassini

Information Systems Department, University of Lausanne, Switzerland
marco.tomassini@unil.ch

Abstract. In this work standard lattice cellular automata and random Boolean networks are extended to a wider class of generalized automata networks having any graph topology as a support. Dynamical, computational, and problem solving capabilities of these automata networks are then discussed through selected examples, and put into perspective with respect to current and future research.

1 Introduction

Cellular automata (CA) have been widely used since their introduction by Ulam and Von Neumann at the beginning of the 1950s. They have turned out to be an extremely flexible and simple model for studying many phenomena in a large variety of fields. Indeed, it would be hard to name a single area of investigation where CA have not been used with some success. This can be seen in two recent books [6,33] in which the focus is either on CA's modeling capabilities [6], or on their intrinsic computational and pattern formation properties [33]. In Wolfram's book the claim is even more ambitious, since CA are seen as the computational model at the source of almost all natural phenomena. Without necessarily accepting such "grand" claims, it should be granted that CA are indeed an extremely useful model. The "secrets" of the wide applicability of CA models are to be found in their structural simplicity, the fact that they can approximate continuous fields by a simpler discrete model which is easier to understand and to implement numerically, and by their universal computational properties. Structural simplicity is apparent in the use of rules that act locally in a regular lattice, and universal computational properties of CA have been known for a long time [33].

On the whole, and although there are many variations on the central theme, CA have been seen in general as simple homogeneous automata laid out on a regular grid, interacting in a small geometrically regular neighborhood. On the other hand, in recent years there has been substantial research activity in the science of networks, motivated by a number of innovative results, both theoretical and applied. Starting from the seminal 1998 paper of Watts and Strogatz [31], networks have been recognized as a central model for the description of countless phenomena of scientific, social and technological interest. Typical examples include the Internet, the World Wide Web, social acquaintance networks, electric power supply networks, biological networks, and many more. The key idea is that most real networks, both in the natural world as well as in man-made structures, have mathematical properties that set them apart from regular lattices and random graphs, which were the two main topologies studied until then. Inspired by previous qualitative observations made by social scientists, Watts and Strogatz

S. El Yacoubi, B. Chopard, and S. Bandini (Eds.): ACRI 2006, LNCS 4173, pp. 14–28, 2006.

introduced an algorithmic construction for *small-world networks* [1] in which pairs of vertices are connected by short paths through the network. The existence of short paths between any pair of nodes has been found since then in real networks as diverse as the Internet, airline routes, the World Wide Web, neural, genetic, and metabolic networks, citation and collaboration networks, and many others [22] . The presence of short paths is also a property of standard random graphs as those constructed according to the Erdös-Rényi model [22], but what sets real networks apart from random graphs is a larger *clustering coefficient*, a measure that reflects the locality of a structure. The topological structure of a network has a marked influence on the dynamical processes that may take place on it, a point that has been strikingly demonstrated, for example, by the fault-tolerant properties of the Internet [2], and by the spreading of epidemics [23].

Regular lattices and random networks (which are also regular in a statistical sense) have been thoroughly studied in many disciplines. For instance, the dynamics of lattices and random networks of simple automata have received a great deal of attention [16,12,6,33]. Starting from the above facts, conceiving of irregular networks of automata does not take a large stretch of imagination and could prove useful. Due to their novelty, and in spite of their potential interest, there have been comparatively few studies of the computational and dynamical properties of automata networks. Notable exceptions are [26,30,24,27,28,19] which mainly deal with extensions of classical CA, and a few recent articles on Boolean automata networks [3,4,21,13].

My intention in the present work is twofold: first, to define in a systematic manner a wider class of CA built on top of general networks, and second, to review recent work on their dynamical and computational properties in the new environment. Thus, I shall first present a graph-theoretic unified view of automata networks, followed by examples taken from the fields of automata computation and dynamics, and random boolean networks. The automata considered will be static, in the sense that the supporting network topology does not change in time. However, this is not a good assumption for many systems either because faults dynamically affect nodes and links, or just because the nature of the interaction between network nodes is itself dynamical as in social networks of interacting agents. Here I shall deal briefly with the effect of network perturbations but not with intrinsically dynamical network systems.

2   Cellular and Networked Automata

Cellular Automata are dynamical systems in which space and time are discrete. A standard d-dimensional cellular automaton consists of a finite or infinite d-dimensional grid of cells, i.e. a regular lattice, each of which can take on a value from a finite, typically small, set of values Σ. The value of each cell at time step t is a function of the values of a small local neighborhood of cells at time $t-1$. The cells update their states simultaneously according to a given local rule. Asynchronous CA with a given sequential update order can also be considered (see section 6).

---

[1] Small-world network is a general term meaning that a graph that has this property has both a small diameter and a clustering coefficient that is larger than that of a corresponding random graph. Watts–Strogatz small-world networks are just one particular family of graphs that possess these properties.

Formally, a cellular automaton A is a quadruple

$$A = (\Sigma, U, d, f),$$

where Σ is a finite set of states, U is the cellular neighborhood, $d \in Z^+$ is the dimension of A, and f is the local cellular interaction rule, also referred to as the transition function.

Given the position of a cell, $\mathbf{i}$, $\mathbf{i} \in Z^d$, in a regular d-dimensional uniform lattice, or grid (i.e., $\mathbf{i}$ is an integer vector in a d-dimensional space), its *neighborhood* U is defined by:

$$U_{\mathbf{i}} = \{\mathbf{i}, \mathbf{i} + \mathbf{r}_1, \mathbf{i} + \mathbf{r}_2, \ldots, \mathbf{i} + \mathbf{r}_{n-1}\},$$

where n is a fixed parameter that determines the neighborhood size, and $\mathbf{r}_j$ is a fixed vector in the d-dimensional space.

The *local transition rule* f

$$f : \Sigma^n \to \Sigma,$$

maps the state $s_{\mathbf{i}} \in \Sigma$ of a given cell $\mathbf{i}$ into another state from the set Σ, as a function of the states of the cells in the neighborhood $U_{\mathbf{i}}$. In uniform CA f is identical for all cells, whereas in non-uniform ones f may differ between different cells, i.e., f depends on $\mathbf{i}$, $f_{\mathbf{i}}$.

For a finite-size CA of size N (such as those treated herein) a *configuration* of the grid at time t is defined as

$$C(t) = (s_0(t), s_1(t), \ldots, s_{N-1}(t)),$$

where $s_{\mathbf{i}}(t) \in \Sigma$ is the state of cell $\mathbf{i}$ at time t. The progression of the CA in time is then given by the iteration of the *global mapping*, also called *evolution operator* Φ

$$\Phi : C(t) \to C(t+1), \qquad t = 0, 1, \ldots$$

through the simultaneous application in each cell of the local transition rule f. The global dynamics of the CA can be described as a directed graph, referred to as the CA's *phase space*.

For one-dimensional CA with two possible states per cell f is a function $f : \{0,1\}^n \to \{0,1\}$, and the neighborhood size n is usually taken to be $n = 2r + 1$ such that:

$$s_i(t+1) = f(s_{i-r}(t), \ldots, s_i(t), \ldots, s_{i+r}(t)),$$

where $r \in Z^+$ is a parameter, known as the *radius*, representing the standard one-dimensional cellular neighborhood. The domain of f is the set of all 2^n n-tuples. For finite-size grids, spatially periodic boundary conditions are frequently assumed, resulting in a circular grid for one-dimensional systems and a torus for two dimensional ones; formally, this implies that cellular indices are computed modulus N.

To visualize the behavior of a one-dimensional CA one can use a two-dimensional space-time diagram, where the horizontal axis depicts the configuration $C(t)$ at a certain time t and the vertical axis depicts successive time steps, with time increasing down the page (for example, see Fig. 1).

We now extend the previous concepts to *Generalized Automata Networks* (GAN). With respect to standard CA, the most important change concerns the network topology: whilst in CA this topology is a d-dimensional regular lattice, GAN can be built on any connected graph. Let $G = (V, E)$ be a graph, where V is a set of vertices and E is a set of edges. E is a binary relation on V; it is either *symmetric* if the edge is unordered, as in undirected graphs, or it is an *ordered* pair, as in directed graphs. Both cases arise in GAN. With these definitions, a GAN on V is a quadruple $(G, \Sigma, U, \{f_i | i \in V\})$. The only change with respect to lattice synchronous CA is in the local transition function f which now depends on the *degree* k_i of vertex i, i.e. the number of neighbors can be different for different $i \in V$. This can be formalized as: $f_i : \Sigma^{k_i} \rightarrow \Sigma$. As in the case of CA, non-uniform GAN can be defined by allowing f_i to depend not only on the degree k_i of vertex i, but also on the position of i in the graph G. Likewise, asynchronous GAN can be defined by explicitly stating a sequence of vertex updates, including random sequences. In this paper I deal with binary, i.e. $\Sigma = \{0, 1\}$, uniform and non-uniform, synchronous and partially asynchronous GAN.

3   Small-World and Scale-Free Graphs

In this section I shall describe the main network types that will be used or referred to in the sequel. Although the following material is well known, I include a succint description for the sake of completeness so as to make the paper more self-contained. The reader is referred to the original works for more details.

The Watts–Strogatz Model. Following Watts and Strogatz [31], a small-world graph can be constructed starting from a regular ring of N nodes in which each node has k neighbors ($k \ll N$) by simply systematically going through successive nodes and "rewiring" each link with a certain probability β. When an edge is deleted, it is re-placed by an edge to a randomly chosen node. If rewiring an edge would lead to a du-plicate edge, the graph is left unchanged. This procedure will create a number of links, called *shortcuts*, that join distant parts of the lattice. Shortcuts are the hallmark of small worlds. While the average path length[2] between nodes scales logarithmically with the number of nodes in a random graph, in Watts-Strogatz graphs it scales approximately linearly for low rewiring probability but goes down very quickly and tends towards the random graph limit as β increases. This is due to the progressive appearance of short-cut edges between distant parts of the graph, which obviously contract the path lengths between many vertices. However, small world graphs typically have a higher clustering coefficient[3] than random graphs, and a degree distribution $P(k)$ close to Poissonian.

The Barabási–Albert Model. Albert and Barabási were the first to realize that real networks grow incrementally and that their evolving topology is determined by the way in which new nodes are added to the network. They proposed an extremely simple model based on these ideas [1]. One starts with a small *clique* of m_0 nodes. At each

---

[2] The average path length L of a graph is the average value of all pairs shortest paths.

[3] The clustering coefficient C of a node is a measure of the probability that two nodes that are its neighbors are also neighbors among themselves. The average $\langle C \rangle$ is the average of the Cs of all nodes in the graph.

successive time step a new node is added such that its $m \leq m_0$ edges link it to m nodes already in the graph. When choosing the nodes to which the new nodes connect, it is assumed that the probability π that a new node will be connected to node i depends on the current degree k_i of i. This is called the *preferential attachment* rule. Nodes with already many links are more likely to be chosen than those that have few. The probability $\pi(k_i)$ of node i to be chosen is given by:

$$\pi(k_i) = \frac{k_i}{\sum_j k_j},$$

where the sum is over all nodes already in the graph. The model evolves into a stationary network with power-law probability distribution for the vertex degree $P(k) \sim k^{-\gamma}$, with $\gamma \sim 3$, which justifies the name *scale-free*. As for Watts–Strogatz small-worlds, scale-free graphs have short average path length and clustering coefficients that are higher than those of the corresponding random graphs with comparable number of vertices and edges.

The Barabási–Albert model is by no means the only way for constructing scale-free graphs. For example, the BA incremental construction introduces historical correlations, due to the non-equilibrium dynamics of the construction process, and also degree correlations to some extent. Other constructions, such as the configuration model, may produce uncorrelated scale-free graphs. It is also possible to build scale-free graphs with a given degree distribution function, i.e. with an exponent $\gamma \neq 3$. Here these distictions are not crucial, although the reader is referred to the specialized literature for details (see [22] and references therein).

4   Dynamics and Pattern Formation in GAN

In a recent work, Marr and Hütt [19] have investigated the connection between network topology and the corresponding impact on network dynamics for binary GAN in a systematic manner. The tools of their analysis were similar to those employed by Wolfram [32] in his study of the emerging spatio-temporal patterns in one-dimensional CA. Although there are other, more rigorous classifications, Wolfram four-classes system, together with Langton's λ parameter [18] are still useful to understand the dynamical behavior of those CA, and an analogous of this classification was used in [19].

Marr and Hütt studied Watts–Strogatz small-world graphs, Barabási–Albert scale-free graphs, and random networks. They defined two main classes of binary GAN $\Omega_1(\kappa)$ and $\Omega_2(\kappa)$, each depending on a single parameter κ. This parameter takes into account the fact that in CA the transition function is defined for a constant number of neighbors while, by definition, this is not the case in GAN. In the first class λ remain constant, while in the second one it varies with κ.

Marr and Hütt showed by numerical simulation that the pattern formation capability of binary GAN strongly depends on the topology of the underlying network and that there are marked differences between GAN belonging to the two classes. By using temporal entropies, they found that in Watts–Strogatz small worlds increasing the rewiring probability progressively destroys local collective behavior, and beyond the small-world regime long-range correlations disappear. In Barabási–Albert scale-free graphs, variation of the degree correlations through rewiring without changing the degree distribution, leads to an inhomogeneous distribution in word entropy of the time series for the symbolic dynamics of individual nodes. From that point of view, nodes with low degree have a far greater entropy than their regular graph counterparts. On average, however, the word entropy is similar to that of CA. There are many other interesting considerations in the paper of Marr and Hütt for which we do not have space here; the reader is referred to the original work for details.

5 Collective Tasks on GAN: Density and Synchronization

The density and the synchronization tasks are prototypical distributed computational problems for binary CA. The design, evolution, and performance evaluation of one-dimensional CA that approximately perform those tasks has a long history; an excellent review appears in [7]. The tasks are briefly described below.

The density Task. The density task for a finite one-dimensional CA of size N is defined as follows. Let $C(0)$ be the *initial configuration* of the CA, i.e. the sequence of bits that represents the state of each automaton at time 0, and let ρ_0 be the fraction of 1s in the initial configuration. The task is to determine whether ρ_0 is greater than or less than $1/2$. If $\rho_0 > 1/2$ then the CA must relax to a fixed-point configuration of all 1's, otherwise it must relax to a fixed-point configuration of all 0's, after a number of time steps of the order of the grid size N. Here N is set to 149, the value that has been customarily used in research on the density task (taking N odd avoids the case where $\rho_0 = 0.5$ for which the problem is undefined).

Fig. 1. The density task. Cell states are represented horizontally (black stands for 1). Time increases down the page. The initial density of ones is 0.416.

This computation is trivial for a computer with a central control: just scanning the array and adding up the number of, say, 1 bits will provide the answer in $O(N)$ time. However, it is nontrivial for a small radius one-dimensional CA since such an automaton can only transfer information at finite speed relying on local information exclusively, while density is a global property of the configuration of states. An example is given in

Fig. 1. It has been shown that the density task cannot be solved perfectly by a uniform, two-state CA with finite radius [17], although a slightly modified version of the task allows perfect solution by such an automaton [5], or by a combination of automata [11].

The *performance* of a CA rule on the density task is defined as the fraction of correct classifications over $n = 10^4$ randomly chosen initial configurations (ICs). ICs are sampled according to a binomial distribution among the 2^N possible binary strings i.e., each bit is independently drawn with probability $1/2$ of being 0. Clearly, this distribution is strongly peaked around $\rho_0 = 1/2$ and thus makes a difficult case for the CA to classify. The best CA found to date either by evolutionary computation or by hand have performances around 0.8 [7].

Using his small-world construction, and thus relaxing the regular lattice constraint, Watts [30] has been able to obtain GAN with performance around 0.85, with the same mean connectivity $\langle k \rangle$ as in the regular CA case. Moreover, given that different nodes may have now different degrees, Watts used a simple majority rule [4] as a transition function, a rule that cannot classify density in a regular CA. In [27] it was shown that such high-performance GAN can be obtained automatically and easily with a simple evolutionary algorithm, starting from either regular or completely random graphs.

The Synchronization Task. The one-dimensional synchronization task was introduced in [9]. In this task the CA, given an arbitrary initial configuration $C(0)$, must reach a final configuration, within $m \simeq 2N$ time steps, that oscillates between all 0s and all 1s on successive time steps, i.e. if $C(m)$ is such a final configuration, and (say) $C(m) = \{0\}^n$, one has $C(m+2k+1) = \{1\}^n$, and $C(m+2k) = \{0\}^n$, $k = 0, 1, \ldots$. Figure 2 depicts the space-time diagram of a CA that solves the task for the given initial configuration.

As with the density task, synchronization also comprises a non-trivial computation for a small-radius CA, and it is thus extremely difficult to come up with CA rules that, when applied synchronously to the whole lattice produce a stable attractor of oscillating all 0s and all 1s configurations. Das et al. were able to automatically evolve very good ring CA rules of radius three for the task by using genetic algorithms [9]. Sipper did the same for quasi-uniform CA, i.e. CA with a few different rules instead of just one [25], attaining excellent performance for radius-one CA. The performance of a CA on this task is evaluated by running it on randomly generated initial configurations, uniformly distributed over densities in the range $[0, 1]$, with the CA being run for $M \simeq 2N$ time steps. Performance values close to 1 have been obtained.

Task Performance on Watts–Strogatz Networks. Figure 3 shows that GAN obtained by artificial evolution of the network topology without including any preconceived design issue, yield high-performance automata networks in the same class of those constructed by Watts and better than ring CA for the density task. The simple majority rule was used at each node. In these figures ϕ is the fraction of shortcuts in the graph; thus $\phi = 0$ corresponds to the ring case while $\phi = 1$ approaches the random graph case.

The results for the synchronization task (not reported here) are similar [28]. Thus, relaxing the regularity condition of the network, one can easily obtain GAN that are at

---

[4] The majority rules attributes to the central cell the state of the majority of neighbors, including the cell itself. In case of tie, the state is chosen uniformly at random.

Fig. 2. A one-dimensional CA correctly performing the synchronization task

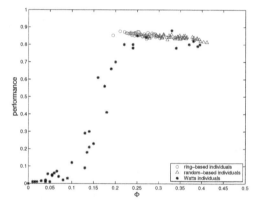

Fig. 3. Density task. The ϕ - performance values of the 50 best individuals found by evolution starting from rings and random graphs. For comparison, Watt's results (redrawn from [30])are also plotted.

least as good as the best designed or evolved CA for the tasks, with a similar average number of neighbors. Besides, if instead of using the simple majority rule the local transition function f was made itself to evolve, results would probably be even better. In fact, in a recent work Mesot and Teuscher [21] shown that randomly interconnected boolean automata using arbitrary boolean functions at the nodes (see section 6) can perform the synchronization and density task with high performance.

Task Performance on Scale-Free Networks. In [8] Albert and Barabási type networks (see section 3) were constructed to be used as support for CA computations with $\langle k \rangle = \{6, 12\}$. Results depicted in Figure 4 show that performance on the density task of CA mapped on scale-free networks are above 0.7 for networks with a smaller m_0, the size of the initial kernel. When a certain threshold is reached (m_0 about 14 for $\langle k \rangle = 6$ and 35 for $\langle k \rangle = 12$), performances drop dramatically. This means that the more the structure of the scale-free network become star-like, with a unique oversized cluster and only small satellites weakly connected ($m \rightarrow 1$), the information circulates with more difficulties. Results for scale-free graphs built using the configuration model are comparable. One can thus conclude that scale-free network topologies are less suitable than Watts–Strogatz small worlds as a substrate for the density task. The results are even worse than those obtained in rings [7] using specialized rules.

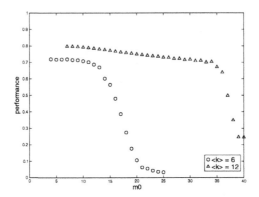

Fig. 4. Performance vs m_0 of scale-free networks (built on the Albert and Barabási model) on the density task. The circles represent the performance of networks with an average connection $\langle k \rangle = 6$ and triangles $\langle k \rangle = 12$.

The relative unsuitability of scale-free nets for collective task solving is confirmed by the numerical study of their behavior under noise for the density task. Using a probabilistic fault model, it appears that Watts–Strogatz type networks are much more robust than scale-free ones, as they tolerate a higher amount of errors without compromising task performance too much [8]. This is a surprising result, given that scale-free networks are notoriously very robust under random node or link failure [2]. Needless to say, Watts–Strogatz small worlds also have much better faul-tolerance capabilities than rings for the same task.

6   Generalized Boolean Networks

Random Boolean Networks (RBN) are directed GAN that have been introduced by Kauffman more than thirty years ago in a landmark paper [15] as a highly simplified model of genetic regulatory networks. In a RBN with N nodes, a node represents a gene and is modeled as an on-off device, meaning that a gene is expressed if it is on (1), and it is not otherwise (0). Each gene receives K randomly chosen inputs from other genes. Initially, one of the possible Boolean functions of K inputs is assigned at random to each gene. The network dynamics is discrete and synchronous: at each time step all nodes simultaneously examine their inputs, evaluate their Boolean functions, and find themselves in their new states at the next time step. Over time, the system travels through its phase space, until a point or cyclic attractor is reached whence either it will remain in that point attractor forever, or it will cycle through the states of the periodic attractor. Since the system is finite and deterministic, this will happen at most after 2^N time steps.

This extremely simple and abstract model has been studied in detail by analysis and by computer simulations of statistical ensembles of networks and it has been shown to be capable of extremely interesting dynamical behavior. We summarize the main results here (a full description is found in [16]).

First of all, it has been found that, as some parameters are varied such as K, or the probability p of expressing a gene, i.e. of switching on the corresponding node's state, the RBN can go through a phase transition. Indeed, for every value of p, there is a critical value of connectivity K such that for values of K below this critical value the system is in the ordered regime, while for values of K above this limit the system is said to be in the chaotic regime. In classical RBN $K = 1$ corresponds to the ordered regime, $K = 2$ is critical, and $K \geq 3$ means that the system is in the chaotic phase. Kauffman found that for $K = 2$ the size distribution of perturbations in the networks is a power law with finite cutoff that scales as the square root of N. Thus perturbations remain localized and do not percolate through the system. The mean cycle length scales at most linearly with N for $K = 2$. Kauffman's suggestion is that cell types correspond to attractors in the RBN phase space, and only those attractors that are short and stable under perturbations will be of biological interest. Thus, according to Kauffman, $K = 2$ RBN lying at the edge between the ordered phase and the chaotic phase can be seen as abstract models of genetic regulatory networks.

RBN are interesting in their own as complex dynamical systems and have been throughly studied as such using the concepts and tools of statistical mechanics. However, I believe that the original view of Kauffman, namely that these models may be useful for understanding real cell regulatory networks, is still a valid one, provided that the model is updated to take into account present knowledge about the topology of real gene regulatory networks, and the timing of events, without loosing its attractive simplicity. In the following I shall describe a couple of ways in which the Kauffman model could be modified in order to take into account a number of experimental observations that were not available at the time (more details of the model can be found in [13]).

The Network Model. Kauffman's RBN model rests on three main assumptions:

- The nodes implement Boolean functions and their state is either on or off;
- The nodes that affect a given node in the network are randomly chosen and are a fixed number;
- The dynamics of the network is synchronous in time.

The binary state simplification could seem extreme but actually it represents quite well "threshold phenomena" in which variables of interest suddenly change their state, such as neurons firing or genes being switched on or off.

Random networks with fixed connectivity degree were a logical generic choice in the beginning, since the exact couplings in networks were generally unknown. Today it is more open to criticism since it does not correspond to what we know about the topology of biological networks. In fact, many biological networks, including genetic regulatory networks, seem to be of the scale-free type or of a hierarchical type (see [29] and references therein) but not random, according to present data. For scale-free networks, this means that the degree distribution function $P(k)$ is a power law $P(k) \sim k^{-\gamma}$, usually with $2 < \gamma < 3$, instead of a Poisson distribution as in a random graph, or a delta distribution as in a classical RBN. Thus the low connectivity suggested by Kauffman for candidate stable systems is not found in such networks, where a wide range of degrees is present instead. The consequences for the dynamics may be important, since in scale-free graphs there are many nodes with low degree and a low, but not vanishing, number of highly connected nodes. Along this line, M. Aldana has recently presented a detailed analysis of Boolean networks with scale-free topology [3]. He definened a phase space diagram for boolean networks, including the phase transition from ordered to chaotic dynamics, as a function of the power law exponent γ. He also made exhaustive simulations for several relatively small values of N, the network size.

The model of [13] has in common with Aldana's the scale-free topology of the networks, although the graphs are constructed in a different way. But, in contrast to Aldana's, a suitable semi-synchronous dynamics is defined for the system, instead of using the customary synchronous update.

As sais above, according to present data many biological networks, including genetic regulatory networks, show a scale-free output distribution $P_{out}(k)$ and a Poissonian input distribution $P_{in}(k)$ [29]. The networks used in Giacobini's et al. work [13] have been generated according to a mixed generalized/poisson random graph : first a sequence of N out-degrees that satisfies a power-law distribution with exponent γ is assigned to N nodes; then, every out-going edge is assigned as input to one of the N nodes chosen at random (excluding self-connections). The resulting networks have a scale-free distribution of the output degrees and a Poisson distribution of the input degrees.

Synchronous, Asynchronous and Semi-Synchronous Network Dynamics. Standard RBN update their state synchronously. This assumption simplifies the analysis, but it is open to discussion if the network has to be biologically plausible. In particular, for genetic regulatory networks, this is certainly not the case, as many recent experimental observations tend to prove. Rather, genes seem to be expressed in different parts of the network at different times, according to a strict sequence (see, for instance, [10]). Thus a kind of serial, asynchronous update sequence seems to be needed. Asynchronous dynamics must nevertheless be further qualified, since there are many ways for serially updating the nodes of the network.

Several researchers have investigated the effect of asynchronous updating on classical RBN dynamics in recent years [14,20]. Harvey and Bossomayer studied the effect of asynchronous updating on some statistical properties of network ensembles, such as cycle length and number of cycles. They used un update sequence in which the next cell to be updated is chosen at random with uniform probability and with replacement. [14]. They found that many features that arise in synchronous RBN do not exist, or are different in non-deterministic asynchronous RBN. Thus, while point attractors do persist, there are no true cyclic attractors, only so-called loose ones and states can be in more than one basin of attraction. Also, the average number of attractors is very different from the synchronous case: even for $K = 2$ or $K = 3$, which are the values that characterize systems at the edge of chaos, there is no correspondence between the two dynamics. Mesot and Teuscher [20] studied the critical behavior of asynchronous RBN and concluded that they do not have a critical connectivity value analogous to synchronous RBN and they behave, in general, very differently from the latter, thus confirming the findings of [14].

Considering the above reults and what is known experimentally from microarray data about the timing of events in genetic networks it seems that neither fully synchronous nor completely random asynchronous network dynamics are suitable models. Synchronous update is implausible because events do not happen all at once, while completely random dynamics does not agree with experimental data on gene activation sequences and the model does not show stable cyclic attractors of the right size. Thus, the activation/update sequence in a RBN should be in some way related to the topology of the network. A topology-driven semi-synchronous update method, called *Cascade Update* (CU) has been proposed in [13]. Such an update scheme is certainly not a faithful model for true biological gene activation sequences which are clearly not the same for different regulatory networks. But the scheme is closer to biological reality than previously proposed ones namely, fully synchronous and various asynchronous policies.

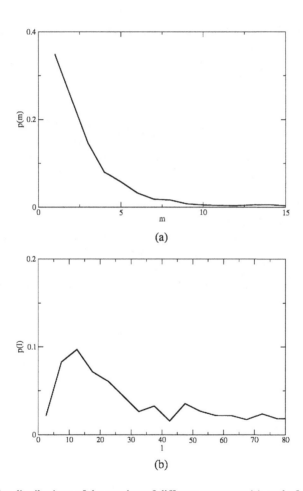

Fig. 5. probability distributions of the number of different attractors (a), and of the length of the attractors (b) for network realizations having $N = 50$ nodes evolving using cascade update

The CU consists in an asynchronous sequence of synchronously updated blocks of nodes. At the beginning of the evolution of the network, a node, say i, is randomly chosen and updated. Then, in the next time step, the block of the nodes to whom i projects is synchronously updated. The process continues, updating at each time step a new block formed by all the nodes in the network to which the nodes updated in the previous time step project. This scheme is deterministic: once the first node is chosen, the sequence of all the successive updates is unique and will reach a cycle, since the dynamical system is finite. As a consequence, the attractors of the dynamics cannot be loose attractors, they have to be true point or cyclic ones.

The results found in [13] by extensive numerical simulation covering Aldana's ordered regime, edge of chaos, and chaotic phase confirm that the behavior of the network model is biologically plausible, showing cyclic attractors of reasonable length. This can be seen in Fig. 5 where average results are reported for a network size $N = 50$ and a power lae exponent $\gamma = 2.48$ which places the system at the edge between the ordered and the chaotic phase. This intermediate regime, the analogous of Kauffman's $K = 2$, is the one where perturbations remain localized, according to Aldana, and thus the system enjoys the necessary stability.

7   Conclusions

Relaxing the regularity constraints in cellular automata gives rise to generalized automata networks (GAN). Although in this way the systems become more complex to describe ant to analyze, they also show a richer set of dynamical behaviors. Here we have reviewed a number of those GAN, ranging from networks for collective task solving, to biological-like Boolean GAN. It has been seen that GAN have better problem solving capabilities than CA, while at the same time offering superior fault-tolerance behavior, except in the scale-free case, which is rather fragile from this point of view. As models of biological regulatory networks, GAN are more credible than customary RBN. They correctly describe the observed network topologies, and their dynamics is also on the right track qualitatively. GAN have been known for a number of years now, but they are still mostly unexplored. The review presented here and the work cited is only a first step toward their characterization.

Acknowledgments. Financial support for this research by the Swiss National Science Fundation under contarct 200021-107419 is gratefully acknowledged.

References

1. R. Albert and A.-L. Barabási. Statistical mechanics of complex networks. *Reviews of Modern Physics*, 74:47–97, 2002.
2. R. Albert, H. Jeong, and L. Barabási. Error and attack tolerance of complex networks. *Nature*, 406:378–382, 2000.
3. M. Aldana. Boolean dynamics of networks with scale-free topology. *Physica D*, 185:45–66, 2003.
4. L. A. N. Amaral, A. Díaz-Guilera, A. Moreira, A. L. Goldberger, and L. A. Lipsitz. Emergence of complex dynamics in a simple model of signaling networks. *Proc. Nat. Acad. Sci. USA*, 101(44):15551–15555, 2004.

5. M. S. Capcarrère, M. Sipper, and M. Tomassini. Two-state, r=1 cellular automaton that classifies density. *Physical Review Letters*, 77(24):4969–4971, December 1996.
6. B. Chopard and M. Droz. *Cellular Automata Modeling of Physical Systems*. Cambridge University Press, Cambridge, UK, 1998.
7. J. P. Crutchfield, M. Mitchell, and R. Das. Evolutionary design of collective computation in cellular automata. In J. P. Crutchfield and P. Schuster, editors, *Evolutionary Dynamics: Exploring the Interplay of Selection, Accident, Neutrality, and Function*, pages 361–411. Oxford University Press, Oxford, UK, 2003.
8. C. Darabos, M. Giacobini, and M. Tomassini. Scale-free automata networks are not robust in a collective computational task. Lecture Notes in Computer Science. Springer, Berlin, 2006. this volume.
9. R. Das, M. Mitchell, and J. P. Crutchfield. A genetic algorithm discovers particle-based computation in cellular automata. In Y. Davidor, H.-P. Schwefel, and R. Männer, editors, *Parallel Problem Solving from Nature- PPSN III*, volume 866 of *Lecture Notes in Computer Science*, pages 344–353, Heidelberg, 1994. Springer-Verlag.
10. E. H. Davidson and et al. A genomic regulatory network for development. *Science*, 295:1669–1678, March1 2002.
11. H. Fukś. Solution of the density classification problem with two cellular automata rules. *Physical Review E*, 55(3):2081–2084, 1997.
12. M. Garzon. *Models of Massive Parallelism: Analysis of Cellular Automata and Neural Networks*. Springer-Verlag, Berlin, 1995.
13. M. Giacobini, M. Tomassini, P. De Los Rios, and E. Pestelacci. Dynamics of scale-free semi-synchronous boolean networks. In L. M. Rocha et al., editor, *Artificial Life X*, pages 1–7, Cambridge, Massachusetts, 2006. The MIT Press.
14. I. Harvey and T. Bossomaier. Time out of joint: attractors in asynchronous random boolean networks. In P. Husbands and I. Harvey, editors, *Proceedings of the Fourth European Conference on Artificial Life*, pages 67–75, Cambridge, MA, 1997. The MIT Press.
15. S. A. Kauffman. Metabolic stability and epigenesis in randomly constructed genetic nets. *Journal of Theoretical Biology*, 22:437–467, 1969.
16. S. A. Kauffman. *The Origins of Order*. Oxford University Press, New York, 1993.
17. M. Land and R. K. Belew. No perfect two-state cellular automata for density classification exists. *Physical Review Letters*, 74(25):5148–5150, June 1995.
18. C. G. Langton. Computation at the edge of chaos: Phase transitions and emergent computation. *Physica D*, 42:12–37, 1990.
19. C. Marr and M.-T.Hütt. Topology regulates pattern formation capacity of binary cellular automata on graphs. *Physica A*, 354:641–662, 2005.
20. B. Mesot and C. Teuscher. Critical values in asynchronous random boolean networks. In W. Banzhaf, editor, *Advances in Artificial Life, ECAL2003*, volume 2801 of *Lecture Notes in Artificial Intelligence*, pages 367–376, Berlin, 2003. Springer.
21. B. Mesot and C. Teuscher. Deducing local rules for solving global tasks with random Boolean networks. *Physica D*, 211:88–106, 2005.
22. M. E. J. Newman. The structure and function of complex networks. *SIAM Review*, 45:167–256, 2003.
23. R. Pastor-Satorras and A. Vespignani. Epidemic spreading in scale-free networks. *Phy. Rev. Lett.*, 86:3200–3203, 2001.
24. R. Serra and M. Villani. Perturbing the regular topology of cellular automata: implications for the dynamics. In S. Bandini, B. Chopard, and M. Tomassini, editors, *Cellular Automata, ACRI 2002*, volume 2493 of *Lecture Notes in Computer Science*, pages 168–177. Springer-Verlag, Heidelberg, 2002.
25. M. Sipper. *Evolution of Parallel Cellular Machines: The Cellular Programming Approach*. Springer-Verlag, Heidelberg, 1997.

26. M. Sipper and E. Ruppin. Co-evolving architectures for cellular machines. *Physica D*, 99:428–441, 1997.

27. M. Tomassini, M. Giacobini, and C. Darabos. Evolution of small-world networks of automata for computation. In X. Yao et al., editor, *Parallel Problem Solving from Nature - PPSN VIII*, volume 3242 of *Lecture Notes in Computer Science*, pages 672–681. Springer Verlag, Berlin, 2004.

28. M. Tomassini, M. Giacobini, and C. Darabos. Evolution and dynamics of small-world cellular automata. *Complex Systems*, 15:261–284, 2005.

29. A. Vázquez, R. Dobrin, D. Sergi, J.-P. Eckmann, Z. N. Oltvai, and A.-L. Barabàsi. The topological relationships between the large-scale attributes and local interactions patterns of complex networks. *Proc. Natl. Acad. Sci USA*, 101(52):17940–17945, 2004.

30. D. J. Watts. *Small worlds: The Dynamics of Networks between Order and Randomness*. Princeton University Press, Princeton NJ, 1999.

31. D. J. Watts and S. H. Strogatz. Collective dynamics of 'small-world' networks. *Nature*, 393:440–442, 1998.

32. S. Wolfram. Universality and complexity in cellular automata. *Physica D*, 10:1–35, 1984.

33. S. Wolfram. *A New Kind of Science*. Wolfram Media, 2002.

On Spiral Glider–Guns in Hexagonal Cellular Automata: Activator–Inhibitor Paradigm

A. Wuensche

Discrete Dynamics Lab., The University of Sussex, 7 Calle Andreita Santa Fe,
New Mexico 87506, USA
andy@ddlab.org

We present a cellular–automaton model of a reaction-diffusion excitable system with concentration dependent inhibition of the activator, and study the dynamics of mobile localizations (gliders) and their generators. We analyze a three–state totalistic cellular automaton on a two–dimensional lattice with hexagonal tiling, where each cell connects with 6 others. We show that a set of specific rules support spiral glider–guns (rotating activator–inhibitor spirals emitting mobile localizations) and stationary localizations which destroy or modify gliders, along with a rich diversity of emergent structures with computational properties. We describe how structures are created and annihilated by glider collisions, and begin to explore the necessary processes that generate this kind of complex dynamics.

S. El Yacoubi, B. Chopard, and S. Bandini (Eds.): ACRI 2006, LNCS 4173, p. 29, 2006.
© Springer-Verlag Berlin Heidelberg 2006

A Structurally Dynamic Cellular Automaton with Memory in the Hexagonal Tessellation

Ramón Alonso-Sanz[1] and Margarita Martín[2]

[1] ETSI Agrónomos (Estadística), C.Universitaria. 28040, Madrid, Spain
ramon.alonso@upm.es
[2] Bioquímica y Biología Molecular IV, UCM. C.Universitaria. 28040, Madrid, Spain
margamar@vet.ucm.es

Abstract. The major features of conventional cellular automata include the inalterability of topology and the absence of memory. The effect of simple memory (memory in cells and links) on a particular reversible, structurally dynamic cellular automaton in the hexagonal tessellation is explored in this paper.

Keywords: Structurally Dynamic, Cellular Automaton, Memory, Hexagonal.

1 A Hexagonal Cellular Automaton

Cellular Automata (CA) are discrete, spatially explicit extended dynamic systems. A CA system is composed of adjacent cells or sites arranged as a regular lattice, which evolves in discrete time steps. Each cell is characterised by an internal state whose value belongs to a finite set. The updating of these states is made simultaneously according to a common local transition rule involving only the neighborhood of each cell. Thus, if $\sigma_i^{(T)}$ is taken to denote the value of cell i at time step T, the site values evolve by iteration of the mapping : $\sigma_i^{(T+1)} = \phi\left(\sigma_j^{(T)} \in \mathcal{N}_i\right)$, where ϕ is an arbitrary function which specifies the cellular automaton *rule* operating on the neighborhood $\mathcal{N}$ of the cell i .

This paper deals with a particular two dimensional totalistic CA rule, the *parity* rule: $\sigma_i^{(T+1)} = \sum_{j \in \mathcal{N}_i} \sigma_j^{(T)} \ mod \ 2$, acting on cells with two possible state values (0 and 1). Despite its formal simplicity, the parity rule exhibits complex behaviour [1]. Figure 1 shows an example of the parity rule operating on a hexagonal tessellation starting from an active cell with its six neighbors also active. This will be the initial configuration all throughout this article.

2 Cellular Automata with Memory

Standard CA are ahistoric (memoryless): the transition function depends on the neighborhood configuration of the cells only at the preceding time step. Historic memory can be embedded in the CA dynamics by featuring every cell by a

S. El Yacoubi, B. Chopard, and S. Bandini (Eds.): ACRI 2006, LNCS 4173, pp. 30–40, 2006.

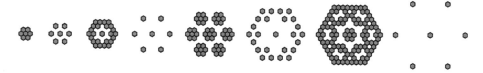

Fig. 1. A hexagonal CA with the parity rule. Evolving patterns up to $T = 8$.

mapping of its states in the previous time steps . Thus, what is here proposed is to maintain the transition rules (ϕ) unaltered, but make them act on the cells featured by a function of their previous states: $\sigma_i^{(T+1)} = \phi(s_j^{(T)} \in N_j)$, $s_i^{(T)}$ being a state function of the series of states of the cell i up to time-step T.

Thus, cells can be featured by a weighted mean value of their previous states:

$$m_i^{(T)}(\sigma_i^{(1)}, \sigma_i^{(2)}, \ldots, \sigma_i^{(T)}) = \frac{\sigma_i^{(T)} + \sum_{t=1}^{T-1} \alpha^{T-t} \sigma_i^{(t)}}{1 + \sum_{t=1}^{T-1} \alpha^{T-t}} \equiv \frac{\omega_i^{(T)}}{\Omega(T)} \qquad [1],$$

and the s values are obtained rounding the m ones: $s_i^{(T)} = round(m_i^{(T)})$, with $s_i^{(T)} = \sigma_i^{(T)}$ if $m_i^{(T)} = 0.5$. Memory becomes operative after $T = 3$, with the initial assignations $s_i^{(1)} = \sigma_i^{(1)}$, $s_i^{(2)} = \sigma_i^{(2)}$.

In the two state scenario, geometrically discounted memory does not affect the scenario if $\alpha \leq 0.5$, but if $\alpha \geq 0.61805$, cells with state history 001 or 110 will be featured after $T = 3$ as 0 and 1 respectively instead of 1 and 0 (last states), and the patterns of the ahistoric and historic models typically diverge from $T = 4$. This is so in Fig.2, which shows the effect of full memory: $\alpha = 1.0$, in which case $s_i^{(T)} = mode(\sigma_i^{(1)}, \ldots, \sigma_i^{(T)})$. Memory *truncates* the expansive evolution of the parity rule, particularly at high values of the memory factor α in which case small size oscillators of short period tend to appear. Thus, in Fig.2 a period two oscillator appears as early as at $T = 4$. But the effect is also dramatic at low values of α: the progression in size turns out restrained and the aspect of the patterns differs notably from that of the ahistoric ones. The effect of memory in cells on CA has been studied in the references by Alonso-Sanz *et al.* .

Fig. 2. Effect of full memory on the parity rule starting as in Fig.1

Note that the memory mechanism here adopted is *accumulative* in its demand of knowledge of past history: to calculate the memory *charge* $\omega_i^{(T)}$ stated in [1], it is not necessary to know the whole $\{\sigma_i^{(t)}\}$ series, while it suffices to (sequentially) proceed as: $\omega_i^{(T)} = \alpha\omega_i^{(T-1)} + \sigma_i^{(T)}$. Let us point out here that the implementation of memory adopted in this work, keeping the transition rule unaltered but applying it to a function of previous states, can be adopted in any dynamical system (see some simple examples in [2]-[5]).

3   Reversible Cellular Automata with Memory

The memory mechanism considered here is different from that of other CA with memory reported in the literature. Typically, higher-order-in-time rules incorporate memory into the transition rule. Thus, in second order in time rules: $\sigma_i^{(T+1)} = \Phi(\sigma_j^{(T)} \in \mathcal{N}_i, \sigma_j^{(T-1)} \in \mathcal{N}_i)$. Particularly interesting is the reversible formulation based on the substraction modulo the number of states (noted $\ominus$): $\sigma_i^{(T+1)} = \phi(\sigma_j^{(T)} \in \mathcal{N}_i) \ominus \sigma_i^{(T-1)}$, reversed as $\sigma_i^{(T-1)} = \phi(\sigma_j^{(T)} \in \mathcal{N}_i) \ominus \sigma_i^{(T+1)}$. Figure 3 shows the evolving patterns of the reversible formulation of the example of Fig.1. As a rule, the pattern at $T = 0$ in the reversible simulations here is the same as that at $T = 1$.

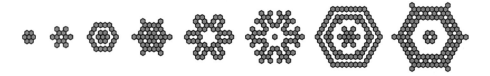

Fig. 3. A reversible hexagonal CA with the parity rule starting as in Fig.1

To preserve reversibility, the reversible formulation with memory must be : $\sigma_i^{(T+1)} = \phi(s_j^{(T)} \in \mathcal{N}_i) \ominus \sigma_i^{(T-1)}$ [7] . Figure 4 shows an example starting as in Fig.3 . The general considerations regarding the *inertial* effect of memory in the irreversible scenario apply in the reversible implementation. Thus starting as in Fig.3 but with full memory, a period four oscillator appears as at $T = 5$.

Fig. 4. A reversible hexagonal CA with $\alpha = 0.6$ memory starting as in Fig.3

For reversing from T it is necessary to know not only $\sigma_i^{(T)}$ and $\sigma_i^{(T+1)}$ but also $\omega_i^{(T)}$ to be compared to $\Omega(T)$, to obtain: $s_i^{(T)} = \begin{cases} 0 & \text{if } 2\omega_i^{(T)} < \Omega(T) \\ \sigma_i^{(T+1)} & \text{if } 2\omega_i^{(T)} = \Omega(T) \\ 1 & \text{if } 2\omega_i^{(T)} > \Omega(T) \end{cases}$.

Then to obtain $s_i^{(T-1)}$, it is necessary to obtain: $\omega_i^{(T-1)} = \dfrac{1}{\alpha}(\omega_i^{(T)} - \sigma_i^{(T)})$. But in order to avoid the division by the memory factor (recall that operations with real numbers are not exact in computer arithmetic), it is preferable to work

with $\gamma_i^{(T-1)} = \omega_i^{(T)} - \sigma_i^{(T)}$, and to compare these values to $\Gamma(T-1) = \sum_{t=1}^{T-1} \alpha^{T-t}$.

This leads to : $s_i^{(T-1)} = \begin{cases} 0 & \text{if } 2\gamma_i^{(T-1)} < \Gamma(T-1) \\ \sigma_i^{(T)} & \text{if } 2\gamma_i^{(T-1)} = \Gamma(T-1) \\ 1 & \text{if } 2\gamma_i^{(T-1)} > \Gamma(T-1) \end{cases}$. Continuing in the

reversing process : $\gamma_i^{(T-2)} = \gamma_i^{(T-1)} - \alpha\sigma_i^{(T-1)}$ and $\Gamma(T-2) = \sum_{t=1}^{T-2} \alpha^{T-t}$. In

general : $\gamma_i^{(T-\tau)} = \gamma_i^{(T-\tau+1)} - \alpha^{\tau-1}\sigma_i^{(T-\tau+1)}$ and $\Gamma(T-\tau) = \sum_{t=1}^{T-\tau} \alpha^{T-t}$, giving:

$$s_i^{(T-\tau)} = \begin{cases} 0 & \text{if } 2\gamma_i^{(T-\tau)} < \Gamma(T-\tau) \\ \sigma_i^{(T-\tau+1)} & \text{if } 2\gamma_i^{(T-\tau)} = \Gamma(T-\tau) \\ 1 & \text{if } 2\gamma_i^{(T-\tau)} > \Gamma(T-\tau) \end{cases} .$$

4 Reversible Structurally Dynamic Cellular Automata

Structurally dynamic cellular automata (SDCA) were suggested by Ilachinski and Halpern [9]. The essential new feature of this model is that the connections between the cells are allowed to change according to rules similar in nature to the state transition rules associated with the conventional CA. This means that given certain conditions, specified by the *link transition rules*, links between rules may be created and destroyed; the neighborhood of each cell is now dynamic rather than fixed throughout the automaton, so state and link configurations of an SDCA are *both* dynamic and are continually interacting.

In the Ilachinski and Halpern model, an SDCA consists of a finite set of binary-valued *cells* numbered 1 to N whose connectivity is specified by an $N \times N$ connectivity matrix in which λ_{ij} equals 1 if cells i and j are connected; 0 otherwise. So, now : $\mathcal{N}_i^{(T)} = \{j / \lambda_{ij}^{(T)} = 1\}$ and $\sigma_i^{(T+1)} = \phi(\sigma_j^{(T)} \in \mathcal{N}_i^{(T)})$. The *distance* between two cells i and j, δ_{ij}, is defined as the number of links in the shortest path between i and j. We say that i and j are *direct neighbors* if $\delta_{ij} \leq 1$, and that i and j are *next-nearest neighbors* if $\delta_{ij} = 2$. There are two types of link transition functions in an SDCA: *couplers* and *decouplers*, the former add new links, the later remove links. The set of coupler and decoupler determines the link transition rule: $\lambda_{ij}^{(T+1)} = \psi(l_{ij}^{(T)}, \sigma_i^{(T)}, \sigma_j^{(T)})$.

Instead of introducing the formalism of the SDCA, we deal here with just one example in which the decoupler rule removes all links connected to cells in which both values are zero ($\lambda_{ij}^{(T)} = 1 \rightarrow \lambda_{ij}^{(T+1)} = 0$ *iff* $\sigma_i^{(T)} + \sigma_j^{(T)} = 0$) and the coupler rule adds links between all next-nearest neighbor sites in which both values are one ($\lambda_{ij}^{(T)} = 0 \rightarrow \lambda_{ij}^{(T+1)} = 1$ *iff* $\sigma_i^{(T)} + \sigma_j^{(T)} = 2$ and $\delta_{ij}^{(T)} = 2$).

Let us consider the case of Fig.5 , in which, again, the initial hexagonal lattice

(with next-nearest neighborhood : ) is seeded as in Fig.1. After the first iteration, most of the lattice structure has decayed as an effect of the decoupler rule, so that the active value cells and links are confined into a small region. After $T = 4$, the link and value structures become a period-two oscillator.

Fig. 5. The ahistoric SDCA described in the text starting as in Fig.1

The Fredkin's reversible construction is feasible in the SDCA scenario extending the $\ominus$ operation also to links: $\lambda_{ij}^{(T+1)} = \psi(\lambda_{ij}^{(T)}, \sigma_i^{(T)}, \sigma_j^{(T)}) \ominus \lambda_{ij}^{(T-1)}$. Figure 6 shows the evolution of the reversible formulation of the SDCA of Fig.5 up to $T = 4$. At variance with what happens in the irreversible formulation in Fig.5, the initial lattice structure does not decay at $T = 2$ (nor at posterior time-steps) because of the adding of the structure at $T = 0$ (at $T - 1$), supposed to be the same that as at $T = 1$. The planar representation of the web of connections may appear ambiguous. Let us mention an example in Fig.6: the central cell seems to be connected to every cell of its neighborhood at $T = 2$ as it is at $T = 1$, but this is not so because of the superposition of webs, which causes the deletion of the links of the central cell at $T = 2$ in Fig.6. The segments that cross the central cell connect only its neighbor active cells, new conexions at $T = 2$ not overlapped. Link transitions rules do not alter auto-connections, but substraction of patterns may. Thus, for example, in Fig.6 every cell is autoconnected at $T = 0$ and $T = 1$, but the substraction of these patterns leads to the complete disappearance of auto-connections at $T = 2$. Auto-connections are not represented in figures, but of course they affect the mass updating.

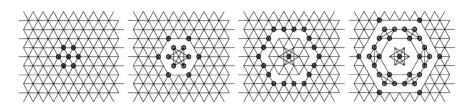

Fig. 6. The reversible structurally dynamic CA starting as in Fig.5, up to $T = 4$

5   A Reversible Structurally Dynamic Cellular Automaton with Memory

Memory can be embedded in links in a similar manner as in state values, so the link between any two cells is featured by a mapping of its previous values :

$$l_{ij}^{(T)} = round(m_{ij}^{(T)}), \; l_{ij}^{(T)} = \lambda_{ij}^{(T)} \; \text{if} \; m_{ij}^{(T)} = 0.5, \; \text{after} \; m_{ij}^{(T)} = \frac{\omega_{ij}^{(T)}}{\Omega(T)} \qquad [2] \, ,$$

with $\omega_{ij}^{(T)} = \lambda_{ij}^{(T)} + \sum\limits_{t=1}^{T-1} \alpha^{T-t}\lambda_{ij}^{(t)} = \omega_{ij}^{(T-1)} + \alpha\lambda_{ij}^{(T)}$

The *distance* between two cells in a historic model (d_{ij}) is defined in terms of the l instead of the λ values, so that i and j are *direct neighbors* if $d_{ij} = 1$, and are *next-nearest neighbors* if $d_{ij} = 2$; $N_i^{(T)} = \{j/d_{ij}^{(T)} = 1\}$. Generalizing the approach to embedded memory introduced in Section 2, the unchanged transition rules (ϕ and ψ) may operate on the featured link and mass values: $\sigma_i^{(T+1)} = \phi(s_j^{(T)} \in N_i)$, $\lambda_{ij}^{(T+1)} = \psi(l_{ij}^{(T)}, s_i^{(T)}, s_j^{(T)})$ [10]. A period-two oscillator is generated at $T = 6$ with full memory in Fig.7.

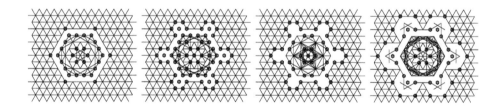

Fig. 7. The SDCA with full memory starting as in Fig.5 from $T = 4$ to $T = 11$

A generalisation of the Fredkin's reversible construction is feasible in the SDCA scenario endowed with memory as: $\sigma_i^{(T+1)} = \phi(s_j^{(T)} \in N_i^{(T)}) \ominus \sigma_i^{(T-1)}$, $\lambda_{ij}^{(T+1)} = \psi(l_{ij}^{(T)}, s_i^{(T)}, s_j^{(T)}) \ominus \lambda_{ij}^{(T-1)}$. Now, for reversing from T it is necessary to know not only $\sigma_i^{(T)}, l_{ij}^{(T)}, \sigma_i^{(T+1)}$, and $l_{ij}^{(T+1)}$, but also $\omega_i^{(T)}$ and $\omega_{ij}^{(T)}$, proceeding for reversing in connections as stated for mass values in Section 3. Figure 8 shows the initial effect of memory with $\alpha = 0.6$ in the initial scenario of Fig.6 .

Fig. 8. The reversible structurally dynamic CA with $\alpha = 0.6$ memory starting as in Fig.6. Evolution from $T = 5$ up to $T = 8$

The evolving patterns in the reversible SDCA model with full memory converge from $T = 7$ to a period-two oscillator, one of whose components has no active mass cell. In the $\alpha = 0.9$ memory model a period-four oscillator is generated at $T = 11$. If $\alpha \geq 0.61805$, the pattern at $T = 4$ has only the central cell alive and the hexagonal web of connections restored, which clearly determines the difference in the evolution compared to that of the ahistoric model.

Figure 9 shows the patterns at $T = 13$ for the ahistoric and $\alpha = 0.6$ reversible SDCA with the initial steps shown in Figs. 6 and 8 . In the ahistoric model, the web of connections is so dense in its central area that it is impossible to discern it. The web appears dramatically cleared in the historic model with the small value of the memory factor $\alpha = 0.6$. The *clearing* of the web of connections together with a restraint in the advance of mass, mark the inertial effect of memory.

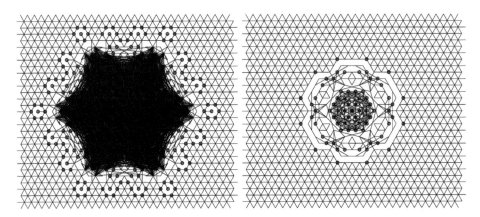

Fig. 9. Patterns at $T = 13$ of the ahistoric and $\alpha = 0.6$ memory SDCAs

Figure 10 shows the evolution of mass density, the average number of nearest neighbors and next-nearest neighbors per site, and the *effective dimension* : the average ratio of the number of next-nearest to nearest neighbors per site (a discrete analogue to the continuous Hausdorff dimension, that in a hexagonal lattice is : 12/7=1.714) in the simulations of Fig.9. The smoothing effect of memory is seen again in Fig.10: *i*) the tendency to grow of the mass and the two neighbor densities is clearly restrained with memory, *ii*) the evolution of the effective dimension is less erratic with memory.

6   Other Memories

Memory may be embedded either in cells but not in connections, or else, only in connections. Figure 11 shows an example in the latter scenario.

Average-like memory models can readily be proposed by generalizing the memory charges as: $\omega_i^{(T)} = \sum_{t=1}^{T} \delta(t)\sigma_i^{(t)}$, $\omega_{ij}^{(T)} = \sum_{t=1}^{T} \delta(t)\lambda_{ij}^{(t)}$, with $\Omega(T) = \sum_{t=1}^{T} \delta(t)$. The geometric discount model considered till now $(\delta(t) = \alpha^{T-t})$ is just one of the many possible weighting functions.

Alternatively, previous states can be pondered with the weight : $\delta(t) = t^c$. Choosing integer c parameter values allows working only with integers by comparing the $2\omega_i$ and $2\omega_{ij}$ figures across the lattice to the factor $\Omega(T)$. For $c = 0$, we have the full historic model, the larger the value of c, the more heavily the recent past is taken into account, and consequently the closer the scenario to the

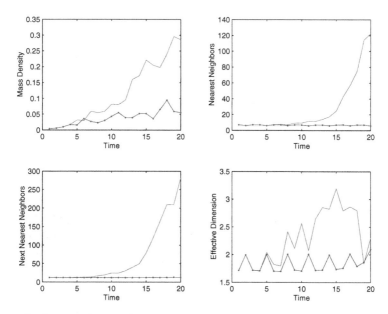

Fig. 10. Evolution of mass density, average number of nearest neighbors and next-nearest neighbors per site, and *effective dimension* in the ahistoric (upper curves) and $\alpha = 0.6$ simulations of Figs. 6 and 8 up to T=20 implemented in a lattice of size 43×43

Fig. 11. The evolving patterns of the SDCA described in text with memory only in connections. Full memory. Evolution from $T = 4$ to $T = 7$ starting as in Fig.6 .

ahistoric one. Figure 12 shows an example of the effect of integer-based memory implementation with $\delta(t) = t$.

Another weight with the same integer-based property, is c^t. This memory weight is not operative with cells and links with two states, but it becomes operative when allowing three states (0,1,2), in which case the $m_i^{(T)}$ and $l_{ij}^{(T)}$ values are to be compared to the hallmarks 1/2 and 3/2, assigning the last state/link value in the case of an equality to any hallmark. In order to work with integers and save computing demands, it is preferable to compare the 2ω values to the hallmarks 1 and 3 [5]. Figure 13 shows the effect of $\delta(t) = 2^t$ memory starting as in Fig. 6 but allowing cells to have three states (links remain two-valued). The cells of the neighborgood of the central cells reach state 2 at $T = 2$ in Fig.13 because $0 \ominus_3 1 = 2$. Memory has effect already at $T = 4$ as the central cell has zero mass value in the ahistoric model.

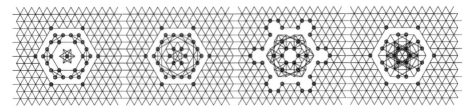

Fig. 12. The evolving patterns of the SDCA described in text, with integer-based memory $\delta(t) = t$. Evolution from $T = 4$ to $T = 7$ starting as in Fig.6.

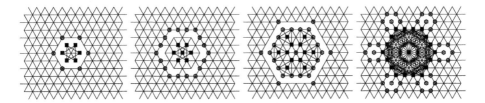

Fig. 13. The evolving patterns of the three-states reversible SDCA described in the text. *Square* cells are at state 2. Evolution with $\delta(t) = 2^t$ memory in cells. Patterns from $T = 2$ up to $T = 5$ starting as in Fig.6.

Reversing is easier in the integer-based memory scenarios than in that of geometric discount as $\omega_i^{(T)} = \omega_i^{(T-1)} + \delta(T)\sigma_i^{(T)}$ and $\omega_{ij}^{(T)} = \omega_{ij}^{(T-1)} + \delta(T)\lambda_{ij}^{(T)}$ readily reverse, without the computational inconvenience of division by α. Working only with integers (*à la CA*) is a clear computational advantage. Nevertheless, the inc^t and t^c , share the same drawback : they *explode* at high values of t.

7   Discussion

The effect of memory embedded in cells and links on a particular reversible structurally dynamic cellular automaton starting from a simple hexagonal scenario is qualitatively (pictorially) studied in this work. As a rule, geometrically discounted memory has been shown to produce an inertial effect that tends to preserve the main features of initial conditions. This notably alters the ahistoric dynamics, even if a low level of memory is implemented.

A complete analysis of the effect of memory on reversible structurally dynamic CA (RSDCA) is left for future work which will develop a phenomenology of RSDCA with memory, i.e. the full analysis of the rule space based on the morphological classification of patterns formed, the intrinsic parameters (e.g. λ and Z), the structure of global transition graphs, the entropy and other dynamics-related issues. Potential fractal features are also to come under scrutiny [11].

Some critics may argue that memory is not in the realm of CA (or even of Dynamic Systems), but we believe that the subject is worth studying. At least CA with memory can be considered as a promising extension of the basic paradigm.

A major impediment to modeling with CA stems from the difficulty of utilizing the CA complex behavior to exhibit a particular behavior or perform a particular function: embedding memory in states and links broadens the spectrum of CA as a tool for modeling.

The SDCA seem to be particularly appropriate for modelling the human brain function (links/synapses connect cells/neurons) in which the relevant role of memory is apparent. Reversibility in this context would avoid the possibility of "reinventing history". Models similar to SDCA have beeen adopted to build a dynamical network approach to quantum space-time physics [12]. Reversibility is an important issue at such a fundamental physics level.

Apart from their potential applications, SDCA with memory have an aesthetic and mathematical interest on their own. The study of the effect of memory on CA has been rather neglected and there have been only limited investigations of SDCA[1]. Nevertheless, it seems plausible that further study on SDCA (and SDLGA [19]) with memory[2] should turn out to be profitable.

Acknowledgement. Supported by CICYT Grant AGL2002-04003-C03-02 AGR.

References

1. Julian,P.,Chua,L.O.: Replication properties of parity CA. Int. J. Bifurcation and Chaos **12** (2002) 477-94
2. Alonso-Sanz,R.: Elementary rules with elementary memory rules: the case of linear rules. J. of Cellular Automata (2006) **1** 71-87
3. Alonso-Sanz,R.,Martin,M.: One-dimensional CA with Memory in Cells of the Most Frequent Recent Value. Complex Systems **15** (2005) 203-236
4. Alonso-Sanz,R.: Phase transitions in an elementary probabilistic CA with memory.Physica A **347** (2005) 383-401
5. Alonso-Sanz,R.,Martin,M.: Three-state one-dimensional CA with memory. Chaos, Solitons and Fractals **21** (2004) 809-834.
6. Alonso-Sanz,R.: One-dimensional, $r = 2$ CA with memory. Int.J. Bifurcation and Chaos **14** (2004) 3217-3248.
7. Alonso-Sanz,R.: Reversible CA with Memory. *Physica D* **175** (2003) 1-30
8. Alonso-Sanz,R.,Martin,M.: Elementary CA with memory. Complex Systems **14** (2003) 99-126, and the references therein.
9. Ilachinski,A.,Halpern,P.: Structurally dynamic CA. Complex Systems **1** (1987) 503-527
10. Alonso-Sanz,R.: A structurally dynamic CA with memory. Chaos, Solitons and Fractals (2006) (in press).
11. Sanchez,J.R.,Alonso-Sanz,R.: Multifractal Properties of R90 CA with Memory. Int.J. Modern Physics C, **15** (2004) 1461-1470
12. Requardt,M.: Cellular networks as models for Plank-scale physics. J. Phys. A **31** (1998) 7797-8021
13. Halpern,P.,Caltagirone,G.: Behaviour of Topological CA. Complex Systems **4** (1990) 623-651
14. Halpern,P.: Sticks and stones: A guide to structurally dynamic CA. Am.J.Phys. **57** (1989) 405-408

---

[1] To the best of our knowledge, the relevant references on SDCA are [9], [13]-[16], together with a review chapter in [17] and a section in [18].

[2] Not only in the basic paradigm scenario, but also in SDCA with random but value-dependent rule transitions (which relates SDCA to genetic networks), and/or in SDCA with the extensions considered in [16], such as unidirectional links.

15. Hillman,D.: Combinatorial Spacetimes. Ph.D. Thesis. Univ. of Pitssburg. (1995)
16. Majercik,S.M.: Structurally Dynamic CA. Univ. of Southern Maine (MsC) (1994)
17. Ilachinski,A.: *Cellular Automata. A Discrete Universe.* (World Scientific, 2000).
18. Adamatzky,A.: *Identification of Cellular Automata* (Taylor and Francis,1994).
19. Love,P.J.,Boghosian,B.M.,Meyer,D.A.: Lattice gas simulations of dynamical geom-
    etry in one dimension. Phil. Trans. R. Soc. London A **362** (2004) 1667-1675

Parallel Simulation of Asynchronous Cellular Automata Evolution*

Olga Bandman

Supercomputer Software Department
ICMMG, Siberian Branch Russian Academy of Sciences
Pr. Lavrentieva, 6, Novosibirsk, 630090, Russia
bandman@ssd.sscc.ru

Abstract. For simulating physical and chemical processes on molecular level asynchronous cellular automata with probabilistic transition rules are widely used being sometimes referred to as Monte-Carlo methods. The simulation requires huge cellular space and millions of iterative steps for obtaining the CA evolution representing the real scene of the process. This may be achieved by allocating the CA evolution program onto a multiprocessor system. As distinct from the synchronous CAs which is extremely efficient, the asynchronous case of parallel implementation is stiff. To improve the situation we propose a method for approximating asynchronous CA by a superposition of a number of synchronous ones, each being applied to locally separated blocks forming a partition of the cellular array.

1 Introduction

The increase of computing power both of individual computers and of multi-processor systems enhance the development of simulation methods for obtaining new knowledge about natural and technological processes. Usually, simulation of spatial dynamics in physics is performed by partial differential equations (PDE) solution. But in case when processes under simulation are nonlinear or have discontinuous behavior PDE are impuissant. Bright manifestation of the situation is kinetics of nano-systems, such that epitaxial growth on silicon crystal [1], autovawes and oscillations during the oxidation of carbon monoxide on catalyst surface [2,3], where the direct modeling of possible movements of particles and their stochastic interactions in a discrete space is used. Due to the stochastic character of the processes the models are sometimes classified as "Random Selection Algorithms of Monte-Carlo methods" [4,5], actually being asynchronous CA with probabilistic transition rules. It is clear, that very small size of real "particles", i.e. molecules or atoms, stipulate the necessity of huge size of the CA, and real speed of their movements requires large simulation time. Thus, the

* Supported by 1)Presidium of Russian Academy of Sciences, Basic Research Program N 14.15 (2006), 2) Siberian Branch of Russian Academy of Sciences, Integration Project 29 (2006).

S. El Yacoubi, B. Chopard, and S. Bandini (Eds.): ACRI 2006, LNCS 4173, pp. 41–47, 2006.
© Springer-Verlag Berlin Heidelberg 2006

capability of simulation is constrained by the performance of modern computers. The situation might be essentially improved by using multiprocessor supercomputers which are available for scientific community nowadays, but as distinct to the synchronous CA parallelization of asynchronous CA evolution is a hard task.

A natural way to achieve acceptable parallelization efficiency is to transform the given asynchronous CA into a synchronous one, which approximate its evolution. The advantages of such an approach is twofold. First, its implementation is faster, because of the decrease of random number generator use. Second, allocation of a CA onto many processors for parallel simulation becomes easier and more efficient. The idea has been already exploited for a particular case of surface reaction simulation [6]. Here we aim at the development of systematic method and present some results of its experimental investigation.

Apart from the Introduction and the Conclusion the paper contains three sections. The second section contains definitions of used concepts. In the third section asynchronous to block-synchronous transformation and its justification are given. The fourth section is dedicated to parallel implementation of of block-synchronous CA.

2   Formal Statement of the Problem

The class of CA under investigation is a mathematical model of the phenomena consisting of elementary actions of *particles*. A particle may be interpreted as a real atom or molecule. Elementary actions are mostly the following: adsorption of particles from the medium (gas) , sublimation, dissociation, diffusion, chemical reaction. The processes are stochastic, probability of each action being conditioned by physical parameters. The class of CA modeling the above processes differs from that of classical cellular automata in the following: 1) transition rules are probabilistic and deal not only with Boolean states, but also with integers and sometimes with symbols, 2) a single transition rule is allowed to update a group of cells at once, being a particular case of *substitution systems*)from [7] or [8], 3) the mode of operation is asynchronous, i.e. each time only one updating act is performed, the cells to be updated being randomly chosen.

A CA with the above features is further referred to as a *kinetic asynchronous CA*, being denoted as CA_α and represented by three concepts $CA = \langle A, M, \theta \rangle$, where A is a *state alphabet*, M – the set of elementary automata names, θ – a transition rule. There is no constraints imposed to the alphabet. As for the set of names, 2D Cartesian lattice $M = \{m : m = i, j, i = 0, \ldots, I; j = 0, \ldots, J\}$, is considered, m being used instead of (i, j) for short. A set $\Omega = \{a, m) : a \in A, m \in M\}$ forms a *cellular arrays*, where a pair (a, m) is called a   *cell*, $a \in A$ and $m \in M$. On the set M naming functions $\varphi : M \to M$ may be defined. If $m_k = \varphi(m)$, then m_k is a neighbor of a cell named m.

A subset of cells

$$S(m) = \{(v_0, m), (v_1, \varphi_1(m)), \ldots, (v_q, \varphi_q(m))\} \tag{1}$$

form a *local configuration*, a cell (v_0, m) being referred to as its *reference cell*, the set of cells names in it

$$T(m) = \{m, \varphi_1(m), \dots, \varphi_q(m)\} \tag{2}$$

being called as an *underlying template*. Two local configurations $S(m)$ and $S'(m)$ with the same reference cells represent an elementary act of cellular array updating,

$$\theta(m) : S(m) \rightarrow S'(m), \quad T'(m) \subseteq T(m), \tag{3}$$

where $S'(m) = \{(u_k, \varphi_k(m)) : k = 0, 1, \dots, p, p \leq q$, is a next-state local configuration, whose cell states $u_k = f_k(v_0, v_1, \dots, v_q), \quad k = 0, 1, \dots, p$, are transition functions values.

Application of $\theta(m)$ to all cells of Ω_t transfers the cellular array into the next *global state* Ω_{t+1}, which is considered as an iteration. In CA_α this transition may be represented as a *transient sequence*

$$\sigma_\alpha(\Omega_t) = (\Omega_t, \dots, \Omega_{t+l\tau}, \dots, \Omega_{t+\mu\tau}), \tag{4}$$

where τ is a micro-step for one updating, and $\Omega_{t+\mu\tau} = \Omega_{t+1}$, $\mu = |M|$. All possible transient evolutions starting from Ω_t and ending at Ω_{t+1} constitute an ensemble $\gamma_\alpha(\Omega)$, whose cardinality is $|\gamma_\alpha(\Omega)| = \mu!$. The sequence $\Sigma(\Omega_0) = (\Omega_0, \dots, \Omega_t, \dots, \Omega_T)$ is referred to as an *evolution*, the set of all possible evolutions of a CA_α starting from an Ω is denoted as $\Gamma_{\mathsf{CA}_\alpha}(\Omega)$.

3   Approximation of an Asynchronous CA by a Block-Synchronous One

Since synchronous CA are preferable for parallel implementation, there is a natural intention to transform a given CA_α into a synchronous one preserving the evolution of CA_α. Unfortunately, there is no exact method known by now how to do this, hence, we make an attempt to obtain an approximate one. The idea used is to impose some order on the random choice of cells to be updated, making this in such a way as to bring no distortion in the evolution progress but only restricting the possible choice of state-transition sequences. Moreover, introducing synchronicity, one should be cautious for conservation behavioral correctness. It is most important because of the fact that in CA_α multicell updating is used, i.e. some cells are updated at once. The correctness condition (in [8] referred to as *noncontradictoryness*) requires that no two simultaneous acts of updating change the same cell state at the same time. Formally, the sufficient correctness condition is as follows.

$$T'(m) \cap T'(\varphi_l(m)) = \emptyset \quad \forall m \in M, \quad \forall l \in 1, \dots, q, \tag{5}$$

where $T'(m)$ and $T'(\varphi_l(m)$ are underlying templates for $S'(m)$ and $S'(\varphi_l(m))$ in (3). It is clear that CA_α are always correct because only a single (although a multicell one) is allowed at a time.

We shall say that a CA_β approximates a CA_α if

$$\Gamma_\beta(\Omega) \subseteq \Gamma_\alpha(\Omega) \quad \forall \Omega \in A \times M. \tag{6}$$

and construct the approximation in the form of a block-synchronous CA (further denoted as CA_β) which operates as follows.

1. On Ω a set of partitions $\Pi = \{\Pi_1, \ldots, \Pi_k, \ldots, \Pi_b\}$ is defined as follows:

$$\Pi_k = \{B_k^1, \ldots, B_k^g, \ldots, B_k^G\}, \quad \bigcup_g B_k^g = \Omega, \quad \bigcap_g B_k^g = \emptyset, \quad G = |M|/b. \tag{7}$$

B_k^g having the underlying template

$$T_B(m_k) = \{m_k, \psi_1(m_k), \ldots, \psi_l(m_k), \ldots, \psi_b(m_k)\} \tag{8}$$

m_k being a reference cell name of a block $B_k^g \in \Pi_k$.

2. A transition $\Omega_t \to \Omega_{t+1}$ is divided into b steps, the resulting arrays forming a sequence:

$$\sigma_\beta(t) = (\Omega_t, \Omega_{t+t'}, \ldots, \Omega_{t+t'k}, \ldots, \Omega_{t+t'b}), \quad t' = \frac{t}{b}, \tag{9}$$

where on k-th step, $k = 1, \ldots, b$, $\theta(m)$ is applied synchronously to reference cells (v_k, m_k) of all blocks $B_k^g \in \Pi_k$, $g = 1, \ldots, G$.

3. Partitions $\Pi_k \in \Pi$ are processed in a random order, the ensemble γ_β of transient sequences in the transitions $\Omega_{t+t'k} \to \Omega_{t+t'(k+1)}$ having the cardinality $|\gamma_\beta| = b!$.

Theorem 1. A $CA_\beta = \langle A, M, \theta \rangle$ is an approximation of an AC_α, if

$$T'(m) \subseteq T_B(m), \tag{10}$$

where $T'(m), T_B(m)$ are underlying templates of $\theta(m)$ and B_k^g, respectively.

Proof. To prove the Theorem it is sufficient to show that the relation $\gamma_\beta(\Omega) \subseteq \gamma_\alpha(\Omega)$ holds for each iteration $\Omega_t \to \Omega_{t+1}$. The latter, according to (9), may be represented as a sequence of synchronous transitions $\Omega_{t+t'k} \to \Omega_{t+t'(k+1)}$ which also belong to the set of cellular arrays included in $\sigma_\alpha(\Omega(t))$ (4). It follows from two facts: 1) condition (10) of the Theorem provides the correctness condition (5) of the synchronous step , and 2) property (7) of CA_β ensures that the result does not depend on the mode of operation. Moreover, in the sequence of synchronous steps the portion of next-state values used as arguments in functions (3), being equal to $\frac{\mu k}{q}$, increases with k in the similar way than it takes place in asynchronous case. So, the whole iteration result is equal to the result of an asynchronous iterative step, which proves the Theorem.

Taking into account the approximation concept (6), the approximation accuracy may be assessed only as the relation between the numbers Q_β of transient sequences $\sigma_\alpha(\Omega(t))$ encapsulated in a transition $\Omega(t) \to \Omega(t + 1)$ of CA_β, and the total numbers of transient sequences in $\gamma_\alpha(\Omega)$, which yields $\varepsilon = \frac{G!b!}{\mu!}$ How serious is the discrepancy from the true process under simulation depends on many factors and may be clarified only by a comprehensive experimental study.

Example 2. The most simple model of epitaxial growth on Silicon (Si) surface is a composition of two following actions: 1) absorption of Si-atoms from the gas with the probability p_a; 2) diffusion of the absorbed atoms over the surface. An atom diffuses to a neighboring cell if it has $n > 0$ neighbors ($n = 1, 2, 3, 4$), whose states is less that that of its own. The probability of the diffusion act is $p' = 0,05^{4-n}$, and the choice among n possible directions to move to is equiprobable, so $p_d = p'/n$. The process may be described by an $CA_\alpha = \langle A, M, \theta \rangle$ where $A = \mathbf{N}$, $M = \{(i, j) : i = 0, \ldots, I, j = 0, \ldots, J\}$. A cell $(a, (i, j))$ corresponds to a site on a Si crystal surface, where the thickness of the adsorbed layer is equal to a atoms. The transition rule $\theta(i, j)$ is a superposition of ϑ_{ads} responsible for absorbtion, and $\vartheta_{diff}(i, j))$ responsible for diffusion.

$$\vartheta_{ads} = \{(v_0, (i, j))\} \xrightarrow{p_a} \{(v_0 + 1, (i, j))\};$$
$$\vartheta_{diff} = \{(v_0, (i, j)), (v_1, \varphi_1(i, j)), (v_2, \varphi_2(i, j)), (v_3, \varphi_3(i, j)),$$
$$(v_4, \varphi_4(i, j))\} \xrightarrow{p_d} \{(u_0, (i, j)), (u_1, \varphi_1(i, j)), (u_2, \varphi_2(i, j)),$$
$$(u_3, \varphi_3(i, j)), (u_4, \varphi_4(i, j))\}, \tag{11}$$

where

$$u_0 = \begin{cases} v_0 & if\ (\forall k : u_k \geq v_0) \wedge (rand > p_n), \\ v_k + 1\ if\ (u_k < v_0) \wedge (rand < p_n) \wedge (1/n \leq k/n \leq (k+1)/n). \end{cases} \tag{12}$$

$rand$ being a random number in the interval [0,1].

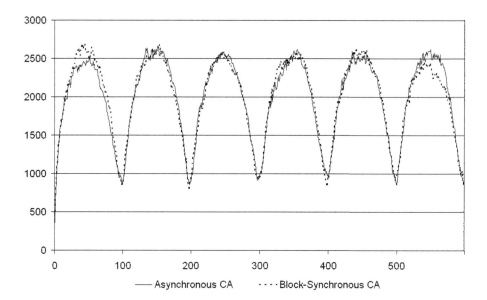

—— Asynchronous CA   ···· Block-Synchronous CA

Fig. 1. The dependence $P(t')$ for AC_α simulating epitaxial growth and its approximation by a CA_β, $|M| = 200 \times 200$, $p_a = 0.2$, $t' = t/500$

The simulation process shows the formation of islands of adsorbed atoms on the Si surface. One of the features under investigation is the dependence of total perimeter $P(t)$ of the islands on time. The perimeter P is computed as a number of cell pairs having different states. During the process this number exhibits oscillations, which are of interest for the researcher. In Fig.1 a few first waves produced both by CA_α and CA_β of such oscillations are shown, CA_β being obtained according to the above method with the block-size 3×3. The mean square error of approximation computed according the above experiment data is $E = 0.0412$. Moreover, CA_β simulation is 1.5 times faster, than CA_α.

4   Parallel Implementation of CA_α

When simulating spatial dynamics on N processors the simulation space is divided into N parts, each allocated and processed in its own processor, the processors exchanging data each iteration. Time for transmitting a data package $T_{trans} = T_{lat} + VT_{bit}$, where T_{lat} is latency time, V-the amount of bits in the package, and T_{bit} - bit transmission time. From the relation $T_{lat} \gg T_{bit}$ it follows, that the exchange efficiency depends directly on package size. That is why parallel implementation of synchronous CA evolution, where all border cells states may be packed in one package, is extremely efficient, the speedup being close to N provided that

$$T_{computation} \gg T_{transmission} \tag{13}$$

Unfortunately, CA_α parallelization allows no package to be formed, because any delay in cell state transmission breaks the correctness condition (5). So, each state change on the border of the array allocated in a processor requires an exchange to be performed. It leads to the slow down instead of speeding up, because (13) cannot be reached even with very large arrays.

The situation is quite different for CA_β, because, border cells states of the results of synchronous steps may be transmitted in a package. The experimental results (Table 1), obtained by running the CA_β simulation program on the cluster MVS-1000/128 of Siberian Supercomputer Center, show quite acceptable speedup for large enough cellular array size.

Table 1. Time T (min), speedup $S = T_N/T_1$, and efficiency $C = T_1/(NT_N)$ in performing 10^4 iterations of CA_β simulation from the Example 1, array size being 6000×6000

N	1	4	9	16	25
T	817.08	212.91	113.66	55.52	41.65
S	1	3.83	7.18	14.78	19.64
C	1	0.95	0.79	0.92	0.78

5   Conclusion

The problem of parallel simulation of kinetic asynchronous CA evolution is considered. It is shown that to make parallel implementation speedup acceptable it is necessary to approximate it by a a block-synchronous CA. An algorithm for constructing a block-synchronous approximation is given and approximation error is assessed. Experimental results are presented which show the approximation error to be admissible for probabilistic algorithms, and speedup of parallel implementation quite acceptable.

References

1. Neizvestny,I.G., Shwartz, N.L., Yanovitskaya, Z.Sh., and Zverev A.V. 3D-model of epitaxial growth on porous {111} and {100} Si surfaces. *Computer Physics Communications,* vol.147, pp.272-275, 2002.
2. Ziff, R.M., Gulari, E., Bershad Y. Kinetic phase transitions in irreversible surface-reaction model. *Physical Review Letters*, vol.56, pp.2553-2558, 1986.
3. Choppard B., Droz M. Cellular automata approach to nonequilibrium phase transition in a surface reaction model; static and and dynamic propereties. *Journ.of Physics. A. Mathenatical and General*, vol.21, pp.205-211, 1988.
4. Elokhin V.I., Latkin E.I., MatveevA.V., and Gorodetskii V.V. Application of Statistical Lattice Models to the Analysis of Oscillatory and Autowave Processes on the Reaction of Carbon Monoxide Oxidation over Platinum and Palladium Surfaces.*Kinetics and Catalysis,* vol.44, N5, pp.672-700, 2003.
5. Makeev A.G. Coarse bifurcation analysis of kinetic Monte Carlo simulations: a lattice-gas model with lateral interactions. *Journ of chemical physics*, vol 117, N18, pp.8229-8240, 2002.
6. Nedea S.V., Lukkien J.J., Jansen A.P.J., and Hilbers P.A.J. Methods for parallel simulations of surface reactions. *arXiv:physics/0209017*, vol.1, N4, pp.1-8, 2002.
7. Wolfram S., A New Kind of Science. - Wolfram Media Inc., Champain, Ill., USA. 2002.
8. Achasova S., Bandman O., Markova V., Piskunov S. Parallel Substitution Algorithm. Theory and Application. - World Scientific, Singapore, 1994.

Regional Analysis of a Class of Cellular Automata Models

A. Bel Fekih[1] and A. El Jai[2]

[1] Mathematical Modeling and Control.
Faculty of Sciences and Technics. Tanger, Morocco
abelfekih@menara.ma
[2] MEPS - Systems Theory Laboratory.
University of Perpignan. France
aej@univ-perp.fr

Abstract. Regional analysis in systems theory has been studied for systems described by partial differential equations [6]. In this paper, we propose an approach based on Cellular Automata (CA) models. The approach is considered for real-valued additive CA. The problem of regional controllability is explored and connected with actuators structures. The so-called rank condition is established. Dual results for the observability of additive CA are developed.

Keywords: Additive real-valued Cellular Automata, Regional controllability, Regional Observability, Actuators, Sensors.

1 Introduction

Amongst the most important problems in systems analysis are the controllability and the observability ones. These concepts have been extensively developed, see [2] and the references therein. For controllability issues, one normally considers a control system on a time interval $[0, T]$ and asks whether some particular target state z_d is reachable. On other hand the observability consists in the state reconstruction based on the knowledge of the system dynamics together with an output function [3]. An extension which is very important in practical applications is that of regional controllability and observability. Regional analysis of DPS is based on the following principle. We consider a given region (sometimes said subregion) ω, as a subdomain of Ω to which we pay a particular attention. That is to say instead of studying an objective problem on the whole Ω, we can focus only on the subregion ω (with the possibility to take $\omega = \Omega$). This allows the generalization of the controllability and different other concepts in systems analysis.

Cellular automata are increasingly being used for representing geographical processes including many applications ranging from urban to environmental systems. They have also been recognized for a long time as an effective way of simulating biological phenomena. They are discrete dynamic systems consisting of similar elements which directly interact with their nearest neighbors. Even if

S. El Yacoubi, B. Chopard, and S. Bandini (Eds.): ACRI 2006, LNCS 4173, pp. 48–57, 2006.

the interaction is based on simple local rules, the resulting structures from the CA evolution may be extremely complex. The aim of this paper is to consider additive cellular automata in the context of systems theory. We propose CA as an alternative modeling approach in the sense that they may be viewed from a mathematical point of view, as discrete counterpart to PDEs, for exploring regional controllability and observability. In [4] an appropriate way to introduce control and observation in CA to make them more useful in systems theory is given. In this paper we consider a simplified approach in the case of real-valued additive cellular automata to explore regional controllability and observability.

2   Considered Systems

2.1   Additive Real-Valued CA Models

In this paper we consider a class of cellular automata models evolving in a space domain $D \subseteq \mathbb{R}^r$ assumed to be unbounded with respect to all the variables.
- The space domain D is represented by a regular lattice $\mathcal{L}$. Each site or cell is denoted c_i with $i = (i_1, i_2, \ldots, i_r) \in \Omega \subseteq \mathbb{Z}^r$.
- The state of the system is updated using a set of rules that take into account the values of the site and its neighboring cells given by $\{c_{i+k} , k \in L\}$, where L is a part of Ω satisfying $-L \subseteq L$ and such that $0 \in L$.

The CA evolves over a succession of time steps and the values of all the sites in the lattice are updated synchronously in time with $t = 0, 1, \ldots, T - 1, T$.
- At time t, the neighborhood of the cell c_i is $V_i = i + L$, assuming that $L = V_0$.
- We denote z_i^t the state of the cell c_i at time t, where the state values range in the state space $\mathcal{E} = \mathbb{R}$. We denote z_i^0 the initial state of the cell c_i (i.e. at time $t = 0$).
- When the system is autonomous, i.e. without control, we assume that the state of the cell c_i is given by the additive transition rule

$$z_i^{t+1} = \sum_{k \in L} \beta_k z_{i+k}^t \quad , \quad i \in \Omega \tag{1}$$

where the coefficients (β_k) are real positive and satisfy the following conservation law

$$\sum_{k \in L} \beta_k = 1 \tag{2}$$

which leads to $\sum_{i \in \Omega} z_i^t = \sum_{i \in \Omega} z_i^0$. When the system is excited by a control ξ_i^t then the state is given by

$$z_i^{t+1} = \sum_{k \in L} \beta_k z_{i+k}^t + \xi_i^t \quad , \quad i \in \Omega , \quad t = 0, 1, 2, \cdots \tag{3}$$

Remark 1

1. In the above hypothesis, we assume that Ω is stable for the addition of $\mathbb{Z}^r$ and $0 \in \Omega$.
2. The hypothesis $V_i = i + L$ means that the neighborhoods of the cell c_i are deduced from each other by translation.
3. The condition $-L \subseteq L$ is a symmetry hypothesis. In the case where the neighborhood are not symmetric one can extend them by symmetry considering $\beta_k = 0$ if $k \notin L$.

2.2   State Explicit Form

We are going to establish a direct calculation rule. For that purpose, we introduce the following generalizing definition.

Definition 1. *Consider a cell c_i. A neighborhood of order t of c_i is the set V_i^t given by*

$$V_i^0 = \{i\}, \quad V_i^1 = V_i, \quad V_i^{t+1} = \bigcup_{j \in V_i^t} V_j$$

Thus we can deduce easily from the above definition that $V_i^{t+1} = V_i^t + L$ and $V_i^t = i + L_t$ for all $t \in \mathbb{N}$ while $L_t = V_0^t$ is the neighborhood of order t of the origin cell 0 defined by

$$L_0 = \{0\}, \quad L_1 = L, \quad L_{t+1} = L_t + L, \quad t = 0, 1, 2, \dots$$

The recursive calculation rule of the state may be generalized in the following result.

Proposition 1. *The state of a cell given by (3) may be calculated using the initial state of the neighboring cells by*

$$z_i^t = \sum_{\ell \in L_t} C_\ell^t z_{i+\ell}^0 + \sum_{s=0}^{t-1} \sum_{\ell \in L_{t-1-s}} C_\ell^{t-1-s} \xi_{i+\ell}^s, \quad t \geq 1 \tag{4}$$

where the coefficients $C_k^t \in \mathbb{R}_+$, assumed to be equal to 0 for $k \notin L_t$, are given by the recursive formula

$$\begin{cases} C_k^0 = \delta_{0k} & \text{if } k \in \Omega \\ \\ C_k^{t+1} = \sum_{\ell \in L} \beta_\ell C_{k-\ell}^t & \text{if } k \in L_{t+1} \ t = 0, 1, 2, \cdots \end{cases}$$

Remark 2

1. If the coefficients depend on time and on the cell c_i, then we have

$$z_i^{t+1} = \sum_{k \in L} \beta_k^{i,t} z_{i+k}^t + \xi_i^t$$

and the state of the system may be expressed by

$$z_i^t = \sum_{k \in L_t} C_k^{i,t} z_{i+k}^0 + \sum_{s=0}^{t-1} \sum_{\ell \in L_{t-1-s}} C_\ell^{i,t-1-s} \xi_{i+\ell}^s, \quad i \in \Omega, \quad t = 0, 1, 2, \cdots$$

where the coefficients $C_k^{i,t}$ ($= 0$ for $k \notin L_t$) may be calculated, for all $i \in \Omega$, by the relations

$$\begin{cases} C_k^{i,0} = \delta_{0k} & \text{if } k \in \Omega \\ C_k^{i,t+1} = \sum_{\ell \in L} \beta_\ell^{i,t} C_{k-\ell}^{i+\ell,t} & \text{if } k \in L_{t+1} \quad t = 0, 1, 2, \cdots \end{cases}$$

2. The coefficients C_k^t can be expressed using the coefficients β_ℓ by

$$C_k^t = \sum_{1 \le j \le t} \sum_{\ell_j \in L} \delta \left(k, \sum_{i=1}^t \ell_i \right) \prod_{i=1}^t \beta_{\ell_i}$$

where $\delta(i, j) = 1$ for $i = j$ and $\delta(i, j) = 0$ otherwise.

3. The coefficients C_k^t satisfy the same conservation law (2) than the (β_k)'s, i.e. $\sum_k C_k^t = 1, \quad t = 0, 1, 2, \cdots$

3   Regional Controllability of Additive CA

3.1   The Controlled System

We assume now that the system is excited on a subregion of the lattice denoted by $\mathcal{L}_1$ with $\mathcal{L}_1 \subset \mathcal{L}$ and indexed in $\Omega_1 \subset \Omega$, by a control $u^t \in U \subseteq \mathbb{R}$. Each cell c_j of Ω_1 is excited, at time t, by a term $u^t g_j$ where the function

$$g : j \in \Omega_1 \to g_j \in \mathbb{R}_+^*$$

defines the space distribution of the control on Ω_1. The cells which are not in Ω_1 are not excited by the control but they also receive the effect of the control via the neighboring cells.

The state of a cell c_i can be calculated by the same rule but some of the cells are augmented by the control effect. For a cell c_i which neighborhood is V_i, two cases may be considered.

Case 1: Consider the case where $\Omega_1 \cap V_i = \emptyset$, then no neighboring cell is excited by the control, and we have

$$z_i^{t+1} = \sum_{\ell \in L} \beta_\ell z_{i+\ell}^t$$

Case 2: In the case where $\Omega_1 \cap V_i \neq \emptyset$, then the cells which are in $\Omega_1 \cap V_i$ are excited (those which are in $\Omega_1^c \cap V_i$ are not). We obtain

$$z_i^{t+1} = \sum_{i+\ell \in \Omega_1 \cap V_i} \beta_\ell \left(z_{i+\ell}^t + g_{i+\ell} u^t \right) + \sum_{i+\ell \notin \Omega_1 \cap V_i} \beta_\ell z_{i+\ell}^t$$

With the convention that $\sum_{\emptyset}(.) = 0$, the last formula may generalize the two cases and written in the form

$$z_i^{t+1} = \sum_{i+\ell \in \Omega_1 \cap V_i} \beta_\ell z_{i+\ell}^t + \sum_{i+\ell \notin \Omega_1 \cap V_i} \beta_\ell z_{i+\ell}^t + u^t \sum_{i+\ell \in \Omega_1 \cap V_i} \beta_\ell g_{i+\ell}$$

$$= \sum_{\ell \in L} \beta_\ell z_{i+\ell}^t + b_i u^t$$

where $b_i = \sum_{i+\ell \in \Omega_1 \cap V_i} \beta_\ell g_{i+\ell}$. In the more general case where p controls u_k^t are applied on p disjoint zones Ω_k we obtain the general formula

$$z_i^{t+1} = \sum_{\ell \in L} \beta_\ell z_{i+\ell}^t + \sum_{k=1}^{p} b_i^k u_k^t \tag{5}$$

with

$$b_i^k = \sum_{i+\ell \in \Omega_k \cap V_i} \beta_\ell g_{i+\ell}^k \tag{6}$$

The initial states z_i^0, $i \in \Omega$, are assumed to be given.

Example 1. Consider the system evolving in $\Omega = \mathbb{Z}$ where the neighborhoods are given by $V_i = \{i-1, i, i+1\}$ and the following state transition rules

$$z_i^{t+1} = \frac{1}{7} \left(2z_{i-1}^t + 3z_i^t + 2z_{i+1}^t \right) = \sum_{\ell=-1}^{1} \beta_\ell z_{i+\ell}^t \tag{7}$$

with $\beta_0 = \frac{3}{7}$, $\beta_1 = \beta_{-1} = \frac{2}{7}$. We excited this system in $\Omega_1 = \{5\}$ (pointwise action) by the control $u^t \in \mathbb{R}$ with $g_5 = 1$ we obtain the coefficient

$$b_i = \sum_{\ell=-1}^{1} \beta_\ell g_{i+\ell} = \frac{2}{7}\delta_{i4} + \frac{3}{7}\delta_{i5} + \frac{2}{7}\delta_{i6}$$

and the following state transition rules of controlled system is

$$z_i^{t+1} = \begin{cases} \frac{1}{7} \left(2z_{i-1}^t + 3z_i^t + 2z_{i+1}^t \right) + \frac{2}{7}u^t & \text{if } i = 4 \text{ or } i = 6 \\ \frac{1}{7} \left(2z_{i-1}^t + 3z_i^t + 2z_{i+1}^t \right) + \frac{3}{7}u^t & \text{if } i = 5 \\ \frac{1}{7} \left(2z_{i-1}^t + 3z_i^t + 2z_{i+1}^t \right) & \text{otherwise} \end{cases}$$

3.2   Actuators

Consider again the controlled system described by (5) with z_i^0 given in $\mathbb{R}$, are equal to 0 except in a finite number of cells. Considering the controls $u_k^t \in \mathbb{R}$, the state of the cell c_i denoted by $z_i^t(u)$ satisfies

$$z_i^{t+1}(u) = \sum_{\ell \in L} \beta_\ell z_{i+\ell}^t(u) + \sum_{k=1}^p b_i^k u_k^t \quad , \quad i \in \Omega, \quad t = 0, 1, \ldots, T-1$$

The controls are $(u_k^t)_{t,k}$ and they are located in a control space

$$\mathcal{U} = \left\{ u = (u_k^t)_{t,k} \ / \ u_k^t \in \mathbb{R} \ ; \ 0 \le t \le T-1, \ 1 \le k \le p \right\} \simeq \mathbb{R}^{pT}$$

We introduce the notion of actuator as stated in [2] for systems governed by partial differential equations.

Definition 2
1. *An actuator is a couple (Ω_1, g) where $\Omega_1 \subset \Omega$ is a sub-lattice of connected cells and $g : j \in \Omega_1 \to g_j \in \mathbb{R}_+^*$.*
2. *Ω_1 is the actuator support and g is the space distribution of the actuator.*
3. *The actuator is said to be pointwise if its support Ω_1 is reduced to one cell. Otherwise the actuator is said to be a zone actuator.*

When the system is excited on p sub-domains Ω_k of Ω, each cell c_j is affected by the term $g_j u_k^t$. The previous definition is generalized as follows.

Definition 3
1. *The sequence of couples $\left\{ (\Omega_k, g^k) \ ; \ k = 1, 2, \ldots, p \right\}$ is said to be a sequence of actuators if each (Ω_k, g^k) is an actuator and $\Omega_k \cap \Omega_\ell = \emptyset$ for $k \ne \ell$.*
2. *The sequence of actuators is pointwise (respectively zone) if each actuator (Ω_k, g^k) is of pointwise (respectively zone) type.*

3.3   Regionally Controllable CA

Consider a given nonempty sub-domain (region) $\omega \subseteq \Omega$ and denote by $|\omega|$ the number of celles of ω. In this section we consider the statement of regional controllability of systems modeled by cellular automata. From the previous section, the state of the controlled system (on p zones Ω_k) may be calculated directly using the initial conditions by the formula

$$z_i^t(u) = \sum_{\ell \in L_t} C_\ell^t z_{i+\ell}^0 + \sum_{k=1}^p \sum_{s=0}^{t-1} \sum_{\ell \in L_{t-1-s}} C_\ell^{t-1-s} u_k^s b_{i+\ell}^k \quad , \quad t = 0, 1, 2, \ldots \quad (8)$$

Definition 4
1. *The system (5) is said to be regionally controllable on ω (or ω-controllable) if*

$$\forall (\xi_i)_{i \in \omega} \subseteq \mathbb{R}, \ \forall (z_i^0)_{i \in \Omega} \subseteq \mathbb{R}, \ \exists u \in U \ / \ z_i^T(u) = \xi_i, \ \forall i \in \omega \quad (9)$$

2. *If the system is ω-controllable, then the sequence of actuators is said to be ω-strategic.*

The relation $z_i^T(u) = \xi_i$, $\forall i \in \omega$ is equivalent to

$$\sum_{k=1}^{p} \sum_{s=0}^{T-1} \left(\sum_{\ell \in L_{T-1-s}} C_\ell^{T-1-s} b_{i+\ell}^k \right) u_k^s = \xi_i - \sum_{\ell \in L_T} C_\ell^T z_{i+\ell}^0$$

Assume that the set ω is ordered by considering the one-to-one mapping σ : $\{1, 2, \ldots, |\omega|\} \subseteq \mathbb{N} \to \omega$ and denote $\eta_i = \xi_i - \sum_{\ell \in L_T} C_\ell^T z_{i+\ell}^0$, thus the relation (9) becomes

$$\sum_{k=1}^{p} \sum_{s=0}^{T-1} \left(\sum_{\ell \in L_{T-1-s}} C_\ell^{T-1-s} b_{\sigma(j)+\ell}^k \right) u_k^s = \eta_{\sigma(j)}, \quad j = 1, \ldots, |\omega|$$

or equivalently $\sum_{k=1}^{p} G_k u_k = \eta$ where

$$G_k = \left(\sum_{\ell \in L_{T-1-s}} C_\ell^{T-1-s} b_{\sigma(j)+\ell}^k \right)_{j,s} \in \mathcal{M}_{|\omega|,T}(\mathbb{R})$$

$$\eta = \begin{pmatrix} \eta_1 \\ \vdots \\ \eta_{|\omega|} \end{pmatrix} \in \mathbb{R}^{|\omega|}, \quad u_k = \begin{pmatrix} u_k^0 \\ \vdots \\ u_k^{T-1} \end{pmatrix} \in \mathbb{R}^T$$

The space $\mathcal{M}_{|\omega|,T}(\mathbb{R})$ is the set of all matrixes with $|\omega|$ rows and T columns. Let us denote

$$u = \begin{pmatrix} u_1 \\ \vdots \\ u_p \end{pmatrix} \in \mathbb{R}^{pT}, \quad G = [G_1, \ldots, G_p] \in \mathcal{M}_{|\omega|,pT}(\mathbb{R})$$

thus the system is ω−controllable if and only if

$$\forall \eta \in \mathbb{R}^{|\omega|} \ \exists \, u \in \mathbb{R}^{pT} \ \text{such that} \ G \, u = \eta$$

which is equivalent to the surjectivity of the mapping $G : \mathbb{R}^{pT} \to \mathbb{R}^{|\omega|}$. This is stated in the following rank condition theorem which is a usual characterization for the controllability in systems theory, both for lumped systems than distributed ones and also in regional analysis [1].

Theorem 1. *Rank condition.*
The system (5) is ω-controllable if and only if

$$rank \, G = |\omega| \tag{10}$$

And we have the immediate following corollary.

Corollary 1. *The system (5) is not ω-controllable if ω is not finite or if $T < \dfrac{|\omega|}{p}$.*

The proof results from the fact that, in these cases, we have $|\omega| = rankG \le \min(|\omega|, pT) \le pT$.

Remark 3

1. In the case of one actuator, one needs the controllability time T such that $T \ge |\omega|$. Whilst in the case of p actuators $p \ge 2$ the ω-controllability can be achieved at time T such that

$$T \ge \frac{|\omega|}{p} \tag{11}$$

2. Notice that the results needs the region ω to be finite even if the actuators support are unbounded.

Corollary 2. *Assume now that the region to be controlled is composed by one cell $c \in \Omega$ or $\omega = \{c\}$, then $|\omega| = 1$. The system (5) is $\{c\}$-controllable if and only if*

$$\left(\bigcup_{k=1}^{p} \Omega_k\right) \cap \left(\bigcup_{1 \le t \le T} W_c^t\right) \ne \emptyset \tag{12}$$

where the sets $W_i^t \subseteq V_i^t$ are given by

$$W_i^t = \{j \ \text{ such that } \ C_{j-i}^t > 0\} \tag{13}$$

4 Regional Observability of Real-Valued Additive CA

Consider again the CA model with the transition rule (1)

$$z_i^{t+1} = \sum_{\ell \in L} \beta_\ell z_{i+\ell}^t \quad , \quad i \in \Omega, \quad t = 0, 1, \ldots, T-1 \tag{14}$$

The initial state z_i^0 is given in $\mathbb{R}$, and supposed to be unknown on a given nonempty finite region $\omega \subseteq \Omega$ and equal to zero out of ω. Consider an output given by the relation

$$y_k^t = \sum_{j \in \Omega_k} h_j^k z_j^t \quad , \quad t = 0, 1, \ldots, T-1, \quad k = 1, \ldots, q \tag{15}$$

The output function gives partial measurements of the state over a subdomain Ω_k.

As for the controllability concept, we consider the observability as stated in the case of continuous systems. We also consider the sensors approach as introduced in [2].

Definition 5

1. A sensor is a couple (Ω_1, h) where $\Omega_1 \subseteq \Omega$ is a set of connected cells and $h : j \in \Omega_1 \rightarrow h_j \in \mathbb{R}_+^*$.
Ω_1 is the support of the sensor and h is the spatial distribution of the sensor.
2. The sensor is said to be pointwise if Ω_1 is reduced to one cell. In the other cases the sensor is said to be a zone sensor.

When the observation is made via q disjoint locations Ω_k of Ω the previous definition is naturally extended. *A sequence of couples $\{(\Omega_k, h^k) \; ; \; k = 1, 2, \ldots, q\}$ is a sequence of sensors if $\Omega_k \cap \Omega_\ell = \emptyset$ for all $k \neq \ell$ and, for all k, (Ω_k, h^k) is a sensor as defined in 5.*

In the case of q sensors, the output is given by the vector function $\{y_k^t\}_{1 \leq k \leq q}$, on the time interval $0, 1, \ldots, T - 1$. Now we consider the problem of regional observability, i.e. the problem of determination of the system state on the cells of a given region ω, based on the measurements given in (15).

Definition 6

1. The system (14) together with the output (15) is said to be observable on the region ω (or ω-observable) if the output $\{y_k^t\}_{1 \leq k \leq q}$ allow a unique reconstruction of the initial states of the cells of ω.
2. When the system is ω-observable, the sequence of sensors is said to be ω-strategic.

Taking into account the system dynamics, the above definition is equivalent to

$$\left[y_k^t = 0 \, , \, t = 0, 1, \cdots, T - 1, \, k = 1, \ldots, q \right] \Longrightarrow \left(z_i^0 = 0, \, \forall i \in \omega \right) \qquad (16)$$

Using (4) and extending by 0 the C_ℓ^t and the h_i^t to all Ω, we obtain

$$y_k^t = \sum_{j \in \Omega_k} h_i^k z_i^t = \sum_{i \in \Omega} h_i^k \left(\sum_{\ell \in \Omega} C_\ell^t z_{i+\ell}^0 \right) = \sum_{m \in \Omega} \left(\sum_{i \in \Omega} h_i^k C_{m-i}^t \right) z_m^0$$

$$= \sum_{j=1}^{|\omega|} \left(\sum_{i \in \Omega_k} h_i^k C_{\sigma(j)-i}^t \right) z_{\sigma(j)}^0$$

where $\sigma : \{1, \ldots, |\omega|\} \rightarrow \omega$ is a one-to-one mapping defined previously. Additionally the relations may be rewritten in the form

$$H_k z^0 = y_k \, , \quad k = 1, \ldots, q$$

with

$$H_k = \left(\sum_{i \in \Omega_k} h_i^k C_{\sigma(j)-i}^t \right)_{t,j} \in \mathcal{M}_{T, |\omega|}(\mathbb{R})$$

$$y_k = \begin{pmatrix} y_k^0 \\ \vdots \\ y_k^{T-1} \end{pmatrix} \in \mathbb{R}^T$$

$$z^0 = \begin{pmatrix} z_{\sigma(1)}^0 \\ \vdots \\ z_{\sigma(|\omega|)}^0 \end{pmatrix} \in \mathbb{R}^{|\omega|} \, ;$$

which can be put in the reduced form $H z^0 = y$ where

$$H = \begin{bmatrix} H_1 \\ \vdots \\ H_q \end{bmatrix} \in M_{qT,|\omega|}(\mathbb{R}), \quad y = \begin{pmatrix} y_1 \\ \vdots \\ y_q \end{pmatrix} \in \mathbb{R}^{qT}$$

The matrix H is of order $(qT, |\omega|)$ and the system is ω-observable if and only if H is injective. Using the identity $\dim(\ker H) + rankH = |\omega|$ we obtain the result.

Theorem 2. *Rank condition.*
The system (14) together with the output (15) is ω-observable if and only if the matrix H is such that

$$rank\ H = |\omega| \tag{17}$$

Corollary 3. *The system (14) together with the output (15) can not be ω-observable on a region ω during the time T if ω is not finite or if $T < \dfrac{|\omega|}{q}$.*

The proof results from the previous theorem because in this case $|\omega| = rankG \leq \min(qT, |\omega|) \leq qT$.

Remark 4. In the case of one sensor, we need the time observation $T \geq |\omega|$, whilst in the case of $q \geq 2$ sensors the observation time must satisfy $T \geq \dfrac{|\omega|}{q}$ and then can be smaller.

Corollary 4. *If we assume that the regional observation is to be done on the region having one given cell $c \in \Omega$, in this case we have $|\omega| = |\{c\}| = 1$. The system (14) augmented with the output (15) is $\{c\}$-observable if and only if*

$$c \in \bigcup_{t=0}^{T-1} \bigcup_{k=1}^{q} \bigcup_{i \in \Omega_k} W_i^t \tag{18}$$

where the sets W_i^t are defined in (13).

References

1. L. Afifi, A. El Jai and E. Zerrik, *Regional approach of dynamical systems*, To appear, 2006.
2. A. El Jai and A. J. Pritchard, *Sensors and controls in the analysis of distributed systems*, J. Wiley, Texts in Applied Mathematics Series, 1988.
3. A. El Jai, E. Zerrik and M. Amouroux. *Regional observability of distributed systems*. Int. J. of System Science. Vol 25, $N°2$, pp 301-313. 1994.
4. S. El Yacoubi, A. El Jai and N. Ammor. *Regional controllability with cellular automata models*, Lecture Notes in Computer Sciences, Springer, LNCS2493, pp 367-375, 2002.
5. S. El Yacoubi & A. El Jaï, *Notes on control and observation in cellular automata models*, WSEAS Transactions on Computers, 2 (2003) 1086-1092.
6. E. Zerrik, A. El Jai and M. Simon. *Regional observability of a thermal process*. IEEE Trans. on Automatic Control. Vol. 40, $N°3$, pp 518-521. 1995.

A Parallel Implementation of the Cellular Potts Model for Simulation of Cell-Based Morphogenesis

Nan Chen[1], James A. Glazier[2], and Mark S. Alber[1]

[1] Department of Mathematics and Center for the Study of Biocomplexity,
University of Notre Dame, Notre Dame, IN 46556, USA
{nchen1, malber}@nd.edu
[2] Department of Physics and Biocomplexity Institute, 727 East Third Street, Swain Hall West
159, Indiana University, Bloomington, IN 47405, USA
glazier@indiana.edu

Abstract. Glazier and Graner's Cellular Potts Model (*CPM*) has found use in a wide variety of biological simulations. However, most current CPM implementations use a sequential modified Metropolis algorithm which restricts the size of simulations. In this paper we present a parallel CPM algorithm for simulations of morphogenesis, which includes cell-cell adhesion, haptotaxis and cell division. The algorithm uses appropriate data structures and checkerboard subgrids for parallelization. Communication and updating algorithms synchronize properties of cells simulated on different computer nodes. We benchmark our algorithm by simulating cell sorting and chondrogenic condensation.

Keywords: Computational biology, morphogenesis, parallel algorithms, Cellular Potts Model, multiscale models, pattern formation.

1 Introduction

Simulations of complex biological phenomena like development, wound healing and tumor growth, collectively known as *morphogenesis*, must handle a wide variety of biological agents, mechanisms and interactions at multiple length scales.

Glazier and Graner's Cellular Potts Model (*CPM*) [1] has become a common technique for morphogenesis simulations because it easily adapts to describe cell differentiation, growth, death, shape changes and migration and the secretion and absorption of extracellular materials. CPM simulations treat many biological and non-biological phenomena, including sorting due to cell-cell adhesion, chicken limb bud growth, Dictyostelium discoideum morphogenesis, liquid drainage in fluid foams and foam rheology [2-6].

The CPM approach to modeling makes several choices about how to describe cells and their behaviors and interactions. First, it describes cells as spatially extended but internally structureless objects with complex shapes. Second, it describes most cell behaviors and interactions in terms of effective energies and elastic constraints. These first two choices are the core of the CPM approach. Third, it assumes perfect

S. El Yacoubi, B. Chopard, and S. Bandini (Eds.): ACRI 2006, LNCS 4173, pp. 58–67, 2006.

damping and quasi-thermal fluctuations, which together cause the configuration and properties of the cells to evolve continuously to minimize the effective energy, with realistic kinetics. Fourth, it discretizes the cells and associated fields onto a lattice. Finally, the classic implementation of the CPM employs a modified Metropolis Monte-Carlo algorithm which chooses update sites randomly and accepts them with a Metropolis-Boltzmann probability.

Since these choices are relatively independent from each other, we can modify some of them to optimize our computation without discarding our basic modeling philosophy. For example, because the acceptance probabilities for updates can be small ($10^{-4} - 10^{-6}$) the classic lattice-based Metropolis algorithm may run slower than continuum off-lattice implementations. Since the typical discretization scale is 2-5 microns per lattice site, CPM simulations of large tissue volumes require large amounts of computer memory. Current practical single-processor sequential simulations can handle about 10^5 cells. However, a full model of the morphogenesis of a complete organ or an entire embryo would require the simulation of $10^6 - 10^8$ cells, or between 10 – 1000 processor nodes.

Clearly, we need a parallel algorithm which implements the CPM and runs on the Beowulf or High Performance Computing Clusters (*HPCC*) [7] available in most universities. Wright *et al.* [11] implemented a parallel version of the original Potts model of grain growth. In this model the effective energy consists only of local grain boundary interactions, so a change of a single pixel changes only the energies of its neighbors.

Gusatto *et al.*'s recent random-walker (*RW*) implementation of the CPM [15] ran approximately six times faster than the standard algorithm on a single processor. In addition, their algorithm parallelizes fairly easily, though a two processor implementation ran only about 15% faster than a one processor version. The standard CPM Metropolis algorithm always rejects spin flips inside a cell, which wastes much calculation time. The RW approach attempts flips only at cell boundaries, reducing the rejection rate and increasing speed. However, the parallel scheme for this algorithm requires shared memory with all processors sharing the same lattice sites, limiting the total lattice size to the memory size of a single computer. Adapting the RW algorithm to accommodate large scale simulations on distributed memory clusters will still require development of an appropriate spatial decomposition algorithm.

The main difficulty in all forms of CPM parallelization is that the effective energy is non-local. The effective energy terms for cell-cell adhesion, haptotaxis and chemotaxis are local, but the constraint energy terms, *e.g.* for cell volume and surface area, have an interaction range of the diameter of a cell. Changing one lattice site changes the volume of two cells and hence the energy associated with all pixels in both cells. For example, if a cell's pixels are divided between the subdomains located on two nodes and the nodes attempt updates affecting the cell simultaneously, without communication, one node has stale information about the state of the cell. If we use a simple block parallelization, where each processor calculates a predefined rectangular subdomain of the full lattice, non-locality greatly increases the frequency of interprocessor communication for synchronization and, because of communication latency, the time each processor spends waiting rather than calculating. To solve this problem, we use an improved data structure to describe cells and decompose the subdomain assigned to each node into smaller subgrids chosen so that corresponding subgrids on different nodes do not interact, a method known as a *Checkerboard Algorithm*. These algorithms are based on those Barkema and his collaborators developed for the Ising model, see, *e.g.* [9]. These methods allow successful parallel implementation of the CPM using MPI [9, 10].

On the other hand, an intrinsic inconvenience of the classical CPM ameliorates one difficulty which Ising model parallelization faces. In MPI parallelization, the larger the number of computations per pixel update, the smaller the ratio of message passing to computation, which results in less latency delay and greater efficiency. In the Ising model, the computational burden per pixel update is small (at most a few floating point operations), which increases the ratio of message passing to computation in a naive partition. However, in the CPM, the ratio of failed update attempts to accepted updates is very large (10^4 or more in some simulations). Only accepted updates change the lattice configuration and potentially stale information in neighboring nodes. The large effective number of computations per update reduces the burden of message passing. However, because we can construct pathological situations which have a high acceptance rate, we need to be careful to check that such situations do not occur in practice.

2 The Glazier-Graner Cellular Potts Model

Glazier and Graner's CPM generalizes the Ising model from statistical mechanics, and shares its core idea of modeling dynamics based on energy minimization under imposed fluctuations. The CPM uses a lattice to describe cells. We associate an integer index to each lattice site (pixel) to identify the space a cell occupies at any instant. The value of the index at a pixel (i, j, k) is l if the site lies in cell l. Domains (*i.e.* collection of pixels with the same index) represent cells. Thus, we treat a cell as a set of discrete subcomponents that can rearrange to produce cell motion and shape changes. As long as we can describe a process in terms of a real or effective potential energy, we can include it in the CPM framework by adding it to the effective energy. The CPM models chemotaxis and haptotaxis by adding a chemical potential energy, cell growth by changing target volumes of cells and cell division by a specific reassignment of pixels. If a proposed change in lattice configuration (*i.e.* a change in the index number associated with a pixel) changes the effective energy by ΔE, we accept the change with probability:

$$P(\Delta E) = 1, \Delta E \leq 0; \qquad P(\Delta E) = e^{-\Delta E / T}, \Delta E > 0 \qquad (1)$$

where T is the *effective temperature* of the simulation in units of energy.

A typical CPM effective energy might contain terms for adhesion, a cell volume constraint and chemotaxis:

$$E = E_{Adhesion} + E_{Volume} + E_{Chemical} \qquad (2)$$

We discuss each of these terms below.

Cell–cell adhesion energy: In Equation 2, $E_{Adhesion}$ phenomenologically describes the net adhesion/repulsion between two cell membranes. It is the product of the binding energy per unit area, $J_{\tau(\sigma)\tau'(\sigma')}$ and the area of interaction of the two cells. $J_{\tau(\sigma)\tau'(\sigma')}$ depends on the specific properties of the interface between the interacting cells:

$$E_{Adhesion} = \sum_{(i,j,k)(i',j',k')} \{J_{\tau(\sigma)\tau'(\sigma')}[1-\delta(\sigma(i,j,k),\sigma'(i',j',k'))]\} \tag{3}$$

where the *Kronecker delta*, $\delta(\sigma,\sigma')=0$ if $\sigma \neq \sigma'$ and $\delta(\sigma,\sigma')=1$ if $\sigma=\sigma'$, ensures that only the surface sites between different cells contribute to the adhesion energy. Adhesive interactions act over a prescribed range around each pixel, usually up to fourth-nearest-neighbors.

<u>Cell size and shape fluctuations:</u> A cell of type τ has a prescribed *target volume* $v(\sigma,\tau)$ and *volume elasticity* λ, *target surface area* $s(\sigma,\tau)$, and *membrane elasticity* λ'. Cell volume and surface area change due to growth and division of cells. E_{Volume} exacts an energy penalty for deviations of the actual volume from the target volume and of the actual surface area from the target surface area:

$$E_{volume} = \sum_{all-cells} \lambda_\sigma (v(\sigma,\tau) - v_{target}(\sigma,\tau))^2 + \sum_{all-cells} \lambda'_\sigma (s(\sigma,\tau) - s_{target}(\sigma,\tau))^2 \tag{4}$$

<u>Chemotaxis and haptotaxis:</u> Cells can move up or down gradients of both diffusible chemical signals (*i.e.* chemotaxis) and insoluble extracellular matrix (*ECM*) molecules (*i.e.* haptotaxis). The energy terms for both chemotaxis and haptotaxis are local, though chemotaxis requires a standard parallel diffusion equation solver for the diffusing field:

$$E_{chemical} = \mu(\sigma)C(\vec{x}) \tag{5}$$

where $C(\vec{x})$ is the local concentration of a particular species of signaling molecule in extracellular space and $\mu(\sigma)$ is the effective chemical potential.

3   Data Structures and Algorithms

System Design Principles
Our parallel CPM algorithm tries to observe the following design principles: to implement the CPM model without systematic errors, to homogeneously and automatically distribute calculations and memory usage among all processor nodes, and to use Object-Oriented programming and MPI to improve portability.

Spatial Decomposition Algorithm
Our parallel algorithm homogeneously divides the lattice among all processor nodes, one subdomain per node. During a CPM simulation some cells cross boundaries between nodes. If nodes attempted to update pixels in these cells simultaneously, cell properties like volume and surface area would stale and energy evaluations would be

incorrect. We use a multi-subgrid checkerboard method to solve this problem: In each node we subdivide the subdomain into four subgrids indexed from 1-4. During the simulation, at all times we restrict calculations in each node to the same index subgrid. Since these subgrids are much larger than a cell diameter, we guarantee that no calculation in one node affects the calculations occurring simultaneously in any other node. In principle, we should switch subgrids after each pixel update to recover the classical algorithm. Since acceptance rates are low, on average, we should be able to make many update attempts before switching between subgrids. However, because acceptance is stochastic, we would need to switch subgrids at different times in different nodes, which is inconvenient. In practice we can update many times per subgrid (which means accepting that we will sometimes use stale positional information from the adjacent subgrids), because the subgrids are large, the acceptance rate small and the effects of stale positional information just outside the boundaries fairly weak. We use a random switching sequence (the switching sequence each time is different and random, for example, 1234, 2341, 4123, 3124 ...) to switch between subgrids frequently enough to make the effect of stale positional information negligible compared to the stochastic fluctuations intrinsic to Monte Carlo methods. Fig. 1 illustrates the algorithm.

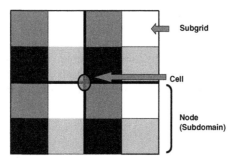

Fig. 1. Spatial decomposition: Each computer node hosts a subdomain which has four subgrids. At any time, each node performs calculations on only one subgrid. At all times, all nodes work on the subgrids with the same index number (indicated by the shading in the figure).

Data Structures

Two basic data structures of the parallel CPM algorithm are the cell and the pixel. During simulations, cells move between subdomains controlled by different nodes. Cells can also appear due to division and disappear due to cell death. In the classical single-processor algorithm, each cell has its own global cell index number. This data structure works efficiently on a single processor. In a parallel algorithm, this data structure for cells requires a Cell Index Number Manager to handle cell division, disappearance and handoff between nodes. For example, when a cell divides in a particular node, the node sends a request to the Manager to obtain a new cell index number and the Manager needs to notify all other nodes about the new cell. Instead, we assign each cell two numbers, a node ID and an index ID. The Node ID is the index number of the node in which the cell was generated and the index ID, like the old index number, is the index number of the cell generation sequence. Since cell IDs are now unique, each node can generate new cells without communicating with other nodes. Since cells may move between nodes, we dynamically allocate the memory for cell data structures on creation or appearance and release it when a cell moves out of the node or disappears. To optimize the usage of memory and speed data access, the index in each pixel is a pointer to the cell data structure.

Communication and Updating

In the spatial decomposition algorithm, when the program switches between different subgrids, the communication algorithm transfers two types of information: lattice configurations and cell volumes. In 2D, each subgrid needs to communicate with 8 neighboring subgrids (in 3D, 26 neighboring subgrids) and the communication algorithm sequentially sends and receives corresponding data according to the spatial organization of the subgrids. Sending and receiving could take place within a node, in which case the algorithm is just a memory copy. Fig. 2 illustrates the communication algorithm. After the communication, the program needs to dynamically update cell structures and buffers. The program also needs to check whether any cells cross between subgrids and implement the corresponding creation or destruction operations.

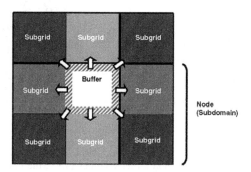

Fig. 2. Communication algorithm: After each change of subgrid, each node needs to transfer data to neighboring nodes. Lattice sites and associated variables (volume, surface area,...) located within the buffer area are transferred so neighboring subgrids contain correct cell configurations and characteristics.

4 Benchmark Results

The following benchmarks used the *Biocomplexity* cluster at the University of Notre Dame. The cluster consists of 64 dual nodes, each of which contains two AMD 64 bit Opteron 248 CPUs (clock frequency 2.2 GHz) and 4GB of RAM.

Cell Sorting

Steinberg's Differential Adhesion Hypothesis (*DAH*), states that cells adhere to each other with different strengths depending on their types [12]. Cell sorting results from random motions of the cells that allow them to minimize their adhesion energy, analogous to surface-tension-driven phase separation of immiscible liquids. If cells of the same type adhere more strongly, they gradually cluster together, with less adhesive cells surrounding the more adhesive ones. Based on the physics of the DAH, we model cell-sorting due to variations in cell-specific adhesivity at the cell level. Fig. 3 shows two simulation results for different adhesivities. All other parameters and the initial configurations of two simulations are the same. In simulation (a), cell type 1 has higher adhesion energy with itself (is less cohesive) than cell type 2 is with itself. The heterotypic (type 1-type 2) adhesivity is intermediate. During the simulation cells of type 2 cluster together and are surrounded by cells of type 1. In simulation (b), the adhesivity of cell type 1 with itself is the same as the adhesivity of cell type 2 with itself and greater than the heterotypic adhesivity. This energy hierarchy results in partial sorting.

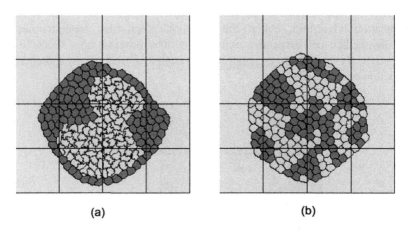

(a)   (b)

Fig. 3. Cell sorting simulation: Cell type 1 (Dark). Cell Type 2 (Light). The two simulations use the same initial cell configuration and target volumes (150), the only differences between (a) and (b) are the different adhesion constants. (a) Adhesion constants: $J_{1-1}=14$, $J_{2-2}=2$, $J_{1-2}=11$, $J_{1,2-ECM}=16$. (b) Adhesion constants: Adhesion energy $J_{1-1}=14$, $J_{2-2}=14$, $J_{1-2}=16$, $J_{1,2-ECM}=16$. The lines indicate the boundaries of the subdomains assigned to each node in a 16 node simulation.

In this simulation the lattice size is (288x288) and we distributed it in homogeneous subdomains of size 72x72 on a 16 node cluster. Each subgrid has 36x36 pixels.

Simulation of Chondrogenic Condensation

Fig. 4 shows the simulation result for a simulation of chondrogenic condensation (cartilage formation) in a chicken limb bud simulation run on 16 nodes with a total lattice size of 1200x1200 sites. In this simulation, we used an externally-supplied chemical pre-pattern (Activator concentration calculated from a pair of coupled reaction-diffusion equations) to control cell differentiation and condensation.

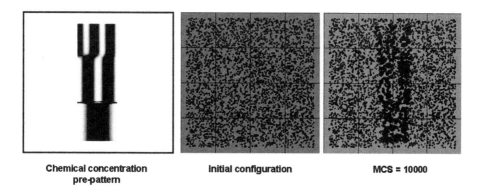

| Chemical concentration pre-pattern | Initial configuration | MCS = 10000 |

Fig. 4. Simulation of chondrogenic condensation during limb-bud formation. The lines indicate the boundaries of the subdomains assigned to each node for a 16 node simulation.

Efficiency of the Parallel Algorithm

We used the cell sorting (lattice size 288x288) and chondrogenesis simulations (lattice size1200x1200) to analyze the efficiency of our parallel algorithm. We ran both simulations on 4, 9 and 16 nodes with switching between subgrids after each Monte Carlo Step (defined as as many lattice update attempts as the number of lattice sites in the subgrid). This switching rate is relatively slow and results in significant effects from stale parameters. Table 1 summarizes the simulation running times. We define the relative efficiency, f:

$$f = \frac{T_4/4}{T_n/n} \tag{6}$$

where T_n is the running time of the simulation on n nodes. Since the smallest cluster on which our program runs uses 4 nodes, we use the running time on 4 nodes as a reference value. Fig. 5 plots the relative efficiency *vs.* the number of nodes. The cell sorting simulation is less efficient than the limb bud simulation because the small (288x288) lattice increases the ratio of communication time to computation time. The larger the subdomain size, the more efficient the calculation.

Table 1. Calculation time for different tests

Tests	Number of Nodes		
	4	9	16
Cell Sorting Simulation. Lattice size 288x288. 10,0000 MCS	3351 Sec.	2352 Sec.	1807 Sec.
Chondrogenesis Simulation. Lattice size 1200x1200. 10,000 MCS	4188 Sec.	2050 Sec.	1305 Sec.

The Gillespie stochastic simulation algorithm acceleration strategy based on "tau-leaping" is a powerful tool for large-scale stochastic biochemical simulations [13][14]. Instead of processing each reaction event, it moves forward in time by "leaps" that include many reaction events. Though it currently applies only to spatially homogeneous models, its extension to parallel simulation of inhomogeneous models would be valuable and could greatly increase the size of feasible CPM simulations.

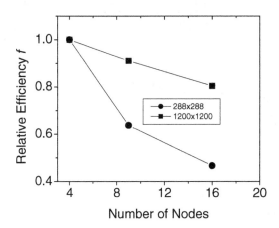

Fig. 5. Relative Efficiency as defined in equation 6 *vs.* the number of nodes used in the calculation. Bullets and solid squares correspond to cell sorting and chondrogenesis simulations respectively.

5 Discussion and Future Work

One issue with our algorithm is whether its results deviate from the classical algorithm significantly. Our switching algorithm works on subgrids one at a time. If the configuration is far from equilibrium, energies and configurations change rapidly and the dynamics of cells at subgrid boundaries could differ from those in the classical algorithm. For instance, if a cell's target volume is much larger than its current volume, the cell should grow rapidly and isotropically, while in our algorithm, a cell at a subgrid boundary might grow anisotropically. A higher switching frequency reduces this problem but also reduces the computational efficiency. In such case, smoothly changing the target value to the equilibrium one would solve this problem.

The parallel algorithm uses the standard CPM site selection algorithm which wastes time by selecting non boundary spins that cannot be updated. We plan to combine our parallel algorithm with the Random Walker algorithm [15] which selects only boundary spins to further improve our simulation efficiency.

6 Conclusions

Sequential versions of the CPM model are extensively used to simulate cell morphogenesis. However, large-scale morphogenesis simulations require a parallel implementation. In this paper, we have proposed a parallel CPM algorithm using appropriate data structures and checkerboard updating. The algorithm reproduces examples of cell sorting and limb bud formation and shows good scalability, which an improved site-selection algorithm like the RW algorithm should be able to improve further.

Acknowledgments. This work was partially supported by NSF Grant No. IBN-0083653 and NIH Grant No. 1R0-GM076692-01: Interagency Opportunities in Multiscale Modeling in Biomedical, Biological and Behavioral Systems NSF 04.6071. Simulations were performed on the Notre Dame Biocomplexity Cluster supported in part by NSF MRI Grant No. DBI-0420980.

References

1. Graner, F. and Glazier, J. A.: Simulation of biological cell sorting using a two dimensional extended Potts model. *Phys. Rev. Lett.* **69**, (1992) 2013–2016.
2. Chaturvedi, R., Huang C, Izaguirre, J. A., Newman, S. A., Glazier, J. A., Alber, M. S.: On Multiscale Approaches to Three-Dimensional Modeling of Morphogenesis, *J. R. Soc. Interface* **2**, (2005) 237-253.
3. Mombach, J., and Glazier, J. A.: Single cell motion in aggregates of embryonic cells. *Phys. Rev. Lett.* **76**, (1996) 3032–3035.
4. Alber, M.S., Kiskowski, M.A., Glazier, J.A., and Jiang, Y., On Cellular Automaton Approaches to Modeling Biological Cells, in J. Rosenthal and D.S. Gilliam (Eds.), Mathematical Systems Theory in Biology, Communication, and Finance, IMA Volume 134, Springer-Verlag, New York, 1-39, 2003.
5. Jiang, Y. and Glazier, J. A.: Foam Drainage: Extended Large-Q Potts Model Simulation. *Phil. Mag. Lett.* **74**, (1996) 119–128.
6. Jiang, Y., Swart, P., Saxena, A., Asipauskas, and Glazier, J. A.: Hysteresis and Avalanches in Two Dimensional Foam Rheology Simulations. *Phys. Rev. E.* **59**, (1999) 5819-5832.
7. See http://www.beowulf.org and links therein for a full description of the Beowulf project, access to the Beowulf mailing list, and more.
8. Barkema, G. T. and MacFarland, T.: Parallel simulation of the Ising model. *Phys. Rev. E* 50, (1994) 1623–1628.
9. Gropp, W., Lusk, E., and Skjellum, A.: *Using MPI: Portable Parallel Programming with the Message Passing Interface, 2nd edition.* MIT Press, Cambridge, MA (1999).
10. Gropp, W., Lusk, E., and Thakur, R.: *Using MPI-2: Advanced Features of the Message-Passing Interface.* MIT Press, Cambridge, MA (1999).
11. Wright, S. A., Plimpton, S. J., Swiler, T. P., Fye, R. M., Young, M. F. and Holm, E. A.: *Potts-model Grain Growth Simulations: Parallel Algorithms and Applications*, SAND Report 97-1925, August (1997).
12. Davis, G. S., Phillips, H. M., and Steinberg, M. S. Germ-layer surface tensions and "tissue affinities" in *Rana pipiens* gastrulae: quantitative measurements. *Dev. Biol.* **192**, (1997) 630-644.
13. Gillespie D. T.: Approximate accelerated stochastic simulation of chemically reacting systems. *J. Chem. Phys.* **115**, (2001) 1716-1733.
14. Lok, L: The need for speed in stochastic simulation. *Nature Biotechnology*, 22, (2004), August, 964
15. Gusatto, E., Mombach, J.C.M., Cercato, F.P., Cavalheiro, G.H.. An efficient parallel algorithm to evolve simulations of the cellular Potts model. *Parallel Processing Letters*, v.15, p. 199-208, 2005.

Classification of CA Rules Targeting Synthesis of Reversible Cellular Automata[*]

Sukanta Das[1] and Biplab K. Sikdar[2]

[1] Dept. of Information Technology, Bengal Engineering & Sc. University, Shibpur,
Howrah, India, 711103
`sukanta@it.becs.ac.in`
[2] Dept. of Computer Sc. & Technology, Bengal Engineering & Sc. University,
Shibpur, Howrah, India, 711103
`biplab@cs.becs.ac.in`

Abstract. This paper reports classification of CA (cellular automata) rules targeting efficient synthesis of reversible cellular automata. An analytical framework is developed to explore the properties of CA rules for 3-neighborhood 1-dimensional CA. It is found that in two-state 3-neighborhood CA, the CA rules fall into 6 groups depending on their potential to form reversible CA. The proposed classification of CA rules enables synthesis of reversible CA in linear time.

1 Introduction

Since the invention of homogeneous structure of Cellular Automata (CA), it has been employed for modeling physical systems with a diversity. The CA structure is significantly simplified with an 1-dimensional CA, each cell having two states (0/1) with uniform 3-neighborhood (self, left and right neighbor) dependencies among the CA cells [8]. However, to model a wide variety of physical systems that are non-homogeneous in nature, non-homogeneous CA structure (also called as *hybrid CA*) is evolved as an alternative to the uniform structure. A number of researchers have directed their attention to hybrid CA [1,2] since 1980s and explored the potential design with 1-dimensional hybrid CA, specially for $VLSI$ (Very Large Scale Integration) domain [2].

A special class of CA, referred to as reversible CA, had attracted the researchers for a long time to model a number of applications in hydrodynamics, dynamical systems, heat conduction, wave scattering, nucleation, dendritic growth, physical modeling, etc. [7]. The dynamical properties of reversible cellular automata were investigated in [6]. For $VLSI$ applications, linear/additive reversible CA structure, had been developed [2]. Due to its importance, we have also focused our work on reversible CA. An analytic scheme has been developed to explore the properties of CA rules. The complete classification of 3-neighborhood CA rules are done depending on their potential to form reversible

[*] This work is supported by sponsored CA Research Projects, Department of CST, Bengal Engineering & Science University, Shibpur, India.

S. El Yacoubi, B. Chopard, and S. Bandini (Eds.): ACRI 2006, LNCS 4173, pp. 68–77, 2006.
© Springer-Verlag Berlin Heidelberg 2006

CA. This classification in effect makes it possible to synthesize reversible CA in linear time. To facilitate further discussion, we introduce the basics of cellular automata in the following section.

2   Cellular Automata Basics

A Cellular Automaton (CA) consists of a number of cells organized in the form of a lattice. In 3-neighborhood, the next state of the ith CA cell is

$$S_i^{t+1} = f_i(S_{i-1}^t, S_i^t, S_{i+1}^t)$$

where f_i is the next state function and S_{i-1}^t, S_i^t & S_{i+1}^t are the states of its neighbors at time t. The $\mathcal{S}^t = (S_1^t, S_2^t, \cdots, S_n^t)$ is the present state of the CA. If the left neighbor of the left most cell and right neighbor of the right most cell are null (0), the CA is null boundary. The f_i is also expressed in the form of a truth table. The decimal equivalent of its output is referred to as the 'Rule' $\mathcal{R}_i$ [8]. Three such rules, in two state (0/1) CA, are illustrated in *Table 1*. The set

Table 1. Truth table for rule 90, 150 and 75

Present state :	111	110	101	100	011	010	001	000	*Rule*
(RMT)	(7)	(6)	(5)	(4)	(3)	(2)	(1)	(0)	
(i) Next State :	0	1	0	1	1	0	1	0	90
(ii) Next State :	1	0	0	1	0	1	1	0	150
(iii) Next State :	0	1	0	0	1	0	1	1	75

of rules $\mathcal{R} = < \mathcal{R}_1, \mathcal{R}_2, \cdots, \mathcal{R}_i, \cdots, \mathcal{R}_n >$ that configures the CA cells is called the *rule vector*. The state transition diagram of a CA may contain *cyclic* and *non-cyclic* states (a state is called *cyclic* if it lies in a cycle). A CA is *reversible* if it contains only cyclic states $(Fig.1)$.

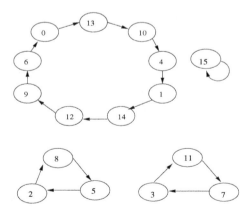

Fig. 1. State transition of a reversible CA with rule vector $< 105, 177, 170, 75 >$

The reversible linear/additive CA forms a cyclic group [2], and so popularly called as *group CA*. In view of the structural similarity with linear/additive group CA in the state transition diagram, we refer reversible CA as group CA.

From the view point of *Switching Theory*, a combination of the present states (1st row of *Table 1*) can be viewed as the *Min Term* of a 3-variable $(S_{i-1}^t, S_i^t, S_{i+1}^t)$ switching function. Therefore, each column of the first row of *Table 1* is referred to as *Rule Min Term (RMT)*. The RMTs of two consecutive cell rules $\mathcal{R}_i$ and $\mathcal{R}_{i+1}$ are related while a CA changes its state [3,5]. Such relation (*Table 2*) among the RMTs is employed to classify the CA rules in characterizing CA behavior.

Definition 1. *A rule is* Balanced *if it contains equal number of 1s and 0s in its 8−bit binary representation; otherwise it is an* Unbalanced *rule.*

Definition 2. *A rule is a* Non-group Rule *if its presence in a rule vector makes the CA non-group (irreversible). Otherwise, the rule is a* Group Rule.

This work concentrates on characterization of group rules. Identification of such rules, out of total 256 rules for two-state 3-neighborhood CA, follows.

3   Identification of Group Rules

The group rules are the basic building blocks of group/reversible CA. The following theorem separates out a section of rules, that are not the group rules.

Theorem 1. *An unbalanced rule is a non-group rule [4].*

Example 1. The $CA < 105, 177, 170, 75 >$ is a group CA (*Fig.1*). Therefore, all of the four rules are group rules. On the other hand, the $CA < 105, 177, 171, 75 >$ is non-group. The presence of the unbalanced rule 171 (binary value 10101011) makes the CA non-group. That is, 171 is a non-group rule.

There are $^8C_4 = 70$ balanced CA rules in 3-neighborhood. However, all of them are not the group rules (balanced non-group rules). For characterization of group rules, the concept of *Reachability Tree* is introduced [3,5].

Reachability Tree: a binary tree, defines the reachability of CA states. Left edge of a node is the 0-edge (0) and 1-edge (1) is the right edge. The nodes of level i are constructed following the selected RMTs of $\mathcal{R}_{i+1}$ for next state computation. The number of leaf nodes denotes the number of reachable states.

Fig.2 represents the reachability tree for a $CA < 90, 15, 85, 15 >$. The RMTs of the CA rules are noted in *Table 3* (ds denote *don't care* bits). The decimal numbers within a node at level i represent the RMTs following which the cell $(i+1)$ changes its state. For example, the root node (level 0) is constructed with RMTs 0, 1, 2 and 3 as cell 1 can change its state following the RMTs 0, 1, 2, and 3. For the RMTs 0 and 2 of rule 90 (*Table 3*), the next states are 0 and it is 1 for the RMTs 1 and 3. Therefore, the node at level 1 after the 0-edge of level 0 contains the RMTs 0, 1, 4 & 5 (*Table 2*).

Table 2. Relationship among RMTs

RMT at i^{th} rule	RMTs at $(i+1)^{th}$ rule
0 or 4	0, 1
1 or 5	2, 3
2 or 6	4, 5
3 or 7	6, 7

Table 3. RMT values of the $CA < 90, 15, 85, 15 >$ rules

RMT	111 (7)	110 (6)	101 (5)	100 (4)	011 (3)	010 (2)	001 (1)	000 (0)	Rule
First cell	d	d	d	d	1	0	1	0	90
Second cell	0	0	0	0	1	1	1	1	15
Third cell	0	1	0	1	0	1	0	1	85
Fourth cell	d	0	d	0	d	1	d	1	15

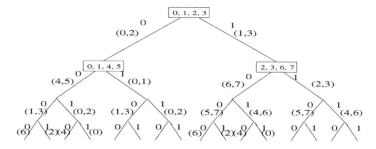

Fig. 2. Reachability tree for the $CA < 90, 15, 85, 15 >$

Definition 3. *Two RMTs are equivalent if both result in the same set of RMTs effective for the next level of reachability tree.*

For example, the RMTs 0 and 4 are equivalent as both results in the same set of effective RMTs $\{0, 1\}$ (*Table 2*) for the next level of reachability tree.

Definition 4. *Two RMTs are sibling at level $i+1$ if they are resulted in from the same RMT at level i of the Reachability Tree.*

The RMTs 0 and 1 are the sibling RMTs as these two are resulted in either from RMT 0 or from RMT 4 (*Table 2*). If a node of Reachability Tree associates an RMT k, it also associates the sibling of k.

Theorem 2. *The reachability tree for a group CA is balanced [5].*

Example 2. The $CA < 90, 15, 85, 15 >$ is group. Its reachability tree (*Fig.2*) is balanced.

Theorem 3. *The reachability tree of a 3-neighborhood null boundary CA is balanced if each edge, except the leaf edges, is resulted from exactly two RMTs of the corresponding rule [5].*

Example 3. Consider the 4-cell group CA of *Fig.2*. Each intermediate edge of the reachability tree is resulted from exactly two RMTs.

Corollary 1. *All the nodes except leaves of the reachability tree for a group CA is constructed with 4 RMTs [3].*

Theorem 4. *At each level, except the root, of the reachability tree for a group* *CA, there are either 2 or 4 unique nodes.*

Proof. Each node of the reachability tree for a group CA is constructed with 4 $RMTs$ (*Corollary 1*) and the sibling $RMTs$ (*Definition 4*) are associated with the same node. Since there are 4 sets of sibling $RMTs$ (0 & 1, 2 & 3, 4 & 5, and 6 & 7), 3 different organizations of $RMTs$ for the nodes are possible – {0, 1, 2, 3} & {4, 5, 6, 7}, {0, 1, 4, 5} & {2, 3, 6, 7} and {0, 1, 6, 7} & {2, 3, 4, 5}. This implies, if a node at level i is constructed with N_1 ={0, 1, 2, 3}, then there exists another node at that level constructed from N_2 ={4, 5, 6, 7}. Therefore, minimum number of unique nodes in a reachability tree of a group CA is 2.

It is obvious from *Theorem 3* that the 2 out of 4 $RMTs$ (*Corollary 1*) of a node in the reachability tree for group CA are d ($d = 0/1$) and the rest 2 are d'. Therefore, 2 $RMTs$ of N_1 or N_2 are d, and the other 2 are d'. So, another two nodes may be possible at level i taking 2 $RMTs$ that produce d from N_1 and another 2 $RMTs$ from N_2. Hence the maximum number of possible nodes in a reachability tree for a group CA is 4.

Theorem 5. *A balanced rule with same value for the RMT set {0, 2, 3, 4} or* *{0, 4, 6, 7} or {0, 1, 2, 6} or {0, 1, 3, 7} is a non-group rule [3].*

Corollary 2. *The number of balanced non-group CA rules in 3-neighborhood* *dependency is 8 [3].*

From *Theorem 5*, it can be identified that the balanced non-group rules are – 29, 46, 71, 116, 139, 184, 209 and 226. Therefore, out of 70 balanced rules the rest 62 are the group rules (listed in *Table 4*). These 62 rules can only form the reversible (group) CA. However, any sequence of such rules in a CA rule vector does not necessarily imply that the resulted CA is group CA.

Theorem 6. *Only a specific sequence of group rules forms a group CA [3].*

Example 4. The $CA < 90, 15, 85, 15 >$ is a group CA. However, the CA $\mathcal{R} =< 90, 85, 15, 15 >$ is a non-group CA even though each $\mathcal{R}' \in \mathcal{R}$ is a group rule.

It directs that the sequence of rules to form a group CA follows a specific relation. The classification of group rules based on the relation is reported next.

4   Classification of Group Rules

This section identifies the relations among group rules and reports classification of 62 group rules to find the sequence of rules for a group CA.

4.1   Formation of Rule Class

Let us consider, the rules $\mathcal{R}_1$, $\mathcal{R}_2$, $\cdots$, $\mathcal{R}_i$ are selected for cell 1, cell 2, $\cdots$, cell i respectively to form an $n-$cell group CA satisfying the theorems 2 and 3. Further, consider S is the set of all group rules ($|S| = 62$). Now, the $(i + 1)$ cell can support a set of rules $S_j \in S$ so that any rule of S_j can be selected as $\mathcal{R}_{i+1}$. We refer the class of $(i+1)^{th}$ cell as C – that is, the class of S_j is C.

Lemma 1: There are 6 possible classes of group CA cells in 3-neighborhood.
Proof: Each node of the reachability tree of a group CA contains 4 $RMTs$ (*Corollary 1*). Since the sibling $RMTs$ are associated with the same node in the reachability tree and there are 4 sets of sibling $RMTs$ (0 & 1, 2 & 3, 4 & 5, and 6 & 7), 3 different organizations of $RMTs$ for the nodes are possible – {0, 1, 2, 3} & {4, 5, 6, 7}, {0, 1, 4, 5} & {2, 3, 6, 7}, and {0, 1, 6, 7} & {2, 3, 4, 5}. Therefore, if the reachability tree contains a node with $RMTs$ {0, 1, 2, 3} at i^{th} level, it also contains a node with $RMTs$ {4, 5, 6, 7}.

Whenever a level is having only 2 unique nodes (*Theorem 4*), the $RMTs$ of the nodes may be organized as one of the 3 possible combinations of $RMTs$. For that case, the rule $\mathcal{R}_{i+1}$ is declared as of class I, II, or III respectively. On the other hand, if the level contains 4 unique nodes, then the $RMTs$ of the nodes may be organized as any two combinations of the 3 possible combinations of $RMTs$. Whenever the nodes are organized like class I & II, I & III, and II & III, the class of that cell is declared as IV, V, and VI respectively. Therefore, there are 6 classes of group rules.

Rules under each class: Since the CA is group, out of 4 $RMTs$ of a node, the two $RMTs$ are 0 and another two are 1 (*Theorem 3*). For class II (RMT partition is {0, 1, 4, 5} & {2, 3, 6, 7}), 0 & 4 (similarly 1 & 5, 4 & 6, and 5 & 7) are the equivalent $RMTs$ (*Definition 3*) and both of these contribute same set of $RMTs$ for the next level. Hence any of the equivalent $RMTs$ may be grouped together to generate a node for the next level. The number of $RMTs$ of that node becomes 2. This results in the CA as non-group (*Corollary 1*). Therefore, equivalent $RMTs$ under the same node can not be grouped to give d ($d = 0/1$) simultaneously. Hence 4 groupings of $RMTs$ out of $^4C_2 = 6$ are possible in each node for class II. Therefore, the number of group rules of class II is $4 \times 4 = 16$. Since equivalent $RMTs$ are not associated with the same node for class I and III, $^4C_2 = 6$ groupings are possible for each node. Hence number of rules for those classes are $6 \times 6 = 36$ (*Table 4*).

4.2   Relationship Between $\mathcal{R}_i$ and $\mathcal{R}_{i+1}$

From the known $\mathcal{R}_i$ and its class, we can find the nodes of the reachability tree that are resulted for $\mathcal{R}_{i+1}$ – that is, the class of $\mathcal{R}_{i+1}$. Let us consider the class of $\mathcal{R}_i$ be I (*Fig.3*). Therefore, two unique nodes having $RMTs$ {0, 1, 2, 3} and {4, 5, 6, 7} are available at the $(i-1)^{th}$ level. Now consider the $RMTs$ of $\mathcal{R}_i$ are clustered as {0, 1, 4, 5} and {2, 3, 6, 7}, where the $RMTs$ of a set are the same, either 0 or 1. In *Fig.3(a)*, the $RMTs$ {0, 1, 4, 5} are considered as 0, and it is 1 for the $RMTs$ {2, 3, 6, 7}. Therefore, the $RMTs$ are grouped as (0, 1), (2, 3), (4, 5) and (6, 7). Each edge of the nodes is resulted from any one of these groups. Hence two edges are connecting the node having $RMTs$ {0, 1, 2, 3} with its children resulted from (0, 1) and (2, 3). Therefore, the two children (for next level) of that node are having $RMTs$ {0, 1, 2, 3} and {4, 5, 6, 7} (*Table 2*) (*Fig.3(a)*).

Table 4. Class Table

Class	RMTs of nodes	Rules
I	{0, 1, 2, 3} {4, 5, 6, 7}	51, 53, 54, 57, 58, 60, 83, 85, 86, 89, 90, 92, 99, 101, 102, 105, 106, 108, 147, 149, 150, 153, 154, 156, 163, 165, 166, 169, 170, 172, 195, 197, 198, 201, 202, 204
II	{0, 1, 4, 5} {2, 3, 6, 7}	15, 30, 45, 60, 75, 90, 105, 120, 135, 150, 165, 180, 195, 210, 225, 240
III	{0, 1, 6, 7} {2, 3, 4, 5}	15, 23, 27, 39, 43, 51, 77, 78, 85, 86, 89, 90, 101, 102, 105, 106, 113, 114, 141, 142, 149, 150, 153, 154, 165, 166, 169, 170, 177, 178, 204, 212, 216, 228, 232, 240
IV	{0, 1, 2, 3} {4, 5, 6, 7} {0, 1, 4, 5} {2, 3, 6, 7}	60, 90, 105, 150, 165, 195
V	{0, 1, 2, 3} {4, 5, 6, 7} {0, 1, 6, 7} {2, 3, 4, 5}	51, 85, 86, 89, 90, 101, 102, 105, 106, 149, 150, 153, 154, 165, 166, 169, 170, 204
VI	{0, 1, 4, 5} {2, 3, 6, 7} {0, 1, 6, 7} {2, 3, 4, 5}	15, 90, 105, 150, 165, 240

Similarly, the children of another node having RMTs {4, 5, 6, 7} are constructed with RMTs {0, 1, 2, 3} and {4, 5, 6, 7} – that is, the nodes are same with the other two nodes of that level. Therefore, the next level of the reachability tree contains two unique nodes having RMTs {0, 1, 2, 3} and {4, 5, 6, 7} (*Fig.3(a)*). Hence the class of $\mathcal{R}_{i+1}$ is I.

Further, if the RMTs of $\mathcal{R}_i$ are grouped as (0, 1), (2, 3), (4, 6), and (5, 7) (*Fig.3(b)*), the nodes of level i, generated from the node of level $(i-1)$ with RMTs {0, 1, 2, 3}, are having RMTs {0, 1, 2, 3} and {4, 5, 6, 7}. The other two nodes at level i, generated from the node with RMTs {4, 5, 6, 7}, are having RMTs {0, 1, 4, 5} and {2, 3, 6, 7}. In this case, the next level of reachability tree contains four unique nodes having RMTs {0, 1, 2, 3}, {4, 5, 6, 7}, {0, 1, 4, 5}, and {2, 3, 6, 7}. Therefore, the organizations of RMTs support the property of both the classes I & II. Therefore, the class of $\mathcal{R}_{i+1}$ is IV.

Table 5 partly displays the relationship among group rules. The first column shows the class of $\mathcal{R}_i$. Column 2 notes the RMTs of unique nodes at level $(i-1)$. Whereas, Column 3 shows the grouping of RMTs for $\mathcal{R}_i$. The RMTs of unique nodes at level i are shown in Column 4. Based on the unique nodes at level i, the class of $\mathcal{R}_{i+1}$ is decided and is reported in Column 5. The details of relationship are reported in *Table 6*. The first and second columns represent the class of ith cell and the $\mathcal{R}_i$ respectively. The class of $(i+1)^{th}$ cell is noted third column.

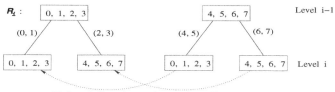

(a) Next rule class is I

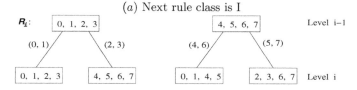

(b) Next rule class is IV

Fig. 3. Determination of class relationship

Table 5. Class Relationship between $\mathcal{R}_i$ and $\mathcal{R}_{i+1}$

(1) Class of $\mathcal{R}_i$	(2) $RMTs$ of unique nodes at level $(i-1)$	(3) Groupings of $RMTs$ at level $(i-1)$	(4) $RMTs$ of unique nodes at level i	(5) Class of $\mathcal{R}_{i+1}$
I	$\{0, 1, 2, 3\}$ $\{4, 5, 6, 7\}$	$(0, 1), (2, 3)$ $(4, 5), (6, 7)$	$\{0, 1, 2, 3\}$ $\{4, 5, 6, 7\}$	I
		$(0, 2), (1, 3)$ $(4, 6), (5, 7)$	$\{0, 1, 4, 5\}$ $\{2, 3, 6, 7\}$	II
		$(0, 3), (1, 2)$ $(4, 7), (5, 6)$	$\{0, 1, 6, 7\}$ $\{2, 3, 4, 5\}$	III
		$\{(0, 1), (2, 3)$ $(4, 6), (5, 7)\}$ or $\{(0, 2), (1, 3)$ $(4, 5), (6, 7)\}$	$\{0, 1, 2, 3\}$ $\{4, 5, 6, 7\}$ $\{0, 1, 4, 5\}$ $\{2, 3, 6, 7\}$	IV
II	$\{0, 1, 4, 5\}$ $\{2, 3, 6, 7\}$	$(0, 1), (4, 5)$ $(2, 3), (6, 7)$	$\{0, 1, 2, 3\}$ $\{4, 5, 6, 7\}$	I
IV	$\{0, 1, 2, 3\}$ $\{4, 5, 6, 7\}$ $\{0, 1, 4, 5\}$ $\{2, 3, 6, 7\}$	$(0, 1), (2, 3)$ $(4, 5), (6, 7)$	$\{0, 1, 2, 3\}$ $\{4, 5, 6, 7\}$	I
		$\{(0, 1), (2, 3)$ $(4, 6), (5, 7)\}$ or $\{(0, 2), (1, 3)$ $(4, 5), (6, 7)\}$	$\{0, 1, 2, 3\}$ $\{4, 5, 6, 7\}$ $\{0, 1, 4, 5\}$ $\{2, 3, 6, 7\}$	IV

First and Last rule: In this work, we have concentrated only on null boundary CA. Therefore, there are $2^{2^2} = 16$ effective rules for $\mathcal{R}_1$ as well as for $\mathcal{R}_n$. The $RMTs$ 4, 5, 6 and 7 are the *don't care* for $\mathcal{R}_1$ and there are only 4 effective

RMTs (0, 1, 2, 3) for $\mathcal{R}_1$. Similarly, the effective RMTs for $\mathcal{R}_n$ are 0, 2, 4 and 6. That is, rule 105 and 9 are equivalent if selected as the $\mathcal{R}_1$.

Corollary 3. *If* $\mathcal{R} = <\mathcal{R}_1, \mathcal{R}_2, \cdots, \mathcal{R}_n>$ *is a group* CA, *then* $\mathcal{R}_1$ *and* $\mathcal{R}_n$ *must be balanced over their effective 4 RMTs [3].*

It signifies that the unbalanced rule 3 is a group rule when it is selected as the $\mathcal{R}_1$. The rule 3 is balanced over its effective (least significant) 4 RMTs. There are $^4C_2 = 6$ rules (out of total 16 effective rules for the $\mathcal{R}_1$) that are balanced over their least significant 4 RMTs. *Table 7* identifies such 6 rules. From similar consideration, *Table 8* lists all such 6 group rules for the $\mathcal{R}_n$.

The classification of CA rules ensures efficient synthesis of the reversible CA in $O(n)$ time. For example, say rule 9 is selected randomly as $\mathcal{R}_1$ from *Table 7* while synthesizing 4-cell reversible CA. Therefore, the class of 2nd cell rule is III. From Class III of *Table 6*, say rule 177 is selected randomly as the $\mathcal{R}_2$. Therefore, the class of $\mathcal{R}_3$ is found to be V (*Table 6*). We select rule 170 as $\mathcal{R}_3$. The class of last cell is, therefore, II. Rule 65 is selected randomly for $\mathcal{R}_4$ from

Table 6. Relationship of $\mathcal{R}_i$ and $\mathcal{R}_{i+1}$

Class of $\mathcal{R}_i$	$\mathcal{R}_i$	Class of $\mathcal{R}_{i+1}$
I	51, 60, 195, 204	I
	85, 90, 165, 170	II
	102, 105, 150, 153	III
	53, 58, 83, 92, 163, 172, 197, 202	IV
	54, 57, 99, 108, 147, 156, 198,201	V
	86, 89, 101, 106, 149, 154, 166, 169	VI
II	15, 30, 45, 60, 75, 90, 105, 120, 135, 150, 165, 180, 195, 210, 225, 240	I
III	15, 51, 204, 240	I
	85, 105, 150, 170	II
	90, 102, 153, 165	III
	23, 43, 77, 113, 142, 178, 212, 232	IV
	27, 39, 78, 114, 141, 177, 216, 228	V
	86, 89, 101, 106, 149, 154, 166, 169	VI
IV	60, 195	I
	90, 165	IV
	105, 150	V
V	51, 204	I
	85, 170	II
	102, 153	III
	86, 89, 90, 101, 105, 106, 149, 150, 154, 165,166, 169	VI
VI	15, 240	I
	105, 150	IV
	90, 165	V

Table 7. First Rule Table

Rules for $\mathcal{R}_1$	Groupings of RMTs	RMTs of nodes for level 2	Class of $\mathcal{R}_2$
3, 12	(0, 1)	{0, 1, 2, 3}	I
	(2, 3)	{4, 5, 6, 7}	
5, 10	(0, 2)	{0, 1, 4, 5}	II
	(1, 3)	{2, 3, 6, 7}	
6, 9	(0, 3)	{0, 1, 6, 7}	III
	(1, 2)	{2, 3, 4, 5}	

Table 8. Last Rule Table

Rule class for $\mathcal{R}_n$	Rule set for $\mathcal{R}_n$
I	17, 20, 65, 68
II	5, 20, 65, 80
III	5, 17, 68, 80
IV	20, 65
V	17, 68
VI	5, 80

Table 8. Therefore, the synthesized reversible (group) CA is $< 9, 177, 170, 65 >$. The synthesis algorithm is reported in [4].

5 Conclusion

This paper reports the classification of CA rules. It is found that there are only 62 rules for two-state 3-neighborhood CA that may form reversible CA. The relation among such rules are identified to ensure synthesis of reversible CA in linear time.

References

1. Kevin Cattel and J. C. Muzio. Synthesis of One Dimensional Linear Hybrid Cellular Automata. *IEEE Trans. on CAD*, 15:325–335, 1996.
2. P Pal Chaudhuri, D Roy Chowdhury, S Nandi, and S Chatterjee. *Additive Cellular Automata – Theory and Applications*, volume 1. IEEE Computer Society Press, California, USA, ISBN 0-8186-7717-1, 1997.
3. Sukanta Das. *Theory and Applications of Nonlinear Cellular Automata In VLSI Design*. PhD thesis, Bengal Engineering And Science University, Shibpur, 2006.
4. Sukanta Das, Anirban Kundu, Biplab K. Sikdar, and P. Pal Chaudhuri. Design of Nonlinear CA Based TPG Without Prohibited Pattern Set In Linear Time. *JOURNAL OF ELECTRONIC TESTING: Theory and Applications*, 21:95–109, January 2005.
5. Sukanta Das, Biplab K Sikdar, and P Pal Chaudhuri. Characterization of Reachable/Nonreachable Cellular Automata States. In *Proceedings of Sixth International Conference on Cellular Automata for Research and Industry, ACRI 2004, The Netherlands*, pages 813–822, October 2004.
6. L Margara, G Mauri, G Cattaneo, and E Formenti. On the dynamical behavior of chaotic cellular automata. *Theoretical Computer Science*, 217:31–51, 1999.
7. T. Toffoli and N. H. Margolus. Invertible cellular automata : A review. *Physica D*, 45:229–253, 1990.
8. S. Wolfram. Statistical mechanics of cellular automata. *Rev. Mod. Phys.*, 55(3): 601–644, July 1983.

On the Dynamics of Some Exceptional Fuzzy Cellular Automata

Darcy Dunne and Angelo B. Mingarelli[*]

School of Mathematics and Statistics, Carleton University,
Ottawa, Canada, K1S 5B6
ddunne@connect.carleton.ca, amingare@math.carleton.ca

Abstract. Over the past 20 years, the study of cellular automata has emerged as one of the most interesting and popular forms of "new mathematics". The study of cellular automata has broadened into many variations of the original concepts. One such variation is the study of one-dimensional fuzzy cellular automata. The evolution and dynamics of the majority of one-dimensional fuzzy cellular automata rules can be determined analytically using techniques devised by the second author. It turns out that only 9 rules (out of 256), three of which are trivial, fail to comply with the techniques given. We give a brief overview of finite cellular automata and their fuzzification. We summarize the method used to study the majority of fuzzy rules and give some examples of its application. We analyze and uncover the dynamics of those few rules which do not conform to such techniques. Using new techniques, combined with direct analysis, we determine the long term evolution of the 4 remaining rules (since two of them were treated in detail elsewhere). We specifically analyze rules 172 and 202 and then, by deriving equivalences to the final two rules, we complete the program, initiated in 2003, of determining the long term dynamics of all 256 one-dimensional fuzzy cellular automata, thereby showing that chaotic dynamics are incompatible with this type of fuzziness, in sharp contrast with boolean cellular automata.

1 Introduction to Cellular Automata

We begin by introducing the definitions and properties of general cellular automata which will allow us to understand the techniques used and results obtained in this paper. In general, a cellular automaton is a regular uniform lattice of cells with each cell containing a discrete variable or value. The lattice may be either finite or infinite and the total state of the automaton is completely specified by the value at each cell. The value or state of the automaton evolves in discrete time steps wherein each new cell value is determined based on the current value of the cells within the automaton. Each cell and its value is updated simultaneously i.e. All new cell values are based solely on those of the previous

---

[*] This research is partially supported by an NSERC Canada Research Grant to the second named author.

S. El Yacoubi, B. Chopard, and S. Bandini (Eds.): ACRI 2006, LNCS 4173, pp. 78–87, 2006.

automaton's state. The majority of studies focus on rules which evolve a cell's value based on the cells within a given neighborhood of the cell, usually the cell's value itself and those immediately adjacent to it. These are referred to as local rules. The most elementary form of cellular automata are one-dimensional boolean cellular automata which consists of a single strip or sequence containing boolean values. The strip is usually considered infinite in both the positive and negative direction and any finite sequence is simply imposed onto an infinite background of zero cells. The neighborhood of each cell consists of itself and its immediately adjacent neighbors (the cell preceding it and the other which follows it). In other words, a local rule is a mapping of the following form: $g : \{0, 1\}^3 \mapsto \{0, 1\}$.

If we then fix a cell in the automaton's evolution and denote it x_0 we may then consider its evolution as an infinite sequence of boolean values where we may access any value of the sequence via its index. This allows us to define a map f (the local rule) for the automaton by mapping each cell x_i via the mapping $f(x_i) = g(x_{i-1}, x_i, x_{i+1})$. Since g maps the set of values in $\{0, 1\}^3$ to the set $\{0, 1\}$, we may describe the map g as follows: $(000, 001, 010, 011, 100, 101, 110, 111) \mapsto (r_0, r_1, ..., r_7)$ where each $r_i = 0$ or 1. This gives us $2^8 = 256$ possible local functions to study. We conveniently name each rule based on the numerical value of the binary string $r_7, r_6, ..., r_0$. In other words, we name the rule via the value of the sum:

$$Rule\ Name = \sum_{i=0}^{7} r_i 2^i.$$

Since we are dealing with binary values, we may express each local rule in a disjunctive normal form (DNF) using the binary operators *and* and *or*, [5]. That is, we write the local rule as an expansion of "ors" and of "ands" of the 3-tuples which generate a 1 under the given local rule i.e., we can always write

$$g(x_1, x_2, x_3) = \vee_{i|r_i=1} \wedge_{j=1}^{3} x_j^{d_{ij}},$$

where d_{ij} is the j-th digit from left to right of the binary representation of i and where x^0 represents $\neg x$ (the negation of x).

For example consider Rule 218: Since $218 = 1 \cdot 2^7 + 1 \cdot 2^6 + 1 \cdot 2^4 + 1 \cdot 2^3 + 1 \cdot 2^1$ it is represented by the binary mapping: $(000, 001, 010, 011, 100, 101, 110, 111) \mapsto (0, 1, 0, 1, 1, 0, 1, 1)$ which gives the following function in DNF.

$$g_{218}(x_1, x_2, x_3) = (\neg x_1 \wedge \neg x_2 \wedge x_3) \vee (\neg x_1 \wedge x_2 \wedge x_3) \vee (x_1 \wedge \neg x_2 \wedge \neg x_3) \vee$$
$$(x_1 \wedge x_2 \wedge \neg x_3) \vee (x_1 \wedge x_2 \wedge x_3). \tag{1}$$

When we apply this rule to any triple $(0, 1, 0), (0, 0, 1)$, etc. starting from a single "1" seed value against a background of zeros its evolution continues indefinitely left and right and may be computed for any finite number of time states. By setting the cells to small colored blocks, black for 1 and white for 0, we can visualize its dynamics as it is normally done these days (cf., [11], [12]).

2   Introduction to FCA's

The properties of binary cellular automata have their origins in works by Von Neumann [9] and Wolfram [11]. We turn our attention to a variation of the elementary binary cellular automaton. We "fuzzify" the automaton by removing the binary restriction and thus allowing the cell values to be any real number in the interval $[0, 1]$. We must then redefine the operations of the binary maps to suit those of our new values. We alter the operations in the DNF of each of the rules for binary cellular automata as follows: $(x \vee y)$ becomes $(x + y)$, $(x \wedge y)$ becomes $(x \cdot y)$ and $(\neg x)$ becomes $(1 - x)$. Since each $x_j^{d_{ij}} \in [0, 1]$ in the DNF we know that the product $\prod_{j=1}^{3} x_j^{d_{ij}}$ is also a positive number in $[0, 1]$. The rule sum

$$g(x_1, x_2, x_3) = \sum_{i=0}^{7} r_i \cdot \prod_{j=1}^{3} x_j^{d_{ij}}$$

is thus maximized when $r_i = 1$ and minimized when $r_i = 0$ for all $i = 0, 1, ..., 7$. These values correspond to fuzzy rules $g_0(x_1, x_2, x_3) = 0$ and $g_{255}(x_1, x_2, x_3) = 1$ respectively. Furthermore, since each of the fuzzy rules are essentially partial sums of fuzzy rule 255, we may bound all the local fuzzy rules above and below which guarantees that for any fuzzy local rule we map back into the interval $[0, 1]$.

For example, let us again consider Rule 218. From above, we recall that the DNF of this rule is given by (1) above. We can fuzzify this using the identifications $x \vee y = x + y$ etc. defined above to find:

$$g_{218}(x, y, z) = (1 - x)(1 - y)z + (1 - x)yz + x(1 - y)(1 - z) + xy(1 - z) + xyz$$
$$= x + z - 2xz + xyz$$

We may then choose a seed value of any $\alpha \in [0, 1]$ and examine the evolution of the automaton over several discrete time steps. Let us choose, for example, $\alpha = 0.5$. This gives an evolution similar to rule 218 above with the number 0.5 scattered about. The space-time diagram is very similar to the one found in the discrete (or boolean) case which does not lead to anything of much interest. In fact, we can show that for any fuzzy rule the space-time diagram produced by an arbitrary seed $\alpha \in (0, 1)$ approaches the boolean space-time diagram

Table 1. Fuzzy rule 218 running on the 3 seeds $(0.25, 0.5, 0.75)$

time	state										
0	0	0	0	0	0.25	0.5	0.75	0	0	0	0
1	0	0	0	0.25	0.5	0.718	0.5	0.75	0	0	0
2	0	0	0.25	0.5	0.699	0.679	0.660	0.5	0.75	0	0
3	0	0.25	0.5	0.687	0.737	0.749	0.724	0.667	0.5	0.75	0
4	0.25	0.5	0.679	0.753	0.786	0.794	0.778	0.741	0.666	0.5	0.75
...					...						

as $\alpha \to 1^-$. However, we may also consider the dynamics of a fuzzy cellular automaton with several seeds on a background of zeros. For example, we now choose three consecutive seeds of 0.25,0.5,0.75. This generates a much more interesting evolution as seen in Table 1.

It is important to note that the above method of fuzzification is not unique. We may choose to transform the binary expressions into functions on the interval using alternative fuzzy logics (cf., [5],[8]).

3   Long Term Dynamics of FCA

By using a powerful enough computer, we may generate any finite number of iterations of a local fuzzy rule. However, it is also interesting to analyze the evolution of an automaton's value as the number of iterations approaches infinity analytically. To study the dynamics of fuzzy cellular automata further, let us adopt a notation which will allow us to manipulate them more easily. We recall that we may reference any cell x_i of an automata via its index i with respect to a chosen cell x_0. Now, let us denote the value of the given cell x_i after t time steps (i.e. t applications of a given local rule) by x_i^t. We denote the *space-time diagram* of a given cell x_i^t as the set of cells $\{x_j^{t+p} | p \geq 0 \text{ and } (i-p) \leq j \leq (i+p)\}$. The space-time diagram of a given cell represents the evolutionary values which are dependent on the vertex value x_i^t. We may then denote any finite fuzzy automaton on a background of 0's via the finite sequence $x_{-k}, ..., x_0, x_q$ for some $k, q \geq 0$. In the simplest case where the automaton acts on a single value $\alpha \in [0,1]$, note that the space-time diagram has vertex $x_0^0 = \alpha$ and $x_{\pm n}^m$ is the n-th cell to the right/left of the seed value at time m.

We examine three types of sequences found in space-time diagrams which are generated by local fuzzy rules. Those which form the positive diagonals, those which form the negative diagonals and those which form the vertical sequences in the space-time diagram. We denote the limits of these sequences as L_i^+, L_i^-, and L_i^0 respectively, where, for the diagonal sequences, i denotes the sequence beginning with the i-th iterate of the x_0 element, x_0^i under the local rule. In the case of vertical sequences, i refers to the sequence beginning with the i-th value left/right of the initial value, i.e. the element x_i^0.

To determine the long term dynamics of a given fuzzy cellular rule we proceed with the method described in [5], a technique which can be summarized as follows: We fix a given seed value which will distinguish both diagonal and vertical sequences. We then use the given rule to derive basic theoretical estimates of the initial diagonal sequences. We proceed by using the continuity of the fuzzified local rule as a function of three variables to prove the existence and value of the initial limits. Finally, when applicable we use an iterative approach to obtain a value for all subsequent limits. To utilize the above scheme to derive the limits of the required sequences we must first enforce the following two conditions on a local rule g_n, $0 < n < 255$: **Condition (I):** The equations: $g_n(x,y,z) - x = 0, g_n(x,y,z) - y = 0$ and $g_n(x,y,z) - z = 0$ can each be solved uniquely for x, y, z respectively, for given values of $(y,z), (x,z), (x,y)$

respectively in $[0,1]^2$. Though not crucial, we also include a second condition, **Condition (II):** The outer most (initial) left/right diagonal sequences converge to the limits L_0^- and L_0^+ respectively.

Without loss of generality, let us consider the right diagonal sequence from the right most value of a finite initial string imposed onto a background of zeros. Let the vertex of the space-time diagram take the value $x_0^0 = \alpha$. We may then compute the values $x_m^m = g_n(x_{(m-1)}^{(m-1)}, 0, 0)$. Now by Condition (II) we know that $\lim_{m\to\infty} x_m^m = L_0^+$ or more appropriately $L_0^+(\alpha)$. We may then proceed to the following sequence immediately below or more precisely $L_1^+(\alpha)$. We know $x_{(m-1)}^m = g_n(x_{(m-2)}^{(m-1)}, x_{(m-1)}^{(m-1)}, 0)$. Thus $L_1^+(\alpha) = \lim_{m\to\infty} x_{(m-1)}^m = g_n(L_1^+(\alpha), L_0^+(\alpha), 0)$. Now, we use Condition (I) to solve for the unique value $L_1^+(\alpha)$. Now that we possess both $L_0^+(\alpha)$ and $L_1^+(\alpha)$, we may continue in a similar manner for the third limit, $L_2^+(\alpha)$. Again, we use the relation

$$x_{(m-2)}^m = g_n(x_{(m-3)}^{(m-1)}, x_{(m-2)}^{(m-1)}, x_{(m-1)}^{(m-1)})$$

and the fact that the limit $L_2^+(\alpha) = \lim_{m\to\infty} x_{(m-2)}^m = g_n(L_2^+(\alpha), L_1^+(\alpha), L_0^+(\alpha))$ can be solved uniquely for $L_2^+(\alpha)$, by Condition (I). We then simply proceed inductively to receive $L_k^+(\alpha) = g_n(L_k^+(\alpha), L_{k-1}^+(\alpha), L_{k-2}^+(\alpha))$ which holds for each $k \geq 2$. Then, by applying Condition (I), we can solve for the limit $L_k^+(\alpha)$ uniquely in terms of the previous 2 limits $L_{k-2}^+(\alpha), L_{k-1}^+(\alpha)$ and thus the induction holds.

We may apply a similar method for the left diagonal sequences using the left most value in the finite automaton as the vertex for the space-time diagram. We note from the above discussion that if we take the limit of both the right and left diagonals, we can obtain an iterative equation for the right/left diagonal limits $L_k^+(\alpha)$ and $L_k^-(\alpha)$. Furthermore, we may take the $\lim_{k\to\infty}$ of both to determine the long term behavior of the limits of the diagonal sequences. We also consider the limits of the vertical sequences in a similar manner and note that not all such sequence must have limit but if so it must be one of the $L_k^\pm$'s, or the limit $\lim_{k\to\infty} L_k^\pm = L^\pm$ itself, where the k generally usually depends on the choice of the column[5].

Returning to the example of Rule 218 above we analyze the 2-seed case. In order to generate a space-time diagram using non-zero adjacent seed values $\alpha, \beta \in (0,1)$, we set the left most seed value as $x_0^0 = \alpha$. We can see easily from its space-time diagram that $L_0^- = \alpha$. This can also be shown easily through derivation by noting $g_{218}(0, 0, z) = z$, thus the left most sequence becomes simply a string of α. A similar argument shows that the second left diagonal sequence is also trivially the second seed value using again the relation $g_{218}(0, \alpha, z) = z$.

By our above conditions and the existence of the first 2 limits, induction of the method on the recurrence $x_j^{k+1} = g_{218}(x_{j-1}^k, x_j^k, x_{j+1}^k)$ shows that the left diagonal sequence $\{x_{-k}^{i+k}\}_{k\geq 0}$ has the limit L_i^- for all $i \geq 2$. Thus, letting $k \to \infty$ in the above recurrence, we obtain

$$\lim_{k\to\infty} x_{-k}^{k+i} = \lim_{k\to\infty} g_{218}(x_{-(k+1)}^{(k+i)-1}, x_{-k}^{(k+i)-1}, x_{-(k-1)}^{(k+i)-1})$$

and this, in turn, implies that $L_i^- = L_{i-2}^- + L_i^- - 2L_{i-2}^- L_i^- + L_{i-2}^- L_{i-1}^- L_i^- = \frac{1}{2-L_{i-1}^-}$. This holds for all $i \geq 2$. From this we can also determine the long term value of the limits. We note that as k increases, so does the value of the limit and as $k \to \infty$ the value $L^- = \lim_{k \to \infty} L_i^-$ approaches the continued fraction $L^- = \frac{1}{2-\frac{1}{2-\dots}} = 1$, (see [10]). To uncover the evolution of the right diagonal sequences, we take advantage of the symmetry property $g_{218}(x,y,z) = g_{218}(z,y,x)$ of this rule. So, setting the right most seed to be $x_0^0 = \beta$ we can simply state that $L_0^+ = \beta, L_1^+ = \alpha$ and then $L_i^+ = \frac{1}{2-L_{i-1}^+}$ for all $i \geq 2$. Again, the limit of these is the continued fraction $L^+ = \frac{1}{2-\frac{1}{2-\dots}} = 1$. Thus, since both the left and right diagonals converge to 1 we can state that the diagonal sequences converge to 1 as well, as per [5].

4   Long Term Dynamics of Exceptional FCA

We note that in order to apply the above techniques to a finite fuzzy cellular automaton on a background of zeros, the local rules must satisfy Conditions (I) and (II). The automata which violate Condition I are precisely those which have the property $g_n(x,x,x) - x = 0$ for all $x \in [0,1]$. (i.e. each point along the diagonal of the cube $[0,1]^3$ is a fixed point of the local rule). We call these *exceptional*. A search shows that only nine fuzzy rules are exceptional, that is, fuzzy rules 170, 172, 184, 202, 204, 216, 226, 228 and 240. However, we need not consider the trivial rules $g_{240}(x_1,x_2,x_3) = x_1$, $g_{204}(x_1,x_2,x_3) = x_2$ and $g_{170}(x_1,x_2,x_3) = x_3$ since they produce trivial evolutions (left, right or zero shifts in their evolution). As for the remaining six local fuzzy rules, the complicated dynamic evolution of fuzzy rule 184 was recently tackled in [4]. However, since the symmetry property $g_{184}(x,y,z) = g_{226}(z,y,x)$ holds for the two rules 184 and 226, it follows (by space-time diagram reflection) that the results in [4] give corresponding results for 226. The remaining 4 rules are now of interest and we find similarities in these rules just as we did in their boolean counterparts. We may first break these 4 rules into two pairs using the reflectional equivalencies: $g_{172}(x,y,z) = g_{228}(z,y,x)$, and $g_{202}(x,y,z) = g_{216}(z,y,x)$. Indeed, we may equate the first two pairs of fuzzy rules with the conjugation equivalencies: $g_{202}(x,y,z) = 1 - g_{172}((1-x),(1-y),(1-z))$ or $g_{216}(x,y,z) = 1 - g_{228}((1-x),(1-y),(1-z))$. Thus, we may restrict our study to a mere two of the four exceptional rules, one per pair. As per custom with boolean rules, we chose those with the lowest rule numbers in each class for the sake of argument.

4.1   Rule 172

The first of the four exceptional rules, rule 172, has binary form 10101100_2 and so the binary mapping: $(000, 001, 010, 011, 100, 101, 110, 111) \mapsto (0,0,1,1,0,1,0,1)$ gives the DNF $g_{172}(x_1,x_2,x_3) = (\neg x_1 \wedge x_2 \wedge \neg x_3) \vee (\neg x_1 \wedge x_2 \wedge x_3) \vee (x_1 \wedge \neg x_2 \wedge x_3) \vee (x_1 \wedge x_2 \wedge x_3)$. Fuzzifying the DNF produces the local rule $g_{172}(x,y,z) = (1-x)y(1-z) + (1-x)yz + x(1-y)z + xyz = y(1-x) + xz$. For our analysis it is helpful to note that $g_{172}(0, y, z) = y$, $g_{172}(x, 0, z) = xz$, and $g_{172}(x, y, 0) = (1 - x)y$.

We note that the one initial seed fuzzy case is similar to the binary case for any initial seed $\alpha \in [0, 1]$ and so we omit it, as there is nothing new. Let us then move forward to the case where we begin with 2 initial adjacent seed values $\alpha, \beta \in [0, 1]$. It is easy to see that its evolution consists in two vertical sequences and no non-trivial diagonal sequences. For our analysis let use denote the left most non-zero value as $x_0^0 = \alpha$. Again, the first sequence, $\{x_0^j\}_{j \geq 0}$, trivially converges to $L_0^0 = \alpha$. The second sequence, $\{x_1^j\}_{j \geq 0}$, can be recursively defined as $x_1^{k+1} = g_{172}(\alpha, x_1^k, 0) = x_1^k(1 - \alpha)$ thus we can derive that $x_1^k = \beta(1 - \alpha)^k$. When $\alpha = 1$ the sequence becomes 0 and when $\alpha \in (0, 1)$ we deduce that $x_1^{k+1} = x_1^k(1 - \alpha) \leq x_1^k$ thus the sequences is decreasing. Since the sequence is bounded, we know that it converges to some limit say L_1^0. We then take the equation $x_1^{k+1} = x_1^k(1 - \alpha)$ and let $k \to \infty$ which gives us $L_1^0 = L_1^0(1 - \alpha)$ and since $\alpha \neq 1$, we have $L_1^0 = 0$. Even more interesting is the case consisting of three initial seeds, say $\alpha, \beta, \gamma \in [0, 1]$ which evolves in a seemingly very complex fashion, very quickly. The terms become increasingly more complicated especially those in the middle sequence. Denoting the left most seed value by $x_0^0 = \alpha$, the first vertical sequence, $\{x_0^j\}_{j \geq 0}$, trivially has the limit $L_0^0 = \alpha$. Furthermore, using an argument similar to the two seed case above, and excluding the trivial case where $\beta = 1$, we can deduce that the right most sequence, $\{x_2^j\}_{j \geq 0}$, is a decreasing sequence. However, we cannot yet claim it converges to the limit $L_2^0 = 0$ since we must compute $\lim_{k \to \infty} x_2^{k+1} = \lim_{k \to \infty} g_{172}(x_1^k, x_2^k, 0)$. Thus we must first show that the sequence $\{x_1^j\}_{j \geq 0}$ itself converges to a limit. Now comes a delicate existence argument.

Let $\alpha, \beta, \gamma \neq 0$, as the other cases are simpler. In order to prove the existence of the limit of $\{x_1^j\}_{j \geq 0}$, we consider the relation $x_1^{k+1} = g_{172}(\alpha, x_1^k, x_2^k) = x_1^k - \alpha(x_1^k - x_2^k)$. Observe that if $(x_1^k - x_2^k) \geq 0$ for all sufficiently large k, we can conclude that the sequence x_1^k is eventually decreasing (and since it is bounded below by zero) it converges to a non-negative limit. To this end, for given k, note the identity $x_1^{k+1} - x_2^{k+1} = x_1^k - \alpha(x_1^k - x_2^k) - x_2^k(1 - x_1^k) = (1 - \alpha)(x_1^k - x_2^k) + x_1^k x_2^k$. Assume, if possible, that as $k \to \infty$, x_1^k actually *increases* to a limit, say, L_1^0. Then $L_1^0 \geq x_1^0 = \beta > 0$. Since $x_1^{k+1} = g_{172}(\alpha, x_1^k, x_2^k) = x_1^k - \alpha(x_1^k - x_2^k)$ and x_2^k is decreasing, it follows that, in the limit, we have $L_1^0 = L_1^0 - \alpha(L_1^0 - L_2^0)$ or $L_1^0 = L_2^0$. On the other hand, $L_2^0 = g_{172}(L_1^0, L_2^0, 0)$ in the limit too, a relation which gives $L_1^0 L_2^0 = 0$. Combining the two equalities regarding the limits we get $L_1^0 = L_2^0 = 0$. But this contradicts the limit relation $L_1^0 > 0$. It follows that x_1^k cannot increase to a limit and thus there exists a subscript, call it k again, such that $x_1^{k+1} < x_1^k$. Thus, for this k, $x_1^k > x_2^k$ on account of the remarks at the opening of this paragraph. This along with the stated identity above, shows that $x_1^{k+1} > x_2^{k+1}$, which in turn gives $x_1^{k+2} > x_1^{k+1}$ and this must hold for every sufficiently large k. Hence x_1^k is eventually decreasing and thus it has a limit. Combining the above arguments we get that its limit $L_1^0 = L_2^0 = 0$.

From here we use induction to handle the general case of n-seeds. If the rule is run on an initial string of size n, say $\alpha_0, \alpha_1, ..., \alpha_{n-1} \in (0, 1)$, we proceed in a similar manner. First, we set the vertex to be $x_0^0 = \alpha_0$ and note that again the left most sequence, $\{x_0^j\}_{j\geq 0}$, is trivially α_0 and thus $L_0^0 = \alpha_0$. We may then prove existence of limits from right to left using arguments similar to those above. Once the existence of limits for all sequences has been determined we may simply use the local rule to deduce that the right most sequence $\{x_{n-1}^j\}_{j\geq 0}$ has limit L_{n-1}^0. Then, as above, we move left along the sequences to deduce that $L_i^0 = 0$ for $i = (n-1), (n-2), ..., 2, 1$.

Now that we have solved Rule 172 for n-seeds, we may use the relationship $g_{172}(x, y, z) = g_{228}(z, y, x)$, to simply invert the entire pattern and run the evolution of Rule 172, then reverse the pattern again to obtain the solution. In other words, the space-time diagrams are refletions of each other and hence the limits do not change. Thus the evolution will consist of only vertical sequences of which, in this case, the right most is the trivial sequence of simply the right most seed value and the remainder of the vertical sequences all tend to zero.

4.2 Rule 202

The final exceptional rule (up to equivalence) is Rule 202. Due to page limitations we need only sketch the process. Since $202 = 11001010_2$, its DNF is
$$g_{202}(x_1, x_2, x_3) = (\neg x_1 \wedge \neg x_2 \wedge x_3) \vee (\neg x_1 \wedge x_2 \wedge x_3) \vee (x_1 \wedge x_2 \wedge \neg x_3) \vee (x_1 \wedge x_2 \wedge x_3).$$
The evolution of the one seed boolean case is a simple left shift. Fuzzification gives the local fuzzy rule $g_{202}(x, y, z) = (1-x)(1-y)z + (1-x)yz + xy(1-z) + xyz$ or $g_{202} = (1-x)z + xy$. As before we identify the special values $g_{202}(0, y, z) = z$, $g_{202}(x, 0, z) = (1-x)z$ and $g_{202}(x, y, 0) = xy$. We again note that the one seed fuzzy case is similar to the boolean case. This has the obvious analysis of containing a single, left diagonal sequence with limit $L_0^0 = \alpha$ and no non-trivial right diagonal or vertical sequences.

In the two-seed case $\alpha, \beta \in (0, 1)$, denote the left most non-zero value as the vertex $x_0^0 = \alpha$. This case now produces several left diagonal sequences. Again, the first left diagonal sequence, $\{x_{-j}^j\}_{j\geq 0}$, trivially converges to $L_0^- = \alpha$. The second sequence is $\{x_{-j}^{j+1}\}_{j\geq 0}$ which because of $x_{-k}^{k+1} = g_{202}(0, \alpha, x_{-(k-1)}^k) = x_{-(k-1)}^k$, continues infinitely as the second seed β and so $L_1^- = \beta$. In general, we may consider the following recurrence relation for the various diagonals:
$$x_{-j}^{j+k} = g_{202}(x_{-(j+1)}^{j+k-1}, x_{-j}^{j+k-1}, x_{-(j-1)}^{j+k-1}) = (1 - x_{-(j+1)}^{j+k-1})x_{-(j-1)}^{j+k-1} + x_{-(j+1)}^{j+k-1}x_{-j}^{j+k-1}.$$

When $k = 0$ we get $L_0^- = \alpha$, when $k = 1$ we have $L_1^- = \beta$. Now, the existence of the subsequent limits is the most delicate problem. However, noting that $x_{-j}^{j+2} - x_{-(j-1)}^{j+1} = \alpha\beta(1-\alpha)^{j+1}$ holds for every $j = 0, 1, ...$, it follows that the sequence x_{-j}^{j+2} is increasing (and it is bounded) and thus has a finite limit, L_2^-. Necessarily, $L_2^- = g_{202}(\alpha, \beta, L_2^-)$. Solving this for L_2^- gives $L_2^- = \beta$ once again. This argument can now be generalized to show that for each k, the sequences x_{-j}^{j+k} are all increasing and so their limit L_k^- exists for each $k \geq 2$, and again $L_k^- = \beta$. It may seem that a more interesting case would arise by extending the number of initial seeds to n seeds. However, mimicking the previous situation shows that the results remain the same. That is, if the seeds are $\alpha, \beta, \gamma, \ldots, \in (0,1)$, in that specific order from left to right, then for a given set of seeds, and for each k, the resulting sequences x_{-j}^{j+k} are increasing and so each L_k^- exists, and $L_k^- = \beta$ for every $k \geq 1$. Thus, the space-time diagram of FCA 202 is deterministic.

The dynamics of rule 202 can then immediately be applied to determine the dynamics of rule 216. Since $g_{202}(x, y, z) = g_{216}(z, y, x)$, the pattern obtained when running rule 216 on n initial seeds, say $\alpha_0, \alpha_1, \ldots, \alpha_{n-1}$, is a simple reflection of the pattern which occurs when we run rule 202 on the reverse of the initial string. Thus, we obtain only right diagonals (no left diagonal or vertical sequences). Setting our initial cell to be the right most seed value or $x_0^0 = \alpha_{n-1}$, the first right diagonal then converges to the right most seed value, or $L_0^+ = \alpha_{n-1}$. All further right diagonal sequences then converge and their limit is the second right most seed value or $L_i^+ = \alpha_{n-2}$ for all $i \geq 1$. By induction, this holds for all $n \geq 2$.

5   Conclusion

In [5] an analytical method was developed for handling fuzzy rules (FCA) as defined in [1]. The technique, however, fails for so-called exceptional FCA. By an *exceptional* rule we mean an FCA whose fixed points consists of a continuum of real numbers. It can be shown that there are only 9 such exceptional FCA out of a total number of 256 (namely FCA 170, 172, 184, 202, 204, 216, 226, 228 and 240). The general method described in [5] combined with work in [3-7], was used to show that all but possibly these 9 FCA admit dynamics at infinity which do not admit sensitive dependence on the initial conditions, that is, for all but possibly these 9 there cannot be chaotic evolution (in the traditional sense) in their space-time diagrams. Now, of these 9 remaining fuzzy rules, the dynamics of 3 of them are trivial, namely FCA 170, 204 and 240. The dynamics of the most complicated exceptional rule namely, FCA 184, considered in [4] did not exhibit sensitive dependence on initial seeds and so no chaos reigns, there is no complexity. Since the space-time diagrams of FCA 184 and FCA 226 are reflections of one another, the same result is true for FCA 226. This left only FCA 172 (its counterpart FCA 228), and FCA 202 (and its counterpart 216) whose dynamic evolution was possibly suspect. In this paper we show that neither FCA 172 nor FCA 202 can admit chaotic space-time diagrams (and so a fortiori nor can FCA 228 and FCA 202), thus completing the study of the general dynamics of all 256 FCA. Finally, we point out that this technique is also applicable under other fuzzy logics, a topic we shall undertake in a future work.

References

1. Flocchini, P., Geurts, F., Mingarelli, A.B., and Santoro, N.: Convergence and Aperiodicity in Fuzzy Cellular Automata - Revisiting Rule 90. Physica D **42** (2000) 20-28
2. Ganguly, N., Sikdar, B., Deutsch, A., Canright, G., and Chaudhuri, P.: A Survey on Cellular Automata. Preprint; Center for High Performance Computing, Dresden University of Technology, 2003

3. Mingarelli, A.B., Beres, E.: The dynamics of general fuzzy cellular automata: Rule 30. WSEAS Trans. Circuits and Systems **10** 3 (2004) 2211-2216
4. Mingarelli A.B., El-Yacoubi, S.: On the decidability of the evolution of the fuzzy cellular automaton, FCA 184. In ICCS 2006, Reading, UK, Lecture Notes in Computer Science (to appear)
5. Mingarelli, A.B.: The global evolution of general fuzzy cellular automata. Journal of Cellular Automata (2006) (to appear)
6. Mingarelli, A.B.: The dynamics of general fuzzy cellular automata. In Proceedings of the International Conference on Computational Science, Emory University, Atlanta, May 22-25, 2005. Springer-Verlag, New York. Lecture Notes in Computer Science **3515** (2005) 351-359
7. Mingarelli, A.B.: Fuzzy rule 110 dynamics and the golden number. WSEAS Trans. Computers **2** (4) (2003) 1102-1107
8. Reiter, C.A.: Fuzzy automata and life. Complexity **7** (3) (2002) 19-29.
9. Von Neumann, J.: Theory of Self-Reproducing Automata. University of Illinois Press, Urbana, 1966
10. Wall, H.S.: Analytic Theory of Continued Fractions. Chelsea Publ., New York, (1948)
11. Wolfram, S.: A New Kind of Science. Wolfram Media Inc, (2002)
12. Wolfram, S.: Cellular Automata and Complexity: Collected Papers. Addison-Wesley Publishing, (1994)

Cellular Automata Modelling of Large Scale Systems and VLSI Implementation Perspectives

Ioakeim G. Georgoudas

Democritus University of Thrace, Department of Electrical and Computer Engineering,
Laboratory of Electronics,
GR 67100 Xanthi, Greece
igeorg@ee.duth.gr
http://www.ee.duth.gr/people/frame.htm

Abstract. Modelling of Large Scale Systems is an interesting research area since it combines issues of risk management and human decision. Strongly related with social, environmental and economic consequences, such issues impel scientific community to investigate for efficient and applicable solutions. To this direction, phenomena involving mass human presence, as crowd panic or extended natural processes, as earthquakes, have been simulated, using a computational intelligent technique, based on Cellular Automata (CA). CA are very effective in simulating physical systems, capturing the essential features of systems where global behaviour arises from the collective effect of simple components which interact locally. Moreover, they are also one of the most suitable computational structures for VLSI realization. The evaluation of each model is based on its response to real data. In both cases, an efficient graphical user interface has been developed, in order to study various hypotheses concerning the prominent features of each model.

1 Introduction

Large-Scale Systems are characterised by a large number of variables and nonlinearities. Such systems, i.e. earthquakes, tsunamis, lava flow, forest fire propagation or crowd movement under panic, cause phenomena of mass destruction. Consequently, economic, environmental as well as social reasons call for their thorough study of high importance. Progress in the area of computer science and electronics provides all necessary tools for the design and implementation of large-scale systems models observing them and control them. Furthermore, the use of suitable computational tools, such as cellular automata (CA) as alternatives to standard simulation methods, enables us to model more accurately distinct features of these dynamical systems.

Alternative CA models that have been developed to model large-scale systems-phenomena are reported in the next two sessions. More specifically, the first one simulates the progress of a mass destruction physical phenomenon, i.e. the earthquake, based on a potential value analysis while the second one simulates issues of risk management and human decision, namely, pedestrian dynamics during the evacuation of a closed area. The efficiency of both models is detected with the use of

S. El Yacoubi, B. Chopard, and S. Bandini (Eds.): ACRI 2006, LNCS 4173, pp. 88–93, 2006.

real data. Both models are supplied with a graphical user interface (GUI) aiming at sufficient investigation.

2 The Earthquake Process Model

The earthquake models presented so far were based on a mass–spring model either in one (1-d) or two (2-d) dimensions. The proposed potential–based model is a 2-d dynamic system constituted of cells–charges [1]. It aims at the simulation of seismic activity with the use of potentials. It simulates earthquake activity in correspondence to the quasi-static 2-d version of the Burridge-Knopoff spring-block model [2], as well as, to the Olami-Feder-Christensen (OFC) model [3].

A new approach towards the reordering and the improvement of the presented models is based on the idea of implementing their capacitor–inductor analogue. The LC circuit resembles a mass–spring system. Energy transformation is similar to the mechanical oscillation that takes place in the mass–spring system, where the potential energy of the spring is converted into the kinetic energy of the mass and vice versa. A step forward is the assumption that each cell of the CA can be well described by the value of its potential. Since the system is conservative every single area of it can be uniquely characterised by a scalar quantity, the potential. Each cell–charge creates around an electrostatic field. The value of the potential that characterises each CA site is the resultant value of the potential if there is taken under consideration only the existence of four (or eight) source charges around (von Neumann/Moore neighbourhood). The system balances through the exercitation of electrostatic Coulomb–forces among charges, without the existence of any other form of interconnection in–between. Such kinds of forces are also responsible for this level to be bonded with a rigid but moving plane below.

From an electronic point of view, it is attempted the presentation of an analogue computer based on a digital platform using CA as the essential intermediate stage. In analogue computers, electrical phenomena are used to model the problem being solved and all computations are performed by using properties of electrical quantities. The 2-d CA model reproduces prominent features of earthquake data, with continuous states and discrete time.

The dynamics of the model is driven by the existence of simple update rules that take place in discrete steps. Specifically, if the potential $V_{i,j}$ of the (i,j) cell exceeds the threshold value V_{th} of the level below, the balance is disturbed. The removal of the cell reorders the values of the potential at its vicinity, driving to a cascade phenomenon, i.e, the model's equivalent to an earthquake [4]. Since the system is conservative the value of the potential of the cell (i,j) is equally shared either to its four or eight neighbours (von Neumann/Moore neighbourhood).This model stores only one real–value field, i.e. the potential. Moreover, the use of closed boundary conditions has been adopted in order the model to present strong forms of in-homogeneity at the boundaries, alike earthquake faults at the surface.

The model has been tested and calibrated with the use of real data. Its effectiveness and reliability are detected by comparing the Gutenberg-Richter law scheme obtained by real data to that resulted through simulation. Recorded data and simulation results quite match, both presenting power-law behaviour with an acceptable divergence [5].

The CA model is structured in a way to provide a variety of measurements [6], such as the "critical state", i.e., the state of the system after a large number of earthquake simulations and the "cascade (earthquake) size", which is defined as the total number of cells that participate in a single earthquake procedure, which stands as long as the condition $V_{i,j} > V_{th}$ is true. This magnitude is a measure of the total energy released during the evolution of the earthquake, hence a measure of the earthquake magnitude.

Finally, the CA model is equipped with a user–friendly interface, enabling interactive simulation. It is enriched with various parameter options as well as with the ability of automatic introduction of real data. It is also provided with the efficiency of monitoring all the aforementioned measurements (Fig. 1).

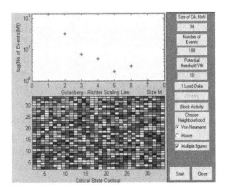

Fig. 1. The GUI of the Earthquake Process CA model

3   The Crowd Dynamics Model

During the last decade, crowd is modelled as composed of discrete individuals rather than being treated as homogeneous mass, like flowing fluid [7]. A major constraint was the enormous number of calculations required. Computational power of modern computers changed this situation. Further simplification of modelling such processes can be achieved by the use of computational techniques such as CA. Regarding the simulation of pedestrian dynamics, 2-d CA models are reported either treating pedestrians as particles subject to long-range forces [8] or using walkers leaving a trace by modifying their paths [9].

A 2-d CA model that aims at the simulation of crowd dynamics during the evacuation of a closed area has been proposed. CA cells obtain discrete values, thus indicating their status; either free or occupied. The grid is uniform and invariant with respect to direction. During each time step, an individual chooses to move in one of the eight possible directions of its vicinity. A particle cannot overcome more than one cell at a time step, meaning that it moves with a maximum velocity of one cell per time step.

Regarding the local CA rule, for each occupied cell a 3x3 matrix is evaluated (Fig.2), pointing the closest direction to an exit. The matrix depends on the reference cell and its eight closest neighbours and the values of its elements indicate the distance from the exit. The distance is defined as the minimum number of cells needed to be covered in order the exit to be reached, moving strictly either vertically or horizontally. Each element represents a possible updated spatial state of the occupied cell at the next time step. All possible routes are detected, and the particle moves towards the shortest one to the next time step. Provided that more than one escaping points exist, the process is repeated, taking place for each exit separately. The particle does not move towards the target unless it is free and it moves if no other particle targets the same cell. In case that more than one particles target the same cell, priority is given to the one that fronts the exit.

A graphical user interface (GUI) based on Matlab® has been developed enhancing the surveillance perspectives of a certain area (Fig. 2). Distinguishing features of the evacuated area are adjustable, incorporating both topological-oriented parameters and parameters that describe the crowd formation. All crowd characteristics are individual dependent. The evacuation process can be demonstrated for several exit locations and it can also be enriched with obstacles at various locations. Moreover, population is adjustable including different types of individuals.

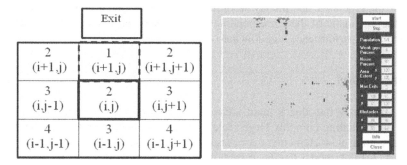

Fig. 2. Left side: A median matrix example. The values of the elements indicate the distance from the exit. Right side: A snapshot of the GUI. Different coloured particles correspond to different groups of individuals. Black dots correspond to obstacles.

Regarding the VLSI architecture of the model, the hardware implementation can be achieved with the translation of the CA algorithm into a synthesizable subset of a hardware description language (HDL), namely VHDL [Very High Speed Integrated Circuit (VHSIC) HDL]. More specifically, the CA rule, described earlier and based on the minimum distance from the exit, is used to produce the interface and the behavioural parts of the VHDL code. The lattice size and the 2-d neighbourhood width (nine cells in the examined case) of the CA model are used to produce the structural part of the resulting VHDL code. The final VHDL code has a mixed behavioural and structural form. Its architecture contains both behavioural and structural parts, such as concurrent statements. Simulation results of the VHDL code are guaranteed to be found in complete agreement with the compilation results of the CA model. The VHDL code would be ready to accomplish the design processes of analysis, elaboration, and simulation; so that the next design process of synthesis (i.e. the translation of register-transfer-level (RTL) design into a gate-level net-list) can take place [10]. The process of design synthesis presupposes the usage of a commercial VLSI CAD system, which will automatically produce, after the completion of the VHDL code

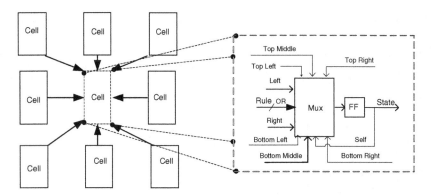

Fig. 3. A 2-d CA structure (left) and the architecture of a single cell of the CA model (right)

synthesis, the schematic and the layout of the corresponding dedicated processor. Fig. 3 depicts the schematic of the corresponding CA cell. Such an implementation achieves high simulation performance with low hardware overhead.

4   Conclusions

This paper shortly introduces main ideas and results of our computational CA approach, for modelling complex large scale systems. These CA models can be further enriched, adding new elementary processes to account situations of increasing complexity. A 2-d CA model has been proposed and calibrated in order to successfully simulate the earthquake activity in a specific region. The study of the seismic activity stands on a potential–based analysis. The advantage of this method is that vector analysis is avoided, also attaining the best use of the current computing power. Hence, this model may be used for risk analysis of endangered areas in terms of long term forecasting of the earthquake activity at various situations. Future research objectives include application of the CA model to new real cases, expecting improvements and extensions towards a more physical and less empirical model.

Furthermore, a 2-d CA pedestrian dynamics model has also been presented. Certain attributes of crowd behaviour, e.g., collective effects, collisions and delaying factors have been successfully encountered during simulation. The developed interface provides the ability for observing various situations of room evacuation process. As future work, based on the flexibility of the proposed model, it could be possible to analyse video sequences related to crowd escaping in order to calibrate the CA model. Data from video monitoring could be supplied to the model to realize whether the model is capable of reproducing phenomena under panic circumstances. In terms of circuit design and layout, silicon-area utilization and maximization of clock speed, CA are efficient computational structures for VLSI realization. Hence, the VLSI implementation of the proposed CA algorithm, translated into a synthesizable subset of a hardware description language (VHDL), is straightforward with low hardware overhead. Consequently, it is feasible the perspective of an integrated surveillance system, with camera based monitoring algorithms that could provide all necessary video data.

References

1. Georgoudas, I.G., Sirakoulis, G.Ch., Andreadis, I.: A Potential-based Cellular Automaton Model for Earthquake Simulation. Int. Conf. on Computational Methods in Sciences and Engineering, Athens, Greece (November 2004) pp. 185-189
2. Burridge, R. and Knopoff, L.: Model and theoretical Seismicity. Bulletin of Seismological Society of America 57 (3) (1967) 341–371
3. Olami, Z., Feder, H.J.S., and Christensen, K.: Self-Organized Criticality in a Continuous, Nonconservative Cellular Automaton Modelling Earthquakes. Phys. Rev. Lett. 68 (8) (1992) 1244–1247
4. Preston, E.F., Sá Martins, J.S., Rundle, J.B., Anghel, M. and Klein, W.: Models of Earthquake Faults with Long-Range Stress Transfer. IEEE Computing in Science and Engineering 2 (2000) 34–41
5. Georgoudas, I.G., Sirakoulis, G.Ch., Scordilis, E.M., Andreadis, I.: Modelling Xanthi's earthquake activity using a two-dimensional cellular automaton. General Assembly 2005 of the European Geosciences Union, Vienna, Austria (April 2005) EGU-A-7603 pp. 456
6. Hernandez, G.: Parallel and distributed simulations and visualizations of the Olami-Feder-Christensen earthquake model. Physica A 313 (2002) 301–311
7. Helbing, D., Farkas, I. Vicsek, T.: Simulating dynamical features of escape panic. Nature 407 (2000) 487–490
8. Aubé, F., Shield, R.: Modeling the Effect of Leadership on Crowd Flow Dynamics. Lecture Notes in Computer Science 3305 (2004) 601–611
9. Burstedde, C., Klauck, K., Schadschneider, A., Zittartz, J.: Simulation of pedestrian dynamics using a two-dimensional cellular automaton. Physica A 295 (2001) 507–525
10. Sirakoulis, G.Ch., Karafyllidis, I., Thanailakis, A., Mardiris, V.: A methodology for VLSI implementation of Cellular Automata algorithms using VHDL. Advances in Engineering Software 32 (2001) 189-202

Merging Cellular Automata for Simulating Surface Effects

Stéphane Gobron[1], Denis Finck[1], Philippe Even[2], and Bertrand Kerautret[2]

[1] Université Henri Poincaré, IUT de St Dié
{Stephane.Gobron, Denis.Finck}@iutsd.uhp-nancy.fr
www.iutsd.uhp-nancy.fr/isn/StGo
[2] LORIA/ADAGIo – Université Henri Poincaré, IUT de St Dié,
11, rue de l'Université, F-88100 Saint-Dié-des-Vosges, France
{Philippe.Even, Bertrand.Kerautret}@loria.fr

Abstract. This paper describes a model of three-dimensional cellular automata allowing to simulate different phenomena in the fields of computer graphics or image processing. Our method allows to combine them together in order to produce complex effects such as automatic texturing, surface imperfections, or biological retina multi-layer cellular behaviours. Our cellular automaton model is defined as a network of connected cells arranged in a natural and dynamic way, which affords multi-behavior capabilities. Based on cheap and widespread computing systems, real-time performance can be reached for simulations involving up to a hundred thousand cells. The efficiency of such an approach is illustrated by a set of CA related to computer graphics –e.g. erosion, sedimentation, or vegetal growing processes– and image analysis –e.g. retina simulation.

Keywords: cellular automata, geometric modeling, image processing, environmental and biological systems, surface effects, fluid simulation.

1 Introduction

This paper presents a model for simultaneous and real-time simulations of surface effects. It refers to the field of Cellular Automata (CA) intended for 3D geometric modeling and image processing and applied to various purposes such as texture synthesis, surface imperfections or simulations of natural phenomena, or retina structure and behaviour simulations as well. We believe that CA are an acceptable solution to deal with the inherent complexity to that domain.

The complex behavior and the diversity that can be observed at a macroscopic level is essentially due to the fact that there are numerous particles with continual interactions. Of course, it is not possible to study all the phenomena coming back at the atomic level. We must consider the right level of abstraction. Although computer *reality* consists of electrons moving through electronic components, their behaviour can be described in terms of electronics, then logic, bits and instructions, algorithms and data structure, languages, software engineering, etc. So when working at a given level, the upper level description can lead to unify

S. El Yacoubi, B. Chopard, and S. Bandini (Eds.): ACRI 2006, LNCS 4173, pp. 94–103, 2006.

phenomena that were previously considered as individual cases. In our case, a level likely to unify the study of surface effects is to consider the surface as a set of small pieces of materials interacting locally –taking into account its thickness, density, color, or elasticity.

Literature about computer graphical CA has become more and more active, especially since Graphics Processing Unit (GPU) became popular [4,20] and since a fundamental book that covers all practical aspects of CA was published by Stephen Wolfram [22]. We mention hereafter some key steps of the CA evolution in this domain. Published in the mid-80s, Thalmann[17] is one of the first computer graphics references directly dealing with the CA issue. In the late 80s and early 90s, CA became quite popular in various fields of computer graphics studies [13,14,16,7,15]. At that time, a work on tumor growth simulation [5] initiated the use of CA for graphical interpretation in biology. In 1991, both Turk [19] and Witkin et al. [21] presented outstanding approaches for texturing; the main idea was to make a texture projection of a 2D reaction-diffusion CA function. In the late 90s, an approach of restricted hyper-texture CA [8] led to a new model, which was called *3DSCA* -for 3D Surface CA-. A series of surface simulations could be generated with this model, unfortunately with many restrictions. In 2003, Tran et al. [18] proposed a CA implemented on GPU, and Harris et al. [12,11] presented even more complex simulations of natural behaviors (boiling fluids) using GPU programming.

Recently, very interesting results were obtained in generating realistic textures with surface imperfections including corrosion, weathered stone, impacts, scratches or even lichen growth. But most of those simulations were designed on a single purpose with a specific and restricted model and the modeled effects require special *ad hoc* data structures. Our present goal is to improve the former *3DSCA* model in order to design a flexible approach, open to any type of multi-behavior surface simulation. This model basically relies on a dynamic data structure combined with CA rules which do not depend on the number of neighbours.

Section 2 describes the general architecture of our model: the generation of initial cells defining the notion of grid type, the way those cells are stored into a non-trivial geometric data structure, and a method for building a regular web of connected cells. Rules of applied cellular automata, design considerations, and corresponding results are detailed in section 3. Finally, section 4 concludes this paper and puts forward some of the related future work emphasizing CA computations based on Graphics Processing Unit (GPU).

2   Merging Cellular Automata

In our approach a surface is a set of cells that are locally interacting together and with the environment of the object they are part of. We show that their limited but non null capabilities can be simulated using the discrete nature of cellular automata. A set of simple rules can produce a wide range of 3D surface simulations. So we define a geometric and dynamic cellular network that has the following advantages: no restriction is made on the input polygon type, any number of vertices, concavities, or holes being accepted; multiple input objects and natural linking between cells of different 3D sources are automatically managed; any type of grids -random, square, triangular or hexagonal- are accepted; cell movements are left possible in all directions; and the cellular structure has no limited number of neighborhood cells or communication types. Our model allows any of the classical natural phenomena to be simulated −e.g.patina/corrosion− and demonstrates the ability to easily code many types of formal CA, such as the famous life game CA [17]. To achieve this aim, we merge and synchronize different cellular automata that are constructed on the same principle. Specific geometrical and CG information on this model are explained in [10].

From polygons to initial cells. The following figure illustrates the cell structure of our new model. This structure is composed of two main areas: two data fields (t) and (t+1) which respectively allow to transmit and to receive information separately, and the four possible cellular states. Note that this kind of meta-state has the advantage of increasing CA computation as only non-

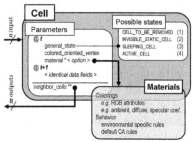

sleeping cells can interact with their neighborhood. Both a random selection of cells position or a pre-selected order can be used to distribute cells over the polygon structure. Harmonious pattern dispositions are restricted to three cases: triangular, square and hexagonal grid. Furthemore, in our model, polygons can be of any type, the cell repartition remains the same, and input polygons and grids are only used for initially positioning the cells.

Dynamic space boxes and cellular network. A new structure called *Dynamic Space Boxes* (DSB) was introduced in order to efficiently determine the neighbor of any cell. This structure relies on a space partition into boxes so that each cell has to be compared with the other cells inside its own box and with all the cell inside the 26-direct neighbor boxes.

The following figure illustrates the 3D relationship between cells and englobing boxes: (a) tested cells are represented by crosses, possible neighbors by squares, and cells that should not be tested by triangles; (b) tested cells are inside the

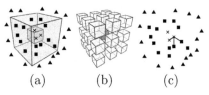

(a)   (b)   (c)

gray box surrounded by the 26 direct neighbor boxes; (c) segments denote successful connections between cell elements and the central tested box. In association with DSB, a special data structure was used to access and store 3D cells. This structure is based on dynamic double-linked-list space tree.

The first step of the connection algorithm consists in traversing the space-structure and connecting every cell C_i to its surroundings making a web of connected cells. For this purpose, we check cells on the 27 boxes (i.e. 26 surrounding + current) that are elements of a sphere of center C_i and radius r_i. The value

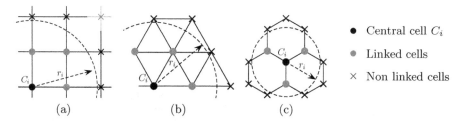

Fig. 1. Radius values r_i of the neighborhood sphere depending on the grid type

r_i is set so that only direct neighbor cells are connected. For the square grid (of size c_s), r_i is set to $2.c_s - \varepsilon$ and for the triangular and hexagonal grids we use $r_i = \sqrt{3}.c_s - \varepsilon$. Figure 1 gives a graphical interpretation for each different grid.

Harmonizing the cellular network. Once a neighbor list has been defined for each cell, the second step is to apply an attraction/repulsion function to the entire system. This function has to repulse cells that are very close or too far from each other and attract the ones that are nearby. After system convergence, the last step consists in keeping only the best links –once again– depending on the type of grid, respectively four or eight for square grids, six for triangular grids, and three for hexagonal grids.

However, this current model presents some limitations. First the harmonization is not trivial and could be improved. For instance, the pre-computation time is very long. Another drawback is that even if a cell knows its neighbor number, the current data structure does not provide the relative positions between neighbors. This property is essential for oriented-rule CA [22], and that is why it is appropriate to call this model *surface cellular network* instead of *surface cellular automaton*. Fortunately, many interesting results can be obtained without harmonizing the connected web or having cellular orientation map. In fact, self-identity and deduced-from-all CA can already be tested; this is what is proposed in the following sections.

3   Current CA Model and Experimental Fields of Study

For a given cell, the number of neighbors is not necessarily constant. Our cellular automaton model thus requires the use of symmetrical rules. Therefore only restricted directional data transfer CA are presented in this section. Nevertheless, the following subsections shows the capabilities and especially the strong potential variety of application field that our model is able to produce.

Results presented in this paper were generated using an AMD Athlon^{TM}64X2 Dual Core 4400+ CPU 2.21GHz with 2Go of RAM and a NVidia^{TM}GeForce 7800 graphical card. For the implementation we used $C++$ language on MS-Visual Studio^{TM}2005 and MS-Windows^{TM}2000 as operating system. Real-time was reached for geometric models composed of less than a hundred thousand cells.

Fig. 2. Multi surface effects on the *Stanford bunny*: (a) fractures, (b) Voronoï diagram and hyper texture, (c) watermap, (d) solvent simulation

This section is organized as follows. Each subsection presents a different level of using our model: subsection 3.1 describes the cell states used to control the cellular network sequences; subsection 3.2 lists graphical applications mainly in the field of automatic texturing and simulations such as cracks and melting; subsection 3.3 illustrates how fluids can be simulated with watercolor or weathering effects such as erosion, sedimentation, or lichen propagation; subsection 3.4 illustrates how non-trivial image analysis processing can be simulated based on the retina pipeline non-linear architecture.

Most subsections present a table showing transition rules with their lexical, logical, and global behavior descriptions using a C-like pseudo-code for conditional gates. Symbol interpretations of equations are: C: current cell; g_s: general state of C; v, v_c, p: cell vertex (*i.e.* position and orientation), cell color, and cell potential; k: active neighbor number at C; k_p k_c: as k with true potential and non-null color attributes.

3.1 General States CA

In our approach, *general states* define the behavior and the existence of a cell: to be or not in terms of geometry and time sequence. The very simple set of rules presented in table 1 are essential for making this model simultaneously flexible, multi-task, and fast computing. The first and second rules maintain initialisation and synchronisation updatings. The third and fourth activate or deactivate a cell so that only useful region of the network is used. The last state transition rule randomly selects seed-cells that can be used for generating Voronoï diagram, fluid and pigment or sediment spring, high pressure region for fracture, etc.

3.2 Automatic Texturing CA

Automatic texturing owns to the field of computer graphics (CG). Although it is not the direct purpose here, it allows to visualize global behaviour of CA. As only few CG plates can be presented in this paper, samples of resulting images or animations can be found at www.iutsd.uhp-nancy.fr/isn/StGo.

Table 1. General state transition rules

Behaviors	State transition rules: $\forall C$	Characteristics
First CA step	$C_{t+1} \leftarrow C_t$	Initialization
CA steps	$C_t \leftarrow C_{t+1}$	Synchronization: updating
Sleeping all	$gs_{t+1} \leftarrow sleepingCell$	Powerless
Active all	$gs_{t+1} \leftarrow activeCell$	Powerful
Random selection	$\forall$ seed type $if(rand_{selected}) \Rightarrow$ $state_{t+1} \leftarrow random_{value}(\text{seed type})$	Seed values

Table 2. Computer graphical automatic texturing CA transition rules

Behaviors	State transition rules: $\forall C$	Characteristics
Spreading color	$vc_{t+1} \leftarrow \frac{vc_t + \sum C_n vc_t}{k_c + 1}$	Propagation
Melting-like	$v_{t+1} \leftarrow \frac{v_t + \sum C_n v_t}{k+1}$	Averaging vert.
Crack-like	$(\exists C_k \neq C)?|v_c : \overline{v_c} \mid gs_{t+1} \leftarrow Sleeping_{cell}$	Derivative
Corrosion	$(p_t > 0)?|p_{t+1} \leftarrow (p_t - \Delta_p)$ $|(p_t \leq 0)?|gs_{t+1} \leftarrow Sleeping_{cell}$ $else(k_p > \frac{k}{2})?|p_{t+1} \leftarrow Max_p$	Destruction
Life game	$(k_k \neq 2)?|(k_p = 3)?|p_{t+1} : \overline{p_{t+1}}$	Reproduction
Maze-like	$(k_p \neq 2 \parallel 4)?|(k_p = 3)?|p_{t+1} : \overline{p_{t+1}}$	Construction
Regrouping	$(p_t)?|((k_p < \frac{k}{2})?|(p_{t+1}) : (\overline{p_{t+1}}))$	Digression-dif.

The first two lines of table 2 propose the *spreading color* –see figure 2(b)– and *melting-like* simulations. These effects are very similar as they simply average the surrounding area respectively in terms of color and vertices (position + normal). However, we can observe that the first one surrounds the surface and the second one drastically changes the 3D topology. To generate a crack-like pattern –see figures 2(a) and 5– we first use a regular color propagation, which provides a Voronoï diagram [2]. We then determine the color derivative to define area edges with a single pass CA. And finally, we associate the resulting derivative potential to fracture the structure of the object. Corrosion as well as patina simulation can be interpreted as a kind or propagation substracting at each time step a potential of each corroded cells and spreading with a random factor proportional to the number of neighbor corroded cells. The last three lines of table 2 present well-known CA where basically, cell behavior depends on the equilibrium of the surroundings –see figure 3. In the first case (*i.e. life game*), we seek a specific number (*2*) for stability, and its tangent (*3*) for sudden state change. Rules of the second case are almost identical to the game of life. Surprisingly, the result is completely different: after a few steps, the system converges to a maze-like pattern with sometimes instable areas. Concerning the "regrouping" CA, it belongs to the family of activation/inhibition.

3.3   Fluid CA

In this subsection, we propose to show how action of fluids can be modeled using our cellular networks model. Of course, as we have a CA approach the

Fig. 3. Three famous CA: (a) life game; (b) maze-like; (c) reaction diffusion

fluid does not "exist" in terms of particle or flow fields; only CA states and CA transition rules remain to simulate fluid interaction on solid, *i.e.* erosion, evaporation, pigment or sediment concentration, and sedimentation. All fluid properties are demonstrated in the following paragraph as we propose an original and non-trivial simulation: *i.e.* watercolor simulation.

Table 3. Fluid CA transition rules

Simulations	State transition rules: $\forall C$	Characteristics
Watercolor	(see detailed formula in the main text)	Erosion, evaporation, and sedimentation
Moss propagation	Only if no-moss:	
	$(min_h < p_t < max_h)?Create(C_{moss})$	Spontaneous seed
	$(rand_{fct(mossAround)})?Create(C_{moss})$	Growth around
	Only if moss:	
	$(p_t < 1)?p_{t+1} \leftarrow (p_t + \delta_{age})$:	Aging
	$gs_{t+1} \leftarrow$ cellToBeRemoved state	Dying

Direct fluid effect, *e.g.* watercolor. The emphasis is on real-time generation of the most salient features of watercolor on a 3D surface within a gravity field. Compared to other works [1] our simulation must be as simple as possible. So we only use two parameters: the potential corresponding to the quantity of water in a cell and the quantity of pigments. The effect we want to obtain consists of pigments spreading in every direction on the surface. The first hypothesis is that at every step, the potential of a cell becomes the average of its potential and the potentials of its neighbor cells. The second hypothesis is that gravity force is partially compensated by viscosity and surface tension. That is why the fluid is not only moving in the direction where the slope is the steepest but also diffusing in every direction proportionally to its slope, and we assume that pigments are moving that way too. The potential of the current cell $C_{p_{t+1}}$ is:

$$p_{c,t+1} = \frac{p_{c,t} \sum_i p_{i,t} \left(1 + \frac{(h_i h_c)}{d(C_i, C_c)}\right)}{1 + k} - \Delta p; \tag{1}$$

where Ci denotes a neighbor cell, $(h_i h_c)/d(C_i, C_c)$ the slope and k the number of neighbors. This phenomena is illustrated in figure 4 and also in figures 2(c) (watermap) and (d) (solvent simulation).

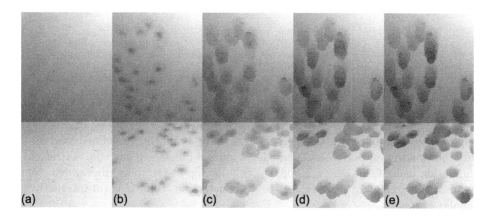

(a)   (b)   (c)   (d)   (e)

Fig. 4. Watercolor simulation: (a) seeds; (b) and (c) watercolor edge darkerning; (d) main spreading due to gravity; (e) drying process

Indirect fluid effects, *e.g.* vegetal growth. In the real world weathering effect of fluid is not limited to erosion and sedimentation, it can also indirectly produce the growth of vegetal such as moss or lichen. To simulate such an effect we must introduce another parameter in the current model: the faculty of a cell to generate another cell. The figure 5 illustrates how powerful can be cellular automata. Based on a simple right-angled parallelepiped (six polygons) we first used a fracture CA simulation in order to generate surface irregularities over the 3D lattice. We then applied a waterflow CA simulation to determine where the humidity would be not too low and not too high to make moss seed appear. Finally we applied a self generated moss CA to make the moss propagate in a natural way over the lattice surface. Details of this model can be found in [6].

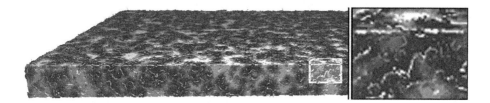

Fig. 5. Auto generated cellular moss covering a simple lattice

3.4   Retina Simulation

The last field of study where we propose to apply our CA model is the architectural modeling of biological retina. Two aspects of the retina are taken into account: a simplified pipeline model of artificial retina based on cellular autotomata, and a 3D cellular network of the cone photoreceptors. Since the study is under way, details can be found in two publications: [3] for the topological 3D

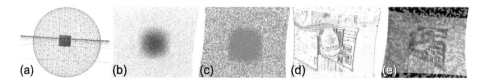

Fig. 6. Retina simulation using cellular network

approach with simple cellular behavior, and [9] for a real-time pipeline based cellular automaton and GPU-based model. Figure 6 illustrates key steps of retina simulation using CA: (a) eye globe; (b) cellular topology around fovea area; (c) corresponding cellular network; (d) contour detection using CA; (e) interactive cellular automata.

4   Conclusion and Future Work

We have presented a model of three-dimensional multi cellular automata allowing to simulate many phenomena in the fields of computer graphics and image processing. We detailed the process for constructing a web of connected cells. We also proposed a way to organise cellular network in any type of grid, and presented different types of CA network. Finally, to show this model capacities for different fields of study, we have applied a series of regular CA to simulate the following phenomena: spreading and diffusion CA, crack-pattern CA, environmental systems such as fluids and vegetation growth, and biological systems such as retina simulation.

From this basis, we are interested in investigating oriented-dependent CA models. Furthermore, we are also convinced that GPU programming has to play a major part in the application of CA. Hence we are studying new approaches in order to take into account the inherent constraints to that type of programming.

References

1. C.J. Curtis, S.E. Anderson, J.E. Seims, K.W. Fleischery, and D.H. Salesin. Computer-generated watercolor. In *SIGGRAPH'97 Conf. Proc.*, volume 24, pages 225–232, 1997.
2. M. de Berg, O. Schwarzkopf, M. van Kerveld, and M. Overmars. *Computational Geometry: Algorithms and Applications, 2nd ed.* Berlin: Springer, 1998.
3. F. Devillard, S. Gobron, F. Grandidier, and B. Heit. Implémentation par automates cellulaires d'une modélisation architecturale de rétine biologique. In *READ'05*. Institut National des Télécommunications, Evry, France, June 1-3 2005.
4. S. Druon, A. Crosnier, and L. Brigandat. Efficient cellular automaton for 2d / 3d free-form modeling. *Journal of WSCG*, 11(1, ISSN 1213-6972), 2003.
5. W. Duchting. Tumor growth simulation. *Computers and Graphics*, 14(3/4):505–508, 1990.
6. P. Even and S. Gobron. Interactive three-dimensional reconstruction and weathering simulations on buildings. In *CIPA 2005 XXth International Symposium*, pages 796–801, Turin, Italy, 2005.

7. M. Gerhardt, H. Schuster, and J.J. Tyson. A cellular automaton model of excitable media including curvature and dispersion. *Science 247*, pages 1563–1566, 1990.
8. S. Gobron and N. Chiba. 3D surface cellular automata and their applications. *The Journal of Visualization and Computer Animation*, 10:143–158, 1999.
9. S. Gobron, F. Devillard, and B. Heit. Real-time contour restoration and segmentation using cellular automaton and GPU programming. in reviewing process, 2006.
10. S. Gobron and D. Finck. Generating surface textures based on cellular networks. In *The Geometric Modeling and Imaging international conference (GMAI06)*. IEEE Computer Society, July 2006.
11. M. Harris. Implementation of a CML boiling simulation using graphics hardware. In *CS. Dept, UNCCH, Tech. Report*, volume 02-016, 2003.
12. M. Harris, G. Coombe, T. Scheueermann, and A. Lastra. Physically-based visual simulation on graphics hardware. *Graphics Hardware*, pages 1–10, 2002.
13. W. Li. Complex patterns generated by next nearest neighbors cellular automata. *Computers and Graphics*, 13(4):531–537, 1989.
14. R. Makkuni. Pixelated structures as a compositional medium. *The Visual Computer*, 2(4):243–254, 1986.
15. W.K. Mason. Art from cellular automata and symmetrized dot-patterns. *Computers and Graphics*, 16(4):439–442, 1992.
16. C. Reynolds. Flocks, herds, and schools: A distributed behavioral model. In *ACM Computer Graphics Conf. Proc.*, volume 21:4, pages 25–33, July 1987.
17. D. Thalmann. A *lifegame* approach to surface modeling and rendering. *The Visual Computer*, 2:384–390, 1986.
18. J. Tran, D. Jordan, and D. Luebke. New challenges for cellular automata simulation on the GPU. *www.cs.virginia.edu*, 2003.
19. G. Turk. Generating texture for arbitrary surfaces using reaction-diffusion. In *SIGGRAPH'91 Conf. Proc.*, volume 25, pages 289–298, 1991.
20. L. Wang, X. Wang, X Tong, S. Lin, S. Hu, B. Guo, and H-Y. Shum. View-dependent displacement mapping. In *SIGGRAPH'03 Conf. Proc.*, volume 22, pages 334–339, 2003.
21. A. Witkin and M. Kass. Reaction-diffusion textures. In *SIGGRAPH'91 Conf. Proc.*, pages 299–308, 1991.
22. S. Wolfram. *A new kind of science*. Wolfram Media Inc., 1st edition, 2002.

Decision Algorithms for Cellular Automata States Based on Periodic Boundary Condition

Byung-Heon Kang, Jun-Cheol Jeon, and Kee-Young Yoo*

Dept. of Computer Engineering, Kyungpook National University,
Daegu, Korea, 702-701
{bhkang, jcjeon33}@infosec.knu.ac.kr,
yook@knu.ac.kr

Abstract. Das et al. have reported characterization of reachable/non-reachable CA states recently. Their scheme has only offered the characterization under a null boundary CA (NBCA). However, in hardware implementation, a periodic boundary CA (PBCA) is suitable for constructing cost-effective schemes such as a linear feedback shift register structure because of its circular property. Thus, this paper provides two decision algorithms for classification of reachable/non-reachable state and group/non-group CA based on periodic boundary condition.

1 Introduction

Study of cellular automata (CA) and its evolutions were initiated in the early 1950s as a general framework for modeling complex structures capable of self-reproduction and self-repair, and the compiled work was reported in [1]. Since then many researchers have taken interest in the study of CA for modeling the behavior of complex system. A new phase of activities started with Wolfram [2], who pioneered the investigation of CA mathematical models for self-organizing statistical systems. He identified several characteristic features of self-organization in uniform three-neighborhood (left, self and right) finite CA with two states (0 or 1) per cell, and has reported one-dimensional, periodic, boundary additive CA with the help of polynomial algebra [3]. Studies of null and periodic boundary CA and some experimental observations have also been reported by Pries et al. [4].

The major CA-based models of a wide variety of applications have been proposed in [5]. Current intensive interest in this field can be attributed to the phenomenal growth of VLSI technology that permits cost-effective realization of the simple structure of local-neighborhood CA. Wolfram has proposed a method to check the non-reachable condition of a state in a uniform CA [3]. Wuensche has proposed a method to compute the predecessors of a CA state that further can be extended to check its non-reachable condition [6]. A group CA has been projected as a generator of pseudo-random patterns of high quality, and a class of non-group CA has been established to be an efficient hashing function generator [5]. In recent years, characterizations of

---

* Corresponding author.

S. El Yacoubi, B. Chopard, and S. Bandini (Eds.): ACRI 2006, LNCS 4173, pp. 104–111, 2006.
© Springer-Verlag Berlin Heidelberg 2006

reachable/non-reachable CA states and group/non-group CA were reported by Das et al. [7]. Their scheme, which has only offered the characterization under a null boundary CA (NBCA), has adopted an approach to find its predecessors. However, in hardware implementation, a periodic boundary CA (PBCA) is suitable for constructing cost-effective schemes such as a linear feedback shift register structure because of its circular property. Thus, we propose an analysis to decide the reachable/non-reachable states and group/non-group CA based on periodic boundary condition.

The rest of the paper is organized as follows. In Section 2, we give a brief description of a CA. Section 3 provides decision algorithm of the reachable/non-reachable states of a PBCA. A distinction to characterize the group/non-group of a PBCA is presented in Section 4, followed by discussion and conclusion in Section 5.

2 Cellular Automata

A CA is a dynamic system in which space and time are discrete. Each cell of a CA consists of a discrete variable. The cells evolve in discrete time steps according to some deterministic rule that depends only on local neighbors. The value of it at time t (the time step) is defined as the present states of the cell. The next state of a cell at $(t+1)$ is estimated from the present states of the cell and in its two neighborhoods (three-neighborhood dependency).

The next state transition of ith cell can be represented as a function of the present states of the $(i-1)$th, ith and $(i+1)$th cells,

$$Q_i(t + 1) = f(Q_{i-1}(t), Q_i(t), Q_{i+1}(t))$$

where f is known as the rule of the CA denoting the combinational logic.

Table 1. State transition for rule 60 and 150

	111	110	101	100	011	010	001	000	Rule
Next state	0	0	1	1	1	1	0	0	60
Next state	1	0	0	1	0	1	1	0	150

For a two-state and three-neighborhood CA, there can be a total of 2^3 distinct neighborhood configurations. If each of these neighborhood configurations is assigned with a Boolean value, there can be a total of 2^{2^3} (256) distinct mappings from all these neighborhood configurations to the next state. Each mapping is called a "rule" of the CA. If the next-state function of a cell is expressed in the form of a truth table, then the decimal equivalent of the output is conventionally called the rule number for the cell. Table 1 specifies two particular sets of transition from a neighborhood configuration to the next state.

The first row gives all eight possible states of the three neighboring cells (the left, itself, and the right neighborhood) at the time instance t. The second and third rows give the corresponding states of the ith cell at time instance $t+1$ for two illustrative CA rules. The combinational logic equivalent for rule 60 and 150 is given as

Rule 60 $\qquad Q_i(t + 1) = Q_{i-1}(t) \oplus Q_i(t)$

Rule 150 $\qquad Q_i(t + 1) = Q_{i-1}(t) \oplus Q_i(t) \oplus Q_{i+1}(t)$

where $\oplus$ denotes XOR (that is, addition modulo-2).

The rule 60 and 150 are involved only XOR logic. In this case, if the rule of a CA cell includes only XOR logic, it is called a linear rule. Otherwise, rule involving XNOR logic is referred to as complement rule. If all the cells of a CA have linear rule, it is called a linear CA. A CA having a combination of XOR and XNOR rules is called an additive CA, whereas a CA having AND-OR rule is non-additive CA.

A CA is called uniform CA if all the CA cells have the same rule, otherwise it is called hybrid CA. If the left (right) neighbor of the leftmost (rightmost) terminal cell is connected to 0-state, then the CA is called a NBCA (Fig. 1 (a)). Otherwise, if the extreme cells are adjacent to each other, the CA is called a PBCA (Fig. 1 (b)).

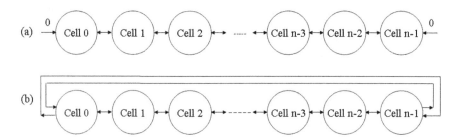

Fig. 1. CA with different boundary conditions (a) null boundary CA, (b) periodic boundary CA

If a CA contains only cyclic states, it is called a group CA. Each state of a group CA has only one predecessor. So, all states of a group CA are reachable state. But if a CA contains both cyclic and non-cyclic states, it is called a non-group CA. Any states of a non-group CA have no predecessor or a number of predecessors. Therefore any states of a non-group CA are reachable or non-reachable state. The proposed two algorithms report the decision of a reachable/non-reachable state and group/non-group CA based on a periodic boundary condition.

3 Classification of Reachable or Non-reachable State

This section investigates that a state of CA is reachable state or non-reachable state based on a PBCA. A state having n cells is presented by $< S_0\ S_1 \cdots S_{n-2}\ S_{n-1} >$. We can consider four cases on the value of the first and last cell of a state as shown in Table 2. A CA is said to be a NBCA if the left (right) neighborhood of the leftmost (rightmost) terminal cell is connected to logic 0-state. That is, the values of the left most cell and the right most cell of NBCA are all 0. Therefore, if those values are 0, then the next value of cell 1 and cell 4 represents d (*don't care*). Rule Min Term (RMT) is the decimal expression of present states [7]. Table 3 offers the set of RMTs S'_{i+1}

Table 2. State transition for a four-cases having rule (90, 204, 60, 102)

RMT	111 (7)	110 (6)	101 (5)	100 (4)	011 (3)	010 (2)	001 (1)	000 (0)	Rule
Cell 1	d	d	d	d	1	0	1	0	90
Cell 2	1	1	0	0	1	1	0	0	204
Cell 3	0	0	1	1	1	1	0	0	60
Cell 4	d	1	d	0	d	1	d	0	102

(a) Case 1 : A state having the first cell (= '0') and last cell (= '0')

RMT	111 (7)	110 (6)	101 (5)	100 (4)	011 (3)	010 (2)	001 (1)	000 (0)	Rule
Cell 1	0	1	0	1	1	0	1	0	90
Cell 2	1	1	0	0	1	1	0	0	204
Cell 3	0	0	1	1	1	1	0	0	60
Cell 4	d	1	d	0	d	1	d	0	102

(b) Case 2 : A state having the first cell (= '0') and last cell (= '1')

RMT	111 (7)	110 (6)	101 (5)	100 (4)	011 (3)	010 (2)	001 (1)	000 (0)	Rule
Cell 1	d	d	d	d	1	0	1	0	90
Cell 2	1	1	0	0	1	1	0	0	204
Cell 3	0	0	1	1	1	1	0	0	60
Cell 4	0	1	1	0	0	1	1	0	102

(c) Case 3 : A state having the first cell (= '1') and last cell (= '0')

RMT	111 (7)	110 (6)	101 (5)	100 (4)	011 (3)	010 (2)	001 (1)	000 (0)	Rule
Cell 1	0	1	0	1	1	0	1	0	90
Cell 2	1	1	0	0	1	1	0	0	204
Cell 3	0	0	1	1	1	1	0	0	60
Cell 4	0	1	1	0	0	1	1	0	102

(d) Case 4 : A state having the first cell (= '1') and last cell (= '1')

Table 3. State transition of RMTS

RMT at ith rule	RMTs at $(i+1)$th rule
0 or 4	0, 1
1 or 5	2, 3
2 or 6	4, 5
3 or 7	6, 7

at($i+1$)th cell rule on which the cell can change its state for an RMT chosen at the ith cell rule for state change.

To check that a state is reachable state or non-reachable state, we define following two properties. At the first, the set of S'_{i+1} is RMTs at $(i+1)$th rule transferred from RMT at ith rule. If RMT at ith rule is m, RMTs at $(i+1)$th rule are changed to $(2m)$

mod 8 and $(2m+1)$ *mod* 8. For instance, if RMT at *i*th rule *m* is 2, RMTs at $(i+1)$th rule are changed to {4, 5}. At the second, the set of S''_{i+1} is the value that the $(i+1)$th bit of a state is equal to the present state in the $(i+1)$th cell. For example, if the third bit of a state is 1, the set of S''_3 is {2, 3, 4, 5} in the case 4. Following Algorithm 1 decides that a state is reachable state or non-reachable state.

Algorithm 1. *FindReachableOrNonreachable_PBCA*

Input : *Rule[n][8]*, *state[n]*, *n*
Output : if non-reachable state, return 1. Otherwise, return 0.
Step 1 : *Select one of the four cases.*
    If state[1] = 0 and state[n] = 0, select and reference case 1.
    Else if state[1] = 0 and state[n] = 1, select and reference case 2.
    Else if state[1] = 1 and state[n] = 0, select and reference case 3.
    Else if state[1] = 1 and state[n] = 1, select and reference case 4.
Step 2 :
    (a) *Find S_1 where Rule[1][j] = state[1],*
        if case 1 or case 3 is selected, j = 1, 2, 3, 4. Otherwise j = 1, $\cdots$, 8.
    (b) *If S_1 has 4, 5, 6 and 7, replace by 0, 1, 2 and 3 respectively.*
    (c) *If $S_1 = \phi$, return 1 as the state is non-reachable.*
Step 3 : *For i = 2 to n−1*
    (a) *Find S'_i such that if $m \in S_{i-1}$, ((2m) mod 8) and ((2m+1) mod 8) are in S'_i.*
    (b) *Find S''_i, where $S''_i = \{j\}$ and Rule[i][j] = state[j], j = 1, $\cdots$, 8.*
    (c) *Find $S_i = S'_i \cap S''_i$.*
    (d) *If S_i has 4, 5, 6 and 7, replace by 0, 1, 2 and 3 respectively.*
    (e) *If $S_i = \phi$, return 1 as the state is non-reachable.*
Step 4 :
    (a) *Find S'_n such that if $m \in S_{i-1}$, ((2m) mod 8) and ((2m+1) mod 8) are in S'_n.*
    (b) *Find S''_n, where $S''_n = \{j\}$ and Rule[i][j] = state[j],*
        If case 1 or case 2 is selected, j = 1, 3, 5, 7. Otherwise j = 1, $\cdots$, 8.
    (c) *Find $S_n = S'_n \cap S''_n$.*
    (d) *If S_n has 4, 5, 6 and 7, replace by 0, 1, 2 and 3 respectively.*
    (e) *If $S_n = \phi$, return 1 as the state is non-reachable.*
Step 5 : *The state is reachable. Return 0.*

For example, let us consider the CA having rule (90, 204, 60, 102) and a state having cell <1 0 0 1>. Assume that a rule (90, 204, 60, 102) as $n \times 8$ two-dimension matrix and a state as *n* one-dimension matrix. The values of the left most cell and the right most cell are '1' and '1', so case 4 is selected and referenced. At the first, we get the first bit '1' from a state. And, find S_1, where rule[1][j] equals to state[1] (= '1'), *j* = 1, $\cdots$, 8. Therefore, S_1 = {1, 3, 4, 6}. As S_1 is not an empty set, a state started with '1' is reachable. And, S'_2 = {0, 1, 2, 3, 4, 5, 6, 7} and S''_2 = {0, 1, 4, 5}. So, $S_2 = S'_2 \cap S''_2$ = {0, 1, 4, 5} = {0, 1}. As S_2 is not an empty set, a state started with '10' is reachable. Similarly, S'_3 = {0, 1, 2, 3} and S''_3 = {0, 1, 6, 7}. So, $S_3 = S'_3 \cap S''_3$ = {0, 1}. S_3

is not an empty set. A state started with '100' is reachable accordingly. Finally, $S'_4 = \{0, 1, 2, 3\}$ and $S''_4 = \{1, 2, 5, 6\}$. So, $S_4 = S'_4 \cap S''_4 = \{1, 2\}$. S_4 is not an empty set. So, the state <1 0 0 1> is reachable state. Fig. 2 shows the state-transition diagram of the rule (90, 204, 60, 102).

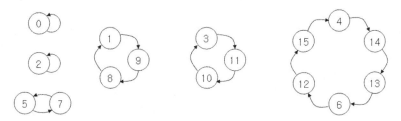

Fig. 2. State-transition diagram of a PBCA having rule (90, 204, 60, 102)

4   Classification of Group or Non-group CA

In this section, we decide that a PBCA is group or non-group. Each cell in a PBCA has only two states with three-neighborhood interconnections. Step 1 finds that $S[i]$ have 0 or 1 with the first rule respectively, where i has 1 and 2. In step 2, we determine 4 RMTs for the next level using Table 3 of $S[j]$. Then, we distribute these rules into $S'[j-1]$ and $S'[j]$, such that $S'[j-1]$ and $S'[j]$ contain 0 and 1 respectively. If the number of $S'[j-1]$ and $S'[j]$ is not same, this PBCA is a non-group. We remove duplicate sets from S' and assign the sets of S' to S for the next step. Finally, if the number of $S[1]$ and $S[2]$ is not same, the PBCA is a non-group. Otherwise, we can find this PBCA is a group. Algorithm 2 checks that the PBCA is group or non-group.

Algorithm 2. *CheckGroupOrNongroup_PBCA*

Input : *Rule[n][8], n*
Output : *if non-group, return 1. Otherwise, return 0.*
Step 1 : *For i = 1 to 2*
      (a) *Find S[i] = {j}, where Rule[1][j] = (i-1), j = 1, ⋯ , 8.*
      (b) *If S[i] has 4, 5, 6 and 7, replace by 0, 1, 2 and 3 respectively.*
Step 2 : *If |S[1]| ≠ |S[2]|, return 1 as a non-group.*
Step 3 : *For i = 2 to n*
   Step 3.1 : *For j = 1 to 2*
      (a) *Determine 4 RMTs for the next level using Table 3 of S[j].*
      (b) *Distribute these 4 RMTs into S'[j-1] and S'[j], such that S'[j-1] and S'[j]*
          contain the RMTs that are 0 and 1 respectively for Rule_i.
      (c) *If |S'[j-1]| ≠| S'[j]|, return 1 as a non-group.*
      (d) *If S'[j-1] and S'[j] have 4, 5, 6 and 7, replace by 0, 1, 2 and 3 respectively.*
      (e) *If (|S'[j-1]| mod 2) = 1 or (|S'[j]| mod 2) = 1, return 1 as a non-group.*
   Step 3.2 : *Remove duplicate sets from S' and assign the sets of S' to S.*
Step 4 : *If |S[1]| ≠ |S[2]|, return 1 as a non-group.*
Step 5 : *The CA is a group. Return 0.*

For example, let consider the PBCA having same rule (90, 204, 60, 102) as remarked above. As we are considering PBCA, Algorithm 2 selects and references case 4 in Table 2. From step 1 of Algorithm 2, we choose $S[1] = \{0, 2, 5, 7\}$ and $S[2] = \{1, 3, 4, 6\}$. In step 3, when $i = 2$, we find $S'[1] = \{0, 1, 4, 5\} = \{0, 1\}$, $S'[2] = \{2, 3, 6, 7\}$ $= \{2, 3\}$, $S'[3] = \{0, 1, 4, 5\} = \{0, 1\}$, $S'[4] = \{2, 3, 6, 7\} = \{2, 3\}$. We can find that each set of S' contains the same number and value respectively, so S' is reduced removing the duplicates and assigned to S. Therefore, $S[1] = \{0, 1\}$ and $S[2] = \{2, 3\}$. When $i = 3$, $S'[1] = \{0, 1\}$, $S'[2] = \{2, 3\}$, $S'[3] = \{6, 7\} = \{2, 3\}$, $S'[4] = \{4, 5\} = \{0, 1\}$. If we should assign S' to S, we get $S[1] = \{0, 1\}$ and $S[2] = \{2, 3\}$. And, when $i = 4$, $S'[1] = \{0, 3\}$, $S'[2] = \{1, 2\}$, $S'[3] = \{0, 3\}$, $S'[4] = \{1, 2\}$. Further, assigning S' to S, we get $S[1] = \{0, 3\}$ and $S[2] = \{1, 2\}$. Finally, the number of $S[1]$ and of $S[2]$ are the same. So, the PBCA having rule (90, 204, 60, 102) is a group.

We show another example of the PBCA having rule (102, 60, 90, 60). From step 1, we choose $S[1] = \{0, 3, 4, 7\} = \{0, 3\}$ and $S[2] = \{1, 2, 5, 6\} = \{1, 2\}$. The number of $S[1]$ and $S[2]$ are the same. So, the PBCA is a group in step 1. In step 3, when $i = 2$, we find $S'[1] = \{0, 1, 6, 7\}$, $S'[2] = \{\phi\}$, $S'[3] = \{\phi\}$, $S'[4] = \{2, 3, 4, 5\}$. We can find that the PBCA having rule (102, 60, 90, 60) is a non-group because the number of $S'[1]$ differs from the number of $S'[2]$.

In order to understand, we present a diagram for decision of group or non-group CA in Fig. 3. Using Fig. 3, we can check the value of S and S' in each step easily. Fig. 3(a) shows that the number of S and S' is same in each step, respectively. Thus we identify that the PBCA having rule (90, 204, 60, 102) is a group, while the PBCA having rule (102, 60, 90, 60) is a non-group because the number of $S'[1] = \{0, 1, 6, 7\}$ differs from $S'[2] = \{\phi\}$.

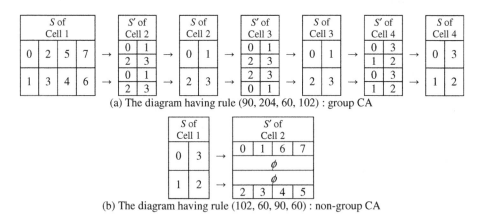

(a) The diagram having rule (90, 204, 60, 102) : group CA

(b) The diagram having rule (102, 60, 90, 60) : non-group CA

Fig. 3. The diagram for classification group or non-group CA

5   Discussion and Conclusion

We have presented two decision algorithms for characterization of reachable/non-reachable state and group/non-group on a PBCA. The proposed schemes have the same time complexity as Das et al.'s scheme which has only offered the characterization under a null boundary condition while our schemes are based on a periodic boundary condition. Moreover, we have reduced the number of loop in comparison with Algorithm 2 of Das et al.'s scheme. We have removed a loop in step 4 by proceeding step 3 and step 4 simultaneously. Therefore, our scheme reduced the program processing time.

A group CA has been projected as a generator of pseudorandom patterns of high quality and a class of non-group CA has been established to be an efficient hashing function generator. Moreover, for hardware implementation, PBCA is suitable for constructing cost-effective schemes such as a linear feedback shift register structure because of its circular property. Thus we expect that our classification can be used as efficient applications on the above mentioned criteria and VLSI technology.

Acknowledgement

The authors in advance would like to thank the anonymous referees for their valuable suggestions on how to improve the quality of the manuscript. This research was supported by the MIC (Ministry of Information and Communication), Korea, under the ITRC (Information Technology Research Center) support program supervised by the IITA (Institute of Information Technology Assessment). This work was also supported by the Brain Korea Project 21 in 2006.

References

1. J. V. Neumann: The Theory of Self Reproducing Automata. A.W. Burks, ed. Univ. of Illinois Press, Urbana and London. (1996)
2. S. Wolfram: Statistical Mechanics of Cellular Automata. Rev. Mod. Phys., 55 (1983) 601-644
3. O. Martin, A. M. Odlyzko, and S. Wolfram: Algebraic properties of cellular automata. Commun. Math. Phys., 93 (1984) 219-258
4. W. Pries, A. Thanailakis, and H. C. Card: Group properties of cellular automata and VLSI application. IEEE Trans. Comput., 12 (1986) 1013-1024
5. P. P. Chaudhuri, D. R. Choudhury, S. Nandi and S. Chattopadhyay : Additive Cellular Automata Theory and Applications. IEEE Computer Society Press, USA (1997)
6. A. Wuensche: Attractor Basins of Discrete Networks. Cognitive Science Research Paper, The University of Sussex, (1997)
7. S. Das, B. K. Sikdar and P. P. Chaudhuri: Characterization of Reachable/Nonreachable Cellular Automata States. Lecture Notes in Computer Science, Vol. 3305. Springer-Verlag, Berlin Heidelberg (2004) 813-822

Qualitative and Quantitative Cellular Automata from Differential Equations

Philippe Narbel

LaBRI, University of Bordeaux 1, France
narbel@labri.fr

Abstract. We give a synthetic and formalized account of relationships between cellular automata (CA) and differential equations (DE): Numerical schemes and phase portraits analysis (via cell-to-cell mappings) can be translated into CA, and compositions of differential operators and phase portraits induce CA compositions. Based on DE, CA can be tuned according to discretization parameters so that faithful CA sequences can be built describing qualitative as well as quantitative solutions.

1 Introduction

Cellular automata (CA) are parallel context-sensitive rewriting processes which are used as computation models and as effective ways of simulating physical, chemical or biological phenomena [20,3,5,26]. With this respect, CA have been mostly considered as tools giving qualitative information, but quantitative information has also been shown reachable [7,6,2,24,23]. This paper generalizes this fact by setting up in a precise way relationships that exist between CA and (systems of) ordinary and partial differential equations (DE). These relationships show how the CA-DE pair can be seen as a generic model to gradually go from qualitative information to quantitative information and vice versa.

We first recall how CA are related to *explicit numerical schemes* to solve DE. Next, we show how *integrated phase portraits of autonomous* DE are transformed into CA (making the link with *cell-to-cell mapping theory* [9]). Compositions of CA can also be based on their relationships with DE : CA are coupled as are differential operators in *splitting techniques* classically used to solve DE [27]; CA can also be coupled as are *invariant regions* of DE phase portraits. The finer (resp. coarser) the involved discretizations in a resolution of a DE, the more quantitative (resp. qualitative) the computations of the induced CA. By tuning discretization levels, qualitative descriptions can be related in a controlled way to quantitative descriptions, yielding what we call here *faithful CA sequences*. Looking for the first terms of these sequences, that is, looking for the simplest meaningful CA, becomes a way of minimizing time and space complexity, but also a way of understanding the model from a *"Kolmogorov complexity point-of-view"*. Based on DE, this search for minimal CA can be driven by studying how and which features are preserved, deformed, smoothed or swept out. In particular, we discuss the existence of *spurious* and *eluded fixed points*, one of the main features indicating that maximum coarseness has been reached.

S. El Yacoubi, B. Chopard, and S. Bandini (Eds.): ACRI 2006, LNCS 4173, pp. 112–121, 2006.

2   Basics

A *cellular automaton* (CA) is a simple context-sensitive rewriting mechanism for which the whole input is processed in parallel using a uniform rewriting rule. Here, we consider CA defined over *lattices* embedded in $\mathbb{R}^n$, i.e. additive subgroups of $(\mathbb{R}^n, +)$ spanned by ordered sets of n independent vectors. A CA is a 4-tuple $\mathcal{A} = (\mathcal{L}_n, \mathcal{Q}, N, \tau)$ where $\mathcal{L}_n$ is a lattice in $\mathbb{R}^n$ whose elements are the *cells*, and where $n \geq 0$ is the CA *dimension*; $\mathcal{Q}$ is a finite set of *states*; $N : \mathcal{L}_n \to 2^{\mathcal{L}_n}$ is a *neighborhood* such that $N(x) = \phi_x(N(x_0))$ where $N(x_0)$ is a set of vectors in $\mathcal{L}_n$ starting at $x_0 \in \mathcal{L}_n$, and ϕ_x is a translation sending x_0 to x (N is such that every x has the same form of neighborhood as x_0); $\tau : \mathcal{Q}^{N(x_0)} \to \mathcal{Q}$ is a *local transition function*. A CA *configuration* f is a global state, that is, an element of $\mathcal{Q}^{\mathcal{L}_n}$. The transition function τ is extended as a *global transition function* $\tilde{\tau} : \mathcal{Q}^{\mathcal{L}_n} \to \mathcal{Q}^{\mathcal{L}_n}$ by applying τ to each cell x as $\tilde{\tau}(f)(x) = \tau(\phi_{-x} \circ f|_{N(x)})$. Applying $\tilde{\tau}$ once is called a *step*. A *run* of a CA is a sequence of consecutive steps starting at an *initial configuration*. Note that these definitions just differ from the classical ones by directly including an CA embedding into $\mathbb{R}^n$.

An *ordinary differential equation* (ODE) is $F(t, u, \frac{du}{dt}, \frac{d^2u}{dt^2}, ..., \frac{d^mu}{dt^m}) = 0$, where the unknown function u is such that $u(t) : \mathbb{R} \to Y$ where Y is a differentiable manifold called the *phase space* or the *state space*. A *partial differential equation* (PDE) is $F(t, x_1, ..., x_n, u, \frac{\partial u}{\partial t}, \frac{\partial u}{\partial x_1}, ..., \frac{\partial^2 u}{\partial x_1 x_2}, ...) = 0$, where the unknown function is such that $u(t, x_1, ...x_n) : \mathbb{R} \times X \to Y$ where X is called the *domain*. Here, Y and X will be restricted to $\mathbb{R}^n$. We shall also only consider *initial-value problems* with exactly one solution, i.e. unique $u(t, \cdot)$ with given prescribed values $u(t_0, \cdot)$ at a given time t_0. When the phase space Y can be decomposed as a Cartesian product $Y_1 \times ... \times Y_p$, one may consider *systems of DE* with an unknown function $u = (u_1, ..., u_p)$.

A numerical method for solving a DE involves three discretization operations respectively applied to the source space of u, the phase space Y, and the differential equation itself: **(1)** Discretizations of the source space generally rely on embedded lattices. For example, regular discretizations of $\mathbb{R}^2$ can be obtained from lattices $\mathcal{L}_2 \subset \mathbb{R}^2$ spanned by two orthogonal vectors of norms δt and δx with an offset shift, i.e. $\{(t, x) \in \mathbb{R}^2 | t = i\delta t + \sigma_t, x = j\delta x + \sigma_x, i, j \in \mathbb{Z}\}$. **(2)** Discretizations of the phase space Y – henceforth denoted by Y_{disc} – are called *quantifications*. Regular discretizations can also be used here, but the most common ones are based on *floating-point numbers* which are non-regular finite quantifications. Sending Y to Y_{disc} is done by *quantification projection functions*. Quantifications and their projection functions lead to *round-off errors*. **(3)** Discretizations of the DE can be obtained by *finite difference schemes* where the differential operators are replaced by difference operators involving only points of the discretized source space (see e.g. [19]). For instance, consider $\frac{du}{dt} = f(t, u)$ with $u : \mathbb{R} \to \mathbb{R}$. Let the source discretization be a lattice $\mathcal{L}_1$ spanned by a δt vector. The so-called *Euler scheme* is based on the two first terms of the *Taylor sequence* of u, i.e. $U(t_0 + \delta t) = U(t_0) + \delta t f(t_0, U(t_0))$, where U is an approximation of u. Solving an initial value problem from $u(t_0)$ for given δt and Y_{disc} is obtained by iterating this scheme: Denoting the i-th time point $i\delta t$ by t_i, we get $U(t_{i+1}) = U(t_i) + \delta t f(t_i, U(t_i))$, $i \geq 0$. As another instance, consider the 2D heat PDE diffusion process $\frac{\partial u}{\partial t} = K(\frac{\partial^2 u}{\partial x^2} + \frac{\partial^2 u}{\partial y^2})$ and a discretization of its source space spanned by vectors of respective norms $\delta t, \delta, \delta$. The *forward-time central-space* finite difference scheme is defined by $U(t_{i+1}, x_j, y_k) = r(U(t_i, x_{j-1}, y_k) + U(t_i, x_{j+1}, y_k) + U(t_i, x_j, y_{k-1})) + U(t_i, x_j, y_{k+1})) + (1 - 4r)U(t_i, x_j, y_k)$ where $r = K\frac{\delta t}{\delta^2}$. These two examples are *explicit numerical schemes*: approximations U of u are built after a map g such that: $U(t_{i+1}) = g(U(t_i, .), ..., U(t_{i-m}, .), t_i, ..., t_{i-m})$, with $0 \leq m < \infty$. In the case that a DE is *autonomous*, which means that the solutions do not depend on time, the scheme can be reduced to $U(t_{i+1}) = g(U(t_i, .), ..., U(t_{i-m}, .))$. Note that a non-autonomous system can be made autonomous by adding the equation $\frac{du_{p+1}}{dt} = 1$. The following first relationship between CA and DE has been informally known for a long time (see e.g. [25]):

Proposition 1. *(Explicit methods and CA). Let $F(u) = 0$ be a (system of) autonomous DE with $u : \mathbb{R} \times \mathbb{R}^n \to Y$, $n \geq 0$. Let Y_{disc} be a finite quantification of Y, and let $\mathcal{L}_1 \times \mathcal{L}_n$ be a discretization of $\mathbb{R} \times \mathbb{R}^n$. Then an explicit numerical scheme g for solving F according to these discretizations can be transformed in a CA $(\mathcal{L}_n, Y_{disc}, N_g, g)$, where N_g is defined by the points in $\mathcal{L}_n$ used in g.*

Euler schemes yield 0-dimensional CA (domain spaces are restricted to a single point)[1]. Heat diffusion processes in n-dimensions lead to n-dimensional CA.

There is another important way of relating DE to CA: When autonomous, a (system of) ODE has a solution space $\mathbb{R} \times Y$ which can be projected without loss of information to the phase space Y as a vector field called *phase portrait*. This vector field can be integrated to obtain a *solution flow*. For a system of p autonomous ODE defined by $\frac{du_i}{dt} = f_i(u_i)$ for which $Y = \mathbb{R}^p$, the phase portrait is $\vec{v}(x_1, ..., x_p) = (f_1(u_1(.)), ..., f_n(u_p(.)))$. For instance, *reaction phenomena* (see e.g. [14]) are captured by autonomous systems of ODE whose phase portraits involve swerving-like behavior around attractive singularities (see Fig. 1). One of these systems is the 2D *Fitzhugh-Nagumo equation* which describes spatial propagation of action potential impulses along the nerve axon by $\frac{du_1}{dt} = (a - u_1)(u_1 - 1)u_1 - u_2$ and $\frac{du_2}{dt} = \epsilon(u_1 - bu_2)$ with $0 < a < 1$, $b > 0$, $\epsilon \in \mathbb{R}$. One can discretize such DE by directly referring to their phase portraits: First, consider a regular discretization Y_{disc} of Y, and let Φ be a numerical method to solve the DE with a fixed integration time $\delta t > 0$. From each point in Y_{disc}, we can integrate the equation by Φ during δt and determine its ending point in Y_{disc}. The result is a relation in $Y_{disc} \times Y_{disc}$, generally studied under the name of *cell-to-cell mappings* [9]. Now, assume that Y includes *invariant bounded sub-domains*, that is, regions $\mathcal{R} \subset Y$ from which the solutions having initial points in $\mathcal{R}$ are strictly contained in $\mathcal{R}$ (a sufficient condition for invariance is that every vector of the vector field on the boundary $\partial\mathcal{R}$ is tangent or entering $\mathcal{R}$). Letting $\mathcal{R}_{disc}$ be the discretization of $\mathcal{R}$ rel. to Y_{disc}, the sub-relation $\mathcal{R}_{disc} \times \mathcal{R}_{disc}$ is finite and defines a possible transition function τ_Φ of a 0D CA. For instance, in the case of the Fitzhugh-Nagumo equation, every bounded rectangular domain

---

[1] Such 0D CA $(\{c\}, \mathcal{Q}, \{c\}, \tau)$ just define finite state paths over a single cell c. They mainly become of interest when composed with nD CA with $n > 0$ (see p. 116).

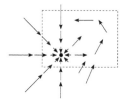

Fig. 1. To the left, the general appearance of the phase portrait of a 2D reaction DE system. The framed region is more precisely represented to the right for a Fitzhugh-Naguino equation with $a = 0.1$, $\epsilon = 0.005$, $b = 4$, together with some integral solutions.

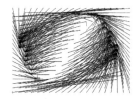

Fig. 2. A CA of 400 states corresponding to the above invariant region (left of Fig. 1), i.e. $[-0.39, 1.1] \times [-0.03, 0.16]$, discretized by a 20×20 grid and integrated by a 4th order Runge-Kutta method with time step $\delta t = 20$ (200 steps of time length 0.1)

containing the parallelogram-like shape of the phase portrait (see Fig. 1) can be proved invariant [4,16,8].

Proposition 2. *(Phase portraits and CA). Let $F(u) = 0$ be a (system of) autonomous ODE. Let $\mathcal{R} \subset Y$ be a bounded invariant region and let $\mathcal{R}_{disc}$ be a regular discretization of $\mathcal{R}$. Let $F(u) = 0$ be such that the solutions of the initial value problems starting from $\mathcal{R}_{disc}$ exist and are unique, and let Φ be a numerical scheme to approximate these solutions. Then there are zero-dimensional CA $(\{c\}, \mathcal{R}_{disc}, \{c\}, \tau_\Phi)$ whose runs also approximate these solutions.*

Note that unlike general *explicit schemes*, Φ has no *a priori* limitations (e.g. *instability*-prone [19]) and can be chosen to be as precise as one wants. Prop. 2 has been already implicitly used to build ad-hoc CA for reaction-diffusion systems (see e.g. [7,6,2]), and also more explicitly [24].

3   DE Coupling and CA Compositions

An effective and direct way of coupling DE consists of adding differential operators. The simplest case is expressed as: $\frac{\partial u}{\partial t} = F(u) = F_1(u) + \dots + F_m(u)$. For instance, the full 2D Fitzhugh-Nagumo *reaction-diffusion* system includes a reaction part and a diffusion part: $\frac{\partial u_1}{\partial t} = [(a - u_1)(u_1 - 1)u_1 - u_2] + K(\frac{\partial^2 u_1}{\partial x^2} + \frac{\partial^2 u_1}{\partial y^2})$ and $\frac{\partial u_2}{\partial t} = \epsilon(u_1 - bu_2)$. One can also add *drift components* [13], for instance wrt the x dimension: $\frac{\partial u_1}{\partial t} = H(\frac{\partial u_1}{\partial x}) + [(a - u_1)(u_1 - 1)u_1 - u_2] + K(\frac{\partial^2 u_1}{\partial x^2} + \frac{\partial^2 u_1}{\partial y^2})$

and $\frac{\partial u_2}{\partial t} = H(\frac{\partial u_2}{\partial x}) + [\epsilon(u_1 - bu_2)]$. Many meaningful DE models can be designed following this composition technique (see e.g. [15]). Now, there exists a classical method to numerically solve such composed DE called *operator splitting* (or *fractional step method*) (see e.g. [27,1]). This method relies on decomposing a DE into its pieces, where each piece is expected to be easier to solve. For instance, the simplest splitting for the above general equation $F(u)$ is to solve the sub-equations $\frac{\partial u}{\partial t} = F_j(u)$ for $j = 1, ..., m$ by distinct numerical schemes g_j, and to get solution approximations by their direct composition: $U(t_{i+1}) = g_m(g_{m-1}(...(g_1(U(t_i), ...))))$. Composing such numerical operators in this way has a counterpart in the CA side:

Proposition 3. *(Splittings and CA). Let $\frac{\partial u}{\partial t} = F(u) = F_1(u) + ... + F_m(u)$ be a DE with $u : \mathbb{R} \times \mathbb{R}^n \to Y$. Let $\mathcal{L}_1 \times \mathcal{L}_n$ be a discretization of $\mathbb{R} \times \mathbb{R}^n$, and let the DE be solvable by an operator splitting for which the sub-equations are $\frac{\partial u}{\partial t} = F_j(u)$, $j = 1, ..., m$. Assume the involved m numerical schemes can be transformed into m distinct CA over the same set of states, i.e. $\mathcal{A}_j = (\mathcal{L}_{n_j}^{(j)}, \mathcal{Q}, N^{(j)}, \tau^{(j)})$ for $j = 1, ..., m$, with $n_j \leq n$, and such that for each j, the lattice $\mathcal{L}_n$ is partitioned into copies of $\mathcal{L}_{n_j}^{(j)}$ according to the variable dimensions involved in the j-th equation. Then a corresponding CA $(\mathcal{L}_n, \mathcal{Q}, N, \tau)$ is defined by sequentially applying the $\mathcal{A}_j$'s to $\mathcal{L}_n$, where τ consists of applying $\tau^{(j)}$ to each copy of $\mathcal{L}_{n_j}^{(j)}$ in $\mathcal{L}_n$.*

A special case occurs when some $n_j = 0$ (i.e. the sub-equation is not a PDE): the corresponding CA is zero-dimensional and the partition of the global reference lattice $\mathcal{L}_n$ consists of its single elements. Reaction-diffusion systems are classic instances taking advantage of the above composition process [7,6,24]: reaction terms are associated to 0D CA, and nD diffusion to nD CA.

There is another way of coupling sets of (systems of) autonomous DE which relies on assembling invariant sub-regions of their phase portraits: Let $\mathcal{R}$ be a region of $\mathbb{R}^n$ (with non-empty interior), let $\mathcal{R}_\epsilon = \{x \in \mathbb{R}^n | \exists y \in \mathcal{R}, \, d(x, y) < \epsilon\}$ where $\epsilon > 0$ and d is the Euclidean metric, and let $\mathcal{R}_{-\epsilon}$ be the region such that $(\mathcal{R}_{-\epsilon})_\epsilon = \mathcal{R}$. A *smooth characteristic function* wrt $\mathcal{R}$ is a continuous monotonic function ψ such that $\psi \equiv 1$ in $\mathcal{R}_{-\epsilon}$, $\psi \equiv 0$ in the complement of $\mathcal{R}_\epsilon$ in $\mathbb{R}^n$, and ψ takes its values in $[0, 1]$ for the other points. Consider M systems of autonomous DE $\frac{du}{dt} = F_j(u)$ acting on the phase space Y, each of them associated to a function ψ_j whose regions $\mathcal{R}_j$ have pairwise disjoint interiors. These systems can be composed by $\frac{du}{dt} = F(u) = \psi_1 F_1(u) + ... + \psi_M F_M(u)$. This can also be reflected in the CA side:

Proposition 4. *(Phase portrait compositions and CA). Consider a DE built according to the above composition technique. Assume there is a zero-dimensional CA $(\{c\}, \mathcal{Q}^{(j)}, \{c\}, \tau^{(j)})$ corresponding to each region $\mathcal{R}_j$. Then the composed CA is defined by $(\{c\}, \mathcal{Q}^{(1)} \cup ... \cup \mathcal{Q}^{(M)}, \{c\}, \tau^{(1)} \circ .... \circ \tau^{(M)})$.*

For instance, reaction equations one can be coupled by composing the invariant regions of their phase portraits. Indeed, let ϕ_x denote a horizontal translation of along the x-axis, let ρ be the reflexion wrt the y-axis and let h_α be a scaling with coefficient α. Let us denote the Fitzhugh-Nagumo equation by *Fitz*. First, we

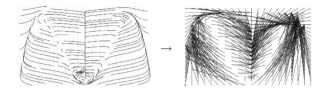

Fig. 3. To the left, the global invariant region of the phase portrait of a Fitzhugh-Nagumo "double reaction". To the right, a corresponding CA with 400 states (a 20×20 grid), built by the same integration method as in Fig. 2.

Fig. 4. A run of the CA obtained by composing the above CA (Fig. 3) and a diffusion CA. This run is sampled every 10 steps from 0 to 60 and only the values of u_1 (horizontal dimension) are shown (the higher the value, the brighter the corresponding point of X). As expected, the white waves have a higher frequency than the black waves.

translate it to the right: $Fitz^{(1)} \equiv \phi_{x_1} \circ Fitz$ with $x_1 \in \mathbb{R}^+$. Second, the system $Fitz^{(1)}$ can be reflected and scaled: $Fitz^{(2)} \equiv h_{\alpha_1} \circ \rho \circ Fitz^{(1)}$ with $\alpha_1 \in \mathbb{R}^+$. If $x_1 > 0$ is large enough, the invariant regions of $Fitz^{(1)}$ and $Fitz^{(2)}$ lie in each side of the y-axis, and they are disjoint except for their attractive fixed point (a case not impairing the composability). DE coupling is then applied by using characteristic functions ψ_1 and ψ_2 for their respective invariant regions: $\frac{\partial u_i}{\partial t} = \psi_1(u_1, u_2) \cdot Fitz^{(1)}(u_1, u_2) + \psi_2(u_1, u_2) \cdot Fitz^{(2)}(u_1, u_2)$ (see Fig. 3). This "double reaction" can be transformed into a CA by composing the CA of each reaction. Note however that when used in a splitting, the invariant regions must be chosen so that all the involved CA are defined over the same set of states (cf. Prop 3). For instance, a double reaction CA composed with a diffusion CA needs a rectangular global invariant region containing a part of the y-axis. When this condition is satisfied, the resulting CA runs show two kinds of traveling waves living together, inducing spirals of two different sizes and frequencies (see Fig. 4).

4   CA Sequences and Tunability

The above constructions establish connections between DE and CA using specific numerical and composition schemes. However, not much has been said about their properties. One of the most important one is *convergence*: Let the source space be $\mathbb{R}$, and consider $F(u) = 0$. Let $\{\mathcal{L}_1^k\}$ be a sequence of regular discretizations of $\mathbb{R}$ spanned by δt_k with $\delta t_k \to 0$ as $k \to 0$. A numerical scheme to solve $F(u) = 0$ is *convergent* iff for every exact solution u wrt an initial condition and for every $T > 0$, the sequence of the computed solutions $\{U_{\delta t_k}\}$ is such that: $\max_{0 \le i \le T/\delta t_k} |U_{\delta t_k}(t_i) - u(t_i)| \to 0$, as $U_{\delta t_k}(t_0) \to u(t_0)$ and $\delta t_k \to 0$.

Proposition 5. *(Convergent numerical schemes and CA sequences). Let $F(u)$ $= 0$ be a (system of) autonomous DE with $u : \mathbb{R} \times \mathbb{R}^n \to Y$ and $n \geq 0$. Let g be any kind of convergent explicit numerical scheme to solve the DE. Then one can associate a CA sequence $\{\mathcal{A}_i\}$ to g which is also convergent.*

Let us discuss the case for which the source space is $\mathbb{R}$. According to their definition, CA need discretizations of the phase space Y, whereas usual convergence definitions – like the above one – do not include them. But clearly, if a discretization of Y does not evolve, $|U_{\delta t_k}(t_i) - u(t_i)|$ could not in general go to zero as $\delta t_k \to 0$. Therefore, one must consider another sequence of finer and finer discretizations of Y. For the sake of simplicity, assume these discretizations are regular and spanned by δy_k. For each discretization of $\mathbb{R}$ based on δt_k, there is a quantification projection function ρ_k sending $U_{\delta t_k}$ to its quantified version $U_{\delta t_k, \delta y_k}$ such that $|\rho_k(U_{\delta t_k}) - U_{\delta t_k, \delta y_k}| < \delta y_k$. Hence, $\{U_{\delta t_k, \delta y_k}\}$ can be defined so as to converge to u. If the associated numerical scheme is explicit, one can translate this sequence into a convergent CA sequence $\{\mathcal{A}_k\}$, where the number of states of each $\mathcal{A}_k$ is determined by δy_k.

Convergence gives a coherent way of tuning CA wrt the numerical discretization parameters. For example, Fig. 5 shows some terms of a CA sequence corresponding to a Fitzhugh-Nagumo reaction resolution. Accordingly, we use finer and finer discretizations of the invariant region of its phase portrait. The runs of the corresponding reaction-diffusion CA yield more and more quantitative features. Exact behaviors and shapes of the solutions are obtained, e.g. *curvatures of the isoclines* or *dispersion effects* [11,6]. Note however that in the general case, convergence is not sufficient to ensure that a numerical scheme – and therefore a CA sequence – converges to the true DE solutions. Concepts as *consistency*, *well-posedness* and *stability* must also be considered (see e.g. [19]).

5   Faithfulness and Qualitativeness

The precedent section emphasizes a fundamental difference between CA and numerical methods: quantification of the phase space Y is an intrinsic part of a CA (a finite sets of states), whereas in numerical methods, quantification is either neglected or considered as a disturbing element. But coarse discretizations of Y may yield results still bearing the main features of the DE's solutions. Thus, we could not only find good solution approximations as discretizations become finer, we could also search for coarse discretizations of Y for which some qualitative aspects of the solutions are preserved. The first terms of a convergent CA sequence become important too. When all the terms of a convergent CA sequence generate some meaningful/qualitative features of the solutions of a DE, this sequence is said to be *faithful* to the DE. Faithfulness indicates how CA could enrich the concept of DE numerical computation by including the idea of reducing, minimizing, optimizing these computations, and not only by

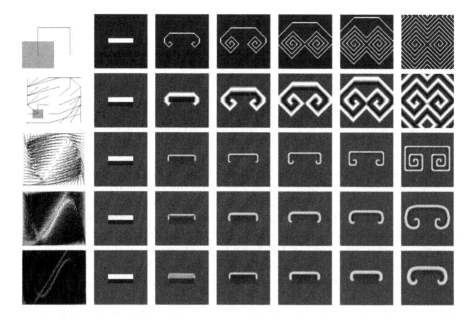

Fig. 5. In the left column, elements of a CA sequence for a Fitzhugh-Nagumo reaction (the representation is the same as in Fig. 2, and small gray rectangles indicate fixed points). From the top to the bottom, the region $\mathcal{R}_{disc}$ has been discretized according to grids of resp. of 2^2, 6^2, 18^2, 54^2 and 162^2 points (multiplication by 3 preserves the offsets). To the right of each reaction CA is shown a run of the corresponding reaction-diffusion CA after 5, 10, 15, 20 and 40 steps. As the integration time δt of the reaction decreases (to be kept proportional to the cell size defined by the discretization and the quantification projection function, see Prop. 2), the wave frequency decreases too.

providing exact computations. The example given in Fig. 5 shows that faithful CA sequences exist, even for non-trivial cases like reaction-diffusion DE: traveling waves occur at very coarse discretization levels of the phase space. Spirals are just more square-like when the phase space is reduced to very few states.

Of course, the qualitative properties of a DE solution space are not easily described in a full general setting. Nevertheless, phase spaces contain some decisive features, like for instance in the autonomous case, *singularities* of their phase portraits – i.e. fixed and periodic points (see e.g. [10]). With this respect, when using coarse discretizations, two main problems may occur: *spurious fixed points* appear or real fixed points are *eluded*. To ensure faithfulness, a natural expected condition is to avoid these. In the case of ODE systems, determining the real fixed points requires to solve $\frac{du_i}{dt}(x) = 0$, for every i. In the Fitzhugh-Nagumo case, this amounts to solve $(a - u_1)(u_1 - 1)u_1 = u_1/b$. When the slope of the linear isocline is steep enough wrt the cubic isocline (e.g. $a = 0.1$ and $b = 4$), there is a unique fixed point at $(0,0)$, and every solution finishes eventually at $(0,0)$ (no cycle exists). Associated CA can be built (cf. Prop. 2) so as to comply with these properties. When the integration time step δt is too short, spurious

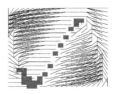

Fig. 6. A CA for the same Fitzhugh-Nagumo reaction as in Fig. 2, but built with a too short integration time $\delta t = 4$: many spurious fixed points occur (gray rectangles).

fixed points mainly occur on the cubic nullcline (see Fig. 6). Tuning δt wrt Y_{disc} has been important to obtain Fig. 5. Note that by continuity, some spurious fixed points may occur in a neighborhood of a real fixed point without much influence. One can also preserve fixed point types like being *attractive, repulsive, stable, unstable*, etc. (see e.g. [10]). For instance, the unique fixed point of the Fitzhugh-Nagumo equation can be shown to be attractive and stable.

This singularity analysis can be difficult to fulfill (and even more when cycles are also considered – see e.g. the results about the *Hilbert's sixteenth problem*). No general method can be expected to be applicable to every situation. Nevertheless, there exist other techniques which help to build faithful CA sequences. First, more classical features of qualitative phase portrait analysis can be used like *attraction basins, funnels*, and *anti-funnels* (see e.g. [10]). One can also apply *index theory* (see in particular *cell-to-cell mapping theory* [9]) or *singular perturbation theory* (see e.g. [22,14]). To ensure the preservation of some global quantities, e.g. the energy of the system, one can consider *conservative numerical schemes* (see e.g. [17]). Finally, *cell-to-cell mapping theory* includes extensions based on Markov chains [9] from which probabilistic CA can be derived.

Summing up, we have seen that DE and CA can be formally related in many respects. Thus, there are cases where DE can be thought of as abstract reference objects to obtain faithful CA sequences, that is, descriptions that include qualitative as well as quantitative features. Qualitative descriptions can be adjusted and compared to quantitative solutions, and DE are used to give insights and tools to produce meaningful CA. As a result, CA can be tuned, DE-based simulations can be optimized (by attempting to find minimal CA), and more generally the qualitativeness of a global model can be studied. As further investigations, other faithful CA sequences could be produced (for instance considering other excitatory systems [18,9,15]). One could also establish connections with *qualitative physics and reasoning* [12] – where quantitative and qualitative descriptions are often mixed –, or with *ultradiscretization methods* [21] – able to transform DE into integrable CA over integers. Coupling invariant regions of phase portraits could lead to new interesting CA behaviors.

Acknowledgment. S. Grivet has been of great help in building the above examples.

References

1. W. F. Ames. *Numerical Methods for Partial Differential Equations (Second edition)*. Academic Press, 1977.
2. D. Barkley. A model for fast computer simulation of waves in excitable media. *Physica D*, 49:61–70, 1991.
3. B. Choppard and M. Droz. *Cellular Automata Modeling of Physical Systems*. Cambridge University Press, 1998.
4. K. Chueh, C. Conley, and J. Smoller. Positively invariant regions for systems of nonlinear parabolic equations. *Indiana Univ. Math. J.*, 26:373–392, 1977.
5. M. Delorme and J. Mazoyer. *Cellular Automata, A Parallel Model*. Kluwer Academic Publishers, 1999.
6. M. Gerhardt, H. Schuster, and J.J. Tyson. Cellular automaton model of excitable media II & III. *Physica D*, 46:392–426, 1990.
7. J.M. Greenberg, B. D. Hassard, and S. P. Hastings. Pattern formation and periodic structures in systems modeled by reaction-diffusion equations. *Bull. of the AMS*, 6:1296–1327, 1978.
8. P. Grindrod. *Patterns and Waves*. Clarendon Press - Oxford, 1991.
9. C. S. Hsu. *Cell-to-Cell Mapping, A Method of Global Analysis for Nonlinear Systems*. Springer-Verlag, 1987.
10. J.H. Hubbard and B.H. West. *Differential Equations. A Dynamical System Approach. Parts I and II*. Springer Verlag, 1995.
11. J.P. Keener. A geometrical theory for spiral waves in excitable media. *SIAM Journ. Appl. Math.*, 46(6):1039–1056, 1986.
12. B. Kuipers. *Qualitative Reasoning*. MIT Press, 1994.
13. P.V. Kuptsov, S.P. Kuznetsov, and E. Mosekilde. Particle in the Brusselator model with flow. *Physica D*, 163:80–88, 2002.
14. J.D. Murray. *Mathematical Biology*. Springer Verlag, 1993.
15. E.S. Oran and J.P. Boris. *Numerical Simulation of Reactive Flow*. Elsevier, 1987.
16. J. Rauch and J. Smoller. Qualitative theory of the Fitzhugh-Nagumo equations. *Adv. in Math.*, 27:12–44, 1978.
17. B. Shadwick, J. Bowman, and P. Morrison. Exactly conservative integrators. *SIAM J. Appl. Math.*, 59, 1999.
18. J. A. Sherratt. Periodic travelling waves in a family of deterministic cellular automata. *Physica D*, 95:319–335, 1996.
19. J.C. Strikwerda. *Finite Difference Schemes and Partial Differential Equations (2nd Edition)*. SIAM, Philadelphia, 2004.
20. T. Toffoli and N. Margolus. *Cellular Automata Machines: a New Environment for Modeling*. MIT Press, 1987.
21. T. Tokihiro, D. Takahashi, J. Matsukidaira, and J. Satsuma. From soliton equations to integrable cellular automata through a limiting procedure. *Physic. Rev. Let.*, 76(18):3247–3250, 1996.
22. J. Tyson. Singular perturbation theory of traveling waves in excitable media. *Physica D*, 32:327–361, 1988.
23. J.R. Weimar. *Simulation with Cellular Automata*. Logos-Verlag, Berlin, 1998.
24. J.R. Weimar and J.P. Boon. Class of cellular automata for reaction-diffusion systems. *Physical Review E*, 49(2):1749–1751, 1994.
25. S. Wolfram. Twenty problems in the theory of cellular automata. *Physica Scripta*, pages 170–183, 1985. Proceedings of the 59th Nobel Symposium.
26. S. Wolfram. *A New Kind of Science*. Wolfram Media Inc., 2002.
27. N.N. Yanenko. *The Method of Fractional Steps*. Springer-Verlag, 1971.

How Does the Neighborhood Affect the Global Behavior of Cellular Automata?*

Hidenosuke Nishio **

Iwakura Miyake-cho 204, Sakyo-ku,
Kyoto, 606-0022, Japan
YRA05762@nifty.com

Abstract. The neighborhood is a fundamental constituent of the cellular automaton (CA) and has been investigated in its own right by H.Nishio, M.Margenstern and F.von Haeseler(2004,2005). In this paper we ask a new question how the neighborhood affects the global behavior of CA and particularly gives some instances of CA where the global behavior *does not* depend on the neighborhood. We also discuss the conjectures that the injectivity is generally preserved from changing the neighborhood but the surjectivity is not.

1 Introduction

The cellular automaton (CA for short) is a uniformly structured information processing system defined on a regular discrete space S, which is typically presented by the Cayley graph of a finitely generated group. The same finite automaton (cell) is placed at every point of the space. Every cell simultaneously changes its state following the local function defined on the neighboring cells. The neighborhood N is also spatially uniform. Most studies on CA assume the historical and standard neighborhoods after John von Neumann and E. F. Moore. The von Neumann neighborhood was used for designing the self-reproducing machine [15], while the Moore neighborhood was defined by E. F. Moore [5] for proving the Garden of Eden Theorem together J. Myhill [6], both neighborhoods being defined in the 2-dimensional Euclidean grid $\mathbb{Z}^2 = \langle a, b \mid ab = ba \rangle$, see Fig.1-2.

The neighborhood is usually crucial for the global behavior of a CA. For example, the Game of Life [1] has been formulated assuming binary states and the Moore neighborhood in $\mathbb{Z}^2$. The local rule is cleverly determined and many interesting behaviors like construction- and computation-universality have been proved to emerge. It would not have been so successful, if it were defined assuming the von Neumann neighborhood.

Changing the point of view, however, we posed an algebraic theory of neighborhoods of CA for clarifying the significance of the neighborhood itself, where

---

* The precursors were presented at the workshops held in Gdansk, September 2005 [7] and in Kyoto, January 2006 [8], respectively.
** Ex. Kyoto University.

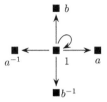

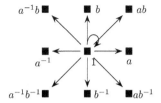

Fig. 1. The von Neumann neighborhood   **Fig. 2.** The Moore neighborhood

the neighborhood N is an arbitrary finite subset of S and recursively generates neighbors as a subsemigroup of S, see H.Nishio, M.Margenstern and F.von Haeseler(2004, 2005) [11][10][12], where particularly the question if N generates (*fills*) S has been discussed.

Based on such a setting, we ask here a new question *how the neighborhood affects the global behavior of a CA*. Most properties of CA are strongly dependent on the neighborhood, while there are several ones which are not. In this paper we show two instances of CA, where the neighborhood *does not* affect the global behavior; the parity of configurations and the surjectivity/injectivity of linear CAs over $\mathbb{Z}_m$. In the last section we discuss the conjecture that the injectivity of global maps is generally preserved from changing the neighborhood but the surjectivity is not.

2 Preliminaries

2.1 Cellular Automaton CA

A CA is defined by a 4-tuple (S, N, Q, f).

- S : *Cellular space* is the Cayley graph $\Gamma(S)$ of a finitely generated group $S = \langle G|R \rangle$ with generators G and relators R. If $G = \{g_1, g_2, ..., g_r\}$, every element of S is presented by a word $x \in (G \cup G^{-1})^*$, where $G^{-1} = \{g^{-1}| \ g \cdot g^{-1} = 1, \ g \in G\}$. The set R of relators is written as

$$R = \{w_i = w_i' \mid w_i, w_i' \in (G \cup G^{-1})^*, i = 1, ..., n\}. \tag{1}$$

  For $x, y \in \Gamma(S)$, if $y = xg$, where $g \in G \cup G^{-1}$, then an edge labelled by g is drawn from vertex x to vertex y. Usually the cellular space is simply denoted by S in stead of $\Gamma(S)$.
- N : *Neighborhood* $N = \{n_1, n_2, ..., n_s\}$ is a finite subset of S. For any cell $x \in S$, the information of cell xn_i reaches x in a unit of time. The set of all neighborhoods is denoted by $\mathcal{N}$. The cardinality $\#(N)$ is called the neighborhood size of CA. The set of all neighborhoods of size s is denoted by $\mathcal{N}_s$.
- Q : *Set of cell states* is assumed to be a finite field $Q = GF(q)$, where $q = p^n$ with prime p and positive integer n, see [13]. The case of the ring $Q = \mathbb{Z}/m\mathbb{Z}$ is also considered.

- f : *Local function* f is a map $Q^N \rightarrow Q$, where an element of Q^N is called a local configuration.
- *Global map* F is a map $C \rightarrow C$, where an element of $C = Q^S$ is called a global configuration. F is uniquely defined by f and N as follows.

$$F(c)(x) = f(c(xn_1), c(xn_2), \cdots, c(xn_s)), \tag{2}$$

where $c(x)$ is the state of cell $x \in S$ for any $c \in C$. When starting with a configuration c, the behavior (trajectory) of CA is given by

$$F^{t+1}(c) = F(F^t(c)) \text{ for any } t \geq 0, \text{ where } F^0(c) = c. \tag{3}$$

When S and Q are understood, the global behavior or the global property of a CA depends on the local function f and the neighborhood N. Furthermore, when the local function f is fixed, we have various CAs or different Fs by changing the neighborhood. That is the definition of a CA depends only on a 2-tuple (f, N). In this sense, this paper treats the dependency of the local function f on the neighborhood N.

2.2   Neighborhood and Neighbors

Given a *neighborhood* $N = \{n_1, n_2, ..., n_s\} \subset S$ for a cellular space $S = \langle G \mid R \rangle$, we recursively define the *neighbors* of CA. Let $p \in S$.

(1) The *1-neighbors* of p, denoted as pN^1, is the set

$$pN^1 = \{pn_1, pn_2, ..., pn_s\}. \tag{4}$$

(2) The *m-neighbors* of p, denoted as pN^m, are given as

$$pN^m = pN^{m-1} \cdot N, \ m \geq 1, \tag{5}$$

where $pN^0 = \{p\}$. *Note that the computation of pn_i has to comply with the relations R which defines $S = \langle G|R \rangle$.* We may say that the information contained in the cells of pN^m reaches the cell p after m time steps.

(3) ∞-*neighbors* of p, denoted as pN^∞, is defined by

$$pN^\infty = \bigcup_{m=0}^{\infty} pN^m. \tag{6}$$

Without loss of generality, we can concentrate on the *m-neighbors of the identity element 1 of S*, which is simply called *m-neighbors* of CA and denoted by N^m. (4) Finally, ∞-neighbors of 1, denoted as N^∞ called the *neighbors of CA*, is given by

$$N^\infty = \bigcup_{m=0}^{\infty} N^m. \tag{7}$$

The *intrinsic m-neighbors* $[N^m] = N^m \setminus N^{m-1}$ are the cells whose information can reach the origin in exactly m steps. Obviously, $N^\infty = \bigcup_{m=0}^{\infty} [N^m]$.

Now we have an algebraic result, which is proved by the fact that the procedure to generate a subsemigroup is the same as the above mentioned recursive definition of N^∞.

Proposition 1

$$N^\infty = \langle N \mid R \rangle_{sg}, \tag{8}$$

where $\langle N \mid R \rangle_{sg}$ means the semigroup obtained by concatenating the words from N with constraints of R.

We also have the following easily proved proposition.

Proposition 2

$$\langle N \mid R \rangle_g = \langle N \cup N^{-1} \mid R \rangle_{sg}, \tag{9}$$

where $\langle N \mid R \rangle_g$ is the smallest subgroup of S which contains N.

If $N = G$, then we have the following lemma as a corollary to Proposition 2.

Lemma 1

$$S = \langle g_1, g_2, ..., g_r | R \rangle_g = \langle g_1, g_2, ..., g_r, g_1^{-1}, g_2^{-1}, ..., g_r^{-1} | R \rangle_{sg}. \tag{10}$$

Example: $\mathbb{Z}^2 = \langle a, b| \ ab = ba \rangle_g = \langle a, b, a^{-1}, b^{-1}| \ ab = ba \rangle_{sg}$.

3 CAs Where the Neighborhood Does Not Affect the Global Behavior

In this section, we show two instances of CA where the neighborhood *does not* affect the global behavior. We also discuss the dependency of the injectivity and surjectivity on the neighborhood.

3.1 Parity function preserves the parity of configurations for any neighborhood.
3.2 As for linear CAs, the surjectivity and the injectivity are independent from the neighborhood.
3.3 Discussions on the injectivity and surjectivity for general cases.

3.1 Parity Function

Let $Q = \{0, 1, ..., p - 1, ...\} = GF(p^n)$ with prime p and positive integer n. As the local function, we consider an s-ary function $f_P : Q^s \to Q$ defined by

$$f_P(x_1, x_2, ..., x_s) = \sum_{i=1}^{s} x_i \mod p. \tag{11}$$

f_P will be called the *(generalized) parity function*. Note that if $Q = \{0, 1\}$ then f_P is the ordinary (binary) parity function.

For the s-ary parity function f_P, choose an arbitrary neighborhood $N \in \mathcal{N}_s$ of size s. Then we have the *parity CA* over Q in S; $CA(f_P, N)$. The global map $F_{P,N}$ of $CA(f_P, N)$ is defined as usual by Equation (2).

Since $f_P(0, , , 0) = 0$, $0 \in Q$ is a *quiescent state*. A configuration $c \in Q^S$ is called *finite* if $\#\{i \mid c(i) \neq 0,\ i \in S\} < \infty$. For a finite configuration c, the finite subset $\{i \mid c(i) \neq 0,\ i \in S\}$ of S is called a *support* of c. Since the finiteness of configurations is preserved by $F_{P,N}$, in the sequel we treat only finite configurations.

The *(generalized) parity* $P(c)$ of a configuration c is defined by

$$P(c) = \sum_{x \in S} c(x) \mod p. \tag{12}$$

Then we have the following theorem.

Theorem 1. *The parity CA preserves the parity of configurations, i.e.*

$$P(F_{P,N}(c)) = P(c), \ c \in Q^S, \tag{13}$$

if and only if $N \in \mathcal{N}_s$, *where* $s = kp + 1, k \geq 0$.

Proof

$$P(F_{P,N}(c)) = \sum_{x \in S} F_{P,N}(c)(x) = \sum_{x \in S} f_P(xn_1, ..., xn_s) \tag{14}$$

$$= \sum_{x \in S} \sum_{i=1}^{s} c(xn_i) = \sum_{i=1}^{s} \sum_{x \in S} c(xn_i). \tag{15}$$

We note here, since the neighborhood is spatially uniform,

$$\sum_{x \in S} c(xn_i) = \sum_{x \in S} c(x), \text{ for any } 1 \leq i \leq s. \tag{16}$$

Then, if $s = kp + 1$, from (15) we have

$$P(F_{P,N}(c)) = \sum_{i=1}^{s} \sum_{x \in S} c(xn_i) = \sum_{x \in S} c(x) = P(c). \tag{17}$$

For the necessity of condition $s = kp + 1$, we can consider a binary parity CA ($p = 2$) having a neighborhood of size $s = 2$. Such a CA maps all configurations into those of parity 0 and does not preserve the parity. ∎

Example 1. Consider the 3-ary binary parity CAs in $\mathbb{Z} = \langle a | \emptyset \rangle$ with neighborhoods of size 3 such as $N_3 = \{a^{-1}, 1, a\}$, $N_3' = \{a^{-2}, 1, a^2\}$ and $N_3'' = \{0, a, a^2\}$. They all preserve the parity, but the binary binary parity CA with neighborhood $N_2 = \{1, a\}$ of size 2 does not. The theorem also holds for finite spaces like $\mathbb{Z}_m = \langle a | a^m = 1 \rangle$.

Note that the binary parity function is not number conserving.

3.2   Linear CA over $\mathbb{Z}_m$

We consider the linear local function f of arity s over $\mathbb{Z}_m = \mathbb{Z}/m\mathbb{Z}$.

$$f(n_1, n_2, ..., n_s) = \sum_{i=1}^{s} a_i n_i, \ a_i \in \mathbb{Z}_m, \ \text{mod } m. \tag{18}$$

Though the linear CA can be defined on an arbitrary cellular space S, we assume here such a space where the Garden of Eden theorem holds, see the remarks below. Then we have the following theorem.

Theorem 2. *For a linear CA on S where the Garden of Eden theorem holds, the surjectivity and the injectivity are independent from the neighborhood.*

Proof. The proof is given owing to the following two lemmas or the theorems established by M.Ito, N.Osato and M.Nasu (1983) [3]. Both lemmas characterize the surjectivity and the injectivity of a linear CA over $\mathbb{Z}_m$, respectively, in terms of the coefficients $a_1, a_2, \cdots, a_s$ and the prime factors of m. Obviously, *the characterization is independent from the neighborhood*. Note that their proofs rely on the result by Richardson(1972) [14], which relies in turn on the Garden of Eden (GOE) theorem for $S = \mathbb{Z}^2$. ∎

Lemma 2 (Theorem 1 of [3]). *A linear CA over $\mathbb{Z}_m$ is surjective if and only if any prime factor of m does not divide all of the coefficients $a_1, a_2, \cdots, a_s$.*

Lemma 3 (Theorem 2 of [3]). *A linear CA over $\mathbb{Z}_m$ is injective if and only if for each prime factor p of m there exists a unique coefficient a_j such that $p \nmid a_j$ and $p \mid a_i$ for $i \neq j$.*

Remarks on the GOE theorem: The Garden of Eden theorem was first established for $S = \mathbb{Z}^2$ by E.Moore (1962) [5] and J.Myhill (1963) [6] and later generalized to groups of faster growth, see A. Machi and F. Mignosi (1993)[4] and M. Gromov (1999) [2]. Inspired by those results, H.Nishio(2006) [9] gives a brief study on the *growth of neighborhoods* of CA.

Theorem 3 (GOE theorem). *F is surjective if and only if F is injective when it is restricted to the finite configurations.*

The *growth function* γ_S of a finitely generated group $S = \langle G|R \rangle$ is defined by the cardinality of the ball of radius n;

$$\gamma_S(n) = \#\{w \mid |w| \le n, \ w \in S\}. \tag{19}$$

The growth function of the 2-dimensional Euclidean grid $\mathbb{Z}^2$ is $2n^2 + 2n + 1$, while the free group $S = \{a, b \mid \emptyset\}$ has an exponential growth function 2^n. Mathematicians have revealed that the GOE theorem holds for the cellular space S of polynomial and subexponential growths [1] but it does not for S of exponential growth. In this context, Theorem 2 would need a different type of the proof for CAs where the GOE theorem does not hold, if it were still correct for them.

---

[1] The subexponential growth is faster than polynomial but slower than exponential growth.

3.3 Injectivity and Surjectivity

We discuss here the dependency of the injectivity and surjectivity on the neighborhood for CAs which are not necessarily linear. In this section we assume that every neighborhood fills S, i.e. $\langle N \mid R \rangle_{sg} = S$.

Let's begin with an example of CA with a nonstandard neighborhood of size 3, say, a 3-horse $N_{3H} = \{n_1, n_2, n_3\} = \{a^2b, a^{-2}b, ab^{-2}\}$ in $\mathbb{Z}^2$. N_{3H} was first discussed by H.Nishio and M.Margenstern(2004,5)[11][10] and particularly shown to fill $\mathbb{Z}^2$ though it does not contain the identity element 1 of $\mathbb{Z}^2$.

Now fix an arbitrary function $f : Q \times Q \times Q \to Q$, $|Q| \geq 2$ of arity 3 and consider a CA $CA_{f,3H}$ with the local function f and the neighborhood N_{3H} in the space $\mathbb{Z}^2$. Depending on f, the global map of $CA_{f,3H}$ can be injective or not injective.

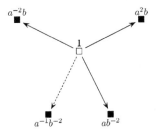

Fig. 3. 3-horse N_{3H} and its variant $N_{3H'}$

Next, consider another CA $CA_{f,3H'}$ with the same f and a slightly different neighborhood $N'_{3H} = \{n_1, n_2, n'_3\} = \{a^2b, a^{-2}b, a^{-1}b^{-2}\}$, which is obtained from N_{3H} by replacing the third element, see Fig. 3. Evidently N'_{3H} is also seen to fill S.

A CA is called injective (res. surjective) if its global map is injective (res. surjective). Then we have the following

Proposition 3. If $CA_{f,3H}$ is injective, then $CA_{f,3H'}$ is injective.

Proof. Assume the contrary. Then there are two different configurations $c_1, c_2 \in C$ such that $F'(c_1) = F'(c_2)$, where F' is the global map of $CA_{f,3H'}$. On the other hand, $c_1 \neq c_2$ implies that there is a point $x \in S$ such that $c_1(x) \neq c_2(x)$. Since $F'(c_1) = F'(c_2)$, the local state transition by $CA_{f,3H'}$ applied to c_1 and c_2 should yield the same result at every point of S. Particularly at $xn_3'^{-1}$, $f(\alpha_1, \alpha_2, c_1(x)) = f(\alpha_1', \alpha_2', c_2(x))$, where αs are the states of the relevant 1-neighbors. It implies that $CA_{f,3H}$ is not injective. A contradiction. ∎

By generalizing, we have

Conjecture 1. The injectivity of CA is preserved from changing the neighborhood.

Conjecture 1 is described more specifically as follows: If a CA with a local function of arity s is injective on a neighborhood $N \in \mathcal{N}_s$, then it is injective on any other neighborhood $N' \in \mathcal{N}_s$ which fills S.

In contrast, as for the surjectivity we have

Conjecture 2. The surjectivity of CA is *not* preserved from changing the neighborhood.

By Thomas Worsch at the Faculty of Informatics, University of Karlsruhe, one of his students is said to have found a 1-dimensional 3 states CA which supports Conjecture 2 [16].

4   Concluding Remarks

In this paper we showed some examples of CAs where the global behavior or the global property is *not* affected by the neighborhood. Theorem 1 holds no matter when the GOE theorem does not hold, but Conjecture 1 seems to need it for its validity. A problem for future research is to establish the general theory for such global properties that are independent from the neighborhood. On the other hand, it will be an interesting research topics to investigate CAs (local functions) so that, by appropriately choosing the neighborhood, the global behavior may become useful from the application point of view.

Many thanks are due to Maurice Margenstern and Thomas Worsch for their interest and discussions on this topics.

References

1. Gardner, M.: The fantastic combinations of John Conway's new game of 'life', *Scientific American*, **223**, 1970, 120–123.
2. Gromov, M.: Endomorphisms of symbolic algebraic varieties, *J. Eur. Math. Soc.*, **1**, 1999, 109–197.
3. Ito, M., Osato, N., Nasu, M.: Linear Cellular Automata over Z(m), *J. Comput. Syst. Sci.*, **27**(1), 1983, 125–140.
4. Machi, A., Mignosi, F.: Garden of Eden Configurations for Cellular Automata on Cayley Graphs of Groups., *SIAM J. Discrete Math.*, **6**(1), 1993, 44–56.
5. Moore, E. F.: Machine models of self-reproduction, *Proc. Symposium in Applied Mathematics*, 14, 1962.
6. Myhill, J.: The converse to Moore's Garden-of-Eden theorem, *Proc. Amer. Math. Soc.*, **14**, 1963, 685–686.
7. Nishio, H.: How does the neighborhood affect the global behavior of cellular automata?, 11th Workshop on Cellular Automata, Gdansk University, September 3-5, 2005, http://iftia9.univ.gda.pl/ CA2005/.
8. Nishio, H.: *How does the neighborhood affect the global behavior of cellular automata?*, Technical Report (kokyuroku) vol. 1489, RIMS, Kyoto University, June 2006, Proceedings of LA Symposium (Jan. 2006).
9. Nishio, H.: *A Note on the Growth of Neighborhoods of Cellular Automata*, Technical Report (kokyuroku) vol. 1503, RIMS, Kyoto University, July 2006, Proceedings of RIMS Workshop on Algebra, Languages and Algorithms (March 22, 2006).
10. Nishio, H., Margenstern, M.: An algebraic Analysis of Neighborhoods of Cellular Automata, Resubmitted to JUCS, 2005.

11. Nishio, H., Margenstern, M.: *An algebraic Analysis of Neighborhoods of Cellular Automata*, Technical Report (kokyuroku) vol. 1375, RIMS, Kyoto University, May 2004, Proceedings of LA Symposium, Feb. 2004.

12. Nishio, H., Margenstern, M., von Haeseler, F.: On Algebraic Structure of Neighborhoods of Cellular Automata –Horse Power Problem–, To appear in Fundamenta Informaticae, 2006.

13. Nishio, H., Saito, T.: Information Dynamics of Cellular Automata I: An Algebraic Study, *Fundamenta Informaticae*, **58**, 2003, 399–420.

14. Richardson, D.: Tessellations with Local Transformations., *J. Comput. Syst. Sci.*, **6**(5), 1972, 373–388.

15. von Neumann, J., Burks(ed.), A. W.: *Theory of Self-reproducing Automata*, Univ. of Illinois Press, 1966.

16. Worsch, T.: Private communication, June 2006.

Simulation of d'-Dimensional Cellular Automata on d-Dimensional Cellular Automata

Christoph Scheben

s_schebe@ira.uka.de

University of Karlsruhe (TH), Germany

Abstract. In this paper a fast and space efficient method for simulating a d'-dimensional cellular automaton (CA) on a d-dimensional CA ($d < d'$) is introduced. For $d' = 2$ and $d = 1$ this method is optimal (under certain assumptions) with respect to time as well as space complexity. Let in this case $t(n)$ be the time complexity and $r(n)$ the side length of the smallest square enclosing all used cells. Then the simulation does not need more than $O(r^2)$ cells and has a running time of $O(r \cdot t)$. In the general case $d' = d + 1$ a version with the time and space complexity of $O(t^2)$ will be presented. Finally it will be shown, how it is possible to simulate a $2d$-dimensional CA on a d-dimensional CA in a similarly efficient way.

1 Introduction

Recently the simulation of a CA of higher dimensionality on a CA of lower dimensionality has received some renewed attention [2]. This problem has been considered before [1]. The constructions in this paper are significantly more efficient than those by Poupet [2] and it is much easier to get a reduction from $2d$ to d dimensions than with the construction by Achilles et al. [1]; furthermore one does not need the constructibility condition required there.

Definition 1 (CA). *A CA is a tuple* $\mathcal{A} = (R, N, Q, \square, \delta)$, *where*

- $R = \mathbb{Z}^d$ *is the underlying grid,*
- $N \subseteq \mathbb{Z}^d$ *is the finite neighborhood;*
  w.l.o.g. we assume von Neumann neighborhood
- Q *is the finite set of states,*
- $\square \in Q$ *is the quiescent state,*
- $\delta : Q^N \to Q$ *is the local transition function.*

The global transition function is defined as usual[1] as

$$\Delta : \begin{cases} Q^R \to Q^R \\ c \mapsto c' \text{ where } c'(z) = \delta\big(n \mapsto c(z + n)\big), \ n \in N \end{cases}$$

---

[1] Because N is subset of $\mathbb{Z}^d$, the mapping $+$ in the definition of the global transition function is the same as in the group $(\mathbb{Z}^d, +)$.

S. El Yacoubi, B. Chopard, and S. Bandini (Eds.): ACRI 2006, LNCS 4173, pp. 131–140, 2006.

We will use the following notion of simulation for this paper:

Definition 2 (Simulation). *A CA $\mathcal{A} = (\mathbb{Z}^d, N_{\mathcal{A}}, Q_{\mathcal{A}}, \Box, \delta_{\mathcal{A}})$ simulates a CA $\mathcal{B} = (\mathbb{Z}^{d'}, N_{\mathcal{B}}, Q_{\mathcal{B}}, \Box, \delta_{\mathcal{B}})$, if there are functions*

$$e : Q_{\mathcal{B}}^{\mathbb{Z}^{d'}} \to Q_{\mathcal{A}}^{\mathbb{Z}^d} \qquad f : \mathbb{Z}^{d'} \to \mathbb{Z}^d$$
$$g : Q_{\mathcal{A}} \to Q_{\mathcal{B}} \qquad h_b : \mathbb{N} \to \mathbb{N} \text{ for each } b \in \mathbb{Z}^{d'}$$

such that for each finite configuration $c_{\mathcal{B}}$, all cells $b \in \mathbb{Z}^{d'}$ and all $t \in \mathbb{N}$ holds:

$$\Delta^t(c_{\mathcal{B}})(b) = g\left(\Delta^{h_b(t)}(e(c_{\mathcal{B}}))(f(b))\right)$$

We require e to always map finite configuration on $\mathbb{Z}^d$ to finite configuration $\mathbb{Z}^{d'}$. Of course, all functions involved should be computable and in fact "simple". We are not going to formalize this aspect, but it will be clear that the constructions described below are simple.

A simulates $\mathcal{B}$ synchronously, if $h_b = h_{b'}$ for all $b, b' \in \mathbb{Z}^{d'}$. A cell $z \in \mathbb{Z}^d$ represents the state $q \in Q_{\mathcal{B}}$ (at the point in time t), if $g(\Delta^t(c_{\mathcal{A}})(z)) = q$ is fulfilled.

The main problems are to find a useful mapping f from the $d'D$-space in the dD-space as well as an algorithm for the transmission of states. If neighboring cells a and b of $\mathcal{B}$ are mapped to distant cells $f(a)$ and $f(b)$ the simulation (at least the obvious one) of one step of $\mathcal{B}$ requires informations to be exchanged between $f(a)$ and $f(b)$ in several steps.

The paper is organized as follows: In Section 2 a simulation method will be explained for the case of $2D \to 1D$ simulation. In Section 3 it will be generalized to $(d+1)D \to dD$ and in Section 4 to the case $d'D \to dD$. Throughout this paper we consider the case $d' > d$. (The opposite direction is considered in [1].)

2   Simulation of 2D on 1D CA

We start with the description of a function f mapping the cells of the 2D-CA to the cells of the 1D-CA (Subsection 2.1). In Subsections 2.2 and 2.3 we will explain, how the 1D-CA simulates one step of the 2D-CA. The computational complexity of the construction will be discussed in Subsection 2.4.

2.1   The Spiral Mapping

Let $f : \mathbb{Z}^2 \to \mathbb{Z}$ denote the "spiral mapping" as depicted in Fig. 1. Obviously f is injective. It is easily seen that $f(n, n)$ grows quadratically with the distance n to the origin: $f(n, n) = (2n + 1)^2 - 1$.

The set of cells of the 2D-CA, which have a distance k to the origin with respect to the maximum norm, is denoted as the *k-th sphere of the 2D-CA*. The images of these cells under f in the 1D-CA, will be called *the k-th 1D-sphere*.

The upper right corner of a 2D-sphere is called the *sphere-exit-cell*, its left neighbor is called the *sphere-entrance-cell*. Sphere-exit-cells in Figure 1 are for example the cells 8, 24, 48 and 80, sphere-entrance-cells are 1, 9, 25, and 49.

56	55	54	53	52	51	50	49	80
57	30	29	28	27	26	25	48	79
58	31	12	11	10	9	24	47	78
59	32	13	2	1	8	23	46	77
60	33	14	3	0	7	22	45	76
61	34	15	4	5	6	21	44	75
62	35	16	17	18	19	20	43	74
63	36	37	38	39	40	41	42	73
64	65	66	67	68	69	70	71	72

| 0 | 1 | 2 | 3 | 4 | 5 | 6 | 7 | 8 | 9 | 10 | 11 | 12 | 13 | 14 | 15 | 16 | 17 | 18 | 19 | 20 | 21 | 22 | 23 | 24 | 25 |

Fig. 1. Mapping of $(a, b) \in \mathbb{Z}^2$ to $\mathbb{Z}$ according to the spiral around the origin

2.2 Shifting States in the 1D-CA

We now turn to the problem of transmission of the 2D-states in the 1D-CA.

A closer look at the mapping f reveals, that in any case two 2D-neighbors are also neighbors in the 1D-CA. If the cells are marked unambiguously according to their position (up, down, left, right) as in figure 2, a 1D-cell is able to identify the 2D-positions of its 1D-neighbors. Thus in the critical moment a cell can read the 2D-states of two of the 2D-neighbors off their 1D-neighbors (exception: sphere-exit-cell and sphere-entrance-cell; see below). The other two 2D-neighbors are located in one or two neighboring spheres. In case of corner-cells, the two 2D-neighbors are located in the outer sphere. For the other cells one is located in the outer and one is located in the inner sphere.

If one shifts for every 1D-sphere the 2D-states in the right way to the cells of the next higher 1D-sphere and afterwards the states of the higher sphere back to the lower one, than every cell knows the 2D-states of the neighbors of their preimage-cell. Sphere-entrance- and sphere-exit-cells have to be treated in a slightly different way.

Algorithm 1 (State shifting)

1. The 1D-image of the entrance-cell of a 2D-sphere starts and sends its 2D-state including its position-marking towards the direction of the next higher sphere. As soon as the signal passes the right neighbor, this one appends a signal with its own 2D-state as well as position marking. All other cells of the sphere behave analogously: They append their 2D-state as well as their marking as soon as the last signal of the arising signal-chain passes.

2. As soon as the first signal reaches the first cell *after* the entrance-cell of the next sphere, which is not a corner-cell, the signal ends in this cell and the cell memorizes the transmitted 2D-state as well as the transmitted marking. All other signals, not coming from a corner, proceed analogously: They ignore the entrance-cell of the next sphere as well as all corner-cells and end, as soon as they find a cell, which has not received a signal yet. Corner-cells

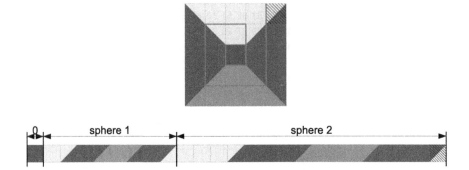

Fig. 2. Mapping $f(a,b)$ for $|a|, |b| \leq 2$ with marked greatest cell. The cells are marked accordingly to their position (up, down, left, right) related to the origin. The corners have two markings and so they are unambiguously identifiable.

behave a bit different, because the state has to be transmitted to two cells. They ignore the sphere-entrance-cell too, but they do not end at the first cells, which has not received a signal yet. In stead they transmit their state and marking to this cell and end at the second cell, which has not received a signal yet (and is not a corner cell).

3. Exception handling: Simultaneously with step 1 the exit-cell of the sphere transmits its 2D-state directly to the entrance-cell of the next sphere. Furthermore the special treatment for corner-cells in step 2 is not applied to the sphere-exit-cell.

   Moreover, the cell at the origin acts in a different way. It behaves similar to a corner-cell, but it transmits its state to the four neighbors positioned in the next sphere. We assume that the cell at the origin knows, that it is the origin.

In the same way, the states are shifted back. The only relevant difference is, that every corner-cell collects two signals.

The algorithm also works, if the next sphere is not constructed yet, because the cells of the next sphere can be marked in a correct way by the transmitted markings. Once again some attention has to be paid to the corner-cells. These have to mark a corner-cell after marking the first normal cell. In addition, the marking of the largest cell has to be shifted.

In oder to prevent constructing too many cells later, the algorithm is "aborted" for the last sphere, if the signal, which was sent at first, notices the following two conditions. First that all cells of the sphere represent the quiescent state of the 2D-CA and second that the sphere is the greatest one. The latter can be recognized by the signal, because the last cell of the sphere is marked as the greatest cell. "Aborting" means that the states are moved indeed but that the new cells will not be marked. This will be of importance in the next section, because the chronological dependencies would be mixed up, if one would abort the shifting directly after reaching the greatest cell.

2.3 Simulation 2D → 1D

Up to now it was shown, how 2D-states can be shifted form one sphere into the next one. Now it shall be explained, how the whole simulation works.

Let the cells of the k-th sphere of the 1D-CA be in the configuration c'_i and let the configuration c'_i represent the i-th 2D-configuration. That means $c'_i(z')$ represents $c_i(z)$ if $z' = f(z)$, $z \in S_k$. Here and in the following S_k denotes the k-th sphere in the 2D-CA, and we also use the abbreviation $K_k = \bigcup_{i \leq k} S_i$ for the "filled" sphere. In addition, the cells of the k-th sphere shall be synchronized and marked according to Figure 2.

Then the $(i + 1)$-th simulation step of the k-th sphere is performed in the following way:

Algorithm 2 (Simulation 2D → 1D)

1. **Shift and wait:** The sphere-entrance-cell starts the algorithm for shifting the 2D-states into the next sphere (sphere $k+1$) as described in the previous subsection. After the states have arrived, they wait until the sphere $k + 1$ synchronizes and switches to the next 2D-state. Now the cells of the sphere $k + 1$ are in the states corresponding to the i-th 2D-configuration.
2. **Exchange:** Sphere $k + 1$ performs two actions: First the cells of the sphere exchange their states with the shifted states of the sphere k and second the sphere starts with step 1 to prepare the next simulation step (for the sphere $k + 1$) itself. The exchange of the states is executed in the following way (compare Fig. 2):
   (a) Upper horizontal cells accept the shifted state as the state of their lower 2D-neighbor.
   (b) Lower horizontal cells accept the shifted state as the state of their upper 2D-neighbor.
   (c) In the same way left and right vertical cells accept the shifted state as the state of their right and left 2D-neighbor respectively.
   (d) The shifted signals accept the states of the cells of the sphere $k+1$ the other way round, i.e. signals of upper cells accept the state of the corresponding $(k+1)$-cell as the state of their upper 2D-neighbor and so on.
   (e) Corner-cells of the sphere $k + 1$ accept no state (that means that they did not got states from the sphere k).
3. **Shift back:** After the states were exchanged, the cell of the last shifted state (meaning the greatest cell of the sphere $k + 1$, which got a state) initiates the shifting back as was described in Subsection 2.2. This cell can identify itself as "last shifted cell", because its right neighbor is marked as upper right corner, which is the sphere-exit-cell.
4. **Exception handling:** Simultaneously to the state shifting in step 1 the entrance-cell of the sphere k sends its current 2D-state to the exit-cells of the same sphere. This one memorizes the state as the state of its left 2D-neighbor. At the same time the sphere-exit-cell sends its 2D-state to the entrance-cell. The sphere-entrance-cell again memorizes the transmitted state as the 2D-state of its right 2D-neighbor.

5. **Synchronization:** After the last state is shifted back (this one belongs to the entrance-cell of the sphere k), the entrance-cell initiates a synchronization of the cells of its sphere.
6. **New states:** If the cells are synchronized, they compute their new 2D-state. This is possible, because the 2D-states either
   (a) have been shifted up from the lower sphere,
   (b) have been acquired from the upper sphere through the own shifting operation,
   (c) the 2D-states are kept ready from the own 1D-neighbors of the cell or
   (d) were transmitted through step (4). This happens in the special case of the entrance- and exit-cell of the sphere (in the 1D-CA).

There is still a special case to be examined: What happens, if the last sphere (w.l.o.g. let this be the sphere i) constructs a new sphere $i+1$? In this case the cells of the sphere $i+1$ know the states of all 2D-neighbors immediately, because all 2D-states, expect the one shifted up, correspond to the quiescent state. Thus the sphere $i+1$ could synchronize and switch to the next state immediately – while simultaneously shifting back the states. But this should not happen, because then the sphere $i+1$ would be approximately half of a simulation phase ahead of sphere i. Therefore the first computation step of the sphere $i+1$ will be delayed artificially until it is ensured, that the sphere i is a computation step in advance of the sphere $i+1$. This can be achieved by initiating the synchronization of the sphere $i+1$ only after the sphere i shifts its states to the sphere $i+1$ again. At this point it becomes clear that the spheres work asynchronously. But the sphere k is maximal one computation step in advance of the the sphere $k+1$, because the sphere k always waits for the sphere $k+1$ at step 1. According to the statement above, the sphere k is always *exactly* one step in advance of the sphere $k+1$.

2.4 Complexity of the 2D → 1D Simulation

We use the same definition for the Landau symbols $O, \Theta, \Omega, o, \omega$ like in [4]. Let t be the time complexity of the 2D-CA and let r denote the side length of the smallest square enclosing all cells which were non-quiescent (hence the space complexity is $O(r^2)$). The time and space complexity of the 1D-CA shall be examined in terms of r and t.

The greatest sphere of the 1D-CA is also the slowest one. That means that the t-th configuration was completely computed, when the greatest sphere – the sphere r – switches to the t-th configuration. Because every step of the described algorithm is bounded by $O(|S_r|)$ and the origin executes $O(r+t)$ computation steps, the runtime of 1D-CA is bounded by $O(|S_r| \cdot (t+r))$, and thus because of $|S_r| = 8r$ and $r \le r_0 + t$ by

$$O(|S_r| \cdot (t+r)) = O(8r \cdot (t+r)) = O(r \cdot t + r^2) = O(r \cdot t) .$$

The space complexity is bounded by $O(f(r,r)) = O((2r+1)^2 - 1) = O(r^2)$ (where $f(a,b)$ is the spiral mapping). So in the 1D-CA most memory is wasted, when the 2D-CA uses only the cells of one direction.

Next, it will be shown, that the algorithm is optimal under certain assumptions with respect to memory as well as time complexity.

Let $f : \mathbb{Z}^2 \to \mathbb{Z}$ be *any* mapping of the cells of a 2D-CA $\mathcal{B}$ on the cells of a 1D-CA $\mathcal{A}$ such that for some constant m the number $|f^{-1}(a)|$ of $\mathcal{B}$-cells simulated by any $\mathcal{A}$-cell a is bounded by m.

Lemma 1. *Under the given assumption, the algorithm for the 2D $\to$ 1D simulation is optimal with respect to the space complexity $\Theta(r^2)$.*

Proof. After assumption a cell of the 1D-CA is able to simulate only a finite number of cells of the 2D-CA, thus the 1D-CA uses at least $\frac{1}{c} \cdot r^2$ cells. But then the space complexity of $\Theta(r^2)$ is optimal.

Define the function $k : \mathbb{N} \to \mathbb{N}$ as

$$k(r) = \max\{|f(a) - f(b)| \mid a, b \in K_r \text{ and } a \text{ and } b \text{ are neighbors}\}$$

where the distance is to be measured as the number of "steps from neighbor to neighbor".

Lemma 2. $k(r) \in \Omega(r)$.

Proof. In the 2D-CA the distance between two cells $a, b \in K_r$ is at most $2r$ cells. Let $a' = max\{f(x) \mid x \in K_r\}$ and $b' = min\{f(x) \mid x \in K_r\}$ the largest and the smallest index respectively of a cell of the 1D-CA $\mathcal{A}$ simulating a cell from K_r.

Assume $k(r) \in o(r)$. Then $|a' - b'| \le 2r \cdot k(r) \in o(r^2)$. But being able to simulate all cells from K_r in $o(r^2)$ cells contradicts Lemma 1.

From this lemma immediately follows that at least all naïve simulation techniques which rely on exchanging $\mathcal{B}$-states between simulating $\mathcal{A}$-cells have to spend $k(r)$ steps for the simulation of one step of a K_r-subcube of $\mathcal{B}$. Hence a running time in $\Theta(r \cdot t)$ cannot be avoided.

To summarize this section we note:

1. The space complexity could be decreased only if one would find a simulation, which does not simply assign a finite number of $\mathcal{B}$-cells to each $\mathcal{A}$-cell.
2. The time complexity could be decreased only if either one could decrease the space complexity or if one would find a way, where the images don't have to exchange their states after a constant number of steps. The second possibility cannot be excluded, but on the other hand one would not expect intuitively, that the simulation could be done faster than in $\Theta(r \cdot t)$.

3   Generalization $(d+1)D \to dD$

We will now show how the simulation method can be extended to d dimensions in an easy way. In this case we define the mapping f as

$$f : \mathbb{Z}^{d+1} \to \mathbb{Z}^d : (a_1, ..., a_{d+1}) \mapsto (a_1, ..., a_{d-1}, f_{spiral}(a_d, a_{d+1})) \, .$$

The $(d+1)D \to dD$ simulation works similar to the $2D \to 1D$ case, because in $\mathcal{A}$ each cell can access $2(d-1)$ $\mathcal{B}$-neighboring states directly the $\mathcal{A}$-neighbors.

The part of the simulation which involves the spiral only has to be changed slightly with respect to the above description:

1. Two cycles after a computation step the 2D-states of a sphere are also transmitted (synchronously) to the $d-1$ parallel neighbor spheres. If such a sphere is not marked yet, then the markings are taken over and a computation step is executed immediately.
2. A new 1D-sphere will be constructed at every step. This construction always takes place and does not depend on whether the sphere will be needed or not. This guarantees, that the parallel spheres always maintain an offset of two cycles.

This way the constructed $(d+1)D \to dD$ simulation has a runtime and a space complexity of $O(t^2)$. It should be mentioned, that it is possible to construct another synchronous $(d+1)D \to dD$ simulation with a space complexity of $O(r^2)$ and a time complexity of $O(r^2 \cdot t)$ (see [3]; because of the page restriction for the paper we leave this out).

4   Generalization $d'D \to dD$

Considering the results from the previous subsection, a (simple-minded) generalization to the case $d'D \to dD$ consists in the application of the demonstrated method $d'-d$ times. But such a simulation is very inefficient for large differences $d'-d$. For example the simulation of a 10D-CA on a 1D-CA would result in a runtime of $O(t^{2^{10}}) = O(t^{1024})$. This is not satisfactory.

The aim of this section is to reduce the running time at least for dimensions $d' = 2^x \cdot d$, $x \in \mathbb{N}$ to $O(t^{2^x})$. With this a 16D-CA as well as a 10D-CA could be simulated on a 1D-CA with a runtime of $O(t^{16})$. This even is optimal for $d' = 2^x \cdot d$, $x \in \mathbb{N}$, if the $d'D$-CA has a space complexity of $O(t)$.

Let f be defined as

$$f : \mathbb{Z}^{d'} = \mathbb{Z}^{2d} \to \mathbb{Z}^d : (a_1, ..., a_{2d}) \mapsto (f_{spiral}(a_1, a_2), ..., f_{spiral}(a_{2d-1}, a_{2d})) .$$

This approach adds one possible source of complications:

The mappings are linked now (Fig. 3). Thus, after constructing a new sphere on one of the axis of the dD-CA and after execution of the first computation step one has to start a new $2D \to 1D$ simulation in the remaining $d-1$ dimensions. At this point it could happen, that a perpendicular started simulation in a domain works faster than the simulation in one of the other directions (e.g. this is the case in the domain $(2, 1)$ in Fig. 3). But a cell is not able to switch to the next 2D-state, until the states of all directions have been received. Thus, the 1D-spheres are no longer synchronized one by one, but they are combined to domains. These domains are synchronized as a whole as soon as the cell, which is the closest to the origin, has received all states (Fig. 3). The domains are chosen in a way, that

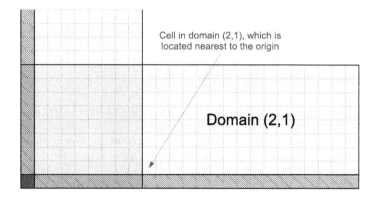

Fig. 3. Simulation $4D \rightarrow 2D$. The cells of the framed areas will be synchronized altogether.

all cells, which are located in every direction in the same 1D-sphere, are merged into one domain.

Also in this simulation, a new 1D-sphere will be constructed at every step. Like above the sphere is always constructed independent of its further use. This guarantees at every time, that the domains are marked completely in one step.

This $2dD \rightarrow dD$ simulation has a time and space complexity of $O(t^2)$ (like the $(d+1)D \rightarrow dD$ simulation). For proving the optimality one considers, that the ratio between the diameter of the $d'D$-CA and the diameter of the dD-CA is quadratic, because it is $l'^{d'} = (2r+1)^{d'} = (2r+1)^{2d} = ((2r+1)^2)^d = (l^2)^d$. Now one uses the same arguments as in Subsection 2.4. Through successive execution one reaches the desired aim.

5   Conclusion

The most suitable method for comparison with the methods presented in this paper, seems to be the $3D \rightarrow 2D$ simulation method of Poupet [2]. Table 1 summarizes the resulting overheads of different methods for the $3D \rightarrow 2D$ simulation.

Table 1. Comparison of simulation methods for the $3D \rightarrow 2D$ simulation

simulation	Achilles [1]	Poupet [2]	present	synchronous [3]
time	$O(t^2)$	$O(t^4)$	$O(t^2)$	$O(r^2 \cdot t)$
space	$O(t^3)$	$O(t^9)$	$O(t^2)$	$O(r^2)$

The algorithm presented in this paper outmatch the one from [2]: Beside the higher speed and the smaller space requirements it is possible to construct a completely synchronous simulation. It also needs less space than the simulation from [1].

Poupet's simulation could be generalized to the $d + 1 \to d$ case (with $d \geq 2$) without difficulties. Table 2 summarizes the resulting overheads for the $(d + 1)D \to dD$ simulation. The results of the comparison with [2] are the same as in the $3D \to 2D$ case. But in addition it shows, that the space efficiency is much better than in [1] – especially for $d \gg 1$.

Table 2. Comparison of simulation methods for the $(d + 1)D \to dD$ simulation

simulation	Achilles [1]	Poupet [2]	present	synchronous [3]
time	$O(t^2)$	$O(t^4)$	$O(t^2)$	$O(r^2 \cdot t)$
space	$O(t^{d+1})$	$O(t^9)$	$O(t^2)$	$O(r^2)$

Furthermore we are able to simulate a d'-dimensional CA on a d-dimensional CA with a time and space complexity of at most $O(t^{2^{\lceil ld(d'/d) \rceil}})$. It is unclear, whether a similar efficiency could be achieved using the simulations in [1] and [2].

In the future we will investigate, whether the principle of the $2D \to 1D$ simulation can be generalized in such a way, that one gets an optimal algorithm for the $(d + 1)D \to dD$ simulation, too. At least in the case of the $3D \to 2D$ simulation one could imagine something like that. In addition a direct $3D \to 1D$ simulation could be useful for improving the idea from Section 4 further.

References

1. Achilles, A.-C., Kutrib, M., Worsch, T.: On relations between arrays of processing elements of different dimensionality, Proc. Parcella 1996, pp. 13–20, Akademie-Verlag, Berlin, 1996.
2. Poupet, V.: Simulating 3D Cellular Automata with 2D Cellular Automata, J. Fiala et al. (Eds.): MFCS 2004, LNCS 3153, pp. 439–450, 2004, Springer-Verlag, Berlin Heidelberg, 2004.
3. Scheben, C.: Simulation von d'-dimensionalen Zellularautomaten auf d-dimensionalen Zellularautomaten, Studienarbeit, Univ. Karlsruhe, 2006.
4. Cormen, T. H., Leiserson, C. E., Rivest, R. L., Stein, C.: Introduction to algorithms, Cambridge, Mass. : MIT Press, 2001.

Cellular Automata Based Encoding Technique for Wavelet Transformed Data Targeting Still Image Compression[*]

Chandrama Shaw[1], Sukanta Das[1], and Biplab K. Sikdar[2]

[1] Dept. of Information Technology, Bengal Engineering & Sc. University, Shibpur,
Howrah, India, 711103
{cshaw, sukanta}@it.becs.ac.in
[2] Dept. of Computer Sc. & Technology, Bengal Engineering & Sc. University,
Shibpur, Howrah, India, 711103
biplab@cs.becs.ac.in

Abstract. This paper reports cellular automata (CA) based efficient encoding technique for wavelet transformed data of still image. The encoding technique handles wavelet coefficients, in transformed domain, and then simulates different classes of transforms with the introduction of CA framework. It ideally suits for low cost implementation of the compression technology for still images. Reported experimental results establish the effectiveness of the proposed scheme.

1 Introduction

The standard methods of lossy compression for still images in frequency domain employ Discrete Cosine Transform [2] and Karhunen-Loeve Transform. Other notable schemes are the Wavelet Transform [3], Pyramid Decomposition and Iterated Function System. Different classes of Cellular Automata (CA) transforms have also been proposed. However, such transforms [6] are highly complex in nature and are obtained through experimentations.

The above scenarios motivate us to design a CA based Vector Quantization (VQ) [5] model for still image compression. The images are taken from the specific domains such as human face, brain MRI, etc. The proposed scheme employs Wavelet Transform and subsequently generates codebook with the help of a CA based clustering model. It ensures effective implementation and searching of codebook. The scheme can also be effective for video telephony to facilitate on-line applications. The basics of CA technology are introduced next.

2 Cellular Automata

An 1-dimensional Cellular Automaton (CA) consists of a number of cells [4]. In 3-neighborhood, the next state of ith cell is assumed to be $q_i(t+1) = f(q_{i-1}(t), q_i(t),$

---

[*] This work is supported by the sponsored CA Research Projects, Department of CST, Bengal Engineering & Science University, Shibpur, India.

S. El Yacoubi, B. Chopard, and S. Bandini (Eds.): ACRI 2006, LNCS 4173, pp. 141–146, 2006.

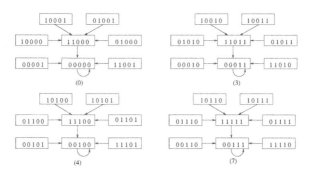

Fig. 1. State transition diagram of a 5-cell MACA $< 102, 60, 204, 204, 170 >$

$q_{i+1}(t))$, where $q_i(t)$ represents the state of the ith cell at t^{th} instant of time. 'f' is the next state function - that is, the rule $\mathcal{R}_i$ of the automata [1]. An n-cell CA is designated by the $\mathcal{R} =< \mathcal{R}_1, \mathcal{R}_2, \cdots, \mathcal{R}_i, \cdots, \mathcal{R}_n >$. The proposed CA based model for VQ employs Multiple Attractor Cellular Automata (MACA) [4].

The state transition graph of an MACA consists of cyclic and non-cyclic states. The non-cyclic states form trees rooted at the cyclic states (attractors). The 5-cell MACA of *Fig.1* having four attractors $\{00000(0), 00011(3), 00100(4), 00111(7)\}$. The states rooted at α forms the α-*basin* (attractor basin).

Theorem 1. *In an n-cell MACA with* $k = 2^m$ *attractors, there exists m-bit positions at which the attractors generate pseudo-exhaustive* 2^m *patterns [4].*

The *modulo-2* sum of two states is a predecessor of *0-state* (pattern with all 0s) iff the two states lie in the same attractor basin. Let consider the two states $\{01010, 01011\}$ of 00011-basin (*Fig.1*). The module-2 sum of the two states is $\{00001\} \in$ 0-basin. Hence, if $\mathcal{P}$ & $\tilde{\mathcal{P}}$ belong to the same basin, the pattern $\mathcal{P}'(= \mathcal{P} \oplus \tilde{\mathcal{P}})$ falls in the 0-basin. $\mathcal{P}'$ is the hamming distance (HD) of $\mathcal{P}$ & $\tilde{\mathcal{P}}$. The distribution of patterns shows that the 0-basin has a definite bias for patterns with lesser weight (the presence of number of 1s in them) [8]. Fig.2 depicts the Expected Occurrence (EO) of a pattern, with weight (w), in the 0-basin. It establishes that (i) the value of EO decreases monotonically with the weight, (ii) a basin contains patterns with low HD, and (iii) pattern pairs with low HD have the high probability of getting covered by a few number of attractor basins. These properties of MACA are exploited in the current design.

3   CA Based Model of Vector Quantization

A vector quantizer $\mathcal{Q}$ of dimension l and size $\mathcal{M}$ is a mapping from $\mathcal{R}^l$ into a finite set $\mathcal{C}$ containing $\mathcal{M}$ reproduction points, called the code vectors. That is, $\mathcal{Q} : \mathcal{R}^l \to \mathcal{C}$, where $\mathcal{C} = \{c_1, \cdots, c_\mathcal{M}\}, c_1 \cdots, c_\mathcal{M} \in \mathcal{R}^l$. The set $\mathcal{C}$ is called the codebook. For the current application, a codebook is generated from the transformed data obtained after Wavelet transformation. We employ the MACA based clustering model for designing such a codebook. Each code vector can be viewed as the centroid or representative of a cluster.

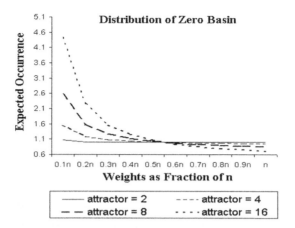

Fig. 2. Expected distribution of patterns in 0-basin of an MACA with n =30

A VQ method consists of an encoder and a decoder [9]. The CA based model [9] addresses the difficulties of generating the codebook from the training set and the high processing overhead at encoding stage. Rather than developing general compression scheme, we concentrate on developing codebook for a specific class of data, that is, still image data on human face. To reduce processing overhead, we introduce MACA based hierarchical clustering algorithm [5].

Design of training set: The bands (LL, LH, HL, HH) of Wavelet coefficients [3] for the input image form the training set. The steps are:

Algorithm 1. Training Set Generation
Input: Set of n images
Output: The training set for different bands
Step 1: Transform input image with Wavelet transform at single level that generates four bands of coefficients LL, LH, HL, HH.
Step 2: Segment each band of Wavelet coefficients into 4×4 blocks.
Step 3: The set of segments, from each band, is the training set for that band.

Codebook design: Separate codebooks are generated for each band with the training set resulted from Algorithm 1. The property of MACA is exploited to identify the clusters among the training set with HD as the metric. An n-bit MACA with k-attractors acts as a natural cluster (*Section 2*). The MACA of Fig.1 can be employed to classify patterns into two clusters, (say [I]= {00011, 00100 and 00111} and [II] = {00000}). The pseudo-exhaustive field yields the address of the memory that stores the cluster information (*Theorem 1*). Therefore, Cluster I attractors yield the memory addresses {01, 10, 11}.

MACA based hierarchical clustering model for codebook: For each node of the binary VQ tree, we genetically evolve an MACA to split the cluster into two sub-clusters with an objective to maximize the self-similarity within a sub-cluster. A leaf node of the MACA tree represents cluster of elements.

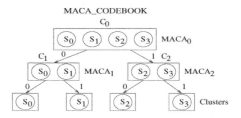

Fig. 3. Structure of MACA based hierarchical clustering scheme

Fig.3 illustrates the design. Suppose, four clusters S_0, S_1, S_2 and S_3 are to be generated from the training set $C_0 = \{\{S_0\}, \{S_1\}, \{S_2\}, \{S_3\}\}$. The MACA, at the first level ($MACA_0$), generates two clusters $C_1 = \{\{S_0\}, \{S_1\}\}$ and $C_2 = \{\{S_2\}, \{S_3\}\}$. The similar process is repeated for C_1 and C_2 to generate the four clusters $\{S_0\}$, $\{S_1\}$ and $\{S_2\}$, $\{S_3\}$, employing $MACA_1$ and $MACA_2$. A leaf node S_i is represented by the centroid $P_i \in S_i$ of the elements in S_i. P_i can be viewed as a codeword in the codebook. Codebook searching: For a given test vector $\acute{P}_i$, we need to identify the codebook entry (the codeword) closest to $\acute{P}_i$. In reference to Fig.3, the $MACA_0$ is loaded with $\acute{P}_i$ and allowed to run. It returns the desired cluster C_1 or C_2. The MACA ($MACA_1$ or $MACA_2$) is then loaded with $\acute{P}_i$ to output the desired cluster S_i and its centroid. The path traversed represents the compressed data (00 for S_0) for the $\acute{P}_i$.

4   Encoding and Decoding Schemes

When an input vector $\acute{P}_i$ is compressed (encoded), it can either be identified as a cluster or non cluster element. A non cluster element is passed through an error analysis process.

Definition 1. *Let $c_i = <x_{i1},...,x_{il}>$ be the ith code vector and $V = <v_1,...,v_l>$ be the input vector mapped to c_i through hierarchical MACA tree, then the error vector $E_i(V) = |\ c_i - V\ | = <e_{i1},...,e_{il}>$, where $e_{ij} = |\ x_{ij} - v_j\ |$ for $j = 1, ...,$ l. The mean square error is defined as $mse_i(V) = \sum_{j=1}^{l} e_{ij}^2$.*

Definition 2. *Let λ_{mse} and λ_{error} are the allowed threshold values for mean square error (mse) and the error value for an input vector V respectively and V maps to the code vector c_i through the hierarchical MACA tree. V is said to be a cluster vector iff $mse_i(V) \leq \lambda_{mse}$ and $e_{ij} \leq \lambda_{error}$ for $j = 1, ..., l$; otherwise, V is said to be a stray (non cluster) vector.*

Algorithm 2. Error Analysis
Step 1: Let V is mapped to the ith code vector c_i. Compute $mse_i(V)$ & $E_i(V)$.
Step 2: Carry out Step 3 and 4 if V is a non-cluster vector.
Step 3: Perform DCT on $E_i(V)$ and c_i to obtain $E_i'(V)$ and c_i' respectively.
Step 4: Encode $E_i'(V)$ through entropy coding with respect to c_i'.

It is found that for a given i^{th} code vector (Wavelet transformed vector) $c_i = x_{i0}, x_{i1}, \cdots, x_{il}$ and error vector $E_i = e_{i0}, e_{i1}, \cdots, e_{il}$ if the DCT of E_i and c_i are $c_i' = x_{i0}', x_{i1}', \ldots, x_{il}'$ and $E_i' = e_{i0}', e_{i1}', \ldots, e_{il}'$ respectively, then $e_{i0}' = - x_{i0}'$.

Algorithm 3. Encoder

Input: A 512×512 two dimensional Gray Image

Output: Compressed image as a bit stream

Step 1: Transform the input image by Wavelet filter into different bands

Step 2: Segment the transformed image of each band into 4×4 blocks

Step 3: For each block, through traversal of MACA tree, find code vector c_i.

Step 4: If the input vector is not a stray vector, then store the index of c_i with flag bit set, to indicate that it is a cluster vector. Goto Step 7.

Step 5: Analyze the error vector (Algorithm 2).

Step 6: Store the encoded bit stream (*Step 3*) with flag bit reset.

Step 7: Store the index in a buffer.

Step 8: Repeat *Step 3* to *Step 7* until all the blocks are processed.

The encoded data has been stored in a bit stream. A decoder check the flag bit and performs a reverse error analysis process on it while decompressing.

5   Experimental Results

The proposed compression technology is developed for human portrait. A large number of test cases are considered. A few of them are reported in *Table 1*. The results depict that the quality of decompressed image is comparable with

(a) The Original image

(a) The Original image

(b) The Decompressed image

Fig. 4. Result1: compression 91%

(b) The Decompressed image

Fig. 5. Result2: compression 91%

that of JPEG 2000 [7] in terms of PSNR for a fixed compression ratio. However, the main achievement of the scheme is it performs faster compression [9]. Fig.4 and Fig.5 display the original and reconstructed images from our *CA* based compression/decompression scheme for comparison.

Table 1. Comparison of results at 91% cmpression ratio

Image File	PSNR of CA Scheme	PSNR of Jpeg2000
face1	42.59	42.09
face2	42.54	42.00
face3	43.04	43.20
face4	42.28	42.97
face5	43.60	43.14
face6	42.46	42.44

6   Conclusion

This paper presents a Cellular Automata (CA) based still image compression technology on transformed data. The CA based transforms have been employed for low cost on-line compression to support efficient data transmission with desired level of image quality.

References

1. S. Wolfram, "A New Kind Of Science," *World Scientific*, 2002.
2. N. Ahmed, T. Natarajan, K. R. Rao, *"Discrete Cosine Transforms"*, IEEE Trans. Comput. C-23, pp-90-93, Jan 1974.
3. I. Daubechies, *" The Wavelet Transform, Time Frequency Localization and Signal Analysis'*, IEEE Trans. on IT, 36(5), pp 961-1005, Sep 90.
4. P. P. Chaudhuri, D. R. Chowdhury, S. Nandi, and S. Chatterjee, "Additive cellular automata, theory and applications, vol. 1," *IEEE Computer Society Press, Los Alamitos, California*, no. ISBN-0-8186-7717-1, 1997.
5. Allen Gresho and Robert M. Gray, *"Vector Quantization and Signal Compression"*, Kluwer Academy Publishers.
6. O. Lafe, *"Data Compression and Encryption Using Cellular Automata Transforms"*, In Proc. of IJSIS, 1996.
7. D. Santa-Cruz, T. Ebrahimi, J. Askelf, M. Larsson and C. Christopoulos. *"JPEG 2000 still image coding versus other standards."*, In Proc. of SPIE, vol 4472, pages 267-275, San Diego, California, Jul. 29-Aug. 3, 2001.
8. P. Maji, C. Shaw, N. Ganguly, B. K. Sikdar, and P. P. Chaudhuri, "Theory and Application of Cellular Automata For Pattern Classification," *Fundamenta Informaticae on Cellular Automata*, 2004.
9. C. Shaw, P. Maji, S. Saha and B. K. Sikdar, "Cellular Automata Based Encompression Technology for Voice Data", *ACRI 2004*, pages 258-267.

An Analytical Formulation for Cellular Automata (CA) Based Solution of Density Classification Task (DCT)

Nirmalya Sundar Maiti, Shiladitya Munshi, and P. Pal Chaudhuri

Cellular Automata Research Lab (CARL), EM 4/1, Salt Lake-V, W.B., India 700091
nirmalya@carltig.res.in, shiladitya@carltig.res.in,
palchau@carltig.res.in

Abstract. This paper presents an analytical solution for Density Classification Task (DCT) with an n cell inhomogeneous Cellular Automata represented by its Rule Vector (RV) $<R_0 R_1 R_2 \cdots R_i \cdots R_{n-1}>$, where rule R_i is employed on i^{th} cell (i=0,1,2,$\cdots$(n-1)). It reports the Best Rule Vector (BRV) for solution of DCT. The concept of Rule Vector Graph (RVG) has provided the framwork for the solution. RVG derived from the RV of a CA can be analyzed to derive the Best Rule Vector (BRV) consisting of only rule 232 and 184 (or 226) for 3-neighborhood CA and their equivalent rules for k-neighborhood CA (k>3). The error analysis of the solution has been also reported.

Keywords: Rule Vector (RV), Rule Vector Graph (RVG), Best Rule Vector (BRV), Rule Min Term (RMT).

1 Introduction

Researchers [4-9] have employed evolutionary computation schemes to arrive at the desired CA for solution of DCT on sample data sets of 149 bit (or higher size) patterns. The current paper reports an analytical formulation for CA based solution of DCT for n bit patterns with k-neighborhood CA (k=3,5,7,$\cdots$). An error analysis has been also presented for the solution derived. The solution has been formulated from the analysis of the Rule Vector Graph (RVG) derived from the Rule Vector (RV) $<R_0 R_1 \cdots R_i \cdots R_{n-1}>$ of an n cell inhomogeneous CA, where Rule R_i is employed in the ith cell (i=0,1,$\cdots$(n-1)). Analysis of CA behavior based on its RVG is next briefly introduced. Periodic boundary CA is employed here for solution of DCT.

2 Derivation of Rule Vector Graph (RVG) from the Rule Vector (RV) of a CA

The next state function of 3-neighborhood CA cell, as defined in Table 1, can be represented as a rule [2]. It represents $2^3 = 8$ possible present states of 3 neighbors

S. El Yacoubi, B. Chopard, and S. Bandini (Eds.): ACRI 2006, LNCS 4173, pp. 147–156, 2006.
© Springer-Verlag Berlin Heidelberg 2006

Table 1. Rule Min Term (RMT) of a Three variable Boolean Function Representing Truth Table of Sample Rule

Present states of 3-neighbours	111	110	101	100	011	010	001	000	Rule
$(i-1), i$, and $(i+1)$ cells	T(7)	T(6)	T(5)	T(4)	T(3)	T(2)	T(1)	T(0)	Number
(Minterms of a 3 variable	(7)	(6)	(5)	(4)	(3)	(2)	(1)	(0)	
boolean function)									
	1	1	1	0	1	0	0	0	232
Next state of ith cell	1	0	1	1	1	0	0	0	184
	1	1	1	0	0	0	1	0	226

of (i-1), i, and (i+1) cells. Each of the eight entries (3 bit binary string) represents a Minterm of a 3 variable boolean function for a 3-neighborhood CA cell. In subsequent discussions, each of the 8 entries in Table 1 is referred to as a Rule Min Term (RMT). The set of all the 8 minterms is noted as T={T(m)},(m=0 to 7); a single RMT is denoted as T(m), while in figures it is simply noted as m for clarity of the diagram. Each of the next three rows of Table 1 shows the next state (0 or 1) of ith cell. A few definitions are next introduced.

Definition 1: Attractor - A cycle in the STG is called an attractor.

Definition 2: Self-loop Attractor (SLA) - A Self Loop State (SLS) with a cycle of length 1 is referred to as SLA. The states 0 and 7 are the SLAs in Fig 1.

Definition 3: Attractor Basin: The set of the states that converge to an attractor cycle form an Attractor Basin. For example in Fig 1, the states 1,2,4 and 0 form an attractor basin with 0 as the attractor while the remaining states form another basin with 7 as the attractor. Both '0' and '7' are SLAs.

Definition 4: 0-RMT, 1-RMT - For a specific CA rule (Table 1), the next state of ith cell is 0 for a subset of RMTs while for other subset it is 1. Thus a CA rule divides the RMTs into two subsets. These two subsets of RMTs is referred to as 0-RMT and 1-RMT of a CA Rule. For rule 184 (Table 1) T(7),T(5),T(4),T(3) are the 1-RMTs while the remaining 4 are the 0-RMTs. The symbol T(T={T(0) to T(7)}) represents all the 8 RMTs of a 3-neighborhood CA cell. The $\{T_{b_i}^i\} \in T$ represents a subset of RMTs for which the next state value of ith cell is $b_i \in \{0,1\}$. While T^i refers to a single RMT, $\{T^i\}$ represents a subset of RMTs corresponding to its ith cell.

2.1 A CA State Expressed as RMT String

A state of n cell CA represented by its binary string $< b_0 b_1 \cdots b_i \cdots b_{n-1} >$ can also be expressed as RMT string $<T^0 T^1 \cdots T^i \cdots T^{n-1}>$ where $T^i \in T$ and T^i $=<b_{i-1} b_i b_{i+1}>$; thus T^i denotes the decimal value of the bit string $<b_{i-1} b_i b_{i+1}>$ where b_{i-1}, b_i, b_{i+1} represents the current state of $(i-1)^{th}, i^{th}, (i+1)^{th}$ cell respectively. In a periodic boundary n cell CA, $T^0 = b_{n-1} b_0 b_1$ and $T^{n-1}= b_{n-2} b_{n-1} b_0$.

Definition 5: Compatible RMT Pair - A pair of RMTs T^i and T^{i+1} in a RMT string $< \cdots T^{i-1}T^iT^{i+1}\cdots >$ (where $T^i \in T, T^i = b_{i-1}b_ib_{i+1}$, and $T^{i+1} = \acute{b_i}\acute{b}_{i+1}\acute{b}_{i+2}$) are compatible if $b_i = \acute{b_i}$ and $b_{i+1} = \acute{b}_{i+1}$. T(2) and T(5) in the string $< \cdots T(2)T(5)\cdots >$ is a compatible pair since T(2) = 010 and T(5) =101.

Definition 6: Valid RMT string - A string of n RMTs $<T^0T^1 \cdots T^i \cdots T^{n-1}>$ is a valid string if each pair T^i and T^{i+1} is a compatible RMT pair.

2.2   Rule Vector Graph (RVG)

The RVG of an n cell CA has n interconnected subgraphs. The ith (i=0 to (n-1)) subgraph corresponds to the one generated for the rule R_i employed on the ith cell. It consists of a set of input nodes and output nodes connected by directed edges (Fig 2) as defined below. The output nodes of ith subgraph serve as the input nodes of $(i+1)^{th}$ subgraph generated for rule R_{i+1}.

Definition 7: Input Node - Each of the ith subgraph input nodes V_1^i, V_2^i, $\cdots$ represent a subset of RMTs, $\{V_{x_i}^i\} \subset$ T=(T(0) to T(7)); x_i=1,2,$\cdots$. The number of RMTs in the subset is assigned as node weight. The RMTs covered by a specific node depends on $(i-1)^{th}$ subgraph. Such a RMT corresponds to the binary string $<b_{i-1}b_ib_{i+1}>$, where b_{i-1}, b_i, and b_{i+1} represents the current state of $(i-1)^{th}$, i^{th}, and $(i+1)^{th}$ cells.

Definition 8: Edge of the ith subgraph - The directed 0-edge and 1-edge outgoing from an input node of ith subgraph refer to 0-RMT $\{T_0^i\}$ and 1-RMT $\{T_1^i\}$ respectively as per the rule R_i employed on the ith cell. The corresponding 0-RMTs and 1-RMTs of input node are assigned as the weight on respective edges.

Definition 9: i^{th} subgraph Output Node $((i+1)^{th}$ subgraph input node) - The successor nodes at the end of the edges are referred to as output nodes represented by $\{V_{x_{i+1}}^{i+1}\} \subset T, x_{i+1} = 1, 2, \cdots$. The output nodes are derived out of RMTs assigned as the edge weight. For the binary pattern $< b_{i-1}b_ib_{i+1}>$ of each such RMT on the edge weight, the left bit b_{i-1} is deleted while appending 0 and 1 bits (as b_{i+2} bit) to the string to derive two RMTs on the output node. That is, all possible 8 RMTs of $(i+1)^{th}$ cell (represented by the string $<b_ib_{i+1}b_{i+2}>$) are grouped as per the weight assigned on the edges of ith subgraph to constitute output nodes which also serve as input nodes of level $(i+1)^{th}$ subgraph. The detailed explanation of the derivation for each of RMTs is reported in Table 2.

Definition 10: Root Node (RN) and Sink Node (SN) - The RN is the input node of the 0th subgraph, while the SN is the output node of the $(n-1)^{th}$ subgraph. Both the RN and SN of a periodic boundary CA is the node $\{T(0)$ to $T(7)\}$ containing all possible RMTs.

2.3   Forward Traversal

This section reports the scheme for identification of all the SLAs (Defn 2) of a CA in linear time through forward traversal of its RVG. This generates the successor state B of A. Algorithm is omitted due to space constraint.

Table 2. Derivation of output nodes in a sub-graph from the RMTs noted as edge weight (Fig 2)

A RMT in $\{T^i_{b_i}\}$ represented by the bit string $<b_{i-1}\ b_i\ b_{i+1}>$ (illustrated as edge weight $w(e_{ab})$ on the edge between input node V_a and output node V_b in Fig 2)	A RMT in the node $\{V^{i+1}_{x_{i+1}}\}$, represented by the bit string $<b_i\ b_{i+1}\ b_{i+2}>$
T(0)(000) and T(4)(100)	T(0)=000(0) and T(1)=001(1)
T(1)(001) and T(5)(101)	T(2)=010(2) and T(3)=011(3)
T(2)(010) and T(6)(110)	T(4)=100(4) and T(5)=101(5)
T(3)(011) and T(7)(111)	T(6)=110(6) and T(7)=111(7)

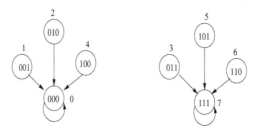

Note : 0(000) and 7(111) are two SLAs

Fig. 1. State transition behaviour of a 3 cell periodic boundary CA <232 232 232>

Each state transition in the STG of Fig 3(a) is representd by a path from Root Node to Sink Node of its RVG (Fig 3(b)). The backward traversal with state B as input generates its previous state A.

Identification of Self-Loop Attractors (SLAs) The following lemma characterizes the path of an SLA (Defn. 1) in the RVG of a CA during its forward traversal.

Lemma 1. *If for each ith (i=0 to (n-1)) level of RVG of a CA, an edge with weight $\{\{T^i_{b_i}\}/b_i\}$ exists where (a) for $T^i_{b_i \acute{q}_i} \in \{T^i\}, T^i_{b_i \acute{q}_i} = < a_{i-1}a_i a_{i+1} >$ and $a_i = b_i \cdots \cdots (1)$ and (b) T^i is compatible with T^{i-1} then the state $B = <b_0 b_1 \cdots b_{n-1}>$ is a SLA.*

The proof is simple & hence omitted.

3   Solution of DCT with Single CA

DCT accepts a binary string of n-bits and generates all 0's or all 1's state as output. If density of 0's is more than that of 1's, it outputs all 0's state, else all 1's state. For the CA based solution of DCT, we need a CA that has two attractor basins (Defn. 2) - one basin (referred to as 0-basin) with all 0's state as the SLA while the other one (1-basin) with all 1's state as the SLA. The states in 0-basin (1-basin) should have more number of 0's (1's).

Definition 11: Best Rule Vector (BRV) - The CA Rule vector (RV) which performs DCT with minimum error. The STG for the BRV should have (i) only

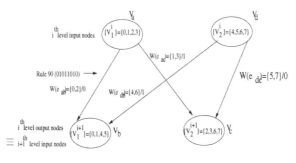

Note: RVG for Rule 90 for two input nodes $V_a = \{ V_1^i \} = \{0,1,2,3\}$ and $V_d = \{ V_2^i \} = \{4,5,6,7\}$

generating two output nodes $V_b = V_1^{i+1} = \{0,1,4,5\}$ and $V_c = \{ v_2^{i+1} \} = \{2,3,6,7\}$

Fig. 2. The subgraph for rule $R_i = 90$

two SLAs with all 0's $(0\cdots0)$ and all 1's $(1\cdots1)$ states; (ii) no attractor cycle of length greater than 1; and (iii) coverage of patterns with more than 50 % of 1's (0's) by 0-basin (1-basin) should be minimum.

For 3-bit patterns, the BRV for 3-neighborhood CA (Fig 1) is the homogeneous RV <232 232 232> with Majority Rule 232 (Table 1) applied on each cell. However DCT on 5 bit patterns with homogeneous RV<232 232 232 232 232> is not the BRV for 5 bit CA. The STG for the CA, as shown in the STG of Fig 3(a), has the states 0(00000) and 31(11111) as the SLAs. In addition, 3(00011), 6(00110), 7(00111), 12(01100), 14(01110), 17(10001), 19(10011), 24(11000), 25(11001), 28(11100) are also SLAs which never reach the attractor 0 or 31 and hence lead to error so far as DCT is concerned. All the SLAs can be identified by forward traversal of the RVG of Fig 3(b). From the analysis of the non all 0's/1's SLAs, it can be observed that the states having minimum of two consecutive 0's (1's) with majority 1's (0's) are SLAs because two consecutive cells having 0's (1's) are locally 0-major (1-major) for the majority rule 232. Consequently, all such states are SLAs for the homogeneous CA <232 232 232 232 232>. In order to remove such error instances we proceed to design inhomogeneous CA for DCT with alternative rules in addition to the majority rule 232. For the first alternative rule (Rule 184) (Table 1), the next state values for RMT 6(110) with two consecutive 1's and RMT 4(100) with consecutive 0's are the inverted values of the corresponding entries (Table 1) for rule 232. In an identical manner rule 226 can be derived by inverting the next state for RMT 3 (011 with two consecutives 1's) and 1 (001 with two consecutive 0's). Introduction of rule 184 (or 226) in place of rule 232 for one cell reduces the number of errors from 10 to 6 for the inhomogeneous CA <232 232 232 232 184> - 4 errors due to wrong SLAs 17(10001), 19(10011), 24(11000), and 25(11001), while two other errors due to wrong coverage of states - 7(00111) covered by 0-basin and 12(01100) covered by the 1-basin. Identical results can be derived by replacing rule 184 by rule 226. The rest of the paper shows the result with rule 184 only.

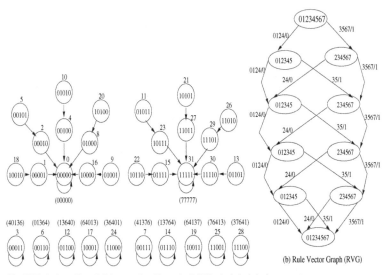

Note: RMT string is noted for each SLA expressed as a binary string & RMT string for its decimal counter part

(a) State Transition Graph of Rule Vector <232 232 232 232 232>

(b) Rule Vector Graph (RVG)

Fig. 3. State Transition Graph of 5 cells 3-neighborhood Periodic Boundary CA with rule Vector<232 232 232 232 232>

3.1 Analysis of Inhomogeneous CA Employing Rules 232 and 184

In the context of earlier discussions, the analysis of this sub-section conforms that there should be just one cell with rule 232 and the remaining cells with rule 184 in the inhomogeneous periodic boundary CAs to arrive at the BRV (Best Rule Vector). It has been shown that the CAs with rule 232 applied on more than one cell results in error due to non-all 0's/1's SLAs or attractor cycle of length greater than 1. The patterns corresponding to each such state is in error so far as DCT is concerned. The properties of Rule Vector Graph (RVG), used for this analysis are formalized in next three lemmas. The formal proof of these results can be derived from the analysis of the RVG and not presented for space constraint. An outline of the proof of such results is noted here. The STG and RVG for the 5 cell CA <232 184 184 184 184> is shown in Fig 4. The RVG has two lanes Lane-0 with edges having weight $\{T_0^i\}/0$ while Lane-1 has edges $\{T_1^i\}/1$. The edges between Lane-0 and Lane-1 are referred to as cross-edges. In general there are two sections - one with cells having rule 184 and other one employing rule 232. The conditions of Lemma 1 get satisfied for each edges of Lane-0 and Lane-1 and thereby generating all 0's and all 1's SLAs. RMT T(0), T(1), T(3), T(7) of rule 184 satisfy condition (a) of Lemma 1, while RMT T(0), T(1), T(3), T(4), T(6), T(7) of rule 232 satisfy the condition. Further, RMT pairs <T(6), T(4)>, <T(7), T(6)>, and <T(4), T(0)> are valid RMT pairs in the path of RVG involving cross-edges. The path for any non all 0's/1's if it exists, utilizes cross-edge.

Lemma 2. *An n cell CA having rule vector* <184 ···184 232 232 184 ···184> *with two consecutive cells configured with rule 232 and remaining cells employing rule 184 has SLAs in addition to all 0's/1's states.*

Lemma 3. *Number of SLAs in a CA varies directly with the number of consecutive cells employing rule 232 in the RV of the CA.*

Hence the CA Rule Vector with consecutive Rule 232 (in any arbitrary position) will generate extra SLAs in addition to all 0's/1's state, thereby violating the basic criteria (Definition 11(i)) of Best Rule Vector (BRV) for solution of DCT problem.

Lemma 4. *An n cell CA with rule 232 employed on two non-consecutive cells and rule 184 on remaining cells has a cycle of length greater than 1 in its State Transition Graph.*

3.2   Best Rule Vector (BRV)

This subsection establishes the fact that the best rule vector for 3 neighborhood CA is the one that employs rule 232 only in one cell and rule 184 in remaining cells. The next theorem utilizes the earlier results to establish the BRV. Only an outline of the proof is noted for shortage of space.

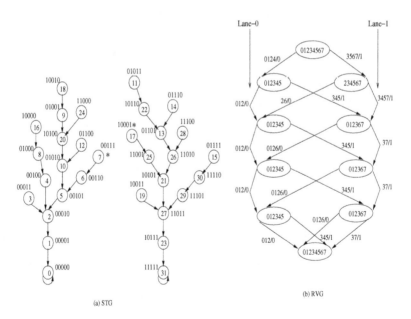

Fig. 4. State Transition Graph (STG) and RVG of 5 cells 3-neighborhood Periodic boundary CA with Rule Vector <232 184 184 184 184>

Theorem 5. *An n cell 3-neighborhood periodic boundary CA with rule vector <232 184 ⋯184> is the best rule vector for DCT on n bit patterns.*

Proof. In order to prove that the RV is the BRV we need to ensure that (a) there are no SLAs other than all 0's/1's state; (b) there is no cycle of length greater than 1; and (c) number of errors due to coverage of a state by a wrong basin is minimum. Each of these issues are treated separately. (a) In order to generate SLAs other all 0's/1's states, it can be shown that SLA other than all 0's/1's states can be generated if cross edge can be inserted between lane-1 to lane-0 with RMT 6 followed by RMT 4 with rule 232 employed on both the cells. But in this rule vector rule 232 is employed only on one cell. So no SLAs other than all 0's/1's with RMT <0⋯0> and <7⋯7> get generated. (b) Generation of a cycle of length 2 demands that there exists a section of cells with rule 184 and rule 232 on either end of this section. Since there exists only one cell with rule 232, no cycle of length 2 can be generated with the RV. Further, from the analysis of the RVG of Fig 4(b) with RV < 232 184 184 184 184 > and by induction it can be shown that there is no cycle of length greater than 1. (c) Error occurs due to coverage of pattern by the wrong basin. Due to presence of 184 which is not the local Best Rule (BR) for DCT in the rule vector, such errors occur. We made changes of the next state value in minimum number of RMTs (RMT 6 and RMT 4) of the majority rule 232 (BR) to generate rule 184. Minimum changes in BR 232 to derive 184 result in minimum error. So Best Rule Vector (BRV) is <184 ⋯184 232 184 ⋯184> for 3-neighborhood CA.

4   Error Analysis of 3-Neighborhood BRV CA

In this section we will derive an expression to calculate the number of errors for 3-neighborhood n-cell CA <232 184 ⋯184>. There are two categories of error: Primary Error (PE) and Secondary Error(SE).

For an n cell CA total number of PEs is given by,

$$NPE = 2 * \sum_{i=0}^{n/2-2} C_i^{n-3} \tag{2}$$

(II) Secondary Error (SE)
There are states which have more no of 0's (1's) and not have RMT 6(4) in 0th cell configured with rule 232. However in intermediate time step, such a state generates a RMT sequence where RMT 6(4) occurs in 0th position and so results in error referred to as secondary error(SE).

$$NSE = 2 * \{\sum_{n/2}^{n-3} C_i^{n-3} - \sum_{i=n/2-2}^{n-5} C_i^{n-5}\} \tag{3}$$

The result for extended neighborhood CA is reported in next section.

5   Extension for k-Neighborhood CA

We need to address following sub-task:

(1) Find majority rule for k-neighborhood CA (equivalent of rule 232 in 3-neighborhood CA) - this is referred to as rule E232. Its derivation is simple.

(2) Find the rule E184 - equivalent of 184 in 3-neighborhood CA. Following the basic principle of derivation of rule 184 for 3-neighborhood CA, E184 for 5 and 7 neighborhood CA have been derived and displayed in Table 3.

(3) Error analysis - implemented following the same principle of Primary Error and Secondary Error as done for 3-neighborhood CA. The Table 4 displays the

Table 3. Rule E184 for 5 and 7 neighborhood

E184 (5 neighbourhood) 32 entries	00000001 00010100 11111101 11010111
E184 (7 neighbourhood) 128 entries	00000000 00000001 00000001 00010101 00000001 00010101 00010101 01010100 11111111 11111101 11111101 11010101 11111101 11010101 11010101 01010111

Table 4. Results of DCT On n Bit Patterns (n= 15, 19, 21, 23, 25) With the BRV of k-neighborhood CA (k=3, 5, 7)

No. of bits	3-neighborhood % of correct result	5-neighborhood % of correct result	7-neighborhood % of correct result
15	77.41	78.43	82.64
19	74.21	74.87	78.87
21	72.96	73.56	77.03
23	71.88	72.33	75.73
25	70.93	71.34	74.62

Table 5. Sample Results On n Bit (n=49, 99, 149, 199) Randomly Generated patterns with 40% to 60% 1's with 7-neighborhood BRV

No. of bits	% of 1's in n bit patterns, % of patterns displaying correct result				
49	(40%, 92.25)	(45%, 86.75)	(50%, 70.50)	(55%, 84.50)	(60%, 90.75)
99	(40%, 90.75)	(45%, 86.25)	(50%, 68.25)	(55%, 85.25)	(60%, 89.75)
149	(40%, 88.25)	(45%, 82.50)	(50%, 62.50)	(55%, 83.75)	(60%, 89.75)
199	(40%, 88.00)	(45%, 85.50)	(50%, 63.00)	(55%, 85.50)	(60%, 87.75)

results on n bit k-neighborhood CAs (k=3,5,7). The results have been derived by running BRV (E232 E232 $\cdots$(k/2 times) E184 E184 $\cdots$ E184 (for rest of the cells)) on 2^n patterns exhaustively. The number of patterns for which the BRV shows the correct results and its percentage are tabulated. The Table 5 shows the sample results of running BRV with 7-neighborhood CA on n bit patterns (n = 49, 99,149,199). The population of 1's in the sample experimental patterns is kept within 40 to 60 %. Percentage of 1's in the sample patterns, and percentage of correct result have been tabulated. We conform that the percentage of correct DCT depends on percentage of 1's and also location of 1's in the experimental patterns. Percentage of correct results, as expected, is minimum with 50% of 1's in the patterns.

6   Conclusion

This paper reports an analytical formulation for solution of DCT problem with a single non-homogeneous CA. Rule Vector Graph (RVG) introduced in this paper has provided the framework for the solution of DCT and it reveals indication of its enormous utility in solving some well known critical problems.

References

1. J. von. Neumann, "The Theory of Self-Reproducing Automata," *A. W. Burks, Ed. University of Illinois Press, Urbana and London,* 1966.
2. S. Wolfram, "Theory and Application of Cellular Automata," *World Scientific,* 1986.
3. P. P. Chaudhuri, D. R. Chowdhury, S. Nandi, and S. Chatterjee "Additive Cellular Automata, Theory and Applications, Vol.1" *IEEE Computer Society Press, Los Alamitos, California,vol. 1.* ISBN-0-8186-7717-1, 1997.
4. Land, M. Belew, R. K. "No Perfect Cellular Automata For Density Classification Exists." *Phyisical Review Letters.*
5. Henryk Funk. "Solution of the Density Classification Problem with Two Cellular Automata Rules." *Phys. Rev.* : E55, R2081 - R2084, Issue 3 - March 1997.
6. Jullie H., J. B. Pollack. "Coevolving the 'ideal'trainer: Application to the discovary of Cellular Automata Rules." *Genetic Programming 1998*: Proceeding of the Third Annual Conference, San Francisco, CA, 1998. Morgan Kaufmann.
7. Das,Mitchel M., J. P. Crutchfield. "A Genetic Algorithm Discovers Practicle-based Computation in Cellular Automata." *Parallel Problem Solving from Nature III,Springer-Verlag.*
8. Ferreira, C. 2001 "Gene Expression Programming: A New Adaptive Algoithm for Solving Problems." *Complex Systems 13 (2) : 87-129*
9. Mitchell, M., P. Crutchfield, and P. T. Hraber. 1994 "Evolving Cellular Automata to Perform Computations : Mechanisms and Impediment." *Physica D* 75 : 361-391.

A Design of Symmetrical Six-State 3n-Step Firing Squad Synchronization Algorithms and Their Implementations

Hiroshi Umeo, Masashi Maeda, and Kazuaki Hongyo

Univ. of Osaka Electro-Communication,
Neyagawa-shi, Hastu-cho, 18-8, Osaka, 572-8530, Japan
{umeo, maeda, hongyo}@cyt.osakac.ac.jp

Abstract. In 1994, Yunès [19] began to explore $3n$-step firing squad synchronization algorithms and developed two seven-state synchronization
algorithms for one-dimensional cellular arrays. His algorithms were so interesting in that he progressively decreased the number of internal states
of each cellular automaton. In this paper, we propose a new symmetrical six-state $3n$-step firing squad synchronization algorithm. Our result
improves the seven-state $3n$-step synchronization algorithms developed
by Yunès [19]. The number *six* is the smallest one known at present in
the class of $3n-$step synchronization algorithms. A non-trivial and new
symmetrical six-state $3n$-step generalized firing squad synchronization
algorithm is also given. In addition, we study a state-change complexity
in $3n$-step firing squad synchronization algorithms. We show that our
algorithms have $O(n^2)$ state-change complexity, on the other hand, the
thread-like $3n$-step algorithms developed so far have $O(n \log n)$ state-
change complexity.

1 Introduction

We study a synchronization problem that gives a finite-state protocol for synchronizing a large scale of cellular automata. The synchronization in cellular
automata has been known as a firing squad synchronization problem since its
development, in which it was originally proposed by J. Myhill to synchronize all
parts of self-reproducing cellular automata [9]. The firing squad synchronization
problem has been studied extensively for more than 40 years [1-5, 7-12, 14-19].

The first synchronization algorithm is a $3n$-step algorithm developed by Minsky and MacCarthy [8]. The optimum-time synchronization algorithm was devised first by Goto [5]. Afterwards, Waksman [18], Balzer [1], Gerken [4] and
Mazoyer [7] also developed an optimum-time algorithm and reduced the number
of states realizing the algorithm, each with 16, 8, 7 and 6 states.

On the other hand, the $3n$-step algorithm is a simple and straightforward
one that exploits a parallel divide-and-conquer strategy based on an efficient
use of $1/1$- and $1/3$-speed of signals. After Minsky and MacCarthy [8] gave
an idea for designing the $3n$-step synchronization algorithm, Fischer [3] implemented the $3n$-step algorithm, yielding a 15-state implementation, respectively.

S. El Yacoubi, B. Chopard, and S. Bandini (Eds.): ACRI 2006, LNCS 4173, pp. 157–168, 2006.

Fig. 1. A one-dimensional cellular automaton

In 1994, Yunès [19] began to explore the $3n$-step firing squad synchronization algorithms and developed two seven-state synchronization algorithms. His algorithms were so interesting in that he progressively decreased the number of internal states of each cellular automaton.

In this paper, we propose several new symmetrical six-state $3n$-step firing squad synchronization algorithms for one-dimensional cellular arrays. Our result improves the seven-state $3n$-step synchronization algorithms developed by Yunès [19]. The number *six* is the smallest one known at present in the class of $3n$−step synchronization algorithms. An important key idea is to increase the number of cells being active during their computation. A non-trivial and new symmetrical six-state $3n$-step generalized firing squad synchronization algorithm is also developed. In addition, we study a state-change complexity in $3n$-step firing squad synchronization algorithms. We show that our algorithms have $O(n^2)$ state-change complexity, on the other hand, the thread-like $3n$-step algorithms developed so far have $O(n \log n)$ state-change complexity.

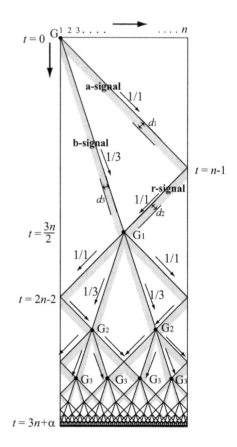

Fig. 2. A time-space diagram for finite-width thread-like $3n$-step firing squad synchronization algorithm

2　A Symmetrical Six-State Synchronization Algorithm

2.1　Firing Squad Synchronization Problem

Figure 1 shows a finite one-dimensional cellular array consisting of n cells. Each cell is an identical (except the border cells) finite-state automaton. The array operates in lock-step mode in such a way that the next state of each cell (except border cells) is determined by both its own present state and the present states of its left and right neighbors. All cells (*soldiers*), except the left end cell (*general*), are initially in the quiescent state at time $t = 0$ with the property that the next state of a quiescent cell with quiescent neighbors is the quiescent state again. At time $t = 0$, the left end cell C_1 is in the *fire-when-ready* state, which is the initiation signal for the array. The firing squad synchronization problem is to determine a description (state set and next-state function) for cells that ensures all cells enter the *fire* state at exactly the same time and for the first time. The set of states and the next-state function must be independent of n.

2.2 A Class of 3n-Step Synchronization Algorithms

The 3n-step algorithm is an interesting class of synchronization algorithms due to its simplicity and straightforwardness and it is important in its own right in the design of cellular algorithms. Figure 2 shows a time-space diagram for the well-known 3n-step firing squad synchronization algorithm. The synchronization process can be viewed as a typical divide-and-conquer strategy that operates in parallel in the cellular space. An initial "*General*" G, located at left end of the array of size n, generates two special signals, referred to as *a-signal* and *b-signal*, which propagate in the right direction at a speed of $1/1$ and $1/3$, respectively. The a-signal arrives at the right end at time $t = n-1$, reflects there immediately, then continues to move at the same speed in the left direction. The reflected signal is referred to as *r-signal*. The b- and the r-signals meet at a center cell(s), depending on the parity of n. In the case that n is odd, the cell $C_{\lceil n/2 \rceil}$ becomes a *General* at time $t = 3\lceil n/2 \rceil - 2$. The *General* is responsible for synchronizing both its left and right halves of the cellular space. Note that the *General* is shared by the two halves. In the case that n is even, two cells $C_{\lceil n/2 \rceil}$ and $C_{\lceil n/2 \rceil + 1}$ become the next *General* at time $t = 3\lceil n/2 \rceil$. Each *General* is responsible for synchronizing its left and right halves of the cellular space, respectively.

Thus at time

$$t = \begin{cases} 3\lceil n/2 \rceil - 2 & n: \text{ odd} \\ 3\lceil n/2 \rceil & n: \text{ even,} \end{cases} \tag{1}$$

the array knows its center point and generates one or two new *General*(*s*) G_1. The new *General*(*s*) G_1 generates the same $1/1$- and $1/3$-speed signals in both left and right directions and repeat the same procedures as above. Thus, the original synchronization problem of size n is divided into two sub-problems of size $\lceil n/2 \rceil$. In this way, the original array is split into equal two, four, eight, ..., subspaces synchronously. In the last, the original problem of size n can be split into small sub-problems of size 2. Most of the 3n-step synchronization algorithms developed so far [3, 8, 19] are based on similar schemes.

2.3 Six-State Implementation: $\mathcal{A}_1$

In the design of 3n-step synchronization algorithms, what is important is to find a center cell(s) of the cellular space to be synchronized. How can we implement those a-, b- and r-signals as a six-state transition table? In the 15-state

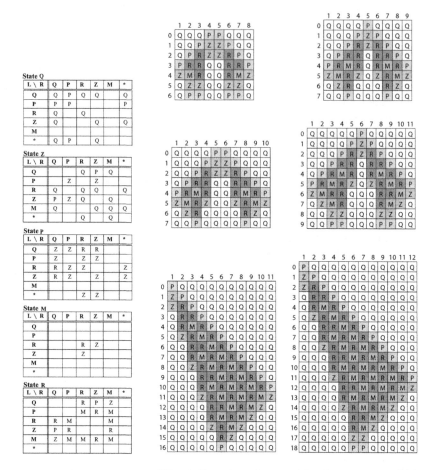

Fig. 3. A five-state transition table $\mathcal{R}_0$ for finding a center cell(s) of cellular arrays

Fig. 4. Snapshots for searching for a center cell(s)

implementation given in Fischer [3], those signals are represented as thread-like signals of width 1. Yunès [19] represented them as thread-like signals of width 2 or 3, thus decreasing the number of states to seven. In addition, a triangle area circled by a-, b-, and r-signals in the time-space diagram in Figure 2 plays an important role in finding the center cell(s). We call the area *zone* $\mathcal{T}$. In the implementations of Fischer [3] and Yunès [19], all cells in zone $\mathcal{T}$ keep quiescent state and are always inactive during the computations.

Now we are going to describe our six-state implementation. A key idea for our six-state implementation is to make all cells inside the zone $\mathcal{T}$ active. It will be shown that five-state cellular automaton can find the center cell(s).

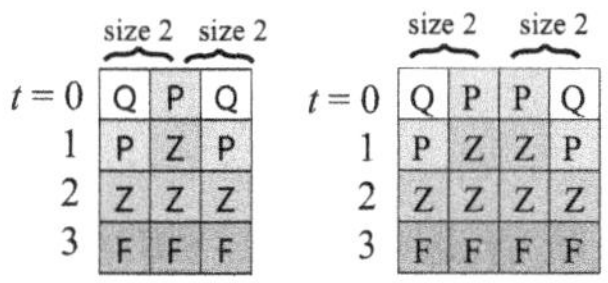

Fig. 5. Snapshots for synchronizing an array of size 2

State Q

L \ R	Q	P	R	Z	M	*
Q	Q	P	Q	Q		Q
P	P	P				P
R	Q		Q			
Z	Q			Q		Q
M						
*	Q	P	Q	Q		

State Z

L \ R	Q	P	R	Z	M	*
Q			Q	P	Q	
P		Z		Z		
R	Q		Q	Q		Q
Z	P	Z	Q	F	Q	F
M	Q			Q	Q	Q
*		Z	Q	F	Q	

State P

L \ R	Q	P	R	Z	M	*
Q	Z	Z	R	R		
P	Z		Z	Z		
R	R	Z	Z			Z
Z	R	Z		Z		Z
M						
*	Z		Z	Z		

State M

L \ R	Q	P	R	Z	M	*
Q						
P						
R			R	Z		
Z			Z			
M						
*						

State R

L \ R	Q	P	R	Z	M	*
Q			R	P	Z	
P			M	R	M	
R	R	M			M	
Z	P	R			R	
M	Z	M	M	R	M	
*						

Fig. 6. A state transition table $\mathcal{R}_1$ for the six-state $3n$-step firing squad synchronization algorithm

First, we consider a special five-state cellular automaton M_0 that can find a center cell(s) of the given array, initially staring from a configuration such that: all of the cells, excluding a center cell(s), are in quiescent state and one or two (depending on the parity of the array) cells located at the center of the array are in special state P. Precisely the center cell(s) is on $\mathrm{C}_{\lceil n/2 \rceil}$, when n is odd, and on $\mathrm{C}_{\lceil n/2 \rceil}$ and $\mathrm{C}_{\lceil n/2 \rceil+1}$, when n is even, respectively. The state P acts as a *General*, which will be described later.

The next state transition function $\mathcal{R}_0$ of M_0, shown in Fig. 3, consists of five sub-tables for each state in {Q, P, R, Z, M}. Each state on the first row (column) indicates a state of right (left) neighbor cell, respectively. The state "*" acts as a border state for the left and right end cells. Each entry of the sub-tables shows a state at the next step. In general the border state "*" is not counted as a number of states.

Let S_i^t denote the state of C_i at time t. We have the following [Lemma 1] on finding a center of the given array.

[Lemma 1] Let M_0 be a five-state cellular automaton of lengh n with the transition tabel $\mathcal{R}_0$. We assume that M_0 has an initial configuration such that:

1. In the case that n is odd: $\mathrm{S}^0_{\lceil n/2 \rceil} = \mathtt{P}$, $\mathrm{S}^0_i = \mathtt{Q}$, for any i such that$1 \leq i \leq n, i \neq \lceil n/2 \rceil$.
2. In the case that n is even: $\mathrm{S}^0_{\lceil n/2 \rceil} = \mathrm{S}^0_{\lceil n/2 \rceil+1} = \mathtt{P}$, $\mathrm{S}^0_i = \mathtt{Q}$, for any i such that $1 \leq i \leq n, i \neq \lceil n/2 \rceil, i \neq \lceil n/2 \rceil + 1$.
   Then, M_0 takes the following configuration.

3. In the case that $\lceil n/2 \rceil$ is odd: At time $t = 3\lceil n/4 \rceil - 2$, $S^t_{\lceil n/4 \rceil} = S^t_{\lceil 3n/4 \rceil} = P$, $S^t_i = Q$, for any i such that $1 \leq i \leq n, i \neq \lceil n/4 \rceil, i \neq \lceil 3n/4 \rceil$.
4. In the case that $\lceil n/2 \rceil$ is even: At time $t = 3\lceil n/4 \rceil$, $S^t_{\lceil n/4 \rceil} = S^t_{\lceil n/4 \rceil + 1} = S^t_{\lceil 3n/4 \rceil} = S^t_{\lceil 3n/4 \rceil + 1} = P$, $S^0_i = Q$, for any i such that $1 \leq i \leq n, i \neq \lceil n/4 \rceil, i \neq \lceil n/4 \rceil + 1, i \neq \lceil 3n/4 \rceil, i \neq \lceil 3n/4 \rceil + 1$.

The a-signal in Fig. 2 is represented by a propagation of P state at $1/1$ speed. Any cell where the P state goes away in the right direction takes a state R and M alternatively at each step until either the b-signal or the r-signal arrives at the cell itself. The b-signal is represented by a propagation of $1/3$ speed signal, where each cell takes a state R, R and Z for each three steps. Only during the first three steps, i.e., for example, from time $t = 0$ to 2, only the *General* cell takes a state P, Z and Z at each step. The r-signal is represented as a $1/1$-speed propagation of the Z state. Figure 4 shows how the cellular automaton M_0 can find the center cell(s) of the cellular space using only five states.

Let M be cellular automaton $M = \{S, \delta\}$. A local transition function $\delta : S^3 \to S$ is said to be *symmetric*, iff for all $a, b, c \in S$, $\delta(a, b, c) = \delta(c, b, a)$, where S is the set of internal states. See [6, 13] for details. Note that the rule set $\mathcal{R}_0$, shown in Fig. 3, has a principal-diagonal line-symmetry. Thus M_0 is symmetric.

A *General* is initially located on the left end of the array in the synchronization problem. The next [Lemma 2] is to ensure the centering of the cellular space, staring from an initial configuration of the problem. To do so, we have to add the following three rules:

$$* \; Q \; R \; \to \; Q; \; * \; Z \; P \; \to \; Z; \; * \; P \; Q \; \to \; Z.$$

Those rules are used only in the first zone $\mathcal{T}$. By adding those rule the set becomes asymmetric.

[**Lemma 2**] Let M_0 be a five-state cellular automaton of length n with the transition table $\mathcal{R}_0$. We assume that M_0 has an initial configuration such that:

1. $S^0_1 = P$, $S^0_i = Q, 2 \leq i \leq n$,
   Then, M_0 takes the following configuration:
2. In the case that n is odd: At time $t = 3\lceil n/2 \rceil - 2$,
   $S^t_{\lceil n/2 \rceil} = P$, $S^t_i = Q$, for any i such that $1 \leq i \leq n, i \neq \lceil n/2 \rceil$.
3. In the case that n is even: At time $t = 3\lceil n/2 \rceil$,
   $S^t_{\lceil n/2 \rceil} = S^t_{\lceil n/2 \rceil + 1} = P$, $S^t_i = Q$, for any i such that $1 \leq i \leq n, i \neq \lceil n/2 \rceil, i \neq \lceil n/2 \rceil + 1$.

A six-state cellular automaton M is defined as follows: The set of internal states of M is $\{Q, P, R, Z, M, F\}$, where Q is the *quiescent* state, P is the *General* state and F is the *firing* state, respectively.

By using the halving [Lemma 1, 2] recursively, the original problem is reduced to many small synchronization problems of size 2. In Fig. 5, we illustrate snapshots for synchronizing an array of size 2. The left figure (in Fig. 5) shows a *General* shared by two sub-arrays of size 2. The *General* is responsible for

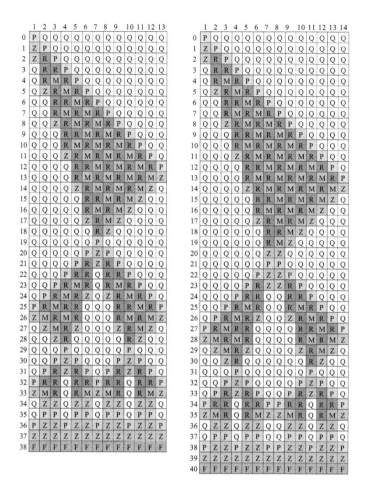

Fig. 7. Snapshots for the 6-state symmetrical firing squad synchronization algorithm on 13 and 14 cells

synchronizing both two subarrays. On the other hand, each *General* in the right figure (in Fig. 5) is responsible for synchronizing each left and right sub-arrays independently. Both of them can be synchronized at exactly three steps. To synchronize them for three steps, we add the following three rules:

$$* \; Z \; Z \rightarrow F; \; Z \; Z \; Z \rightarrow F; \; Z \; Z \; * \rightarrow F.$$

In Fig. 6 we give our final transition rule set for synchronizing cellular arrays in $3n$-steps. Three rules within shaded squares in the table are asymmetric due to asymmetry of the original synchronization problem being with the general at one left end. Figure 7 shows snapshots for the 6-state symmetrical firing squad synchronization algorithm on 13 and 14 cells. Let $T(n)$ be time complexity for synchronizing an array of size n. Then we have:

$$T(n) = \begin{cases} T(\lceil n/2 \rceil) + 3\lceil n/2 \rceil - 2 & n\text{: odd} \\ T(\lceil n/2 \rceil) + 3\lceil n/2 \rceil & n\text{: even,} \end{cases} \tag{2}$$

The recurrence equation can be expressed as $T(n) = 3n + O(1) + \eta(n)$, where $\eta(n)$ is the number of odds appearing $\{n, \lceil n/2 \rceil, \lceil n/4 \rceil, \lceil n/8 \rceil, ..., 2\}$. Since $\eta(n)$ is of $O(\log n)$, $T(n) = 3n + O(\log n)$. Thus we have:

[**Theorem 3**] There exists a 6-state symmetrical cellular automaton that can synchronize any n cells in $3n + O(\log n)$ steps.

3 A Symmetrical Six-State Generalized Synchronization Algorithm

In this section, we consider a generalized firing squad synchronization problem, in which the general can be initially located at any position on the array. The generalized firing squad synchronization problem has been studied by several researchers [10, 11, 12, 14, 16]. Moore and Langdon[10], Szwerinski[12] and Varshavsky, Marakhovsky and Peschansky [16] developed an optimum-time firing algorithm with 17, 10 and 10 internal states, respectively, that fires n cells in $n - 2 + \max(k, n - k + 1)$ steps, where the general is located on C_k. Recently, Umeo, Hisaoka, Michisaka, Nishioka and Maeda [14], and Settle and Simon [11] developed an optimum-time firing algorithm with 9 states. Settle and Simon [11] also studied a $3n$-step generalized synchronization algorithm and gave a seven-state implementation based on Mazoyer's six-state algorithm. The algorithm was a trivial one in a sense that an arbitrary-positioned *General* emits a 1/1-speed signal to the left end to initiate the Mazoyer's six-state optimum-time synchronization algorithm. An additional new state is used for the propagation of the signal in the construction [11].

Now we are going to design a symmetrical six-state generalized firing squad synchronization algorithm $\mathcal{A}_2$ with the transition rule set $\mathcal{R}_2$. The rule set $\mathcal{R}_2$ can be obtained from $\mathcal{R}_1$ with the following modifications.

- The initial *General*'s state P is changed by M.
- The next two rules: * P Q → Z; * Z P → Z are deleted from $\mathcal{R}_1$.
- The following rule set $\mathbf{r}_g$, given in Table 1, is added to $\mathcal{R}_1$.

A six-state cellular automaton M_2 is defined as follows: The set of internal states of M_2 is completely same as of M such that {Q, P, R, Z, M, F}, where Q is the *quiescent* state, M is the *General* state and F is the *firing* state, respectively. The next-state transition function $\mathcal{R}_2$ is given in Fig. 8. Note that M_2 is symmetric.

Figure 9 illustrates a time-space diagram for searching a center cell(s) of the initial cellular space and snapshots for its 6-state implementation. Note that , after finishing the first halving, synchronization processes in the generalized firing squad synchronization are completely same as of the processes of the previous

Table 1. The rule set $\mathbf{r_g}$ to be added to $\mathcal{R}_1$

Rule set $\mathbf{r_g}$:

R , Q , * → Q	Q , M , M → M	M , M , Z → Z
Q , Q , M → M	Q , M , * → R	M , M , * → Z
M , Q , Q → M	P , M , Q → M	Z , M , P → Z
M , Q , * → M	P , M , M → M	Z , M , M → Z
* , Q , M → M	P , M , Z → Z	* , M , Q → R
M , P , M → P	P , M , * → Z	* , M , P → Z
M , P , Z → R	R , M , Q → R	* , M , R → Z
Z , P , M → R	R , M , M → R	* , M , M → Z
M , R , * → Z	R , M , * → Z	Q , Z , Q → P
* , R , M → Z	M , M , Q → M	Q , Z , P → Q
Q , M , Q → P	M , M , P → M	* , Z , P → Q
Q , M , P → M	M , M , R → R	P , Z , Q → Q
Q , M , R → R	M , M , M → M	P , Z , * → Q

State Q

L\R	Q	P	R	M	Z	*
Q	Q	P	Q	M	Q	Q
P	P	P				P
R	Q		Q			Q
M	M					M
Z	Q				Q	Q
*	Q	P	Q	M	Q	

State Z

L\R	Q	P	R	M	Z	*
Q	P	Q	Q	Q	P	
P	Q	Z			Z	Q
R	Q		Q		Q	Q
M	Q			Q	Q	Q
Z	P	Z	Q	Q	F	F
*		Q	Q	Q	F	

State M

L\R	Q	P	R	M	Z	*
Q	P	M	R	M		R
P	M			M	Z	Z
R	R		R	R	Z	Z
M	M	M	R	M	Z	Z
Z			Z	Z	Z	
*	R	Z	Z	Z	Z	

State P

L\R	Q	P	R	M	Z	*
Q	Z	Z	R		R	
P	Z		Z		Z	
R	R	Z	Z			Z
M				P	R	
Z	R	Z		R	Z	Z
*			Z		Z	

State R

L\R	Q	P	R	M	Z	*
Q			R	Z	P	
P			M	M	R	
R	R	M		M		
M	Z	M	M	M	R	Z
Z	P	R		R		
*				Z		

Fig. 8. A state transition table $\mathcal{R}_2$ for the six-state $3n$-step generalized firing squad synchronization algorithm

synchronization problem with a *General* at left end. At time $t = max(k, n - k + 1) + 1 + \lceil n/2 \rceil$, a center cell(s) can be found, where n is array size and k is the *General*'s position from left end. In Fig. 10 we give some snapshots for the 6-state generalized firing squad synchronization algorithm on 15 cells with a *General* on C_5.

[**Theorem 4**] There exists a symmetrical 6-state cellular automaton that can solve generalized firing squad synchronization problem in $max(k, n - k + 1) + 2n + O(\log n)$ steps.

4   State-Change Complexity in $3n$-Step Synchronization Algorithms

Vollmar [17] introduced a state-change complexity in order to measure the efficiency of cellular algorithms and showed that $\Omega(n \log n)$ state changes are re-

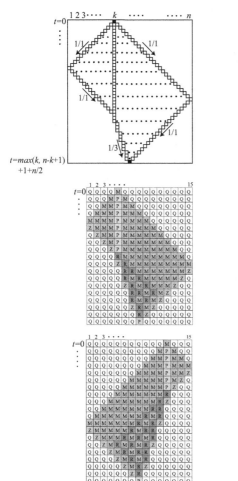

Fig. 9. A time-space diagram for searching a center of the cellular space and snapshots for its 6-state implementation

Snapshots for the 6-state generalized firing squad synchronization algorithm on 15 cells with a *General* on C_5:

	1	2	3	4	5	6	7	8	9	10	11	12	13	14	15
0	Q	Q	Q	Q	M	Q	Q	Q	Q	Q	Q	Q	Q	Q	Q
1	Q	Q	Q	M	P	M	Q	Q	Q	Q	Q	Q	Q	Q	Q
2	Q	Q	M	M	P	M	M	Q	Q	Q	Q	Q	Q	Q	Q
3	Q	M	M	M	P	M	M	M	Q	Q	Q	Q	Q	Q	Q
4	M	M	M	M	P	M	M	M	M	Q	Q	Q	Q	Q	Q
5	Z	M	M	M	P	M	M	M	M	M	Q	Q	Q	Q	Q
6	Q	Z	M	M	P	M	M	M	M	M	M	Q	Q	Q	Q
7	Q	Q	Z	M	P	M	M	M	M	M	M	M	Q	Q	Q
8	Q	Q	Q	Z	P	M	M	M	M	M	M	M	M	Q	Q
9	Q	Q	Q	Q	R	M	M	M	M	M	M	M	M	M	Q
10	Q	Q	Q	Q	Z	R	M	M	M	M	M	M	M	M	M
11	Q	Q	Q	Q	Q	R	R	M	M	M	M	M	M	M	Z
12	Q	Q	Q	Q	Q	R	M	R	M	M	M	M	M	Z	Q
13	Q	Q	Q	Q	Q	Z	R	M	R	M	M	M	Z	Q	Q
14	Q	Q	Q	Q	Q	Q	R	R	M	R	M	Z	Q	Q	Q
15	Q	Q	Q	Q	Q	Q	R	M	R	M	Z	Q	Q	Q	Q
16	Q	Q	Q	Q	Q	Q	Z	R	M	Z	Q	Q	Q	Q	Q
17	Q	Q	Q	Q	Q	Q	Q	R	Z	Q	Q	Q	Q	Q	Q
18	Q	Q	Q	Q	Q	Q	Q	P	Q	Q	Q	Q	Q	Q	Q
19	Q	Q	Q	Q	Q	Q	P	Z	P	Q	Q	Q	Q	Q	Q
20	Q	Q	Q	Q	Q	P	R	Z	R	P	Q	Q	Q	Q	Q
21	Q	Q	Q	Q	P	R	R	Q	R	R	P	Q	Q	Q	Q
22	Q	Q	Q	P	R	M	R	Q	R	M	R	P	Q	Q	Q
23	Q	Q	P	R	M	R	Z	Q	Z	R	M	R	P	Q	Q
24	Q	P	R	M	R	R	Q	Q	Q	R	R	M	R	P	Q
25	P	R	M	R	M	R	Q	Q	Q	R	M	R	M	R	P
26	Z	M	R	M	R	Z	Q	Q	Q	Z	R	M	R	M	Z
27	Q	Z	M	R	R	Q	Q	Q	Q	Q	R	R	M	Z	Q
28	Q	Q	Z	M	R	Q	Q	Q	Q	Q	R	M	Z	Q	Q
29	Q	Q	Q	Z	Z	Q	Q	Q	Q	Q	Z	Z	Q	Q	Q
30	Q	Q	Q	P	P	Q	Q	Q	Q	Q	P	P	Q	Q	Q
31	Q	Q	P	Z	Z	P	Q	Q	Q	P	Z	Z	P	Q	Q
32	Q	P	R	Z	Z	R	P	Q	P	R	Z	Z	R	P	Q
33	P	R	R	Q	Q	R	R	P	R	R	Q	Q	R	R	P
34	Z	M	R	Q	Q	R	M	Z	M	R	Q	Q	R	M	Z
35	Q	Z	Z	Q	Q	Z	Z	Q	Z	Z	Q	Q	Z	Z	Q
36	Q	P	P	Q	Q	P	P	Q	P	P	Q	Q	P	P	Q
37	P	Z	Z	P	P	Z	Z	P	Z	Z	P	P	Z	Z	P
38	Z	Z	Z	Z	Z	Z	Z	Z	Z	Z	Z	Z	Z	Z	Z
39	F	F	F	F	F	F	F	F	F	F	F	F	F	F	F

Fig. 10. Snapshots for the 6-state generalized firing squad synchronization algorithm on 15 cells with a *General* on C_5

quired for the synchronization of n cells in $(2n - 2)$ steps.

[Theorem 5][17] $\Omega(n \log n)$ state-change is necessary for synchronizing n cells.

Let $S(n)$ be total number of state changes for synchronization algorithms on n cells. In the case of $3n$-step finite-width thread-like algorithms with time-space diagram is shown in Fig. 2, we see that $S(n) = \alpha n + 2S(n/2) = O(n \log n)$. Thus we have:

[Theorem 6] Any $3n$-step finite-width thread-like algorithm with the time-space diagram shown in Fig. 2 has an $O(n \log n)$ state-change complexity.

[**Theorem 7**] Each linear-time $3n$-step synchronization algorithm developed by Fischer [3], Minsky and MacCarthy [8], and Yunés [19] has an $\theta(n \log n)$ state-change complexity, respectively.

As for the synchronization algorithms $\mathcal{A}_1$ and $\mathcal{A}_2$, we have $S(n) = \alpha n^2 + 2S(n/2) = O(n^2)$. Thus we have:
[**Theorem 8**] The six-state synchronization algorithm $\mathcal{A}_1$ and $\mathcal{A}_2$ have $O(n^2)$ state-change complexity, respectively.

5 Conclusions

We have proposed a new symmetrical six-state $3n+O(n \log n)$-step firing squad synchronization algorithm for one-dimensional cellular arrays. Our result presented is an improvement over the seven-state $3n$-step synchronization algorithms developed by Yunés [19]. The number *six* is the smallest one known at present in the class of non-trivial $3n$-step synchronization algorithms. A non-trivial and new symmetrical six-state $3n$-step generalized firing squad synchronization algorithm is also given. By increasing the number of working cells from $O(n \log n)$ to $O(n^2)$, state-efficient synchronization algorithms have been obtained. In addition, a state-change complexity in $3n$-step firing squad synchronization algorithms is also studied. It is shown that our algorithms have $O(n^2)$ state-change complexity, on the other hand, the finite-width thread-like $3n$-step algorithms developed so far have $O(n \log n)$ state-change complexity. Here, in the last, we present Table 2 based on a quantitative comparison of $3n$-step synchronization protocols with respect to the number of internal states of each finite state automaton, the number of transition rules realizing the synchronization and state-change complexity.

Table 2. A comparison of $3n$-step firing squad synchronization algorithms

Algorithm	# States	# Rules	Time complexity	State-change complexity	Generals's position	Type	Notes	Ref.
Minsky and MacCarthy [1967]	13	–	$3n + \theta_n \log n + c$	$O(n \log n)$	left	thread	$0 \le \theta_n < 1$	[8]
Fischer [1965]	15	–	$3n - 4$	$O(n \log n)$	left	thread	–	[3]
Yunès I [1994]	7	105	$3n \pm 2\theta_n \log n + c$	$O(n \log n)$	left	thread	$0 \le \theta_n < 1$	[19]
Yunès II [1994]	7	107	$3n \pm 2\theta_n \log n + c$	$O(n \log n)$	left	thread	$0 \le \theta_n < 1$	[19]
Settle and Simon I [2002]	6	134	$3n + 1$	$O(n^2)$	right	plane	–	[11]
Settle and Simon II [2002]	7	127	$2n - 2 + k$	$O(n^2)$	arbitrary	plane	–	[11]
this paper $\mathcal{A}_1$	6	78	$3n + O(\log n)$	$O(n^2)$	left	plane	–	–
this paper $\mathcal{A}_2$	6	115	$\max(k, n - k + 1) + 2n + O(\log n)$	$O(n^2)$	arbitrary	plane	–	–

References

1. R. Balzer: An 8-state minimal time solution to the firing squad synchronization problem. *Information and Control*, vol. 10 (1967), pp. 22-42.

2. A. Berthiaume, T. Bittner, L. Perkovic, A. Settle and J. Simin: Bounding the firing squad synchronization problem on a ring. *Theoretical Computer Science*, 320 (2004), 213-228.
3. P. C. Fischer: Generation of primes by a one-dimensional real-time iterative array. *J. of ACM*, vol.12, No.3 (1965), pp.388-394.
4. Hans-D., Gerken: Über Synchronisations - Probleme bei Zellularautomaten. *Diplomarbeit*, Institut für Theoretische Informatik, Technische Universität Braunschweig, (1987), pp. 50.
5. E. Goto: A minimal time solution of the firing squad problem. *Dittoed course notes for Applied Mathematics* 298, Harvard University, (1962), pp. 52-59.
6. Y. Kobuchi: A note on symmetrical cellular spaces. *Information Processing Letters*, 25 (1987), 413-415.
7. J. Mazoyer: A six-state minimal time solution to the firing squad synchronization problem. *Theoretical Computer Science*, vol. 50 (1987), pp. 183-238.
8. M. L. Minsky: *Computation: Finite and infinite machines*. Prentice Hall, (1967), pp. 28-29.
9. E. F. Moore: The firing squad synchronization problem. in *Sequential Machines, Selected Papers* (E. F. Moore, ed.), Addison-Wesley, Reading MA.,(1964), pp. 213-214.
10. F. R. Moore and G. G. Langdon: A generalized firing squad problem. *Information and Control*, vol. 12(1968), pp. 212-220.
11. A. Settle and J. Simon: Smaller solutions for the firing squad. *Theoretical Computer Science*, 276 (2002), 83-109.
12. H. Szwerinski: Time-optimum solution of the firing-squad-synchronization-problem for n-dimensional rectangles with the general at an arbitrary position. *Theoretical Computer Science*, vol. 19(1982), pp. 305-320.
13. H. Szwerinski: Symmetrical one-dimensional cellular spaces. *Information and Control*, vol. 67(1982), 163-172.
14. H. Umeo, M. Hisaoka, K. Michisaka, K. Nishioka and M. Maeda: Some new generalized synchronization algorithms and their implementations for a large scale of cellular automata. *Proc. of International Conference on Unconventional Models of Computation*, LNCS 2509(2002), pp.276-286.
15. H. Umeo, M. Hisaoka and T. Sogabe: A Survey on Firing Squad Synchronization Algorithms for One-Dimensional Cellular Automata. International Journal of Unconventional Computing, Vol.1, pp.403-426, (2005).
16. V. I. Varshavsky, V. B. Marakhovsky and V. A. Peschansky: Synchronization of interacting automata. *Mathematical Systems Theory*, Vol. 4, No. 3(1970), pp. 212-230.
17. R. Vollmar: On cellular automata with a finite number of state changes. *Computing, Supplementum*, vol. 3(1981), 181-191.
18. A. Waksman: An optimum solution to the firing squad synchronization problem. *Information and Control*, vol. 9 (1966), pp. 66-78.
19. J. B. Yunès: Seven-state solution to the firing squad synchronization problem. *Theoretical Computer Science*, 127(1994), pp.313-332.

State-Efficient Firing Squad Synchronization Protocols for Communication-Restricted Cellular Automata

Hiroshi Umeo, Takashi Yanagihara, and Masaru Kanazawa

Univ. of Osaka Electro-Communication,
Neyagawa-shi, Hastu-cho, 18-8, Osaka, 572-8530, Japan
{umeo, yanagihara, masaru}@cyt.osakac.ac.jp

Abstract. In this paper, we study a trade-off between internal states and communication bits in firing squad synchronization protocols for k-bit communication-restricted cellular automata (CA_{k-bit}) and propose several time-optimum state-efficient bit-transfer-based synchronization protocols. It is shown that there exists a 1-state CA_{5-bit} that can synchronize any n cells in $2n - 2$ optimum-step. The result is interesting, since we know that there exists no 4-state synchronization algorithm on *conventional* $O(1)$-*bit communication* cellular automata. A bit-transfer complexity is also introduced to measure the efficiency of synchronization protocols. We show that $\Omega(n \log n)$ bit-transfer is a lower-bound for synchronizing n cells in $(2n - 2)$ steps. In addition, each optimum-time/non-optimum-time synchronization protocols, presented in this paper, has an $O(n^2)$ bit-transfer complexity, respectively.

1 Introduction

Cellular automata (CA) are considered to be a good model of complex systems in which an infinite one-dimensional array of finite state machines (cells) updates itself in a synchronous manner according to a uniform local rule. In the long history of the study of CA, generally speaking, the number of internal states of each cell is finite and the local state transition rule is defined in a such way that the state of each cell depends on the previous states of itself and its neighboring cells. Thus, in the finite state description of the CA, the number of communication bits exchanged in one step between neighboring cells is assumed to be $O(1)$ bits. However, such inter-cell bit-information is hidden under the definition of the conventional automata-theoretic finite state description.

In the present paper, we study a firing squad synchronization problem on a very restricted model of cellular automata, CA_{k-bit}, for which inter-cell communication at one step is restricted to k-bit, where k is any positive integer such that $k \geq 1$. We hereinafter refer to the model as k-bit CA (CA_{k-bit}). The number of internal states of CA_{k-bit} is assumed to be finite in the usual sense. The next state of each cell is determined by the present state of the cell and two binary k-bit inputs from its left- and right-neighbor cells. A 1-bit CA model,

S. El Yacoubi, B. Chopard, and S. Bandini (Eds.): ACRI 2006, LNCS 4173, pp. 169–181, 2006.

where $k = 1$, can be thought of as being one of the simplest CAs to have a low computational complexity. On the k-bit CA we consider the firing squad synchronization problem that has studied extensively on the conventional CA model and propose several optimum-time firing squad synchronization protocols together with its implementation on a computer. Although many researchers have examined various aspects of the conventional cellular automata [1-5, 7, 8, 11-14, 21-23], studies focusing on the amount of bit-information exchanged in inter-cell communications are few. Mazoyer [6] first studied this model under the name of CAs with *channels* and proposed a time-optimum firing squad synchronization algorithm in which only one-bit information is exchanged. Umeo [15] and Umeo et al. [17, 19] have studied algorithmic design techniques for sequence generation and connectivity recognition problems on CA_{1-bit}. In addition, Umeo and Kamikawa [16, 18] showed that infinite non-regular sequences such as $\{2^n | n = 1, 2, 3, ..\}$, $\{n^2 | n = 1, 2, 3, ..\}$ and Fibonacci sequences can be generated in real-time and the prime sequence in twice real-time by CA_{1-bit}. Worsch [24] established a computational hierarchy between one-way 1-bit CAs.

First, in Section 2, we introduce a class of bit-communication-restricted cellular automaton having k-bit inter-cell communication and define the firing squad synchronization problem on CA_{k-bit}. In Section 3, we propose several state-efficient bit-transfer-based synchronization protocols for CA_{k-bit}. It is shown that there exists a 1-state CA_{5-bit} that can synchronize any n cells in $2n - 2$ optimum-step. A bit-transfer complexity is also introduced to measure the efficiency of synchronization protocols. We show that $\Omega(n \log n)$ bit-transfer is a lower-bound for synchronizing n cells in $(2n - 2)$ steps. In addition, each optimum-time/non-optimum-time synchronization protocols, presented in this paper, has an $O(n^2)$ bit-transfer complexity, respectively. Due to space constraints, we do not present the detailed proofs of the theorems presented herein.

2   Cellular Automaton Having k-Bit Inter-cell Communication

2.1   Bit-Communication-Restricted Cellular Automaton

A one-dimensional k-bit inter-cell communication cellular automaton consists of an infinite array of identical finite state automata, each located at a positive integer point (See Fig. 1). Each automaton is referred to as a cell. A cell at point i is denoted by C_i, where $i \geq 1$. Each C_i, except for C_1, is connected to its left- and right-neighbor cells via a left or right one-way communication link. These communication links are indicated by right- and left-pointing arrows in

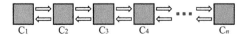

Fig. 1. One-dimensional cellular automaton having k-bit inter-cell communication links

Fig. 1, respectively. Each one-way communication link can transmit k bits at each step in each direction. A cellular automaton with k-bit inter-cell communication (abbreviated by CA_{k-bit}) consists of an infinite array of finite state automata $A = (Q, \delta)$, where

1. Q is a finite set of internal states.
2. δ is a function, defining the next state of any cell and its binary outputs to its left- and right-neighbor cells, such that $\delta: Q \times \{0,1\}^k \times \{0,1\}^k \to Q \times \{0,1\}^k \times \{0,1\}^k$, where $\delta(p, x_1, x_2, ..., x_k, y_1, y_2, ..., y_k) = (q, x'_1, x'_2, ..., x'_k, y'_1, y'_2, ..., y'_k)$, $p, q \in Q$, $x_i, x'_i, y_i, y'_i \in \{0,1\}, 1 \le i \le k$, has the following meaning. We assume that at step t the cell C_i is in state p and is receiving k binary inputs x_i and $y_i, 1 \le i \le k$, from its left and right communication links, respectively. Then, at the next step, $t+1$, C_i assumes state q and outputs x'_i and $y'_i, 1 \le i \le k$, to its left and right communication links, respectively. Note that k binary inputs to C_i at step t are also outputs of C_{i-1} and C_{i+1} at step t. A quiescent state $q \in Q$ has a property such that $\delta(q, \overbrace{0, 0, ..., 0}^{k}, \overbrace{0, 0, ..., 0}^{k}) = (q, \overbrace{0, 0, ..., 0}^{k}, \overbrace{0, 0, ..., 0}^{k})$.

Thus, the CA_{k-bit} is a special subclass of *normal* (i.e., *conventional*) cellular automata. Let N be any normal cellular automaton having a set of states Q eand a transition function $\delta : Q^3 \to Q$. The state of each cell on N depends on the previous states of the cell and its nearest neighbor cells. This means that the total information exchanged per one step between neighboring cells consists of $O(1)$ bits. By encoding each state in Q with a binary sequence of length $\lceil \log_2 |Q| \rceil$, sending the sequences sequentially bit by bit in each direction via each one-way communication link, receiving the sequences bit-by-bit again, and then decoding the sequences into their corresponding states in Q, the CA_{1-bit} can simulate one step of N in $\lceil \log_2 |Q| \rceil$ steps. This observation yields the following computational relation between the normal CA and CA_{1-bit}.

[**Lemma 1**] Let N be any *normal* cellular automaton having time complexity $T(n)$. Then, there exists a CA_{1-bit} which can simulate N in $kT(n)$ steps, where k is a positive constant integer such that $k = \lceil \log_2 |Q| \rceil$ and Q is the set of internal states of N.

In addition, the next lemma can be stated in the case where each cell can transfer k-bits at each step.

[**Lemma 2**] Let N be any s-state *normal* cellular automaton. Then, there exists an s-state CA_{k-bit} which can simulate N in *real time*, where k is a positive integer such that $k = \lceil \log_2 s \rceil$.

2.2   Firing Squad Synchronization Problem on CA_{k-Bit}

In this section, we study a famous firing squad synchronization problem on the newly introduced CA_{k-bit} model for which solution gives a finite-state protocol for synchronizing a large scale of cellular automata. The problem was originally proposed by J. Myhill to synchronize all parts of self-reproducing cellular automata [8]. The firing squad synchronization problem has been studied extensively in more than 40 years [1-20, 22-24].

The firing squad synchronization problem is formalized in terms of the model of cellular automata. All cells (*soldiers*), except the left end cell, are initially in the *quiescent* state at time $t = 0$ and have the property whereby the next state of a quiescent cell having quiescent neighbors is the quiescent state. At time $t = 0$ the left end cell (*general*) is in the *fire-when-ready* state, which is an initiation signal to the array. The firing squad synchronization problem is stated as follows. Given an array of n identical cellular automata, including a *general* on the left end which is activated at time $t = 0$, we want to give the description (state set and next-state function) of the automata so that, *at some future time*, all of the cells will *simultaneously* and, *for the first time*, enter a special *firing* state. The set of states must be independent of n. Without loss of generality, we assume $n \geq 2$. The

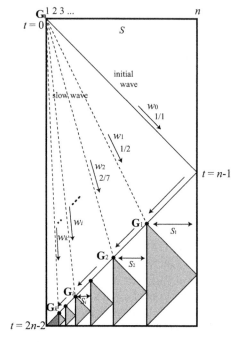

Fig. 2. A time-space diagram for Mazoyer's optimum-time synchronization scheme

difficult part of the problem is that the same types of soldier having a fixed number of states must be synchronized, regardless of the length n of the array.

2.3   A Brief History of the Developments of Optimum-Time Firing Squad Synchronization Algorithms

The problem known as the *firing squad synchronization problem* was devised in 1957 by J. Myhill, and first appeared in print in a paper by E. F. Moore [8]. This problem has been widely circulated, and has attracted much attention. The firing squad synchronization problem first arose in connection with the need to simultaneously turn on all parts of a self-reproducing machine. The problem was first solved by J. McCarthy and M. Minsky who presented a $3n$-step algorithm. In 1962, the first optimum-time, i.e. $(2n - 2)$-step, synchronization algorithm was presented by Goto [4], with each cell having several thousands of states.

Waksman [23] presented a 16-state optimum-time synchronization algorithm. Afterward, Balzer [1] and Gerken [3] developed an eight-state algorithm and a seven-state synchronization algorithm, respectively, thus decreasing the number of states required for the synchronization. In 1987, Mazoyer [5] developed a six-state synchronization algorithm which, at present, is the algorithm having the fewest states on the conventional model of CA.

2.4   An Overview of Mazoyer's Synchronization Algorithm

Figure 2 is a time-space diagram for Mazoyer's optimum-time synchronization scheme. The *General* G_0 generates an infinite number of signals $w_0, w_1, w_2, ..$, to generate new *Generals* $G_1, G_2, ..$, by dividing the array recursively with the ratio $1/2$. Propagation speed of the i-th signal w_i, $i \geq 1$ is as follows:

$$1/3^i(1 + \sum_{l=1}^{i} 2^{l-1}/3^l).$$

When the first signal w_0 hits the right end of the array, a return r-signal is generated that propagates at speed $1/1$ in the left direction. The w_1- and r-signals meets on cell C_m, $m = \lceil n/3 \rceil$, and a special mark is printed as a new *General* G_1. The G_1 does the same procedures as G_0 to the subspace between C_m and C_n. The ith collision of the w_i- and r-signals yields the ith new *General* G_i. The i-th *General* $G_i(i \geq 2)$ does the same operations as G_1 does. Mazoyer [5] successfully implemented the scheme on a conventional cellular automaton with only six states.

[**Theorem 1**][5] There exists a 6-state normal cellular automaton that can synchronize any n cells in $2n - 2$ optimum steps.

3   A Trade-Off in Firing Squad Synchronization Protocols for CA_{k-bit}

In this section, we present four synchronization protocols on CA_{k-bit} where $k = 1, 2, 3$ and 4. All of the protocols presented are designed on the basis of Mazoyer's synchronization scheme.

3.1 $\mathcal{P}_1$: A Non-optimum-Time Synchronization Protocol on CA_{1-bit}

The next theorem is our first implementation of the Mazoyer's synchronization scheme on CA_{1-bit}. An optimum-time implementation seems to be difficult, since the original $O(1)$-bit w_i-signal carries n_i mod 3 with traveling at a unit-speed, where n_i is the size of the subspace for which the i-th General is responsible. To carry two bits information: n_i mod 3 on a 1-bit signal in real-time, we delay the whole synchronization processes by one step.

[**Theorem 2**] There exists a 54-state CA_{1-bit} that can synchronize any n cells in $2n - 1$ steps.

Figure 3 (right) illustrates the snapshots of our 54-state $(2n - 1)$-step synchronization protocol on CA_{1-bit}. The small black triangles ▶ and ◀ indicate a 1-bit signal transfer in the right or left direction, respectively, between neighboring cells. A symbol in a cell shows internal state of the cell. For ease of understanding of the synchronization processes and for the reference, we usually (below) provide snapshots of the Mazoyer's 6-state synchronization processes of the same size on conventional cellular automata. See Fig. 3 (left).

3.2 $\mathcal{P}_2$: An Optimum-Time Six-State Synchronization Protocol on CA_{2-bit}

By combining [Lemma 2] and [Theorem 1], it is easily seen that there exists a 6-state CA_{3-bit} that can synchronize n cells in $2n - 2$ optimum-step. The next theorem shows an improvement over the communication bits. Figure 4 (right) illustrates the snapshots of our 6-state $(2n - 2)$-step synchronization protocol on CA_{2-bit}.

[**Theorem 3**] There exists a 6-state CA_{2-bit} that can synchronize any n cells in $2n - 2$ optimum-step.

3.3 $\mathcal{P}_3$: An Optimum-Time Four-State Synchronization Protocol on CA_{3-bit}

As for the number of internal states in firing squad synchronization protocol on conventional cellular automata, the following three distinct states:

- quiescent state Q such that Q Q Q → Q
- general state: G, and
- firing state: F

are required in order to define the firing squad synchronization problem on conventional cellular automaton. In addition, the following theorem has been established by Balzer [1], Berthiaume [2] and Sanders [11].

[**Theorem 4**] [1,2,11] There is no four-state conventional cellular automata that can synchronize any n cells in optimum-step.

The question that remains is: "What is the minimum number of states for an optimum-time solution of the problem?". At present, that number is *five or six* on the conventional cellular automata. On the CA_{3-bit} model, we can establish the following theorem.

[**Theorem 5**] There exists a 4-state CA_{3-bit} that can synchronize any n cells in $2n - 2$ optimum-step.

Figure 5 illustrates the snapshots of our 4-state $(2n - 2)$-step synchronization protocol on CA_{3-bit}.

Fig. 3. Snapshots for Mazoyer's synchronization processes (left) and those for the 54-state $(2n-1)$-step protocol (right) on 24 cells

3.4 $\mathcal{P}_4$: An Optimum-Time Three-State Synchronization Protocol on CA_{4-bit}

An additional 1-bit yields the following 3-state synchronization protocol. Figure 6 illustrates the snapshots of our 3-state $(2n-2)$-step synchronization protocol on CA_{4-bit}.

[**Theorem 6**] There exists a 3-state CA_{4-bit} that can synchronize any n cells in $2n-2$ optimum-step.

3.5 $\mathcal{P}_4^*$: An Optimum-Time Two-State Synchronization Protocol on CA_{4-bit}

In our previous design the firing state is defined as a unique internal state that appears simultaneously and for the first time on each cell. We can observe that

Fig. 4. Snapshots for the 6-state $(2n - 2)$-step firing squad synchronization algorithm operating on CA_{2-bit} with 24 cells (right)

the quiescent state with two 3-bit binary outputs $0, 0, 1$ can act as the firing state in the Protocol $\mathcal{P}_4$. By regarding the firing state as a product of the quiescent state and two 3-bit binary outputs $0, 0, 1$ to each neighbor at the final step we can reduce the internal states by one. Figure 7 illustrates the snapshots of our 2-state $(2n - 2)$-step synchronization protocol on CA_{4-bit}.

[**Theorem 7**] There exists a 2-state CA_{4-bit} that can synchronize any n cells in $2n - 2$ optimum-step.

3.6 $\mathcal{P}_5$: An Optimum-Time Single-State (State-Less) Synchronization Protocol on CA_{5-Bit}

A single state can be removed by a similar method used in the previous section. In tha last we can establish the following theorem. In some sense we need no state to synchnize the whole array.

[**Theorem 8**] There exists a 1-state CA_{5-bit} that can synchronize any n cells in $2n - 2$ optimum-step.

Fig. 5. Snapshots for 4-state $(2n-2)$-step firing squad synchronization algorithm operating on CA_{3-bit} with 24 cells

Fig. 6. Snapshots for 3-state $(2n-2)$-step firing squad synchronization algorithm operating on CA_{4-bit} with 24 cells

Figure 8 illustrates the snapshots of the 1-state $(2n-2)$-step synchronization protocol on CA_{5-bit}.

3.7   Bit-Transfer Complexity on CA_{k-bit}

Vollmar [21, 22] introduced a state-change complexity in order to measure the efficiency of cellular algorithms for the conventional cellular automata model and showed that $\Omega(n \log n)$ state changes are required for the synchronization of n cells in $(2n-2)$ steps. Gerken [3] and Umeo, Hisaoka and Sogabe [20] have studied the state-change complexity for optimum-time synchronization protocols proposed so far.

[Theorem 9] [21,22] $\Omega(n \log n)$ state-change is necessary for synchronizing n cells in $(2n-2)$ steps.

[Theorem 10] [3,20] Each optimum-time synchronization algorithm developed by Balzer [1], Gerken [3], Mazoyer [5] and Waksman [23] has an $O(n^2)$ state-change complexity, respectively.

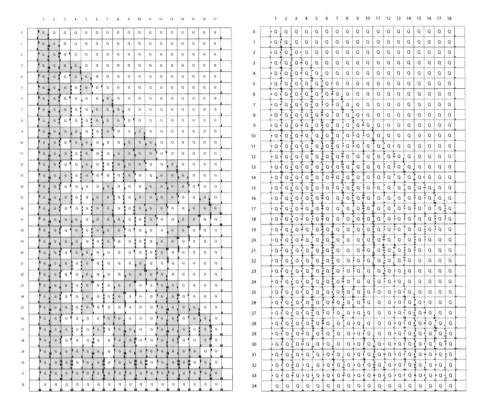

Fig. 7. Snapshots for 2-state $(2n - 2)$-step firing squad synchronization algorithm operating on CA_{4-bit} with 17 cells

Fig. 8. Snapshots for 1-state $(2n - 2)$-step firing squad synchronization algorithm operating on CA_{5-bit} with 18 cells.

Let $BT(n)$ be total number of bits transferred needed for synchronizing n cells on CA_{k-bit}. By using the similar technique developed by Vollmar [21, 22], we can establish a lower-bound on bit-transfer complexity for synchronizing n cells on CA_{k-bit} in a way such that $BT(n) = \Omega(n \log n)$. In addition, it is shown that each synchronization protocol $\mathcal{P}_i, 1 \leq i \leq 5$, presented above has an $O(n^2)$ bit-transfer complexity, respectively.

[Theorem 11] $\Omega(n \log n)$ bit-transfer is a lower bound for synchronizing n cells on CA_{k-bit} in $(2n - 2)$ steps.

[Theorem 12] Each optimum-time/non-optimum-time synchronization protocols $\mathcal{P}_i, 1 \leq i \leq 5$, presented in this paper, has an $O(n^2)$ bit-transfer complexity, respectively.

3.8 A Comparison of Quantitative Aspects of Optimum-Time Synchronization Algorithms

Here, we present Table 1 based on a quantitative comparison of optimum-time synchronization protocols with respect to the number of internal states of each finite state automaton, the number of transition rules realizing the synchronization, and the number of communication bits transferred on the array. Firing squad synchronization algorithms have been designed on the basis of parallel divide-and-conquer strategy that calls itself recursively in parallel. Those recursive calls are implemented by generating many *Generals* that are responsible for synchronizing divided small areas in the cellular space.

Table 1. Quantitative and qualitative comparison of optimum-time/non-optimum-time firing squad synchronization protocols

Synchronization Protocol	Communication Bits Transferred	# of States	# of Transition Rules	Time Complexity	One-/Two-sided Recursiveness
$\mathcal{P}_1$	1	54	207	$2n - 1$	One-Sided
$\mathcal{P}_2$	2	6	60	$2n - 2$	One-Sided
$\mathcal{P}_3$	3	4	76	$2n - 2$	One-Sided
$\mathcal{P}_4$	4	3	87	$2n - 2$	One-Sided
$\mathcal{P}_4^*$	4	2	88	$2n - 2$	One-Sided
$\mathcal{P}_5$	5	1	114	$2n - 2$	One-Sided
Mazoyer [1996]	1	58	-	$2n - 2$	Two-Sided
Mazoyer [1996]	12	3	-	$2n - 2$	-
Nishimura et al. [2000]	1	78	208	$2n - 2$	Two-Sided

If all of the recursive calls for the synchronization are issued by *Generals* located at one (both two) end(s) of partitioned cellular spaces for which the *General* is responsible, the synchronization algorithm is said to have *one-sided* (*two-sided*) recursive property. We call the synchronization algorithm with one-sided (two-sided) recursive property as one-sided (two-sided) recursive synchronization algorithm. It is noted that optimum-time synchronization algorithms developed by Balzer [1], Gerken [3] and Waksman [23] are two-sided ones and an algorithm proposed by Mazoyer [5] is only one synchronization algorithm with the one-sided recursive property. Each synchronization protocol $\mathcal{P}_i, 1 \leq i \leq 5$, presented in this paper, has one-sided property, since they are basd on Mazoyer's algorithm. A detailed definition of the one- and two-sided recursiveness can be found in Umeo, Hisaoka and Sogabe [20].

4   Conclusions

We have made an investigation into a trade-off between internal states and communication bits in firing squad synchronization protocols for communication-restricted cellular automata and proposed several time-optimum state-efficient bit-transfer-based synchronization protocols. It has been shown that there exists a 1-state CA_{5-bit} that can synchronize any n cells in $2n - 2$ optimum-step. The result is interesting, since we know that there exists no 4-state synchronization algorithm on conventional O(1)-bit communication cellular automata. A bit-trasnfer complexity has been also introduced. We have shown that $\Omega(n \log n)$ bit-transfer is a lower-bound for synchronizing n cells in $(2n - 2)$ steps. In addition, it has been shown that each optimum-time/non-optimum-time synchronization protocols, presented in this paper, has an $O(n^2)$ bit-transfer complexity, respectively. As for the protocols with $\Omega(n \log n)$ bit-transfer, it might be possible to design those protocols based on Gerken's or Goto's algorithm developed on conventional model, each of them has $\Omega(n \log n)$ state-change complexity. The CA_{k-bit} is confirmed to be an interesting computational subclass of CAs that merits further study. We conclude with the following questions for further investigations.

- What is the minimum number of states for protocols on each CA_{k-bit}, $k = 1, 2, 3, 4$ and 5?

References

1. R. Balzer: An 8-state minimal time solution to the firing squad synchronization problem. *Information and Control*, vol. 10 (1967), pp. 22-42.
2. A. Berthiaume, T. Bittner, L. Perković, A. Settle and J. Simon. (2004): Bounding the firing synchronization problem on a ring. *Theoretical Computer Science*, 320, pp. 213-228.
3. Hans-D., Gerken. (1987): Über Synchronisations - Probleme bei Zellularautomaten. *Diplomarbeit*, Institut für Theoretische Informatik, Technische Universität Braunschweig, pp. 50.
4. E. Goto: A minimal time solution of the firing squad problem. Dittoed course notes for Applied Mathematics 298, Harvard University, (1962), pp. 52-59.
5. J. Mazoyer: A six-state minimal time solution to the firing squad synchronization problem. *Theoretical Computer Science*, vol. 50 (1987), pp. 183-238.
6. J. Mazoyer: On optimal solutions to the firing squad synchronization problem. *Theoretical Computer Science*, vol. 168(1996), pp. 367-404.
7. M. Minsky: *Computation: Finite and infinite machines*. Prentice Hall, (1967), pp. 28-29.
8. E. F. Moore: The firing squad synchronization problem. in *Sequential Machines, Selected Papers* (E. F. Moore ed.), Addison-Wesley, Reading MA., (1964), pp. 213-214.
9. J. Nishimura, T. Sogabe and H. Umeo. (2003): A design of optimum-time firing squad synchronization algorithm on 1-bit cellular automaton. *Proc. of the 8th International Symposium on Artificial Life and Robotics*, Vol.2, pp. 381-386.
10. J. Nishimura and H. Umeo: An Optimum-Time Synchronization Protocol for 1-Bit-Communication Cellular Automata. *Proc. of The 9th World Multi-Conference on Systemics, Cybernetics and Informatics*, (2005).
11. P. Sanders. (1994): Massively parallel search for transition-tables of polyautomata. In *Proc. of the VI International Workshop on Parallel Processing by Cellular Automata and Arrays*, (C. Jesshope, V. Jossifov and W. Wilhelmi (editors)), Akademie, 99-108.
12. A. Settle and J. Simon. (1998): Improved bounds for the firing synchronization problem. In *SIROCCO 5: Proc. of the 5th International Colloquium on Structural Information and Communication Complexity*, Carleton Scientific, 66-81.
13. A. Settle and J. Simon. (2002): Smaller solutions for the firing squad. *Theoretical Computer Science*, 276, 83-109.
14. S. L. Torre, M. Napoli and M. Parente: A compositional approach to synchronize two dimensional networks of processors. *Theoretical Informatics and Applications*, 34 (2000) pp. 549-564.

15. H. Umeo: Linear-time recognition of connectivity of binary images on 1-bit inter-cell communication cellular automaton. *Parallel Computing*, 27, pp. 587-599, (2001).

16. H. Umeo and N. Kamikawa: A design of real-time non-regular sequence generation algorithms and their implementations on cellular automata with 1-bit inter-cell communications. *Fundamenta Informaticae*, 52 (2002) 255-275.

17. H. Umeo, K. Michisaka and N. Kamikawa: A synchronization problem on 1-bit-communication cellular automata. Proc. of International Conference on Computational Science-ICCS2003, LNCS 2657, pp.492-500, (2003).

18. H. Umeo and N. Kamikawa: Real-time Generation of Primes by a 1-Bit-Communication Cellular Automaton. *Fundamenta Informaticae*, 58(2003) 421-435.

19. H. Umeo, M. Kanazawa, K. Michisaka and N. Kamikawa: State-Efficient 1-Bit-Communication Solutions for Some Classical Cellular Automata Problems. Proc. of the International Workshop on Tilings and Cellular Automata (Ed. M. Margenstern), pp.1-12, (2004).

20. H. Umeo, M. Hisaoka and T. Sogabe: A Survey on Firing Squad Synchronization Algorithms for One-Dimensional Cellular Automata. International Journal of Unconventional Computing, vol.1(2005), pp. 403-426.

21. R. Vollmar. (1981): On Cellular Automata with a Finite Number of State Change. *Computing, Supplementum*, vol. 3(1981), pp. 181-191.

22. R. Vollmar. (1982): Some remarks about the "Efficiency" of polyautomata. *International Journal of Theoretical Physics*, vol. 21, no. 12, pp. 1007-1015.

23. A. Waksman: An optimum solution to the firing squad synchronization problem. *Information and Control*, vol. 9 (1966), pp. 66-78.

24. T. Worsch: Linear time language recognition on cellular automata with restricted communication, *Proc. of LATIN 2000:Theoretical Informatics* (Eds. G. H. Gonnet, D. Panario and A. Viola), LNCS 1776, pp.417-426, (2000).

Discrete Baker Transformation for Binary Valued Cylindrical Cellular Automata

Burton Voorhees

Center for Science - Athabasca University, 1 University Drive
Atahbasca, AB, CANADA T9S 3A3
burt@athabascau.ca

Abstract. Recently, the discrete baker transformation has been defined for linear cellular automata acting on multi-dimensional tori with alphabet of prime cardinality. Here we specialize to binary valued cylindrical cellular automata and generalizing the discrete baker transformation to non-linear rules. We show that for a cellular automaton, defined on a cylinder of size $n = 2^k m$ with m odd, the equivalence classes of rules that map to the same rule under the discrete baker transformation fall into equivalence classes labeled by the set of 2^m cellular automata defined on a cylinder of size m. We also derive the relation between the state transition diagram of a cellular automata rule and that of its baker transformation and discuss cycle periods of the baker transformation for odd n.

1 Baker Transformation of Additive Rules

In [1] the discrete baker transformation for linear cellular automata (LCA) acting on multidimensional tori was defined and shown to produce exponential speed-up of rule evolution. This provided a number of significant results on rule behavior, including sharp estimates of parameters such as maximal tree heights and cycle periods. Here attention is restricted to binary valued one-dimensional cylindrical cellular automata [2]. For these CA the discrete baker transformation is generalized to non-linear rules. This is a first step in a study of general index permutations of CA rules.

Let $C(n)$ be the set of n-site binary valued CA rules defined on cylinders of size n and $AD(n) \subset C(n)$ the subset of additive rules. If a rule $X \in AD(n)$, it can be expressed in terms of the left shift operator σ as:

$$X = \sum_{s=0}^{n-1} a_s \sigma^s \qquad (1)$$

where σ is defined by its action on strings μ:

$$[\sigma(\mu)]_i = \mu_{i+1 \bmod(n)} \qquad (2)$$

The rule table for a CA is given by its neighborhood components: $x_i = X(i_0 \ldots i_{k-1})$ for neighborhoods of size k [3]. In what follows, maximal neighborhoods (k = n) are assumed. Components of rules in $AD(n)$ satisfy an additivity condition [3]

S. El Yacoubi, B. Chopard, and S. Bandini (Eds.): ACRI 2006, LNCS 4173, pp. 182–191, 2006.

$$x_i = \sum_{s=0}^{n-1} i_{n-s-1} x_{2^s} \bmod(2) \tag{3}$$

The component index i is just the denary form of the binary number $i_0 \ldots i_{n-1}$. The coefficients a_s in equation (1) are related to the rule components by

$$a_s = \begin{cases} 1 & x_{2^{n-s-1}} = 1 \quad 0 \le s \le n-1 \\ 0 & otherwise \end{cases} \tag{4}$$

Example: Rule 90, n = 5
In this case, with maximal neighborhoods, there are 32 rule components given by the rule table

x_0–x_3	x_4–x_7	x_8–x_{11}	x_{12}–x_{15}	x_{16}–x_{19}	x_{20}–x_{23}	x_{24}–x_{27}	x_{28}–x_{31}
0	1	0	1	1	0	1	0

This yields the coefficients for equation (1) as

s	0	1	2	3	4
$x_{2^{n-s-1}}$	$x_{16} = 1$	$x_8 = 0$	$x_4 = 1$	$x_2 = 0$	$x_1 = 0$
a_s	1	0	1	0	0

Thus, rule 90 has the form $X = I + \sigma^2$.
For additive binary valued rules, the baker transformation $X \rightarrow BX$ is defined by

$$a_s \rightarrow \sum_{r:\, s=2r \bmod(n)} a_r \bmod(2) \tag{5}$$

and in [1] it was shown that in this case $BX = X^2$ and more generally, $B^k X = X^{2^k}$.

The transformation of equation (5) can be expressed in terms of the n-dimensional vector $\vec{a} = (a_0, a_1, \ldots, a_{n-1})$ and the 2^n-dimensional vector $\vec{x} = (x_0, x_1, \ldots, x_{2^{n-1}})$:

$$\vec{a} \rightarrow b \cdot \vec{a}$$
$$\vec{x} \rightarrow B \cdot \vec{x} \qquad x_i \rightarrow x_{i \cdot b} \tag{6}$$

Where

$$b_{rs} = \begin{cases} 1 & 2s = r \bmod(n) \\ 0 & otherwise \end{cases}$$
$$B_{ij} = \begin{cases} 1 & j = i \cdot b \\ 0 & otherwise \end{cases} \tag{7}$$

2 Baker Transformation for Arbitrary Rules

The second form of the baker transformation in equation (6) is independent of the coefficients a_s. This indicates that the transformation can be applied to all CA rules. That is, for an arbitrary rule, the transformation acts on the indices of rule components defined with respect to maximal neighborhoods and this action is defined in terms of the way that the baker transformation of additive rules acts on component indices of these rules.

Example: Rule 18, n = 6

i	X	BX	i	X	BX	i	X	BX	i	X	BX
0	0	0	16	0	0	32	1	1	48	0	1
1	0	0	17	0	0	33	1	1	49	0	1
2	0	1	18	0	1	34	1	0	50	0	0
3	0	1	19	0	1	35	1	0	51	0	0
4	0	0	20	0	0	36	1	1	52	0	1
5	0	0	21	0	0	37	1	1	53	0	1
6	0	1	22	0	1	38	1	0	54	0	0
7	0	1	23	0	1	39	1	0	55	0	0
8	1	0	24	0	0	40	0	0	56	0	0
9	1	0	25	0	0	41	0	0	57	0	0
10	1	0	26	0	0	42	0	0	58	0	0
11	1	0	27	0	0	43	0	0	59	0	0
12	1	0	28	0	0	44	0	0	60	0	0
13	1	0	29	0	0	45	0	0	61	0	0
14	1	0	30	0	0	46	0	0	62	0	0
15	1	0	31	0	0	47	0	0	63	0	0

If X is additive $BX = X^2$ but this is not the case when X is non-linear. The example of rule 18 for n = 5 demonstrates this: the string 00100, for example, becomes 00110 under X^2 but 00101 under BX.

Proof of the next theorem follows directly from equation (7).

Theorem 1
1. If n is odd the matrices b and B are permutations.
2. If $n = 2^k m$ with m odd and k > 0 then, labeling the rows of the matrix b^r from 0 to n-1 (starting at the top), if $s \neq 2^r h$ ($0 \leq h \leq 2^{k-r}m-1$) the s-th row of b^r consists entirely of 0s. For $s = 2^r h$ the s-th row of b^r consists of identical blocks of length $2^{k-r}m$, each block containing a single 1 in the h-th position.

Thus, $B^s X$ ($0 \leq s \leq k$) is determined by $2^{2^{k-s}m}$ of the 2^n components of X.

Corollary
If X is in C(n) and $n = 2^k m$ ($0 \leq k$) then $B^k X$ is completely determined by the set of components $\{x_{i(c)} | 0 \leq c \leq 2^m - 1\}$ where

$$i(c) = c \sum_{s=0}^{2^k-1} 2^{(2^k-s-1)m} \tag{8}$$

Example: n = 5.

If n = 5 the matrices b and B are permutations. The matrix b is given by

$$b = \begin{pmatrix} 1 & 0 & 0 & 0 & 0 \\ 0 & 0 & 0 & 1 & 0 \\ 0 & 1 & 0 & 0 & 0 \\ 0 & 0 & 0 & 0 & 1 \\ 0 & 0 & 1 & 0 & 0 \end{pmatrix} \tag{9}$$

and B is determined by entries in Table 1.

Table 1. Index transformation for n = 5

i	i·b	i	i·b	i	i·b	i	i·b
0	0	8	2	16	16	24	18
1	4	9	6	17	20	25	22
2	1	10	3	18	17	26	19
3	5	11	7	19	21	27	23
4	8	12	10	20	24	28	26
5	12	13	14	21	28	29	30
6	9	14	11	22	25	30	27
7	13	15	15	23	29	31	31

Examination of this table shows that there are four fixed points (1,15,16,31), two period 2 cycles (6,9) and (22,25) with the remaining indices showing period 4 cycles. Orbits of the baker transformation on CA rule space for n = 5 consists of cycles having these periods. For example, $I + \sigma \rightarrow I + \sigma^2 \rightarrow I + \sigma^4 \rightarrow I + \sigma^3 \rightarrow I + \sigma$.

Example: n = 6.

For n = 6 the matrix b is not a permutation matrix, but has all odd numbered rows consisting entirely of zeros. Thus, the 64 components of a 6-site rule reduce to only eight components under the baker transformation. The index transformation matrix b is

$$b = \begin{pmatrix} 1 & 0 & 0 & 1 & 0 & 0 \\ 0 & 0 & 0 & 0 & 0 & 0 \\ 0 & 1 & 0 & 0 & 1 & 0 \\ 0 & 0 & 0 & 0 & 0 & 0 \\ 0 & 0 & 1 & 0 & 0 & 1 \\ 0 & 0 & 0 & 0 & 0 & 0 \end{pmatrix} \begin{matrix} h = 0 \\ \\ h = 1 \\ \\ h = 2 \\ \\ \end{matrix} \tag{10}$$

Giving the transformation of the B matrix as indicated in Table 2.

Table 2. Index transformations for n = 6

i	$i \cdot b$	i	$i \cdot b$	i	$i \cdot b$	i	$i \cdot b$
0	0	16	0	32	36	48	36
1	0	17	0	33	36	49	36
2	9	18	9	34	45	50	45
3	9	19	9	35	45	51	45
4	0	20	0	36	36	52	36
5	0	21	0	37	36	53	36
6	9	22	9	38	45	54	45
7	9	23	9	39	45	55	45
8	18	24	18	40	54	56	54
9	18	25	18	41	54	57	54
10	27	26	27	42	63	58	63
11	27	27	27	43	63	59	63
12	18	28	18	44	54	60	54
13	18	29	18	45	54	61	54
14	27	30	27	46	63	62	63
15	27	31	27	47	63	63	63

Thus, for n = 6, BX is determined by eight components of X: x_0, x_9, x_{18}, x_{27}, x_{36}, x_{45}, x_{54}, and x_{63}. Further, examination of this table shows that $B^3X = BX$ indicating that the baker transformation on cylinders of size 6 has maximum period 2.

Example: n = 12.
For n = 12 the matrices b and b^2 are given by

$$
b = \begin{pmatrix}
1 & 0 & 0 & 0 & 0 & 0 & 1 & 0 & 0 & 0 & 0 & 0 \\
0 & 0 & 0 & 0 & 0 & 0 & 0 & 0 & 0 & 0 & 0 & 0 \\
0 & 1 & 0 & 0 & 0 & 0 & 0 & 1 & 0 & 0 & 0 & 0 \\
0 & 0 & 0 & 0 & 0 & 0 & 0 & 0 & 0 & 0 & 0 & 0 \\
0 & 0 & 1 & 0 & 0 & 0 & 0 & 0 & 1 & 0 & 0 & 0 \\
0 & 0 & 0 & 0 & 0 & 0 & 0 & 0 & 0 & 0 & 0 & 0 \\
0 & 0 & 0 & 1 & 0 & 0 & 0 & 0 & 0 & 1 & 0 & 0 \\
0 & 0 & 0 & 0 & 0 & 0 & 0 & 0 & 0 & 0 & 0 & 0 \\
0 & 0 & 0 & 0 & 1 & 0 & 0 & 0 & 0 & 0 & 1 & 0 \\
0 & 0 & 0 & 0 & 0 & 0 & 0 & 0 & 0 & 0 & 0 & 0 \\
0 & 0 & 0 & 0 & 0 & 1 & 0 & 0 & 0 & 0 & 0 & 1 \\
0 & 0 & 0 & 0 & 0 & 0 & 0 & 0 & 0 & 0 & 0 & 0
\end{pmatrix}
\begin{matrix}
h = 0 \\ \\ h = 1 \\ \\ h = 2 \\ \\ h = 3 \\ \\ h = 4 \\ \\ h = 5 \\ \\
\end{matrix}
\tag{11}
$$

$$b^2 = \begin{pmatrix} 1 & 0 & 0 & 1 & 0 & 0 & 1 & 0 & 0 & 1 & 0 & 0 \\ 0 & 0 & 0 & 0 & 0 & 0 & 0 & 0 & 0 & 0 & 0 & 0 \\ 0 & 0 & 0 & 0 & 0 & 0 & 0 & 0 & 0 & 0 & 0 & 0 \\ 0 & 0 & 0 & 0 & 0 & 0 & 0 & 0 & 0 & 0 & 0 & 0 \\ 0 & 1 & 0 & 0 & 1 & 0 & 0 & 1 & 0 & 0 & 1 & 0 \\ 0 & 0 & 0 & 0 & 0 & 0 & 0 & 0 & 0 & 0 & 0 & 0 \\ 0 & 0 & 0 & 0 & 0 & 0 & 0 & 0 & 0 & 0 & 0 & 0 \\ 0 & 0 & 0 & 0 & 0 & 0 & 0 & 0 & 0 & 0 & 0 & 0 \\ 0 & 0 & 1 & 0 & 0 & 1 & 0 & 0 & 1 & 0 & 0 & 1 \\ 0 & 0 & 0 & 0 & 0 & 0 & 0 & 0 & 0 & 0 & 0 & 0 \\ 0 & 0 & 0 & 0 & 0 & 0 & 0 & 0 & 0 & 0 & 0 & 0 \\ 0 & 0 & 0 & 0 & 0 & 0 & 0 & 0 & 0 & 0 & 0 & 0 \end{pmatrix} \begin{matrix} h=0 \\ \\ \\ \\ h=1 \\ \\ \\ \\ h=2 \\ \\ \\ \\ \end{matrix} \qquad (12)$$

From these the determining components of BX and B^2X are given by Table 3.

Table 3. Index transformations for $n = 6$ for b and b^2

$i \cdot b$	$i \cdot b^2$	$i \cdot b$	$i \cdot b^2$	$i \cdot b$	$i \cdot b^2$	$i \cdot b$	$i \cdot b^2$
0	0	1040	0	2080	2340	3120	2340
65	0	1105	0	2145	2340	3185	2340
130	585	1170	585	2210	2925	3250	2925
195	585	1235	585	2275	2925	3315	2925
260	0	1300	0	2340	2340	3380	2340
325	0	1365	0	2405	2340	3445	2340
390	585	1430	585	2470	2925	3510	2925
455	585	1495	585	2535	2925	3575	2925
520	1170	1560	1170	2600	3510	3640	3510
585	1170	1625	1170	2665	3510	3705	3510
650	1755	1690	1755	2730	4095	3770	4095
715	1755	1755	1755	2795	4095	3835	4095
780	1170	1820	1170	2860	3510	3900	3510
845	1170	1885	1170	2925	3510	3965	3510
910	1755	1950	1755	2990	4095	4030	4095
975	1755	2015	1755	3055	4095	4095	4095

The 64 components listed first in each column determine BX, and the 8 components listed second in each column determine B^2X.

Returning to the n = 6 example, BX is determined by the eight digit binary string $(x_0, x_9, x_{18}, x_{27}, x_{36}, x_{45}, x_{54}, x_{63})$ which also defines a 3-site rule. Thus, the set of 256 3-site rules acts as a classifying set for these equivalence classes of 6-site rules. All n = 6 rules having the same values for the eight determining components map to the same rule under the baker transformation. There are 2^{64} rules for n = 6, thus specification of the values for these eight components characterizes a class of 2^{56} rules.

Restricting attention to additive rules, the 64 6-site additive rules partition into equivalence classes of eight rules each with rules X and Y equivalent if BX = BY:

Table 4. Equivalence classes of 64 6-site additive rules

0	I	$\sigma^2+\sigma^4$	$I+\sigma^2+\sigma^4$
$\sigma+\sigma^4$	$I+\sigma^2+\sigma^5$	$\sigma+\sigma^5$	$\sigma^2+\sigma^3+\sigma^4$
$\sigma^2+\sigma^5$	σ^3	$\sigma^4+\sigma^5$	$\sigma^3+\sigma^4+\sigma^5$
$I+\sigma^3$	$I+\sigma+\sigma^4$	$I+\sigma^3+\sigma^4+\sigma^5$	$I+\sigma^4+\sigma^5$
$I+\sigma+\sigma^2+\sigma^3+\sigma^4+\sigma^5$	$\sigma+\sigma^2+\sigma^3+\sigma^4+\sigma^5$	$I+\sigma^2+\sigma^3+\sigma^4$	$\sigma+\sigma^3+\sigma^5$
$I+\sigma^2+\sigma^3+\sigma^5$	$\sigma+\sigma^3+\sigma^4$	$I+\sigma+\sigma^3+\sigma^5$	$I+\sigma+\sigma^5$
$I+\sigma+\sigma^3+\sigma^4$	$I+\sigma+\sigma^2+\sigma^4+\sigma^5$	$I+\sigma+\sigma^2+\sigma^3$	$I+\sigma+\sigma^2$
$\sigma+\sigma^2+\sigma^4+\sigma^5$	$\sigma^2+\sigma^3+\sigma^5$	$\sigma+\sigma^2$	$\sigma+\sigma^2+\sigma^3$

$I+\sigma^4$	$I+\sigma^2$	σ^4	σ^2
$\sigma+\sigma^3$	$\sigma^2+\sigma^3$	$\sigma^2+\sigma^4+\sigma^5$	$\sigma+\sigma^4+\sigma^5$
$I+\sigma+\sigma^2+\sigma^5$	$\sigma+\sigma^2+\sigma^3+\sigma^4$	$\sigma+\sigma^2+\sigma^5$	σ^5
$\sigma^2+\sigma^3+\sigma^4+\sigma^5$	$\sigma^3+\sigma^5$	σ	$\sigma+\sigma^2+\sigma^4$
$\sigma+\sigma^2+\sigma^3+\sigma^5$	$\sigma+\sigma^3+\sigma^4+\sigma^5$	$I+\sigma+\sigma^2+\sigma^3+\sigma^5$	$I+\sigma+\sigma^3+\sigma^4+\sigma^5$
$I+\sigma$	$I+\sigma+\sigma^2+\sigma^4$	$I+\sigma^2+\sigma^3+\sigma^4+\sigma^5$	$I+\sigma^3+\sigma^5$
$\sigma^3+\sigma^4$	$I+\sigma^5$	$I+\sigma^3+\sigma^4$	$I+\sigma+\sigma^2+\sigma^3+\sigma^4$
$I+\sigma^2+\sigma^4+\sigma^5$	$I+\sigma+\sigma^4+\sigma^5$	$I+\sigma+\sigma^3$	$I+\sigma^2+\sigma^3$

Note that under the baker transformation $I+\sigma^2 \leftrightarrow I+\sigma^4$ and $\sigma^2 \leftrightarrow \sigma^4$. Thus, in the lower half of Table 4 the first and third columns map under the baker transformation to $I+\sigma^2$ and σ^2 respectively while the second and fourth columns map respectively to $I+\sigma^4$ and σ^4. In the first part of the table, all rules in a column map under the baker transformation to the rule at the top of the column.

3   Transformations of the State Transition Diagram

For any given rule X, basic information such as cycle periods and tree heights is exhibited in the structure of the state transition diagram STD(X). This information is given by the adjacency matrix A(X) of this diagram:

$$A_{ij}(X) = \begin{cases} 1 & X(i_0 \ldots i_{n-1}) = j_0 \ldots j_{n-1} \\ 0 & otherwise \end{cases} \qquad (13)$$

The natural question is how the state transition diagram of the baker transformations of a rule relates to the state transition diagram of the rule itself. For odd values of n the relation is straight forward. When n is even, however, a more complicated construction is required.

Theorem 2
Let $n = 2^k m$ with m odd and let $A(X)$ be the adjacency matrix for STD(X).

1. If $k = 0$ then

$$A(BX) = BA(X)B^{-1} \tag{14}$$

2. If $k \neq 0$ let $A(X)$ be written in the form

$$A(X) = \begin{pmatrix} A*(X) & C \\ 0 & A_m(X) \end{pmatrix} \tag{15}$$

Where $A_m(X)$ is indexed by all sequences with spatial period a divisor of m. Then

$$A_m(BX) = B_m A_m(X) B_m^{-1} \tag{16}$$

with B_m the baker matrix for strings of length m.

Given the importance of the state transition diagram, it is useful to find a means of constructing $A(BX)$ when n is even. The procedure for doing so utilizes the $2^{n-1} \times 2^{n-1}$ de Bruijn fragment matrix $d_1(X)$ [3,4] defined in terms of the components of X by

$$[d_1(X)]_{\alpha\beta} = \begin{cases} x_j & j = \alpha * \beta, \beta = 2\alpha \text{ or } 2\alpha + 1 \\ 0 & otherwise \end{cases} \tag{17}$$

$0 \leq \alpha, \beta \leq 2^{n-1} - 1$. Here the binary forms of α and β are n-1 length strings and the concatenation of these, $\alpha * \beta = \alpha_0 \alpha_1 \ldots \alpha_{n-2} \beta_{v-2}$ when $\beta = 2\alpha$ or $2\alpha+1$, is just the n-site neighborhood that maps to the rule component x_j.

Theorem 3: Generation of $A(X)$ From $d_1(X)$
For $i = i_0 \ldots i_{n-1}$ define the numbers $i'(s) = i_s i_{s+1 \bmod(n)} \ldots i_{s+n-2 \bmod(n)}$ $0 \leq s \leq n - 1$ as the denary form of the indicated binary strings. Then, for $j = j_0 \ldots j_{n-1}$

$$[A(X)]_{ij} = \begin{cases} 1 & j_s = [d_1(X)]_{i'(s)i'(s+1 \bmod(n))} & 0 \leq s \leq n - 1 \\ 0 & otherwise \end{cases} \tag{18}$$

Example: Let X be rule 18 with $n = 3$. The matrix $d_1(X)$ for $n = 3$ is

$$d_1(X) = \begin{pmatrix} x_0 & x_1 & 0 & 0 \\ 0 & 0 & x_2 & x_3 \\ x_4 & x_5 & 0 & 0 \\ 0 & 0 & x_6 & x_7 \end{pmatrix} \quad d_1(18) = \begin{pmatrix} 0 & 1 & 0 & 0 \\ 0 & 0 & 0 & 0 \\ 1 & 0 & 0 & 0 \\ 0 & 0 & 0 & 0 \end{pmatrix} \tag{19}$$

With $i = i_0 i_1 i_2$, $i'(0) = i_0 i_1$, $i'(1) = i_1 i_2$, $i'(2) = i_2 i_0$ so that

$$j_0 = [d_1(18)]_{i_0 i_1, i_1 i_2}, \quad j_1 = [d_1(18)]_{i_1 i_2, i_2 i_0}, \quad j_2 = [d_1(18)]_{i_2 i_0, i_0 i_1}$$

From equation (12) this yields

$i_0i_1i_2$	000	001	010	011	100	101	110	111
j_0	x_0	x_1	x_2	x_3	x_4	x_5	x_6	x_7
j_1	x_0	x_2	x_4	x_6	x_1	x_3	x_5	x_7
j_2	x_0	x_4	x_1	x_5	x_2	x_6	x_3	x_7

From equation (18) and the rule table for rule 18

$$A(X) = \begin{pmatrix} 1 & 0 & 0 & 0 & 0 & 0 & 0 & 0 \\ 0 & 0 & 0 & 0 & 0 & 1 & 0 & 0 \\ 0 & 0 & 0 & 1 & 0 & 0 & 0 & 0 \\ 1 & 0 & 0 & 0 & 0 & 0 & 0 & 0 \\ 0 & 0 & 0 & 0 & 0 & 0 & 1 & 0 \\ 1 & 0 & 0 & 0 & 0 & 0 & 0 & 0 \\ 1 & 0 & 0 & 0 & 0 & 0 & 0 & 0 \\ 1 & 0 & 0 & 0 & 0 & 0 & 0 & 0 \end{pmatrix} \qquad (20)$$

Theorem 4

Let X be in C(n). Then

$$\left[d_1(BX) \right]_j = \sum_{r,s=0}^{2^{n-1}-1} \Gamma_{ij}^{rs} \left[d_1(X) \right]_{rs} \qquad (21)$$

where the object Γ is generated from the matrix B as follows:

1. Label rows and columns of B from 0 to $2^{n-1}-1$ in the pattern $0,1,\ldots, 2^{n-1}-1$, $0,1,\ldots, 2^{n-1}-1$.
2. In front of each row and column label write the numbers from 0 to $2^{n-1}-1$ in the pattern $0,0,1,1,\ldots, 2^{n-1}-1, 2^{n-1}-1$.

The i,j,r,s element Γ_{ij}^{rs} is the entry of B having row label i,j and column label r,s. All other elements of Γ are 0.

Example: n = 3. The matrix B, with rows appropriately labeled, is

$$B = \begin{array}{c} \\ \\ \begin{pmatrix} 1 & 0 & 0 & 0 & 0 & 0 & 0 & 0 \\ 0 & 0 & 1 & 0 & 0 & 0 & 0 & 0 \\ 0 & 1 & 0 & 0 & 0 & 0 & 0 & 0 \\ 0 & 0 & 0 & 1 & 0 & 0 & 0 & 0 \\ 0 & 0 & 0 & 0 & 1 & 0 & 0 & 0 \\ 0 & 0 & 0 & 0 & 0 & 0 & 1 & 0 \\ 0 & 0 & 0 & 0 & 0 & 1 & 0 & 0 \\ 0 & 0 & 0 & 0 & 0 & 0 & 0 & 1 \end{pmatrix} \end{array} \begin{array}{l} 0,0 \\ 0,1 \\ 1,2 \\ 1,3 \\ 2,0 \\ 2,1 \\ 3,2 \\ 3,3 \end{array} \qquad (22)$$

$$\begin{array}{cccccccc} 0,0 & 0,1 & 1,2 & 1,3 & 2,0 & 2,1 & 3,2 & 3,3 \end{array}$$

Thus $\Gamma_{00}^{00} = \Gamma_{01}^{12} = \Gamma_{12}^{01} = \Gamma_{13}^{13} = \Gamma_{20}^{20} = \Gamma_{21}^{32} = \Gamma_{32}^{21} = \Gamma_{33}^{33} = 1$ and all other elements are 0. From equation (21) this yields

$$d_1(BX) = \begin{pmatrix} x_0 & x_2 & 0 & 0 \\ 0 & 0 & x_1 & x_3 \\ x_4 & x_6 & 0 & 0 \\ 0 & 0 & x_5 & x_7 \end{pmatrix} \tag{23}$$

For fixed n, the baker transformation is a mapping of CA rule space for rules with neighborhoods of size $k \leq n$. Since this space is finite, there must be cycles. The matrix b used here is a form of the index projection defined in [6]. There it is proved that for odd n the lengths of all cycles of this projection (and hence, of b) have periods that divide $\text{ord}_n 2$. The actual cycle structure for b with n odd is determined by the solutions of the homogeneous equation $(I - b) \cdot \vec{a} = 0$. For example, for n = 7 this yields the conditions ($a_1 = a_4 = a_2$) and ($a_3 = a_5 = a_6$) with a_0 free. Taking the possible values for these conditions yields eight fixed points: 0000000, 0110100, 0001011, 0111111, 1000000, 1110100, 1001011, and 1111111. In addition, $\text{ord}_7 2 = 3$ and the two period three cycles are ($a_1 \rightarrow a_4 \rightarrow a_2 \rightarrow a_1$) and ($a_3 \rightarrow a_5 \rightarrow a_6 \rightarrow a_3$). Since for additive rules $BX = X^2$ the corresponding well-known result [1,7] is that the cycle periods of an additive rule on a cylinder of size n must divide $2^{\text{ord}_n 2} - 1$.

Acknowledgements

This paper has benefited from a number of comments and suggestions made by Valeriy Bulitko. It was supported by NSERC Discovery Grant OGP 0024871 and by grants from the Athabasca University Research Committee.

References

1. Bulitko, V, Voorhees, B., & Bulitko, V. (2006) Discrete baker transformation for linear cellular automata analysis. Journal of Cellular Automata 1(1) (to appear).
2. Jen, E. (1988) Cylindrical cellular automata. Communications in Mathematical Physics 118 569 – 590.
3. Voorhees, B. (1995) Computational Analysis of One Dimensional Cellular Automata Singapore: World Scientific.
4. Golomb, Solomon W. (1967) Shift Register Sequences San Francisco: Holden-Day.
5. Ralston, A. (1982) De Bruijn sequences—a model example of the interaction of discrete mathematics and computer science. Mathematics Magazine 55 131 – 143.
6. Bulitko, V. (2004) Discrete baker transformation and estimation of heights and cycle lengths for additive cellular automata. (unpublished manuscript)
7. Martin, O., Odlyzko, A.M., & Wolfram, S. (1984) Algebraic properties of cellular automata. Communications in Mathematical Physics 93 219 – 258.

CA Models of Myxobacteria Swarming

Yilin Wu[1], Nan Chen[1], Matthew Rissler[1], Yi Jiang[2], Dale Kaiser[3], and Mark Alber[1]

[1] Department of Mathematics and Center for the Study of Biocomplexity,
University of Notre Dame, Notre Dame, IN 46556-5670
{Yilin.Wu.34, NAN.Chen.93, Matthew.Rissler.4, malber}@nd.edu
[2] Theoretical Division, Los Alamos National Laboratory, Los Alamos, NM 87545
jiang@lanl.gov
[3] Department of Biochemistry, Stanford University, Stanford, CA 94305
kaiser@pmgm2.stanford.edu

Abstract. We develop two models for Myxobacteria swarming, a modified Lattice Gas Cellular Automata (LGCA) model and an off-lattice CA model. In the LGCA model each cell is represented by one node for the center of mass and an extended rod-shaped cell profile. Cells check the surrounding area and choose in which direction to move based on the local interactions. Using this model, we obtained a density vs. expansion rate curve with the shape similar to the experimental curve for the wild type Myxobacteria. In the off-lattice model, each cell is represented by a string of nodes. Cells can bend and move freely in the two-dimensional space. We use a phenomenological algorithm to determine the moving direction of cells guided by slime trail; the model allows for cell bending and alignment during collisions. In the swarming simulations for A+S-Myxobacteria, we demonstrate the formation of peninsula structures, in agreement with experiments.

Keywords: probabilistic cellular automata, lattice and off-lattice models, bacteria swarming, slime guidance, pattern formation.

1 Introduction

Myxobacteria (Myxococcus xanthus) are social bacteria that live in the soil; they exhibit complex multi-cellular behavior and provide many useful insights to multicellular morphogenesis. They are rod shaped with an aspect ratio of roughly 10:1. When growing on a solid medium with sufficient nutrient, Myxobacterial cells grow as a swarm that spreads outwards from the origin, forming rafts and group of cells that project from the edge of the swarm (peninsula structures) [1] (see Figure 1). When nutrient is depleted, the starved Myxobacteria stop growing and build fruiting bodies [2, 3].

Myxobacteria moves by gliding on surfaces, it cannot swim in liquid [4]. It has two types of motility, S(social)-motility and A(adventurous)-motility that are driven by different engines. S-motility is due to pilus extension from the front end of the cell, attachment of the pilus tip to a group of cells ahead, and pilus retraction, drawing the cell up to the leading group [4]. A-motility is due to secretion of polysaccharide slime from the rear of the cell. The hydration-driven swelling of the slime gel is suggested

S. El Yacoubi, B. Chopard, and S. Bandini (Eds.): ACRI 2006, LNCS 4173, pp. 192 – 203, 2006.

to generate the propulsive force for A-motility [5]. A+S- mutants of Myxobacteria have only A-motility but no S-motility , while those with S-motility but no A-motility are called A-S+ mutants [1]. Individual Myxobacteria cells reverse their gliding direction roughly once every 10 min, and the mglA mutants which are unable to reverse normally are unable to swarm [2, 4, 12].

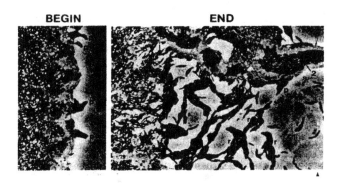

Fig. 1. The swarming patterns of wild-type A+S+ Myxobacteria (Picture taken from [1], by Kaiser, D. and C. Crosby (1983)). On the upper-left part of the END picture, a large peninsula projected outwards from the colony edge. There were also smaller peninsulas and rafts of cells.

Isolated cells move along their long axis and may bend slightly [1, 2]. When a cell is less than a pilus length from other cells, S-motility can be active because the pili can reach groups of other cells that are ahead [2]. As the cells move, they leave a slime trail behind which pushes the cells forward (A-motility). Experimental observations showed that when cells meet a slime trail, they tend to turn at the acute angles to follow the trail [8].

Swarming of Myxobacteria has been modeled using a continuous model with partial differential equations (PDE) [9], which treats the radial swarming pattern expansion as a one-dimensional problem and assumes a rate at which peninsulas merge.

In this paper, we first present a modified two-dimensional LGCA model, and investigate the expansion rate as well as the peninsula formation in wild type Myxobacteria during swarming. We then present an off-lattice model, which is the first computational model based on slime guidance for cells and motility engine reversal. We describe preliminary simulations for the swarming of A+S- Myxobacteria, which successfully reproduce the peninsula pattern.

2 Lattice Gas Cellular Automata (LGCA) Model

2.1 Description

Unlike classical LGCA [10], in our model each cell is not simply a point particle, it has an extended domain (profile) that encompasses several lattice sites. (Notice that the extended profiles have been used previously, amongst others, for modeling collective cell movement in *Dictyostelium discoideum* [11].) Each cell is defined by the position of its center of mass on the two dimensional hexagonal lattice, direction of movement (when it is moving), its length and the extent of its bending. From these five state variables we determine the extended domain (profile) of the cell. Cell direction is updated using a Monte Carlo algorithm.

Three representative cells and the surrounding search area of one of the cells are displayed in Figure 2. Each cell has a length of 7 sites and a width of 1 site. The sites of the cell are indexed from the back of the cell to the front of the cell. The center of mass of the cell is always at half of the cell length. The dark grey spot is the center of mass, and the black ones are the rest of the body of the cell. The shaded spots are to show the search area for S-motility. The length of the cell changes as the cell absorbs a diffusing nutrient until it reaches a maximum value. Then the cell divides into two equal halfs.

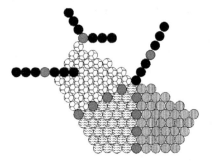

Fig. 2. Three representative cells and the surrounding search area of one of the cells. The three cells are represented by the groups of black circles with the center of mass node in light gray. The three areas below the cell on the right represent the search areas for the S-motility algorithm. The four sites that are shaded dark between two searching areas belong to both areas.

Cells choose which direction to turn at each time step based on three components, slime, S-motility, and physical contact with other cells. Cells tend to align with the direction of previous cells that have passed and deposited slime. S-motility is pili driven, and we model it by favoring cells to be pulled towards areas of higher local cell density. Physical contact accounts for side-to-side alignment due to adhesion, deflections by collisions with other cells, and physical obstacles to turning caused by nearby cells.

We assign a weight, α_i to each effect listed above. For each cell we collect data pertaining each of them, $f_i^{\,j}(x)$, where x is the current system state and $f_i^{\,j}$ is the function describing the strength of an effect in the jth direction. The detailed explanations for $f_i^{\,j}$ are listed in Table 1.

Table 1. The local information collected to model each effect for determining cell turning and bending

	Effect modeled	Data collected
f_1	A- motility	The amount of slime deposited on the three lines passing through the center of mass of the cell.
f_2	S- motility	The number of occupied sites in each of the three regions of Illustration 1.
f_3	Cell-Cell alignment	The number of sites that will contain a parallel cell beside this cell if it turns in this direction.
f_4	Collisions	The number of cells one lattice site in front of the current cell that are not aligned with this cell
f_5	Crowding	The negative of the number of occupied lattice sites that are in the triangle formed between the current cell and the cell if it turns this direction.

The cell is only allowed to bend 60° to the left or right. After these function values are collected we assign each of the possible outcomes a probability $P(j)$ calculated as follows:

$$P(j) = \frac{\sum_{i=1}^{5} e^{\frac{\alpha_i f_i^j(x)}{\beta}}}{Z}, \text{ where } Z = \sum_{j=1}^{3} \sum_{i=1}^{5} e^{\frac{\alpha_i f_i^j(x)}{\beta}}$$

This choice of probability function provides a good separation of similar states, with β corresponding to the amount of separation. The new direction for the cell is determined by this probability. To model motility mutants, A⁺S⁻ and A⁻S⁺, we set $\alpha_2 = 0$ and $\alpha_1 = 0$ respectively.

A cell moves one step forward and straightens as long as this does not cause it to overrun another cell, otherwise it stalls, and stays bent. All cells turn or bend simultaneously, so collisions that involve two cells moving into an unoccupied space are not prevented. After that all cells move simultaneously. After movement, cells can grow, deposit slime, or reverse with a preset period. The time step and lattice spacing are matched to produce the appropriate velocity for the motilities of the cells.

2.2 Simulation Results

We simulated circular colonies of A+S+ wild type Myxobacteria of initial radius 60 μm and varying initial densities. We first calculate the radial distribution function of cell density for the entire colony. Then define the edge of the colony by a cell density threshold of the distribution. The rate of expansion was then calculated from the linear fit for the distance to the colony edge versus time.

The expansion rates from simulations were plotted against the initial density of the colony, the plot was fit by this function:

$$f(x) = A + B\left(1 - \exp\left(\frac{x}{C}\right)\right)$$

where x is the initial density, as in [1]. From simulation data, a fit of A=-0.1±0, B=0.5±0.2, C=50±20 was found for wild-type cells. In the experiment with an initial radius of 1.5 mm [1], the fit of the same form for wild type cells was A=0.1, B=1.48, C=48±6, with A+B=1.58±0.06. While the length scale between the simulation and experiment differ by 3 orders of magnitude, the expansion rate was constant over two orders of magnitude for the simulation.

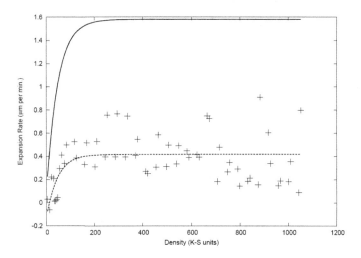

Fig. 3. Density (X-axis,) vs. Growth Rate (Y-axis,) curves for experiment (upper) and simulation (lower). The density is in Klett-Summerson unit [1], and the growth rate is in unit of microns per minute. The exes are simulation results.

Figure 4 shows the peninsulas that formed from an initial smooth colony edge. The peninsulas appear mostly in the areas of the initial circle of cells where the radius aligned with a direction of the lattice. This agrees with experimental observation that cells are initially aligned perpendicularly to the colony boundary.

Fig. 4. The initial condition and a representative snapshot of a myxobacteria colony after 300 time steps. The snapshot demonstrates peninsulas that curve and merge, as well as rafts of cells. Five peninsulas exist in this snapshot.

From our simulations, we find that the exponent, C, in the expansion function agrees with experimental measurements within error; we also observe the peninsulas forming.   But the overall expansion rate is much lower than the experimental measurements. This is due to several artifacts in our model.   The first is that peninsulas form mostly at the corners of a hexagon centered at the center of the colony, since this is the only point on the boundary where a direction normal to the boundary is allowed. If a cell attempts to leave the colony at another point, the local rules for S-motility turn it back into the colony, since pili are modeled to prefer areas of higher cell density.   This S-motility effect also causes a negative expansion rate at low densities. Secondly, due to the rigidity of the cells, cells collide with each other and cannot easily free themselves from the current configurations.   Therefore in the high density area in the initial colony, cells become entrapped and can not move. We overcome these difficulties by introducing an off-lattice model, which is described in the next section.

3   Off-Lattice Model

3.1   Modeling Individual Cell

To incorporate into the model the elastic properties of the Myxobacteria cell body as described in [12], we adopt an off-lattice cell representation to allow for more flexible cell shape and mechanical properties [13]. An individual cell's configuration is represented by a string of N nodes (Figure 5) which can occupy any positions in two-dimensional space. The first node is called the head-node, and the N-th node is called the end node. The vector pointing in the direction from the end-node to the head-node determines the cell's orientation. There are (N-1) segments of length r each between every two neighboring nodes. There are also (N-2) angles θ between every two neighboring segments. We define the Hamiltonian for an individual cell (see Figure 5) as follows:

$$H = E_{stretching} + E_{bending}$$

Stretching and bending energies are defined as a quadratic function of segment length r between nodes and the angles θ between two segments respectively, i.e. we approximate the cell body as having simple elastic stretching and bending energies:

$$E_{stretching} = \sum_{i=0}^{N-1} K_b (r_i - r_0)^2, \qquad E_{bending} = \sum_{i=0}^{N-2} K_\theta \theta_i^2$$

Here K_b and K_θ are parameters analogous to the spring constants in Hooke's Law; they determine the extent to which the segment lengths and angles can change in the presence of external forces, respectively. They are the same for all segments and angles. r_0 is the target length of the segment.

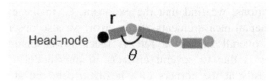

Fig. 5. A cell body of Myxobacteria is represented by N=4 nodes. The black solid dot is the head-node. The length to width ratio of the cell is 10:1.

The relative positions of nodes can change during the configuration updates in our algorithm, so the cell body is flexible.

The Monte Carlo approach is used for configuring the position of the nodes at every time step. We first move the head-node to a new position, denoting the magnitude of the displacement as Δx, and then repeat the following steps for a sufficient number of times (we choose this number as 2.5N): 1. Randomly choose a node within the same cell, for instance, node i, and move it in the direction from node i to node $(i-1)$ for a distance of Δx, with a small random fluctuation; 2. Calculate the energy change ΔE due to the relative position change of the nodes; 3. Use the Metropolis algorithm [14] to determine the acceptance probability for the positional change of a node:

$$P(\Delta E) = 1, \Delta E \leq 0;$$
$$P(\Delta E) = e^{-\Delta E / kT}, \Delta E > 0$$

Here k is a Boltzmann constant; T is a parameter that characterizes the system's tendency to statistically fluctuate from the equilibrium. The cells in the model can bend elastically due to the random fluctuation during the updating of nodes configurations while keeping their lengths within certain range.

3.2 Modeling Cell Motion

In our off-lattice model, cells are allowed to move freely in any direction in the two-dimensional space. This is a significant improvement compared to the lattice models where cells move on a fixed lattice.

Biologically, wild type A+S+ Myxobacteria cells move by using pulling force from pili retraction at the head and pushing force from slime secretion at the end. We focus on the global motion of a large number of cells during swarming instead of studying details of motility mechanisms of an individual cell. Therefore, we model the cell's effective motion by using simplified assumption about the motion of a cell being led by the head. That is, the head of a cell pulls the whole cell body to move forward. We distinguish cells with different types of motility through a variable magnitude of the head velocity. In this preliminary model, we only include the A-motility and fix the magnitude of the head velocity at about 4 microns per minute.

In experiment, an isolated cell moves along the direction of its long axis and keeps roughly straight. When meeting a slime trail, cells tend to turn at the acute angles to follow the trail [8]. When cell density is high, as they are at the colony's edge at early stage of Myxobacteria swarming, cells are packed layer by layer, and they can move on top of other cells. In this case, there will be a lot of intersecting slime trails and cells may not follow a particular slime trail. On the other hand, collisions between cells are more important than cell-slime interactions at high cell densities. For these reasons, we define a searching circle centered at the head node of each cell (Figure 6), and define a local slime field density $D(s)$ for each cell as the total area covered by slime within the divided by the area of searching circle (Figure 6):

$$D(s) = \frac{(\text{area covered by slime})}{(\text{area of searching circle})}$$

We then let the cell follow a particular slime trail only if the slime field density is below a certain threshold. Because the width of a slime trail is close to cell-width, while the radius of searching circle is defined to be about half of a cell-length, then the slime field density for a searching circle with single slime trail will be:

$$\frac{2 \cdot (\text{radius of searching circle}) \cdot (\text{width of slime trail})}{\pi \cdot (\text{radius of searching circle})^2} \approx \frac{4 \cdot (\text{cell-width})}{\pi \cdot (\text{cell-length})}$$

A typical cell's width-to-length ratio is 1:10, so we choose the threshold of slime field density to be 0.2, which corresponds to only a few slime trails in the simulation domain.

Based on experimental observations of cell motion, we develop a phenomenological algorithm to determine the direction of head node velocity, which we call the head-sensing slime guidance algorithm (see Figure 6):

(1) Search the circlar area ahead of the cell for slime trail and calculate the local slime field density $D(s)$;
(2) If no slime trail is found, or if $D(s)>0.2$, choose the cell orientation as head velocity direction and go to step (6) (The cell's orientation is defined by the vector pointing in the direction from end to head). If $D(s) \leqslant 0.2$, go to next step;
(3) Approximate the direction of the slime trail as a line segment (from point A to B);
(4) Transform the coordinate of point A and B from XOY to the cell's local coordinate system (X'O'Y');
(5) If Y' of one point is less than that of the other one, for instance, Y'(A) < Y'(B), then choose the new direction as O'→B because cells tend to turn at the acute angles to follow slime trails; if the new direction opposes the cell direction and thus may reduce the cell length, choose the new direction as A→B. In the case of Y'(B) < Y'(A), simply change O'→B (or A→B) to be O'→A (or B→A).
(6) Tentatively advance the cell using the head velocity obtained through the above procedures. If it collides with another cell, choose the collided cell's orientation as the new head-velocity direction, so that cells can align with each other when collision happens.

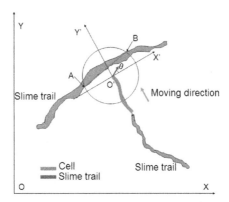

Fig. 6. A schematic description of head-sensing slime guidance for Myxobacteria cells. The orange lines represent a part of cell body, which meets with a slime trail. The head of the cell is defined as O' point, the origin of the cell's local coordinate system X'O'Y'. The cell orientation is along the direction of O'Y'. The cell will turn to a new direction at an angle θ with O'X' axis when it meets the slime trail.

In our simulation, cells move at most 0.8 micron every time step, so 5 simulation time steps correspond to one minute of real time. At each time step, we do the following for each cell in the order of numbering of cells: First, find out the moving direction for its head node by the head-sensing slime guidance algorithm. If no collision happens in the direction, move the head node for a distance of 0.8 microns; otherwise the cell stalls and waits until next time step for a new moving direction. Next, apply the Monte Carlo algorithm described in section 3.1 to re-configure the positions of the rest nodes. Besides, cells reverse polarity every 50 time steps. We also include cell divisions. Typically cells divide after more than 10 times reversals [6]. The division rate is set in such a way that the total number of cells approximately doubles after about 3 hours, which is the typical duoubling time of the swarming stage.

3.3 Simulation Results

We first run simulations to demonstrate the head-sensing slime guidance algorithm for cells. As shown in Figure 7(a-d), the cells could efficiently orient along slime trails. Initially 10 cells were randomly distributed in space. The black dots and lines represent slime (cells are not shown in the figure).

In swarming experiments, tens of thousands of cells form a solid wall at the edge of a circle with a radius of about 1.5 mm [1]. Due to the computation limit, we first look at a small curved section which is 167 microns in length and 17 microns in width. The length is about 1/60 of the perimeter of circle. Because the length of the section is much smaller than the radius of circle, the small section can be approximated as a rectangular area. We use a 1000×1000 square as the simulation domain as shown in Figure 8, and the rectangular area is indicated as "Initial Area of Cells". 1000 units of length are equivalent to 167 microns, so 6 units of length are equivalent to 1 micron. We distribute 1111 cells randomly in the rectangular area,

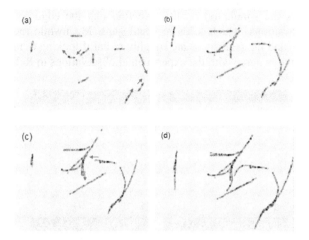

Fig. 7. (a) At 10 time steps, cells have not yet interacted with the slime trails deposited by other cells. The red arrows indicate directions of moving cells (cells are not shown in the figure). (b) At 25 time steps, some cells begin to follow the existing slime trails in the arrow-indicated areas. (c, d) At 40 and 55 time steps, more cells have been following and gliding on slime trails. The cell on the left does not meet any slime trail deposited by other cells, so it keeps gliding and reversing on its own slime trail.

which corresponds to the case of close-packing of cells, because the average area occupied by one cell is 2.5 square-microns, the same as the area of one cell body. The sides a and c in Figure 8 are set to be periodic boundaries, and the upper side of "Initial Area of Cells" acts as a reflecting boundary, that is, when a cell crosses the boundary upwards, it will disappear, while another cell will emerge and cross the boundary downwards. The reason of doing this is that we only simulate a small section of the edge of cell colony, and the cell population in simulation region should keep roughly the same if not considering cell division.

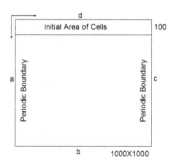

Fig. 8. The simulation region is a 1000×1000 square. Cells are initially distributed in the "Initial Area of Cells" as indicated. Sides a and c are periodic boundaries, while side d acts as a reflecting boundary.

Figure 9 shows the simulation results. We find that the edge solid with cells is broken in some positions, which leads to small gaps. Meanwhile raft and peninsula structures emerge, and the peninsulas are roughly radial if looking at the whole colony circle. These behaviors agree with the experimental observations in Reference [1].

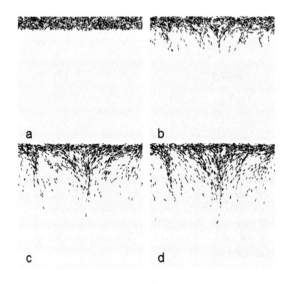

Fig. 9. (a). Initially 1111 cells are randomly distributed in a rectangle area 167 microns in length and 17 microns in width. (b) At 20 minutes, some cells start to move outwards the edge and some small peninsulas form. (c) At 60 minutes and 80 minutes, gaps appear on the initial edge and larger peninsula structures form by merging of smaller ones. The peninsulas point downwards, corresponding to pointing outwards in radial direction if looking at the whole colony circle. The peninsulas are similar to the structures shown in the experimental Figure 1 (END picture).

4   Discussion

Both the modified LGCA model and the off-lattice model presented in this paper can simulate the peninsula formation during Myxobacteria swarming. We have also used modified LGCA model to obtain a quantitative result of the relationship between expansion rate and initial density with the exponential coefficient being within experimental error. However, several artifacts in the LGCA model became apparent while running simulations. The primary one is that a perpendicular direction for peninsula formation only occurred in a few points on the perimeter of the colony. The advantage of this model is that it can model up to tens of thousands of cells, and does produce initial patterns similar to that of experiment.

The off-lattice representation for cells does not have geometric constraints. It allows for bending at small angles and stretching, and incorporates easily a detailed mechanism for slime guidance. Therefore, we expect that the off-lattice model can provide more accurate results for swarming stage. With the off-lattice approach, we plan to model in detail the quantitative properties of the swarming process, such as the expansion rate and the peninsula dynamics. We are also currently developing parallel algorithms to overcome the computational limitations of this approach.

Acknowledgments. This work was partially supported by NSF Grant No. IBN-0083653 and NIH Grant No. 1R0-GM076692-01: Interagency Opportunities in Multiscale Modeling in Biomedical, Biological and Behavioral Systems NSF 04.6071, and partially supported by US DOE contract number W-7405-ENG-36. Simulations were performed on the Notre Dame Biocomplexity Cluster supported in part by NSF MRI Grant No. DBI-0420980.

References

1. Kaiser, D. and Crosby, C.: Cell movement and its coordination in swarms of Myxococcus xanthus. Cell Motility **3** (1983) 227-245
2. Kaiser, D.: Coupling Cell Movement to Multicellular Development in Myxobacteria. Nature Reviews Microbiology **1** (2003) 45-54
3. Sozinova, O., Jiang, Y., Kaiser, D., Alber, M.: A three-dimensional model of myxobacterial aggregation by contact-mediated interactions. Proc. Natl. Acad. Sci. U.S.A. **102** (2005) 11308-11312
4. Hodgkin, J. & Kaiser, D.: Genetics of gliding motility in M. xanthus (Myxobacterales): two gene systems control movement. Mol. Gen. Genet. **171** (1979) 177-191
5. Wolgemuth, C., Hoiczyk, E, Kaiser, D., Oster G.: How Myxobacteria Glide. Curr. Biol. **12** (2002)369-377
6. Kaiser, D., and Yu, R.: Reversing cell polarity: evidence and hypothesis. Cur. Opin. Microbiol. **8** (2005) 216-221
7. Kaiser, D. Signaling in Myxobacteria. Annu. Rev. Microbiol. **58** (2004) 75-98
8. Burchard, R. P.: Trail following by gliding bacteria. J. Bacteriol. **152** (1982) 495-501
9. Gallegos, A., Mazzag, B., Mogilner, A.: Mathematical analysis of the swarming behavior of myxobacteria. Bulletin of Mathematical Biology (In Print)
10. Hardy, J., Pazzis, O., Pomeau, Y.: Molecular dynamics of a classical lattice gas: Transport properties and time correlation functions. Phys. Rev. A **13** (1976) 1949-1961
11. Palsson, E., Othmer, H. G.: A model for individual and collective cell movement in Dictyostelium discoideum. Proc. Natl. Acad. Sci. USA. **97** (2000) 10448–10453
12. Spormann, A. M., Kaiser, D.: Gliding movements in Myxococcus xanthus. J. Bacteriol. **177** (1995) 5846–5852
13. Newman, T. J.: Modeling Multicellular systems using subcellular elements. Mathematical Biosciences and Engineering **2** (2005) 611-622
14. Newman, M. E. J., Barkema, G. T.: Monte Carlo Methods in Statistical Physics. Clarendon Press, Oxford (1999)

A Cellular Automata Based Approach for Generation of Large Primitive Polynomial and Its Application to RS-Coded MPSK Modulation

Debojyoti Bhattacharya[1], Debdeep Mukhopadhyay[2], and D. RoyChowdhury[3]

[1] IIT-Kharagpur, Kharagpur, India
deba@vlsi.iitkgp.ernet.in
[2] IIT-Kharagpur, Kharagpur, India
debdeep@vlsi.iitkgp.ernet.in
[3] IIT-Kharagpur, Kharagpur, India
drc@iitkgp.ac.in

Abstract. Generation of large primitive polynomial over a Galois field has been a topic of intense research over the years. The problem of finding a primitive polynomial over a Galois field of a large degree is computationaly expensive and there is no deterministic algorithm for the same. In this paper we present an new recursive algorithm based on cellular automata for generation of very large primitive polynomial over finite fields. The motivation for cellular automata based construction comes into play as it has an excellent regular structure and efficient hardware representation. At the end we give an application of this new construction in a RS-encoded MPSK Modulation in Rayleigh fading channel. But the general construction given here can be extended to any area like cryptography, coding theory etc. having application of sufficiently large Galois field.

Keywords: Cellular Automata, Galois field, Primitive polynomial, MPSK Modulation, RS-encoding.

1 Introduction

Over the years Galois field has found its application in many areas such as number theory, algebraic geometry, coding theory, cryptography, polynomial equations, computational biology etc [1,2]. A Galois field is completely characterized by its primitive polynomial. A polynomial $p(x)$ of degree m over the finite field $GF(q)$ is primitive if it is irreducible (having no non-trivial factor) and the smallest positive integer n for which $p(x)$ divides $x^n - 1$ is $n = q^m - 1$. One can generate every field $GF(q^m)$ using a primitive polynomial over $GF(q)$, and the arithmetic performed in the $GF(q^m)$ field is modulo this primitive polynomial [1]. However, for several years it has been a problem to generate large primitive polynomial of a given degree over a Galois field. In the present work we have explored construction of primitive polynomial over large Galois field of the form $GF(2^m)$. A novel Cellular Automata (CA) based construction methodology has

S. El Yacoubi, B. Chopard, and S. Bandini (Eds.): ACRI 2006, LNCS 4173, pp. 204–214, 2006.

been presented which generates primitive polynomials over fields like $GF(2^m)$, where m is in the form of $m = 2^p n$. The motivation behind using CA is its excellent correspondence with Galois field [3]. We have used 3-neighbourhood linear CA, which also reduces the interconnects of our design. This linear CA represents a linear finite state machine [4] which is characterized by the characteristics polynomial of its state transition matrix. The characteristics polynomial of an n-cell maximum length CA is a primitive polynomial of degree n over $GF(2)$. Hence a maximum length cellular automata structure can be employed to represent primitive polynomial over a given Galois field. In this work we show how maximum length CA of a base field $GF(2^n)$ can be combined to generate a maximum length CA of a higher field $GF((2^n)^2)$ and so on. The characteristics polynomial of the composed CA is the primitive polynomial of the higher field and the CA structure can generate all the elements in the field. This algorithm can find applications in several areas where Galois field of very high order is needed. We present such an example application of the above construction in Reed-Solomon coded MPSK modulation scheme in Rayleigh fading channel.

The rest of the paper is organized as follows. In section 2: we give a brief description of basic cellular automata theory, section 3 explores novel and generic CA based primitive polynomial generation algorithm of large Galois field. Section 4 describes basic of RS-coded MPSK modulation scheme in rayleigh fading channel. Section 5 discusses the application of our proposed hardware and a brief comparative analysis. Section 6 concludes our paper.

2   Cellular Automata Theory and Galois Field

A Cellular Automata (CA) consists of a number of cells arranged in a regular manner, where the state transition of each cell depends on the states its neighbors. For a three neighborhood CA the state q of the ith cell at time $(t+1)$ is given as $q_i^{t+1} = g(q_{i-1}^t, q_i^t, q_{i+1}^t)$ where g is the *rule* of the automata [5]. As g is a three variant function, it can have 2^8 or 256 outputs. The decimal equivalent of the output column in the truth table of g denotes the rule number. The next state function of Rule 90 and Rule 150 are given below :

Rule 90 : $q_i^{t+1} = q_{i-1}^t \oplus q_{i+1}^t$ and **Rule** 150 : $q_i^{t+1} = q_{i-1}^t \oplus q_i^t \oplus q_{i+1}^t$
The CA preliminaries where the CA is in $GF(2)$ are noted in [6]. For an n-cell one dimensional CA, the linear operator can be shown to be an $n \times n$ matrix [6], whose i-th row corresponds to the neighborhood relation of the i-th cell. The next state of the CA is generated by applying the linear operator on the present state. The operation is simple matrix multiplication, but the addition involved is modulo-2 sum. The matrix is termed as the characteristics matrix of the CA and is denoted by T. If f_t represents the state of the automata at t^{th} instant of time, then the next state, i.e., the state at $(t+1)^{th}$ instant of time, is given by $f_{t+1} = T * f_t$. If for a CA all states in a state transition graph lies in some cycle, it is called a group CA; otherwise it is a non-group CA. It has been shown in [6] that for a group CA its T matrix is non-singular, i.e., $det[T] = 1$ ($det[T]$ = determinant of T). An n-cell CA can be characterized by a $n \times n$ **characteristics matrix** T as follows :

$$T[i, j] = 1 (\text{if next state of i-th cell}$$
$$\text{depends on the present state of j-th cell})$$
$$= 0 (\text{otherwise})$$

The associated characteristics polynomial $(p(x))$ can be obtained as determinant $det([T] + x[I])$. If the characteristics polynomial of an n-cell group CA (for which $detT = 1$) is primitive, then a repetitive application of the linear operator T generates a cycle of length $(2^n - 1)$ with all non-zero states [6]. This CA is called maximum length group CA. It has been noted that a spatial combination of rule 90 and rule 150 generates a maximum length group CA which ensures that some combination of these two rules can generate all the non-zero elements of a Galois field of order n. For an n-cell maximum length group CA, if T is its characteristics matrix, $T^{2^n - 1} = I$(identity matrix).

A 2-cell null boundary hybrid CA over $GF(2)$ with rule vector $< 150, 90 >$ is given in (Fig 1) [6]. This CA can also be regarded as a 1-cell CA over $GF(2^2)$. This 2-cell CA can be characterized by the following characteristics matrix :

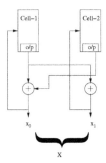

Fig. 1. 2-cell CA with rule vector $\langle 150, 90 \rangle$

$$T = \begin{pmatrix} 1 & 1 \\ 1 & 0 \end{pmatrix}$$

Characteristics polynomial of the matrix is $m(x) = x^2 + x + 1$ which is a primitive polynomial over $GF(2^2)$. The element $X = (X_0, X_1) \in GF(2^2)$. If the characteristics polynomial of a CA is primitive over $GF(2^n)$, then repeated application of the transformation matrix T generates all the non-zero states of that field [6]. T can be termed as *primitive matrix* as repeated application of this matrix generates all states repesenting the field. The corresponding CA rule can be termed as *primitive rule*.

3   CA Based Approach to Generate Primitive Polynomial for Large Galois Field

The current section focusses on a hierarchical construction of composite Galois field using the theory of cellular automata. An n-bit maximum length CA is characterised by a primitive polynomial of degree n over $GF(2)$. This is an n-cell CA over $GF(2)$, where each cell is of 1-bit. This can be visualised as a 1-cell CA over $GF(2^n)$ where the characteristics polynomial is a primitive polynomial over $GF(2^n)$. In our construction we will use this 1-cell CA as basic building block. Primitive rules can be applied on this basic cell to generate primitive polynomial of higher order Galois field. Combining two basic cells one can generate primitive polynomial over $GF((2^n)^2)$ (isomorphic to $GF(2^{2n})$), which will serve as the basic cell for the next stage. Combining two basic cells of order $2n$ one can generate primitive polynomial for Galois field of order $4n$ and so on. We have applied this construction recursively to generate primitive polynomial of large Galois field. The field generated will be of the form of $GF((((2^n)^2)\cdots)^2)$, which is isomorphic to $GF(2^m)$, where $m = 2^p n$.

To explain the theory behind this hierarchical construction we first develop some background results.

Definition 1. *[7] Given a binary primitive polynomial $g(x)$ of degree b, the companion matrix A corresponding to $g(x)$ is defined as the following $b \times b$ non-singular matrix.*

$$A = \begin{bmatrix} 0 & \cdots & 0 & g_0 \\ & \cdots & & g_1 \\ \vdots & I_{b-1} & \vdots & \vdots \\ & \cdots & & g_{b-1} \end{bmatrix} \tag{1}$$

$g(x) = \sum_{i=0}^{b} g_i \cdot x^i, g_0 = g_1 = 1,\ I_{b-1} : (b-1) \times (b-1)$ *identity matrix.*

The set of powered elements of A including zero element, i.e., $0, A, A^2, A^3, \ldots,$ $A^{q-1} = I$, where I is an identity element, makes Galois field of $q = 2^b$ elements, i.e., $GF(q = 2^b)$. As all the elements can be represented as different powers of A, matrix A can be thought of as a primitive element of the field.

Theorem 1. *If T represents a primitive element of $GF(2^n)$ then any power of T, e.g. $T^q = T_1$ represents another primitive element of that field if $gcd(q, 2^n - 1) = 1$.*

Proof. Since, T is a primitive element $T^{2^n-1} = I$ and $T^q = T_1$ (as given). Now $T_1, T_1^2, T_1^3, \ldots T_1^{2^n-1}$ represents $T^q, T^{2q}, T^{3q}, \ldots, T^{(2^n-1)q}$ respectively. As $gcd(q, 2^n - 1) = 1, T^q, T^{2q}, T^{3q}, \ldots, T^{(2^n-1)q}$ all are distinct elements. $\therefore T^q = T_1$ has order $2^n - 1$, which implies T^q is another primitive elements.

Theorem 2. *[8] Two matrices A and B represent the same linear operator T if, and only if, they are similiar to each other .*

Theorem 3. *[8] Similiar matrices have the same characteristics polynomial .*

Theorem 4. *[9] If two matrices A and A' are similiar nonsingular state-transition matrices, then their state graphs have identical cycle structures and differ only in the labeling of the states .*

Theorem 5. *If T be the state transition matrix of a maximum length n-cell CA, then the set of powered elements of T including zero element, i.e., $0, T, \ldots, T^{2^n-1} = I$, where I is an identity element, makes Galois field of 2^n elements, i.e., $GF(2^n)$.*

Proof. Let A denotes the companion matrix of a binary primitive polynomial $g(x)$ over $GF(2^n)$ and T denotes the state transition matrix of a maximum length n-cell CA, whose characteristics poynomial is $g(x)$. As per theorem 2 and 3, A and T are similiar matrices and represent the same linear operator. A and T have identical cyclic structures and differ only in the labeling of the states as per theorem 4. Therefore set of powers of T and A has one-to-one correspondence. Now the set of powers of matrix A including zero element makes Galois field of 2^n elements (theorem 1) which implies that the set of powers of T also makes Galois field of 2^n elements. Matrix T can be thought of as the primitive element of this field.

3.1   Proposed CA Based Approach for Composite Galois Field of the Form $GF((2^n)^2)$

Primitive polynomial of composite Galois field of the form $GF((2^n)^2)$ can be generated using 2-cell CA, where each cell is an n-bit maximum length CA. We state an theorem below for that construction.

Theorem 6. *Composite Galois field of the form $GF((2^n)^2)$ can be formed by applying primitive rule to a 2-cell CA where each basic cell is itself an n-cell CA. Each n-cell CA is configured with a primitive rule. One n-cell CA is being operated for $2^n - 1$ cycles and the other n-cell is being operated for q cycles where $gcd(q, 2^n - 1) = 1$.*

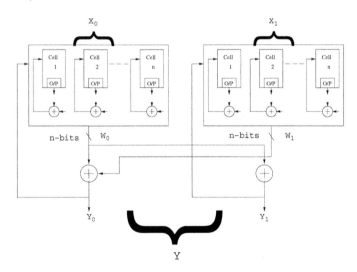

Fig. 2. CA construction for composite galois field of the form $GF((2^n)^2)$

Proof. Let the same rule vector be applied on X_0 and X_1 where both are n-cell CA (Fig 2). The rule is *primitive rule* such that the characteristics polynomial of the CA state-transition matrix is primitive over $GF(2^n)$. Let the characteristics matrix be T. Hence, T is a primitive matrix and a primitive element of $GF(2^n)$. Therefore, $T^{2^n-1} = I$. Let p cycles are applied to X_0 and q cycles are applied to X_1. Therefore W_0 and W_1 can be written as $W_0 = T^p X_0$ and $W_1 = T^q X_1$. Now X_0 and X_1 can be considered as two cells. A rule vector $R = < 150, 90 >$ be applied. The characteristics matrix is :

$$T = \begin{pmatrix} 1 & 1 \\ 1 & 0 \end{pmatrix} \tag{2}$$

Therefore,

$$\begin{pmatrix} Y_0 \\ Y_1 \end{pmatrix} = \begin{pmatrix} 1 & 1 \\ 1 & 0 \end{pmatrix} \begin{pmatrix} T^p X_0 \\ T^q X_1 \end{pmatrix} \tag{3}$$

This can be written as $Y = MX$, where

$$M = \begin{pmatrix} T^p & T^q \\ T^p & 0 \end{pmatrix} \tag{4}$$

Characteristics polynomial of M is

$$m(x) = |M + Ix| = x^2 + T^p x + T^p T^q \tag{5}$$

p can be chosen as $p = 2^n - 1$. Therefore, $m(x) = x^2 + x + T^q = x^2 + x + p_0$ $((p_0 \in GF(2^n)))$. There always exists a primitive polynomial of this form over composite field $GF((2^n)^2)$, where p_0 is a primitive element of the base field [10]. According to Theorem 1 this is true for all q for which $gcd(q, 2^n - 1) = 1$. Hence the element $Y = (Y_0, Y_1) \in GF((2^n)^2)$. Repeated application of matrix M generates all the non-zero elements of $((2^n)^2)$. Moreover the polynomial $m(x)$ is not unique, as it depends on the choice of q., i.e., on the choice of element p_0.

Extension of the proposed construction to generate higher order fields
The construction given above can be used recursively to generate primitive polynomials of higher order fields by using the shown hierarchical CA structure as basic cell and applying the construction in the same way. The CA based construction for generation of $GF(((2^n)^2)^2)$ is shown below (Fig 3) and the proof is given along with it. For higher order extensions, circuit of the subfield is taken as 1 basic cell and 2-cells of the subfield are joined using the same rule vector $R = (150, 90)$. Cycles applied to each cells are p and q, where q is chosen suitably and $p = 2^n - 1$ at sub-cell and $p = 2^{2n} - 1$ at outermost cell. Using the result of the previous section Y_0, Y_1, Y_2, Y_3 can be written as,

$$\begin{pmatrix} Y_0 \\ Y_1 \end{pmatrix} = \begin{pmatrix} 1 & 1 \\ 1 & 0 \end{pmatrix} \begin{pmatrix} T^{2^n-1} X_0 \\ T^q X_1 \end{pmatrix} = \begin{pmatrix} T^{2^n-1} & T^q \\ T^{2^n-1} & 0 \end{pmatrix} \begin{pmatrix} X_0 \\ X_1 \end{pmatrix} \tag{6}$$

$$\begin{pmatrix} Y_2 \\ Y_3 \end{pmatrix} = \begin{pmatrix} 1 & 1 \\ 1 & 0 \end{pmatrix} \begin{pmatrix} T^{2^n-1}X_2 \\ T^q X_3 \end{pmatrix} = \begin{pmatrix} T^{2^n-1} & T^q \\ T^{2^n-1} & 0 \end{pmatrix} \begin{pmatrix} X_2 \\ X_3 \end{pmatrix} \tag{7}$$

$Z_0 = (Y_0, Y_1), Z_1 = (Y_2, Y_3) \in GF((2^n)^2)$ (proved). From Fig. 3, L can be written as

$$\begin{pmatrix} L_0 \\ L_1 \end{pmatrix} = \begin{pmatrix} 1 & 1 \\ 1 & 0 \end{pmatrix} \begin{pmatrix} M^{2^{2n}-1}Z_0 \\ M^q Z_1 \end{pmatrix} = \begin{pmatrix} M^{2^{2n}-1} & M^q \\ M^{2^{2n}-1} & 0 \end{pmatrix} \begin{pmatrix} Z_0 \\ Z_1 \end{pmatrix} \tag{8}$$

or, $L = AZ$ where,

$$A = \begin{pmatrix} M^{2^{2n}-1} & M^q \\ M^{2^{2n}-1} & 0 \end{pmatrix} \tag{9}$$

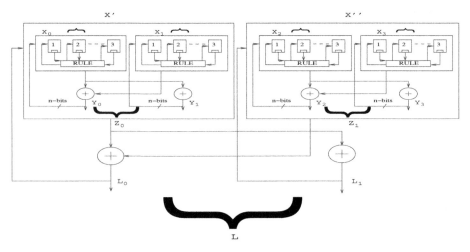

Fig. 3. CA construction for generation of $GF(((2^n)^2)^2)$

Characteristics polynomial of matrix A is given by $a(x) = |A + Ix| = x^2 + M^{2^{2n}-1}x + M^{2^{2n}-1}M^q$. Similiar to the previous construction q is chosen such that $gcd(q, 2^{2n} - 1) = 1$. As $M^{2^{2n}-1} = I$, $a(x)$ is primitive polynomial over $GF(((2^n)^2)^2)$ which can generate the whole field. This concept can be extended infinitely in powers of 2 to generate higher order fields taking the previous sub-fields as basic cell and applying the CA rule and cycles in the same way.

Complexity Analysis : Cell and time complexities of the above construction are given below. We consider a field $GF(2^m)$, where $m = 2^p n$ for some p and n and n is the order of the base block.

Cell complexity

Field	Xor-gates	cells
$GF(2^n)$	n	n
$GF((2^n)^2)$	$2n + 2$	$2n$
$GF(((2^n)^2)^2)$	$2^2n + 2^2 + 2$	2^2n
$GF(((2^n)^{\cdots})^2) = (2^n)^{2^p})$	$2^p n + 2^p + \ldots + 2 = 2^p n + 2^{p+1} - 2$	$2^p n$

Time complexity. In the proposed construction $GF(2^m)$ is based on $GF(2^{m/2})$, as it acts as the basic cell for next stage. The basic cell must go through all the non-zero states, i.e. through $2^{m/2}$ cycles. Hence the time complexity is of the order of $O(2^{m/2})$.

The above CA based algorithm gives an easy and efficient way of generating primitive polynomial of large galois field. This CA based construction can easily be implemented in VLSI circuits as it has a very regular and structural construction which is very suitable for VLSI circuits. The limitation of our methodology is that it can be used for only even ordered field. The method can be used in application areas where large primitive polynomials over even ordered Galois fields are nedded. The following section reports such an application area where the CA based construction of generating large primitive polynomial can be very well suited.

4   RS Coded MPSK Modulation Scheme

In recent years RS-MPSK has been proved to be an attractive scheme for wireless mobile communication systems [11]. Here we put forward a design for the same using our novel cellular automata based field generator.

4.1   RS Coding Scheme

Reed Solomon codes are an important subclass of BCH codes defined over $GF(q)$. It is based on groups of bits, such as bytes, rather than individual 0s and 1s, making it particularly good at dealing with bursts of errors. Thus, even a double-error-correction version of a Reed-Solomon code can provide a comfortable safety factor. A Reed-Solomon code is specified as RS (n, k) with s-bit symbols. This means that the encoder takes k data symbols of s bits each and adds parity symbols to make an n symbol codeword. There are $n - k$ parity symbols of s bits each. A Reed-Solomon decoder can correct up to t symbols that contain errors in a codeword, where $2t = n - k$. More importantly a message for an $[n, k]$ Reed-Solomon code must be a k-column Galois array in the field $GF(2^n)$ [12]. Each array entry must be an integer between 0 and $2^n - 1$. The code corresponding to that message is an n-column Galois array in $GF(2^n)$. The codeword length must be between 3 and $2^n - 1$. A Reed-Solomon codeword is generated using a special generator polynomial. All valid code words are exactly divisible by the generator. The codeword is constructed using $c(x) = g(x).i(x)$, where $g(x)$ is the generator polynomial, $i(x)$ is the information block, $c(x)$ is a valid codeword.

RS-MPSK scheme primarily employs a RS code with large code-length. It couples the RS code defined over $GF(2^{lm})$ with 2^m PSK modulation scheme, where each code symbol is represented by the concatenation of l channel symbols [13]. At high signal to noise ratio (E_b/N_o), the symbol error rate of MPSK signal in Rayleigh fading channel can be written approximately as [14]

$$P_s = 1 - \sqrt{1/(1/x + 1)}, \tag{10}$$

where $x = mR_c sin^2(\pi/2^m)E_b N_o$, m = channel bits, R_c= coding rate
E_b = energy per information bit, N_0 = PSD of noise

From Eq. 10 it is observed that P_s decreases with increasing x. Now, the only varying term in x is $msin^2(\pi/(M = 2^m))$, which increases with m. Hence with the increase in bit-width(m) channel reliability increases. Large sized Galois field is needed in this context.

5   The Proposed Encoder Architecture

In a high gain, low error probability providing RS-MPSK based scheme the code length has to be on the higher side [15]. In our paper we have proposed a cellular automata based novel scheme, which, for any given value n generates all the elements in 2^n Galois field. The proposed architecture consists of a generator polynomial block, a field generator block, an n-bit Xor gate block and a decision control block. The connections are as shown in Fig. 4. The generator polynomial block (a conventional one) generates the codewords. The field generator generates the whole field in composite field form, instead of generating the parity words only. Each codeword from the generator polynomial are compared with the word coming from the field generator block. If the word from generator polynomial block does not match with the word from field generator block then the word from the field generator is a parity word and it is passed to generated code block. The Xor gate and the decision control block is used for this checking purpose. The decision control block is basically a tristate buffer which is controlled by the the output of the Xor gate. It passes the input if the output from Xor gate is 0.

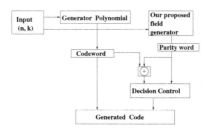

Fig. 4. Proposed architecture

6   Comparison of Complexity

The following diagram shows an architecture for a systematic RS$(255, 249)$ encoder [16]. Each of the six registers carry 8-bits. And the arithmatic operators carry out addition and multiplication operations. In case of a normal Reed-Solomon coding scheme the codeword is generated using the following scheme $C(x) = i(x) * g(x)$ Where $i(x)$ is the input message stream, $g(x)$ is the generator polynomial. The fact that the codeword is generated with the help of a

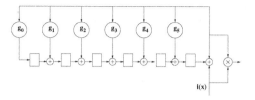

Fig. 5. A RS $(255, 249)$ Encoder

uni-variate multiplier circuit makes the conventional circuit cited in Fig. 5 a complex one. The proposed design is devoid of any conventional multiplier circuit. The CA based core of the architecture directly generates the extensive Galois field elements and the decision maker circuit, generates the parity words using a nominal set of hardware. The $2t$ parity symbols in a systematic Reed-Solomon codeword are given by

$$p(x) = i(x)x^{n-k} mod g(x) \tag{11}$$

Now, for each of power operation and modulo multiplication, we need 2 multipliers and 1 conditional block comprised of a shifter and Xor gate. Thus, for RS$(255, 249)$ with generator polynomial $g(x) = \sum_{m=1}^{6} x^m g_m$ we need 8 multipliers, 1 shifter and 8 Xor gates. In general, for $2t$ parity symbols we need, $2(t+1)$ multipliers, 1 shifter and $2(t+1)$ Xor gates, which increases hardware complexity. Our scheme employs cellular automata which is devoid of any sort of multiplier and comprises of only Xor gates and flipflops. Thereby it reduces the hardware complexity drastically.

7   Conclusion

Generation of large primitive polynomial over Galois field is considered to be a hard problem, as there is no deterministic algorithm for this. The paper proposes a hierarchical methodology to generate primitive polynomials of higher order Galois fields of the form $GF(2^n)$, where n is even. The proposed construction may find several applications in fields like cryptography and communication. We have shown an application of our construction in RS-coded MPSK modulation scheme over Rayleigh fading channel.

References

1. R. Lidl, H.N. In: Introduction to finite fields and their applications. Cambridge University Press (1986)
2. Sanchez, R., Grau, R., Morgado, E.R.: A new dna sequence vector space on a genetic code galois field. MATCH Commun. Math. Comput. Chem. **54** (2005) 3–28

3. Cattell, K., Muzio, J.C.: Analysis of one-dimensional linear hybrid cellular automata over gf(q). IEEE Transactions on Computers **45** (1996) 782–792
4. Sun, X., Kontopidi, E., Serra, M., Muzio, J.C.: The concatenation and partitioning of linear finite state machines. Int. J. Electronics **78** (1995) 809–839
5. S.Wolfram: Statistical Mechanics of Cellular Automata. Rev. Mod. Phys **55** (1983) 601–644
6. Chaudhuri, P.P., RoyChowdhury, D., Nandi, S., Chattopadhyay, S. In: Additive Cellular Automata Theory and its Application. Volume 1. IEEE Computer Society Press (1997)
7. E.Fujiwara, M.: Single b-bit byte error correcting and double bit error detecting codes for high-speed memory systems. In: IEEE Computer Society Press, Proceedings International Symposium on Fault-Tolerant Computing (FTCS) (1992) 494–501
8. S.Lipschutz. In: Linear algebra. Mcgraw-Hill, New York (1968) 155–202
9. H.S.Stone. In: Discrete Mathematical Structures and Their Applications. Science Research Associates, New York (1973) 307
10. Paar, C. In: Efficient VLSI Architecture for Bit-Parallel Computation in Galois Fields. Institute for Experimental Mathematics,University of Essen, Germany (1994)
11. Jamalipur, A. In: The Wireless mobile Internet Architectures,Protocols and Services. John Wiley & Sons, The Atrium,West Sussex,England (2003)
12. Rao, T., E.Fujiara: 3. In: Error-Control Coding for Computer Systems. Prentice-Hall (1989)
13. Zhang, L., Cao, Z., Gao, C.: Application of RS-Coded Modulation Scenarios to Compressed Image Communication in Multi Fading Channel. Volume 3., 52nd IEEE Vehicular Technology Conference (2000) 1198–1203
14. Peterson, W., E.J. Weldon, J. In: Error-correcting codes. 2nd edn. MIT Press, Cambridge (1971)
15. S.H.Jamali, T.Le-Ngoc. In: Coded Modulation Techniques for Fading Channels. Kluwer Academic Publishers, Boston (1994)
16. http://www.4i2i.com/reed_solomon_codes.htm (2004)

Introducing Reversibility in a High Level JJL Qubit Model According to CAN2 Paradigm

C.R. Calidonna[1] and A. Naddeo[2]

[1] CESIC - NEC Italia, Via P. Bucci Cubo 22b, 87036 Rende, (CS), Italy
[2] Dipartimento di Fisica "E. R. Caianiello", Universitá degli Studi di Salerno and
CNISM, Unità di Ricerca di Salerno, 84081 Baronissi (SA), Italy
Claudia.Calidonna@cesic.neceur.com, naddeo@sa.infn.it

Abstract. Reversibility is a concept widely studied in physics as well as in computer science. Reversible computation is characterized by means of invertible properties [1]. Quantum systems evolution is described by the time evolution operator U, which is unitary and invertible; therefore such systems can implement reversibility. Reversible/invertible Cellular Automata (CA) [1] are one of the most relevant reversible computational models. Here we introduce a model for a Josephson junction ladder (JJL) device addressing reversibility: it is based on a hybrid Cellular Automata Network (CAN), the CAN2 one [2][3][4].

1 Introduction

Reversibility is a concept widely studied in physics as well as in computer science. In particular, reversible computation is characterized by means of invertible properties. In the past Bennett [5] theoretically showed how it were possible to design machines based on reversible logic. In order to make computation logically reversible, each state of the machine must have only one possible predecessor state that could be reached during the computation. In the past several studies were performed on the connection between reversible classical functions and computation without loss of energy as a solution to the Maxwell demon paradox [5]. In particular it was shown that any classical function can be represented as a reversible function which can be computed by many elementary reversible steps; in fact the corresponding unitary matrix is decomposable into a sequence of many elementary unitary operations. The evolution of a quantum system is described by the time evolution operator U, which is unitary and then invertible; therefore such systems can implement reversibility. Reversible/invertible cellular automata [1] have been growing as one of the most relevant reversible computational models in the last thirty years. In particular, it has been shown that it is always possible to transform an arbitrary cellular automaton in a reversible one [6] as well as to simulate any irreversible one dimensional cellular automaton, endowed with a finite number of configurations, with a one dimensional reversible one. Recently, also the concept of a CA with memory has been introduced [7]. In the following we introduce a new model of JJL device which incorporates reversibility: a model based on a reversible hybrid CA with memory. The paper

S. El Yacoubi, B. Chopard, and S. Bandini (Eds.): ACRI 2006, LNCS 4173, pp. 215–221, 2006.

is organized as follows. In Section 2 we briefly describe a fully frustrated JJL. Section 3 introduces a particular CA hybrid model, i.e. the CAN2 one, and then gives the description of the implemented model in terms of such a formalism while in Section 4 reversibility is introduced. Finally in Section 5 some closing remarks and future perspectives of our work are presented.

2   Josephson Junction Ladders

The subject of our study is a Josephson junction ladder [8] built of N plaquettes closed in a ring with a half flux quantum ($\frac{1}{2}\Phi_0 = \frac{1}{2}\frac{hc}{2e}$) threading each plaquette. The number of plaquettes must correspond to the number of junctions on the vertical links of the ladder, so that each plaquette contains two junctions on the left and right link respectively. Such a condition is fulfilled when each plaquette of the ring contains an odd number of the so called π-junctions [9] (a π-junction is characterized by a current-phase relation of the kind $I = I_c \sin(\phi + \pi)$), one in our case, or putting the array in a transverse magnetic field. The first choice is the best in view of a feasibility study of a "protected" qubit because it avoids the switching of an external uniform magnetic field at least at the earliest stage of the definition of the ground states. With each site i we associate a phase φ_i and a charge $2en_i$, representing a superconducting grain coupled to its neighbors by Josephson couplings; n_i and φ_i are conjugate variables satisfying the usual phase-number commutation relation. The system is described by the quantum phase model Hamiltonian [10]:

$$H = -\frac{E_C}{2}\Sigma_i \left(\frac{\partial}{\partial\varphi_i}\right)^2 - \Sigma_{\langle ij\rangle} E_{ij} \cos\left(\varphi_i - \varphi_j - A_{ij}\right), \tag{1}$$

where E_C is the charging energy at site i, while the second term is the Josephson coupling energy between sites i and j and $A_{ij} = \frac{2\pi}{\Phi_0}\int_i^j A\cdot dl$, with Φ_0 the superconducting flux quantum. The gauge invariant sum around a plaquette is $\Sigma_p A_{ij} = 2\pi f$ with $f = \frac{\Phi}{\Phi_0}$, where Φ is the flux of the external magnetic field threading each plaquette. When $f = \frac{1}{2}$ and $E_C = 0$ the ground state of the $1D$ frustrated quantum XY model displays – in addition to the continuous $U(1)$ symmetry of the phase variables – a discrete Z_2 symmetry associated with an antiferromagnetic pattern of plaquette chiralities $\chi_p = \pm 1$, measuring the two opposite directions of the supercurrent circulating in each plaquette. For small E_C there is a gap for creation of kinks in the antiferromagnetic pattern of χ_p and the ground state has quasi long range chiral order. Our ladder has a ground state twofold degenerate with antiferromagnetic ordering, hence it can be mapped into a linear antiferromagnetic chain of half–integer spins. Furthermore it can acquire, in addition to superconducting quasi long range order, a topological order parameter due to its peculiar geometry, as it has been shown recently [11]. It is now possible to construct symmetric and antisymmetric linear combinations of such degenerate ground states and then to control their amplitude and relative phase: such operations are needed in order to prepare the qubit in a definite state [12]. In fact it can be shown that the tunnelling between the two ground states corresponds to the physical process of creation and annihilation of kink–antikink pairs [13].

3 The Cellular Automata Network v.2 (CAN2) Model and a Qualitative JJL Qubit Description

The CAN2 model [2,3,4] extends the standard CA model introducing the possibility to have a hybrid network of standard cellular automata components and global operators. It provides the possibility to simulate a two-level evolutionary process in which the local cellular interaction rules evolve together with some global functions according to network connections. Each automaton of the network represents, for instance, a component of the physical system to be simulated, the global operator represents global behavior and/or control capabilities and the network connections represent an evolving law which characterizes the physical system evolution. A more formal definition of a CAN2 network is given in [2,3,4]. Briefly we define a CAN2 network as the tuple

$$\langle \mathcal{L}, X, S, G, P, P_{var}, f, g, F \rangle \tag{2}$$

where:

- $\mathcal{L}$ is the the finite region where the system evolves;
- X is the neighborhood set as union of the neighborhoods of all components;
- S is a finite set of states;
- G is a finite set of global variables;
- P is a finite set of parameters, $P = \{p : p \in \mathcal{R}\}$;
- P_{var} is the set of global parameters;
- f is the set of the cellular automata transition functions;
- g is the set of global operator functions;
- $F : S^{\#Ntot} \rightarrow S$ is the transition for all the cells in $\mathcal{L}$.

In order to define the total transition function for the whole system it could be useful to separately define the CA component and the global operator components. Precedence relations occur if one cellular automaton needs to know the value/s of a global variable (or inverse) at the same step in order to evolve, and the execution of the g functions must precede (succeed) the execution of the transition functions f. We obtain the following definition

$$F : \circ_{i,j=1}^{M,K} [g_j] \circ [f_i] \tag{3}$$

and the $[g_j]$ ($[f_i]$) symbol implies that its presence could be optional and the corresponding precedence relations must be expressed according to it. Now, according to our CAN2 based qualitative model introduced in [4], we have the following formal definition of the JJL system [2]:

$$\langle \mathcal{L}, X, S, G, P, Pvar, f, g \rangle \tag{4}$$

- $\mathcal{L} = x|x \in N$ is the lattice grid, that is a finite linear array where each point identifies a cell.
- X includes $x - 2, x + 2$ for each cell x.

- $S = S_1 \times S_2 \times S_3 \times S_4$ is the set of state values. The substates are respectively: Pseudo_S (assuming $(-1, 1)$ values), the fixed magnetic pulse Mp, LABEL to identify the cell, and FLIP to register if the pseudospin flips.
- G is the set of global variables, where B_{tot} is the total applied magnetic pulse and $Start_C$ is the number of the corresponding starting cell.
- P is the set of global constant parameters: I (current) and C (capacitance).
- Pvar includes STEP, the step iterator to trigger the evolution.
- $f : S \rightarrow S$ is the deterministic state transition to determine the pseudospin state and values.
- $g : S_2 \rightarrow G$ expresses the global operator which controls the total magnetic pulse applied on the system.
- $g_s : G \rightarrow G$ is the global operator which chooses randomly the driving cell.

In order to implement a protected qubit (see Section 2) the boundary condition topology is annular. In order to get a transition between the two ground states the magnetic pulse period is equal to the pulse period. The flipping procedure between the input and output states implements a tunnelling between the two ground states which corresponds to the physical processes of creation and annihilation of kink-antikink pairs [13]. In general, for N cells, $(N/2)$ double flips are needed to switch from $|0 >$ to $|1 >$. We choose to use a double step for the CA transition component, with each time step equal to the half of the single sawtooth magnetic pulse period. The CA component has, as initial condition, the pseudospin configuration obtained in the precedent stage since it must obey to an antiferromagnetic arrangement and the flipping state is zero. At the initial time, our device is in a steady state, in one of the two possible ground states. Each parameter is fixed and the LABEL values are fixed for all transition steps, but the variable STEP is initialized to each macrostep T. The general transition function takes into account the coupling factor, adding an external frustration, as a single sawtooth magnetic pulse acting on each lattice cell. The system transition is assumed to be given by the possible simultaneous application of the two global operators followed by the transition function. The evolution of the model obeys to the following function $F : S\_f \times G \times P \times Pvar \rightarrow S\_f \times G \times Pvar$. The transition function scheme shows two global operators, the pulse application and the random starting cell chooser, in the first formulation of the model [2]. The transition function applies repeatedly the cellular automata component according to the multiplicity related to the double flips.

4   Introducing Reversibility in the JJL Qualitative Model

In 1961 Landauer [14] discussed the limitation of the efficiency of a computer imposed by physical laws. He argued that, according to the second law of thermodynamics, the erasure of one bit of information requires a minimal heat generation $k_B T \ln 2$, where k_B is Boltzmann's constant and T is the temperature at which one erases. Inspired by such studies, a considerable amount of work has been made on the thermodynamics of information processing [5][15]. Bit erasure is the simplest logically irreversible process because it requires a one bit input and always returns the null state as the output, so making impossible to recover the input value from just the output value. Landauer provided a method [14] for building up a logically reversible erasure in a bistable potential by taking into account the value of the bit being erased. In the context of cellular automata, such a process involving a "demon" cell can be used to copy the bit stored in a cell and then perform a logically reversible erasure process according to the value of the stored bit. So, it is clear that a logically reversible erasure process corresponds to the sequence *copy bit to the demon, then erase bit*. Now, in order to build up a reversible computer new logic gates must be used which are reversible. Reversible gates are such that the input of the gate can be reconstructed starting from its output. Toffoli and Fredkin [15] introduced such devices for the first time. They showed how to implement in a reversible way the AND and XOR gates through only one gate, a three-bit one. In particular, the *Fredkin Gate* is a device which operates following a conservative logic: signals are unalterable objects which can be moved during the course of computation but never created or destroyed. Now the idea is to implement a *copy, than erase* sequence in order to obtain a reversible qualitative qubit. In order to build up such a device, literature tells us that reversibility could be addressed avoiding the bit erasure and considering its addition to the actual values state. The evolution of the Toffoli and Fredkin gate may be viewed as the foundations of the actual reversible logic and computation. Deutsch [16] showed how to obtain a universal quantum computation, defined as an arbitrary unitary transformation on a discrete Hilbert space spanned by the set of all the states of a collection of bits, by means of a simple generalization of the scheme for building a reversible classical network. There exists a close connection between classical reversible computation and quantum computation because all unitary quantum operations need to be reversible: so, classical gates can be implemented quantumly by making the computation reversible and reversible computing can be conceived as a subset of quantum computing. All the above considerations are our starting point for the introduction of reversibility in our device. According to the classical definition CA are memoryless: no knowledge about the value of the previous states (substates) is required but only about the neighborhood states (sub-states) values. The memory concept introduced in Ref. [7] can be viewed as a *historic* one, i.e. the CA state is updated, being regularly augmented with the cell state at the previous time step: this means that CA need to be defined just by featuring every cell by its most frequent (mode) state. The most frequent mode implies that we have to consider a weight by applying a geometric discounting process, which is obtained from the rounded weighted average of all the time steps before [7]. According to [7], in order to reverse the state of a Fredkin gate the memory concept should be introduced; this implies that we need to consider the system at the $t-1$ and $t+1$ evolution time steps. Following the approach sketched above it could be feasible to use a double address space in order to store the state value at the previous time step and at the actual one. On the other side it could be useful to store the values of the global variable representing the driving

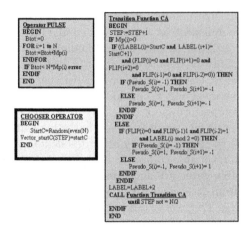

Fig. 1. The JJL system components according to a CAN2 vision: the shaded box is the modified operator

cell at the actual as well as at the previous time step in order to be able to fulfill the reversibility requests. This is enough to mimic the unitary transformation effect between two subsequent system transitions requested by the reversibility constraint but it leads to the doubling of the requested memory space. In order to simplify the memory space requests we specify a condition without considering any state addition. The solution consists in storing the sequence of the driving flipping cells in order to capture the computing properties of the model at each time step. Let us now explain in more detail our approach. In our case the Chooser Operator has a crucial role and it must be modified in the following way in order to achieve our reversibility goal: a further global variable must be considered in order to store the sequence of chosen cells at each time step for the whole system evolution. This is enough for our model in order to recover all the states since the starting point and not only the previous one. The new procedure is depicted in Fig. 1, included in the lower small box called *Chooser Operator*. This operator is equipped with a global vector (a global variable which is able to store more values) which stores at each time step the starting cell for the evolution, so it is much more simple to recover the previous values. In fact for each time step directly accessible, the first evolution cell can be recovered. This approach has two main advantages: 1) we recover all the previous states as each starting cell is stored and, in this case, the previous system state is exactly the negation; 2) we avoid to store all the cells values, what could be very cumbersome in the case of a device with a high number of cells; instead we restrict to the storage of one value for each time step evolution. The simulation of the reversible CA component is now trivially accomplished by reducing the step of the variable as well as by changing the direction of the cyclic function. The new operator does not modify the precedence relations and the components within the CAN network.

5   Conclusions and Outlooks

In this contribution we addressed the reversibility issue in the context of a generalized JJL qubit device. It was shown how it is possible to view reversibility, in whole generality, by considering a quasi-probabilistic model behavior. The advantage in considering such a scheme relies strongly in avoiding the memory waste and the consequent energy dissipation. We need to store only one variable per step instead of a set of values (which depends strongly on the number of the array cells). Further reversibility issues will be addressed in the future, such as the consideration of no erasing operations but only of the state selection while performing the memory doubling.

References

1. Toffoli, T. et al.: Invertible cellular automata. Physica D **45** (1990) 229-253.
2. Calidonna, C. R., Naddeo, A.: Using a hybrid CA based model for a flexible qualitative qubit simulation: fully frustrated JJL application. Computing Frontiers 2005, ACM Press, New York (2005), 145-151.
3. Calidonna, C. R., Naddeo, A.: Towards a CA model for quantum computation with fully frustrated Josephson junction arrays. Phys. Lett. A **327** (2004) 409-415.
4. Calidonna, C. R., Naddeo, A.: A basic qualitative CA based model of a frustrated linear Josephson junction array. Lect. Not. Comp. Sci. **3305** (2004) 248-257.
5. Leff, H. S., Rex, A. F.: Maxwell's Demon: Entropy, Information, Computing, Princeton University Press, Princeton (1990).
6. Toffoli, T.: Cellular Automata Mechanics, Ph.D. Thesis, Univ. of Michigan (1977).
7. Alonso-Sanz, R., Martin, M.: Three-state one-dimensional cellular automata with memory. Chaos Sol. Frac. **21** (2004) 809–834.
8. Granato, E.: Phase transitions in Josephson junction ladders in a magnetic field. Phys. Rev. B **42** (1990) 4797-4799.
9. Fulde, P., Ferrel, R. A.: Superconductivity in a strong spin–exchange field. Phys. Rev. **135** (1964) A550-A563.
10. Blanter, Y.: Duality in Josephson junction arrays. Nucl. Phys. B **S58** (1997) 79-90.
11. Naddeo, A., et al.: A conformal field theory description of magnetic flux fractionalization in Josephson junction ladders. Eur. Phys. J. B **49** (2006) 83-91.
12. Galindo, A., Martin-Delgado, M. A.: Information and computation: classical and quantum aspects. Rev. Mod. Phys. **74** (2002) 347-423.
13. Goldobin, E., et al.: Ground states in $0 - \pi$ long Josephson junctions. Phys. Rev. B **67** (2003) 224515/1-9.
14. Landauer, R.: Irreversibility and heat generation in the computing process. IBM J. Res. Dev. **5** (1961) 183-191.
15. Fredkin, E., Toffoli, T.: Conservative logic. Int. J. Theor. Phys. **21** (1982) 219-253.
16. Deutsch, D.: Quantum computational networks. Proc. R. Soc. London A **425** (1989) 73-90.

Analysis of Hybrid Group Cellular Automata*

Sung-Jin Cho[1], Un-Sook Choi[2],
Yoon-Hee Hwang[3], and Han-Doo Kim[4]

[1]Division of Mathematical Sciences, Pukyong National University
Busan 608-737, Korea
sjcho@pknu.ac.kr
[2] Department of Multimedia Engineering, Tongmyong University
Busan 626-847, Korea
choies@tu.ac.kr
[3] Department of Information Security, Graduate School, Pukyong National
University, Busan 608-737, Korea
yhhwang@pknu.ac.kr
[4] Institute of Mathematical Sciences and School of Computer Aided Science
Inje University, Gimhae 621-749, Korea
mathkhd@inje.ac.kr

Abstract. In this paper, we analyze a Linear Hybrid Group Cellular
Automata(LHGCA) **C** and the complemented group CA derived from
C with rules 60, 102 and 204. And we give the conditions for the comple-
ment vectors which determine the state transition of the CA dividing the
entire state space into smaller spaces of equal maximum cycle lengths.
And we show the relationship between cycles of complemented group
CA. Our results extend and generalize Mukhopadhyay's results.

1 Introduction

Biological self-reproduction was first investigated in terms of Von Neumann's cellular automaton capable of universal computation and construction([1]).
Wolfram([2]) suggested the use of a simple two-state, 3-neighborhood one-
dimensional cellular automata(CA) with cells arranged linearly in one dimension. Each cell is essentially comprised of a memory element and a combinatorial
logic that generates the next-state of the cell from the present-state of its neighboring cells(left, right and self). Various researchers([3] $\sim$ [5]) have carried out
extensive study in the modeling of CA and finding out better applications of
the automata. Later Das et al.([6]) proposed a versatile matrix algebraic tool
for the analysis of state transition of CA with linear next state functions. CA
have been employed in several applications([7] $\sim$ [11]). Especially, Cho et al.([12]
$\sim$ [14]) and many researchers([15] $\sim$ [17]) analyzed CA to study hash function,
data storage, cryptography and so on.

A group CA has nonsingular state transition matrix. The state transition
diagram of such a CA consists of a set of cycles. Furthermore group CA can

---

* This work was supported by grant No. (R01-2006-000-10260-0) from the Basic Research Program of the Korea Science and Engineering Foundation.

S. El Yacoubi, B. Chopard, and S. Bandini (Eds.): ACRI 2006, LNCS 4173, pp. 222–231, 2006.

be divided into two classes: maximum-length CA and non maximum-length CA. All $(2^n - 1)$ nonzero states of a linear n-cell maximum-length group CA form a single cycle. Such a group CA has been projected as a generator of pseudorandom patterns of high quality. The states of a non maximum-length group CA form multiple cycles. Recently many researchers have identified the CA as the core of security algorithms([16], [17]). Mukhopadhyay et al.([9]) investigated the state spaces of the fundamental transformations of a group CA and proved properties which relate the state spaces of the CA for the development of new encryption and key distribution protocols. And they asserted that an essential requirement for identifying the CA as the core of security algorithms is that the cycle length of a group CA has to be small, so that ciphering (or deciphering) is performed at the expense of few clock cycles. Moreover the length of the machines has to be equal so that the number of cycles required to encrypt or decrypt is predecided. So we need the analysis of group CA with special rules. In 2005 Cho et al.([15]) analyzed the complemented group CA derived from a uniform group CA with rule 60 or 102.

In this paper, by using the results in [15] we analyze a LHGCA **C** and the complemented group CA derived from **C** with rules 60, 102 and 204. And we give the conditions for the complement vectors which determine the state transition of the CA dividing the entire state space into smaller spaces of equal maximum cycle lengths. And we show the relationship between cycles of complemented group CA. Our results extend and generalize Mukhopadhyay's results([9]).

2   CA Preliminaries

A CA consists of a number of cells. In a 3-neighborhood dependency, the next state $q_i(t + 1)$ of a cell is assumed to be dependent only on itself and on its two neighbors (left and right), and is denoted as

$$q_i(t + 1) = f(q_{i-1}(t), q_i(t), q_{i+1}(t))$$

where $q_i(t)$ represents the state of the i-th cell at the t-th instant of time. f is the next state function and referred to as the rule of the automata. The cells evolve in discrete time steps according to some deterministic rule that depends only on logical neighborhood.

$rule \ \ 60 : q_i(t + 1) = q_{i-1}(t) \oplus q_i(t)$ $rule \ 195 : q_i(t + 1) = \overline{q_{i-1}(t) \oplus q_i(t)}$
$rule \ 102 : q_i(t + 1) = q_i(t) \oplus q_{i+1}(t)$ $rule \ 153 : q_i(t + 1) = \overline{q_i(t) \oplus q_{i+1}(t)}$
$rule \ 204 : q_i(t + 1) = q_i(t)$ $rule \ \ 51 : q_i(t + 1) = \overline{q_i(t)}$

The following results are necessary for proving some results in the following sections.

Lemma 2.1([15]). Let **C** be an n-cell linear uniform group CA with rule 60 (resp. 102), where $2^{k-1} < n \le 2^k$. Let T (resp. S) be the state transition matrix of **C**. Then $T^{2^k} = S^{2^k} = I$, $T^{2^{k-1}} = (t_{ij})$ and $S^{2^{k-1}} = (s_{ij})$, where

$$t_{ij} = s_{ji} = \begin{cases} 1, & \text{if } i = j \ \text{ or } \ i = j + 2^{k-1} \\ 0, & \text{otherwise} \end{cases}$$

Lemma 2.2([15]). Let **C** be an n-cell linear uniform group CA with rule 60 or 102 and R be a rule vector. Let T be the state transition matrix of **C**. Let $X = (x_1, \cdots, x_n)^t$ be a state in **C**. Then

$$(T \oplus I)^{m-1}X = \begin{cases} (0, 0, \cdots, \overset{m}{x}_1, x_2, \cdots, x_{n-m+1})^t, & \text{if } R = < 60, 60, \cdots > \\ (x_m, \cdots, x_{n-1}, x_n, 0, \cdots, 0)^t, & \text{if } R = < 102, 102, \cdots > \end{cases}$$

3   Analysis of LHGCA and Complemented Group CA Derived from LHGCA

In this section we analyze LHGCA **C** and the complemented group CA derived from **C** with rules 60, 102 and 204.

Theorem 3.1. Let **C** be a linear hybrid n-cell CA with rule vector R and state transition matrix T, where R is a combination of rules 60, 102 and 204. Then **C** is a LHGCA if and only if rule 60 is not followed immediately by rule 102.

By Theorem 3.1 **C** having the rule vector which is the only combination of the rule vectors $RV_i(i = 1, \cdots, 5)$ in Theorem 3.3 is a LHGCA.

Theorem 3.2. Let **C** be an n-cell LHGCA with rule vector R and state transition matrix T, where R is a combination of rules 60, 102 and 204. Then the characteristic polynomial of T is $(x + 1)^n$.

The following theorem characterizes the order and the minimal polynomial of the state transition matrix T of an n-cell LHGCA.

Theorem 3.3. Let **C** be an n-cell LHGCA and let $m(x)$ be the minimal polynomial of the state transition matrix T of **C**. Then $m(x) = (x+1)^p$ in the following cases:

(1) $RV_1 = <\overset{a}{\overline{60, \cdots, 60}}, \overset{b}{\overline{102, \cdots, 102}}>$, $p = \max\{a, b\}$

(2) $RV_2 = <\overset{a}{\overline{60, \cdots, 60}}, 204, \overset{b}{\overline{60, \cdots, 60}}>$, $p = \max\{a, b+1\}$

(3) $RV_3 = <\overset{a}{\overline{60, \cdots, 60}}, 204, \overset{b}{\overline{102, \cdots, 102}}>$, $p = \max\{a, b\}$

(4) $RV_4 = <\overset{a}{\overline{102, \cdots, 102}}, 204, \overset{b}{\overline{60, \cdots, 60}}>$, $p = \max\{a+1, b+1\}$

(5) $RV_5 = <\overset{a}{\overline{102, \cdots, 102}}, 204, \overset{b}{\overline{102, \cdots, 102}}>$, $p = \max\{a+1, b\}$

Proof. We only prove for the case (4). Let $a + 1 \geq b + 1$. Partition $T \oplus I$ into 2×2 block matrices of the form

$$T \oplus I = \begin{pmatrix} T_1 & O \\ A & T_2 \end{pmatrix} = (a_{ij}),$$

where T_1 is a $(a+1) \times (a+1)$ matrix and

$$a_{ij} = \begin{cases} 1, & \text{if } (i = j - 1, i < a + 1) \text{ or } (i = j + 1, i > a + 1), \\ 0, & \text{otherwise} \end{cases}$$

Then

$$(T \oplus I)^q = \begin{pmatrix} T_1^q & O \\ T_2^{q-1}A & T_2^q \end{pmatrix}$$

Here $T_1^{a+1} = O$, $T_1^j \neq O$ $(j < a + 1)$ and $T_2^b = O$. Since $T_2^{q-1}A = (b_{ij})$, where

$$b_{ij} = \begin{cases} 1, & \text{if } i = q, \; j = a + 1 \\ 0, & \text{otherwise} \end{cases}$$

for $1 \leq q \leq b$, $T_2^b A = O$. Therefore

$$(T \oplus I)^{a+1} = O, \qquad (T \oplus I)^j \neq O \; (j < a + 1) \qquad \cdots \qquad (1)$$

Let $a + 1 < b + 1$. Partition $T \oplus I$ into 2×2 block matrices of the form

$$T \oplus I = \begin{pmatrix} S_1 & B \\ O & S_2 \end{pmatrix} = (a_{ij}),$$

where S_1 is a $a \times a$ matrix and

$$a_{ij} = \begin{cases} 1, & \text{if } (j = i + 1, \; j < a + 2) \text{ or } (j = i - 1, \; j > a), \\ 0, & \text{otherwise} \end{cases}$$

Then

$$(T \oplus I)^q = \begin{pmatrix} S_1^q & S_1^{q-1}B \\ O & S_2^q \end{pmatrix}$$

Here $S_1^a = O$ and $S_2^{b+1} = O$ but $S_2^j \neq O$ $(j < b + 1)$. Since $S_1^{q-1}B = (c_{ij})$ for $1 \leq q \leq a$, where

$$c_{ij} = \begin{cases} 1, & \text{if } i = a + 1 - q, \; j = 1 \\ 0, & \text{otherwise} \end{cases}$$

and $S_1^a B = O$,

$$(T \oplus I)^{b+1} = O, \qquad (T \oplus I)^j \neq O \; (j < b + 1) \qquad \cdots \qquad (2)$$

By (1) and (2), $m(x) = (x + 1)^p$.

Remark. From Theorem 3.3 and Lemma in [18], we obtain $ord(T) = 2^r$, where $2^{r-1} < p \leq 2^r$.

Theorem 3.4. Let $\mathbf{C}$ be an n-cell LHGCA with rule vector $RV_i (i = 1, \cdots, 5)$ in Theorem 3.3 and state transition matrix T. Let $\mathbf{C}'$ be the complemented group

CA derived from **C** with complement vectors $F_i (i = 1, \cdots, 5)$ which are in below and state transition operator $\overline{T}$.

(1) $RV_1:$ $F_1 = \begin{cases} (1, f_2, f_3, \cdots)^t, & \text{if } a \geq b \\ (f_1, \cdots, 1)^t, & \text{if } a < b \end{cases}$

(2) $RV_2:$ $F_2 = \begin{cases} (1, f_2, \cdots, f_n)^t, & \text{if } a \geq b+1 \\ (f_1, \cdots, f_a, 1, f_{a+2}, \cdots, f_n)^t, & \text{if } a < b+1 \end{cases}$

(3) $RV_3:$ $F_3 = \begin{cases} (1, f_2, \cdots, f_n)^t, & \text{if } a \geq b \\ (f_1, \cdots, f_{n-1}, 1)^t, & \text{if } a < b \end{cases}$

(4) $RV_4:$ $F_4 = \begin{cases} (f_1, \cdots, f_a, 1, f_{a+2}, \cdots, f_n)^t, & \text{if } a+1 \geq b+1 \\ (f_1, \cdots, f_a, 1, f_{a+2}, \cdots, f_n)^t, & \text{if } a+1 < b+1 \end{cases}$

(5) $RV_5:$ $F_5 = \begin{cases} (f_1, \cdots, f_a, 1, f_{a+2}, \cdots, f_n)^t, & \text{if } a+1 \geq b \\ (f_1, \cdots, f_{n-1}, 1)^t, & \text{if } a+1 < b \end{cases}$

where $f_1, \cdots, f_n \in \{0, 1\}$.

Let the minimal polynomial $m(x)$ of T be $(x+1)^p$. If $ord(T) = 2^r$, then the following hold:

(a) All the lengths of cycles in **C'** are the same.

(b) $ord(\overline{T}) = \begin{cases} 2^r, & \text{if } 2^{r-1} < p < 2^r, \\ 2^{r+1}, & \text{if } p = 2^r \end{cases}$

Proof. We only prove for the case (2) with $a \geq b+1$. Let $X = (x_1, \cdots, x_n)^t$ be a state in **C'**. Then

$$\overline{T}^{2^{r+1}} X = T^{2^{r+1}} X \oplus (T^{2^{r+1}-1} \oplus \cdots \oplus T \oplus I)F$$
$$= X \oplus \{T^{2^r}(T^{2^r-1} \oplus \cdots \oplus T \oplus I) \oplus (T^{2^r-1} \oplus \cdots \oplus T \oplus I)\}F = X.$$

Therefore $ord(\overline{T})(:= l)$ divides 2^{r+1}. Since $X = \overline{T}^l X = T^l X \oplus (T^{l-1} \oplus \cdots \oplus T \oplus I)F$ for all X, $T^l X = X$ and $(T^{l-1} \oplus \cdots \oplus T \oplus I)F = 0$. Therefore $ord(T)$ divides l. Thus $l = 2^r$ or 2^{r+1}.

Case I. Let $p = 2^r$. Then $(T \oplus I)^{2^r-1} = (a_{ij})$, where

$$a_{ij} = \begin{cases} 1, & \text{if } i = a, \ j = 1 \\ 0, & \text{otherwise} \end{cases}$$

Thus

$$\overline{T}^{2^r} X = T^{2^r} X \oplus (T \oplus I)^{2^r-1} F = X \oplus (0, \cdots, 0, \overset{a}{1}, 0, \cdots, 0)^t \neq X$$

for all X. Therefore $ord(\overline{T}) = 2^{r+1}$ and thus all the lengths of cycles in **C'** are the same.

Case II. Let $2^{r-1} < p < 2^r$. Then $(T \oplus I)^{2^r-1} = O$. Thus

$$\overline{T}^{2^r} X = T^{2^r} X \oplus (T \oplus I)^{2^r-1} F = X$$

Therefore $ord(\overline{T}) = 2^r$. To show that all the lengths of cycles in $\mathbf{C}'$ are the same, suppose that $X = (x_1, \cdots, x_n)^t$ is a state lying on a cycle in $\mathbf{C}'$ whose length is 2^c $(c < r)$. Then

$$\overline{T}^{2^c} X = \overline{T}^{2^{c+1}} X = \cdots = \overline{T}^{2^{r-1}} X = \overline{T}^{2^r} X = X$$

and

$$(T \oplus I)^{2^{r-1}-1} F = (0, \cdots, 0, \overset{2^{r-1}}{1}, \cdots)^t$$

First, let X be a state lying on a cycle in $\mathbf{C}$ whose cycle length is less than 2^r. Then

$$\overline{T}^{2^{r-1}} X = T^{2^{r-1}} X \oplus (T^{2^{r-1}-1} \oplus \cdots \oplus T \oplus I) F$$
$$= X \oplus (T \oplus I)^{2^{r-1}-1} F \neq X$$

This is a contradiction.

Second, let X be a state lying on a cycle in $\mathbf{C}$ whose cycle length is 2^r. Partition T into 2×2 block matrices of the form

$$T = \begin{pmatrix} T_1 & O \\ O & T_2 \end{pmatrix},$$

where T_1 and T_2 are the state transition matrices of uniform group CA with rule 60. Therefore by Lemmas 2.1 and 2.2

$$\overline{T}^{2^{r-1}} X = T^{2^{r-1}} X \oplus (T^{2^{r-1}-1} \oplus \cdots \oplus T \oplus I) F$$
$$= T^{2^{r-1}} X \oplus (T \oplus I)^{2^{r-1}-1} F$$
$$- \begin{pmatrix} T_1^{2^{r-1}} & O \\ O & T_2^{2^{r-1}} \end{pmatrix} X \oplus \begin{pmatrix} (T_1 \oplus I)^{2^{r-1}-1} & O \\ O & (T_2 \oplus I)^{2'-1-1} \end{pmatrix} F$$
$$= (\cdots, \overset{2^{r-1}}{x_{2^{r-1}}}, \cdots)^t \oplus (\cdots, \overset{2^{r-1}}{1}, \cdots)^t \neq X$$

This is a contradiction. Therefore all the lengths of cycles in $\mathbf{C}'$ are the same.

By the similar method we can prove for the case (2) with $a < b + 1$.

Let $\mathbf{C}$ be an n-cell LHGCA with rule vector $RV_i(i = 1, \cdots, 5)$ in Theorem 3.3 and state transition matrix T. Let $\mathbf{C}'$ be the complemented CA derived from $\mathbf{C}$ with complement vector F_i in Theorem 3.4 and state transition operator $\overline{T}$. Let $m(x) = (x + 1)^p, (p = 2^r)$ and $ord(T) = 2^r$. Then there exists F such that $ord(\overline{T}) = 2^r$ (not 2^{r+1}). For example, let $\mathbf{C}$ be an n-cell LHGCA with rule vector $RV_2(a \geq b + 1), F = (0, f_2, \cdots, f_n)^t$ and $p = 2^r$. Then all the lengths of cycles in $\mathbf{C}'$ are the same and $ord(\overline{T}) = 2^r$ because $\overline{T}^{2^r} X = X \oplus O = X$.

4   Relationship Between Cycles of Complemented Group CA

In this section we construct several operators which are different from R_1 and R_2 and analyze the properties of these operators.

Theorem 4.1. Let **C** be an n-cell LHGCA with rule vector $RV_i(i = 1, \cdots, 5)$ in Theorem 3.3 and state transition matrix T. Let **C'** be the complemented group CA derived from **C** with complement vector F_i which is in Theorem 3.4 and state transition operator $\overline{T}$. Then the following hold:

(1) X and $X \oplus \overline{T}X \oplus \overline{T}^2 X$ lie on different cycles.
(2) X and $X \oplus \overline{T}X \oplus \overline{T}^3 X$ lie on different cycles.
(3) X and $X \oplus \overline{T}^2 X \oplus \overline{T}^3 X$ lie on different cycles.

Proof. We only prove for the case (1) and $RV_4(a + 1 \geq b + 1)$.

Let T be the 2×2 block matrix of the form

$$T = \begin{pmatrix} T_1 & O \\ Q & T_2 \end{pmatrix},$$

where T_1 is a $(a + 1) \times (a + 1)$ matrix. Then T_1 is the state transition matrix of $(a + 1)$-cell uniform CA with rule 102 and T_2 is the state transition matrix of b-cell uniform CA with rule 60, and

$$Q = \begin{pmatrix} 0 & 0 & 0 & \cdots & 0 & 0 & 1 \\ 0 & 0 & 0 & \cdots & 0 & 0 & 0 \\ & \cdots & & & \cdots & & \\ 0 & 0 & 0 & \cdots & 0 & 0 & 0 \end{pmatrix}_{b \times (a+1)}$$

Let $B = X \oplus \overline{T}X \oplus \overline{T}^2 X$ and $X = (x_1, x_2, \cdots, x_n)^t$. Then

$$B = (I \oplus T \oplus T^2)X \oplus TF = \begin{pmatrix} \vdots \\ x_a \oplus x_{a+1} \\ \overline{x_{a+1}} \\ x_{a+1} \oplus x_{a+2} \\ x_{a+1} \oplus x_{a+2} \oplus x_{a+3} \\ \vdots \end{pmatrix} \quad a + 1$$

and

$$\overline{T}^v X = \begin{pmatrix} \vdots \\ {}_vC_0 x_a \oplus {}_vC_1 x_{a+1} \oplus {}_vC_2 \\ {}_vC_0 x_{a+1} \oplus {}_vC_1 \\ {}_vC_1 x_{a+1} \oplus {}_vC_0 x_{a+2} \oplus {}_vC_2 \\ {}_vC_2 x_{a+1} \oplus {}_vC_1 x_{a+2} \oplus {}_vC_0 x_{a+3} \oplus {}_vC_3 \\ \vdots \end{pmatrix} \quad a + 1$$

for a positive integer v. Suppose that there exists an integer v such that $\overline{T}^v X = B$.

Case I. v is even:

Since $B = (\cdots, \overset{a+1}{\overline{x_{a+1}}}, \cdots)^t$ and $\overline{T}^v X = (\cdots, \overset{a+1}{x_{a+1}}, \cdots)^t, \overline{T}^v X \neq B$.

Case II. v is odd: (i) $v = 4m + 1$.

Since $B = (\cdots, \overset{a+2}{\overline{x_{a+1} \oplus x_{a+2}}}, \cdots)^t$ and $\overline{T}^v X = (\cdots, \overset{a+2}{x_{a+1} \oplus x_{a+2}}, \cdots)^t, \overline{T}^v X \neq B$.

(ii) $v = 4m + 3$.

Since $B = (\cdots, \overset{a+3}{x_{a+1} \oplus x_{a+2} \oplus x_{a+3}}, \cdots)^t$ and $\overline{T}^v X = (\cdots, \overset{a+3}{\overline{x_{a+1} \oplus x_{a+2} \oplus x_{a+3}}}, \cdots)^t, \overline{T}^v X \neq B$.

This is a contradiction. By the similar method we can prove for the case (1) and $RV_4(a + 1 < b + 1)$. This completes the proof.

Define the operators R_i as follows:

$$R_1(X) = X \oplus \overline{T} X \oplus \overline{T}^2 X, \qquad R_2(X) = X \oplus \overline{T} X \oplus \overline{T}^3 X,$$
$$R_3(X) = X \oplus \overline{T}^2 X \oplus \overline{T}^3 X.$$

Since

$$\overline{T}(X_1 \oplus X_2 \oplus \cdots \oplus X_{2n-1}) = T(X_1 \oplus X_2 \oplus \cdots \oplus X_{2n-1}) \oplus F$$
$$= (TX_1 \oplus F) \oplus (TX_2 \oplus F) \oplus \cdots \oplus (TX_{2n-1} \oplus F)$$
$$= \overline{T}X_1 \oplus \overline{T}X_2 \oplus \cdots \oplus \overline{T}X_{2n-1},$$

$\overline{T}$ acts as a linear operator on any sum of odd states. Also $\overline{T}^v(X_1 \oplus X_2 \oplus \cdots \oplus X_{2n-1}) = \overline{T}^v X_1 \oplus \overline{T}^v X_2 \oplus \cdots \oplus \overline{T}^v X_{2n-1}$, where v is a positive integer.

Lemma 4.2. Let $\mathbf{C}$ be an n-cell LHGCA with rule vector $RV_i(i = 1, \cdots, 5)$ in Theorem 3.3 and state transition matrix T. Let $\mathbf{C}'$ be the complemented group CA derived from $\mathbf{C}$ with complement vector F_i which is in Theorem 3.4 and state transition operator $\overline{T}$.

Then the following hold:

$$(1) \qquad \overline{T}^v(R_\alpha R_\beta(\overline{T}^u(X))) = \overline{T}^u(R_\beta R_\alpha(\overline{T}^v(X)))$$

for all integers α and β $(1 \leq \alpha, \beta \leq 3)$, where v and u are positive integers.

$$(2) \qquad R_\alpha(X_1 \oplus \cdots \oplus X_{2n-1}) = R_\alpha(X_1) \oplus \cdots \oplus R_\alpha(X_{2n-1})$$

for each integer α $(1 \leq \alpha \leq 3)$.

Lemma 4.3. Let $\mathbf{C}$ be an n-cell LHGCA with rule vector $RV_i(i = 1, \cdots, 5)$ in Theorem 3.3 and state transition matrix T. Let $\mathbf{C}'$ be the complemented group CA derived from $\mathbf{C}$ with complement vector F_i which is in Theorem 3.4 and state transition operator $\overline{T}$. Then for each nonnegative integer v,

$$\overline{T}^{\alpha \cdot 2^v} R_\alpha^{2^v}(X) = \{(T \oplus I)^{3 \cdot 2^v}(T^\alpha \oplus T \oplus I)^{2^v} \oplus I\} X \oplus (T \oplus I)^{3 \cdot 2^v - 1}(T^\alpha \oplus T \oplus I)^{2^v} F,$$

where $1 \leq \alpha \leq 3$.

The following theorem can be proved by Lemmas 4.2 and 4.3.

Theorem 4.4. Let $\mathbf{C}$ be an n-cell LHGCA with rule vector $RV_i(i = 1, \cdots, 5)$ in Theorem 3.3 and state transition matrix T. Let $\mathbf{C}'$ be the complemented group CA derived from $\mathbf{C}$ with complement vector F_i which is in Theorem 3.4 and state transition operator $\overline{T}$. Then the following hold:

   (1) $\overline{T}^{\alpha \cdot 2^v} R_\alpha^{2^v}(X) = X$

   (2) $\overline{T}^{(\alpha+\beta) \cdot 2^v} (R_\alpha R_\beta)^{2^v}(X) = X$ for $\alpha \neq \beta$

   (3) $\overline{T}^{6 \cdot 2^v} (R_1 R_2 R_3)^{2^v}(X) = X$

for $\alpha, \beta = 1, 2, 3$, where v is a nonnegative integer satisfying $3 \cdot 2^{v-1} \leq p < 3 \cdot 2^v$ and p is in Theorem 3.3.

5   Conclusion

In this paper we analyzed LHGCA $\mathbf{C}$ and the complemented group CA derived from $\mathbf{C}$ with rules 60, 102 and 204 by using the results in [15]. And we gave the conditions for the complement vectors which determine the state transition of the CA dividing the entire state space into smaller spaces of equal maximum cycle lengths. And we showed the relationship between cycles of complemented group CA. Our results extended and generalized Mukhopadhyay's results([9]).

References

1. J. Von Neumann, *The theory of self-reproducing automata*, A.W. Burks ed. (Univ. of Illinois Press, Urbana and London) (1966)
2. S. Wolfram, *Statistical mechanics of cellular automata*, Rev. Mod. Phys., **55** (1983) 601–644
3. J. Thatcher, *Universality in Von Neumann cellular model*, Tech. Rep. 03105-30-T, ORA, University of Michigan (1964)
4. Ch. Lee, *Synthesis of a cellular universal machine using 29-state model of Von Neumann*, in The University of Michigan Engineering Summer Conferences (1964)
5. F.C. Hennie, *Iterative arrays of logical circuits*, Academic, Nework (1961)
6. A.K. Das and P.P. Chaudhuri, *Efficient characterization of cellular automata*, in Proc. IEE (Part E), **137** (1964) 81–87
7. A.K. Das and P.P. Chaudhuri, *Vector space theoretic analysis of additive cellular automata and its application for pseudo-exhaustive test pattern generation*, IEEE Trans. Comput., **42** (1993) 340–352
8. S. Nandi, B.K. Kar and P.P. Chaudhuri, *Theory and applications of cellular automata in cryptography*, IEEE Trans. Computers, **43** (1994) 1346–1357
9. D Mukhopadhyay and D.R. Chowdhury, *Characterization of a class of complemented group cellular automata*, ACRI 2004, Lecture Notes in Computer Science, **3305** (2004) 775–784
10. S. Chakraborty, D.R. Chowdhury and P.P. Chaudhuri, *Theory and application of nongroup cellular automata for synthesis of easily testable finite state machines*, IEEE Trans. Computers, **45** (1996) 769–781
11. S. Nandi and P.P. Chaudhuri, *Analysis of periodic and intermediate boundary 90/150 cellular automata*, IEEE Trans. Computers, **45(1)** (1996) 1–12

12. S.J. Cho, U.S. Choi, Y.H. Hwang, Y.S. Pyo, H.D. Kim, K.S. Kim and S.H. Heo, *Computing phase shifts of maximum-length 90/150 cellular automata sequences*, ACRI 2004, *Lecture Notes in Computer Science*, **3305** (2004) 31–39

13. S.J. Cho, U.S. Choi and H.D. Kim, *Analysis of complemented CA derived from a linear TPMACA*, Computers and Mathematics with Applications, **45** (2003) 689–698

14. S.J. Cho, U.S. Choi and H.D. Kim, *Behavior of complemented CA whose complement vector is acyclic in a linear TPMACA*, Mathematical and Computer Modelling, **36** (2002) 979–986

15. S.J. Cho, Y.H. Hwang, U.S. Choi, H.D. Kim and Y.S. Pyo, *Characterization of a class of the complemented CA derived from linear uniform CA*, Submitted

16. S. Sen, C. Shaw, D.R. Chowdhury, N. Ganguly and P.P. Chaudhuri, *Cellular automata based cryptosystem*, ICICS 2002, *Lecture Notes in Computer Science*, **2513** (2002) 303–314

17. M. Mukherjee, N. Ganguly and P.P. Chaudhuri, *Cellular automata based authentication*, ACRI 2002, *Lecture Notes in Computer Science*, **2493** (2002) 259–269

18. B. Elspas, *The theory of autonomous linear sequential networks*, TRE Trans. on Circuits, CT-6(1), (1959) 45–60

Behaviors of Single Attractor Cellular Automata over Galois Field $GF(2^p)^\star$

Sung-Jin Cho[1], Un-Sook Choi[2], Yoon-Hee Hwang[3],
Han-Doo Kim[4], and Hyang-Hee Choi[5]

[1]Division of Mathematical Sciences, Pukyong National University
Busan 608-737, Korea
sjcho@pknu.ac.kr
[2] Department of Multimedia Engineering, Tongmyong University
Busan 626-847, Korea
choies@tu.ac.kr
[3] Department of Information Security, Graduate School, Pukyong National
University, Busan 608-737, Korea
yhhwang@pknu.ac.kr
[4] Institute of Mathematical Sciences and School of Computer Aided Science
Inje University, Gimhae 621-749, Korea
mathkhd@inje.ac.kr
[5] Department of Applied Mathematics, Pukyong National University
Busan 626-847, Korea
choihhee@pknu.ac.kr

Abstract. In this paper, we analyze behaviors of state transitions of
a linear Single Attractor Cellular Automata(SACA) $\mathbf{C}$ and the complemented SACA $\mathbf{C}'$ derived from $\mathbf{C}$ over Galois Field $GF(2^p)$. And we
propose the algorithm for the construction of the state transition dia-
gram of $\mathbf{C}$ and $\mathbf{C}'$ over $GF(2^p)$ by using the new concept of basic path.
These results extend the results over $GF(2)$ of Cho et al. for SACA.

1 Introduction

Cellular Automata(CA) introduced by Von Neumann([1]) have been used for
diverse applications such as modelling biological self-reproduction, modelling
problems of number theory, parallel processing computation etc. Wolfram([2])
pioneered the investigation of CA as mathematical models for self-organizing statistical systems and suggested the use of a simple two-state, three-neighborhood
CA with cells arranged linearly in one dimension.

Das et al.([3], [4]) developed a matrix algebraic tool capable of characterizing
CA. CA have been employed in several applications([5] $\sim$ [9]). Cho et al.([10]
$\sim$ [12]) analyzed CA to study hash function, data storage, cryptography and so
on. In particular, they proposed an algorithm for the construction of the state
transition diagram of two predecessor multiple attractor CA over $GF(2)$. Also

* This work was supported by grant No.(R01-2003-000-10663-0) from the Basic Research Program of the Korea Science and Engineering Foundation.

S. El Yacoubi, B. Chopard, and S. Bandini (Eds.): ACRI 2006, LNCS 4173, pp. 232–237, 2006.
© Springer-Verlag Berlin Heidelberg 2006

they analyzed behaviors of the state transition of the complemented nongroup $GF(2)$ CA corresponding to two predecessor nongroup CA.

Sikdar et al.([13]) used group CA over $GF(2^p)$ with hierarchical structure([14]) for a test pattern generation. Also they used $GF(2^p)$ multiple attractor CA for the diagnosis of the defect of VLSI circuits.

In this paper, we characterize a linear Single Attractor CA(SACA) **C** and the complemented SACA **C′** derived from **C** over $GF(2^p)$ and propose the algorithm for the effective construction of the state transition diagram of **C** and **C′**. These results extend the results over $GF(2)$ of Cho et al.([11], [12]) for SACA. This algorithm reduces the time-complexity by changing multiplications of matrices into additions of vectors. Also these results will be helpful to study data storage, hashing by $GF(2^p)$ SACA and so on.

2 $GF(2^p)$ CA Preliminaries

$GF(2^p)$ CA can be viewed as an extension of $GF(2)$ CA. It consists of an array of cells, spatially interconnected in a regular manner, each cell being capable of storing an element of $GF(2^p)$ (Figure 1). In effect, each $GF(2^p)$ CA cell has p number of memory elements. Figure 1 shows a general $GF(2^p)$ CA structure.

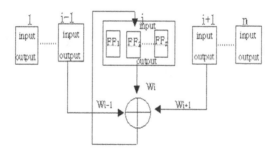

Fig. 1. General structure of a $GF(2^p)$ CA

Under three neighborhood restriction, the next state of the i-th cell is a function of the weighted combination of the present states of the $(i-1)$-th, the i-th and the $(i+1)$-th cells (Figure 1), the weights being elements of $GF(2^p)$. Thus if $q_i(t)$ represents the state of the i-th cell at the t-th instant, then

$$q_i(t+1) = \phi(w_{i-1}q_{i-1}(t), w_iq_i(t), w_{i+1}q_{i+1}(t)),$$

where ϕ denotes the local transition function of the i-th cell and w_{i-1}, w_i and $w_{i+1} \in GF(2^p)$ specify the weights of interconnections; the **addition** and **multiplication** operations follow the addition and multiplication over $GF(2^p)$.

3   Behaviors of Linear $GF(2^p)$ SACA

Let **C** be a linear n-cell $GF(2^p)$ SACA. Then **C** is a nongroup $GF(2^p)$ CA and the state transition matrix T of **C** is singular. In this case the attractor is the only zero state and the depth of state transition diagram of **C** is n. The number of all states of **C** is 2^{np} and the number of the immediate predecessors of any reachable state is 2^p.

The following theorem shows the property of the state transition matrix of a linear n-cell $GF(2^p)$ SACA.

Theorem 3.1. Let T be the state transition matrix of a linear n-cell $GF(2^p)$ SACA. Then T satisfies the following properties.
   (1) $rank(T) = n - 1$.
   (2) $rank(T + I) = n$.
   (3) The characteristic polynomial and the minimal polynomial of T are x^n.

Theorem 3.2. Let **C** be a linear n-cell $GF(2^p)$ SACA. Then the sum of distinct two immediate predecessors of any reachable state in **C** is a nonzero immediate predecessor of the zero state.

Definition 3.3. Let **C** be a linear $GF(2^p)$ SACA with depth d and let T be the state transition matrix of **C**. Then we call

$$x \to Tx \to \cdots \to T^d x (= \alpha)$$

an α-basic path of the α-tree in **C**, where x is a nonreachable state of the α-tree in **C**.

Theorem 3.4. Let **C** be a linear n-cell $GF(2^p)$ SACA. Given a 0-basic path of the 0-tree in **C**, we can construct the state transition diagram of the 0-tree of **C** as the following. If the states of the state transition diagram of **C** are labeled such that $S_{l,k}$ is the $(k+1)$-th state in the l-th level, then

$$S_{l,k} = (b_l + 1)S_{l,0} + \sum_{i=1}^{l-1} b_i S_{i,0},$$

where $k = b_l b_{l-1} \cdots b_1{}_{(2^p)} (\, 0 \le k \le (2^p)^{l-1}(2^p) - 1)$ is the base 2^p expansion of k.

4   Complemented $GF(2^p)$ SACA

The next state function of the complemented CA is given by $y = \overline{T}x = Tx + F$. Here we call F *inversion vector*. For example, consider the 4-cell $GF(2^2)$ CA **C** with the following state transition matrix T :

$$T = \begin{pmatrix} 1 & 2 & 0 & 0 \\ 0 & 1 & 3 & 0 \\ 0 & 0 & 1 & 2 \\ 0 & 0 & 0 & 1 \end{pmatrix}$$

Let $F = (3201)^t$ and $x = (3123)^t$. Then $y = (2232)^t$.

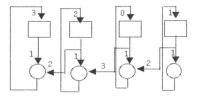

Fig. 2. Structure of 4-cell complemented $GF(2^2)$ CA of **C**

Figure 2 shows the structure of the complemented CA of **C**.

Theorem 4.1. Let **C** be a linear n-cell $GF(2^p)$ SACA and let **C**′ be the complemented $GF(2^p)$ SACA derived from **C** with the inversion vector F whose level is $l(1 \leq l \leq n)$. Then, in the state transition diagram of **C**′,

(a) all states at levels higher than l in the state transition diagram of **C** remain unaltered,

(b) all states at levels up to $(l-1)$ in the state transition diagram of **C** are located in level l,

(c) some states at level l of **C** are rearranged in levels lower than l and the other states at level l are located in the remaining part of level l,

(d) F lies at the level $(l-1)$.

The following Table 1 shows alteration of states of a linear SACA over $GF(2^p)$.

Table 1. Alteration of the states of a linear SACA over $GF(2^p)$

Linear SACA over $GF(2^p)$	Complemented SACA over $GF(2^p)$
States at levels higher than level l	The level is unchanged
States at levels lower than level l	Rearranged at level l
Complement vector F	F lies at level $(l-1)$
States at level l	Rearranged at levels lower than or equal to l

Theorem 4.2. Let **C** be a linear n-cell $GF(2^p)$ SACA and let **C**′ be the complemented $GF(2^p)$ SACA derived from **C**. Given a 0-basic path of the 0-tree in **C**, we can construct the state transition diagram of the 0-tree of **C**′ as the following. If the states of the state transition diagram of **C**′ are labeled such that $\overline{S}_{l,k}$ is the $(k+1)$-th state in the l-th level, then

$$\overline{S}_{l,k} = \overline{S}_{l-1,0} + (b_l + 1)S_{l,0} + \sum_{i=1}^{l-1} b_i S_{i,0},$$

where $k = b_l b_{l-1} \cdots b_1 {}_{(2^p)} (\; 0 \leq k \leq (2^p)^{l-1}(2^p) - 1)$ is the base 2^p expansion of k.

5   Algorithm for the Tree Construction of $GF(2^p)$ SACA

From Theorems 3.4 and 4.2, we propose the following algorithm for the construction of state transition diagrams of n-cell SACA **C** and **C′** over $GF(2^p)$.

Tree_Construction_Algorithm

/* Tree construction of a linear n-cell SACA **C** */

Step 1. For the state transition matrix T of **C** find a nonreachable state x
in the 0-tree satisfying $T^n x = 0$ and $T^{n-1} x \neq 0$.

Step 2. Find the following basic path of the 0-tree by using x.

$$x(= S_{n,0}) \rightarrow Tx(= S_{n-1,0}) \rightarrow \cdots \rightarrow 0$$

Step 3. Construct the 0-tree by the equation

$$S_{l,k} = (b_l + 1)S_{l,0} + \sum_{i=1}^{l-1} b_i S_{i,0}$$

/* Tree construction of the complemented SACA **C′** derived from **C** */

Step 4. Find the attractor $\overline{S}_{0,0}$ of **C′**.

$$\overline{S}_{0,0} = \overline{T}^{l-1} F,$$ where l is the level of the inversion vector F in **C**.

Step 5. We construct the tree of **C′** by using the equation

$$\overline{S}_{l,k} = \overline{S}_{l-1,0} + (b_l + 1)S_{l,0} + \sum_{i=1}^{l-1} b_i S_{i,0}$$

6   Conclusion

In this paper we investigated properties of a linear n-cell $GF(2^p)$ SACA **C** and analyzed behaviors of the state transition of the complemented $GF(2^p)$ SACA **C′** derived from **C**. And we proposed the algorithm for the construction of the state transition diagram of **C** over $GF(2^p)$ by using the basic path of **C** and **C′**. Using this algorithm the time-complexity is diminished by $\frac{1}{n^2}$ by changing multiplications of matrices into additions of vectors. These results extended the results over $GF(2)$ of Cho et al. for SACA. In the generation of CA-based hashing functions the behavior of state transition is very important. So this work will be helpful for the generation of CA-based hashing functions by using $GF(2^p)$ SACA.

References

1. J. Von Neumann, *Theory of self-reproducing automata*, University of Illinois Press Urbana, (1966)
2. S. Wolfram, *Statistical mechanics of cellular automata*, Rev. Modern Physics, **55** (1983) 601–644

3. A.K. Das and P.P. Chaudhuri, *Efficient characterization of cellular automata, Proc. IEE(Part E)*, **137** (1990) 81–87

4. A.K. Das and P.P. Chaudhuri, *Vector space theoretic analysis of additive cellular automata and its application for pseudo-exhaustive test pattern generation, IEEE Trans. Comput.*, **42** (1993) 340–352

5. P. Tsalides, T.A. York and A. Thanailakis, *Pseudo-random number generators for VLSI systems based on linear cellular automata, IEE Proc. E. Comput. Digit. Tech.*, **138** (1991) 241–249

6. S. Nandi, B.K. Kar and P.P. Chaudhuri, *Theory and applications of cellular automata in cryptography, IEEE Trans. Computers*, **43** (1994) 1346–1357

7. K. Paul, *Theory and application of $GF(2^p)$ cellular automata*, Ph. D. Thesis, B.E. College (Deemed University), Howrah, India, (2002)

8. C. Chattopadhyay, *Some studies on theory and applications of additive cellular automata*, Ph. D. Thesis, I.I.T., Kharagpur, India, (2002)

9. S. Sen, C. Shaw, D.R. Chowdhury, N. Ganguly and P.P. Chaudhuri, *Cellular automata based cryptosystem*, ICICS 2002, *Lecture Notes in Computer Science*, **2513** (2002) 303–314

10. S.J. Cho, U.S. Choi, Y.H. Hwang, Y.S. Pyo, H.D. Kim and S.H. Heo, *Computing phase shifts of maximum-length 90/150 cellular automata sequences*, ACRI 2004, *Lecture Notes in Computer Science*, **3305** (2004) 31–39

11. S.J. Cho, U.S. Choi and H.D. Kim, *Analysis of complemented CA derived from a linear TPMACA, Computers and Mathematics with Applications*, **45** (2003) 689–698

12. S.J. Cho, U.S. Choi and H.D. Kim, *Behavior of complemented CA whose complement vector is acyclic in a linear TPMACA, Mathematical and Computer Modelling*, **36** (2002) 979–986

13. B.K. Sikdar, P. Majumder, M. Mukherjee, N. Ganguly, D.K. Das and P.P. Chaudhuri, *Hierarchical cellular automata as an on-chip test pattern generator, VLSI Design, Fourteenth International Conference on 2001*, (2001) 403–408

14. B.K. Sikdar, N. Ganguly, P. Majumder and P.P. Chaudhuri, *Design of multiple attractor $GF(2^p)$ cellular automata for diagnosis of VLSI circuits, VLSI Design, Fourteenth International Conference on 2001*, (2001) 454–459

Measures for Transient Configurations of the Sandpile-Model

Matthias Schulz

University of Karlsruhe, Department for Computer Sciences
Am Fasanengarten 5, 76128 Karlsruhe, Germany
schulz@ira.uka.de

Abstract. The Abelian Sandpile-Model (ASM) is a well-studied model for Self-Organized Criticality (SOC), for which many interesting algebraic properties have been proved. This paper deals with the process of starting with the empty configuration and adding grains of sand, until a recurrent configuration is reached.

The notion studied in this paper is that the configurations at the beginning of the process are in a sense very far from being recurrent, while the configurations near the end of the process are quite close to being recurrent; this leads to the idea of ordering the transient configurations, such that configurations closer to being recurrent generally are greater than configurations far from recurrent. Then measures are defined which increase monotonically with respect to these orderings and can be interpreted as "degrees of recurrence". Diagrams for these measures are shown and briefly discussed.

1 Introduction

The concept of Self-Organized Criticality (SOC) was suggested by Bak, Tang and Wiesenfeld in [1], introducing the Sandpile-Model (or the Abelian Sandpile-Model (ASM)): Considering a lattice with a boundary on whose vertices are placed grains of sand, a vertex shall topple if it contains more than three grains, i.e. the vertex loses four grains of sand and to each of the four adjoining vertices a grain is added; if a vertex lies next to the boundary, grains are lost. Now, starting with the empty configuration and adding grain after grain, at first there are very little vertices that topple per added grain, but after some time, a critical state is reached where there are avalanches of topplings of every possible size, distributed according to a power law, and the system will stay in this critical state as the process goes on.

Much research has been done on the configurations of the critical state, called recurrent configurations, for which Dhar proved in [2] that these configurations together with the addition of configurations form a group. There has also been established a connection between the set of recurrent configurations and the set of spanning forests of the lattice rooted in the boundary (e.g. in [3]), which leads to a formula for the number of recurrent configurations on a given lattice (cf. [4]).

S. El Yacoubi, B. Chopard, and S. Bandini (Eds.): ACRI 2006, LNCS 4173, pp. 238–247, 2006.

There also have been suggested several approaches towards explaining the power law distribution of the sizes of avalanches, as well as methods to analyze and measure avalanches; one key concept is the concept of decomposing avalanches into several waves of activity (cf. [5]).

Recently, the structure of the neutral element in the group of recurrent configurations has been studied in [6].

So far, the structure of the set of transient, i.e. non-recurrent, configurations has hardly been investigated. In this paper, partial orderings are considered, such that every transient configuration is smaller than another recurrent configuration. We find measures for transient configurations that increase monotonically in respect to these orderings, and observe an influence of the boundary of the lattice on the way these measures behave near the critical state when grains are added randomly to the actual configuration.

2   Definitions

Let $Z \subset \mathbb{Z}_n \times \mathbb{Z}_m$ be a proper non-empty subset of the torus of dimension $n \times m$, $S = \mathbb{Z}_n \times \mathbb{Z}_m \setminus Z$ be the boundary.

A function $c \in \mathbb{N}_0^Z$ is called a *configuration*; for each vertex $z \in Z$, $c(z)$ denotes the number of grains z contains.

A configuration is called *stable*, if each vertex contains at most three grains of sand; else c is *critical*. Let $\mathcal{C}$ be the set of all stable configurations.

If a configuration is critical, then there is at least one vertex in Z which can topple, losing four grains to the adjoining vertices; in a stable configuration, there exists no such vertex. If, starting with a critical configuration c, in each time step a vertex containing at least four grains topples, eventually a stable configuration is reached; this configuration does not depend on the order of the vertices that toppled and is denoted by c_{rel}; the process of iterated topplings until a stable configuration is reached is called *relaxation*, and $Rel(c)$ is an abbreviation for the relaxation of c.

For two configurations c and d, let $c \oplus d = (c+d)_{rel}$; then a stable configuration c is called *recurrent*, if there exists a non-empty configuration e, such that the equation $c \oplus e = c$ holds; a stable configuration is called *transient*, if it is not recurrent. Let $\mathcal{R}$ be the set of all recurrent configurations.

3   Recurrent Configurations

Let b denote the configuration such that each vertex $z \in Z$ contains as many grains as z has neighbors that belong to the boundary S; b is called the *burning configuration*.

For a (possibly critical) configuration c, let $A_c \subseteq Z$ be the set of all vertices that toppled at least once during $Rel(c + b)$. Then $c_{rel|A_c}$ is a recurrent configuration (possibly for another lattice); this implies that c_{rel} is recurrent if each vertex topples at least once during $Rel(c + b)$, and it is a well known fact that the opposite also is true, i.e. c_{rel} is transient if there is at least one vertex $z \in Z$ which does not topple during $Rel(c + b)$.

If c is a stable recurrent configuration, then each vertex topples exactly once during $Rel(c+b)$ and $(c+b)_{rel} = c$ holds (cf. [7]).

It is a well known fact that $(\mathcal{R}, \oplus)$ is an Abelian group (cf. [2]); let id denote the neutral element of this group.

4   Orderings

4.1   The Ordering $\leq$

Let $c, d \in \mathcal{C}$; a natural idea for ordering the configurations is to say that $c \leq d$ iff d can be reached from c by adding sand to c, which is the same as saying that there exists a configuration e such that $c \oplus e = d$. It can be shown straightforward that, if restricted to the transient configurations, $\leq$ is reflexive, transitive and anti-symmetric; $\leq$ is also compatible with $\oplus$, i.e. if $c \leq d$ holds, then for every $e \in \mathcal{C}$ $c \oplus e \leq d \oplus e$ holds, too.

Note that for every recurrent configuration c and every stable configuration d, there exists a configuration e such that $d \oplus e = c$ holds and thus $d \leq c$ holds for every configuration $d \in \mathcal{C}$. In particular, for two different recurrent configurations c and d, $c \leq d$ holds as well as $d \leq c$, which contradicts $\leq$ being an ordering on the whole of $\mathcal{C}$.

Let $\mathbf{3}$ be the configuration which assigns to each vertex three grains of sand. To check for two transient configurations c and d whether or not $c \leq d$ holds, the configuration

$$diff(c, d) = \mathbf{3} - (c \oplus (\mathbf{3} - d)) \tag{1}$$

called the *difference from c to d* is defined. The following equivalence is shown in [8]:

$$c \leq d \iff c \oplus diff(c, d) = d. \tag{2}$$

4.2   The Ordering $\sqsubseteq$

Consider the equivalence $\sim_{id}$, defined by

$$c \sim_{id} d \iff c \oplus id = d \oplus id. \tag{3}$$

This equivalence is compatible with $\oplus$, i.e. if $c \sim_{id} d$, then $c \oplus e \sim_{id} d \oplus e$ for every configuration e. Also, if c is recurrent, then the configurations d_1 and d_2 are equivalent iff $c \oplus d_1 = c \oplus d_2$.

Another ordering is the relation $\sqsubseteq$, defined by

$$c \sqsubseteq d \iff diff(d, c) = \mathbf{0}, \tag{4}$$

where $\mathbf{0}$ denotes the empty configuration. It is shown in [8] that $\sqsubseteq$ is an ordering on every equivalence class $[c]_{\sim_{id}}$ compatible with $\oplus$, and the following statements hold:

a) If $c \sqsubseteq d$, then $c \sim_{id} d$ holds.
b) If $c \sim_{id} d$ and $c \leq d$, then $c \sqsubseteq d$ holds.
c) If $c \sqsubseteq d$, then the total number of grains on the vertices given by c is less than or equal to the total number of grains on the vertices given by d; these numbers are denoted by $s(c)$ respectively $s(d)$.
d) For every stable configuration c the relation $c \sqsubseteq c \oplus id$ holds; thus in every equivalence class $[c]_{\sim_{id}}$, the greatest element is the only recurrent element in this class, namely $c \oplus id$.

4.3   Calculation Rules

Further, there are some "calculation rules" regarding the operations $\oplus$ and $diff$ as well as the relation $\sqsubseteq$:

$\forall c, d, e \in \mathcal{C}$:

a) $diff(c, diff(d, e)) = diff(c \oplus d, e)$;
b) $d \sqsubseteq c \oplus diff(c, d)$;
c) $diff(c \oplus e, d \oplus e) \sqsubseteq diff(c, d)$;
d) $diff(diff(d, e), diff(c, e)) \sqsubseteq diff(c, d)$;
e) $diff(diff(e, c), diff(e, d)) \sqsubseteq diff(c, d)$.

5   Measures for Transient Configurations

In the previous section two orderings of the transient configurations were introduced; this section deals with values assigned to transient configurations in such a way that, for a configuration c that is greater than configuration d with respect to $\leq$ or $\sqsubseteq$, the value assigned to c is greater than the value assigned to d. This value can roughly be interpreted as a *"degree of recurrence"*.

A function $m : \mathcal{C} \longrightarrow \mathbb{R}_0^+$ is called a *compatible measure with respect to* $\leq$ respectively a *compatible measure with respect to* $\sqsubseteq$, iff $m(c) \leq m(d)$ holds whenever $c \leq d$ respectively $c \sqsubseteq d$ holds. A function m is called a *fully compatible measure*, iff m is compatible as well with respect to $\leq$ as with respect to $\sqsubseteq$.

Let m be a compatible measure with respect to $\leq$; since for all recurrent configurations c and d, the relation $c \leq d$ holds as well as the relation $d \leq c$, it follows that $m(c) \leq m(d)$ and $m(d) \leq m(c)$, i.e. $m(c) = m(d)$. Since for each configuration $c \in \mathcal{C}$ and each recurrent configuration d the relation $c \leq d$ holds, each compatible measure with respect to $\leq$ takes its maximum at each recurrent configuration.

5.1   Examples for Compatible Measures

a) For each stable configuration c let $D(c)$ be the minimal number of grains that have to be added to c in order to get a recurrent configuration; formally expressed:

$$D(c) = \min\{n \in \mathbb{N} : \exists e \in \mathcal{C} : s(e) = n \wedge c \oplus e \in \mathcal{R}\}; \tag{5}$$

then the function $m_1 : \mathcal{C} \longrightarrow \mathbb{N}$ with

$$m_1(c) = 3|Z| - D(c) \tag{6}$$

is a fully compatible measure.
b) The function $m_2 : \mathcal{C} \longrightarrow \mathbb{N}$ with

$$m_2(c) = s(id) - s(\mathit{diff}(c, c \oplus id)) \tag{7}$$

is a fully compatible measure.
c) The function $m_3 : \mathcal{C} \longrightarrow \mathbb{N}$ which assigns to each configuration c the largest possible size of a subset $A \subseteq Z$ such that $c_{|A}$ is recurrent, is compatible with respect to $\leq$.
d) The function $m_4 : \mathcal{C} \longrightarrow \mathbb{N}$ which assigns to each configuration c the largest possible size of a connected subset $A \subseteq Z$ such that $c_{|A}$ is recurrent, is compatible with respect to $\leq$.

Proof

a) Let $c \leq d$ and let e be a configuration such that $c \oplus e$ is a recurrent configuration and e contains $D(e)$ grains, i.e. every configuration e' satisfying $c \oplus e' \in \mathcal{R}$ contains at least as many grains as e.

Since $\leq$ is compatible with respect to $\oplus$, the relation $c \oplus e \leq d \oplus e$ holds. $c \oplus e$ is a recurrent configuration, and so $d \oplus e$ has to be a recurrent configuration too; so $s(e) = D(c)$ is obviously an upper bound for $D(d)$, and it follows that $D(d) \leq s(e) = D(c)$ holds, from which relation we get $m_1(c) \leq m_1(d)$.

So m_1 is compatible with respect to $\leq$.

Now consider the configurations c and d with $c \sqsubseteq d$; let e be again a configuration satisfying $s(e) = D(c)$ and $c \oplus e \in \mathcal{R}$. Since $\sqsubseteq$ also is compatible with respect to $\oplus$, we get $c \oplus e \sqsubseteq d \oplus e$; there is only one recurrent configuration in every equivalence class $[c]_{\sim_{id}}$, and since $c \oplus e$ is recurrent, we get $c \oplus e = d \oplus e \in \mathcal{R}$. This leads again to the relation $D(c) \geq D(d)$, and again $m_1(c) \leq m_1(d)$ holds.

So m_1 is compatible with respect to $\sqsubseteq$ and thus fully compatible.
b) Let c be a stable configuration, e be a configuration such that $e \oplus c = id$ holds. We get the chain of equations

$$id \oplus \mathit{diff}(c, c \oplus id) = e \oplus c \oplus \mathit{diff}(c, c \oplus id) = e \oplus c \oplus id = id \oplus id. \tag{8}$$

From this we get $\mathit{diff}(c, c \oplus id) \sim_{id} id$; since id is recurrent, the equations $\mathit{diff}(c, c \oplus id) \sqsubseteq id$ as well as $s(\mathit{diff}(c, c \oplus id)) \leq s(id)$ hold. So $m_2(c) \geq 0$ for each stable configuration c.

Let $c \leq d$; then there exists a configuration e, such that $c \oplus e = d$. Then the calculation rule c) from 4.3 yields

$$\mathit{diff}(c \oplus e, c \oplus e \oplus id) = \mathit{diff}(c \oplus e, c \oplus id \oplus e) \sqsubseteq \mathit{diff}(c, c \oplus id), \tag{9}$$

which leads to $s(\mathit{diff}(d, d \oplus id)) \leq s(\mathit{diff}(c, c \oplus id))$; thus, we get the inequality $m_2(c) \leq m_2(d)$.

If $c \sqsubseteq d$, we know that $c \sim_{id} d$ holds and thus we get $c \oplus id = d \oplus id$; this configuration shall be denoted by e. According to the definition of $\sqsubseteq$ the equation $\mathit{diff}(d, c) = \mathbf{0}$ holds.

The calculation rule d) from 4.3 yields

$$\mathit{diff}(\mathit{diff}(c, e), \mathit{diff}(d, e)) \sqsubseteq \mathit{diff}(d, c) = \mathbf{0}, \tag{10}$$

from which we get

$$\mathit{diff}(d, d \oplus id) = \mathit{diff}(d, e) \sqsubseteq \mathit{diff}(c, e) = \mathit{diff}(c, c \oplus id), \tag{11}$$

and as above the relation $m_2(c) \leq m_2(d)$ can be shown.

It follows that m_2 is fully compatible.

c) Let c and d be stable configurations, such that $c \leq d$ holds. It is shown in [8] that in this case for every subset A of Z, $c_{|A} \leq d_{|A}$ holds. So, if there is a subset A of Z such that $c_{|A}$ is a recurrent configuration, then $d_{|A}$ is recurrent too, since $c_{|A} \leq d_{|A}$. The size of the largest subset A of Z such that $c_{|A}$ is recurrent is therefore a lower bound for size of the largest subset A' of Z, such that $d_{|A}$ is recurrent, and $m_3(c) \leq m_3(d)$ follows.

Thus, we get $m_3(c) \leq m_3(d)$.

d) The proof that $m_4(c) \leq m_4(d)$ whenever $c \leq d$ is just analogous to the proof of c).

Only m_2 is defined by an explicit formula. Considering m_1, it is shown in [8] that the problem of computing $D(c)$ for a given stable configuration c is NP-complete in case of a three-dimensional Sandpile-Model, and there is no efficient way known to the author of computing $D(c)$ for a configuration c in a two-dimensional Sandpile-Model. As similar problems arise for the computation of m_3 and m_4, approximations m_1', m_3' and m_4' are considered.

5.2   Approximations for m_1, m_3 and m_4

Approximation for m_1. Let c be a stable configuration, b be the burning configuration. Consider the configuration $c_0 = c + b$:

If there are vertices that do not topple during $Rel(c + b)$, let z_1 be a vertex such that z_1 has not toppled yet, at least one grain of sand has been added to z_1 and there is no vertex z' satisfying these two conditions and containing more grains than z_1. We add to z the necessary amount of grains such that z_1 becomes critical to get the configuration c_1.

Again, if there are vertices that neither toppled during $Rel(c_0)$ nor during $Rel(c_1)$, we choose a vertex z_2 satisfying the analogous conditions z_1 satisfied, i.e. z_2 has neither toppled during $Rel(c_0)$ nor during $Rel(c_1)$, there has been added at least one grain to z_2 and each z' satisfying these two conditions contains at most as many grains as z_2. We add grains to z_2, such that z_2 becomes critical, and get accordingly the configuration c_2.

This step is repeated until all vertices have toppled during one of the relaxations $Rel(c_0), \ldots, Rel(c_k)$; the stable configuration $(c_k)_{rel}$ is recurrent, and the total number of grains added to the vertices after $Rel(c+b)$ is an upper bound fr $D(c)$. Let $D'(c)$ denote this number; then $3|Z| - D'(c)$ is a lower bound for $m_1(c)$.

Note that this approximation depends on the choices for the vertices grains of sand are added to; while different choices can lead to different results for $D'(c)$, the results are qualitatively the same.

Approximations for m_3 and m_4. Starting from a (possibly critical) configuration c, the subset $A \subseteq Z$ is defined as the set of all vertices that toppled during $Rel(c+b)$. Then $(c_{rel})|_A$ is recurrent, and $|A|$ is a lower bound for $m_3(c_{rel})$; finding the largest connected subset of A yields a lower bound for $m_4(c_{rel})$.

6   Diagrams for Measurements

Starting with the configuration $c_0 = \mathbf{0}$, in each time step t a grain of sand is added to a uniformly distributed randomly chosen vertex z_t, thus getting the configuration c'_{t+1} and the configuration $c_{t+1} = (c'_{t+1})_{rel}$. We stop once a recurrent configuration is reached.

This process was simulated for a lattice of size 501×501 with the boundary being all vertices (x, y) with $xy = 0$; thus, the lattice is a square of side length 500, on whose boundary grains of sand get lost.

Another lattice studied is a torus of size 500×500 with one single vertex belonging to the boundary.

For the approximation of $m_3(c_t)$ and $m_4(c_t)$, the vertices that toppled during the relaxation of $(b + \sum_{i=0}^{t-1} e_{z_t})$ are used as described above. (e_z denotes the configuration, which assigns one grain to the vertex z and no grains to every other vertex).

In figure 1 diagrams are shown, where the values of $m_i(c_z)$ are plotted versus t, both for the square lattice as well as the torus lattice; because of the greater time complexity for computing m_2, for m_2 the process was simulated on a square of side length 200 and a torus of side length 200.

6.1   Discussion

Except for the rightmost part, the corresponding diagrams for the square and the torus are very similar; however, for the torus a recurrent configuration is reached quite some time before a recurrent configuration is reached for the square, so that there is a delay in the diagrams for the square, when the maximum of the measure is almost reached, although the observed configuration is not yet recurrent.

A closer look at the vertices that do not topple during $Rel(c_t + b)$ for large t shows them to lie near a corner of the square; for these vertices, the probability of change when a grain of sand is added to the lattice is very low, since they are protected from two sides against any avalanches of topplings. So, there is little change for the number of grains on these vertices, and since on these vertices

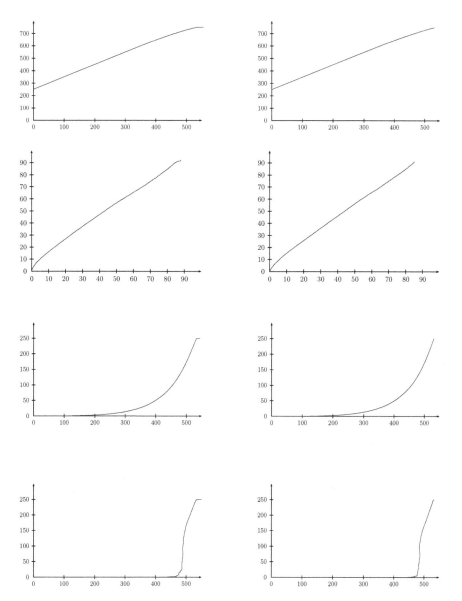

Fig. 1. Diagrams for m_1 (first row) to m_4 (last row) for the process of adding sand to an initial empty configuration, run on a 500×500 square (left diagram) respectively torus (right diagram), except for m_2, for which the process is run on a 200×200 square respectively torus. All axes are scaled down by the factor 1000.

the initial configuration is transient, it takes a longer time to reach a recurrent configuration on these vertices than on other subsets of Z. This explains the observed delay compared to the case of the lattice being a torus, where there are no such "protected" vertices.

Except for the delay in case of the lattice being a square, m'_1 and m_2 increase nearly linearly, while m'_3 increases nearly exponentially in the interval from $t = 3 \cdot 10^5$ to $t = 5 \cdot 10^5$.

One can see a phase transition in the diagram for m'_4: For $t < 450000$ the values of $m'_4(c_t)$ are very small, near $t = 480000$ the value of $m'_4(c_t)$ increases drastically, and afterwards the values increase nearly linearly. This behavior can be explained as follows:

At first, there are very few vertices that have toppled, and they are isolated. Around $t = 480000$, these isolated vertices get connected to a large cluster; once nearly all vertices that toppled during the process are in one cluster contained, the size of the cluster increases nearly linearly until it contains the whole of Z.

In Figure 2 the gradient of $m'_4(c_t)$ is plotted against t for the lattice being a square; there is a clear peak near $t = 480000$.

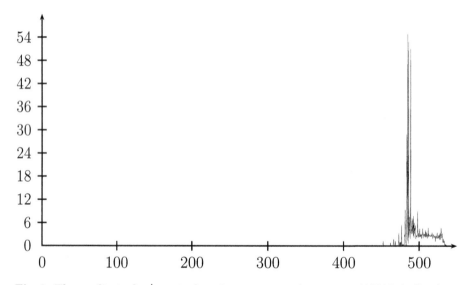

Fig. 2. The gradient of m'_4 vs. t; there is a strong peak near $t = 480000$, indicating a phase transition. The x-axis is scaled down by the factor 1000.

7 Conclusion

The concept of compatible measures for transient measures has been introduced, thus allowing to specify a notion of " more recurrent " and " less recurrent " configurations.

Four such measures have been discussed. One important observation is that the choice of the boundary has an influence on the behavior of the measures, as there is an interval during which each measure is near its maximum but stays nearly constant if the lattice is a square, while there is no such delay in case of the lattice being a torus. Here it would be of interest to explore more deeply the relation between the choice of the lattice and the behavior of the measures near the time a recurrent configuration is reached.

Another important observation is the fact that there are measures compatible with respect to $\leq$ which clearly show a phase transition, which is in accordance with observations of other global observables, especially the average size of an avalanche when a grain of sand is added to a vertex. However, the phase transition happens some time before these other observables change their behavior, so that other measures should be considered and studied.

References

1. Bak, P., Tang, C., Wiesenfeld, K.: Self-organized criticality: An explanation of the 1/f noise. Phys. Rev. Lett. **59** (1987) 381–384
2. Dhar, D., Ruelle, P., Sen, S., Verma, D.N.: Algebraic aspects of abelian sandpile models. J.PHYS.A **28** (1995) 805
3. Chung, F., Ellis, R.: A chip-firing game and dirichlet eigenvalues. Discrete Mathematics **257** (2002) 341–355
4. Creutz, M.: Cellular automata and self-organized criticality. In G. Bhanot, S.C., Seiden, P., eds.: Some new directions in science on computers. World Scientific, Singapore (1996) 147–169
5. E. V. Ivashkevich, D.V.K., Priezzhev, V.B.: Waves of topplings in an abelian sandpile. Physica A: Statistical and Theoretical Physics **209** (1994) 347–360
6. Dartois, A., Magnien, C.: Results and conjectures on the sandpile identity on a lattice. In Morvan, M., Rémila, É., eds.: Discrete Models for Complex Systems, DMCS'03. Volume AB of DMTCS Proceedings., Discrete Mathematics and Theoretical Computer Science (2003) 89–102
7. Majumdar, S.N., Dhar, D.: Equivalence between the abelian sandpile model and the $q \longrightarrow 0$ limit of the potts model. Physica A: Statistical and Theoretical Physics **185** (1992) 129–145
8. Schulz, M.: Untersuchungen am sandhaufen-modell. Master's thesis, University of Karlsruhe (2006)

From Cells to Islands: An Unified Model of Cellular Parallel Genetic Algorithms

David Simoncini, Philippe Collard, Sébastien Verel,
and Manuel Clergue

Université Nice Sophia-Antipolis/CNRS
{simoncin, pc, verel, clerguem}@i3s.unice.fr

Abstract. This paper presents the Anisotropic selection scheme for cellular Genetic Algorithms (cGA). This new scheme allows to enhance diversity and to control the selective pressure which are two important issues in Genetic Algorithms, especially when trying to solve difficult optimization problems. Varying the anisotropic degree of selection allows swapping from a cellular to an island model of parallel genetic algorithm. Measures of performances and diversity have been performed on one well-known problem: the Quadratic Assignment Problem which is known to be difficult to optimize. Experiences show that, tuning the anisotropic degree, we can find the accurate trade-off between cGA and island models to optimize performances of parallel evolutionary algorithms. This trade-off can be interpreted as the suitable degree of migration among subpopulations in a parallel Genetic Algorithm.

Introduction

In the context of cellular genetic algorithm (cGA), this paper proposes the Anisotropic selection as a new selection scheme which accurately allows to adjust the selective pressure and to control the exploration/exploitation ratio. This new class of evolutionary algorithms is supervised in a continuous way by an unique real parameter α in the range [-1..1]. The work described in this paper is an attempt to provide a unified model of parallel genetic algorithms (pGA) from fine grain massively parallel GA (cGA) to coarse grain parallel model (island GA). As extreme cases, there are the cGA that assumes one individual resides at each cell, and at the opposite, a pGA where distinct subpopulations execute a standard GA; between them we find models of pGA where migration allows to exchange to some extend genetic information between subpopulations. Thus the search dynamics of our family of pGA can vary from a diffusion to a migration process. To illustrate our approach we used one well-known problem: the Quadratic Assignment Problem (QAP). We study the performances of our class of parallel evolutionary algorithms on this problem and we show that there is a threshold for parameter α according to the average performances. Section 1 gives a description of the cGA and the island models. Section 2 introduces the anisotropic parallel Genetic Algorithms (apGA) and the anisotropic selection scheme. Section 3 is a presentation of the test problem: the QAP, and gives the performances of the apGA on the QAP. Finally, a study on population genotypic diversity is made in section 4.

S. El Yacoubi, B. Chopard, and S. Bandini (Eds.): ACRI 2006, LNCS 4173, pp. 248–257, 2006.

1 Background

This section introduces the concepts of Cellular and Island Models of parallel genetic algorithms.

1.1 Cellular Genetic Algorithms

The Cellular Genetic Algorithms are a subclass of Evolutionnary Algorithms in which the population is generally embedded on a two dimensional toroidal grid. In this kind of algorithms, exploration and population diversity are enhanced thanks to the existence of small overlapped neighborhoods [9]. An individual of the population is placed on each cell of the grid and represents a solution of the problem to solve. An evolutionnary process runs simultaneously on each cell of the grid, selecting parents from the neighborhood of the cells and applying operators for recombination, mutations and replacement for further generations. Such a kind of algorithms is especially well suited for complex problems [5]. One of the interests of cGA is to slow down the convergence of the population among a single individual. Complex problems often have many local optima, so if the best individual spreads too fast in the population it will improve the chances to reach a local optimum of the search space. Slowing down the convergence speed can be done by slowing down the selective pressure on the population.

1.2 Island Model of pGA

Cellular genetic algorithms and Island Model genetic algorithms are two kinds of Parallel genetic algorithms. The first one is a *fine grain* massively parallel implementation that assumes one individual resides at each cell. The second one, using distinct subpopulations, is a *coarse grain* parallel model; Each subpopulation executes as a standard genetic algorithm, and occasionally the subpopulations would exchange a few strings: *migration* allows subpopulations to share genetical material [4]. Many topologies can be defined to connect the islands. In the basic island model, migration can occur between any subpopulations, whereas in the *stepping stone* model islands are disposed on a ring and migration is restricted to neighboring islands.

2 Anisotropic Parallel Genetic Algorithms

This section presents the *anisotropic parallel Genetic Algorithms*, which is a family of parallel genetic algorithms based on cellular GA in which anisotropic selection is used.

2.1 Definition

The Anisotropic selection is a selection method in which the neighbors of a cell may have different probabilities to be selected. The Von Neumann neighborhood of a cell C is defined as the sphere of radius 1 centered at C in manhattan distance. The Anisotropic selection assigns different probabilities to be selected to the cells of the Von Neumann neighborhood according to their position. The probability to choose the center cell C remains fixed at $\frac{1}{5}$. Let us call p_{ns} the probability of choosing the cells North (N) or

South (S) and p_{ew} the probability of choosing the cells East (E) or West (W). Let $\alpha \in [-1; 1]$ be the control parameter that will determine the probabilities p_{ns} and p_{ew}. This parameter will be called the *anisotropic degree*. The probabilities p_{ns} and p_{ew} can be described as:

$$p_{ns} = \frac{(1 - p_c)}{2}(1 + \alpha)$$

$$p_{ew} = \frac{(1 - p_c)}{2}(1 - \alpha)$$

Thus, when $\alpha = -1$ we have $p_{ew} = 1 - p_c$ and $p_{ns} = 0$. When $\alpha = 0$, we have $p_{ns} = p_{ew}$ and when $\alpha = 1$, we have $p_{ns} = 1 - p_c$ and $p_{ew} = 0$.

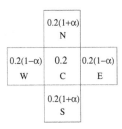

Fig. 1. Von Neumann neighborhood with probabilities to choose each neighbor

Figure 1 shows a Von Neumann Neighborhood with the probabilities to select each cell as a function of α.

The Anisotropic Selection operator works as follows. For each cell it selects k individuals in its neighborhood ($k \in [1; 5]$). The k individuals participate to a tournament and the winner replaces the old individual if it has a better fitness or with probability 0.5 if the fitnesses are equal. When $\alpha = 0$, the anisotropic selection is equivalent to a standard tournament selection and when $\alpha = 1$ or $\alpha = -1$ the anisotropy is maximal and we have an uni-dimensional neighborhood with three neighbors only. In the following, considering the grid symmetry we will consider $\alpha \in [0; 1]$ only: when α is in the range [-1;0] making a rotation of 90° of the grid is equivalent to considering α in the range [0;1]. When the anisotropic degree is null, there is no anisotropy in selection method, the apGA corresponds to the standard cellular GA. When the anisotropic degree is maximal, selection is computed between individuals in the same column only, the apGA is then an island model where each subpopulation is a column of the grid structured as a ring of cells with no interactions between subpopulations. When the anisotropic degree is set between low and maximum value, according to selection, a number of individuals can be copied from one subpopulation (i.e. column) to the adjacent columns. Thus the anisotropic degree allows to define a family of parallel GA from a cellular model to an island model.

In standard island model, the migration rate is defined as the number of individuals which are swap between subpopulations and migration intervals is the frequency of migration. In apGA, the migration process is structured by the grid. Only one parameter (the anisotropic degree) is needed to tune the migration policy. There is a difference between migration in a standard island model and migration in an apGA. In an apGA it can only happen (when the anisotropic degree allows it) between nearest neighbors in adjacent columns. Migration in that latter case is diffusion as it happens in the standard cGA model, except that the direction is controllable. In the following sections, we study the influence of this parameter on selection pressure, performances and population diversity.

2.2 Takeover Times and apGAs

The selective pressure is related to the population diversity in cellular genetic algorithms. One would like to slow down the selective pressure when trying to solve multi-modal problems in order to prevent the algorithm from converging too fast upon a local optimum. On the opposite side, when there is no danger of converging upon a local optimum, one would like to increase the selective pressure in order to obtain a good solution as fast as possible. A common analytical approach to measure the selective pressure is the computation of the takeover time [8] [10]. It is the number of generations needed for the best individual to conquer the whole grid when the only active operator is the selection [3]. Figure 2 shows the influence of the anisotropic degree on the takeover time. This figure represents the average takeover times observed on 1000 runs on a 32×32 grid for different anisotropic degrees. It shows that the selective pressure is decreasing while increasing anisotropy. These results confirm that the anisotropic selection gives to the algorithm the ability to control accurately the selective pressure. They are fairly consistent with our expectation that selection intensity decreases when the anisotropic degree increases. However, the correlation between takeover and anisotropy is not linear; it fast increases after the value $\alpha = 0.9$.

3 Test Problem

This section presents tests on one well-known instance of the Quadratic Assignment Problem which is known to be difficult to optimize. Our aim is to study the dynamics of the apGA for different tunings, and not to obtain better performances than other optimization techniques. Still, the apGA is implicitly compared to a cellular genetic algorithm when the anisotropic degree is null ($\alpha = 0$).

3.1 The Quadratic Assignment Problem

We experimented the family of apGAs on a Quadratic Assignment Problem (QAP): Nug30. Our purpose here is not to obtain better results with respect to other optimization methods, but rather to observe the behavior of apGAs. Especially we go in the search of a threshold for the anisotropic degree.

The QAP is an important problem in theory and practice as well. It was introduced by Koopmans and Beckmann in 1957 and is a model for many practical problems [6]. The QAP can be described as the problem of assigning a set of facilities to a set of locations with given distances between the locations and given flows between the facilities. The goal is to place the facilities on locations in such a way that the sum of the products

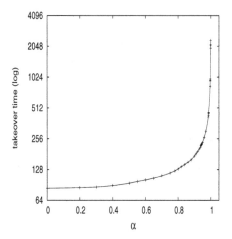

Fig. 2. Average of the takeover time as a function of the anisotropic degree α

between flows and distances is minimal. Given n facilities and n locations, two $n \times n$ matrices $D = [d_{ij}]$ and $F = [f_{kl}]$ where d_{ij} is the distance between locations i and j and f_{kl} the flow between facilities k and l, the objective function is:

$$\Phi = \sum_i \sum_j d_{p(i)p(j)} f_{ij}$$

where $p(i)$ gives the location of facility i in the current permutation p. Nugent, Vollman and Ruml proposed a set of problem instances of different sizes noted for their difficulty [2]. The instances they proposed are known to have multiple local optima, so they are difficult for a genetic algorithm. We experiment our algorithm on the 30 variables instance called Nug30.

3.2 Setup

We use a population of 400 individuals placed on a square grid (20×20). Each individual represents a permutation of $\{1, 2, ..., 30\}$. We need a special crossover that preserves the permutations:

- Select two individuals p_1 and p_2 as genitors.
- Choose a random position i.
- Find j and k so that $p_1(i) = p_2(j)$ and $p_2(i) = p_1(k)$.
- exchange positions i and j from p_1 and positions i and k from p_2.
- repeat $n/3$ times this procedure where n is the length of an individual.

This crossover is an extended version of the UPMX crossover proposed in [7]. The mutation operator consist in randomly selecting two positions from the individual and exchanging those positions. The crossover rate is 1 and we do a mutation per individual. We perform 500 runs for each anisotropic degree. Each run stops after 1500 generations.

3.3 Experimental Results

Figure 3 shows the average performance of the algorithm towards α on the QAP: for each value of α we average the best solution of each run. The purpose here is to minimize the fitness function values. The performances are growing with α and then fall down as α is getting closer to its limit value. The best average performance is achieved for $\alpha = 0.86$. This threshold probably corresponds to a good exploration/exploitation trade-off: the algorithm favors propagation of good solutions in the vertical direction with few interactions on the left or the right sides. This kind of dynamics is well adapted to this multi-modal problem as we can reach local optima on each columns of the grid and then migrate them horizontally to find new solutions. The worst average performance is observed for $\alpha = 0$ when the apGA is a cellular GA. $\alpha = 0.86$ corresponds to the optimal trade-off between cellular and island models for this problem, with the best migration rate between subpopulations. In our model, the migration rate is not the number of individuals which are swap between subpopulations, but the probability for the selection operator to choose two individuals from separate columns: two individuals from separate subpopulations would then share information. We can tell that there is an optimal migration rate that is induced by the value of the anisotropic degree α. Performances would probably improve if the migration rate did not stay static during the search process. As in [1], we can define some criteria to self-adjust the anisotropic degree along generations.

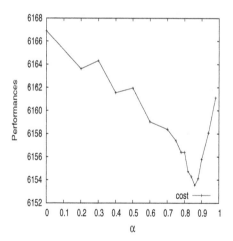

Fig. 3. Average costs as a function of α for the QAP

4 Diversity in apGAs

To understand better why we observe influence of the anisotropic parameter on performances, we felt it is important to measure genetic diversity during runs. We studied changes in diversity during runs according to the whole grid, the rows and the columns.

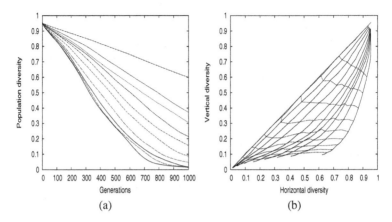

Fig. 4. Global population diversity against generation, with increasing α from bottom to top (a) and vertical diversity against horizontal diversity, with increasing α from left to right (b)

This section presents measures on population diversity in an apGA for the QAP. We conducted experiences on the average population diversity observed along generations on 100 independent runs for each anisotropic degree. We made three measures on the population diversity. First, we computed the global population diversity gD:

$$gD = (\frac{1}{\sharp r \sharp c})^2 \sum_{r_1, r_2} \sum_{c_1, c_2} d(x_{r_1 c_1}, x_{r_2 c_2})$$

where $d(x_1, x_2)$ is the distance between individuals x_1 and x_2. The distance used is inspired from the Hamming distance: It is the number of locations that differs between two individuals divided by their length n.

Then, we made measures on diversity inside subpopulations (vertical diversity) and diversity between subpopulations (horizontal diversity). The vertical (resp. horizontal) diversity is the sum of the average distance between all individuals in the same column (resp. row) divided by the number of columns (resp. rows):

$$vD = \frac{1}{\sharp r} \frac{1}{\sharp c^2} \sum_{r} \sum_{c_1, c_2} d(x_{r c_1}, x_{r c_2})$$

$$hD = \frac{1}{\sharp c} \frac{1}{\sharp r^2} \sum_{c} \sum_{r_1, r_2} d(x_{r_1 c}, x_{r_2 c})$$

where $\sharp r$ and $\sharp c$ are the number of rows and columns in the grid.

Figure 4(a) shows the average global diversity observed on the 1000 first generations during 100 runs on the QAP. The curves from bottom to top correspond to increasing values of α from zero to nearly one. Experiments measuring genetic diversity show that small migration rate (α close to one) causes islands to dominate others and retain global diversity without being able to exchange solutions to produce better results. At the opposite, for the cellular model, as α is closed to zero, global diversity falls near to zero after 800 generations causing premature convergence and negatively affects performances (see figure 3). Analysis on the QAP show the necessity of maintaining diversity to produce new results and the necessity to have enough information exchanges between columns.

Figure 4(b) represents the vertical diversity against the horizontal diversity. The contour lines plotted every 100 generations give some information on the speed of decrease of diversity. The more the migration rate decreases (i.e. α increases), the more the diversity is maintained on each row and subpopulations converge in each column. The vertical and horizontal diversities are decreasing with the same speed for the cellular model ($\alpha = 0$) and lower number of interactions between subpopulations helps the algorithm to maintain diversity on the rows when α is high.

Figure 5 shows snapshots of the population diversity during one single run at different generations. The snapshots are taken from left to right at generations 1, 200, 500, 1000 and 2000. The parameter α takes values in $\{0, 0.5, 0.7, 0.86, 0.98\}$ from top to bottom. Each snapshot shows the genotypic diversity in the neighborhoods of all cells on the grid. Color black means maximum diversity and color white means that there is no more diversity in the cell's neighborhood. Those snapshots help to understand the influence of the anisotropic selection on the genotypic diversity. First, we can see that the anisotropic degree influences the dynamic of propagation of good individuals on the grid. This propagation is the cause of the loss of diversity in the population. In the standard cellular model ($\alpha = 0$), good individuals propagate roughly circularly. If we slightly privilege the vertical direction ($\alpha = 0.5$) the circles become elliptical. As α increases, the dynamic changes and good individuals propagate column by column. For extreme values of the anisotropic degree (α close to 1) the migration rate is so low that good individuals are stuck in the subpopulations and the sharing of genetic information with other subpopulations is seldom observed. In that case, the selective pressure is too low and it negatively affects performances. The crossover operator doesn't have any effect in the white zones, since they represent cells with no more diversity in their neighborhoods. For the standard cellular case, interactions between cells may have some effects on performances only at the frontier between the circles. It represents a little proportion of cells on the grid after a thousand generations. For $\alpha = 0.86$, we can see vertical lines of diversity, which means that good individuals appear in each subpopulations. For example, when we see two adjacent columns colored in grey it means that those columns have been colonized by two different individuals. At generation 2000, a good individual has colonized the left of the grid but he still can share information with individuals in the grey zones. This means that the migration rate between subpopulations is strong enough to guarantee the propagation of the genetic information through the whole grid. This study showed that the dynamic of the propagation of individuals on the grid is strongly related to the anisotropic degree. Once again, it would be interesting to see what kind of dynamic appears if we define a local criteria to auto-adapt α during a run. This parallel model of GA allows to tune separately the anisotropic degree for each cell on the grid and measures during the search process can help to adjust locally the selective pressure.

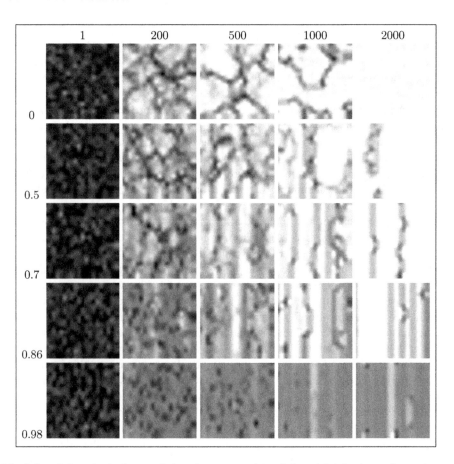

Fig. 5. Local diversity in the population along generations (left to right) for increasing α (top to bottom)

5 Conclusion and Perspectives

This paper presents a unified model of parallel Genetic Algorithms where granularity can be continuously tuned from fine grain to coarse grain parallel model. This family is based on the new concept of anisotropic selection. We analysed the dynamics of this class of pGAs on the well-known QAP problem. We have shown that the anisotropic degree plays a major role with regard to the average fitness found. Performances of the apGA increases with α until a threshold value ($\alpha = 0.86$). After this threshold, the migration rate between subpopulations in columns may be too small to generate good solutions. A study on local diversity shows the interactions between cells for different tunings of the apGA. The dynamic of propagation of individuals, which is strongly related to the genotypic diversity in the population, is dependent from the anisotropic degree of the apGA. Propagation of good individuals is done in circles for low values of α and turns to vertical lines for high values of α. Diversity is maintained in the population when the anisotropic degree is high, but when it reaches values close to the extreme case the few interactions between columns penalize the performances of the algorithm. These experimental results lead us to suggest to adjust dynamically the migration ratio during a run: by tuning the control parameter α, it would be possible to make the algorithm to self-adjust the migration level, depending on global or local measures. While theorical and experimental studies on island models are difficult due to their complexity, the apGA model could be used as a simple framework for calculations on parallel GA. Naturally it would be worth seeing how properties described in this paper extend for even more complex problems.

References

1. E. Alba and B. Dorronsoro. The exploration/exploitation tradeoff in dynamic cellular genetic algorithms. In *IEEE transactions on Evolutionnary Computation*, volume 9, pages 126–142, 2005.
2. J. R. C.E. Nugent, T.E. Vollman. An experimental comparison of techniques for the assignment of techniques to locations. *Operations Research*, 16:150–173, 1968.
3. D. E. Goldberg and K. Deb. A comparative analysis of selection schemes used in genetic algorithms. In *FOGA*, pages 69–93, 1990.
4. M. Gorges-Schleuter. Explicit parallelism of genetic algorithms through population structures. In *PPSN*, pages 150–159, 1991.
5. K. A. D. Jong and J. Sarma. On decentralizing selection algorithms. In *ICGA*, pages 17–23, 1995.
6. T. Koopmans and M. Beckmann. Assignment problems and the location of economic activities. *Econometrica*, 25(1):53–76, 1957.
7. V. V. Migkikh, A. P. Topchy, V. M. Kureichik, and A. Y. Tetelbaum. Combined genetic and local search algorithm for the quadratic assignment problem.
8. G. Rudolph. On takeover times in spatially structured populations: Array and ring. *Proceedings of the SecondAsia-Pacific Conference on Genetic Algorithms and Applications (APGA '00)*, pages 144–151, 2000.
9. P. Spiessens and B. Manderick. A massively parallel genetic algorithm: Implementation and first analysis. In *ICGA*, pages 279–287, 1991.
10. J. Sprave. A unified model of non-panmictic population structures in evolutionary algorithms. *Proceedings of the congress on Evolutionary computation*, 2:1384–1391, 1999.

Neutral Fitness Landscape in the Cellular Automata Majority Problem

S. Verel[1], P. Collard[1], M. Tomassini[2], and L. Vanneschi[3]

[1] Université de Nice-Sophia Antipolis/CNRS
{verel, pc}@i3s.unice.fr
[2] University of Lausanne
Marco.Tomassini@unil.ch
[3] University of Milano
vanneschi@disco.unimib.it

Abstract. We study in detail the fitness landscape of a difficult cellular automata computational task: the majority problem. Our results show why this problem landscape is so hard to search, and we quantify the large degree of neutrality found in various ways. We show that a particular subspace of the solution space, called the "Olympus", is where good solutions concentrate, and give measures to quantitatively characterize this subspace.

1 Introduction

Cellular automata (CAs) are discrete dynamical systems that have been studied for years due to their architectural simplicity and the wide spectrum of behaviors they are capable of [1]. Here we study CAs that can be said to perform a simple "computational" task. One such task is the so-called *majority* or *density* task in which a two-state CA is to decide whether the initial state contains more zeros than ones or vice versa. In spite of its apparent simplicity, it is a difficult problem for a CA as it requires a coordination among the automata. As such, it is a perfect paradigm of the phenomenon of *emergence* in complex systems. That is, the task solution is an emergent global property of a system of locally interacting agents. Indeed, it has been proved that no CA can perform the task perfectly i.e., for any possible initial binary configuration of states [2]. However, several efficient CAs for the density task have been found either by hand or by using heuristic methods, especially evolutionary computation [3,4,5]. For a recent review see [6].

All previous investigations have empirically shown that finding good CAs for the majority task is very hard. However, there have been no investigations, to our knowledge, of the reasons that make this particular fitness landscape a difficult one. In this paper we statistically quantify in various ways the degree of difficulty of searching the majority CA landscape.

The paper proceeds as follows. The next section summarizes some known facts about CAs for the density task. A description of its fitness landscape follows, focusing on the hardness and neutrality aspects. Next we identify and analyze

S. El Yacoubi, B. Chopard, and S. Bandini (Eds.): ACRI 2006, LNCS 4173, pp. 258–267, 2006.

a particular subspace of the problem search space called the Olympus. Finally, we present our conclusions and hints to further works and open questions.

2   The Majority Problem

The density task is a prototypical distributed computational problem for CAs. For a finite CA of size N it is defined as follows. Let ρ_0 be the fraction of 1s in the *initial configuration* (IC) s_0. The task is to determine whether ρ_0 is greater than or less than $1/2$. In this version, the problem is also known as the *majority* problem. If $\rho_0 > 1/2$ then the CA must relax to a fixed-point configuration of all 1's that we indicate as $(1)^N$; otherwise it must relax to a fixed-point configuration of all 0's, noted $(0)^N$, after a number of time steps of the order of the grid size N. Here N is set to 149, the value that has been customarily used in research on the density task (if N is odd one avoids the case $\rho_0 = 0.5$ for which the problem is undefined).

This computation is trivial for a computer having a central control. Indeed, just scanning the array and adding up the number of, say, 1 bits will provide the answer in $O(N)$ time. However, it is nontrivial for a small radius one-dimensional CA since such a CA can only transfer information at finite speed relying on local information exclusively, while density is a global property of the configuration of states. It has been shown that the density task cannot be solved perfectly by a uniform, two-state CA with finite radius [2].

The lack of a perfect solution does not prevent one from searching for imperfect solutions of as good a quality as possible. In general, given a desired global behavior for a CA (e.g., the density task), it is extremely difficult to infer the local CA rule that will give rise to the emergence of the computation sought. This is because of the possible nonlinearities and large-scale collective effects that cannot in general be predicted from the sole local CA updating rule, even if it is deterministic. Since exhaustive evaluation of all possible rules is out of the question except for elementary $(d = 1, r = 1)$ and perhaps radius-two automata, one possible solution consists in using evolutionary algorithms, as first proposed by Packard in [7] and further developed by Mitchell et al. [3,6].

The *standard performance* of the best rules (with $r = 3$) found at the end of the evolution is defined as the fraction of correct classifications over $n = 10^4$ randomly chosen ICs. The ICs are sampled according to a binomial distribution (i.e., each bit is independently drawn with probability $1/2$ of being 0).

Mitchell and coworkers performed a number of studies on the emergence of synchronous CA strategies for the density task (with $N = 149$) during evolution [6,3]. Their results are significant since they represent one of the few instances where the dynamics of emergent computation in complex, spatially extended systems can be understood. As for the evolved CAs, it was noted that, in most runs, the GA found unsophisticated strategies that consisted in expanding sufficiently large blocks of adjacent 1s or 0s. This "block-expanding" strategy is unsophisticated in that it mainly uses local information to reach a conclusion. As a consequence, only those IC that have low or high density are classified correctly since they are more likely to have extended blocks of 1s or 0s. These

CAs have a performance around 0.6. A few runs yielded more sophisticated CAs with performance (around 0.77) on a wide distribution of ICs. However, high-performance automata have evolved only nine times out of 300 runs of the genetic algorithm. This clearly shows that the search space is a very difficult one, even there exists some recent works on coevolutionary algorithm [8] which able to find a number of "block expanding" strategies.

These sophisticated strategies rely on traveling signals ("particles") that transfer spatial and temporal information about the density in local regions through the lattice, and have been quantitatively described with a framework known as "computational mechanics" [9,10]. The GKL rule [11] is hand-coded but its behavior is similar to that of the best solutions found by evolution. Das and Davis solutions are two other good solutions that have been found by hand [6]. Other researchers have been able to artificially evolve a better CA (*ABK*) by using genetic programming[4]. Finally, Juillé *et al* [5] obtained still better CAs (*Coe*1 and *Coe*2) by using a coevolutionary algorithm. Their coevolved CA has performance about 0.86, which is the best result known to date. We call the six best local optima known, with a standard performance over 0.81, the *blok* (tab. 1).

In the next section we present a study of the overall fitness landscape, while section 4.2 concentrates on the structure of the landscape around the *blok*.

Table 1. Description in hexadecimal and standard performance of the 6 previously known best rules (*blok*) computed on sample size of 10^4

GKL 0.815	Das 0.823
005F005F005F005F005FFF5F005FFF5F	009F038F001FBF1F002FFB5F001FFF1F
Davis 0.818	ABK 0.824
070007FF0F000FFF0F0007FF0F310FFF	050055050500550555ΓΓ55ΓΓ55ΓΓ55ΓΓ
Coe1 0.851	Coe2 0.860
011430D7110F395705B4FF17F13DF957	1451305C0050CE5F1711FF5F0F53CF5F

3   Fitness Landscape and Neutrality of the Majority Task

First we recall a few fundamental concepts about fitness landscapes [12]. A *fitness landscape* is a triplet $(\mathcal{S}, \mathcal{V}, f)$ such that : $\mathcal{S}$ is the set of potential solutions, $\mathcal{V} : \mathcal{S} \to 2^{\mathcal{S}}$ is the neighborhood function which associates to each solution $s \in \mathcal{S}$ a set of neighbor solutions $\mathcal{V}(s) \subset S$, $f : \mathcal{S} \to \mathbb{R}$ is the fitness function which associates a real number to each solution.

Within the framework of metaheuristic by local search, the local operators allow to define the neighborhood $\mathcal{V}$. If the metaheuristic only uses one operator *op*, the neighborhood of a solution s is often defined as $\mathcal{V}(s) = \{s' \in \mathcal{S} \mid s' = op(s)\}$. If more than one operator are used, it is possible to associate one fitness landscape to each operator or to define the set of neighbors as the set of solutions obtained by one of the operators. A neighborhood could be associated to a distance; for example, in the field of genetic algorithms, when the search space is the set of bit strings of fixed size, the operator which change the value of one bit defines the neighborhood. Thus, two solutions are neighbors if their Hamming distance is equal to 1.

The notion of neutrality has been suggested by Kimura [13] in his study of the evolution of molecular species. According to this view, most mutations are either neutral (their effect on fitness is small) or lethal. In the analysis of fitness landscapes, the notion of neutral mutation appears to be useful [12]. Let us thus define more precisely the notion of neutrality for fitness landscapes.

A *test of neutrality* is a predicate $isNeutral : S \times S \rightarrow \{true, false\}$ that assigns to every $(s_1, s_2) \in S^2$ the value $true$ if there is a small difference between $f(s_1)$ and $f(s_2)$.

For example, usually $isNeutral(s_1, s_2)$ is $true$ if $f(s_1) = f(s_2)$. In that case, $isNeutral$ is an equivalence relation. Other useful cases are $isNeutral(s_1, s_2)$ is $true$ if $|f(s_1) - f(s_2)| \leq 1/M$ with M is the population size. When f is stocastic, $isNeutral(s_1, s_2)$ is $true$ if $|f(s_1) - f(s_2)|$ is under the evaluation error.

For every $s \in S$, the *neutral neighborhood* of s is the set $\mathcal{V}_{neut}(s) = \{s' \in \mathcal{V}(s) \mid isNeutral(s, s')\}$ and the *neutral degree* of s, noted $nDeg(s)$ is the number of neutral neighbors of s, $nDeg(s) = \sharp(\mathcal{V}_{neut}(s) - \{s\})$.

A fitness landscape is neutral if there are many solutions with high neutral degree. In this case, we can imagine fitness landscapes with some plateaus called *neutral networks*. There is no significant difference of fitness between solutions on neutral networks and the population drifts around on them.

A *neutral walk* $W_{neut} = (s_0, s_1, \ldots, s_m)$ is a walk where for all $i \in [0, m-1]$, $s_{i+1} \in \mathcal{V}(s_i)$ and for all $(i, j) \in [0, m]^2$, $isNeutral(s_i, s_j)$ is $true$.

A *Neutral Network*, denoted NN, is a graph $G = (V, E)$ where the set V of vertices is the set of solutions belonging to S such that for all s and s' from V there is a neutral walk W_{neut} belonging to V from s to s', and two vertices are connected by an edge of E if they are neutral neighbors.

3.1   Statistical Measures of Neutrality

H. Rosé et al. [14] develop the *density of states* approach (DOS) by plotting the number of sampled solutions in the search space with the same fitness value. Knowledge of this density allows to evaluate the performance of random search or random initialization of metaheuristics. DOS gives the probability of having a given fitness value when a solution is randomly chosen. The tail of the distribution at optimal fitness value gives a measure of the difficulty of an optimization problem: the faster the decay, the harder the problem.

To study the neutrality of fitness landscapes, we should be able to measure and describe a few properties of NN. The following quantities are useful. The *size* $\sharp NN$ i.e., the number of vertices in a NN, the *diameter*, which is the maximum distance between two solutions belonging to NN. The *neutral degree distribution* of solutions is the degree distribution of the vertices in a NN. Together with the size and the diameter, it gives information which plays a role in the dynamics of metaheuristic [15]. Another way to describe NN is given by the *autocorrelation of neutral degree* along a neutral random walk [16]. At each step s_i of the walk, one neutral solution $s_{i+1} \in \mathcal{V}(s_i)$ is randomly chosen such as $\forall j \leq i$, $isNeutral(s_j, s_j)$ is true. From neutral degree collected along this neutral walk, we computed its autocorrelation. The autocorrelation measures the correlation structure of a NN. If the correlation is low, the variation of neutral degree is low ; and so, there is some areas in NN of solutions which have nearby neutral degrees.

4   Neutrality in the Majority Problem Landscape

In this work we use a performance measure, the *standard performance* defined in section 2, which is based on the fraction of n initial configurations that are correctly classified from one sample. Standard performance is a hard measure because of the predominance in the sample of ICs close to 0.5 and it has been typically employed to measure a CA's capability on the density task.

The error of evaluation leads us to define the neutrality of the landscape. The standard performance cannot be known perfectly due to random variation of samples of ICs. The ICs are chosen independently, so the fitness value f of a solution follows a normal law $\mathcal{N}(f, \frac{\sigma(f)}{\sqrt{n}})$, where σ is the standard deviation of sample of fitness f, and n is the sample size. For binomial sample, $\sigma^2(f) = f(1 - f)$, the variance of Bernouilli trial. Thus two neighbors s and s' are neutral neighbors $(isNeutral(s, s')$ is $true)$ if a t-test accepts the hypothesis of equality of $f(s)$ and $f(s')$ with 95 percent of confidence. The maximum number of fitness values statistically different for standard performance is 113 for $n = 10^4$, 36 for $n = 10^3$ and 12 for $n = 10^2$.

4.1   Analysis of the Full Landscape

Density Of States. It has proved difficult to obtain information on the Majority Problem landscape by random sampling due to the large number of solutions with zero fitness. From 4.10^3 solutions using the uniform random sampling technique, 3979 solutions have a fitness value equal to 0. Clearly, the space appears to be a difficult one to search since the tail of the distribution to the right is non-existent. Figure 3-a shows the DOS obtained using the Metropolis-Hastings technique for importance sampling. For the details of the techniques used to sample high fitness values of the space, see [17]. This time, over the 4.10^3 solutions sampled, only 176 have a fitness equal to zero, and the DOS clearly shows a more uniform distribution of rules over many different fitness values. It is important to remark a considerable number of solutions sampled with a fitness approximately equal to 0.5. Furthermore, no solution with a fitness value superior to 0.55 has been sampled.

Computational costs do not allow us to analyse many neutral networks. In this section we analyse two important large neutral networks (NN). A large number of CAs solve the majority density problem on only half of ICs because they converge nearly always on the final configuration $(O)^N$ or $(1)^N$ and thus have performance about 0.5. Mitchell et al. [3] call these "default strategies" and notice that they are the first stage in the evolution of the population before jumping to higher performance values associated to "block-expanding" strategies (see section 2). We will study this large NN, denoted $NN_{0.5}$ around standard performance 0.5 to understand the link between NN properties and GA evolution. The other NN, denoted $NN_{0.76}$, is the NN around fitness 0.7645 which contains one neighbor of a CA found by Mitchell et al. The description of this "high" NN could give clues as how to "escape" from NN toward even higher fitness values.

Diameter. In our experiments, we perform 5 neutral walks on $NN_{0.5}$ and 19 on $NN_{0.76}$. Each neutral walk has the same starting point on each NN. We try to explore the NN by strictly increasing the Hamming distance from the starting solution at each step of the walk. The neutral walk stops when there is no neutral step that increases distance. The maximum length of walk is thus 128. On average, the length of neutral walks on $NN_{0.5}$ is 108.2 and 33.1 on $NN_{0.76}$. The diameter of $NN_{0.5}$ is thus larger than the one of $NN_{0.76}$.

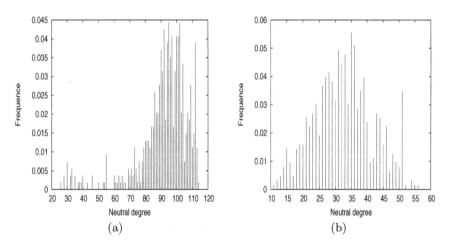

Fig. 1. Distribution of Neutral Degree along all neutral walks on $NN_{0.5}$ in (a) and $NN_{0.76}$ in (b)

Neutral Degree Distribution. Figure 1 shows the distribution of neutral degree collected along all neutral walks. The distribution is close to normal for $NN_{0.76}$. For $NN_{0.5}$ the distribution is skewed and approximately bimodal with a strong peak around 100 and a small peak around 32. The average of neutral degree on $NN_{0.5}$ is 91.6 and standard deviation is 16.6; on $NN_{0.76}$, the average is 32.7 and the standard deviation is 9.2. The neutral degree for $NN_{0.5}$ is very high : 71.6 % of neighbors are neutral neighbors. For $NN_{0.76}$, there is 25.5 % of neutral neighbors. It can be compared to the average neutral degree of the neutral NKq-landscape with $N = 64$, $K = 2$ and $q = 2$ which is 33.3 % .

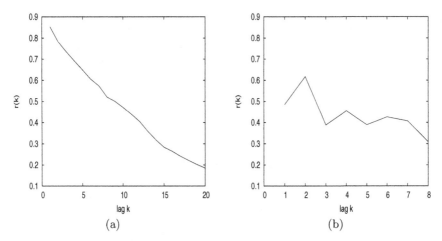

Fig. 2. Estimation of the autocorrelation function of neutral degrees along neutral random walks for $NN_{0.5}$ (a) and for $NN_{0.76}$ (b)

Autocorrelation of Neutral Degree. Figure 2 gives an estimation of the autocorrelation function $\rho(k)$ of neutral degree of the neutral networks. The autocorrelation function is computed for each neutral walk and the estimation $r(k)$ of $\rho(k)$ is given by the average of $r_i(k)$ over all autocorrelation functions. For both NN, there is correlation. The correlation is higher for $NN_{0.5}$ ($r(1) = 0.85$) than for $NN_{0.76}$ ($r(1) = 0.49$). From the autocorrelation of the neutral degree, one can conclude that the neutral network topology is not completely random, since otherwise correlation should have been nearly equal to zero. Moreover, the variation of neutral degree is smooth on NN; in other words, the neighbors in NN have nearby neutral degrees. So, there is some area where the neutral degree is homogeneous.

This study give us a better description of Majority fitness landscape neutrality which have important consequence on metaheuristic design. The neutral degree is high. Therefore, the selection operator should take into account the case of equality of fitness values. Likewise the mutation rate and population size should fit to this neutral degree in order to find rare good solutions outside NN [18]. For two potential solutions x and y on NN, the probability p that at least one solution escaped from NN is $P(x \notin NN \cup y \notin NN) = P(x \notin NN) + P(y \notin NN) - P(x \notin NN \cap y \notin NN)$. This probability is higher when solutions x and y are far due to the correlation of neutral degree in NN. To maximize the probability of escaping NN the distance between potential solutions of population should be as far as possible on NN. The population of an evolutionary algorithm should spread over NN.

4.2   Study on the Olympus Landscape

In this section we show that there are many similarities inside the *blok* (see section 2), and we use this feature to define what we have named the *Olympus*

Landscape, a subspace of the full landscape in which good solutions are found. Next, we study the relevant properties of this subspace. Before defining the Olympus we study the two natural symmetries of the majority problem.

The states 0 and 1 play the same role in the computational task; so flipping bits in the entry of a rule and in the result have no effect on performance. In the same way, CAs can compute the majority problem according to right or left direction without changing performance. We denote S_{01} and S_{rl} respectively the corresponding operator of $0/1$ symmetry and *right/left* symmetry. Let $x = (x_0, \ldots, x_{\lambda-1}) \in \{0,1\}^\lambda$ be a solution with $\lambda = 2^{2r+1}$. The $0/1$ symmetric of x is $S_{01}(x) = y$ where for all i, $y_i = 1 - x_{\lambda-i}$. The *right/left* symmetric of x is $S_{rl}(x) = y$ where for all i, $y_i = x_{\sigma(i)}$ with $\sigma(\sum_{j=0}^{\lambda-1} 2^{n_j}) = \sum_{j=0}^{\lambda-1} 2^{\lambda-1-n_j}$. The operators are commutative: $S_{rl}S_{01} = S_{01}S_{rl}$. From the 128 bits, 16 are invariant by S_{rl} and none by S_{01}.

Two optima from the *blok* could be distant whereas some of theirs symmetrics are closer. Here the idea is to choose for each *blok* one symmetric in order to broadly maximize the number of joint bits.

The optima GKL, Das, Davis and ABK have 2 symmetrics only because symmetrics by S_{01} and S_{rl} are equal. The optima Coe1 and Coe2 have 4 symmetrics. So, there are $2^4.4^2 = 256$ possible sets of symmetrics. Among these sets, we establish the maximum number of joint bits which is possible to obtain is 51. This "optimal" set contains the six *Symmetrics of Best Local Optima Known (blok$'$)* which are GKL$'$ = GKL, Das$'$ = Das, Davis$'$ = S_{01}(Davis), ABK$'$ = S_{01}(ABK), Coe1$'$ = Coe1 and Coe2$'$ = S_{rl}(Coe2).

The Olympus Landscape is defined from the *blok$'$* as the subspace of dimension 77 defined by the string S':

```
000*0*0* 0****1** 0***00** **0**1** 000***** 0*0**1** ******** 0*0**1*1
0*0***** *****1** 111111** **0**111 ******** 0**1*1*1 11111**1 0*01*111
```

Density Of States. The DOS is more favorable in the Olympus with respect to the whole search space by sampling the space uniformly at random, only 28.6% solutions have null fitness in the random sample. Figure 3-a shows the DOS on the Olympus which has been obtained by sampling with the Metropolis-Hastings method. Only 0.3% solutions have null fitness value in this sample, although the tail of the distribution is fast-decaying beyond fitness value 0.5 the highest solution for M-H is 0.68. The DOS thus justifies the favours to concentrate the search in the Olympus landscape.

Neutral Degree. The figure 3-b gives the neutral degree of solutions from Olympus as a function of their performance. The solutions below performance 0.5 are randomly chosen in Olympus. The solutions over performance 0.5 are sampled with 2 runs of a GA during 10^3 generations. This GA is based on GA defined by Mitchell [3] where the operators are restricted to Olympus subspace and the selection is a tournament selection of size 2 taking into account the neutrality. This GA allows to discover a lot of solutions between 0.80 and 0.835 and justified

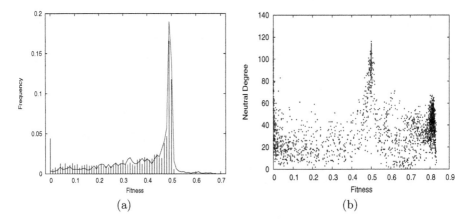

Fig. 3. (a) DOS using Metropolis-Hasting technique to sample the whole space (impulse) and the Olympus Landscape (line). (b) Neutral degree on Olympus as a function of the performance.

the useful of Olympus[1]. Two important NN are located around fitnesses 0 and 0.5 where the neutral degree is over 70. For solutions over 0.5, the average of neutral degree is 37.6 which is a high neutral degree.

5   Discussion and Conclusion

The landscape has a considerable number of points with performance 0 or 0.5 which means that investigations based on sampling techniques on the whole landscape are unlikely to give good results. The neutrality of the landscape is high, and the neutral network topology is not completely random. Exploiting similarities between the six best rules and symmetries in the landscape, we have defined the *Olympus* landscape as a subspace of the Majority problem landscape. This subspace have less solutions with performance 0 and it is easy to find solutions over 0.80 with a simple GA. We have shown that the neutrality of landscape is high even for solution over 0.5.

References

1. Wolfram, S.: A New Kind of Science. Wolfram Media (2002)
2. Land, M., Belew, R.K.: No perfect two-state cellular automata for density classification exists. Physical Review Letters **74** (1995) 5148–5150
3. Mitchell, M., Crutchfield, J.P., Hraber, P.T.: Evolving cellular automata to perform computations: Mechanisms and impediments. Physica D **75** (1994) 361–391

---

[1] Over 50 runs, average performances are 0.832 with standard deviation 0.006 which is higher than $0.80_{0.02}$ of coevolutionary algorithm of Pagie [8].

4. Andre, D., Bennett III, F.H., Koza, J.R.: Discovery by genetic programming of a cellular automata rule that is better than any known rule for the majority classification problem. In Koza, J.R., Goldberg, D.E., Fogel, D.B., Riolo, R.L., eds.: Genetic Programming 1996: Proceedings of the First Annual Conference, Cambridge, MA, The MIT Press (1996) 3–11

5. Juillé, H., Pollack, J.B.: Coevolutionary learning: a case study. In: ICML '98 Proceedings of the Fifteenth International Conference on Machine Learning, San Francisco, CA, Morgan Kaufmann (1998) 251–259

6. Crutchfield, J.P., Mitchell, M., Das, R.: Evolutionary design of collective computation in cellular automata. In Crutchfield, J.P., Schuster, P., eds.: Evolutionary Dynamics: Exploring the Interplay of Selection, Accident, Neutrality, and Function. Oxford University Press, Oxford, UK (2003) 361–411

7. Packard, N.H.: Adaptation toward the edge of chaos. In Kelso, J.A.S., Mandell, A.J., Shlesinger, M.F., eds.: Dynamic Patterns in Complex Systems. World Scientific, Singapore (1988) 293–301

8. Pagie, L., Mitchell, M.: A comparison of evolutionary and coevolutionary search. In Belew, R.K., Juillè, H., eds.: Coevolution: Turning Adaptive Algorithms upon Themselves, San Francisco, California, USA (2001) 20–25

9. Das, R., Mitchell, M., Crutchfield, J.P.: A genetic algorithm discovers particle-based computation in cellular automata. In Davidor, Y., Schwefel, H.P., Männer, R., eds.: PPSN III. Volume 866 of LNCS., Springer-Verlag (1994) 344–353

10. Hanson, J.E., Crutchfield, J.P.: Computational mechanics of cellular automata: An example. Technical Report 95-10-95, Santa Fe Institute Working Paper (1995)

11. Gacs, P., Kurdyumov, G.L., Levin, L.A.: One-dimensional uniform arrays that wash out finite islands. Problemy Peredachi Informatsii **14** (1978) 92–98

12. Reidys, C.M., Stadler, P.F.: Neutrality in fitness landscapes. Applied Mathematics and Computation **117** (2001) 321–350

13. Kimura, M.: The Neutral Theory of Molecular Evolution. Cambridge University Press, Cambridge, UK (1983)

14. Rosé, H., Ebeling, W., Asselmeyer, T.: The density of states - a measure of the difficulty of optimisation problems. In: Parallel Problem Solving from Nature. (1996) 208–217

15. Van Nimwegen, E., Crutchfield, J., Huynen, M.: Neutral evolution of mutational robustness. In: Proc. Nat. Acad. Sci. USA 96. (1999) 9716–9720

16. Bastolla, U., Porto, M., Roman, H.E., Vendruscolo, M.: Statiscal properties of neutral evolution. Journal Molecular Evolution **57** (2003) 103–119

17. Vanneschi, L., Clergue, M., Collard, P., Tomassini, M., Verel, S.: Fitness clouds and problem hardness in genetic programming. In: Proceedings of GECCO'04. LNCS, Springer-Verlag (2004)

18. Barnett, L.: Netcrawling - optimal evolutionary search with neutral networks. In: Proceedings of the 2001 Congress on Evolutionary Computation CEC2001, COEX, World Trade Center, 159 Samseong-dong, Gangnam-gu, Seoul, Korea, IEEE Press (2001) 30–37

Stability Analysis of Harvesting Strategies in a Cellular Automata Based Predator-Prey Model

Qiuwen Chen, Jingqiao Mao, and Weifeng Li

State Key Lab for System Ecology, Research Centre for Eco-Environmental Sciences,
Chinese Academy of Sciences, China
{qchen, mao.jq, li.wf}@rcees.ac.cn

Abstract. The stability properties of different harvesting strategies are an important aspect of predator-prey system. Most of the previous studies applied a non-spatial approach such as Lotka-Volterra model. In this paper, a stochastic cellular automata based predator-prey model (EcoCA) was developed and verified by the classical Lotka-Volterra model. The EcoCA was then used to investigate the statistical stabilities of different harvesting strategies of the predator-prey complex. Four groups of numerical experiments have been conducted: (1) no harvesting, (2) harvesting prey only, (3) harvesting predator only and (4) harvesting prey and predator jointly. Two harvesting methods, constant quota versus constant effort, are examined for each group. The effects of harvesting criterion are studied as well, which imposes a limit of population density when execute a harvest. The simulation results showed that constant effort leads to statistically more stable behaviors than constant quota. The joint harvesting of prey and predator with a reasonable constant effort can improve system stability and increase the total yields. In addition, it once again confirmed that space places a significant role in the stability properties of the predation and harvesting system, which indicates the importance to use spatially explicit model in conservation ecology.

1 Introduction

Qualitative and quantitative understanding of interactions between different species is crucial for population management where predation, competition and harvesting are the most influential factors [1, 2]. The competition and predation effects reflected by functional response have been substantially studied [3]. Much research effort has also been put into investigating the yields of different harvesting strategies [2, 4-5]. One of the basic concepts in the analysis of harvesting populations is maximum sustainable yield [1]. The usefulness of this measure is reduced when there are several interconnected species that are harvested, and this limitation was well discussed by May et al [6] on the management of multispecies fisheries. Beddington and Cooke [7] further studied the stability properties of various management regimes including constant quota versus constant effort, especially the joint harvesting of predators and prey. They found that constant quota cannot be achieved for small population size in order to prevent extinction. They also showed that the maximum stable sustainable yield cannot be fully exploited because any disturbance in that case could lead to system

S. El Yacoubi, B. Chopard, and S. Bandini (Eds.): ACRI 2006, LNCS 4173, pp. 268–276, 2006.

collapse. Costa Duarte [8] claimed on the basis of numerical simulations that constant quota is more stable than constant effort, which was contrary to what is often believed and was argued by Azar et al [5].

These studies usually applied a non-spatial model such as the Lotka-Volterra model. Some semi-spatial predation models were developed based on coupled map and coupled ordinary differential equations, where the coupled terms represents the migration of individuals between different patches [9]. These researches indicated that space plays an important role in stability properties of predation system. Another important property of the semi-spatial models is synchrony which will increase the probability of regional extinction and reduce metapopulation persistence. Spatially explicit models using cellular automata [10] and individual based paradigms [11] further proved the importance of space in stability properties of population dynamics.

This paper concentrates on investigation of statistical stabilities of different harvesting strategies of the predator-prey complex through a spatially explicit model. The stochastic cellular automata based model EcoCA [10] was updated to incorporate the capability of simulating harvesting processes. Four groups of experiments have been studied: (1) no harvesting, (2) harvesting prey only, (3) harvesting predator only and (4) harvesting prey and predator jointly. Two harvesting methods constant quota and constant effort are tested. The updated EcoCA is also compared with spatially lumped model to investigate space effects. The simulation results showed that constant effort leads to more statistically stable behaviours than constant quota. The joint harvesting of prey and predator with reasonable constant effort can improve system stability and increase the total yield, while harvesting predator only usually results in predator extinction. Space places a significant role in the stability of predation system, so that spatially explicit model is more advantageous in understanding ecosystem conservation.

2   Model Development

EcoCA is a two dimensional cellular automata model which has been developed for simulation of predator-prey system [10, 12]. The model has up to three possible cell states: empty, prey and predator; and the state of each cell is exclusive, namely that at each time step only one of the three states can exist in one cell. The boundary conditions are fixed in such a way that the neighbourhoods are completed with cells taking the state of empty [13]. The initial conditions are randomly defined, but as uniform as possible, by specifying the densities of prey and predator. The cell size can be subdivided or aggregated for investigating the effects of spatial scale. The neighbourhood configuration can be Von Neumann or Moore or extended Moore. The evolutions for each cell (i, j) applies stochastic rules that are dependent on the current state of the cell, the number of the neighbouring cells that are occupied by predator, N_{pd}, and the number of cells occupied by prey, N_{py}. These rules define a probability that a cell will become prey, P_{py} or predator, P_{pd} or empty 0 at next time step (Eq. 1).

$$P_k = f(S_{i,j}^t, N_{py}^t, N_{pd}^t) \qquad k \in (py, \ pd) \tag{1}$$

where f are evolution rules. These rules take into account reproduction, food availability, overcrowded and loneliness (Appendix). After the probability is calculated, a random selection process is used to determine the transition of the cell sate. Several runs of this system with various initial conditions all led to a very similar pattern of results as exemplified by the plots of Fig 1. These plots show respectively the population dynamics and phase dynamics of a 40×40 CA system with the initial conditions of prey = 400 and predator = 120. Although the dynamics of EcoCA model is not as strictly periodic as Lotka-Voterra model, the cyclic behaviours are well captured. The verification of EcoCA and comparison of statistical descriptors with Lotka-Voterra model were provided in Chen [12].

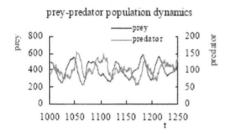
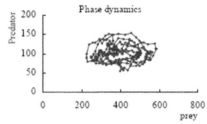

Fig. 1. Population dynamics (left) and phase dynamics (right) of EcoCA simulation; the square grids is 40×40; initial condition is prey = 400 and predator = 120; neighbourhood is Moore scheme

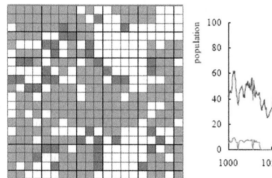
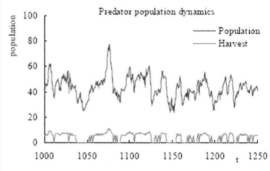

Fig. 2. Snapshot of population dynamics at t=1050 (left); predator population dynamics and harvest (right). Simulation results of the updated EcoCA model; the square grids is 20×20; initial condition is prey = 100 and predator = 100; neighbourhood is Moore scheme; jointly harvesting of prey and predator at the same constant effort 15%; harvesting criterion is 10%.

To investigate the stability properties of different harvesting strategies of a spatially explicit predation system, the EcoCA model is updated to be capable of simulating harvesting processes. The extended function consists of various options such as constant quota and constant effort, regional harvest and random harvest. In addition, a criterion can be specified so that a pre-scheduled harvesting is suspended when the population density is lower than the threshold.

The results of an exemplified simulation of the updated EcoCA model are presented in Fig 2. In the simulation, a square grid of 20×20 is used. The initial condition is prey = 100 and predator = 100, and the neighbourhood is Moore scheme. The harvesting strategy is to jointly take prey and predator at a same constant effort of 15% in a random way, and the harvesting criterion is defined as 0.1. It is seen from the results that the updated EcoCA is able to model the harvesting processes.

3 Design of Experiments

The updated EcoCA model is then used as an instrument to study the stability properties of a predation system with respects to harvesting strategies and spatial effects. To achieve the objective, a series of simulation experiments are systematically designed and implemented.

The first aspect is to test harvesting on different species that include no harvesting, harvesting of prey only, harvesting of predator only and joint harvesting of prey and predator. For each experiment, constant effort and constant quota are both examined. The second aspect is to investigate the space effects on system stability with different harvesting strategies. The EcoCA is a spatially explicit model; therefore comparisons with spatially lumped model should be conducted. In this study, the modified Lotka-Volterra (MLV) model is applied (Eq. 2).

$$\frac{dN}{dt} = aN - bN^2 - \alpha NP - H_1 \tag{2.1}$$

$$\frac{dP}{dt} = -cP + \beta NP - H_2 \tag{2.2}$$

where N: population of prey, P: population of predator; a: growth rate of prey; b: loading capacity limits (loading capacity $K = a/b$); c: mortality rate of predator; α: functional response of prey on predator; β: functional response of predator on prey; H_i is the harvesting that is defined as:

$$H_i = \begin{cases} C_i & \text{for constant quota} \\ r_i N \text{ or } r_i P & \text{for constant effort} \end{cases} \quad i = 1, 2 \tag{3}$$

in which r_i is constant effort. The MLV model is numerically resolved through a 4th-order Runge-Kutta method. The MLV model evolves in rich behaviours that include periodic, chaotic and centre point ($b{\neq}0$) depending on initial conditions and the parameters. However, in this paper the cyclic behaviour is of interests.

The third aspect is to study the difference between constant effort and constant quota. To keep them comparable, the mean harvests of constant effort is used as the constant quota. In addition to harvesting strategies and space, the effect of harvesting criterion is studied as well. In the present experiments, a threshold population density of 0.15 is selected and then compared with no criterion. However, comparison between regional harvesting and random harvesting is not conducted in the present study although the updated EcoCA model has the capability for such investigation.

In principal, there are totally 32 (2×4×2×2) cases to be investigated. But to focus on the key features, only 7 scenarios are selected that are given in the Table 1. The scenarios 1 to 4 are to test species effect, and the scenarios 4 and 5 are to test space effect, and the scenarios 4 and 6 are to test constant effort versus constant quota and the scenarios 4 and 7 are to test criterion effect. The EcoCA used exactly the same initial condition, which is defined by randomly distribute 100 preys and 100 predators in the domain, i.e. a population density of 0.25. The simulation period is 2000 time-steps. The parameters used in MLV model are $N_0 = 202$, $P_0 = 41$, $dt = 0.2$, $a = 0.95$ d^{-1}, $b = 0$, $c = 0.7$ d^{-1}, $\alpha = 0.0085$, $\beta = 0.0018$.

Table 1. Simulation scenarios of the experiments

Scenarios	Model	Harvest species	Harvest strategy	Harvest ratio	Criterion
1	EcoCA	No harvest			
2	EcoCA	Prey only	Constant effort	0.1	0.15
3	EcoCA	Predator only	Constant effort	0.1	0.15
4	EcoCA	Joint	Constant effort	both 0.1	both 0.15
5	MLV	Joint	Constant effort	both 0.1	both 0.15
6	EcoCA	Joint	Constant quota	Mean of constant effort	both 0
7	EcoCA	Joint	Constant effort	both 0.1	both 0

Table 2. Simulation scenarios of the experiments

Scenarios	Dynamics behaviours			M_{prey}	$M_{prdator}$	Var_{prey}	$Var_{predator}$
1	Stable	Not stationary	Coexistence	199	45	2824	149
2	Stable	Stationary	Coexistence	202	38	3339	157
3	Stable	Stationary	Coexistence	199	45	2215	164
4	Stable	Stationary	Coexistence	202	41	2288	116
5	Stable	Periodic	Coexistence	168	50	14342	915
6	Unstable	--	Prey dominant	--	--	--	--
7	Stable	Stationary	Coexistence	225	45	1461	102

The experiment results are analysed by using the similar methods that are applied in the previous researches [10]. The overall behaviours such as single species extinction, both species extinction and coexistence are first examined. Following that, stationarity [2] and chaotic dynamics [14] are analysed by using the procedure for screening time series data. For stationary dynamics, the stability properties will be further quantified in terms of statistical descriptors [15] since the EcoCA is a stochastic model. The square variance of population densities is chosen to be the major indicator of stability in the study.

The dynamics at the beginning are dominated by the effects of random initialisation. However, after sufficient time steps, it is then governed by evolution rules. Therefore, the results of the first 500 steps are excluded in the time series analyses.

4   Experiment Results

Several repeated runs of each scenario with the same initial condition lead to a very similar statistical behaviour that is summarized in Table 2.

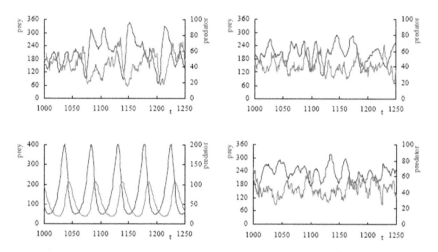

Fig. 3. Populations of scenarios 1 (top left), 4 (top right), 5 (bottom left) and 7 (bottom right)

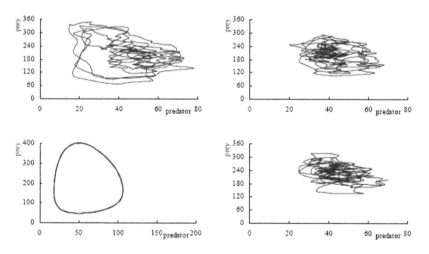

Fig. 4. Phase trajectories of scenarios 1 (top left), 4 (top right), 5 (bottom left) and 7 (bottom right)

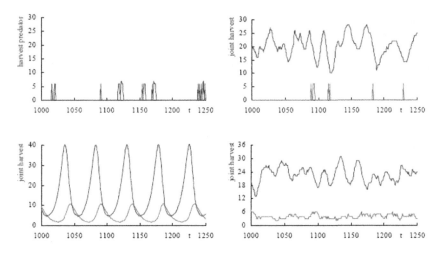

Fig. 5. Harvest of scenarios 3 (top left), 4 (top right), 5 (bottom left) and 7 (bottom right)

The population dynamics and phase trajectory of scenarios 1, 4, 5 and 7 are plotted in the Fig 3 and Fig 4. In addition, the harvesting results of scenario 3, 4 and 7 are presented in Fig 5. Since scenario 6 is unstable, a further statistical analysis is unnecessary.

5 Discussions

It is seen from the phase trajectories and statistical analyses (Table 2) that joint harvesting leads to the most stationary behaviour, while harvesting on prey alone has the least stationary dynamics. By comparing scenario 4 with 1, an interesting point is that a reasonable joint harvesting makes the system more stationary than no harvesting.

With respect to constant quota and constant effort, the simulations indicate that constant quota easily leads to system collapse, while constant effort usually evolves stationary. This result is consistent with the previous findings.

Comparing scenario 7 and 4, it is found that a jointly harvesting without restriction can lead to the system more stationary and productive. However, it is valid only when the constant efforts are reasonably small, which is 0.22 for predator in the presented experiment. Otherwise, the system will collapse. Due to the setting of harvesting criterion, the predator yields in scenario 3 and 4 are sporadic (Fig 4).

The study once again demonstrates that the spatially explicit EcoCA model has more stable dynamics than spatially lumped MLV model. The reason is that in lumped model, predators can pursuit preys globally, which results in large oscillations and sometimes chaotic behaviours or even extinction. In the EcoCA model, predation is limited to local area so that patches are emerged (Fig 2). This not only reduces the oscillation, but also increase the probability for the system to recover from one/more patches and thus improve the stability. This kind of feature of structural stability indicates the importance of spatially explicit methods.

It is concluded from the study that (1) joint harvesting on prey and predator with a rational effort can improve the stability and productivity of a predation system; (2) constant effort usually leads to more stable behaviours than constant quota; (3) space places an important role in the stability of a predation and harvesting system that need to be taken into account in the ecosystem conservation.

Acknowledgement

The research is partly funded by 973 National Basic Research Program of China (No. 2005CB121107) and the Ministry of Education.

References

1. Beddington, J.R., May, R.M.: Maximum Sustainable Yields in Systems Subject to Harvesting at More Than One Tropic Level. Mathematic Biosciences 15 (1980) 261-281
2. Azar, C., Holmberg, J., Lindgern, K.: Stability Analysis of Harvesting in a Predator-Prey Model. Journal of Theoretical Biology 174 (1995) 13-19
3. Beddington, J.R.: Mutual Interference between Parasites or Predators and its Effect on Searching Efficiency. Journal of Animal Ecology 51 (1975) 331-340
4. Brauer, F., Soudach, A.C.: Stability Region in Predator-Prey Systems with Constant Rate Prey Harvesting. Journal of Mathematic Biology 8 (1979) 55-71
5. Azar, C., Lindgern, K., Holmberg, J.: Constant Quota versus Constant Effort Harvesting. Environmental and Resource Economics 7 (1996), 193-196
6. May, R.M., Beddington, J.R., Clark, C.W., Holt, S.J., Laws, R.M.: Management of Multispecies Fisheries. Science 205 (1979) 267-277
7. Beddington, J.R., Cooke, J.G.: Harvesting from a Prey-Predator Complex. Ecological Modelling 14 (1982) 155-177
8. Costa Duarte, C.: Renewable Resource Market Obeying Difference Equations: Stable Points, Stable Cycles, and Chaos. Environmental and Resource Economics 4 (1994) 353-381
9. 9 Jasen, V.A.A.: The Dynamics of Two Diffusively Coupled Predator-Prey Populations. Theoretical Population Biology 59 (2001) 119-131
10. Chen, Q., Mynett, A.E.: Effects of Cell Size and Configuration in Cellular Automata Based Prey-Predator Modelling. Simulation Modelling Practice and Theory 11 (2003) 609-625
11. Nowak, M.A., Sasaki, A., Taylor, C., Fudenberg, D.: Emergence of Cooperation and Evolutionary Stability in Finite Populations. Nature, 428 (2004) 646-650
12. Chen, Q.: Cellular Automata and Artificial Intelligence in Ecohydraulics Modeling, Taylor & Francis Group plc, London UK (2004)
13. Chopard, B., Droz, M.: Cellular automata modelling of physical systems. Cambridge University Press, ISBN: 0-521-46168-5 (1998)
14. Hirota, R., Iwao, M., Ramani, A., Takahashi, D., Grammaticos, B., Ohta, Y.: From Integrability to Chaos in a Lotka-Volterra Cellular Automaton. Physics Letters A 236 (1997) 39-44
15. Mynett, A.E., Chen, Q.: Cellular automata as a paradigm in ecological and ecohydraulics modeling. Lecture Notes in Computer Science, Springer-Verlag Press, Germany (2004)
16. Thompson, J.M.T., Hunt, G.W.: Instabilities and Catastrophes in Science and Engineering. John Wiley & Sons, London, ASIN: 0471100714 (1982)

Appendix: Rules of the EcoCA

if cell is empty	if cell is prey

if Npy = 0, 1 and Npd = 0, 1 then
# not enough to reproduce 	
  Ppy = 0
  Ppd = 0
if Npd = 0, 1 and Npy ≥ 2 then
# prey will reproduce 	
  Ppd = 0
  Ppy = k1 * Npy / (Npy + Npd)
else
# predator will reproduce 	
  Ppy = 0
  Ppd = k2 * Npy / (Npd+1)
	if Npy = 0 and Npd = 0 then
	# prey may die (loneliness)
	  Ppy = p1 = 0.9
	if Npy = 0 and Npd • 0 then
	# prey will probably be eaten
	  Ppy = p2 = 0.1
	elseif Npd > Npy+1 then
	# prey will be eaten
	  Ppy = 0
	else
	# survival depends on Npy and Npd
	  Ppy = 1 – k3 * Npd / (Npy+1)

if cell is predator	Harvest

if Npy = 0 and Npd = 0 then
# no food & loneliness 	
  Ppd = p3 = 0.2
elseif Npy = 0 and Npd ≠ 0 then
# no food & competition 	
  Ppd = p4 = 0.1
elseif Npy ≠ 0 and Npd = 0 then
# predator may die (loneliness) 	
  Ppd = p5 = 0.8
elseif Npy > Npd + 1 then
# predator will survive 	
  Ppd = 1
else
# survival depends on Npy and Npd 	
  Ppd = k4 * Npy / (Npd + 1)
	1. compute Npy and Npd at t+1
	2. compute Hpy and Hpd
	3. random harvest Hpy and Hpd
	4. compute final Npy and Npd at t+1

Several probability constants and 'adjustment' parameters are included in the above rules that affect the evolutionary process:

p1 the probability that a prey will survive in the absence of any neighbours
p2 the probability that a single prey will survive in the presence of predators
p3 the probability that a predator will survive on its own with no food
p4 the probability that a predator will survive in a group with no food
p5 the probability that a single predator will survive in the presence of prey.
k1 adjustment factor for reproduction rate of prey
k2 adjustment factor for reproduction rate of predator
k3 adjustment factor for effect of predators upon prey survival
k4 adjustment factor for effect of prey upon predator survival

A Cellular Automata Model for Species Competition and Evolution

Bastien Chopard and Daniel Lagrava

Computer Science Department, University of Geneva, Switzerland
bastien.chopard@cui.unige.ch,
lagrava1@etu.unige.ch

Abstract. We propose a inhomogeneous cellular automata (CA) model in which several species compete for their territory and can co-evolved in regions where several of them coexist. Our model has as few parameters as possible. Each cell represent an individual and the associated CA rule represents its genome. The state evolution of each cell is interpreted as a phenotype. The fitness is defined as the cell activity, i.e. the variability of the state over time. Individuals of low fitness evolves by copying part of the genomes of neighboring high fitness individuals. We then consider a computer experiment implementing the competition-evolution of two species (two rules) each populating initially half of cellular space.

1 Introduction

Cellular Automata (CA) offer a powerful interaction paradigm to model many complex, spatially extented dynamical systems [3]. Artificial life and computer simulations of idealized ecosystems is a domain which has attracted a lot of research activities and, among them, the simulation of species evolutions, speciation and extinction [4,1,7,5,8] is of importance.

A difficulty which arises when modeling an ecosystem in which several species are competing and evolving is how to compute the fitness of each individual as a function of its genome. Ideally we would like that the fitness takes into account the performance of the genome in the actual environment. This is complex because the environment is affected by the presence of other individuals and other species. Thus, computing the fitness as the distance to a fixed "master" sequence in the genome space [4,2] amounts to assuming that the environment is completely static.

Here we propose a model in which most evolution parameters are naturally embedded in the basic model components and has a natural way to link the fitness value to the adaptablity of the individuals to their dynamically changing environment.

Our model represents a geographical area divided in many cells, each of them being populated by an individual identified by its genome. As will be discussed in section 2, this genome corresponds to a CA rule. In addition, each individual has a state (the sate of each CA cell) representing its current response to the environment and its interaction with neighboring individuals. The way this response

S. El Yacoubi, B. Chopard, and S. Bandini (Eds.): ACRI 2006, LNCS 4173, pp. 277–286, 2006.

evolves over time determines the phenotype and the fitness of each individual. During time evolution, individuals are allowed to mate with their neighbors. During this crossover phase, low fitness individuals will tend to borrow genetic code from high fitness individuals.

The problem we want to investigate is how a system, initially populated with only two different species, will evolve. As an illustration, fig. 1 shows the initial stage where two species are separated in space and the stable situation obtained after many iterations of our evolution-competition process. We can observe that new species have emerged and that homogeneous regions coexist with regions where no single species can dominate. This rich behavior is not due to a specific

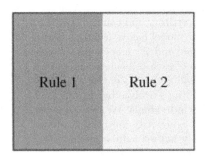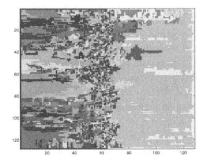

Fig. 1. *Left:* the initial configuration with two species occupying adjacent spatial regions. *Right:* after many rounds of interaction and hybridization, a new spatial distribution is observed, with many new species coexisting in some form of equilibrium. Here, the rule originally on the left is the so-called `Parity` rule (see below). On the right, the initial rule is built as a random lookup table.

choice of parameters but to the complexity of the spatial interactions and the large variety of species that can exist in our model. On the other hand, in spite of this huge evolution space, some structures emerge as the result of the competition and co-evolution process, indicating that collective organization counteracts the expected increase of entropy.

2   A CA Evolution-Competition Model

2.1   Environment Dynamics

Our model is based on a rather simple and intuitive CA dynamics. We consider a spatial region represented as $n_x \times n_y$ cells organized as a square lattice. In what follows we choose $n_x = n_y = 128$. In our model we assume that each of these cell host an individual.

Each cell c_{ij}, $1 \leq i \leq n_x$ and $1 \leq j \leq n_y$, is characterized by a lookup table T_{ij} and a state s_{ij}. T_{ij} is at the same time the CA rule of the cell and the genome of the corresponding individual. The state s_{ij} is the state of the cell and its time evolution is interpreted as the phenotype of the individual.

According to the standard definition of a CA, the time evolution of the states s_{ij} is given by

$$s_{ij}(t + 1) = T_{ij}(N_{ij}(t))$$ (1)

for $1 \leq i \leq n_x$ and $1 \leq j \leq n_y$. Here N_{ij} denotes an index to access the lookup table T_{ij}. It is built from the values the cell states in the neighborhood of c_{ij}. Note that here we allow for a inhomogeneous CA as the rule T_{ij} can be different on each cell.

In a general implementation, we may have z-bit states, i.e. $s_{ij} \in \{0, 1, \ldots, 2^z - 1\}$ and a neighborhood containing N cells. Therefore all possible CA rules T_{ij} can be coded by a lookup table with 2^{zN} entries. The return values are z-bit numbers. Since we consider a inhomogeneous CA, each cell must store its own lookup table T_{ij}. This may cause memory overflow for large n_x and n_y values, or for large neighborhood size N and large z. For this reason, we shall restrict to $z = 2$ and a von Neumann neighborhood with $N = 5$. Thus 32-entry lookup table are sufficient on each cell.

The boundary condition of our inhomogeneous CA can be chosen as desired. Here, for the sake of simplicity, we have considered periodic boundary conditions along the direction of the initial interface between species (vertical direction in fig. 1). In the perpendicular direction, we assume a reflexive boundary condition: $s_{i-1,j} = s_{i+1,j}$ on the left side and $s_{i+1,j} = s_{i-1,j}$ on the right.

2.2   Fitness Definition

Equation 1 together with the chosen boundary conditions define the behavior of each cell within the current environment. The time evolution of each cell depends on its local rule and of the states of the neighboring cells. Therefore, a cell will respond differently as a function of the type of the other individuals (cells) sharing the same neighborhood.

In order to describe the time evolution of each state or, in other words, to quantify the interaction between each individual and its environment, we define a fitness value F_{ij} at each CA cell. In our ecological interpretation, F_{ij} should reflect the level of adaptation of an individual to its environment. There is no obvious way to define this fitness value. Here we consider an arbitrary choice without any claim that it is biologically meaningful.

We assume that the phenotype of each individual is related to its behavior in the environment. A natural way to quantify this behavior is to measure the activity of each individual in a time window. We will arbitrarily decide that cells whose state s_{ij} often changes from one iteration to the next are more adapted (more alive) than those which are constant over long time intervals and appear to be "dead". Therefore, in our interpretation, active cells are more fit than inactive ones. Again, this is biologically questionable but beyond the scope of this paper.

Consequently, we define our time-dependent fitness function as the amount of change of the cell state over a given time T. In our case we will choose $T = 200$ iterations of the CA:

$$F_{ij}(t) = \sum_{\tau=T-t}^{t-1} |s_{ij}(\tau+1) - s_{ij}(\tau)| \tag{2}$$

With this definition some neighboring CA rules may coexist in a symbiotic way if the output of the first feeds the second one so as to increase its activity. On the other hand, some rules may have a negative interaction when their mutual activity is decreased when sharing a common neighborhood. Note that, in general, the interaction may be asymmetrical: one rule may gain in activity while the other decreases.

Using definition 2 we can easily exhibit an individual (or rule) of maximum fitness

$$s(t+1) = \begin{cases} s_{max} & \text{if } s(t) = s_{min} \\ s_{min} & \text{if } s(t) = s_{max} \end{cases}$$

where s_{min} and s_{min} are the min and max possible values of the set of state. With 2-bit states, we have $s_{min} = 0$ and $s_{max} = 1$.

2.3   Crossover

Once a fitness is defined, we can use it to drive an evolution process. We can for instance decide that low fitness cells will modify their genome in the hope to be better adapted to the current environment. Every $T = 200$ CA iterations, we shall perform such an evolution step by which individuals may change their lookup table. This approach is probably more inspired from an evolutionary computation framework such as Genetic Algorithms than biology. But, this choice can be easily modified in order to consider a specific biological case.

In order to select the individuals which will be subject to genetic evolution, we compare the fitness of each cell to that of the rest of the system. The average fitness $\bar{F} = 1/(n_x n_y) \sum_{ij} F_{ij}$ is first computed and if $F_{ij}(t) < \bar{F}(t)$, cell c_{ij} will hybridize with its highest fitness neighbor c_{kl}. We assume a uniform crossover of probability p_{ij} computed as

$$p_{ij} = \frac{F_{ij}}{F_{ij} + F_{kl}}$$

This means that entry ℓ of the genetically modified lookup table T_{ij} will be constructed as

$$T_{ij}(\ell) \leftarrow \mu_{ij}(\ell)T_{ij}(\ell) + \mu_{kl}(\ell)T_{kl}(\ell)$$

where $\mu_{ij}(\ell) = 1 - \mu_{kl}(\ell)$ are Boolean quantities. For each values of ℓ, $\mu_{ij}(\ell)$ will be 1 with probability p_{ij} and 0 with probability $1 - p_{ij}$. In this way, the best rule T_{lk} will be more represented than T_{ij} in the new individual c_{ij}. Figure 2 illustrates this genetic transformation. The above crossover process is applied synchronously to all cells after the T iterations. From an implementation point of view, this requires that every cell has actually two lookup tables: the current one which can be used in the crossover phase by a neighbor and the new one.

Note also that a cell surrounded by identical rules cannot be modified. Our crossover rule will only create new genomes when several different species are

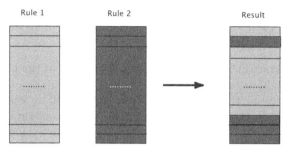

Fig. 2. Genetic transformation of a CA lookup table by a uniform crossover biased toward the fittest lookup table

neighbors. In our simulations, we shall assume that the left and right boundaries of the CA space are not subject to genetic evolution. The individuals on these two lines will keep their initial lookup table all along the simulation.

3   Simulation Results

We consider several simulations of our competition-evolution model with different initial pairs of rules. The typical initial condition is displayed in fig. 3 (left). A rules R_1 is chosen for the cells on the left part of the system and a rule R_2 for the cells on the right. We also have to specify the initial values of the state s_{ij}.

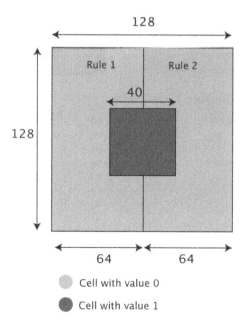

Fig. 3. Initial setup of the simulations

Here we assume, somehow arbitrarily, a central square of 1's surrounded by a sea of 0's. The possible rule candidates we shall consider here as the initial pair of left and right rules are

- **Parity:** The state at time $t + 1$ is the sum modulo 2 of the north, east, west and south neighbors at time t.
- **East:** The state at time $t + 1$ is the value of the cell on the left at time t: $s_{i,j}(t+1) = s_{i-1,j}(t)$. Thus, this rule translate any configuration eastwards,
- **Sup:** The state at time $t + 1$ is obtained by adding 1 modulo 2 to itself: $s(t + 1) = s(t) \oplus 1$.

The last rule is called *Sup* because it maximizes fitness given in eq. 2 by producing the sequence of states $0 \rightarrow 1 \rightarrow 0 \rightarrow 1 \ldots$, independently of the neighbors.

In fig. 4 we show the result of a run in which rules *Parity* and *East* are chosen as the initial pair. Our goal is to measure which new rules (or individuals) are generated during the iterations of the CA and how they populate the cellular space. For this purpose we need to associate an identifier with each individual.

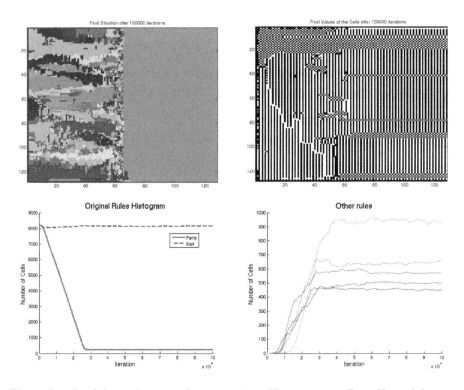

Fig. 4. Result of the evolution and competition of*Parity* versus *East. Upper left:* population after 1×10^5 steps; the color represent the lookup table at each cell. *Upper right:* the state of each cell after 1×10^5. *Lower left:* Number of individuals with the original rules. *Lower right:* Dominant emerging rules: each curve shows the number of individuals with a given new rules.

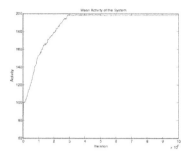

Fig. 5. Average fitness (or activity) as a function of time for the *Parity* versus *East* co-evolution

A way is to take the $z \times 2^{zN}$ bits of the lookup tables T_{ij}. This is by far too much information if we want to display a population dynamics, even with small values of z and N. This problem can be solved by applying a hash function to the content of the lookup tables. We chose Pearson function [6] which maps a string of symbols of arbitrary length onto an integer value between 0 and 255. The pseudo-code is

```
value := 0;
For i=0 to table_size
        value := table[value XOR LUT[i]];
return value;
```

where LUT contains the lookup table and table is an array containing an arbitrary permutation of $\{0, \ldots, 255\}$. An interesting property of this hash function is that table can be chosen so that our three basic rules have a different color when value is used as an index to a color map.

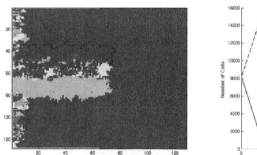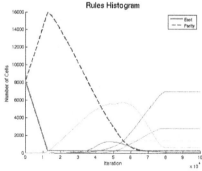

Fig. 6. The behavior of *East* versus *Parity*. *Left:* Situation after 20 000 generations. *Parity* has almost completely replaced *East* and then new rules start to appear from the left boundary. *Right:* Histogram of the rule distribution until the stationary regime is reached. We observe the growth of *Parity* at the expense of *East* and then the creation of new rules. Again, only the dominant rules are shown here. the situation changes.

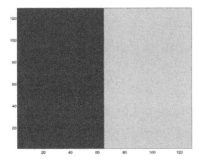 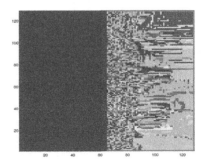

Fig. 7. *Left:* Result of the evolution and competition of *Sup* versus *East* after 200 000 iterations. The two rules coexist. *Right:* Result of the evolution and competition of *Sup* versus *Parity*, after 200 000 iterations. *Parity* is destroyed but other emerging rules develop on a smaller scale.

In the numerical experiments we show the CA configuration after 1×10^5 steps and give, for each cell, a color level corresponding to the quantity `value` obtained as explained above. In addition, we show, as a function time, the number of individuals using some of the emerging new rules. The new rules which are shown are those covering at least 10% of the total area (i.e. at least $128^2/10$ individuals belong to this species). As shown in fig. 5 the evolution corresponds to an increase of the average fitness of the whole system.

If the initial rules are swapped, i.e. *East* is on the left and *Parity* on the right, the behavior is quite different. This is due to the fact that *East* moves information from left to right and thus works differently if placed on the left or on the right of its competitor. When *East* is on the left of *Parity*, with the initial condition given in fig. 3, it does not generate activity and will disappear at the expense of *Parity* which quickly progresses in the left part of the

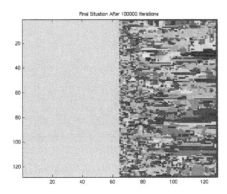 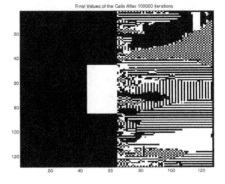

Fig. 8. Another run of the evolution and competition of *Sup* versus *Parity*. *Left:* Population distribution after 1×10^5 steps. *Right:* Corresponding states of the cells.

system. When the left boundary is reached, *East* activity resumes because of the chosen reflexive boundary conditions. New species are created, as illustrated in fig. 6.

On the other hand, rule *East* is very robust if, on its left side, a random sequence of 0 and 1 are produced. This is likely to occur when a mix of different rules are created beyond the interface. This situation also occurs in fig. 7 (left) where the *Sup* rule is on the left of *East*. We see that such a pair of rules is in an equilibrium situation or collaboration state. On the other hand, fig. 7 (right) shows that *Parity* does not coexist with *Sup*. To illustrate the reproducibility of the evolution process, fig 8 shows another run of the *Sup* and *Parity* interaction. The pattern is qualitatively similar to that of fig. 7 (right) but the details are of course different.

4   Conclusion

Our model proposes a simple abstraction of a ecosystem in which several species compete and interact with an environment which is dynamically shaped by the spatial distribution of the species. By associating local CA rules with the genome of an individual, we have a natural way to define the phenotype and the fitness of each individual from the dynamics of the cell states.

We considered the evolution of a population initially made of only two species occupying adjacent spatial regions. We show that, depending on the initial pair of rules representing each of the two species, different behaviors can be observed. The most interesting one is the emergence of new rules which populate significantly large contiguous area of cells and can coexist over time, even though some other regions are populated by a fast changing and uncorrelated individuals. Finally we also exhibit patterns of collaboration between rules or, on the contrary, situations where one rule overcome the other one.

From a biological point of view, we may argue that the choices we have made are not representing a realistic species evolution. At this stage we have mostly exploited the ecosystem metaphor to propose and discuss the behavior of a complex dynamical system. We do hope, however, that in a near future, the ideas proposed in this paper will indeed be applicable to describe the interactions and evolutions of living organisms.

References

1. F. Bagnoli and M. Bezzi. Punctuated equilibrium and criticality in a simple model of evolution. *Phys. Rev. Lett.*, 71:1593–1599, 1993.
2. F. Bagnoli and M. Bezzi. Speciation as pattern formation by competition in a smooth fitness landscape. *Phys. Rev. Lett.*, 79:3302–3305, 1997.
3. B. Chopard and M. Droz. *Cellular Automata Modeling of Physical Systems*. Cambridge University Press, 1998.
4. W. Eigen and P. Schuster. *Naturwissenshaften*, 64:541, 1977.
5. M.E.J. Newman. Simple models of evolution and extinction. *Computing in Science and Engineering*, 2:80–86, 2000.

6. Peter K. Pearson. Fast hashing of variable-length test strings. *CACM*, 33(6):677–680, 1990.
7. L. Peliti. Fitness landscape and evolution. Technical report, 1995. http://xxx.lanl.gov/abs/cond-mat/9505003.
8. D. Stauffer and M.E.J. Newman. Dynamics of simple evolutionary process. *Int. J. Mod. Phys. C*, 12:1375–1382, 2001.

A Cellular Automata Model for Adaptive Sympatric Speciation

Samira El Yacoubi and Sebastien Gourbière

MEPS/ASD - University of Perpignan
52, Paul Alduy Avenue, 66860 Perpignan, Cedex, France
{yacoubi, gourbier}@univ-perp.fr
http://www.univ-perp.fr/see/rch/cef/index.html

Abstract. The emergence of new species is one of the trickiest issues of evolutionary biology. We propose a cellular automata model to investigate the possibility that speciation proceeds in sympatry, focusing on the importance of the structure of the landscape on the likelihood of speciation. The conditions for speciation are shown to be limited whatever the landscape being considered, although habitat structure best favours the emergence of new species.

1   Introduction

Understanding the origin and maintenance of diversity is a fundamental problem in biology. Ecology and genetics usually focus on the maintenance of diversity addressing essential theoretical issues and trying to answer major questions of applied biology related to the harmful impact of human activities on the current biodiversity. More romantically, evolution is also concerned by the appearance of new forms of life on earth.

The emergence of new species is among the most controversial topics in evolution, whose origin is usually tracked back to Darwins seminal The Origin of species (1859). Several definitions of species have been provided (see [3], Ch. 1 for review), all fitting parts of the complexity of the process. Surely, the most used definition of species is related to the biological species concept; *species are groups of interbreeding natural populations that are reproductively isolated from other such groups* [18]. Starting from this definition, theoreticians investigate speciation as the emergence of two sets of individuals from one and the evolution of reproductive isolation between them.

Different scenarii have been proposed to account for such a diversification process. The most approved one is allopatric speciation, in which pools of individuals of a single initial population get geographically isolated because of an external event (like mountains formation). Sub-populations then differentiate, simply because they evolve separately. Sympatric speciation, the emergence of two species within a set of individuals living and reproducing in the same place, is much more tricky and has long been seen as a purely and unlikely theoretical hypothesis. The difficulty with sympatric speciation is that the continual mixing

S. El Yacoubi, B. Chopard, and S. Bandini (Eds.): ACRI 2006, LNCS 4173, pp. 287–296, 2006.

due to reproduction between individuals of the two incipient species (referred to as gene flow by evolutionary biologists) opposites the differentiation process.

Adaptive sympatric speciation provides an appealing answer to this issue. The basic idea is that, if splitting of the population is due to adaptation of the two pools of individuals to different ecological resources, then every single individual (whatever the pool it belongs to) has an advantage to mate with a partner using the same resource as it. This is simply because mating with an individual exploiting another resource eventually leads to produce unfit offsprings, which are unable to live on either resource. Also intuitive, this verbal argument calls for quantitative investigations under the many different ecological and genetic situations observable in the diversity of biological organisms.

In this contribution, we use cellular automata as a simple formalism to investigate adaptive sympatric speciation. Some work on sympatric speciation has been done in the past in the framework of CA's [1]. We focus in this paper on the importance of habitat structure on the probability of speciation by habitat specialization and evolution of assortative mating through a one-locus two-allele model (see [3], Ch. 4).

2   The Proposed Cellular Automata Model

2.1   Cellular Automata Approach

Cellular automata (CA) are a class of spatially and temporally discrete mathematical systems characterized by local interaction and an inherently parallel form of evolution. First introduced by von Neumann in the early 1950s to act as simple models of self-reproduction in biological systems, CA are considered as models for complex systems in computability theory, mathematics, and theoretical biology [4,15,16,22,24,25]. In addition to these theoretical aspects of CA, there have been numerous applications to physics, biology, chemistry, biochemistry among other disciplines. The studied phenomena include fluid and chemical turbulence, plant growth, ecological theory, DNA evolution, propagation of infectious diseases, urban social dynamics and forest fires. CA have also been used as discrete versions of partial differential equations in one or more spatial variables [2,8,9,12,23].

A cellular automaton consists generally of a regular array of identically programmed units called "cells" which interact with their neighbours subject to a finite set of prescribed rules for local transitions. Each cell is characterized by a particular state taken in a discrete set of values. Time progresses in discrete steps. The state of a cell at time $t + 1$ is a function only of its own state and of the states of its neighbours at time t.

In a mathematical formalism, a cellular automaton is defined as the quadruple $\mathcal{A} = (\mathcal{L}, \mathcal{S}, N, f)$, where $\mathcal{L}$ is a regular lattice which consists of a periodic paving of a d-dimensional space domain, $\mathcal{S}$ is a discrete state set, N is the neighbourhood of size n defined by the mapping

$$N : \mathcal{L} \longrightarrow \mathcal{L}^n$$
$$c \longrightarrow N(c) = \{c_1, c_2, \ldots, c_n\} \tag{1}$$

and f is a function which specifies the transition rule defined by

$$f: \quad \mathcal{S}^n \quad \longrightarrow \quad \mathcal{S}$$
$$s_t(N(c)) \longrightarrow s_{t+1}(c) \tag{2}$$

where $s_{t+1}(c)$ is the state of the cell c at time $t+1$.

The dynamics definition is augmented with initial and boundary conditions which depend on the considered application.

2.2 Biological Background

We considered a haploid population with discrete and non-overlapping generations living in a landscape including two types of habitat. Life-cycle involves a viability selection stage followed by reproduction. During the viability selection stage, each individual survives according to its adaptation to the habitat it is living in. All the surviving individuals are allowed to reproduce. Individuals first enter a mating pool according to some preferences they have and then mate randomly within the pool. Offsprings are laid close to the place occupied by their mother before mating. The genetic underlying ecological adaptation and mating pool preferences are as simple as possible. One ecological locus with two alleles, A and a, provides adaptation to the first and second type of habitat, respectively. One mating locus with two alleles, B and b, provides preferences for a first and a second mating pool, respectively.

In this background, we are interested in the joint evolution of habitat specialization and reproductive isolation. Speciation will be achieved if the two groups of individual adapted to each of the habitat get reproductively isolated by choosing different pools of mating. That is if the genetic structure of the population evolves towards one of the two following sets of genotypes $\{AB, ab\}$ or $\{Ab, aB\}$. This scenario, where individuals tend to mate assortatively with respect to genes non-involved in ecological adaptation, has been called *Assortative mating genes* by Maynard-Smith [17], who recognized it as the most plausible scenario for species to emerge in sympatry. It has received much attention leading to several modelling attempts (see [3,6,11] for reviews), none of them considering space explicitly as will be done using our cellular automata model.

2.3 Model Description

To model the spatiotemporal changes in the population, we propose a model based on a two-dimensional cellular automaton. It is defined on a square lattice where a cell can be either empty or occupied by a single individual which is assumed to carry one of the two ecological alleles (A or a) and one of the two mating alleles (B or b). We then consider four categories of individuals : AB, Ab, aB, ab which will be associated with the state values represented by a couple (x, y) where $x \in \{A, a\}$ and $y \in \{B, b\}$. A cell is given by its coordinates (i, j) in the square lattice $\mathcal{L}$ and its state at time t is denoted by $s_t(i, j)$ which takes values in the discrete state set $\mathcal{S} = \{A, a\} \times \{B, b\} \cup \{*\}$, where $*$ represents an empty cell. The cell (i, j) also has a characteristic of habitat denoted by $c_{i,j} \in \{H_1, H_2\}$ corresponding to the two types of habitat.

Each transition step is divided on three processes : survival which depends on the ecological allele A or a and the site occupation H_1 or H_2, mating depending on the second allele B or b and a local dispersal process of offsprings.

Survival is based on the following transition rules. An individual $(A, .)$ survives with probability s_A^1 if it lives in habitat H_1 and with probability s_A^2 if it lives in H_2. An individual $(a, .)$ survives with probability s_a^1 if it lives in H_1 and with probability s_a^2 if it lives in H_2, with $s_A^1 > s_A^2$ and $s_a^1 < s_a^2$.

For simplicity, we restrict ourselves throughout this paper to the case :

$$s_A^1 = s_a^2 = s \text{ and } s_A^2 = s_a^1 = 1 - s \text{ with } s \geq 0.5.$$

Let us denote by $\tilde{s}_t(i, j)$ the intermediate state of cell (i, j) after the survival phase which is applied only to occupied cells. For each cell (i, j) such that $s_t(i, j) \neq *$, the survival step is expressed by :

$$\tilde{s}_t(i, j) = \begin{cases} s_t(i, j) \text{ with probability} & \begin{array}{l} s_A^1 \text{ if } c_{i,j} = H_1 \text{ and } s_t(i, j) = (A, .) \\ s_A^2 \text{ if } c_{i,j} = H_2 \text{ and } s_t(i, j) = (A, .) \\ s_a^1 \text{ if } c_{i,j} = H_1 \text{ and } s_t(i, j) = (a, .) \\ s_a^2 \text{ if } c_{i,j} = H_2 \text{ and } s_t(i, j) = (a, .) \end{array} \\ * \qquad\qquad \text{otherwise} \end{cases} \quad (3)$$

Mating. We assume that individuals mate randomly within two pools they join with some preferences defined by the mating allele, B or b, they carry. It is important to note that mating process is independent on the spatial localization of individuals, which conforms to Gavrilets definition of sympatric speciation [11]. Let S_1 and S_2 be the mating pools, we denote by p $(p \geq 0.5)$ the preference probability of $(., b)$ to be in S_1 and $(., B)$ in S_2.

Let $S_i^{(x,y)}$ be the set of individuals xy belonging to S_i, $i = 1, 2$. We have then $S_i = S_i^{(a,b)} \cup S_i^{(a,B)} \cup S_i^{(A,b)} \cup S_i^{(A,B)}$ and we can calculate the different mating probabilities as :

$$p_1(a, b) = \frac{p}{|S_1|}(|S_1^{a,b}| + \frac{1}{2}|S_1^{a,B}| + \frac{1}{2}|S_1^{A,b}| + \frac{1}{4}|S_1^{A,B}|) +$$
$$\frac{1-p}{|S_2|}(|S_2^{a,b}| + \frac{1}{2}|S_2^{a,B}| + \frac{1}{2}|S_2^{A,b}| + \frac{1}{4}|S_2^{A,B}|)$$
$$p_2(a, b) = \frac{p}{2|S_1|}(|S_1^{A,b}| + \frac{1}{2}|S_1^{A,B}|) + \frac{1-p}{2|S_2|}(|S_2^{A,b}| + \frac{1}{2}|S_2^{A,B}|) \quad (4)$$
$$p_3(a, b) = \frac{p}{2|S_1|}(|S_1^{a,B}| + \frac{1}{2}|S_1^{A,B}|) + \frac{1-p}{2|S_2|}(|S_2^{a,B}| + \frac{1}{2}|S_2^{A,B}|)$$
$$p_4(a, b) = \frac{p}{4|S_1|}|S_1^{A,B}| + \frac{1-p}{4|S_1|}|S_2^{A,B}|$$

In the same way, we obtain the probabilities $p_i(a, B)$, $p_i(A, B)$ and $p_i(A, b)$, for $i = 1..4$. They represent all the mating probabilities in a set S_i, $i = 1, 2$, with a given category of individuals ab, aB, AB or Ab. Each individual xy has a probability $p_1(x, y) + p_2(x, y) + p_3(x, y) + p_4(x, y)$ of mating and can produce one of the fourth categories :

$$(a,b) \longrightarrow \begin{cases} (a,b) & \text{with } p_1(a,b) \\ (A,b) & \text{with } p_2(a,b) \\ (a,B) & \text{with } p_3(a,b) \\ (A,B) & \text{with } p_4(a,b) \end{cases} \qquad (A,b) \longrightarrow \begin{cases} (A,b) & \text{with } p_1(A,b) \\ (a,b) & \text{with } p_2(A,b) \\ (A,B) & \text{with } p_3(A,b) \\ (a,B) & \text{with } p_4(A,b) \end{cases}$$

$$(a,B) \longrightarrow \begin{cases} (a,B) & \text{with } p_1(a,B) \\ (A,B) & \text{with } p_2(a,B) \\ (a,b) & \text{with } p_3(a,B) \\ (A,b) & \text{with } p_4(a,B) \end{cases} \qquad (A,B) \longrightarrow \begin{cases} (A,B) & \text{with } p_1(A,B) \\ (a,B) & \text{with } p_2(A,B) \\ (A,b) & \text{with } p_3(A,B) \\ (a,b) & \text{with } p_4(A,B) \end{cases}$$

$$(5)$$

Dispersal. To describe offsprings dispersal, we will be interested in empty cells after the survival process. We construct an offsprings matrix produced after the mating step and denoted by $(r(i,j))_{i,j}$. The considered rule consists for each cell (i,j) whose state is given by $\tilde{s}_t(i,j) = *$ in selecting randomly one of its neighbouring mated individuals and taking its offspring. Let $N : \mathcal{L} \longrightarrow \mathcal{L}^n$ define the neighbourhood type in the considered CA model and $n = |N(i,j)|$ its size defined by its cardinality. Consider for each cell (i,j) the number $m_t(i,j) \leq (n-1)$, of neighbouring cells occupied by a mated organism at time t. Each offspring produced in the neighbourhood has a probability $\dfrac{1}{m_t(i,j)}$ to colonize the empty cell (i,j). It will die if it is surrounded only by occupied cells. The rule summarizing this step is expressed by :

$$s_{t+1}(i,j) = \begin{cases} \tilde{s}_t(i,j) & \text{if } \tilde{s}_t(i,j) \neq * \\ r(i',j') \text{ with probability } \dfrac{1}{m_t(i,j)} & \text{if } m_t(i,j) \neq 0 \\ * & \text{otherwise} \end{cases} \qquad (6)$$

where s_{t+1} denotes the final state after a complete transition, $(i',j') \in N(i,j)$ and $r(i',j') \neq *$.

3 Simulation Results

The landscape is represented by a square grid of 50×50 cells. Accordingly, the maximal population size is 2 500 individuals. Three matrixes are then constructed : habitat matrix which is given or randomly generated and is unchanged during the simulation. Individuals occupation matrix representing the ecological and mating characters which are initially randomly generated. The individuals ab, aB, Ab and AB are represented by 0, 1, 2 and 3 respectively. An empty cell is represented by 4. An offsprings matrix which is initialized at each iteration after the mating process.

We used two types of landscape either a highly or a non-spatially structured habitat as shown in Fig. 1. In both cases, we varied the strength of disruptive selection s and the strength of assortative mating p between 0.5 and 1. We followed the evolution of the genetic structure in space and time.

To make the understanding of our theoretical results easier, we first observe the different types of outcome while varying the model parameters : *Extinction,*

(a) Structured landscape   (b) Non-structured landscape

Fig. 1. Highly and non- spatially structured considered landscapes

Fixation, *Genetic Polymorphism* and *Speciation*. We then present the set of parameter values allowing for these possible outcomes.

The first pattern we obtain is called *Extinction*. The numbers of individuals of the different genotypes go down to 0.

The second obtained pattern is what we call *Fixation*. In this case, after a few generations, all the individuals tend to have the same genotype.

The more interesting cases are the ones where individuals of different genotypes persist. In these cases, simulations end up with either genetic polymorphism or speciation. To make the difference between these two potential outcomes, we used a common quantity called linkage disequilibrium (LD), and defined as :

$$LD(t) = \frac{N_0(t) * N_3(t) - N_1(t) * N_2(t)}{(|\mathcal{L}| - N_4(t))^2} \tag{7}$$

where $N_i(t)$ is the number of cells in state i at time t and $|\mathcal{L}|$ designates the total number of lattice cells.

Since genetic polymorphism corresponds to one of the two following structures $\{AB, aB\}$ or $\{Ab, ab\}$, we expect LD to tend towards 0. On the contrary, when speciation proceeds, LD is expected to converge to 0.25. More specifically, the simulation stop criterion for speciation corresponds to the following fulfilled condition :

$$|LD(t) - 0.25| < \varepsilon , \quad \text{for } t > T \tag{8}$$

when ε is a given tolerance and T is chosen to be big enough.

The first two patterns observed in Fig. 2 are called *Genetic Polymorphism* and were obtained with the two types of landscape of Fig. 1. In this case, two pools of individuals persist, each limited to the part of the landscape it is adapted to. As exemplified in Fig. 2a,b, individuals bearing allele a and A leave in habitat H_1 and H_2, respectively. But, these two pools of individuals do not correspond to two species since they are still reproducing one with another. This can be seen looking at the locus encoding for reproductive isolation. At this locus either allele b or allele B is fixed, so that all the individuals (whatever their ecological phenotype) enter the same mating pools. Which of allele b or allele B get fixed depend on initial conditions. Both cases correspond to genetic polymorphism as indicated by the null value of LD.

The two following pattern we observed in Fig. 2c,d, correspond to *speciation*. In this case the two pools of individuals are fixed for alternative alleles at both the ecological and the mating loci. For instance, the upper part of the landscape is occupied by ab individuals while the lower part is occupied by AB individuals. We also observed a spatial splitting between aB and Ab individuals, which also is identified as an instance of speciation.

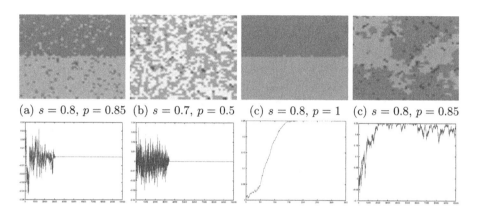

(a) $s = 0.8$, $p = 0.85$ (b) $s = 0.7$, $p = 0.5$ (c) $s = 0.8$, $p = 1$ (c) $s = 0.8$, $p = 0.85$

Fig. 2. Final patterns for different probabilities s and p and the corresponding linkage disequilibrium graphes

Interestingly, speciation is much faster in a highly structured landscape. Furthermore, in a random landscape the LD goes on varying in a large range of values while it does not when the habitat is structured. This is because in the former case the border between the areas occupied by the two species are much bigger. This gives opportunities for the frequency of the two genotypes to vary and, consequently, for the LD to fluctuate.

One important biological implication of these results is that completion of speciation (when it happens) depends on the structure of the landscape.

These phenomena are illustrated by implementing the CA rule given by eq (6) starting from an arbitrary initial condition and considering a von Neumann neigbourhood of radius $r = 1$. The tolerance ε is equal to 0.05. The codes are written in Matlab using its graphical interface for visualization. In Table 1 and 2, we give the probabilities values for which the speciation hold in the two types of landscape.

Clearly, selectivity for the mating pool has to be very high for speciation to happen, while requirements on the strength of disruptive selection are much lower. We proceed to the same sensitivity analysis considering a non-structured landscape where habitat H_1 and habitat H_2 are randomly attributed to each cell of the grid.

Table 1. Survival and mating probabilities for speciation with highly structured landscape

Mating probability p	Survival probability s	Speciation time
0.95	0.65	2243
0.95	0.7	1043
0.95	0.75	624
0.95	0.8	535
0.95	0.85	466
0.95	0.9	578
0.95	0.95	995
1	0.55	299
1	0.6	246
1	0.65	263
1	0.7	274
1	0.75	277
1	0.8	307
1	0.9	549
1	0.95	676

Table 2. Survival and mating probabilities for speciation with non-spatially structured landscape

Mating probability p	Survival probability s	Speciation time
1	0.5	1345
1	0.55	1881
1	0.6	5175

When the landscape is non spatially structured, the set of parameters allowing for speciation is even lower. Especially, speciation requires a perfect choice for each of the mating pools.

It should be noted that the obtained results in Table 1 and 2 for speciation time which corresponds to the first time the condition 8 has met, are very sensitive to the initial condition which is random for soil occupation and population distribution. Nevertheless, the values of s and p allowing speciation did not change between several simulations.

4   Discussion

In the *Assortative mating genes* scenario we investigated, individuals tend to mate assortatively with respect to genes non-involved in ecological adaptation. Different models have been set up to investigate the joint evolution of ecological specialization and reproductive isolation, all including different refinements in the description of the survival and mating processes (see [3,6,11] for reviews).

Our cellular automata model confirms that speciation is hard under the *Assortative mating gene* scenario since it requires (when the landscape is highly structured) a very high level of mating pool preferences ($p > 0.9$). Nevertheless, in those conditions, the required level of disruptive selection (that is the level s of adaptation of the two morphs to each type of habitat) is not as high as previously reported.

An important feature of our modelling is that the spatial distributions of two types of habitat are modelled explicitly and that individuals do not choose the habitat where their offspring will grow up. This differs from previous models where females are assumed to preferentially lay their eggs in the habitat where they were raised (e.g., Maynard-Smith [17]) or where other types of niche preferences are allowed to evolve [7,10,13,14]. Evolution of such preferences is shown to be an important requirement for speciation to proceed. In our model, offspring are more likely to live in the same habitat as their parents, although we did not model it explicitly. This can happen because we assumed offspring to occupy one of the neighbouring cells around the spatial location occupied by female before mating. A typical example of such process is reproduction of plants where seeds are passively dispersed around the trees where they come from. Whether an offspring is likely to live in the same habitat as its mother then depends of the structure of the landscape. A highly structured landscape is expected to produce an involuntary habitat preference while a random habitat is expected to result in no such by product of limited dispersal.

Indeed, speciation occurs more easily and faster when a strong spatial structure is included in the model, but it still occurs even in landscape when both types of habitat are randomly distributed. In this case, unexpectedly, there are strong spatial genetic structures which do not match with the random distribution of the two type of environment each species is adapted to. These results provide us with interesting perspectives to explain sympatric speciation in plants by adaptive processes as recently demonstrated for palm trees [21].

References

1. Bagnoli F., Bezzi M.: Speciation as Pattern Formation by Competition in a Smooth Fitness Landscape. Phys. Rev. Lett. 79, (1997) 3302–3305
2. Chopard B., Droz M.: Cellular Automata Modeling of Physical Systems. Cambridge University Press, (1998)
3. Coyne, J.A. and Orr, H.A.: Speciation. Sinauer Associates Sunderland, MA (2004)
4. Culik K., Hurd L. P., S. Yu.: Computation theoretic aspects of cellular automata. Physica D, 45, (1990) 357-378
5. Darwin, C. On the Origin of Species by Means of Natural Selection, or The Preservation of Favoured Races in the Struggle for Life. John Murray, London, (1859)
6. Dieckmann U, Doebeli M, Metz JAJ& Tautz D (eds): Adaptive Speciation. Cambridge University Press (2004)
7. Diehl, S. R., Bush G. L.:The role of habitat preference in adaptation and speciation. In D. Otte and J. A. Endler (eds.), Speciation and its consequences. Sinauer Associates, Sunderland, Massachusetts (1989) 345-365

8. El Yacoubi S., El Jai A.: Cellular automata and spreadability. Mathematical and Computational Modelling, vol. 36, (2002) 1059–1074

9. Ermentrout G. B., Edelstein-Keshet L.: Cellular automata approaches to biological modeling. Journal of Theoretical Biology, 160, (1993) 97–133

10. Fry, J. D.: Multilocus models of sympatric speciation: Bush versus Rice versus Felsenstein. Evolution 57 (2003) 1735–1746

11. Gavrilets, S.: Fitness Landscapes and the Origin of Species. Princeton Uiversity Press, Monographs in Population Biology, vol 41, (2004)

12. Green D. G.: Simulated effects of fire, dispersal and spatial pattern on competition within forest mosaics, Vegetation, Vol.82 (1989) 139–153

13. Kawecki, T.J.: Sympatric Speciation Driven by Beneficial Mutations. Proceedings Royal Society of London Vol. 265 (1996) 1515–1520

14. Kawecki, T.J.: Sympatric Speciation via Habitat Specialization Driven by Deleterious Mutations. Evolution 51 (1997) 1751–1763

15. Mange D., Tomassini M. (Eds.): Bio-Inspired Computing Machines, Presses Polytechniques et Universitaires Romandes (1998)

16. Margolus N.: Physics-like models of computation. Physica D, 10 (1984) 81–95

17. Maynard Smith J.: Sympatric speciation. Am. Nat. 100 (1966) 637-650

18. Mayr, E.: Systems of ordering data. Biol. Phil. 10 (1995) 419–434

19. Murray J.D.: Mathematical Biology, Biomathematics Texts. Springer (1993)

20. Perrier J.Y., Sipper M., Zahnd J.: Toward a viable, self-reproducing universal computer. Physica D, Vol.97 (1996) 335–352.

21. Savolainen V., Anstett M.C., Lexer C., Hutton I., Clarkson J.J., Norup M.V., Powell M.P., Springate D., Salamin N. and Baker W.J.: Sympatric speciation in palms on an oceanic island. Nature 441 (2006) 210–213

22. Sipper M.: Non-Uniform Cellular Automata: Evolution in Rule Space and Formation of Complex Structures. In R. A. Brooks and P. Maes, editors, Artificial Life IV, The MIT Press (1994) 394–399

23. Toffoli T.: Cellular automata as an alternative to (rather than an approximation of) differential equations in modeling physics. Physica D, Vol. 10 (1984) 117–127

24. Vichniac G.:Simulating physics with cellular automata. Physica D 10 (1984) 96–115

25. von Neumann J.: Theory of Self-Reproducing Automata. University of Illinois Press, Illinois, Edited and completed by A.W. Burks (1966)

26. Wolfram S.: Cellular automata and complexity: collected papers. Addison-Wesley Publishing Company (1994)

Combination of the Cellular Potts Model and Lattice Gas Cellular Automata for Simulating the Avascular Cancer Growth

Mehrdad Ghaemi[1] and Amene Shahrokhi[2]

[1] Department of Chemistry, Teacher Training University, Tehran, Iran
ghaemi@tmu.ac.ir
[2] District Health Center Shahre Ray, Vice-Chancellor for Health,Tehran University of Medical Science, Tehran, Iran
amene_shahrokhi@hotmail.com

Abstract. The advantage of Cellular Potts Model (CPM) is due to its ability for introducing cell-cell interaction based on the well known statistical model i.e. the Potts model. On the other hand, Lattice gas Cellular Automata (LGCA) can simulate movement of cell in a simple and correct physical way. These characters of CPM and LGCA have been combined in a reaction-diffusion frame to simulate the dynamic of avascular cancer growth on a more physical basis.The cellular automaton is evolved on a square lattice on which in the diffusion step tumor cells (C) and necrotic cells (N) propagate in two dimensions and in the reaction step every cell can proliferate, be quiescent or die due to the apoptosis and the necrosis depending on its environment. The transition probabilities in the reaction step have been calculated by the Glauber algorithm and depend on the K_{CC}, K_{NC}, and K_{NN} (cancer-cancer, necrotic-cancer, and necrotic-necrotic couplings respectively). It is shown the main feature of the cancer growth depends on the choice of magnitude of couplings and the advantage of this method compared to other methods is due to the fact that it needs only three parameters K_{CC}, K_{NC} and K_{NN} which are based on the well known physical ground i.e. the Potts model.

1 Introduction

Perhaps the most destructive phenomenon in natural science is the growth of cancer cells. The qualitative and quantitative comparison of simulated growth patterns with histological patterns of primary tumors may provide additional information about the morphology and the functional properties of cancer. Understanding the dynamics of cancer growth is one of the great challenges of modern science. The interest of the problem has led to the formulation of numerous growth models. Mathematical cancer modeling has been going on for many years. These models all included cancer cells and healthy cells to compete for space and nutrients, or drug. These progressed to Partial Differential Equation (PDE) models that generally modeled the tumor using diffusion of the cells [1]. Previous modeling techniques for the invasion process have included using sets of coupled reaction–diffusion equations for the cells and important groups of extracellular proteins and nutrients [2-5]. Today's model is typically a three

S. El Yacoubi, B. Chopard, and S. Bandini (Eds.): ACRI 2006, LNCS 4173, pp. 297 – 303, 2006.

dimensional PDE model with diffusion and advection for the cells, with scalar modifications based on nutrient and drug concentrations [6]. The PDE models can be numerically difficult to implement, however, due to a potentially high degree of coupling, besides the complex moving boundary problems. The inclusion of adhesion has been proven problematic in this type of model, although there have been some attempts [7, 8]. In addition, the reaction–diffusion approach makes the inclusion of the stochastic behavior of individual cells difficult to treat.

One way to circumvent this is to use a Cellular Automata (CA) model. CA approaches to biological complexity by describing specific biological models using two different types of cellular automata [9]: Lattice-Gas Cellular Automata (LGCA) and the Cellular Potts model (CPM).

LGCA can model a wide range of phenomena including the diffusion of fluids [10], reaction-diffusion processes [11], and population dynamics [12]. Dormann at al used LGCA for simulating dynamic of tumor growth [13]. In their model the dynamic of cancer growth can be explained as a reaction-diffusion process with three steps in each update. The reaction step contains mitosis, apoptosis, necrosis, and no change. In the diffusion step each cell moves to adjacent node according to it's velocity and in the redistribution step the occupation of channels in each site change according to preference weight. Dormann et al used phenomenological equations with adjustable parameters for the reaction part of the automata [14].

The Potts models [15] are general extension of the Ising model with q-state spin lattice, i.e., the Potts model with $q = 2$ reduces to Ising model. It attracted intense research interest in the 1970s and 1980s because it has a much richer phase structure and critical behavior than the Ising model [14]. In the cellular Potts model (CPM) [16-18] of cancer growth, each site contains one cell and considers necrotic, quiescent, and proliferating tumor cells as distinct cell types, in addition to healthy cells, with different growth rates and volume constraints for each type. In the CPM, transition probabilities between site states depend on both the energies of site-site adhesive and cell-specific non-local interactions.

The advantage of CPM is due to its ability for introducing cell-cell interaction in a correct and well known physical way. On the other hand LGCA can simulate movement of cell in a simple and correct physical way. In this article as explained in the next section, these characters of CPM and LGCA has been combined to simulate the dynamic of cancer growth on the more understandable and physical basis.

2 Method

The basic biological principles included in the model are cell proliferation, motility, necrosis, and apoptosis. The main body of the model is similar to the LGCA used for simulating reactive-diffusion systems. The cellular automaton evolves on a square lattice on which tumor cells (C) and necrotic cells (N) propagate in two dimensions. Each cell has associated with a velocity, which indicates the direction and the distance the cell will move in one time step. There are five velocity channels in each lattice site:

$$V_0=(0,0) , V_1 = (1,0), V_2 = (0,1), V_3 = (-1,0), V_4 = (0,-1),$$

where V_0 is resting channel and V_1, V_2, V_3, and V_4 represent moving to right, up, left, and down, respectively. In each lattice site, we allow at most one cell (N or C) with each velocity, or maximum five cells in each lattice site. The dynamic is built from the following three basic steps: 1- the reaction step that consists of mitosis, apoptosis, necrosis, and no change, 2- the propagation step, and 3- the velocity redistribution step.

2.1 Reaction Step

Every cell can proliferate, be quiescent, or die due to the apoptosis and the necrosis, depending on its environment. We have not enough and detailed information about the cell (cell itself is a complex system) and its interaction with other cells and materials, so deterministic prediction about the evolution of the cell is impossible and it is better to treat the cell dynamic as a stochastic dynamic. Cells adhere to each other by cell adhesion molecules (CAMs) which are present in the cell membrane. Usually cells of the same type have the same CAMs and adhere to each other more strongly than the cells of different types. Glazier and Graner [19] incorporated this type-dependent adhesion into the Potts model by assigning different coupling energies to different pairs of types.

Assume $C_{i,j}$ and $N_{i,j}$ are the number of cancer cells and necrotic cells in site (i,j), respectively, and K_{CC}, K_{NC} and K_{NN} are cancer-cancer, necrotic-cancer and necrotic-necrotic couplings, respectively. For the sake of simplicity it is assumed that all cells in the same site interact with each others but there is no interaction between adjacent sites. Although it seems unrealistic but in the diffusion step the cells will move to the adjacent sites, and in the next time step each cell will interact with the cells which coming from the neighbours sites. So by evolving cellular automata each cell will experience the entire micro environment. The configuration energy of the lattice can be written as;

$$\frac{E_{\text{conf}}}{kT} = \sum_{i,j} E_{i,j,\text{conf}} \tag{1}$$

$$E_{i,j,\text{conf}} = -\left\{ \tfrac{1}{2} \left(C_{i,j}(C_{i,j}-1)K_{CC} + N_{i,j}(N_{i,j}-1)K_{NN} \right) \right\} + C_{i,j}N_{i,j}K_{NC} \tag{2}$$

where $E_{i,j,\text{conf}}$ is the configuration energy of the site i, j and k is the Boltzmann constant.   Cell-cell interactions are adhesive, thus the couplings are positive (note that there is a minus sign before bracket in the Eq. 2) . Now in each lattice site one of the following reactions can occur at each time step;

Quiescent :
$$\begin{cases} C_{i,j} \longrightarrow C_{i,j} \\ N_{i,j} \longrightarrow N_{i,j} \end{cases}$$

Proliferation:

$$\begin{cases} C_{i,j} \longrightarrow C_{i,j} + 1 \\ N_{i,j} \longrightarrow N_{i,j} \end{cases} \text{ if and only if } (C_{i,j} + N_{i,j} < 5 \text{ and } C_{i,j} \geq 1)$$

Apoptosis:

$$\begin{cases} C_{i,j} \longrightarrow C_{i,j} - 1 \\ N_{i,j} \longrightarrow N_{i,j} \end{cases} \text{ if and only if } (C_{i,j} \geq 1)$$

Necrosis:

$$\begin{cases} C_{i,j} \longrightarrow C_{i,j} - 1 \\ N_{i,j} \longrightarrow N_{i,j} + 1 \end{cases} \text{ if and only if } (C_{i,j} \geq 1)$$

By replacing the right hand side variables of each reaction with the previous one in eq. 2 we can compute the corresponding configuration energy and by method use the Glauber algorithm [20] the probability of each reaction in the each lattice site can be computed. For example

$$P_{\text{apoptosis}} = \frac{e^{\frac{-E_{\text{apoptosis}}}{kT}}}{e^{\frac{-E_{\text{quiescent}}}{kT}} + e^{\frac{-E_{\text{prolifrations}}}{kT}} + e^{\frac{-E_{\text{apoptosis}}}{kT}} + e^{\frac{-E_{\text{necrosiss}}}{kT}}}, \qquad (3)$$

where each term in the right hand side of eq. 3 is a Boltzmann factor. According to restriction of maximum five cells in each lattice site and non negative values of $C_{i,j}$ and $N_{i,j}$, in some cases one or more of the reactions cannot be occur. For these cases we set the corresponding Boltzmann factor equal to zero.

2.2 Propagation and Redistribution Steps

In the propagation step each cell will move to neighbor site according to its velocity. Because the cells collide with each other the velocity of the cell should be changed. In addition, according to the chemotaxic effect, the cancerous cell will move toward the source of the chemotaxic materials i. e. the necrotic cells. We can include these effects in the redistribution step. In this step the velocity of the cancerous cells and the necrotic cells are changed according to the following rules:

a) Because the necrotic cells are less motile compared to the cancerous cells, first the velocity of the necrotic cells is redistributed then the cancerous cells are redistributed over the remainder channels.

b) Due to the adhesion effect the resting channel (V_5) is filled first and the remainder cells are distributed among the channels V_1 to V_4 according to the probability of occupation of channels. This probability is proportional to the gradient of the concentration of the chemotaxic materials. So in the simplest case we can assume that the relative magnitude of these probabilities is equal to the relative number of the necrotic cells in the adjacent sites:

$$\frac{P_i}{P_j} = \frac{n_i}{n_j},$$

(4)

where P_i is the probability of occupation of the channel V_i, and n_i is the number of necrotic cells in the adjacent site conjugate to channel V_i.

3 Results and Discussion

The simulation is conducted on a 600 × 600 square lattice with central site initially defined to contain five cancerous cells. The size of the lattice is chosen sufficiently large such that the boundaries do not influence the tumor growth within the considered time interval. Multicellular spheroids have a well-established characteristic structure. There is an outer rim of proliferating cells (a few hundred μm thick) and an inner core of necrotic cells. Between these there is a layer of quiescent cells, which are not dividing but are alive, and can begin dividing again if environmental conditions change. The choice of coupling parameters values ($K_{CC} = 3$, $K_{NC} = 1.5$ and $K_{NN} = 3$) are determined in such a way to produce multicellular spheroids shape (Fig. 1). The results show that by increasing the value of K_{NC}, the diameter of the layer of quiescent cells will decrease more rapidly and simultaneously the rate of growing of the inner core of necrotic cells will increase. The future of tumor strongly depend on the values of K_{CC} and K_{NN}. For the values of $K_{CC} = K_{NN} < 2.5$ the tumor initially grow up and after some time step the layers of proliferating and quiescent cell will be destroyed .

The average number of cancerous cell versus time step is calculated for 20 different samples with the coupling parameters $K_{CC} = 3$, $K_{NC} = 1.5$ and $K_{NN} = 3$ (Fig. 2). After an initial exponential growth phase, growth significantly slows down.

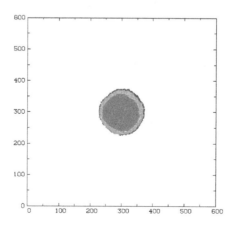

Fig. 1. The pattern of cancer growth on the 600 × 600 square lattice using coupling parameters $K_{CC} = 3$, $K_{NC} = 1.5$ and $K_{NN} = 3$ after 150 time steps. Red, green and blue colors correspond to necrotic, quiescent and proliferating shells respectively.

The advantage of this method compared to other simulation of cancer growth is that the present method needs only three parameters K_{CC}, K_{NC} and K_{NN} based on the well known physical ground i.e. the Potts model. The main aim of this work was to show the possibility of combination of the two fundamentally different methods i.e. CPM and LGCA, so the simulation has been greatly simplified by neglecting some crucial effects such as: interaction of healthy cells with cancerous cells, the effect of nutrients concentrations and limited volume space for tumor. We expect addition of these effects may be introduced in the reaction part of the automata which is still under investigation.

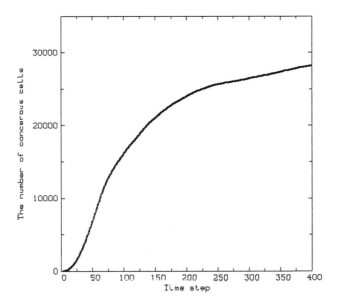

Fig. 2. The average number of cancerous cell versus time step for 20 different samples using coupling parameters $K_{CC} = 3$, $K_{NC} = 1.5$ and $K_{NN} = 3$

Acknowledgment

We acknowledge Prof. R. Islampour for his useful comments.

References

1. Adam, J. A. and Bellomo, N. " A Survey of Models for Tumor-Immune System Dynamics", Birkhäuser : Boston, (1997).
2. Anderson, A. R. A., Chaplain, M. A. J., Newman, E. L., Steele R. J. C. and Thompson, A. M.: J. Theor. Med. 2, (2000), 129−154.
3. Chaplain, M. A. J.: Acta Biotheoret. 43, (1995), 387−402.
4. Orme, M. E. & Chaplain, M. A. J.: IMA J. Math. Appl. Med. Biol. 14, (1997), 189−205.

5. Perumpanani, A. J., Sherratt, J. A., Norbury, J. and Byrne, H. M.: Invasion Metastasis 16, (1996), 209–221.
6. Breward C. J. W.; Byrne, H. M. and Lewis, C. E.: Euro. Jnl. of Applied Mathematics, 26, (2001), no pages.
7. Byrne, H. M. & Chaplain,M. A. J.: Math. Comp. Modell. 24, (1996), 1–17.
8. Byrne, H. M.: IMA J. Math. Appl. Med. Biol. 14, (1997), 305–323.
9. Alber, M.; Kiskowski, M.; Glazier, J. and Jiang, Y.: "On Cellular Automaton Approaches to Modeling Biological Cells", in IMA: Mathematical systems theory in biology, communication, and finance. Springer-Verleg, New York. 134, (2002), 12.
10. Kadanoff, L.P. McNamara, G.R. and Zanetti, G.: Phys. Rev. A, 40, (1989), 4527–4541.
11. Chen, S. Dawson, S. P. Doolen, G. D. Janecky, D. R. and Lawniczak,: Computers & Chemical Engineering, 19, (1995), 617–646.
12. Ofria, C. Adami, C. Collier T. C., and Hsu, G. K.: Lect. Notes Artif. Intell., 1674, (1999), 129–138.
13. Dormann, S. and Deutsch, A.: In Silico Biology 2, (2002), 0035.
14. Potts, R.: Proc. Cambridge Phil. Soc., 48, (1952), 106–109.
15. Wu, F.: Rev. Mod. Phys., 54, (1982), 235–268.
16. Stott, E. L., Britton, N. F., Glazier, J. A., and Zajac, M. :Math. Comput. Modell. 30, (1999), 183–198.
17. Graner, F. & Glazier, J. A.: Phys. Rev. Lett. 69, (1992), 2013–2016.
18. Turner, S. and Sherratt, J. A.: J. theor. Biol. 216, (2002), 85–100.
19. Glazier, J.A. and Graner, F.: Phys. Rev. E, 47, (1993), 2128–2154.
20. Glauber, R.J.: J. Math. Phys. 4, (1963), 294.

A Model Based on Cellular Automata to Simulate Epidemic Diseases

A. Martín del Rey[1], S. Hoya White[2], and G. Rodríguez Sánchez[3]

[1] Department of Applied Mathematics, E.P.S. de Ávila, Universidad de Salamanca
C/Hornos Caleros 50, 05003-Ávila, España
delrey@usal.es
[2] Department of Applied Mathematics, Universidad de Salamanca
sarahw@usal.es
[3] Department of Applied Mathematics, E.P.S. de Zamora, Universidad de Salamanca
Avda. Requejo 33, 49022-Zamora, España
gerardo@usal.es

Abstract. The main goal of this work is to introduce a mathematical model, based on two-dimensional cellular automata, to simulate epidemic diseases. Specifically, each cell stands for a square portion of the ground where the epidemic is spreading, and its state is given by the fractions of susceptible, infected and recovered individuals.

1 Introduction

As is well known, the disease that spread through a large population yields serious health and economic threats. Then, public health issues have a lot of importace in our society. Some examples of epidemics are the Black Death during the mid-14th century, the so-called Spanish Flu pandemic in 1918, the Severe Acute Respiratory Syndrome in 2002, or more recently, the Avian Influenza.

As a consequence, since the first years of the last century, an interdisciplinary scientific effort to study the spreading of a disease in a social system has been made. In this sense, mathematical epidemiology is concerned with modeling the spread of infectious disease in a population. The aim is generally to understand the time course of the disease with the goal of controlling its spread. The work due to W.O. Kermack and A.G. McKendrick in 1927 (see [7]) can be considered as the first one in the design of modern mathematical models. One can consider some types of mathematical models depending on the division of the population into classes. So, we have the SIR models where susceptible (S), infected (I), and recovered (R) individuals are considered. The susceptible individuals are those capable to contracting the disease; the infected individuals are those capable of spreading the disease; and the recovered individuals are those immune from the disease, either died from the disease, or, having recovered, are definitely immune to it. For many infections there is a period of time during which the individual has been infected but is not yet infectious himself. During this latent period the individual is said to be exposed. In this case we have the SEIR model

S. El Yacoubi, B. Chopard, and S. Bandini (Eds.): ACRI 2006, LNCS 4173, pp. 304–310, 2006.

in which the new class of exposed individuals (E) must be considered. Some infections, for example the group of those responsible for the common cold, do not confer any long lasting immunity. Such infections do not have a recovered state and individuals become susceptible again after infection. Then we have the SIS models. Moreover, there are another variants of these models such as the SIRS model or the SEIRS model.

Traditionally, the majority of existing mathematical models to simulate epidemics are based on ordinary differential equations. These models have serious drawbacks, for example: They fail to simulate in a proper way the individual contact processes, the effects of individual behaviour, the spatial aspects of the epidemic spreading, and the effects of mixing patterns of the individuals.

Cellular automata (CA for short) can overcome these drawbacks and have been used by several researches as an efficient alternative method to simulate epidemic spreading (see, for example, [1, 2, 3, 4, 5, 6, 8, 9, 10, 11, 13]). Usually, when a model based on cellular automata to simulate an epidemic spreading is considered, individuals are assumed to be distributed in the cellular space such that each cell stands for an individual of the population. Nevertheless, some models have been appeared in the literature with the assumption that each cell of the cellular space contain a large number of individuals (see, for example, [12]).

The main goal of this work is to introduce a new CA model to simulate epidemic spreading based on the work due to Sirakoulis et al. (see [12]) in which the state of the cell is obtained from the fraction of the number of individuals which are susceptible, infected, or recovered from the disease.

The rest of the paper is organized as follows: In section 2 the basic results about cellular automata are introduced; the model to simulate the epidemic spreading is presented in section 3; in section 4 a simulation using laboratory parameters is shown, and, finally, the conclusions are introduced in section 5.

2 Cellular Automata

Bidimensional cellular automata are discrete dynamical systems formed by a finite number of $r \times c$ identical objects called cells which are arranged uniformly in a two-dimensional cellular space. Each cell is endowed with a state (from a finite state set Q), that changes at every step of time accordingly to a local transition rule. In this sense, the state of a particular cell at time t depends on the states of a set of cells, called its neighborhood, at the previous time step $t - 1$. More precisely, a CA is defined by the 4-uplet (C, Q, V, f), where C is the cellular space: $C = \{(i, j), 1 \leq i \leq r, 1 \leq j \leq c\}$; Q is the finite state set; $V = \{(\alpha_k, \beta_k), 1 \leq k \leq n\} \subset \mathbb{Z} \times \mathbb{Z}$, is the finite set of indices defining the neighborhood of each cell, such that the neighborhood of the cell (i, j) is $V_{ij} = \{(i + \alpha_1, j + \beta_1), \ldots, (i + \alpha_n, j + \beta_n)\}$. In this work, we will consider the Moore neighborhood consisting of the cell itself and its eight nearest neighbor cells. Finally, f is the local transition function: $s_{ij}^t = f\left(s_{i+\alpha_1, j+\beta_1}^{t-1}, \ldots, s_{i+\alpha_n, j+\beta_n}^{t-1}\right) \in Q$, where s_{ij}^t stands for the state of the cell (i, j) at time t.

As is mentioned above, the CA evolves deterministically in discrete time steps, changing the states of the cells by means of the local transition function f. As the cellular space is considered to be finite, in this work null boundary conditions must be considered in order to assure a well-defined dynamics of the CA.

3 Description of the Model

In this section, we introduce the CA-based model to simulate the spreading of a general epidemic. It is suppose that the ground where the epidemic is spreading stands for the cellular space of the CA, which is divided into identical square areas, each one of them representing a cell of the CA. In our work different cells can have different populations: differing densities and different "across cell" traversal or mobility properties. The main features of the epidemic and the environment where it is spreading are the following: (1) The epidemic is not lethal, and no birth, immigration or emigration is considered; consequently, the total amount of population is constant and, as a consequence, the population of each cell is always the same; (2) The population distribution is inhomogeneous, and the total population of the (i, j)-th cell is N_{ij}; (3) The way of infection is the contact between an infected individual and a healthy one; (4) Once the healthy individuals have contracted the disease and have recovered from it, they acquire immunity, that is, it is impossible for them to be susceptible again; (5) People can move from one cell to another cell (if there is some type of way of transport), that is, the individuals are able to go outside and come back inside their cells during each time step; and (6) It is suppose that when an infected individual arrives at a cell, the fraction of healthy individuals contacted by him/her is the same independently of the total amount of population of the cell. Let $S_{ij}^t \in [0, 1]$ be the portion of the healthy individuals of the cell (i, j) who are susceptible to infection at time t; set $I_{ij}^t \in [0, 1]$ the portion of the infected population of the cell who can transmit the disease to the healthy ones; and let $R_{ij}^t \in [0, 1]$ be the portion of recovered individuals from the disease at time t that will be permanently immunised. As the population of each cell is constant then $1 = S_{ij}^t + I_{ij}^t + R_{ij}^t$, for every time step t and every cell (i, j). The state of each cell is a three-coordinate vector specifying the susceptible, infected and recovered individuals of the cell at each time step. As these three states are real numbers between 0 and 1, and the state set must be finite, then a suitable discretization of such parameters must be included. In this work we will consider $0 \leq N_{ij} \leq 100$, and consequently, the state set used will be $Q \times Q \times Q$, where $Q = \{0.00, 0.01, 0.02, \ldots, 0.99, 1.00\}$, that is, the discretization represents the finiteness of population. As a consequence, the state of the cell (i, j) is $s_{ij}^t = \left(DS_{ij}^t, DI_{ij}^t, DR_{ij}^t \right)$, with

$$DS_{ij}^t = \left[100 \cdot S_{ij}^t \right] / 100, \ DI_{ij}^t = \left[100 \cdot I_{ij}^t \right] / 100, \ DR_{ij}^t = \left[100 \cdot R_{ij}^t \right] / 100, \quad (1)$$

where $[x]$ is the nearest integer to x.

The local transition function of the CA-based model is the following:

$$I_{ij}^t = (1 - \varepsilon)I_{ij}^{t-1} + S_{ij}^{t-1}vI_{ij}^{t-1} + S_{ij}^{t-1} \sum_{(\alpha,\beta)\in V^*} \frac{N_{i+\alpha,j+\beta}}{N_{ij}} \mu_{\alpha\beta}^{(i,j)} I_{i+\alpha,j+\beta}^{t-1}, \qquad (2)$$

$$S_{ij}^t = S_{ij}^{t-1} - S_{ij}^{t-1}vI_{ij}^{t-1} - S_{ij}^{t-1} \sum_{(\alpha,\beta)\in V^*} \frac{N_{i+\alpha,j+\beta}}{N_{ij}} \mu_{\alpha\beta}^{(i,j)} I_{i+\alpha,j+\beta}^{t-1}, \qquad (3)$$

$$R_{ij}^t = R_{ij}^{t-1} + \varepsilon I_{ij}^{t-1}. \qquad (4)$$

where $V^* = V - \{(0,0)\}$, and the real parameter $\mu_{\alpha\beta}^{(i,j)}$ is defined as the product of three factors: $\mu_{\alpha\beta}^{(i,j)} = c_{\alpha\beta}^{(i,j)} m_{\alpha\beta}^{(i,j)} v$, where $c_{\alpha\beta}^{(i,j)}$ and $m_{\alpha\beta}^{(i,j)}$ are the connection factor and the movement factor between the main cell (i,j) and the neighbour cell $(i + \alpha, j + \beta)$, respectively, and $v \in [0,1]$ is the virulence of the epidemic. Moreover, the parameter $\varepsilon \in [0,1]$ stands for the portion of recovered infected individuals at each time step.

The equations (2)-(4) reflect that every loss in the infected population is due to a gain in the recovered population, while every gain in the infected population is due to a loss in the susceptible population. Roughly speaking, the equation (2) can be interpreted as saying that the portion of infected individuals of a cell (i,j) at a particular time step t is given by the portion of infected individuals of this cell which have not been recovered from the disease (first sum of the summation); by the portion of susceptible individuals of the same cell at time $t - 1$ which have been infected by the infected individuals at time $t - 1$ of the cell (second sum of the summation) taking into account the virulence of the disease; and finally note that some susceptible individuals of the cell can be infected by infected individuals of the neighbour cells which have traveled to the cell (third sum of the summation). Obviously, it depends on some parameters involving the virulence, the nature of the connections between the cells, the possibilities of an infected individual to be moved from one cell to another, and the relation between the population of the cells. Finally, due to assumption (6) stated above we have to apply the normalization factor $N_{i+\alpha,j+\beta}/N_{ij}$. Moreover, equation (3) gives the portion of susceptible individuals of the cell (i,j) at time t as the difference between the portion of susceptible individuals at the previous time step and the portion of susceptible individuals which have been infected. Finally, equation (4) gives the portion of recovered individuals of the cell (i,j) at time t as the number of recovered individuals of the cell at the previous time step plus the fraction of infected individuals of the cell which have been recovered in one step of time. Note that $S_{ij}^t + I_{ij}^t + R_{ij}^t = 1$.

As is mentioned above, the way of infection of the epidemic to be modeled is the contact between a sick individual and a healthy one. As a consequence, the healthy individuals of a particular cell can be infected by the infected individuals of this cell or by the infected individuals of the neighbour cells that have traveled to the main cell. The first case, that is, when an individual is infected by another individual of his/her cell, is reflected in the first sum of the summation given in (2). In the other case, given by the second sum of the summation of

(2), when the infection is carried out by individuals belonging to neighbour cells, some type of connection between the cells must be exist in order to allow the epidemic spreading. For example, we can consider the following ways of transport between two neighbor cells: airplane, train or car. This connection is given by the coefficients $c_{\alpha\beta}^{(i,j)} \in [0,1]$. Obviously, this assumption is a strong simplification since, for example, airplains or trains could connect distant cells. The parameter $m_{\alpha\beta}^{(i,j)}$ stands for the probability of an infected individual belonging to the neighbour cell $(i+\alpha, j+\beta)$ to be moved to the main cell (i,j). Note that this parameter must be given by the main features of the disease to be modeled.

The effect of population vaccination can be also considered in this model. In this case, a vaccination parameter, $\omega \in [0,1]$, must be considered in the local transition functions of the model. Such parameter stands for the portion of susceptible individuals at each time step which are vaccinated. Consequently, equations (3) and (4) are:

$$S_{ij}^t = (1-\omega)S_{ij}^{t-1} - S_{ij}^{t-1}vI_{ij}^{t-1} - S_{ij}^{t-1} \sum_{(\alpha,\beta)\in V^*} \frac{N_{i+\alpha,j+\beta}}{N_{ij}} \mu_{\alpha\beta}^{(i,j)} I_{i+\alpha,j+\beta}^{t-1}, \quad (5)$$

$$R_{ij}^t = R_{ij}^{t-1} + \varepsilon I_{ij}^{t-1} + \omega S_{ij}^{t-1}. \quad (6)$$

Finally, it is very important to decide whether or not the outbreak disease occurs. In this sense, we will obtain the values of the parameters for which the epidemic spread from one cell to its neighbor cells. Suppose that in the initial configuration there is only one cell with infected individuals: $O = (i,j)$, and set $P = (i+\alpha, j+\beta)$ one of its neighbor cells. Then the infected individuals of this neighbor cell at time step $t = 1$ is given by the following expression: $I_P^1 = N_O c_O^P m_O^P v I_O^0 / N_P$. In our model, we suppose that there are infected individuals in the cell P at a particular time step t when $I_P^t \in Q - 0$, that is, when $I_P^t \geq 0.01$ Consequently, as a simple calculus shows, the following equation must hold: $I_O^0 \geq N_P / \left(100 N_O c_O^P m_O^P v\right)$.

4   A Simple Simulation

We have used the computer algebra system Mathematica to implement the algorithm stated in the last section. Specifically, the cellular space in the simulation will be formed by a two-dimensional array of 50×50 cells. The initial configuration is formed by only one cell with infected population: the cell $(25, 25)$, with $s_{25,25}^0 = (0.7, 0.3, 0)$. For the sake of simplicity, we will use the following artificially chosen parameters: $\varepsilon = 0.4$, $v = 0.6$, and $m_{\alpha\beta}^{(i,j)} = 0.5$ for every cell (i,j). Moreover, each cell is connected with all of its neighborhoods with the same parameter: $c_{\alpha\beta}^{(i,j)} = 1$ for every cell (i,j), and $(i+\alpha, j+\beta)$. Finally, it is suppose that the population in each cell is the same, that is, $N_{ij} = N = 100$ for every cell (i,j). The evolution of the number of susceptible, infected and recovered individuals are shown in Figure 1-(a). Note that the infected population grows from $t = 0$, when only one cell has infected inviduals, to $t = 28$ and, then it decreases to zero.

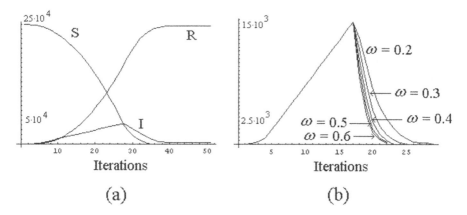

Fig. 1. (a) Evolution of the susceptible, infected and recovered individuals. (b) Evolution of infected population with vaccination effect.

Finally, in Figure 1-(b) the evolution of infected individuals is shown when the vaccination process is considered. We suppose that the initial configuration is formed by only one cell with infected individuals: the cell $(25, 25)$, with $s^0_{25,25} = (0.7, 0.3, 0)$. Moreover $\varepsilon = 0.6, v = 0.6, m^{(i,j)}_{\alpha\beta} = 0.5, c^{(i,j)}_{\alpha\beta} = 1$ for every cell (i, j). Five different values of w are considered: $w = 0.2, 0.3, 0.4, 0.5, 0.6$, and the vaccination process starts at $t = 16$. Note that as w increases, the number of infected individuals decreases. Moreover, the results obtained show that the vaccination efficiency decreases with increasing w (curves for $w = 0.5$ and 0.6 are much closer than those for 0.2 and 0.3).

5   Conclusions and Further Work

In this work a new mathematical model to simulate the spreading of an epidemic is introduced. It is based on the use of two-dimensional cellular automata endowed with a suitable local transition function. Each cell stands for a portion of the land in which the epidemic is spreading and the population is divided into three classes: susceptible, infected and recovered individuals.

Traditionally, the CA-based epidemiological models consider only one individual in each cell. In the proposed model a large population can "live" in each cell of the cellular space. Consequently, the main feature of the model is the definition of the state of each cell as a 3-coordinate vector representing the portion of its population which is susceptible, infected and recovered at each time step. Moreover, although the total amount of population is constant, it could not be uniformly distributed between the cells. As the model is based on two-dimensional CA, the spreading of the epidemic disease is simulated both in time and space. In this sense, it is simplest than models based on PDEs. The simulation obtained (using artificially chosen parameters) seem to be in agreement with the expected behaviour of a real epidemic. Consequently, this model can be used to analyse the impact of real epidemic diseases.

Future work aimed at designing a more complete CA-based epidemic model taking into account the effect of births, deaths, etc., and involving additional effects such as the effect of virus mutation, etc. Moreover, a more detailed study of the effect of vaccination must be carried out since as the costs of any vaccination program will certainly increase with ω, there seems to be an optimum value of such parameter such that any other increase of ω will bave a marginal and inefficient effect.

Acknowledgements

The authors thank the anonymous referees for their valuable suggestions. This work has been partially supported by the Consejería de Sanidad (Junta de Castilla y León, Spain), and by "D. Samuel Solórzano Barruso" Memorial Foundation (Universidad de Salamanca, Spain) under grant FS/3-2005.

References

1. Ahmed, E., Agiza, H.N.: On modeling epidemics. Including latency, incubation and variable susceptibility, Physica A **253** (1998) 247–352.
2. Beauchemin, C., Samuel, J., Tuszynski, J.: A simple cellular automaton model for influenza A viral infections, J. Theor. Biol. **232** (2005) 223–234.
3. Boccara, N., Cheong, K.: Critical behaviour of a probabilistic automata network SIS model for the spread of an infectious disease in a population of moving individuals, J. Phys A-Math. Gen. **26** (1993) 3707–3717.
4. Boccara, N., Cheong, K., Oram, M.: A probabilistic automata network epidemic model with births and deaths exhibiting cyclic behaviour, J. Phys A-Math. Gen. **27** (1994) 1585–1597.
5. Fuks, H., Lawniczak, A.T.: Individual-based lattice model for spatial spread of epidemics, Discrete Dyn. Nat. Soc. **6** (2001) 191–200.
6. Fuentes, M.A., Kuperman, M.N.: Cellular automata and epidemiological models with spatial dependence, Physica A **267** (1999) 471–486.
7. Kermack, W.O., McKendrick, A.G.: Contributions to the mathematical theory of epidemics, part I, Proc. Roy. Soc. Edin. A **115** (1927) 700–721.
8. Quan-Xing, L., Zhen:, J. Cellular automata modelling of SEIRS, Chinese Phys. **14** (2005) 1370–1377.
9. Ramani, A., Carstea, A.S., Willox, R., Grammaticos, G.: Oscillating epidemics: a discrete-time model, Physica A **333** (2004) 278–292.
10. Rousseau, G., Giorgini, G., Livi, R., Chaté, H.: Dynamical phases in a cellular automaton model for epidemic propagation, Physica D **103** (1997) 554–563.
11. Satsuma, J., Willox, R., Ramani, A., Grammaticos, B., Carstea, A.S.: Extending the SIR epidemic model, Physica A **336** (2004) 369–375.
12. Sirakoulis, G. Ch., Karafyllidis, I., Thanailakis, A.: A cellular automaton model for the effects of population movement and vaccination on epidemic propagation, Ecol. Model. **133** (2000) 209–223.
13. Willox, R., Grammaticos, B., Carstea, A.S., Ramani, A.: Epidemic dynamics: discrete-time and cellular automaton models, Physica A **328** (2003) 13–22.

FlySim: A Cellular Automata Model of *Bactrocera Oleae* (Olive Fruit Fly) Infestation and First Simulations

Pierre Pommois[1], Pietro Brunetti[2], Vincenzo Bruno[1], Antonio Mazzei[2], Valerio Baldacchini[2], and Salvatore Di Gregorio[3]

[1] University of Calabria, Department of Physics, Arcavacata,
87036 Rende (CS), Italy
{vbruno, pommois}@fis.unical.it
[2] University of Calabria, Department of Ecology, Arcavacata,
87036 Rende (CS), Italy
{pbrunetti, amazzei}@unical.it, valerio@baldacchini.it
[3] University of Calabria, Department of Mathematics, Arcavacata,
87036 Rende (CS), Italy
dig@unical.it

Abstract. The Cellular Automata model FlySim was developed for simulating life and reproduction cycles of olive fruit flies (*Bactrocera Oleae*) and their behaviour, especially when they infest olive (*Olea europaea*) groves. This serious agricultural problem can be partially tackled in many ways, but not all the methods look sustainable, e.g., by using chemical agents at the first signs of the infestation. Sustainable solutions could be adopted with the use of interactive simulation tools in order to permit developing scenarios and testing different strategies. This paper outlines the model and exhibits a first partial application.

1 Introduction

An important and difficult problem for olive groves farmers (mainly *Olea europaea*, but also *Olea verrucosa*, *Olea chrysophylla*, and *Olea cuspidata*) in the Mediterranean area is the infestation of olive fruit flies (*Bactrocera Oleae* also called *Dacus Oleae*) [5], [10]. The olive oil production worsens in quantity and quality compared with the plague gravity [9].

The life cycle of the olive fruit fly is linked to the seasonal development of olive trees and to the local climate. A generation (egg, larva, pupa, adult) can be completed in 30 days in optimum weather conditions, while larvae produced during late fall pupate in the soil in winter or in olives remaining on trees in spring [7]. Before the drupe maturation, females enter a state of reproductive diapause in which few or no eggs are produced [5]. Flies may disperse to new locations during this period. When quite mature olive fruits (receptive drupes) appear, females are attracted to the fruit and begin to produce eggs abundantly and to deposit them in the receptive drupes [8].

This ecological frame isn't easy to be focused; it is a complex dynamical system, whose evolution depends on climatic, territorial and biological factors [6], [7]. Olive fruit fly behaviour may be described efficaciously by its interaction with the environment at local level; as a consequence, such a type of system looks a good candidate to

S. El Yacoubi, B. Chopard, and S. Bandini (Eds.): ACRI 2006, LNCS 4173, pp. 311 – 320, 2006.

be modelled and simulated by Cellular Automata (CA), because it evolves mainly on the basis of local interactions of its constituent parts. Nonetheless, CA modelling was yet applied to a similar problem concerning outbreaks of mountain pine beetle [2].

CA are a paradigm of parallel computing [11]; they involve a regular division of the space in cells, each one characterised by a state s, which represents the actual conditions of the cell. The state changes according to a transition function τ that depends on the states of neighbouring cells and of the cell itself; the transition function and the neighbourhood pattern are invariant in time and space. At time $t=0$, cells are in states that describe initial conditions; the CA evolves changing the state of all the cells simultaneously at discrete times, according to its transition function.

FlySim is a CA model for the territorial dynamics of olive fruit flies (*Bactrocera Oleae*) populations; it is the evolution of a forecasting model, developed by the researchers of the *Dip. di Agrobiotecnologie* (*ENEA*, Roma, Italy) [1] [3]. It was applied in diverse programs for integrated control of the olive fruit flies infestation.

1.1 CA Empirical Method

The proposed preliminary CA model FlySim is mixed, deterministic-probabilistic; it is related to olive fruit fly behaviour [1], [5], [6], [7], [10] and is based on an empirical method [4], which may be applied to some macroscopic phenomena in order to produce a proper CA model. It is based on an extension of the classical CA definition for permitting a straight correspondence between the system with its evolution in the physical space/time and the model with the simulations in the cellular space/time. The main points of the method are here illustrated shortly:

- Global parameters (their values are invariant in time or space or space/time) must be made explicit: primarily, the size of the cell p_{ce} and the time correspondence to a CA step p_{time} must be fixed; they are constant in space/time.
- The state of the cell must account for all the characteristics, relevant to the evolution of the system and relative to the space portion corresponding to the cell; e.g. number of flies. Each characteristic must be individuated as a substate. The substate value is considered constant in the cell.
- As the state of the cell can be decomposed in substates, the transition function may be also split in many components, the "elementary" processes. We distinguish two types of elementary processes: internal transformations, depending on the substates of the cell (e.g., flies depositing eggs in the receptive drupes, depending on substates "number of flies" and on the "maturation degree of drupes") and local interactions, depending on the substates of the cells in the neighbouring. Local interactions may account for the transfer of quantity or propagation of properties from a cell to another one in the neighbouring, in terms of flows towards the neighbouring cells, e.g. flies moving toward areas with larger concentration of receptive drupes.
- Some cells represent a kind of input from the "external world" to the CA; it accounts for describing external influences which cannot be described in terms of CA rules; e.g. entrance points of olive fruit flies.
- Special functions supply the history of "external influences" on the CA cells, e.g. the climatic conditions. Such functions affect all the cells or some special cells.

The model FlySim is illustrated in the next section; the CA transition function is described in the successive section; both sections treat the features of the olive fruit fly, olive trees and olive groves. The fourth section illustrates the model implementations and first results of applications; at the end, comments conclude the paper.

2 The Model FlySim

FlySim = <R, X, S, P, τ, I, Γ> is a two-dimensional CA with square cells, where:

- $R = \{(x, y) \mid x, y \in \mathcal{N}, 0 \leq x \leq l_x, 0 \leq y \leq l_y\}$ is a rectangular region of square cells, individuated by integer co-ordinates; $\mathcal{N}$ is the set of natural numbers; each cell corresponds to a portion of territory, where the phenomenon evolves.
- $X = <(0,0), (0,1), (0,-1), (1,0), (-1,0), (1,1), (-1,-1), (1,-1), (-1,1)>$ is the neighbourhood relation; the co-ordinates of the cells in the neighbourhood of a cell c are obtained adding the c co-ordinates; they are the cell itself (called the central cell) with index 0 and the eight surrounding cells with indices 1, 2, ... , 8.
- S is the finite set of states $S = S_{territory} \times S_{drupe} \times S_{fly}$, where $S_{territory}$ regards the substates associated to the terrain and climate features of the cell (e.g. temperature), S_{drupe} regards the substates that accounts for the drupes conditions in the cell (e.g. maturation degree) and S_{fly} regards the substates that accounts for the general conditions of olive fruit flies in the cell (e.g. stage of development). The complete specifications of such substates are reported in the Table 1, 2 and 3.

Table 1. List of the substates names (to be used as variables) and their meaning for $S_{territory}$

$S_{territory} = S_T \times S_{avT} \times S_{T1} \times S_{T2} \times ... \times S_{Tm} \times S_{cT} \times S_w \times S_{C0} \times S_{C1} \times ... \times S_{Cm}$	
NAME	MEANING
T	actual temperature
avT	average temperature in the day
T_i, $1 \leq i \leq m$	average temperatures of the last m days
cT	thermal accumulation (average temperature for last m days)
w	quantity of present water
C_j $0 \leq j \leq n$	ratio of the n cultivars in the cell (*0* for no cultivar)

Table 2. List of the names (to be used as variables) of the substates and their meaning for S_{drupe}

$S_{drupe} = S_{maxD1} \times ... \times S_{maxDn} \times S_{recD1} \times ... \times S_{recDn} \times S_{damD1} \times ... \times S_{damDn}$	
NAME	MEANING
$maxD_j$ $1 \leq j \leq n$	maximum number of drupes (for the j-th cultivar)
$recD_j$ $1 \leq j \leq n$	number of receptive drupes (for the olive fruit fly)
$damD_j$ $1 \leq j \leq n$	number of damaged drupes (by the olive fruit fly)

Table 3. List of the names (to be used as variables) of the substates and their meaning for S_{fly}

$$S_{fly}= S_e{\times}S_{l1}{\times}S_{l2}{\times}S_{l3}{\times}S_p{\times}S_a{\times}S_{ed}{\times}S_{l1d}{\times}S_{l2d}{\times}S_{l3d}{\times}S_{pd}{\times}S_{ad}{\times}S_{mf1}{\times}S_{mf2}{\times}...{\times}S_{mf8}$$

NAME	MEANING
e, l_1, l_2, l_3, p, a	number of flies at different stages of maturity in order: egg, larva$_1$ larva$_2$, larva$_3$, pupa, adult
$ed, l_1d, l_2d, l_3d, pd, ad$	degree for each maturity stage
maf_k $1{\le}k{\le}8$	number of adults migrating to the neighbourhood cell k

- P is the finite set of global parameters of the CA, which affect the transition function. All the parameters are always global in space/time except when it is specified differently. The size of the cell edge and the time corresponding to a FlySim step are the fundamental parameters to match FlySim to the real phenomenon. The hour+date specification is a space global parameter. The determination of the maximum number of drupes in a cell is dependent by a density parameter for each cultivar. The determination of the receptive drupes is very complex, it must account for climatic history in order to determine the ratio (receptivity parameter) of the not receptive drupes, which reach a maturity degree to become receptive for the flies after the time interval p_{time}. The receptivity parameters are space global. Progress (step rate) for each maturity stage is described by a couple of temperature connected logistic curves (the former is increasing, the latter is decreasing); therefore, six parameters are necessary for each stage, except for the adult stage. The relaxation rate and attractor parameters are needed for the fly diffusion algorithm. The parameters are reported in the Table 4.
- $\tau.S^9{\rightarrow}S$ is the transition function; it must account for the average daily temperature, thermal accumulation (important for the fly growth), number of receptive drupes (depending on the drupe growth), number of deposited eggs, growth of the olive fruit flies for each maturity stage (except the adult stage), death rate and diffusion of the adult olive fruit fly from a cell to the other cells of the neighbourhood. Corresponding elementary processes are specified in the next section.

Table 4. List of the set P of parameters and their meaning

$$P=\{p_{ce},p_{time},p_{cl},p_m,p_n,p_{d1}..p_{dn},p_{r1}..p_{rn},p_{aaf},p_{ec1}..p_{ec6},p_{l1c1}..p_{l3c6},p_{c1}..p_{c6},p_{sr1}..p_{sr6},p_{a1}..p_{a3},p_{b1}..p_{b3},p_r\}$$

NAME	MEANING
$ce, time$ (= 1 hour)	size of the cell edge, time corresponding to a FlySim step
cl	internal clock (hour and date specification)
m	number of days for historical temperatures
n	number of cultivars
d_j, r_j $1{\le}j{\le}n$	density and receptivity parameter for each cultivar
aaf	adult aging factor
$ec_h, l_1c_h, l_2c_h, l_3c_h, pc_h, sr_h$ $1{\le}h{\le}6$	six constants of logistic functions for: egg, larva$_1$ larva$_2$, larva$_3$, pupa and spawning rate
$a_1, a_2, a_3, b_1, b_2, b_3$	couple of constants for the three cell attractors
rel	relaxation rate for fly diffusion

- $I \subset R$ individuates the border cells, if any, where part of adult olive fruit flies pene-
trates in the territory.
- $\Gamma = \{\gamma_1, \gamma_2, \gamma_3, \gamma_{r1}, .. \gamma_{rn}\}$ accounts for the external influences: $\gamma_1 : p_{cl} \rightarrow p_{cl}$ updates hourly
p_{cl} ; $\gamma_2 : \mathcal{N} \rightarrow S_T$ updates hourly the substate temperature from a value average of
around weather stations, $\gamma_3 : \mathcal{N} \hat{\times} I \times S_a \rightarrow I \times S_a$ updates the substate S_a in border cells,
where adult olive fruit flies can penetrate according to a probabilistic rule;
$\gamma_{ri} : \mathcal{N} \hat{\times} S_{avT} \times p_{rj} \rightarrow p_{rj}$ update the value of the receptivity parameters for each cultivar. $\mathcal{N}$ is referred to the FlySim steps. The Γ functions are applied in order at each
step before the τ function.

3   The FlySim Transition Function

The following subsections describe the elementary processes of FlySim. The new
values of substate or parameter for the next step are indicated with the name of the
substate or parameter, followed by the prime sign. Neighbourhood indices are placed
in square brackets.

3.1   Temperature

The new average temperature avT' is computed for each hour by the following formula: $avT' = (T + avT(hour-1))/hour$; the variable $hour$ ($1 \leq hour \leq 24$) is deduced by the
parameter cl and represents the day hour. When the day last value is computed, then
$T_1' = avT'$, $T_i' = T_{i-1}$ for $2 \leq i \leq m$, and $cT' = \sum_{1 \leq i \leq m} T_i' / m$ [3].

3.2   Drupes and Egg Deposition

The maximum number of drupes in a cell may be considered in first approximation
dependent on drupe density for different cultivars, considering the olive coverage of
each cultivar: $maxD_j' = ce^2 \cdot d_j \cdot C_j$ for $1 \leq j \leq n$.

The number of receptive drupes (rD) [10] is computed by the following formula:
$rD = \sum_{1 \leq j \leq n}((recD_j + (maxD_j - recD_j - damD_j) \cdot r_j)$. It increases step by step for each cultivar
until r_j takes the value 1.

The damaged drupes [5] are receptive drupes, where olive fruit flies lay eggs (usually no more than one egg for drupe). The number of possible damaged drupes
($pdamD$) in a step is depending on the number of adult flies in the cell (only 20% of
flies are spawning female flies): $pdamD = a \cdot srate \cdot time$, where $srate$ is the spawning
rate, which is computed according to two correlated logistic functions of temperature
T with parameters sr_h for $1 \leq h \leq 6$ (the former $sr_1/(1 + sr_2 \cdot \exp(sr_3 \cdot T))$ is increasing, the
latter $sr_4/(1 + sr_5 \cdot \exp(-sr_6 \cdot T))$ is decreasing).

Three values of temperatures are deduced: T_{switch} is obtained by the equation
$sr_1/(1 + sr_2 \cdot \exp(sr_3 \cdot T_{switch})) = sr_4/(1 + sr_5 \cdot \exp(-sr_6 \cdot T_{switch}))$ and represents the "middle"
value; T_{min} is obtained by the equation $sr_1/(1 + sr_2 \cdot \exp(sr_3 \cdot T_{min})) = 0$; T_{max} is obtained by
the equation $sr_4/(1 + sr_5 \cdot \exp(-sr_6 \cdot T_{max})) = 0$; $srate$ is computed according the former
logistic function for $T_{min} \leq T \leq T_{switch}$; $srate$ is computed according the latter logistic

function for $T_{switch} \leq T \leq T_{max}$; *srate* is null out of range $T_{min} \leq T \leq T_{max}$ because the adult flies die.

If $rD \leq pdamD$, then all the receptive drupes are damaged, $recD_j'=0$ for $1 \leq j \leq n$ and $damD_j'=damD_j+recD_j+(maxD_j-recD_j-damD_j) \cdot r_j$ for $1 \leq j \leq n$.

If $rD > pdamD$, then $recD_j'=((recD_j+(maxD_j-recD_j-damD_j) \cdot r_j)/(1-pdamD/rD)$ for $1 \leq j \leq n$ and $damD_j'=damD_j+(recD_j+(maxD_j-recD_j-damD_j) \cdot r_j)/(pdamD/rD)$ for $1 \leq j \leq n$.

Not integer values may be used for *pdamD* , *rD*, etc, in support of a more refined computation of the phenomenon.

3.3 Growth and Death Rate of Olive Fruit Flies

The olive fruit flies maturation rate *mrate* is depending mainly from the temperature and is computed for each maturity stage (in time order: egg, larva$_1$, larva$_2$, larva$_3$ and pupa [6], [7]) except the last one (adult) according to two correlated logistic functions of temperature T with six parameters each. The computation for each stage is performed according to the considerations of the previous subsection on the use of the logistic function with the determination of the "middle" temperature T_{switch} and the temperature range $T_{min} \leq T \leq T_{max}$. Note that the flies die out of that temperature range.

The maturity degree for each stage has 0 as initial value, while 1 represents the end of the stage and the beginning for the next one (the death for the adult fly).

The increase of maturity degree (*degree*) for each stage, except the adult one, is computed by the general formula *degree'=mrate·time+degree* . Of course, the value of *mrate* changes for each maturity stage (it would be properly referred to own maturity stage) and d*egree* substituted by the appropriate substate name, e.g. $l_2'=l_2 mrate·time+l_2$.

The maturity degree for the adult stage *ad* may be updated at each step by a simple formula *ad'=ad+aaf·T* . Note that the range of survival temperature for the adult fly $T_{min} \leq T \leq T_{max}$ was determined in the previous subsection: $a'=0$ out of this range.

3.4 Diffusion of Adult Olive Fruit Flies

An attraction weight [10] *aw* (*aw*≤0) is attributed to each cell; it is related to its olive coverage $1-C_0$, number of its receptive drupes $rD=\sum_{1 \leq j \leq n} recD_j$, its water quantity w : $aw=a_1 \cdot (1-C_0) \cdot \exp b_1 + a_2 \cdot rD \cdot \exp b_2 + a_3 \cdot w \cdot \exp b_3$.

Fly diffusion is a local interaction and is modelled according to a minimisation algorithm [4], which determines the movement of flies from the central cell to the other cells of the neighbourhood so that the sum of the differences of the "indicator" *aw+ad* among the cells is minimised. It involves that cells with more attraction weight (more convenient conditions) "capture" more flies and that flies diffuse little by little towards cells with higher attraction weight.

More precisely, two quantities are identified in the central cell: a "mobile" part (*ad*[0]), which can originate migration flows (*maf*[k], 1≤k≤8) toward the other 8 cells of the neighbourhood and a "not mobile" part *aw*[0]; *ad*[k] and *aw*[k] 1≤k≤8 are the corresponding quantities for the neighbourhood other cells; *ind*[k]=*ad*[k]+*aw*[k], 0≤k≤8 is defined.

The migration flows alter the situation: $ind^*[0]=ad[0]-\sum_{1\leq k\leq 8}maf[k]+aw[0]$, while $ind^*[k]=ad[k]+maf[k]+aw[k]$, $1\leq k\leq 8$. The minimisation algorithm application determines $maf[k]$, $1\leq k\leq 8$, such that the quantity $\sum_{0\leq k1<k2\leq 8}|ind^*[k1]-ind^*[k2]|$ is minimum.

Number of flies in a cell is obtained trivially by a balancing equation, adding migration inflows and subtracting migration outflows to the number of flies in the cell at the previous step.

All the adult flies are imposed to have the same age in a cell in this preliminary model; therefore, the weighted average maturity degree value is adopted for *ad* ; such an approximation is not so rough, if we consider that there is no large *ad* difference.

4   First FlySim Implementation and Simulations

FlySim, as described in the previous sections, is a preliminary model. The substates and the elementary processes represent a strong abstraction for more complex real situations; e.g. the pheromone (fly attractor) produced by the mature drupes can overcome significantly the limits of the cell [10], so that the only olive coverage factor (which is strictly bound by the cell) may be insufficient sometimes to account for this type of attraction.

All the elementary processes of type "internal transformations" have been tested separately with a large number of instances. This was easily performed because internal transformations imply a part of the transition function applied to a single cell.

Results look good within limits of verifying a phenomenon fragment: the qualitative behaviour was always ascertained, but a good quantitative response depends on the value of the parameters, which must be tuned by comparison with the data of real phenomena in complete simulations involving all the transition function.

The crucial point is the validation of all the elementary processes of type "local interactions", because the significant "properties" of the system emerge mainly by the application of such elementary processes.

4.1   Movement of the Flies

The only local interaction of FlySim for this release is the "diffusion of adult olive fruit flies".

The diffusion, in absence of attractors, is a plain diffusion with spurious symmetries effects. In order to account for a stochastic noise in diffusion and for the number of flies (which is an integer and cannot give rise to fractional number), a probabilistic correction (less than 10%) was introduced in the computation.

Diffusion of olive fruit flies was observed to produce an important "shield" effect: flies migrate toward more attractive areas but, when many contiguous attractive cells form a dense cluster, flies attack the more external olive trees and penetrate very slowly inside the cluster. This property is exploited by farmers, which surround clusters of olive trees with precocious olive trees, in order to prevent in time the flies' diffusion (at olive fruit maturing) inside the cluster by preparing opportune actions.

We present two cases, which have been specifically planned in order to individuate the peculiar characteristics emerging by the local interactions in the evolution of the phenomenon. The number of steps for both cases was selected to 100 (each step is 1 hour); note that this time period isn't so long to dilute emergent features in a final and almost steady state and isn't so short to lose the evolution prospect.

The first case represents a conceptual "experiment" (Fig.1): the CA region (in the fact a toroidal surface) is divided in eighteen identical rectangles of cells (10×20). The initial configuration considers that a rectangle with olive trees doesn't contain flies and vice versa, so that a chequer is built (it isn't realistic). The edge of the cell is 4 metres. The number of attractive drupes is 90 for the cells with the olive trees; the same number 90 of flies is present for the infested cells.

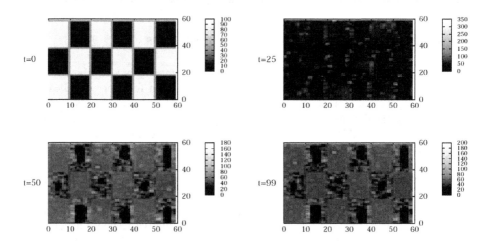

Fig. 1. The figure represents the evolution of an instance of FlySym at the end of the steps 0, 25, 50 and 99. The cellular region is a 60×60 cells torus (note that there is an image distortion: double space in the horizontal direction). The grey tones scale is referred to the number of flies and changes at each step of simulation for a better visualisation.

The attack of the flies "erodes" little by little the edges of the olive trees rectangles, whose cells, free of flies in the subsequent steps, take an irregular shape of cluster. It is possible to individuate an intact central area of different form (stochastic effect) for the clusters at step 99 (the last one in our simulation). Note that there is no large difference between step 50 and 99 in comparison between step 0 and 25, because of the larger shield effect when the flies distribution causes a reduction in average of the flies difference between contiguous cells.

The second case represents a more realistic situation (Fig.2): the initial configuration of 60×60 cells (a toroidal surface) is the same of the previous case for the trees distribution, while the flies are concentrated (3600 for cell) only in a rectangle (5×10) of cells, which is the infestation source.

The larger number of flies overwhelm the cells around almost independently of the presence of attractive drupes (Fig.2, t=25).

The shield effect appears also in this case when the flies' distribution causes a reduction in average of the flies' difference between contiguous cells. Still, it is evident

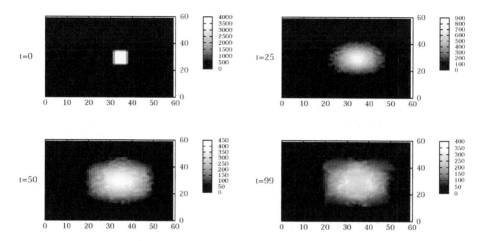

Fig. 2. The figure represents the same cellular region of Fig.1 with the same image distortion and the evolution of a different instance of FlySym at the end of the steps 0, 25, 50 and 99. The grey tones scale is referred to the number of flies.

at the step 50 and more manifestly at step 99, that there is a different condition for rectangles with drupes, which are strongly attacked at the border, while flies penetrate in depth for rectangles without drupes. This behaviour agrees with field observations.

5 Conclusions

This first qualitative validation of the model is very encouraging; the next necessary step is a quantitative validation of the entire model. This involves an organisation at farm level in order to obtain daily significant data, defining reliable interpretation protocols for such data; e.g. traps to capture flies must be opportunely disposed in order to evaluate the most accurately possible the movements of the flies (direction, number and so on).

Moreover, the proposed model needs an accurate selection of the real cases to be used for the validation phase; in fact, particularly complicate situations may require an excessive number of parameters, e.g. many different cultivars. An expedient could be to consider initially simple cases, limited in time where the system evolution isn't affected severely by the necessity to know precisely the value of some parameters, while the remaining could be accurately evaluated.

The whole simulation can be based in the future on a real environment represented by a Geographical Information System (GIS) which contains data about morphology of the territory, distribution of olive trees, rivers, roads and so on, all spatially referenced and superimposed to orthophotos of the territory. The GIS contains also time-dependent information such as: meteorological data taken from fixed station, number of flies captured by traps, maturation degree of the fruit and other biological information taken by agronomists.

Simulation of olive fruit fly attacks is very important in order to establish optimal intervention strategies. Efficacy and selection of different chemical treatments depends in correctly forecasting the attack extent and the crop imminence. Alternative use of proteinic baits represents a preventive method, based on long-term prediction.

Acknowledgements

The authors are grateful to Dr Maria Francesca De Franceschis for her contribution to the model implementation and to Prof. Beatrice Bitonti for the useful suggestions for the development of the model. This research has been partially funded by the Italian Ministry of Instruction, University and Research, project P.O.N. AGRO-TRACE.

References

1. Baldacchini, V., Gazziano, S.: Environmental Monitoring and Forecasting, Chap. 8 in Olive Pest Management, final report of the project ECLAIR 209(CEE AGRE 0013-C) "Development of Environmentally Safe Pest Control System for European Olives" (1998)
2. Bone, C., Dragicevic, S., Roberts A.: A Fuzzy-Constrained Cellular Automata Model of Forest Insect Infestations. Ecological Modelling, 192 (2006) 107–125
3. Cirio, U., Baldacchini, V., Gazziano, S., Santella, A.: Un Modello di Simulazione Previsionale/Decisionale per la Lotta Guidata al Dacus Oleae, 7° Simposio Chimica degli Antiparassitari, Università Cattolica del Sacro Cuore, Facoltà di Agraria. Piacenza 8-9 Giugno (1989)
4. Di Gregorio, S., Serra, R.: An Empirical Method for Modelling and Simulating Some Complex Macroscopic Phenomena by Cellular Automata. FGCS, 16 (1999) 259-271
5. Dominici, M., C. Pucci, and G. E. Montanari: Dacus Oleae (Gmel.) Ovipositing in Olive Drupes (Diptera, Tephrytidae). J. Appl. Entomol. 101 (1986) 111-120
6. Eskafi, F., Fernandez, A.: Larval-pupal mortality of Mediterranean fruit fly (Diptera: Tephritidae) from interaction of soil, moisture and temperature. Environ. Ent. 19, (1990) 1666–1670.
7. Fletcher, B.S., Kapatos E.T.: The Influence of Temperature, Diet and Olive Fruits on the Maturation Rates of Female Olive Flies at Different Times of the Year. Entomol. Exp. Appl., 33 (1983) 244-252
8. Haniotakis, G.E.: Sexual attraction in the olive fruit fly, Dacus oleae (Gmelin). Environmental Entomology 3 (1974) 82–86
9. Neuenschwander, P., Michelakis S.: The Infestation of Dacus Oleae (Gmel.) (Diptera, Tephritidae) at Harvest Time and Its Influence on Yield and Quality of Olive Oil in Crete. Z. Ang. Entomol. 86 (1978) 420-433
10. Neuenschwander, P., Michelakis, S., Holloway, P., Berchtold, W.: Factors affecting the susceptibility of fruits of different olive varieties to attack by Dacus oleae (Gmel.) (Dipt., Tephritidae). Z. Ang. Ent. 100, (1985) 174–188
11. Worsch, T.: Simulation of Cellular Automata. FGCS, 16 (1999) 157-170

The Influence of Risk Perception in Epidemics: A Cellular Agent Model

Luca Sguanci[1], Pietro Liò[2], and Franco Bagnoli[1]

[1,*]Dept. Energy, Univ. of Florence, Via S. Marta 3, 50139 Firenze, Italy
[2] Computer Laboratory, University of Cambridge, CB3 0FD Cambridge, UK
luca.sguanci@unifi.it,
pietro.lio@cl.cam.ac.uk,
franco.bagnoli@unifi.it

Abstract. Our work stems from the consideration that the spreading of a disease is modulated by the individual's perception of the infected neighborhood and his/her strategy to avoid being infected as well. We introduced a general "cellular agent" model that accounts for a heterogeneous and variable network of connections. The probability of infection is assumed to depend on the perception that an individual has about the spreading of the disease in her local neighborhood and on broadcasting media. In the one-dimensional homogeneous case the model reduces to the DK one, while for long-range coupling the dynamics exhibits large fluctuations that may lead to the complete extinction of the disease.

1 Introduction

In "Les rois thaumaturges: étude sur le caractère surnaturel attribué à la puissance royale particulièrement en France et en Angleterre" the historian Marc Bloch [1] wrote that until about 1700, sick people in England and France tried to be touched by the king who they believed was a miraculous physician whose mere touch would cure physical illness. Since then, much time has passed, we do no more touch the king but we still have to face with illness and different pathologies. Now that we know viruses and bacteria, we are addressing the issue of studying the mutual influences between collective behaviour, disease spreading and viral evolution. In fact, HIV epidemics has changed many of our sexual and social behaviors [2] and selection on viral strains has been in act by social groups [3, 4]. Zanotto and collaborators [5] have shown that viral evolution depends on differences in modes of dispersal, propagation, and changes in the size of host populations. They also suggest a link between the growing and fluidity of the human population and its exposure to an expanding range of increasingly diverse viral strains.

Understanding the role of social behaviour has potentiality of giving better answers to the pressing public health questions about whether and how we can contain or slow the spread of an emerging epidemics to give time for vaccine

---

* Also CSDC and INFN, sez. Firenze.

S. El Yacoubi, B. Chopard, and S. Bandini (Eds.): ACRI 2006, LNCS 4173, pp. 321–329, 2006.

development. Moreover, the understanding of key properties of contact networks may allow to reduce disease transmission, avoid both costly and time consuming universal vaccination or leaving hidden pockets of poor coverage that will seed again the epidemics.

Previous epidemiological models have investigated the effect of a wide variety of parameters, such as use of antiviral agents, super spreaders and individual variation [6], quarantine and pre-vaccination to contain the spread of disease at source. However, an outmost important factor that has been ignored so far is how the perception of the epidemics, as perceived from a neighborhood (short range information contacts) or from the media (long range), will change the diffusion parameters.

Here we concentrate on the study of the risk perception on disease spreading in the case of a homogeneous population. Although spatial variables can play a major role, it is important to study average statistical properties (mean field analysis) before taking into consideration more complex geometries. In general, populations do not experience full-mixing condition. However, well-stirred conditions are recovered whenever conditions of people crowdedness are considered or if it is possible to focus on a given scale of observation. Noteworthy the former conditions occur very frequently in urban contexts, for example in tubes and buses at peak times and aerial spreading of cold-related virus particles from coughing and sneezing disregards the casual contact. Other examples are children in a nursery who have large number of contacts during the day. On the other hand, we can concentrate on a homogeneous scale of observation if we study disease spreading in the hubs constituted by airports and train stations. Similarly, if we are interested in the interplay between cities and the countryside in disease evolution, we may address the problem considering the interaction between those two distinct entities, each characterized by homogeneous properties.

Different models for spreading of epidemics have been proposed, either considering homogeneous populations [7, 8], or in the framework of complex networks [9]. This kind of approach allows assessing the relative importance of local and long-range contacts not only in spreading the infection but also in spreading information on the infection risk and thus potentially stand as a very useful tool for public health managing and decision making processes.

The paper is organized as follows. In the next section we present a general *cellular agent* model for the study of the perceptive dynamics of a disease spreading. In section III we present the mean field approximation of the model, then we present the results of the performed simulations and finally we draw our conclusions.

2   The Model: Partying with Your Neighbors or Stay Home, Spy Them and Read the News?

We shall develop a quite general agent-based model, allowing age classes (progression of the illness) and different types of communication networks. We propose to use the term *cellular agent* for it, since it reduces to cellular automata for a regular lattice of connections, but connections may also change in time.

The single agent i (representing an individual or a group of strongly connected individuals like a family) is implemented as a set of (directional) incoming connections, an internal state and an output state. Let us denote as M_{ij} the connection from site j to site i. In our model a connection represents the propensity of being infected, which is proportional to the fraction of time spent together by the two individuals i and j, but also depends on the type of contact. For this last reason, the connection needs not to be symmetric: while it may be true for friendly contacts, the risk of being infected is quite asymmetrical for professionals (nurses, physicians, etc.) and also for parents vs. children, and so on. In the simplest case of unweighted connection, $M_{ij} \in \{0, 1\}$, $k_i = \sum_j M_{ij}$ is the number of neighbors and $s_i = \sum_j M_{ij}[\sigma_j \neq 0]$ is the number of infected neighbors[1]. In the case of weighted connections, s and k are no more integers. The network of connections may be fixed, or evolving in time. The degree (or connectivity) of a node is defined as the number of the incoming/outcoming links, while the degree distributions of a network, $P(k)$, represents the fraction of nodes with degree k. Many social networks have a scale-free structure [10], and this kind of networks can only be *grown* using a connection rule. So, it is natural to assume that new connections may be established, and old one removed, following a dynamical rule. Actually, one could work with a fully-connected network, and implement the evolution of connection as a rule for the intensities M_{ij} (possibly introducing a threshold value for the efficacy of a connection), but this would be quite expensive in computer terms. We limit the present investigations to fixed connection all of the same intensity.

We represent the internal state (progression of illness) of the individual i as a bitstring σ_i. Each bit in σ (represented as a base-2 number) indicates the presence of a given strain. In this way we can account for the geographic distribution of different strains (important for immunization strategies), multiple infections (co-infection or delayed re-infection) and recombination among strains. To each possible value of σ is associated an infection probability (infectivity) $\tau(\sigma)$, with $\tau(0) = 0$. The internal state contains also a time counter, for timing the progression of the illness. In the present model, we simply assume that the individual becomes healthy after a certain interval from the last infection. We do not consider here immunization, nor the internal dynamics between infective pathogens and the immune system [11].

The output state indicate if an individual is infective, and if it is visibly ill. In this way we can represent incubation periods. In this first study, we assume that the illness become visible the unit of time (day) after infection, thus obtaining a parallel evolution.

We assume that the probability of infection is proportional to the frequency of contacts M_{ij}, but that it is also modulated by the individual's *perception* of the percentage of infected people in her neighborhood as well as by the strategy

---

[1] We use the notation [*statement*] to indicate the truth function, which gives 1 if *statement* is true and 0 otherwise.

for avoiding being infected. If an individual realizes that a large fraction of her neighbors is infected, or is alerted by broadcasting media, then she may change her habits. She may rise the level of precautions (thus lowering the effective infectivity of the illness) or alter her connection patterns. Since this last choice implies a large rearrangement of individual lifestyle, this dramatic change is assumed to take place only in extreme cases. However, even without changing lifestyle it is possible to lower the infection probability by simply taking elementary precautions. We assume this to be the most common reaction. Therefore we keep M_{ij} constant during the simulation, but make the infection probability of a single contact to vary according with the fraction of infected people among the neighbors (weighted with the connection strengths) and with the influence by media information. We also assume that the recovering is immediate, and that the individual becomes immediately susceptible.

The perception (information) about the disease is written ass $I(s,k) = \exp[-(H + Js/k)]$. The parameter J modulates individual's response to the the local infection load. The role of the intensity of the external fields, like public healths alerts and media influences, is accounted for by the H parameter. In the following we assume $H = 0$, but it's worth noting that this parameter can play a major role in scenarios of low perception of the risk of infection. This could be the case of infections characterized by a long-asymptomatic phase, in which many contacts occurs without the perception of any risk of being infected. In such scenarios, H turns out to be the only mean to downregulate the spreading of the disease.

The microscopic infection process is the following: for all the contacts of the individual i, the bitstring σ_i is OR-ed with σ_j, the bitstring representing the neighboring individual j, if the contact is effective in propagating the infection. This happens with a probability $M_{ij}I(s_i, k_i)\tau(\sigma_j)$.

The total infection probability $p_i(s_i, k_i)$ of an individual i facing s_i infected neighbors among the k_i, is therefore

$$p_i(s_i, k_i) = 1 - \prod_j \left[1 - M_{ij}I(s_i, k_i)\tau(\sigma_j)\right]. \tag{1}$$

In the unweighted case, with single-valued connectivity, $P(k') = \delta_{k,k'}$, and assuming the same infectivity τ for all strains, equation (1) becomes:

$$p_i(s_i) = 1 - [1 - I(s_i, k)\tau]^{s_i}, \tag{2}$$

In summary, the algorithm for the microscopic dynamics is as follows. Given the status of the network at time t, all the nodes of the network are sequentially considered. According to the infected neighbors and to the influence of long-rance interactions the probability of infection of each node is calculated and thus the evolution rule is applied in order to get the status of the network at time $t+1$. At the same time a check is made whether infected individuals recover from disease and become susceptible again.

3   Results

3.1   One Dimensional Case

Here we consider the simplest case where M_{ij} defines a 1D regular lattice with $k = 2$ (nearest neighbors), and where all the contacts have the same strength. The status of node i is represented by a single bit, $\sigma_i = \{0, 1\}$ and the infectivity parameter, τ, is single valued.

This case can be mapped on the Domany-Kinzel model [12]. This latter is defined as a one-dimensional totalistic cellular automaton with $k = 2$, and its evolution rule depends on two parameters: p_1, the probability becoming infected if only one of the neighbors is infected, and p_2, the probability of being infected if both neighbors are infected. The correspondence with our model is therefore $p_1 = p(1, 2)$ and $p_2 = p(2, 2)$.

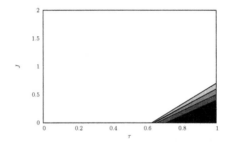

Fig. 1. Percentage of asymptotic infected population for the one-dimensional, $k = 2$ case (1000 sites). White: no individual is infected, black: all individuals are infected.

We have obtained the phase space $(H = 0)$ using the (τ, J) parameters. The results are shown in Fig. 1. The model exhibits a continuous transition (second-order) from a healthy state to the complete infection, as the infectivity increases. As far as J is subsequently increased over a threshold value, the infection can no longer subsist and the population recovers completely from the disease.

3.2   Long-Range Case

Mean-Field Approximation. The average asymptotic behavior of networks can be investigated by means of mean field approach. Given N the number of nodes, let us call $N_k = NP(k)$ the number of nodes with connectivity k; $\Omega_{k,k'}$, the probability of a node with connectivity k being connected to a node with connectivity k'; $N_k c_k$, the number of nodes with connectivity k being infected; m, the average frequency of contact between two individuals. We refer to the probability of being infected of a node with connectivity k at time t with c_k.

Now, if only one infective strain is considered, i.e. $\tau(\sigma_j) = \tau$, the probability of being infected at time $t + 1$, c'_k, is given by:

$$c'_k = \sum_{s=1}^{k} \binom{k}{s} \left(\sum_{k'_1, k'_2, \ldots, k'_s} (\Omega_{kk'_1} c_{k'_1}) \ldots (\Omega_{kk'_s} c_{k'_s}) \right) \times$$

$$\left(\sum_{k'_{s+1}, \ldots, k'_{k-s}} (\Omega_{kk'_{s+1}} (1 - c_{k'_{s+1}})) \ldots (\Omega_{kk'_{k-s}} (1 - c_{k'_{k-s}})) \right) \left[1 - (1 - m\, I(s,k)\tau)^s \right] =$$

$$\sum_{s=1}^{k} \binom{k}{s} \left(\sum_{k'} \Omega_{kk'} c_{k'} \right)^s \left(\sum_{k'} \Omega_{kk'} (1 - c_{k'}) \right)^{k-s} \left[1 - (1 - m\, I(s,k)\tau)^s \right] \tag{3}$$

If a non assortative network is considered, i.e. $\Omega_{k,k'} = N_{k'}/N = P(k')$:

$$c'_k = \sum_{s=1}^{k} \binom{k}{s} \left(\sum_{k'} P(k') c_{k'} \right)^s \left(\sum_{k'} P(k')(1 - c_{k'}) \right)^{k-s} \left[1 - (1 - m\, I(s,k)\tau)^s \right] \tag{4}$$

and, if k is fixed, i.e. $P(k') = \delta_{k',k}$,

$$c' = \sum_{s=1}^{k} \binom{k}{s} c^s (1 - c)^{k-s} \left[1 - (1 - m\, I(s,k)\tau)^s \right] \tag{5}$$

Estimation of the infection reproductive rate. A meaningful epidemiological parameter is the basic reproductive rate, R_0, which is defined as the mean number of infections caused by an infected individual in a susceptible population [13, 6]. This parameter can be considered an epidemiological threshold. When $R_0 < 1$, each person who contracts the disease will infect fewer than one person before dying or recovering, so the outbreak will cease. When $R_0 > 1$, each person who gets the disease will infect more than one person, so the epidemic will spread.

A more careful investigation of this parameter can lead to a better insight in the dynamics of the epidemics, at the same time allowing to assess the efficacy of different strategies of containment on the spreading of the disease. For example Lloyd-Smith and colleagues have shown that the distribution of individual infectiousness around R_0 is often highly skewed [6]. Longini and collaborators have investigated bird flu pandemia scenarios. They found that if R_0 was below 1.60, a prepared response with targeted antivirals would have a high probability of containing the disease. If pre-vaccination occurred, then targeted antiviral prophylaxis could be effective for containing strains with an R_0 as high as 2.1. Combinations of targeted antiviral prophylaxis, pre-vaccination, and quarantine could contain strains with an R0 as high as 2.4 [13].

With reference to the model we propose, we can derive the expression of the basic reproductive ratio, by considering the variation of c' with respect to c, when a small fraction of infected population is considered, i.e.

$$R_0 = \lim_{c \to 0} \frac{\partial c'}{\partial c} = k[I(1,k)\tau] \tag{6}$$

In this way we recover the expression of the basic reproductive ratio, when a unitary mean time of infectivity per individual is considered. From this we derive the critical value of J, below which the fraction of infected individuals is different from zero, i.e. $R_0 > 1$,

$$J_c = k \ln(k\tau) \tag{7}$$

Numerical Simulations. To better characterize the role of the mean connectivity of individuals k (randomly chosen), we plot the value of the fraction of infected individuals, c, as a function of J, for different values of k. In Fig.2 we report the results of the numerical simulations for the mean field approximation of the model, plot (a), and for the microscopic dynamics, plot(b). We can first

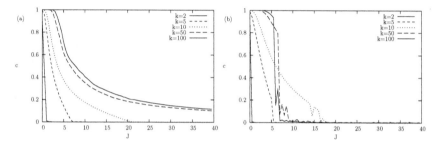

Fig. 2. The value of the fraction of infected individuals c, is plotted as a function of J. The results of the numerical simulations are shown for the mean field model (a) and for the microscopic dynamics (b, 100 sites).

notice that, for a growing number of neighbors, the fraction of infected individuals increases. This suggest that if we consider bounded the strength of the individual perception of the disease, an ever growing influence of the external field is necessary to keep low the number of infected individuals. By comparing the mean field model with the microscopic dynamics a good agreement is shown for small values of J (depending on k). For larger values of J, the infected population exhibits large coherent oscillations, that may lead to a complete recover from the infection and to the disappearing of the epidemics. In the mean field approximation, for increasing values of k, the model begins to show a high variation in the fraction of infected individuals, without reaching extinction.

By keeping fixed the value of the mean connectivity and setting $H = 0$, we analyzed the mean-field phase space. In Fig.3, the case for $k = 50$ is reported. The results of the numerical simulations display either stable solutions and oscillatory behaviours. Moreover chaotic dynamics arise for particular values of the parameters. It is worth noticing that the huge variety of social behaviours is well reflected by the model outcomes.

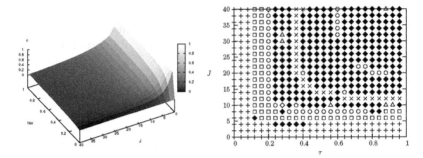

Fig. 3. Mean field asymptotic value of the fraction of infected sites (left) and bifurcation diagram for $k = 50$, $N = 100$. Pluses: fixed points, empty squares: period-2, crosses: period-3, empty circles: period-4, empty triangles: period-5, empty pentagons: period-6, empty diamonds: period-8, filled diamonds: chaotic orbits.

4   Conclusions

Our model represents a general framework that enables us to make predictions and to compare different scenarios of disease spreading management.

The model can be also useful to investigate the effect that the lack of information from neighbors and media can have on the disease spreading. Indeed this can be comparable to the disease incubation period i.e. the lack of symptoms when the virus is not demonstrable. Similarly we can analyze how a chronic disease, which represent a latent but infectious state, may reduce the level of surveillance as well as continuous media and neighborhood alarm.

Viral diseases have different intrinsic biological characteristics which become coupled with different social and psychological behaviors of the neighborhood, generating a vast combinatorial of dynamics, as shown by the results of the phase-space analysis reported in the previous section.

The probability of contacts leading to infection can be calibrated against seasonal or environmental effects and total and age-specific illness attack rates of data in past pandemics. In fact, by including age dependent distributions we can take into account whether an infected person becomes ill or remains asymptomatic and, if symptomatic, when (if ever) the person withdraws to household-only contacts [14]. Glass and collaborators [15] found that heterogeneity in measles vaccination coverage can lead to an increased rate of infection among non-vaccinated individuals, with a simultaneous drop in the average age at infection.

A major factor is the correct identification of target age groups. Recent works show that pre-scholar children aged 3 to 4 drive influenza epidemics and are most strongly linked with mortality in the vulnerable groups (elderly) and general population than other children [16]. In fact they present flu-like respiratory illness as early as late September, while children aged 0-2 began arriving a week or two later and older children first arrived in October and adults began arriving only in November. This example points to the difference between high-risk individuals, for example babies under 24 months or the elderly, and those who are transmitting the disease to everyone else . The former should be vaccinated first [17].

The above examples show that the field is at the early stage and will benefit from an interdisciplinary approach and from a methodic and careful analysis of the contribution of each parameter.

References

1. M. Bloch, *The Royal Touch: Monarchy and Miracles in France and England* (Dorset Press, New York 1990).
2. Fredrik Liljeros, Christofer R. Edling, Luis A. Nunes Amaral Sexual networks: implications for the transmission of sexually transmitted. infections Microbes and Infection 5 (2003) 189–196
3. P. Schliekelman, C. Garner and M. Slatkin, Nature **411**, 545 (2001).
4. J. Novembre, A.P. Galvani and M. Slatkin, PLoS Biol.**3** 339 (2005).
5. P.M. Zanotto, E.A. Gould, G.F. Gao, P.H. Harvey and E.C. Holmes, *Population dynamics of flaviviruses revealed by molecular phylogenies*, Proc. Natl. Acad. Sci. USA. **93**, 548 (1996).
6. J.O. Lloyd-Smith, S. J. Schreiber, P. E. Kopp and W.M. Getz, Nature **438**, 355 (2005).
7. J.D. Murray, *Mathematical biology* (Springer-Verlag, NY 2002).
8. R.M. Anderson and R.M. May, *Infectious Diseases of Humans: Dynamics and Control* (Oxford Univ. Press, Oxford, 1991).
9. R. Pastor-Satorras and A. Vespignani, Phys. Rev. Lett. **86**, 3200 (2001); R. Pastor-Satorras and A. Vespignani, Phys. Rev. E **63**, 066117 (2001). A. L. Lloyd and R.M. May, Science **292**, 1316 (2001).
10. A.L. Barabasi and R. Albert, Science **286**, 509 (1999); R. Albert and A.L. Barabasi, Rev. Mod. Phys. **74**, 47 (2002); S. Boccaletti, V. Latora, Y. Moreno, M. Chavez and D.U. Hwang, Phys. Rep. **424**, 175 (2006).
11. F. Bagnoli, P. Lió and L. Sguanci, Physica A, In Press, Corrected Proof, Available online 28 November 2005.
12. E. Domany and W. Kinzel, Phys. Rev. Lett. **53**, 311 (1984).
13. I.M. Longini, A. Nizam, S. Xu, K. Ungchusak, W. Hanshaoworakul, D.A.T. Cummings and E.M. Halloran, Science **309**, 1083 (2005).
14. T.C. Germann, K. Kadau, I.M. Longini, and C.A. Macken Proc. Natl. Acad. Sc. USA **103**, 15 (2006)
15. K. Glass, K. Kappey and B.T. Grenfell Epidemiol Infect. **132**, 675 (2004).
16. J.S. Brownstein, K.P. Kleinman and K.D. Mandl, Amer. J. Epidemiol. **162** 686 (2005).
17. M.B. Aldous AAP Grand Rounds **15**, 6 (2006).

Spreadable Probabilistic Cellular Automata Models: An Application in Epidemiology

Redouane Slimi and Samira El Yacoubi

MEPS/ASD - University of Perpignan
52, Paul Alduy Avenue, 66860 Perpignan, Cedex, France
{slimi, yacoubi}@univ-perp.fr
http://www.univ-perp.fr/see/rch/cef/index.html

Abstract. Many important physical processes reveal spreadable phenomena which describe the expansion with time of a given spatial property. The general spreadability concept have been studied using models based on partial differential equations (PDE's). These spreadable dynamics are generally non linear and then difficult to simulate particularly in 2 dimensions. A cellular automata approach have been used as an alternative modelling tool to model and simulate spreadable systems in the deterministic case.

We propose in this paper a probabilistic cellular automaton model that exhibits the growth with time of a spatial property. The obtained local dynamics are directly implemented and the numerical results are performed to illustrate spreadable phenomena. An example to epidemic propagation is given to illustrate the considered phenomena.

1   Introduction

The investigation of phenomena involving spatial growth has gone through a spectacular development in the last decade. A wide variety of real processes in physics, biology, urban environment or medicine has been shown to be related to and raised interest in spatial modelling. These systems usually exhibit an expansion phenomenon that can be difficult to describe by classical approaches. The concept of spreadability was then introduced in order to find the suitable dynamics for which a certain spatial property can survive inside increasing domains.

First introduced by El Jai and Kassara [1,2] in 1994, the spreadability and spray control concepts have been studied using partial differential equations (PDE's) and tested essentially for transport and diffusion systems [2,4]. Spreadable distributed parameter systems provide a mathematical framework for modelling and control expansion phenomena [3,4]. However, these studies were restricted to linear systems while the most of growth processes are non linear. Recent works devoted to feedback spreading control has been studied using semi-linear PDE's in [9,10].

Cellular automata (CA) models which are often described as a counterpart to PDE's offer a simple and powerful approach to study spatio-temporal systems which exhibit complex phenomena by means of simple local rules.

S. El Yacoubi, B. Chopard, and S. Bandini (Eds.): ACRI 2006, LNCS 4173, pp. 330–336, 2006.

The mathematical formulation in terms of CA models which aimed at capturing the main features of spreadable phenomena has been considered in [5]. A study of spreadable systems by means of deterministic CA dynamics has been done in [6]. We consider in this paper, the probabilistic case which seems to be more realistic. We numerically illustrate the growth of the domains ω_t where the property is satisfied at time t. The result concerning the convergence of these sets to a limit L is also emphasized. A simple epidemic model is given to illustrate the studied phenomenon.

The paper is organized as follows, section 2 is devoted to the description of spreadable phenomena by means of probabilistic CA rules defined in terms of birth and survival functions. The given simulation example show the convergence of the domains Ω_t to a limit set when the probabilities are close to one as shown in the deterministic case [6]. In section 3, an application in the context of epidemic dynamics is considered and illustrated with a simulation example.

2   Spreadability of Two-Dimensional Probabilistic Cellular Automata

A CA is an aggregation of identically programmed cells which interact with each others. Every cell is characterized by a state belonging to a finite set. CA evolves through a sequence of discrete time steps. The automata state is updated every step according to a finite set of prescribed rules for local transitions.

The essential elements of a cellular automaton are : its global state, its neighborhood and its dynamics. These features must be specified for each application. CA models constitute suitable tools for modelling and simulating spatial properties of a large variety of biogeographical applications. They are discrete in nature so that they are quite analogous with digital computers. This analogy is the main reason of our interest in such an approach particularly regarding the spreadability phenomenon.

We built in this section a class of CA rules which describe spreading effects. Let us first define the spreadability by means of CA models.

2.1   Spreadability Concept

General concept of spreadability, see [1,2], concerns distributed systems defined on an open bounded domain Ω, governed by a given dynamics and whose state at time $t \in I =]0,T[$ and position $x \in \Omega$ is denoted by $z(x,t)$. Let us consider a spatial property $\mathcal{P}$ which aims to be spread or resorbed with time. It may be a vegetation cover, a pollution area or a zone of infected population. The spradability is equivalent to the growth with time of domains where $\mathcal{P}$ is satisfied by the system's state $z(x,t)$, starting from an initial state z_0 which is assumed to be known in a given subregion $\Omega_0 \subset \Omega$. Let us now express this notion in terms of CA approach defined on an infinite space.

Consider a two-dimensional lattice $\mathcal{L}$ the elements (cells c) of which are represented by their coordinates (i,j). The state of a cell c is taken in the cyclic ring $\mathcal{S} = \{s_1, s_2, \cdots, s_k\}$ of cardinality k. Let N denotes the cell's neighborhood and f the transition function which allows to calculate the cell's state at time $t+1$ given the neighborhood's state at time t. If $s_t(c)$ designates the c cell state at time t and let us define a sequence of domains Ω_t where the property $\mathcal{P}$ is satisfied at time t :

$$\Omega_t = \{c \in \mathcal{L} \mid \mathcal{P}s_t(c)\} \tag{1}$$

We recall the following definition [5]:

Definition 1. *The CA defined by the quadruple* $(\mathcal{L}, \mathcal{S}, f, N)$ *is said to be* $\mathcal{P}$-*spreadable from an initial domain*

$$\Omega_0 = \{c \in \mathcal{L} \mid \mathcal{P}s_0(c)\}$$

where s_0 *is an initial CA configuration if the sequence* $\{\Omega_t\}_{t\geq 0}$ *is increasing :*

$$\Omega_t \subseteq \Omega_{t+1} \tag{2}$$

2.2   Spreadable Cellular Automata Rules

We shall built in what follow, a class of simple CA rules capable to maintain the property $\mathcal{P}$ on increasing subdomains. Let us associate to $\mathcal{P}$, a mapping π defined on the state set $\mathcal{S}$ by :

$$\begin{aligned} \pi : \mathcal{S} &\longrightarrow \{0,1\} \\ x &\longrightarrow \begin{cases} 1 & \text{if } x \text{ satisfies the property } \mathcal{P} \\ 0 & \text{otherwise} \end{cases} \end{aligned} \tag{3}$$

and denote by K the support of π given by $K = \{x \in \mathcal{S} \mid \pi(x) = 1\}$. We can write

$$\Omega_t = \{c \in \mathcal{L} \mid s_t(c) \in K\} \tag{4}$$

Since the spreadability describes the survival of the property $\mathcal{P}$, it is natural to define a mapping $\sigma : K \longrightarrow K$ to be related to the survival of $\mathcal{P}$.

In order to study the spatial spreading of $\mathcal{P}$, we shall examine the impact of the local environment on the generation of domains growth. The presence of $\mathcal{P}$ in the neighbourhood $N(c)$ of cell c at each time t, is given by the quantity $[0, 1[\ni p_t(c) = \dfrac{y_t(c)}{n}$ which expresses the local density of π where $y_t(c) = \sum\limits_{c' \in \dot{N}(c)} \pi(s_t(c'))$, with $n = |N(c)|$ the neighborhood size and $\dot{N}(c) = N(c) - \{c\}$.

Let us now consider a mapping $\nu : [0, 1[\longrightarrow \{0, 1\}$ where for all $y = p_t(c) \in [0, 1[$:

$$\nu(y) = \begin{cases} 1 & \text{if } y \geq \theta_1 \text{ with probability } p_1 \\ 0 & \text{otherwise} \end{cases} \tag{5}$$

which defines the birth of the property inside a cell c according to what happens around. We then establish the following generic rule :

$$s_{t+1}(c) = (\delta_1(x)\nu(y) + \delta_2(x)(1 - \nu(y)))(1 - \pi(x)) + \sigma(x)\pi(x) \tag{6}$$

where $\delta_1 : \mathcal{S} \longrightarrow K$ and $\delta_2 : \mathcal{S} \longrightarrow K^c$ are two arbitrary mappings and the variables x and y denotes $s_t(c)$ and $p_t(c)$ respectively.

Suppose that there exists $t_0 \geq 0$ such that the CA configuration s_{t_0} satisfies the property $\mathcal{P}$. Then the local dynamics defined by eq. (6) describes a $\mathcal{P}$-spreadable phenomenon from the initial domain Ω_{t_0}. The sequence $\{\Omega_t\}_{t>t_0}$ given in (4) becomes :

$$\Omega_{t+1} = \Omega_t \cup \{c \in \Omega_t{}^c \mid \nu(p_t(c)) = 1\} \tag{7}$$

which are increasing by construction.

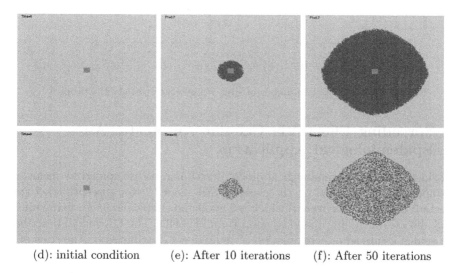

(d): initial condition   (e): After 10 iterations   (f): After 50 iterations

Fig. 1. Evolution of spreadable CA starting from an initial condition composed of 10×10 occupied cells placed at the middle of a 200×200 lattice and considering a Moore neigbourhood of radius $r = 2$. For (a): $\theta_1 = 0.16$ and $p_1 = 0.7$. For (d) $\theta_1 = 0.16$, $\theta_2 = 0.64$, $p_1 = 0.7$ and $p_2 = 0.9$.

The rule given by eq. (6) has been implemented with $\mathcal{S} = \{0, 1\}$ and a given property defined by $\pi : \mathcal{S} \longrightarrow \{0, 1\}$ of support $K = \{1\}$ with $\delta_1 \equiv 1$, $\delta_2 \equiv 0$ and $\sigma \equiv 1$. We illustrate the spreadable phenomenon which was generated from the same initial condition. The codes are written in C language and the visualization uses the graphical interface of Matlab. The simulation results are obtained in a two-dimensional space with square cells and periodic boundary conditions. The three first pictures in Fig. 1 illustrate the spreadable phenomenon with a probabilistic birth function ν defined in eq. (5) while the other ones consider the case where the survival function $\sigma : K \longrightarrow \mathcal{S}$ is also probabilistic and defined through a threshold parameter as follows :

$$\sigma(s_t(c)) \in \begin{cases} K & \text{if} \qquad p_t(c) - \frac{1}{n} \geq \theta_2 \text{ with probability } p_2 \\ K^c & \text{otherwise} \end{cases} \tag{8}$$

where $0 \leq \theta_1 \leq 1$ represents the survival threshold of the property $\mathcal{P}$. One plots in each case, the variation with time of $|\Omega_t|$. The corresponding curves are depicted in Fig. 2.

The case of probabilistic survival function correspond to a new approach of spreadability which consists in considering the increase of measure of domains Ω_t instead of the classical definition as shown in Fig. 2(b).

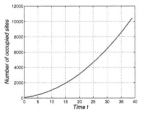
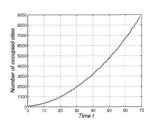

(a) $\theta_1 = 0.16$ and $p_1 = 0.7$ (b) $\theta_1 = 0.16$, $\theta_2 = 0.64$, $p_1 = 0.7$ and $p_2 = 0.9$

Fig. 2. Variation of the number of sites whose states satisfy the property

3   Spreading Effect Via Cellular Automata: An Epidemiological Application

Consider a simple epidemiological model describing disease spread by means of CA approach. It is based on the classical SIR model S (for susceptible), I (for infected) and R (for recovered) which is a good and simple model for many infectious diseases including measles, mumps and rubella. The CA model describes the epidemic spread of a population of individuals distributed on the sites of a fixed array of $L \times L$ cells which interact with each other according to a given neighbourhood. Individuals are born susceptible, then may acquire the infection and finally recover. The model is probabilistic as these transitions are performed with given probabilities. Each site may be occupied by a susceptible, infected or recovered individual, associated with the state value 0, 1 or 2 respectively. The dynamic evolution of the population is described, step by step, by the following set of interaction rules :

1. Susceptible individuals become infected with probability p_i if the local density of infected individuals is greater than a threshold θ_1.
2. Infected individuals remain in state 1 with probability p_s if the local density of infected individuals is greater than a threshold θ_2. Otherwise they recover.
3. Recovered individuals remain in state 2 with probability p_r or become susceptible.

The simulated example is concerned with a square lattice of 200×200 cells with a Moore neighbourhood of radius $r = 2$. The property to be spread corresponds to the infection associated with the state value 1.

In both cases, the increase of the infected zones is observed and the influence of initial condition is clearly shown. The whole domain is filled after 150 iteration for fixed initial seed while it is done in 50 iterations in the random case.

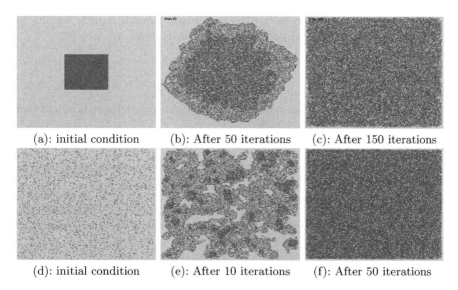

(a): initial condition   (b): After 50 iterations   (c): After 150 iterations

(d): initial condition   (e): After 10 iterations   (f): After 50 iterations

Fig. 3. Evolution of the epidemic spread starting from: (a)-(c) a seed of square shape of 62×62 infected sites, (d)-(f) a random initial seed with density 0.1 corresponding to the same number of infected sites as in (a)-(c). Susceptible, Infected and Recovered sites are presented in green, blue and pink respectively with $r = 2$, $\theta_1 = 0.16$, $\theta_2 = 0.40$, $p_i = 0.7$, $p_s = 0.8$ et $p_r = 0.9$.

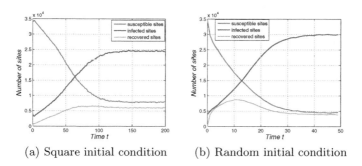

(a) Square initial condition   (b) Random initial condition

Fig. 4. Variation of the number of susceptible, infected and recovered sites with $r = 2$, $\theta_1 = 0.16$, $\theta_2 = 0.40$, $p_i = 0.7$, $p_s = 0.8$ and $p_r = 0.9$

4   Conclusion and Future Work

In this paper, we have investigated an efficient model for spreadability defined as the ability of some geographic properties to spread from one defined area to increasing subdomains. The given probabilistic rule have been implemented and used to model an epidemic dynamics.

The presented model will be concerned in a future work with the spread of Chagas disease transmitted by non-domiciliated triatomines in the Yucatan peninsula (Mexico). It will integrate the space heterogeneity and time delay. A simulation tool will be developed for the presented epidemic model. An efficient control strategy for disease spread has to be investigated.

References

1. EL Jai, A., Kassara, K.: Spreadable distributed systems. Mathematical and Computer Modelling, vol. 20, n. 1 (1994) 47–64
2. EL Jai, A., Kassara, K.: Spreadability of transport systems. International Journal of Systems Science, vol. 27, n. 7 (1996) 681–688
3. EL Jai, A., Kassara, K., Cabrera O.: Spray Control. International Journal of Control, vol. 68 (1997) 709–730
4. El Yacoubi, S., El Jai A., Karrakchou, J.: Spreadability and spray actuators. Journal of Applied Mathematics and Computer Science, vol. 8, n. 2 (1998) 367–379
5. El Yacoubi, S., El Jai A.: Cellular automata and spreadablility. Mathematical and Computer Modelling, vol. 36 (2002) 1059–1074
6. El Yacoubi S., Slimi R.: Spreadable cellular automata: Modelling and simulations. Int. Journal of Systems Analysis Modelling Simulation, to appear.
7. Gravner, J., Griffeath, D.: Thershold Growth Dynamics. Trans. Amer. Math. society, (1993) 837–870
8. Jacewicz, P.: Modélisation Et Simulation Des Systèmes distribués Par Automates Cellulaires. Application En Ecologie. Thèse de doctorat, Université de Perpignan (2002)
9. Kassara K.:Feedback spreading controls for semilinear parabolic systems. J. Comp. Appl. Math. 114 (2000) 41–54
10. Kassara K.:Feedback spreading control laws for semilinear distributed parameter systems. Systems control lett. 40 (2000) 269–276
11. von Neumann, J.: Theory of Self-Reproducing Automata. Edited and completed by Arthur Burks, University of Illinois Press (1966)
12. Toffoli, T.: Cellular automata as an alternative to differential equation in modeling physics. Physica D, vol. 10 (1984) 117–127

Towards a Two-Scale Cellular Automata Model of Tumour-Induced Angiogenesis

Paweł Topa

AGH University of Science and Technology, al. Mickiewicza 30,
30-059 Kraków, Poland
topa@agh.edu.pl

Abstract. This paper presents a new framework for modelling tumour-induced angiogenesis. Classical Cellular Automata approach is employed to model cellular and intracellular processes that occur in cancer tissue and neighbourhood. Vascular system is modelled by using Graph of Cellular Automata, which combines graph theory with Cellular Automata paradigm. A new model is proposed as a starting point for further investigations on multiscale model covering wide range of spatio-temporal scales including blood flow processes. The basis of the model with the algorithms are presented. Preliminary results with short discussion are also included.

1 Introduction

Angiogenesis is the process of formation of blood vessels. It occurs in embryogenesis after the vasculogenesis stage. During vasculogenesis, primary, chaotic network of capillaries are formed from the endothelial precursors [1]. Next, during the angiogenesis stage, the network is rebuilt into a fully functional network of arteries, capillary vessels and veins.

In adulthood angiogenesis is rigorously controlled by wide range of stimulators and inhibitors [2]. Their very precise balance makes this process quiescent except tissue healing, placenta forming during pregnancy and in the cycling ovary. The angiogenic process can be activated by metabolic stress e.g. low O_2 (hypoxia), low pH or hypoglycemia. Other conditions such as mechanical stress (pressure generated by proliferating cells), immune response and genetic mutations [2] can activate angiogenesis too.

Oxygen and nutrients penetrate the tissue only in a certain distance from the vessel. Distant cells, influenced by metabolic stress, synthesise angiogenesis stimulators such as VEGF (Vascular Endothelial Growth Factor) and bFGF (Basic Fibroblast Growth Factor) [2], [3]. Stimulators migrate towards the nearest blood vessels. When they reach the vessel, the endothelial cells (ECs) that lines the wall of this vessel are activated. They start to proliferate and migrate towards the tumour cell attracted by VEGF and other stimulators. The wall of the parent blood vessel becomes degraded and it opens to a new capillary. Migrating and proliferating ECs form a hollow tube-like cavity (the lumen), which are stabilised later by smooth muscle cells and perycites. Finally a new capillary vessel becomes fully functional.

S. El Yacoubi, B. Chopard, and S. Bandini (Eds.): ACRI 2006, LNCS 4173, pp. 337–346, 2006.

Uncontrolled proliferation of tumour cells makes that existing blood vessels cannot supply them with oxygen and nutrients. In consequence "starving" tumour cells produce VEGF, bFGF and other stimulators of angiogenesis described in this case as Tumour Angiogenesis Factors (TAFs). Neighbouring vessels, activated by TAFs, start sprouting, and develop toward tumour tissue. Due to imbalance of angiogenic factors new vessels form a highly chaotic and disorganised network [6]. Moreover, their walls have a pathological form, i.e. they are thin and permeable, their diameter changes abruptly etc.

Inhibition of tumour-induced angiogenesis is the most promising strategy in anti–cancer therapy [2], [1], [5]. Most of the currently tested therapies targeted endothelial cells. The inhibitors not only suppress ECs proliferation but also initiate their death what follows to vessels regression. Anti-VEGF treatment also normalises chaotic structure and abnormal architecture of tumour induced vessels what improves drug delivery to tumour tissue.

However, clinical tests show that none of the tested inhibitors did success in broad range types of cancers [1]. Monotherapies fail because angiogenesis is controlled by very complex balance of stimulators and inhibitors. Therefore, further investigations have to concentrate on researches including wider range of angiogenic factors.

1.1   Models of Angiogenesis

Angiogenesis is modelled by using continuous and discrete approaches [3]. Continuous models employ Partial Differential Equations in order to reflect distributions of endothelial cells and angiogenic factors. Stochastic movement of endothelial cells are represented by diffusion equation. Other factors are included as additional terms to the original diffusion equation. Anderson and Chaplain [7] simulate diffusion of ECs governed by angiogenic stimulators and fibronectin influence. Plank et al. [8] meets wider range of angiogenic stimulators including angiopoetins to their model.

Discrete approach assumes that modelled molecule as endothelial cells or angiogenic factors are treated individually. Anderson and Chaplain proposed one of the most often cited discrete model of angiogenesis [7]. They assume that growth of the single vessel is governed by move of the endothelial cell located at the sprout tip. This cell moves across regular, rectangular network according to defined rules. At each step of simulation the cell moves in one of the four directions or stays with a certain probability. The probabilities are calculated by using continuous approach, i.e. diffusion equation supplied with terms reflecting VEGF and fibronectin influence. Additional rules which model vessels branching and anastomosing are also defined.

Stokes and Lauffenberg presented a bit different approach [9]. They also model sprouting vessels as separate structures. Each sprout is described by the position and velocity of its tip at a given time step of simulation. The velocity is calculated by using stochastic differential equation that combines viscous damping term, random motion term and chemotactic term (models TAFs influence).

Recent researches focus on multiscale model that are able to cover all phenomena contributing to cancer development. Alacorn et al. [10], [11] presented model that couples processes occurring on different spatio-temporal scales:

- vascular scale that includes vascular network adaptation and blood flow,
- cellular scale: cell-cell interaction (e.g. tumour-normal competition) and cell spatial distribution,
- intracellular scale: cell division, TAFs secretion and apoptosis.

Alacorn et al. [10] focuses on modelling whole cancer rather than on angiogenic processes, thus their vascular network has a form of simple hexagonal mesh.

In this paper a new framework for modelling tumour–induced angiogenesis is proposed. The presented model is regarded as a test for this framework, therefore, some problems connected with angiogenesis were substituted by their simplifications. The investigation is targeted on building a modelling environment that besides wide spectrum of angiogenesis factors, is able to consider blood flow processes and their influence on vascular system development.

2   The Model of Tumour-Induced Angiogenesis

The model is founded upon the concept of transportation network and consuming (or producing) environment [12], [13]. The network delivers certain resources to the system, where they are absorbed and changed into progress of the environment. Changes in the environment influence network structure. The system leads to the state of dynamic balance, when the whole environment is equally supplied. An anastomosing river [14] as well as a vascular system are good examples of such the phenomenon. We can also consider the system in which the resources are transported in the opposite direction i.e. the resources are collected from the environment and transported outside. Branching network formed by a river and its tributaries fits this scheme.

This approach postulates partial separation of the two time scales represented by formation of the channel and the environmental factor, respectively. Instead of modelling local relations between the endothelial cells, blood, nutrients and oxygen, we consider now the global interactions between the blood vessels network and tissue. The network edges (vessels) can be added or removed accordingly to the local distribution of TAFs. Conversely, the nutrients distribution is formed by the entire river network. The feedback between environmental changes and evolution of the network should be faster allowing for modelling vessels over larger spatial scales.

The tissue is represented by a mesh of cellular automata. The distribution of oxygen, nutrients and TAFs is modelled by using Cellular Automata rules of local interaction [15]. The transportation network is represented by the Graph of Cellular Automata (GCA) which is built over the CA mesh [12], [13]. The graph is constructing by choosing some cells from the regular mesh, and connecting them with edges that represent the sections of the vessels.

The angiogenesis is an extremely complex process which is still not fully understood. Therefore, the following assumptions had to be made to this model:

- tumour cells do not migrate nor proliferate,
- "hungry" tumour cells produce TAFs at constant rate,
- TAFs migrating through the tissue establish gradient of TAFs concentration,
- TAFs concentration exceeding certain threshold activate endothelial cells in existing vessels,
- only "mature" vessels are able to create sprouts,
- sprouts grow attracted by TAFs concentration,
- new vessel have to "mature" before it can be able to fulfil they function — it corresponds to the process of covering endothelial cells by smooth muscle cells an perycites.

Most of these assumptions are based on real observations, however some of them are only hypothesis or they were included for the sake of clarity of the algorithms.

The model can be defined in a more formal way as follows:

$$CA_{ANG} =< Z^2, G_{CA}, X_K, S, \delta >, \quad \text{where :}$$

- Z^2 — a collection of cells ordered as a square mesh of $Z \times Z$ cells,
- G_{CA} — a planar and acyclic graph defined as (V_G, E_G), where $V_G \subset Z^2$ and $E_G \subset Z^2 \times Z^2$ are a finite set of vertices and a finite set of edges, respectively,
- $X_K(i,j)$ — neighbourhood for the (i,j) cell in regular mesh of automata,
- S — is the set of state vectors corresponding to each cell: $S = S_m \times S_g$,
  - S_m — represents states corresponding to all cells in the mesh:
    * t_{ij} — state of a single tumour cell, two possible values: "`full`" and "`hungry`",
    * f_{ij} — TAFs concentration,
    * n_{ij} — nutrient (oxygen) concentration,
  - S_g — represents states corresponding to the cells that belong to the Graph of Cellular Automata:
    * a_{ij} — "age", maturation level,
    * p_{ij} — indicate "tip" cell (boolean),

The cells which form the graph are the sources of nutrients (e.g. oxygen). Nutrients are distributed to the surrounding cells, providing certain gradient of concentration. Tumour cells with nutrients concentration below the certain value turn their state into "hungry" and start producing TAFs. TAFs distribute through the mesh of automata and establish certain gradient of concentration, in a similar way as in case of nutrients.

When the TAFs concentration in cell that belongs to the graph exceed certain threshold, a new branch is initiated. The vessel grows attracted by higher TAFs concentration. Similarly to the discrete Chaplain and Anderson model [7], growth of the single vessel is governed by the move of its tip. The consecutive tip cells are calculated based on local TAFs gradient.

Initially a new vessel is not mature enough to be able to supply nutrients. The maturation level of each cell in the graph is increased at each step of simulation until it reach the state "mature". The "mature" cells become the source of nutrients.

Vessel forks when the local condition (TAFs concentration exceed certain threshold and cell is mature enough) are fulfilled. When growing vessel meet other vessel, it joins them creating anastomosis.

The set of the parameters that tune the model is as follows:

- ρ_{TAF} — gradient of TAFs distribution,
- ρ_N — gradient of nutrient(oxygen) distribution,
- T_b — TAFs threshold that triggers branch forming,
- N_t — nutrients threshold that triggers production of TAFs in tumour cells,
- M_s — maturation speed,
- P_b — branch probability.

2.1   The Algorithm

Fig. 1 presents an outline of the algorithm. At each step of simulation, procedures that implement the defined rules are applied to cellular automata and graph of cellular automata.

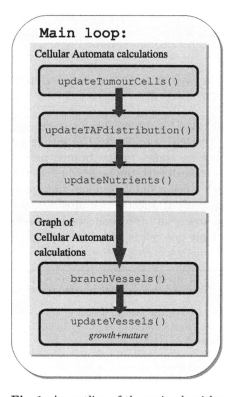

Fig. 1. An outline of the main algorithm

Procedure `updateTumourCells()` tests the nutrients concentration in the cells that represent tumour and triggers the production of TAFs if necessary.

Procedure 1 An outline of the `updateTumourCells()` procedure

---
for all cell in the mesh **do**
  if $n_{ij} < N_t$ **then**
    $t_{ij} \Leftarrow$ "hungry";
  else
    $t_{ij} \Leftarrow$ "full";

Procedures `updateNutrients()` and `updateTAFdistribution()` distribute nutrients and TAFs, respectively, and they have very similar form. New values of nutrients and TAFs concentrations are calculated based on maximum concentration within their neighbourhoods. C_{ij} denotes a cell identified by using indexes i, j.

Procedure 2 Procedures `updateTAFdistribution()` and `updateNutrients()`

TAFs distribution	*Nutrients distribution*
for all cell in the mesh **do**	**for all** cell in the mesh **do**
if $t_{ij} =$ "hungry" **then**	**if** $C_{ij} \in V_G$ and $a_{ij} =$ "mature" **then**
$f_{ij} \Leftarrow 1.0$;	$n_{ij} \Leftarrow 1.0$;
else	**else**
$f_{ij} \Leftarrow \rho_{TAF} \max(f_{X_K(ij)})$;	$n_{ij} \Leftarrow \rho_O \max(n_{X_K(ij)})$;

Procedure `updateVessels()` is responsible for vessels growth and maturation (see Procedure 3). If "tip cell" marker (p_{ij}) is set, procedure `addNextTip()` calculates which cell will be added to the branch next. Growing vessels are attracted by TAFs thus the cell with the largest increase of the t_{ij} value will be added. If there is no such a cell a simple random-walk procedure is applied. An new cell becomes a "tip cell". If selected cell already belongs to other branch, the "tip" marker p_{ij} is unset, and the branches join creating anastomosis. At each step of simulation only one cell is added to each sprout.

Procedure 3 An outline of `updateVessels()` procedure

---
for all cell $C_{ij} \in V_G$ **do**
  if p_{ij} **then**
    addNextTip(C_{ij});
  if $a_{ij} <$ "mature" **then**
    $a_{ij} \Leftarrow a_{ij} + M_s$;

Procedure `branchVessels()` tests whether the conditions for branching occur. If necessary it initiates a new sprout with probability P_b, by setting "tip cell" marker — p_{ij}. New sprout starts to grow on the next run of the `updateVessels()` procedure.

Procedure 4 An outline of the `branchVessels()` procedure

for all cell $C_{ij} \in V_G$ **do**
　　if $f_{ij} > T_b$ and $a_{ij} =$ "mature" and $random() < P_b$ **then**
　　　　$p_{ij} \Leftarrow 1$;

3 Results

We present preliminary results obtained by using described model. The model was implemented in C++ language as a sequential program and run on workstation under Linux operation system. Results were postprocessed and visualized by using Amira program (www.tgs.com).

Fig. 2 presents snapshot taken after 200 steps of simulation performed on mesh 100×100 cell. Apart the vascular network, the TAFs distribution is visualized. Single sprouts grow attracted by higher TAFs concentrations. The nodes of Graph of Cellular Automata were intentionally emphasised.

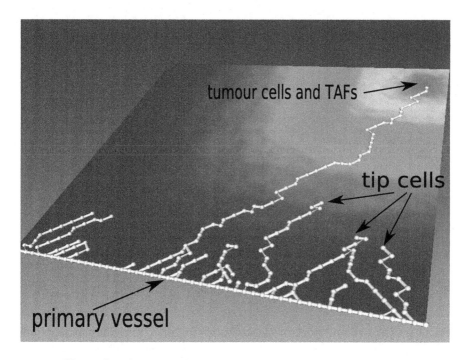

Fig. 2. Simulation results: vessels network and TAFs distribution

Fig. 3 presents snapshots taken after 100, 120, 220 and 1200 steps of simulation. Simulations were performed on 100×100 mesh. The vascular network is presented together with the TAFs distribution. The algorithm of branch growth neglects random motion and considers only the TAFs influence. It results in the

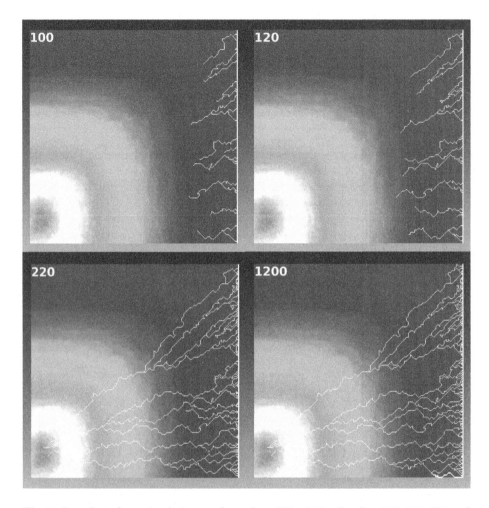

Fig. 3. Snapshots from simulation performed on 100×100 cells after 100, 120, 220 and 1200 steps. Primary vessel is located on the right edge of the mesh.

clearly visible direction of growth. The assumption that only "mature" vessels can branch makes that we observe anastomosing vessels without branching at all.

Fig. 4 presents the network of blood vessels together with the nutrients and the TAFs distribution. Simulation was performed on mesh 100×100 cells and snapshot was taken after 1200 steps. Compared with Fig. 3 simulations were performed with higher maturation speed M_s. As a result most of the sprouts are already mature enough to supply nutrients and the network has much more complex structure. Single sprouts have already reached tumour cells, however they are still not mature enough to supply oxygen and nutrients to starving cells.

Fig. 4. Network of blood vessels growing towards tumour cells. Primary vessel is located on the bottom edge of the mesh. Green area represents tumour cells producing TAFs. Yellow-to-red area represents nutrients.

4   Conclusions

The general framework combining Cellular Automata and Graph of Cellular Automata seems to be suitable for modelling tumour-induced angiogenesis. The preliminary results are promising, however at this stage it is pure phenomenological model, and it has numerous oversimplifications. Future investigations have to carefully revise the rules, defined for this model and include the new ones that will be able to consider other factors and subprocesses that contributes to angiogenesis.

One of the major simplification is the assumption that nutrients can be supplied by any mature vessel. In fact it is not true if the vessel is not a part of closed circuit. Thus, the further work on this model will be targeted on considering blood flow processes in capillary vessels and their influence on cancer development [16]. Moreover, the investigations on blood flow in tumour induced vessels are another very promising area in anti-cancer researches e.g. improved drug delivery increases chemotherapy efficiency.

Another issue, which is going to be investigated deeply is quantitative comparison of real and simulated vessels networks. Graph representation of vessels networks facilitates calculating the descriptors for the simulation results. Network descriptors for real vascular networks will be obtained from pictures with tumour tissue through the pattern recognition process.

Acknowledgements

The author thanks Prof. A. Dudek (University of Minnesota Cancer Center), Prof. D.A. Yuen (Minnesota Supercomputing Institute), Prof. W. Dzwinel,

T. Arodź (AGH University of Science and Technology) and Dr. M. Paszkowski (Polish Academy of Science) for valuable comments and discussions on the model assumptions. Dr. J. Tyszka and Dr. W. Alda kindly revised this paper. This research is partially supported by Polish Ministry of Education and Science (grant no. 3 T11F 010 30).

References

1. Carmeliet P., Angiogenesis in life, disease and medicine, Nature, vol.438, 2005.
2. Carmeliet P., Jain R.K., Angiogenesis in cancer and other disease, Nature, vol.407, 2000.
3. Mantzaris N.V., Webb S., Othmer H.G., Mathematical modeling of tumour-induced angiogenesis, J.Math.Biol., 2004.
4. Coultas L., Chawengsaksophak K., Rossant J., Endothelial cells and VEGF in vascular development, Nature, vol. 438, 15 December 2005.
5. Ferrar N., Kerbel R.S., Angiogenesis as a therapeutic target, Nature, vol.438, 2005.
6. Tonini T., Rossi F., Claudio P.P., Molecular basis of angiogenesis and cancer, Oncogene, vol.22 pp.6549-6556, 2003.
7. Anderson A.R.A., Chaplain M.A.J., Continuous and discrete mathematical models of tumour-induced angiogenesis, Bull.of Math.Biol., vol.60, pp. 857-900, 1998.
8. Plank M.J., Sleeman B.D., Jones P.F., A mathematical model of tumour growth, regulated by vascular endothelial growth factor and the angiopoietins, J.of Theor. Biology, vol.229, pp.435-454, 2004.
9. Stokes C.L., Lauffenburger, Analysis of the roles of microvessel endothelial cell random motility and chemotaxis in angiogenesis, J.Thoer.Biol., vol.152, 1991.
10. Alacorn T., Byrne H.M., Maini P.K., Towards whole-organ modeling of tumour growth, Progress in Biophysics & Molecular Biology, vol.85, pp. 451-472, 2004.
11. Alacorn T., Byrne H.M., Maini P.K., A multiple scale model for tumour growth, Multiscale Model.Simul. vol. 3, no. 2, pp. 440-475, 2005.
12. Topa P., Dzwinel W., Consuming Environment with Transportation Network Modelled Using Graph of Cellular Automata, LNCS 3019, pp. 513-520, 2004.
13. Topa P., Dzwinel W., Yuen D., A multiscale cellular automata model for simulating complex transport systems, Int.J.Mod.Phys.C (accepted for publication), 2006.
14. Topa, P., and Paszkowski, M., Anastomosing transportation networks. LNCS 2328 pp.904-911, 2002.
15. Chopard B., Droz M., Cellular Automata Modeling of Physical Systems, Cambridge University Press, 1998
16. Dzwinel W., Boryczko K., Yuen D., A discrete-particle model of blood dynamics in capillary vessels, J.Colloid Int.Sci., 258/1, pp.163-173, 2003.

Online Marking of Defective Cells
by Random Flies

Teijiro Isokawa[1], Shin'ya Kowada[1], Ferdinand Peper[2,1], Naotake Kamiura[1],
and Nobuyuki Matsui[1]

[1] Division of Computer Engineering, Graduate School of Engineering,
University of Hyogo, 2167 Shosha, Himeji, 671-2280, Japan
{isokawa, kamiura, matsui}@eng.u-hyogo.ac.jp,
er05j019@steng.u-hyogo.ac.jp
[2] Nanotechnology group, National Institute of Information and Communications
Technology, 588-2 Iwaoka, Iwaoka-cho, Nishi-ku, Kobe, 651-2492, Japan
peper@nict.go.jp

Abstract. Defect-tolerance, the ability to overcome unreliability of
components in a system, will be essential to realize computers built by
nanotechnology. This paper presents a novel approach to defect-tolerance
for nanocomputers that are based on self-timed cellular automata, a type
of asynchronous cellular automaton. According to this approach, defective cells are detected and isolated by configurations of *random flies* that
move around in cellular space. We show that detection and isolation are
realized in an on-line manner, i.e., while computation takes place.

1   Introduction

The trend towards nanometer-scale logic devices may lead to computers with
high speed and low power consumption, but this will require new techniques and
architectures. Such nanocomputers may require a regular structure, like in cellular arrays [1, 2, 3], to allow mass manufacturing based on molecular self-assembly.
Another important issue for nanoscale integration densities is the reduction of
power consumption, and, related to it, heat dissipation. Getting rid of the clock,
i.e., using asynchronous timing, has been suggested as a promising way toward
this end, especially when done in the context of cellular automata (CA) [2, 3].

A major obstacle to the realization of nanocomputers is the reduced reliability
of nanodevices as compared to their VLSI counterparts, due to noise, quantum
effects, etc. Discarding chips that have defects, as done in VLSI manufacturing,
is inefficient and, moreover, it cannot deal with defects occurring during computations. So, other approaches need to be explored to achieve defect-tolerance,
self-repair, and/or self-healing. In the context of CA, defect-tolerance has been
investigated in [4, 5], but the detection of defects is done in an off-line way,
i.e., detection takes place before computation starts. A set of CA-like processors
called *Embryonic arrays*, capable of self-repair and self-healing, is implemented
in hardware in [6]. The BioWatch, which is implemented by embryonic arrays,
can inactivate faulty component (cells) and replace them by spare ones during its

S. El Yacoubi, B. Chopard, and S. Bandini (Eds.): ACRI 2006, LNCS 4173, pp. 347–356, 2006.

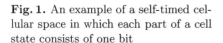

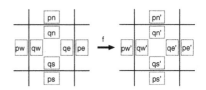

Fig. 1. An example of a self-timed cellular space in which each part of a cell state consists of one bit

Fig. 2. Transition rule in accordance with the function f

operation [7]. This model, however, requires a self-checking mechanism for each of the embryonic arrays that needs to be fault-free. Alternatively, *Immunotronics* uses an external layer monitoring the status of embryonic arrays to check faults [8, 9], but this makes the system more complex.

This paper presents an asynchronous CA that can detect and isolate cells with stuck-at fault defects in an on-line manner, i.e., during computation. We first establish the computational universality of the underlying CA by embedding a so-called Toggle Switch Element [10] onto it. Detection and isolation of defects are then realized by having configurations of *random flies* move around in the cellular space and attach to faulty cells. Key to distinguishing a faulty from a non-faulty cell is the latter's propensity to eat flies as part of its ability to undergo state changes. All the tasks including computation and detection and isolation of faults are accomplished within the CA model, i.e., no external or off-line detection mechanisms are required.

2   Preliminaries

2.1   Self-Timed Cellular Automata

A self-timed cellular automaton (STCA)[11, 3] is a two-dimensional asynchronous CA of identical cells, each of which has a state that is partitioned into four parts in one-to-one correspondence with its neighboring cells. For example, if each part of a cell state consists of 1 bit, a cell can be in one of 16 states encoded by 4 bits, and the cellular space is an array like in Fig. 1, where a filled circle denotes a 1-bit, and a open circle denotes a 0-bit. Each cell undergoes transitions in accordance with a transition function f that operates on the four parts of the cell q_n, q_e, q_s, q_w and the nearest part of each of its four neighbors p_n, p_e, p_s, p_w. The transition function f is defined by

$$f(q_n, q_e, q_s, q_w, p_n, p_e, p_s, p_w) = (q_n', q_e', q_s', q_w', p_n', p_e', p_s', p_w'), \tag{1}$$

where a state symbol to which a prime is attached denotes the new state of a partition after update (see Fig. 2). Dummy transitions are not included in the transition function (1), so we assume that the left-hand side of Fig. 2 differs from the right-hand side. Furthermore, we assume that transition rules on an STCA are rotation-symmetric, thus each of the rules has four rotated analogues.

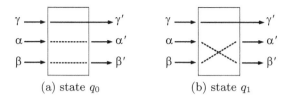

Fig. 3. Toggle Switch Element in states (a) q_0 and (b) q_1

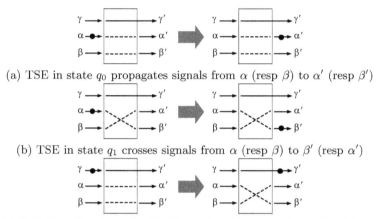

(a) TSE in state q_0 propagates signals from α (resp β) to α' (resp β')

(b) TSE in state q_1 crosses signals from α (resp β) to β' (resp α')

(c) Switching the state of a TSE is achieved by inputting a signal to γ

Fig. 4. Operations of a TSE, where a blob on a line denotes a signal

In an STCA, transitions of the cells occur at random times, independent of each other. Furthermore, it is assumed that neighboring cells never undergo transitions simultaneously to prevent a situation in which such cells write different values in shared bits at the same time (write conflict). Compared to conventional CAs, an STCA transition rule lacks strict locality in the sense that a cell may change states that belong to its neighbors. The lack of locality is very limited, however: every partition of a cell can only be changed by two cells, that is, the cell to which the partition belongs and the cell to which the partition is adjacent.

There are several approaches to perform computation on STCAs, such as simulating synchronous CA[11] and embedding delay-insensitive circuits on STCAs [2, 12], of which we use the latter. To ensure computational universality, we embed a so-called *Toggle Switch Element* (TSE) on the STCA used in this paper.

2.2   Toggle Switch Element and Its Implementation on STCA

A TSE is a logic element with 3 input lines, 3 output lines and 2 states [10]. Figure 3 shows TSEs with states q_0 and q_1, where input lines are denoted by the symbols α, β and γ, and output lines are denoted by the symbols α', β' and γ'. When a TSE in state q_0 accepts a signal on input line α (resp. β), it passes the signal through to the output line α' (resp. β') (see Fig. 4(a)). If a TSE is in

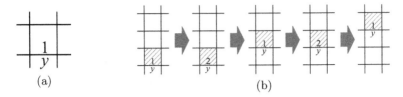

(a)   (b)

Fig. 5. (a) A signal configuration and (b) its move forward. The dark cell in each step is the cell to which a transition rule is applied.

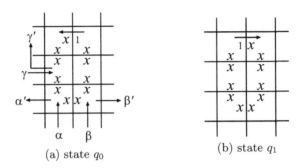

(a) state q_0 (b) state q_1

Fig. 6. A TSE configuration in states q_0 and q_1

state q_1 and a signal on input line α (resp. β) arrives at it, it outputs a signal on the output line β' (resp. α') (see Fig. 4(b)). The state of a TSE is changed from q_0 to q_1 or the other way around by inputting a signal on input line γ, after which a signal is output to line γ' (see Fig. 4(c)). TSE has been proven to be computationally universal [10] in the sense that a network of TSEs, consisting of signals, TSEs and signal lines, can compose a *Rotary Element* (RE) [13], from which a universal Turing Machine can be constructed.

To embed a network of TSEs on an STCA, we define signals and their paths between TSEs. A cell is divided in partitions, each of which can be in one of 9 states, denoted by the set of symbols $\{\ , 1, 2, 3, x, y, z, B, W\}$. Figure 5(a) shows a signal toward the north on an STCA, whereby the signal is represented by the partition pair '$1y$'. To move the signal forward, this state pair is first changed into '$2y$' according to the transition rules (see Fig. 5(b)). Signal paths are represented by cells of which all the partitions have the state ' '. Since the STCA is rotation symmetric, a signal going to the south, east, or west can be defined by rotating the cell configuration in Fig. 5(a).

A TSE is represented on an STCA as a loop structure (Fig. 6) through which an internal signal is continuously moving, whereby the direction of the signal denotes the state of the element, clockwise corresponding to state q_1 and counterclockwise to state q_0.

The internal signal in a TSE, denoted by the partition pair '$x1$' or '$x2$', moves along the 'xx' loop of the TSE in a similar way as with the propagation of a signal, i.e., two stages are used to move a signal forward by one step. Figure 7 shows how an internal signal in a TSE in state q_0 propagates along the loop.

Fig. 7. An internal signal propagating in a TSE in state q_0. Only part of the TSE loop is shown to save space.

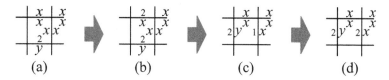

Fig. 8. A TSE in state q_0 operating on a signal from α

Fig. 9. Operation of a TSE in state q_1 after an input signal is input to it on β

The input and output ports of the TSE, denoted by arrows in Fig. 6, are arranged differently as compared to the original TSE, to ensure that the internal signal of the TSE can easily interact with input signals. A TSE in state q_0 processes signals on its input lines as follows. When an input arrives on line α, as in Fig. 8(a), it waits at the lower-left part of the TSE until the internal signal arrives from the cell to the right (Fig. 8(b)), after which an intermediate state is assumed (Fig. 8(c)). This is followed by output to the port α' (Fig. 8(d)), whereas the internal signal continues its journey inside the TSE-loop, without changing its direction. Signal on β is processed in a similar way.

The operation of a TSE in state q_1 is more complicated than when it is in state q_0, since signals need to be crossed in that case. Figure 9 shows the transitions in this case when a signal is input to port β. When the internal signal meets the input signal on input port β (Fig. 9(a)), the partition pair '21' appears at the bottom of the TSE (Fig. 9(b)). This pair changes to '22' (Fig. 9(c)), after which the signal appears on output port α' and the internal signal continues its journey inside the TSE-loop (Fig. 9(d) and (e)).

Finally, when a signal is input to port γ the state will be flipped from q_0 and q_1 or the other way around (see Figs. 10(a) and (b)).

The reason why almost all the transitions of signals and elements need two stages to proceed by one step is to cope with the stuck-at faults of partitions of cells; this occurs when the state of the partition itself can be referred to and used by neighboring cells but cannot be changed by any transition rules. Consider the case in which the transition rule to move a signal forward contains only one stage, as shown in Fig. 11(a), and the cellular space contains stuck-at faults in the partitions of a lowest cell in Fig. 11(b). When this transition rule

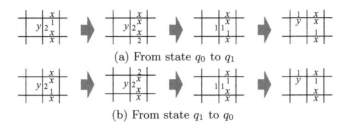

(a) From state q_0 to q_1

(b) From state q_1 to q_0

Fig. 10. Switching the state of the TSE

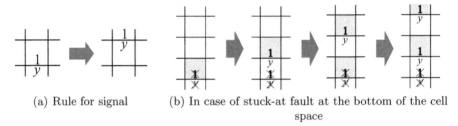

(a) Rule for signal   (b) In case of stuck-at fault at the bottom of the cell space

Fig. 11. Example of a stuck-at fault. Cross marks on partitions represent stuck-at faults.

is applied to the lowest cell, a new signal appears on its north, but the signal configuration at the lowest cell is not annihilated due to the faults. So, this configuration becomes a signal generator that produces an unlimited number of signals. Such a situation can be prevented by checking whether the partitions are stuck in a particular state, and this is implemented easily by propagating signals according to a 2-step protocol: in this case signal propagation always fails when there is a stuck-at fault at one or more cells involved.

3   Wrapping Defects by Random Flies

A useful strategy towards defect-tolerance is to wrap defects in a layer of isolating cells that are all in a special state assigned for this purpose. Isolation of defects creates a uniform environment: instead of having to deal with defective cells being stuck in a great variety of states, there is only one state associated with defective cells to take into account, and this significantly simplifies avoidance of defects or creating roundabouts around them at a later stage. A similar strategy is used in [5], be it that in that paper isolation around defects is done off-line, before computation takes place. Here we conduct isolation on-line, by using 'random flies'.

3.1   Random Flies

A random fly is a signal-like cell configuration, represented by the partition pair '33'. It has no preferred direction as it is symmetric, and it is designed to move around in cellular space in random directions. This is accomplished by changing the partition pair '33' into the pair '3z' in accordance with the transition rules. Due to the symmetry of '33' and the randomness associated with asynchronous updating, this transition into pair '3z' can take place in two different ways, as shown in Fig. 12. We have designed the transition rules of our cellular automaton such that the partition pair '3z' subsequently changes back into pair '33', but only so in combination with a left turn (see Fig. 12). The netto result is that in the end the fly has moved forward to the left, or backward to the right.

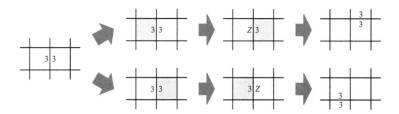

Fig. 12. Possible transitions of a random fly

3.2   Checking Living Configurations by Random Flies

A collision of a random fly with a signal or a working TSE or other random flies results in the annihilation of the fly. Figure 13 shows a random fly that collides with a signal, after which an intermediate state is reached as the precursor of the final annihilation of the fly. It is also possible that two or more random flies collide with a signal, TSE, or other fly at a time, and also in these cases annihilation of the flies takes place. For example, when a random fly attaches to the input (or output) port of a working TSE, it stays at this port until an internal signal circulating in the TSE arrives, after which the fly is annihilated. If another fly also attaches to the same output (or input) port before the internal signal arrives, a situation like in Fig. 14 will occur, and the two random flies will disappear in accordance with the transition rules, with the internal signal continuing its path in the TSE. Other situations concerning collision of random flies with TSEs are treated in similar ways.

Important is that random flies stuck to a TSE are annihilated whenever the TSE is working, i.e., to annihilate these random flies it is necessary that an internal signal flows in the TSE. When the internal signal of a TSE stops, for example due to a defect, random flies will no longer be annihilated and will wrap this TSE completely (see Fig. 15). These flies remain in the state '3z', so all the partitions pointing outwards of this TSE will assume this state, forming an isolation layer.

3.3   Random Fly Generation

The process of wrapping defects by flies and annihilating flies can only continue if there are enough flies. So, where do flies come from? It is tempting to generate them by some external source, but this implies the necessity of a mechanism to control their density. Rather, we have opted for a self-regulating mechanism, in

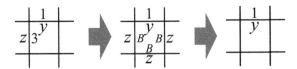

Fig. 13. Random fly colliding with a signal, resulting in an intermediate state, and finally the fly's annihilation

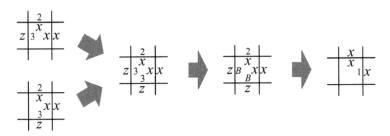

Fig. 14. Two random flies colliding with a signal in a TSE. Eventually, both flies are annihilated.

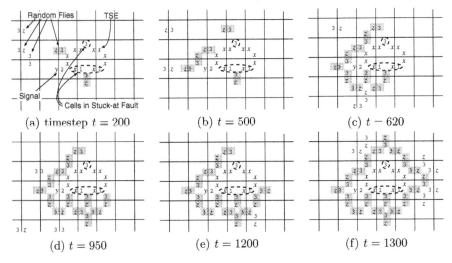

Fig. 15. Isolation of defective TSE by random flies. Shaded random flies represent the ones stuck to cells that no longer undergo transitions. This may be faulty cells, but also cells that become inactive as a result of defects in cells near them.

which flies are only generated around where they are needed, that is near TSEs, because there is where defect cells compromise the correctness and continuation of the computation process. Such a self-regulating mechanism is implemented by equipping TSEs with the inherent ability to generate flies as part of their behavior as defined by the transition rules. Fig. 16 shows transition rules that are used for this purpose. According to these rules, random flies are generated around

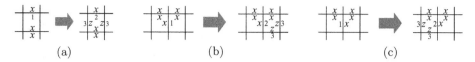

Fig. 16. Extended transition rules for generating random flies originating from TSEs

the input and output ports of a TSE. Flies are also generated and annihilated inside TSE loops, but this is only for keeping transition rules simple.

4 Conclusion

The defect-tolerant self-timed cellular automata proposed in this paper can detect and mark stuck-at faults of cells during computation in a self-contained way. Our model adopts random flies that are produced in the cellular space, check whether cells are defective by utilizing the ability of cells to change their states, and isolate those cells that are unable to do so (the defective cells) from non-defective cells. Cells becoming defective due to some permanent stuck-at fault occurring at the time of computation will be automatically wrapped in flies and isolated from healthy cells. This creates a uniform environment of the states in which cells can be, which can then be dealt with in a follow-up strategy, like the one in [5], to reconfigure circuits around wrapped defects.

The model employs 154 transition rules.[1] Many of these rules are used to describe the collisions of random flies with signals and TSEs, suggesting that a relatively large overhead is required by the defect-tolerance mechanism, as compared to the computation mechanism. Implementation at molecular scales may therefore be less practical in its current form. In this sense, the situation is perhaps similar to that with the self-repairing systems mentioned in the introduction [4, 5, 6, 7, 8, 9]. Our method, however, has still room for improvement: for example, the number of rules can be reduced by limiting the variety of situations in which random flies are annihilated. Moreover, different asynchronous models of cellular automata may enable more efficient implementations of the defect-tolerance mechanism.

We finish with noting that the random fly mechanism in itself may serve as an illustration how the power of randomness associated with asynchronous updating can be exploited for the design of relatively simple and localized algorithms.

References

1. Durbeck, L.J.K., Macias, N.J.: The cell matrix: an architecture for nanocomputing. Nanotechnology **12** (2001) 217–230
2. Peper, F., Lee, J., Abo, F., Isokawa, T., Adachi, S., Matsui, N., Mashiko, S.: Fault-Tolerance in Nanocomputers: A Cellular Array Approach. IEEE Transaction on Nanotechnology **3**(1) (2004) 187–201

---

[1] The list of transition rules and videos of this model are shown in the website of http://www.eng.u-hyogo.ac.jp/eecs/eecs12/research/acri06/.

3. Peper, F., Lee, J., Adachi, S., Mashiko, S.: Laying out circuits on asynchronous cellular arrays: a step towards feasible nanocomputers? Nanotechnology **14** (2003) 469–485
4. Isokawa, T., Abo, F., Peper, F., Kamiura, N., Matsui, N.: Defect-tolerant computing based on an asynchronous cellular automaton. In: Proceeding of SICE Annual Conference. (2003) 1746–1749
5. Isokawa, T., Kowada, S., Takada, Y., Peper, F., Kamiura, N., Matsui, N.: On Defect-Tolerance in Cellular Computers. In: Proceedings of the 5th IEEE Conference on Nanotechnology. (2005) TU–P7–5
6. Mange, D., Sipper, M., Marchal, P.: Embryonic electronics. BioSystems **51**(3) (1999) 145–152
7. Stauffer, A., Mange, D., Tempesti, G., Teuscher, C.: A Self-Repairing and Self-Healing Electronic Watch: The BioWatch. In: Proc. 4th International Conference on Evolvable Systems: From Biology to Hardware (ICES2001). Volume LNCS 2210. (2001) 112–127
8. Bradley, D., Ortega-Sanchez, C., Tyrrell, A.: Embryonics + Immunotronics: A Bio-Inspired Approach to Fault Tolerance. In: The Second NASA/DoD workshop on Evolvable Hardware. (2000) 205–224
9. Canham, R., Tyrrell, A.: A Multi-layered Immune System for Hardware Fault Tolerance within an Embryonic Array. In: Proc. 1st International Conference on Artificial Immune Systems. (2002) 3–11
10. Ueno, R.: Universal reversible logic elements with 3 inputs, 3 outputs and 2 states. Master's thesis, Hiroshima University (2006) (in Japanese).
11. Peper, F., Isokawa, T., Kouda, N., Matsui, N.: Self-timed cellular automata and their computational ability. Future Generation Computer Systems **18**(7) (2002) 893–904
12. Lee, J., Peper, F., Adachi, S., Morita, K., Mashiko, S.: Reversible computation in asynchronous cellular automata. In Calude, C.S., Dinneen, M.J., Peper, F., eds.: Third International Conference on Unconventional Models of Computation 2002, Springer (2002) 220–229
13. Morita, K.: A simple universal logic element and cellular automata for reversible computing. In: MCU. Volume 2055 of LNCS. (2001) 102–113

Modeling of Sound Absorption by Porous Materials Using Cellular Automata

Toshihiko Komatsuzaki and Yoshio Iwata

Graduate School of Natural Science and Technology, Kanazawa University,
Kakuma-machi, Kanazawa, 920-1192, Japan
{toshi, iwata}@t.kanazawa-u.ac.jp

Abstract. In the present study, acoustic wave propagation in acoustic tube in-corporating sound absorbing material is simulated using Cellular Automata (CA). CA is a discrete system which consists of finite state variables, arranged on a uniform grid (cell). CA dynamics is described by a local interaction rule, which is used for computation of new state of each cell from the present state at every time step. In this study an acoustic tube model is introduced in which ab-sorbing material is characterized by direct modeling of porosity and flow resis-tance. Direct numerical simulation CA model is performed and evaluated by absorption coefficient using standing wave ratio measure. The results showed good correspondence with analytical solutions.

1 Introduction

The vibrating structures and various kinds of machineries often cause serious noise problems to humans within an environment. The passive sound attenuation method is generally employed using resonators, isolation walls and sound absorbing treatment. Among various kinds of sound absorption materials, porous materials such as glass wool quilting and polyurethane foams are the most common and significant technique which are widely used for room acoustics and various electric devices. However, the recent designing of compact and lightweight devices put limits on the application of such dissipative materials in conjunction with saving costs. Hence the material itself, amount and placement must be determined carefully that can realize high performance damping and low cost. The development of numerical model which can predict sound propagation and attenuation effect of those materials is then important for realizing efficient and suitable engineering design.

Before predicting desired sound absorption effect in a practical environment, material properties such as acoustic propagation constant and the absorption coefficient must be determined either numerically or experimentally. The more precise measurement system has been developed for the latter approach. On the other hand, theoretical prediction of sound absorbing mechanism of porous materials has long been investigated which coincides with basic experimental results[1]. The finite element and also the boundary element methods may be reliable and useful approach for exploring more realistic situations. However,

S. El Yacoubi, B. Chopard, and S. Bandini (Eds.): ACRI 2006, LNCS 4173, pp. 357–366, 2006.
© Springer-Verlag Berlin Heidelberg 2006

on setting properties and shapes of porous materials with these models certain approximation must be incorporated which may lead to the lack of micro structure and the essential mechanism of sound absorption of materials itself. Also, obtaining transient response of the system with these models require elaborate modeling procedure.

In this paper, the acoustic wave model is developed using Cellular Automata. CA is a kind of discrete computations which has been developed for modeling wide range of phenomena including many physical processes described generally by partial differential equations[7]. Specifically the wave propagation models have been studied by researchers based on Cellular Automata[3]-[8]. The works include Chopard et al.[8] who had modeled wave propagation by Lattice Boltzmann approach applicable for practical situations such as the radio wave transmission in complex urban environments. The authors have also developed an acoustic wave propagation model for two dimensional acoustic problems for simulating sound source movement, sound diffraction by the presence of barriers and reflection due to inhomogeneity of acoustic media[9]. Due to its easiness and simplicity of modeling procedure, the modeling approach also seems suitable for the problems concerned. However, the preceding work does not include energy dissipating mechanisms which is nessesary for producing sound absorption effect. In the present study, the modified version of the acoustic wave propagation model is numerically developed using CA for understanding fundamental sound absorption mechanism of porous materials and evaluating sound absorption performance, where the details of porous material structure is considered in the model. The acoustic waveguide incorporating sound absorbing porous material is constituted and the sound absorption effect is predicted. The theoretical approach for obtaining absorption coefficient is also presented for comparison.

2 Theoretical Description of One-Dimensional Acoustic Field

In this section, theoretical description of one-dimensional acoustic field is shown, and the material property related to acoustic characteristics which is commonly known as the sound absorption coefficient is also derived. Moreover, the parameter known as standing wave ratio (SWR) and used for determining absorption coefficient by numerically measured sound pressure amplitude is presented.

2.1 The Wave Equation

The generated pressure oscillation in an acoustic medium is observed as sound, which is described by a set of linear equations for one dimensional field under the presence of absorbing material[1]:

$$\frac{\rho_0}{\sigma} \frac{\partial \dot{u}(x,t)}{\partial t} = -\frac{\partial p(x,t)}{\partial x} - R_f \dot{u}(x,t) \tag{1}$$

$$\frac{\sigma}{\kappa} \frac{\partial p(x,t)}{\partial t} = -\frac{\partial \dot{u}(x,t)}{\partial x} \tag{2}$$

where $p(x,t)$ is a sound pressure and $\dot{u}(x,t)$ a particle velocity, ρ_0 density, κ volume elasticity, σ porosity of porous material and R_f flow resistance constant respectively. Equation (1) corresponds to equation of motion of the continuum per unit volume, and also (2) satisfies continuity of the medium. The solution to (1) and (2) without porous material is given by setting $\sigma = 1.0$ and $R_f = 0.0$, on the assumption that the wave is harmonic:

$$p(x,t) = j\omega\rho Ae^{j(\omega t - kx)} + Be^{j(\omega t + kx)} \tag{3}$$

where A and B are constants determined by boundary conditions, ω the sound source frequency, k the wave number respectively. The first term of (3) expresses a progressive wave, and the second a regressive wave.

If we employ acoustic tube model which has a sound source on one edge, the pressure distribution inside tube is then calculated by giving boundary conditions $\dot{u}(0,t) = \dot{u}_0 e^{j\omega t}$, and also $\dot{u}(l,t) = 0$ for the another edge closed:

$$p(x,t) = -j\rho c\dot{u}_0 \frac{\cos k(l-x)}{\sin kl} e^{j\omega t} \tag{4}$$

In the above (4), l stands for the tube length, $\dot{u}_0$ the driving source velocity.

2.2 Definition of Propagation Constant and Characteristic Impedance

Sound absorbing materials are usually characterized by acoustic properties known as propagation constant and characteristic impedance. The absorption coefficient is then determined by those constants. The characteristic impedance is defined by the ratio between acoustic pressure and particle velocity while the wave travels along the media, described as:

$$Z_c = \frac{p}{u} = \rho c_m \tag{5}$$

In (5), p and u denotes sound pressure and particle velocity, c_m sound speed along material and ρ the density of material, respectively. The propagation constant γ is defined by the damping the phase chance along the unit length of material axis, which is given by a complex form:

$$\gamma = \alpha + \beta, \quad \beta - \omega/c_m \tag{6}$$

In the above (6), α and β signifies damping and phase constant.

Sound propagation model inside acoustic waveguide incorporating absorbing materials is shown in Fig. 1. The sound wave propagating through the material 1 with thickness d is described by the following (7) with respect to the incoming sound pressure P_{i0} traveling through the air,

$$p_{1d} = p_{1i}e^{-\gamma d} \tag{7}$$

In the case material 1 is backed by another material 2, the inhomogenous boundary between these two materials is characterized by acoustic impedance Z_2. In

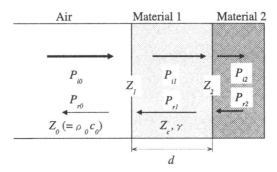

Fig. 1. Sound propagation model inside acoustic waveguide incorporating absorbing material. In this figure, three kinds of acoustic media exist. Hence two boundaries between air and material 1, and also between materials 1 and 2 are present. P denotes sound pressure, and Z acoustic impedance.

the same way the acoustic impedance Z_1 with respect to the boundary between air and material 1 is given by the following equation using Z_2.

$$Z_1 = Z_c \frac{Z_2 \cosh(\gamma d) + Z_c \sinh(\gamma d)}{Z_2 \sinh(\gamma d) + Z_c \cosh(\gamma d)} \tag{8}$$

Before calculating sound absorption coefficient α, the reflection constant r_p must be determined using acoustic impedance Z_1. The constant r_p is defined as follows.

$$r_p = \frac{Z_1 - \rho_0 c_0}{Z_1 + \rho_0 c_0} \tag{9}$$

In (9), ρ_0 and c_0 denotes density and sound speed of air, respectively. The absorbing coefficient α is then calculated using (9), according to the following (10).

$$\alpha = 1 - |r_p|^2 \tag{10}$$

As already described above, in order to obtain absorption coefficient the acoustic impedance Z_1 must be determined, however, Z_1 also depends on another impedance Z_2. Therefore, Z_2 must be first determined by setting the layer behind the target material become air, or directly backed by the rigid wall before calculating Z_1. (In the latter case Z_2 become zero.) The rest of the unknown parameter, propagation constant γ and characteristic constant Z_c, are usually determined by measurements. They are also derived analytically by solving (1) and (2), for the case the porous material is backed directly by the wall described as follows.

$$\gamma = \frac{\omega}{c_0} \sqrt{1 - j \frac{\sigma R_f}{\omega \rho_0}} \tag{11}$$

$$Z_c = \frac{\rho_0 c_0}{\sigma} \sqrt{1 - j \frac{\sigma R_f}{\omega \rho_0}} \tag{12}$$

Equations (11) and (12) are used for the comparison with results obtained by the Cellular Automata acoustic model in subsequent section. γ, Z_c and Z_1 are the important parameters for characterizing the property of porous materials. However, the measurement process as well as parameter calculation seem rather complex.

2.3 Determining Absorption Coefficient by Standing Wave Ratio Method

One of the most fundamental approaches for determining absorption coefficient experimentally is known as the standing wave ratio (SWR) method. Due to its simple idea and constitution, and also the needless for complex calculation, the method is suitable for the direct numerical approach such as the CA model dealt in the present study. As illustrated in Fig. 2, the progressive wave propagates into the material and a wave reflected at the face of material interferes and forms standing wave distribution. The standing wave ratio (SWR) is defined by the ratio between the maximum and the minimum peaks of standing wave. Practically, in an experimental situation, these peaks are explored by scanning microphone along acoustic tube axis. The SWR, n, is defined as follows.

$$n = \frac{|P_i| + |P_r|}{|P_i| - |P_r|} \tag{13}$$

The reflection constant r_p is then determined by the following equation and further absorption coefficient by (10), as well.

$$r_p = \frac{|P_r|}{|P_i|} = \frac{n}{n+1} \cdot \frac{1}{} \tag{14}$$

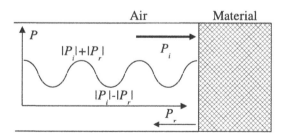

Fig. 2. Standing wave distribution inside an acoustic tube. The progressive wave propagates into the material and a wave reflected at the face of material interferes and forms standing wave distribution. The standing wave ratio (SWR) is defined by the ratio between the maximum peak and the minimum peak of the standing wave.

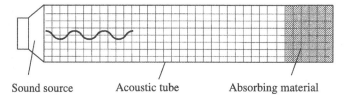

Sound source   Acoustic tube   Absorbing material

Fig. 3. Simulation model of acoustic tube incorporating absorbing material. A sound source is located at left hand side of the tube, whereas the porous material located on the other side.

3   The Cellular Automata Model

In this section, Cellular Automata model is developed for simulation of acoustic wave propagation in a media incorporating porous material. The simple finite difference scheme obtained by linear wave equation is referenced for developing local interaction rule, in a sense that discretized wave equation yields to an expression of local relationship of wave amplitudes. The rule is then extended to a more practical case, yet time and space are treated as discrete integers. The Cellular Automata approach to such a wave propagation problem was discussed for two dimensional models comparing with analytical solutions. Definitions for state variables and local interaction rules are presented in the following subsections.

3.1   Space Partitioning and State Definition

Figure 3 shows two dimensional space discretized into rectangular cells. Each one of the cell is distinguished for its state by three numbers; i) zero for acoustic media (air), ii) 1 for rigid wall , and iii) 2 for portion of absorbing material. Additionally, two variables which express the sound pressure and particle velocity are defined for the first acoustic medium state. These variables are updated at each simulation step according to the local interaction rules explained in the next subsection. In advance to composition of local rules, the definition of neighbor is specified as shown in Fig. 4. For the two dimensional model, cross-located four cells are neighbors which is conventionally called Neumann Style neighbors. In each medium state cell the sound pressure variable is assigned as well as particle velocities in four neighboring directions. Following Cellular Automata convention, time and space are treated as integers. In order for the model to be comparable with analytical solution, we assign unit cell length $dx = 0.001$[m], and also the sound speed $c = 344$[m/s]. Table 1 shows comparative listing between CA space and physical parameter.

3.2   Foundation of Local Rules

State parameters given in each one of the cells is updated every discrete time step according to a local interaction rule which is described in this section.

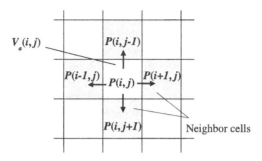

Fig. 4. Definition of neighbor in two dimensional acoustic model. Two state variables, sound pressure P and particle velocity V, are placed in each cell.

Table 1. Table 1. Equivalent system parameters. Parameters defined in the CA model are com-pared with those in physical system.

	Sound speed	Unit time step	Unit space size
Physical system	$c = 344$ [m/s]	$dt = 1/344$ [sec]	$dx = 0.001$ [m]
2-dim CA model	$c = 1/\sqrt{2}$ [cell/step]	$dt = 1$ [step]	$dx = 1$ [cell]

First, the particle velocities in four directions are updated in time with respect the difference of sound pressure between adjacent cells, whose update rule is described explicitly as,

$$V_a(\mathbf{x}, t+1) = V_a(\mathbf{x}, t) - \{P(\mathbf{x} + \mathbf{dx}_a, t) - P(\mathbf{x}, t)\} \qquad (15)$$

V_a represents particle velocity of media and P the sound pressure. Two dimensional cell position is expressed as a vector $\mathbf{x}$ and discrete time step as t. A suffix a in (15) signifies index of four neighbors. The particle velocity further obeys (16), which expresses energy dissipation by the flow resistance due to presence of porous material.

$$V_a(\mathbf{x}, t) = (1 - n \cdot d)V_a(\mathbf{x}, t) \qquad (16)$$

In the above (16), n represents number of porous material cells in neighbor, d a damping constant per unit cell. The pressure is then updated according to the rule described by (17),

$$P(\mathbf{x}, t+1) = P(\mathbf{x}, t) - c_a^2 \sum_a V_a(\mathbf{x}, t+1) \qquad (17)$$

where c_a denotes the wave traveling speed in CA space. Sound pressure and particle velocities are updated according to the local rule described by above three equations.

Since calculation will be carried out between nearby cells that are separated only a unit length at every single step, any physical quantities cannot have the transport speed exceed to this calculation limit. This applies directly to one dimensional CA model with maximum speed condition $c_a \leq 1$, whereas not for two dimensional case. Since wave is assumed to propagate isotropically despite the square compartment of space and cross-style definition of neighbors, an effective traveling speed must be considered. It is known that the maximum wave speed becomes $c_a = 1/\sqrt{2}$ for two dimensional case, therefore the wave front travels $1/\sqrt{2}$ of unit cell length per calculation step. These conditions can also be obtained by the CFL condition, which provides requirement for numerical stability of finite difference scheme expressed explicitly as,

$$c = \frac{\Delta t}{\Delta x} \leq \begin{cases} 1 & \text{for one dimension} \\ 1/\sqrt{2} & \text{for two dimension} \end{cases} \tag{18}$$

where Δt and Δx are unit time step and unit length in difference scheme, respectively. By setting Δt and Δx be unity, we get $c \leq 1$ as one dimensional stability condition, and also $1/\sqrt{2}$ for another. It is straightforward to say that upper limit condition of propagating speed can be derived not numerically, but physically in the CA model.

4   Simulation of Wave Propagation

In this section, simulation of acoustic wave propagation is performed for the acoustic tube model incorporating porous material as shown in Fig. 3, which is described by the Cellular Automata. Analytical solution is also calculated using set of equations explained in section 2.

In the CA model, the space inside acoustic tube is divided into 100 x 1000 cells, where the unit size of a cell is assumed to be 1 [mm] for the comparison with physical system. Hence the size of acoustic tube corresponds to 100 [mm] in diameter and 1000 [mm] in length respectively. The sound source is provided by giving forced particle velocity to cells which are located on the left edge of the tube, whereas the sound absorbing material with certain thickness is located on the other side by assigning cell state as porous material.

Two cases of simulation are performed in the following subsections. The first case calculates acoustic field inside sound tube without porous material, where the resonance characteristic is investigated comparing with analytical solution. In the second case the CA model is tested for the presence of absorbing material, where the result is compared with analytically calculated absorbing coefficient.

4.1   Acoustic Tube Model Without Porous Material

The acoustic field inside sound tube model without porous material is calculated. Analytical pressure distribution caused by pulse excitation at the sound source can be obtained by (4). The resonance characteristic of the acoustic tube with length 1 [m] is shown in Fig. 5. The first and the second resonant frequencies for the tube are 172 and 344 [Hz], respectively. From Fig. 4, it is known that frequency response obtained by CA model well corresponds to analytical one.

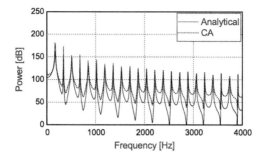

Fig. 5. Frequency response of acoustic tube. The CA model well coincides with analytically calculated response.

4.2   Acoustic Tube Incorporating Porous Material

The second case deals with an acoustic field inside sound tube under the presence of porous material. Two cases of porous material with thickness 50 and 100 [cells] are considered in the present simulation. Hence the thickness of material becomes 50 [mm] and 100 [mm] in the actual physical system, respectively. The damping parameter with respect to the (16) in the CA model is set to $d = 0.2$, and the inner pores of the material is expressed by randomly locating cell states by the mixture of medium and material state, so that the porosity becomes 0.8 apparently. Sinusoidal excitation at the sound source whose frequency varies from 10 to 4000 [Hz] is generated at the left end of the tube. The absorption coefficient is processed according to the SWR method depicted in section 2.3 by the measured standing wave amplitudes.

The absorption coefficient is also calculated analytically by using set of equations mentioned in section 2. In calculating propagation constant and characteristic

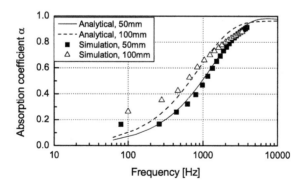

Fig. 6. Absorption coefficient obtained by the CA model. The absorption coefficient is determined according to the SWR method. The solid and dashed curve signifies analytically calculated absorption coefficient for the respective material thickness 50mm and 100mm.

impedance using (11) and (12), the flow resistance R_f is set 5000 [Ns/m^4], and the porosity $\sigma = 0.8$, respectively.

Calculation results obtained by both CA and analytical model are illustrated in fig-ure 6. The results calculated by the CA model well coincides with analytical one for two cases of material thickness except for considerable difference in relatively low and high frequency regions, which is due to the inadequate formation of standing wave for extremely low frequency in such an short distance of the present acoustic tube model, and also insufficient partition of space compared to the wave length in higher frequency.

5   Conclusions

In the present paper, the two dimensional acoustic wave propagation model is devel-oped using Cellular Automata. Moreover, the sound absorbing model incorporating porous material is investigated. It is shown that the CA model well illustrated results which are consistent with analytical solutions.

Acknowledgements

We thank Professor Shin Morishita at Yokohama National University for his advice and support to the present work.

References

1. Morse, P. M. and Ingard, K. U.: Theoretical Acoustics. Princeton University Press (1986)
2. Doolen, G. D.: Lattice Gas Methods. MIT Press (1991)
3. Frisch, U., Hasslacher, B.and Pomeau, Y.: Lattice-Gas Automata for the Navier-Stokes Equation. Phys. Rev. Lett. **56** (1986) 1505–1508
4. Chen, H., Chen, S., Doolen, G., and Lee, Y. C.: Simple Lattice Gas Models for Waves. Complex Systems **2** (1988) 259–267
5. Chen, H., Chen, S. amd Doolen, G. D.: Sound Wave Propagation in FHP Lattice Gas Automata. Phys. Lett. A **140** (1989) 161–165
6. Sudo, Y. and Sparrow, V. W.: Sound Propagation Simulations Using Lattice Gas Methods. AIAA J. **33** (1995) 1582–1589
7. Chopard, B. and Droz, M.: Cellular Automata Modeling of Physical Systems. Cambridge University Press (1998)
8. Chopard, B., Luthi, P. O. and Wagen, J.-F.: A Lattice Boltzmann Method for Wave Propagation in Urban Microcells. IEE Proceedings - Microwaves, Antennas and Propagation, **144**, 4 (1997) 251-255.
9. Komatsuzaki, T., Sato, H., Iwata Y. and Morishita, S.: Simulation of Acoustic Wave Propa-gation using Cellular Automata. Trans. JSCES **1** (1999) 135–140

Simulation of the Evolution of Band Structures in Polycrystals on the Basis of Relaxation Element Method and Cellular Automata

G.V. Lasko[1,2], Ye.Ye. Deryugin[1], and S. Schmauder[2]

[1] Institute of Strength Physics and Material Science, SB RAS (ISPMS SB RAS),
pr.Akademicheskii 2/1, 634021 Tomsk, Russian Federation
dee@ispms.tsc.ru
[2] Institute for Material Testing, Material Science and Strength of Materials (IMWF)
Universität Stuttgart, Pfaffenwaldring 32, D-70569, Germany
{Galina.Lasko, Siegfried.Schmauder}@mpa.uni-stuttgart.de

Abstract. The development of a new scientific trend - physical mesomechanics gave a stimulus to elaboration of new methods of simulation of the self-organization phenomenon in solids under loading. One such method, is the relaxation element method, which maintains an unambiguous connection between the stress-drop in the local volume of a solid with plastic deformation in it. Based on this method and with combination of cellular automata approach a simulation of the evolution of band structures in polycrystals has been studied. The model can be referred to the class of geometrical models, known as cellular automata. Physical principles, laid on the basis of the model, allowed to reveal in the simulated polycrystals self-organization of the band structures and the regularities of the development of localization patterns, observed in experiments. The fundamental property of a solid: "plastic deformation in the local volumes of solid is accompanied by stress relaxation in it" lies in the basis of the method.

1 Introduction

It was experimentally proved and theoretically grounded that the evolution of band structures in polycrystalline metals reveals the phenomenon of self-organization. Neither theory of dislocations, nor the mechanics of solids can explain such phenomena adequately. That is why necessary prerequisites have been created for the appearance of the new scientific trend-physical mesomechanics [1,2], filling the gap between two extreme approaches: micro- and marcolevels. From the point of view of physical mesomechanics the development of the band structures in deformable solid under loading is governed by stress relaxation of the stress concentrators on the different scales. The difficulty of the description of the phenomenon of strain localization lies in the fact that it is not possible to formulate a universal physical law of the connection between the plastic deformation and the stresses in the solid because of the relaxation nature of the former. One of the ways to resolve such kind of problems is to apply a new method of description of the stress-strain state of the material under loading-Relaxation Element Method [3-7]. The fundamental property of a solid: "plastic

S. El Yacoubi, B. Chopard, and S. Bandini (Eds.): ACRI 2006, LNCS 4173, pp. 367–372, 2006.

deformation of solid under loading is accompanied by stress relaxation in the local volumes of solid" lies in the basis of the method. Because the approach represented in this paper is based on two methods - REM and Cellular Automata, let us concentrate first on the first one. In the next section of this paper the basic equations of the method are demonstrated.

2 Physical Principles and Algorithm of the Model

2.1 Constitutive Equations and Postulates of Continuum Theory of Defects

The dependence of the plastic deformation on the stresses in the local volume of the solid is defined by the statements and postulates of continuum theory of defects. Following the procedure, described in [4], we obtain the system of equations

$$\sigma_{ij,j} + f_i = C_{ijkl}\varepsilon^e_{kl,j} - C_{ijkl}\varepsilon^p_{mn,j} = 0, \text{ or}$$

$$C_{ijkl}\varepsilon^e_{kl,j} = C_{ijmn}\varepsilon^p_{mn,j}. \tag{1}$$

The above equations are enough to unambiguously define the connection between incompatible plastic deformation and stresses within a volume of solid. The Relaxation Element Method (REM) simplifies the solution of the problems, connected with theoretical calculation of the stress fields in the continuous medium and the sites of plastic deformation.

2.2 The Stress Field Components for Relaxation Elements

In [10] it was shown that in the system of origin of coordinates at the center of a circle and Oy-axis along the tensile stresses, the components of the stress field beyond the round contour [8,9] are equal:

$$\Delta\sigma_y = \frac{\Delta\sigma a}{4r^2}\left(1 + \frac{3a^2 + 10y^2}{r^2} - \frac{8y^2(3a^2 + 2y^2)}{r^4} + \frac{24a^2y^4}{r^6}\right) + \Delta\sigma;$$

$$\Delta\sigma_x = \frac{\Delta\sigma a}{4r^2}\left(1 - \frac{3a^2 + 18y^2}{r^2} + \frac{8y^2(3a^2 + 2y^2)}{r^4} - \frac{24a^2y^4}{r^6}\right); \tag{2}$$

$$\Delta\sigma_{xy} = \frac{\Delta\sigma a yx}{4r^4}\left(3 - \frac{2(3a^2 + 4y^2)}{r^2} + \frac{12a^2y^2}{r^4}\right).$$

This is the known solution of Kisch's problem [8,9]. However, in the present case the analogous stress state of the plane is caused by plastic deformation of the material in the circle, and the region without stresses should not be considered as a region where there is no material. It is not difficult to prove that at that time beyond the round region the non-homogeneous stress field will exist (2) without $\Delta\sigma$ stress. Within the site of plastic deformation the material will be in compression state $-\Delta\sigma$.

Shown in Fig. 1a is the spatial distribution of the σ_y component of the stress field in the plane with the site of plastic deformation of the considered type. (see equation (2)).

It is seen, that inhomogeneous stress fields exist beyond the site. The stresses break at the round contour. Stress relaxation σ by the value $\Delta\sigma$ creates around itself the zone of elevated stress concentration, while maximum value of stress σ_y ($3\Delta\sigma$) exceeds the value of external applied stress.

We have proved that the prescription of the value of stress relaxation $\Delta\sigma$ within the zone of plastic deformation allows to define the stress-strain state beyond this zone with the method of theory of elasticity. As a result the stress field in the whole volume of solid with the site of plastic deformation became known.

3 Model

Application of relaxation elements as defects, characterizing the interaction between plastic deformation and stresses allows to simulate the process of plastic strain localization and to obtain the dependency of flow stress on the sequence of separate structural elements involvement into plastic deformation. Developed on the basis of REM model operates on the basis of uniform synchronous cellular automata [10].

We followed here the same procedure as in [11]. The calculational field is divided into a large number of cells, playing the role of elements of structure. Each element of the simulated medium posseses the ability to switch the state by a discrete jump of plastic deformation, setting by a definite relaxation element. This procedure means that the element of structure can periodically increase its degree of plastic deformation and as a stress concentrator influences the change $\Delta\sigma$ of the stress field in the whole volume of solid. The involvement of structural elements into plastic deformation is realized by definite rules of transition (for example, at the instance of time of achieving of critical value of shear stress).

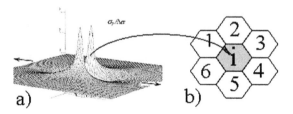

Fig. 1. a) Stress field distribution of the component σ_y, which is obtained as the critical shear stress is attained in some hexagonal cell; b) Neighbourhood pattern in the proposed model: the coloured cell

Interaction of the stress fields from the various structural elements, which have undergone plastic deformation, proceeds automatically according to the procedure, described above. The orientation of slip plane in each crystallite was set by generator of random numbers from 0 to 360°. The second slip system was chosen to be oriented at an angle of $\pi/3$ with respect to the previous one.

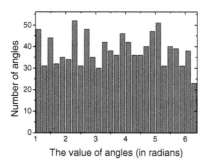

Fig. 2. The distribution of angles, generated by a random numbers generator

Resolved shear stress in each crystallite was defined according to the equation:

$$\tau = (\sigma_y - \sigma_x)\sin\alpha\cos\alpha + \sigma_{xy}(\cos^2\alpha - \sin^2\alpha) \qquad (10)$$

rule: it changes the filed of stresses inside the hexagon and outside of it by placing the stress field from plastic site inside the circular region inside the hexagon. Then the value of critical shear stress is calculated in the neighbouring grains, the maximum of shear stress, corresponding to the minimum of external applied stress is calculated. For the case of rigid inclusion, the simulation starts in the similar way as in the case without the inclusion.

The implementation was developed in the programming language C++. The visualization was performed in Java language.

4 Results and Discussion

Using the above approach, the simulation of the propagation of the sites of localized plastic deformation has been performed for the case of an aluminum polycrystal under tensile loading without and with the presence of a rigid inclusion. Shown in Fig. 3 are the patterns of plastic shear band evolution in an aluminium polycrystal.

As can be seen in Figure 3, the grains one after another are involved into plastic deformation, consequently embracing the whole specimen grid. The external applied stress oscillates around some average value (Fig 3 a).

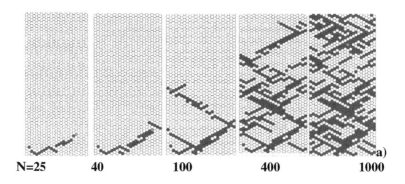

N=25   40   100   400   1000

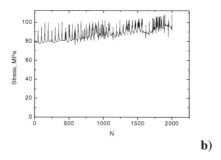

b)

Fig. 3. a) Self-organization of the bands of localized plastic deformation in a polycrystalline aluminum under tensile loading; b) Loading curve

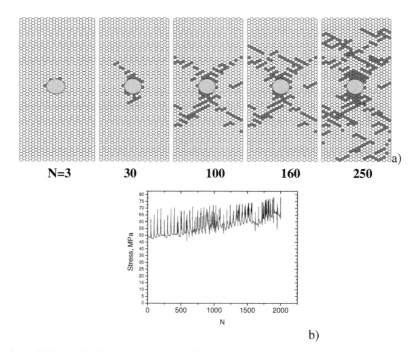

N=3   30   100   160   250

a)

b)

Fig. 4. a) Self-organization of the bands of localized plastic deformation in a polycrystalline aluminum with a rigid inclusion under tensile loading; b) Loading diagram

Each stress drop on the loading curve matches the intersection of the cross-section of the specimen by deformation bands.

As can be seen from the diagram, the same regularities in its behaviour are detected. With the only difference that it oscillates around lower value than in the case without presence of the inclusion. The value is different because, the internal stress field from the inclusion makes contribution.

5 Conclusions

In the present paper the self-organization of the bands of plastic deformation in poly-crystalline aluminium without and with rigid Al_2O_3 inclusions is simulated within the framework of the combination of two methods-cellular automata method and relaxation element method. LPD bands-evolution in a polycrystals with round inclusions have been performed. The simulation shows the qualitative difference of the development of plastic strain localization in pure aluminium polycrystal and in one with a rigid inclusion. The model could be used for the prediction of the evolution of the bands of localized plastic deformation in polycrystals with inclusions. Future work needs to concentrate on a more sophisticated description of plastic strain localization.

Acknowledgements

The authors are thankful for the financial support from German Research Foundation (DFG) under project Schm 746/52-2.

References

1. Panin, V.E., Yu.V. Grinyaev, V.I. Danilov et al. Structural level of plastic deformation and fracture (in russian)-Novosibirsk: Nauka, 1990
2. Panin, V.E.,. Egorushkin, V.Ye, Makarov, P.V., Grinyaev, Yu.V., Popov V.L. et. al. Physical mesomechanics of Heterogeneous Media and computer-Aided Design of Materi-als, Ed. V.E. Panin., Cambridge International Science Publishing, Cambridge (UK)1998, 440 p.
3. Deryugin, Ye.Ye., Lasko, G.V. Relaxation element method in the problem of mesome-chanics and calculations of band structures, in: V.E. Panin (Ed.), Physical mesomechanics and computer-aided designing of materials, in two volumes, Novosibirsk, Nauka, Siberian book-publishing firm SB RAS, Vol.1 (1995), p. 131-161.
4. Deryugin, Ye. Relaxation element method, Monograph. Novosibirsk, Nauka, Siberian book-publishing firm SB RAS, 1998
5. Deryugin, Ye.Ye., Lasko, G.V., Schmauder, S. Relaxation element method, Computa-tional Materials Science (1998) 11 (3), 189-203
6. Lasko, G.V., Deryugin, Ye.Ye., Schmauder, S., Saraev, D., Determination of stresses near multiple pores and rigid inclusions by relaxation element method, Theoretical and Applied Fracture Mechanics, 34 (2000) 93-100
7. Deryugin Ye.Ye., Lasko G.V., Smolin Yu. E., Russian Physician J., 38(5) (1995) 15-18
8. de Wit, R., Continuum Theory of disclinations, Mir, Moscow (1977)
9. Timoshenko, S.P., Goodier, J.N., Theory of elasticity, 3d edn. New York:McGraw-Hill, (1970)
10. Gould, H., Tobochnik, Ya. An introduction to computer simulation methods. Pt. 2:   Ap-plication to physical systems. Moscow, Mir, 1990.
11. Lasko, G.V., Deryugin, Y.Y., and S. Schmauder Plastic Deformation Development in Polycrystals based on the Cellular Automata and Relaxation Element Method, LNCS 3305 2004, pp.375-384.

A Bi-fluid Lattice Boltzmann Model for Water Flow in an Irrigation Channel

Olivier Marcou[1,2], Samira El Yacoubi[1], and Bastien Chopard[2]

[1] MEPS/ASD - University of Perpignan
52, Paul Alduy Avenue, 66860 Perpignan, Cedex, France
{marcou, yacoubi}@univ-perp.fr
http://www.univ-perp.fr/see/rch/cef/index.html
[2] University of Geneva, Computer Science Department,
24 rue General-Dufour, CH-1211 Geneva 4, Switzerland
Bastien.Chopard@cui.unige.ch

Abstract. This paper is devoted to modelling of water flow dynamics in open-channels for the goal of controlling irrigation systems. We expose and validate a methodology based on Lattice Boltzmann models as an alternative to the commonly used Saint-Venant equations. We adapt a bi-fluid model to the case of a free surface water flow. A gravity force is applied to the heaviest fluid as to maintain it at the bottom. The considered boundary conditions take into account the control actions provided by the two underflow gates located at the left and right ends of the reach. Numerical results for density profiles are given to validate our approach.

1 Introduction

The control and management of water resources has become an increasingly important problem in the world and have attracted a strong interest. Irrigation (water for agriculture, or growing crops) is probably the most important use of water. Traditional irrigation systems still waste too much water, especially during transport from the rivers, lakes or reservoirs, to the crop fields. Recent researches were focused on regulated river systems and developed automatic dam gate controller for water flow in order to improve the performance of irrigation systems. Different methods and controllers have been reported in literature in which a flow, level or volume variable is controlled by acting with a discharge or gate opening control variable [18,12,13].

The controller design (i.e. the determination of control actions leading to a desired dynamic behaviour of the controlled system) is an important step in control theory. It requires a model that captures the main features of the system. Open-channels dynamics are commonly described using non-linear partial differential equations based on the so-called Saint-Venant (SV) system (see [4,8,11] and the references therein). The SV system is a well-known approximation of the incompressible Navier-Stokes equations for shallow water flows with gravity and

S. El Yacoubi, B. Chopard, and S. Bandini (Eds.): ACRI 2006, LNCS 4173, pp. 373–382, 2006.
© Springer-Verlag Berlin Heidelberg 2006

a free moving boundary. Its derivation relies on the hydrostatic approximation where the role of viscosity and friction at the bottom is considered.

SV equations are known to provide an accurate description of the canal dynamic behaviour [6,7]. Nevertheless, the problem is that these equations are very complex and highly non-linear. They cannot be solved analytically except for very simple situations. Furthermore, the various numerical methods used to solve SV equation (finite-difference and finite-element methods, collocation method [19,5]) need a large amount of spatial discretization points in order to obtain realistic solutions.

We propose in this paper an approach based on lattice Boltzmann (LB) models which have been successfully used for modelling and simulating several complex fluid flows [2,3,20]. The LB method, which is an extension of the cellular automata approach, solves the fluid motion based on the mesoscopic dynamics of pseudo-fluid particles evolving on a discrete space-time universe (the lattice). It is especially useful for flows around complex geometries and naturally accommodates a variety of boundary conditions such as the pressure drop across the interface between two fluids and wetting effects at a fluid-solid interface.

The present study focuses on the behavior of the water level in a reservoir with upstream and downstream gates and the effect of various conditions on the reservoir boundaries. We consider the Shan-Chen two-fluid model [16] to simulate an open channel with a free water level.

The paper is organized as follows: section 2 gives a brief introduction to lattice Boltzmann (LB) models, presents the main features of our model and discusses various boundary conditions. Section 3 is dedicated to numerical simulations and model validation. The paper ends with some concluding remarks.

2   System Description

In general irrigation canals can be a complicated structure made up of several reaches delimited by underflow gates. The gate opening is used as the control actions. Here we restrict our study to a canal partitioned as a single reach consisting of a single pool with two gates, G_{up} and G_{down}, located at its upstream and downstream ends, respectively, as depicted in Fig. 1. A one-dimensional portion of a canal is shown. It is assumed to be horizontal with one reach of length L. The flow dynamics in such open canals are usually described by the so-called Saint-Venant equations [4,8,11], a set of nonlinear partial differential equations expressed as

$$\frac{\partial A}{\partial t} + \frac{\partial Q}{\partial x} = 0 \qquad (1)$$

$$\frac{\partial Q}{\partial t} + \frac{\partial A}{\partial x} \cdot \left(\frac{gA}{B} - \frac{Q^2}{A^2} \right) + \frac{\partial Q}{\partial x} \cdot \frac{2Q}{A} + gA \cdot (S_f - \bar{S}) = 0 \qquad (2)$$

for all $(x,t) \in]0, L[\times R^+$ where x is the spatial location and t is the temporal variable; A is the flow cross-section, Q the discharge, g the gravity, h the water elevation ($A = h \cdot B$, where B is the width of the channel), $\bar{S}$ the channel slope and S_f the friction slope. These equations are completed with initial conditions $h(x,0)$ and $Q(x,0)$. The associated boundary conditions are given by a standard discharge relationship for under flow gates defined as follows :

$$Q_{in} = \alpha_{in} \cdot B \cdot \theta_{in} \sqrt{2g(h_{up} - h(0,t))} \tag{3}$$

$$Q_{out} = \alpha_{out} \cdot B \cdot \theta_{out} \sqrt{2g(h(L,t) - h_{down})} \tag{4}$$

where h_{up} and h_{down} are the left and right water level respectively, outside the reach, with $h_{\mathrm{up}} > h_{\mathrm{down}}$. The quantities θ_{out} and θ_{in} are respectively the openings of the downstream and upstream gates. The constants α_{out} and α_{in} are gates-specific coefficients.

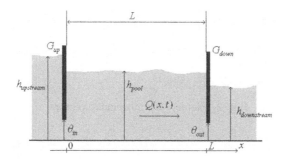

Fig. 1. Channel diagram

3 Proposed Lattice Boltzmann Model

3.1 Lattice Boltzmann Approach

Lattice Boltzmann (LB) models constitute an efficient tool to model and simulate realistic fluid flows obeying the Navier-Stokes equations. They derive from Lattice-Gas cellular automata models as they describe, on a Cartesian grid, the fluid motion by an equivalent mesoscopic dynamics that still contains the sufficient physics to allow accurate recovery of the desired macroscopic behavior.

Let us consider a discrete space made up of a Cartesian lattice of spacing Δ_r, with a discrete clock of time step Δ_t. At any discrete time t, we assume that particles are entering every lattice site $\boldsymbol{r}$ according to the possible lattice directions $i = 0, \ldots, z$. By definition, direction $i = 0$ refers to particles at rest.

In the LB approach, the particle populations are described by densities distribution $N_i(\boldsymbol{r}, t)$. As in any kinetic approach, the fluid density ρ and fluid velocity $\boldsymbol{u}$ are given by the moments of the N_i (see for instance [3,20,2])

$$\rho = \sum_{i=0}^{z} m_i N_i(\overrightarrow{r}, t) \tag{5}$$

$$j = \rho \vec{u} = \sum_{i=0}^{z} m_i \vec{v}_i N_i(\vec{r}, t) \qquad (6)$$

where j is the local momentum. The m_i are specific weights associated with each direction and $\vec{v}_i$ denotes the velocity associated with each population. By defining the ratio between the lattice spacing and time step as $v = \frac{\Delta_r}{\Delta_t}$, we obtain $\vec{v}_i = v \cdot \vec{c}_i$.

The dynamics is divided in two steps that alternate over time: propagation and collision. During the propagation step the N_i from each r move towards a nearest neighbor site $r + c_i$, in a direction given by the $z + 1$ vectors c_i. Fig. 2 shows an example for $z = 8$. The collision phase amounts to transforming the incoming distributions N_i at each lattice site into outgoing distributions.

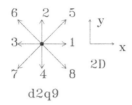

Fig. 2. Elementary movement vectors

In the case of the well-known BGK model (Bhatnager, Gross and Krook, see [15,3,20]), the collision operator is a relaxation towards prescribed local equilibrium distributions N_i^{eq}. The equation combining the collision and propagation steps is then

$$N_i(\vec{r} + \Delta_r, t + \Delta_t) = N_i(\vec{r}, t) - \frac{1}{\tau}(N_i(\vec{r}, t) - N_i^{eq}(\vec{r}, t)) + \frac{\Delta_t}{v^2 C_2}\vec{v}_i \cdot F \quad (7)$$

The quantity τ is a relaxation time which allows to control the system viscosity and C_2 is a model parameter whose value is based on tensors isotropy considerations. The equilibrium populations $N_i^{eq}(\vec{r}, t)$ are given functions of the local density and velocity [3,20]. It can be shown that the LB dynamics is, in some limits, equivalent to the Navier-Stokes equation. A particularity of the LB approach is that the pressure p is related to the density ρ as in an ideal gas $p = c_s^2\rho$, where c_s is the speed of sound.

3.2   The Irrigation Canal Model

In order to model two fluids (water, air) in the channel, we consider the so-called Shan-Chen model (see [14,16,16]) which implements the interaction of two immiscible fluids. In this model, each lattice cell contains two types of populations, denoted $R_i(\vec{r}, t)$ and $B_i(\vec{r}, t)$, describing the often called red and blue fluids, respectively. The calculation of the total momentum at each location has to take into account the momentum of each of the two components

$$u \cdot \left(\frac{\rho_R}{\tau_R} + \frac{\rho_B}{\tau_B}\right) = \frac{j_R}{\tau_R} + \frac{j_B}{\tau_B} = \frac{1}{\tau_R} \cdot \sum_{i=0}^{z} m_i \vec{v}_i R_i(\vec{r}, t) + \frac{1}{\tau_B} \cdot \sum_{i=0}^{z} m_i \vec{v}_i B_i(\vec{r}, t) \quad (8)$$

where $m_i, i = 0 \ldots z$ are the weights of each lattice direction.

In the Shan-Chen model, an interaction force is introduced between the particles of different kind to mimic their mutual repulsion. The result is the existence of a surface tension between the two fluids. This interaction force is supposed to occur only within the nearest neighbours, and can be expressed as follows :

$$F_R(\vec{r}) = -\psi^R(\vec{r}) G_{RB} \sum_{i=0}^{z} \psi^B(\vec{r} + \Delta_t \vec{v}_i) \vec{v}_i \quad (9)$$

$$F_B(\vec{r}) = -\psi^B(\vec{r}) G_{RB} \sum_{i=0}^{z} \psi^R(\vec{r} + \Delta_t \vec{v}_i) \vec{v}_i \quad (10)$$

Here $\psi^\sigma = f_\sigma(\rho_\sigma(\vec{r}))$ (with $\sigma = R, B$) is a function of the local density and G_{RB} defines the importance of the interaction potential. These two expressions are then used in equation 7 as the value of F and thus couples the R_i and B_i evolution. In what follows, we choose the following form for the function $\psi^\sigma(\vec{r}) = \rho_\sigma(\vec{r})$.

For the case of the canal application (see Fig. 1), we assume that the red fluid represents the water and the blue fluid the air. The water must stay at the bottom of the pool and exhibit a hydrostatic pressure variation. This can be achieved by applying a gravity force to the red fluid only.

Two types of boundary conditions were tested so far for modelling the left, right and bottom walls of the pool : the bounce-back and the Zou-He boundary conditions. In the bounce-back case the collision step consists in giving each population the value of the population of its opposite direction. The Zou-He boundary condition applies a given velocity at the boundary and is described in detail in [9,10]. The upper boundary is a pressure flow boundary condition, which sets the density of each fluid at a fixed value at the boundary.

The gate boundary sites are considered as having a Zou-He boundary condition with a specified velocity. The velocity is derived from the discharge expression of the SV model according to the following formula :

$$u_x^{upstream} = \alpha_{in} \cdot \sqrt{2(h_{upstream} - h_{pool})} \quad (11)$$

$$u_x^{downstream} = \alpha_{out} \cdot \sqrt{2(h_{pool} - h_{downstream})} \quad (12)$$

where α_{in} and α_{out} are gate-specific parameters. The left part of figure 3 shows where the different boundary conditions are applied.

The numerical experiment consists in having an initial set of values for $h_{upstream}$, h_{pool} and $h_{downstream}$ and let the system reach an equilibrium of water level between the three regions. The question will be then whether this equilibrium corresponds to the prediction of SV equations.

We see on Fig. 3 (right) the density (or the pressure) of both fluids as a function of the elevation above the canal bottom, once the equilibrium is reached.

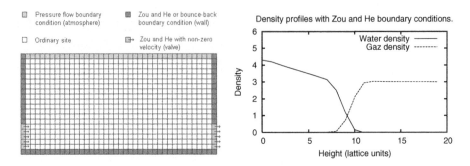

Fig. 3. Left : diagram of lattice Boltzmann model for a free-surface irrigation channel. - Right : Density profiles of the water and air fluid. The intersection between the two profiles is arbitrarily defined as the water level.

As the air-water interface is not sharp we define the water level as the height for which the densities of the two fluids are equal.

4   Simulation Results

Simulations with the our model are carried out as follows: at $t = 0$, the lattice is initialized with completely closed boundary conditions (the wall boundary conditions are either Zou-He or bounce-back) until the system has reached equilibrium. At $t = 20000$, the wall condition at the top is replaced by our constant pressure boundary condition. At $t = 40000$, one or both gates are opened. The wall condition (whether Zou-He or bounce-back) on the sites belonging to a gate are replaced with the imposed velocity Zou-He boundary condition, with velocity taken from eqs. 11 and 12. At $t = t_{end}$, the simulation ends.

4.1   Simulation with Opened Upstream Gate

In a first simulation we observe the filling of the pool while only the upstream gate is opened. The wall boundary condition we used for the first simulation is the Zou-He boundary condition. The size of the lattice is 40×20, with 20 being the height of the lattice. Fig. 4 shows the density (or pressure) profiles of both fluids at times $t = 40000$ (when the upstream gate is opened) and $t = 100000$, which is the end of the simulation. We observe, as expected, that the water level has increased while keeping the same the pressure gradient as well as the same air pressure.

The Zou-He boundary condition does not ensure a perfect mass conservation for any value of the incoming population densities. It is thus necessary to verify whether it results or not in a significant global mass loss (or increase) in the system. To do so, we evaluate and compare both the global mass increase m_{system} of the system after the gate is opened and the actual mass m_{in} which was introduced in the system through the gate. We obtain the left part of Fig. 5 with Zou-He boundary condition and the right part with the bounce-back boundary condition.

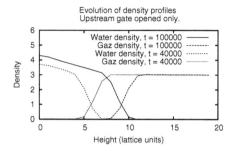

Fig. 4. Evolution of the density profiles of the water and air fluid when the upstream gate is opened

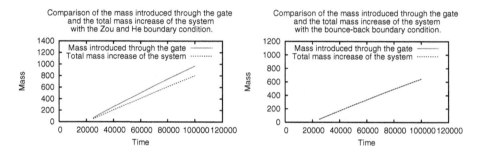

Fig. 5. Comparison between the mass of water in the system and the mass of water introduced through the upstream gate, with either Zou and He and bounce-back boundary condition at left, right, and bottom walls

With Zou-He condition, there is a significant mass loss. On the other hand, with bounce-back wall conditions, the conservation of mass is much better obeyed (see Fig. 5, right). The evolution of the relative error $|m_{in} - m_{system}|/m_{in}$ for the bounce-back case is shown in the Fig. 6 (left). We explain this small error by the fact that the top boundary was not replaced by a bounce-back condition. The constant pressure condition at the upper sites is implemented in the same way as in the Zou-He condition. Therefore a small mass loss is likely to be observed at these sites.

Even if the bounce-back boundary condition seems better at keeping in the system the mass which was introduced at the gate, it shows severe drawbacks when we observe the density profiles. Fig. 6 (right) shows an example the density profiles obtained with the bounce-back wall conditions. The pressure drop seen at the bottom of the lattice, as well as the presence of the second fluid is unphysical.

We believe it is due to the fact the the density is not well calculated in a bounce-back condition. Density is the sum of all populations but, on a wall, only half of the populations are present. This results in a bad calculation of the two-fluid interaction force in the sites which are neighbours to the boundaries.

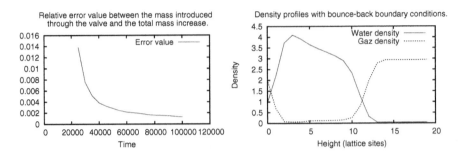

Fig. 6. Left : Relative error between the mass of water in the system and the total mass of water introduced through the upstream gate with the bounce-back boundary condition. - Right : Density profiles in the case of a bounce-back boundary condition applied to the left, right and bottom boundaries.

4.2 Simulation with Both Opened Underflow Gates

The next simulation concern a system where both upstream and downstream gates are opened. The water level is then supposed to converge to an equilibrium value. Both gates are opened at $t = 40000$. Fig. 7 (left) shows the evolution of the mean water level compared to the expected equilibrium value, when the upstream and downstream water levels are imposed. The expected equilibrium water level is the one which, in eqs. 11 and 12 makes the inlet and outlet flows identical.

The mean water level stabilizes at a value close to the theoretical equilibrium value. After performing several simulations with the two types of boundary conditions as well as different values of the gates coefficients α_{in} and α_{out} (which are equal in our simulations), we conclude that the simulated water level is closer to its theoretical value when the bounce-back boundary condition is used and when the gate coefficients are small. Fig. 7 (right) shows the results of the measurements.

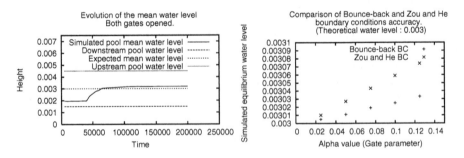

Fig. 7. Left : Stationary water level obtained when both gates are open: comparison with the expected equilibrium level. - Right : Distance to equilibrium water level, for bounce-back and Zou-He wall conditions and different values of gates coefficients.

The fact that the mean water value is better with the bounce-back than with Zou-He condition suggests that the water level issue may be related to the mass conservation issue. It is likely that the influence of the gate coefficients on the mean water level is also related to the mass conservation. Indeed, the mass loss which happen with a Zou-He boundary condition is related to how far the system is from its equilibrium. Increasing the gate coefficients implies that a stronger flow in the system and thus flow conditions more distant from the local equilibrium state.

Note also that since the air-water interface is not sharp, an error in the estimation of the water level could occur.

5   Concluding Remarks

We have proposed a two-fluid LB model in order to describe free surface flows in irrigation canals. At this stage of our project, we have been concerned with the validation of the very basic property of such system. In particular we have simulated the water level in a pool subject to an inlet and outlet flow.

On the one hand, we obtained promising results as the simulated water level is consistent with its expected value. However, we have shown that non truly mass conserving boundary conditions cannot be used in the present context, probably due to the fact that gravity induces a density gradient which amplifies mass loss on the walls. On the other hand, it is expected that the problem with the bounce-back wall condition at the bottom wall can be overcome with a more clever calculation of the density.

Finally, a conceptual difficulty of our approach is related to the fact that, here, the water fluid is compressible. Although this produces a correct hydrostatic pressure, compressibility introduces a difference between the mass of water in the pool and its level over the bottom wall. This question will be investigated more thoroughly in a forthcoming study.

This research is supported by the Swiss National Science Foundation.

References

1. Bhatnager, P., Gross, E., Krook, M. : A model for collision process in gases, Phys. Rev. 94, 511, 1654.
2. Chen, S., Doolen, G.D. : Lattice Boltzmann method for fluid flows. Ann. Rev. Fluid Mech. 30 (1998), pp. 329364. H. Chen, S. Chen and W. Matthaeus, Recovery of the NavierStokes equations using a lattice-gas Boltzmann method. Phys. Rev. A 45 (1992), pp. R5339R5342.
3. Chopard, B., Luthi, P., Masselot, A., A. Dupuis, A. : Cellular automata and lattice Boltzmann techniques: An approach to model and simulate complex systems, Advances in Complex Systems 5 (2002), no. 2.
4. Chow, V. T. : Open-channels Hydrolics, (International Students Ed. New York : Mc Graw-Hill, 572 pages (1954).
5. Colley, R. L., Moin, S. A. : Finite element solution of St Venant equation, Journal of hydraulical engineering. Division ASCE, vol. 102, N HY6, 759-775 (1976).

6. Cunge J.A. : Simulation des coulements non permanents dans les rivires et canaux, Ecole Nationale Suprieure d'Hydraulique de Grenoble, 173 p. (1988).
7. Cunge J.A., Holly F.M., Verwey A. : "Practical aspects of computational river hydraulics", Pitman Advanced Publishing Program, 420 p. (1980).
8. Graf, W.H. : Hydraulique fluviale, Collection traité de genie civil. Ecole polytechnique federale de Lausanne. Presses polytechniques et universitaire romandes (1993).
9. He, X., Zou, Q. : Analysis and boundary condition of the Lattice Boltzmann BGK Model with two velocities components, Los Alamos preprint, LA-UR-95-2293.
10. He, X., Zou, Q. : On pressure and velocity flow boundary conditions for the lattice Boltzmann BGK model, Cellular Automata and Lattice Gases, abstract comp-gas/9508001, http://arxiv.org/abs/comp-gas/9508001 (1995).
11. Mahmood, M. A., Yevjevich, V. : Unsteady Flow in Open Channels, Vols. 1 and2- Fort Collins USA: Water Ressources Publications.
12. Malaterre, P.-O. ,Baume, J.-P. : Modeling and regulation of irrigation canals : ongoing researches.
13. Malaterre, P.-O. ,Rogers, D., Schuurmans, J. : Classification of canal control algorithms, Journal of irrigation and drainage engeneering, **98** I24(1), 3-10.
14. Martys, N. S., Chen, H. : Simulation of multi-components fluids in complex three-dimensional geometries by the Lattice Boltzmann method, Phys. Review E, Volume 53, number 1 (1996).
15. Qian, Y., d'Humières, D., Lallemand, P. : Lattice BGK models for Navier-Stokes equations, Europhys. Lett. 17(6), 470-84 (1992) 94, 511, 1654.
16. Shan, X., Chen, H. : Lattice Boltzmann model for simulating flows with multiple phases and components, Phys. Review E, Volume 47, number 3 (1993).
17. Shan, X., Chen, H. : Simulation of nonideal gases and liquid-gas phase transitions by the lattice Boltzmann equation, Phys. Review, Volume 49, number 4 (1994).
18. Shand, M.J. : Automatic downstreem control systems for irrigation canals, PhD, University of California, Berkley, 159 p, (1971).
19. Strelkoff, T. : Numerical solution of St Venant equation, Journal of hydraulical engineering. Division ASCE, vol. 96, N HY1, 223-252 (1970).
20. Succi, S. : The Lattice Boltzmann Equation for Fluid Dynamics and Beyond, Oxford Science Publications (2001).

A Flow Modeling of Lubricating Greases Under Shear Deformation by Cellular Automata

Shunsuke Miyamoto, Hideyuki Sakai, Toshihiko Shiraishi, and Shin Morishita

Yokohama National University,
Graduate School of Environment and Information Sciences
79-7 Tokiwadai, Hodogaya-ku, Yokohama 240-8501 Japan
{miyamoto, sakai}@neuman.jks.ynu.ac.jp,
{shira, mshin}@ynu.ac.jp

Abstract. A Cellular Automata modeling of the lubricating grease flow under the shear deformation is proposed. Lubricating greases are composed of thickening agent, liquid lubricant and various kinds of additives. The thickening agent forms fibrous microstructures in liquid lubricant, and lubricating greases present their special feature due to this microstructure. Though they are widely used in mechanical components, there is little understanding on the lubrication mechanism including the contribution of the fibrous microstructure. There have been proposed no other theoretical model except for the average flow model based on the fluid lubrication theory in tribology field. In the present paper, the flow modeling of lubricating greases under shear deformation was proposed by Cellular Automata, where aggregated thickening agent and liquid lubricant were represented by virtual particles movable on the two-dimensional cell space. It was assumed that the fibrous microstructure was composed of multiple particles, and external stress induces the flow of grease where the particles interacts one another.

1 Introduction

Lubricating greases are widely used in mechanical components of various kinds of machines. Greases are solid or semi-fluid lubricant. They basically consist of liquid lubricant and thickening agent which constructs fibrous microstructures in lubricant. Other ingredients which produce special properties may be included[1-3]. Because of this two-phase system, the special features of greases such as the long interval of lubricant supply or the simple sealing mechanism are induced.

The typical properties of lubricating greases have been investigated through mainly experimental methods by lots of authors. According to previous literatures, the fibrous microstructure in lubricating greases might be observed by electron microscope, and they revealed various static-state microstructures depending on the kinds of thickening agent. Theoretical approach has also been made by several authors[4], in which the liquid lubricant including fibrous microstructure has been treated as homogeneous fluid presenting the feature of Bingham plastic fluid. But, for more than fifty years, the dynamic mechanism of microstructures in lubricating greases has not been revealed, and that no theoretical model has been proposed to investigate it.

S. El Yacoubi, B. Chopard, and S. Bandini (Eds.): ACRI 2006, LNCS 4173, pp. 383–391, 2006.

In the present paper, the flow modeling of lubricating greases under shear deformation was proposed by Cellular Automata (CA), where the aggregated thick fibers constructing networks of microstructures in greases, the short fibers of thickening agent and liquid lubricant were represented by virtual particles movable on the two-dimensional cell space. It may be the first proposal by the authors even in tribology field that, according to the experimental observation, there exist two kinds of fibers; aggregated thick fibers and short fibers of thickening agent. It was assumed that the fibrous microstructure was composed of multiple particles, and external stress induces the flow of grease where the particles interacts one another due to friction and absorption effect.

2 Grease

General features of lubricating greases and visualized procedure of the fibrous microstructure under shear deformation are presented in this chapter[1-5]. To the best of our knowledge, it may be the first observation of dynamic behavior of thickening agent in lubricating greases. Further, the observation may be the most important procedure in defining the local neighbor rules in modeling by CA.

2.1 General Description of Lubricating Greases

Lubricating greases are basically composed of gelling or thickening agent, lubricating oil and various kinds of additives. It looks like a gel or a solid. The accepted definition of lubricating greases, published by the American Society of Testing Materials (ASTM), is "a solid to semi-fluid product of a thickening agent in a liquid lubricant. Other ingredients imparting special properties may be included." Though the amount of lubricating greases used in industry is relatively small compared with the amount of lubricating oil, it is widely used in mechanical components. The main advantages of greases to lubricating oils are; long interval of lubricant supply, small amount for sufficient lubrication, and simple mechanism of sealing system. On the contrary, disadvantages are; large energy loss caused by friction force, lower limit of shear velocity, or little cooling capacity.

Lubricating greases may be classified into two types in reference to the kinds of thickening agent: soap or non-soap type greases. Further classification of non-soap type greases may be made by urea, organic, and inorganic type greases. Mineral oils and synthetic lubricants are used as the base oil for greases. In each type of greases, most thickening agent has a fibrous form and constructs a microstructure in liquid phase.

The fibrous microstructure in lubricating grease governs its typical properties. It has been said that lubricating greases show elasticity, plasticity and fluidity in response to its environment. The magnitude of applied force determines the strain reaction of grease. Up to a particular value of applied stress, the grease will exhibit elastic properties; and beyond that value, the grease will deform plastically. With further increase in stress, the flow will be accelerated.

A schematic view of fibrous microstructure is shown in Fig.1. It has been believed that lots of fibers form mesh-type microstructure and lubricating oil is comprised by the gap of mesh structure. The microstructure is deformable by the external stress to some degree. When a shear deformation is applied to lubricating grease, the mesh-type microstructure is forced to deform and liquid lubricant comprised in the structure is separated into the lubricated space. After the external stress to the structure is removed, then liquid lubricant is comprised again into the gap of microstructure. This procedure is shown schematically in Fig.2.

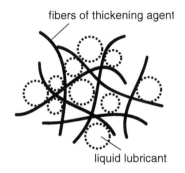

fibers of thickening agent

liquid lubricant

Fig.1. Schematic model of fibrous microstructure

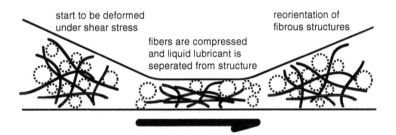

start to be deformed under shear stress

reorientation of fibrous structures

fibers are compressed and liquid lubricant is seperated from structure

Fig. 2. Deformation of microstructure

2.2 Experimental Observation

It is important to know the physical phenomena in detail to build up a new dynamic model of the target. It is well known that there exist fibrous microstructures composed of thickening agent in lubricating greases, and lots of photographs were taken by electron microscope. But most of them reveal the static feature of microstructure, not the dynamic one. In order to make a flow model of lubricating greases, we need to know the dynamic behavior of microstructure in the flow state of greases.

Various attempts were made by the authors to understand the dynamic behavior of fibrous microstructure in lubricating greases, and we finally succeeded in visualizing the flow by means of phase-contrast microscope developed for biological research. Figure 3 shows the visualized microstructure in the test sample of urea-type grease. In the close view of Fig.3, there were two kinds of fibers; short fibers whose length was several micrometers, and long and thick fibers lying in coils clearly observed in Fig.3.

According to the tribologist specialized for grease, the two kinds of fibers, short and long one, might be produced in the manufacturing process of grease, and they have not been reported in the past literatures.

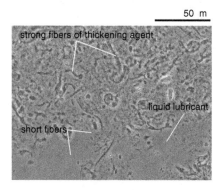

Fig. 3. Visualized fibrous structures in lubricating grease

The dynamic flow visualization experiments were conducted in a simplified plain bearing system set on the microscope, as shown schematically in Fig.4. The time series of visualized flow in a wedge is shown in Fig.5. Among the various phenomena observed in this experiment, the following three special features were conspicuous:

(1) The flow of lubricating greases is composed of the cluster of strong micro-structures of fibers, short fibers, and liquid lubricant. The size of clusters lubricant seems to flow among the clusters of structures.

(2) There exists some slipping boundary of lubricating greases in the wedge area almost parallel to the moving surface. Though the experiment gives us two-dimensional view parallel to the moving surface, the slipping boundary may be observed by adjusting the focus of microscope. This slipping boundary between fixed and moving surface may have been clearly observed in a simple experiment.

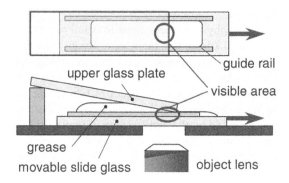

Fig. 4. Experimental set up on the stage of phase-contrast microscope

edge of upper plate

50 m

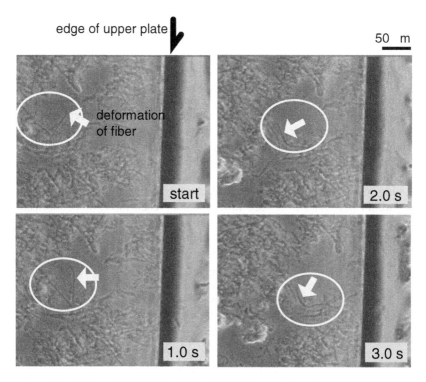

Fig. 5. Dynamic behavior of visualized microstructures in urea grease

(3) Reverse flows of lubricant were excited among the clusters of microstructure at several points in the visual field of microscope. It is not understood clearly that the reverse flow was observed in lubricating greases, but this may be caused by local pressure gradient in the lubricant.

3 Modeling by Cellular Automata

The main purpose of this research is to construct a flow model of lubricating greases including the fibrous microstructures by Cellular Automata[6,7]. Because lubricating grease is typically two-phase (or multi-phase) system, it is not easy to propose a precise flow model including the cluster of microstructures, the slipping boundary and reverse flow of lubricant. For more than fifteen years, the average flow model has generally been adopted in the simulation of grease flow, and it has been thought to be almost impossible to simulate the flow of lubricating greases including microstructure in detail.

3.1 Definition of State

The simulation was conducted in two-dimensional space perpendicular to the moving surface along the sliding direction. The flow of grease in a wedge was essentially three-dimensional one, but a two-dimensional space was set in simplicity. This simulation space was not the same as the one shown in Fig.5, but perpendicular to the experimental observation space. From the tribological viewpoint, the flow in the selected space for the simulation was more important, because the flow into a wedge produces the pressure supporting the load to the bearing. In fact, it was almost impossible to observe the flow in the present two-dimensional space in the experiment. The space was divided into triangular cells, and four kinds of particles representing each state of cells were prepared: wall or boundary surface, strong fibers for microstructures, short fibers, and lubricant. Each particle had the state of mass and velocity.

Lubricant was represented by particles and rest areas of cell having no particles. Because lubricant was generally thought to be incompressible fluid, all the cells representing lubricant should be filled with the lubricant particles. But, the flow of particles would not realized in such full condition. Then the flow of lubricant was visualized by the combination of particles and vacant area. The flow velocity should be estimated from the average velocity of particles representing lubricant.

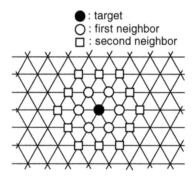

Fig. 6. Cell division and local neighbor definition

3.2 Local Neighbor Rules

The local neighbor was defined as the first and second neighbor, corresponding to the degree of influence to the target cell, as shown in Fig.6. The interactions between surrounding cells concerned in this simulation were the friction effect and the absorption effect among particles.

The friction effect, indicated by the parameter α, appeared in the interaction among particles and between particles and moving surface. In case of the interaction among particles, the friction parameter α_{pp} had the effect on the velocity of the target particle when the particles have different velocity. When a particle exists in a cell near the moving surface, the particle was given induced velocity from the moving surface caused by the friction parameter α_{pw}. The degree of influence corresponded to the distance from the surface.

It was assumed that a particle in the target cell might have absorption effect from surrounding particles in the local neighbor. This effect was indicated by the parameter β. In this simulation, the absorption effect was considered from the surface β_s, from the particle constructing fibrous microstructure β_{fm}, from the particle of short fibers

β_{sf}, and from the particles of lubricant β_l. Each effect was determined by a parameter set given as input data. The degree of absorption effect also corresponded to the distance from the target particle.

After the velocity of the target particle was estimated and it exceeded the threshold value v_{th} given as input data, then the particle moved to the neighboring cell. The cell to move was determined due to the direction of velocity vector and the position of the cell. When more than one particle was determined to move to the same cell, the particle having maximum velocity was selected to move and the state of the other particles were changed not be able to move.

4 Simulation Results and Discussions

Examples of simulation results are shown in Figs.7 and 8. The parameter set representing the friction and absorption effect is shown in Table 1.

Figure 7 shows the case where the lubricating grease is placed between a pair of parallel plates, and the bottom surface moves at a constant speed in the shear direction. The dynamic behavior of cluster formation of microstructures and the slipping boundary may be simulated qualitatively in reference to the experimental results shown in Section 2.2. The strong fibrous structure indicated inside of dotted circle moves along the direction changing the form and main direction in the flow of lubricating grease.

Table 1. Friction and absorption parameters

Friction parameters :	pp = 1.0							
	pw = 0.6 (for 1st neighbor)							
	pw = 0.3 (for 2nd neighbor)							
Absorption parameters :	{ s	fm	sf	l }	{ s	fm	sf	l }
fibrous structure	{0.1	0.1	1.5	0.0}	{0.1	0.1	1.5	0.0}
short fiber	{0.5	0.1	0.1	0.0}	{0.2	0.1	0.1	0.0}
lubricant	{-0.1	0.5	0.1	0.0}	{-0.1	0.2	0.1	0.0}
	1st neighbor				2nd neighbor			

The flow under shear deformation in wedge area is shown in Fig.8. In this case, the slipping boundary is clearly observed, and the reverse flow of lubricant can be simulated at several points in the wedge area. As described in the previous section, it is necessary to simulate dynamic behavior under shear deformation in two-dimension space parallel to the moving boundary in comparison with the experimental observation. But the tree-dimensional simulation would be a future plan.

The parameters representing the friction and absorption effect were determined by trial and error based on the experimental observation in this simulation. And it should be noted that these results may be the first simulation which shows the flow of lubricating greases including the dynamic behavior of clusters of thickening agent. It may be required to give the physical background to the degree of parameters in the next step of this research.

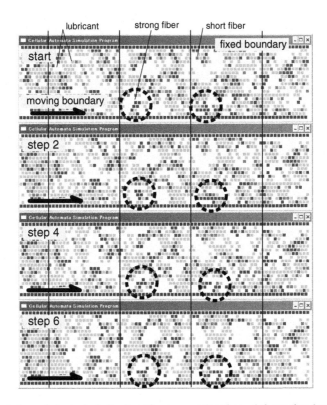

Fig. 7. Simulation of dynamic behavior of grease under shear deformation between parallel plates

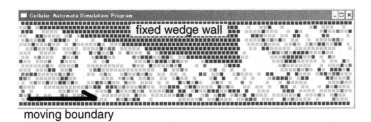

Fig. 8. Simulation of dynamic behavior under shear deformation in wedge-shape pathway

5 Conclusions

In this paper, a dynamic flow modeling of lubricating greases by Cellular Automata was proposed, in which the thickening agent and liquid lubricant as the component of greases are represented by virtual particles movable in simulation space. The microstructures of thickening agent were represented by the aggregation of particles, and dynamic behavior of microstructure was simulated under shear deformation of greases. Introducing the friction effect between the boundary wall and lubricating grease, and also among the particles, a slipping boundary appeared in the simulation. There is still little understanding as for the degree of the friction and absorption effects introduced in this simulation, and it is necessary to give physical background to the parameters expressing friction and absorption effects.

References

1. Braithwaite, E.R.: Lubrication and Lubricants, Elsevier Publishing Company (1967) 197-240
2. Cameron, A.: Principles of Lubrication, Longmans Green (1966) 528-541
3. Hoshino, M.: Theory of Grease Lubrication, Journal of Japanese Society of Tribologist, Vol.47, No.1 (2002) 8-14
4. Mori, Y.(ed): Theory of Grease Lubrication, Journal of Japanese Society of Lubrication, Vol.13, No.3 (1968) 146-151
5. Bondi, A., Cravath, A.M., Moore R.J. and Peterson,W.H.: Basic Factors Determining the Structure and Rheology of Lubricating Greases, The Institute Spokesman, March (1950) 12-18
6. Ilachinski,A.: Cellular Automata, World Scientific (2001) 463-506
7. Shiraishi,T., Morishita,S. Gavin,H.: Estimation of Equivalent Permeability in MR Fluid Considering Cluster Formation of Particles, Transaction of ASME, Journal of Applied Mechanics, Vol.71, No.2 (2004) 201-207

Interactive Terrain Simulation and Force Distribution Models in Sand Piles

Marta Pla-Castells[1], Ignacio García-Fernández[2], and Rafael J. Martínez[2]

[1] Previfor Simulation S.L. Alava, Spain
Marta.Pla@uv.es
[2] LSyM. Instituto de Robótica. Universidad de Valencia
P.O. Box 2085, 46071 Valencia, Spain
{Ignacio.Garcia, Rafael.Martinez}@uv.es

Abstract. This paper presents an application of Cellular Automata in the field of dry Granular Systems modelling. While the study of granular systems is not a recent field, no efficient models exist, from a computational point of view, in classical methodologies. Some previous works showed that the use of Cellular Automata is suitable for the development of models that can be used in real time applications. This paper extends the existing Cellular Automata models in order to make them interactive. A model for the reaction to external forces and a pressure distribution model are presented and analyzed, with numerical examples and simulations.

1 Introduction

Granular systems dynamics has been widely studied during the last decades. The traditional approach uses fluid models and particle system models for describing the flow of granular material and the formation of heaps [1]. However, granular systems show characteristics, such as the appearance of macroscopic patterns or avalanches, that cannot be properly modelled using this approach. For this reason, Cellular Automata (CA) have been used to model and study the statistical properties of these systems [2,3,4].

When simulating the behaviour of a granular system in a computer graphics application, the visualization of the system's external surface and its evolution is crucial [5]. The classical models employ fluid dynamics or discrete element modelling (DEM) to study the systems. Such techniques are not appropriate, since their computational cost makes them difficult to be included in real time simulations. In contrast, CA based models are simple and describe the granular system as a grid, so they can be very efficiently rendered by graphics processors [6].

This paper deals with modelling of dry, low cohesive, granular systems for real time computer simulation of terrain manipulation (tillage, excavation, mining,...). In this context, a simulation is considered to run in real time if computing a time interval of Δt seconds takes less than Δt using an standard personal computer.

S. El Yacoubi, B. Chopard, and S. Bandini (Eds.): ACRI 2006, LNCS 4173, pp. 392–401, 2006.

1.1   Granular Systems Modelling

A dry, low cohesive, granular system can be considered as a system with two layers; the standing layer, that forms the slope or the heap of the system, and the rolling layer, that is a thin layer that flows on the surface of the slope [1]. This behaviour can be modelled by means of a set of partial differential equations [8] that describe the evolution of these layers' thickness.

The model can be formulated as follows [8,9]: the system has two state variables, the height of the static layer, $s(x, y, t)$ and the height of the rolling layer, $r(x, y, t)$. The variation of these variables along time is expressed by the set of equations

$$r_t = v\nabla(r\nabla s) - \gamma(\alpha - |\nabla s|)r \qquad (1)$$
$$s_t = \gamma(\alpha - |\nabla s|)r$$

where α is the so called angle of repose of the system, γ is a parameter that expresses the rate of matter transfer between layers and v is the speed of the rolling layer, that is considered constant.

1.2   Description of the CA Model

In [7], some simplifications are taken upon this model in order to define an update rule for a CA model that reflects the behaviour of a granular system. The rolling layer is considered of constant width and the update rule is defined so that matter flows in the direction of maximum slope, indicated by the vector field $-\nabla h(x, y)$.

According to the model presented in [7], a CA on an $L \times L$ square grid is considered. This grid represents the plane on which a granular system with constant density ρ is laying. The value of each cell $h(i, j) \in \mathbb{R}$ represents the height of the system on the cell's centre (x_i, y_j). The set of points $\{(x_i, y_j, h(i, j))\}_{ij}$ is a discretization of the surface $\{(x, y, h(x, y))\}$.

For each cell, (i, j), an approximation to the gradient $\nabla h(x_i, y_j)$ is computed. When the slope angle obtained from this gradient $\arctan(|\nabla h|)$ is lower than the repose angle of the system α, the value of cell (i, j) remains unchanged. On the other case, if $\arctan(|\nabla h|) > \alpha$, the following update is done:

$$h(i, j) \leftarrow h(i, j) - z_+ \cdot (h_x(i, j) + h_y(i, j))$$
$$h(i + 1, j) \leftarrow h(i + 1, j) + z_+ \cdot h_x(i, j)$$
$$h(i, j + 1) \leftarrow h(i, j + 1) + z_+ \cdot h_y(i, j) \qquad (2)$$

where z_+ indicates the velocity of flowing matter, and h_x, h_y are the partial derivatives of $h(x, y)$ respect to x and y, computed numerically. For further detail on how the parameters of model (1) relate to the CA model, refer to [7].

The main advantages of this model are that it can be run in real time and that it can be easily managed in a 3D graphics environment. However, it lacks the possibility of interaction, which is a very important aspect in many virtual reality and simulation applications like a driving or civil heavy machine simulator.

The goal of this paper is to derive from (2) some models that allow to perform an interactive simulation of a granular system. Firstly, in Sect. 2, a CA model that will be able to consider the effect of the application of vertical forces in the system will be defined. Then, in Sect. 3, a model for the computation of pressure under the granular system, based on the CA representation will be developed. Finally, in Sect. 4 a brief analysis about computational issues will be done.

2   Interactive CA Model

In order to provide interactivity to the model (2), a brief analysis of the stress propagation behaviour within a granular system will be done. Following, and taking into account the main properties observed, a CA model to consider the effect of applying vertical forces to the surface of the system will be proposed.

In order to maintain the constant density condition, we will assume that our system is formed by a cohesionless material, with low compressibility. Examples of such systems are dry sand, or many fertilizers formed by dry, hard particles.

2.1   Stress Distribution in Granular Systems

A well stated granular systems property, observed both in real systems and in simulations, is the fact that the internal stress it is not exclusively propagated vertically within the system. It also spreads horizontally, and forming some angle ϵ with the vertical line axis [10,11,12,13]. In that way, if we consider the application of a vertical force at a point x on the top of the surface, the stress will be propagated not only downwards, but also horizontally pushing some material away.

In the case the force be strong enough, the pressure transmitted from point x to the surroundings will make some part of the material to move up, as this is the direction where the pressure offers less resistance. After all, when the whole process ends, the result is that the height of the material at the surrounding of x should have raised.

2.2   The Model

If we now discard any discussion about the granular system internal properties, the behaviour depicted above can be summarized as follows. If an strong enough force, f, is applied at a point x, a movement of material from point x to the points surrounding it happens. This system dynamics description is analogous to the model of the granular system presented by (2), where an increase of the material in cell i causes a displacement of material from that cell to its neighbours.

The new model proposed here is a modification of the original one, in which the displacement of material can be fired both, by a large difference in height, and by a big difference among the vertical forces applied to two neighbouring cells.

Let's consider a granular system on a square plane and the CA representation defined in [7]: an $L \times L$ grid with a variable $h(i,j)$ representing the height of the system at the centre of cell (i,j). Let $f(i,j)$ be the scalar value of the vertical force applied on each cell, and let F be a real function $F : \mathbb{R} \to \mathbb{R}$. We define two new variables for the CA: h_f as the composition $h_f(i,j) := F(f(i,j))$, and the sum $h' := h + h_f$.

For each cell (i,j), $\nabla h'$ is computed. Then, in the cells where $\arctan(|\nabla h'|)$ is higher than the resting angle of the system α, the state of the automata is updated according to the following rule:

$$
\begin{aligned}
h(i,j) &\leftarrow h(i,j) - z_+ \cdot (h'_x(i,j) + h'_y(i,j)) \\
h(i+1,j) &\leftarrow h(i+1,j) + z_+ \cdot h'_x(i,j) \\
h(i,j+1) &\leftarrow h(i,j+1) + z_+ \cdot h'_y(i,j)
\end{aligned}
\tag{3}
$$

where, again, z_+ represents the velocity of flowing matter, and h'_x, h'_y are approximations to the partial derivatives of $h'(x,y)$.

A first approximation to F is to consider the height of a square column of material that weights exactly f. That is

$$
F(f) = \eta \frac{f}{d^2 \rho g}
\tag{4}
$$

where g is the acceleration of gravity, ρ is the density of material, d^2 is the area of a cell of the automata and $\eta > 0$ is a parameter that allows to define how easily the force causes matter displacement.

The force function F defined by (4) integrates very well with contact force models based on spring-damper equations. These models are very common in real-time applications and avoid large object interpenetrations by means of applying forces proportional to their overlapping [14,15]. In case of a collision between a rigid object and a granular system modelled by (3), the force defined by (4) will cause the granular system deformation, allowing some object advance until the deformation be large enough to eventually stop it.

2.3   Numerical Simulations

Figure 1 shows two examples of the use of the proposed models with this contact force computation strategy. A ball has been left fall onto two system configurations; a plane, and a heap. The pictures correspond to the final equilibrium state, for a value of $\eta = 1$, with $d = 0.5$, $\alpha = 30^\circ$ and $z_+ = 0.05$ for the system's parameters. During the simulations, it has been observed that, as expected, if the value of η is increased, matter flow is higher. Thus lower resistance to penetration is offered, and higher terrain deformation can be observed. This effect has not been shown in figures for space reasons.

Although the proposed model does not reproduce the inner processes that drive the interaction between a granular system and a rigid object, the effect of the interaction is the observed behaviour [16,17], extending the application range of the one presented in [7], by allowing its use in interactive real time simulations.

Fig. 1. A ball thrown on two different configurations of the system. The parameters of the simulation are $\eta = 1$, with $d = 0.5$, $\alpha = 30°$ and $z_+ = 0.05$.

3   Pressure Distribution Model

In this section, an expression to compute the pressure supported by a cell i in the base of the automata, according to the state of the system, will be obtained. In order to simplify the resulting expressions, the developments will be firstly done over a unidimensional automata. Then, the way to extend the calculus to the general case will be shown.

Consider a unidimensional granular system, whose state is given by function $h(x)$, which indicates the height of every point. According to the discretization shown in [7], this system can be represented by means of a unidimensional CA, where every cell represents a point of the base. The cell value indicates the height of the system in that point.

Upon this system representation, we will split the automata in vertical slices, in such a way that the material existing over the i cell will be considered as a pile of blocks of height H (see Fig. 2). Let m_i^n be the weight of the n-th block located over the i cell, and let p_i^n be the total pressure existing on the base of the n-th block situated over the i cell.

In order to calculate the pressure over the base of one cell, we will consider, apart from the own block m_{i+j}^n, the pressure received by a finite number of blocks in the upper level[13], all of them centred over the i cell, $\{p_{i+j}^{n+1} : j = -r, \ldots, r\}$. For simplicity we will only consider the closest blocks $\{m_j^{n+1} : j = -1, 0, 1\}$, although the development for the general case is analogous.

The way pressure of layer n blocks propagates to layer $n-1$ will be expressed by means of a symmetric function $\phi : \mathbb{Z} \to [0, 1]$, accomplishing

$$\phi(k) = 0 \ \forall k : |k| > 1; \qquad \phi(-1) + \phi(0) + \phi(1) = 1 \qquad (5)$$

so that $\phi(t)$ indicates the rate of the pressure received by the base of block i in layer n which is propagated to block $i + t$ in layer $n - 1$.

For seek of simplicity, we will denote $\phi(i) = \phi^i$, and we will use the index summation convention, for which any repeated index i is summed over its range, $a^i b_i := \sum_i a^i b_i$. Using this notation the pressure over the base of the block at height n on cell i is

$$p_i^n = m_i^n + \sum_{k=-1}^{1} \phi^k p_{i+k}^{n+1} = m_i^n + \phi^k p_{i+k}^{n+1} \qquad (6)$$

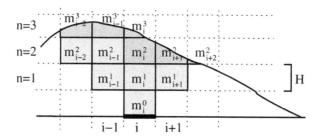

Fig. 2. Scheme of the system vertical decomposition in blocks of height H. The pressure that acts on the base of block m_i^n depends on the weight of blocks that are at the sides above it (see text).

From this relation among the weight on a level and the weight on the immediately superior level, after recursive substitution, the total weight over a cell in the base is

$$
\begin{aligned}
p_i^0 = m_i^0 &+ \phi^{k_1} m_{i+k_1}^1 + \phi^{k_1}\phi^{k_2} m_{i+k_1+k_2}^2 + \cdots \\
&+ \phi^{k_1}\cdots\phi^{k_{n-1}} m_{i+k_1+\cdots k_{n-1}}^{n-1} + \phi^{k_1}\cdots\phi^{k_n} p_{i+k_1+\cdots k_n}^n \qquad (7)
\end{aligned}
$$

where l again takes values in $\{-1, 0, 1\}$. This sum ends when the top of the system is reached, since if $N \in \mathbb{N}$ is such that NH overpasses the system's top, $m_i^n = 0, \forall i, \forall n > N$.

Equation (7) expresses a pressure model that can be applied to a granular system represented by a CA. This expression does not depend on the update rule of the CA, but only on its state. For this reason, it can be applied both to the original CA and to the one defined in Sect. 2. Note that, when considering the action of an external force f, it is only necessary to add equivalent weight to the block where the force is applied.

However, (7) involves the computation of a large summation whenever the system is updated, i.e. when one of the top m_i^n blocks is modified. This is unaffordable in real time applications, where a set of cells must be updated several times per second. For this reason, a rearrangement of (7) will be done to allow a more efficient pressure distribution update after a local change affecting a few cells.

Sorting the terms in (7), it can be rewritten as

$$
p_i^0 = \sum_{n=0}^{N} \sum_{j=-n}^{n} a_{jn} m_{i+j}^n \qquad (8)
$$

where

$$
a_{jn} = \sum_{k_1+\cdots+k_n=j} \phi^{k_1}\cdots\phi^{k_n}; \qquad a_{00} = 1. \qquad (9)
$$

Generalization of this model to a bi-dimensional system is straightforward, from (6), and using a bi-dimensional weight expression ϕ^{ij}. Total weight over

(i, j) cell is obtained as

$$p_{ij}^0 = \sum_{n=0}^{N} \sum_{s=-n}^{n} \sum_{t=-n}^{n} a_{stn} m_{i+sj+t}^n \tag{10}$$

where

$$a_{stn} = \sum_{k_1+\cdots+k_n=s} \sum_{l_1+\cdots+l_n=t} \phi^{k_1 l_1} \cdots \phi^{k_n l_n}; \qquad a_{000} = 1. \tag{11}$$

Therefore, from (10) and (11) it is possible to calculate pressure exerted by the system over every cell in the base.

This model depends of two parameters: the local distribution function ϕ, and the block height, H. Election of function ϕ determines how the material is distributed from one layer to the immediately lower. As indicated before, and according to several experimental and simulation studies [12,13], load is distributed towards the sides. Thus, it is recommended to take ϕ as $\phi(-1) = \phi(1) = \epsilon, \phi(0) = 1 - 2\epsilon$, with $\frac{1}{3} < \epsilon < \frac{1}{2}$. This makes that most of the load distribution will be addressed to the neighbour cells, and not to the one located just below.

By the other side, election of parameter H determines the angle with respect to the vertical in which the load is propagated, $\delta = \arctan \frac{d}{H}$. This angle depends on the characteristics of each system and should be obtained experimentally. However, and according to experimental and simulation results by several authors [11,12,13,19] most frequent values oscillate between 30° and 45° with respect to the vertical, which yields $d < H < 2d$.

3.1   Numerical Simulations

The model described previously has been implemented and simulated in order to be compared to other simulations and experimental observations. Numerical simulations have been performed, starting from an unidimensional system like the one used in the model developments. These simulations have used a system with $d = 0.5$, $\alpha = 30^o$ and $z_+ = 0.05$, with density $\rho = 1$, taking 30°, 34° and 45° for δ, and ϕ with $\epsilon = 0.4$. The most common experiment used in the literature has been reproduced, consisting on forming a heap by dropping material in a circular area over an horizontal plane. As results, the pressure distributions in the base of the automata, once the system reach the steady state, have been obtained.

In Fig. 3, simulation results show a curve that smoothly follows the heights of the system. This result is the same that the one obtained from other authors that have studied the case of material with constat density with numerical simulations [11], and furthermore, our results do not vary significantly from some other experimental results [10], except just in the fact that they show fluctuations that can not be viewed in our results due to the uniformity of our system.

It can be seen in Fig.3 that no substantial difference can be observed upon the election of parameter δ, which indicates robustness on the procedure followed to develop the model.

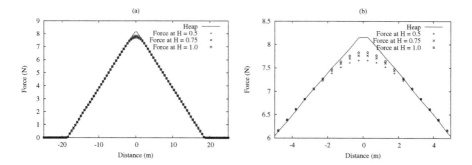

Fig. 3. Pressure distribution under a heap formed by deposition of material. The y axis represents the pressure over each point of the base of the heap, that has been formed by deposition of material at point $x = 0$. (a) Pressure distribution for different values of H. (b) Detail of the central region of the heap.

4   Computational Cost Analysis

In this work, the computational properties of the implemented algorithms are of great importance. The main motivation for developing CA based models has been the possibility to solve such models in the computer in real time, allowing their incorporation to graphics and simulation applications. Therefore we will focus in a detailed analysis of their computational cost, to show that they are efficient enough to make possible their inclusion in such kind of applications.

The new CA defined in this paper (3), has the same computational cost that the one described in [7]. This was predictable, since the new interactive model just incorporates four additions and two divisions per cell. Both offer a maximum cost of order L^2 for an automata $L \times L$, but an implementation sufficiently optimized offers a cost of order L [6]. As a result, they have been successfully used in real time graphic applications [7].

It is also necessary to evaluate the influence of the pressure model calculation in the overall performance of the new algorithm. Calculating the coefficients a_{stn} from (10) implies, if using a recursive algorithm and dynamic programming, a cost of order N^3. However, it is not necessary to make this computation every time (10) is computed, since they can be calculated only once for the chosen function ϕ.

Once the coefficients have been calculated, pressure over a cell computation, using (10), requires $(2n + 1)^2$ products for every level, $n = 1, \ldots, N$. However, the computation of the pressure for the whole system should be done just before the simulation starts, according to the system initial state.

As of that moment, only those cells that are modified by external causes will produce changes in the pressure distribution, affecting a square area centred in the cell. This square side will be the number of blocks of height H that are occupied on that cell. In these cells, only those terms involving the modified block need to be calculated.

Summarizing, we can state that, by one side, the CA model described in this paper has a computational cost that, with the appropriate implementation, can be reduced to be of order one respect to the side of the automata L. By the other side, the pressure distribution model in the base of the CA, although it requires a costly initialization, it can be done previously to the simulation. Once the model has been set up, the cost of the pressure update after a system modification is bounded by the square of the number of blocks of height H in which the system is split, N. This number is usually one order of magnitude below L.

Therefore, the given computational costs allow the use of the automata model in the realistic simulations included in interactive real time applications.

5   Conclusions

In this paper, an application of CA models to interactive simulation of granular systems is presented. The main goal has been to develop efficient models of a complex system, for which the usual modelling methodologies are computationally expensive.

The proposed models complement the work previously done [7], widening it use range, and allowing CA as a valid alternative to classical models in granular systems simulation. They improve the previous model by adding two modes of interactivity. On the one hand, a model of the system response to an external force is proposed. On the other hand, a model for pressure distribution at the base of the system is developed.

The models have a realistic behaviour, according to granular systems bibliography. The response model of Sect. 2 behaves properly from a qualitative point of view according to the numerical tests performed, and the force distribution obtained accomplishes the main properties shown by experimentation and other simulation methodologies.

Furthermore, it has been shown that both models offer a reduced computational cost during the simulation, which makes them suitable for real time interactive applications such as computer graphics applications and simulation applications.

As a future research, some of the aspects of this work will be studied in more detail. Different expressions for the force function f_h will be analyzed, according to several equilibrium conditions. Within this work, the pressure model has only been numerically investigated for the case $\phi(k) = 0$ if $|k| > 1$. Numerical experiments have to be done for the more general case. Also, some research has to be done in order to obtain revisions of the pressure model that reproduce effects observed in real and simulated systems, and that are not reproduced by the current model. In addition, new models for tool-terrain interaction will be developed in order to consider additional situations, such as the horizontal forces that appear on a vertical system-tool interface.

Acknowledgements

This work is supported by Universitat de València, project H-TERRAIN n. 20060238. Authors would also like to thank Prof. F. Ferri for the discussion about computational cost analysis.

References

1. Aradian, A., Raphael, E., de Gennes, P. G.: Surface flows of granular materials: a short introduction to some recent models. Comptes Rendus Physique. **3** (2002) 187–196.
2. Chen, C. C., den Nijs, M.: Directed avalanche processes with underlaying interface dynamics. Physical Review E. **66** (2002).
3. Prado, C., Olami, Z.: Inertia and break of self-organized criticality in sandpile cellular-automata models. Phys. Rev. A **45** (1992) 6665–6669
4. Nerone, N., Gabbanelli, S.: Surface fluctuations and the inertia effect in sandpiles. Granular Matter. **3** (2001) 117–120
5. Müller, M., Charypar, D., Gross, M.: Procedural modeling and animation: Particle-based fluid simulation for interactive applications. ACM SIGGRAPH/Eurographics Symposium on Computer Animation (2003) 154–159
6. Pla-Castells, M.: Nuevos modelos de sistemas granulares basados en autómatas celulares para simulación en tiempo real. MSc Thesis. Escuela Técnica Superior de Ingeniería, Universidad de Valencia. (2003)
7. Pla-Castells, M., et al.: Approximation of Continuous Media Models for Granular Systems Using Cellular Automata. Lec. Not. in Comp. Sc. (2004) 230–237.
8. Bouchaud, J. P., Cates, M. E, Prakash, J. R., Edwards, S. F.: A Model for the Dynamics of Sandpile Surfaces. J. Phys. I France. **4** (1994) 1383–1410.
9. Hadeler, K. P., Kuttler, C.: Dynamical models for granular matter. Granular Matter. **2** (1999) 9–18.
10. Geng, J., Longhi, E., Behringer, R. P., Howell, D. W.: Memory in two-dimensional heap experiments. Physical Review E. **64** (2001).
11. Liffman, K., Nguyen, M., Metcalfe, G., Cleary, P.: Forces in piles of granular material: an analytic and 3D DEM study. Granular matter. **3** (2001) 165–176.
12. Snoeijer, J. H., van Hecke, M., Somfai, E., van Saarloos, W.: Force and weight distributions in granular media: Effects of contact geometry. Physical Review E. **67** (2003).
13. Snoeijer, J. H., van Hecke, M., Somfai, E., van Saarloos, W.: Packing geometry and statistics of force networks in granular media. Physical Review E. **70** (2004).
14. Stewart. D. E.: Rigid-body dynamics with friction and impact. SIAM Review, **42** (1) (2000) 3–39.
15. García-Fernández, I., Pla-Castells, M., Martínez, R. J.: New models for fast contact force computation. Industrial Simulation Conference (2003) 401–407.
16. Maciejewski J., A. Jarzebowski, A.: Experimental analysis of soil deformation below a rolling rigid cylinder. Journal of Terramechanics. **41** (2004) 223–241.
17. Fukami K., et al.: Mathematical models for soil displacement under a rigid wheel. Journal of Terramechanics. **43** (2006) 287–301.
18. Geng, J., et al. : Footprints in Sand: The Response of a Granular Material to Local Perturbations. Physical Review Letters. **87** (2001).
19. Nouguier, C., Bohatier, C., Moreau, J. J., Radjai, F.: Force fluctuations in a pushed granular material. Granular matter. **2** (2000) 171–178.

A Linear Cellular Automaton over a Vector Space and Its Application to a Generalized Special Relativity

Tadakazu Sato

Toyo University, 2100 Kujirai Kawagoesi, Japan
tsato@cs.toyo.ac.jp

Abstract. The theory of special relativity is based on matrix theory. We generalize matrix theory from the viewpoint of cellular automata, and using this theory, we propose a new principle of special relativity.

1 Introduction

Special relativity is stated mathematically that fundamental laws of physics are invariant by the Lorentz transformation, where the Lorentz transformation is expressed as

$$L(\beta) = \frac{1}{\sqrt{1-\beta^2}} \begin{pmatrix} 1 & -\beta \\ -\beta & 1 \end{pmatrix}, \beta = \frac{\nu}{c}.$$

By $L(\beta)$, the distance $ds^2 = c^2 dt^2 - dx^2$ is preserved. However, this condition is too strict. Cellular automata are transformations with local interaction, and can thus be used to generalize $L(\beta)$ by regarding the matrix as a linear cellular automaton with no interaction (i.e., scope-1). $L(\beta)$ is consequently obtained as a special case given by $L_X(\beta, 0) = L(\beta)$, where $L_X(\beta, \gamma)$ is the generalized form of $L(\beta)$ including local interaction based on the concept of linear cellular automata. This case leads to a new principle of special relativity.

2 A Linear Cellular Automaton

A linear cellular automaton consists of a quadruplet $\langle Z, V_2, N, f \rangle$, where Z is the set of all integers (one-dimensional cell space), V_2 is a two-dimensional vector space (state set), N is a neighbor frame with $N = \{-r, \cdots, -1, 0, 1, \cdots, r\} \subset Z$, and f is a local map with scope $2r+1$, that is, f is a linear map from V_2^{2r+1} to V_2 such that $f = \sum_{j=-r}^{r} A_j x_j$, $A_j \in M_2(R)$ where $M_2(R)$ is a set of all matrices of 2×2 size over real field R.

For a local map, the parallel map f_∞ from V_2^Z to itself is defined as follows. For any $u_\infty, v_\infty \in V_2^Z$,

$$f_\infty(u_\infty) = v_\infty \Leftrightarrow v_i \equiv v_\infty(i) = f(u_{i-r}, \cdots, u_{i-1}, u_i, u_{i+1}, \cdots, u_{i+r}), \ i \in Z,$$

$$= \sum_{j=i-r}^{i+r} A_j u_j. \tag{1}$$

S. El Yacoubi, B. Chopard, and S. Bandini (Eds.): ACRI 2006, LNCS 4173, pp. 402–406, 2006.

From the theory of linear cellular automata, the parallel map can be expressed by a polynomial representation $F(X) = \sum\limits_{j=-r}^{r} A_j X^j$ and note that $V(X) = F(X)U(X)$ from (1), where $U(X) = \sum\limits_{i \in Z} U_i X^{-i}$ and $V(X) = \sum\limits_{j \in Z} U_j X^{-j}$.

Definition 1. *For $F(X)$, the transposed matrix A is defined as ${}^t F(X) = \sum\limits_{j=-r}^{r} {}^t A_j X^{-j}$.*

1. *In Euclidean space,*
   $F(X)$ *is orthogonal $\Leftrightarrow {}^t F(X) F(X) = I$.*
2. *In Minkowski space,*
   $F(X)$ *is orthogonal $\Leftrightarrow {}^t F(X) \Lambda F(X) = \Lambda$, where $\Lambda = \begin{pmatrix} 1 & 0 \\ 0 & -1 \end{pmatrix}$.*

3   A Generalization of a Matrix

1. The case of Euclidean space.

   Definition 2. *A generalization $A_X(\gamma_1, \cdots, \gamma_n)$ of a matrix A is defined as*

   $$A_X(\gamma_1, \cdots, \gamma_n) = U_X(\gamma_1, \cdots, \gamma_n) A U_X(\gamma_1, \cdots, \gamma_n)^{-1}$$

   where $U_X(\gamma_1, \cdots, \gamma_n)$ satisfies the following three conditions.
   (a) $U_X(0, \cdots, 0) = I$ (Identity matrix).
   (b) $U_X(\gamma_1, \cdots, \gamma_n)$ is orthogonal.
   (c) $U_X(\gamma_1, \cdots, \gamma_n)$ is continuous on each parameter.
   We simply write this generalization as $A \to A_X(\gamma_1, \cdots, \gamma_n)$. When the scope of $U_X(\gamma_1, \cdots, \gamma_n)$ increases, the number of the parameter also increases and the form of $U_X(\gamma_1, \cdots, \gamma_n)$ becomes more complicated. Therefore, finding $U_X(\gamma_1, \cdots, \gamma_n)$ with minimum scope except scope-1, we obtain $U_X(\gamma)$,where

   $$U_X(\gamma) = \frac{\gamma}{1+\gamma^2} \begin{pmatrix} 0 & 1 \\ 0 & \gamma \end{pmatrix} X^{-1} + \frac{1}{1+\gamma^2} \begin{pmatrix} 1 & -\gamma \\ \gamma & 1 \end{pmatrix} + \frac{\gamma}{1+\gamma^2} \begin{pmatrix} \gamma & 0 \\ -1 & 0 \end{pmatrix} X, \quad (-\infty \le \gamma \le \infty).$$

   Then $U_X(\gamma)$ has the following four conditions.
   (a) $U_X(0) = I$.
   (b) ${}^t U_X(\gamma) U_X(\gamma) = I$.
   (c) $U_X(\gamma)$ is continuous on γ.
   (d) $U_X(\gamma)$ has a minimum scope-3.

   Therefore, when $A \to A_X(\gamma)$, $A_X(\gamma)$ satisfies the following four conditions.
   (a) $A_X(0) = A$.
   (b) The generalization preserves algebraic property of A.
   (c) $A_X(\gamma)$ is continuous on γ.
   (d) $A_X(\gamma)$ has a minimum scope-5.

2. The case of Minkowski space.

Definition 3. *A generalization* $A_X(\gamma_1, \cdots, \gamma_n)$ *of a matrix* A *is defined as*

$$A_X(\gamma_1, \cdots, \gamma_n) = U_X(\gamma_1, \cdots, \gamma_n)AU_X(\gamma_1, \cdots, \gamma_n)^{-1}$$

where $U_X(\gamma_1, \cdots, \gamma_n)$ satisfies the following three conditions.
(a) $U_X(0, \cdots, 0) = I$ (Identity matrix).
(b) $U_X(\gamma_1, \cdots, \gamma_n)$ is orthogonal.
(c) $U_X(\gamma_1, \cdots, \gamma_n)$ is continuous on each parameter.
We simply write this generalization as $A \rightarrow A_X(\gamma_1, \cdots, \gamma_n)$.
Therefore, finding $U_X(\gamma_1, \cdots, \gamma_n)$ with minimum scope except scope-1, we obtain $U_X(\gamma)$, where

$$L_X(\beta, \gamma) = U_X(\gamma)L(\beta)U_X(\gamma)^{-1},$$

$$U_X(\gamma) = \tfrac{-\gamma}{1-\gamma^2}\begin{pmatrix} 0 & 1 \\ 0 & \gamma \end{pmatrix}X^{-1} + \tfrac{1}{1-\gamma^2}\begin{pmatrix} 1 & -\gamma \\ \gamma & 1 \end{pmatrix} + \tfrac{-\gamma}{1-\gamma^2}\begin{pmatrix} \gamma & 0 \\ 1 & 0 \end{pmatrix}X, \quad (-1 < \gamma < 1).$$

Then $U_X(\gamma)$ has the following four conditions.
(a) $U_X(0) = I$.
(b) ${}^tU_X(\gamma)\Lambda U_X(\gamma) = \Lambda$.
(c) $U_X(\gamma)$ is continuous on γ.
(d) $U_X(\gamma)$ has a minimum scope-3.

Therefore, when $A \rightarrow A_X(\gamma)$, $A_X(\gamma)$ satisfies the following four conditions.
(a) $A_X(0) = A$.
(b) The generalization preserves algebraic property of A.
(c) $A_X(\gamma)$ is continuous on γ.
(d) $A_X(\gamma)$ has a minimum scope-5.

4   A Generalization of $L(\beta)$

Let $L(\beta) \rightarrow L_X(\beta, \gamma)$, that is, $L_X(\beta, \gamma) = U_X(\gamma)L(\beta)U_X(\gamma)^{-1}$.

Properties of $L(\beta)$.

1. It has no local interaction.
2. It has a one parameter.
3. ${}^tL(\beta)\Lambda L(\beta) = \Lambda$.
4. It preserves the distance $ds^2 = c^2dt^2 - dx^2$.

Properties of $L_X(\beta, \gamma)$.

1. It is locally interactive.
2. It has 2-parameters.
3. ${}^tL_X(\beta, \gamma)\Lambda L_X(\beta, \gamma) = \Lambda$, $\quad \Lambda = \begin{pmatrix} 1 & 0 \\ 0 & -1 \end{pmatrix}$.
4. It preserves the distance $ds^2 = \sum_{i \in Z} c^2dt_i^2 - dx_i^2$.
5. $L_X(\beta, \gamma)$ has a minimum scope-5 with local interaction.
6. $L_X(\beta, \gamma)$ is continuous on γ.
7. $L_X(\beta, 0) = L(\beta)$.

Clearly, $L_X(\beta, \gamma)$ is weaker than $L(\beta)$, hence, the inclusion of the extra parameter γ.

5   A Physical Meaning of the Parameter γ

The parameter γ has no dimension physically, and hence, must express the ratio of some physical quantity such as length to length, time to time, mass to mass, energy to energy, or velocity to velocity (in which case it has already appeared in $L(\beta)$). The case of time to time, reduces to the case of length to length from the relation "$x = ct$". Other cases are similar. It is thus assumed that γ represents a length-to-length ratio. Since γ is bounded by 1, the following two possibilities exist:

(1) $\gamma = \frac{l}{l_{\max}}$, (2) $\gamma = \frac{l_{\min}}{l}$,

where l ,$l_{\min}$ and $l_{\max}$ are the length of the target object, the minimum length and the maximum one in the inertial system respectively.

Case (1) does not appear valid, since the universe is considered to be expanding. In case (2), it is considered that the Plank length is the smallest. The hypothesis is then $\gamma = \frac{l_{\min}}{l}$.

Therefore, (1) $L_X(\beta, \gamma) \to L(\beta)$ if $l \to \infty$ ($\gamma \to 0$), in other words, $L_X(\beta, \gamma)$ $\approx L(\beta)$ when $\gamma \approx 0$. (2) $L_X(\beta, \gamma)$ is gradually shifted away from $L(\beta)$ as l tends $l_{\min}$ and it exhibits remarkable features as $\gamma \to 1$.

Given the relation "$x = ct$", the new transformation suggests that there exists a minimal size or unit in space-time.

6   Role of β and γ

We next consider the effect of Lorentz contraction seen from other inertia systems. Since $l_{\min}$ and l are contracted at the same rate, we conclude that γ is invariant.

Therefore, the roles of β and γ in $L(\beta)$ and $L_X(\beta, \gamma)$ are as follows.

1. In $L(\beta)$, C(velocity of light) is invariant for two different inertia systems, whereas the parameters v and β are not.
2. In $L_X(\beta, \gamma)$, the parameter γ is invariant for two different inertia systems, whereas l_{min} and l are not.

7   A New Principle of Special Relativity

Since $L(\beta)$ approximates $L_X(\beta, \gamma)$ and does not contain the parameter γ, $L(\beta)$ and $L_X(\beta, \gamma)$ diverge remarkably as γ tends toward 1. Can $L_X(\beta, \gamma)$ thus be applied to micro space-time? Correction of the principle of conventional special relativity then leads to a new principle of special relativity as follows.

Proposal
"The fundamental laws of physics are invariant by the Lorentz transformation $L_X(\beta, \gamma)$ with local interaction".

In the conventional theory, space-time is considered to be divisible into small pieces endlessly. However, the present theory suggests that there exists a minimal size or unit in space-time. The physical validity of this theory will need to be determined experimentally.

References

[1] A. Einstein, The principle of relativity, Dover, New York, 1958.
[2] M. Ito, N. Osato and M. Nasu, Linear cellular automata over Z , J. Comput. System Sci. 27 No. 2 (1983) 125-140.
[3] T. Sato, Cellular automata and their applications to mathematics, Comp 2003-68, Technical report of IEICE, 2003.
[4] T. Sato, Matrix theory from the viewpoint of cellular automata, RIMS Koukyuroku, 1437, 2005.
[5] T. Sato, Linear cellular automata and their applications to physics, International Workshop Automata 2005, Poland, 2005.
[6] T. Sato, A new Lorentz transformation, The IEICE Society Conference, 2005.

A Cellular Automata Model for Ripple Dynamics

Luca Sguanci, Franco Bagnoli, and Duccio Fanelli

*Dept. Energy, Univ. of Florence, Via S. Marta 3, 50139 Firenze, Italy
luca.sguanci@unifi.it,
franco.bagnoli@unifi.it,
duccio.fanelli@cmb.ki.se

Abstract. We present a simple cellular automata model to address the issue of aeolian ripple formation and evolution. Our simplified approach accounts for the basic physical mechanisms and enables to reproduce the observed phenomenology in the framework of a near-equilibrium statistical mechanics formulation.

1 Background

The complex interaction between a granular material and a fluid gives rise to erosion patterns, dunes and ripples. Such collective phenomena are particularly influenced by the distribution of the fluid velocity, that may vary widely in space and time, and by the shape of the grains and their relative density, that gives origin to buoyancy. Importantly, the instantaneous fluid velocity field depends on the profile of the sand bed, which is modified by erosion and deposition, and on the shielding effect of saltating particles.

As reported in Ref. [1], ripples are characterized as being asymmetric and their formation and persistence is determined by flux intensity. Small ripples are observed to travel faster than large ones and the temporal evolution of the maximum ripple height is limited and not linear. Theoretical studies aim at reproducing some of these relevant aspects.

To address the erosion/deposition process, continuum models of mechanics can be employed [2,3,4]. Alternatively, accurate hydrodynamical descriptions have been proposed and deeply investigated [9,5,6,7]. The latter allows to quantitatively study the process of ripple formation by incorporating a detailed representation of the fluid flow via Navier-Stokes equation, and/or facing the problem of considering the flow near the soil. However, these approaches are computationally expensive and difficult to treat analytically in presence of complex and time-dependent boundaries, or when turbulence and other fluctuating aspects play an active role. Linear stability analysis [2,3,8] enables to predict the instability regime of a flat surface and quantifies its associated growth rate.

To gain more insight into the crucial interplay between erosion and deposition, beyond the linear approximation, a series of simplified theoretical frameworks

---

* Also Center for the Study of Complex Systems (CSDC) and INFN, sezione di Firenze.

S. El Yacoubi, B. Chopard, and S. Bandini (Eds.): ACRI 2006, LNCS 4173, pp. 407–416, 2006.

(toy models) have been developed, focusing only on those aspects supposed to be the relevant ones. Following these lines, it is customary to replace the complex fluid velocity distribution with a limited number of aggregated data, like the average shear velocity and the associated fluctuations.

Simple models of sand ripples dynamics were first introduced by Anderson [10,11] for grain segregation and stratigraphy. A discrete stochastic model was further proposed about a decade ago by Werner and Gillespie [12]. Another minimal model, widely adopted in the relevant literature, was proposed the same year by Nishimori and Ouchi [13] and therefore termed NO model. Within this scenario, the saltation and reptation are accounted for and shown to produce the spontaneous formation of characteristic ripple patterns. Though it represents a significant step forward in the comprehension of the basic mechanism underlying the phenomenon, the NO model allows for non realistic structures of infinite heights, since in this model there is no explicit or implicit mechanism that leads to the appearance of a critical angle of repose. Recently, Caps and Vandewalle [14] modified the preexisting scheme by including explicitly the effect of avalanches (SCA model: Saltation Creep and Avalanches). This modification results in asymmetric ripple profiles and induces a saturation for the maximal height.

Cellular automata modeling of sand transportation was pionereed by Anderson and Bunnan [15] and by Werner and Gillespie [12]. In these models, the driving mechanism for sand transport is the saltation/reptation dynamics, eventually complemented by toppling, that corresponds to diffusion in a continuous model. Masselot and Chopard [17,16] also introduced a cellular automata for snow and sand transportation. They explicitly modeled the fluid flow by means of lattice Boltzmann methods, while the granular phase is represented as a probabilistic cellular automaton. The erosion mechanism here is modeled by a constant probability of detachment, and local rearrangements are again achieved by a toppling mechanism.

The elementary building blocks of these stochastic models, like the erosion, deposition and toppling steps, have a phenomenological nature, implying that the probability of their occurrence has to be measured experimentally.

In this paper, we shall investigate the process of pattern (ripple) formation, emerging due to the interactions between a fluid (air) flow and a granular material (sand). More precisely, we propose to adopt a standard statistical mechanics approach to account for the evolution of the system, coupled to an external forcing that drives it out of equilibrium. The role of temperature is here played by the fluctuations of the velocity field.

This local-equilibrium dynamics enables to reproduce the main characteristics of ripple dynamics, like the observed stable states and the saturation of ripple height, without including an explicit mechanism for toppling or other local rearrangements. Finally, it is worth emphasizing that this simple scheme can be straightforwardly extended to accommodate a more detailed description of a real fluid. In fact, starting from this model, it is possible to develop a two-dimensional model in which the pattern constituted by the heights of the particles composing

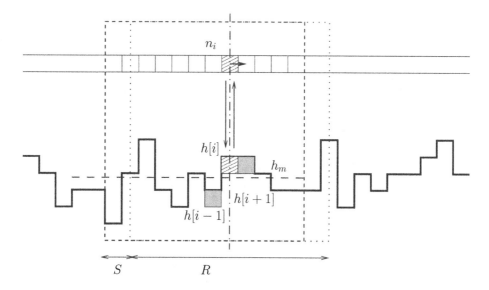

Fig. 1. Sand bed schematization in the 1D model. For a given site i of height h_i, the symmetric interval of neighbors of amplitude R is shown (dotted line). In order to account for flux asymmetry the interval considered is shifted by an amount S (dashed line).

the ripples acts like a boundary condition and the fluid flow evolution is computed according to the Lattice Boltzmann Equation. By doing this it is also possible to compute in an approximate way the fluid drag in a given point of the bottom, and also the trajectory of an entrained particle. This extension is very similar to that used in [16].

2   The Theoretical Framework

We consider a one dimensional discrete model, L being the extension of the segment partitioned in N equally spaced intervals, and assuming periodic boundary conditions, Fig. 1.

Label with h_i the number of particles constituting the ith slice of the *sand bed*. In other words h_i represents the height of the ith site. Further, we consider a bunch of n_i particles flowing over the bed. The system is therefore constituted of two interacting layers of particles.

The two processes governing the dynamical evolution of the system are respectively *erosion*, which occurs when a resting grain belonging to the surface of the sediment layer is entrained by the fluid and *deposition*, that mimics the deposition of a flowing grain.

More precisely, the following scheme is put forward. First the bunch of flowing particles it is shifted forward at every time step. Then focusing on the ith site, we select an interval of R neighbors, asymmetrically shifted by an amount S, see

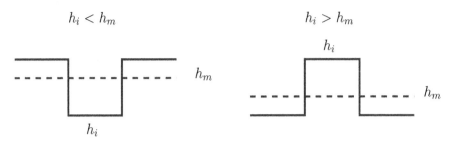

Fig. 2. In order to account for bed geometry and hydrodynamics effects, we suppose a grain on the bed surface to experience a force proportional to the difference between its height and the mean height of a local interval of neighbors. In particular, the erosion (deposition) probability increases as the height of the site being considered is higher (lower) than the mean height of the neighboring sites.

Fig. 1. The amplitude of the interval accounts for the range of local interactions and is shown to be correlated to the shape of the ripple. The quantity S is introduced to model hydrodynamics effects, such as lift and drag forces [18,8,9], which result in an asymmetry of the flow.

We then calculate the mean height of the selected interval, h_m. As a reasonable hypothesis, assume that the probability to experience an erosion event increases when augmenting the gap between h_i and h_m, under the constraint $h_i > h_m$. Conversely, the deposition will most probably occur when the positive difference $h_m - h_i$ gets larger, Fig. 2.

Following the previous reasoning, as a first approximation, we suppose the force acting on a particle to depend on the difference between the height of the site being considered and the mean height of the neighbors. The energy scales therefore as:

$$E_i = (h_m - h_i)^2 . \tag{1}$$

The erosion and deposition processes are hence characterized by means of the following change in energy:

Erosion	Deposition
$h_i(t+1) = h_i(t) - 1$	$h_i(t+1) = h_i(t) + 1$
$\Delta E_{er,i} = 2(h_m - h_i + 0.5)$	$\Delta E_{dep,i} = 2(h_i - h_m + 0.5)$

Consequently, it is reasonable to assume the erosion and deposition probabilities [19]:

$$P_{er,i} = \begin{cases} 1 & \text{if } \Delta E_{er,i} < 0, \\ \exp(-\beta_e \Delta E_{er,i}) & \text{otherwise;} \end{cases}$$

$$P_{dep,i} = \begin{cases} 1 & \text{if } \Delta E_{dep,i} < 0, \\ \exp(-\beta_d \Delta E_{dep,i}) & \text{otherwise.} \end{cases}$$

where β_e and β_d are constant parameters, analogous to the inverse of effective temperatures $1/T_e$, $1/T_d$. The system is out of equilibrium, and these temperatures are assumed to be related to the amplitude of the fluctuations of the velocity field in correspondence with the typical erosion and deposition events.

The local evolution rule is based on a Metropolis Monte Carlo dynamics [19]: first the deposition takes place followed by the subsequent erosion step. We decided to use this kind of Monte Carlo dynamics as a starting point. Indeed we are experimenting with other dynamics and also trying to extract the transition probabilities from a more detailed model, that explicitly accounts for the evolution of the fluid flow.

Focusing on the ith site, the deposition step yields:

1. for each of the n_i flowing particles a uniformly distributed random number r is extracted;
2. if $r < P_d$ deposition occurs and the height of the site is increased by one, $h_i(t+1) = h_i(t) + 1$, while the bunch of flowing particles is decreased by one, $n_i(t+1) = n_i(t) - 1$,

Analogously, the erosion is characterized by:

1. a uniformly distributed in the unit interval random number r is generated;
2. the site is eroded if $r < P_e$; in this case the height of the site is decreased by one, $h_i(t+1) = h_i(t) - 1$, and the pool of eroded particle is increased by one, $n_i(t+1) = n_i(t) + 1$.

The procedure is iterated and the evolution of the heights monitored.

3   Numerical Results

In our simulation we assumed an initial uniformly random generated river-bed. Small inhomogeneities are magnified as time evolves, and eventually result in macroscopic ripples that display a characteristic asymmetric profile.

A sequence of successive snapshots of the dynamics is presented in Fig. 3 and allows to qualitatively investigate the process of formation of coherent structures.

The displacement of a ripple is a consequence of the combined effects of erosion and deposition: the grains are eroded in the stoss side and deposited in the lee one. This is indeed a dynamical mechanism: there is a continuous exchange between the particles at rest and the ones belonging to the flowing population. The net effect is that the lower end of the stoss side is eroded and this matter deposes in the lee part, leading to the displacement of the ripple with a velocity that decreases with size.

The interaction mechanism of two ripples is rather complex, as illustrated by the "collision" of two ripples of similar size reported in Fig. 4. In order for the collision to occur, the front ripple has to be larger than the rear one, which is consequently faster. When the two ripples approach, the lower part of the stoss side of the front ripple is not eroded anymore. Such an effect is determined (in the model) by the increasing average height, that includes the contribution of the approaching rear ripple. In the reality, this corresponds to the reduction in erosion due to the shielding effect of the rear ripple.

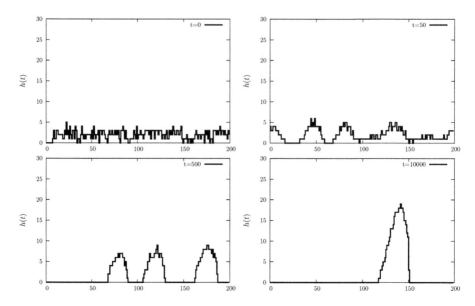

Fig. 3. Time snapshots of ripple dynamics. Note that the scales of the two axes are different.

The region of the stoss side next to this one becomes the source of eroded particles, thus forming a local sink. The size of the front ripple is decreased and its speed increased. If the relative difference of velocity of the two ripples is low enough (*i.e.* for similar ripples of similar size) this depression may proceed so to make the front ripple detach from the rear one, Fig. 4.

If the rear ripple is small, the sinking region is continuously moved downwind and finally the two ripples coalesce. This mechanism is illustrated in Fig. 5. In the third panel ($t = 825$) one can still recognize a signature of this process: focusing on the right ripple, originated by the interaction of two ripples of different size (see first panel), one can still identify the protruding bump on the lee side. This is the relic of the highest peak displayed by the right ripple in the second panel, that experienced a reduction in size and consequently proceeded faster. However, this bump is eventually screened by the rear portion of the ripple. As a consequence it stops and is therefore engulfed in the incoming massive agglomeration.

These observations are in agreement with direct measurements and provide a first validation of our simplified interpretative framework [1].

Label with l the linear size of a typical ripple and assume h to represent its characteristic height. By tuning the parameter R, *i.e.* varying the extension of the segment that defines the interacting region, one modulates the ratio h/l and operates an a priori selection among various types of structures (ripples, megaripples, giantripples) based on their intrinsic geometry. The crucial role of R has been investigated through a dedicated campaign of simulations: by assigning larger values to R corresponds to generating less peaked structures, which translates into a systematic reduction of the quantitative indicator h/l.

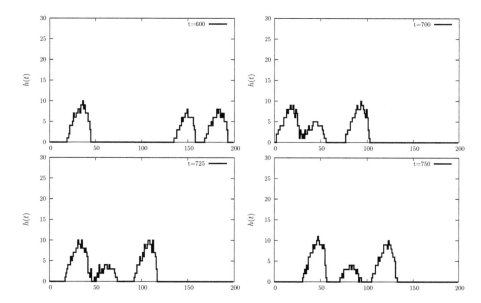

Fig. 4. When two ripples of similar sizes encounter, an exchange in their relative positions occur (take into account periodic boundary conditions)

Focusing on ripples, we assume $R = 32$, and speculate on the role of the remaining parameters S (the asymmetry of the interval being considered) and β_d in the formation of the ripple [20]: few quantities of paramount importance are monitored and compared with analogous predictions reported in the classical literature [13,14].

As already anticipated, within our simplified scheme, the ripples present an asymmetric shape which can be measured by introducing the *aspect ratio* σ ($\sigma > 0$):

$$\sigma = \frac{x_s}{x_l}, \qquad (2)$$

where x_s (resp. x_l) stands for the projection of the stoss (resp. lee) slope on the horizontal axis, as depicted in Fig. 6. If $\sigma = 1$ the ripples are symmetric, while $\sigma \neq 0$ implies an asymmetry. In the main panel of Fig. 7, the evolution of the ripple aspect ratio σ is plotted as function of time for different values of the ratio S/R. An initial growth is observed, followed by a subsequent saturation towards an asymptotic plateau, σ_{as}. A self-consistent selection mechanism is therefore operated by the system and eventually only one specific class of ripples arises and occupies the one dimensional lattice. The ansatz, $\sigma = \sigma_{as} (1 - \exp(-\alpha t))$ is numerically fitted to the simulated profiles of Fig. 7 and shown to interpolate well the data. To better visualize the tendency of enhancing the degree of asymmetry for increased values of the local distortion S (working at constant R), σ_{as} is represented versus the ratio S/R in the top-left inset of Fig. 7. Further, to provide a complete characterization of the morphology of the ripple, we calculate the angle of repose θ_r. This is defined as follows: if a bunch of particles is poured

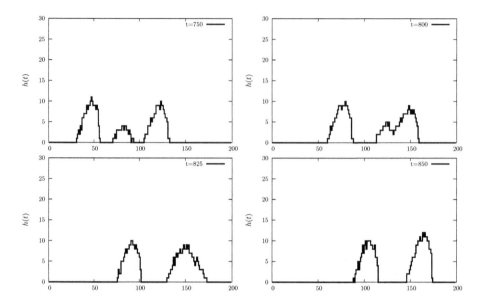

Fig. 5. An encounter between ripples of different sizes results in the merging of the structures

onto a flat surface, a conical pile will form. The angle between the edge of the pile and the horizontal surface is the angle of repose. We calculate it as the angle between the segment linking the right-extreme grain of the ripple base with the grain having the maximum height and the horizontal. This angle is dynamically selected within our proposed approach, as function of the control quantity S/R.

The time evolution of σ was previously monitored in Ref. [14] for both the NO and SCA models. The original NO formulation predicts almost symmetric profiles which in turn implies $\sigma \simeq 1$. Conversely, for the case of the SCA σ grows linearly in time and then relaxes to a final value. This remarkable improvement was achieved by Caps and Vandewalle by postulating the existence of a repose angle θ_r and modeling the process of avalanches, not included in the NO philosophy. It is worth emphasizing that a similar mechanism is reproduced here without invoking a priori the existence of a limiting angle. Note that the saturation for σ is exponentially approached, as obtained in Ref. [14].

Further, simulations are performed to shed light into the role of β_d. The normalized density of particles ρ is calculated as a function of the deposition distance, for different values of β_d. Results (not displayed here) suggest that for larger values of β_d, the particles spend more time in the surrounding halo and retard the deposition event. We are therefore led to conclude that β_d controls the characteristic length of the reptation process.

Finally, we investigated the dynamical evolution of the maximum ripple height h_{max}. In [14] the SCA model was shown to reproduce the non linear evolution of the ripple amplitude h_{max}, this success being ascribed to the new ingredients introduced with respect to the NO scenario. Results of our simulations are

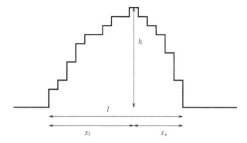

Fig. 6. Ripple schematization, where x_l (x_s) is the projection of the lee (stoss) slope and h is the ripple height

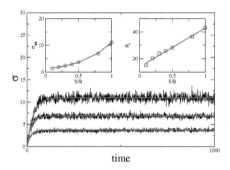

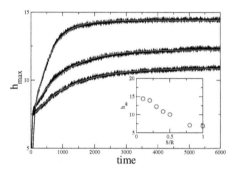

Fig. 7. Time evolution of ripple asymmetry σ as a function of the ratio S/R. Left-inset: asymptotic value of ripple asymmetry as a function of S/R. Right-inset: plot of the dynamic angle of repose θ_r against the ratio S/R (circles: numerical values; solid line: numerical fit).

Fig. 8. Exponential increase of the maximum ripple height h_{max} with time for different values of the ratio S/R. Small inset: The asymptotic height h_{as} is plotted as a function of the ratio S/R.

displayed in Fig. 8: as for the SCA an exponential growth law is found, thus reinforcing the validity of our probabilistic approach as an alternative tool to address the relevant issue of ripple formation. The asymptotic height, h_{as}, is plotted in the small inset, as function of the ratio S/R.

4   Conclusion

In this paper we propose a local-equilibrium model to study the dynamics of aeolian ripple. The model is shown to successfully reproduce key observed features, despite its intrinsic simplicity. In particular, the irreversible and not trivial coarsening dynamics with merging and scattering of structures, the saturation of the maximum height of the ripples and the asymmetry of ripple structures have been reproduced. The results are critically compared with the classical literature [13,14], outlining the role of the parameters involved in our formulation and their physical interpretation. This simple theoretical picture can be further extended to accommodate a more detailed description of the fluid flow and include a more complete representation of the granular phase.

References

1. R.A. Bagnold, *The Physics of Blown Sand and Desert Dunes* (Chapman and Hall, London, 1941).
2. O. Terzidis, P. Claudin, and J.-P. Bouchaud, Eur. Phys. J. B **5**, 245 (1998).
3. A. Valance and F. Rioual, Eur. Phys. J. B **10**, 543 (1999).
4. L. Prigozhin, Phys. Rev. E **60**, 729 (1999).
5. A. Valance, Eur. Phys. J. B **45**, 433 (2005).
6. P.-Y. Lagree, Phys. Fluids **15**, 2355 (2003).
7. Z. Csahók , C. Misbah, F. Rioual, A. Valance, Eur. Phys. J. E **3**, 71 (2000).
8. B. Andreotti, P. Claudin, S. Douady, Eur. Phys. J. B **28**, 321 (2002).
9. K. Kroy, G. Sauermann, H.J. Herrmann, Phys. Rev. Lett. **88**, 54301 (2002).
10. R. S. Anderson, Sedimentology **34**, 943 (1987).
11. R. S. Anderson, Earth Sci. **29**, 77 (1990).
12. B. T. Werner and D. T. Gillespie, Phys. Rev. Lett. **71**, 3230 (1993).
13. H. Nishimori, N. Ouchi, Phys. Rev. Lett. **71**, 197 (1993).
14. H. Caps, N. Vandewalle, Phys. Rev. E, **64**, 041302 (2002).
15. R. S. Anderson, K. L. Bunan, Nature **365**, 740 (1993).
16. A. Dupuis, From a lattice Boltzmann model to a parallel and reusable implementation of a virtual river. PhD thesis, University of Geneva, June 2002, http://cui.unige.ch/spc/PhDs/aDupuisPhD/phd.html
17. A. Masselot and B. Chopard, Europhys. Lett. **42**, 259 (1998); B. Chopard, A. Masselot and A. Dupuis, Comp. Phys. Comm. **129**, 167, (2002).
18. W. Graf, *Hydraulics of sediment transport*, (McGraw-Hill, New York, 1971).
19. N. Metropolis, A.W. Rosenbluth, M.N. Rosenbluth. A.H. Teller and E. Teller, J. Chem. Phys. **21**, 1087 (1953).
20. The quantity β_e refers to the granular material selected and indirectly measure its degree of packing and internal cohesion. In the present study we assume $\beta_e = 1$.

A Cellular Automata Simulation Tool for Modelling and Automatic VLSI Implementation of the Oxidation Process in Integrated Circuit Fabrication

Georgios Ch. Sirakoulis

Democritus University of Thrace, Department of Electrical and
Computer Engineering, Laboratory of Electronics,
GR 67100 Xanthi, Greece
gsirak@ee.duth.gr
http://utopia.duth.gr/~gsirak

Abstract. As device lots become more and more expensive, the importance of technology computer-aided design (TCAD) is increasing. TCAD can be used to simulate device fabrication and performance and to avoid processing experimental lots. Cellular Automata (CAs) have been applied successfully to the simulation of several physical systems and semiconductor processes, and have been extensively used as VLSI architecture. This paper describes a TCAD system for the simulation of the two-dimensional oxidation process in integrated circuit fabrication. The TCAD system is fully automated and is also able to support, the hardware implementation of the corresponding CA algorithm, leading to its execution by dedicated parallel processor. The simulation results are in good qualitative and quantitative agreement with experimental data reported in literature. The proposed system produces as output the corresponding VHDL code, which leads directly to the FPGA implementation of the CA algorithm.

1 Introduction

In the semiconductor industry, device densities have grown exponentially in the last three decades. With each new generation of integrated circuit (IC) manufacturing technology, the complexities of IC fabrication processes and devices are increasing significantly [1]. Process modelling is an integral portion of technology computer-aided design (TCAD) and can be used to predict device structures and doping. Truly predictive process modelling has proven to be a demanding goal, because the controlling physics is complicated and difficult to investigate experimentally [1]. As a result, TCAD that accurately predicts the process and device characteristics of anticipated wafer fabrication technology is indispensable for future IC fabrication technology and device development.

Oxidation and selective oxidation is an important process in IC fabrication. Layers of SiO_2 are used as insulators, dielectrics, protective films, and, at several fabrication stages, as masks, passivators, and inhibitors. The kinetics of oxidation of Si is fairly well understood for one-dimensional problems [2-4]. Whereas, oxidation simulation

S. El Yacoubi, B. Chopard, and S. Bandini (Eds.): ACRI 2006, LNCS 4173, pp. 417–426, 2006.

in one dimension has been successful, there are many difficulties in simulating the oxidation in two dimensions [2], because of the advancement of the Si-SiO$_2$ and SiO$_2$-air fronts during oxidation, particularly in bounded domains. Numerical techniques for the oxygen diffusion with moving oxidation fronts on unbounded domains have been successfully developed [3], but these methods can not be applied to the cases of oxidation of non-planar surfaces, and oxidation through a mask, which are common in IC fabrication.

In order to develop an efficient TCAD system for the modelling of the oxidation fabrication process for which the hardware implementation will be straightforward Cellular Automata (CAs) were chosen as the simulation and implementation method. CAs have been applied successfully to IC fabrication processes, such as photolithography [5-6], oxidation [7] and deposition [8]. On the other hand, CAs have been extensively used as a VLSI architecture. CAs are one of the computational structures best suited for a VLSI realization [9]. The CA architecture offers a number of advantages and beneficial features such as simplicity, regularity, ease of mask generation, silicon-area utilization, and locality of interconnections.

The proposed TCAD system, named "*CA_OXIDA_TCAD*", is an interactive tool offering the power of automated modelling and VLSI implementation of oxidation process with CAs, while hiding architecture and programming issues from the user. It is both, a computational tool for modelling oxidation process and an automated producer of Very High Speed Integrated Circuit (VHSIC) Hardware Description Language (VHDL) synthesizable code for the hardware implementation of the CA algorithms that model oxidation process. More specifically, the user inputs to the TCAD system are: the CA lattice size, the maximum process time and the initial and boundary conditions imposed by the oxidation process, namely process geometry, mask presence, defects presence and defects temperature. The user can change any one or all of the above input parameters until the CA best models the oxidation process. Then, the TCAD system produces the graphical simulation results of the CA algorithm. The obtained simulation profiles of the oxidation process are found in very good qualitative agreement with experimental and simulation results found in the literature [2]. However, it should be mentioned that these simulation profiles are not yet calibrated with experimental results. After that, *CA_OXIDA_TCAD* using a translation algorithm, that checks the CA parameters values previously determined by the user, automatically produces the synthesizable VHDL code that describes the CA algorithm. This VHDL code can be fed either into a commercial VLSI CAD system, and, as a result, the layout of the dedicated hardware that executes the CA algorithm can be designed, too, or to any FPGA Programmer. Furthermore, research workers could use the *CA_OXIDA_TCAD* simulation interface to calibrate and validate the CA algorithm of oxidation model using experimental data and produce the corresponding dedicated hardware. Another attractive possible feature of *CA_OXIDA_TCAD* presented here is the implementation of the resulting VHDL code in a FPGA, able to perform some real experiments, and to serve as a powerful "virtual lab" dedicated to the modelling of the oxidation process.

2 The Oxidation Process and the Corresponding CA Algorithm

In the oxidation process oxidant from the gas phase interacts with the Si surface, and SiO_2 is formed. After the oxidation of Si surface, the oxidant diffuses through holes in SiO_2 towards the Si-SiO_2 interface to form new SiO_2 material. This interaction is accompanied by a large volume increase. The reaction is aided by viscoelastic flow of the oxide film towards the surface. Therefore two interfaces are formed: the Si-SiO_2 and the SiO_2-air interface, which advance at different rates in opposite directions [2].

Oxidation is a nonequilibrium process, with the driving force being the deviation of concentration from equilibrium. According to the Deal and Grove model [2, 4], the oxidant is transported from the bulk of the gas phase to the gas-oxide interface with a flux F_1, is transported across the existing oxide towards the Si with a flux F_2, and reacts with Si at the Si-SiO_2 interface with a flux F_3. The steady state is reached when:

$$F_1 = F_2 = F_3 \qquad (1)$$

The fluxes are given by:

$$F_1 = h_G \left(C_G - C_s \right), \ F_2 = -D \frac{dC}{dx}, \ F_3 = k_s C_i \qquad (2)$$

where h_G is the gas-phase mass-transfer coefficient, C_G is the oxidant concentration in the bulk of the gas, C_S is the oxidant concentration adjacent to the oxide surface, D is the oxidant diffusion coefficient, C is the oxidant concentration in the oxide, k_S is the rate of the silicon oxidation surface reaction, and C_i is the oxidant concentration at the oxide-Si interface.

Solving equations (1)-(2), the following solution is obtained:

$$d = \frac{A}{2} \left(-1 + \sqrt{1 + \frac{4B(t+\tau)}{A^2}} \right) \qquad (3)$$

where d is the oxide thickness and the constants A, B, and τ are fitting parameters of the mathematical model described above. The values of these parameters, which are determined by fitting the model results to experimental results, can be found in any textbook on IC fabrication technology [1]. To produce an oxide of thickness d_o, a Si layer with thickness $0.44 \, d_o$ must be consumed. The Deal-Grove model describes very well the oxidation process in one dimension, but its extension to two dimensions is very difficult. More specifically, as described analytically in [7], if the Deal-Grove model is used, an unphysical discontinuity will appear at the air-Si interface.

If unit time is small enough (i.e. when $[4B(t+\tau)/A^2 < 1]$), then equation (3) becomes:

$$d \approx \frac{B}{A} \left(t + \tau \right) \qquad (4)$$

CAs are able to produce a variety of fronts, if the proper local rules are used. To simulate the two-dimensional oxidation process using CAs, a local rule must be found that produces fronts like the ones which are provided by the Deal-Grove model. The area that contains the Si, the SiO_2, and the air is divided into a matrix of identical square cells with side length a, as shown in Fig. 1, and it is represented by a CA by assuming that each cell is a CA cell. The algorithm becomes more accurate as the side length a is reduced, because the number of cells is increased, but this leads to greater computation times and memory requirements. The value of a is user defined and should be a compromise between accuracy and computer time and memory. The local state of the (i, j) CA cell at time t, $S^t_{i,j}$, is given by:

$$S^t_{i,j} = \{F^t_{i,j}, E^t_{i,j}\}, \text{ where } E^t_{i,j} = \frac{A_o}{A_t} \tag{5}$$

$E^t_{i,j}$ is the ratio of the oxidized area, A_o, to the total cell area, A_t, at time t. The state of a fully oxidized cell is 1, whereas the state of a non-oxidized cell is 0. $E^t_{i,j}$ may take any value between 0 and 1. $F^t_{i,j}$ is a one-bit flag. If $F^t_{i,j}$ equals to 0, the cell is located at or above the SiO_2-air boundary, whereas if $F^t_{i,j}$ equals to 1, the cell is located at or beneath the SiO_2-Si boundary. Some examples are given: (a) $S^t_{i,j}=\{0, 0\}$, (b) $S^t_{i,j}=\{1, 0.55\}$, and (c) $S^t_{i,j}=\{\#, 1\}$. The state given by example (a) indicates a non-oxidized cell located above the SiO_2-air boundary. The state given by (b) indicates that the cell is located at the SiO_2-Si boundary, and that the 55% of its area is oxidized. Finally, the state given by (c) indicates that the cell is fully oxidized and, therefore, it is located in the bulk of the oxide and its flag value is not considered.

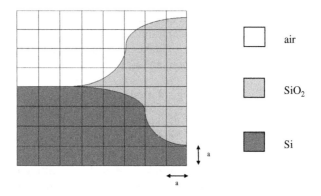

air

SiO_2

Si

Fig. 1. Representation of the Si-SiO$_2$-air system by a CA. The two interfaces, the SiO$_2$-air interface and the SiO$_2$-Si interface form the well-known "bird's beak".

The neighbourhood of the (i, j) cell is chosen to be Moore neighbourhood. Several CA local rules have been tested and found that the local rule that produces fronts of the form of Fig. 1 is:

$$S^{t+1}_{i,j} = S^t_{i,j} + n S^t_{i-1,j} + s S^t_{i+1,j} + e S^t_{i,j+1} + w S^t_{i,j-1} +$$
$$nw S^t_{i-1,j-1} + sw S^t_{i+1,j-1} + ne S^t_{i-1,j+1} + se S^t_{i+1,j+1} \tag{6}$$

$S^t_{i,j}$ is the local state of the (i, j) cell, at time step t, and $S^{t+1}_{i,j}$ is the local state of the (i, j) cell, at time step $t+1$. n, s, e, w, nw, sw, ne, and se are weights that multiply the states of the neighbouring cells. The oxidation of the (i, j) cell due to oxidant incoming from the upper cell [i.e. the $(i-1, j)$ cell] is described by $(n S^t_{i-1,j})$, whereas the oxidation of the (i, j) cell due to oxidant incoming from the lower cell [i.e. the $(i+1, j)$

cell] is described by (s $S^t_{i+1,j}$). To produce an oxide thickness equal to d_o, a Si film with thickness 0.44 d_o will be consumed. Therefore, the relation of weights s and n is:

$$\frac{s}{n} = \frac{0.56}{0.44} \qquad (7)$$

The CA was found to produce the desired fronts, i.e. the fronts shown in Fig. 1, when the following relations hold between the weights:

$$e > ne > se, \, w > nw > sw \text{ and } e = w, \quad ne = nw, \quad se = sw \qquad (8)$$

The weights n, s, e, w, nw, sw, ne, and se are the fitting parameters of the model. They are related as described by equation (8), and their values can be determined by fitting the simulation results to experimental data, in analogy with the A, B, and τ parameters of the mathematical model described earlier.

3   The Proposed TCAD System

The *CA_OXIDA_TCAD* system is able of automated modelling and VLSI implementation of oxidation process with CAs. In modelling of semiconductor processes, graphic output is a necessary tool for rapid and clear understanding of the computation results. Thus user-friendly tools allowing users to interact with the system is a basic part of the *CA_OXIDA_TCAD* environment. *CA_OXIDA_TCAD* user interface has been implemented using Matlab® GUI facilities, enabling interactive simulation.

The simulation profiles are produced using two CA oxidation algorithms (one with discrete state space and one with continuous state space). The necessity of using two CA algorithms that differ only in state space stems from the hardware implementation, which is much facilitated using the CA algorithm with discrete state space. These CA parameters are maximum number of CA cells, maximum number of time steps, process geometry, mask presence, presence of defects and defects' temperature, and their coordinates or predefined initial and boundary conditions, depicted on *CA_OXIDA_TCAD* simulation interface. The aforementioned parameters remain unchanged during the simulation. It should be mentioned that *CA_OXIDA_TCAD* does not impose any *a priori* limitations on these parameters. All parameters are modifiable, can be changed interactively, and the resulting simulations can be looked at in graphical form. The main system parameter during the simulation phase is the choice of the CA state space (i.e. discrete or continuous). Whatever the user's choice is, the TCAD produces, except the graphical output of the simulation results, a txt file that gives the area covered by oxidation process during time evolution.

As mentioned before a crucial question is for which reason the proposed system provides the user with two CA algorithms that differ only at state space. It is proven that each one of the two algorithms with proper parameters' values can model oxidation process as good as the other. The reason is that the translation algorithm of *CA_OXIDA_TCAD*, no matter which state space the user selects, uses the discrete CA algorithm as its input and as the basis for producing the synthesizable VHDL code. It should be emphasized that in case of continuous CA algorithm, the CA cell takes continuous values over the range (0) and (1) with accuracy of three decimal digits. Moreover the continuous CA rule is rather simple constructed with the usage of algebraic operators +, * and / and implemented on a Moore neighbourhood. On the other hand, in the case of the discrete CA algorithm, the CA cell takes only two values (0) and (1), in correspondence, while the discrete CA rule is a lot more complex than the previous continuous one and is implemented on a extended Moore neighbourhood. As a result the continuous CA algorithm is offered to the user, during the modelling of oxidation process, in order to lead him in comparable conclusions in short time.

To achieve discrete oxidation simulation profiles of same accuracy with the ones produced by the continuous CA, the number of discrete CA cells should be increased. Due to the fact that the increment of the number of discrete CA cells is analogous to the delay production of simulation profiles, the user should find the golden mean with several tests. The user will be helped to find the proper parameters values by two ways: first by the optical similarity between the produced profiles of continuous and discrete CA algorithms appeared in *CA_OXIDA_TCAD* modelling screen; and second by the minimization of the difference between the areas covered by oxidation process using the two CA algorithms (i.e. comparison of the equivalent txt files).

After the performance and the functional correctness of CA oxidation algorithm is checked with the help of animated visualization of the environment developed in this research work, the *CA_OXIDA_TCAD* translation algorithm, written in a high-level scripting language, is used. This translation algorithm receives the CA algorithm with discrete state space as its input, and automatically produces, as output, a synthesizable VHDL code. The final VHDL code produced by translation algorithm, including both the behavioral and structural parts, addresses the basic VHDL concepts (i.e. inter-faces, behavior, structure, test benches) included in the IEEE Standard 1076-2002. To achieve its goal, the translation algorithm collects information from the discrete CA algorithm by checking its primary parameters. After the CA algorithm is read, the translation algorithm searches the discrete CA code to detect the CA rule in order to produce the VHDL code for the main component, i.e. the CA cell. This will be the behavioral part of the final VHDL code, containing process and signal assignment statements. To be more specific, the entity declaration of a CA cell describes the in-put/output ports of the module, which happens to be the main component in our VHDL code. In other words, this part describes the functional part of the CA code. The architecture body of the behavioral part of VHDL code displays the implementa-tion of the entity CA cell. Subsequently, the translation algorithm searches the CA code to detect the lattice size, the boundary and initials CA conditions, in order to construct the structural part of the final VHDL code. The structural part implements the final module as a composition of subsystems, like the aforementioned main com-ponent. It contains signal declarations for internal interconnections, where the entity ports are also treated as signals. In addition, it includes component instances of previ-ously declared entity/architecture pairs, port maps in components, meaning to connect signals to component ports, and wait statements. It is clear, that the translation algo-rithm operates in a dynamical way depending on the previous definitions made by the user.

The VHDL codes produced by *CA_OXIDA_TCAD* are automatically saved in the hard disk, as VHDL files. The VHDL code of the main component is named ca.vhd, while four other VHDL codes, referred to the implementation of four counters, are saved as counter5.vhd, counter8. vhd, counterup.vhd and counterdown.vhd, in corre-spondence. These four counters are needed to construct the main component of the VHDL code, since they are integral part of the VHDL implementation of the discrete CA local rule. The entity name of the overall CAs is oxidacas.vhd. The final CA cell states will be transferred through multiplexers to the outputs of the future produced FPGA. The VHDL code for the multiplexer component is also produced automati-cally by the *CA_OXIDA_TCAD* system and saved in the hard disk, as a VHDL file. This file's name is multxoxida.vhd, and it is implemented in the final VHDL code, namely oxidacas.vhd, as a VHDL component. There is always a possibility, if the user wishes so, of functional simulation of VHDL code with the help of the appropriate test benches. The translation algorithm automatically produces these test benches using the final VHDL code and the initial and boundary conditions of the CA algo-rithm, plus its termination condition. In other words, the test benches depend on the surface geometry of the oxidation process, on the presence or absence of masks, on the presence or absence of defects and on defects' temperature. The file of the test benches is also saved as VHDL file in the hard disk, namely as casoxidatest.vhd. The results of the simulation of VHDL code are guaranteed to be found in complete agreement with the compilation results of CA oxidation algorithm.

These VHDL codes, after being synthesized by means of a VLSI CAD tool, can produce the schematic of the corresponding expression. The design processing of the finally produced VHDL code, i.e. analysis, elaboration and simulation, has been checked out with the help of the Quartus II, v. 5.1® design software of the ALTERA® Corporation. Test benches were automatically constructed by our system, for the simulation needs of the VHDL code, and the Simulator of Quartus® was used to simu-late the operation of the dedicated processor described by the VHDL code obtained. As a result, the VHDL code is applied as input to the Quartus® FPGA system, which in turn produces the layout of the corresponding dedicated parallel FPGA that exe-cutes the oxidation process simulation algorithm.

An example of *CA_OXIDA_TCAD* application in the simulation and automatic generation of VHDL code for the oxidation process is presented in Fig. 2. The simula-tions to be presented are only a few of the several possible cases that can be handled by the proposed TCAD system. However, these simulations are just characteristic working cases of the oxidation process and the oxidation simulation profiles obtained are in very good qualitative and quantitative agreement with the experimental and simulation results found in the literature [2]. In Fig. 2 oxidation simulation profiles obtained in the cases of: (a) a planar Si surface using continuous CA, (b) a planar Si surface using discrete CA, (c) a rectangular Si line (step) using continuous CA, (d) a rectangular Si line (step) using discrete CA and (e) through a metal mask using con-tinuous CA. The dashed line is the initial Si-air interface before the onset of oxida-tion. Solid lines beneath the dashed line represent the advancement of the SiO2-Si interface at successive time steps. Solid lines above the dashed line represent the advancement of the SiO2-air interface at the same successive time steps. These work-ing case simulations, resulting from both continuous and discrete CA oxidation algo-rithms, are used for reasons of simplicity, convenience, and statistical comparison, in order to check the ability of the discrete CA to produce oxidation profiles of the same accuracy with the ones produced by the continuous CA.

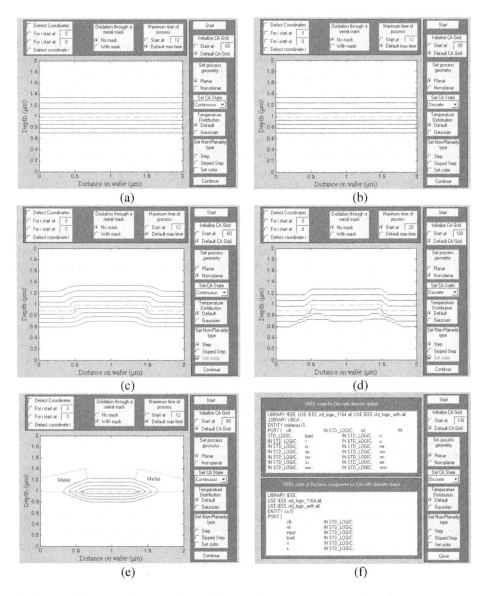

Fig. 2. Oxidation simulation profiles obtained in the cases of: (a) a planar Si surface using continuous CA, (b) a planar Si surface using discrete CA, (c) a rectangular Si line (step) using continuous CA, (d) a rectangular Si line (step) using discrete CA and (e) through a metal mask using continuous CA. (f) *CA_OXIDA_TCAD* VHDL code production screen.

The maximum simulation time and the maximum cell number for each grid side of the continuous CA algorithm were chosen equal to 12 and 60, respectively, for all the aforementioned working cases studied. As mentioned before, the difference between the state spaces of the CA algorithms leads to different evolution times and different grid sizes. Consequently, the values of these algorithm parameters should be increased in the case of discrete state space, so as to simulate the oxidation process with the same accuracy, as in case of continuous state space. As a result, the maximum simulation time and the maximum grid size are chosen to be 20 and 100, respectively, in order to achieve the best combination of computational accuracy and computational time-memory, for working case (d). In case (b), these parameters are chosen to be 12 and 60, respectively, i.e. exactly the same as in the case of the continuous CA. The main difference between cases (b) and (d) is induced by the lack of curvature in the simulation profiles obtained, arising from the planarity of Si surface.

The comparison of simulation results on the oxidation profiles in the cases of continuous state space [Fig. 2(a) and 2(c)] and discrete state space [Fig. 2(b) and 2(d)] leads to the conclusion that the proposed binary CA simulates successfully the oxidation process. The qualitative agreement between the oxidation profiles of continuous and discrete state space is confirmed by the results of statistical comparison calculations of the oxidation areas in both cases. Indeed, in all working cases of oxidation simulation, as well as the ones not mentioned here for readability reasons, the final difference between the covered oxidation areas of the two CAs with discrete and continuous state space is never greater than 11%. Furthermore, it should be mentioned, that the CA local rule in case of continuous state space includes multiplications, divisions, and square roots, and its hardware implementation using VHDL would result in an integrated circuit with a larger silicon area, and consequently, smaller maximum operational frequency compared to the discrete state space VHDL code. As a result this implementation would not only be expensive to fabricate, but also its power consumption should be taken under serious consideration. Finally, the computational complexity of the produced hardware that implements the discrete CA algorithm is infinitely smaller than the corresponding complexity of the dedicated hardware that would implement the continuous one.

After the simulation of the oxidation process, the VHDL codes of the main component (CA cell) and of the entire CA are depictured automatically on the lower and upper window of Fig. 2(f), in correspondence by pressing the "Continue" button on Fig. 2(c) or Fig. 2(d). The proposed system produces automatically, in addition to the aforementioned VHDL codes, the necessary VHDL codes for the counters and the multiplexers needed for the synthesis of the final VHDL code and the VHDL codes of the test benches. The main parameter for the generation of the final VHDL code is the maximum number of cells per CA grid size, which depended on the choice previously made by the user. The only VHDL code that would change because of different initial and boundary CA conditions (surface geometry, mask's presence, defects' presence and defects' temperature) is the VHDL code of test benches. The functional simulation of the final VHDL code is accomplished using of the above test benches. The produced results are in very good agreement with the simulation results of CA algorithm with binary state space. After the comparison of the simulation results for each of the *CA_OXIDA_TCAD* system operations, the hardware implementation of the corresponding parallel-specified FPGA is done with other proper VLSI CAD tools except the proposed system. For hardware implementation, ALTERA® Cyclone series FPGAs were chosen due to their desirable features but mostly because they provide the scalable platform with highest densities than most commercial FPGAs. These chips also support small designs, up to 20K logic gates, and are suitable for reducing interconnection time delay and thus increasing performance. Functional simulation revealed a maximum frequency of operation of 218 MHz of the chosen EP1C12 FPGA Cyclone device. Inputs to the dedicated processor are the lines through which the initial conditions are transferred to the CA, the clock, reset and load control signals, the boundary condition signals, as well as the power and ground connections. The final CA cell states are transferred through multiplexers to the FPGA outputs.

4 Conclusions

An efficient TCAD system, named "*CA_OXIDA_TCAD*", for the automated modelling and VLSI implementation of oxidation process using VHDL, has been presented in this paper. A user-friendly interface that enables easy and effective interaction between the user and the TCAD system in every stage of the modelling procedure has been developed using MATLAB® GUI facilities. The produced profiles of oxidation process modelling obtained by *CA_OXIDA_TCAD* were found to be in very good qualitative and quantitative agreement with experimental and simulation results cited in literature. In the proposed system, a translation algorithm, written in high scripting language, is used to automatically produce synthesizable VHDL code. An example of successful modelling and VLSI implementation leading to a FPGA device that models oxidation process has been given. As a result, the aforementioned FPGA could serve as a powerful "virtual lab" dedicated to the modelling of the oxidation process.

References

1. Semiconductor Industry Association: The International Technology Roadmap for Semiconductors. SIA Press, http://www.itrs.net/Common/2005ITRS/Home2005.htm, (2005)
2. Sze, S.M. (ed.): VLSI Technology. McGraw-Hill, Singapore (1988)
3. Law, M.E.: Grid adaption near moving boundaries in two dimensions for IC process simulation. IEEE Transactions on Computer Aided Design 14 (1995) 1223–1230
4. Deal, B.E., Grove, A.S.: General relationship for the thermal oxidation of silicon. Journal of Applied Physics 36 (1965) 3770–3784
5. Sirakoulis, G.Ch., Karafyllidis, I., Mardiris, V., Thanailakis, A.: Study of lithography profiles developed on non-planar Si surfaces. Nanotechnology 10 (1999) 421–427
6. Sirakoulis, G.Ch., Karafyllidis, I., Mardiris, V., Thanailakis, A.: Study of the effects of photoresist surface roughness and defects on developed profiles. Semiconductor Science and Technology 15 (2000) 98–107
7. Sirakoulis, G.Ch., Karafyllidis, I., Soudris, D., Georgoulas, N., Thanailakis, A.: A new simulator for the oxidation process in integrated circuit fabrication based on cellular automata. Modelling and Simulation in Materials Science and Engineering 7 (1999) 631–640
8. Karafyllidis, I., Georgoulas, N., Hagouel, P.I., Thanailakis, A.: Simulation of deposition-topography granular distortion for TCAD Modelling and Simulation in Materials Science and Engineering 6 (1998) 199–210
9. Chopard, B., Droz, M.: Cellular Automata Modeling of Physical systems. Cambridge University Press, Cambridge (1998)

Automatic Detection of Go–Based Patterns in CA Model of Vegetable Populations: Experiments on *Geta* Pattern Recognition

Stefania Bandini, Sara Manzoni, Stefano Redaelli, and Leonardo Vanneschi

Dept. of Informatics, Systems, and Communication
University of Milano–Bicocca
{bandini, manzoni, redaelli, vanneschi}@disco.unimib.it

Abstract. The paper presents an empirical study aiming at evaluating and comparing several Machine Learning (ML) classification techniques in the automatic recognition of known patterns. The main motivations of this work is to select best performing classification techniques where target classes are based on the occurrence of known patterns in configurations of a forest system modeled according to Cellular Automata. Best performing ML classifiers will be adopted for the study of ecosystem dynamics within an interdisciplinary research collaboration between computer scientists, biologists and ecosystem managers (Cellular Automata For Forest Ecosystems - CAFFE project). One of the main aims of the CAFFE project is the development of an analysis method based on recognition in CA state configurations of spatial patterns whose interpretations are inspired by the Chinese Go game.

1 Introduction

The paper presents an experimental work to evaluate and compare Machine Learning (ML) classification techniques for the automatic recognition of known patterns that can occur in the dynamic behavior of a vegetable population model based on Cellular Automata (CA). This work is part of an ongoing research collaboration (Cellular Automata For Forest Ecosystems - CAFFE project) between the Computer Science Department of University of Milano–Bicocca, and biologists and ecosystem managers of the Systems Research Department of Austrian Research Center (ARC). CAFFE project aims at supporting ecosystem management in the study of forest systems according to a modeling and simulation approach based on CA. To this aim a CA–based model of vegetable populations competing on resources has been developed and validated by good results in reproducing real conditions in an empirical study on vegetable populations consisting of robiniae (black locust), oaks, and pine trees on the foothills of the Italian Alps. The CAFFE model is based on two–dimensional Cellular Automata, whose cells represent portions of a given area in terms of available resources and trees. Each cell can host a tree where its specie, size, the amount of resources it needs to survive, grow, and/or reproduce itself are represented. Interested readers can refer to [1] for a detailed description of this part of the research.

S. El Yacoubi, B. Chopard, and S. Bandini (Eds.): ACRI 2006, LNCS 4173, pp. 427–435, 2006.
© Springer-Verlag Berlin Heidelberg 2006

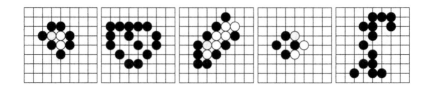

Fig. 1. From left to right: *Geta*, *Iki*, *Shicho*, *Ko*, and *Tsugi* patterns that can occur on a Go board during a game and whose interpretation can be exploited to interpret similar structures that can occur on configurations of cell states in the CAFFE forest model

In order to support ecosystem managers in studying the dynamics of the CA–based forest model, the *Go–based pattern detection method* has been recently proposed [2]. The latter suggests to interpret known spatial patterns that can be recognized in CA configurations mediating their interpretations from the Go game. Figure 1 shows the structure of *Geta*, *Iki*, *Shicho*, *Ko*, and *Tsugi* patterns, a subset of patterns that can occur on a Go board during a game [3] and that expert players interpret in terms of competition between adversary stones on the spatial structure of the board. The patterns shown in the figure have been selected as the ones whose occurrence in configurations of CA cell states' can be interpreted as the related Go pattern that is, the Go pattern with the same spatial structure). For instance, when a *Geta* pattern occurs during a game, it is interpreted as the *local capture of a group of stones* by a set of adversary stones that surrounds it. Due to the central role of the concept of *liberty* in Go rules, the captured group is considered as lost and it is removed from the board.

Similarly within the competition of vegetable populations on available resources, when a small group of trees is surrounded by trees of other species, it is considered by ecosystem experts to be in not favorable conditions due the scarcity of needed resources. Figure 2 shows a *Geta* pattern that in the following time steps disappear together with all trees belonging to the captured group. Unfortunately, the automatic detection of the occurrence of a *Geta* pattern in

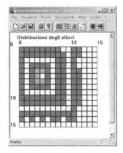
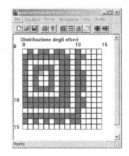
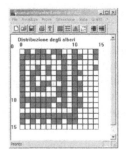

Fig. 2. Three configurations of the CA forest model in which a *Geta* pattern disappears together with all trees belonging to the captured group

the CA cells' configuration is not a simple task. For instance, Figure 3 shows
three configurations of the CA–based forest model in which the local capture of a
small group of trees can be recognized, but it is evident that pattern dimensions
and positions can vary. Moreover, it is not necessary to have a group of trees
completely surrounded by trees of other species to recognize the occurrence of
Geta. All this elements thus do not allow us to simply design a formal method
for pattern detection within CA configurations.

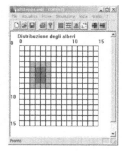 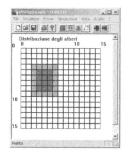 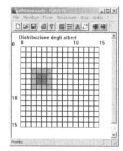

Fig. 3. Three configurations of the CA–based forest model in which the local capture
of a group of trees (*Geta* pattern) can be recognized. Cell colors indicate different tree
specie (no tree in the case of white cells).

In the following, we present the results of an empirical study aiming at selecting the best performing ML classification techniques in recognizing *Geta* pattern
in configurations of the CA–based model of forest systems. In particular, after
an overview of our reference forest model, in Section 3 we will introduce the
experimented classifier, data filters, and the data set we built with a selection
of CA configurations. Classification performances and experiment results in detecting *Geta* pattern will conclude the paper with on outline of next steps in
CAFFE research collaboration.

2 CA–Based Forest Model

The Cellular Automata For Forest Ecosystems (CAFFE) model is based on two–
dimensional Cellular Automata, whose cells, arranged on a square grid, represent
portions of a given area. Some resources are present on the area, divided among
the cells. A cell can host a tree, represented in the model by a set of parameters
defining its species, its size, the amount of each resource it needs to survive,
grow, and/or reproduce itself.

The CA has been defined as [1]:

$$\mathbf{CA} = \langle R, N, Q, f, I \rangle$$

where:

1. $R = \{(i,j)|1 \leq i \leq N, 1 \leq j \leq M\}$ is a two–dimensional $N \times M$ lattice;
2. H is the neighborhood, that can be either the von Neumann or Moore neighborhood;
3. Q is the finite set of cell state values;
4. $f : Q \times Q^{|H|} \rightarrow Q$ is the state transition function;
5. $I : R \rightarrow Q$ is the initialization function.

2.1 Cells' State

Each cell of the automaton reproduces a square portion of terrain with a side ranging from three to five meters. Each cell contains some resources, and can host a tree. The possible states of each cell (Q) represents:

1. The type of terrain the cell reproduces;
2. The resources present in the cell;
3. The amount of resources the cell produces at each update step, and the maximum amount of resources it can contain, according to its type;
4. Whether a tree is present in the cell, or not;
5. If a tree is present:
   (a) the size of the tree;
   (b) the amount of each resource it needs at each update step to survive and grow;
   (c) the amount of each resource stored by the tree at previous update steps;
6. Seeds scattered by trees living in the area.

2.2 Update Rule

At each update step of the automaton, the tree present in each cell (if any) takes the resources it needs from the cell itself and uses them to survive, grow (if enough resources are available), and produce seeds. Moreover, we defined the update rule in order to reproduce the increasing influence that a growing tree can have on neighboring cells. We modeled the impact of a tree in a given position on its neighborhood by making resources flow from richer cells to poorer ones. In other words, a cell hosting a large tree is poor on resources, since the tree at each update step takes most (or all) of them. If the neighboring cells are vacant, their resources remain unused, and thus are richer than the one hosting the tree. Therefore, if we let resources flow from richer cells to poorer neighbors, the effect is that in practice a large tree starts to collect resources also from neighboring cells.

3   Empirical Pattern Recognition Study on *Geta* Pattern

In order to evaluate classification performances of several ML classifiers when target classes are based on the occurrence of *Geta* pattern, we have built a data set composed by 50 entries. Each entry represents a cell state configuration of the CA–based forest model where a 7×6 grid with Moore neighborhood has been considered. *Geta* pattern occur in 26 entries of the data set that differ according to pattern size (i.e. the size of the captured group ranges from 1 to 5 cells); pattern position (i.e. translations and rotations of *Geta* pattern within the CA grid have been considered); size of involved trees; type of terrain on which patterns occur; presence of other trees in the neighborhood of surrounding group; number of surrounding trees: if k is the size of the captured group neighborhood, the size of the surrounding group can range from $k - 2$ to k.

Each data set entry represents a CA configuration at a given time step, and it can be defined as:

$$C(t) =< s_0, s_1, ..., s_n, p >$$

where

- p is a boolean attribute that indicates the occurrence of *Geta* pattern (in our experiments we considered the occurrence of *Geta* pattern in a given CA configuration, if after a maximum of 20 simulation time steps we can observe the disappearance of the whole group of surrounded trees);
- $s_i \in T \times P \times Z$ (for $i = 0 \ldots 41$) indicates the state of the i–th CA cell, where $T = \{\text{water,rock,wet,arid}\}$ refers to the type of terrain represented by the cell; $P = \{\text{noTree,Pine,Fir}\}$ is the type of tree in the given cell (if any); and Z can assume, according to tree biomass, one of the following values:

$$\begin{cases} verybig & \text{if } biomass < 600; \\ big & \text{if } 450 < biomass \leq 600; \\ highmedium & \text{if } 320 < biomass \leq 450; \\ medium & \text{if } 230 < biomass \leq 320; \\ lowmedium & \text{if } 180 < biomass \leq 230; \\ small & \text{if } 150 < biomass \leq 180; \\ verysmall & \text{if } 0 < biomass \leq 150; \\ \bot & \text{if no tree is present.} \end{cases}$$

In the following, after introducing the set of ML classification techniques we experimented, we report the results of their performance evaluation both with no preprocessing and with three different filters on data (introduced in Section 3.2). Tests have been performed using the 10–*folds cross validation* evaluation method [4].

3.1   Experimented Classifiers

ML techniques we experimented to classify CA configurations in which at least a *Geta* pattern occurs are:

- **Naive Bayes:** A widely used framework for classification based on a simple theorem of probability known as Bayes' theorem (see for instance [5]). For a detailed description of this classifier, see for instance [6,7].
- **Multilayer Perceptron:** A neural network that computes a single output from multiple real-valued inputs by forming a linear combination according to its input weights and then possibly putting the output through

some nonlinear activation function. For a detailed description, see for instance [8,9,10,11].

– **Support Vector Machines with Sequential Minimal Optimization:** A method for creating functions from a set of labeled training data, which operates by finding a hypersurface in the space of possible inputs [12,13]. Sequential Minimal Optimization (SMO) is a training method described in [14,15].
– **K* Classifier:** An instance-based classifier which belongs to the class of k–nearest neighbors classifiers [16,4].
– **The ID3 Decision Tree Induction Algorithm:** Its aim is to describe an algorithm whose input is a collection of instances and their correct classification and whose output is a tree that can be used to classify each instance [17,18].
– **Random Tree Classifier:** A different variant of decision tree induction algorithm, much simpler than ID3, with a usually faster training phase. They are described in [19,20].

3.2   Filters on Data Set

Classifier performances have been studied both with no preprocessing technique and with the following three filters on data set:

– *Resample Filter*: produces a random subsample with replacement of the dataset and maintains the class distribution in the subsample.
– *Remove Useless Filter*: removes constant attributes, along with nominal attributes that vary too much.
– *Attribute Selection Filter*: a supervised filter which evaluates the worth of a subset of attributes by considering the individual predictive ability of each feature along with the degree of redundancy between them. Subsets of features that are highly correlated with the class while having low inter-correlation are preferred. The space of attribute subsets is searched by greedy hill climbing augmented with a backtracking facility.

3.3   Performance Evaluation

For each class G in which data have to be partitioned by classifiers (i.e. the occurrence or non–occurrence of *Geta* pattern), let:

– $x(G)$ be the number of instances belonging to class G which have been classified as belonging to class C by the classifier system;
– $y(G)$ be the number of instances that have been classified as belonging to class G the classifier;
– $z(G)$ be the number of instances which really belong to class G.

The classification performance of the system reports values on *correctly* and *incorrectly classified instances* to quantify classifier performance independently from data classes. They report the number of CA configurations in the test set which have correctly or incorrectly been classified, in terms of:

- *precision* on class G, defined by $p(G) = x(G)/y(G)$;
- *recall* on class G, defined by $r(G) = x(G)/z(G)$;
- *F–measure*, defined as: $F(G) = \frac{2 \times p(G) \times r(G)}{p(G) + r(G)}$

3.4   Results on *Geta* Pattern

Table 1,Table 2, Table 3, and Table 4 summarize the results of our experiments with no filter on data and with the Resample, Remove Useless and Attribute Selection filters, respectively.

Table 1. Results with no filter on data

Classifiers	Corr.Cl.Ist. Yes	Corr.Cl.Ist. No	Prec. Yes	Prec. No	Rec. Yes	Rec. No	F-means Yes	F-means No
Naive Bayes	25 (50%)	25 (50%)	0.514	0.462	0.731	0.25	0.603	0.324
MLP	31 (62%)	19 (38%)	0.613	0.632	0.731	0.5	0.667	0.558
SMO	30 (60%)	20 (40%)	0.594	0.611	0.731	0.458	0.655	0.524
KStar	27 (54%)	23 (46%)	0.543	0.533	0.731	0.333	0.623	0.41
Id3	21 (42%)	17 (34%)	0.538	0.583	0.737	0.368	0.622	0.452
RandomTree	25 (50%)	25 (50%)	0.514	0.462	0.731	0.25	0.603	0.324

Table 1 clearly shows that if no preprocessing is used on data, performances of all classifiers are poor: only the MLP and the SMO perform significantly better than a random classifier in this case. From Table 2, Table 3, and Table 4 we can observe that all filters improve performances of all classifiers, except Random Projection, which slightly degradates all classifiers performances. Nevertheless, only the Resample filter remarkably improves the performances of all classifiers. We hypothesize that this is due to the fact that randomly sampling the dataset, this filter automatically reduces noise on data.

When the Resample filter is used (Table 2), SMO has very good performances (all performance measures reported have a value over 0.9). MLP performs slightly worse than SMO, but still very well (precision and recall are over 0.9 for the class *yes* and over 0.8 for the class *no*). In conclusion, we can state that Resample

Table 2. Results with Resample Filter on data

Classifiers	Corr.Cl.Ist. Yes	Corr.Cl.Ist. No	Prec. Yes	Prec. No	Rec. Yes	Rec. No	F-means Yes	F-means No
NaiveBayes	28 (56%)	22 (44%)	0.561	0.556	0.852	0.217	0.676	0.313
MLP	43 (86%)	7 (14%)	0.833	0.9	0.926	0.783	0.877	0.837
SMO	46 (92%)	4 (8%)	0.926	0.913	0.926	0.913	0.926	0.913
KStar	40 (80%)	10 (20%)	0.84	0.76	0.778	0.826	0.808	0.792
Id3	34 (68%)	7 (14%)	0.857	0.8	0.818	0.842	0.837	0.821
RandomTree	38 (76%)	12 (24%)	0.759	0.762	0.815	0.696	0.786	0.727

Table 3. Results with Remove Useless Filter on data

Classifiers	Corr. Cl. Ist. Yes	Corr. Cl. Ist. No	Prec. Yes	Prec. No	Rec. Yes	Rec. No	F-means Yes	F-means No
NaiveBayes	25 (50%)	25 (50%)	0.514	0.462	0.731	0.25	0.603	0.324
MLP	29 (58%)	21 (42%)	0.581	0.579	0.692	0.458	0.632	0.512
SMO	30 (60%)	20 (40%)	0.594	0.611	0.731	0.458	0.655	0.524
KStar	27 (54%)	23 (46%)	0.543	0.533	0.731	0.333	0.623	0.41
Id3	21 (42%)	17 (34%)	0.538	0.583	0.737	0.368	0.622	0.452
RandomTree	25 (50%)	25 (50%)	0.514	0.467	0.692	0.292	0.59	0.359

Table 4. Results with Attribute Selection Filter on data

Classifiers	Corr. Cl. Ist. Yes	Corr. Cl. Ist. No	Prec. Yes	Prec. No	Rec. Yes	Rec. No	F-means Yes	F-means No
NaiveBayes	28 (56%)	22 (44%)	0.556	0.571	0.769	0.333	0.645	0.421
MLP	29 (58%)	21 (42%)	0.581	0.579	0.692	0.458	0.632	0.512
SMO	30 (60%)	20 (40%)	0.594	0.611	0.731	0.458	0.655	0.524
KStar	31 (62%)	19 (38%)	0.6	0.667	0.808	0.417	0.689	0.513
Id3	23 (46%)	14 (28%)	0.615	0.636	0.8	0.412	0.696	0.5
RandomTree	29 (58%)	21 (42%)	0.564	0.636	0.846	0.292	0.677	0.4

filter is the most suitable for our data set and Support Vector Machines seems a reasonable pattern detection strategy for our application.

4   Concluding Remarks and Future Works

The presented work has been conducted within an interdisciplinary research collaboration aiming at designing a method for the analysis of forest ecosystems. Cellular Automata have been adopted as modeling approach and the Go–based pattern detection method is under design in order to support the analysis CA dynamic behavior. Go–based pattern detection method proposes to automatically detect in CA configurations a set of patterns whose interpretations have been inspired by Chinese Go game. In particular, in this paper we have shown the empirical work we conducted in order to select best performing Machine Learning classification techniques in the recognition of the occurrence of *Geta* pattern in CA configurations (i.e. in Go jargon, *Geta* indicates the local capture of a group of stones by adversary stones). Performed experiments suggest Resample filter and Support Vector Machines as pattern detection strategy for this pattern.

Future experimental works on ML classification techniques will concern similar studies on other Go–based patterns. In particular, we will focus on *dynamic patterns* that, despite *Geta* and other *static patterns*, require the analysis of a sequence of CA configurations in order to be recognized.

References

1. Bandini, S., Pavesi, G.: Simulation of vegetable populations dynamics based on cellular automata. In Bandini, S., Chopard, B., Tomassini, M., eds.: Cellular Automata, Proceeding of 5th International Conference on Cellular Automata for Research and Industry (ACRI 2002), Geneva (Switzerland), October 9-11, 2002. Volume 2493 of Lecture Notes in Computer Science., Berlin, Springer-Verlag (2002)
2. Bandini, S., Manzoni, S., sand S. Redaelli, G.M.: Emergent pattern interpretation in vegetable population dynamics. To appear in Internal Journal of Unconventional Computing - special issue on selected papers from AUTOMATA 2005 workshop (To appear)
3. Soletti, G.: Note di Go. FIGG (Federazione Italiana Giuoco Go) (Avaiable for download at www.figg.org)
4. Mitchell, T.: Machine Learning. McGraw Hill, New York (1996)
5. Duda, R.O., Hart, P.E.: Pattern Classification and Scene Analysis. Wiley-Interscience, New York (1973)
6. McCallum, A., Nigam, K.: A comparison of event models for naive bayes text classification. In: AAAI-98 Workshop on Learning for Text Categorization. (1998)
7. Rish, I.: An empirical study of the naive bayes classifier. In: IJCAI 2001 Workshop on Empirical Methods in Artificial Intelligence. (2001)
8. Rosenblatt, F.: Principle of Neurodynamics. Spartan Books, Washington (1958)
9. Gallant, S.I.: Perceptron-based learning algorithms. In: IEEE Transactions on Neural Networks. (1990) 179–191
10. Hornik, K., Stinchcombe, M., White, H.: Multilayer feedforward networks are universal approximators. Neural Networks **5** (1989) 359–366
11. Gelman, A., Carlin, J.B., Stern, H.S., Rubin, D.B.: Bayesian Data Analysis. Chapman & Hall/CRC, Boca Raton (1995)
12. Vapnik, V.: Statistical Learning Theory. Wiley-Interscience, New York (1998)
13. Burges, C.J.: A tutorial on support vector machines for pattern recognition. Data Mining and Knowledge Discovery **2** (1998) 121–167
14. Platt, J.C.: Fast training of support vector machines using sequential minimal optimization. In: Advances in Kernel Methods - Support Vector Learning. (1998)
15. Keerthi, S., Shevade, S., Bhattacharyya, C., Murthy, K.: Improvements to Platt's SMO algorithm for SVM classifier design. (1999)
16. Cleary, J.G., Trigg, E.L.: K*: an instance-based learner using an entropic distance measure. In: Proc. of 12th International Conference on Machine Learning, Morgan Kaufmann (1995) 108–114
17. Quinlan, J.R.: Induction of decision trees. Machine Learning (1986) 81–106
18. Breiman, L., Friedman, J., Olshen, R.A., Stone, C.J.: Classification and regression trees. Wadsworth (1984)
19. Cutler, A.: Fast classification using perfect random trees. Technical Report 5/99/99, Department of Mathematics and Statistics, Utah State University, USA (1999)
20. Breiman, L.: Random forests - random features. Technical Report 576, Statistics Department, U. C. Berkeley, USA (1999)

Urban Sprawl: A Case Study for Project Gigalopolis Using SLEUTH Model

Matteo Caglioni, Mattia Pelizzoni, and Giovanni A. Rabino

DIAP, Department of Architecture and Planning, Polytechnic of Milan,
piazza Leonardo da Vinci 32, 20132 Milan, Italy
giovanni.rabino@polimi.it

Abstract. A brief approach through a CA-based model is perfect for modelling of different urban phenomena at different observation scales. SLEUTH model, situated in Project Gigalopolis, is a powerful tool for description of urban agglomeration and spatial dynamics. In this paper, new applications of this model, other methodological analyses, and sensitivity studies allow us to improve our comprehension of model parameters, taking advantage of this type of synthetic description of reality. Many deductions are possible thanks to the comparison of our studies with other precious databases, already existent, about results of this model.

1 Introduction

We can consider Cellular Automata (CA) like analysis tools for complex systems, because the city and its land-use can be seen like a mechanism, or parts interacting between themselves, in a sort of autonomous systems [1]. Cell changes in a CA are spatially and temporally self-correlated, and they simulate some properties of urban decision process, subdivided in different zones (i.e. zoning policies). A particular really interesting phenomenon that we want to study is the so called urban sprawl, which is an uncontrolled and really ungovernable growth of urbanized areas with a low density level, that acts outside the cities or among different close cities, with several territorial and environmental consequences. To avoid the effort in building different models for the same subject, not really different one from the others, the idea of the *Project Gigalopolis* was born from a collaboration between the University of California of Santa Barbara and United States Geological Survey, which proposed to apply, on a large range of different territories, a CA-based model, already developed: SLEUTH [2][3].

We purpose the first completely autonomous application in Europe, with a critical approach about the use of this model: in particular we want to go deep in the meaning of the parameters, used to describe urban dynamics if different phases of growth, and we want also to individualize the effects through specific simulations and other sensitivity analyses for parameters. The goal of this paper is a contribution for the ambitious Project Gigalopolis, investigating the meaning of the parameters of the model, and the common aspect among different type of urbanized area, so it's possible to build a "DNA of city" through the analysis of the outgoings produced by SLEUTH. Experiences and results come out from previous applications are the main resource for a deep comprehension of the urban and spatial problems.

S. El Yacoubi, B. Chopard, and S. Bandini (Eds.): ACRI 2006, LNCS 4173, pp. 436–445, 2006.

2 SLEUTH Model and Project Gigalopolis

In order to characterize urban dynamics SLEUTH works with a strict structure based on different layers: as we can see from its name, which is the acronym of input data that this model needs, the growth of the city is driven, conditioned, or limited by five factors: Slope, Land use, Excluded areas (where the development of urban areas is forbidden), Urban areas, Transportation network; this factors are represented through different layer, and Hillshade, used as background in visualization.

This model is located inside the recent panorama of the urban modelling as a flexible, robust, reliable tool which can be compared and can be competitive with the other CA models. SLEUTH is an evolution of Urban Growth Model, an AC-based built for the first time in 1998 by Keith Clarke. So it is structured in two different modules, which can be activated independently: UGM (Urban Growth Model), that simulate the urban growth, and Deltatron, that allow observing the changes in land uses [4]. In its main module, SLEUTH is a probabilistic CA with Boolean logic (for example a cell can be only urbanized or not urbanized), and with only five parameters; this approach justify the use of "*brute force*" calibration based on the research of parameters in determinate ranges which are progressively reduced. This model is valued for the parameters ability in adjusting and representing, in a careful way, different phenomena of various areas and regions; then theoretically there isn't any limit in dimension of the studied area: there are case studies about a whole region and other application about a single city.

2.1 Model Parameters and Growth Rules

The time unit of the urban growth simulation is the growth cycle, and it corresponds to one year. Urban growth dynamics in UGM module (which provides probabilistic information) are modeled using four sequential rules, like four steps of a cycle; all the cells which constitute the whole automata are update on the whole grid after each rule application.

Five parameters (with values between 0 and 100) influence the way how the transition rules, which describe growth and transformation of the city, can be applied.

1. *Dispersion coefficient* (DI): it controls the number of time that a cell is randomly selected to be urbanized during the application of spontaneous growth law.
2. *Breed coefficient* (BR): it determines the probability of an urbanized cell, in the spontaneous growth phase, to become a new urban core which has the possibility to evolve (new spreading centre). Moreover BR is used road-influenced growth phase, determining the spread along a road.
3. *Spread coefficient* (SP): it defines the probability that a cell, which is part of a spreading centre (a cluster with at least two urbanized cells, in a 3x3 neighbourhood), generates another urbanized cell in its neighbourhood.
4. *Slope resistance* (SR): Slope above 21% can't be urbanized. The slope coefficient determines the weight of the probability that a location may be built up.
5. *Road gravity coefficient* (RG): it defines the maximum influence distance for each road on urbanization probability. It depends also from input map dimension.

The urban growth dynamic, implemented in UGM sub-model, is defined by four steps, depending on the previous parameters: *Spontaneous Growth*, *New Spreading Center Growth*, *Edge Growth*, *Road-influenced growth*. After these phases, there is the self-modification process; without it the model produces linear or exponential growth, which is quite far from reality: growth coefficients do not necessarily remain static throughout an application. In response to rapid or depressed growth rates, the coefficients may be increased or decreased to further encourage system wide growth rate trends.

In order to perform Deltatron module is necessary to predispose input data about land use changes. Dynamics we have already seen start from assumption that the urbanization process is the engine of changes in non-urbanized land cover. Land cover modelling is based on changes of virtual entities, called Deltatron (which represent different type of classes we can consider) described in 4 phases: *Initiate change, Cluster Change, Propagate change, Age Deltatron.*.

2.2 Project Gigalopolis

Project Gigalopolis deals with the problem of the modelling of urban growth dynamics, which nowadays have overcome the regional scale to take a global dimension, studying the sprawled city phenomenon. Applying SLEUTH model at the greatest number and different types of territories (this software is freeware at http://www.ncgia.ucsb.edu/projects/gig.html) it's possible to analyze the urban sprawl phenomenon at a global scale and derive some conclusions, with general validity, about the trend of urban development and of urbanized areas.

In whole theory at the base of this project there is the vision of the urban development as driving force of the spatial changes. Project Gigalopolis offers the possibility to compare results among a large number of case studies in Cellular Automata field applied to spatial analysis: it is allowed the access to database composed by parts of results coming from previous application of SLEUTH model.

Use of this model on a large and heterogeneous range of case studies is made to compare the results and understand the real possibility to build new realistic scenarios of urban development, creating in a long period an efficient modelling system, as swell as to realize shared and updated database to drive local communities in clever and responsible development for urban growth. Generalization and contextualization of obtained results, also for heterogeneous territories, can allow identifying the "DNA of the cities", as different combination of parameters.

3 Methodological Analysis, Sensitivity Studies and Applications

Validity of simulations made with a CA-based urban model directly depends on its capability, after a suitable calibration of parameters, to well fit the system we want to study. So, to evaluate critically the ability of SLEUTH in simulating urban systems, we did a study on an ideal territory characterized by a population distributed according the very general Zipf's rank-size rule, and a simulation of a hypothetical case of urban sprawl. But, first of all, we show the behaviour of the model in respect to the values of its parameters.

3.1 Sensitivity Analysis of Parameters

In general it is not possible to associate one parameter with one growth process in an explicit and univocal way, because the growth parameters BR, DI and RG are highly correlated between themselves. This makes difficult to understand each growth cycle in urban evolution, and we can observe only the reproduction of the overall urban complexity. In order to better define the parameter role, we performed some simulations with representative sets of different urban centres (highly constrained for development, prevalence of the diffusion effect, sprawl effect, etc.), both in ideal and actual territories.

In case of an ideal territory, characterized by spatial isotropy and by absence of previous urban structures (20 years of simulation), given initial conditions, we obtain the greatest growth assigning an high value (80-100) to SP parameter rather than to BR and DI. This allows the urbanization of cells in the neighbourhood of other cells previously urbanized: we can observe exponential growths of urbanized area. With high values of BR we obtain with a good approximation a linear growth in urbanization processes (high values of DI lead to similar results but with a lower velocity in respect to BR). RG shows only a qualitative effect, influencing only the localization of new urbanized cells, but not their amount. If we isolate the effect of one parameter, minimizing values of the others, we observe an opposite situation compared to what we have explained before: the highest urbanization growth is obtained with high values of DI parameter. Moreover SP is quantitatively important, if and only if either BR and DI values are negligible, or there are previous urban agglomerations with a relevant extent (like many urban cores in a metropolitan area).

For real territories, where we have done the calibration using four years of data input (with the possibility to compare the effect produced by a set of parameters with a reference situation), maximizing BR, SP, and DI, we obtained a confirmation of the previous results.

This analysis shows that maximization of RG parameter leads to an high urbanization of more accessible areas in connection to road network, with equal growth rate (due to the values of the other parameters).

3.2 Ideal Behaviours at Two Extremes: Hierarchic Structure and Urban Sprawl

The rank-size rule (power law distribution) describes the emergent attitude of urban systems, which have the tendency of self-organization: the law relates the population of a city classified at one level with the level itself, and it comes from the observation of the real behaviour of territorial systems [6]. Generally, distribution of population among the cities is such that there are few big centres, and a lot of smaller urban cores.

Even though SLEUTH model has been efficiently used in simulation of urban dynamics, it's possible to apply it also to evolution of territorial systems on large scale. The principles which rule the urban development (described by SLEUTH parameters) can be seen also in a higher observation level: for example, generation of a new urbanized cell, due to dispersion or spread, could represent one or more buildings of the same city, or a new urban centre which will grow thanks to the effect of breed coefficient; in the same way, the systems of cities take into account, for their growth, slope and road network proximity. The decision to consider the power law in order to simulate those territories can be well understood when we consider one of its main proprieties, that scale invariance, and as for urban development mechanisms, discussed previously, its validity is independent from the considered scale.

Simulation of a territory to verify Zip's rule (rank-size) refers to a spatial pattern produced by an iterative process with a mechanism of allometric (differentiated) growth: we followed this logic for building the model input layers. Observing simulation output (calibration set is DI=0, BR=1, SP=0, SR=7 and RG=60), it's possible to notice how it respects territorial organization described by the law: we observe to the growth of a lot of very little centres equal-spaced from each others, and gravitating, in an ordered way, around big dimension "cores" situated in accessible places reached by the road network (radial transportation network, according to Wu's road model [7]).

We have also the possibility to verify how this experiment fits the law using a numerical analysis. As size we can use the extension of the cities, and not population anymore (but they are proportional, so we can exchange one with the other). Through a graphical and numerical analysis of the map we can extract the empirical data for rank-size rule.

We can observe 67 clusters on our ideal territory, and the rank will go from 0 for the largest mass, to 66 for the smallest mass (We can recognise just 4 different class of size of cities – masses - , but we will have much more differences in size, considering other iterations in the process of territory building). Plotting rank and size together in a bi-logarithmic graph we have a definitive confirmation about how the functioning of SLEUTH can recognise and interpret a rank-size structure in a good way: the number of centres grows in a power way with rank (using logarithms this relationship becomes linear, and an example of scale invariance).

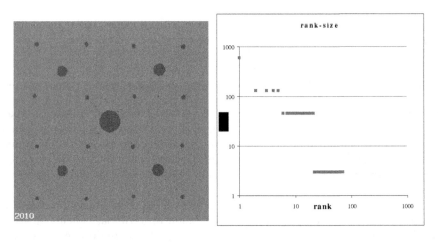

Fig. 1. Left: output image of the last year of prediction: it's possible to distinguish different level of urban centres dimensions (simulation date range: 1990-2010). Right: rank- size rule on the data of the ideal case study in logarithmic coordinates.

Having verified the ability of the model to represent and reproduce a hierarchically organized territory, it's also interesting to see how parameters combination can reproduce a hypothetic urban sprawl.

In this analysis, input layers were realized "ad hoc" for this type of simulation; and some hypothesis are necessary [8]: morphologically homogeneous territory (to guarantee an equal development probability for each cell at the beginning); no urban restrictions and constraints; "star shaped" urbanized area, which generally derives from the radial distribution of the road of transportation network. Calibration for this input gives values of DI, BR, SP, SR and RG parameters equal to 2, 6, 26, 1 and 1 respectively. The main parameters which can give an idea of urban sprawl phenomenon are BR, DI and SP; but even the road disposition and the resultant accessibility have influence upon it. Output suggests that urban area (dis)organization, which is typical of urban sprawl, is effectively reproduced in a quite good way. In the simulation the SP parameter, in spite of its predominant effect, can't replicate by itself alone urban sprawl phenomenon: it has to be associated with non-irrelevant BR and DI values.

The diffusion phenomenon, part of the sprawl, causes the presence of a high number of clusters. They decrease in number progressively, but remain - in average - very small.

3.3 Italian and European Case Studies

Results of Italian and European real territories are proposed to make the Project Gigalopolis database more consistent: in this way the comparison between real cases parameters values is easier and it's possible to trace general characteristics of urban growth phenomenon. In order to create land-use input layer, for case studies on real territories, we have assumed as opportune to convert our classification (Corine land cover) in the American one named Anderson Level I Classification System, also to conform ourselves to the classification system used in many other application of this model, in order to make the results much more shareable.

New applications are representing very different case studies: for geographic position, territory morphology and urban story and settlements types (one city or metropolitan area, more towns and municipalities together...).

Case studies are heterogeneous overall about technical details, such as input image dimensions and precision (cell size).

Table 1. Precision and parameters values for European and Italian applications

Region/area	cell [ha]	DI	BR	SP	SR	RG
Padova-Mestre, Italy	0,85	2	9	3	1	79
Palermo, Italy	0,25	2	26	38	70	100
Helsinki, Finland	1,07	2	100	11	1	62
Bilbao, Spain	0,45	6	22	22	12	53

The case study about the corridor between Padova and Mestre (near Venice) is quite different respect the others because we are analysing not a single city, but a territorial system, with an area of 51578 ha and 18 municipalities. The simulation made on 20 years (1997- 2017) shows a constant growth rate and a consequent linear growth of the urbanized areas, especially along road network: these results are confirmed by demographic analyses, which show a growth of the number of inhabitants in those municipalities and consequently of their extension.

The prevision made for Palermo from 1997 to 2017, otherwise, can be considered as a typical example of urban expansion "for contiguity". This effect is given by an high value of SP parameter, higher than Italian and European mean, and this behaviour is explained by two reasons: the constraint factor, that is the topological structure of the areas outside the city; and the phenomenon of the suburban growth, confirmed by a parallel analysis of commuters and residence transfers of people.

The case of Helsinki, instead, it's an example of the saturation of urbanized areas; whereas the simulation on the future of Bilbao shows a moderate growth near the city boundaries.

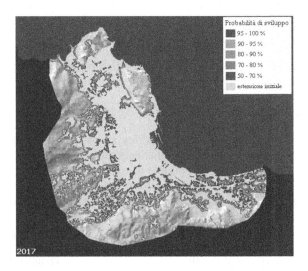

Fig. 2. Urban growth (1997-2017) and associate probabilities in Palermo, Italy

4   Remarks and Observations

The comparison with results from other cases can be performed integrating our results with Project Gigalopolis available database. So it's possible to understand SLEUTH strength theoretical and methodological bases and to individualize, in a concise way, common characteristics of urban expansion phenomena in different areas, identifying "DNA of world and cities", based on parameters values. The aim is to realize a regression that allows not only to describe city growth with a parametric combination, but also to deduce city or territory expansion by knowing the intrinsic effects of different parameters set. An opposite direction than calibration is ideally followed. Which actions and types of growth can a certain combination describe?

A comparison can be affected among parameters based on different geographic location case studies to understand how they can be distinguished in different territory. It's undeniable that social-economic, building and urban differences exist among different continents: they can emerge by this comparison. Instead the resistance parameter based on slope is difficult to generalize because it's typical of a land and can be traced back social-economic factors.

From it follows that: 1) a low value of DI is noticed in historical cities and metropolitan areas; in Italy and Europe there is a different space competition than in USA (max ID values); 2) BR is maximum in Europe because there is a very rational land use: when an installation occurs, its possibilities are exploited at its maximum; 3) the more the cities development is quick and recent (a growth that spreads at first from the edges), the more SP reaches high values: the maximum SP values are referred to cities which have known an economic and social boom (Mexico City, Houston, Tijuana); this is attested by the fact that minimum SP values are registered in Italian and European cities; 4) RG is often maximum in Italy and decreasing respectively in Europe, USA and other Asian and African countries. BR high and DI low values can be associated to planned and monitored territorial systems (Netherlands, Helsinki, lands which are also very flat too). There is a difference between the coastal and inland cities attitude: the firsts seem to be associated to highest DI values, the seconds refer to lower RG.

From these qualitative speculations, general principles are deduced and these can be used to describe different types of urbanization according to various parameters combination, performing the so called "parameters - real case" regression (Tab. 2). Using these methods, an effort to reproduce urban growth in Milan (between 1980 and 1997) was performed. According to the previous considerations, a set of DI=8, BR=100, SP=17, SR=1, RG=100 was chosen; results validation is possible thanks to the known situation in 1997. The obtained results are qualitatively good (right location of new settlements), but there is a trend to underestimate (-1%) the urban area, due to the presence in the Exclusion input layer of constraints representing the South Milan Agricultural Park from 1980 (but funded in 1990).

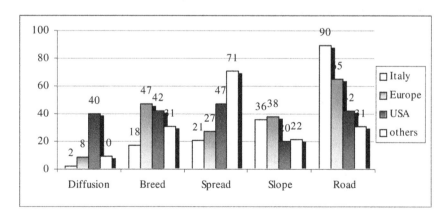

Fig. 3. Comparison between parameters values in different counties and cities in the world

Table 2. Parameters values ranges for the description of different urban development kinds

kind of urban area	hypothetical parameters values			
	DI	BR	SP	RG
recently developed metropolis	25-40	>50	>80	>50
urban sprawl	10-20	10-30	10-30	>50
well-established, planned city	<5	>90	<10	40-60
strongly restricted zone	<<5	100	<10	<10
metropolis with 'satellite cities'	5-10	30-40	10-30	>90

5 Conclusions

Parameters manipulating is the most synthetic approach to control urban dynamics. Being SLEUTH a trend extrapolator (using a historic database), it's possible to intuitively understand which parameter combination can describe urban dynamics for an urban complex typology (town, cities, metropolitan areas); it's possible to overcome absence of bi-univocal correspondence between parameters and growth phases using this kind of regression. Contextualizing real new case studies and methodological analysis permits to trace an inductive experimental approach, of which validity is confirmed by Milan application.

In the future, the intensive use of SLEUTH model for wide areas can be realized overcoming the computational problems, due to input images dimension and the large number of states explored by the automaton, thanks to parallel computing techniques, that is using multi-processor endowed pc or with workstations group. The whole CA cells space can be investigated dividing it in subset or subspaces and allocating these parts of study area to different computers. In this direction the intent is to integrate SLEUTH uses with the so called Computational Grid [9]. So the research continues in two directions: on one hand using the model as a tool improving performances; on the other hand investigating proprieties, using sensitivity analysis.

References

1. Couclelis H.: From cellular automata to urban models: new principles for model development and implementation. Environment and Planning B vol.24 n° 2 (1997) 165-174.
2. Candau J.T., Clarke K.C., Rasmussen S.: A coupled cellular automaton model for land use/land cover dynamics. 4th International Conference on Integrating GIS and Environmental Modeling (GIS/EM4) Alberta, Canada n° 94 (2000) 1-13.
3. Clarke K.C., Gaydos L.: Loose-coupling a cellular automaton model and GIS: long-term urban growth prediction for San Francisco and Washington/Baltimore. International Journal of Geographical Information Science vol 12 n° 7 (1998) 699-714.
4. Dietzel C., Clarke K.C.: Replication of Spatial-temporal Land Use Patterns at Three Levels of Aggregation by an Urban Cellular Automata. Cellular Automata – International Conference on Cellular Automata for Research and Industry – ACRI LNCS 3305 (2004) 523-532.

5. Candau J.T.: Temporal Calibration Sensitivity of the Sleuth Urban Growth Model. University of California, Santa Barbara (2002).
6. Camagni A.: Le ragioni della coesione territoriale: contenuti e possibili strategie di policy. Scienze Regionali n. 2 (2004) 97-111.
7. Wu F.: Calibration of cellular automata parameters using tabu search: an application to urban spatial structure. 9th Computers in Urban Planning and Urban Management n° 324 (2005) 1-19.
8. Caglioni M., Rabino G.: Contribution to fractal analysis of the cities: a study of metropolitan area of Milan. Cybergeo: Revue européenne de géographie ISSN 1278-3366 n° 260 (2004).
9. Clarke K.C.: Geocomputation's future at the extremes: high performances computers and nanoclients Parallel Computing 29 (2003) 1281-1295.

A Full Cellular Automaton to Simulate Predator-Prey Systems*

Gianpiero Cattaneo, Alberto Dennunzio, and Fabio Farina

Università degli Studi di Milano–Bicocca
Dipartimento di Informatica, Sistemistica e Comunicazione,
Via Bicocca degli Arcimboldi 8, 20126 Milano, Italy
{cattang, dennunzio, farina}@disco.unimib.it

Abstract. A Cellular Automaton (CA) describing a predator–prey dynamics is proposed. This model is fully local, i.e., without any "spurious" Monte Carlo step during the movement phase. A particular attention has been addressed to the comparison of the obtained simulations with the discrete version of the Lotka–Volterra equations.

1 Introduction

Nonlinear ordinary differential equations are still a fundamental tool in the analysis of Predator-Prey systems [5, 8]. The limit due to lack of information about the spatial distribution during the time evolution of the populations have pushed the research, since the early 1990's, toward lattice models. These systems evolves in discrete time steps by means of the application of some rules to the lattice sites. Most of the proposed lattice models are based on Monte Carlo (MC) simulation methods [9, 7, 11, 4, 1, 6, 10]. This approach is usually paired with mean-field equation analysis. The rules used to define the hunting process, i.e. the strictly local predator-prey interaction, are in many cases deterministic. Sometimes this local interaction does not assume the exclusion principle, so many entities may stay in the same lattice site [6, 11, 7]. More important, in the MC methods the movement phase of the species is a non local process. Let us stress that the random unbounded jumps between lattice sites may be unlikely w.r.t. the real movement capabilities of the individuals. In effects in many MC lattice models the focus on the biological semantics of the predation is somehow considered a secondary aspect. In [2] the predation phase is suitably treated but the MC modelling of the movement is not completely satisfactory from a biological point of view.

Cellular Automata (CA) models [12, 3] give a better biological approach to simulate predator-prey interactions. In the CA context all the lattice sites are updated in a synchronous way and, generally, the local evolution rule is simpler than the MC versions. The small cardinality of the CA neighborhood grants to model properly the individual movements.

---

* This work has been supported by the MIUR PRIN project "Formal Languages and Automata: Mathematical and Applicative Aspects".

S. El Yacoubi, B. Chopard, and S. Bandini (Eds.): ACRI 2006, LNCS 4173, pp. 446–451, 2006.

We propose a CA model to simulate predator-prey systems. The probabilistic predation rule, inspired by [2], has been designed by ecological motivations. We have defined a truly local movement phase, where wishes and fears of each species have been taken into account. A comparison between the simulations obtained by our CA approach and dynamical systems is exposed.

2   Discrete Time Dynamical Systems

Let us consider a single population within a closed environment. We denote by the variable $x(t) \in \mathbb{R}_+$ the population magnitude at time $t \in \mathbb{N}$ and by $r : \mathbb{N} \mapsto \mathbb{R}$ the growth rate function of the population. The system evolves according to the equation $x(t+1) - x(t) = r(t) \cdot x(t)$. We consider the logistic case where $r(t) = k\,(1 - x(t)/L)$ with $k \geq -1$ and $L \in \mathbb{R}_+$. The parameter L is the capacity, i.e., the maximum number of individuals allowed by the system in order to maintain the population in equilibrium. The variation of the parameter k in the domain $-1 < k < 3$ determines different dynamical behaviors modifying the features of the equilibrium points 0 and L.

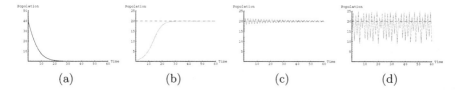

(a)   (b)   (c)   (d)

Fig. 1. Dynamics in the cases: (a) $-1 < k = -0.2 < 0$ (0 attracting, $L = 100$ repelling), (b) $0 < k = 0.23 < 1$ (0 repelling, $L = 20$ attracting), (c) $1 < k = 1.98 < 2$ (0 repelling, $L = 20$ attracting with possible oscillations) and (d) $2 < k = 2.6 < 3$ (0 and $L = 20$ repelling)

On the other hand, the behavior of two species $x_1(t) \geq 0$ (preys) and $x_2(t) \geq 0$ (predators) in competition in the same environment is summarized by the following discrete time difference equation generalization of the standard Lotka–Volterra differential equations system with $a_{ij} \geq 0$

$$\begin{cases} x_1(t+1) = x_1(t)[(1+k_1) - a_{11}x_1(t)] - a_{12}x_1(t)x_2(t) \\ x_2(t+1) = x_2(t)[(1+k_2) - a_{22}x_2(t)] + a_{21}x_1(t)x_2(t) \end{cases} \tag{1}$$

The study of the equation 1 shows that prey and predator populations exhibit an evolution consisting of oscillations.

3   The CA Model of Predator–Prey Dynamics

The automaton we consider in this paper is based on the $2D$ discrete rectangular lattice space $\mathcal{L} = \{0, \dots, M-1\} \times \{0, \dots, N-1\}$ consisting of M cells in the

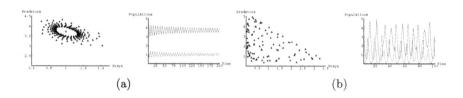

Fig. 2. (a) and (b): dynamics for $k_1 = 2.8$, $k_2 = 0.5$, $a_{12} = a_{21} = 0.5$. (c) and (d): dynamics for $k_1 = 2.8$, $k_2 = 0.5$, $a_{12} = a_{21} = 0.7$.

horizontal direction and N cells in the vertical one with periodical boundary conditions (toroidal geometry). Each cell can assume a value in $Q = \{0a, 1, 2a\}$, where $0a$, 1 and $2a$ mean that either the cell is empty, it contains a prey or it contains a predator, respectively. A *configuration* $\underline{c}$ of the automaton is a function $\underline{c} : \mathcal{L} \mapsto Q$ which assigns to each cell $(x, y) \in \mathcal{L}$ a state $\underline{c}(x, y) \in Q$, implemented as a $M \times N$ two dimensional array. In this paper we present two CA models. The second model, as an improvement of the first one, corresponds to better (and in some sense optimal) results in comparison with the difference equations discussed in section 2. The enhancement regards the possibility of prey death in cells whose neighborhood contains a great number of other preys in absence of predators. The uniformly applied local transition CA rule consists of two steps: *reaction* and *movement*.

The reaction step is composed by two sub-phases: the attack and the reproduction (including also death processes). They depend on the following 4 parameters: b_p (prey birth probability), d_p (prey natural death probability), b_h (predator birth probability), and d_h (predator death probability). In both these sub-steps the involved neighborhood is the Von Neumann one. Let us introduce two temporary further states: $0b$ which means that the cell becomes empty after the attack sub-step and $2b$ meaning the cell contains a predator which ate. In this way, we have obtained a new state set $Q_0 = \{0a, 0b, 1, 2a, 2b\}$. For the attack we consider a cell state $s \in Q$ in the position $(x, y) \in \mathcal{L}$. If it is a prey $(s = 1)$ we have two possible transitions towards a new state $s' \in Q_0$. If there are no predators in its neighborhood the cell remains prey $(s' = 1)$. Otherwise, it alive $(s' = 1)$ with probability $(1 - d_p)^{n_{pt}(x,y)}$ where $n_{pt}(x, y)$ is the number of predators in its neighborhood. If the prey dies the state of the cell becomes $s' = 0b$. If the cell is a predator $(s = 2a)$, the predator fails the hunt (and in this case $s' = 2a$) with probability $(1 - d_p)^{n_{pr}(x,y)}$ where $n_{pr}(x, y)$ is the number of preys in its neighborhood. If the hunt succeeds the state of the cell becomes $s' = 2b$. Let us consider now a cell of state $s \in Q_0$ in the position $(x, y) \in \mathcal{L}$. During the reproduction sub-step if the cell is a prey $(s = 1)$, its state does not change $(s' = 1)$. If the cell is a predator $(s = 2a/2b)$, it can die with probability d_h. In this case the cell becomes empty $(s' = 0a)$, otherwise the new state is $s' = 2a$. Let us now trait the situation of an empty cell $s = 0a$. If either there are some predators or there are no preys in its neighborhood, the cell remains empty $(s' = 0a)$. Otherwise it becomes prey $(s' = 1)$ with probability $(1 - b_p)^{n_{pr}(i)}$. In the case $s = 0b$ (corresponding to the fact that in the previous sub-phase the cell

Fig. 3. The 4 quadrants of the radius 2 Moore neighborhood of a cell

was occupied by a prey and in its neighborhood there was predators) the cell remains empty (with $s' = 0a$) with probability $(1 - b_h)^{n_{pt2}(x,y)}$, where $n_{pt2}(x, y)$ is the number of predators which have eaten. Otherwise the cell becomes predator ($s' = 2a$).

In order to describe the movement phase let us introduce the mapping $T : Q \times \mathcal{L} \mapsto \{0, 1\}$ defined as follows:

$$T(v; x, y) = \begin{cases} 1 & \text{if the state of the cell } (x, y) \text{ is } v \in Q \\ 0 & \text{otherwise} \end{cases} \tag{2}$$

We can associate to any cell of position (x, y) and to each state $v \in Q$ the following quantities

$$n_N^{(r)}(v; x, y) = \sum_{i=1}^{r} \sum_{j=-i}^{i} T(v, x + j, y + i) \quad n_S^{(r)}(v; x, y) = \sum_{i=1}^{r} \sum_{j=-i}^{i} T(v, x + j, y - i)$$

$$n_E^{(r)}(v; x, y) = \sum_{i=1}^{r} \sum_{j=-i}^{i} T(v, x + i, y + j) \quad n_W^{(r)}(v; x, y) = \sum_{i=1}^{r} \sum_{j=-i}^{i} T(v, x - i, y + j)$$

which represent the number of cells of state v in the North, South, Est, and West, respectively, quadrant of the radius r Moore neighborhood centered in the cell (x, y) (see figure 3). On the basis of these numbers it will be possible to determine the movement intentions of the individuals. If a cell contains a prey, the associated direction is the one corresponding to the quadrant containing the minimum number of predators. If many quadrants contain the same minimum value, then the direction is chosen with uniform probability. If there are not predators in the whole Moore neighborhood there is no movement. Analogously, a predator cell direction is directed toward the quadrant with the maximum prey number. Once the intentions are set, the movement is modelled so that the individuals move towards available empty cells in their Von Neumman neighborhood. If the same available empty cell is pointed by many creatures then a random choice is performed.

4   Simulations

In order to make a first test about the validity of the proposed model, we have considered the two opposite situations of preys without predators and vice versa. In the former (see the fig. 4b), the simulations show an increase of the population which is similar to the behavior of the logistic difference equation under

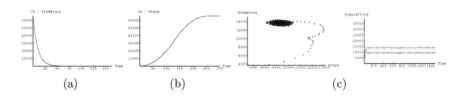

(a)   (b)   (c)

Fig. 4. CA dynamics of (a) predators in absence of preys and (b) preys in absence of predators. (c) CA dynamics with prey and predators ($b_p = .6, d_p = .7, b_h = .3, d_h = .2$).

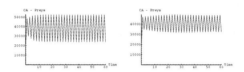

Fig. 5. CA prey dynamics with cosine function (left) and exponential function (right)

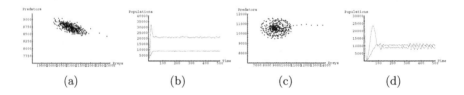

(a)   (b)   (c)   (d)

Fig. 6. CA dynamics of an interacting predator–prey system with cosine function

$0 < k < 1$ (compare with the fig. 1b). In the latter (see the fig. 4a) the decrease of predators is comparable to the logistic difference equation under $-1 < k < 0$ (compare with the fig. 1a).

These behaviors occur in any performed simulation independently by the CA parameters. Differently from the difference logistic equation behavior no oscillations appear. The figure 4b shows a simulation of a predator-prey interaction.

An improvement of the first CA model

The above discussion, with the inadequacy in obtaining oscillatory dynamics in the case of a single prey population, led us to modify the attack sub-phase for cells (x, y) containing a prey ($s = 1$). **If** *either* there is some predator in the Von Neumann neighborhood of the given cell and the prey is alive to the attack *or* there is no predator in its Moore neighborhood of radius r, **then** it dies ($s' = 0a$) with probability $n'_{pr}(x, y) \cdot f(b_p)/(2r+1)^2$, where $n'_{pr}(x, y)$ is the number of preys in the Moore neighborhood of radius r and f is a pre-assigned mapping on the interval $[0, 1]$. In this paper we have adopted the two following different choices $f_1(b_p) = (1 - \cos(\pi/2 \cdot b_p))$ (cosine) and $f_2(b_p) = 1 - e^{-e \cdot b_p}$ (exponential). The figure 5 shows two oscillating prey dynamics and the figures 6 and 7 propose some simulations of interacting populations obtained by the modified model.

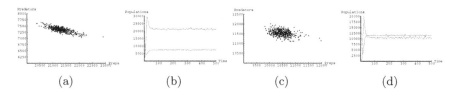

$$(a) \qquad\qquad (b) \qquad\qquad (c) \qquad\qquad (d)$$

Fig. 7. CA dynamics of an interacting predator-prey system with exponential function

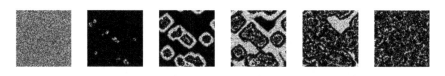

Fig. 8. Different lattice evolution steps

5   Conclusions

We have presented a full CA model of predator–prey systems whose fit with the logistic discrete time results about the dynamical evolution of the total number of individuals is very promising. Furthermore, the information about the "spatial strategies" adopted by the two species during these dynamics, information non available in the difference (but also differential) equation case, can be obtained.

References

[1] T. Antal and M. Droz, *Phase transitions and oscillations in a lattice prey-predator model*, Physical Review E **63** (2001), 056119(11).
[2] N. Boccara, O. Roblin, and M. Roger, *Automata network predator-prey model with pursuit and evasion*, Physical Review E **50** (1994), 4531–4541.
[3] B. Chopard and M. Droz, *Cellular automata modelling of physical systems*, Cambridge University Press, Cambridge, 1998.
[4] M. Droz and A. Pekalski, *Coexistence in a prey-predator system*, Physical Review E **63** (2001), 051909(5).
[5] M. W. Hirsch and S. Smale, *Differential equations, dynamical systems, and linear algebra*, Accademic Press, NY, 1974.
[6] M. Kovalik, A. Lipowski, and A.L. Ferreira, *Oscillations and dynamics in a two-dimensional prey-predator system*, Physical Review E **66** (2002), 066107(5).
[7] A. Lipowski, *Oscillatory behaviour in a lattice prey-predator system*, Physical Review E **60** (1999), 5179–5184.
[8] J.D. Murray, *Mathematical biology*, Springer Verlag, Berlin, 1993.
[9] J.E. Satulovsky and T. Tomè, *Stochastic lattice gas model for a predator-prey system*, Physical Review E **49** (1994), 5073–5079.
[10] G. Szabò and G.A. Sznaider, *Phase transition and selection in a four-species cyclic predator-prey model*, Physical Review E **69** (2004), 031911(5).
[11] T. Antal, M. Droz, A. Lipowski and G. Òdor, *Critical behaviour of a lattice prey-predator model*, Physical Review E **64** (2001), 036118(6).
[12] S. Wolfram, *A new kind of science*, Wolfram Media, 2002.

Lava Invasion Susceptibility Hazard Mapping Through Cellular Automata

Donato D'Ambrosio[1], Rocco Rongo[2], William Spataro[1],
Maria Vittoria Avolio[2], and Valeria Lupiano[2]

[1] Department of Mathematics and High Performance Computing Center,
University of Calabria, 87036 Rende, Italy
{d.dambrosio, spataro}@unical.it
[2] Department of Earth Sciences and High Performance Computing Center,
University of Calabria, 87036 Rende, Italy
{rongo, valeria.lupiano, avoliomv}@unical.it

Abstract. This work deals with a new methodology for the definition of volcanic susceptibly hazard maps through Cellular Automata and Genetic Algorithms. Specifically, the paper describes the proposed approach and presents the first results to the South-Eastern flank of Mt. Etna (Sicily, Italy). In particular, resulting hazard maps are characterized by a high degree of detail and allow for a punctual and accurate evaluation of the risk related to lava invasion.

1 Introduction

Cellular Automata (CA) are discrete dynamical systems, widely utilised for modelling and simulating complex systems, whose evolution can be described on the basis of local interactions. Well known examples are Lattice Gas Automata and Lattice Boltzmann models (cf. [1]), which are particularly suitable for modelling fluid dynamics at a microscopic level. However, many natural phenomena are difficult to be modelled at such scale, as they generally evolve on very large areas, thus needing a macroscopic level of description. Moreover, they may be also difficult to be modelled through standard approaches, such as differential equations (cf. [2]), and Macroscopic Cellular Automata [3] can represent a valid alternative.

Among the above mentioned phenomena, lava flows may involve serious dangers for people security and property, and their forecasting could significantly decrease this hazard, for instance by simulating lava paths and evaluating the effects of control works (e.g. embankments or channels). SCIARA [4] is a family of deterministic Macroscopic CA models, specifically developed for simulating lava flows, in particular for the Etnean "aa" type, which are characterised by a relatively high viscosity degree. Numerous versions have been proposed, ranging from mainly empirical [5] up to models which embed a proper physical description of the phenomenon and a more accurate control of its development [6]. However, experience showed that these latter allow for not considerable improvements in terms of simulation results, in spite of a notably increase of computational requirements. Consequently, the more sophisticated models may represent the better choice for studies needing the high possible accuracy, while even a simplest version can be considered for preliminary analysis, especially in

S. El Yacoubi, B. Chopard, and S. Bandini (Eds.): ACRI 2006, LNCS 4173, pp. 452–461, 2006.

case the execution time is a critical factor. Accordingly, the SCIARA-fv version (derived from SCIARA-hex1 [5]) was considered in this study, as it permits satisfying simulations of real events and is characterised by low computational times, allowing for the execution of an elevated number of simulations, needed for the scope of this work.

Concerning model calibration and validation, the former was performed through Genetic Algorithms on a well known case of study, and results then validated on different ones. By applying the model to the simulation of an adequate number of "possible" events, a preliminary hazard map was obtained for the South-Eastern flank of Mt Etna (Italy), based on a new methodology, as described in the following sections.

2 The SCIARA-fv CA Model

The Macroscopic CA model SCIARA-fv can be simply thought as a region partitioned into hexagonal cells of uniform size, each one embedding an identical finite automaton (*fa*). Input for each *fa* is given by the states of the *fa* in the adjacent cells. The state specifies the physical conditions (altitude, lava thickness, flows, temperature, etc.) of the corresponding space portion. At time t=0, the states of the *fa* are specified according to the initial conditions of the phenomenon to be simulated; the CA then evolves by simultaneously updating the state of all the *fa* at discrete time steps, in accordance with the *fa* transition function. The SCIARA-fv formal definition is given by

$$SCIARA\text{-}fv = <R, L, X, S, P, \tau, \gamma>$$

where:

- R is the set of hexagonal cells covering the finite region where the phenomenon evolves;
- L⊂R specifies the lava source cells;
- X = {Center, NW, NE, E, SE, SW, W} identifies the hexagonal pattern of cells that influence the cell state change. They are the cell itself, "*Center*", and the "*North-West*", "*North-East*", "*East*", "*South-East*", "*South-West*" and "*West*" neighbors;
- $S = S_a \times S_t \times S_T \times S_f^6$ is the finite set of states of the *fa*, considered as Cartesian product of "substates". Their meanings are: cell altitude, cell lava thickness, cell lava temperature, and outflows lava thickness (from the central cell toward the six adjacent cells), respectively;
- $P = \{p_s, p_{tv}, p_{tsol}, p_{adv}, p_{adsol}, p_{cool}, p_a\}$ is the finite set of SCIARA-fv parameters (invariant in time and space), which affect the transition function. Their meaning are: time corresponding to a CA step, lava temperature at the vent, lava temperature at solidification, lava adherence at the vent, lava adherence at solidification, the cooling parameter and cell apothem, respectively;
- $\tau : S^7 \to S$ is the deterministic *fa* transition for the cells in R;
- $\gamma : S_t \times N \to S_t$ specifies the emitted lava from the source cells at each step $k \in N$.

Even though principally derived from SCIARA-hex1 [5], SCIARA-fv embeds a better management of several aspects with respect to the original version, as a more adequate lava adherence evaluation (which considers the effective relation with temperature - cf. [2]). Refer to [5] for a detailed description of the model. Moreover, from a computational point of view, SCIARA-fv introduces many optimizations (e.g. [7]) and a thread-based multiple simulation feature (based on the portable OpenThreads cross-platform library), allowing for the simultaneous execution of multiple experiments. In particular, SCIARA-fv showed a linear scalability with respect to employed processors on both shared memory and NUMA (Non-Uniform Memory Access) machines, as the ones adopted in this work. This represents a significant computational improvement with respect the previous version, as it permits to reduce the overall execution time of a factor equal to the number of available processing elements.

2.1 Model Calibration and Validation

In general, once that a Macroscopic CA model has been defined, two stages are needed to assess its reliability: the calibration and validation phase. The former searches a set of parameters able to adequately reproduce a considered case; the latter tests the model on a sufficient number of cases (which should be different of those considered in the calibration phase, though similar in terms of physical and geological properties), permitting to give a final response on its goodness.

Genetic Algorithms (GAs, [8]), adaptive heuristic search algorithms inspired to Natural Selection and Genetics, were here adopted for the calibration phase, as they demonstrated to be a good choice in case of Macroscopic CA [9].

In brief, a solution to a problem is encoded as a genotype (or individual), and the set of all possible values it can assume is named search space. At the beginning, the GA randomly creates a population of individuals (candidate solutions), each one evaluated by means of a fitness function. Subsequently, the selection operator, which represents a metaphor of Darwinian Natural Selection, chooses individuals that undergo reproduction, by means of genetic operators (generally crossover and mutation, representing a metaphor of sexual reproduction), to form a new population of offspring. The evolution towards a good solution is typically obtained by the iterative application of selection and genetic operators to the initial population. The iterative process continues until a termination criterion is met, such as a known optimal or acceptable solution is attained, or the maximum number of steps is reached. The convergence to a good solution is stated by the "Fundamental Theorem of GAs" [8].

In this work, the employed GA was a Master-Slave parallel model (cf. [13]), exactly defined as in [10], except for the number of individuals forming the initial population (which was set to 256), and for the number individuals to be replaced at each step (set to 16). Importantly, the e_1 fitness function was unchanged; it is defined as:

$$e_1 = \sqrt{\frac{m(R \cap S)}{m(R \cup S)}} \ .$$

Table 1. The best set of SCIARA-fv parameters, together with their explored ranges, as obtained through calibration and validation phases. Note that parameter p_{tv} was set to a prefixed value, which corresponds to the typical temperature of Etnean lava flows at vents. Parameter p_a was also prefixed, as it was imposed by the detail of the considered topographic data.

Millions of m^3 / Duration (*days*)	$0 \div 32$	$32 \div 64$	$64 \div 96$	$96 \div 128$	$128 \div 160$
$0 \div 15$	19	3	0 (*4.18*)	0*	0*
$15 \div 30$	6	3	1	0 (*2.3*)	0*
$30 \div 60$	3	0 (*2.89*)	1	0 (*1.33*)	1
$60 \div 90$	1	2	0 (*1.37*)	1	0 (*1.05*)
$90 \div 120$	3	0 (*1.49*)	1	0 (*1.08*)	0 (*1.01*)
$120 \div 150$	1	1	1	0 (*1.03*)	0 (*1.01*)
$150 \div 180$	0 (*1.27*)	0 (*1.13*)	1	1	1
$180 \div 210$	0 (*1.16*)	1	0 (*1.02*)	0 (*1.06*)	1
$210 \div 240$	0*	0 (*1.11*)	0 (*1.05*)	0 (*1.06*)	0 (*1.15*)
$240 \div 270$	0*	0*	0 (*1.08*)	0 (*1.14*)	0 (*1.23*)
$270 \div 300$	0*	0*	0 (*1.12*)	1	0 (*1.36*)
$300 \div 500$	0*	0*	1	0 (*1.32*)	2

Note that the function e_1 gives values belonging to the interval $[0, 1]$. Its value is 0 if the real and simulated events are completely disjoint, being $m(R \cap S) = 0$; it is 1 in case of a perfect overlap, being $m(R \cup S) = m(R \cap S)$. As a consequence, the goal for the GA is to find a set of CA parameters that maximise e_1.

Calibration was performed on a Nec TX7 NUMA machine composed by 4 quadri-processors Itanium class nodes, with an overall RAM memory of 32 GB and a peak performance of 64 GFLOPS. On the basis of previous empirical attempts, ranges within which the values of the CA parameters are allowed to vary were individuated in order to define the GA search space (cf. Table 1), and a set of 10 experiments iterated for 100 steps. The best result allowed to satisfactorily reproduce the considered case of study, the 2001 Nicolosi Etnean lava flow, giving rise to a fitness equal to 0.71.

However, as already discussed in [9], a validation phase is generally needed in order to assess the goodness of the devised parameters, especially in case the fitness function only considers areal comparisons. Moreover, as calibration was performed on a "short" event (in terms of extension and duration), results had to be confirmed on more general cases, which must be considered for the scope of the work. As a consequence, the validation phase was carried out by testing the obtained parameters to other well-known real cases of study: the first 28 days of the 1991-93 Valle del Bove and the 2002 Linguaglossa events. In this phase, some parameters were slightly refined, and the definitive "best" set, listed in Table 1, permitted a satisfactorily reproduction of the considered phenomena. In quantitative terms, the obtained fitness was 0.78 and 0.72, respectively. A further experiment was also performed for evaluating the ability of the model in reproducing lava fields on longer events (in terms of duration), and the 1792 Etnean lava flow (developed in 90 days) was well reproduced (even if only from a qualitative point of view as the pre-event morphological data was obviously not available). Eventually, it is worth to note that, on the basis of the above results and by considering that Etnean lava flows may be essentially considered as characterised by the same rheological features (cf. [11]), the model can be confidently adopted for simulating new cases on the same study area.

3 A New Methodology for Hazard Map Creation

The main goal of this work is the definition of a methodology for the compilation of a new kind of map showing the hazard related to lava invasion in predefined study areas. Differently to standard approaches, in which the hazard is generally based on statistical studies of past events [12] or on the application of probabilistic simulation models (e.g. [13]), the one here proposed relies on a deterministic "virtual laboratory" (i.e. the SCIARA-fv framework) where new events are simulated on present morphological data, which implicitly embeds the effects of past events. A grid of vents is defined in the study area, and a prefixed number of simulations is executed for each of them, each one characterised by its own effusion rate and duration. Moreover, a probability of activation is assigned to each vent in the grid (*activation probability*), based on historical, prehistoric and geological data, and a probability is assigned to each type of considered effusion rate and duration (*event probability*), devised on the basis of the emission behaviour analysis of the study area. Eventually, on the basis of other considerations, more additional probabilities can be also considered (e.g. a higher probability can be assigned to an event on the basis of the minor distance of the vent with respect to the summit craters - *altitude probability*). The resulting hazard map is thus compiled by taking into account both information on lava flows overlapping, and their occurrence probability.

Accordingly, the definition of the hazard map can not prescind from the following requirements: 1) a reliable simulation model, well calibrated and validated, needed to perform the simulations; 2) an adequately detailed topography representing the study area, together with locations of vents and their probability of activation; 3) a set of eruptive histories, together with their probability of occurrence; 4) further probabilities of occurrence (e.g. the altitude probability), if any. Once these requirements are satisfied, a simulation is executed for each combination of vent location and event history, by storing results in a database. The resulting map is obtained by evaluating the hazard at each point in the study area as follows: 1) for each simulation, the hazard related to a generic point in the study area is computed as the product of the defined probabilities of occurrence (conditioned probability) if it is affected by the simulated lava flow, zero otherwise; 2) for each point, the conditioned probabilities are added over all the performed simulations. Note that, in such a way some areas will be characterised by very low hazard values (even zero), while others by high ones. Depending on the number of performed simulations and morphological conditions, the hazard of remaining areas may range in a quasi-continuous manner between the two extremes. As a consequence, it may be possible to compile hazard maps with a high level of description even if, in general, few hazard classes are considered adequate for many practical applications.

The accuracy of the results strictly depends on the reliability of the simulation model, on the quality of input data and on the hypotheses on assigning the different probabilities of occurrence. Thus, if some of such aspects should not be sufficiently adequate, it could be possible (and desirable) to improve them in order to compile a resulting hazard map with a higher level of accuracy. For instance, in case of uncertainty in assigning the probabilities of occurrence, a different map can be obtained by simply re-processing the simulations database and by just considering a more reliable criterion of analysis. Finally, note that if an equal probability of occurrence is assigned to each simulation, a more classical criterion of hazard mapping is obtained, which only considers the number of simulated events which affect a given area.

4   First Application to the South-Eastern Flank of Mt Etna

The South-Eastern flank of Mt Etna (Sicily, Italy) was chosen as the study area since previous studies describe it as one of the most dangerous in terms of possible fracture reactivation. Fig. 1 shows the considered area, together with the location of vents subdivided in 4 classes of activation probabilities (corresponding to 4/10, 3/10, 2/10 and 1/10), these latter derived by a statistical study on lava events occurred over the last 400 years and on geological considerations [12]. The grid of vents consists of 340 points, each one located 500 m apart from each other, in order to uniformly cover the interested area. Note that, events generated by fractures are not considered. However, by also considering the high density of vents in the grid, they can be ignored, at least in a first analysis.

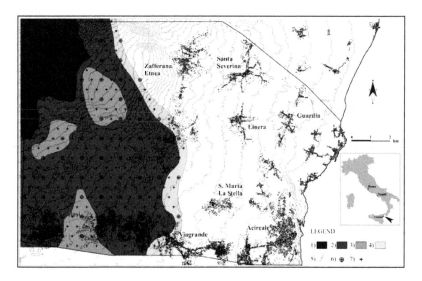

Fig. 1. The South-Eastern flank of Mt Etna. Key: 1-4) vent activation probability, in decreasing order, corresponding to 4/10, 3/10, 2/10 and 1/10, respectively; 5) study area limits; 6) the 88 vents considered in the present work; 7) remaining 252 vents

Moreover, by analysing historical records (also dating back to the last 400 years – cf. [12]), eruptions were classified in 50 different typologies, each one characterised by its own range of duration and of emitted lava. The worst case (i.e. the most dangerous) was chosen as representative for each class, and its event probability assigned by simply dividing its class frequency (i.e. the number of events in the class – cf. Table 2) by the overall number of occurred events.

Eventually, the altitude probability (conjectured significant for the considered study area [12]) was computed by considering the relation between the topographic altitudes of vents and the lava flows occurred in the last 400 years (cf. Fig. 2). However, in order to provide information over the entire range of altitudes for the study area, the tendency line was considered in spite of real data.

Table 2. Frequencies of events occurred on Mt Etnean during the last 400 years, grouped in terms of duration and emitted lava. Numbers in brackets show interpolated data (considered for evaluating the event probabilities), useful to gather information on "missing" events. Events with asterisk were not considered as they represent not realistic cases (i.e. high volume vs. short duration, low volume vs. long duration).

Duration (days) \ Millions of m^3	0 ÷ 32	32 ÷ 64	64 ÷ 96	96 ÷ 128	128 ÷ 160
0 ÷ 15	19	3	0 (4.18)	0*	0*
15 ÷ 30	6	3	1	0 (2.3)	0*
30 ÷ 60	3	0 (2.89)	1	0 (1.33)	1
60 ÷ 90	1	2	0 (1.37)	1	0 (1.05)
90 ÷ 120	3	0 (1.49)	1	0 (1.08)	0 (1.01)
120 ÷ 150	1	1	1	0 (1.03)	0 (1.01)
150 ÷ 180	0 (1.27)	0 (1.13)	1	1	1
180 ÷ 210	0 (1.16)	1	0 (1.02)	0 (1.06)	1
210 ÷ 240	0*	0 (1.11)	0 (1.05)	0 (1.06)	0 (1.15)
240 ÷ 270	0*	0*	0 (1.08)	0 (1.14)	0 (1.23)
270 ÷ 300	0*	0*	0 (1.12)	1	0 (1.36)
300 ÷ 500	0*	0*	1	0 (1.32)	2

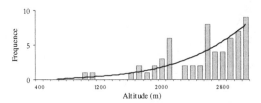

Fig. 2. Relation between the elevation of vents (a.s.l.) and the number of occurred lava flows for the set of lava flows listed in Table 2. Tendency line is also reported.

As regards the simulation phase, 50 events (i.e. the representative cases of each considered class – cf. data without asterisk in Table 2) must be simulated for each of the 340 considered vents (cf. Fig. 1), and therefore a total of 17000 experiments must be executed for an exhaustive study. By considering the extent of the study area (a map of 2272×1790 hexagonal cells, each with a 5 m apothem, derived from a 1:10000 scale topography) and the duration of the considered events (which ranges from 15 to

500 days), the adoption of Parallel Computing is mandatory to reduce the execution time. Accordingly, the simulation phase is being performed (it is currently in progress) on two parallel machines: a 16 Itanium processor Nec TX7 shared memory super computer and an 8 processor Apple Xserve G5.

Results here presented are therefore only preliminary, and specifically refer to a total of 1056 simulations on a sub-grid of vents (88 vents, key 6 of Fig. 1) and on a subset of event typologies (the 12 most probable typologies, first 3 rows of Table 2).

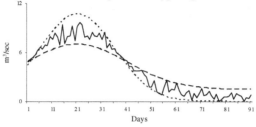

Fig. 3. An example of effusion rate randomly generated by considering the Etnean lava flows trend, where dotted lines define the variation range for a typical real event. The example refers to a case of 90 days and a peak of about 10 m^3/s.

As regards the effusion rates of the considered events (cf. Table 2), these were randomly generated on the basis of a representative trend of Etnean lava flows [12]; an example is shown in Fig. 3 for a case of 90 days and a peak of about 10 m^3/s.

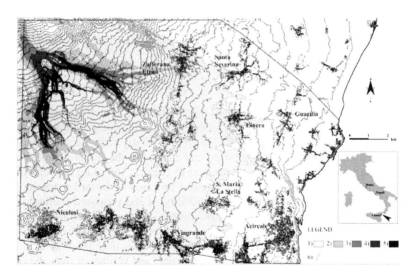

Fig. 4. Hazard map of the study area based on the 1056 executed simulations and the criterion described in Section 3. Key: 1-5) hazard classes, in increasing order; 6) study area limits

The resulting hazard map, obtained as described in section 3, is shown in Fig. 4. Eventually, a further map was also compiled by only considering flows overlapping (Fig. 5), which is in accordance with a more classical hazard mapping criterion. It is worth to note that results are quite different: in particular the hazard map which only considers flows overlapping does not take into account the very low probability of occurrence for the events which originate at low elevations, thus determining high risk areas even in zones which never were interested by lava flows in the last 400 years. At the contrary, the map compiled by applying the methodology here proposed seems more reliable, as it is more likely that higher risk areas are located at higher altitudes, near the summit crater.

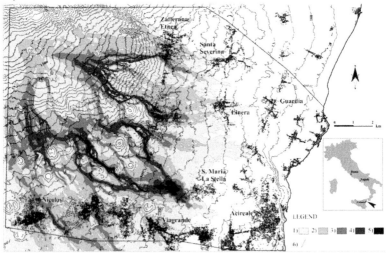

Fig. 5. Hazard map of the study area obtained by simply considering the overlapping of the 1056 executed simulations. Key: 1-5) hazard classes, in increasing order; 6) study area limits.

5   Conclusions

The "a priori" knowledge of hazard related to lava invasion is a crucial aspect for risk mitigation in volcanic areas. A new kind of criterion for the compilation of lava invasion susceptibly maps, based on Cellular Automata, jointly with Genetic Algorithms and Parallel Computing, has been proposed and applied to the South-Eastern flank of Mt Etna. Results, even if preliminary, seemed to confirm the more reliability of the approach when compared with a more classical criterion of hazard mapping. However, a more rigorous assessment of the reliability of the proposed methodology is certainly desirable for effective usage in civil defense. A possible solution could simply consist awaiting for next events in the study area but this could, obviously, require an unpredictable time. An alternative could consist in compiling the map on a subset of sample events (e.g. occurred in the first 300 years) and validate it over the remaining ones, on condition to dispose of a proper "past" topography. Other alternatives are also currently being conjectured, which will be certainly taken into account in future works.

Acknowledgements

This work is sponsored by the Italian Ministry for University and Research, FIRB project n° RBAU01RMZ4 *Lava flow simulations by Cellular Automata*". Geological data and topographic maps have been provided by Dr. S. Calvari, Dr. M. Neri and Dr. B. Behncke of the INGV (National Institute for Geophysics and Volcanology) of Catania (Italy). The authors are also grateful to Prof. G. M. Crisci, Prof. S. "Toti" Di Gregorio, Dr. G. Niceforo and Dr. G. Iovine for the common researches.

References

1. Succi, S.: The Lattice Boltzmann Equation for Fluid Dynamics and Beyond. Oxford University Press (2004)
2. McBirney A.R., Murase T.: Rheological properties of magmas. Ann. Rev. Ear. Plan. Sci., 12 (1984) 337–357
3. Di Gregorio, S., Serra, R.: An empirical method for modelling and simulating some complex macroscopic phenomena by cellular automata. Fut. Gener. Comp. Syst. 16 (1999) 259–271
4. Barca D., Crisci G.M., Di Gregorio S., Nicoletta F.: Cellular Automata for simulating lava Flows: A method and examples of the Etnean eruptions. Transp. Theory Stat. Phys. 23, (1994) 195–232
5. Crisci G.M., Rongo R., Di Gregorio S., Spataro W.: The simulation model SCIARA: the 1991 and 2001 lava flows at Mount Etna. J. Vol. Geo. Res., 132 (2004) 253–267
6. Avolio M.V., Crisci G.M., Di Gregorio S., Rongo R., Spataro W., Trunfio G.A.: SCIARA $\gamma2$: An improved cellular automata model for lava flows and applications to the 2002 Etnean crisis. Computers and Geosciences, in press
7. Walter R., Worsch T.: Efficient Simulation of CA with Few Activities. In: P.M.A. Sloot, B. Chopard and A.G.Hoekstra (Eds.), LNCS 3305. Springer-Verlag, Berlin (2004) 101–110
8. Holland J.H.: Adaption in Natural and Artificial Systems. University of Michigan Press, Ann Harbor (1975)
9. D'Ambrosio D., Spataro W., Iovine G.: Parallel genetic algorithms for optimising cellular automata models of natural complex phenomena: an application to debris-flows. Comput. Geosci-UK, in press
10. Spataro W., D'Ambrosio D., Rongo R., Trunfio G.A.: An Evolutionary Approach for Modelling Lava Flows through Cellular Automata. In: P.M.A. Sloot, B. Chopard and A.G.Hoekstra (Eds.), LNCS 3305. Springer-Verlag, Berlin (2004) 725–734
11. Chester D.K., Duncan A.M., Guest J.E., Kilburn C.R.J., Mount Etna: The anatomy of a volcano. Chapman and Hall, London, UK (1985)
12. Behncke, B., Neri, M., Nagay, A.: Lava flow hazard at Mount Etna (Italy): New data from a GIS-based study. In M. Manga, and G. Ventura (Eds.), Kinematics and dynamics of lava flows: Geological Society of America Special Paper 396 (2005) 189–208
13. Damiani, M.L., Groppelli, G., Norini, G., Bertino, E., Gigliuto, A., Nucita A.: A lava flow simulation model for the development of volcanic hazard maps for Mount Etna (Italy) Comput. Geosci-UK, 32 (2006) 512–526
14. Cantù-Paz E.: Efficient and accurate Parallel Genetic Algorithms. Kluwer Academic Publishers, Dordrecht, The Netherlands (2000)

Exploring the DNA of Our Regions: Classification of Outputs from the SLEUTH Model

Nicholas Gazulis and Keith C. Clarke

University of California, Santa Barbara, 3611 Ellison Hall, University of California, Santa Barbara, CA, 93106
{ngazu, kclarke}@geog.ucsb.edu

Abstract. The SLEUTH urban growth model is a cellular automata model that has been widely used by geographers to examine the rural to urban transition as a physical process and to produce forecasts of future urban growth [1]. Previous SLEUTH applications have generally been limited to individual model applications, with little to no comparison of model results [2]. Building upon research by Silva and Clarke [3], and borrowing from their metaphorical comparison of urban growth characteristics to genetic DNA, this research distills a combination of actual city and model behavior in a controlled environment to provide for comparisons between disparate model applications. This work creates a digital "petri dish" capable of producing normalized model forecasts from previously incomparable results. Results indicate that despite the inherent differences between actual model results, sufficient similarities were observed among the forecasts to warrant the creation of an urban behavioral taxonomy, providing for direct comparison of the results.

1 Introduction

Cellular Automata (CA) models are increasingly being used for representing geographical processes, including many applications within the field of urban and regional modeling [1], [4]. Spatial processes, such as urban growth, exploit the natural analogy between two-dimensional CA and time-sequenced grid representations of two-dimensional geographic space. As geographer Waldo Tobler realized [5], the grid cells of a CA lattice can represent the "state" in areas of land while the lattice of the CA can foster geographical processes such as distance decay and spatial autocorrelation. While the idea of simulation with CA in the field of geography can be traced to Tobler [5], a more formal declaration of the use of CA applicability for representing urban systems was by Couclelis [6], leading to a major new modeling paradigm in recent years [7]. More recently, CA models have broadened to multiple states, and so to land-use change modeling [8].

Innovation within the computer and geographical sciences, coupled with increased access to quality and affordable remotely sensed data, has led to the use of these new urban growth models in both a policy and theoretical context [9]. Responding to heavy criticism of the first generation of urban computer models [10], [11], CA models have demonstrated practical success in urban planning. Due to data-driven

S. El Yacoubi, B. Chopard, and S. Bandini (Eds.): ACRI 2006, LNCS 4173, pp. 462–471, 2006.
© Springer-Verlag Berlin Heidelberg 2006

issues, such as inconsistent scale and resolution, urban and regional models are generally limited to specific policy situations where little emphasis is placed on comparisons between successive applications. Urban areas exhibit extremely different characteristics due to the complexity of the processes underlying urban growth. Consequently, modeling results produced from heterogeneous applications are generally incomparable [12].

Silva and Clarke [3] suggest that despite overwhelming differences between urban areas, there exist fundamental elements that are common to each urban area. This variability manifests itself in unique patterns of urban growth for each particular city as determined by the local environment or site. Many of these common elements relate to an area's particular dependence on transportation, how technologically feasible construction is on steep slopes, to what extent new urban centers develop within a system, how likely new spreading centers are to develop their own growth cycle, and how quickly spreading centers are to grow. Silva and Clarke [3] further suggest that many of these common elements can be empirically quantified for individual urban systems. The reduction of the characteristics that describe an urban area's uniqueness bears a resemblance to the biological notion of genetic DNA, a complete set of which fully describes a living organism's growth and development cycle, and as such, can metaphorically be considered to be the "DNA of our Regions". Like individual creatures, all cities are unique, yet share common building-blocks that permit replication and growth.

Given the DNA analogy, an experiment was created to distill a combination of actual city and model behavior in a controlled environment out of the data-dependent context of typical applications. DNA fragments were selected from cities and then grown under controlled circumstances in a digital "Petri dish." As in the work by Silva and Clarke [3], the SLEUTH urban growth and land use change model was used to quantify differences among worldwide urban areas. To do this, two sets of input data were used, including an anisotropic plane representing geographic variability and individual parameter sets as fit to various real cities. The anisotropic plane was held fixed throughout the experiments while only the SLEUTH control parameter sets were varied. The overall goal of this work was to create an experiment that allowed for comparison of previously incomparable results. As a means for comparing the results, a simple taxonomy was created based on visual and quantitative model results.

2   The SLEUTH Model

SLEUTH is capable of modeling the complex dynamics of any urban growth or land use change system given a set of historical input data. SLEUTH is an acronym for the six required data inputs, **S**lope, **L**anduse, **E**xclusion, **U**rban extent, **T**ransportation, and **H**illshade, and simulates land use dynamics as a physical process [13].

During forecasting with SLEUTH, the model is initialized with the most recent data as the "seed" layer. SLEUTH then executes a finite set of transition rules that influence state changes within the CA. The transition rules involve selecting cells at random and investigating the spatial properties of that cell's neighborhood. Based on an urbanization probability derived from the local characteristics of a particular cell, that cell is either urbanized or not urbanized. Monte Carlo simulation is employed to reduce stochastic bias, and it has been shown that a large number of iterations does not always result in improved results [14]. As such, users typically define between 15 and 30 iterations.

Before forecasting, the model must account for the physical differences that exist among individual study areas. To do so, SLEUTH employs a calibration routine that examines the historical data input to derive a set of parameters representing past urbanization trends for each unique region. As the CA iterates, a dozen statistical descriptors are computed that relate model behavior to the known historical data. The calibration phase of SLEUTH produces a set of five coefficients, each of which describes an individual growth characteristic of an urban area, plus their statistical goodness of fit to the historical data. A complete set of five calibration coefficients (each with an integer value ranging from 0 to 100) influences the degree to which each of the four growth rules influences urban growth in the system. These coefficients include:

1. *Dispersion* – controls the overall dispersive nature of the distribution.
2. *Breed* – determines the likelihood that an urbanized cell will start its own growth cycle.
3. *Spread* – determines the likelihood that the pixels that comprise a new spreading center will continue to generate new urban pixels.
4. *Slope* – influences the likelihood that a cell will be urbanized on a slope.
5. *Road Gravity* – a factor that encourages growth along the road network.

This set of parameters drives the four transition rules that govern urban growth within the system, which simulate *spontaneous* growth in suitable urban areas, *diffusive* growth in new spreading centers, *organic* growth in infill and edge areas, and *road-influenced* growth along the transportation network.

Calibration of the model is based on comparing model output and initial model inputs for a variety of parameter combinations. The model is initialized with the earliest available time period and "forecasts" urban extent using a coefficient set for the time period corresponding to the distance between the first and last data inputs. Images of urban extent are produced using many different parameter combinations and compared to the control data available for "goodness of fit". The degree of similarity between the simulated images and the control years is determined through a set of metrics that are calculated and stored in a log file. The analyst must examine the log file to determine the optimal set of parameters based on the calculated metrics, deducing which set of parameters produces an image that most closely resembles the control data images. Recent work has determined an optimal metric of fit, known as the Optimal SLEUTH Metric (OSM) specifically for use in determining best fit [15]. As a substitute for an exhaustive search, SLEUTH employs a 'Brute Force' method of coefficient optimization, which explores the parameter space in successively finer intervals. This structured brute force approach has been shown to reduce model overfit. Computation time is still a major factor in calibration, and other methods have been explored such as genetic algorithms [16].

3 Input Data

The data inputs for this research are twofold, including (1) a set of simulated images, and (2) a set of calibration parameters derived from the twenty SLEUTH model applications in the data repository for which parameters were reported.

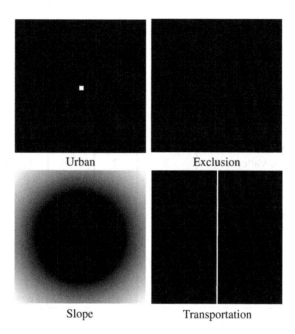

Fig. 1. Inputs: GIS images used in exploring the SLEUTH model parameters

For the first input, Nystuen [17] suggests that geographical problems must be assessed in a uniform representation of abstract space devoid of geographic variability, a surface he refers to as the isotropic plane. Contrary to Nystuen's [17] experimental isotropic data space, this work proposes that the isotropic plane, while preferable for some applications, is not preferable for others, and as such, cannot be considered to be a uniform standard for the modeling of geographic processes.

Due to the continually variable conditions of the Earth's surface, urban areas necessarily develop under sub-optimal conditions. As a result, the reduction of urban growth behavior into a set of parameters requires a variable surface from which a forecast can be derived. Otherwise, modeling results would only yield information about the overall spread and growth rates of the system. To allow for a robust comparison of the results, input data was created that mimicked the variable conditions experienced in actual urban systems.

The initial urban input consists of a single urban cell in the middle of the image with all other cells beginning as non-urban (see figure 1). The exclusion layer is divided lengthwise from east to west, with the southern portion bearing no resistance

Table 1. SLEUTH parameters derived from studies documented in the SLEUTH repository

Application Location	Diffusion	Breed	Spread	Slope	Road
Atlanta, GA	55	8	25	53	100
Austin, TX	47	12	47	1	59
Chiang Mai, Thailand	1	4	88	1	25
Colorado Front Range	11	35	41	1	91
Houston, TX	1	3	100	22	17
Lisbon, Portugal	19	70	62	38	43
Mexico City, Mexico	24	100	100	1	55
Netherlands	2	80	5	4	5
New York, NY	100	38	41	1	42
Oahu, HI	5	96	12	1	50
Porto, Portugal	25	25	51	100	75
San Joaquin Valley, CA	2	2	83	10	4
Santa Barbara, CA	40	41	100	1	23
Santa Monica Mts, CA	31	100	100	1	33
Seattle, WA	87	60	45	27	54
Sioux Falls, SD	1	1	12	34	29
Tampa/S. Florida	90	95	45	50	50
Tijuana, Mexico	3	8	70	42	22
Washington, DC	52	45	26	4	19
Yaounde, Cameroon	10	12	25	42	20

to urbanization and the northern portion bearing 50% resistance. No portion of the exclusion layer was 100% excluded from urbanization. The center of the slope layer has a slope of 0% while the far diagonal corners have the maximum slope of 100%. The slope increments radially, appearing as a spherical depression centered at the initial urban area with a slope of 0 %. There is a threshold above which urbanization cannot occur due to a high degree of slope, resulting in an effective circular constraint on growth (the edges of the Petri dish). A threshold was included to represent the physical barrier of increased slope, above which urbanization is rarely permitted, or even possible. The slope threshold was defined as 23% in this study. The transportation layer consists of a single road running north-south through the center of the image. The hill-shade layer, which consists of a simple white background, adds only to the visual output of SLEUTH.

For the second input, a collection of parameters from the approximately one-hundred papers, presentations, theses, and dissertations about the more than 80 domestic and international SLEUTH applications was performed. Recently, studies completed by Gazulis et al. [18] and Clarke et al. [2] have sought to compile, catalog, and analyze this wealth of information, resulting in the creation of the SLEUTH online data repository, http://www.ncgia.ucsb.edu/projects/gig/.

4 Results

Initial modeling of each parameter set with the hypothetical anisotropic plane resulted in more than 2000 SLEUTH output images for the twenty unique parameter sets included in this study. Each parameter set produced time-series images in one year increments, displaying the probability of urbanization over twenty-five Monte Carlo iterations. The result was 100 probabilistic images of urban growth for each parameter set outside of the specific data driven environment that usually underlies disparate SLEUTH applications.

The results indicate that the anisotropic plane defined for this study was capable of producing conditions to which each parameter set must adapt in order to grow. Each unique parameter set adapted differently, producing a distinct urbanization pattern both spatially and temporally. However, despite the heterogeneous results produced by each parameter set, some spatial and temporal similarities did arise among particular applications.

Based on an analysis of the growth rates of individual regions, and coupled with the spatial distribution of urban pixels in each image, sufficient similarities were observed among the resulting forecasts to warrant the creation of an urbanization behavioral taxonomy. The latter was tabulated by counting growth pixels by quadrant in the four principal directions. The initial conditions of the anisotropic plane were identical for the east and west quadrants, and as a result, the relative population of these two quadrants was averaged, giving three growth dimensions. Growth rates were calculated for each of the regions and averaged over the user-specified twenty-five Monte Carlo iterations. These growth rates were plotted and examined for similarities among the individual regions.

Plots of relative quadrant counts for each of the forecasts were created and examined for clustering. A three dimensional plot of north, south, and average east/west quadrant population revealed a distinct cluster of points with high values in the southern quadrant relative to both the north and average east/west quadrants as well as a cluster of points at or near the origin (see figure 2).

A third cluster appeared with relatively high values in the north and average east/west quadrants, as well as near complete urbanization of the southern quadrant. However, within this cluster were three parameter sets that produced results that never reached full saturation in the southern quadrant – indicating a separate cluster of points.

Each of these clusters represented a different urban growth behavior dependency, characteristic, or constraint that could be easily determined through a visual inspection of the time series images. As a result, each cluster was given a name representing the dependency, characteristic, or constraint that best described the cluster's urban behavior: these were (1) slope resistant growth; (2) transportation network dependent growth; (3) little to no growth; or (4) full build out growth.

An examination of the growth rates for each model application revealed that the clusters indicated above tended to have similar growth rates. Growth rates were calculated by dividing the number of newly urbanized pixels at each time step by the total number pixels urbanized during the simulation and then converted to a percent increase. Growth rates for slope resistant regions tapered off exponentially but

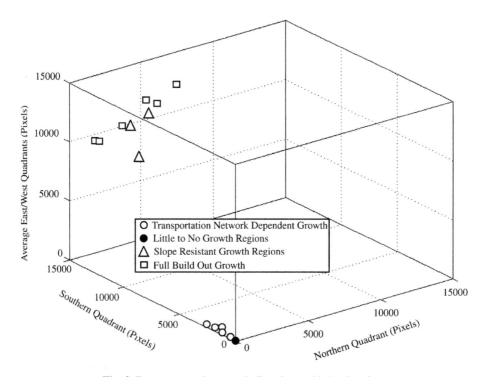

Fig. 2. Parameter set by growth direction and behavior class

generally did not drop to zero by model year 100. Growth rates for transportation network-dependent parameter sets also tapered off exponentially, but not in a smooth fashion. Year to year variability was extremely high relative to the other classes, especially in the initial growth stage between model years 0 and 30. In all fully-built-out parameter sets, growth rates dropped to zero by model year 100 and experienced little to no growth after model year 75. Finally, growth rates of little to no growth parameter sets were highly variable in all regions over the course of all 100 model years, with extreme year to year variability in the early model years. Rates for these sets dropped close to zero by model year 100 and also became less variable.

Of some interest is the little or no growth class. An interpretation of this group is that these are cities which are unable to sustain growth at all given the starting conditions for the geographical location. Of course the actual conditions differ from those we used as hypothetical examples, but nevertheless, these could be interpreted as cities that required some other impetus than normal growth to get started, perhaps planning, government incentives, or a convergence of factors such as existence of a port, railhead or other factor, including chance. Houston, for example, had the advantage of oil finds in the surrounding area adding an external impetus to growth.

The piece of information that has been missing thus far is the direct influence of time on the different categories of urbanization. The model runs allow temporal

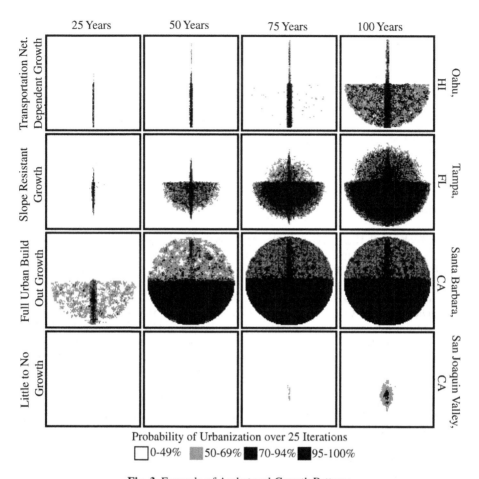

Fig. 3. Example of Archetypal Growth Patterns

comparison. For example, the sprawl category seems to accelerate early, while the slope resistant class begins sprawl-like infill only after all the available flat land is taken, about half way through the model run.

5   Conclusion

This research has shown that the output from SLEUTH calibration can provide for data-independent modeling of the urban growth of individual areas. In separating the behavior of urban growth from the city environment into a set of parameters, we gain the ability to experiment with the growth form in time and space using the SLEUTH model. An advantage of the approach is that the growth behavior is then directly comparable, and, as we have shown, is subject to classification and generalization. Exactly why these cities fall into the classes remains the topic of future research. Similarly, a more robust analysis would have hundreds or thousands of parameter sets to compare and contrast. Nevertheless, the study shows that models can be used above and beyond their traditional role (i.e. forecasting), and we have added a new role as experimental platforms for abstract behavior characterization. CA behaviors (e.g. extinction, stability, dynamic stability, growth) were expected from a CA model, nevertheless we were not aware prior to the analysis that cities could be grouped in this way.

Uninvestigated in this research were the impacts of resolution, temporal sensitivity, data sensitivity, or land use. Some of these factors have been the topic of research work on SLEUTH and other urban models, yet we feel that these issues can now be the topic of further work.

References

1. Clarke, K. C., S. Hoppen, et al. (1996). Methods And Techniques for Rigorous Calibration of a Cellular Automaton   Model of Urban Growth. Third International Conference Workshop on Integrating GIS and Environmental Modeling, Santa Fe, New Mexico, National Center for Geographic Information and Analysis.
2. Clarke, K. C., N. Gazulis, et al. (2006). A Decade of SLEUTHing: Lessons Learned from Applications of a Cellular Automaton Land Use Change Model. Twenty Years of the International Journal of Geographic Information Science and Systems. T.& F. London.
3. Silva, E. and K. C. Clarke (2005) Complexity, emergence and cellular urban models: lessons learned from applying SLEUTH to two Portuguese metropolitan areas. European Planning Studies January 2005, vol. 13, no. 1, pp. 93-115 (23).
4. Agarwal, G., Grove, Evans, Schweik (2003). A review and assessment of land-use change models: Dynamics of space, time, and human choice. UFS Technical Report NE-297. Burlington, VT, U.S. Department of Agriculture Forest Service, NE Research Station.
5. Tobler, W. (1979). Cellular Geography. Philosophy in geography. S. Gale and G. Olsson. Dordrecht; Boston, D. Reidel Pub. Co.: 379-386.
6. Couclelis, H. (1985). "Cellular worlds: a framework for modeling micro-macro dynamics." Environment and Planning A 17: 585-596.
7. Batty, Michael, Helen Couclelis, and M. Eichen. 1997. Special issue: urban systems as cellular automata. Environment and Planning B 24 (2).
8. Verburg, P. H. (2006) Modeling Land-Use and Land-Cover Change. Chapter 5 in Lambin, E. F. amd Geist, H. (eds) Land-Use and land-Cover Change: Local Processes, Global Impacts. Springer-Verlag: Berlin, Heidelberg.
9. Brail and Klosterman (2001). Planning Support Systems: Integrating Geographic Information Systems, Models, and Visualization Tools. Redlands, CA, ESRI Press.
10. Lee, J. D. B. (1973). "Requiem for Large-Scale Models." AIP Journal May: 163-77.
11. Lee, J. D. B. (1994). "Retrospective on Large-Scale urban Models." Journal of the American Planning Association 60(1): 35-40.
12. Benenson, I. and P. M. Torrens (2004). Geosimulation: automata-based modelling of urban phenomena. Hoboken, NJ, John Wiley & Sons.
13. Clarke, K. C., and L. Gaydos (1998) "Loose Coupling A Cellular Automaton Model and GIS: Long-Term Growth Prediction for San Francisco and Washington/Baltimore" International Journal of Geographical Information Science, vol. 12, no. 7, pp. 699-714.
14. Goldstein, N., Dietzel, C., Clarke, K.(2005) Don't Stop 'Til You Get Enough - Sensitivity Testing Of Monte Carlo Iterations For Model Calibration. Proceedings, 8th International Conference on GeoComputation University of Michigan, Eastern Michigan University.

15. Dietzel, C. (2005). From Parameters to Scenarios: Using the Behavior of CA to Create New Features. Geography. Santa Barbara, University of California, Santa Barbara. **PhD:** 166.
16. Goldstein, N. C. (2005). Brains versus Brawn - Comparitive Stratagies for the Calibration of a Cellular Automata-Based Urban Growth Model. GeoDynamics. P. M. Atkinson. Boca Raton, CRC Press: 249-272.
17. Berry, B. J. L. and D. F. Marble (1968). Spatial analysis; a reader in statistical geography. Englewood Cliffs, N.J., Prentice-Hall.
18. Gazulis, N., N Goldstein, and K. C. Clarke (2005). The SLEUTH Online Data Repository. Annual Meeting of the Association of American Geographers. Denver, CO.

Improved Cell-DEVS Models for Fire Spreading Analysis

Matthew MacLeod, Rachid Chreyh, and Gabriel Wainer

Dept. of Systems and Computer Engineering
Carleton University. 1125 Colonel By Dr. Ottawa, ON. K1S 5B6. Canada
{mmacleod, rchreyh, gwainer}@sce.carleton.ca

Abstract. The spread of fire is a complex phenomenon that many have tried to study over the years. As one can imagine, the spread of fire depends on many different variables such as the material being burned, the geography of the area, and the weather. Here, we will show a Cell-DEVS model based on an existing model to speed up the simulation. We use Quantized DEVS and 'dead reckoning' to vary the length of the time steps taken by each cell. This paper explores how using one or both of the methods together can sometimes decrease the number of messages sent (and hence the execution time).

1 Introduction

The spread of fire is a complex phenomenon that many have tried to study over the years. As one can imagine, the spread of fire depends on many different variables such as the material being burned, the geography of the area, and the weather. It has been determined that finding an analytical solution for mathematical models of fire spread is almost impossible, and therefore many have looked to simulation as an attractive alternative. Simulations have been found that accurately represent the way in which fire spreads, and are now generally the preferred solution for predicting the behavior of fire. This goal of predicting fire behavior is important to firefighters (for example), because having a tool that is able to predict where the fire will be and how it will move will enable them to better plan strategies to control the fire quickly and safely. An aspect of great importance in such a tool is that it has to be able to predict the fire behavior at the very minimum faster than the fire itself moves, preferably much faster. In a real life situation, if we want to use a tool to help us predict how the fire will spread we have to be confident that it will give us a reasonable result on the order of minutes. Otherwise, valuable time will be lost as the fire spreads further.

The complexity of how fire spreads has made it the target of study in the modeling and simulation field. Mathematical models for this phenomenon are too complex to give an analytical solution; therefore, simulations have been used to study it and there has been some success in predicting fire behavior using cellular models. Although Cellular Automata have been used in defining the kind of models of our interest [1, 2, 3] CA poses precision constraints and extra computation time. Cell-DEVS [4] was proposed to solve these problems by defining cell spaces as DEVS (Discrete Events systems Specifications) models [5]. Using Cell-DEVS, a cell space is described as a discrete event model in which explicit delays can be used to model accurately the cell

S. El Yacoubi, B. Chopard, and S. Bandini (Eds.): ACRI 2006, LNCS 4173, pp. 472–481, 2006.

timing properties. CD++ [6] allows implementing DEVS and Cell-DEVS models, while providing remote access to a high performance DEVS simulation server [4].

Here, we will show improvement to previously developed fire spreading model using Cell-DEVS [7]. In this model, the physical area of interest is divided into cells, with each cell exhibiting the same behavior. The model uses a simple set of equations to determine the temperature of each cell at regular time intervals. The temperature of a non-burning cell is an averaging function of its own temperature and that of its neighbors. Once ignited the temperature of burning cells, on the other hand, is also a function of time – the cell's temperature increases to a peak and then falls back down, modeling the exhaustion of fuel in the cell.

As all the cells are activated on every timestep, performance can be poor (especially for large models). Here, we explore modifications to the existing model to speed up the simulation. This can be done in several ways, including both using Quantized DEVS (Q-DEVS) to quantize the model output [8], and using 'dead reckoning' to vary the length of the time steps taken by each cell. By using Q-DEVS we will be able to reduce the number of messages exchanged between the cells so that messages are only sent when the output of a cell passes a quantization threshold. The use of dead reckoning contrasts with the traditional method of using an equation (fit from experimental data) that determines the temperature of a cell as a function of time. In the dead reckoning approach, we find an equation (or set of equations) that determines the time the next quanta will be passed as a function of the current temperature. In other words, we will only update the temperature of the cells at the quantum boundaries, by using an equation that determines at what time the next quantum will be reached. This paper explores how using one or both of the methods together can sometimes decrease the number of messages sent (and hence the execution time).

2 Background

A real system modeled using the DEVS formalism [5], can be described as a hierarchy of submodels. Each of them can be behavioral (atomic) or structural (coupled). A DEVS atomic model is described as $M = < X, S, Y, \delta_{int}, \delta_{ext}, \lambda, D >$. The interface is composed of input and output ports (X, Y) to communicate with other models. The input external events (those coming from other models) are received in input ports. The model specification defines the behavior of the external transition function under such inputs (δ_{ext}). Each state has an associated duration time (D). When this time is consumed, the output function (λ) is triggered, and then the internal transition function (δ_{int}) is activated to produce internal state changes. A DEVS coupled model is defined as: $CM = < I, X, Y, D, \{M_i\}, \{I_i\}, \{Z_{ij}\} >$. Here X is the set of input events, and Y is the set of output events. **D** is an index of components, and for each i ∈ D, M_i is a basic DEVS model (atomic or coupled). I_i is the set of influencees of model i. For each j ∈ I_i, Z_{ij} is the i to j translation function. Each coupled model consists of a set of basic models connected through the input/output ports. The influencees of a model will determine to which models one send the outputs. The translation function is in charge of translating outputs of a model into inputs for the others. To do so, an index of influencees is created for each model (I_i). For every j in this index, outputs of the model M_i are connected to inputs in the model M_j.

Cell-DEVS allows defining complex cellular models that can be integrated with other DEVS. Each cell of a space is defined as an atomic DEVS. Transport and inertial delays allow defining timing behavior of each cell in an explicit and simple fashion. Cell-DEVS atomic models can be specified as TDC = < X, Y, S, N, delay, d, δ_{int}, δ_{ext}, τ, λ, D >. X represents the external input events, Y the external outputs. **S** is the cell state definition, and **N** is the set of input events. **Delay** defines the kind of delay for the cell, and **d** its duration. Each cell uses a set of N input values to compute the future state using the function τ. These values come from the neighborhood or other DEVS models, and they are received through the model interface. A delay function can be associated with each cell, allowing deferring the outputs. A Cell-DEVS coupled model is defined by GCC = < X_{list}, Y_{list}, X, Y, n, $\{t_1,...,t_n\}$, N, C, B, Z >. Here, Y_{list} is an output coupling list, X_{list} is an input coupling list. X are the external input events and Y the external outputs. The **n** value defines the dimension of the cell space, $\{t_1,...,t_n\}$ is the number of cells in each dimension, and **N** is the neighborhood set. **C** is the cell space, **B** is the set of border cells and **Z** the translation function. The cell space defined by this specification is a coupled model composed of an array of atomic cells. Each of them is connected to the cells defined by the neighborhood. As the cell space is finite, the borders should have a different behavior than the remaining cells. Finally, the Z function allows one to define the internal and external coupling of cells in the model. This function translates the outputs of m-eth output port in cell Cij into values for the m-eth input port of cell Ckl. The input/output coupling lists can be used to transfer data with other models.

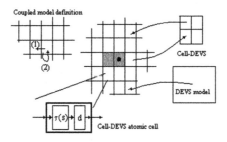

Fig. 1. Informal definition of a Cell-DEVS model

Recently, DEVS has been used recently for continuous systems simulation. In most cases, the techniques are based on Q-DEVS [8], whose main idea is to represent continuous signals by the crossing of an equal spaced set of boundaries. This approach requires a fundamental shift in thinking about the system as a whole. Instead of determining what value a dependant variable will have (its state) at a given time, we must determine at what time a dependant variable will enter a given state.

In [7], we showed how Cell-DEVS and CD++ could be used to model fire spread. Below is a simplified diagram of the temperature curve used in the original model. The temperature curve is divided into four stages, and, at any given instant, each cell in the model will be in one of these stages. The first is the inactive stage, when a cell has no neighbors with a temperature higher than the ambient temperature (T_a). The second is the unburned stage in which the temperature of the cell is increasing due to heat from the neighboring cells; during this stage, the cell's temperature is between the ambient temperature and the ignition temperature (300°C). The third is the burning stage in which the cell has reached the ignition temperature and fuel in the cell starts to burn. The cell's temperature increases until it reaches a peak temperature, and then begins to fall back down to 60°C. The fourth and final stage is the burned stage in which a burning cell's temperature has fallen below 60°C. Because it has exhausted its fuel, it can no longer reignite and it is considered inactive.

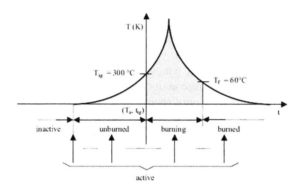

Fig. 2. Simplified Temperature curve [1]

The Cell-DEVS model contains two planes of cells. The first represents the fire spread itself, in which each cell calculates its temperature. The additional plane is used to store the ignition times for the cells (this can be considered merely a state variable of the true cells of interest). The cells in the ignition temperature plane have a simple rule – record the current simulation time when the corresponding cell in the fire spread plane reaches the ignition temperature. The cells in the fire spread plane compute fire spreading. When a cell is in the unburned phase, its temperature is calculated as the weighted average of the current cell's temperature with its neighbors' temperatures. When a cell is in the burning phase, its temperature is calculated as an exponential function of time that describes the fire's behavior, taking into account the same weighted average. In the other two phases (inactive and burned), the cell's temperature does not change, and thus these cells remain in the passive state (the inactive cells will of course respond to any temperature changes in their neighborhood, so they may eventually ignite). One of the advantages of using Cell-DEVS is that all cells in the inactive or burned phase will remain passive, and thus the calculations will be confined to the fire front. This saves on the simulation's execution time.

The reason for the slow execution time of the simulation is mainly due to the high number of messages being exchanged between cells. In the simplest version of the model, each cell in the unburned or burning phase will update its temperature once every millisecond and will as a result send messages to its neighbors. To remedy this problem a solution must be found that decreases the number of messages exchanged.

3   Quantizing the Fire Spread Cell-DEVS Model

In order to increase the speed of the simulation, we propose two simplifications. Firstly, if we are able to keep the unburned cells completely in the passive state until they reach the ignition temperature, we would reduce the number of cells that send out messages to their neighbors. The second is to use quantization to reduce the number of messages exchanged among the cells. This is explained in more detail below.

The model we propose will still have the same four phases of inactive, unburned, burning and burned. The main difference, however, is that in our model, in addition to the inactive and burned phase, the unburned cells also remain passive. We have found that a cell in the unburned phase will reach the ignition temperature when: a) one of its neighbors has reached a temperature above 650 °K , or b) two of its neighbors have reached a temperature above 474 °K. Using this result, we are able to keep all cells in the passive state until their neighbors meet these conditions, rather than constantly calculating weighted averages. When running the original model, we found that all cells more or less exhibit the same temperature curve when they are in the burning phase, implying that the temperatures of neighboring cells do not have a big impact on a burning cell's temperature. As a result, when a cell reaches the ignition temperature it can calculate its temperature by following only the temperature curve determined from experimentation, rather than taking into account its neighbors at every step. By doing this we have restricted the majority of calculations to the cells in the burning phase, and removed the need for messages from the neighbors in many cases.

The other method of reducing the messaging between cells is quantization [8, 9]. There are two quantization ideas that we have implemented in our model. The first is to use Q-DEVS to automatically quantize the model. In Q-DEVS, all cells in the model have a fixed quantum size and each cell has a quantizer. Each cell will only send output to its neighbors if its temperature has exceeded the next quantum threshold. The quantizer acts as the detector that decides when a threshold has been crossed, and it sends out the output only in that case. By implementing quantization as described here, the number of messages exchanged between cells will be reduced, thus increasing the speed of the simulation. However, the accuracy of the simulation will also be reduced. The key is to select a quantum size that gives a good performance increase for a small reduction in accuracy. The second method of quantization involves calculating time based on temperature, rather than temperature as a function of time. The first task was to find the inverse of the temperature curve for a typical cell [10]. Given such a function $f(T)$, we can calculate the amount of time it will take to reach the next quantum level as a simple difference $f(T_2)-f(T_1)$. By doing this, cells can be kept quiescent until they reach the next quantum threshold. After this time has passed, they will wake up, calculate the next time at which they will cross a threshold, and return to the quiescent state. This saves unnecessary calculation, as cells will only become active when a significant change in temperature occurs. To obtain the required function f, we started with a typical temperature curve of a cell in the burning phase.

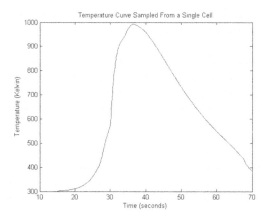

Fig. 3. Burning Cell's Temperature Curve

This function fails the horizontal line test, and therefore is not directly invertible. So, it must be divided into increasing and decreasing components, giving us two invertible functions. A state variable can then be used to choose between them during execution. We found two functions that approximate the two curves reasonably well. Note that for the scope of this paper we are not overly concerned about the accuracy of these functions, as the focus of this study is to analyze the performance of our proposed model, which if successful could be refined by fire experts to the desired level of accuracy. Collecting data for this version of the model would also be more efficient, as instead of sampling every cell of the real model every millisecond, samples would only have to be recorded at threshold crossings. This could potentially save much data storage, and make better use of network bandwidth in the test bed.

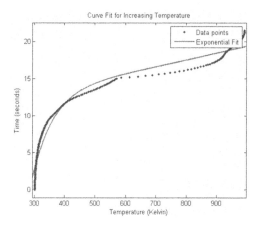

Fig. 4. Inverted increasing temperature function

The fit for the increasing temperature portion of the curve is shown above in figure 4. It uses a sum of two exponential functions:

$$f(T) = 11.56 * e^{0.0005187*T} - 784.7 * e^{-0.01423*T} \tag{1}$$

Where T is the temperature in degrees Kelvin. This will be used for cells in there "Burning Up" phase, i.e. the phase in which they are burning with increasing temperature. Similarly, the decreasing portion (or "Burning Down" phase) is fit with the linear function:

$$f(T) = 0.052 * T \tag{2}$$

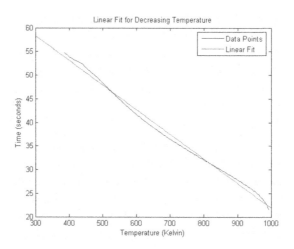

Fig. 5. Inverted decreasing temperature function

There are a few things to notice: although we found higher order functions that fit the functions with greater accuracy, these had issues related to local maxima and minima. As time is necessarily monotonically increasing, it is not acceptable for the functions to decrease at any point. Therefore, any function of time must also pass the horizontal line test, and therefore be invertible. As a consequence, we cannot model any up and down fluctuations in temperature within any of our piecewise curves, and we will need a new state for any change in direction. This restriction causes the obtained functions to be linear or near-linear in most regions (the exponential curve shown has two nearly linear regions joined by a knee). These functions will be used to develop the time advance portion of the model rules, which is easily implemented in Cell-DEVS delay functions.

3.1   Cell-DEVS Model Definition

In our Cell-DEVS model, temperatures remain on the first plane, and ignition times are in the second plane, and a third plane stores information about each cell that will help us determine which rule to apply. The second plane has a value of 0 by default, and the following values as indicated below:

- -100: If the temperature of the cell is between 301 and 474, meaning it is burning but not hot enough to cause a neighbor to ignite.
- -200: If the temperature of the cell is between 474 and 650, meaning it is burning and hot enough to cause a neighbor to ignite if another neighbor is in this state.
- -300: If the temperature of the cell is above 650, meaning it is burning and is by itself hot enough to cause a neighbor to ignite.
- -400: If the temperature has reached the peak temperature (992) from our data curve, and is now starting to burn with a decreasing temperature.
- -500: When the cell has burned out.

The neighborhood is as follows: Looking at a cell in the first plane (the fire spread plane) each cell has its corresponding cell in the second plane (the supporting info plane) and the Von Neumann neighborhood of that cell as its neighbors. The local computing function described below:

- **A cell whose neighbor in above plane has values of -100, -200 or -300:** Cells in the Burning Up phase; they have not yet reached their peak temperature. These cells will calculate (according to the burning up function) the time delay after which they should increment their temperature by the quantum amount and then sleep for this time.
- **A cell whose neighbor in other plane has values of - 400:** Cells in the Burning Down phase; they are still burning but have reached their peak temperature and their temperature is falling from here on in. These cells will calculate (according to the burning down function) the time delay after which they should decrement their temperature and then sleep for this time.
- **A cell whose value is 0 and its neighbor in other plane has a value between 301 and 474:** cells in the "Supporting Info" Plane. After a short time delay, they are to get a value of -100 indicating that their corresponding cell has ignited but is still below 474 °K.
- **A cell whose value is 0 or -100, and its neighbor in other plane has a value > 474:** cells are in the "Supporting Info" Plane. After a short time delay, they are to get a value of -200 indicating that their corresponding cell has ignited and has reached 474 °K. Two of these cells can cause a neighbor to ignite.
- **A cell whose value is 0 or -200, and its neighbor in other plane has a value > 650:** cells are in the "Supporting Info" Plane. After a short time delay, they are to get a value of -300 indicating that their corresponding cell has ignited and has reached 650 °K. This cell alone can cause a neighbor to ignite.
- **A cell whose value is -300 and its neighbor in other plane has a value > 992:** cells in the "Supporting Info" Plane. After a short time delay, they are to get a value of -400 indicating that their corresponding cell has just reached the peak temperature and should use the burning down equation.
- **A cell whose value is -400 and its neighbor in other plane has a value < 332:** cells in the "Supporting Info" Plane. After a short time delay, they are to get a value of -500 indicating that their corresponding cell has Burned out.
- **Ignition Rules:** A cell in the "fire spread plane" that has not ignited yet (i.e. has a value of 300 °K) will ignite if at least two of its neighbors have a value of -200 or at least one neighbor with a value of -300. The cell will ignite by being assigned a temperate of 301 °K.

4 Simulation Results

We ran the fire spread simulation in CD++ using our proposed model in comparison with the original model. The initial values used represented a line ignition scenario (i.e. the initial burning cells are in a straight line).

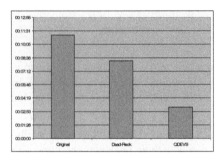 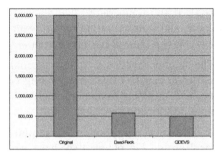

Fig. 6. (a) Execution times (b) Number of messages passed

As we had noted earlier the aim of our model is to reduce the execution time of the simulation without reducing the accuracy. Our model successfully reduced the simulation execution time. The following figure shows the execution time and the number of messages involved in the simulation of the original model and the two new versions here presented. As we can see, the reduction in the number of messages involved is exponential, thus providing an excellent technique for execution in parallel/distributed environments, in which message passing between the components are the cause of most of the execution time of the model. Gains were greater when only a few cells were initially activated.

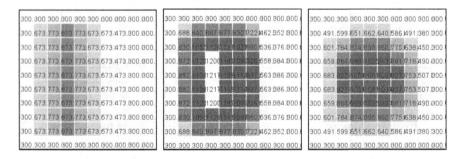

Fig. 7. Execution results at 0, 300 and 1000 time units

The previous diagrams depict the results we obtained using our model, which were similar to the original model. The cumulative average weighted error for the simulations was below 2%, following the trend presented in multiple studies on DEVS quantization [8, 9].

5 Conclusion

Our study concurred that the original model was too slow in execution time, due to the large number of messages exchanged among the cells in the model. Our techniques were able to improve performance. Our first proposed model used quantization to reduce the number of messages between the cells and thus increase the speed of the simulation. Quantization was implemented by calculating the time steps between temperatures, instead of the temperatures at time steps. This achieved the goal of keeping all cells "asleep" until a significant event takes place. The effect of neighboring cells was ignored, as in previous test runs all cells were seen to develop similarly. Another modification was to keep cells in the unburned state "passive" until they are seen to reach the ignition temperature. This increased performance, but had problems with accuracy, and required some prior knowledge of how the fire would develop to obtain good equations. We found that the general direction and speed of fire spread was maintained by our model, although some finer details such as peak temperatures and temperatures of cells at the fire front lost accuracy.

References

1. Rothermel, R.C.: A Mathematical Model for Predicting Fire Spread in Wasteland Fuels. USDA Forestry Service Research Paper, INT-115 (1972)
2. Barros, F., Ball, G.L.: Fire Modelling Using Dynamic Structure Cellular Automata. In: III International Conference On Forest Fire Research. 14th Conference on Fire and Forest Meteorology. Luso, Portugal (1998)
3. Balbi, J.; Santoni, P.; Dupuy, J.: Dynamic Modelling of Fire Spread Across a Fuel Bed. In: International Journal of Wasteland Fire. Vol. 9 (1999) 275-284
4. Wainer, G.; Giambiasi, N.: N-dimensional Cell-DEVS. In: Discrete Events Systems: Theory and Applications. Kluwer, Vol. 12, No. 1 (2002) 135-157
5. Zeigler, B.; Kim, T.; Praehofer, H.: Theory of Modeling and Simulation: Integrating Discrete Event and Continuous Complex Dynamic Systems. Academic Press (2000)
6. Wainer, G: CD++: a Toolkit to Define Discrete-Event Models. In: Software, Practice and Experience. Wiley, Vol. 32, No.3 (2002) 1261-1306
7. Muzy, A., Innocenti, E., Aiello, A., Santucci, J., Wainer, G.: Specification of Discrete Event Models for Fire Spreading. In: Transactions of the Society for Modeling and Simulation International, Vol.81, Issue 2 (2005)
8. Wainer, G., Zeigler, B.: Experimental Results of Timed Cell-DEVS Quantization. In: Proceedings of AIS'2000. Tucson, Arizona. USA (2000)
9. Zeigler, B.: DEVS Theory of Quantization. DARPA Contract N6133997K-007: ECE Dept., University of Arizona, Tucson, AZ (1998)
10. Lin, K.-C.: Dead Reckoning and Distributed Interactive Simulation. In: Distributed Interactive Simulation Systems for Simulation and Training in the Aerospace Environment; Proceedings of the Conference. Orlando, FL, USA (1995) 16-36.

A Cellular Automata Approach for Modelling Complex River Systems

Paweł Topa

AGH University of Science and Technology, al. Mickiewicza 30,
30-059 Kraków, Poland
topa@agh.edu.pl

Abstract. Rivers can be treated as transportation networks which supply or collect and remove certain resources from the surrounding environment. A positive feedback between environment and river network both reshapes the configuration of the terrain and produces dynamically stable web of river channels. Anastomosing rivers exemplify such interactions very clearly. In case of this specific type of river, nutrients carried by water disseminate to the surrounding soil and stimulate growth of peat-forming plants. Vertical accumulation of peats changes the shape of terrain and influence river network. We present a model of anastomosing river system based on Cellular Automata paradigm. Principal phenomena that contribute to evolution of such a river system are encoded as rules of local interactions. We discuss extensively the parameters and their influence on simulation results.

1 Introduction

Transportation networks are unique structures occurring only in highly organised dissipative systems, such as biological organisms, geological structures and evolving animal colonies. Functionality of these networks is the principal factor of evolution. Transportation networks can play two different roles. They can supply the necessary nutrients, which are consumed by the environment. Transportation networks can also collect and remove some products from productive environment. These two functions are usually performed simultaneously, as in the vascular tissue (arteries and veins), road and railway networks and river systems.

Rivers and river systems have been investigated for years as an important environmental aspect of human life and as the largest natural transportation network. Dynamics of river system is a good example of both self-organising complex system [1] and the source of natural fractals [2]. As shown in [3], a wide range of natural objects and phenomena possess a fractal–like structure. Examples of these so-called fractal trees include actual trees in gardens, plants, such as cauliflowers, river and cardiovascular systems. Unlike transportation networks in biological organisms, the growth factors influencing river systems can be directly observed and scrutinised. One can distinguish both global environmental factors such as terrain configuration, geology, ecological features, climate and local ones, e.g., erosion, deposition and sedimentation [4].

S. El Yacoubi, B. Chopard, and S. Bandini (Eds.): ACRI 2006, LNCS 4173, pp. 482–491, 2006.

The existence of diverse topological, biological, geomorphological degrees of freedom, sharp interfaces between interacting components, multifaceted boundary conditions and self-organised criticality phenomena driving the system dynamics, make the river topology intrinsically complex. Consequently, it seems the phenomena cannot be placed in an appropriate integrable function space and therefore the classical approaches involving partial or ordinary differential equations cannot be used in modelling of such the systems. The existing models prefer statistical methods (e.g., Monte-Carlo simulations, diffusion limited aggregation) and the cellular automata (CA) [13], which employs rules instead of equations (see [5], [7], [6]).

"Anastomosing river" term refers to river system that possess extremely complex network of forking and joining channels (see Figure 1). Anastomosing rivers are usually formed by repeated avulsions i.e. sudden change of route by whole or part of the stream. Avulsions are primarily driven by aggradation of the channel belt and/or loss of channel capacity and throughput by in-channel deposition [14]. Both processes are triggered by a low floodplain gradient.

Fig. 1. Part of the Narew River in eastern Poland with clearly visible anastomosing pattern (illustration courtesy Prof. Gradziński [8])

The area of the river valley, with growing layer of peat bog represents a typical consuming environment. The nutrients (nourishing resources as ions of nitrogen, phosphorus and potassium), supplied by river, penetrate the soil surrounding the riverbeds and stimulate the vegetation of peat-forming plants. Products of their partial decay accumulates as a peat, what results in gradual raising the level of terrain. Gradient of nutrients saturation, which appears mainly as a result of suction of root system, decreases the rate of peat accumulation proportionally to the distance from the channel. At the same time, sedimentation of organic and mineral material decreases the throughput of river channels. Water level fluctuations or jams occurring in channels can lead to avulsion, when part of stream leaves the main channel. The route of new channel is determined by the local terrain topography. The new channels usually merge with the others, creating a complex network composed of splitting and merging water channels and small lakes (see Fig. 1). An example of such the river is Narew (Poland, shown in Fig. 3A). There are many other examples such as the fragments of: upper Columbia River (south eastern British Columbia, Canada), Ob (Siberia), Okawango (Africa) and more. The detailed description of the factors, which govern the evolution of the anastomosing river can be found in [8] and [14].

The hypothesis of "starving environment" [12] is a focal point of transportation networks expansion. In the anastomosing river system the peat bog environment is "starving". It means that the supply of nutrients is insufficient, they are consumed very fast and the peat bog growth is restrained. These factors fuel up the expansion of the river network towards "hungry" areas. Conversely, "starving" plant explores productive environment by the huge network of roots in search for water and minerals. The positive feedback interaction between two factors: the network and environment, results in a mutual growth. While dysfunction in mechanisms stimulating the network expansion causes the death of the entire system.

In this paper we propose the Cellular Automata approach for modelling river networks in consuming environment. The CAMAN model ((CAMAN stands for Cellular Automata Model of Anastomosing Networks) is extended and modified version of older SCAMAN model [12]. We present the definition of Cellular Automata and outline of the main algorithm. The results are presented and discussed extensively.

2   Cellular Automata Model of Anastomosing River

For modelling a river, which is undergoing anastomosis we shall construct the algorithm of water distribution in terrain of a predefined topography. We use the modified version [9] of the algorithm described by Di Gregorio and Serra in [10], which was used for modelling lava and mud flow. The model of water spreading can be easily extended on anastomosing rivers. According to the definition of anastomosing river given in the Introduction, we have supplemented the model with the rules of both nutrients distribution and vertical growth of the peat bog.

Let us define this cellular automata model as follows :

$$CA_{CAMAN} = < Z^2, A_{in}, A_{out}, X, S, \delta >$$

where:

- Z^2 — is the $Z \times Z$ square mesh of cellular automata,
- $A_{in} \subset Z^2$ — collection of cells modelling sources - inlets,
- $A_{out} \subset Z^2$ — collection of cells modelling outlets,
- $X(ij)$ — defines the collection of neighbouring cells for an (i, j) cell,
- $S_{ij} = (g_{ij}, w_{ij}, n_{ij}, p_{ij}), i, j = 1, ..., Z$ — the vector describing state of an (i, j) cell:

- g_{ij} — the height of the terrain,
- w_{ij} — the height of water,
- n_{ij} — concentration of nutrients,
- p_{ij} — the peat-bog thickness,
- δ — is a transition function defined as follows:

$$\delta((g_{ij}^t, w_{ij}^t, n_{ij}^t, p_{ij}^t)) = (g_{ij}^{t+1}, w_{ij}^{t+1}, n_{ij}^{t+1}, p_{ij}^{t+1}).$$

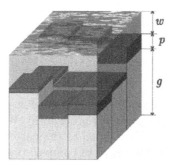

Fig. 2. The heights of columns on the cellular automata lattice represent the elevation of the terrain g and the thickness of both water w and peat-bog layers p

The terrain is modelled by a rectangular mesh $Z \times Z$ of cellular automata. The Moore neighbourhood and the fixed boundary conditions are applied [13]). The borders of the mesh are simulated as extremely high barriers, which prevent horizontal dissipation of water from the simulation domain. The only exceptions are "inlets" (sources) — from which water is added and "outlets" where water is removed from the system.

We defined the following parameters that tune the model:

- γ — gradient of nutrient distribution,
- ρ — peat bog vertical growth rate,
- μ — sedimentation rate.

Main loop of the algorithm consists of three procedures that implement the rules of CAMAN model (see Algorithm 1). The procedure `calculate_flows()` deals with water flow simulation by using method of difference minimising in the neighbouring cells [9]. The rule is homogeneous for the whole CA system and it mimics the process of water distribution due to gravitation.

The procedure `calculate_nutrient_dist()` calculates the concentration of nutrients in the neighbourhood of cells with non-zero water amount ($w_{ij} > 0$). We assume that the cells flooded by water have the maximum concentration of nutrients. This concentration decreases proportionally to the distance from the nutrient source. The value of γ is the nutrients concentration gradient. The procedure for each cell calculates maximum concentration in its neighbourhood and decrease by γ coefficient (see Algorithm 2).

Algorithm 1. The algorithm of CAMAN model

for all step of simulation do
  calculate_flows();
  calculate_nutrient_dist();
  calculate_peat_growth();

Procedure 2. Outline of the `calculate_nutrient_dist()` procedure

for all cell in the mesh do
  if $w_{ij} > 0$ then
    $n_{ij} \Leftarrow 1.0$;
  else
    $n_{ij} \Leftarrow \gamma \max(n_{X(ij)})$;

The nutrients concentration influences the thickness of the peat bog layer in "dry" cells (`calculate_peat_growth()` procedure). We assume that each time-step its growth increment is proportional to the current concentration of nutrients with proportionality coefficient ρ. In comparison to SCAMAN model [12], the rule of growth of peat layer has been extended and now it distinguish between cells with and without water. Areas covered by water elevate with rate described by μ parameter what reflects the process of sedimentation occurring on the bottom of channels. "Dry" areas grow with ρ rate. Difference between μ and ρ parameters has substantial influence on resulting patterns (see Figure 7).

Procedure 3. Outline of the `calculate_peat_growth()` procedure

for all cell in the mesh do
  if $w_{ij} > 0$ then
    $p_{ij} \Leftarrow \mu\, n_{ij}$;
  else
    $p_{ij} \Leftarrow \rho\, n_{ij}$;

2.1   Results

To speed up calculations, our model was parallelised and implemented under MPI environment on SGI/Altix cluster. The results has been postprocessed and visualised using Amira package (www.tgs.com). In Table 1 we present the parameters used in our simulations.

In Fig. 3A we illustrate the snapshots from simulations for cellular automata mesh of size 530×530 grid points. The snapshot is compared with a small section of Narew River (Figure 3B). The terrain is slightly inclined (the slope is 0.05%) and rough. However, vertical random amplitude of roughness is assumed to be small and less than 1% of the distance between neighboring cells. Water is supplied to the system by a single source cell. We can observe the creation of small floods in the two pictures and similar backbone structure.

Table 1. Simulation parameters for presented results

Fig. no.	γ	ρ	μ	slope	mesh
Fig.3A	0.02	0.0002	0.00014	0.05% (0.5m/km)	530×530
Fig.4	0.02	0.0005	0.0004	0.2% (2m/km)	730×730
Fig.5	(A,B) 0.02 (C,D) 0.08	0.0005	0.0004	0.05%	330×330
Fig.6	0.04	(A) 0.0005 (B) 0.001	(A) 0.0004 (B) 0.0009	0.05%	330×330
Fig.7	0.04	(A) 0.0009 (B) 0,0009	(A) 0.00075 (B) 0.00085	0.05%	330×330
Fig.8	0.03	0.00003	0.00002	0.05%	330×330

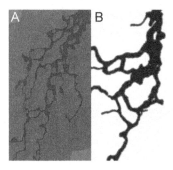

Fig. 3. Comparison of modelled river network (A) to small fragment of real anasto-mosing pattern (B, the Narew River from Figure 1)

In comparison to the previous run, the snapshots shown in Fig. 4 represent the terrain of a greater inclination (0.2%) and greater number of source cells. Therefore, despite we used larger system of cellular automata (730×730 grid points), the river system develops faster. The situation from Fig.4A was obtained after 10^3 timesteps. As displayed in Fig.4B, after about 2×10^4 timesteps the environment saturates and the landscape pattern stabilizes in an equilibrium state.

Figs. 5 and 6 illustrate the various influences of the simulation parameters, such as gradient of nutrients distribution γ and peat bog growth factor ρ, respectively, on the evolution of river networks. Large value of γ and small value of peat bog growth factor ρ, cause that smaller area of the terrain is penetrated by the nutrients. Thus the environment is "starving". As a consequence, the complexity of the river system, as measured by the number of channels and bifurcations, increases [14]. Irregular distribution of nutrients stimulates creation of more complex river networks. This confirms the hypothesis that "starving environment" is a driving force developing transportation networks [12].

Third parameter μ, which represents growth of sedimentation layer, has to be slightly smaller than the gradient of nutrients spreading. Greater differences between them result in formation of river networks with deep and narrow channels

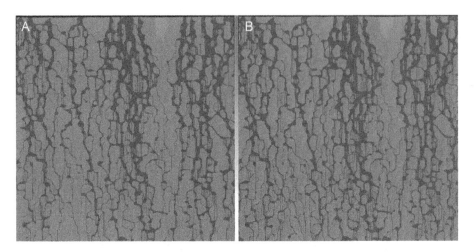

Fig. 4. The river system after A) 10^3 and B) 2×10^4 time-steps. The saturation of the environment can be observed.

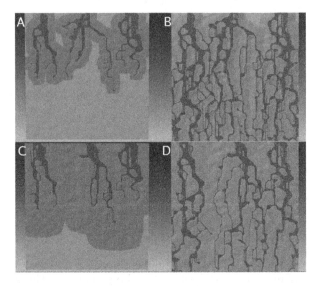

Fig. 5. The snapshots from simulations of river networks performed on 330×330 point mesh. After 500 (A,C) and 4×10^3 (B,D) time-steps, illustrate influence of nutrient gradient parameter γ: 0.02 (A,B) and 0.08 (C,D). Areas covered by peat-bogs are depicted by using dark green colour.

(see Fig.7A). This increases considerably the total volume of the river system, decreasing simultaneously the probability of new channels formation and branching. Conversely, by diminishing the difference between γ and μ, frequent floods produce deeper river networks.

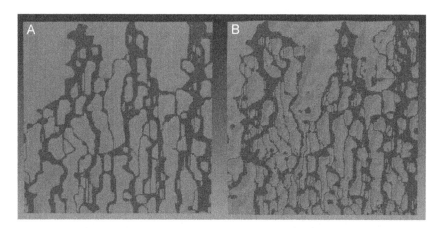

Fig. 6. The snapshots from simulations of river networks after 2×10^4 (mesh 330×330 points) for two different values of the peat bog growth rate ρ: 0.0005 (A) and 0.001 (B)

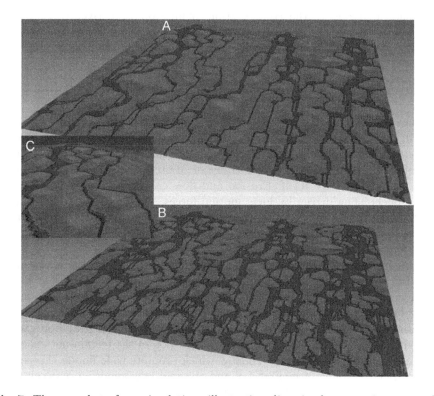

Fig. 7. The snapshots from simulations illustrating diversity between river networks obtained for large (A) and small (C) differences between peat bog growth rate ρ and sedimentation rate μ. In B) a fragment from Fig A) is presented under different angle to show better the terrain configuration.

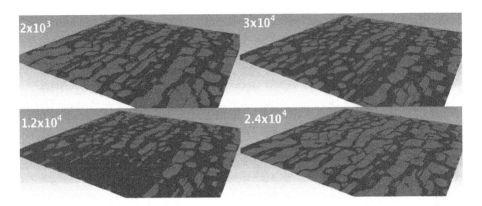

Fig. 8. The landscape changes with time (number of time-steps is given for each picture) produced for variable outputs of water sources. This figure illustrate periodic floods in anastomosing river basin.

As shown in Fig. 8, the configuration of anastomosing river basin is also influenced by periodical changes of water level e.g., spring floods and summer droughts — modelled by high and low water output from the source cells.

3   Conclusions

The classical synchronous cellular automata paradigm is a perfect tool for modelling drainage systems and dendric rivers [15] such as those created by erosion [http://fd.alife.co.uk]. We have shown that CA can be used as a fine grained model for simulating more complex transportation networks. Their role is very different from drainage itself. Erosion and flow can be simulated as two concurrent phenomena driven by local mutual forces. The transportation network distributes nutrients to the environment. The slow changes in the environment (e.g. peat bog growth and changes in terrain configuration) feedbacks the growth of the network.

The main disadvantage of our CA model is its low computational speed for simulating more disparate spatio-temporal scales. This is mainly due to the high degree of spatial and temporal disparity between the processes modelling the evolution of anastomosing rivers. The flow speed of the river is orders of magnitude greater than environmental changes, such as the peat bog growth and sedimentation. This results in the configuration of the terrain not changing too much. The channels are too shallow which prompts wide floods. Therefore, the simulated systems from Figs.4–8 and the real anastomosing network from Fig.1 represent different scales. Modelling realistic anastomosing networks with our CA model would involve $10^6 - 10^8$ cells and a similar number of time-steps. This would be very demanding in terms of CPU time.

Acknowledgements

The author thanks Prof. D.A. Yuen (Minnesota Supercomputing Institute) and Prof. W. Dzwinel (AGH University of Science and Technology) for valuable comments and discussions on the model assumptions. This work is partially supported by Polish Ministry of Education and Science (grant no. 3 T11F 010 30).

References

1. Rodriguez-Iturbe I., and Rinaldo, A., Fractal River Basins. Chance and Self-Organization. Cambridge University Press, 1997.
2. Turcotte, D.L., Fractals and Chaos in Geology and Geophysics, University of Cambridge,, 1997.
3. Mandelbrot, B., The Fractal Geometry of Nature, 1982.
4. Murray, A.B., and Paola, C., A new quantitative test of geomorphic models, applied to a model of braided streams: Water Res.Research. 32:2579-2587, 1996.
5. Murray, A.B., and Paola, C., A cellular model of braided streams: Nature. 371:54-57, 1994.
6. Chase, G., Fluvial landsculpting and the fractal dimension of topography. Geomorphology 5:39-57, (1992).
7. Kramer, S., and Marder M., Evolution of river networks. Phys.Rev.Lett. 68:205-209, (1992).
8. Gradziński, R., Baryła J., Danowski W., Doktor M., Gmur D., Gradziński M., Kędzior A. Paszkowski M., Soja R., Zieliński T., Żurek S., Anastomosing System of Upper Narew River, Ann.Soc.Geologorum Poloniae, 70:219-229, 2000.
9. Topa, P., River flows modeled by cellular automata, Proc. of The First Worldwide SGI Users Conference, Kraków, 2000.
10. Di Gregorio, S., Serra R., An empirical method for modeling and simulating some complex macroscopic phenomena by cellular automata, FGCS, 16:259-271, 1999.
11. Topa P, Computational models of growth in selected problems of geology, PhD thesis (in polish), AGH University of Science and Technology, 2005.
12. Topa P., Paszkowski M., Anastomosing Transportation Networks, LNCS 2328,p.904 ff., Springer-Verlag,2002.
13. Chopard B., Droz M., Cellular Automata Modeling of Physical Systems, Cambridge University Press, 1998.
14. Makaske B., Anastomosing Rivers: Forms, Processes and Sediments, The Royal Dutch Geographical Society, Utrecht University, 1998.
15. Wittmann, R., Kautzky, T., Hübler, A., Lüscher, E. A simple Experiment for the Examination of Dendritic River Systems, Naturwissenschaften 78:23–25, 1991.

Social Distances Model of Pedestrian Dynamics

Jarosław Wąs[1], Bartłomiej Gudowski[1], and Paweł J. Matuszyk[2]

[1] Institute of Automatics
[2] Department of Modelling and Information Technology,
AGH University of Sciences and Technology,
al. Mickiewicza 30, 30-059 Kraków, Poland
{jarek, bart, pjm}@agh.edu.pl

Abstract. The knowledge of phenomena connected with pedestrian dynamics is desired in the process of developing public facilities. Nowadays, there is a necessity of creating various models which take into consideration the microscopic scale of simulation. The presented model describes pedestrian dynamics in a certain limited area in the framework of inhomogeneous, asynchronous Cellular Automata. The pedestrians are represented by ellipses on a square lattice, which implies the necessity of taking into account some geometrical constraints for each cell. An innovative idea of social distances is introduced into the model — dynamics in the model is influenced by the rules of proxemics. As an example, the authors present a simulation of pedestrian behavior in a tram.

1 Introduction

The modeling of pedestrian behavior has been very popular over the last years. Scientists and engineers have become interested in methods, which give more and more realistic results of simulation. As a result of wide research, Cellular Automata have become one of the most useful approaches to pedestrian dynamics. Let us mention some interesting recent works.

In the model by Burstedde et al. [2], a concept of static and dynamic floor fields is proposed. Dynamic floor field makes it possible to track and indicate the most attractive cells on the basis of selected criteria. Thus, simulated pedestrians can follow each other in the evacuation process.

Dijkstra et al. [3] present a model, which combines Cellular Automata and Multi-Agent Systems. Agents in the model have the possibility of perceiving their local neighborhood and affecting their environment. It makes it possible to simulate pedestrian traffic in streets or commercial centers.

A model of tourist activity in the Alps is presented in the work by Gloor et al. [6]. Tourists are understood as agents. Each agent makes certain decisions such as: excursion destination, route choice etc. In the model, an additional lattice of nodes (graphs) is added to the basic Cellular Automata lattice. The shortest way in the network is calculated for all Alpine paths simulated in the model.

Another problem is presented by Narimatsu et al. [11]. In their works, authors present an algorithm of collision avoidance for bi-directional pedestrian

S. El Yacoubi, B. Chopard, and S. Bandini (Eds.): ACRI 2006, LNCS 4173, pp. 492–501, 2006.

movement. Pedestrians walk along a corridor in two opposite directions and they learn some patterns to avoid collisions.

In this paper, the authors present a Cellular Automata model of pedestrian dynamics applying the sociological theory of *Social Distances* introduced by E. T. Hall [8,9]. As an example a passenger movement in a tram is discussed.

2   Social Distances Theory

The issues of the space requirements of people and optimal distances among them became a subject of research of sociologists and anthropologists long time ago. In 1959, Edward Hall popularized spatial research on human beings. In his book: "The Silent Language" [8], he introduced the term *proxemics*. He formulated the basic law of proxemics as follows: *We may not go everywhere as we please. There are cultural rules and biological boundaries.* Hall mentioned some interesting facts concerning *personal space* among people [8,9]. In proxemics, one can differentiate four sorts of distances:

Intimate distance ranges from body contact to approximately 40–50 cm. It can appear between couples, parents and children, friends etc. Intimate distance is different in various cultures. The infringement of intimate distance zone by another person causes discomfort and could be perceived as painful. Already 3 seconds of eye contact in closer distance is perceived as an intrusion or expression of pressurization [5].

Personal distance ranges approximately from 40–50 cm to 150 cm. Hall identifies a close and a far phase [9]. The close phase: 50 to 90 cm permits one person to touch the other, while the far phase of personal distance: 90 cm to 150 cm "an arm's length" does not permit this [1]. The close phase is typical, for instance, for people, who know each other very well. It is sometimes called "a shaking hand distance". The wider personal distance is the limit of the personal area of domination. This is the distance which people usually accept when they meet each other unexpectedly (i.e. in the street). Such distancing expresses the message that someone is prepared for an open and neutral conversation [5].

Social distance ranges approximately from 150 cm to 3 m. It is the casual interaction-distance between acquaintances and strangers. It is common for business meetings, classrooms and impersonal social affairs [1].

Public distance (above 300 cm) is observed between strangers and in audiences. This distance is also called a public speaking distance.

It is important to emphasize that these distances could vary according to *personality* and *environmental factors* since an abnormal situation could bring people closer than they usually are [8].

3   General Assumptions

The presented model is based on 2-dimensional Cellular Automata. In the model, space is represented as a lattice with square cells. The size of each cell

d_g equals 0.25 cm. A formalization for this type of inhomogeneous CA could be found in [4].

3.1   Pedestrian Representation

Each person in the model is represented by an ellipse, whose center concides with the center of the cell occupied by that person. The size of each ellipsis equals $a = 0.225$ cm (semimajor axis) and $b = 0.135$ cm (semiminor axis) which is assumed the average size of a person (*WHO* data). A pedestrian can transfer to another cell in Moore neighborhood of radius 1. A person occupying the cell can take one out of four allowed positions: H, R, V and L which correspond to the action of turning the ellipsis around by: ± 0, ± 45, ± 90 and ± 135 degrees respectively. Thus, in each time-step-slice, we determine a combination of allowed positions for each cell on the basis of the neighborhood configuration.

The crucial issue is to establish the set of forbidden and allowed positions for all cells in Moore neighborhood of radius 1, each cell being occupied by one person. The calculation of the allowed/forbidden positions is based upon simple geometrical dependencies. It takes into account: the orientations of two ellipses occupying two adjacent cells and the size of their crossection. It is assumed that the position is allowed, if the ratio of the calculated crossection (for this position) to the size of the ellipsis is smaller than imposed tolerance $\epsilon_N \in [0, 1]$. For a square lattice, with eight neighbor cells and four possible positions in each cell one has to investigate only 14 combinations (Fig. 1). The remaining combinations can be obtained on the basis of the mentioned ones due to the existing symmetries.

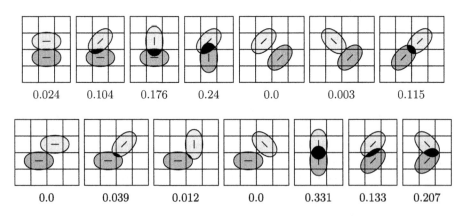

0.024	0.104	0.176	0.24	0.0	0.003	0.115

0.0	0.039	0.012	0.0	0.331	0.133	0.207

Fig. 1. Reciprocal orientations of two persons (represented by grey ellipses) and calculated ratios of crossections (black) and ellipse size for cell size $d_g = 0.25$ cm

As an example, Fig. 2 presents allowed states for neighbor-cells for different tolerance parameters.

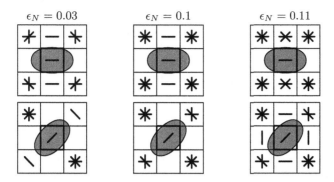

Fig. 2. Allowed neighborhood configurations for different tolerance parameters

3.2   Social Distances Representation

People in the model are represented by ellipses, thus social areas are represented similarly. However the eccentricities of both ellipses can differ. The authors suggest that social distances are asymmetric due to the fact that "social configuration" in front of the person has much more influence on them behavior than the configuration behind them. Therefore geometrical centers of both the ellipses are not identical: usually ellipse representing the social area is shifted forward along line of vision of the considered pedestrian by some distance t (see Fig. 3). Due to

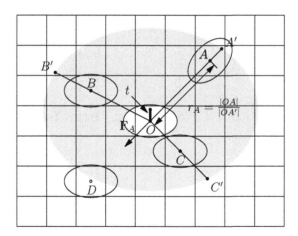

Fig. 3. Social area ellipse: semimajor axis equals $4a$ and semiminor axis equals $5b$. Shift t equals $0.7b$. Parameters a and b defined in subsection 3.1.

the mentioned asymmetry, the model has to distinguish the front and the back of the person which results in 8 possible orientations: N, NE, E, SE, S, SW, W and NW. Fig. 3 presents the method of calculating the distance between the "observer" O and "intruders" (A, B, C and D). If the intruder enters the social area of the observer (on Fig. 3 only A, B and C) the normalized distance r within the social area is calculated as a ratio of the distance between the centers of persons (e.g. $|OA|$) to the distance between the observer and the point of projection of the intruder's center on the boundary of the social area (respectively $|OA'|$). The normalized distance belongs to the interval $[0, 1]$.

The interaction between the observer and a single intruder is described by "social distance force" $\mathbf{F}_s$. The absolute value of $\mathbf{F}_s$ depends only on the normalized distance between them, $\mathbf{F}_s = F_i(r)$ where F_i is one of some assumed models for social distance force (presented in Fig. 4). $\mathbf{F}_s$ has reverse sense than the vector observer-intruder. Total social force affecting the observer is calculated simply as a vector sum of social forces calculated for each intruder (in the presented case: $\mathbf{F}_s = \mathbf{F}_A + \mathbf{F}_B + \mathbf{F}_C$).

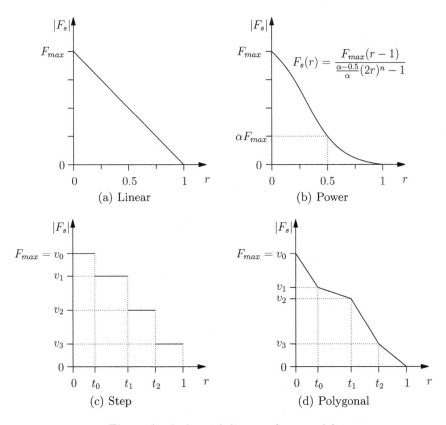

Fig. 4. Applied social distance force models

3.3   Movement Algorithm

The presented model proposes three possible pedestrians states: *Go to*, *Wait in intermediate aim (tarpit)* and *Wait*. The general movement algorithm is shown in Fig. 5.

A pedestrian's orientation can be changed only during movement to the next cell. The new orientation is determined according to the following rules: firstly, the pedestrian tries to adjust his/her orientation to the movement direction (face directed forward), otherwise the pedestrian takes one out of the allowed positions randomly. Social forces do not affect changing the orientation directly.

Depending on their state, pedestrians proceed according to different movement algorithms. Passengers having particular aims (tarpits) in "mind" try to move towards descending values of potential field. It is possible that in an actual time-step a passenger has more than one neighbor cell to choose. In this case a passenger selects the next cell randomly from among them. If a passenger is blocked, that is in their radius 1 Moore neighborhood there is no cell with a potential field value better than the potential value of the field occupied by the passenger, they try to move randomly to one of the cells with equal potential value.

Sitting passengers only wait for their tramstop. When the tram reaches their desired destination they run to the exits using movement algorithm described above.

The only state, when social distances have a direct influence on pedestrians is the *Wait* state. Every pedestrian in this state is under the influence of all other pedestrians. If the value of social force influencing the pedestrian exceeds the assumed threshold, he/she calculates the new target cell on the basis of resultant social force vector and changes his/her state to *Go to*.

4   Model Application in a Tram Simulation

As an example of the model described above, the authors consider passenger dynamics in a tram NGT–6 used by Public Transport Company in Kraków, Poland [7]. We take into account a movement algorithm from the previous section (Fig. 5). Let us analyze some important elements of this algorithm.

Resources and intermediate aims in the model like: seats, validators, exits etc. are understood as "tarpits" [7,14]. These tarpit cells are aims of *Go to* action and simultaneously they are objects of *Wait in intermediate aim*. Pedestrians, behaving according to social distances rules, try to get to intermediate aims. If their trip is short or if they have not defined any intermediate aims, they are in the third state: *Wait*. This state causes pedestrian's behavior to be passive, that is if she/he does not violate any strangers' territory but if her/his social area is violated, pedestrian recedes the others with greater priority.

5   Implementation

The model has been implemented with the use of C++ programming language. All features of the model are enclosed into several C++ classes, which represent: grid, grid cells, passengers, a set of allowed configurations, the geometric model of social areas and considered variants of social distance forces. The application has two main parts: the part representing the model and Graphical User Interface.

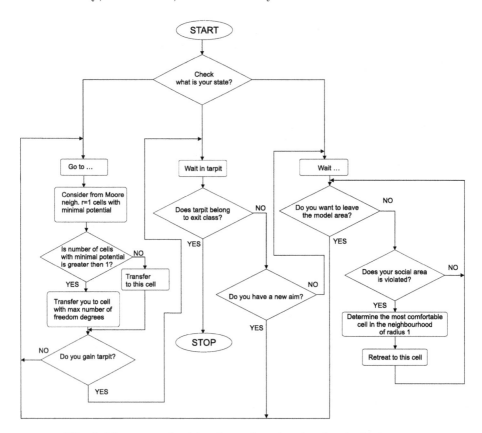

Fig. 5. Movement algorithm for each pedestrian for single time step

The most important module of the simulation part of the program is the *executive* [12], which controls the simulation progress. The *executive* has to control time flow in the model and has to ensure that every passenger is handled in every time-step-slice. Each passenger is enqueued in one of the three lists: the list of passengers getting off, the list of boarding passengers and the list of passengers who are standing inside the vehicle. Every list has assigned priority. The *executive* examines the lists of passengers in a descending order of priority. In every time-step-slice all lists are examined. Passengers getting off are handled first, then boarding passengers or passengers moving towards their intermediate aims, and finally — passengers standing inside the vehicle. Moving passengers do not care about the violation of their social distance areas. However, standing passengers try to find the most comfortable place inside the vehicle. Therefore the executive examines lists in the described order.

It is worth noting supplementary classes performing key computations. *Field-Pattern* class is used to determine the templates of allowed configurations inside a passenger's neighborhood, depending on his orientation in the space and his geometric dimensions. *SocialField* class computes vector of the "repulse" force coming from the intruder who violates the passenger's social distance area.

Simulation program is an application working under Windows 2000/XP operating system. Therefore the Microsoft Visual C++ 6.0 compiler was used. GUI implementation uses classes of standard MFC library.

6   Simulation Results

In the presented simulation we can observe how the social distance force idea works. First, let us consider situation with two pedestrians: the first one is in the state *Go to* (Action: *Go to* exit) and the second one is in the state *Wait*. The second pedestrian stand on the way of the first one. In this situation the first one is the "intruder" for the second one.

In Fig. 6 one can observe a situation in which the pedestrian marked grey goes to the exit (cells also marked grey). The "grey" pedestrian (in the state *Go to*) influences two others, marked black (in the state *Wait*). The third, pedestrian marked black (in the bottom right-hand corner of Fig. 6) is too far from the grey "intruder" to experience any influence.

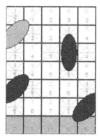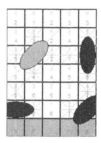

Fig. 6. Two consecutive phases of the simulation. Pedestrian marked grey, which get off the vehicle, violates the social distances of two other pedestrians marked black. Pedestrians marked black recede and make get off possible.

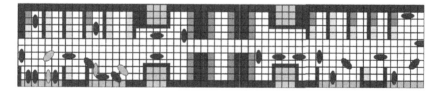

Fig. 7. Pedestrian proxemics across a vehicle

In Fig. 7 the pedestrian allocation in a part of vehicle is shown. It presents a typical situation at the tram stop. Some passengers (marked grey) get off the vehicle, while the majority (marked black) stay inside. Dark grey cells represent unoccupied seats and light grey cells represent occupied seats. In the population of travelling passengers (marked black) one can see a tendency towards regular, equilibrated allocation. Proposed wall representation is connected with pedestrian movement possibilities.

7   Conclusions

An innovative idea of introducing social distances to the CA pedestrian dynamics model, contributes to a significant growth of realism of the simulation. Social distances mechanisms make simulated interactions among passengers more realistic. The authors propose several models of social distances forces. One of the presented models was called *Step* (Fig. 4) and it corresponds directly to E.T. Hall theory. The remaining models of social distance forces seem to be more precise in interactions simulation.

The second profit resulting from the application of social distances theory is the explanation of passenger distribution inside a considered area (vehicle). It is a practical application of proxemics.

To illustrate practical application of the theory of social distances, the authors have created CA modeling pedestrian behavior inside a tram. Space in the model is represented as square, regular lattice. Pedestrians are represented by ellipses. A center of an ellipse coincides with the cell center. In one time-step-slice, pedestrian can transfer into another cell in Moore neighborhood of radius $r = 1$.

In one of the previous models [7] the authors presented another pedestrian representation, where each pedestrian was similarly represented by an ellipse. The difference is that the ellipse occupied two or four adjacent cells of the lattice. In such case, the movement algorithm was much more complicated.

The main limitation of the current model is lack of strategical abilities of pedestrians. Actually, pedestrians always approach the closest aim (in the sense of potential), while such choice is not necessarily globally optimal (e.g. one could faster reach another equivalent aim).

Instead of the necessity of computing social distances, discrete character of simulation allows its to be effective. Simulations based on Molecular Dynamics (e.g. Social Forces by Helbing and Molnar [10]) gives possibilities of more detailed simulation, but computational effectiveness of this method is probably lower.

References

1. Arias, I.: Proxemics in the ESL Classroom, Forum Vol. **34** No. 1, Costa Rica (1996)
2. Burstedde C.K., Klauck K., Schadschneider A., Zittartz J.: Simulation of Pedestrian Dynamics using a 2-dimensional Cellular Automaton, Phys. Rev. **A 295** (2001) 507–525.
3. Dijkstra J., Jessurun A.J., Timmermans H.: A Multi-Agent Cellular Automata System for Visualising Simulated Pedestrian Activity, Proceedings of ACRI, (2000) 29–36.
4. Dudek–Dyduch E., Wąs J.: Knowledge Representation of Pedestrian Dynamics in Crowd. Formalism of Cellular Automata. Proceedings of ICAISC, Lecture Notes in Artificial Intelligence (2006) (accepted)
5. Geisler L.: Doctor and patient – a partnership through dialogue. Pharma Verlag, Frankfurt (1991)
6. Gloor C., Stucki P., Nagel K.: Hybrid Techniques for Pedestrian Simulations, Proceedings of 6th ACRI, LNCS **3305**, Amsterdam (2004) 581–590

7. Gudowski B., Wąs J.: Modeling of People Flow in Public Transport Vehicles, Proceedings of PPAM, LNCS **3911**, (in print)
8. Hall E.T.: The Silent Language. Garden City, New York (1959)
9. Hall E.T.: The Hidden Dimension. Garden City, New York (1966)
10. Helbing D., Molnar P.: A Social Force Model for Pedestrian Dynamic, Phys. Rev. **E 51**, 4284–4286
11. Narimatsu K., Shiraishi T., Morishita S.: Acquisiting of Local Neighbour Rules in the Simulation of Pedestrian Flow by Cellular Automata, Proceedings of 6th ACRI, LNCS **3305**, Amsterdam (2004) 211–219
12. Pidd M.: Computer Simulation in Managment Science, Wiley (1994)
13. Wąs J., Gudowski B.: The Application of Cellular Automata for Pedestrian Dynamics Simulation., Automatyka Journal AGH-UST, Kraków (2004) 303–313
14. Wąs J., Gudowski B.: Simulation of Strategical Abilities in Pedestrian Movement using Cellular Automata, Proceedings of 24th IASTED MIC Conference, Innsbruck (2005) 549–553

Cellular Automata and Its Application to the Modeling of Vehicular Traffic in the City of Caracas

Angel Aponte[1] and José Alí Moreno[2]

[1] Centro de Investigación y Desarrollo de Ingeniería (**CIDI**)
Facultad de Ingeniería. Universidad Católica Andrés Bello. Caracas, DC. Venezuela
aaponte@ucab.edu.ve
[2] Laboratorio de Computación Emergente (**LACE**)
Facultad de Ingeniería. Universidad Central de Venezuela. Caracas, DC. Venezuela
jose@neurona.ciens.ucv.ve

Abstract. In this paper an emergent microscopic traffic model based on a cellular automaton is presented. The model is part of a vehicular traffic study recently initiated in the city of Caracas in Venezuela. The proposed simulation model is an extension of the Nagel and Schreckenberg model for identical vehicles incorporating several important features: Velocities of cars are picked from a Gaussian distribution to take into account that not every car driver honors velocity limits. The model is validated by fitting measured normalized average vehicle flows by means of an iterative unconstrained optimization algorithm. For this purpose mean and variance of the velocity distribution are considered as optimization parameters together with other model parameters. Objective Functions quantifying the mean square deviations of the differences of measured and simulated normalized averages flows, are defined. The results show that the proposed simulation models reproduce satisfactorily the general features of empirical flow measurements.

Keywords: Cellular Automata, Traffic Modeling, Emergent Behavior, Nonlinear Optimization.

1 Introduction

In the last decades the study of vehicular traffic has become an area of research of great interest and activity in statistical mechanics, condensed matter physics, emergent computing, traffic engineering and urban planning.

Traffic models that incorporate in their implementation, what is called an Emergent Microscopic Model Based on a Cellular Automaton (EMMBCA) [1], are of particular interest. An EMMBCA consists on a binary cellular automaton with few sets of simple rules and the most essentials ingredients sufficient for the emergence of the general common features of typical real traffic. In this way elementary local interactions, defined by the rules, lead to the emergence of the global complex traffic behavior.

In the city of Caracas in Venezuela, no great scale vehicular traffic study, including a massive recollection of information and traffic modeling and simulation, has been yet carried out. As a contribution to fill this gap, preliminary results of a vehicular

S. El Yacoubi, B. Chopard, and S. Bandini (Eds.): ACRI 2006, LNCS 4173, pp. 502–511, 2006.
© Springer-Verlag Berlin Heidelberg 2006

traffic study recently initiated, including modeling, simulation and validation with real data, are presented in this paper. The proposed model incorporates several important features: a) velocities of cars are picked from a Gaussian distribution to take into account that not every car driver honors velocity limits established to the motorways; b) model validation is carried out by fitting to empirical data through an iterative unconstrained optimization algorithm. For this propose mean and variance of the velocity distributions are considered as optimization parameters; and c) for the optimization, objective functions which quantify the mean square deviations of the difference of the measured and simulated normalized average flows, are introduced.

The paper is structured as follow. Section 2 describes the main ingredients that constitute an EMMBCA in the context of traffic modeling. Section 3 describes model implementation and validation. In Section 4 results are presented and discussed. Finally in Section 5 some conclusions and final comments are exposed.

2 Cellular Automata (CA) and Traffic Models

Traffic models that incorporate an EMMBCA in their implementations are of particular interest, because they are developed bottom up by including the most simple and essential ingredients and defining just a few sets of elementary rules, necessary to describe the general features of typical real traffic. Nagel and Schreckenberg [2] presented one of the most simple and successful emergent traffic models based on a cellular automaton. It can be said that most contribution on EMMBCA traffic modeling are based on this original model.

Nagel and Schreckenberg [2] modeled the dynamic of vehicular traffic on a single-lane freeway. They represented the road by a one-dimensional array of length L, subdivided in n lattice cells. Each lattice site can be occupied by a car or it is empty. Car density (number of cars per length unit) is given by $\rho = n_{ocp}/L$, where n_{ocp} is the total number of occupied lattice cells. Vehicles move in time from left to right.

It is clear that the dynamical model is totally discrete, velocity and the position of a car are discrete variables and time is also considered discrete. Vehicle dynamic is modeled according to the following four-step process executed each time step:

1. Acceleration: If the velocity v of a vehicle is lower than v_{max}, where v_{max} is the maximum velocity possible in the system, the speed is advanced by one $[v = v+1]$.
2. Slowing down: (due to other cars): If the distance D to the next car ahead is not larger than v $(D \leq v)$ the speed is reduced to $D-1$ $[v = D-1]$.
3. Randomization: With probability p, the velocity of a vehicle (if greater than zero) is decreased by one $[v = v-1]$.
4. Car motion: Each vehicle is advanced v sites.

In the model specifications and definition of boundary conditions for the cellular automaton are also required. They can be either Open Boundary Conditions (OBC) or Periodic Boundary Conditions (PBC).

In the above four dynamic rules defined in the Nagel-Schreckenberg model all the elementary actions and interactions of and between vehicles, sufficient to emulate the basic features of real traffic are included. However in order to capture more complex behavior additional rules need to be formulated and incorporated such as for example for lane changing and vehicle overtaking maneuvers. Also, it is necessary to take into account aspects related to drivers behavior, which tremendously influences traffic dynamics [3]. Huge Traffic Information Systems like *OLSIM* [4,5] and *MITSIMLab* [6], incorporate in their implementations these and other important features in order to model more realistic situations.

3   Model Implementation and Validation

This section describes the implementation and validation of an EMMBCA, proposed to model and simulate dynamic and performance of traffic in two situations: a two-lane rectilinear motorway where vehicles move in the same direction along both lanes, and, a two-lane curved road where cars move in opposite directions along each lane. The model proposed elaborates from the basic rules of the Nagel-Schreckenberg model.

The motorway is modeled as two parallel one-dimensional arrays of length L, each one subdivided in n lattice cells. Lane-change rules, based on algorithms presented in previous CA models [7,8], are incorporated. The curved road is modeled as two one-dimensional arrays, each one of total length $L_{cr} = 2l + S$. Each side of the road consist of two identical rectilinear segments of length l joined together by a circular arc of radius $R = l f_{long}$ and length $S = R\Theta$. Here, Θ is the angle of curvature of the circular arc, and f_{long} is a scaling factor introduced to explore possible influences of the road configuration on the traffic dynamic due to variation of R vs. l ratio. The length l is calculated from the equation

$$l = \frac{n}{2 + \Theta f_{long}} . \tag{1}$$

here n is the total number of cells dividing each road-lane. In both motorway and road, incentive and security criteria are included. These are essential to avoid car collisions. For the road, no overtaking maneuvers are allowed along the curve itself.

Simulations are performed as follow. First of all, values for the total parameters involved in the model are given. These parameters include the number of cells n, number of time steps n_{ts}, the lane density ratio df_{21} (i.e., $df_{21} = \rho_2/\rho_1$, with ρ_1 and ρ_2 as the lane-1 and lane-2 car densities), ρ_1, randomization probabilities p_{c_1}, p_{c_2}, the total number of experiments n_R, the longitudinal factor f_{long}, initial cars velocities, etc. Values for ρ_1 are generated using the formula

$$\rho_1 = 0.001 + \sqrt{n_{count}/(n_R - n_{count})} . \tag{2}$$

where n_{count} is an integer variable with values ranging from zero to $n_R - 1$. In this way the values for ρ_1 range from low densities (free traffic) to high densities (congested traffic), spanning a half of a typical labor-day range, i.e., from midnight to noon. Then, for each density value, cars positions and velocities are assigned randomly. To take into account that not every car driver honors velocity limits established to the motorway, velocities are picked from a Gaussian distribution. The mean of the distribution is taken as v_{max}. For the cellular space Periodic Boundary Conditions (PBC) are assumed in both the motorway and the curved road. Lane change and overtaking maneuvers are performed in parallel at each time step, as referred in [7,8]. The four-step procedure of acceleration, slowing down, randomization and car conduction, is then applied and car positions and velocities are updated. After each n_{ts} time steps average velocity and traffic flow (number of vehicles per unit time), for each lane, are evaluated. In this way, simulated flow values, average velocities, lane-occupancy (lane use percentage), and the corresponding car densities, will be available for comparison with empirical data.

It was found that the emergent model proposed here reproduces satisfactorily the general features of typical real traffic: from the free flow to formation and propagation of traffic jams. Additionally, characteristics of *Fundamental Diagrams* – Flow vs. Density, Mean Velocity vs. Density, Mean Velocity vs. Flow, and, Lane-Occupancy vs. Density– derived from simulations are qualitatively consistent with the characteristics shown by empirical-generated Fundamental Diagrams for similar situations. Due to space limitations and since it is not relevant for the rest of the discussion, these qualitative comparison are not shown here.

For a quantitative validation of the model, real data measured on location with geometric configurations like those implemented, is required. In the city of Caracas not too much traffic data has been collected and in most cases is not completely reliable or easy available. However, in 2002 the city municipal government contracted a traffic study [9] in Las Mercedes (a south-east suburb). Only traffic flow measurements were performed. Fortunately, two locations with the required geometric configurations were considered in this study: a two-lane bridge (Las Mercedes' Bridge at the end of Rio de Janeiro Avenue), where cars move from east to west on both lanes, and a curved section of the two-lane Baruta's Old Road where cars move from west to east on one lane and in the opposite direction along the other lane. The availability of this data makes possible a vis-à-vis comparison between flow real measurements and those obtained from the simulations. Hence, due to the lack of empirical data on density, mean velocity, occupancy, etc., results and discussions presented ahead will be based only on traffic flows.

The data made available in the traffic study consisted on, for the Las Mercedes' bridge, the two-lane average of traffic flows, and for the curved section of Baruta's Old Road, flow measurements on each individual lane. Measurements were carried out from Wednesday February 20th 2002 (WedFeb20/2002) to Tuesday February 26th 2002 (TueFeb26/2002), five labor days and the weekend. Each day, twenty-four vehicular average flow data points were reported, from 1:00 am in the morning to the next-day-midnight hour, so N_{ed} – the number of empirical flow data available for comparison– will be 24 or less.

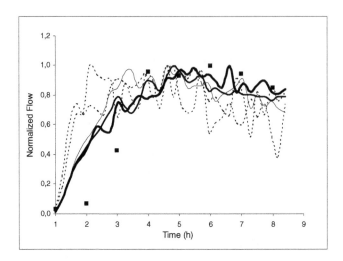

Fig. 1. Empirical Data vs. Numerical Simulation. Evolution in time of average normalized flows for the two-lane Las Mercedes' Bridge.

In a labor day, variation of traffic flow in the time interval from eve hours to hours around midday is a consequence of the progressive increase of the number of vehicles driving on the motorway. At certain critical value of the density, flow reaches a maximum. For densities greater than this value, flow reduces progressively until it reaches a minimum around the rush hour, when car density is maxima. So, process exhibits a typical phase transition from a "free-flow" phase toward a "congested-flow" phase [1]. In the afternoon, things reverse. Density now reduces progressively due to gradual reduction in the number of vehicles on the motorway. At some time point, density and flow start increasing again until another critical value of the car density maximizes flow. Then it reduces again when the next rush hour approaches, and the system goes through a second phase transition. Process described repeats until eve hours are reached, when ones again, flow has a minimum, and so on. The EMMBCA presented here was implemented in such a way that it simulates just the first phase transition described, as stated by Eq. (2). In this sense, after sorting in increasing order, the five labor-day data sets, vis-à-vis comparisons between simulated and empirical data were performed only for a twelve-hour time interval, setting N_{ed} equal to 12.

In the following section it is shown how the proposed model satisfactorily reproduces the general features of typical real traffic.

4   Results and Discussion

First, let's consider the model for the bridge. As mention, it was modeled as a two-lane rectilinear motorway. The seven adjustable parameters: lane-density ratio (df_{21}), randomization probabilities (p_{c_1}, p_{c_2}), and, mean and variance of the velocities

Gaussian distributions functions ($v_{\max_1}$, S_{v_1}, $v_{\max_2}$, S_{v_2}), are used as fitting parameters to the empirical data.

In Fig.1, the results of a trial and error fitting process are presented. The figure shows the time evolution of normalized empirical average flow. The eight data points presented, shown as solid squares, correspond to eight hours of traffic performance on WedFeb20/2002, from 5:00 am in the morning to 12 at noon. Simulation results are shown as dashed and solid lines. Dashed lines correspond to simulated flows obtained when mean and variance of the velocity distribution are not included among the fitting parameters. Simulation represented by the three solid curves (thin, medium and thick), resulted from using the full set of seven fitting parameters. It can be appreciated that in this former case a considerable improvement in the quality of the fit is attained. The cumbersome trial-and-error process eventually leads to a reasonable fit of the data (thick curve).

A more effective way of producing the values of the fitting parameters consists on the application of a general optimization technique to a properly chosen objective function that quantifies the quality of he fit. To do so, an Objective Function σ is introduced, defined by

$$\sigma = \sum_{j} (f_j^{\exp} - f_j^{sim})^2 . \tag{3}$$

where $j = 1,2,3,......, N_{ed}$, and N_{ed} is the number of empirical flow data. The quantities $f_j^{\exp}$ and f_j^{sim} are, respectively, average empirical (WedFeb20/2002) and simulated normalized flows. Values of f_j^{sim} are obtained after sampling the "continuous" curves generated using the simulation model.

The optimization algorithm applied to find the optimal values of the seven parameters involved incorporates a well-known unconstrained optimization technique, the Down-Hill Simplex Method [10]. Since it is an unconstrained algorithm, optimal parameters might take arbitrary real values. On the other hand, p_{c_1}, p_{c_2} represent randomization probabilities, and must be positive real numbers smaller than one. Then, in order to guarantee acceptable values for these probabilities, the transformation $p = r/(1+r)$ [11] is applied. Another approach is to use constrained optimization techniques of the type reported in references [12].

An iterative process, incorporating the Down-Hill Simplex Method and that uses the proposed emergent traffic model for the bridge as generator of the values f_j^{sim} in the objective function to optimize, was implemented. It requires a $8x7$ matrix P and an 8-dimensional vector Y. Each row of matrix P was obtained after giving eight arbitrary values to the seven fitting parameters, say, $df_{21}^1, p_{c_1}^1, p_{c_2}^1, v_{\max_1}^1, S_{v_1}^1, v_{\max_2}^1, S_{v_2}^1; df_{21}^2, p_{c_1}^2, p_{c_2}^2, v_{\max_1}^2, S_{v_1}^2, v_{\max_2}^2, S_{v_2}^2; \ . \ . \ . \ ;$ $df_{21}^8, p_{c_1}^8, p_{c_2}^8, v_{\max_1}^8, S_{v_1}^8, v_{\max_2}^8, S_{v_2}^8$. Each set of values represents the coordinates of a point in a 7-dimensional Euclidean Space, and are thought to correspond to the eight vertices of a 7-d tetrahedron or *simplex*. The superscript labels the eight vertices of the tetrahedron. Values occurring in vector Y are obtained by evaluating the Objective Function σ at the 8 vertices of the simplex. Fig.2 shows a 3-d example where df_{21}, p_{C_1} and p_{C_2} are the fitting parameters. The structure of the corresponding matrix P and vector Y for this particular case, are shown as well.

At every stage of the iterative process the coordinates of the vertices of the simplex, are modified sequentially with a relaxation dynamics so that the shape of the 7-d tetrahedron is conserved and the value of σ is decreased at the same time. After a large number of iterations, σ reaches a minimum value. This state defines the values of the fitting parameters for the traffic model.

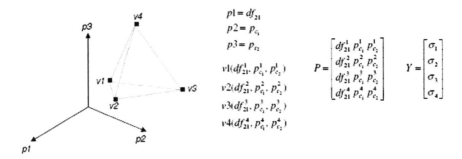

Fig. 2. Tetrahedron (*simplex*) used in the Down-Hill Method (3-d case)

Fig.3 shows the results obtained with the described procedure on the bridge data corresponding to the 5 labor days. The figure depicts the time evolution of simulated normalized and empirical flow values. The former values are represented by solid and empty squares, empty triangles, diamonds and circles. The simulation result, depicted by the solid curve, was obtained using the optimal values of the fitting parameters, listed as well in the figure. The minimum value of the Objective Function was $\sigma = 0.0912$, so that the values of f_j^{sim} are quite close to those of f_j^{exp}. In summary the model parameters obtained by the fitting procedure produces a traffic simulation that reproduces quite well the general features of empirical flow data reported for Las Mercedes' Bridge.

In considering the model for the curved road, the objective function to optimize now depends on 9 variables: lane-density ratio df_{cg} (i.e. $df_{cg} = \rho_c/\rho_g$, where ρ_g is the west-to-east-lane car density and ρ_c is the east-to-west-lane car density), randomization probabilities (p_{C_g}, p_{C_c}), means and variances of lane-velocity Gaussian distributions (v_{max_g}, S_{v_g}, v_{max_c}, S_{v_c}), the angle of curvature (Θ), and the longitudinal factor f_{long}.

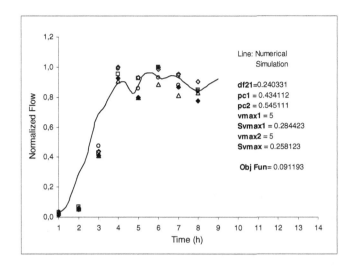

Fig. 3. Empirical Data vs. Numerical Simulation. Evolution in time of average normalized flows for the two-lane Las Mercedes' Bridge. Optimal values of the fitting parameters and Objective Function, are shown.

In order to quantify simultaneously the mean square deviations of the differences between averages normalized empirical and simulated flows values, an aggregate Objective Function of the form

$$\sigma_{gc} = \frac{1}{2}(\sigma_g + f_{long}\sigma_c).$$ (4)

is proposed. Here, σ_g and σ_c are individual-lane objective functions, defined as in Eq. (3). Both objective functions were evaluated using WedFeb20/2002 measurements.

An iterative process, similar to the one implemented for the case of the bridge, was used to find the optimal values of the nine fitting parameters. Again, after a large number of iterations, the Objective Function σ_{gc} reached its lowest value. Results for each lane are shown in Fig.4. Normalized flow data for the 5-labor-days are represented, as before, by solid and empty squares, empty triangles, diamonds and circles. Solid curves in both figures are simulations performed using the obtained optimal values of the 9 fitting parameters. The minimum value of the aggregate Objective Function was $\sigma_{gc} = 0.27$, indicating that in this case, values of f_j^{sim} are not very close to those of f_j^{exp}.

These results clearly indicate the need of further research. Two important facts must be taken into account. First, the aggregate Objective Function σ_{gc} given by Eq. (4), depends on a two functions σ_g and σ_c; its complexity requires that it be defined and handled in a more careful way. Secondly, it is necessary to enhance the road simulation model, including additional relevant aspects that influence traffic

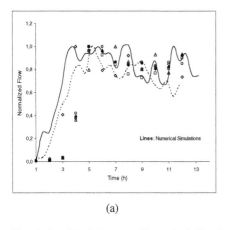
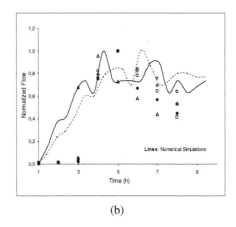

(a)   (b)

Fig. 4. Empirical Data vs. Numerical Simulation. Evolution in time of normalized flows: (a) West-to-East lane; (b) East-to-West lane, of the two lane Baruta's Old Road. Lines (dashed and solid) represent simulation results.

dynamic. In spite of all these facts, it can be say that the proposed emergent traffic model reproduces the general features of typical real traffic on the considered sector of the Baruta's Old road.

5   Conclusions and Finals Comments

An EMMBCA to simulate traffic dynamics and performance on two locations of the city of Caracas – a two-lane rectilinear bridge, and, a sector of a two-lane curved road with cars moving in opposite directions– was implemented. The model is a generalization of the well-known Nagel and Schreckenberg model for identical vehicles.

To take into account some aspects related with car drivers' behavior, i.e., that some of them do not honors velocity limits established for the motorways, car velocities were picked from a Gaussian distribution.

Model validation was carried out through an iterative process which incorporates an unconstrained optimization technique to find the minimum of multivariable functions. Objective Functions which quantifies the mean square deviations of the differences of measured and simulated normalized flow, were defined. Mean and variance of velocities distributions were considered as optimization parameters together with other model parameters.

The proposed emergent traffic model describes quantitatively, the general features of empirical mean flows measured along a week in two specific locations of the city of Caracas in Venezuela. Incorporation of mean and variance of the velocity Gaussian distributions as optimization parameters substantially improved the fitting. To improve it even further, particularly in the road case, a more appropriate definition of the aggregate objective function and additional enhancements in the emergent traffic model including additional aspects that influence traffic dynamic, must be incorporated. This research is in progress.

References

1. D. Chowdury, L. Santen and A. Schaschneider. Statistical physics of vehicular traffic and some related systems. *Physics Report* 329, 199 (2000). Institut für Theoretische Phisik, Universität zu Köln. Germany. August 2002.
2. K. Nagel and M. Schreckenberg. A cellular automaton model for freeway traffic. *J. Physique* I 2, 2221-2229. 1992.
3. H. M. Zhang and T. Kim. Understanding and modeling driver behavior in dense traffic flow. *University of California Transportation Center*. October 2002.
4. A. Pottmeier, R. Chrobok, S. F. Hafstein, F. Mazur and M. Schreckenberg. *OLSIM:* Up-to date traffic information on the Web. *Proceeding of the Third IASTED. St. Thomas, US Virgin Islands.* November 22-24 2004.
5. J. Esser and M. Schreckenberg. Microscopic Simulation of Urban Traffic Based on Cellular Automata. *International Journal of Modern Physics C.* Vol. 8, No.5 (1997) 1025-1036.
6. M. Ben-Akiva, M. Cortes, A. Davol, H. Koutsopoulos and T. Toledo. *MITSIMLab* Enhancements and applications for urban networks. Intelligent transportation system program. *Massachusetts Institute of Technology. Civil and Environmental Engineering Topic Area Code: C4.* Cambridge Massachsetts, USA. November 1999.
7. K. Nagel, D. Wolf, P. Wagner and P. Simon. Two-lane traffic rules for cellular automata: a systematic approach. *Phys. Rev. E*, Vol. 58, No. 2. August 1998.
8. A. Daoudia and N. Moussa. Numerical simulations of a three-lane traffic model using cellular automata. *CHINESE JOURNAL OF PHYSICS* Vol. 41, NO. 6. December 2003.
9. URVISA. *Urbanismo y Vialidad URVISA.* Estudio de Circulación y Diagnóstico, Alcaldía de Baruta. Caracas, Venezuela. Jun 2002.
10. *Numerical Recipes in C. THE ART OF SCIENTIFIC COMPUTING.* Cambridge University Press. 1986-1992.
11. H. Martínez. *Personal Communication.* November 2005.
12. S. Buitrago. Aplicaciones de técnicas de optimización en sistemas de producción de petróleo II. *Memorias del VI Congreso Internacional de Métodos Numéricos en Ingeniería y Ciencias Aplicadas (CIMENICS).* Porlamar. Venezuela, March 2006.

Scale-Free Automata Networks Are Not Robust in a Collective Computational Task

Christian Darabos, Mario Giacobini, and Marco Tomassini

Information Systems Department, University of Lausanne, Switzerland
{christian.darabos, mario.giacobini, marco.tomassini}@unil.ch

Abstract. We investigate the performances and collective task-solving capabilities of complex networks of automata using the density problem as a typical case. We show by computer simulations that evolved Watts–Strogatz small-world networks have superior performance with respect to scale-free graphs of the Albert–Barabási type. Besides, Watts–Strogatz networks are much more robust in the face of transient uniformly random perturbations. This result differs from information diffusion on scale-free networks, where random faults are highly tolerated.

1   Introduction

Networks are a central model for the description of countless phenomena of scientific, social and technological interest. Typical examples include the Internet, the World Wide Web, social acquaintances, electric power supply networks, neural networks, and many more [1]. In recent years there has been substantial research activity in the science of networks, motivated by a number of innovative results, both theoretical and applied. The key idea is that most real networks, both in the natural world as well as in man-made structures, have mathematical properties that set them apart from regular lattices and random graphs, which were the two main topologies studied until then. In 1998, Watts and Strogatz introduced an algorithmic construction for *small-world networks* [2], in which pairs of vertices are connected by short paths through the network. The existence of short paths between any pair of nodes has been found in networks as diverse as the Internet, airline routes, neural networks, or metabolic networks, among others. The presence of short paths is also a property of random graphs, but what sets real networks apart from these latter is a larger *clustering coefficient*, a measure that reflects the locality of a structure.

The topological structure of a network has a marked influence on the processes that may take place on it. Regular and random networks have been thoroughly studied from this point of view in many disciplines. For instance, the dynamics of lattices and random networks of simple automata have received a great deal of attention [3,4]. On the other hand, there are very few studies of the computational properties of networks of the small-world type. Notable exceptions are Watts' book [5] and [6] in which cellular automata (CAs) computation on small-world networks is examined. In these works the automata networks were designed by a prescribed algorithm. Recently, we have shown that evolutionary algorithms can be an effective way for obtaining high-performance computational networks in the small-world region without explicit prior design [7].

S. El Yacoubi, B. Chopard, and S. Bandini (Eds.): ACRI 2006, LNCS 4173, pp. 512–521, 2006.

Indeed, many man-made networks have grown, and are still growing, incrementally. The Internet is a case, for which a *preferential attachment* growth rule was proposed as a model, giving good results [8]. The kind of graphs that are obtained in this way are called *scale-free*, a term that will be clarified below. Scale-free graphs also share the small world property.

In this work we study in detail some computational behaviors of automata networks of the small-world and scale-free types. As a typical example of a collective computational task we take the *density task*, which is briefly described below. As natural computational systems often have a degree of stochasticity, it is particularly important to investigate their behavior in a noisy environment. We shall see the behavior in the presence of perturbations strongly depends on the network topology, and we shall draw some conclusions on the suitability of these topologies for collective computation.

In the following section we give a brief account of the Watts–Strogatz small-world and Barabási-Albert scale-free networks used here, as well as a description of the density task. Next we will discuss the experimental performance of generalized networks on the task. After that we study in detail their fault-tolerance capabilities and, finally, we present our conclusions and ideas for future extensions.

2   Small-World and Scale-Free Graphs

The Watts–Strogatz Model. Following Watts and Strogatz [2], a small-world graph can be constructed starting from a regular ring of N nodes in which each node has k neighbors ($k \ll N$) by simply systematically going through successive nodes and "rewiring" each link with a certain probability β. When an edge is deleted, it is replaced by an edge to a randomly chosen node. If rewiring an edge would lead to a duplicate edge, it is left unchanged. This procedure will create a number of links, called *shortcuts*, that join distant parts of the lattice. Shortcuts are the hallmark of small worlds. While the average path length[1] between nodes scales logarithmically with the number of nodes in a random graph, in Watts-Strogatz graphs it scales approximately linearly for low rewiring probability but goes down very quickly and tends towards the random graph limit as β increases. This is due to the progressive appearance of shortcut edges between distant parts of the graph, which obviously contract the path lengths between many vertices. However, small world graphs typically have a higher clustering coefficient[2] than random graphs, and a degree distribution $P(k)$ close to Poissonian.

The Barabási-Albert Model. Albert and Barabási were the first to realize that real networks grow incrementally and that their evolving topology is determined by the way in which new nodes are added to the network. They proposed an extremely simple model based on these ideas [8]. One starts with a small *clique* of m_0 nodes. At each successive time step a new node is added such that its $m \leq m_0$ edges link it to m nodes already in the graph. When choosing the nodes to which the new nodes connect, it is assumed that the probability π that a new node will be connected to node i depends

---

[1] The average path length L of a graph is the average value of all pairs shortest paths.

[2] The clustering coefficient C of a node is a measure of the probability that two nodes that are its neighbors are also neighbors among themselves. The average $\langle C \rangle$ is the average of the Cs of all nodes in the graph.

on the current degree k_i of i. This is called the *preferential attachment* rule. Nodes with already many links are more likely to be chosen than those that have few. The probability $\pi(k_i)$ of node i to be chosen is given by:

$$\pi(k_i) = \frac{k_i}{\sum_j k_j},$$

where the sum is over all nodes already in the graph. The model evolves into a stationary network with power-law probability distribution for the vertex degree $P(k) \sim k^{-\gamma}$, with $\gamma \sim 3$, which justifies the name *scale-free*. As for Watts–Strogatz small-worlds, scale-free graphs have short average path length and clustering coefficients that are higher than those of the corresponding random graphs with comparable number of vertices and edges.

3   The Density Task on Generalized Networks

The density task is a prototypical distributed computational problem for binary CAs. For a finite one-dimensional CA of size N it is defined as follows. Let s_0 be the *initial configuration* of the CA, i.e. the sequence of bits that represents the state of each automaton at time 0, and let ρ_0 be the fraction of 1s in the initial configuration. The task is to determine whether ρ_0 is greater than or less than $1/2$. If $\rho_0 > 1/2$ then the CA must relax to a fixed-point configuration of all 1's, otherwise it must relax to a fixed-point configuration of all 0's, after a number of time steps of the order of the grid size N, usually $2N$. Here N is set to 149, the value that has been customarily used in research on the density task (if N is odd one avoids the case where $\rho_0 = 0.5$ for which the problem is undefined).

   This computation is trivial for a computer with a central control: just scanning the array and adding up the number of, say, 1 bits will provide the answer in $O(N)$ time. However, it is nontrivial for a small radius one-dimensional CA since such a CA can only transfer information at finite speed relying on local information exclusively, while density is a global property of the configuration of states. It has been shown that the density task cannot be solved perfectly by a uniform, two-state CA with finite radius [9], although a slightly modified version of the task can be shown to admit perfect solution by such an automaton [10], or by a combination of automata [11].

3.1   Task Performance on Different Network Structures

The design, evolution, and performance evaluation of one-dimensional CAs that approximately perform the density task has a long history; an excellent review appears in [12]. The *performance* of a CA rule on the density task is defined as the fraction of correct classifications over $n = 10^4$ randomly chosen initial configurations (ICs). These are sampled according to a binomial distribution among the 2^N possible binary strings i.e., each bit is independently drawn with probability $1/2$ of being 0. Clearly, this distribution is strongly peaked around $\rho_0 = 1/2$ and thus making a difficult case for the CA to classify. The best CAs found to date either by evolutionary computation or by hand have performances around 0.8 [12].

Using his small-world construction, and thus relaxing the regular lattice constraint, Watts [5] has been able to easily obtain automata networks with performance around 0.85, with the same mean connectivity $\langle k \rangle$ as in the regular CA case.

Task Performance on Watts–Strogatz Networks. In [7,13], inspired by the work of Watts on small-world cellular automata, we have used an evolutionary algorithm to evolve networks that have similar computational capabilities. Each individual represents a network topology, and the automaton rule is the generalized majority rule described by Watts [5]: at each time step, each node will assume the state of the majority of its neighbors in the graph, and, in case of a draw the next state is assigned at random with equal probability. We have evolved network topologies starting from populations of slightly modified regular one-dimensional lattices, and from populations of random graphs. For the evolutions, we have used two different fitness functions, in order to obtain two different classes of networks, with small and high number of shortcuts (captured by the measure of the ϕ value, which is the fraction of edges in a graph that are shortcuts), and with different average degrees. Without including any preconceived design issue, the evolutionary algorithm has been consistently able to find high-performance automata networks in the same class of those constructed by Watts (see figure 1).

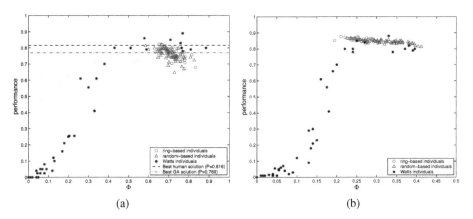

(a)   (b)

Fig. 1. Density task. The ϕ - performance values of the 50 best individuals found by evolution starting from rings and random graphs. For comparison, Watt's results are also plotted (redrawn from [5]). (a): using a fitness function that does not favor low ϕ networks, thus obtaining networks comparable with Watts' hand-constructed networks with $\langle k \rangle = 6$. (b): using a fitness function that favors low ϕ networks, thus obtaining networks comparable with Watts' hand-constructed networks with $\langle k \rangle = 12$.

Task Performance on Scale-Free Networks. In accordance to the Albert and Barabási model, we constructed networks to be used as support for CA computations. Knowing that the average degree must remain comparable to our work on the small-world graphs [13], we generated scale-free graphs with $\langle k \rangle = \{6, 12\}$. Following the model, we then defined the range of m_0 values for each k using the derived equation for m. These values of m_0 must respect the constraints $m \leq m_0$ and $m \geq 1$ to ensure the graph is connected. For $\langle k \rangle = 6$, $m_0 \in [4, 25]$ and for $\langle k \rangle = 12$, $m_0 \in [7, 40]$. We assure that even though m is not always an integer, the exact global number of edges in the graph, thus $\langle k \rangle$, is respected in all cases.

Results as represented in Figure 2 show that performance on the density task of CAs mapped on scale-free networks are above 0.7 for networks with a smaller m_0. When a certain threshold is reached (m_0 about 14 for $\langle k \rangle = 6$ and 35 for $\langle k \rangle = 12$), performances drop dramatically. This means that the more the structure of the scale-free network become star-like, with a unique oversized cluster and only small satellites weakly connected ($m \rightarrow 1$), the information circulates with more difficulties. One can conclude from these results that scale-free network topologies are less suitable than Watts–Strogatz small worlds as a substrate for the density task. The results are even worse than those obtained in rings [12] using specialized rules.

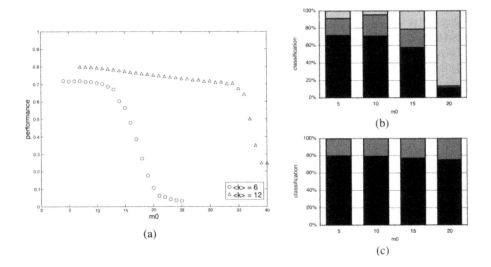

(a)

(b)

(c)

Fig. 2. (a) Performance vs m_0 of scale-free networks (build on the Albert and Barabási model) on the density task. The circles represent the performance of networks with an average connection $\langle k \rangle = 6$ and triangles $\langle k \rangle = 12$. On the right, the average percentages of correctly classified ICs (black), incorrectly classified ICs (dark gray) and unclassified ICs (light gray) for sizes of the initial clique in [5,20] by scale-free networks with (b) $\langle k \rangle = 6$ and (c) $\langle k \rangle = 12$. Results are averages over 50 graph realizations.

4   The Effects of Noise

Noisy environments are the rule in the real world. Since these automata networks are toy examples of distributed computing systems, it is interesting and legitimate to ask questions about their fault-tolerance aspects. A network of automata may fail in various ways when random noise is allowed. For instance, the cells may fail temporarily or they may die altogether; links may be cut, or both things may happen. In this section, we shall compare the robustness of standard lattice-CAs to that of small-world and scale-free CAs with respect to a specific kind of transient perturbation, which we call *probabilistic updating*. It is defined as follows: the CA rule may yield the incorrect output bit with probability p_f, and thus the probability of correct functioning will be $(1 - p_f)$. Furthermore, we assume that errors are uncorrelated. This implies that, for a network with N vertices, the probability $P(N, m)$ that m cells (vertices) are faulty at any given time step t is binomially distributed. It should be noted that we do not try to correct or compensate for the errors, which is important in engineered system but very complicated and outside our scope. Instead, we focus on the "natural" fault-tolerance and self-recovering capabilities of the systems under study.

4.1 Evolved Watts–Strogatz Networks Under Probabilistic Updating Perturbation

To observe the effects of probabilistic updating on the CA dynamics, two initially identical copies of the system are maintained. One proceeds undisturbed with $p_f = 0$, while the second is submitted to a nonzero probability of fault. We can then measure such things as Hamming distances between unperturbed and faulty configurations, which give information on the spreading of damage [14].

Figure 3(a) shows that, for our evolved Watts-Strogatz small-world networks with $\langle k \rangle = 6$ (results for $\langle k \rangle = 12$ are similar and thus are not shown), the amount of disorder is linearly related to the fault probability. This is an excellent result when compared with ring CAs where already at $p_f = 0.001$ the average Hamming distance is about 20 [13], and tends to grow linearly. At $p_f = 0.1$ it saturates at about 95, while it is still only about 20 for the small-world CA.

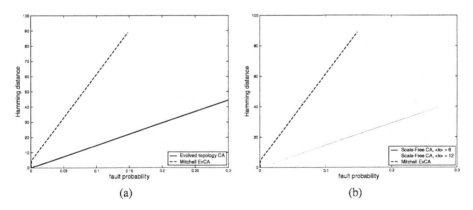

(a)   (b)

Fig. 3. Hamming distance (y-axis) vs. fault probability (x-axis): rule-evolved [12] (Mitchell EvCA) ring CAs (dashed lines) are compared (a) to evolved small-world topology networks (the two classes of networks, with $\langle k \rangle \approx 6$ and $\langle k \rangle \approx 12$, show very similar behaviors, thus a single curve is plotted), and (b) to hand-made scale-free CA with $\langle k \rangle = 6$ and $\langle k \rangle = 12$. The curves are averages over 10^4 distinct initial configurations, each configuration running for $2N$ time steps.

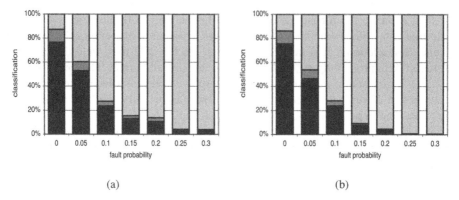

(a)   (b)

Fig. 4. Percentages of correctly classified (black), incorrectly classified (dark gray) and unclassified (light gray) as the fault probability increases for (a) ring-based networks and (b) random-based networks with a fitness function not favoring low ϕ values, thus $\langle k \rangle = 6$. Results are averages over 50 graph realizations.

As described in Section 3.1 we have extracted the best individual of 50 independent evolutionary runs for both considered starting points (ring-based and random-based). In this first experiment individuals had evolved freely towards shortcut proportions ϕ between 0.6 and 0.8. We have studied the performance (or classification abilities) variation of these networks under probabilistic updating for fault probabilities f_p evenly scattered over $[0, 0.3]$. Figure 4 show how percentages of initial configurations that are correctly classified (in black), incorrectly classified (in dark gray), and not classified at all (in light gray) change as the fault probability increases. These percentages are averaged out over all contributing individuals to that classification category. Figure 4(a) depicts the behavior of networks having evolved from perturbed rings, whereas Figure 4(b) shows that of networks having emerged from random networks.

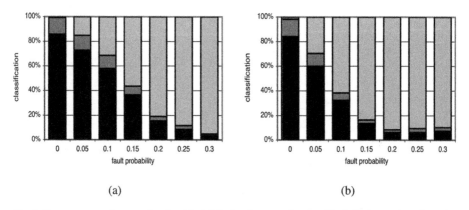

(a)   (b)

Fig. 5. Percentages of correctly classified (black), incorrectly classified (dark gray) and unclassified (light gray) with increasing fault probability for (a) ring-based networks and (b) random-based networks evolved using a fitness function favoring low ϕ values, thus $\langle k \rangle = 12$. Results are averages over 50 graph realizations.

As pictured in Figure 4 although the fault probability increases rapidly, our evolved networks show interesting fault tolerance capabilities up to 10% of faulty outputs. Moreover we note that the proportion of correctly classified ICs compared to the incorrectly classified ones is around 10:1, and this ratio remains almost constant despite the increase in the fault probability. This is especially interesting considering that identifying unclassified ICs is trivial ($2N$ steps and no convergence to a steady state) whereas distinguishing correct from incorrect classification is impossible without knowing the solution beforehand. We conclude that although an increasing number of ICs will not reach a fixed point, the ratio between correctly classified and misclassified ICs remains comparable.

Figure 5 shows classification abilities of networks evolved using a fitness function favoring low values of ϕ resulting in networks with higher average degrees and generally better performances. In fact, we can see that where the approximate 10:1 proportion of correctly vs. incorrectly classified is respected, the percentage of unclassified ICs drops significantly for both networks evolved starting from ring and from random structures.

4.2   Scale-Free Networks Under Probabilistic Updating Perturbation

To investigate the effects of noise on scale-free automata networks we have used populations of 50 scale-free networks with $m_0 = 9$ to perform the density task for 7 values of fault probability $f_p \in [0.0, 0.3]$ equally scattered over the interval. Figure 3(b) illustrates the random faults for both $\langle k \rangle = 6$ and $\langle k \rangle = 12$ compared to the results of the rule evolved for a ring [12]. The curves for both values of $\langle k \rangle$ are practically overlapping. Results show that the robustness of scale-free and small-world (Figure 3(a)) CAs is comparable for all values of f_p.

The performance under noise of the above scale-free automata networks is shown in Figure 6. The ratio of correctly to incorrectly classified ICs is close to 1:5. Figure 6 shows that as the fault probability increases, the ability of performing the collective task is lost. When one compares these results to the small-world case in the above section, we conclude that the fault tolerance is significantly lower in the scale-free case. Figure 6(a) shows classification details for scale-free networks with an average degree of $\langle k \rangle = 12$ and an initial clique size $m_0 = 5$ and Figure 6(b) for $m_0 = 10$, for increasing fault probability. The two cases present the same qualitative behavior.

These results raise an interesting issue concerning the fault-tolerance of scale-free graphs. Indeed, a recent widely publicized result states that scale-free graphs are extremely robust against random node failures, while they have been shown to be fragile when the failures concern highly connected nodes (hubs), a fact that is particularly relevant for the Internet [15]. Thus, scale-free networks are good for information dissemination, i.e. when what counts is that alternative paths remain available in spite of random noise. However, we find that the same structures do not offer such resilience when a task is to be solved in a collective, coordinated way, such as the density task studied here; the results would be even worse if the faults were unrecoverable. We have performed similar computer experiments with scale-free graphs starting from larger *cliques*. The results, not shown to save space, confirm the findings described above.

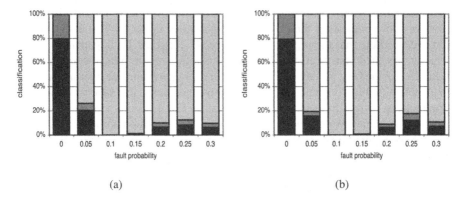

(a)   (b)

Fig. 6. Percentages of correctly classified (black), incorrectly classified (dark gray) and unclassified (light gray) as the fault probability increases for (a) an initial clique size of 5 and (b) and initial clique size of 10. Results are averages over 50 graph realizations.

5   Conclusions

In this work we have empirically investigated the performances and collective task-solving capabilities of complex networks of automata using the density problem as a typical case. We have shown by computer simulations that previously evolved Watts–Strogatz small-world networks have superior performance with respect to scale-free graphs of the Albert–Barabási type. Then we have investigated in some detail the fault-tolerance capabilities of both network families against transient uniformly random errors. The main, and relatively surprising, result is that Watts–Strogatz networks are much more robust in the face of that type of perturbations. On the contrary, scale-free graphs are extremely vulnerable with respect to this kind of random failures. In the light of well known results concerning information diffusion on scale-free networks, where random faults do not impact performance up to a point, our results seem to indicate that the kind of computation performed "by" the network, as opposed to "on" the network is very sensitive to network integrity. Nevertheless, both Watts–Strogatz and scale-free graphs are much more fault-tolerant than standard regular lattice CAs for the task.

Acknowledgements. Ch. Darabos and M. Tomassini gratefully acknowledge financial support by the Swiss National Science Foundation under contract 200021-107419/1.

References

1. M. E. J. Newman. The structure and function of complex networks. *SIAM Review*, 45:167–256, 2003.
2. D. J. Watts and S. H. Strogatz. Collective dynamics of 'small-world' networks. *Nature*, 393:440–442, 1998.
3. M. Garzon. *Models of Massive Parallelism: Analysis of Cellular Automata and Neural Networks*. Springer-Verlag, Berlin, 1995.

4. S. A. Kauffman. *The Origins of Order*. Oxford University Press, New York, 1993.
5. D. J. Watts. *Small worlds: The Dynamics of Networks between Order and Randomness*. Princeton University Press, Princeton NJ, 1999.
6. R. Serra and M. Villani. Perturbing the regular topology of cellular automata: implications for the dynamics. In S. Bandini, B. Chopard, and M. Tomassini, editors, *Cellular Automata, ACRI 2002*, volume 2493 of *Lecture Notes in Computer Science*, pages 168–177. Springer-Verlag, Heidelberg, 2002.
7. M. Tomassini, M. Giacobini, and C. Darabos. Evolution of small-world networks of automata for computation. In X. Yao et al., editor, *Parallel Problem Solving from Nature - PPSN VIII*, volume 3242 of *Lecture Notes in Computer Science*, pages 672–681. Springer Verlag, Berlin, 2004.
8. R. Albert and A.-L. Barabási. Statistical mechanics of complex networks. *Reviews of Modern Physics*, 74:47–97, 2002.
9. M. Land and R. K. Belew. No perfect two-state cellular automata for density classification exists. *Physical Review Letters*, 74(25):5148–5150, June 1995.
10. M. S. Capcarrère, M. Sipper, and M. Tomassini. Two-state, r=1 cellular automaton that classifies density. *Physical Review Letters*, 77(24):4969–4971, December 1996.
11. H. Fukś. Solution of the density classification problem with two cellular automata rules. *Physical Review E*, 55(3):2081–2084, 1997.
12. J. P. Crutchfield, M. Mitchell, and R. Das. Evolutionary design of collective computation in cellular automata. In J. P. Crutchfield and P. Schuster, editors, *Evolutionary Dynamics: Exploring the Interplay of Selection, Accident, Neutrality, and Function*, pages 361–411. Oxford University Press, Oxford, UK, 2003.
13. M. Tomassini, M. Giacobini, and C. Darabos. Evolution and dynamics of small-world cellular automata. *Complex Systems*, 15:261–284, 2005.
14. M. Sipper, M. Tomassini, and O. Beuret. Studying probabilistic faults in evolved non-uniform cellular automata. *International Journal of Modern Physics C*, 7(6):923–939, 1996.
15. R. Albert, H. Jeong, and L. Barabási. Error and attack tolerance of complex networks. *Nature*, 406:378–382, 2000.

Simulation of Heterogeneous Motorised Traffic at a Signalised Intersection

Puspita Deo and Heather J. Ruskin

School of Computing, Dublin City University, Dublin9, Ireland
{dpuspita, hruskin}@computing.dcu.ie

Abstract. The characteristics of heterogeneous traffic (with variation in vehicle length) are significantly different from those for homogeneous traffic. The present study describes an overview of the development and validation of a stochastic heterogeneous traffic-flow simulation model for an urban single-lane two-way road, with controlled intersection. In this paper, the interaction between vehicle types during manoeuvres at the intersection are analysed in detail. Two different motorised vehicle types are considered, namely cars and buses, (or similar length vehicles). A two-component cellular automata (CA) based model is used. Traffic flow data, captured manually by Dublin City Council at a local intersection, are analysed to give a baseline on how the distribution of short and long vehicles affect throughput. It is anticipated that such detailed studies will aid traffic management and optimisation strategies for traffic flow.

Keywords: Heterogeneous, motorised traffic, two-component cellular automata.

1 Introduction

Studies of road traffic characteristics are necessary for planning, design and operation of road facilities, in addition to regulation and control of traffic. In Western countries, specifically Ireland, car and heavy goods vehicle (HGV) traffic volumes have increased dramatically over the past 30 years [1], and this trend is likely to continue, at least in the short term.

Field observations of traffic flow can be difficult and time consuming to obtain. Frequently, such experiments in the field must cover a wide range of traffic volume and composition to provide practical benefits. Computer simulation models offer a viable alternative for in-depth study and a practical tool for understanding traffic dynamics.

There are three different conceptual frame works for modelling traffic. A fluid dynamical model [2], the car- following model [3], [4] and [5] and cellular automata models [6],[7] and [8] for modelling traffic on both highways and urban networks. These cellular automata (CA) traffic models represent a single lane road as a one-dimensional array of cells of certain length, with each cell either empty or occupied

S. El Yacoubi, B. Chopard, and S. Bandini (Eds.): ACRI 2006, LNCS 4173, pp. 522–531, 2006.

by a single vehicle. Vehicle movement is updated according to a given rule set, which applies to all constituent units.

Typical urban roads support mixed traffic with a variety of motorised vehicle types, using the same right of the way. As an extreme case, traffic composition in South Asian countries, specifically India, is mixed with both motorised and non motorised vehicles and with e.g. little or no lane discipline [9], whereas traffic in Western European countries consists of a mix of mainly motorised vehicles of different length. The features that characterise mixed traffic systems, otherwise known as *heterogeneous traffic*, mainly reflect the wide variation in size, manoeuvrability, and static and dynamic properties.

Much of the work on heterogeneity in traffic flows has been done in India for widely diverse units [10], [11], [12] and [13]. As such, these include motorised and non-motorised flows. These models cannot be used for a comprehensive study of mixed motorised traffic flow characteristic in a "single-lane", due to different patterns of road usage, e.g. multiple occupation of cells. The work presented thus aims at the development of an appropriate traffic simulation model for Western European roads. The Western European model is a simplified model, which excludes multiple and shared occupation, (unlike e.g. Indian characteristic road-usage patterns). We propose and developed a simplified and novel heterogeneous *two-component cellular automata* model that allows for two classes of vehicle, long and short. The model was designed to describe stochastic interaction between individual vehicles and is independent of headway distribution [14]. In this heterogeneous model space mapping rules are used for each vehicle type, namely long and short vehicles, where the former equal a multiple of two of the latter. The detailed description of the update rules of the different vehicle types is given in the following section.

2 Methodology

The To describe the state of a road using a CA, the street is first divided into cells of length 7.5m [8]. This corresponds to the typical space (car length + distance to the preceding car) occupied by a car in a dense jam. Each cell can either be empty or occupied by exactly one car. A speed say, v=5, means that the vehicle travels five cells per time step or 37.5 m/s (135 km/h).

In our model, each cell is occupied by one particle per cell corresponding to a standard car of length less then or equal to 7.5metrs. Long vehicles (LV) are taken, for simplicity, to be double the length of a standard car i.e. two cells are required for one LV. A short vehicle (SV) is understood to be a car of length 1, while a LV is of length 2. Both SV and LV will move exactly one cell in the next time step if the cell in front is vacant.

The update rules are as follows.

C_n^t designates the state of the nth cell at time step t. If $C_n^t > 0$, there is a vehicle in n^{th} cell at time step t. The updates of the cells are on a vehicle- by- vehicle basis i.e. if the $C_n^t = 1$ (SV) in this time step and the cell in front is vacant then the SV will move one cell otherwise the SV will stay in the same cell in the next time step. Similarly, if

$C^t_n = C^t_{n+1} = 2$ (LV) in this time step and the cell in front is vacant then the LV will move one cell in next time step otherwise the LV will not move. In general, if either a given LV or SV is considered in this time step and the cell in front is occupied either by a SV or LV, then the given vehicle will not move in the next time step. Otherwise, it will move by one cell. In the two-component cellular automata model described, the states of the cells update simultaneously, in each cell is examined in the same time. In the case of a LV a single cell clearance is needed for the vehicle to move as a whole (22 designation) through half its length.

The algorithm is:

- If $C^t_n = 1$ and $C^t_{(n+1)} = 0$, then $C^{(t+1)}_{(n+1)} = C^t_n$ and $C^{(t+1)}_n = 0$

- If $C^t_n = 1$ and $C^t_{(n+1)} > 0$, then $C^{(t+1)}_n = C^t_n$

- If $C^t_n = C^t_{(n-1)} = 2$ and $C^t_{(n+1)} = 0$, then $C^{(t+1)}_{(n+1)} = C^t_n$ and $C^{(t+1)}_n = C^t_{(n-1)}$ and $C^{t+1}_{(n-1)} = 0$

- If $C^t_n = C^t_{(n-1)} = 2$ and $C^t_{(n+1)} > 0$, then $C^{(t+1)}_n = C^{(t+1)}_{(n-1)} = 2$

2.1 Traffic Light Controlled Intersection

In Fig.1, roads are labelled road-1, road-2, road-3, road-4, with major and minor as indicated. The shaded area is the intersection area and the junction is control by traffic light and a pre-determined cycle of green, yellow and red lights, with the yellow light occurring twice per cycle. This is common in most European countries including Ireland.

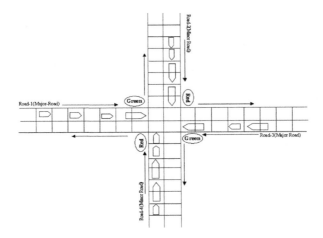

Fig. 1. A schematic traffic flow at a single-lane two-way signalised intersection

Signalisation of Traffic Light: Fixed Time Scheme. In this scheme, the traffic flow is controlled by a set of traffic lights, which are operated in a *fixed cycle* manner. Fixed-cycle intersections operate with a constant period of time T= 100 seconds for each cycle, where this is divided into a green, yellow and red periods for each phase. For road-1 and 3 Green= 55 seconds, yellow= 5 seconds and Red= 40 seconds where as road- 2 and 4, Green= 35 seconds, yellow= 5 seconds and Red= 60 seconds.

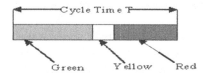

Fig. 2. Break down of a single fixed cycle

In our model we consider two phases for controlling the four roads. In *phase-1* the traffic light is green for major road-1 and road-3 (simultaneously red for road-2 and road-4). In the second part, the lights change colour to yellow for major road-1 and road-3 and simultaneously change to red for road-2 and road-4. In phase-2 the cycle repeats i.e. road-2 and road-4 become green and road-1 and road-3 red and the light changes colour to yellow for road-2 and road-4 and simultaneously red for road-1 and road-3.

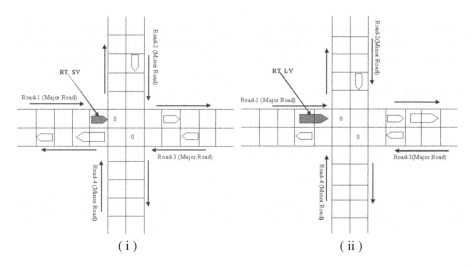

Fig. 3. A right turning (RT) vehicle from major road (i) SV (ii) LV

Vehicle Manoeuvring at the Intersection. Fig. 3 shows the requirements in terms of free cells for right turning vehicles from both major and minor road in a controlled intersection. Right turning short vehicles and long vehicles require 2 marked free cells for manoeuvring. "0" means that the cell is free or vacant whereas left turning (LT) and straight through vehicles need one free cell before entry into the intersection. In previous work [14], right turning SVs and LVs check only one free cell for manoeuvring. In the situation when two vehicles, travelling in the opposite direction, have entered the intersection to turn right, both vehicles wait for an indefinite period of time i.e. there is a deadlock condition. In this paper we present an improved version of our previous model, which requires clearance to complete the manoeuvre once commenced and which should be more realistic where intersection controls are observed.

CA models have considerable flexibility in terms of modelling urban road feature and a *one-dimensional two-component deterministic automata model*, can be used to simulate the interactions between various types of vehicles. The speed of the vehicle is taken simply to be either 0 or 1.

3 Simulated Results

Simulation was carried out for 36000 time steps (equivalent to 10 hours) for a road length of 100 cells for all approaches and under different values of traffic parameters, such as arrival rate, turning rate and proportion of short and long vehicle in each of the four roads. The basic inputs that are necessary to underpin and validate the simulation are given in Section 3.3. This is a base line and we would expect to vary the base line values, which underpin the sensitivity analysis, enabling us to determine how robust the model is to different assumptions and values. The intersection chosen for developing the model in this study is a single lane two-way signalised intersection. Based on the assumptions given in Section 2 we studied *throughput* (the number of vehicles, which cross the intersection in a given time) and *entry capacity or capacity of the intersection* (the number of vehicles passing from an entrance road on to the intersection per unit time). In each of these scenarios the simulation ran for 10 hours and we have averaged the result over 10 independent runs of the program unless otherwise specified.

3.1 Overall Throughput of the Intersection

Table 1 illustrates effects of different SV: LV proportions on overall throughputs. In each scenario, the turning rates of all approaches are based on analysis of the field data. For road-1, left turn (LT): straight through (ST): right turn (RT) =0.1:0.85:0.05, for road-2, LT: ST: RT=0.16=0.65:0.19, for road-3, LT: ST: RT=0.03:0.09:0.07 and for road-4, LT: ST: RT= 0.23: 0.71: 0.06. The arrival rate of the two major roads and minor roads are taken to be equal and vary from 0.1 to 0.3 (equivalent to 360 vph to 1800 vph). It is found that the average throughput of the intersection increases when arrival rate increases both in homogeneous (100 percent SV) and heterogeneous (SV+LV) traffic. In contrast, heterogeneous traffic throughput decreases with increased proportion of LV in the traffic mix.

Table 1. Avg. throughput Vs. arrival rate and long-vehicle proportion

SV: LV	Arrival Rate ($AR_{1=2=3=4}$)				
	0.1	0.2	0.3	0.4	0.5
1: 0	14405	28744	38411	44781	47874
0.9:0.1	14249	28143	36308	42153	44517
0.8:0.2	14031	27352	34509	39497	41052
0.7:0.3	13984	26171	32865	36557	37690
0.6:0.4	13793	24905	31327	33573	34464
0.5:0.5	13707	23855	29624	30809	31720
0.4:0.6	13534	22461	27320	28453	28995
0.3:0.7	13411	21762	25576	26301	26709
0.2:0.8	13272	20913	23786	24138	24601
0.1:0.9	13145	20109	22177	22396	22580
0: 1	12997	19280	20303	20248	20242

3.2 Capacity of Major Road

Right-turning vehicles from the major-road in a shared lane,(where RT, ST and LT vehicles are on the one lane), can block ST and LT vehicles behind and on the same road. RT rates (RTR) of the major-roads thus have great impact on capacities of these roads. In order to examine the capacity, we varied major- road1 right turning rate (RTR1) from 0.1 to 0.2, with major-road3 RTR3=0. Arrival rates of AR1 = AR2 =AR4 = 0.15, (equivalent to540 vph), were used initially, with the arrival rate of major road 3 varied from 0.05 to 0.55, (i.e. equivalent to 180 vph to 1980vph).

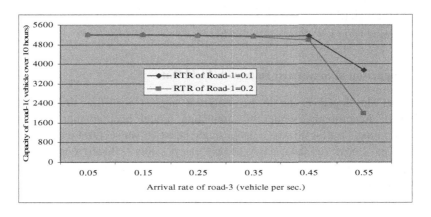

Fig. 4. Capacity of major road-1, there is no RT vehicles of major road-3

Fig 4 shows, unsurprisingly, that the capacity of the major-road 1 declines as RTR of road-1 and arrival rate of oncoming traffic in major-road-3 increases. Here we conclude that capacity of the major road declines when the percentage of RTR increases and /or the arrival rate of the oncoming major- road-3 increases.

4 Validation of the Model with Real Data

4.1 Field Data

The data for SV: LV ratios are studied for one local single lane two-way intersection (Rathgar Road/ Frankfort Avenue) in Dublin, Ireland. The intersection is controlled by signals, with basic characteristics and composition of flow at the intersection as detailed in Table 2. The traffic flow data were collected on 17th December 1997 by Dublin City Council, Ireland over a 10 hours period at every 15-minute intervals; weather was fair.

Table 2. Field Data collected by Dublin City Council 1997, total for 10 hours

Road number ⟶	Road-1	Road-2	Road-3	Road-4
Totals (SV+LV) for 10 hours	4937	2428	4941	2138
Averages per seconds	0.14	0.07	0.14	0.06
Total SV	4703	2391	4678	2111
Total LV	234	31	263	27
Left turning (LT) SV	523	378	137	497
Straight through (ST) SV	3941	1545	4173	1504
Right turning (RT) SV	239	468	368	128
Left turning (LT) LV	9	9	3	2
Straight through (ST) LV	219	24	254	22
Right turning (RT) LV	6	4	6	3

4.2 Comparison of Simulated Data with Field Data

The model developed needs to be validated against real life situations (field conditions). Accordingly, while the simulation model may attempt to replicate directly the mixed traffic flow on a given single lane two-way control intersection, for which we have observed data, this is clearly one possible realization only. The field data represents an average day's traffic and so it makes sense to validate our model using an average run. For 50 runs of ten hours, and the parameter values observed, the average results are presented in Tables 3 and 4 and Figure5. The model was run 50 times to ensure convergence of the average and this average was used in validation.

Table 3. Comparison results of our model and field data

Road Number	Turn	Short vehicle (SV)		Long vehicle (LV)	
		Obs Data	Avg. Sim. Data	Obs . Data	Avg. Sim. Data
Road-1	LT	523	478.12	9	21.42
	ST	3941	4057.68	219	184.9
	RT	293	240.8	6	10.34
Road-2	LT	378	395.04	9	7.74
	ST	1545	1596.74	24	29.66
	RT	468	464.34	4	9.32
Road-3	LT	137	149.32	3	6.48
	ST	4173	4458.44	254	203.98
	RT	368	163.02	6	7.7
Road-4	LT	497	510.1	2	5.06
	ST	1504	1578.06	22	14.68
	RT	128	49.24	3	0.32

Obs.= Observed, Avg. Sim= Average simulated

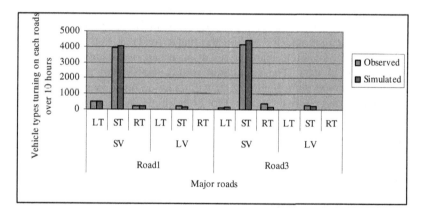

Fig. 5. Model validation (comparison of observed and simulated turning data of SV and LV from two major roads)

From the Figure and table, it appears that the simulation model reproduces, accurately, observed behaviour at the intersection.

Table 4 presents the comparison of observed and average simulated entry capacity or capacity of each approach of the study intersection. Simulated capacity matches the corresponding observed value with low % error. The highest relates to road2 and may be due to variation of cycle time with respect to the real time situation.

Table 4. Comparison of observed and simulated entry capacity or capacity of the intersection over 10 hour

Intersection entry capacity (vehicle in 10 hours)			
Road number	Obs. Data	Avg. sim. Data	% Error
Road-1	4937	4993.26	+1.13
Road-2	2428	2502.84	+3.08
Road-3	4941	4988.92	+0.96
Road-4	2138	2157.46	+0.91

5 Conclusions

In this paper, we have described a prototype two- component cellular automata model, which attempts to simulate heterogeneous motorised traffic flow at a single-lane two way signalised intersection. Importantly, we consider vehicles of different length, (true to real life situations). In order to achieve a more realistic microscopic simulation, various vehicle arrival and turning rates, as well as different vehicle types are built into our model.

On investigating the throughput of mixed (SV+LV) traffic and comparison with the homogeneous (SV or LV), our model clearly reproduces the decrease in throughput observed when traffic is mixed (proportion of LV increases).

Secondly, the major road capacity is clearly shown to depend on the arrival rate of the opposing major road and RT rate of the major roads as well as LV proportion. Finally, our model of vehicle manoeuvres at an urban road configuration has been validated using field data. The simulation results show good agreement between simulated and observed data. Future work will examine other features such as delay time, queue length and congestion period for both simple and complex intersections.

References

1. Future year growth forecasts for Ireland, Future traffic forecasts 2002-2040 final report, prepared by TRL Limited for the National Roads Authority, June, (2003),6-38
2. Lighthill, M.J., Whitham G.B.: On Kinematics waves: II. A theory of traffic flow on long crowded roads, proceeding of Royal Society of London series A, Vol. 229, (1995), 317-345
3. Pipes, L. A.: An Operational analysis of traffic dynamics, Journal of Applied Physics, Vol. 24, (1953), 274-281
4. Herman, R. and Ardekani, S.: Characterising traffic conditions in urban areas, Transportation Science, 18 (2),(1984),101-140
5. Jiang, R., Wu, Q., Zhu, Z.: A new continuum model for traffic flow and numerical tests, Transportation Research Part B,Vol. 36, (2002), 405-419
6. Nagel, K., Schreckenberg, M.: A cellular automaton model for freeway traffic, J.Phys. I France 2, (1992), 2221-2229
7. Chopard, B., Luthi P. O., and Queloz P-A.: Cellular automata model of car traffic in a two-dimensional street network, to appear in J. Phys. A,(1996),1-14

8. Nagel, K., Cellular automata models for transportation application, ACRI, LNC 2493, (2002), 20-31

9. Koshy, R. Z., and Arsan. V. T.: Modelling Stochasticity of Heterogeneous Traffic, Proceedings of the Fourth International Symposium on Uncertainty Modelling and Analysis (ISUMA' 03), IEEE Computer Society, (2003).

10. Marwah, B.R., and Singh, B.: Level of service classification for urban heterogeneous traffic: A case study of Kanpur metropolis, Transp. Res Circular E-C018: Proc., 4th International Symp. on Highway Capacity, Maui, Hawaii,(2000), 271-286

11. Khan, S.I., and Maini, P., Modelling heterogeneous traffic flow, Transportation Research Record, 1678,Transportation Research Board, Washington, D.C., (2000), 234-241

12. Tiwari G., Fazio J. and Pavitravas S., Passenger car units for heterogeneous traffic; a modified density method, Trans. Res. Circular E-C018: Proc., 4th International Symp. on Highway Capacity, Maui, Hawaii, (2000), 246-257

13. Arsan, V. T. and Koshy, R. Z.: Methodology for Modelling Highly Heterogeneous Traffic Flow, Journal of Transportation Engineering, Vol. 131, No. 7, July 1, (2005), 544-551

14. Deo, P. and Ruskin, H. J., Comparison of Homogeneous and Heterogeneous Motorised Traffic at Signalised and Two-way Stop control Single lane Intersection, International Conference on Computational Science and Its Applications - ICCSA, Glasgow, UK, May 8-11, LNCS 3980, (2006), 622-632.

Some Applications and Prospects of Cellular Automata in Traffic Problems

Boris Goldengorin[1], Alexander Makarenko[2], and Natalia Smelyanec[2]

[1] University of Groningen, Faculty of Economics, P.O. Box 800 9700AV,
Groningen, The Netherland
b.goldengorin@rug.nl
[2] Institute for Applied System Analysis at
National Technical University of Ukraine (KPI),
37 Pobedy Avenue, Kiev, 03056, Ukraine,
makalex@i.com.ua, smelyana@bk.ru

Abstract. In this paper we deal with mathematical modeling of participants' movement based on cellular automata (CA). We describe some improvements of CA models of pedestrian motion taking into account the real geometrical constraints induced by a specific restricted space. Also some presumable optimization problems in traffic modeling based on CA are discussed. Besides some general problems of cellular modeling are discussed which are related to the accounting of mentality of traffic participants.

1 Introduction

Recently Cellular Automata approach (CA) explicitly and sometimes implicitly expands the fields of applications [1, 2, 3]. The CA has been applied to car traffic [4,5] and pedestrian movements [1,2,3] including pedestrian flows [6,7,8] and fire evacuation [9]. There is a gap between real world applications and theoretically known solutions since some essential elements are not incorporated in CA, for example, the real world geographical and geometrical constraints.

Although some optimization traffic problems are studied in the framework of quantitative logistics [10] and network flows [11], sometimes leading to computationally difficult (NP-hard) problems. All above mentioned models do not taking into account the dynamical laws of CA, namely the evolution of models based on CA as well as some mentality properties of traffic participants. An unrealistic assumption is done by imposing that a single car driver could be simulated as a simple cell. Note that an elementary model of the driver itself is a more complex model than the classical cellular automata model. For example, the mechanical movement of human requires very complicated models [12]. Taking into account essential properties of mentality is a fundamental task for many scientific areas such as informatics, psychology, and management science. Hence it will be important to incorporate the mentality properties into CA.

The purpose of this paper is twofold. (i) We have incorporated the real world geometrical requirements into the CA for the pedestrian movement problem including

S. El Yacoubi, B. Chopard, and S. Bandini (Eds.): ACRI 2006, LNCS 4173, pp. 532–537, 2006.

some optimization versions for crowd flows and have simulated them for understanding the fire evacuation in restricted areas like buildings, stadiums, supermarkets, concert halls, etc.; (ii) we have transferred a frame of models with the associative memory into CA and suggest to incorporate the Hopfield neural network as an internal structure of cells representing some mentality properties of participants in traffic.

2 Model Based on Cellular Automata

We assume that each pedestrian in a group of pedestrians tries to move in the predefined direction which is the same for all participants [9, 13, 14]. If it is impossible to move in that direction, for example there is an obstacle represented by either another tight concentration of pedestrians or a wall, the pedestrian tries to change the moving direction by choosing a direction with a smallest concentration of obstacles along the chosen direction. The field of a cellular automaton is represented by a homogeneous lattice and the state of each cell is coded by either 1 (occupied by either an obstacle or pedestrian) or 0 (not occupied by an obstacle or pedestrian). It is clear that the state of a cell occupied by a wall cannot be changed in contrast to a cell occupied by another pedestrian. At each step we define all single available pedestrian movements within the fixed neighbourhood. In case of the Neumann's neighbourhood we compute the probabilities of participant's movement into one of four neighbouring cells as follows. We set this probability to zero if a neighbouring cell is occupied by a wall, and assign non-zero probabilities to cells of all other directions. By increasing the probability in a chosen direction we model an intention of each participant and the crowd to move in that direction simultaneously decreasing the probabilities in all remaining directions such that the sum of all involved probabilities will be unchanged. By combining the weights of probabilities along a chosen direction for the fixed number of successive cells (predicts a movement depending on states of r cells) we are able to model some predefined super-positions of different types of neighbourhoods. For example, a sequence of Neumann's neighbourhoods can be embedded (combined) in (with) a sequence of Moore's neighbourhoods. The described above rules predefine the dynamic properties of our model such that all participants are able to move with different speeds taking into account both types of possible obstacles.

3 Some Simulation Results of Crowd Movement

By means of developed software it is possible to solve a wide class of problems. Many of them concern pedestrian movements. Here we pose a brief description of such examples.

One of the advantages of applied software is the possibilityy to consider the real geometry of the movement space: buildings, street networks, transportation infrastructure etc. The plans or maps of geometry of the space region may be prepared separately in different computer files with the help of usual tools for design and visualization (see MATCAD, GIS, and MatLab etc.). The geometry can be presented by a simple variant or more complex one. Also different conditions for movements may be preconditioned. For example, the pedestrians may move into one or two directions.

The first simulated example was the problem on width of pass, which is narrowed at obviously set characteristics of a stream of pedestrians. We have simulated the calculations of the width of pass, beginning from which the movement of pedestrians will be comfortable. The results are as follows. At narrower pass the pedestrian stream is unstable and non-uniform on different zones of movement (before pass and after it); sometimes before pass the condensations are observed which do not dissipate for a long time; that testifies an occurrence of a jam on the way of movements.

Other problems consist the finding of optimal (that is such, that does not lead to a jam at probably big density of a people flow) configuration and arrangement of obstacles in the pass (one, or several identical objects, which block itself half of pass area). We shall make an optimal choice with three existing variants, namely with 1, 2, or 3 obstacles. The results are as follows. The best data it is received at the quantity of gaps n_g =2. The worst results are obtained at a lot of obstacles, which testifies that it is the worst variant. The jams arise before obstacle from time to time. Results can be compared also, being looked on the graph.

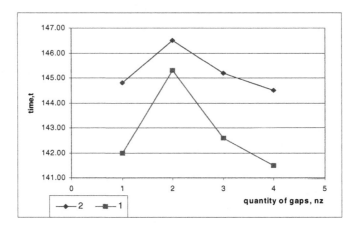

Fig. 1. Dependence of average achievement time for two pedestrian streams from number of gaps in pass

In third example we describe the problem of evacuation of the staff from office the plan of which is depicted in Fig.2. The ways of evacuation are pre-determined. The plan is represented as a suitable for simulation (black cells are walls and other obstacles - an accessories, computers, etc.). 30% of the office space is occupied by people. Iterations of evacuation are presented in Fig.2. The full output of all staff has required less than 300 iterations. Basic numerical characteristics in this case are: (1) average time of reaching an output by pedestrians; (2) general evacuation time.

The obtained results may be useful for specific applications (created software will be useful for simulation of traffics, evacuations from buildings, ships, fire emergency, antiterrorist actions, holidays planning etc.). The next natural step is an attempt to optimize the simulated processes. Some combinatorial optimization models and methods could be useful for such problems.

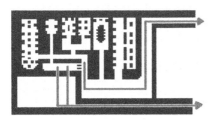 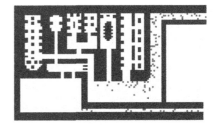

Fig. 2. Application of the approach in modeling of evacuation. Results of simulation. We show the plan of the office, the ways of evacuation and iteration 10 and 150 (left and right).

4   The Problems of Mentality Accounting in Trafficking

In Sections 2 and 3 we have presented results restricted by the classical approach of CA without taking into account the mentality properties for pedestrian movements. This problem is also new for other approaches: multi-agent systems, master equation, non-linear differential equations.

The accounting of mentality of the participants of social processes (including trafficking) is one of the main tendencies in developing more adequate models. There are many presumable ways of doing such accounting – from the attempts to model the human consciousness and decision – making in artificial intelligence to the simplest statistical roles. Earlier in the frame of the models with associative memory we have found a particular way and new prospects in accounting and interpretation of mentality in the models of large socio–economical systems [15]. As the first step of mentality accounting we suggest to incorporate the Hopfield neural network model as the internal structure of cells (elements). Such representation is useful for the stock market dynamics. A part of approach could be incorporated into the CA traffic models.

Of course many aspects related to the mentality accounting should be represented in the complicated models of the traffic: monitoring and recognition of traffic situation; decision – making process on movement direction, velocity and goals; possibilities of movement implementation etc. In principle in the context of CA modelling it should follow to the complication of cell states description, introducing non - homogeneous rules for cell state changes and some portion of non-locality in the models.

One of the most interesting properties in social systems is the anticipation property. The anticipation property is the property that the individual makes a decision accounting the prediction of future state of the system [15, 16]. Concerning the specific case of the traffic problems we stressed that the anticipatory property is intrinsic for traffic. At the local level each participant of the traffic process tries to anticipate the future state of traffic in local neighbourhood when he makes the decision on movement. Also the macro neighbourhood of traffic participants might be accounted for the common radio information). The adequate accounting of anticipatory property in the CA methodologies is a difficult problem because it requires also complication of CA models by introducing the internal states of CA cells and special internal dynamical laws for mental parameters. Right now we are able to propose some consequences for traffic considerations. One of the consequences is that the accounting of anticipatory property might be done for mathematical models of differences equations type.

For example, the CA model is represented as the following discrete time equation

$$s_i(t+1) = G_i(\{s_j(t)\}|j \in N(i), R), i = 1, 2, ..., M \tag{1}$$

where R – the set of parameters for cell's rules, N(i) - the set of neighbours of i –th cell in CA, $s_j(t)$ sets of states in neighbours of i – th cell, M – the number of cells in CA. The anticipation may have different types depending on the prediction horizon in time and the scales of mentality accounting. But in the simplest case the anticipating on one time step in the neighbourhood of cell follows to counterpart of (1):

$$s_i(t+1) = G_i(\{s_j(t)\}, \{s_j(t+1)\}|j \in N(i), R), i = 1, 2, ..., M \tag{2}$$

The difference between (1) and (2) is that in the equations (2) the possible states at the next time step (the term $s_j(t+1)$) is taken into considerations. That is the rules of such CA should depend on the next states in the neighbourhood of i – th cell.

The main peculiarities of the equation is that such equations may have multivalued solutions for some range of parameters. For example we have found the multivaluedness in solutions for anticipating neural networks. In our case the multivaluedness origins by branching the solutions of models at each time step. The multivalued solutions correspond to possibilities of different scenarios in the evolution of systems with anticipation. In traffic problems it may correspond on many possible routes of traffic movements at each time moment. Remark that the 'anticipative' modification may be introduced just in game 'Life'. The suggested generalizations are open investigations of the anticipatory cellular automata (ACA).

Investigation of ACA is the matter of future. But here we would like to remark some general new possibilities. A new class of research problems is the investigation of self–organization processes in the anticipating media, in particular in discrete chains, lattices, networks constructed from anticipating elements. In such a case the main problems are self–organization, emergent of structures including dissipative, bifurcations, synchronization and chaotic behaviour.

The extension of the results described in the present paper to new traffic models would open new possibilities for exploring behaviour of traffic participants. As it is follows from our investigations anticipation and multivaluedness also may serve as the source of uncertainty in the systems. Thus potential new tools for managing such uncertainty will follow from mathematical modelling of anticipatory traffic systems.

5   Conclusions

In this paper we have presented some ways and tools for improvement the CA based models and their software. The presented results are interesting for practical applications. Described models may be used as the polygon for testing new developments and ideas in the field of cellular automata investigations. A further research tasks include some of the discussed optimization problems. Also some absolutely new possibilities for CA properties are proposed which are connected with the accounting of anticipatory properties of traffic participants. The main new possibility is the multivaluedness of solutions of CA models with anticipation.

References

1. Toffoli T., Margolis N.: Cellular automata computation. Mir, Moscow (1991)
2. Gilbert N., Troitzsch K.: Simulation for the social scientist. Open University press, Surrey, UK (1999)
3. Wolfram S.: New kind of science. Wolfram Media Inc., USA (2002)
4. Benjamin S. C., Johnson N. F. Hui P. M.: Cellular automata models of traffic flow along a highway containing a junction. J. Phys. A: Math Gen **29** (1996) 3119-3127
5. Nagel K., Schreckenberg M.: A cellular automation model for freeway traffic. Journal of Physics I France **2** (1992) 2221- 2229
6. Schreckenberg M., Sharma S.D. (eds.): Pedestrian and evacuation dynamics. Springer–Verlag, Berlin (2001) 173-181
7. Helbing D., Molnar P., Schweitzer F.: Computer simulations of pedestrian dynamics and trail formation. Evolution of Natural Structures, Sonderforschungsbereich 230, Stuttgart (1998) 229-234
8. Thompson P.A., Marchant E.W.: A computer model for the evacuation of large building populations. Fire Safety Journal **24** (1995) 131 -148
9. Stepantsov M.E.: Dynamic model of a group of people based on lattice gas with non-local interactions. Applied nonlinear dynamics (Izvestiya VUZOV, Saratov) **5** (1999) 44-47
10. Wang F.Y. et al.: A Complex Systems Approach for Studying Integrated Development of Transportation Logistics, and Ecosystems. J. Complex Systems and Complexity Science 2. **1** (2004) 60–69
11. Ahuja R.K., Magnanti T.L., Orlin J.B.: Network Flows: Theory, Algorithms, and Applications. Prentice Hall (1993)
12. Kreighbaum E., Barthels K.M.: A Qualitative Approach for Studying Human Movement, Third Edition, Biomechanics. Macmillan, New York (1990)
13. Klupfel H.: A Cellular Automaton Model for Crowd Movement and Egress Simulation. PhD Thesis, Gerhard-Mercator-Universitat, Duisburg-Essen (2003)
14. Kirchner A., Schadschneider A.: Simulation of evacuation processes using a bionics-inspired cellular automaton model for pedestrian dynamics. Physica A **312** (2002) 260-276
15. Makarenko A.: Anticipating in modeling of large social systems - neuronets with internal structure and multivaluedness. International .Journal of Computing Anticipatory Systems **13** (2002) 77 - 92
16. Rosen R.: Anticipatory Systems. Pergamon Press, London (1985)

Stochastic Cellular-Automaton Model for Traffic Flow

Masahiro Kanai[1], Katsuhiro Nishinari[2], and Tetsuji Tokihiro[1]

[1] Graduate School of Mathematical Sciences, The University of Tokyo, 3-8-1
Komaba, Tokyo 153-8914, Japan
{kanai, toki}@ms.u-tokyo.ac.jp
[2] Department of Aeronautics and Astronautics, Faculty of Engineering,
The University of Tokyo, 7-3-1 Hongo, Tokyo 113-8656, Japan
tknishi@mail.ecc.u-tokyo.ac.jp

Abstract. In recent studies on traffic flow, cellular automata (CA) have
been efficiently applied for simulating the motion of vehicles. Since each
vehicle has an exclusion volume and moves by itself not being ruled by the
Newton's laws of motion, CA is quite suitable for modelling traffic flow.
In the present paper, we propose a stochastic CA model for traffic flow
and show the availability of CA modelling for the complex phenomena
that occur in real traffic flow.

1   Introduction

Traffic flow has been attracting much attention from physicists, engineers and
mathematicians as a complex, nonequilibrium and self-driven many-particle system. Studies of traffic flow expands in a wide variety of fields and now includes
general transport phenomena [1,2,3]. In real traffic, each vehicle is not ruled by
the Newton's laws of motion because it is equipped with an engine and determines its motion by itself, i.e., *self-driven.* Therefore, one needs to have another
look at this subject taking a distance from traditional approaches in physics. In
the present work, we exclusively focus on a one-lane traffic, which is essential in
traffic dynamics, and accordingly, only one-dimensional *cellular automata* (CA)
are considered.

A number of different approaches to traffic flow have been made from various
viewpoints such as microscopic and macroscopic, continuous and discrete, deterministic and stochastic [1,2,3]. According to these approaches, a number of models have been introduced thus far. We shall pick up three representative examples
and review a theory that unifies the three models via the ultra-discretization
method and the discrete Euler-Lagrange transformation. The Burgers equation,
expressed as

$$\rho_t = 2\rho\rho_x + \rho_{xx}, \tag{1}$$

is known as an elementary model of traffic flow. Here, we denote the density
of vehicles on a road by ρ and use subscript notation for partial derivatives as
usual. It formulates the evolution of density distribution of vehicles, i.e., it is a

S. El Yacoubi, B. Chopard, and S. Bandini (Eds.): ACRI 2006, LNCS 4173, pp. 538–547, 2006.

macroscopic, continuous model. Recent studies show that the Burgers equation is directly connected with other basic models of traffic flow [4]. The Burgers equation is, at first, transformed into a CA model (a microscopic discrete one) through *ultra-discretization* [5]. It provides a method to reveal another profile of models, and enables us to return from macroscopic to microscopic. From the Burgers equation, we thereby obtain the so-called *Burgers cellular automata* (BCA), which is an extension of the Rule-184 CA [4]. Rule-184 CA has a very simple update rule, i.e., if the adjacent site is not occupied, the vehicle move ahead with a given probability, but otherwise it does not. Each site in Rule-184 CA contains one vehicle at most, and the rule is generally called *the hard-core exclusion rule*. Meanwhile, each site in BCA allows multiple occupations.

Moreover, BCA can be transformed into another basic model, i.e., the *Optimal Velocity (OV) model*, through the *discrete Euler-Lagrange (E-L) transformation*. The discrete E-L transformation is made on fully discrete variables, and then field variables change to particle variables [4]. The OV model is a continuous, microscopic model, and is expressed as

$$\frac{d^2 x_i}{dt^2} = a\left[V(x_{i+1} - x_i) - \frac{dx_i}{dt}\right], \tag{2}$$

where $x_i = x_i(t)$ denotes the position of the i-th vehicle at time t and the function V is called the *Optimal Velocity (OV) function* [6,7]. The OV function gives the optimal velocity of a vehicle in terms of the headway $x_{i+1} - x_i$, where the i-th vehicle follows the $(i+1)$-th in the same lane, and then the OV function, in general, is monotonically increasing. Parameter a presents the sensitivity of the driver to accelerate or decelarate. In particular, the OV model obtained from BCA has OV function which is a step function. This suggests that the OV model with a step function is essential as well as elementary.

Cellular automaton models are efficient and flexible compared to those described by differential equations, and they have been used to model complex traffic systems such as ramps and crossings [2]. The Nagel-Schreckenberg (N-S) model, a well-known CA model, successfully reproduces typical properties of real traffic [8]. What makes it sophisticated is a *random braking rule*, which is a plausible mechanism to simulate the motion of vehicles in a single lane. Nevertheless, the N-S model does not succeed in reproducing the so-called *metastable state*, i.e., an unstable state which breaks down to the lower-flux stable state under some perturbations.

Extensive study of traffic flow has revealed that the metastable property, appearing in the medium density region, is universal in real traffic flows, and accordingly that property is essential in modelling [9]. Moreover, it is quite distinct among non-equilibrium statistical systems [1]. In other words, this metastable property plays a critical role in characterizing traffic flow from the viewpoint of dynamics, and it is hence required for traffic models to exhibit this property. Thus far, one needs the *slow-start rule* to reproduce a metastable state in existing CA models [9,10,11,12]. It introduces a delay for vehicles to respond to the changing traffic situation, i.e., if a vehicle stops due to the hard-core exclusion rule, the slow-start rule forces it to stop again at the next time step. In contrast, due to the second-order derivative, the OV model naturally includes a similar mechanism to the slow-start rule.

In the next section, we introduce a stochastic CA model following [14,15], and then we show that the model inherits the sophisticated features from the OV model.

2   The Stochastic Optimal Velocity Model

First of all, we explain the general framework of our stochastic CA model for one-lane traffic. The roadway, being divided into cells, is regarded as a one-dimensional array of L sites, and each site contains one vehicle at most. Let M_i^t be a stochastic variable which denotes the number of sites through which the i-th vehicle moves at time t, and $w_i^t(m)$ be the probability that $\mathsf{M}_i^t = m$ ($m = 0, 1, 2, \ldots$). Then, we assume a principle of motion that the probability $w_i^{t+1}(m)$ depends on the probability distribution $w_i^t(0), w_i^t(1), \ldots$, and the positions of vehicles $x_1^t, x_2^t, \ldots, x_N^t$ at the previous time. The updating procedure is as follows:

- Calculate the next intention w_i^{t+1} ($i = 1, 2, \ldots, N$) from the present, intention $w_i^t(0), w_i^t(1), \ldots$ and positions $x_1^t, x_2^t, \ldots, x_N^t$;

$$w_i^{t+1}(m) = f(w_i^t(0), w_i^t(1), \ldots; x_1^t, \ldots, x_N^t; m) \tag{3}$$

- Determine the number of sites M_i^{t+1} through which a vehicle moves (i.e. the velocity) probabilistically according to the intention w_i^{t+1}.
- The new position of each vehicle is

$$x_i^{t+1} = x_i^t + \min(\Delta x_i^t, \mathsf{M}_i^{t+1}) \quad (\forall i), \tag{4}$$

where $\Delta x_i^t = x_{i+1}^t - x_i^t - 1$ denotes the headway. (Headway is defined to be the clear space in front of the vehicle, and thus in a CA model we need to subtract 1 to take account of the site occupied by the vehicle itself.)

The hard-core exclusion rule is incorporated through the second term of the right hand side of (4).

We call the probability distribution w_i^t *the intention* because it is an intrinsic variable of the vehicle. It brings uncertainty of operation into the traffic model and has no physical counterpart. In what follows, we assume $w_i^t(m) \equiv 0$ for $m \geq 2$. It is notable that $\sum_{m=0}^{\infty} w_i^t(m) = 1$ by definition and the expectation value $\langle \mathsf{M}_i^t \rangle = \sum_{m=0}^{\infty} m w_i^t(m)$, and hence, setting $v_i^t = w_i^t(1)$, we have $w_i^t(0) = 1 - v_i^t$ and $\langle \mathsf{M}_i^t \rangle = v_i^t$. From (3) we have

$$\begin{cases} w_i^{t+1}(1) = v_i^{t+1} = f(v_i^t; x_1^t, x_2^t, \ldots; 1) \\ w_i^{t+1}(0) = 1 - v_i^{t+1}, \end{cases} \tag{5}$$

and we therefore express the intention by v_i^t in stead of w_i^t. As long as vehicles move separately (i.e. $\Delta x_i^t \gg 0$), the positions are updated according to the simple form

$$x_i^{t+1} = \begin{cases} x_i^t + 1 & \text{with probability } v_i^{t+1} \\ x_i^t & \text{with probability } 1 - v_i^{t+1}, \end{cases} \tag{6}$$

and consequently we have

$$\langle x_i^{t+1} \rangle = \langle x_i^t \rangle + v_i^{t+1} \tag{7}$$

in the sense of expectation value. This equation expresses the fact that the intention v_i^{t+1} can be regarded as the average velocity at time t.

Let us take an evolution equation

$$v_i^{t+1} = (1-a)v_i^t + aV(\Delta x_i^t), \tag{8}$$

in (3), where a $(0 \leq a \leq 1)$ is a parameter and the function V takes the value in $[0,1]$ so that v_i^t should be within $[0,1]$. Equation (8) consists of two terms, i.e., a term turning over the intention v_i^t into the next, and an effect of the situation (the headway Δx_i^t). The intrinsic parameter a indicates the sensitivity of vehicles to the traffic situation, and the larger a is, the less time a vehicle takes to change its intention.

A discrete version of the OV model is expressed as

$$x_i(t + \Delta t) - x_i(t) = v_i(t)\Delta t, \tag{9}$$
$$v_i(t + \Delta t) - v_i(t) = a\Big[V(\Delta x_i(t)) - v_i(t)\Big]\Delta t, \tag{10}$$

where $\Delta x_i(t) = x_{i+1}(t) - x_i(t)$, and Δt is a time interval. Due to the formal correspondence between (8) and (10), we call a stochastic CA model defined by (8) the *Stochastic Optimal Velocity (SOV) model*, hereafter.

3   The SOV Model with a Step OV Function

In this section, we take a step function

$$V(x) = \begin{cases} 0 & (0 \leq x < d) \\ 1 & (x \geq d) \end{cases} \tag{11}$$

as the OV function. Here, d is the smallest safe distance to move forward. Then, we impose a periodic boundary condition and adopt the parallel updating as usual. We denote the density of vehicles to sites by $\rho = N/L$ (L is the number of sites, and N the number of vehicles), which is a macroscopic variable, and a conserved quantity of motion under the periodic boundary condition, no entrances or exits. Another macroscopic variable flux, $Q = \rho v$, is defined using the average velocity in a steady state;

$$v := \frac{1}{N}\sum_{i=1}^{N}(x_i^T - x_i^{T-1}), \tag{12}$$

where time T should be taken large enough for the system to reach a steady state.

A *fundamental diagram*, a plot of the flux versus the density, illustrates how traffic conditions depend on density. It represents the characteristics of a traffic

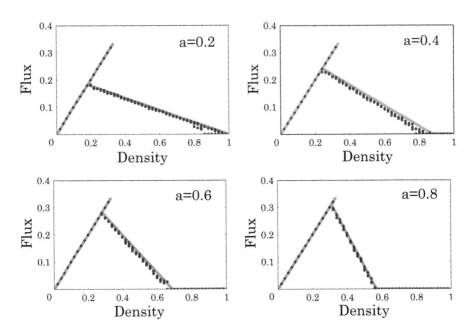

Fig. 1. The fundamental diagram of the SOV model with the step OV function (11) plotted at each value of sensitivity parameter a. The smallest safe distance (i.e. the discontinuous point of the OV function) is $d = 2$, the initial value of the intention is $v_i^0 = 1$. Theoretical curve (gray) illustrated from (14) and (16) has a complete agreement with simulated data (dots). The system size is $L = 1000$.

model, and hence traffic models are required to reproduce a fundamental diagram observed in real traffic flow.

Figure 1 shows the fundamental diagram of the SOV model with the step OV function (11). We find that the diagram consists of two lines corresponding respectively to *free-flow* phase (positive slope) and *jam* phase (negative slope). It is remarkable that there is a region of density where two states (a free-flow state and a jam state) coexist. The second-order difference allows the model to show this property, so-called *hysteresis*. The free-flow line in the fundamental diagram has a slope of 1, i.e., all the vehicles are moving deterministically (i.e. $v_i^t = 1$) without jamming. This kind of state can be implemented in the uniform state; equal spacing of vehicles and the initial velocity $v_i^0 = 1$ for all i. As can be seen from (8), the intention changes

$$\begin{cases} v_i^t = 1 - (1 - v_i^0)(1 - a)^t & (\Delta x_i^t \geq d), \\ v_i^t = v_i^0 (1 - a)^t & (\Delta x_i^t < d), \end{cases} \tag{13}$$

and consequently the uniform states constitute a line segment

$$Q = \rho \qquad (0 \leq \rho \leq \rho_h) \tag{14}$$

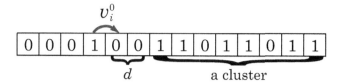

Fig. 2. Schematic picture of the case that a free vehicle reduces its intention $v_i^0 = 1$ approaching a cluster, and finally comes to be in the cluster. The vehicle stops with a headway to the cluster ahead, which is estimated from the OV function.

in the fundamental diagram. The maximum-flux density ρ_h, at which the vehicles take the minimum value d of equal spacing, is given as follows:

$$\rho_h = \frac{1}{1+d}. \tag{15}$$

In Figure 1, we see that the formula (15) is in the complete agreement with the simulated results in the case of $d = 2$.

The flux of traffic flow increases in proportion to the density of vehicles while the density is small. However, as the density becomes bigger, close-range interaction between vehicles makes a wide, strong correlation over them, and consequently gives rise to a jam. Then, there appears a turning point at which the flux declines for the first time. Around that point (the so-called *critical point*), the states of traffic flow bifurcates into a stable branch and a metastable branch, and moreover phase transition occurs between them. In order to estimate the critical point, we consider that the jam line should be expressed by

$$Q = \frac{\rho_c}{\rho_{max} - \rho_c}(\rho_{max} - \rho), \tag{16}$$

where ρ_{max} and ρ_c denote respectively the density at which flux vanishes and that of the critical point. From (16) and $Q = \rho v$, we have

$$\frac{1-\rho}{\rho} = \frac{1-\rho_{max}}{\rho_{max}}(1-v) + \frac{1-\rho_c}{\rho_c}v. \tag{17}$$

Equation (17) suggests that the spatial pattern divides into two kinds, i.e., clustering ($v = 0$) and free flow ($v = 1$). Then, since the vehicles move at velocity 1 or 0 in the present model, v just indicates the ratio of those in free flow, and moreover total average headway $\langle \Delta x \rangle = (1-\rho)/\rho$ is calculated from the average headway of the clustered vehicles $\langle \Delta x_J \rangle = (1-\rho_{max})/\rho_{max}$ and that of the vehicles in free flow $\langle \Delta x_F \rangle = (1-\rho_c)/\rho_c$. These two values reflect a macroscopic property of the SOV model with the OV function (11), but we should estimate them from a microscopic viewpoint. In what follows, we consider the case of $d = 2$, following [16].

First, we think of ρ_{max} as the limit density at which all free-flow domains of the roadway close up and no vehicle can move then. Let us consider the situation illustrated in Figure 2 that a free vehicle with its intention 1 is going into a

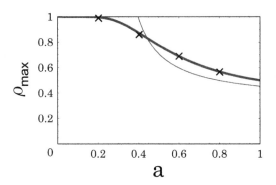

Fig. 3. The theoretical curve of the maximum density ρ_{max} (thick line) at which the flux vanishes with the corresponding numerical results (cross). They have perfect agreement. We also show a corresponding curve of the original OV model (thin line) by use of (20).

cluster. Then, taking the time $t = 0$ when the headway firstly gets equal to d, the intention decreases as $v_i^t = (1 - a)^t$. Since it gives the probability of the vehicle moving at t, the average headway, while in cluster, amounts to

$$\langle \Delta x_J \rangle = \prod_{t=1}^{\infty}(1 - v_i^t) = \left[\frac{\vartheta_4(0, 1 - a)^4 \vartheta_2(0, 1 - a)\vartheta_3(0, 1 - a)}{2(1 - a)^{1/4}}\right]^{1/6}, \tag{18}$$

where $\vartheta_k(u, q)$ $(k = 1, 2, 3, 4)$ are the elliptic theta functions. Consequently, we obtain the density of clustering vehicles

$$\rho_{max} = \frac{1}{1 \mid \langle \Delta x_J \rangle}, \tag{19}$$

as a function of the sensitivity parameter a. Note that $0 \leq \langle \Delta x_J \rangle \leq 1$ since $d = 2$, and $\langle \Delta x_J \rangle$ is equivalent to the probability of Δx_i^t taking the value of 1.

Figure 3 shows the graph of ρ_{max}, and it has a perfect agreement with the numerical results read off from Figure 1. In [16], they give the explicit formula of Δx_J, the uniform headway with which vehicles stop in a jam. It reads

$$\Delta x_J = d - \frac{v_{max}\sigma}{2a}, \tag{20}$$

where $d = 2$ and $v_{max} = 1$ in the present case, and $\sigma \simeq 1.59$. By use of (20), we illustrate the corresponding graph in Fig. 3 as well. Since the original OV model does not incorporate a hard-core exclusion rule, the sensitivity parameter a is limited in the scope of $\Delta x_J \geq 0$ so as to avoid any collision. In contrast, the maximum density of the SOV model is retained, due to that rule, not to diverge within $0 \leq a \leq 1$.

Next, in order to estimate $\langle \Delta x_F \rangle$ we consider that two vehicles in the front of a cluster are getting out of it as illustrated in Figure 4. Then, as described above, there occur two cases since $d = 2$; $\Delta x_i^0 = 1$ with probability $\langle \Delta x_J \rangle$ and $\Delta x_i^0 = 0$

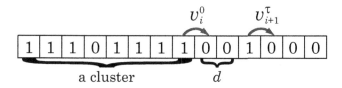

Fig. 4. Schematic picture of the situation that two adjacent vehicles in the front of a cluster recover their intention and get out of the cluster. We estimate the headway with which the two vehicles finally come to move free.

with probability $1 - \langle \Delta x_J \rangle$, where we again take the time $t = 0$ when Δx_i^t becomes d. Corresponding to $\Delta x_i^0 = 0$ and 1, we describe $\langle \Delta x_F \rangle$ respectively as $\langle \Delta x_F \rangle_0$ and $\langle \Delta x_F \rangle_1$, and accordingly our main result is expressed as follows:

$$\rho_c = \frac{1}{1 + \langle \Delta x_F \rangle}, \tag{21}$$

where

$$\langle \Delta x_F \rangle = \langle \Delta x_F \rangle_1 \langle \Delta x_J \rangle + \langle \Delta x_F \rangle_0 (1 - \langle \Delta x_J \rangle). \tag{22}$$

Let τ denote the interval of time for the front vehicle to get out of the cluster. Provided that clusters are large enough to take approximately $v_i^0 = 0$ and that the second vehicle leaving the cluster maintains a headway of at least d, we conclude that $v_i^0 = 0$, $v_{i+1}^0(\tau) = 1 - (1 - a)^\tau$, $v_i^t = 1 - (1 - a)^t$, and $v_{i+1}^t(\tau) = 1 - (1 - a)^{\tau + t}$ from (13). Note that τ is a stochastic variable, and hence v_{i+1}^0 and v_{i+1}^t are dependent on τ.

In the case of $\Delta x_i^0 = 1$: Since v_i^t indicates the probability of moving ahead at one site, the probability of $\tau = t$ amounts to

$$P_1(\tau = t) = v_i^t \prod_{s=1}^{t-1} (1 - v_i^s) \tag{23}$$

and moreover, the distance which the two make in free flow amounts to

$$\sum_{t=1}^{\infty} \left[v_{i+1}^t(\tau) - v_i^t \right] = \frac{1 - a}{a} v_{i+1}^0(\tau). \tag{24}$$

Consequently, we have $\langle \Delta x_F \rangle_1$ in a convenient form for computation:

$$\langle \Delta x_F \rangle_1 = d + \sum_{\tau=1}^{\infty} \frac{1 - a}{a} v_{i+1}^0(\tau) P_1(\tau) = 1 + \frac{\vartheta_2(0, \sqrt{1 - a})}{2(1 - a)^{1/8}}. \tag{25}$$

In the case of $\Delta x_i^0 = 0$: The probability of $\tau = t$ amounts to

$$P_0(\tau = t) = v_i^t \sum_{s=1}^{t-1} \left[v_i^s \prod_{r=1, \neq s}^{t-1} (1 - v_i^r) \right] \tag{26}$$

Consequently, from (13) we have

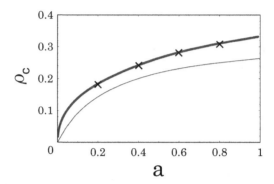

Fig. 5. The theoretical curve of the critical density ρ_c (thick line) at which the flux bifurcates into a metastable branch and a stable jam branch (i.e. hysteresis), with the corresponding numerical results (cross). They also have a perfect agreement. The corresponding curve (thin line) of the original OV model is illustrated by use of (28).

$$\langle \Delta x_F \rangle_0 = d + \sum_{\tau=1}^{\infty} \left[\frac{1-a}{a} v_{i+1}^0(\tau) P_0(\tau) \right], \qquad (27)$$

and finally $\langle \Delta x_F \rangle$ is formulated as a function of the sensitivity parameter a from (18), (22), (25) and (27).

The formula of Δx_F in the corresponding case of the OV model, given in [16], reads

$$\Delta x_F = d + \frac{v_{\max}\sigma}{2a}, \qquad (28)$$

where $d = 2$, $v_{\max} = 1$, and $\sigma = 1.59$. Figure 5 shows the critical density ρ_c versus the sensitivity parameter a. It also has a perfect agreement with the numerical results read out from Fig. 1. By use of (28), we illustrate the corresponding graph in Fig. 5 as well. We find that the two theoretical curves present a qualitative agreement, while there are some quantitative differences due to the choice of unit car size.

4   Conclusion

The Stochastic Optimal Velocity model was introduced in the preceding paper [14] as a stochastic cellular automaton model extending two exactly solvable models (the Asymmetric Simple Exclusion Process and the Zero Range Process). Moreover, since it has the same formulation as the Optimal Velocity model, the SOV model can be regarded as a stochastic extension of the OV model.

In the present paper, we focus on the stochastic effects on the stability of the spatial-temporal patterns. For that purpose, we take the Optimal Velocity function to be a step function, and analytically estimate the critical point where the stability of solutions changes. In this model, the sensitivity parameter presents the strength of stochasticity. Then, as the stochasticity increases, there appears a density region where two different states coexist. A detailed investigation reveals that the high-flux state consists of the uniform configuration and the low-flux states does of the other configurations. We show that the stochasticity introduced into CA breaks some steady patterns and induces phase transitions.

References

1. Helbing, D.: Traffic and related self-driven many-particle systems. Rev. Mod. Phys. **73** (2001) 1067-1141
2. Chowdhury, D., Santen, L., Schadschneider, A.: Statistical physics of vehicular traffic and some related systems. Phys. Rep. **329** (2000) 199-329
3. Nagatani, T.: The physics of traffic jams. Rep. Prog. Phys. **65** (2002) 1331-1386
4. Matsukidaira, J., Nishinari, K.: Euler-Lagrange correspondence of cellular automata for traffic-flow models. Phys. Rev. Lett. **90** (2003) 088701-1 - 088701-4
5. Tokihiro, T., Takahashi, D., Matsukidaira, J., Satsuma, J.: From Soliton Equations to Integrable Cellular Automata through a Limiting Procedure. Phys. Rev. Lett. **76** (1996) 3247-3250
6. Bando, M., Hasebe, K., Nakayama, A., Shibata, A., Sugiyama, Y.: Dynamical model of traffic congestion and numerical simulation. Phys. Rev. E **51** (1995) 1035-1042
7. Bando, M., Hasebe, K., Nakanishi, K., Nakayama, A., Shibata, A., Sugiyama, Y.: Phenomenological Study of Dynamical Model of Traffic Flow. J. Phys. I France **5** (1995) 1389-1399
8. Nagel, K., Schreckenberg, M.: A cellular automaton model for freeway traffic. J. Phys. I France **2** (1992) 2221-2229
9. Nishinari, K., Fukui, M., Schadschneider, A.: A stochastic cellular automaton model for traffic flow with multiple metastable states. J. Phys. A **37** (2004) 3101-3110
10. Takayasu, M., Takayasu, H.: 1/f noise in a traffic model. Fractals **1** (1993) 860-866
11. Schadschneider, A., Schreckenberg, M.: Traffic flow models with 'slow-to-start' rules. Ann. Physik **6** (1997) 541-551
12. Nishinari, K.: A Lagrange representation of cellular automaton traffic-flow models. J. Phys. A **34** (2001) 10727-10736
13. Newell, G. F.: Nonlinear effects in the dynamics of car flowing. Oper. Res. **9** (1961) 209-229
14. Kanai, M., Nishinari, K., Tokihiro, T.: Stochastic optimal velocity model and its long-lived metastability. Phys. Rev. E **72** (2005) 035102(R)
15. Kanai, M., Nishinari, K., Tokihiro, T.: Analytical study on the criticality of the stochastic optimal velocity model. Phys. Rev. E **39** (2006) 2921-2933
16. Sugiyama, Y., Yamada, H.: Simple and exactly solvable model for queue dynamics. Phys. Rev. E **55** (1997) 7749-7752
17. Nakanishi, K., Itoh, K., Igarashi, Y., Bando, M.: Solvable optimal velocity models and asymptotic trajectory. Phys. Rev. E **55** (1997) 6519-6532

Coupled Random Boolean Network Forming an Artificial Tissue

M. Villani[1], R. Serra[1], P. Ingrami[1], and S.A. Kauffman[2]

[1] DSSC, University of Modena and Reggio Emilia,
via Allegri 9, I-42100 Reggio Emilia
villani.marco@unimore.it, serra.roberto@unimore.it,
pingrami@gmail.com
[2] Institute for Biocomplexity and Informatics, University of Calgary 2500
University Drive NW, Calgary AB T2N 1N4, Canada
skauffman@ucalgary.ca

Abstract. Random boolean networks (shortly, RBN) have proven useful in describing complex phenomena occurring at the unicellular level. It is therefore interesting to investigate how their dynamical behavior is affected by cell-cell interactions, which mimics those occurring in tissues in multicellular organisms. It has also been suggested that evolution may tend to adjust the parameters of the genetic network so that it operates close to a critical state, which should provide evolutionary advantage ; this hypothesis has received intriguing, although not definitive support from recent findings. It is therefore particularly interesting to consider how the tissue-like organization alters the dynamical behavior of the networks close to a critical state. In this paper we define a model tissue, which is a cellular automaton each of whose cells hosts a full RBN, and we report preliminary studies of the way in which the dynamics is affected.

1 Introduction

A very interesting line of research on the study of biological organization is the "ensemble approach", pioneered several years ago by one of us [1][2] in the study of genetic networks. According to this line the emphasis is placed on the typical properties of networks which are supposed to capture some characteristics of real biological systems, instead of concentrating upon the study of specific cases. While the detailed study of specific organisms and specific genetic circuits is of the utmost importance, it is claimed here that the ensemble approach provides a useful complement to it. The search for typical (often called "universal") behaviors has proven very useful also in the study e.g. of phase transitions and dynamical systems

Random boolean networks (RBN) have been proposed as a model of genetic regulatory networks, precisely with the aim of devising a model which should be manageable enough to draw conclusions about its generic behaviors, which should be compared with experimental data. Many excellent presentations of the model exist [2][3], and we will only very briefly outline it below (section 2).

S. El Yacoubi, B. Chopard, and S. Bandini (Eds.): ACRI 2006, LNCS 4173, pp. 548 – 556, 2006.

In most cases, the RBN model has been used to model a single cell, or a population of single cells, and it has proven able to capture some of their properties, including the response to perturbations in gene knock-out experiments [4][5]. It has also been suggested that evolution may tend to adjust the parameters of the genetic network so that it operates close to a critical state, which should provide evolutionary advantage; this hypothesis has received intriguing, although not definitive support from recent findings [6][7].

On the other hand, multicellular organisms are organized in tissues composed by similar cells which are often close in space, and it is natural to ask whether the multicellular organization affects the dynamics. Does interaction lead to a higher order, or rather the contrary? Kauffman recently suggested that it is likely that the whole tissue operates close to the critical state, and that the single cells might be slightly more ordered than if they were alone. While some work addressing this issue in the context of scale-free RBN has been performed [8], in this paper we investigate on the effects of interactions among neighboring cells using "classical" random boolean networks (precisely defined in section 2).

In particular, we set up a 2D CA model, described in section 3, where each lattice site is occupied by a RBN, and introduce a mechanism whereby neighboring RBN can influence each other.

Section 4 describes the experiments which have been performed with this model, in order to analyze the effects of coupling on the dynamics. Finally, in section 5 we draw some brief conclusions and indications for further work.

2   A Brief Description of RBN

There exist some different realizations of the idea of a random boolean network, which may differ in the network topology, the choice of the set of boolean functions, the updating strategies [2][3][9]. We will described here only the model which we used in our study, which is the same as that originally proposed by Kauffman, and which will be briefly called the "classical" RBN.

Let us consider a network composed of N genes, or nodes, which can take either the value 0 (inactive) or 1 (active). Let $x_i(t) \in \{0,1\}$ be the activation value of node i at time t, and let $X(t) = [x_1(t), x_2(t) \ldots x_N(t)]$ be the vector of activation values of all the genes (for simplicity, it will be assumed that activations are boolean).

Real genes influence each other through their corresponding products and through the interaction of these products with other chemicals, by promoting or inhibiting the activation of target genes. In the corresponding model network these relationships are lumped in directed links (directed from node A to node B, if the product of gene A influences the activation of gene B) and boolean functions (which model the response of each node to the values of its input nodes). In a classical RBN each node has the same number of incoming connections k_{in}, and its k_{in} input nodes are chosen at random with uniform probability among the remaining N-1 nodes. The probability that a particular combination of input activities gives the response "1" is the same for all the nodes and is specified by the value p. Both the topology and the boolean function associated to each gene do not change in time (i.e. we use the so-called quenched model). The network dynamics therefore is discrete and synchronous, so all the nodes update their values at the same time: once the connections and the boolean functions of each node have been specified, X(t) uniquely determines X(t+1).

A careful analysis of some known real biological control circuits has shown that

a) Boolean functions with a low probability of activation (i.e. a relatively high number of outputs which are 0) are more frequent than the others
b) In most cases the functions are limited to those which are canalizing

In this preliminary work we take (a) into account, while the set of boolean functions is built, as usual, by choosing one with probability p and 0 with probability 1-p (therefore these functions are not necessarily canalizing).

The model shows two main dynamical regimes: by observing for example how the average number of attractors and the average cycle length scales with the number of nodes N we can note that these variables could increase their values as a power law (ordered region) or could diverge exponentially (disordered region), depending upon the value of the parameter k_{in} and the bias p (see Figure 1a). Systems near the interface between the two regions (i.e. in the "critical" region) show a particularly interesting behavior, as described in the introduction.

Several observations (summarized in [2][10]) indicate that biological cells, because of this biological constraints, tend to be found in the ordered region not too far from the border between ordered and disordered regimes (the "edge of chaos") thus allowing both control and evolution.

In this work we are interested in understanding what happens when the cells are grouped in a higher order organization like a tissue, asking what is the influence (if any) of this grouping on the ordered/chaotic behavior of cells.

A priori, it could be argued that cells in tissues should be rather more ordered than isolated ones, thus simplifying system-level control, but also the opposite, i.e. that the additional interactions could introduce more constraints, leading to a more frustrated (and disordered) system. These hypotheses need testing, and this can be done in a disciplined way using particular models.

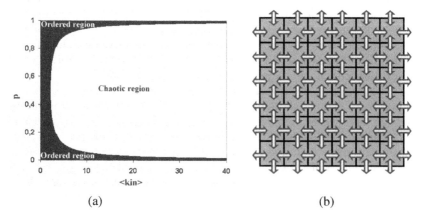

(a)	(b)

Fig. 1. (a) Ordered and disordered regions for a single random boolean network; the border between the two region is given by the formula $(k_{in})^{-1}=2p(1-p)$[3] (b) the mathematical idealization of a tissue utilized in this article: each square cell is a complete random boolean network; a subset of its nodes interacts with the first four neighbors RBNs

3   A Model Tissue

Now we have to define a mathematical analogue of a generic tissue. This requires to define:

(a) a topology of the tissue
(b) the kind of random boolean networks present on each cell of the tissue
(c) the rules of interaction among the cells of the tissue

A simple topology like that of Figure 1b, where square cells interact with their first four neighbors inside a two dimensional world, represents a schematization of the spatial topology of some tissues, and will be used here.

Each tissue is composed by homogeneous cells, and in general all the cells of a given multicellular individual share the same genetic material, therefore in each cell we have to consider a copy of the same random boolean network (same topology of the RBN and same boolean function).

The rules of interaction among cells are very important. It is possible to take into account several possibilities, however the physics of the problem provides useful suggestions. A gene in cell A can influence another gene in cell B by synthesizing a protein which (may trigger a cascade of reactions some of whose products) may cross the cell membrane. Therefore, if a gene is active in A (so that its value is 1) it may affect B, but if it is inactive it has no effect.

Therefore we assume that:

- only a subset of the total number of nodes that define the RBN can be influenced by neighboring cells (not all the proteins cross membranes) (described by a parameter fraction of interacting nodes, *frin*)
- the effective input given to the other nodes by node a_{ij} (activity of node j belonging to cell i), whose protein can diffuse through the membrane, is "1" if at least one of the four nodes with the same value of j , belonging to the RBNs present in the four neighboring cells of cell i , is "1"
- the interactions are limited to nearest neighbors (we adopted the von Neumann neighborhood N,S,E,W)

The model defined above is clearly a square cellular automaton, where each cell has a fairly complicated behavior, since it hosts a full RBN.

4   Results

4.1   Description of Parameters and Methods

In our initial testing of this system, we concentrated on networks which are close to their critical point. This choice should allow us to better detect the effects of embedding them in a higher order system. Therefore, taking into account the fact that in nature those activation functions which (in the boolean approximation) show a bias towards the value 0 seems to be preferred, we chose $k_{in}=3$ and p close to 0.21 (the critical value for $k_{in}=3$, cfr the legend to Figure 1a). Incidentally, this choice implies a large presence of canalizing functions (as it is found in biology [11]): also with the highest *p* value we utilized (*p*=0.22), more that 78% of boolean functions are canalizing in at least one input.

The initial condition is chosen at random for every RBN, independently from those of the other cells.

The number of nodes of every RBN (N) is 100, and the dimension of our artificial tissue is a square of 20x20 elements (so the total number of genes in the tissue is 40.000); the global topology is that of a torus.

In order to find the attractors of each RBN, we run the system for 1600 steps (a step being a complete update of each node of each RBN present in the system), and check the presence of an attractor in each RBN belonging to the tissue during the last 200 steps (therefore, we are not able to find attractors whose period is higher than 200 steps, nor those which are reached after a very long transient). When each RBN reaches an attractor (or when the system reaches 1600 step) the search ends.

For each level of the intensity of interaction *frin* (the fraction of nodes whose outcome can affect neighboring cells) we made a series of 1000 runs, each run involving a different RBN (same kin and p, but different topology and boolean functions) and different initial conditions.

We consider the following variables. For each series of runs:

- the fraction of runs α where all the cells of the system reach the same attractor (out of 1000 runs)
- the fraction of runs β where all the cells of the system reach an attractor (out of 1000 runs)
- the fraction of runs γ where no cell reaches an attractor (out of 1000 runs)

and, for each run of each series:

- the number of different attractors present at the end of the run
- the number of different periods present at the end of the run
- the average length of the 20x20 RBN periods at the end of the run
- the structural factor *sfct* (see below) at the end of the run

sfct is an aggregate variable we utilize as a first indicator of presence of homogeneous zones inside the artificial tissue. For each RBN_i, we compute the number of nearest neighboring RBNs that are in the same attractor of RBN_i, and sum all the 20x20 quantities. If all the RBN share the same attractor (the idealized situation where all the cells of the system belong to only one kind of tissue) this variable reaches its maximum value 1600 (20x20x4), otherwise the cells self organize in more sparse structures.

4.2 Experimental Results

First of all, we analyze the behavior of the aggregate variables α, β and γ as function of the interaction intensity. As the strength of this interaction grows, the fraction of runs β where all the cells of the system reaches an attractor decreases; contemporarily, the fraction of runs γ where no cell reaches an attractor increases. Obviously, these measures are influenced by the search parameters we utilized, but this general behavior seems to happen for many sets of parameters. This indicates that the increase of interaction strength introduces more and more disorder into the systems.

But this is not the whole story of the phenomenon: as the strength of this interaction grows, the fraction of runs α where all the cells of the system reach the same attractor increases. What's more, if we consider the fraction of runs (out of the runs where all the cells of the system reach an attractor) where all the cells of the system reach the same attractor, this increase is even more evident. This is an evidence that the increase of interaction strength introduces more and more order into the systems, *if the system is already prone to the order* (Figure 2a).

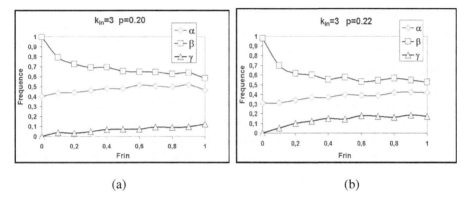

(a)   (b)

Fig. 2. Fraction of runs where all the cells of the system reach the same attractor (α),where all the cells of the system reach an attractor (β) and where no cell reach an attractor (γ). (a) Tissue constituted by ordered RBN (k_{in}=3, **p**=0.20); (b) tissue constituted by slightly disordered RBN (k_{in}=3, **p**=0.22).

A tentative explanation may be based on the observation that, also for RBN well inside the ordered region, exists a small but finite subset of networks that are chaotic [12]. That is, a possible interpretation of our result is that the increasing strength of interaction among neighboring RBNs amplifies the already present tendencies (or at least the already present tendencies of the majority of RBN present inside the tissue). Networks prone to disorder are more disordered, and networks already prone to order can reinforce their tendency and are more ordered.

This description is enforced by a new series of simulations (Figure 2b), where the RBN are more slightly into the chaotic region (this series has **p**=0.22; we remember that the border between order and chaos for systems with k_in=3 is approximately **p**=0.211). The runs where all the cells reach an attractor decrease in a more evident way, but the system is still able to increase the fraction of cases where all the cells reach the same attractor (phenomenon again more evident if we consider the fraction of cells that reach the same attractor out the fraction of runs where all the cells reach an attractor).

Then, what happens to fairly ordered systems? We have to carefully interpret, or select, the data we produced: how we can compare systems where all the cells reach an attractor and systems where only 30% (5%, 75%, …) of the cells do it? As a first step we decided to take into account only the systems where all the cells reach an attractor (but a survey of some less conservative cases shows that the general conclusions could be quite similar).

Therefore, we extract from our data (k_{in}=3 and p=0.20) all the systems where all the cells reach an attractor; the data are very noisy (the number of possible different RBNs and the number of possible different initial conditions are enormous, and therefore any realistic set of runs is always an undersampling), nevertheless some interesting trends are visible (see Figure 3). The most tangible changes are evident on the distributions of the number of different periods and of the average period (Figure 3b and Figure 3c): the higher the strength of the interaction among neighboring cells, the narrower are the distributions. That is, the system decrease the number of different periods that are present on the artificial tissue at the end of the runs, and their average becomes smaller; on average, the RBNs are compelled to share some characteristics. A second observation is that a large part of the effect is already present at the first "switch on" of the interaction: the further strengthening of the interaction results in changes of smaller entity.

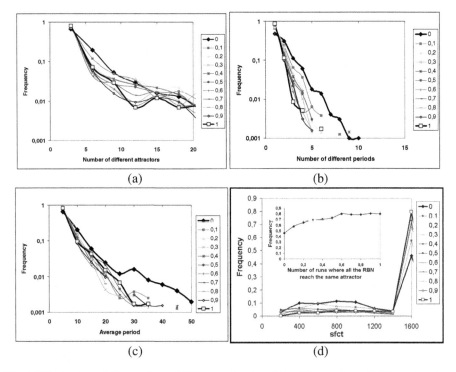

Fig. 3. Distribution of the number of different attractors (a), of the number of different periods (b), of the average of periods presents on the artificial tissue (c) and of the structural parameter *sfct* (d) as function of the strength of interaction coupling (spanning from 0.0 to 1.0 – see the legends). The involved RBNs are ordered networks (k_{in}=3 and p=0.20); the total number of RBNs that normalize the distributions is shown by line α in Figure 2a.

Let us now consider the number of attractors present inside the artificial tissue. Figure 3a (the distribution of the number of different attractors present at the end of each run) shows that there is a small effect due to the growing strength among neighboring RBN, but this distribution doesn't allow us to observe, for example, the formation of "islands" of attractors inside the matrix (which might be an interesting phenomenon). Therefore we need another indicator: as a first attempt, we propose the quantity *sfct* discussed above. The *sfct* distribution has an evident peak on it maximum value (that is, the cells tend to reach the same attractor); moreover, this peak grows hardly as the interaction strength increases (Figure 3d and its insert). When the system doesn't reach this so homogeneous situation, it could be found in a very high number of situations (the long tails at the left of the peaks), but the importance of these tails decreases as the strength of interaction becomes more intense. That is, the presence of homogeneous zones inside the system is more and more intense as the interaction strength grows up (see Figure 4 for an example of association between the presence of homogeneous zones and the value of *sfct*).

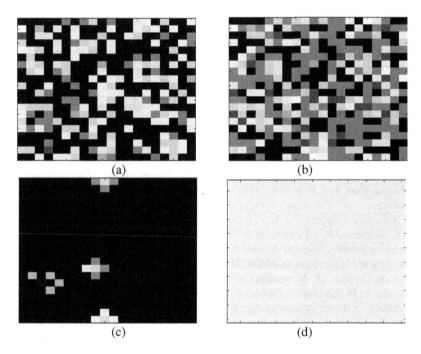

Fig. 4. Emerging of homogeneous zones inside the artificial tissue; the variable shown is the kind of attractor. (a) interaction strength at 0 and *sfct*=323; (b) interaction strength at 0.1 and *sfct*=308; (c) interaction strength at 0.3 and *sfct*=1138; (d) interaction strength at 0.7 and *sfct*=1600. This last case shows a complete homogeneous tissue, with only one attractor.

There is another more subtle and interesting issue: in Figure 4 we are observing the kind of attractors, but this is not NECESSARILY WHAT MATTERS FROM A FUNCTIONAL VIEWPOINT. If we consider one node (whose product can pass through the cell membrane) of one particular RBN and if its activation is "0", this doesn't means that the real effect of this activation is "0". It is enough that one of its neighboring RBNs has the same node with activation "1", that under all the functional aspects this node behaves as the state "1". That is, it is possible that a part of differences we are now observing among the cells doesn't exists as functional difference. And, for a tissue, it is important that all the cells be similar under the functional aspect. This aspect of the problem will be the subject of further analysis.

5 Conclusions

This work is a preliminary study of the effects of the interactions among several RBN: an intriguing phenomenon has been observed, i.e. that the interaction, as it has been modeled here, can have different effects on different kinds of RBN. In particular, the fraction of networks which do not reach an attractor increases, indicating a growth of dynamical disorder. But, limiting our considerations to those networks which reach an attractor within the time limits of our simulations, we observe that they tend to more homogeneous attractors. It is interesting to speculate about the possible implications of this finding from the viewpoint of evolution theory; since a certain degree of order is needed to allow robust functionality, those networks which reach an attractor might have been selected, and in this case the ordering effect of interaction would prevail – a finding which seems biologically plausible. Further work has to been done in order to investigate, *inter alia*, the effect of different coupling interactions, different values of parameters, and to investigate the interaction between genomic and functional differences.

References

1. Kauffman, S.A.: Gene Regulation Networks: A Theory of their Global Structure and Behavior. Curr. Top. Dev. Biol 6 (1971), 145-182
2. Kauffman, S. A.: The origins of order. Oxford University Press (1993)
3. M. Aldana, S. Coppersmith, L. P. Kadanoff, Boolean Dynamics with Random Couplings, in E. Kaplan, J.E. Marsden, K.R. Sreenivasan (eds), Perspectives and Problems in Nonlinear Science. Springer Applied Mathematical Sciences Series (2003). Also available at http://www.arXiv:cond-mat/0209571
4. Serra, R., Villani, M. & Semeria, A.: Robustness to damage of biological and synthetic networks. In W. Banzhaf, T. Christaller, P. Dittrich, J.T. Kim & J. Ziegler (eds): Advances in Artificial Life. Berlin: Springer Lecture Notes in Artificial Intelligence 2801, (2003) 706-715
5. Serra, R., Villani, M. & Semeria, A.: Genetic network models and statistical properties of gene expression data in knock-out experiments. J. Theor. Biol. 227 (1) (2004) 149-157
6. P.Ramo, J.Kesseli, O. Yli-Harja 2005 Perturbation avalanches and criticality in gene regulatory networks Journal of Theoretical Biology, submitted
7. Shmulevich, I. and Kauffman, S.A. Activities and Sensitivities in Boolean Network Models, Phys Rev. Lett. 93(4), 048701 (1-4) (2004)
8. S.Kauffman, C.Peterson, B.Samuelsson, C.Troein Genetic networks with canalyzing Boolean rules are always stable PNAS vol. 101 no.49 (2004)
9. Harvey, I., and Bossomaier, T. Time out of joint: Attractors in asynchronous random boolean networks. In Husbands, P., and Harvey, I., eds., Proceedings of the Fourth European Conference on Artificial Life (ECAL97) MIT Press (1997) 67-75
10. Kauffman, S.A.: Investigations. Oxford University Press (2000)
11. Harris, S.E., Sawhill, B.K., Wuensche, A. & Kauffman, S.A.: A model of transcriptional regulatory networks based on biases in the observed regulation rules. Complexity 7 (2002) 23-40
12. U. Bastolla and G. Parisi The modular structure of Kauffman networks Physica D 115 (1998) 219-233

Dynamics of Emergent Flocking Behavior

Masaru Aoyagi and Akira Namatame

Dept. of Computer Science,
National Defense Academy, Yokosuka, Japan
{g45074, nama}@nda.ac.jp

Abstract. Flocking behavior is widely used in virtual reality, computer games, unmanned vehicle, robotics and artificial life. However, coordination of multiple flocking behaviors to accomplish such tasks remains a challenging problem. This paper reports some progress for implicit coordination and gets swarm intelligence as works based on the flocking behavior. It consists of two parts. In the first part, we study on the pattern formation problem with avoiding complex constraints, that is how can a group of agents be controlled to get into and maintain a formation. The second part considers the studies that use adaptation strategies in controlling multiple agents based on probabilistic methods. Specifically we investigated (1) how probabilistic method is used to reorganize generate group (flocking) behaviors, and (2) how adaptation at the individual level is used to make multiple agents respond to obstacles in the environment.

1 Introduction

To creatures a large number of objects by hand would be a tedious job. To make the job easier, we would like to try to automate as much of the process as possible. For the case of flocks or herds of creatures, Reynolds [1,2] introduced a simple agent-based approach to animate a flock of creatures through space. In this method, each creature makes its own decisions on how to move, according to a small number of simple rules that consider the neighboring members of the flock. In nature, aggregations of large numbers of mobile organisms are also faced with the problem of organizing themselves efficiently. This selective pressure has led to the evolution of behavior such as flocking of birds or herding of land animals and schooling of fish. The reasons why organisms form flocks are varied and include protection from predation, improved food search and improved social cohesion. However, the actual dynamics of the flocking behavior are essentially constrained by the dynamics of the individual organisms and the flock is relatively limited in the types of behavior it can exhibit. This gives a flock of a given organism, be it fish or bird, its characteristic look and feel.

Boids models are considered and accepted or rejected on the basis of how well observed phenomena can be imitated. The scientific approach has very different objectives the goal is not just to produce realistic simulations but also to understand and explain the local mechanisms that control patterns. As such the wealth of behavioral data available can be incorporated. We show appropriate spatial and

S. El Yacoubi, B. Chopard, and S. Bandini (Eds.): ACRI 2006, LNCS 4173, pp. 557–563, 2006.

temporal statistics that need to be applied to evaluate the conditions of models. Perhaps, most importantly analytical methods can be used to translate the local mechanisms into macroscopic dynamics.

First, in this paper, we present a theoretical analysis for emergence mechanism of flocking behavior in steady-state. Secondary, we suggest two effective methods, with "probabilistic method" and "adaptive change of action rules to combine multiple parallel action rules agents have. Finally, we investigate the theoretical analysis results and the method with 3D multi-agent simulation.

2 Literature on Flocking Behavior

A flock may be loosely defined as a clustered group of individuals with a common velocity vector. Note that flocking of aircraft is different from formation flying. In the latter, aircraft are arranged according to predefined relationships that generally remain fixed during the flight. With flocking flight, there are no predefined relation-ships and the flock members may constantly change their position within the group. The fixed relationships within aircraft formations make them relatively difficult to maneuver, whereas the fluid nature of a flock allows relatively rapid changes in flock direction.

Reynolds first demonstrated the viability of obtaining coherent flocking behavior from simple rules. The primary application for this work was in developing realistic motions of groups of agents in computer simulation. For large numbers of agents, for example a flock of birds, the process was cumbersome and did not produce realistic results. This led to the use of relatively simple flocking rules that would automatically govern the dynamic behavior.

The dynamics and stability of multi-robot formations have drawn recent attention by Wang and by Chen and Luh. Wang [3] developed a strategy for robot formations where individual robots are given specific positions to maintain relative to a leader or neighbor. Sensory requirements for these robots are reduced since they only need to know about a few other robots. Wang's analysis centered on feedback control for formation maintenance and stability of the resulting system. It did not include integrative strategies for obstacle avoidance and navigation. In work by Chen and Luh [4] formation generation by distributed control is demonstrated. Large groups of robots are shown to cooperatively move in various geometric formations. Chen's research also centered on the analysis of group dynamics and stability, and does not provide for obstacle avoidance. In the approach forwarded in this article, geometric formations are specified in a similar manner, but formation behaviors are fully integrated with obstacle avoidance and other navigation behaviors.

Flierl, Grunbaum, Levin and Olson analyses the processes by which organisms form groups and how social forces interact with environmental variability and transport [5]. They discuss the transformation of individual based models into continuum models for the density of organisms. A number of subtle difficulties arise in this process however we find that a direct comparison between the individual model and the continuum model is quite favorable. They examine the dynamics of group statistics and give an example of building an equation for the spatial and temporal variations of the group size distribution from individual based simulations.

We have suggested that agent has multi action rules with "probabilistic method" and "adaptive change of action rules" [6]. The flock breaks away form a box-type obstacle and goes toward the destination.

3   Agent Based Simulation for Flocking Behavior

A method is presented for flocking behavior of creatures, birds, fishes and so on, that can form herds by evading obstacles in airspace, terrain or ocean floor topography in 3D space while being efficient enough to run in real-time. This method involves making modifications to Reynolds' flocking algorithm as following.

- Cohesion: steer to move toward the average position of local flockmates
- Separation: steer to avoid crowding local flockmates
- Alignment: steer towards the average heading of local flockmates

The agent is individual and it is behavior determines how it reacts to others in its local neighborhood. An agent outside of the local neighborhood is ignored. A Flock often consists of multi local interactions of each agent.

Simulations show that reasonable flocking behavior can be obtained using just cohesion and alignment rules. Left unchecked, the cohesion rules will tend to lead to flock overcrowding. To balance this, a separation rule is used, where the active flock member tries to translate away from the local flock centroid.

Each agent has direct access to the whole scene's geometric description, but flocking requires that it react only to flockmates within a certain small neighborhood around itself. That the relative position vector to an agent's position and the relative velocity vector to an agent's velocity characterize the neighborhood. The evading obstacles rule added to the flocking algorithm has a constant parameter that can be adjusted to produce different behaviors.

4   Theoretical Analysis of Emergent of Flocking Behavior

The flocking algorithm works as follows: For a given agent, centroids are calculated using the sensor characteristics associated with each flocking rule. Next, the velocity vector the given agent should follow to enact the rule is calculated for each of the rules. These velocity vectors are then weighted according to the rule strength and summed to give an overall velocity vector demand. Finally, this velocity vector demand is resolved in to a heading angle, pitch attitude and speed demand, which is passed to the control system. The control system then outputs an actuator vector that alters the motion of the aircraft in the appropriate manner. Each agent recognizes two physical values. One is the position to flockmates from the agent. The other is the relative velocity of flockmates.   Agent i acquires the flockmate agent j in visual sensor range.   Agent i can recognize vector $\vec{d}_{ij}$ that is the position vector to the flockmate agent j. It also recognizes vector $\vec{v}_{ij} = d\vec{d}_{ij} / dt$ that is the relative velocity vector.

Cohesion force vector $\vec{F}_{ci}$, separation force vector $\vec{F}_{si}$ and alignment force vector $\vec{F}_{ai}$ are defined from these two physical values, flocking force vector $\vec{F}_{fi}$ expression is defined as liner combination of cohesion, separation and alignment force.

$$\vec{F}_{fi} = \vec{F}_{ci} + \vec{F}_{si} + \vec{F}_{ai}$$

$$= \left(w_{ci} - \frac{w_{si}}{\left| \sum_{j}^{n_i} \vec{d}_{ij} \right|} \right) \frac{\sum_{j}^{n_i} \vec{d}_{ij}}{\left| \sum_{j}^{n_i} \vec{d}_{ij} \right|} + w_{ai} \frac{\sum_{j}^{n_i} \vec{v}_{ij}}{\left| \sum_{j}^{n_i} \vec{v}_{ij} \right|} \tag{1}$$

Where coefficient w_{ci}, w_{si} and are weights each force and positive. If flocking force vector $\vec{F}_{fi} = \vec{0}$, then, the flock moving becomes steady-state. In this case, both first and second term in Eq.(1) has to equals $\vec{0}$.

The condition of first term in Eq. (1) is

$$\left| \sum_{j}^{n_i} \vec{d}_{ij} \right| = \frac{w_{si}}{w_{ci}} \tag{2}$$

Eq. (2) shows the distance between agent and flockmates in steady-state. If w_{si} is smaller or w_{ci} is larger, then the absolute value of the sum of the position vector $\sum_{j}^{n_i} \vec{d}_{ij}$ becomes shorter. The steady-state condition of second term, alignment term, in Eq.(1) is

$$\sum_{j}^{n_i} \vec{v}_{ij} = \sum_{j}^{n_i} \frac{d\vec{d}_{ij}}{dt} = \vec{0} \tag{3}$$

Eq. (3) shows the velocity of both agent and flockmates is same in steady-state. If w_{ai} is larger, then recognizes vector $\vec{v}_{ij}$ comes to zero more quickly, and the velocity of agent comes to the velocity of flockmates more quickly.

Here, we make agents have a new action rule; "go toward a destination". The propulsion toward a destination is defined $\vec{F}_{di}$. The new action rule is in parallel with and conflict "flocking behavior". We combine the new action rule to "flocking behavior" with a "Probabilistic Method". The method is that an agent recalls to go toward the destination by probability p. Total force of the whole flock $\vec{F}_{total}$ is

$$\vec{F}_{total} = \vec{F}_f + p\vec{F}_d = \frac{1}{n}\left(\sum_i^n \vec{F}_{fi} + p\sum_i^n \vec{F}_{di}\right) \tag{4}$$

where $\vec{F}_f$ is the average of flocking behavior force of agents, and $\vec{F}_d$ is average force that agents want to go toward a destination. We combine the two actions rules with a probabilistic method. Then, it emerges that the flock follows a horizontal circular path around the destination. To solve the equation of motion of circular movement, L is an average distance from agent to the destination and is estimated as a follow equation.

$$L = \frac{mv^2}{\left|\langle\vec{F}_d\rangle\right|} = \frac{mv^2}{p\dfrac{1}{N}\displaystyle\sum_{i=1}^N w_d\dfrac{\vec{L}(t)}{\left|\vec{L}(t)\right|}} = q\frac{mv^2}{pw_d} \tag{5}$$

Where $\langle\vec{F}_d\rangle$ is the average of $\vec{F}_d$ by time scale, m is a mass of agents, q is a coefficient come from spatial distribution of each agent, v is the magnitude of sum of all agents' velocity vector. Eq. (5) shows L is proportional to m and v^2, and is inversely proportional to p and w_d.

5   Simulation Results on Purposive Flocking Behavior

Each agent is homo and has parallel and conflict two action rules; "flocking behavior" and "go toward a destination". Amount of agents is 100.

The simulation result is shown in Fig 1. The flock follows a horizontal circular path around the destination. Fig.2 is a graph about SD and L versus time t, where SD is the standard deviation of positions of agents' position and L is the distance form the center of the positions of agents to the destination. When t = 2000, SD becomes constant. It indicates that flocking behavior become in steady-state in this time. L becomes also constant same time. It indicates that the flock's track become in circular orbit.

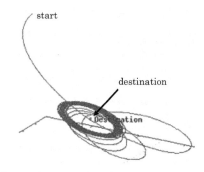

Fig. 1. The track of the flock. It is a circular orbit. (recall probability: $p = 0.15$) All agents that construct the flock are bound in a plane: $z = -0.220\,x - 0.181\,y$.

Fig.3 shows that SD and L versus p. An approximate equation about L and p is follow.

$$L = 1.30/p + 0.0709 \tag{6}$$

Eq.(6) indicates L is inversely proportional to p. This result matches Eq.(5) very well.

Next step we put an obstacle in front of agents. A flock is closing to it. Each agent in the flock wants to avoid an obstacle. In the case of conventional Boids model, a flock is split three flocks. On the other hand, in the case of "adaptive change of action rules", the flock members don't disjoined. Fig.4 shows R-m curve, where R is the distance from the agent to the center of all agents position and m is agent density that define as the density of number that an agent recognizes other agents in his visual range. In the case of conventional Boids model as shown in Fig.4(b), R-m curve splits three clusters. On the other hand, in the case of "adaptive change of action rules", R-m curve keeps its shape as shown in Fig.4(c).

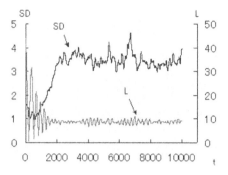

Fig. 2. Standard deviation: *SD* and the distance form the flock to the destination: *L* vs times: *t*. (recall probability: *p = 0.15*).

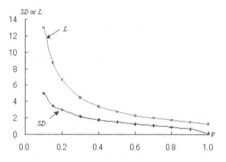

Fig. 3. Standard deviation: *SD* and the distance form the flock to the destination: *L* vs recall probability: *p*

6   Conclusions

We usually ascribe agents' behaviors as if they are oriented toward a goal. Agents or a group of agents pursue their own goals. We might characterize these behaviors as purposive behaviors. On the other hand, agents also often behave by reacting to others. Therefore, what we also have is a mode of contingent behavior that depends on what other agents are doing

Therefore, we have to look closely at agents who are adapting to other agents. In this way, the behavior of one agent affects the behaviors of the other agents. How well agents accomplish what they want to accomplish depends on what other agents are doing. What makes this kind of interactive situation interesting and difficult is that the aggregate outcome is what has to be evaluated, not merely how agents behave within the constraints of their own environments.

We analyzes theoretically for emergence mechanism of flocking behavior in steady-state. We have investigated the problem how an agent has combined two action rules; both "flocking behavior" and "go toward a destination". We have suggested "probabilistic method" as a solution for the problem. Then, it emerges that the flock follows a horizontal circular path around the destination. All agents are bound

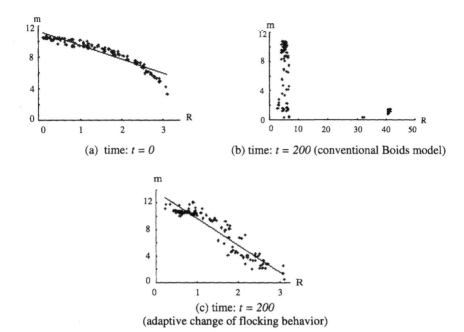

(a) time: $t = 0$

(b) time: $t = 200$ (conventional Boids model)

(c) time: $t = 200$

(adaptive change of flocking behavior)

Fig. 4. *R-m* curve. *R* is the distance from the agent to the center of all agents' position. *m* is agent density that define as the density of number that an agent recognizes other agents in his visual range.

in circular track plane. As the time scales increase, we investigated the statistical properties of flocking behavior and show theoretically analysis matches the simulation result very well. We also challenged the problem how the flock don't disjoin when avoiding an obstacle. We have suggested "adaptive change of action rules" as a solution for this problem and ensured the effectiveness of the method in a simulation.

References

1. Reynolds, C. W.: "Flocks, Herds, and Schools: A Distributed Behavioral Model," in Computer Graphics, 21(4) (SIGGRAPH '87 Conference Proceedings) (1987) 25-34.
2. Reynolds, C. W.: "Steering Behaviors For Autonomous Characters," in the proceedings of Game Developers Conference 1999 held in San Jose, California. Miller Freeman Game Group, San Francisco, California (1999) 763-782.
3. Wang, P. K. C.: "Navigation strategies for multiple autonomous robots moving in formation," J. Robot. Syst., vol. 8, no. 2 (1991) 177-195.
4. Chen, Q. and J. Y. S. Luh.: "Coordination and control of a group of small mobile robots," in Proc. IEEE Int. Conf. Robot. Automat., San Diego, CA, 1994 (1991) 2315-2320.
5. Flierl, G., D. Grunbaum, S. Levin, D. Olson: "From individuals to aggregations: the interplay between behavior and physics," J. Theoret. Biol. 196 (1999) 397-454.
6. Aoyagi, M. and A. Namatame: "Massive Multi-Agent Simulation in 3D", Soft Computing as Trans-disciplinary Science and Technology Proceedings of the 4th IEEE International Workshop (WSTST'05) (2005) 295-305.

A Maze Routing Algorithm Based on Two Dimensional Cellular Automata

Shahram Golzari[1] and Mohammad Reza Meybodi[2]

[1] Computer Engineering Department, Hormozgan University, Bandarabbas, Iran
golzari@hormozgan.ac.ir
[2] Computer Engineering Department, Amir Kabir University, Tehran, Iran
mmeybodi@aut.ac.ir

Abstract. This paper propose a maze routing algorithm based on cellular automata. The aim of this algorithm is find the shortest path between the source cell and the target cell , so that the path does not pass from the obstacles. Algorithm has two phases, exploration and retrace. In exploration phase a wave is expanded from source cell and it puts token on cells which it passes via them while expanding. In the retracing phase , we start from target cell, follow the wave and arrive to source cell; the path created in this phase is desirable. Propose algorithm is simple and it's transactions are local and follow the cellular automata properties. This algorithm find the desirable path in $m \times m$ two dimensional CA in $O(m^2)$ time step.

Keywords: cellular automata, routing, maze routing algorithm, physical design, parallel algorithm.

1 Introduction

Maze routing algorithm find the smallest path between the source and target point in a planner rectangular graph. For doing routing by these algorithms, at first entire plan (the place where we want to do routing operation) is simply modeled by grid cells. For doing it , entire plan is displayed by a set of square cells with unit surface which are placed in a two dimensional form just as we have thrown a grid on the plan.

Now, by using these cells and relationship between them, the graph is obtained. In this Manner , each c_i cell is displayed by v_i node in graph. The nodes similar the cells which have obstacle are called closed nodes and other nodes are called non closed ones. If c_i and c_j cells are neighborhood, there will be one edge between v_i and v_j nodes in graph. The weight of each edge in graph equals one, except those edges related to closed nodes, whose weight equals zero.

In the planner rectangular grid graph , each node has four neighbor nodes. The nodes similar to those area of plan which routing can be done by them , are displayed in the non closed form and the another nodes are displayed in the closed form. The aim of maze routing algorithms is to find a path between source and target nodes that this path does not pass any closed nodes and it has also the shortest length. This types of algorithms has two phases: exploration and retrace and algorithm start from

S. El Yacoubi, B. Chopard, and S. Bandini (Eds.): ACRI 2006, LNCS 4173, pp. 564–570, 2006.

exploration phase. In this phase we start from source node , consider all possible paths that start from it, and continue all of them so that one of those paths arrive at target nodes.

When path arrives to target nodes, the retrace phase will start. In this phase by using the way of back tracking it is recognized that which nodes of graph settle in the connective path between target and source node. After this phase algorithm is finished. For doing the retrace phase, it is necessary to set some information about paths in exploration phase, then by using this information the retrace phase is done[7,8,11,15]. Maze routing algorithms used in robot path planning and routing phase of VLSI physical design[8,15].

The first algorithm of this type algorithms is introduced by Lee. Which find the shortest path in one grid graph with $h \times w$ dimensions in $O(h \times w)$ [8], then several algorithms based on Lee's algorithm for improving the way of path extension and run time of algorithm, are reported such as algorithms of Soukup[14] and Hadlock[7]. One of the interesting properties of maze routing algorithms is parallelism that hidden on it. This case has caused that these algorithms are simply maps on the parallel structures and in spite of constancy of algorithm complexity, the run time of algorithm, because of doing algorithm by suitable hardware and being reduced the number of instruction done by every processor, are decreased to a large extent. Some of these maps have done by Sagar and Massaka[19].

In this paper, one maze routing algorithm on CA is proposed. The proposed algorithm is so simple. In this algorithm, each cell of CA perform little transactions which cause to reduce the run time of algorithm. The used structure also is simple, parallel and local which is suitable for maze routing algorithm. In this algorithm at first the plan maps on the two dimensional Ca; then by using the simple, local and suitable rules, routing phase is implemented. In this paper we describe the basic concepts of CA in section 2, then explain and implement it by CA in section 3.

2   Cellular Automata(CA)

Suppose a regular network of finite state machine. Each machine called cell. According to a fixed and uniform pattern each cell is related to some of it's adjacent cells. This relationship is local and uniform for all cells. The Cell and all cells related to it are neighbors of cell. Each cell can have one state from limited state at each time step. The states are similar for all cells. At each time step state of all cells update simultaneously and according to uniform rule. This rule is function of states of cell's neighborhood. Therefore in any time next state of cell is dependent on the current state of it's neighborhood. This network start from an initial configuration, at any time step by using the rule for all cells, the configuration is updated and finally the network produce a complex and interest behavior.

According to the explanation the differentiation of CA and other automata network is: simplicity of structure, local communication between cells, establishing a uniform communicative pattern for all cells, simultaneously update of cells, updating cells by uniform rule and producing the complex, interesting behavior from simple cells and rules. According to these properties, CA is referred as a parallel, local and uniform structure in most of literatures, which can simulation the behavior that have these properties[4,6,6,15,18].

Today CA has been used in several areas, such as random pattern generation, computation theory, physical and biological system simulation and applied science[3,5,6,9,12,15,16,18].

So far, by using several method has proved that CA is universal computing model [1,2], but in real world , this model is often used to simulate physical phenomena and this model   has drawn attention of researcher of some sciences such as physics and biology rather than that of researcher of computer science. They simulate the evolution of physical phenomena by CA rules step by step. Whereas according the definition , a computational model is not a mechanism for describing the evolution of phenomena; but it is a structure to perform computing on the input data.

In this paper CA is seen as general computing machine and an algorithm is proposed to solve one problem by CA. To solve the computational problems, a data structure and a procedure are needed. The data structure saves input and output data and procedure convert input data to output. The stage of processing and convert input to output in CA done state transmission of CA. Although in the definition of standard CA the memory isn't used but if CA like to play a role of a general computing machine, each automate cell needs several memories to save the values of input and output and also the automata should have the ability to read   the values of input and the ability to write the values of output(from-to) memory. The definition proposed follow , which is considered as the definition of CA in this paper, is the extended definition of Mealy Automata[5].

Definition 1: CA is a seven-tuple as $\{Q, d, v, \Sigma, \Delta, \delta, \lambda\}$ when:

1. **Q**: the set of states that each cell can be have.

2. **d**: define the dimension of cell's space. If d=2 , we will have   a two dimensional CA.

3. For each cell **x** in CA , vector **V** specify k+1 neighbors that is directly communicate to cell.

4. Σ : the input alphabet of CA.

5. Δ : the output alphabet of CA.

6. δ: the transmission function in the form $\delta : (Q \times \Sigma^n)^{k+1} \rightarrow Q$. According to the function, next state of a cell is dependent on state and values of input memories of all neighbors in the current step. N is the number of input and output registers of cell.

7. λ: the transducer relation which is a finite subset of $(Q \times \Sigma^n)^{k+1} \times \Delta^n$. This transducer defines the value of each output memory according to state and value of input memories of it's neighborhood. Here each cell of CA writes on those memories that reads from them, therefore $\Sigma = \Delta$.

3 A Maze Routing Algorithm Based on CA

3.1 Algorithm Implementation by CA

In this section , the implementation of algorithm by CA is explained. In order to do that, first entire plan should be mapped in a two dimensional CA with von Neumann neighborhood. In this way, entire plan is considered as e set of cells with have unit area. Those cells that cover the obstacles of the plan are considered with the Block(B) initial state. The initial state of cells that equivalent to the source and target points are considered respectively Source(S) and Target(T) and initial state of other cells are considered Free(F). It is clear that desirable path passes among the cells with F state. Therefore ,the memory variable(state) is needed for save the state of cell. Hereafter we use B-cell, S-cell, T-cell, and F-cell respectively for the cell with state B, cell with state S, cell with state T and cell with state F.

As it described, a wave must be produced from the source cell. For implementation the wave production the below method is used. In the first step, the wave arrives at just cells in the neighborhood of source cell. Now the F-cells that wave arrive to them, update their states to Mark(M). In the next step, wave includes all F-cells which have a M-cell neighbor, that these cells also update their states to M. Expanding the wave continues so and by this way, the exploration phase is implemented. According to this scenario, we can do the wave expanding by simple rule: each F-cell has at least one M-cell or S-cell neighbor update it's state to M.

As it is explained in the idea of algorithm, the wave should put a token in places where it passes, so that the path is made regarding that in retrace phase. While the above scenario does not do this and only expands the wave. Now, the scenario must be verified to save the affect of wave expanding in cells.

As maintained, in each step that the wave expands, number of F-cells change to M-cells, in fact those F-cells that are in the neighborhood of M-cells or S-cell update to M-cells. Then to save the affect of wave, it is sufficient to know that which neighbor of F-cell is M-cell or S-cell and save this information in a memory variable. In order to do this, we use a memory variable called "direction". This variable can save one of the Right, Left, Down up and null values. In initial configuration, the value of this variable is null for all F-cells and T-cell and it is don't care for another cells.

Now, each F-cell which is in the neighborhood M-cells or S-cell, checks that which side cell that neighbor is placed, and regarding that, it assigns value to it's Direction variable. If the M-cell or S-cell is placed at up, down, left and right of cell, the value of Direction variable respectively will update to Up, Down, Right and Left. If cell has more than one M-cell neighbor, it's Direction variable choice one of them randomly. T-cell is also doing operation such as M-cell, but it's state isn't update and only it's Direction variable gets value.

When the wave arrives at T-cell (the Direction variable of this cell gets value that isn't equal to null) exploration phase is finished and retrace phase start. In this phase, the path must be specified from T-cell to S-cell step by step and the cells is placed in the path must be change to P-cells. But how this path is made? To explain this, first we define the following concept:

Definition 2: pointing to: Cell A points to cell B if one of the following cases has been happened:

- Cell A is down neighbor of cell B and Direction value of cell A is equal to Up.
- Cell A is up neighbor of cell B and Direction value of cell A is equal to Down.
- Cell A is left neighbor of cell B and Direction value of cell A is equal to Right.
- Cell A is right neighbor of cell B and Direction value of cell A is equal to Left.

In retrace phase, if T-cell or P-cell has a M-cell neighbor and in addition point to M-cell neighbor, then that neighbor changes to P-cell. The result of using the scenario will be so: when the Direction variable of T-cell gets value against null (that is when wave arrives at T-cell) retrace phase has been started. Therefore , in the first step of new phase, that M-cell which T-cell points to it changes to P-cell; and the next step the M-cell which points to new P-cell changes to P-cell, this operation continues to arrive at S-cell. The desired path involves P-cells. When the path arrives at S-cell the algorithm is finished(That is S-cell has a T-cell or P-cell neighbor).

3.2 Structure of Cells

In the proposed algorithm, each cell has two memory variables called State and Direction. State variable specifies the stat of cell and can get one of the following values:

- Source(S): the source cell has S state.
- Target(T): the target cell has T state.
- Block(B): the cells which the path can't pass through them, have B state.
- Free(F): the cells which the path can pass through them, have F state.
- Mark(M): the cells which the wave arrives at them, have M state.
- Path(P): the cells which placed in the final path, have P state.

Direction variable: this variable specifies the affect of wave expanding in each cell and can get one of the following variables:

- Up: the cells which the wave arrives at them via up neighbor, the value of their Direction variable equals to Up.
- Down: the cells which the wave arrives at them via down neighbor, the value of their Direction variable equals to Down.
- Left: the cells which the wave arrives at them via left neighbor, the value of their Direction variable equals to Left.
- Right: the cells which the wave arrives at them via right neighbor, the value of their Direction variable equals to Right.
- Null: the cells which the wave doesn't arrive at them' the value of their Direction variable equals to Null.

3.3 Initial Configuration of CA

In the initial configuration, the plan must be mapped on CA. To do it, the cells which have obstacles, are being B-cell. The cells similar to source and target respectively get S and T state and state of others cells will be F. The value of Direction variable for F-cells and T-cell equals null in initial configuration and for other cells will be don't care.

3.4 Final Configuration of CA

At the end of algorithm, the cells which place on the path have P state (p-cells). The cells which state of them equal T, B or S in the initial configuration, remain fix.

3.5 Rules of CA

- If State variable of cell equals S, it remains fix in the next step.
- If State variable of cell equals B, it remains fix in the next step.
- If State variable of cell equals F, one of the following cases is done:
- If cell dos not have M-cell or S-cell between neighbors, it remains fix in the next step.
- If cell has only one M-cell or S-cell neighbor, the State variable of cell gets M value and cell points to suitable neighbor(if the M-cell or S-cell neighbor has been placed at up, down, left and right of the cell, Direction variable of cell gets Up, Down, Left and Right value respectively.)
- If cell has some M-cell or S-cell neighbors, the State variable of cell gets M value and cell points to one of them randomly.
- If State variable of cell equals T, the cell follows the rule of F-cell but State variable of cell remains fix.
- If State variable of cell equals M, one of the following cases is done:
- If cell dos not have P-cell or T-cell between neighbors, it remains fix in the next step.
- If cell has at least one P-cell or T-cell neighbors and cell points to one of them, the State variable of cell gets P value.
- If State variable of cell equals P, it remains fix in the next step.

3.6 Complexity of Algorithm

The path from source to target in a $m \times m$ two dimensional CA, can't have a length more than m^2, because the path can't pass each cell more than one time and the number of cells is also m^2. Therefore, time complexity of algorithm is $O(m^2)$.

4 Conclusion

In this paper a maze routing algorithm based on two dimensional cellular automata was proposed. This algorithm find a smallest path from source cell to target cell and path doesn't pass the obstacles. The proposed algorithm is simple and has local transactions that match with properties of cellular automata. Each cell of CA also has simple structure and accesses only the contents of neighbor cells in each time and VLSI circuit of it can be designed easily. This algorithm find the desirable path in $m \times m$ two dimensional CA in $O(m^2)$ time step.

References

1. Bruks, W.: Essay on Cellular Automata. Urbana. IL:University of Illinois Press (1970)
2. Conway, J.H., Berlekamp, E., Guy, R.: Wining Ways for Your Mathematics Plays. Vol. 2. Academic Press (1982)
3. Culik, K., Hurd, L., Yu, S.: Computation Theoritic Aspects of Cellular Automata. Physica D. Vol. 45. (1990) 357-378
4. Farmer, D., Toffoli, T., Wolfram, S. (eds.): Cellular Automata Proceedings of An Interdisciplinary Workshop. Amsterdam. North Holland (1984)
5. Gordillo, L., Lunna, V.: Parallel Sort on Linear Array of Cellular Automata. IEEE Transaction on Computers (1994) 1904-1910
6. Gutowitz, A.H.: Cellular Automata. Cambridge. MA:MIT Press (1990)
7. Hadlock, F.O.: A Shortest Path Algorithm for Grid Graph. Networks (1997)
8. Lee, C.Y.: An Algorithm for Path Connection and it's Application. IRE Transaction on Electronic Computers (1961)
9. Mitchel, M.: Computation in Cellular Automata: A Selected Review. Technical Report. Santa Fe Institute. Santa Fe. New Mexico (1996)
10. Packard , N.: Two Dimensional Cellular Automata. Journal of Statistical Physics. Vol. 30. (1985) 901-942.
11. Pan, Y., Hsu, Y.C., Kubitz, W.J.: A Path Selection Global Router. Proceedings of Design Automation Conference (1987)
12. Sarkar, P.: Brief History of Cellular Automata. ACM Computing Surveys. Vol. 32. No. 1. (2000)
13. Sherwani, N.A.: Algorithm for VLSI Physical Design Automation. Western Michigan University. Kluwer Academic Publishers (1993)
14. Soukup, J.: Fast Maze Router. Proceedings of 15th Design Automation Conference (1987) 100-102
15. Toffoli, T., Margolus, N.: Cellular Automata Machines: A New Environment for Modeling. Cambridge. MA:MIT Press (1987)
16. Wolfram, S.: Statistical Mechanics of Cellular Automata. Review of Modern Physics. Vol. 55. (1983) 601-644
17. Wolfram , S.: Computation Theory of Cellular Automata. Communication in Mathematical Physics. Vol. 96. (1984) 15-57
18. Wolfram, S.: Theory and Application of Cellular Automata. Singapor: World scientific (1986)
19. Sagar, V.K., Masara, R.E.: General Purpose Parallel Hardware Approach to the Routing Problems of VLSI Layout. IEEE Proceedings G. Vol. 140. Issue. 4. (1993) 294-304

Optimal 6-State Algorithms for the Behavior of Several Moving Creatures

Mathias Halbach, Rolf Hoffmann, and Lars Both

TU Darmstadt, FB Informatik, FG Rechnerarchitektur
Hochschulstraße 10, D-64289 Darmstadt, Germany
Phone: +49 6151 16 {3713, 3606}; Fax: +49 6151 16 5410
{halbach, hoffmann}@ra.informatik.tu-darmstadt.de, ra@lboth.de

Abstract. The goal of our investigation is to find automatically the absolutely best rule for a moving creature in a cellular field. The task of the creature is to visit all empty cells with a minimum number of steps. We call this problem *creature's exploration problem*. The behaviour was modelled using a variable state machine represented by a state table. Input to the state table is the current state and the neighbour's state in front of the creature's moving direction. The problem is that the search space for the possible rules grows exponentially with the number of states, inputs and outputs. We could solve the problem for six states, two inputs and two outputs with the aid of a parallel hardware platform (FPGA technology). The set of all possible n-state algorithms was first reduced by discarding equivalent, reducible and not strongly connected ones. The algorithms which showed a certain performance for five initial configurations during simulation were extracted by the hardware and send to the host PC. Additional tests for robustness and the behaviour of several creatures was carried out in software. One creature with the best algorithm can visit 99.92 % of the empty cells of 26 test configurations. Several creatures up to 16 can perform the task more efficiently for the tested initial configuration.

1 Introduction

The general goal of our project is to optimize the individual and cooperative behavior of moving creatures in order to fulfill a certain global task in an artificial environment. The simulation and optimizing procedures of such problems are very time consuming and therefore require support by special hardware or multiprocessor systems or at least optimized software if non-trivial problems have to be solved.

The CA model was chosen because its modeling capabilities are well suited to such problems with local interactions and also it is inherently massively parallel which allows an easy and efficient mapping to hardware structures.

There are many applications for such artificial worlds:

- *Synthetic Worlds*: Games, genetic art, optimization of the behavior of the creatures to reach global goals, social behavior, self organization.

S. El Yacoubi, B. Chopard, and S. Bandini (Eds.): ACRI 2006, LNCS 4173, pp. 571–581, 2006.

- *Computational Worlds*: Creatures are considered as active moving objects. Passive objects contain data. Creatures are programmed or are able to learn to solve a complex algorithmic problem.

With this approach also real world problems can be addressed as soon as the features of the creature and the features of the environment come close to the real world features of interest.

The problem of finding optimal solution of moving agents using a state machine has also been addressed in [1], and the problem has practical applications like mowing a lawn [2] or exploring an unknown environment by robots. Results of our preceding investigations were presented in [3,4,5,6] and were addressing the hardware architectures for acceleration. In contrast, this contribution is focused on the evaluation of the found algorithms for one creature, the robustness of these algorithms and the behaviour of several creatures.

2   CA Model for Moving Creatures

The Task: Visit all Empty Cells in Shortest Time. We have studied a simplified problem in order to perceive the open questions and to find some first solutions in the context of optimizing the behavior of creatures. The problem is defined as follows.

Given is a two-dimensional grid of cells which are of type OBSTACLE, EMPTY, or CREATURE. All these cells together define the *artificial world*. The *environment* is the fixed part of the world defined by the obstacles and the empty cells. Border cells and obstacles are both modeled as OBSTACLE. CREATURE is a more complex type with a simple brain and it is able to move around. It has associated an actual moving direction and can look forward one space unit in that direction. The cell in front of the creature is called *front cell* and its location is called *front position*. A creature will move forward to the front position if the front cell is empty and no other creature intends to move to it at the same time.

Initial Configuration. At the beginning the number and the placement of the obstacles are given. Also the creatures are placed in certain start positions with defined directions.

Goal. The goal is to find an optimal and simple local algorithm for the creatures to visit a maximum number of empty cells with a minimum number of time steps for a given set of initial configurations.

The Actions. The creature may perform four different actions: R (turn Right), L (turn Left), Rm (turn Right and move, i.e. move forward and simultaneously turn right), Lm (turn Left and move, i.e. move forward and simultaneously turn left).

The action R/L is performed if the front cell signals *not free* ($m = 0$) because of an obstacle, a creature or a collision conflict. The action Rm/Lm is performed if the front cell signals *free* ($m = 1$).

The Rule. Each cell stores in its state the information (Type, Direction). We call "My" the cell which is acting according to the uniform CA rule.

The sub rule for **My.Type=CREATURE** is
  if (My.FrontCell.Type=EMPTY) and (My.FrontCell.SignalsFree) then
    My.Type=EMPTY // *delete because of moving, case b in fig. 1*
  else
    My.Direction:= TurnRight/Left(My.Direction)
    // *only turn R/L, cases a1, a2 in fig. 1*
The sub rule for **My.Type=EMPTY** is
  n = Number of Creatures in the Neighbourhood with direction to My
  if (n=1) then
    My.Type:=CREATURE // *create, move by copy, case b in fig. 1*
    My.Direction:= TurnRight/Left(My.NeighbourCreature.Direction)

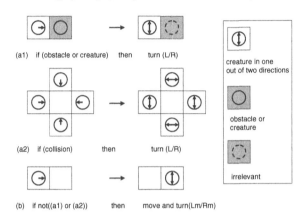

Fig. 1. The rule for the moving creatures

In the case (a1) (fig. 1) a creature can only turn right or left because either
an obstacle or another creature is in front. If more than one creature wants to
visit the same cell (they have a common front cell) we have the conflict/collision
case (a2). We have solved this problem by forbidding all creatures to move on. A
creature will move only if the front cell is empty and no other creature wants to
move to it. Note that the moving of a creature in a CA is a coordinated action
between two cells. The source cell is deleting the creature whilst the destination
cell is copying the creature.

Conflict Resolution in Detail. Different ways of detecting and resolving conflicts are possible. One way is to use a two phase algorithm [7]: In the first phase
the cell to be visited selects one creature and copies it in a hidden place. In the
second phase the creature which was already copied deletes itself and the hidden
creatures becomes a real creature.

In our approach we resolve the conflict in one phase (during the current clock
cycle). Each creature which wants to visit the same empty front cell sends a request
signal and awaits a grant signal. The front cell analyses the requests and generates
only one grant signal which is send back to the selected creature. In our current
implementation no grant signal is send back if more than one creature requests.

Our implementation is an extension of the CA model with von-Neumann
neighborhood. Each cell contains logic (from the hardware view) or an additional function (from the mathematical view) which generates feedback signals
for arbitration (fig. 2). By this technique the neighborhood of the creature (the

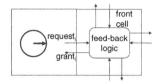

Fig. 2. Asynchronous feed-back logic used for arbitration

current front cell) can be extended to all neighbors of the front cell. Therefore a creature can indirectly be informed that another creature is either two cells ahead or diagonal in front. The arbitration signal is only influencing the next state of the creature but is not further propagated to avoid very long propagation chains and possible asynchronous oscillations.

Behavior of the Creatures. For the reason of simplification we have assumed that all creatures act according to the same algorithm. In our first approach we use a state machine for that purpose. The state machine can also be seen as control logic, intelligence or brain of the creature. The state machine is based on a programmable state table stored in the control memory. To study the basic problems thoroughly we reduced the intelligence to a minimum.

The state table for our problem consists of two tables called *TableFree* and *TableNotFree* (fig. 3a). Input to the state machine is the current control state s and the moving condition m. Output of the state machine is the next control state and the action signal d. The state s is a value between 0 and $n - 1$. The moving condition is either true or false. The action signal is $d = 0$ if the action R (for $m = 0$) or Rm (for $m = 1$) shall be performed. The action signal is $d = 1$ if the action L (for $m = 0$) or Lm (for $m = 1$) shall be performed.

We consider the state machine as a MEALY automaton with inputs (m, s), next state s' and output d. The state table consists of two parts. The part for $m = 0$ is called *TableNotFree* and the part for $m = 1$ is called *TableFree*. *TableNotFree* is selected if the creature cannot move, *TableFree* is selected if the creature is able to move. An algorithm is defined by the contents of the table. We are coding an algorithm by concatenating the contents line by line to a string or a corresponding number, e. g.

> 1L2L0L4R5R3R-3Lm1Rm5Lm0Rm4Lm2Rm   *string representation*
> = 1L2L0L4R5R3R-3L1R5L0R4L2R   *simplified string representation*

The state table can be represented clearer as a state graph (fig. 3b). If the state machine uses n states, we call such an algorithm *n-state algorithm*. Note that the number of states of the state machine considered as a MOORE automaton is the product $n \times \#r$, where $\#r$ is the number of possible directions (4 in our case).

3   Results

The Number of Algorithms. In the general case that the different values of the states, inputs and outputs are not restricted to powers of two, the number

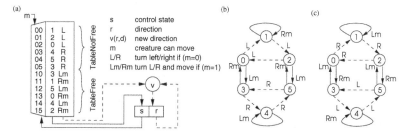

Fig. 3. A state machine (a) models the behavior of a creature. Corresponding 6-state algorithm G6 (b) and the secondary robust algorithm C6 (c).

of M of all algorithms which can be coded by a table oriented state machine is

$$M = (\#s \times \#y)^{(\#s \times \#x)}$$

where $n = \#s$ is the number of states, $\#x$ is the number of different input states and $\#y$ is the number of different output actions. Note that M increases dramatically, especially with $\#s$, which makes it very difficult or even impossible to check the quality of all algorithms in reasonable time.

We are trying to reduce the number of algorithms which shall be checked for their performance. One sub goal is to generate only such algorithms which fulfill certain properties. Therefore we have analyzed the algorithms. The set of M algorithms were divided into the following main classes:

- **P** (without prefix): Each state reachable from initial state 0 is able to return to the initial state.
- **N** (normalized): Equivalent algorithms which only differ in their state encodings are represented in a unique form. Only the representatives are in that class.
- **R** (irreducible): Algorithms in this class are true n-state algorithms which cannot be reduced to algorithms with less than n states.
- **V** (all reachable): All states can be reached from the initial state 0 for each algorithm in this class.

The set of relevant algorithms we are interested in is the intersection $Q = P \cup N \cup V \cup R$. The number of algorithms has been evaluated in software until $n = 5$ and in hardware for $n = 6$, represented as Karnaugh-Veitch diagram (fig. 4). The percentage of relevant algorithms relatively to all algorithms is decreasing from 100 % ($n = 1$) to 1.0 % ($n = 5$) and 0.2 % ($n = 6$).

Finding the Optimal Rules. We have generated and evaluated all relevant n-state algorithms for $n \in \{2, 3, 4, 5, 6\}$ using simulation and statistics. The optimal rules until $n = 5$ could be detected by software using optimized C++. The optimal rules for $n = 6$ could only be found by the use of programmable hardware (FPGA technology).

R

0	0	0	0
12	36	99	49
103100	350580	765912	137916
10898226	45101310	95631945	14257227
0	0	**4**	0
1124	3228	**8124**	1348
10126168	45419688	**98869740**	10115604
1315683540	6797296428	**14762149668**	1420458204
0	0	0	0
1124	3228	8124	1348
232901864	1044652824	2274004020	232658892
156566341260	808878274932	1756695810492	169034526276
0	0	0	0
1260	2148	10653	4751
550770052	1241288268	3349882248	907953124
517736994894	1364111256450	3351700968375	766914799029

N (left), V (right), P (bottom)

(a) 1 state
(b) 3 states
(c) 5 states
(d) 6 states

Fig. 4. The number of algorithms in the different classes

The procedure in general to discover the best algorithms is

for all relevant algorithms do
    for all configurations do
        count the cells which are visited and how many steps are needed
        evaluate the quality

All relevant algorithms were simulated and evaluated for the five initial configurations shown in fig. 5 for one creature. Algorithms were discarded during simulation if the creature showed a bad behavior, especially if the number of visited cells did not increase after a certain number of generations. There are different parts in the whole evaluation process which consume different amounts of time for

- the enumeration of the next algorithm,
- picking out a relevant algorithm (discarding non relevant algorithms),
- the simulation with a set of configurations,
- discarding algorithms which show insufficient performance during simulation,
- selecting the best algorithms (candidates),
- further testing if the candidates do not behave weak under other initial configurations (test for robustness),
- further testing how the candidates perform for more than one creature.

In order to evaluate the creatures' behavior the following questions are of interest. Is the creature able to visit all or almost all cells for a given set of configurations? Is the algorithm *robust*, meaning that it will perform also well

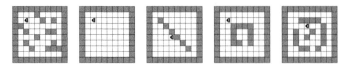

Fig. 5. The initial configurations 1 to 5 from left to right

under different configurations? How fast is the creature? How many cells are visited in a time period (number of generations)? What is the speed-up if p creatures are used instead of one?

The following definitions and metrics are used in order to qualify the performance of an algorithm

- $R :=$ number of empty cells,
- $g :=$ generation (time step),
- $r(g) :=$ number of visited cells in generation g,
- $r_{\max} :=$ the maximum number of cells which can be visited for $g \to \infty$,
- $g_{\max} :=$ the first generation in which $r_{\max}$ is achieved,
- $e := \frac{r_{\max}}{R}$ [%], the *coverage* or *exploration rate*, i. e. $\frac{visited\ cells}{all\ empty\ cells}$,
- $successful := true$, if $e = 100\ \%$,
- $speed := \frac{R}{g_{\max}}$, i. e. only defined for successful algorithms,
- *mean step rate* := $\frac{1}{speed}$, i. e. the mean number of cells visited per generation.

The initial configuration plays an important role and it influences significantly the results. The mean step rate to visit n cells during g generations is greater or equal than one, because at least one more generation is necessary to visit a cell which was not visited before. An optimal algorithm would yield a mean step rate of 1, if each cell is visited once only (remember space filling curves, *HILBERT* curve [8], *PEANO* curve [9]). Such optimal algorithms can only be found for certain configurations and a sufficient intelligent creature. Our simplified creature is not able to move directly forward, therefore a mean step rate of around 2 would already be a good result.

If a particular algorithm showed a bad behavior (no improvement between generation g and generation $g + \Delta$), the time consuming simulation process was abandoned and the algorithm was excluded from the set of possible solutions. Only solutions which exceeded a certain degree of performance were taken into account and they formed the set of *candidates*. The candidates were sent from the simulation hardware platform to a host PC. In a post processing step on a PC the candidates were checked again for their quality using 21 additional initial configurations in order to test for robustness. At least the best algorithms which showed the best behavior on average were selected.

Less than 6-state Algorithms. We have evaluated all 2-state, all 4-state and all 5-state algorithms. The best 2-state algorithm was 0R1L-1R0L. With this algorithm the creature was able to visit 61 % of all empty cells of the 5 initial configuration.

The best 4-state algorithms were A4 = 0R1L2R3R-1L3L1R2L and B4 = 1L3L2R0R-2L0L3R1R. Both were able to visit 97 % of all empty cells of the 5 initial configurations.

Exactly six 5-state algorithms were found which have been successful (100 % coverage) for all 5 initial configurations. Two of those are A5 = 2R1L3R4R0R-1R0L3L2L4L and B5 = 0L4R2L1R3R-1L2R3L4L0R. The fastest algorithm is A5 with a mean step rate of 4.26 (speed = 0.234). Although these results are good, it should be noted that these algorithms may be less performant under different initial configurations.

6-State Algorithms. The best 6-state algorithms were discovered by the aid of configurable logic (FPGA). A first set of 312 948 of relevant algorithms with a minimum level of performance (coverage, speed) was elaborated by the hardware and send to the host PC for further processing. By the application of further tests a second set of 64 061 algorithms was generated, which belong to the class of relevant algorithms Q. This set was used for further simulations and evaluation.

In order to sort out the best algorithms, a robustness test with 21 additional initial configuration was performed in software. They differ from the 5 primary configurations in their size, distribution of obstacles and the start position/direction of the creature. For the whole set of 26 initial configurations the following 10 best algorithms with respect to (1.) success, (2.) coverage and (3.) speed were discovered:

1. G6: 1L2L0L4R5R3R-3L1R5L0R4L2R   6. E6: 1R2L0R4L5L3L-3R4R5R0L1L2R
2. B6: 1R2R0R4L5L3L-3R1L5R0L4R2L   7. F6: 1R2L0L4R5R3R-3L4L5L0R1L2R
3. C6: 1R2R0R4L5L3L-3R4R2L0L1L5R   8. H6: 1L2L3R4L2R0L-2L4L0R3L5L4R
4. A6: 0R2R3R4L5L1L-1R5R4R0L2L3L   9. I6: 1L2L3L4L2R0L-2L4L0R3R5L4R
5. D6: 1R2R3R1L5L1L-1R0L2L4R3L1L   10. J6: 1R2R3R0R4L5L-4R5R3L2L0L1L

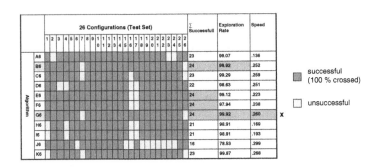

Fig. 6. Evaluation

The best algorithm G6 (fig. 3) can visit 99.9197 % of all empty cells of all the 26 test configurations. The mean speed for the successful visited configurations is 0.26. A surprise was that G6 cannot visit two cells of configuration 7. J6 visits only 78.529 % of all the 26 test configurations but J6 is the fastest for the successful configurations.

The most robust algorithm G6 (fig. 3) shows a noticeable symmetry. A creature turns left (L), if it starts in state 0 and cannot move (dotted transition). If the creature can move after 2 or 3 L turns it changes into the lower half of the automaton with the action Lm. In the lower half of the automaton the actions are inverted compared to the upper half. The algorithm B6 differs from G6 only by exchanging R and L. C6 (fig. 3) differs from G6 by inverting the actions and inverting the directions of the state transitions.

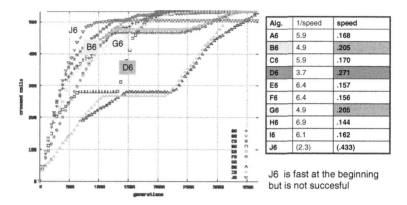

Alg.	1/speed	speed
A6	5.9	.168
B6	4.9	.205
C6	5.9	.170
D6	3.7	.271
E6	6.4	.157
F6	6.4	.156
G6	4.9	.205
H6	6.9	.144
I6	6.1	.162
J6	(2.3)	(.433)

J6 is fast at the beginning
but is not succesful

Fig. 7. Visited cells vs. number of generations

The speed of an algorithm depends not only on the algorithm itself but also on the actual initial configuration. For one of the initial configurations (empty environment of size 40×16 with no obstacles, start position of the creature in the middle, direction to the right) the speed of the 10 candidates are shown in fig. 7. It can be observed that the algorithm D6 is the fastest for that configuration, followed by B6 and D6. J6 is slightly faster than C6 between generation 500 and 1200, but is at least not able to visit all empty cells.

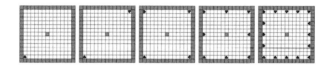

Fig. 8. Initial configurations used to evaluate the behavior of several creatures

Several Creatures. The 6-state algorithms which were found for one creature were tested for their performance for 2, 4, 8, 16 creatures. The initial configurations are shown in fig. 8.

The results are shown in the tables of fig. 9. If the number of creatures is doubled the number of needed generations g_{max} can be less than the half (1043 $\rightarrow$ 286), as can be seen for algorithm D6. This means that a group of n creatures may do better than n times under certain circumstances (effect of synergy). Another

Number of generations g_{max}						Speed per creature				
Algo-	Number of creatures					Algo-	Number of creatures			
rithm	1	2	4	8	16	rithm	1	2	4	8	16
A6	not succ.	272	79	80	39	A6		0.31	**0.53**	0.26	0.27
B6	337	311	143	138	38	B6	0.50	0.27	0.29	0.15	0.28
D6	**1043**	**296**	176	136	**31**	D6	0.16	0.28	0.24	0.15	0.34
J6	322	280	140	102	34	J6	**0.52**	0.30	0.30	0.21	0.31

Fig. 9. Generations and Speed for a different number of creatures

effect can be noticed if the speed per creature is considered: Four creatures with algorithm A6 work relatively faster than one creature with algorithm J6 $(0.53 \rightarrow 0.52)$. In other words: Several creatures may do the job more efficiently (with less work units $= g_{\max} \times$ creatures) than one creature.

4   Conclusion

The creature's exploration problem was modelled as a cellular automaton (CA) because CAs are massively parallel and can be perfectly supported by hardware. The brain of the creature was modelled using a state table driven state machine. The number of n-state algorithms is exploding with the number of states, inputs, and outputs. The evaluation of a single algorithm needs a check for relevance, simulation with a number of configurations, robustness tests, and statistics. Therefore the whole process is very time consuming. We found and evaluated the best 6-state algorithms for one creature and checked them for robustness. These algorithms were also applied to a configuration with up to 16 creatures. Several creatures can perform the given task more efficiently in some cases, meaning that the work (generations $\times$ creatures) can be minimized using more than one creature.

References

1. Mesot, B., Sanchez, E., Pena, C.A., Perez-Uribe, A.: SOS++: Finding Smart Behaviors Using Learning and Evolution. In Standish, Abbass, Bedau, eds.: Artificial Life VIII, MIT Press (2002) 264ff.
2. Koza, J.R.: Genetic Programming: On the Programming of Computers by Means of Natural Selection. MIT Pres (1992) ISBN 0-262-11170-5.
3. Halbach, M., Heenes, W., Hoffmann, R., Tisje, J.: Optimizing the Behavior of a Moving Creature in Software and in Hardware. In: Sixth International conference on Cellular Automata for Research and Industry (ACRI 2004). Number 3305 in LNCS (2004) 841 – 850
4. Halbach, M., Hoffmann, R.: Optimal Behavior of a Moving Creature in the Cellular Automata Model. In Malyshkin, V., ed.: Parallel Computing Technologies. Number 3606 in LNCS, Krasnoyarsk, Springer (2005) 129 – 140 ISBN 3-540-28126-6.
5. Halbach, M., Heenes, W., Hoffmann, R.: Implementation of the Massively Parallel Model GCA. In: Parallel Computing in Electrical Engineering (PARELEC), Parallel System Architectures. (2004)
6. Halbach, M., Hoffmann, R.: Implementing Cellular Automata in FPGA Logic. In: International Parallel & Distributed Processing Symposium (IPDPS), Workshop on Massively Parallel Processing (WMPP), IEEE Computer Society (2004)
7. Hochberger, C.: CDL – Eine Sprache für die Zellularverarbeitung auf verschiedenen Zielplattformen. PhD thesis, TU Darmstadt (1998) Darmstädter Dissertation D17.
8. Hilbert, D.: Ueber die stetige Abbildung einer Linie auf ein Flachenstück. In: Mathematische Annalen. Volume 38., Springer (1891) 459 – 460
9. Peano, G.: Sur une courbe, qui remplit une aire plane. In: Mathematische Annalen. Volume 36., Springer (1890) 157 – 160

10. Halbach, M., Hoffmann, R.: Minimising the Hardware Resources for a Cellular Automaton with Moving Creatures. In: PARS Newsletter. (2006)
11. Hoffmann, R., Ulmann, B., Völkmann, K.P., Waldschmidt, S.: A Stream Processor Architecture Based on the Configurable CEPRA-S. In: Field-programmable Logic: The Roadmap to Reconfigurable Systems (FPL 2000). Number 1896 in LNCS, Villach, Austria, Springer Verlag (2000)
12. Waldschmidt, S., Hochberger, C.: FPGA synthesis for cellular processing. In: IEEE/ACM International Workshop on Logic Synthesis. (1995) 9–55 – 9–63

Evolutionary Learning in Agent-Based Combat Simulation

Tomonari Honda, Hiroshi Sato, and Akira Namatame

Dept of Computer Science, National Defense Academy,
Yokosuka, 239-8686, Japan
{g44038, hsato, nama}@nda.ac.jp

Abstract. In this paper, we consider one of old-age problems about trade-off relation between homogeneity and diversity. We investigate combat based on agent-based simulation, not conventional mathematical model based on attrition. By introducing synthetic approach and adapting evolutionary learning to action rules that are expressed by a combination of parameters in combat simulation, we focus on the interaction between sets of action rules. For searching how many sets of action rules does work well, we change the number of sets of action rules. And we make statistical analysis and show that there is good intermediate stage between high homogeneity and high diversity in group.

1 Introduction

It is quite often the case that an organization which has proper and reliable people does not work at all. It is also quite normal that a professional sports team made from first-class players does not achieve the excellent results.

In the society, neither the group that consist only of leaders nor the group that consist only of followers perform well. Leaders and followers must coexist in one group. When a group consists of same type of people, homogeneity of the group will be high and diversity will be low. On the contrary, when a group consists of totally different people, diversity is high and homogeneity is low. Assume that a scale of a group to be constant, homogeneity and diversity of a group are trade-off relation.

Extremely high homogeneity or extremely high diversity is not preferable for a group. The middle state, in which character of people is basically similar and yet somehow different, is preferable. Trade-off between homogeneity and diversity is one of the age-old problems in social science.

Making social group (e.g. governments or company and so on) and cooperating with each other, we can accomplish what we cannot achieve by only one power.

In this study, we treat military forces, which are the most typical yet the simplest social groups. Analyzing a mathematical model based on Lanchester equation is a conventional way of the military study. Lanchester equation describes a process of attrition, however it can treat only simple force-on-force attrition.

In recent years, synthetic approach using agent-based simulation starts to gaining attention. Flexibility of the model gives an advantage on the synthetic approach. [2,3]

S. El Yacoubi, B. Chopard, and S. Bandini (Eds.): ACRI 2006, LNCS 4173, pp. 582–587, 2006.
© Springer-Verlag Berlin Heidelberg 2006

By synthetic approach, we show that the total gain of a group is maximum at the stage that homogeneity and diversity are middle.

This paper is organized as follows. Next section reviews combat simulation. EINSTein, the subject of our study, is presented in section 3. In section 4, the scenario is introduced. We explain EINSTein GA in section 5. Section 6 provides simulation result and compares performance. Section 7 concludes.

2 Modelling Combat Using the Statistics of Scaling Systems

Combat simulations are often used for analysis and training. However, traditional linear models of combat such as Lanchester equations treat attrition as a continuous function of time. However, recent thinking on the nature of warfare has it that combat is an inherently nonlinear situation. Attrition is during duels followed by maneuver in space and time. Tactics will try to concentrate duels for all individuals. If the statistical moments of the data scale, it can be expected that the variance relative to the size of the force will increase as the size of the force decreases. The dependence of the statistical variance on the size of the force results from using an attrition rate which is not continuous. The interesting question is then, what happens to the statistics if the opposing forces are allowed to position themselves in a dynamically evolving and non-linear way?

Experience in a wide range of fields for which complex adaptive systems exist has shown that increasing the detail of the model does not necessarily improve its ability to reproduce reality, but often simply reflects the emphasis placed on various aspects by the designer. This complexity makes modeling of a combat situation difficult, particularly because the model designer must assume knowledge of how the participants will behave in a given situation. Thus there is a real danger that the model will simply reproduce the preconceived ideas of the modeler.

With the growing acceptance of agent-based models as a method for simulating combat, which are designed to incorporate behavior which adapts to the situation, it may be that a clearer link between fractal statistics and the non-linear dynamics of combat can be established. Combat must generally be considered to be a complex adaptive system that evolves in an unpredictable way. Complex networks in many fields have been shown to generate discontinuous functions to describe various quantities as functions of space and time, which often show scaling similarities. The modern combat simulation be modeled with simplified agent-based models combined with complex networks, in which an agent's behavior is determined by some set of rules, which are also constrained by the networks of friends and enemies.

3 The Outline of EINSTein Combat Simulation

As main subject of this study, we use EINSTein developed by the Center for Naval Analyses. [1]

EINSTein is a multi-agent artificial war simulation consisting of 2 dimensional lattice-shaped battlefield and agents of two groups, which are red force and blue force, fighting in the battlefield. There are a red flag and a blue flag in a battlefield.

Agents act based on local information that they obtained from their own sensor. Agents use the flags' position as landmark of action. Parameters to govern an action of agents are classified into basic capability, personality and meta-rules.

Basic capability contains states, fire range r_F, firepower, sensor range r_S, combat threshold range r_T, movement range r_M, defense, maximum simultaneous targets number and so on. Through simulation, the constraint condition of range is $r_F \leq r_T \leq r_S$. Depending on the attacked degree, agents takes one of three states, alive, injured or killed.

Agent personality is also modeled using by 6-componet weight vector $\vec{w}$.

$$\vec{w} = (w_{AF}, w_{IF}, w_{AE}, w_{IE}, w_{FF}, w_{EF}) \quad st. -1 \leq w_X \leq 1, \sum |w_X| = 1 \tag{2.1}$$

Each weight shows how much agents are attracted or repulsed by other friendly and enemy agents or flags.

Agents decide where to move by calculating minimum value of penalty function given by:

$$z(B_{xy}) = \frac{1}{\sqrt{2}r_s} \left[\frac{w_{AF}}{N_{AF}} \sum_{i \in AF}^{N_{AF}} D_{i,B_{xy}} + \frac{w_{AE}}{N_{AE}} \sum_{j \in AE}^{N_{AE}} D_{j,B_{xy}} + \frac{w_{IF}}{N_{IF}} \sum_{i \in IF}^{N_{IF}} D_{i,B_{xy}} + \frac{w_{IE}}{N_{IE}} \sum_{j \in IE}^{N_{IE}} D_{j,B_{xy}} \right]$$
$$+ w_{FF} \frac{D_{FF,B_{xy}}^{new}}{D_{FF,B_{xy}}^{old}} + w_{EF} \frac{D_{EF,B_{xy}}^{new}}{D_{EF,B_{xy}}^{old}} \tag{2.2}$$

Where B_{xy} is the (x, y) coordinate of battlefield B; AF, AE, IF and IE represent the sets of alive friends, alive enemies, injured friends and injured enemies within the agent's sensor range r_s; N_X is the total number of elements of type X within the agent's sensor range; $D_{A,B}$ is the distance between elements A and B; FF and EF denote the friendly and enemy flags; and $D_{x,y}^{new}$ and $D_{x,y}^{old}$ represent new and current distance of x and y.

Meta-rule represents condition modifier. If a certain condition was satisfied, then penalty function is changed over partly. Take "Advance", for an example, if enough friendly agents do not exist nearby, then do not advance to the enemy flag.

4 Simulation

The baseline scenario is that red force breaks through a defence line of blue force and seizes landmark area around the flag at top right corner. Figure 1 shows appearance of the scenario. Size of a battlefield is (50, 50).

Blue force:

- Make defence line at distance 25 from blue flag.
- Have single shot hit probability 10 times superior to red.
  ($k_B = 0.05$, $k_R = 0.005$)
- Have equal or shorter sensor range to red ($r_S = 3$) and have shorter fire range ($r_F = 2$).
- Escape from red, if blue agent senses disadvantage.
- Consist of a single squad. (All members has same action rule.)

Red force:

- Have mission to seize top right-hand corner within 50 time step.
- Initial 60 strong, equal to blue. Consist of single squad or multi squads.

For a common point, blue and a red agent can move eight neighbourhoods by one step. Through a study blue parameters are fixed, and red parameters are changed to fit the mission except sensor and fire range and single shot hit probability. We use genetic algorism for change of parameters.

Fig. 1. Screenshot of the scenario The landmark area is around the flag at top right corner

5   Evolutionary Learning in Combat Simulation

Genetic algorism (GA) is one of probabilistic optimal value searchings based on natural selection. A chromosome which has a tendency to lead success of survival is stayed in, and a chromosome of other properties to bring unsuccessful disappears. To apply this property to real problems, candidates of problem solution are expressed with some rows of symbol and considered to be chromosome. To search for the chromosome that degree of fitness is high, operations of selection / crossover / mutation with chromosome are repeated. [5]

In EINSTein, sets of parameters are regarded as chromosome and adapt GA. Degree of fitness is replaced with mission fitness. Mission in this scenario is "maximize number of red agents $(=R_t(D))$ within distance D of blue flag", so mission fitness function in this scenario is given by:

$$f = \frac{1}{T - t_{\min}} \sum_{t=t_{\min}}^{T} \left(\frac{R_t(D)}{R_{\max}} \right)^n \qquad (5.1)$$

Where $t_{\min}$ is earliest possible time that red agents could move to within distance D of blue flag, $R_{\max}$ is maximum possible value, and T is termination time for the run. The mission fitness is given by time average.

In our study, we use multiple-squad personality search mode. GA searches over set of personality parameters. And the number of squads and the size of each squad remain fixed throughout GA. Note that squad called in EINSTein is a group of agents who have same set of personality parameters, and is not combatant group acting together. GA in EINSTein is summarized as follows. By learning evolutionarily, set of parameters (set of action rules) which make mission fitness high could be found.

6 Effect of Evolutionary Learning

To compare achievement of the mission in the scenario, we change the squad numbers of red force from 1 to 6, and carry out GA for each case. The number of agents of each squad is 60 / (number of squad). At case of 6 squads, for instance, red force has six 10-strong squads and 10 agents in one squad share same action rule. Parameter n in mission fitness function f is 2.GA is carried out for 500 generations. 100 populations per 1 generation, 10 initial conditions per 1 population. GA solutions in each case are saturated around 300 generations.

To compare performance of GA solutions in each case, plot time steps in horizontal axis and the number of agents which arrived at landmark area in vertical axis. As red line in time-series plot moves to left-top, mission fitness could become higher.

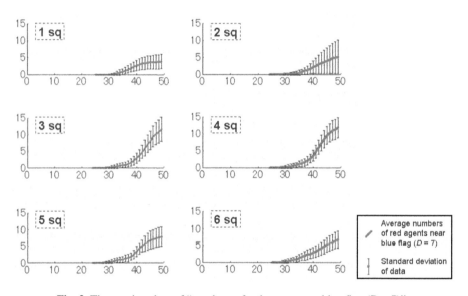

Fig. 2. Time-series plots of "numbers of red agents near blue flag (D = 7)"

Figure 2 shows performance of GA solutions in each case, "sq" means squad.

Characteristic common point of Figure 2 is that red agents begin to arrive from time step 25, and number of average arrived agents is around 2 or 3 to time step 40. On the contrary, characteristic different point of Figure 2 is that 3 or 4 squads case is most success, over 10 red agents can arrive on average, and average number is less than 10 in other cases.

By this characteristic, too much or too little squad number does not make good result. Just good squads number can get good performance. Remember that squad in this study means sharing same action rule, the case that some action rules are interlaced make strong positive interaction than the case all member have the same action rule. On the contrary, tendency that ties of interaction weaken comes out with many action rules.

To make specific mention of action rule, set of parameters of each squad of GA solution are common to about a point to move towards blue flag basically, but details of if then rule are slightly different.

7   Conclusion and Future Works

In this study, we treat trade-off between homogeneity and diversity by synthetic approach using agent-based combat simulation and bear out that the middle stage of homogeneity and diversity make good result for social group.

Expressing metaphorically, when red forces are compared to one boss and several squads are compared to several subordinate, there is just good number of subordinate to carry out some task.

In this study, we treat single purpose military unit. In future works, we will treat multi purpose military unit. In other words, for organizing military force to achieve multi purposes at the same time, our concern is which one is better, gathering up military unit of the specialist group adapted each single purpose, or preparing single military unit achieving multiple purpose, or the combination that is neither.

References

1. Andrew Ilachinski. Artificial War: Multiagent-Based Simulation of combat, World Science, 2004
2. Ang Yang, Hussein A, Abbass, Ruhul Sacker, Michael Barlow. Network Centric Multi-Agent Systems: A Novel Architecture, TR-ALAR-200504004, 2005
3. Lauren, M. K. Firepower Concentration in Cellular Automata Models –An Alternative to the Lanchester Approach, DOTSE Report 172, NR 1350. Defence Operational Technology Support Establishment, New Zealand, 2000
4. Lauren, M.K. Fractal Methods Applied to Describe Cellular Automaton Combat Models, Fractal, Vol.9, No.2, 2002
5. Lawrence Davis. Handbook Of Genetic Algorithms, International Thomson Computer Press, 1991
6. Mandelbrot, B. B. Fractals and Scaling in Finance. Springer-Verlag, New York, 1997

Cellular Automata Based Role-Delegation in RBAC*

Jun-Cheol Jeon and Kee-Young Yoo**

Department of Computer Engineering, Kyungpook National University,
Daegu, 702-701 Korea
jcjeon33@infosec.knu.ac.kr,
yook@knu.ac.kr

Abstract. In this paper, we present Cellular Automata (CA) based conflict-resolution in Role-based Access Control (RBAC). In RBAC, delegation of role is necessary for scalability of general computing environments. However, this practical principle can lead to conflicts at compile time and run time. Thus we propose a policy for Separation of Duty (SoD), and demonstrate role-delegation without any conflicts. Our delegation scheme based on a special class of CA such as Multiple-Attractor CA (MACA) can be efficiently used for granting strategy in complex automatic system within RBAC.

Keywords: Multiple-Attractor Cellular Automata, Role-based Access Control, Separation of Duty, Role-Delegation.

1 Introduction

Cellular automata (CA), as introduced by John Von Neumann [1], have been accepted as a good computational model for the simulation of complex physical systems, and have been used in evolutionary computations for over a decade. They can readily simulate complex growth patterns and have been used in various applications, such as parallel processing computations and number theory [2]. Various studies have presented the characteristics of CA based on a group and non-group CA [3, 4]. While in the state-transition graph of a group CA all states belong to some disjoint set of cycles, non-group CA are characterized by the presence of some non-reachable states in the state- transition graph.

Role-based access control (RBAC) emerged rapidly in the 1990s as a proven technology for managing and enforcing security in large-scale enterprise-wide systems. Its basic notion is that permissions are associated with roles, and users are assigned to appropriate roles. This greatly simplifies security management. Two significant areas of extensions to the RBAC96 model have been proposed; one

---

* This research was supported by the MIC (Ministry of Information and Communication), Korea, under the ITRC (Information Technology Research Center) support program supervised by the IITA (Institute of Information Technology Assessment). This work was also partially supported by the Brain Korea 21 Project in 2006.
** Corresponding author.

S. El Yacoubi, B. Chopard, and S. Bandini (Eds.): ACRI 2006, LNCS 4173, pp. 588–594, 2006.

concentrates on the specification of constraints [5, 6], the other describes a framework for role-based delegation [7, 8]. However, these two extensions create a new range of problems within a role-based access control model. The main concern is that specified separation of duty (SoD) can conflict with a model allowing for the delegation of authority through role transfer.

Thus, the current study proposes two kinds of exclusion clarified by role, i.e. exclusion specified by role sets and role pair, and divides the exclusion into two types, positive and negative. How to detect conflict in role delegations is demonstrated based on linear non-group CA such as multiple-attractor CA (MACA). We propose two algorithms for setup and activation and show how CA computation is used for the proposed schemes.

2   Characterization of RBAC and CA

This section covers the basic concept and background of RBAC and CA.

2.1   Role-Based Access Control

A significant body of research on RBAC models and experimental implementations has developed [9]. RBAC is a proven alternative to traditional discretionary and mandatory access controls; it ensures that only authorized users are given access to certain data or resources. It also supports three well-known security principles: information hiding, least-privilege, and SoD.

Under the core RBAC model, users are assigned to roles based on their competencies, authority, and responsibilities. User assignments can be easily revoked, and new assignments established as job assignments dictate. With RBAC, users are not granted permissions to perform operations on an individual basis; instead, permissions are assigned to their roles. System administrators can update roles without updating the permissions for every user on individual basis [9].

A role is a semantic construct forming the basis of access control policy. With RBAC, system administrators can create roles, grant permissions to those roles, and then assign users to the roles on the basis of their specific job responsibilities and policy. In particular, role-permission relationships can be predefined, making it simple to assign users to the predefined roles. Without RBAC, it is difficult to determine what permissions have been authorized for which users.

Users create sessions during which they may activate a subset of roles to which they belong. Each session can be assigned to many roles, but it maps only one user. The concept of a session corresponds to the traditional notion of subject in the access control literature. Constraints are an effective mechanism to establish higher-level organizational policy. They can apply to any relation and function in an RBAC model. When applied, constraints are predicates that return a value of acceptable or not acceptable.

In short, a delegation from one entity to another either gives the later some rights or obligation. A delegation of right in security systems causes the delegatee to gain some additional access rights, whereas a delegation of responsibility causes the delegatee to gain some new responsibility. Both theses delegations are based on 'role'. Thus we focus on the mapping users and roles except permission onto a CA at the first stage.

2.2 Cellular Automata

A CA is a collection of simple cells arranged in a regular fashion. CAs can be characterized based on four properties: cellular geometry, neighborhood specifications,
number of states per cell, and the rule to compute to a successor state. The next state
of a CA depends on the current state and rules [10]. Only 2-state and 3-neighborhood
CAs are considered in this paper. Each mapping is called a 'rule' of the CA.

The next state transition for the ith cell can be represented as a function of the present states of the ith, $(i+1)$th, and $(i-1)$th cells for a 3-neighborhood CA: $Q_i(t+1) =$
$f(Q_{i-1}(t), Q_i(t), Q_{i+1}(t))$, where '$f$' represents the combinational logic function as a CA
rule implemented by a combinational logic circuit (CL), and $Q(t+1)$ denotes the next
state for cell $Q(t)$.

Using the logic function defined in the above, it is also represented by the characteristic polynomial $p(x)$ by determinant of characteristic matrix T so that the state at
the next instant can be represented by $Q_i(t+1) = T \cdot Q_i(t)$. The state- transition diagram
of a four-cell linear CA is shown in Fig. 1. It has attractors 0000, 0001, 1000 and
1001, and its characteristic polynomial is $p(x) = x^2(x^2 + 1)$. The state-transition diagram of such a CA consists of multiple (single-cycle) attractors and trees rooted on
such attractors.

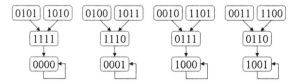

Fig. 1. State- Transition Diagram of a Four-Cell Linear Null Boundary CA with Rule <102,
102, 60, 60>

The following Theorem 1 indicates that there are enough available MACAs.

Theorem 1 [11]. For any two integer n and m ($0 \le m \le n$) there exists an n-cell MACA
with 2^m attractors.

3 MACA Based Role-Delegation

SoD is dividing right for critical operations so that no user acting alone can compromise the security of the data processing system. Existing systems typically rely on
mutual exclusion of roles to enforce SoD polices and the policy is usually interpreted
using mutual exclusion rules between roles [9]. However, there still remain difficult
problems related to how strictly the policy is interpreted and how this SoD policy
should be implemented in distributed computing environment.

To remedy the problems, we classify the policy of SoD rule and present a detailed explanation of the policy of SoD rules in section 3.1. We also demonstrate an efficient role-delegation algorithm without any conflicts in section 3.2.

3.1 Policy of SoD Rules

We classify two kinds of mutual exclusion clarified by role, i.e. a role set based exclusion and role pair based exclusion. Each kind is divided into two types, positive and negative.

Definition 1. (Role-set (pair) based mutual exclusion: SE (PE)) Positive type, PSE (PPE) is clarified based on mutually exclusive role-set (pair) while negative type, NSE (NPE) is clarified based on mutually non-exclusive role set (pair).

It is possible to declare a set of roles that are mutually exclusive or not. This feature is particularly desirable if the application requires elaborate SoD requirements. Meanwhile, role-pair based mutual exclusion is a more complex feature since the number of pairs is $n(n-1)/2$ for n roles.

Example 1. Assume that there are four roles, R_1 through R_4, and a mutual exclusion relationship exists as followings; PSE: $R_1(R_2, R_3)$, $R_2(R_1, R_3)$, $R_3(R_1, R_2, R_4)$, $R_4(R_1, R_3)$, NSE: $R_1(R_4)$, $R_2(R_4)$, $R_3(\phi)$, $R_4(R_2)$, PPE: (R_1, R_2), (R_1, R_3), (R_2, R_3), (R_3, R_4) and NPE: (R_1, R_4), (R_2, R_4).

In PSE and NSE, the roles in parentheses represent exclusive sets or non-exclusive sets, respectively, e.g. a user with R_2 cannot have R_3 at the same time, but R_4. In PPE and NPE, all roles are tied by pair, and each pair shows that two roles are mutually exclusive or not. As shown in the above example, PSE and NSE always have the same number of sets as the number of roles. However, if the number of mutually exclusive roles is more than half of them, NSE can reduce the initialization time but both cases have a similar searching time for finding exclusion. It is better to use NPE when the number of mutually exclusive roles is more than $n(n-1)/4$. This can minimize both the initialization time and searching time.

3.2 Role Delegation

We consider two occasions, setup and activation, for the whole procedure. Setup is the point of time when mutually exclusive roles are set to the system, and activation is the point of time when role delegations occur among users. We demonstrate how to detect conflicts corresponding to PSE, NSE, PPE, and NPE based on CA mechanism. As shown in Fig. 1, the graph consists of a set of distinct components; each component is an inverted tree containing an equal number of states. The CA states and attractors can be viewed as the addresses connecting user nodes and roles, respectively.

We assume that there are four roles for distribution such as the above example in section 3.1. We could assign one role to each of the four users, but is it essential to have four, or could fewer users suffice? Using graph theory, there is an easy way to determine this number. The chromatic number, $\chi(G)$, of a graph is the minimum number of colors that are required to color vertices so that no two adjacent vertices are the same color [9].

Table 1. Mutual exclusion relationships among states in MACA according to Example 1

Types	0000	0001	1000	1001
PSE	0001, 1000	0000, 1000	0000, 0001, 1001	0001, 1000
NSE	1001	1001	-	0001
PPE	(0000, 0001), (0000, 1000), (0001, 1000), (1000, 1001)			
NPE	(0000, 1001), (0001, 1001)			

For the sake of comprehension, we explain our procedures using Example 1. Only three colors are needed to ensure that no edge is connected to one vertex of the same color; therefore, SoD requirements can be maintained by assigning roles R_1 through R_4 to three different users, corresponding to the three colors. In initialization procedure, R_1 through R_3 should be assigned to the different users while R_4 can be assigned to U_1 or U_2, since they have only the roles, R_1 or R_2 that are not mutually exclusive with R_4. However, R_3 cannot be assigned to U_2 since the two roles, R_2 and R_3, are mutually exclusive. The setup procedure illustrates the assignment of role and user onto MACA as following.

(1) Determines the minimum number of users by chromatic number, $\chi(G)$.
(2) Constructs an n-cell MACA with 2^m attractors where $n \geq \chi(G)$ and $2^m \geq$ the number of roles.
(3) Assigns each role and user to each attractor and leaf state, respectively.
(4) The remained roles are assigned to the users who belong to roles which are not mutual exclusive with the remained roles according to the given SoD constraints.

After the setup procedure, Current roles and users are assigned to role-tree without any conflicts. If the CA is loaded with a particular address and allowed to run for a number of cycles equal to the depth of such trees, it will evolve through a number of states before reaching the root of the corresponding tree. Thereafter, the evolved state always reaches the attractor autonomously.

Hence, by autonomous evolution from the CA state of user node, we can obtain the role corresponding to a user. In the activation procedure, there are two possible approaches for delegation. One is that a user wants to delegate a role to a non-specific user; the other is that a user wants to delegate a role to a particular user.

In the former case, our scheme firstly finds a role that is a non-exclusive relationship with the role that a user wants to delegate, and checks if the user assigned the role is assigned a role which is mutually exclusive relationship with the previous role. If not, the user is assigned to the role-tree; otherwise, it is regarded as conflict and a new user is generated and assigned to the role-tree. The next procedure illustrates a role delegation when a user, U_i wants to delegate a role, R_j,

(1) Finds attractors (roles) that are in a non-mutual exclusion relationship with R_j according to NSE or NPE.
(2) Checks if the users assigned the roles found in (1) have been assigned to a role which is mutually exclusive with R_j according to PSE or PPE.
(3) Assigns the user to the R_j-tree; otherwise, conflict occurs, and optionally a new user, U_k, can be created and assigned to the R_j-tree.

In the above example, we assume that U_2 wants to delegate R_2 to another user. We can find that R_4 (1001) is in a non-mutual exclusion relationship with R_2 (0001) according to Table. 1, but U_1 assigned R_4 has already been assigned to R_1 which is in a mutual exclusion relationship with R_2. Hence, a new user, U_4, can be created and assigned to R_2.

In the latter case, if a user wants to delegate a role to a particular user, then we can simply obtain the result by checking the relationship of two roles associated with two users. In this case, we can simply obtain the result by checking whether two roles are mutually exclusive or not. For example, we assume that U_2 wants to delegate R_2 to U_3. We can find that R_2 (0001) is in a mutual exclusion relationship with R_3 (1000) according to Table. 1 so that conflict occurs. However, if U_1 wants to delegate R_4 to U_2 then we can get the result with R_4-tree assigning U_2.

Through the whole proposed algorithms, we could simply find conflict by checking relationships between attractors based on evolution of user nodes. A user node should evolve for a number of cycles equal to the depth of trees then the evolved state always reaches the attractor. After the whole procedures, the previous user node can be deleted from the graph according to the administration policy.

4   Analysis and Discussion

For elaborate granting rights, we have realized SoD requirements by exclusion of role. In this case, assignment of roles in a SoD environment can become complex. To accomplish this task safely and automatically, a system must first ensure that no single user has all roles needed to accomplish a critical task and then ensure that roles are assigned to individuals in such a way that no individual will have all of these roles through some combination of roles. Users also must be assigned to roles in such a way that no user can violate SoD rules through a combination of roles. The following items show the superiority of our policy and role-delegation mechanism.

- *Positive and negative type on role-set and role-pair*: We propose two types of policy for SoD requirements according to the number of mutually exclusive relationships. It is a practical alternative plan if the system does not provide enough capability.
- *Role-delegation based on MACA*: We find each role by evolution from each user node so that conflicts among users and roles can be simply found by proposed scheme. Thus, setup and activation can be achieved without any conflicts.
- *Algorithm classification*: The setup algorithm should be performed at the first stage, and the activation algorithm can be divided into two types. One is that a user wants to delegate his/her role to whoever he/she is, and the other is that a user needs to delegate his/her role to a particular user. Both cases occur frequently in a distributed computing environment so that operating two procedures separately offers much better system performance and capacity.

5   Conclusion

Since multiple subjects can grant authorizations and the problem of cascading and cyclic authorization may arise, administration in RBAC is more difficult to control. Thus, we have proposed an efficient delegation mechanism based on the policies of an SoD requirement and MACA computation. The proposed policy for SoD requirement and delegation scheme can block that user acting alone can compromise the security of the data processing system, and it also minimizes frequent granting operations without any conflicts. Thus, we expect that our mechanism can be effectively used for granting strategy in complex automatic system within RBAC.

References

1. J. Von Neumann: The theory of self-reproducing automata, University of Illinois Press, Urbana and London (1966)
2. J.C. Jeon and K. Y. Yoo: Design of Montgomery Multiplication Architecture based on Programmable Cellular Automata. Computational intelligence 20 (2004) 495-502
3. M. Seredynski, K. Pienkosz, and P. Bouvry: Reversible Cellular Automata Based Encryption. Lecture Notes in Computer Science, Vol. 3222. Springer-Verlag, Berlin Heidelberg New York (2004) 411-418
4. S. Das, B. K. Sikdar, and P. Pal Chaudhuri: Charaterization of Reachable/Nonreachable Cellular Automata States. Lecture Notes in Computer Science, Springer-Verlag, Berlin Heidelberg New York 3305 (2004) 813-822
5. F.Chen and R.Sandhu: Constraints for RBAC" 1st ACM Workshop on Role-Based Access Control, Gaithersburg, MD (1995) 39-46
6. G.Ahn: RCL 2000, ph.d dissertation, George Mason University (2000)
7. E. Barka and R. Sandhu: Framework for Role-Based Delegation Models. 16th Annual Computer Security Applications Conference, New Orleans, Louisiana (2000)
8. Z. Longhua, G. Ahn, and Chu. B.: A Rule-based Framework for Role-Based Delegation. ACM SACMAT, Chantilly, VA, USA (2001)
9. David Ferraiolo, Richard Kuhu, Ramaswamy Chandramouli: Role-Based Access Control, Artech house (2003)
10. O. Lafe, Cellular Automata Transforms: Theory and Applications in Multimedia Compression, Encryption, and Modeling, Kluwer Academic Publishers (2000)
11. P. P. Chaudhuri, D. R. Chowdhury, S. nandi, and S. Chattopadhyay: Additive Cellular Automata Theory and Applications Vol. 1, IEEE Computer Society Press (1997)

Modeling Robot Path Planning with CD++

Gabriel Wainer

Department of Systems and Computer Engineering. Carleton University.
1125 Colonel By Dr. Ottawa, Ontario, Canada
gwainer@sce.carleton.ca

Abstract. Robotic systems are usually built as independent agents that collaborate to accomplish a specific task. Analysis of robot path planning consists of route planning and path generation. We will show how to apply the Cell-DEVS formalism and the CD++ toolkit for these tasks. We present a Cell-DEVS model for route planning, which, based on the obstacles, finds different paths available and creates a Voronoi diagram. Then, we show route planning using the Voronoi diagram to determines an optimal path free of collision. Finally, we introduce a Cell-DEVS model that can be applied to the routing of self-reconfigurable robots.

1 Introduction

The analysis of robot path planning in general include a multirobot system in cooperative environments (all mobile agents interact, trying to achieve a common goal). In most cases, the environment under study consists of a physical environment, a number of robots, objects in the environment, a set of predefined tasks, a task distribution scheme (specifying what to do at every moment), and intercommunication mechanisms. Path planning typically refers to the design of specifications of the positions and orientations of robots in the presence of obstacles. Path planning can be static or dynamic, depending on the mode in which the obstacle information is available. In order to follow the movement of robots in the work area, we need a spatial planner which must find a path free of obstacles to follow a predefined trajectory. In general, this consists of two phases:

- Route planning: a route is defined as a sequence of sub-goals that must be reached by the robots before reaching the final goal.
- Path generation: once the plan has been created, different heuristics (for instance, the shortest path) could be used to reach the predefined goal.

Cellular models provide an advantage to carry out these tasks. Route planning using Voronoi diagrams can be easily constructed using simple 2D cellular models (without needing to compute distance or intersections, sorting distances, and or explicit modeling of objects). Since cellular models only use local rules, any proposed algorithm can be applied to objects of arbitrary size/shape. Cell-DEVS [1] allows defining cell spaces using the DEVS (Discrete Events systems Specification) formalism [2] to define a cell space.

We present a Cell-DEVS model for route planning, which, based on the obstacles, finds different paths available and creates a Voronoi diagram. Then, we provide an

S. El Yacoubi, B. Chopard, and S. Bandini (Eds.): ACRI 2006, LNCS 4173, pp. 595–604, 2006.

algorithm for route planning, and we present an algorithm that takes the Voronoi diagram and determines an optimal path free of collision (considering the size of the robot). We apply this heuristics to create a Cell-DEVS model able to solve the route planning phase. Finally, we introduce an advanced Cell-DEVS model that can be applied to the routing of self-reconfigurable robots.

2 Background

Cell-DEVS improves execution performance of cellular models by using a discrete-event approach. It also enhances the cell's timing definition by making it more expressive. Each cell, defined as $TDC=< X, Y, S, N, delay, d, \delta_{INT}, \delta_{EXT}, \tau, \lambda, D >$, uses N inputs to compute its next state. These inputs, which are received through the model's interface (X, Y), activate the local computing function (τ). State (s) changes can be transmitted to other models, but only after the consumption of a delay (d). Once the cell behavior is defined, a coupled Cell-DEVS is created by putting together a number of cells interconnected by a neighborhood relationship. A coupled Cell-DEVS is composed of an array of $t_1 x \ldots x t_n$ atomic cells, defined as $GCC=< Xlist, Ylist, X, Y, n, \{t_1,\ldots,t_n\}, N, C, B, Z >$. Each cell is connected to its neighborhood (N) through DEVS ports. Border cells (B) can have a different behavior or be "wrapped". Finally, the model's external couplings can be defined in the Xlist and Ylist. Each cell in a Cell-DEVS is a DEVS atomic model, and the cell space is a DEVS coupled model. DEVS is a formalism based on generic dynamic systems, including well defined coupling of components and hierarchical modular construction. A DEVS model is described as a composite of submodels, each of them being behavioral (atomic) or structural (coupled). Each atomic model, defined by $AM=< X, Y, S, \delta_{ext}, \delta_{int}, \lambda, ta>$, has an interface (X, Y) to communicate with other models. Every state (S) is associated to a time advance (ta) function, which determines its duration. Once this time is consumed, the model generates results by activating an output function (λ), and the internal transition function (δ_{int}) is fired. Input external events activate the external transition function (δ_{ext}). Coupled models are defined as a set of basic components (atomic or coupled), which are interconnected through the model's interfaces.

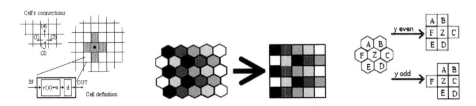

Fig. 1. Informal definition of Cell-DEVS, and shift mapping to the square lattice

CD++ [3, 4] was developed following the definitions of the Cell-DEVS formalism. Cell-DEVS are described using a built-in specification language, which provides a set of primitives to define the diferent parameters of the model. The behavior of a cell (τ function) is defined using a set of rules of the form: *RESULT DELAY CONDITION*.

When an external event is received, the rule evaluation process is triggered to calculate the new cell value. The CONDITION is evaluated; if satisfied, the new cell state is obtained by evaluating the RESULT expression. The cell will transmit these changes after a DELAY. A Lattice Translator allows using different topologies, which are translated into square CD++ rules, using the mechanism depicted in Fig. 1.

The algorithms here presented are based on Voronoi diagrams, which use the idea of proximity to a finite set of points in the plane P={$p1...pn$} (n ≥2). The diagram associates every point pj to their closest points pi (i ≠j), conforming covering sets [5, 6]. Points equidistant to two elements in P define the *border* of a region. The resulting sets define a tessellation of the plane (exhaustive, as every point belongs to a set, and they are mutually exclusive). Voronoi diagrams can be used to study the movement of a robot of a given size, describing paths surrounding the obstacles (and indicating the distance to them). These indicators allow a robot to determine if the path is feasible to pass through the path.

Fig. 2. Voronoi Diagram

We are also interested in models of self-reconfiguring robots. These systems are versatile in both their structure and the tasks they perform [7]. These robots are composed of a number of modules that can reshape according to the task to be carried out. Each robot is independent of the rest, and they act as parallel entities. The ability of reconfiguration leads to flow-based locomotion algorithms (allowing the robots to conform to the terrain on which they have to travel), which can be nicely modeled as cellular models.

3   Route Planning Models

Our path-planning model is based on [5] where CA are used to process a "top down" bitmap of a diamond-shaped area including a robot of arbitrary shape. The algorithm produces a Voronoi diagram that can be used to determine a path equidistant from obstacles in the space. Paths are calculated by marking the intersections of expanding "wavefronts" propagated by cellular expansion from given starting points. The input is an array of cells with values 1 (obstacle) or 0. The model executes in two stages:

1. Object boundary detection: cells and their neighborhoods are examined and compared to a set of 12 "edge code" templates. Each cell matching a configuration in the template uses the corresponding code (1-12) for the second stage.
2. Cells with edge codes are expanded in free space. Where expansions intersect, the cell of the intersection is given a timestamp and considered part of the final Voronoi diagram. The final state contains the Voronoi diagram.

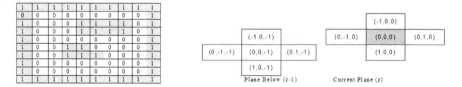

Fig. 3. (a) Input bitmap; (b) 3D neighborhood

The following state variables are required for every cell: the *original encoding* of detected obstacles (0 or 1); the *calculated edge* code for the cell (1-12); a *flag* value used during the "wavefront expansion", and the point on the *Voronoi diagram* representing this cell's position. We put each state variable on a separated plane in a 3D Cell-DEVS. Plane 0 (x, y, 0) contains the original bitmap representing the space, Plane 1 (x,y,1) contains the edge codes, Plane 2 (x,y,2) includes the propagation of edge codes over time, and Plane 3 (x,y,3) stores the final Voronoi diagram. The 3D neighborhood is shown in Figure 3.b).

```
[Path-Finding]
dim : (10, 10, 4)   delay : transport localtransition : nothing-rule
neighbors:(-1,0,0)(0,-1,0)(0,0,0)(0,1,0)(1,0,0)(0,-1,-1) ... (0,1,-1)
zones : bound-rule { (0,0,1)..(9,9,1) } plane2-rule {
(0,0,2)..(9,9,2) }
                plane3-rule { (0,0,3)..(9,9,3) }
[nothing-rule]
rule: { (0,0,0) } 10 { t }
[bound-rule]
rule: 1 10 { (0,0,-1)=1 and (0,-1,-1)=1 and (-1,0,-1)=1 and (0,1,-
1)=1 and (1,0,-1)=1 }
...
rule: 12 10 { (0,0,-1)=1 and (0,-1,-1)=1 and (-1,0,-1)=0 and (0,1,-
1)=0 and (1,0,-1)=1 }
[plane2-rule]
rule: {(0,0,-1)+0.1} 10 { (0,0,-1) >4 and (0,0,-1)<13 }
...
rule: {(0,1,0)} 10 { fr((0,1,0))=0.1 and isint((0,-1,0)) and isint((-
1,0,0)) and isint((1,0,0)) }
[plane3-rule]
rule: {(time)} 10 { (0,0,0)=0 and %check and (-1,0,-1)!=(0,1,-1) }
...
rule: {(time)} 10 { (0,0,0)=0 and %check and (0,-1,-1)!=(0,1,-1) }
```

Fig. 4. Cell-DEVS model definition in CD++

Fig. 4 describes the model definition in CD++. The model specification defines a 10x10x4 Cell-DEVS (a surface grid of size 10x10 and the four data planes). Four sets of rules which are used on each plane. The 3D cell model is effectively divided into four 2D models by using separate zones consisting of plane regions. The rule sets are:

- **nothing-rule:** used by the original data plane to keep the values from being changed.
- **bound-rule:** coding of edge directions. Patterns of cell values in each cell and its neighborhood are classified as one of 12 edge codes. The rules in this section perform the classification if the cells in the data plane correspond to one of 12 templates.

- **plane2-rule:** Cells with edge codes from 1-4 must be discarded. Cells with edge codes 5-12 are copied into a new grid and given a flag value for propagation in the third stage. The rules in this section carry over the values from the second plane which satisfy the criteria (4 < edge_code < 13).
- **plane3-rule:** the Voronoi diagram. In the previous plane, cells receive data values from their immediate neighbors and propagate the data out from any given starting point (points where these data wavefronts collide are those farthest away and equidistant from the starting obstacles; these are the points of interest when plotting a path for a robot). This plane examines the values in the plane below. If more than has its flag is set (and they do not contain the same values), the cell belongs to the Voronoi diagram. The Voronoi diagram is given the iteration number at which the cell was added to the diagram.

The first example here presented shows the execution of the model using a partial boundary and two obstacles.

```
    +----------+      +----------+      +----------+      +----------+
0|1111111111|     0|          |     0|          |     0|          |
1|111       |     1| 57       |     1|          |     1|          |
2|          |     2|    222222 |     2|          |     2|          |
3|          |     3| 22222222  |     3|          |     3|          |
4|          |     4| 222    22 |     4|          |     4|          |
5|    111   |     5| 22 192 2  |     5|          |     5|          |
6|    111   |     6| 22 857 2  |     6|          |     6|          |
7|          |     7| 222    22 |     7|          |     7|          |
8|          |     8|          |     8|          |     8|          |
9|1111111111|     9|          |     9|          |     9|          |
    +----------+      +----------+      +----------+      +----------+

...

    +----------+      +----------+      +----------+      +----------+
0|1111111111|     0|          |     0|          |     0|          |
1|111       |     1| 57       |     1| 57777    |     1| 33   55  |
2|          |     2|    222222 |     2| 57   92  |     2| 33 455   |
3|          |     3| 22222222  |     3| 57 1922  |     3| 444444   |
4|          |     4| 222    22 |     4| 5  192 2 |     4| 54 333   |
5|    111   |     5| 22 192 2  |     5| 11119222 |     5| 54322234 |
6|    111   |     6| 22 857 2  |     6| 88885777 |     6| 54322234 |
7|          |     7| 222    22 |     7| 8 857 7  |     7|   333    |
8|          |     8|          |     8|  88577   |     8|   444    |
9|1111111111|     9|          |     9|          |     9|          |
    +----------+      +----------+      +----------+      +----------+
```

Fig. 5. Partial boundary and two obstacles

The inputs describe a boundary on the upper and lower horizontal edges of the 10x10 space, as well as two small obstacles inside the space. The input values in the first plane remain unchanged, and the edge codes in the second plane are generated after one iteration. The third plane is initially populated with edge codes >4, and these values are successively propagated across their neighborhoods (note the are "holes" where cells were out of reach of their neighbors). Propagation stops when cells have no more non-flagged neighbors. The final plane is the Voronoi diagram, where "for a diamond shape of diagonal size d, the path planning process selects those Voronoi edges that consist of points with labels of value $\ell \geq d+\frac{1}{2}$". Since the first values on the diagram are 2's, one should add that offset to find the desired values. In this case, for a robot of diagonal size 2, the points on the graph of value 4 or 5 represent viable travel paths which can be used by a robot of diagonal size 2 to travel avoiding the two obstacles.

```
+----------+   +----------+   +----------+   +----------+
0|1111    11|  0|          |  0|          |  0|          |
1|1111    11|  1|          |  1|          |  1|          |
2|111    111|  2|          |  2|          |  2|          |
3|111    111|  3|          |  3|          |  3|          |
4|111    111|  4|          |  4|          |  4|          |
5|111    111|  5|          |  5|          |  5|          |
6|111    111|  6|          |  6|          |  6|          |
7|111    111|  7|          |  7|          |  7|          |
8|11    1111|  8|          |  8|          |  8|          |
9|11    1111|  9|          |  9|          |  9|          |
+----------+   +----------+   +----------+   +----------+

  . . .

+----------+   +----------+   +----------+   +----------+
0|1111    11|  0|          |  0|          |  0|          |
1|1111    11|  1| 117 22 0 |  1| 6 7771 0 |  1|  2   442 |
2|111    111|  2| 16 22 11 |  2| 66 7111  |  2|   244332 |
3|111    111|  3| 16 22 01 |  3| 66660000 |  3|    4432  |
4|111    111|  4| 16 22 01 |  4| 66660000 |  4|   44     |
5|111    111|  5| 16 22 01 |  5| 66660000 |  5|   44     |
6|111    111|  6| 16 22 01 |  6| 66660000 |  6|  2344    |
7|111    111|  7| 17 22 01 |  7|  7771 00 |  7| 233442   |
8|11    1111|  8| 6 22 111 |  8| 6 7111 0 |  8|  244  2  |
9|11    1111|  9|          |  9|          |  9|          |
+----------+   +----------+   +----------+   +----------+
```

Fig. 6. Two large obstacles

Once we find the Voronoi diagram, we obtain a number of possible paths. We can find the shortest path based using a flooding technique like in [6]. We built a Cell-DEVS model to generate the shortest path: a cell is considered to be part of a valid path if its value is larger or equal to the robot size (*valid* cells). A cell with more than 2 valid neighbors is called a *node*. An *output node* is a cell where the robot is located before moving, and an *end node* is the destination. The shortest path to the end node is based on the Manhattan distance. The algorithm consists of two phases: flooding and selection. The *flooding* algorithm explores all possible paths starting on the output node in parallel, choosing only valid cells. When a node is found, the path is divided in parallel. If during the exploration two paths are crossed, only the one with the best value continues. *Selection* starts when we get to the end node; we backtrack, looking for the minimum cost according to the chosen criteria. In this way, we can find a minimal path, as seen in the following figure.

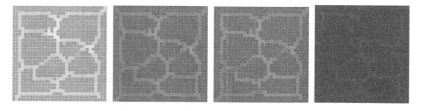

Fig. 7. (a) Initial Voronoi Diagram; (b-c) Flooding; (d) Selection

Our Cell-DEVS implementation encodes the distance to the objects at the beginning of the process (obtained by the Voronoi diagram selection presented in previous section). The following figure shows two examples of execution based on the original Voronoi diagrams. On Fig. 8.b), we see a modification, in which we have added an extra connection in the bottom-left part of the diagram (which affects the shortest path found).

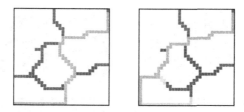

Fig. 8. (a) Shortest path (b) Shortest path with modified Voronoi diagram

4 Modeling Self-reconfiguring Robots

In this section we will show how to model self-reconfiguring robots, based on the work presented in [7]. Self-reconfiguring robots are composed identical modules that can autonomously reshape. The problem we will use as our case study is that of robotic locomotion in the two-dimensional plane, following a flow-like locomotion pattern. The model is capable of: (1) linear motion on plane of modules; (2) convex transitions into a different plane; and (3) concave transitions into a different plane [1]. The control algorithm uses local rules and it is constructed as a cellular model. We will show the behavior of a self-reconfiguring robot moving in a non-structured space, avoiding the obstacles presented. Ten different states can be defined for each cell: empty (0), occupied by a non-moving module (1), occupied by an obstacle, or occupied by a robot moving in N/S/E/W direction (3-9). The model uses a modified Moore Neighborhood. The model consists of 27 rules controlling the full behavior of a cell. Each cell can be in a specific state, from a total of 10 states. The basic idea behind the model is that locomotion is produced from a two-phase mechanism, in which in the first phase each cell determines if it has to change its state, and the new state it will

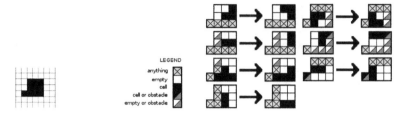

Fig. 9. (a) Neighborhood shape; (b) Model's rules

reach. On the second phase, depending on the state of each neighbor, a cell might decide to cancel its decision, or to go ahead as planned.

The following figure shows some of the execution results obtained when using a square topology. Particularly noteworthy is the fact that the robot climb obstacles with a relative height of 3 units, and when it climbs down, it follows the shape of the terrain.

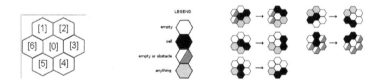

Fig. 10. Model execution

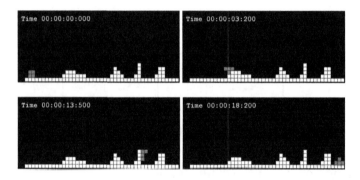

Fig. 11. (a) Hexagonal Neighborhood definition; (b) Model's rules

The model was extended to a hexagonal topology, resulting is on the same two-phase mechanism, but fewer rules (21). The amount of possible states is also reduced (8). The following figure shows a graphical representation of the model, showing the local rules. The following figure shows the model representation using hexagonal Cell-DEVS in CD++ (notation in Fig. 7a)

```
[reconfig-robot-hexa]
dim : (15,45)                    delay : transport    border : wrapped
neighbors :  (-1,-1)(-1,0)(-1,1)(0,-1)(0,0)(0,1)  (1,-2)  (1,-1)  (1,0)
(1,1)

[reconfig]
rule: 1 100 {[0]=0 and [4]=1 and [5]=3 and ([6]=0 or [6]=2)}
rule: 1 100 {[0]=3}
rule: 4 0 {[0]=1 and [1]=0 and [2]=0 and [3]=0 and [4]=1}
rule: 0 100 {[0]=4 and [1]=0 and [2]=0 and [3]=0 and [4]=1}
rule: 1 100 {[0]=0 and [1]=0 and [5]=1 and [6]=4}
rule: 1 100 {[0]=4}
rule: 5 0 {[0]=1 and [1]=0 and [2]=0 and [3]=0 and [4]=0 and [5]=1}
rule: 0 100 {[0]=5 and [1]=0 and [2]=0 and [3]=0 and [4]=0 and [5]=1}
rule: 1 100 {[0]=0 and [1]=5 and [2]=0 and [6]=1}
rule: 1 100 {[0]=5}
...
```

Fig. 12. (a) Hexagonal Neighborhood definition; (b) Model's rules

The following figure shows the model's execution. As we can see, the results obtained are similar to those presented in Figure 12, using the hexagonal topology. Nevertheless, using a square topology required 18.2 seconds to travel across all obstacles, while the second robot, modeled with a hexagonal topology required only 15.8 seconds.

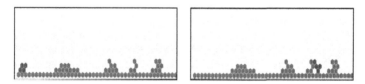

Fig. 13. Model execution

5 Conclusion

We have introduced the use of CD++ for applications of path planning in robotic applications. We first presented a model that correctly simulates the behavior of path-finding algorithms, creating a Voronoi diagram as a result. The map describes paths surrounding the obstacles, and indicating the distances between them, allowing determining if a robot can pass through the path. After, we presented an algorithm that takes the Voronoi map and determines a shortest path between the robot and the destination. The use of hexagonal topology, with fewer rules, resulted in faster movement. The cellular models presented show the feasibility of this approach in solving complex application using very simple rules, permitting observation of emerging behavior. In this way, one can develop algorithms that can execute parallel searches and improve the quality and speed in the determination of the paths.

The use of cellular models is very efficient, as it can operate extremely quickly (in just a few cycles of evolution) and every cell is being solved in parallel, in contrast to more traditional, mathematical approaches which require more complex calculations of distances and angles. The downside is that it does require a full knowledge of the obstacle. In addition, the model does not provide a complete solution in the case where there is not one distinct solution path.

Acknowledgments

This work was partially funded by Precarn and NSERC. Different students participated in developing the models here presented: Javier Ameghino, Alejandro Baranek, Ricardo Kirkner, Kevin Lam, Maximiliano Polimeni and Marcela Ricillo.

References

1. Wainer, G., Giambiasi, N.: N-dimensional Cell-DEVS. Discrete Events Systems: Theory and Applications, Kluwer, Vol.12. No.1 (2002) 135-157.
2. Zeigler, B., Kim, T., Praehofer, H.: Theory of Modeling and Simulation: Integrating Discrete Event and Continuous Complex Dynamic Systems. Academic Press (2000).
3. López, A., Wainer, G. Improved Cell-DEVS model definition in CD++. In: P.M.A. Sloot, B. Chopard, and A.G. Hoekstra (Eds.): ACRI 2004, LNCS 3305. Springer-Verlag. 2004.
4. Wainer, G.: CD++: a toolkit to develop DEVS models. Software - Practice and Experience. vol. 32, pp. 1261-1306. (2002).
5. P. Tzionas, A. Thanailakis and P. Tsalides. Collision-Free Path Planning for a Diamond-Shaped Robot Using Two-Dimensional Cellular Automata", IEEE Trans. On Robotics and Automation. Vol. 13, No. 2. pp. 237-246 (1997).
6. Behring, C., Bracho, M. Castro, M., Moreno, J. A.: An Algorithm for Robot Path Planning with Cellular Automata. Proceedings of ACRI 2000. Karlsruhe, Germany. (2000).
7. Butler, Z., Kotay, K., Rus, D., Tomita, K.: Generic Decentralized Control for a Class of Self-Reconfigurable Robots. Proceedings of 2002 IEEE International Conference on Robotics and Automation, ICRA 2002. Washington, DC, USA. (2002).

Authentication Based on Singular Cellular Automata*

Jun-Cheol Jeon and Kee-Young Yoo**

Department of Computer Engineering, Kyungpook National University,
Daegu, 702-701 Korea
jcjeon33@infosec.knu.ac.kr,
yook@knu.ac.kr

Abstract. One-Time Password (OTP) authentication schemes have been grown based on the time synchronization or one-way hash functions, although they can be trouble some and have a high computational complexity. In order to remedy the problems, the current paper provides a low-complexity authentication scheme which is only composed of logical bitwise operations such as XOR, AND, OR, and NOT. Our scheme highly minimizes the computational and transmission complexity and solves the time or sequence synchronization problems by applying singular CA based on the non-reversibility and uniqueness of the state configuration. Thus, our secure authentication scheme can be effectively used for other applications requiring authentication that is secure against passive attacks based on replaying captured reusable passwords.

Keywords: One-Time Password, Cellular Automata, Singular Operation, Authentication, Hash function.

1 Introduction

One-Time Password (OTP) authentication was first proposed by Leslie Lamport [1], and Bellcore's S/KEY system, from which the OTP is derived, was proposed by Neil Haller [2]. Recently, Ben Soh and A. Joy addressed an efficient OTP scheme based on a web service evaluation model [3]. However, all these schemes have practical difficulties such as high hash overhead, additional transmission complexity, and the time / sequence synchronization since there is not an alternative solution.

A natural progression from fixed password schemes to challenge-response identification protocols may be observed by considering OTP schemes. Variations include [4]: shared lists of one-time passwords, sequentially updated one-time passwords, and one-time password sequences based on a one-way function. However, their drawbacks are the maintenance of the shared list, the synchronization of sequences, and the high hash overhead [1, 5].

* This research was supported by the MIC (Ministry of Information and Communication), Korea, under the ITRC (Information Technology Research Center) support program supervised by the IITA (Institute of Information Technology Assessment). This work was also partially supported by the Brain Korea 21 Project in 2006.
** Corresponding author.

S. El Yacoubi, B. Chopard, and S. Bandini (Eds.): ACRI 2006, LNCS 4173, pp. 605–610, 2006.
© Springer-Verlag Berlin Heidelberg 2006

Cellular automaton (CA), introduced by John Von Neumann [6], have been accepted as a good computational model for the simulation of complex physical systems, and have been used in evolutionary computations for over a decade. It can readily simulate complex growth patterns and it has also been used for in various applications, such as parallel processing computations and number theory [7].

Various studies have presented the reversibility and non-reversibility of CA based on a non-singular and singular CA [8, 9]. The non-singular CA contains only cyclic states while the singular CA contains both cyclic and non cyclic states. In order to satisfy the characteristics of the OTP scheme, the CA should provide the non-reversibility and uniqueness of the state configuration - that is, the previous state is not reachable from the present state of the CA, and there is no duplicate state in a CA.

Thus, this current study finds the CA which satisfies the non-reversibility and uniqueness of the state configuration, and constructs the OTP scheme based on the mentioned properties. The proposed OTP scheme, based on singular CA, eliminates the computational and transmission overhead and time/sequence synchronization problems. It provides also sufficient security satisfaction.

2   Cellular Automata

A CA is a collection of simple cells arranged in a regular fashion. CAs can be characterized based on four properties: cellular geometry, neighborhood specification, the number of states per cell, and the rules to compute to a successor state. The next state of a CA depends on the current state and rules [6]. A CA can also be classified as linear or non-linear. If the neighborhood is only dependent on an XOR operation, the CA is linear, whereas if it is dependent on another operation, the CA is non-linear. If the neighborhood is only dependent on an XOR or XNOR operation, then the CA can also be referred to as an additive CA.

According to the conditions, they are divided into three types: null boundary CA, periodic boundary CA, and intermediate boundary CA [7]. A CA is said to be a Null Boundary CA (NBCA) if the left neighbor of the leftmost cell and right neighbor of the rightmost cell are regarded to be 0. A CA is said to be a Periodic Boundary CA (PBCA) if the leftmost cell and rightmost cell are regarded to be adjacent to each other, i.e., the left neighbor of the leftmost cell becomes the rightmost cell, and the right neighbor of the rightmost cell becomes the leftmost cell. A CA is said to be an Intermediate Boundary CA (IBCA) if the left neighbor of the leftmost cell is regarded to be the second right neighbor, and right neighbor of the rightmost cell is regarded to be the second left neighbor.

A one-dimensional CA consists of a linearly connected array of n cells, each of which takes the value of 0 or 1, and an evolutionary function $F(s)$ on the state configuration, s, with q variables. The value of the cell state s_i is updated in parallel using this function in discrete time steps as $s_i(t+1) = F(s_{i+j}(t))$ where $-r \leq j \leq r$ [8]. The parameter q is usually an odd integer, i.e. $q = 2r+1$, where r is often named the radius of the function F; the possible configuration and the total number of rules for radius r neighborhood are 2^q and 2^n, where $n = 2^q$. The evolutionary function $F(s)$ on the state configuration, s, is also expressed as Ts by a characteristic matrix, T on the transition rule.

The new value of the ith cell is calculated using the value of the ith cell itself and the values of r neighboring cells to the right and left of the ith cell. If a non-singular rule is applied to a CA then the CA is called a non-singular CA (NCA), otherwise the CA is a singular CA (SCA). In a two state 3-neighborhood CA, there are 256 rules [10].

The success of the OTP authentication to protect host systems is dependent on the non-reversibility property. A CA provides both reversible and non-reversible properties by F. In a non-singular CA, the previous state can be easily found by computing the inverse of a rule, but it is computationally infeasible to find the inverse of a rule in a SCA [11]. The current paper only considers the singular 3-neighbour CA with null boundary condition based on the non-reversible properties.

3   SCA Based Authentication

The security of our scheme is based on the *non-reversibility* and *uniqueness of the state configuration*. Such a function must be tractable to compute in the forward direction, but computationally infeasible to invert, and the evolved states must be distinctive. In order to achieve the conditions, a system should compute and save the singular rule and the length according to the given initial state. A length represents the number of the unique states in a CA.

Theorem 1. (SCA) A CA is a singular CA if and only if the determinant $det\ T \neq 1$, where T is the characteristic matrix for the CA.

Proof. If the CA under the transition operation with T forms a cyclic non-singular, then for all states, s, there should exist an integer m such that $T^m = I$ and $s = T^m s = s$ where I indicates the identity matrix. The necessary condition to have an m such that $T^m = I$, is $det\ T = 1$. This follows because if $T^m - I$, then $[det\ T]^m = 1$ so that $det\ T = 1$. The contraposition also holds, hence the proof.

Definition 1. The rule applied on a uniform non-singular CA is called *a non-singular rule*, otherwise, called *a singular rule*.

Remark 1. (non-reversibility) Since SCA are associated with singular T matrices, characterization of such CA in terms of the inverse matrices is impossible. The forward state transition is represented as $s(t+1) = Ts(t)$. However, there does not exist the reverse state transition, i.e. $s(t)$ can not be found from the given $s(t+1)$ and T because of its singular property.

Fig. 1 shows the transition-configurations and lengths when the initial state is a 4-bits vector (1011). The non-singular CAs, that applied rules 90 and 150, have the cyclic property that the initial state appears after a certain number of evolutions. The singular CAs, that applied rules 171 and 129, have the property that an indefinite state appears after a certain period which is called a length, L. It shows that each CA has the unique states as many as its length.

Remark 2. (Uniqueness of the state configuration) In our scheme, we have defined and utilized the states in length which is composed of distinctive states. Thus there are no overlapped states in the given length so that it guarantees the uniqueness of the state configuration. The number of unique states is exactly equal to its length.

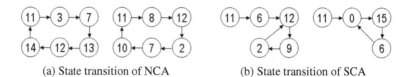

(a) State transition of NCA   (b) State transition of SCA

Fig. 1. The state transition diagram of (a) NCA applied nonsingular rules 90 and 150 and (b) SCA applied singular rules 171 and 129. [rule 90: $s_i(t+1) = s_{i-1}(t) \oplus s_{i+1}(t)$, rule 150: $s_i(t+1) = s_{i-1}(t) \oplus s_i(t) \oplus s_{i+1}(t)$, rule 171: $s_i(t+1) = (\neg(s_{i-1}(t) \lor s_i(t))) \oplus s_{i+1}(t)$ rule 129: $s_i(t+1) - \neg((s_{i-1}(t) \oplus s_i(t)) \lor (s_{i-1}(t) \oplus s_{i+1}(t)))$, where the notations '$\oplus$', '$\lor$', and '$\neg$' indicate the bitwise XOR operation, OR operation, and NOT operation respectively.]

Registration phase

S-1. A user, A chooses a pass-phrase, ρ, and transmits it to the system, B.

S-2. The pass-phrase is concatenated with a seed, ς, by B ($\delta = \rho \| \varsigma$). B decides a singular rule, ω, and finds the length, τ, of the singular CA. Then it computes and saves $\delta_0 = T_\omega^\tau(\delta)$, and initializes its counter for A to $C_A = 1$.

S-3. B transfers ω, τ, and δ to A.

Authentication phase

L-1. A computes $\delta_i = T_\omega^{\tau-i}(\delta)$, and transmits A, i, and δ_i to B.

L-2. B checks $i = C_A$, and $T_\omega(\delta_i) = \delta_{i-1}$. If both checks succeed, B accepts the password, sets $C_A \leftarrow C_A + 1$, and saves δ_i for the next session verification.

The proposed scheme consists of two phases: The registration phase and authentication phase. In the registration phase, the information is exchanged by secure channel while the authentication message is sent to the system through insecure channel. The proposed efficient OTP authentication is operated as above.

In the setup phase, ρ may be of any length within 64 bits to 96 bits, and ς should be remainder bits, 32 bits to 64 bits, so that the secret, δ, is initialized as 128 bits length. The notations '$\|$' indicates the concatenation operation. In S-2, ω can be just one singular rule or the combination of rules, e.g., <107, 230> - That is the rules are applied to the CA alternately. The password for the ith identification session, $1 \leq i \leq \tau$, is defined to be $\delta_i = T_\omega^{\tau-i}(\delta_0)$. In the login phase, for the ith session, B already has the user's identity and counter, along with the verifier, δ_{i-1}, so that B simply checks the user's authentication by applying the transition function T_ω once. After use of all state configurations during the τ times, the singular rule ω should be changed into another rule ω'.

4 Discussion and Analysis

In order to solve the high hash computation problem, our scheme has taken advantage of the CA characteristics that the computation only consists of logical bitwise operations such as XOR, AND, OR, and NOT, while the hash function is composed of not only the logical bitwise operations but also padding, appending length, and additional operations. Moreover the CA computations are performed in parallel.

Our scheme has a minimal path to check whether a user is certified in a login phase, and it does not need the synchronization of time. If A and B have gotten out of synchrony because of unstable computer network – A sends δ_i and B uses $T_\omega(\delta_j)$ to authenticate it, with $i \neq j$ – then this can be detected by repeatedly applying ω to B's authenticating value until a match is obtained.

We recommend that the whole size of the state configuration, $|\delta|$ is 128 bits which consists of ρ and ς. To reduce the risk from techniques such as exhaustive search or dictionary attacks, the user's secret pass-phrase should be between 64 bits and 96 bits. This is believed to be long enough to be secure and short enough to be entered manually. We also recommend 3-neighbor CA which has $r = 1$ since a longer neighbor CA does not ensure better safety but adds to the complexity of the computations.

Meanwhile, the length, τ, should be reasonably long enough but not too long. If the τ of a CA is too short or too long, it causes the frequent renewal of the rule or password guessing from the attacker. Thus we recommended that the length of CA should be in the several hundreds to several thousands. Table 1 shows the length when the rules are applied to the initial value, 'evolutionry1234'. Only the CAs applied the singular rules have relatively shorter length, 657 and 127, which correspond to rules 107 and 230. Meanwhile the CAs applied the combinations of non-singular rule and singular rule <90, 129>, <171, 90> have sufficient lengths, 2,524 and 2,471. There are a number of the combination rules which are sufficient in length.

Table 1. The length corresponds to the singular rule and the combination of a non-singular rule and singular rule with the initial state as mentioned in section 3

	singular rule		combination of non-singular rule and singular rule	
rule no.	107	230	90, 129	171,90
length	657	127	2,524	2,471

The following criteria are crucial for the robust security of authentication schemes.

- *Password guessing attack*: It is computationally infeasible for the attacker to choose a password which is same as the current δ_i from the previous session keys δ_{i-j}, where $1 \leq j \leq i\text{-}1$.
- *Replay attack*: Though the attacker replays δ_i to B in the login phase, the request will be rejected, since δ_i is used only once.
- *Impersonating A*: It is also infeasible that the attack can acquire a shared secret δ_0 since he cannot extract it from any information which he obtains.
- *Stolen verifier attack*: Though the attacker has stolen the verifier, $T_\omega^{\tau-i}(\delta_0)$, in ith session, $T_\omega^{\tau-(i+1)}(\delta_0)$ can not be computed by any method since it is infeasible to find the inverse in the SCA.

Table 2. CPU time comparison among our singular CA and typical hash schemes according to the number of one-time passwords

			(unit: sec.)
functions	500	1000	5000
MD5	1.1	2.2	28.4
SHA-1	1.3	2.6	33.2
SCA	0.8	1.5	19.7

We implemented and measured CPU times of a singular CA, MD5 and SHA-1 according to the number of one-time passwords in order to prove the better performance of CA computation using a Pentium 4, CPU 2.60GHz. Table 2 shows the performance comparison of CPU time among SCA computation and typical hash schemes. In software computing, we have implemented it in serial, however, our scheme has had better time complexity than the other hash schemes. As shown in Table 2, our SCA computation has more than about 30% and 40% lower time complexity compared to MD5 and SHA-1, respectively. Based on hardware implementation or parallel computing technique, it is obvious that our scheme would be much faster than the other schemes because of its parallel property and simple computation.

5   Conclusions

One-time password schemes provide significant additional protection but their use is limited due to the complexity and inconvenience regarding week networks. Our simple scheme provided not only minimal computational complexity and transmission path but also safety guarantees. We have shown that only our scheme has logical bitwise operations and one path for authenticating purposes, and it can resist the above mentioned attacks. In addition, our CA computation is much faster than hash schemes in both software and hardware implementations, so that we believe that our authentication scheme is suitable and practical for low power network environments because of its light computation and simple transaction.

References

1. L. Lamport: Password Authentication with Insecure Communication. Communication of ACM 24 (1981) 770-772
2. N. Haller: The S/KEY One-Time Password System. Proc. of the ISOC Symposium on Network and Distributed System Security (1994)
3. B. Soh and A. Joy: A Novel Web Security Evaluation Model for a One Time Password System. Proc. of the IEEE/WIC International Conference on Web Intelligence (2003)
4. A.J. Menezes, P.C. Oorschot, S.A. Vanstone: Handbook of Applied Cryptography, CRC Press (1997)
5. W. C. Ku and S. M. Chen: Weaknesses and Improvement of an Efficient Paword Based Remote User Authentication Scheme Using Smart Cards. IEEE trans. On Consumer electronics 50 (2004) 204-207
6. J. Von Neumann: The theory of self-reproducing automata. University of Illinois Press, Urbana and London (1966)
7. J.C. Jeon and K. Y. Yoo: Design of Montgomery Multiplication Architecture based on Programmable Cellular Automata. Computational intelligence 20 (2004) 495-502
8. M. Seredynski, K. Pienkosz, and P. Bouvry: Reversible Cellular Automata Based Encryption. LNCS Vol. 3222 (2004) 411-418
9. S. Das, B. K. Sikdar, and P. Pal Chaudhuri: Charaterization of Reachable / Nonreachable Cellular Automata States. LNCS Vol. 3305 (2004) 813-822
10. C.K. Koc, A.M. Apohan: Inversion of cellular automata iterations. IEE Proc. Comput. Digit. Tech. 144 (1997) 279-284
11. M. Seredynski and P. Bouvry: Block Encryption Using Reversible Cellular Automata. LNCS Vol. 3305 (2004) 785-792

Concatenated Automata in Cryptanalysis of Stream Ciphers[*]

A. Fúster-Sabater[1] and P. Caballero-Gil[2]

[1] Institute of Applied Physics, C.S.I.C., Serrano 144, 28006 Madrid, Spain
amparo@iec.csic.es
[2] Faculty of Maths, D.E.I.O.C., University of La Laguna, 38271 Tenerife, Spain
pcaballe@ull.es

Abstract. This work shows that sequences generated by a class of linear cellular automata equal output sequences of certain nonlinear sequence generators. A simple modelling process for obtaining the automata from a partial description of such generators is here described. Furthermore, a method that uses the linearity of these cellular models for reconstructing some deterministic bits of the keystream sequence is presented.

Keywords: Stream cipher, cellular automata, linear model, cryptography.

1 Introduction

Most keystream generators are based on Linear Feedback Shift Registers (LF-SRs) [5] whose output sequences, the so-called PN-sequences, are combined in a nonlinear way. Such generators are easy to implement and produce keystreams with high linear complexity, long period and good statistical properties [8].

Cellular Automata (CA) [2] have been proposed as an alternative to LF-SRs [3] [7] as every sequence generated by a LFSR can be obtained from one-dimensional CA too. Moreover, it has been proved [9] that linear one-dimensional CA are isomorphic to conventional LFSRs. This work uses CA in such a way that generators designed as nonlinear structures in terms of LFSRs preserve linearity when they are expressed under the form of CA. The specific generators that may be linearized in this way are those made out of one or more LFSRs plus a feed-forward nonlinear function, such as the Clock-Controlled, Cascade-Clock-Controlled and Shrinking generators, or the generators producing Kasami, GMW, No and Klapper sequences etc. [8]. These sequences belong to the class of *interleaved sequences* [6], which are pseudorandom sequences such that each sequence can be decomposed into a collection of shifts of an unique PN-sequence. It will be shown that these sequences can be obtained from CA made out of a basic structure concatenated a number of times. Once one of these generators has been linearized, a method for reconstructing unknown bits of the output sequence based on intercepted keystream bits has been developed. In this sense, linearity of the cellular models is used for the cryptanalysis of the generators.

[*] Research supported by the Spanish Ministry of Education and Science and the European FEDER Fund under Projects SEG2004-02418 and SEG2004-04352-C04-03.

S. El Yacoubi, B. Chopard, and S. Bandini (Eds.): ACRI 2006, LNCS 4173, pp. 611–616, 2006.
© Springer-Verlag Berlin Heidelberg 2006

2   Basic Structures

Next some aspects of the two basic structures used in this work are described.

This work deals only with one-dimensional linear null hybrid 90/150 CA. A natural way to specify such CA is an L-tuple $M = [R_1, R_2, ..., R_L]$, where $R_i = 0$ if the i-th cell satisfies rule 90 while $R_i = 1$ if the i-th cell satisfies rule 150.

The characteristic polynomial $P_i(x)$ of any CA $[R_1, R_2, ..., R_i]$ can be computed in terms of the characteristic polynomials of the previous sub-automata according to the recurrence relationship where $P_{-1}(x) = 0$ and $P_0(x) = 1$:

$$P_i(x) = (x + R_i)P_{i-1}(x) + P_{i-2}(x), \ \ 0 < i \le L \tag{1}$$

A Multiplicative Polynomial Cellular Automaton is defined as a cellular automaton whose characteristic polynomial is of the form $P_M(x) = (P(x))^p$ where p is a positive integer. If $P(x)$ is a primitive polynomial, then the automaton is called a Primitive Multiplicative Polynomial Cellular Automaton.

The Cattell and Muzio synthesis algorithm [1] computes two 90/150 CA for each input characteristic polynomial. It takes as input an irreducible polynomial $Q(x) \in GF(2)[x]$ defined over a finite field and computes two reversal linear CA whose output sequences have $Q(x)$ as characteristic polynomial.

The Shrinking Generator (SG) is composed by two LFSRs [4]: a control register R_1 that decimates the sequence produced by the other register R_2. L_j ($j = 1, 2$) denote their corresponding lengths with $(L_1, L_2) = 1$ and $L_1 < L_2$, while $C_j(x) \in GF(2)[x]$ ($j = 1, 2$) denote their corresponding characteristic polynomials. The sequence $\{a_i\}$ produced by R_1 controls the bits of the sequence $\{b_i\}$ produced by R_2 which are included in the output sequence $\{z_j\}$ according to the following rule: If $a_i = 1$, then $z_j = b_i$, while if $a_i = 0$, then b_i is discarded. Long period, high linear complexity and good distributional statistics are properties satisfied by the shrunken sequence [4]. Therefore, this scheme is suitable for practical implementation of stream ciphers and pattern generators.

3   Linear Modelling by Concatenation of CA

Now the particular form of the automata that will be used to linearize the class of interleaved sequence generators is analyzed. Since the characteristic polynomial of these automata is $P_M(x) = (P(x))^p$, it seems quite natural to construct a multiplicative polynomial cellular automaton by concatenating p times a basic automaton (or its reverse version). In this way, the construction of a linear model based on CA is carried out by the following generic algorithm:

Input: The parameters of a nonlinear keystream generator producing an interleaved sequence.

- *Step 1:* Determine the irreducible factor $P(x)$ of the characteristic polynomial of each interleaved sequence.
- *Step 2:* Compute the pair of basic CA whose characteristic polynomial is $P(x)$ by means of the Cattell and Muzio algorithm.

- *Step 3:* For each one of these basic CA, construct by successive concatenations a longer cellular automaton able to generate the original interleaved sequence. The concatenation of the basic automaton can be realized with complementation of any extreme bit.

Output: Two linear CA producing the corresponding keystream sequence.

The SG is a typical example of cryptographic generator with characteristic polynomial of the form $P_M(x) = (P(x))^p$. In particular, in this case $P(x)$ is a primitive polynomial of degree L_2 and $p = 2^{(L_1-1)}$. Moreover, $P(x)$ is the characteristic polynomial of the cyclotomic *coset* E given by:

$$P(x) = (x + \lambda^E)(x + \lambda^{2E}) \ldots (x + \lambda^{2^{L_2-1}E}) \tag{2}$$

with $E = 2^0 + 2^1 + \ldots + 2^{L_1-1}$ and λ the generator element of $GF(2^{L_2})$.

4 Cryptanalytic Application

Since CA-based linear models describing the behavior of sequence generators have been derived, a cryptanalytic attack that exploits the weaknesses of these models has been developed too. The proposed attack is here applied to the SG, but it can be extended to any interleaved sequence generator. Starting from bits of the intercepted sequence and using the CA-based linear models, additional bits of the shrunken sequence can be reconstructed.

Given r bits of the shrunken sequence $z_0, z_1, z_2, ..., z_{r-1}$, we can assume without loss of generality that this sub-sequence has been generated at the most left extreme cell of its corresponding pair of CA. That is $x_1^t = z_0$, $x_1^{t+1} = z_1, ..., x_1^{t+r-1} = z_{r-1}$. From r bits of the shrunken sequence, it is always possible to reconstruct $r - 1$ new sub-sequences $\{x_i^t\}$ of lengths $r - i + 1$ at the i-th cell of each automaton such as follows:

$$x_i^t = \Phi_{i-1}(x_{i-1}^t, x_i^{t+1}, x_{i-2}^t) \quad (1 < i \leq r), \tag{3}$$

where Φ_{i-1} corresponds to either rule 90 or 150 depending on the value of R_{i-1}. For instance, if $r = 10$, $\{z_i\} = \{0, 0, 1, 1, 1, 0, 1, 0, 1, 1\}$ and $R_1 = R_2 = R_3 = 0$, the application of the equation (3) gives rise to the first sub-triangle, notated $\Delta 1$, in Table 1. Now, if any sub-sequence $\{x_i^t\}$ is placed at the most left extreme cell, then $r - 2i + 2$ bits are obtained at the i-th cell in the second chained sub-triangle, notated $\Delta 2$. Repeating recursively n times the same procedure, $r - ni + n$ bits are obtained at the i-th cell in the n-th chained sub-triangle Δn. Table 1 shows the succession of 4 chained sub-triangles constructed from 10 intercepted bits of the shrunken sequence. In fact, the 10 initial bits $z_0, z_1, z_2, ..., z_9$ generate 8 bits at the third cell in $\Delta 1$. These 8 bits are placed at the most left extreme cell producing 6 new bits at cell 3 in $\Delta 2$. With these 6 bits, we get 4 additional bits in $\Delta 3$. Finally, 2 new bits are obtained at cell 3 in the sub-triangle $\Delta 4$. Since rules 90 and 150 are additive, for any R_i the corresponding generated sub-sequence will be the sum of elements of the shrunken sequence. General expressions can be deduced for the elements of any sub-sequence in any chained sub-triangle. In fact, the i-th sub-sequence in the n-th chained sub-triangle includes the bits z_j corresponding to the exponents of $P_{i-1}(x)^n$ where $P_{i-1}(x)$ is the characteristic polynomial of the sub-automaton $R_1R_2...R_{i-1}$, see the equation (1). More precisely, for the previous example the characteristic polynomial of the sub-automaton R_1R_2 is $P_2(x) = x^2 + 1$. Thus, x_3^t in the different sub-triangles will take the form:

$$x_3^t = z_0 + z_2 \ in \ \Delta 1; \qquad x_3^t = z_0 + z_4 \ in \ \Delta 2;$$
$$x_3^t = z_0 + z_2 + z_4 + z_6 \ in \ \Delta 3; \quad x_3^t = z_0 + z_8 \ in \ \Delta 4; \ ...$$

Table 2 shows the general expressions of the sub-sequence elements in $\Delta 1$ and $\Delta 2$ for the example under consideration.

Table 1. Reconstruction of chained sub-triangles from 10 shrunken bits

$\Delta 1 : R_1\ R_2\ R_3\ ...$	$\Delta 2 : R_1\ R_2\ R_3\ ...$	$\Delta 3 : R_1\ R_2\ R_3\ ...$	$\Delta 4 : R_1\ R_2\ R_3\ ...$
0 0 1 ...	1 1 1 ...	1 0 1 ...	1 1 1 ...
0 1 1	1 0 0	0 0 1	1 0 1
1 1 0	0 1 0	0 1 0	0 0
1 1 1	1 0 1	1 0 0	0
1 0 0	0 0 0	0 1	
0 1 0	0 0 1	1	
1 0 0	0 1		
0 1 1	1		
1 1			
1			

On the other hand, in [6] it is shown that the shrunken sequence is the interleaving of $2^{(L_1-1)}$ different shifts of an unique PN-sequence of length $2^{L_2} - 1$ whose characteristic polynomial $P(x)$ is given by the equation (2). Consequently, the elements of the shrunken sequence indexed z_{di}, with $i \in \{0, 1, \ldots, 2^{L_2} - 2\}$ and $d = 2^{(L_1-1)}$, belong to the same PN-sequence. Thus, if the elements of the i-th sub-sequence in the n-th chained sub-triangle take the general form: $x_i^t = z_{k_1} + z_{k_2} + \ldots + z_{k_j}$, with

$$k_l \equiv 0 \ mod \ 2^{(L_1-1)} \quad (l = 1, \ldots, j), \qquad (4)$$

then such a sub-sequence can be written as $x_i^t = z_{k_m}$, with z_{k_m} satisfying the equation (4). Therefore, $\{x_i^t\}$, the i-th sub-sequence in the n-th chained sub-triangle, is just a sub-sequence of the shrunken sequence shifted a distance δ from the r bits of the intercepted sequence. The value of δ depends on the extension field $GF(2^{L_2})$ generated by the roots of $P(x)$. In brief, the chained sub-triangles enable us to reconstruct additional bits of the shrunken sequence from bits of the intercepted sequence.

The number of reconstructed bits depends on the amount of intercepted bits (proportional to 2^{L_1-1}). Indeed, if we know N_l bits in each one of the

Table 2. General expressions for sub-sequences in $\Delta 1$ and $\Delta 2$ with $R_1 = R_2 = R_3 = 0$

$\Delta 1:$ R_1	R_2	R_3	$\dots$	$\Delta 2:$ R_1	R_2	R_3	$\dots$
z_0	z_1	$z_0 + z_2$ $\dots$		$z_0 + z_2$	$z_1 + z_3$	$z_0 + z_4$ $\dots$	
z_1	z_2	$z_1 + z_3$		$z_1 + z_3$	$z_2 + z_4$	$z_1 + z_5$	
z_2	z_3	$z_2 + z_4$		$z_2 + z_4$	$z_3 + z_5$	$z_2 + z_6$	
z_3	z_4	$z_3 + z_5$		$z_3 + z_5$	$z_4 + z_6$	$z_3 + z_7$	
z_4	z_5	$z_4 + z_6$		$z_4 + z_6$	$z_5 + z_7$	$z_4 + z_8$	
z_5	z_6	$z_5 + z_7$		$z_5 + z_7$	$z_6 + z_8$	$z_5 + z_9$	
z_6	z_7	$z_6 + z_8$		$z_6 + z_8$	$z_7 + z_9$		
z_7	z_8	$z_7 + z_9$		$z_7 + z_9$			
z_8	z_9						
z_9							

PN-sequence shifts, then the total number of reconstructed bits is given by

$$\sum_{l=1}^{2^{(L_1-1)}} \sum_{k=2}^{N_l} \binom{N_l}{k}.$$

In order to compare the proposal with known related results, note that on the one hand, both reconstructed bits and their positions on the shrunken sequence are known with absolute certainty, and on the other hand, the off-line phase is to be executed before intercepting sequence. The off-line computational complexity of the proposed attack is $O(L_A{}^2 * 2^{L_S})$ whilst its on-line complexity is $O(L_A * 2^{L_S-2})$. If we compare it with the one of known attacks on SG, we find that all of them are actually exponential in L_S or in L_A.

Let us consider now as an illustrative example a SG with the following parameters: $L_1 = 4$, $L_2 = 5$, $C_2(x) - 1 + x + x^3 + x^4 + x^5$. According to the equation (2), we can compute the polynomial $P(x) = 1 + x + x^2 + x^4 + x^5$ while the two basic automata $1\ 0\ 0\ 0\ 0$ and $0\ 0\ 0\ 0\ 1$ are obtained from the algorithm of Cattell and Muzio. The corresponding CA of length $L = 40$ are computed via the algorithm developed in sub-section 3.1. Indeed, they are $CA_1 = 0060110600$ and $CA_2 = 8C0300C031$ in hexadecimal notation. In addition, let α be a root of $P(x)$ that is $\alpha^5 = \alpha^4 + \alpha^2 + \alpha + 1$ as well as a generator element of the extension field $GF(2^{L_2})$. The period of the shrunken sequence is $T = (2^{L_2} - 1) \cdot 2^{(L_1-1)} = 248$ and the number of interleaved PN-sequences is $2^{(L_1-1)} = 8$. Finally, the intercepted sequence of $r = 24$ is: $\{z_0, z_1, \dots, z_{23}\}$ $= \{1, 0, 1, 0, 0, 0, 0, 1, 1, 0, 0, 1, 1, 1, 0, 0, 1, 1, 0, 1, 0, 0, 1, 1\}$. With the previous premises, we accomplish the reconstruction process.

For CA_1: The chained sub-triangles provide the following reconstructed bits. For $i = 3$, sub-automaton $R_1 R_2$ and $P_2(x) = x^2 + 1$.

- In $\Delta 4$, $x_3^t = z_0 + z_8$, $x_3^{t+1} = z_1 + z_9$, $\dots$, $x_3^{t+15} = z_{15} + z_{23}$. Considering z_0, z_8 as the first and second element of the PN-sequence and keeping in mind that in $GF(2^{L_2})$ the equality $1 + \alpha = \alpha^{19}$ holds, we get $x_3^t = z_{19 \cdot 8} = z_{152}$, $x_3^{t+1} = z_{153}$, $\dots$, $x_3^{t+15} = z_{167}$. Thus, 16 new bits of the shrunken sequence have been reconstructed at positions $152, 153, \dots, 167$.

- In $\Delta 8$, $x_3^t = z_0 + z_{16}$, $x_3^{t+1} = z_1 + z_{17}$, $\ldots$, $x_3^{t+7} = z_7 + z_{23}$. As before keeping in mind that the equality $1 + \alpha^2 = \alpha^7$ holds, we get $x_3^t = z_{7 \cdot 8} = z_{56}$, $x_3^{t+1} = z_{57}$, $\ldots$, $x_3^{t+7} = z_{63}$. Thus, 8 new bits of the shrunken sequence have been reconstructed at positions $56, 57, \ldots, 63$.

For CA_2: The chained sub-triangles provide the following reconstructed bits. For $i = 3$, sub-automaton $R_1 R_2$ and $P_2(x) = x^2 + x + 1$.

- In $\Delta 8$, $x_3^t = z_0 + z_8 + z_{16}$, $x_3^{t+1} = z_1 + z_9 + z_{17}$, $\ldots$, $x_3^{t+7} = z_7 + z_{15} + z_{23}$. As before, keeping in mind that the equality $1 + \alpha + \alpha^2 = \alpha^{23}$ holds, we get $x_3^t = z_{23 \cdot 8} = z_{184}$, $x_3^{t+1} = z_{185}$, $\ldots$, $x_3^{t+7} = z_{191}$. Thus, 8 new bits of the shrunken sequence have been reconstructed at positions $184, 185, \ldots, 191$.

In brief, from 24 intercepted bits a total of 32 new bits have been reconstructed.

5 Conclusions

In this work, it is shown that wide classes of LFSR-based sequence generators with cryptographic application can be described in terms of CA-based structures. In this way, sequence generators conceived and designed as complex nonlinear models can be written in terms of simple linear models. Based on the linearity of these cellular models a method of reconstructing with absolute certainty unknown bits of the generated sequence is also presented.

References

1. K. Cattell and J. Muzio, *Synthesis of One-Dimensional Linear Hybrid Cellular Automata,* IEEE Trans. on Computer-Aided Design of Integrated Circuits and Systems **15** (3) (1996), 325-335.
2. P.P. Chaudhuri, D. R. Chowdhury, S. Nandi and S. Chatterjee, *Additive Cellular Automata- Theory and Applications,* Vol.1. IEEE Computer Society Press (1997).
3. S. Cho, C. Un- Sook and H. Yoon- Hee, *Computing Phase Shifts of Maximum-Length 90/150 Cellular Automata Sequences,* Proc. of ACRI 2004. LNCS **3305**, Springer, (2004), 31-39.
4. D. Coppersmith, H. Krawczyk and Y. Mansour, The Shrinking Generator. Proc. of CRYPTO'93. LNCS **773**, Springer, 22-39 (1994).
5. S.W. Golomb, Shift Register-Sequences, Aegean Park Press, Laguna Hill (1982).
6. G. Gong, Theory and Applications of q-ary Interleaved Sequences, IEEE Trans. on Information Theory, Vol. 41, No. 2, 400-411 (1995).
7. O. Martin, A.M. Odlyzko and S. Wolfram, *Algebraic Properties of Cellular Automata,* Commun. Math. Phys. **93** 219-258 (1984).
8. Rueppel, R.A.: Stream Ciphers, in Gustavus J. Simmons, Editor, Contemporary Cryptology, The Science of Information. IEEE Press 65-134 (1992)
9. M. Serra, T. Slater, J. C. Muzio and D. M. Miller. The Analysis of One-dimensional Linear Cellular Automata and Their Aliasing Properties, IEEE Trans. on Computer-Aided Design, Vol. 9, No. 7, 767-778 (1990).

Discrete Physics, Cellular Automata and Cryptography

Stephane Marconi and Bastien Chopard

Computer Science Department, University of Geneva, Switzerland
stephane.marconi@cui.unige.ch,
bastien.chopard@cui.unige.ch

Abstract. This paper aims at showing that Physics is very close to the substitution-diffusion paradigm of symmetric ciphers. Based on this analogy, we present a new Cellular Automata algorithm, termed `Crystal`, implementing fast, parallel, scalable and secure encryption systems. Our approach provides a design principle to ensure an invertible dynamics for arbitrary neighborhood. Thus, several variants of our CA can be devised so as to offer customized encryption-decryption algorithms. Considering larger data blocks improve both security and speed (throughput larger than 10Gbps on dedicated hardware).

1 Introduction

As introduced by Shannon [7], symmetric block ciphers are usually based on r rounds of diffusion and confusion operations applied to a plain text message M. This transformation is usually considered in a purely mathematical framework, with no reference to any physical process despite the fact that the term diffusion actually refers to a well known physical phenomena.

It seems that the contribution of physics to **classical** cryptography (quantum cryptography thus excluded) has been only to provide some vocabulary but no design principles and the few physical devices that have been proposed to encode a message are usually rather exotic and their security hard to prove [6].

Here we claim that the analogy between classical physics and symmetric block cipher is strong, natural and useful. This claim is made very clear when considering discrete physical models such lattice gases automata (LGA) used to model fluids [1].

These models consist of a discrete space time abstraction of the real world. N point-particles move on a regular lattice in D spatial dimensions. The possible velocities of each particle are restricted by the lattice topology: the propagation P moves, in one time step Δt, a particle from one site to one of its neighbor. Thus, if z is the lattice coordination number, particles may have z possible velocities. A collision C occurs between particles entering the same site from different directions. The result of such a collision is to create new particles in some directions and to remove some particles in others. Particle motion and collision are repeated alternatively for any chosen amount of time. Mathematically, the dynamics of our discrete fluid can be described by

$$M(t + \Delta t) = PCM(t)$$

S. El Yacoubi, B. Chopard, and S. Bandini (Eds.): ACRI 2006, LNCS 4173, pp. 617–626, 2006.

where $M(t)$ is the configuration of the particles over the full lattice at iteration t. This dynamics is structurally identical to the diffusion-confusion paradigm of cryptography. Diffusion is produced by an operator P and operator C implements a substitution box.

The other relevant ingredient from Physics is the second principle of thermodynamics which states that all configurations evolve to a final state which seems to contain no more memory of the initial situation. As such, this process is a good encryption mechanism. Deciphering, fortunately, is possible since the microscopic laws of physics are fully symmetrical with respect to past and future. Theoretically then, there is a way to come back. It is however highly impractical with real physical systems: one would have to reach every single particle of the system and to reverse its microscopic velocity with arbitrary precision.

On the contrary, with LGA systems, this time reversal is possible since the calculation is Boolean and performed without truncation error. We can thus reverse the arrow of time by simply inverting the direction of motion of each particles: $M(t) = RM(t)$, where R is the so-called time-reversal operator. Therefore, a deciphering mechanism is already embedded in a system obeying $CRC = R$ and $PRP = R$. It is then identical to the ciphering steps because

$$(CP)^r R(PC)^r = (CP)^{r-1} CPRPC(PC)^{r-1}$$
$$= (CP)^{r-1} R(PC)^{r-1} = R \qquad (1)$$

It is well known that time-reversibility in a physical system is highly sensitive to any small perturbation. Thus, the keying mechanism for the cipher may be viewed as errors that are deliberately introduced to prevent an attacker to reverse time.

Due to their properties of producing a complex behavior, cellular automata (CA) have been considered by several authors as a way to build cryptographic devices [5,9,4]. Several of the proposed CA are designed to produce a sequence of bits out of a secrete key and, as such, provide a stream cipher in which a sender and a receiver can both produce the same complex sequence of bits starting from an initial state given by the key.

However, when symmetric block ciphers are devised, it is necessary that encryption can be inverted in order to be able to decipher an encoded message. Therefore, a central question arises about how to build invertible CA's.

The standard definition of CA uses the so-called "gather-update" paradigm [1] (first get the neighbor values and then update the cell). It is well known that finding the inverse of a CA rule when the gather-update paradigm is used is a difficult task [3]. A procedure to produce a reversible CA rule (the rule is its own inverse) is the so-called technique of Fredkin [8]: a reversible cellular automata can be constructed by using the following rule:

$$s(r, t+1) = f(s(N(r), t)) \oplus s(r, t-1)$$

where f is arbitrary and N designate the neighborhood of cell r. This rule is said to be of second order since it requires state t and $t-1$ to compute the evolution.

Another approach to produce invertible CA uses the so-called block-permutation CA [3]. The central idea is to partition the CA cells into adjacent blocs of size $w \times w$, with respect to origin (ox, oy), and to define a function F applying the block to itself. By changing the partition offset (ox, oy), one obtains a family of different transformations of the cell space. Several of these transformation can be composed so as to produce a CA rule. Within this paradigm of block-partition CA, an invertible CA can be designed by taking the function F invertible. This approach however is restricted to regular, Cartesian grids and is non-local.

Finally, a last paradigm to implement a CA rule is the collision-propagation paradigm of LGA discussed above to model discrete physical systems. In this approach, it has been noted that the dynamics is reversible (i.e. is its own inverse) when the collision operator implements a reversible physical processes.

Our approach exploits this last paradigm to build a general reversible CA in a possibly irregular topology, of arbitrary dimension, through the introduction of three inter-related operators P, R and C. The main advantage of this formulation is that it offers an effective way to build both a hardware and a software device, with high scalability. In addition, it reconciliates the well admitted Shannon generic model of symmetric cryptography (confusion and diffusion) with the promising domain of complex dynamical systems (e.g CA) that are often considered as exotic and non-reliable cryptographic methods.

2   Description of the Algorithm

We first discuss a simple instance of the algorithm and then we formalize a general approach. Let us consider a 2D square periodic lattice with z bits per site and containing a N-bit message. With N bits distributed over the z directions, the lattice size must be $\sqrt{N/z} \times \sqrt{N/z}$.

When $z = 8$, each lattice site has eight neighbors, four along the main lattice directions, as well as four along the diagonals. This so-called D2Q8 topology defines the action of P. Note that the z links are two-way between the interconnected neighbors; they are labeled by a direction index $j = 0, ..., (z - 1)$ so that opposite directions j and j' are such that $j' = j + (z/2) \mod z$. By definition, the reverse operator R swaps the content of direction j and j'. By construction, we thus have $R^2 = 1$, i.e. $R^{-1} = R$.

The collision C is implemented as lookup table. In order to ensure $CRC = R$, the following randomized algorithm is used (here $z = 8$):

```
for all a=0 to 255, such that C(a) is still undefined
  do b=rand(0,255)
  until C(R(b)) is undefined
  C(a)=b;  C(R(b))=R(a);
endfor
```

The cipher key K is a N-bit string. It can be easily constructed from a N'-bit string, with $N' \leq N$, using any acceptable padding procedure.

With these ingredients, we propose the following block cipher algorithm

```
algorithm Crystal(M,K)  // M is the message, K the key
  reverse(M), reverse(K)
  propagation(M), propagation(K)
  repeat r times
    M=M+K
    collision(M), collision(K)
    propagation(M), propagation(K)
  end repeat
  M=M+K
  return M, K
end algorithm
```

Note that operators R, C and P act locally but, by extension we also use the same symbols to denote the synchronous action of R, C and P at all sites.

It can be shown that Crystal both encodes and decodes the blocks. Indeed the above algorithm can be expressed in a matrix formulation

$$\begin{pmatrix} M' \\ K' \end{pmatrix} = \begin{pmatrix} 1 & 1 \\ 0 & 1 \end{pmatrix} \left[PC \begin{pmatrix} 1 & 1 \\ 0 & 1 \end{pmatrix} \right]^n PR \begin{pmatrix} M \\ K \end{pmatrix}$$

in which we assume a modulo 2 algebra so that

$$\begin{pmatrix} 1 & 1 \\ 0 & 1 \end{pmatrix} \begin{pmatrix} M \\ K \end{pmatrix} = \begin{pmatrix} M \oplus K \\ K \end{pmatrix}$$

In addition, we define the product of the operator PC by a matrix as

$$PC \begin{pmatrix} 1 & 1 \\ 0 & 1 \end{pmatrix} = \begin{pmatrix} PC & PC \\ 0 & PC \end{pmatrix}$$

In order for our scheme to be reversible, we need

$$\begin{pmatrix} 1 & 1 \\ 0 & 1 \end{pmatrix} \left[PC \begin{pmatrix} 1 & 1 \\ 0 & 1 \end{pmatrix} \right]^n PR \begin{pmatrix} 1 & 1 \\ 0 & 1 \end{pmatrix} \left[PC \begin{pmatrix} 1 & 1 \\ 0 & 1 \end{pmatrix} \right]^n PR = \begin{pmatrix} 1 & 0 \\ 0 & 1 \end{pmatrix}$$

This is achieved provided that

$$PRP = R^{-1} \qquad CR^{-1}C = R$$

The proof follows by applying the same procedure as used in eq. 1 and by the fact that, in a modulo 2 algebra

$$\begin{pmatrix} 1 & 1 \\ 0 & 1 \end{pmatrix}^2 = \begin{pmatrix} 1 & 0 \\ 0 & 1 \end{pmatrix}$$

Note that in simple and regular topologies we have $R = R^{-1}$. However, the above formulation shows that any topology of interconnected cells for which

$PRP = R^{-1}$ and $CR^{-1}C = R$ hold can be used to implement the Crystal algorithm.

Such a topology can be constructed in a very general way, with possibly a different number of neighbors for each cell. The key condition is to distinguish the input and output links of the cell and to impose a suitable symmetry relation between them. This is detailed below.

Let R be a one-to-one mapping from the inputs to the output, as shown for instance in fig. 1 (a). So, within a cell there must be the same number of input and output ports. The collision operator C is also a one-to-one transformation of the the input data into the output data. This mapping is constructed so that $CR^{-1}C = R$. The propagation operator P transfers these output data to the input ports of the corresponding neighboring cells, as illustrated in fig. 1 (b). In order to build a reversible CA rule the following must be true: for each link connecting output j of cell r to input ℓ of cell r', there is a second link connecting output ℓ' of cell r' to input j' of cell r. If j and ℓ are such that $j = R(j')$ and $\ell' = R(\ell)$ (see fig. 1) then, by construction $PRP = R^{-1}$.

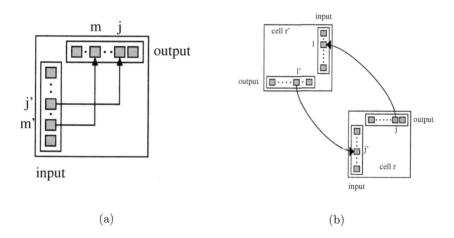

(a)   (b)

Fig. 1. (a) Illustration of the reverse operator R. (b) Illustration of the propagation operator P.

Therefore, any irregular interconnection topology obeying this pairwise symmetry can be devised to obtained a *reversible* dynamics. More generally, an *invertible* dynamics can be obtained by having two collision operators C and C' such that $C'R^{-1}C = R$. Thus, we can also think of our algorithm as a way to connect different processors, each running locally an invertible encryption process C and whose decryption is C'.

Within this relatively large framework, we can easily imagine several keying mechanisms, such as a secret topology, a secret collision or the more classical choice of secret bit string K.

3   Throughput and Security

We derive some properties of our cryptographic system in the case of the D2Q8 topology. These properties allow us to quantify both the security and the performances of the Crystal algorithm.

(1) A required property of a cipher is a high sensitivity to a little modification in the initial message M. We observe in fig. 2 that, after a number r of rounds equals to the lattice diameter $d = (1/2)\sqrt{N/z}$, a single bit error causes an avalanche of the full lattice size. The average Hamming distance between two messages initially differing only by one bit is $(1/2)N$ as expected for two random messages. Based on the speed at which information travels in the lattice, the

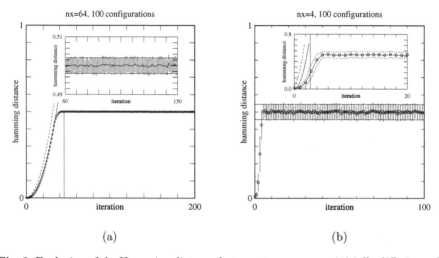

Fig. 2. Evolution of the Hamming distance between two messages initially differing only by one bit. In (a) we have $N = 64 \times 64 \times 8 = 32768$ bits and in (b) $N = 4 \times 4 = 128$ bits. Comparison with the ideal curve (eq. 2 is given with the doted parabola. The solid line parabola is the theoretical estimate of eq. 3). Finally, the vertical line show the iteration $r = (\sqrt{2}/2)\sqrt{N/z}$ at which the plateau should be reached.

Hamming distance can at best evolve as (see [2])

$$H(r) = \frac{1}{2}z(2r + 1)^2 \tag{2}$$

In numerical experiments, the speed at which the $1/2$ plateau is reached is less than predicted by eq. 2 because after a collision, only about $z/2$ bits differ from the reference configuration. From fig. 3, we can assume that the error propagates roughly as a disk. Its diameter grows on average by one lattice site at each iteration. Thus, during the first $r = \sqrt{N/z}/2$ rounds, H behaves as

$$H(r) = \frac{z}{2}\pi r^2 \tag{3}$$

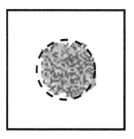
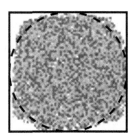

Fig. 3. Snapshot of the error propagation region, after 16 and 32 iterations, in a system of size 64×64. The non-blank regions indicates where the two configurations differ. The darker the gray, the more are the bits that differ. The dashed-line disks have radius 16 and 32, respectively; thus, the error propagates at speed one for this topology.

Therefore the minimal number r of rounds needed to mix the information all over the system must be $r = \alpha d$ where α is some constant larger than 1.

(2) Once the number of round is determined, we may compute the throughput of the algorithm. As any CA model, the dynamics of our system can be fully parallelized so that propagation and collision take a constant time for any N. Then, the time T needed to encrypt is proportional to the number of rounds but independent of the block size

$$T \propto r = \alpha d \propto \sqrt{N/z} \tag{4}$$

and therefore the encryption throughput W is

$$W = \frac{N}{T} \propto \sqrt{N} \tag{5}$$

Thus, when large data blocks are encrypted, the throughput increases although the number of round increases. The reason is that the number of rounds grows slower than the amount of data. Implementation studies on FPGA indicates that $W > 10Gb/s$ can be achieved with reasonable resources.

(3) It is commonly accepted that increasing the number of round r increases security. Therefore, with a full parallel implementation and large data blocks, both security and throughput are improved when `Crystal` is used.

Security can be assessed quantitatively by a differential cryptanalysis approach. The goal is to obtain information on the key K by considering how two plain text messages M_1 and M_2 get encrypted into M_1' and M_2'.

With $M_i^{(m)}$ and $K^{(m)}$ denoting the state of the messages and the key after m rounds, the algorithm `Crystal` gives

$$M_i^{(m)} = PC \left(M_i^{(m-1)} \oplus K^{(m-1)} \right) \tag{6}$$

for $i = 1, 2$. By XORing the above relation for $i = 1$ and $i = 2$ and applying inverse propagation, we obtain

$$P^{-1}\left(M_1^{(m)} \oplus M_2^{(m)}\right) = C\left(M_1^{(m-1)} \oplus K^{(m-1)}\right) \oplus C\left(M_2^{(m-1)} \oplus K^{(m-1)}\right) \quad (7)$$

It is now convenient to define $\mathcal{F}^{-1}$ as

$$a_1 \oplus a_2 \in \mathcal{F}^{-1}(b) \qquad \text{iff} \qquad b = C(a_1) \oplus C(a_2) \quad (8)$$

For a given collision operator C, $\mathcal{F}^{-1}$ can be computed easily by an exhaustive search [2]. With definition 8, we can rewrite eq. 7 as

$$\mathcal{F}^{-1}P^{-1}\left(M_1^{(m)} \oplus M_2^{(m)}\right) = M_1^{(m-1)} \oplus K^{(m-1)} \oplus M_2^{(m-1)} \oplus K^{(m-1)}$$
$$= M_1^{(m-1)} \oplus M_2^{(m-1)} \quad (9)$$

By repeating this relation, one obtains

$$M_1^{(1)} \oplus M_2^{(1)} = \left(\mathcal{F}^{-1}P^{-1}\right)^{r-1}\left(M_1^{(r)} \oplus M_2^{(r)}\right) \quad (10)$$

where r is the number of rounds. In [2] we show that if $M_1^{(1)} \oplus M_2^{(1)}$ is known to the attacker, it is rather easy to obtain the secret key K with an extra 2^z operations.

Below we compute how much computational effort is required to obtain $M_1^{(1)} \oplus M_2^{(1)}$ from $M_1^{(r)} \oplus M_2^{(r)}$ which, by hypothesis, is known since attackers are supposed to have access to any pairs (M, M') they want.

Since we assume that $r > d$, where d is the lattice diameter, $M_1^{(r)}$ and $M_2^{(r)}$ differ over all N/z lattice sites. In order to perform the backward scheme indicated in eq. 9, one has to find all possible pre-images of $P^{-1}\left(M_1^{(m)} \oplus M_2^{(m)}\right)$ by $\mathcal{F}^{-1}$. Empirically we observe that the number of pre-image of a given b is larger than $2^z/4$. Of course this depends on the choice of C, but this seems to be a minimal value for a C constructed with our randomized procedure.

Therefore, for each lattice site, at least 2^{z-2} values are possible for $M_1^{(r-1)} \oplus M_2^{(r-1)}$. This requires to select $(N/z)2^{z-2}$ candidates for $M_1^{(r-1)} \oplus M_2^{(r-1)}$. The same argument can be repeated $r - d$ times. After that, we can quickly exclude some possibilities. Indeed, at this point, we know that the error has not been able to propagate up to the outer boundary of the lattice. For these lattice sites, $M_1^{(d-1)} \oplus M_2^{(d-1)}$ must be zero. Thus the number of sites for which the exploration continues is $(\sqrt{N/z} - 2)^2$. If we undo one more step, even more possibilities can be excluded and the pre-images of "only" $(\sqrt{N/z} - 4)^2$ sites must be investigated.

Following this idea for the $d - 1$ steps, one has to explore $3^2 \times 5^2 \times \ldots \times (\sqrt{N/z} - 1)^2$ possible configurations[1], each with $2^z/4 = 2^{(z-2)}$ possible values.

---

[1] For a D2Q8 topology.

An inferior bound for this number is (see [2])

$$\left(3^2 \times 5^2 \times \dots \times (\sqrt{N/z} - 1)^2\right) 2^{z-2} > (d/2)^{2d} 2^{z-2} = \frac{1}{4}\left(\frac{N}{z}\right)^d 2^{z-2}$$

Thus, in total (undoing the rounds beyond and below the diameter) implies to investigate

$$\mathcal{N} > (N/z)^{r-d} 2^{(z-2)(r-d)} (N/z)^d 2^{z-4} = (N/z)^r 2^{(z-2)(r-d)+(z-4)} \tag{11}$$

candidates for $M_1^{(1)} \oplus M_2^{(1)}$.

Let us define the security measure S as the logarithm of our estimate of $\mathcal{N}$

$$S = \log_2 \mathcal{N} \tag{12}$$

A security of $S = 128$ is usually considered as safe. Eq. 11 can be shown as a graph. In figure 4 (a), we show how r must change with respect to N, for a given security level S. In figure 4 (b) we show how security S increases with N when we take the number of round r as twice the diameter d.

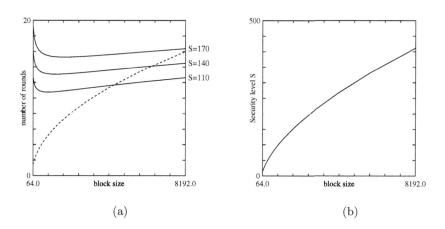

(a)   (b)

Fig. 4. (a) Number of rounds r as a function of block size N, to keep a given security level S. Note that r must be larger than the diameter d. The limit $r = d$ is shown by the dashed curve. (b) Security S as a function of block size N, for $r = 2d$.

4   Conclusion

A first specificity of Crystal with respect to standard block ciphers is that it is made of many fully identical components (the sites). Hence, it is local, scalable, fully parallel and fits naturally on silicon.

Second, Crystal can be tailored in many different variants, so as to provide each user with a unique encryption-decryption method, whose details can be kept secret in addition to the key. The simplest way to customize `Crystal` is to choose a personal substitution box C. Indeed a large number of C's can be generated with the same level of security. Other ways to customize the algorithm is to have a main substitution box C and a second one C' active only at some secrete cells. Finally the shape of the encryption domain can be a secrete information.

In conclusion, we have described a new cipher which is cost effective to develop and implement, simple to analyze and which efficiently addresses the increasing needs for high throughput, high security and high level of versatility.

References

1. B. Chopard and M. Droz. *Cellular Automata Modeling of Physical Systems*. Cambridge University Press, 1998.
2. B. Chopard and S. Marconi. Discrete physics: a new way to look at cryptography. Technical report, University of Geneva, 2005.
   http://arXiv.org/abs/nlin.CG/0504059.
3. Jerome Durand-Lose. Representing reversible cellular automata with reversible block cellular automata. *Discrete Mathematics and Theoretical Computer Sciences Proceedings AA (DM-CCG)*, pages 145–154, 2001.
4. E. Franti, S. Goschin, M. Dascalu, and N. Catrina. Criptocel: Design of cellular automata based cipher schemes. In *Communications, circuits and systems*, volume 2, pages 1103–1107. ICCCAS, IEEE, 2006.
5. Howard Gutowitz. Cryptography with dynamical systems. In E.Goles and N.Boccara, editors, *Cellular Automata and Cooperative phenomena*. Kluwer Academic Press, 1993.
6. Pour la Science: dossier hors srie, editor. *L'Art du Secret*, 2002.
7. Claude Shannon. Communication theory of secrecy systems. *Bell Syst. Tech. Journal*, 28:656–715, 1949.
8. T. Toffoli and N. Margolus. *Cellular automota machines: a new environment for modelling*. MIT Press, 1987.
9. Stephen Wolfram. Cryptography with cellular automata. In *Advances in Cryptology: Crypto85*, volume 218 of *Lectures Notes in Computer Science*, pages 429–432. Springer Verlag, 1986.

A Protocol to Provide Assurance of Images Integrity Using Memory Cellular Automata

A. Martín del Rey

Department of Applied Mathematics, E.P.S., Universidad de Salamanca
C/Hornos Caleros 50, 05003-Ávila, Spain
delrey@usal.es

Abstract. In this work, the use of memory cellular automata to design a cryptographic protocol to provide assurance of digital images integrity is studied. It is shown that the proposed protocol is secure against the adequate cryptanalytic attacks. As a consequence, memory cellular automata seems to be suitable candidates to the design of hash functions.

1 Introduction

The rapid development of new technologies for the fast provision of commercial multimedia services yields a strong demand for reliable and secure copyright protection for multimedia data. In this sense, digital image protection is one of the most important problems that have arisen with the use of internet. As is well known, digital images can be easily altered by using common suitable software. Consequently, it is of special importance to decide whether a given image is authentic or has been modified subsequent to capture by some available digital image processing tools. That is an important question in, for example, legal applications, news reporting, medical images, etc., where we want to be sure that the digital image truly reflects the original image used. Another important application arises in the e-commerce where the digital images of the goods to be sold are stored into a data base with free-access for the buyers. Obviously, the buyer wants to be sure that the digital image is genuine and no modification has been done. To address these issues several protocols have been proposed in the literature (see, for example [8,11,18,19]).

The main goal of the protocol proposed in this paper is to guarantee the authenticity of digital images stored into a data base. The protocol is based on the use of memory cellular automata (see, for example, [1,3]). Basically, the proposed protocol consists of computing for each image, I, a fingerprint, F_I, such that minimum changes in I yields a different fingerprint. As a consequence, if one suspects that an image has been modified, then its fingerprint must be computed and compared with the derived from the original one which is securely stored. If both fingerprints are equal, the image is the original, otherwise, the image has been changed. Note that, the proposed protocol does not define a hash function. Nevertheless, it can serve as a basis for the development of message authentication codes (MAC protocols).

S. El Yacoubi, B. Chopard, and S. Bandini (Eds.): ACRI 2006, LNCS 4173, pp. 627–635, 2006.

Roughly speaking, memory cellular automata are delay discrete dynamical systems formed by a one-dimensional array of cells, which are endowed with a particular state at each time. These states change at every step of time according to a local transition rule. The main characteristic of cellular automata is that they are very simple models of computation capable to simulate complex behavior (see, for example, [24]). Several cryptographic protocols based on cellular automata have been proposed in the last years not only for text data (see, for example [4,7,9,10,12,13,15,16,17,21,22,23]), but also for images (see, for example, [5,6]). Nevertheless, any cryptographic protocol based on cellular automata to guarantee the integrity of digital images has not been proposed.

The rest of the paper is organized as follows: In Section 2, the basic theory of cellular automata is introduced; in Section 3, the model to guarantee the authenticity of digital images is shown and an example is also given; in Section 4, the security analysis of the algorithm is performed; and finally the conclusions and the further work are presented in Section 5.

2   Overview of Cellular Automata

In this section an overview of the theory of memory cellular automata is presented. Moreover, the interpretation of a digital image in terms of memory cellular automata is also shown.

A cellular automata (CA for short) is a special class of discrete dynamical system which is formed by a finite one-dimensional array of n identical objects called cells. Each one of them can assume a state from a finite state set S. The i-th cell of the bidimensional lattice is denoted by (i), and the state of such cell at time t is s_i^t.

The CA evolves deterministically in discrete time steps, changing the states of all cells according to a local transition function, $f : S^m \rightarrow S$. The updated state of each cell depends on the m variables of f, which are the states at previous time steps of a set of cells, including the cell itself, and called its neighbourhood. The set of indices defining the neighborhood of the CA is the ordered finite subset $V \subset \mathbb{Z}$, with $|V| = m$, such that for every cell (i), its neighborhood, V_i, is the set of m cells given by

$$V_i = \{(i + l) : l \in V\}. \tag{1}$$

In this work, symmetric neighbourhoods of radius p are considered; that is, the neighbourhood of each cell is formed by its p nearest cells at left, its p nearest cells at right and the cell itself. Note that it is given by the following set of indices:

$$V = \{-p, -p + 1, \ldots, -1, 0, 1, \ldots, p - 1, p\}. \tag{2}$$

Consequently, the evolution of the state of the cell (i) is given by $s_i^{t+1} = f(V_i^t)$, where V_i^t stands for the states of the neighbour cells of (i) at time t. The vector $C^t = (s_1^t, \ldots, s_n^t) \in S \times \overset{(n}{\ldots} \times S$, is called the configuration at time t of the CA. The set of all configurations of a CA is denoted by $\mathcal{C}$. As the number of cells is finite, boundary conditions must be considered in order to assure the well-defined dynamics of the cellular automata. In this paper, periodic boundary conditions are taken: if $i \equiv j \pmod{n}$, then $s_i^t = s_j^t$.

Moreover, the global function of the CA is a map, $\Phi\colon \mathcal{C} \to \mathcal{C}$, that yields the configuration at the next time step during the evolution of the cellular automaton, that is, $\Phi(C^t) = C^{t+1}$. If Φ is bijective then the CA is called reversible (RCA for short) and the evolution backwards is possible by means of the inverse CA whose global transition function is Φ^{-1} (see [20]).

The standard paradigm for cellular automata considers that the state of every cell at time $t+1$ depends on the state of its neighbour cells at time t. Nevertheless, one can consider cellular automata for which the state of every cell at time $t+1$ not only depends on the states of the neighbour cells at time t, but also on their states at previous time steps: $t-1, t-2$, etc. This is the main feature of memory cellular automata, MCA for short (see [1]). Specifically, a k-th order MCA is defined by a global transition function given by

$$\Phi\colon \mathcal{C} \times \overset{(k}{\ldots} \times \mathcal{C} \to \mathcal{C}, \tag{3}$$

where

$$C^{t+1} = \Phi\left(C^t, C^{t-1}, \ldots, C^{t-k+1}\right). \tag{4}$$

Finally, remark that every image defined by $r \times c$ pixels and by a palette of 2^b colors (where $b = 1$ stands for black and white images, $b = 8$ stands for grey-level images, and $b = 24$ stands for general color images) can be interpreted as a set of r configurations of a MCA with c cells, by simply considering each row of pixels as a configuration, and each pixel as a cell of the configuration. The i-th coefficient of such configuration, that is, the state of the i-th cell, is the numeric value associated to the color of the i-th pixel of the row. As a consequence, the state set of the MCA is given by $S = \mathbb{Z}_{2^b}$.

3 The Protocol to Authenticate Digital Images

3.1 Description of the Protocol

In this section the model based on MCA to authenticate digital images is presented. Let I be a digital image defined by a palette of 2^b colors and $r \times c$ pixels. Basically, the protocol consists of computing a fingerprint, $F_I = (f_1, \ldots, f_c) \in S \times \overset{c}{\ldots} \times S$ using a $(r+1)$-th order MCA. This fingerprint must be securely stored using another protocol (see, for example, [14]). Consequently, if we want to check the authenticity of the image I, we have to compute its fingerprint by means of the same protocol and compare the result with the fingerprint securely stored. If both fingerprints are the same, then the original image is authentic; otherwise, it has been changed.

Specifically, the proposed protocol is as follows: Let I be an image defined by $r \times c$ pixels and by a palette of 2^b colors. Let $C^1, \ldots, C^r$, be the r configurations obtained from the r rows of pixels of the image I. Then $C^t \in \mathbb{Z}_{2^b} \times \overset{c}{\ldots} \times \mathbb{Z}_{2^b}$ for each $1 \le t \le r$. Moreover, the initial configuration, C^0, must be computed at random and it is the secret key of the protocol.

Let us consider the $(r+1)$-th order RMCA with c cells and $S = \mathbb{Z}_{2^b}$, defined by the following local transition function:

$$s_i^{t+1} = f\left(V_i^t, \ldots, V_i^{t-r+1}\right) + s_i^{t-r} \pmod{2^b}, \tag{5}$$

where $1 \leq i \leq c$. Recall that this RMCA is reversible (see, for example [2]) and the local transition function of its inverse is the following:

$$s_i^{t+1} = -f\left(V_i^t, \ldots, V_i^{t-r+1}\right) + s_i^{t-r} \pmod{2^b}. \tag{6}$$

Note that, in terms of the global transition function, it yields:

$$C^{t+1} = \Phi\left(C^t, \ldots, C^{t-r}\right). \tag{7}$$

Now, computing the sucessive configurations of the MCA given by (5) and starting from $C^0, C^1, \ldots, C^r$, we obtain the following sequence of configurations:

$$C^0, C^1, \ldots, C^r, C^{r+1}, C^{r+2}, \ldots, C^{2r+2}. \tag{8}$$

The last configuration computed, that is: C^{2r+2} is considered the fingerprint of the image I.

3.2   An Example

In this section, a MCA-protocol with a simple local transition function is introduced. Let us consider the image shown in Figure 1 which is given by 128×128 pixels and $2^8 = 256$ gray-level colors.

Fig. 1. Gray-level image defined by 128×128 pixels

For the sake of simplicity, let us consider a 129-th order MCA whose local transition function is as follows:

$$s_i^{t+1} = f_0\left(V_i^t\right) + \ldots + f_{r-1}\left(V_i^{t-r+1}\right) + s_i^{t-r} \pmod{2^b}, \tag{9}$$

with $1 \leq i \leq 128$. Furthermore, the function f_k is defined as follows:

$$f_k\left(V_i^{t-k}\right) = s_{i-\alpha_k}^t + \ldots + s_{i-1}^t + s_i^t + s_{i+1}^t + \ldots + s_{i+\alpha_k}^t \pmod{2^b}, \tag{10}$$

where $1 \leq \alpha_k < c/2$. Note that this function can be considered as the local transition function of a (non-memory) cellular automata endowed with symmetric neighborhoods of radius α_k. Set

$$
\begin{aligned}
C^0 = \{ & 155, 160, 141, 85, 20, 214, 81, 121, 95, 92, 236, 20, 251, 94, 49, \\
& 205, 234, 218, 2, 255, 162, 15, 198, 25, 205, 200, 204, 78, 4, \\
& 189, 52, 28, 247, 135, 208, 124, 199, 40, 232, 63, 119, 25, 46, \\
& 98, 93, 243, 66, 156, 77, 112, 0, 115, 72, 38, 115, 127, 136, 214, \\
& 6, 65, 173, 166, 141, 101, 163, 33, 94, 129, 60, 190, 200, 64, 12, \\
& 130, 239, 118, 59, 227, 52, 186, 7, 182, 253, 38, 74, 4, 237, 246, \\
& 6, 61, 91, 68, 33, 248, 31, 9, 158, 144, 129, 81, 56, 102, 181, 65, \\
& 82, 83, 18, 83, 114, 202, 39, 192, 56, 224, 15, 123, 144, 104, 168, \\
& 8, 199, 165, 142, 130, 71, 33, 188, 111 \},
\end{aligned}
\tag{11}
$$

the initial configuration. Let us consider the following artificially chosen $\Omega = \{\alpha_1, \ldots, \alpha_{128}\}$:

$$
\begin{aligned}
\Omega = \{ & 1, 3, 3, 2, 3, 1, 1, 1, 2, 2, 1, 2, 2, 2, 2, 2, 1, 2, 1, 2, 3, 3, 2, 1, 1, 1, 2, 2, 3, 2, \\
& 2, 1, 2, 2, 3, 1, 2, 3, 3, 3, 1, 2, 2, 2, 2, 1, 1, 2, 1, 1, 2, 3, 2, 2, 1, 2, 1, 1, 2, 2, \\
& 2, 1, 3, 2, 1, 1, 1, 1, 3, 1, 1, 3, 1, 1, 1, 1, 1, 3, 3, 2, 1, 2, 3, 1, 2, 2, 2, 3, 3, 2, \\
& 1, 3, 1, 1, 3, 1, 3, 3, 2, 1, 1, 2, 2, 2, 2, 1, 3, 1, 2, 2, 2, 2, 1, 3, 2, 1, 3, 2, 3, 2, \\
& 3, 1, 1, 2, 2, 3, 2, 3 \}.
\end{aligned}
\tag{12}
$$

Then, if we compute the evolution of the MCA, the configuration C^{258} is the fingerprint. Specifically, it is:

$$
\begin{aligned}
F_I = \{ & 0, 221, 55, 206, 204, 185, 47, 125, 97, 173, 243, 37, 154, 150, 239, 137, 244, 51, \\
& 105, 61, 190, 197, 0, 216, 28, 208, 138, 85, 133, 196, 123, 242, 122, 26, 31, 70, \\
& 197, 119, 203, 169, 44, 213, 204, 36, 57, 175, 108, 163, 136, 95, 202, 35, 87, \\
& 82, 232, 62, 12, 91, 105, 229, 202, 247, 96, 132, 174, 217, 44, 227, 104, 94, \\
& 129, 54, 166, 13, 161, 35, 106, 128, 193, 153, 154, 7, 176, 89, 203, 13, 178, \\
& 8, 152, 11, 172, 132, 31, 150, 253, 237, 63, 70, 38, 192, 180, 168, 66, 179, \\
& 72, 52, 193, 158, 79, 24, 222, 207, 134, 3, 225, 78, 126, 153, 226, 123, 147, \\
& 204, 139, 228, 26, 59, 183, 94 \}.
\end{aligned}
\tag{13}
$$

In Figure 2 the graphic representation of the fingerprint is shown.

Fig. 2. Fingerprint of the original image

Remark that, taking into account the diffusion process, it is sufficient to consider $\alpha_k < c/2$. Moreover, in this sense, in order to obtain higher diffusion the configuration at time $2r + 2$ is considered as the fingerprint.

4   Security Analysis

In this section the security of the protocol introduced in the last section is analyzed. Specifically, for evaluating its security, some properties are studied: The sensitivity to initial conditions and the preimage resistant, second-preimage resistant and collision resistance properties. Moreover, the complexity of the proposed protocol is computed.

4.1   Sensitivity to Initial Conditions

A desirable property of any cryptographic protocol is that a small change in the inputs should result in a significant change in the ciphertext. That is, in our case, changing value of one randomly pixel in the original image I should produce a great change of the pixels of the fingerprint.

Then suppose that only one pixel is modified in the original image of the example I, say for example the 64-th pixel of the first row that passes from the gray level given by the number 100 to the grey level defined by the numeric value 101 (note that the human eye does not detect such change). If its fingerprint is calculated using the same MCA as in the example above, then the following result is obtained:

$$F_I = \{36, 63, 14, 81, 69, 26, 183, 165, 162, 103, 111, 50, 237, 204, 165, 46,$$
$$33, 226, 241, 159, 236, 185, 13, 41, 165, 206, 201, 27, 69, 50, 104, 173,$$
$$135, 115, 158, 239, 159, 107, 90, 141, 184, 208, 17, 208, 201, 74, 135,$$
$$174, 147, 128, 168, 50, 181, 74, 223, 107, 84, 79, 107, 94, 177, 204, 99,$$
$$202, 177, 174, 19, 92, 106, 82, 201, 99, 157, 5, 0, 50, 72, 161, 204, 164,$$
$$181, 161, 65, 6, 16, 8, 63, 235, 39, 254, 134, 46, 158, 239, 11, 168, 44,$$
$$179, 229, 134, 243, 166, 203, 4, 85, 40, 239, 1, 215, 199, 11, 116, 60, 57,$$
$$53, 91, 249, 83, 36, 163, 28, 45, 4, 103, 240, 156, 219, 16\}, \tag{14}$$

and as a simple calculus shows, all pixels are different from the original fingerprint.

In this sense, note that if only one pixel is changed in the i-th row of the original image, then $2 \cdot \alpha_{r-i}$ pixels are changed in the configuration C^{r+1}, $2 \cdot \alpha_0 + 2 \cdot \alpha_{r-i}$ pixels are changed in the configuration C^{r+2}, $2 \cdot \alpha_1 + 2 \cdot \alpha_1 + 2 \cdot \alpha_{r-i}$ pixels are changed in the configuration C^{r+3}, and so on. Consequently, if $\alpha_0, \dots, \alpha_{r-1}$ are sufficient large, then in a few iterations the change of only one pixel yields the change of all pixels of the fingerprint.

4.2   Collision Resistance

The main feature of the proposed algorithm is that it satisfies some desirable properties for data integrity protocols: The preimage resistant property, the second-preimage resistant property and the collision resistant property (see [14]).

The preimage resistant property states that for essentially all pre-specific outputs, it is computationally infeasible to find any input which yields to that output. This property holds in our case since if we have a fixed fingerprint $F_I = C^{2r+2}$, to obtain the image $I = \{C^1, \ldots, C^r\}$, it is necessary to solve the following system of equations:

$$
\begin{cases}
C^{2r+2} = \Phi\left(C^{2r+1}, \ldots, C^{r+1}\right) \\
C^{2r+1} = \Phi\left(C^{2r}, \ldots, C^r\right) \\
\cdots \\
C^{r+1} = \Phi\left(C^r, \ldots, C^0\right)
\end{cases}
\tag{15}
$$

Then, by substituting recursively, the following system is obtained:

$$
C^{2r+2} = \Psi\left(C^r, \ldots, C^0\right),
\tag{16}
$$

which is formed by c equations with $(r+1)\, c$ unknown variables:

$$
\{s_i^t,\ 1 \le i \le c, 0 \le t \le r\}.
\tag{17}
$$

Moreover, the protocol also satisfies the second-preimage resistant property which establishes that it must be computationally infeasible to find any second image $\bar{I} = \{\bar{C}^1, \ldots, \bar{C}^r\}$ which has the same fingerprint, F_I, as a specific image $I = \{C^1, \ldots, C^r\}$. In this case one has to solve the following system of equations:

$$
\Psi\left(C^{r-1}, \ldots, C^0\right) = \Psi\left(\bar{C}^{r-1}, \ldots, \bar{C}^0\right),
\tag{18}
$$

which is formed by c equations with $(r+1)\, c$ unknown variables:

$$
\{\bar{s}_i^t,\ 1 \le i \le c, 0 \le t \le r\}.
\tag{19}
$$

Finally, the proposed protocol is a collision resistance model, that is, it is computationally infeasible to find two distinct images, I and $\bar{I}$, which yield to the same fingerprint. In this case, the system of equations obtained is similar to the last one but with $2\,(r+1)\, c$ unknown variables: $s_i^t, \bar{s}_i^t$ with $1 \le i \le c, 0 \le t \le r$.

4.3 Computational Complexity

The complexity of execution of the cryptographic protocol introduced in this paper, depends on the local functions used. A simple computation shows that the complexity of the MCA proposed in the example is $O\left(r \cdot c \cdot \log\left(2^b + 1\right)\right)$.

5 Conclusions and Further Work

In this work the study of the use of memory cellular automata in the design of protocols to guarantee the integrity of digital images has been introduced. Specifically, a very simple local transition function is proposed and it is shown to be secure against the most important cryptanalytic attacks.

The main features of proposed protocol are the following:

- It is very easy to compute the fingerprint of each image.
- It is very easy to verify whether or not a digital image has been modified.
- No external adversary can be able to efficiently produce the fingerprint for any digital image of his/her choice.

Further work aimed at studying another suitable local transition functions with the same security level and with the same (or less) computationally complexity. Also, it will be very important to design a RMCA-based algorithm with a lesser and fixed fingerprint and with the same security level. Moreover, this work can serve as a basis for the development of MCA-based hash functions. In this case, some specific cryptanalysis of the local transition functions employed will be studied rather than brutte-force attacks.

Acknowledgements

This work has been partially supported by the Consejería de Educación y Cultura of Junta de Castilla y León (Spain), by "D. Samuel Solorzano Barruso" Memorial Foundation (Universidad de Salamanca, Spain) under grant FS/3-2005, and by the Ministerio de Educación y Ciencia (Spain) under grant SEG2004-02418.

References

1. Alonso-Sanz, R., Martín, M.: One-dimensional cellular automata with memory: patterns from a single seed, Internat. J. Bifur. Chaos **12** (2002) 205–226.
2. Alonso-Sanz, R.: Reversible cellular automata with memory: patterns starting with a single site seed, Physica D, **175** (2003) 1–30.
3. Alonso-Sanz, R., Martín, M.: Elementary cellular automata with memory, Complex Systems **14** (2003) 99–126.
4. Álvarez Marañón, G., Hernández Encinas, A., Hernández Encinas, L., Martín del Rey, A., Rodríguez Sánchez, G.: Graphic cryptography with pseudorandom bit generators and cellular automata, Proceedings of the Seventh International Conference on Knowledge-Based Intelligent Information & Engineering Systems, LNAI **2773** (2003) 1207–1214.
5. Álvarez Marañón, G., Hernández Encinas, L., Martín del Rey, A.: A new secret sharing scheme for images based on additive 2-dimensional cellular automata, Proceedings of the 2nd Iberian Conference on Pattern Recognition and Image Analysis, LNCS **3522** (2005) 411-418.
6. Álvarez, G., Hernández Encinas, A., Hernández Encinas, L., Martín del Rey, A.: A secure scheme to share secret color images, Comput. Phys. Comm. **173** (2005) 9–16.
7. Bao, F.: Cryptanalysis of Partially Known Cellular Automaton Cryptosystem, IEEE Trans. Comput. **53** (2004) 1493–1497.
8. Barni, M., Bartolini, F., Cappellini, V., Piva, A.: Copyright protection of digital images by embedded unperceivable marks, Image and Vision Computing **16** (1998), 897–906.

9. Dasgupta, P., Chattopadhyay, S., Sengupta, I.: Theory and application of non-group cellular automata for message authentication, J. Syst. Architecture **47** (2001) 383–404.

10. Fúster-Sabater, A., de la Guía-Martínez, D.: Cellular automata applications to the linearization of stream cipher generators, Proceedings of ACRI 2004, LNCS **3305** (2004) 612–621.

11. Lin, Ch. and Tsai, W.: Secret image sharing with steganography and authentication, J. Syst. Soft. **73** (2004) 405–414.

12. Martín del Rey, A.: Design of a Cryptosystem Based on Reversible Memory Cellular Automata, Proc. of 10th IEEE Symposium on Computers and Communications, 482–486, 2005.

13. Martín del Rey, A., Pereira Mateus, J., Rodríguez Sánchez, G.: A secret sharing scheme based on cellular automata, Appl. Math. Comput. **170** (2005) 1356–1364.

14. Menezes, A., van Oorschot, P., Vanstone, S.: Handbook of Applied Cryptography, CRC Press, Boca Raton, FL, 1997.

15. Mihaljevic, M., Zheng, Y., Imai, H.: A family of fast dedicated one-way hash functions based on linear cellular automata over $GF(q)$, IEICE Trans. Fundamentals **E82-A** (1999) 40–47.

16. Mukherjee, M., Ganguly, N., Chaudhuri, P.P.: Cellular automata based authentication, Proc. of ACRI 2002, LNCS **2493** (2002) 259–269.

17. Nandi, S., Kar, B.K., Chaudhuri, P.P.: Theory and applications of cellular automata in cryptography, IEEE Trans. Comput. **43** (1994) 1346–1357.

18. Page, T.: Digital watermarking as a form of copyright protection, Computer Law & Security Report **14** (1998) 390–392.

19. Queluz, M.: Authentication of digital images and video: Generic models and a new contribution, Signal Processing: Image Communication **16** (2001) 461–475.

20. Richardson, D.: Tessellation with local transformations, J. Comput. Syst. Sci. **6** (1972) 373–388.

21. Seredynski, M., Bouvry, P.: Block encryption using reversible cellular automata, Proc. of ACRI 2004, LNCS **3305** (2004) 785–792.

22. Wolfram, S.: Random sequence generation by cellular automata, Adv. Appl. Math. **7** (1986) 123–169.

23. Wolfram, S.: Cryptography with cellular automata, Advances in Cryptology: Crypto'85, LNCS **218** (1986) 429–432.

24. Wolfram, S.: A New Kind of Science, Wolfram Media, Inc., 2002.

Generation of Expander Graphs Using Cellular Automata and Its Applications to Cryptography

Debdeep Mukhopadhyay[1] and Dipanwita RoyChowdhury[2]

[1] PhD Student, Department of Computer Science and Engg., Indian Institute of
Technology, Kharagpur, India
debdeep@cse.iitkgp.ernet.in
[2] Associate Professor, Department of Computer Science and Engg., Indian Institute
of Technology, Kharagpur, India
drc@cse.iitkgp.ernet.in

Abstract. The paper proposes a methodology to generate family of
expander graphs based on Two Predecessor Single Attractor Cellular
Automata (TPSA-CA). The construction is finally applied to develop a
one-way function whose security lies on the combinatorial properties of
the expander graph. It is shown that while the forward transformation
of the one-way function is computationally efficient the inverse operation appears to be intractable. Such a one-way function can be an ideal
candidate for one-way functions and thus help to develop fast and secure
key establishment protocols.

Keywords: Expander Graphs, Cellular Automata, One-way functions,
Security, Efficiency.

1 Introduction

Expander Graphs have been a significant tool both in theory and practice. It
has been used in solving problems in communication and construction of error
correcting codes as well as a tool for proving results in number theory and computational complexity. The combinatorial properties of the expander graphs can
also lead to the construction of one-way functions [1]. Informally, the one-way
functions are a class of functions in which the forward computation is easy, but
the inverse is hard to find. The one-way functions form an important core of all
key agreement algorithms which are an important step in secure electronic communication. The well known Diffie-Hellman key exchange algorithm [2] provides
a ground-breaking solution to the problem of secured key distribution. However the security of the algorithm depends on the one-wayness of the modular
exponentiation, which is a costly process in terms of computational resources.
Since the seminal paper of Diffie-Helmann, there has been efforts in developing key exchange protocols whose security lies on one-way functions which are
computationally efficient. However designing a strong one-way function which is
computationally strong and yet efficient is a challenging task.

The present paper uses a special class of Cellular Automata (CA) [3], known as
the *Two Predecessor Single Attractor Cellular Automata* (TPSA-CA) to generate

S. El Yacoubi, B. Chopard, and S. Bandini (Eds.): ACRI 2006, LNCS 4173, pp. 636–645, 2006.

expander graphs on the fly. The elegance of the scheme is that it uses regular, cascadable and modular structures of CA to generate random d regular graphs of good expansion property with very less storage. The state transitions of each TPSA is captured in a single state, which is known as the graveyard of the CA. Finally, the expander graphs have been used to construct the one-way function according to the proposal of [1].

The paper is organized as follows: *Section 2* presents the preliminaries of the expander graphs. The TPSA-CA has been used to generate a family of expander graphs in *section 3*. *Section 4* presents the final composition of the one-way function based on the TPSA-CA based expander graphs. The work is concluded in *section 5*.

2   Preliminaries on Expander Graphs

Informally *expander graphs* are a class of graphs $G = (V, E)$ in which every subset S of vertices expands quickly, in the sense that it is connected to many vertices in the set $\overline{S}$ of complementary vertices. It may be noted that the graph may have self loops and multiple edges in the graph. The following definition states formally the *expansion property* of these class of graphs [4].

Definition 1. *The edge boundary of a set $S \in G$, denoted $\delta(S)$ is $\delta(S) = E(S, \overline{S})$ is the set of outgoing edges from S. The* expansion parameter *of G is defined as $h(G) = min_{S:|S| \leq n/2} \frac{|\delta(S)|}{|S|}$ where $|S|$ denotes the size of a set S.*

There are other notions of expansion, the most popular being counting the number of neighbouring vertices of any small set, rather than the number of outgoing edges. Following is an example of expander graph [5].

Example 1. *Let G be a random d-regular graph, in which each of n vertices is connected to d other vertices chosen at random. Let S be a subset of atmost $n/2$ vertices. Then a typical vertex in S will be connected to roughly $d \times |\overline{S}|/n$ vertices in $\overline{S}$, and thus $|\delta S| \approx d \times |S||\overline{S}|/n$, and so $\frac{|\delta(S)|}{|S|} \approx d\frac{|\overline{S}|}{n}$. Since, $|\overline{S}|$ has its minimum at approximately $n/2$ it follows that $h(G) \approx d/2$, independently of the size n.*

Although d-regular graph random graphs on n vertices define an expander, for real life applications it is necessary to have more explicit constructions on $O(2^n)$ vertices, where n is the parameter defining the problem size. This is because to store a description of a random graph on so many vertices requires exponentially much time and space. Two well known constructions are given in [6,7,8].

The properties of the eigenvalue spectrum of the adjacency matrix $A(G)$ can be used to understand properties of the graph G. The **adjacency matrix** of a graph G, denoted by $A(G)$ is an $n \times n$ matrix that each (u, v) contains the number of edges in G between vertex u and vertex v. For a d-regular graph, the sum of each row and column in $A(G)$ is d. By definition the matrix $A(G)$ is symmetric and therefore has an orthonormal base $v_0, v_1, \ldots, v_{n-1}$, with eigenvalues

$\mu_0, \mu_1, \ldots, \mu_{n-1}$ such that for all i we have $Av_i = \mu_i v_i$. Without loss of generality we assume the eigenvalues sorted in descending order $\mu_0 \geq \mu_1 \geq \ldots \geq \mu_{n-1}$. The eigenvalues of $A(G)$ are called the spectrum of G. The following two results are important in estimating the expansion properties of the graph.

1. $\mu_0 = d$
2. $\frac{d-\mu_1}{2} \leq h(G) \leq \sqrt{2d(d - \mu_1)}$

Thus, the parameter $d - \mu_1$, also known as the *Spectral Gap* gives a good estimate on the expansion of the graph G. The graph is an expander if the spectral gap has a lower bound, i.e, $d - \mu_1 > \epsilon'$.

A graph G_1 has better expansion properties than graph G_2, implies that for any subset S, $|S| \leq n/2$ of the graph G_1 has a larger number of neighbouring elements outside the set S, compared to that in G_2. Mathematically, the value of $h(G_1) > h(G_2)$. Informally, it implies that the graph G_1 expands faster compared to graph G_2. The hardness of inverting the one-way function based on expander graphs increases with the expansion of the expander graph [1]. A random regular graph has good expansion properties. However the problem of realising such a graph is in its description which grows exponentially with the number of vertices. In the following section we show a construction of a family of random d regular graph using the properties of a special class of CA, known as the Two Predecessor Singe Attractor Cellular Automaton (TPSA CA). It has been shown that the graph has good expansion properties. The merit of the construction lies in the fact that the generation is extremely simple and leads to efficient one-way functions.

3   Expander Graphs Using TPSA CA

TPSA CA are a special class of non-group CA in which the state transition graph forms a single inverted binary routed tree at all zero state. Every reachable state in the state transition graph has exactly two predecessors. The only cyclic state is the all zero state (for a non-complemented TPSA CA), which is an attractor (or graveyard). If T_n is the characteristic matrix of an n cell automaton then the necessary and sufficient conditions to be satisfied by the Transition matrix for the CA to be TPSA CA is: (i) Rank$(T_n)=n-1$, (ii) Rank$(T_n + I_n)=n$, I_n being an $n \times n$ identity matrix (iii) Characteristic Polynomial $= x^n$, (iv) Minimal Polynomial $= x^n$[3]. For an n cell TPSA CA with characteristic polynomial x^n and minimal polynomial x^n, (i) the number of attractors is 1, the all zero state, (ii) the number of states in the tree is 2^n. For an n cell TPSA CA having minimal polynomial x^n the depth of the tree is n. Following is an example of a 4 cell non-complemented TPSA CA.

Example 2. *The state transition matrix for the CA is denoted by:*

$$T_4 = \begin{pmatrix} 1 & 1 & 0 & 0 \\ 1 & 1 & 0 & 0 \\ 0 & 1 & 1 & 1 \\ 0 & 0 & 1 & 1 \end{pmatrix}$$

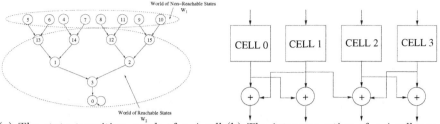

(a) The state transition graph of a 4 cell (b) The interconnection of a 4 cell non-non-complemented TPSA CA   complemented TPSA CA

Fig. 1. A 4 cell non-complemented TPSA CA

The state transition diagram of a 4 cell TPSA is shown in **Fig. 1(a)**. *As an example let us compute the next state of* 14, *which in binary form is* $X =$

$$(1110)^T. \text{ Thus the next state is obtained as } Y = T_4 \begin{pmatrix} 1 \\ 1 \\ 1 \\ 0 \end{pmatrix} = \begin{pmatrix} 0 \\ 0 \\ 0 \\ 1 \end{pmatrix} = 1 \text{ Thus}$$

the next state of 14 *is* 1, *which may be observed in* **Fig. 1(a)**. *Here* {0} *is the* attractor *or* graveyard *state. The states* {5, 6, 4, 7, 8, 11, 9, 10} *make the* non-reachable *world, while the states* {13, 14, 12, 15, 1, 2, 3, 0} *make the* reachable *world. The corresponding interconnection is given in* **Fig. 1(b)**. *As may be observed that the structure comprises of local interconnections leading to efficient designs.*

Next, we present an method to recursively synthesize an n cell TPSA. The state transition matrix of the n cell TPSA is denoted by T_n and is generated from an $n-1$ cell TPSA CA characterized by the matrix T_{n-1}. The following theorem describes the property exploited in the construction.

Theorem 1. *Given that* T_{n-1} *is the chararacteristic matrix of an* $(n-1)$ *cell TPSA, the matrix* T_n *denoted by:*

$$T_n = \left(\begin{array}{ccccc|c} & & & & & 0 \\ & & & & & 0 \\ & & & & & \vdots \\ & & T_{n-1} & & & 0 \\ & & & & & \vdots \\ & & & & & 0 \\ & & & & & 0 \\ \hline 0 & \cdots & 0 & 1 & & 0 \end{array} \right)$$

represents the characteristic matrix of an n *cell TPSA.*

Proof. It is evident that since the element at the nth row and $(n-1)^{th}$ column is 1 and by the construction methodology all the rows have 0 in the $(n-1)^{th}$ columns the row added is linearly independent from the other rows of T_n. Hence it adds by 1 to the rank of T_{n-1}. Thus, $rank(T_n) = rank(T_{n-1})+1 = n-1+1 = n$ Similarly, using the fact that $rank(T_{n-1} \oplus I_{n-1}) = n-1$ (where I_{n-1} is the identity matrix of order $n-1$), we have $rank(T_n \oplus I_n) = n$. The characteristic polynomial of the matrix T_n, denoted by $\phi_n(x)$ is evaluated as $det(T_n \oplus xI_n)$, where det denotes the determinant. Thus we have, $\phi_n(x) = x\phi_{n-1}(x) = x.x^{n-1} = x^n$. ($\phi_{n-1}(x)$ denotes the characteristic polynomial of T_{n-1}).

In order to evaluate the minimal polynomial we make use of the following proposition.

Lemma 1. *Let $\phi_n(x)$ and $\psi_n(x)$ be the characteristic polynomial and the minimal polynomial of the matrix T_n, respectively. Let the greatest common divisor (gcd) of the matrix $(T_n \oplus I_n x)^\vee$ that is the matrix of algebraic complements of the elements of the matrix $(T_n \oplus I_n x)$ be $d(x)$. Then, $\phi_n(x) = d(x)\psi_n(x)$.*

From the matrix $(T_n \oplus I_n x)^\vee$ it may be observed that the element at the position $(0, n)$ is 1 and thus the gcd $d(x)$ is also 1. Thus the minimal polynomial is equal to the characteristic polynomial which is x^n. Thus, we observe that the construction follows all the four necessary and sufficient requirements of a TPSA CA. This completes the proof.

Example 3. *Given the fact that $T_2 = \begin{pmatrix} 1 & 1 \\ 1 & 1 \end{pmatrix}$ is the characteristic matrix of a 2 cell TPSA CA. Thus, using the above theorem it is evident that $T_3 = \begin{pmatrix} 1 & 1 & 0 \\ 1 & 1 & 0 \\ 0 & 1 & 0 \end{pmatrix}$ is the characteristic matrix of a 3 cell TPSA CA.*

We have seen above that the state transition in the above class of TPSA CA is governed solely by the characteristic matrix. This class of CA is known as the non-complemented TPSA CA. On the contrary when the next state is obtained by the application of the characteristic matrix and then xoring with a $0-1$ vector F, the CA is known as the complemented TPSA-CA. The following results show how complementing the state transition function of the non-complemented CA generates a class of automaton with the same properties as the original TPSA CA.

Lemma 2. *Corresponding to a non-complemented TPSA CA M_1 and a state Z, there exists a complemented CA M_2 with state Z as an attractor. If the characteristic matrix M_1 be indicated by T_n and it is required to build a complemented TPSA CA such that Z is the graveyard (attractor) then the characteristic matrix of the complemented CA, $\overline{T}_n$ is related to T_n by*

$$\overline{T}_n(X) = T_n(X) \oplus (I_n \oplus T_n)Z$$

where X is the seed to the CA and I_n is the identity matrix of order n.

Lemma 3. *A complemented TPSA CA has the same structure as a non-compl emented TPSA CA. To emphasize*

- *Number of attractors in the complemented CA is the same as that in the original non-complemented CA.*
- *Number of reachable states and non-reachable states are same as that in the original non-complemented CA.*

Lemma 4. *If any state Z in the non-reachable world of a non-complemented CA is made the graveyard in a complemented TPSA, then the non-reachable elements become elements of the reachable world in the commplemented CA and viceversa. Thus the reachable world (W_1) and the non-reachable world (W_2) exchange themselves.*

Proof. Let X and Z be two non-reachable elements in the n cell non-complemented CA with characteristic matrix T_n. Let X be the lth level sister of Z. In all cases $l < n$. Thus, we have:

$$T_n^l(X) = T_n^l(Z)$$

Let us consider the state transition diagram of the complemented CA with Z as the graveyard. The state transition of the complemented CA is indicated by $\overline{T}_n$. We shall prove that in this state transition graph X is a reachable state. Let, the depth of X in the graph of the complemented CA be t. If t is less than n then X is a reachable state. Since, Z is the graveyard of this graph we have:

$$\overline{T}_n^t(X) = Z$$
$$T_n^t(X) \oplus (I_n \oplus T_n^t)Z = Z$$
$$T_n^t(X) = T_n^t(Z)$$

Thus, X and Z are t^{th} level sisters in the state transition graph of the non-complemented CA. But we know that they are l^{th} level sisters. Thus $t = l < n$. Thus, the depth of X is lesser than n and hence X is a reachable state in the state transition graph of the complemented CA.

3.1   Construction of Expander Graph Using the TPSA CA

The TPSA CA can be effectively used to generate a random d regular graph on the fly. It may be noted that the entire nature of the graph is stored in the graveyard state, thus leading to a very compact storage of the graph. This is because given the graveyard state, the entire transition graph can be obtained.

In order to construct the d regular graph we proceed as follows: Let $Z_1 \in W_1$ (non-reachable world in the non-complemented TPSA CA) and $Z_2 \in W_2$ (reachable world in the non-complemented TPSA CA). Let, G_1 and G_2 be the state transition graphs with Z_1 and Z_2 as the graveyards respectively.

Clearly, in G_1 if $X \in W_1$, $degree(X) = 3$ and if $X \in W_2$, $degree(X) = 1$. Similarly, in G_2 if $X \in W_1$, $degree(X) = 1$ and if $X \in W_2$, $degree(X) = 3$.

Here *degree* is defined as the sum of the *indegree* and the *outdegree* in the corresponding graph.

Thus, in the graph G obtained by a union operation in the graphs G_1 and G_2, allowing multiple edges and self loops, we have for $X \in G$, $degree(X) = 4$. If we continue the union operation in the above method we have $degree(X) = 2(t+1)$, where t is the number of union operations. **Table 1** shows the result of an experimentation performed with the TPSA based regular graph. It measures the value of the two largest eigen values for random TPSA based graphs for degree $4, 8, 12$ and 16. The difference between the largest two eigen values is known as the spectral gap and should be large for good expansion of the graph. Results show that the spectral gap and hence the expansion increases proportionately with the number of union operations (t).

Table 1. Spectrum of a 4 cell TPSA based regular graph

No. of Union (t)	Graveyards	Degree	First Eigen Value	Second Eigen Value	Spectral Gap (g)	g/t
1	{0},{4}	4	4	3.2361	0.76	0.76
3	{0,15},{4,8}	8	8	4.899	3.10	1.03
5	{0,15,3},{4,8,10}	12	12	6.3440	5.66	1.14
7	{0,15,3,2},{4,8,10,9}	16	16	5.2263	10.77	1.54

3.2   Setting Parameters of the d Regular TPSA Based Graph for Good Expansion Properties

In the present section we compute the expansion obtained in the d regular TPSA based graph in terms of the parameters of the graph G. Let the number of nodes in the graph be n and the degree of each node is d. Let, us consider a random d regular graph which has a subset A with αn vertices $(0 < \alpha < 1)$.

For the graph G to have good expansion properties the set A should have more than βn $(0 < \beta < 1)$ neighbours outside A. The probability of such an event should be high.

Equivalently, we may state that the probability that the number of neighbours of the vertices of A outside A is less than βn is negligible. Let us fix A and B such that $|A| = \alpha n$ and $|B| = \beta n$.

It is required that the vertices of A be matched to $N(A)$ (neighbours of A outside A) s.t $N(A) \subset B$. If we first consider a single matching αn vertices can have maximum αn neighbours in $N(A)$. The probability that the neighbours of A are in B is :

$$p = \frac{\text{no. of ways in which N(A) can lie inside B}}{\text{no. of ways in which N(A) may be chosen outside A}} = \frac{\binom{\beta n}{\alpha n}}{\binom{n - \alpha n}{\alpha n}}$$

Hence, if we consider a d-matching, assuming all the edges to be independent we have

$$\Pr[N(A) \subset B] = \left(\frac{\binom{\beta n}{\alpha n}}{\binom{n - \alpha n}{\alpha n}} \right)^d \approx \left(\frac{\beta}{1-\alpha} \right)^{\alpha n d}$$

Thus, we have the following probability:

$$\Pr[\exists A \in G \text{ s.t } |A| = \alpha n, |N(A)| \leq \beta n] \leq \sum_{|A|=\alpha n} \sum_{|B|=\beta n} \left(\frac{\beta}{1-\alpha} \right)^{\alpha n d}$$

$$\leq \binom{n}{\alpha n} \binom{n}{\beta n} \left(\frac{\beta}{1-\alpha} \right)^{\alpha n d}$$

Next, we use the following approximations: $\binom{n}{\alpha n} = 2^{nH(\alpha)}, \binom{n}{\beta n} = 2^{nH(\beta)}$.

Here, $H(\alpha) = -\alpha \log_2 \alpha - (1-\alpha) \log_2 (1 - \alpha)$. Thus, setting $\alpha = \frac{1}{m}$ and $\beta = \frac{1}{2}$ and some simplifications we have:

$$\Pr[\exists A \in G \text{ s.t } |A| = \alpha n, |N(A)| \leq \beta n] \leq 2^{n[\log_2 m - (1 - \frac{1}{m}) \log_2 (m-1) + 1 + \frac{d}{m} \log \frac{m}{2(m-1)}]}$$

$$\approx 2^{-cn}$$

Hence in order to make the probability negligible we may choose parameters m and d such that c becomes positive. The value of d gives us an estimate of the number of union operations t to be performed.

3.3 Mathematical Formulation of Adjacency in the TPSA Based Graph

The graph $G(V, E)$ can thus be described as a union operation between the graphs G_1 and G_2 where $Z_1 \in W_1$ and $Z_2 \in W_2$ are the respective graveyard states. Hence the degree in this case is $d = 2(1+1) = 4$.

The following algorithm computes the four neighbours of a given state in the graph G.

Algorithm 1. Computing neighbourhood of a vertex in G
  Input: Z_1, Z_2, a state $X \in G$
  Output: *The four neighbours of X (U, V, W, Y)*
  Step 1: *Clearly,*

$$U = T_n(X) \oplus (I_n \oplus T_n)Z_1$$
$$V = T_n(X) \oplus (I_n \oplus T_n)Z_2$$

  Step 2: *Compute,* $X \oplus (I_n \oplus T_n)Z_1 = (x_1, x_2, \ldots, x_n)^T$
    If$(x_1 = x_2)\{/ * X \in G_1 * /$
    set $w_n = 0$, Compute $w_{n-1} = x_n, w_{n-2} = x_{n-1}, \ldots, w_2 = x_3, w_1 = w_2 \oplus x_1$
    set $y_n = 1$, Compute $y_{n-1} = x_n, y_{n-2} = x_{n-1}, \ldots, y_2 = x_3, y_1 = y_2 \oplus x_1$
  Step 3: }
    *else{/ * X \in G_2 * /*
    repeat Step 2 with Z_2 replacing Z_1
    }

It is evident that the distribution of the neighbourhood is identical to that of Z_1 or Z_2 which are randomly chosen. Thus, we have a four regular pseudo-random graph when we have only one union operation. The degree may be increased with the number of union operations. The advantage lies in the fact that in general the description of a random graph grows exponentially with the number of vertices. However, using the TPSA based construction one may generate graphs which exhibit randomness and also may be described using polynomial space, as we require to store only the graveyard state. For an N cell TPSA, in order to compute the neighbourhood of any state, Algorithm 1 is applied in constant time, as each of the steps $1, 2$ and 3 may be applied in constant time parallely on the N bit input vector. Herein lies the efficacy of the TPSA based expander graphs.

4   Application of TPSA Based Expander Graphs in Constructing One-Way Functions

The one-way function using the d-regular graph generated by the TPSA is based on the construction proposed in [1]. The one-way function maps a string in $\{0,1\}^n$ to another in $\{0,1\}^n$. The algorithm is based on a d regular graph generated by the TPSA. As already mentioned the graveyard states are from W_1 and W_2. Let Z_1 denotes the graveyard states from W_1 and Z_2 denotes the graveyard states from W_2. If there are i elements in Z_1 and Z_2 then the number of union operations required to generate the d regular graph is $2i - 1$ and so we have $d = 2(2i - 1 + 1)$. Thus we arrive at the number of graveyard states required as $i = \frac{d}{4}$.

The evaluation of the one-way function is as follows:

Algorithm 2. One-way function (f) **using the state transitions of a TPSA**

    Input: $Z_1 \in W_1$, $Z_2 \in W_2$, a state $X \in \{0,1\}^n$.

    Output: *The one-way output* $Y \in \{0,1\}^n$ *such that* $Y = f(X)$

    Step 1: *Consider an N cell TPSA, where $N = \log_2(n)$. Generate a collection C, which constitutes of the neighbours of each node in the regular graph generated by the state transitions of the TPSA using* **Algorithm 1**. *Mathematically, $C = \{S_i, if\ v \in S_i, E(v,i) = 1, i \in \{1, \ldots, n\}\}$.*

    Step 2: *For $i = 1$ to n, project X onto each of the subsets S_i. If $S_i = \{i_1, i_2, \ldots, i_d\}$, then the projection of X on S_i denoted by X_{S_i}, is a string of length d indicated by $\{X_{i_1}, X_{i_2}, \ldots, X_{i_d}\}$.*

    Step 3: *Evaluates a non-linear boolean function Π on each of the n projections thus giving an n bit output, $\{\Pi(X_{S_1}), \Pi(X_{S_2}), \ldots, \Pi(X_{S_n})\}$. The non-linear function Π is*

$$\Pi(z_1, z_2, \ldots, z_d) = \left(\sum_{i=1}^{d/2} z_i z_{i+d/2} \right) \bmod 2.$$

The forward transformation is very efficient as the total time required is $O(n)$. This may be observed as the time required to perform **Step 1** is due to that required to apply Algorithm 1 at all the 2^N vertices. Hence the total time is also proportional to $2^N = n$. The time required to apply **Step 2** and **Step 3** is also proportional with n and hence the total time required. However computing the inverse seems to be intractable even when the collection C is known. As proved in [1] the complexity of a proposed inverting algorithm is atleast exponential in $min_\pi \{max_i \{| \cup_{j=1}^{i} S_{\pi(j)}| - i\}\}$.

We have shown in *section 3.2* that the probability that the size of the neighbourhood of any subset S is proportional with n is very high. Thus for all cases the value of $min_\pi \{max_i \{| \cup_{j=1}^{i} S_{\pi(j)}| - i\}\}$ is $O(n)$ and hence the complexity of a possible inverting algorithm proposed in [1] is atleast exponential in $O(n)$. Thus the problem of inverting the one-way function seems to be intractable.

5   Conclusion

The paper proposes a novel method to generate expander graphs with good expansion properties based on the state transitions of a special class of Cellular Automata, known as the Two Predecessor Single Attractor CA (TPSA-CA). The expander graphs has been finally used to compose an efficient one-way function whose security lies on the combinatorial properties of the expander graphs. The one-way function may be an ideal candidate for use in key establishment protocols.

References

1. Oded Goldreich, "Candidate One-Way Functions Based on Expander Graphs," Cryptology ePrint Archive, Report 2000/063, 2000.
2. W.Diffie and M.Hellman, "New Directions in Cryptography," in *IEEE Transactions on Information Theory (22).* 1976, pp. 644–654, IEEE.
3. P. Pal Chaudhuri, D.Roy Chowdhury, Sukumar Nandi, and Santanu Chattopadhyay, *Additive Cellular Automata Theory and its Application,* vol. 1, chapter 4, IEEE Computer Society Press, 1997.
4. Nati Linial and Avi Wigderson, "Expander graphs and their applications," , 2003.
5. Michael A. Nielsen, "Introduction to expander graphs," , 2005.
6. A. Lubotzky, R. Phillips, and P. Sarnak, "Ramanujan graphs," *Combinatorica,* vol. 8, no. 3, pp. 261–277, 1988.
7. G. A. Margulis, "Explicit constructions of expanders," *Problemy Peredači Informacii,* vol. 9, no. 4, pp. 71–80, 1973.
8. G. A. Margulis, "Explicit group-theoretic constructions of combinatorial schemes and their applications in the construction of expanders and concentrators," *Problemy Peredachi Informatsii,* vol. 24, no. 1, pp. 51–60, 1988.

Minority Gate Oriented Logic Design with Quantum-Dot Cellular Automata

Samir Roy[1] and Biswajit Saha[2]

[1] Dept. of Computer Science & Engineering
National Institute of Technical Teachers' Training & Research (NITTTR), Kolkata
Block – FC, Sector – III, Salt Lake City, Kolkata – 700106, India
roysamir_cst@yahoo.co.in
[2] Dept. of Computer Science & Technology, Polytechnic Institute, Narsingarh,
P.O.- Agartala Aerodrome, Tripura West, India
sahabiswajit@yahoo.com

Abstract. This paper presents novel combinational logic designs with plus-shaped quantum-dot cellular automata (QCA) using minority gate as the fundamental building block. Present CMOS technology of VLSI design is fast approaching its fundamental limit, and researchers are looking for a nano-scale technology for future ICs in order to continue the pace of circuit miniaturization predicted by Moore's law even beyond 2016. QCA is considered to be a promising technology in this regard. This paper provides the fundamentals of QCA followed by the proposed QCA structure realizing a minority gate, given by the Boolean expression $m(x_1, x_2, x_3) = x_1.x_2' + x_2'.x_3' + x_3'.x_1'$. Universality of minority gate is established, and minority gate oriented design principles are provided. Minority gate oriented designs for XOR and full adder are presented. Simulation results show the effectiveness of the proposed designs.

Keywords: Nano-computing, Quantum-dot Cellular Automata, Minority Gate.

1 Introduction

Gordon Moore of INTEL predicted in 60's that the packing density of IC chips would double every two years. This is known as the famous Moore's law. Thanks to the ceaseless efforts of the VLSI research community, Moore's law was more or less obeyed for the last fifty years. However, as the present CMOS technology of VLSI design is fast approaching its fundamental limit, reality is gradually deviating from Moore's prediction (Fig.1). It seems that further reduction in device size will produce quantum mechanical effects that hinder device functionality. However, it is quantum mechanics that provides hope for further development in IC technology.

Quantum-dot cellular automata (QCA) [1-6] is projected as a promising nano-technology for future ICs. It offers a new way of information processing which is conceptually simple. Unlike conventional electronics, QCA stores logic states as positions of individual electrons rather than voltage levels. Although QCA is still in the research stages, it has been experimentally verified [7-9] and practical issues in

S. El Yacoubi, B. Chopard, and S. Bandini (Eds.): ACRI 2006, LNCS 4173, pp. 646–656, 2006.
© Springer-Verlag Berlin Heidelberg 2006

the realization of QCA have been investigated [10]. In [11] Niemier *et al* proposed a potentially implementable field programmable gate array (FPGA) for QCA. Fault-tolerant computing with QCA is dealt with in [12-14].

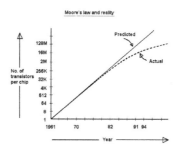

Fig. 1. Progress in IC technology

This paper presents novel minority gate oriented designs of combinational circuits. The flow of information through the circuits is controlled by four clock signals [15, 16] each shifted in phase by 90 degrees. The design and simulation is carried out in the QCADesigner [17] environment.

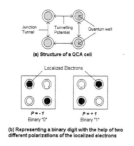

Fig. 2. Structure of a QCA cell

Rest of the paper is organized as follows. Section 2 presents the fundamentals of QCA. The structure of the minority gate and its characterization are presented in Section 3. The minority gate based logic designs are given in Section 4, which is followed by the simulation results given in Section 5. Section 6 concludes the paper.

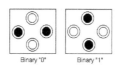

Fig. 3. Diagonal (plus-shaped) QCA cell

2 Preliminaries

The following subsections present a brief overview of the fundamentals of QCA.

2.1 Cell Structure

A QCA is an array of structures known as quantum-dots. Computing with QCA is achieved by the tunneling of individual electrons among the quantum-dots inside a cell and the classical Coulombic interaction among them. A quantum-dot is a region where an electron may be localized. It acts like a well, because once an electron is trapped inside the dot, it cannot escape due to lack of adequate energy. However, when sufficiently energized, the electron may tunnel to another quantum-dot. A QCA cell consists of four of such dots, positioned at the four corners of a square. Fig. 2 shows the structure of a QCA cell and the way of storing a single bit within such a cell. Each cell contains two extra electrons. They can tunnel among the dots but cannot go out of the cell. Moreover, these are subject to electrostatic repulsion so that they are forced to settle into the opposite corners. The corresponding polarizations $P = -1$ and $P = +1$, represent the logic values of "0" and "1" respectively. Depending on the relative position of the quantum-dots within a cell, QCA cells are classified as either normal (or, cross-shaped), or diagonal (i.e., plus-shaped). The structure of a plus-shaped cell and the way to represent a single bit with it are shown in Fig. 3.

2.2 Wire

QCA cells retain their electrons but inter-cell electrons interact electrostatically. Hence, the electrons rearrange among the dots through tunneling so that the whole cell-arrangement acquires ground energy level. If a cell C_1 is fixed at polarization P, the adjacent cell C_2 will be induced to the same polarization P. A binary wire (Fig.4) is an array of QCA cells. Once a logic "0" or "1" is fixed at one end of the array, the other cells acquire the same logic value. In other words, one bit of information may be instantaneously propagated from one end of a QCA wire to the other end.

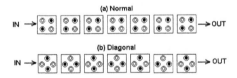

Fig. 4. QCA wires

Depending on the category of constituent cells, there can two kinds of binary wires, viz., normal, and diagonal. A diagonal wire consists of diagonal cells. A bit, while passing through a diagonal wire, toggles itself at each successive cell.

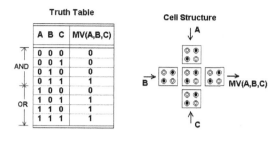

Fig. 5. Majority Voter Logic

2.3 Logic Gates

Logic gates are realized by appropriate arrangement of QCA cells. The basic logic operation in QCA circuits is majority voting, MV (Fig.5). A 3-input MV outputs a logical one whenever there are more than one logical ones at the inputs. The AND/OR operations can be realized with the majority gate by keeping $x_3=0$, and $x_3=1$, respectively. However, the majority voter is not functionally complete because it cannot realize logical NOT. Separate cell arrangements are required for this.

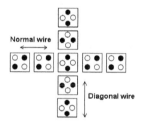

Fig. 6. Co-planer wire crossing

Interestingly, QCA have the unique property of being able to create co-planer wire crossings. This is shown in Fig. 6. A normal QCA wire can cross a diagonal QCA wire on the same plane without interfering one another. Hence, interconnection in a QCA wire is easier than in conventional electronic circuits. In principle, the majority voter, inverter, and wire crossing, are sufficient to create any complex digital circuit.

2.4 Clocking

The basic QCA cell has no inherent directionality for information flow. Therefore, in an arbitrary arrangement of QCA cells, information may propagate in uncontrollable directions. Four clock signals, each shifted in phase by 90^0, are used to retain control over the flow of information in a QCA circuit (Fig.7). When the clock signal is low the cells are latched, i.e., the electrons settle in their respective quantum-dots. When it is high, they are relaxed. This implies that they are equally likely to exist in any of the four quantum-dots and consequently, have no polarization. During the transition periods, the cells are in the process of either being latched or relaxed.

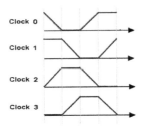

Fig. 7. QCA clocking scheme

QCA clocking is realized by controlling the potential barriers between the cells. A high tunneling potential makes the electron wave function de-localized resulting in indefinite polarization. When the potential barrier is raised, tunneling potential is decreased and the electrons localize. This, in turn, gives a definite polarization to the QCA cell. The entire process is completely adiabatic. Four clocking zones, each 90^0 out of phase, are employed to bypass the problems associated with thermal excitation. The phases through which a single clocked QCA cell undergoes attached to a certain clocking zone is shown in Fig. 8(a). A QCA wire with different clocking zones to facilitate information flow in a predefined direction is shown in Fig. 8(b).

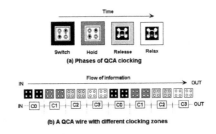

Fig. 8. Information flow through clocking zones

3 Minority Gate

The logic of a 3-input minority gate is expressed as $m(x_1,x_2,x_3) = x_1'.x_2'+x_3'.x_1'+x_2'.x_3'$. It outputs a logical one whenever there are two or more logical zeros at the inputs. A 4-cell realization of a minority gate [18] is shown in Fig.9. The structure uses plus-shaped QCA cells instead of the conventional cross-shaped cells. Fig.10 shows the simulation results obtained through QCADesigner. The simulation results confirm that the proposed structure follows the desired logic of minority gate.

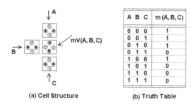

(a) Cell Structure   (b) Truth Table

Fig. 9. Minority gate with QCA

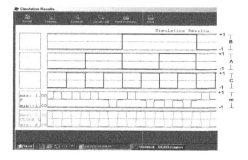

Fig. 10. Simulation results for minority gate

Minority gate is universal. The following derivations prove this.

NAND	: $(x_1.x_2)' = x_1'+ x_2' = x_1'.x_2' + x_1'+ x_2' = m (x_1, x_2, 0)$
NOR	: $(x_1+x_2)' = x_1'.x_2' = m (x_1, x_2, 1)$
NOT	: $x_1' = m (x_1, 0, 1)$
AND	: $x_1.x_2 = ((x_1.x_2)')' = m (m (x_1, x_2, 0) , 0, 1)$
OR	: $x_1+x_2 = ((x_1+x_2)')' = m (m (x_1, x_2, 1), 0, 1)$

As the expressions show, 2 minority gates are needed to implement AND/OR logic. However, only one is sufficient for this purpose. This can be achieved in two ways :

  i) By configuring the minority gate as MV and obtaining the AND/OR logic as specific cases of majority voting.

  ii) By applying complementary values of the input variables through proper selection of the length of the diagonal wires leading to the inputs of the minority gate.

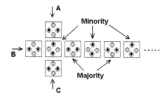

Fig. 11. Dual function realization

Majority voter can be realized with minority gate by positioning a diagonal cell next to the output cell (Fig.11). Evidently, minority and majority outputs are available at successive cells of the diagonal wire at the output of the minority gate. This is due to the toggling property of logic values at alternative cells of a diagonal wire.

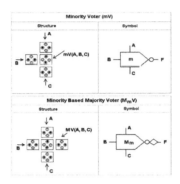

Fig. 12. Schematic symbols for minority/majority gate

4   Logic Design

For the purpose of minority gate oriented logic design, two symbols, one for minority gate, another for majority voter realized with minority gate, are introduced in this paper (Fig.12). The symbols manifest the fact that the I/O lines of the device must be perpendicular to each other. This inherent property of QCA circuit building blocks plays an important role during complex circuit design. The proposed schematic symbols help the process of QCA circuit design by bringing out the hidden layout constraint and making the designer aware of it. Fig.13 depicts the schematic diagrams and the corresponding cell structures of the basic gates realized with minority gate.

Logic Operation	AND	OR	NOT
Schematic	B — M_m ⟩⟨ A.B, "0"	B — M_m ⟩⟨ A+B, "1"	B — M_m ⟩ $\bar{B}$, "0", "1"
Cell Arrangement	B ▭ A.B, P = -1.0000	B ▭ A+B, P = +1.0000	B ▭ $\bar{B}$, P = +1.0000

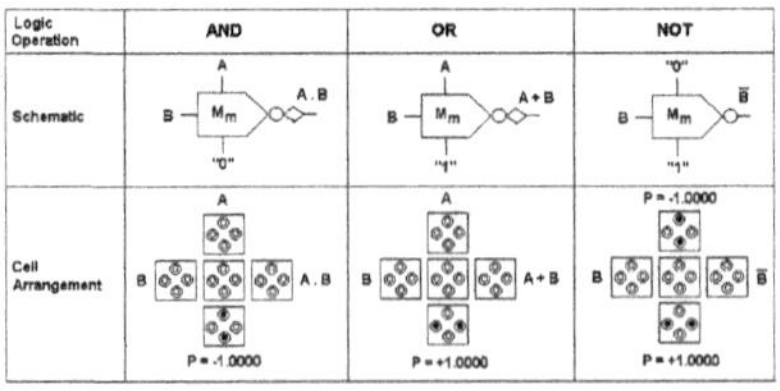

Fig. 13. Universality of minority gate

Various minority gate oriented combinational circuits are designed and tested with the QCADesigner tool. Among them, an XOR gate and a full adder are presented here because of their importance in combinational circuit design. Fig.14 and 15 show the schematic diagram and the QCADesigner implementation of the XOR gate.

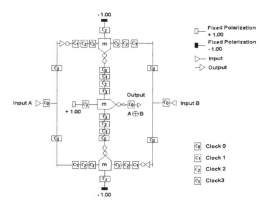

Fig. 14. Schematic diagram of minority oriented XOR

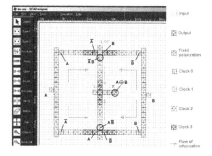

Fig. 15. Minority gate oriented XOR with QCADesigner

Fig.16 and 17 show the schematic diagram and the QCADesigner implementation of the full adder. The rectangles with C_0, C_1, C_2, and C_3 represent a series of consecutive cells belonging to the respective clocking regions. The arrows indicate the direction of flow of information. The present design employs two full cycles of QCA clocking between the input and the final output. This is because both XOR and

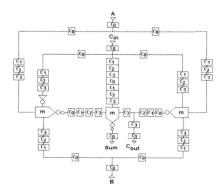

Fig. 16. Schematic diagram of minority oriented Full Adder

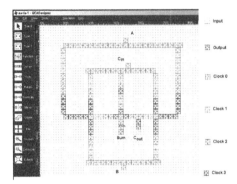

Fig. 17. Minority gate oriented Full Adder with QCADesigner

full adder are two level logic functions. In order to synchronize the input to the second level logic, the outputs of the first level should be at the same clock region.

5 Simulation Results

This section reports the simulation results for the designs under QCADesigner. It consists of various CAD features required for complex circuit design with QCA cells. The simulation steps are as follows:

a) Input vectors are applied to the corresponding input cells, so that the cells are polarized to the input values.
b) Then, the polarization of the cells are iteratively calculated by the simulation engine until each cell converges to a polarization within the preset tolerance.
c) Polarization of the output cells are recorded and then a new iteration starts.

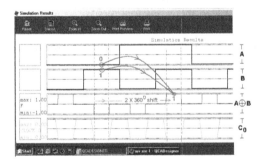

Fig. 18. Simulation results for XOR

Fig.18 and Fig.19 show the simulation results for the XOR and the full adder circuits respectively. The simulator engine was setup to bi-stable approximation with exhaustive verification type. Here, outputs for every possible input sequence are produced. To control the flow of information, 4 clock signals, each shifted in phase by

90^0 are used. There are 8 clocked regions from the input to the output. Hence, the output is 2×360° out of phase from the input. Considering the phase lag, we find that the truth tables of XOR and full adder are satisfied. The results for simulation engine set to bi-stable approximation are shown. Similar results are obtained for the other models, viz., non-linear approximation, digital simulation, and coherence vector.

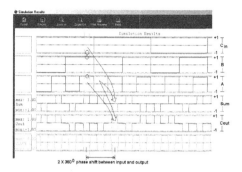

2 X 360^0 phase shift between input and output

Fig. 19. Simulation results for Full Adder

6   Conclusions

Novel combinational circuits with plus-shaped quantum-dot cellular automata (QCA) using minority gate as the fundamental building block are presented in this paper. QCA is a promising nano-technology for continuing the pace of miniaturization of IC-chips even beyond the year 2016. The fundamentals of QCA are discussed, followed by the proposed QCA structure realizing the minority gate, given by the expression $m(x_1,x_2,x_3) = x_1'.x_2 + x_2'.x_3 + x_3'.x_1$. Universality of minority gate is proved and minority gate oriented design principles are provided. The designs for XOR gate and full adder are presented that employs only plus-shaped QCA cells and uses minority gate as the basic building block. Simulation results are reported that manifest the effectiveness proposed designs.

References

1. Lent, C. S., Tougaw, P. D., and Prod, W., "Quantum Cellular Automata: The physics of computing with quantum dot molucules,," in *Proc. of Workshop on Physical Computing*, PhysComp 94, IEEE Computer Society Press, (1994).
2. Tougaw, P. D., and Lent, C. S., "Logical device implementation using quantum cellular automata," *Journal of Applied Physics*, Vol. 75, pp. 1818, (1994).
3. Lent, C. S., and Tougaw, P. D., "A device architecture for computing with quantum dots," in *Proc. IEEE*, Vol. 85(4), (1994).
4. Amlani, I., Orlov, A. O., Bernstein, G. H., Lent, C. S., and Snider, G. L., "Realization of a functional cell for quantum-dot cellular automata," *Science*, Vol. 277, pp. 289, (1997).
5. Amlani, I., Orlov, A. O., Toth, G., Lent, C. S., Bernstein, G. H., and Snider, G. L., "Digital logic gate using quantum-dot cellular automata," *Applied Physics Letters*, Vol. 74, pp. 2875, (1999).

6. Fijany, A., and Armstrong, C. D., "Systematic approach for the design of novel computing architecture and applications based on arrays of quantum-dot cellular automata," in *Proc. of Nanospace 2002*, (2002).

7. Orlov A. O., *et al.*, "Experimental demonstration of a binary wire for quantum-dot cellular automata," *Applied Physics Letters*, Vol. 74, No. 19, pp. 2875-2877, (1999).

8. Amlani, I., *et al.*, "Experimental demonstration of a leadless quantum-dot cellular automata cell," *Applied Physics Letters*, Vol. 77, No. 5, pp. 738-740, (2000).

9. Orlov A. O., *et al.*, "Experimental demonstration of clocked single-electron switching in quantum-dot cellular automata," *Applied Physics Letters*, Vol. 77, No. 2, pp. 295-297, (2000).

10. Bernstein, G. H., *et al.*, "Practical issues in the realization of quantum-dot cellular automata," *Superlattices and Microstructures*, Vol. 20, No. 4, pp. 447-459, (1996).

11. Niemier, M. T., Rodrigues, A. F., and Kogge, P. M., "A potentially implementable FPGA for quantum dot cellular automata," in *Proc. of 1st Workshop on Non-Silicon Computation*, Boston, (2002).

12. Armstrong, C. D., Humphreys, W. M., and Fijany, A., "The design of fault tolerant quantum dot cellular automata based logic," in *Proc. of NASA Symposium on VLSI Design*, (2003).

13. Tahoori, M. B., Momenzadeh, M., Huang J., and Lombardi, F., "Defects and faults in quantum cellular automata at nano scale," in *Proc. of the 22nd IEEE VLSI Test Symposium*, (VTS 2004), (2004).

14. Momenzadeh, M., Tahoori, M. B., Huang, J., and Lombardi, F., "Quantum cellular automata : New defects and faults for new devices," in *Proc. of the 18th Intl. Parallel and distributed processing symposium*, (IPDPS'04), (2004).

15. Toth G., and Lent, C. S., "Quasiadabatic switching for metal-island quantum dot cellular automata," *Journal of Applied Physics*, Vol. 85, No. 5, pp. 2977-2984, (1999).

16. Hennessy, K., and Lent, C. S., "Clocking of molecular quantum-dot cellular automata," *Journal of Vac. Sci. Technol. B.*, Vol. 19, No. 5, pp. 1752-1755, (2001).

17. Walus, K. *et al.*, "ATIPS lab. QCADesigner homepage," *http://www.atips.ca/projects/qcadesigner*, ATIPS laboratory, Univ. of Calgary, Canada, (2002).

18. Roy, S., "A Universal Logic for Quantum-Dot Cellular Automata," in *Proc. of VLSI Design and Test Workshops*, pp. 386-389, (2005).

In Search of Cellular Automata Reproducing Chaotic Dynamics Described by Logistic Formula

Witold Dzwinel

AGH University of Science and Technology, Institute of Computer Science,
Al. Mickiewicza 30, 30-059 Krakow, Poland
dzwinel@agh.edu.pl

Abstract. Two-dimensional cellular automata (CA) systems are widely used for modeling spatio-temporal dynamics of evolving populations. Conversely, the logistic equation is a 1-D model describing non-spatial evolution. Both clustering of individuals on CA lattice and inherent limitations of the CA model inhibit the chaotic fluctuations of average population density. We show that crude mean-field approximation of stochastic 2-D CA, assuming untied, random "collisions" of individuals, reproduces full logistic map ($2 \leq r \leq 4$) only if infinite neighborhood is considered. Whereas, the value of the growth rate parameter r obtained for this CA system with the Moore neighborhood is at most equal to 3.6. It is interesting that this type of behavior can be observed for diversity of microscopic CA rules. We show that chaotic dynamics of population density predicted by the logistic formula is restrained by the motion ability of individuals, dispersal and competitions radiuses and is rather exception than the rule in evolution of this type of populations. We conclude that the logistic equation is very unreliable in predicting a variety of evolution scenarios generated by the spatially extended systems.

Keywords: spatially extended systems, cellular automata, logistic equation, chaotic dynamics.

1 Introduction

The individuals from evolving populations are usually distributed in space. This generates at least two potentially important consequences for their dynamics. First, individuals interact more frequently with neighbors than with more distant individuals creating rich collection of spatial structures. Second, individuals at different locations may experience different environmental interactions influencing their birth and death rates. Therefore, creation of spatial patterns and heterogeneity of the environment have been suggested in [1] as an explanation of substantial differences between behavior generated by simple ecological models e.g., by the logistic equation, and real evolution of many organisms.

Of course, there are other reasons why the logistic equation may fail to give an adequate description of population growth [2]. The per capita effect of density on population growth may not increase linearly with density or there may be a time delay

S. El Yacoubi, B. Chopard, and S. Bandini (Eds.): ACRI 2006, LNCS 4173, pp. 657–666, 2006.
© Springer-Verlag Berlin Heidelberg 2006

in the operation of density dependence. Time delays can occur in structured populations when density affects vital rates at particular ages or sizes. Similarly, spatial patterns produced by colonies of organisms can be treated not only as a consequence of population dynamics, the effect of energy minimization or dissipation but also as a built-in, self-control mechanism of further evolution.

In [1] the authors discussed how great an effect does spatial structures generated by evolving population have on the total logistic growth. They employ an individual-based model (IBM) with spatially localized dispersal and competition. From a deterministic approximation to the IBM, describing the dynamics of the first and second spatial moments, they concluded that populations may grow slower or faster than would be expected from the non-spatial logistic model. Moreover, they may reach their maximum rate of increase at densities other than half of the carrying capacity as states the logistic formula. These types of behavior can be controlled both by values of dispersal/competition radiuses and their ratio.

Surprisingly, the methodology proposed in [1] explains the evolution of only stable colonies, i.e., the situations when the total number of individuals converges to a fixed point. Other types of dynamics including chaos are not discussed in [1] at all. Therefore, the important questions arise. Can spatially distributed population reveal the chaotic behavior similar to this predicted by non-spatial logistic equation? Which factors decide about transition from a stable to chaotic population and vice versa? What is the role of spatial structures in controlling chaos? These problems can be addressed within a modeling formalism best matched to the type of investigated population.

The attempts to decide the role of spatial component of population dynamics has inspired a variety of modeling formalisms, which differ in grain and detail. Space, time, and local population state may be treated as discrete or continuous variables. Local processes and spatial locations of population individuals may or may not be explicitly modeled. For example, IBM method, mentioned above, is continuous in time and space. Population is defined by discrete objects moving in space. In PDE based models [3] population density is a continuous function of time and spatial coordinates. Both models describe nonlinear local population dynamics and include explicit space. Conversely, the approaches based on coupled logistic map treat space in an implicit way [2,4].

To compare chaotic modes of logistic model and spatially extended system we use 2-D stochastic cellular automata system, which simulates evolution of a discrete population in a discrete space and time. In the first section we introduce and discuss stochastic CA model representing spatially correlated and uncorrelated populations. We also derive its limitations in simulating chaotic behavior. Then we show that for similar but motionless systems only fixed point behavior is observed. At the end we summarize our findings.

2   Logistic and 2-D Stochastic CA Systems

Non-spatial population dynamics is governed by the logistic map:

$$x' \rightarrow r \cdot x(1 - x) \qquad (1)$$

The variable x represents the current population density while x' denotes the density of the following generation. This is obvious that x (and x') $\in [0,1]$. The dynamics of this map is well understood. If the growth rate parameter (biotic potential) r is between 0 and 1, the equilibrium at $x=0$ is stable. If $1<r<3$, $x=1-1/r$ is the fixed point of iteration (1). At $r=3$ there is a period-doubling bifurcation, starting a period-doubling cascade that leads to the onset of chaos at $r>3.5699$. If $r>4$ the map generates negative numbers and is no longer interpretable as an ecological model.

The random collision of individuals assumed in the logistic equation, often referred to as the "mean-field" assumption, may not represent interactions among organisms well. It is obvious how unsatisfactory this assumption is observing plant populations. Spatially localized colony of plants develops clumped structures. In such the structures, individuals can experience strong effects of competition with their neighbors, even though unexploited resources are located nearby. To define the conditions for which a spatially extended system mimics well the logistic equation and when their behaviors become different, let us define a simple 2-D cellular automata model of evolving population.

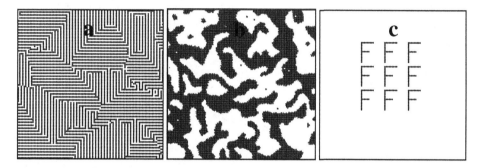

Fig. 1. Snapshots from a few specific examples of 2-D automata based on the model a) spin glasses, b) annealing rule, c) Fredkin parity rule automata.

We consider species living on a two-dimensional discrete, squared lattice $\mathfrak{I}=\{X(k,l),\ k=1,...,M;l=1,...,M\}$. The lattice is periodic, homogeneous, limited but large enough for edge effects to be neglected. In all simulations we used $M=200$ because larger lattices do not change considerably the results obtained. Moreover, the structures with correlation lengths < 100 produce adequate statistics. We consider binary CA, i.e., if an individual resides at node (k,l) then $X(k,l)=1$, otherwise $X(k,l)=0$. Every (k,l) node "sees" only its closest neighbors from $\Omega(k,l)$ vicinity, e.g., for the Moore neighborhood, only $N_m=8$ adjacent nodes. Initially, the lattice is populated randomly with density $x=x^0$. The population evolves in space and time. The CA system is updated synchronously according to the following rule:

$$X'(k,l)\rightarrow R(X(k,l),N(k,l)) \qquad (2)$$

where $X'(k,l)$ denotes the (k,l) node state in the following generation and $0\leq N(k,l)\leq N_m$ is the number of individuals in $\Omega(k,l)$. We define the stochastic rule R as a set of probabilities:

$$A(X,N) = \{0<a_{X,N}<1,\ X\in\{0,1\},\ N=1,...N_m : X'(k,l)=0\}, \qquad (3)$$

where $a_{X(k,l),N(k,l)}$ corresponds to the probability that in the following generation the $X(k,l)$ node with $N(k,l)$ neighbors becomes/remains unpopulated (i.e., $X'(k,l)=0$). For example, $a_{1,8}=1$ means that the (k,l) individual surrounded by $N(k,l)=8$ other individuals will die in the following generation (i.e., $X'(k,l)=0$), while $a_{0,8}=0.6$ indicates that the unpopulated (k,l) node surrounded by $N(k,l)=8$ individuals (in its closest neighborhood) will remain empty in the following generation with the probability equal to 0,6. This type of CA represents broad class of 2-D cellular automata, including totalistic CAs as well as many known specific automata [5] such as "game of life", Fredkin, parity rule automata, Vichniac annealing rule, spin glasses, and many others. In Fig.1 we show a few examples.

Let us assume that we are not interested in a restricted behavior of the model, e.g., generated by specific initial conditions or anisotropic rules. As displayed in Fig.2, a very feeble stochastic term may change the CA evolution substantially. On the one hand, it destroys regular patterns produced by evolving population. On the other, the chaotic fluctuations of population density calms down and the population becomes stable. The same transition occurs by violating randomly the symmetry of the pattern from Fig.2a.

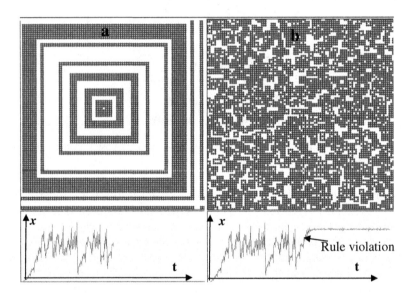

Fig. 2. a) Regular spatial patterns producing the chaotic time evolution of the average population density x for deterministic 2-D CA defined as follows: $a_{1N(k,l)}=1$ for $0<N(k,l)<8$ and $a_{1N(k,l)}=0$ elsewhere, and $a_{0N(k,l)}=1-a_{1N(k,l)}$. The population starts from a single individual located in the lattice center. b) Fixed point behavior obtained during the same simulation but after a slight modification of the CA rule specified in a). After this modification the rule reads as follows: $a_{1N(k,l)}=0.99$ for $0<N(k,l)<8$ and $a_{1N(k,l)}=0$ elsewhere, and $a_{0N(k,l)}=1-a_{1N(k,l)}$.

We are looking for a local rule R, for which the 2-D CA system as a whole will mimic the logistic formula from Eq.(1). Particularly, we expect observing the chaotic behavior such as this generated by Eq.(1) for $r=4$.

2.1 Uncorrelated Population

We consider here a CA model of "uncorrelated" populations. The random collisions and untied motion of individuals – being the assumptions of the logistic model - we simulate by their random scatter over the CA lattice after each evaluation round. That is, our CA model is realized in two steps which repeat in time. After employing the rule R synchronously in all the lattice nodes, each individual is moved randomly to an optional, unoccupied node. Then the number of neighbors $N(k,l)$ of each lattice node undergoes the Bernoulli distribution. Therefore, the average population density x evolves in time according to the following formula:

$$x' \rightarrow px\left[1-\sum_{k=0}^{N_m}a_{1k}\binom{N_m}{k}x^k(1-x)^{N_m-k}\right]+q(1-x)\left[1-\sum_{k=0}^{N_m}a_{0(N_m-k)}\binom{N_m}{k}x^{N_m-k}(1-x)^k\right] \quad (4)$$

where
$$x = \sum_{k,l}^{M}X(k,l)/M^2$$

$0<p<1$ and $0<q<1$ are "environmental" probabilities of survival of both existing individuals and newborns to the next round, respectively. The expressions in brackets represent the competition terms. We are looking for rules R (i.e., $A(X,N)$ sets) which can reduce Eq.4 to Eq.1. After some algebra we get the following relationships:

$$p\cdot\left(\frac{N_m}{N_m-i}\right)\cdot(1-a_{1i})+q\cdot\left(\frac{N_m}{i+1}\right)\cdot(1-a_{0i+1})=r; \quad \wedge \quad a_{1N_m}=a_{00}=1 \quad (5)$$

$$\text{for} \quad i=0,..., N_m-1$$

where r is the biotic potential from Eq.1. The maximum value of r, i.e., r_{max} can be computed from (5) for $a_{0i}=a_{1i}=0$ and $i=N_m/2$, thus:

$$r_{max}=4\cdot\left(\frac{N_m\left(\frac{p+q}{2}\right)+p}{N_m+2}\right) \quad \wedge \quad \lim_{N_m\to\infty}(r_{max})=4\cdot\left(\frac{p+q}{2}\right). \quad (6)$$

Therefore, only for infinite neighborhood $N_m\to\infty$ - i.e., infinite dispersal and competition radiuses - one can obtain fully developed chaotic fluctuations, the same as produced by the logistic equation for $r=4$. A few exemplar rules of 2-D CA rules yielding chaotic populations (in respect to x) are collected in Table.1. Projections on (a_1,i) and (a_0,i) planes of allowed solutions of Eq.5 are shown in Fig.3. Despite these microscopic rules are not perfect copies of the resulting macroscopic behavior, they are of a very similar nature. Except of the third set in Table 1, the remaining sets mimic dispersal and competition rules from the logistic equation. As shown in Fig.4, our CA model exactly reproduces the logistic map for $r\in[2,3.6]$.

Let us reduce the number of possible solutions of Eq.5 focusing on the totalistic cellular automata. Then the subsequent state of each (k,l) node depends on the probability $a_{N'(k,l)}\in(0,1)$ computed for all $N'(k,l)=N(k,l)+X(k,l)$ individuals in $\Omega(k,l)$ neighborhood including the $i=(k,l)$ node.

Table 1. A few examples of stochastic rules computed from Eqs.5,6 and producing chaotic behavior for "uncorrelated" CA populations ($N_m=8$, $p=q=1$) corresponding to the logistic equation with $r=r_{max}=3,6$

No neig $i=$	I		II		III		IV	
	a_{1i}	a_{0i}	a_{1i}	a_{0i}	a_{1i}	a_{0i}	a_{1i}	a_{0i}
0	100 %	100 %	60 %	100 %	0 %	100 %	100 %	100 %
1	100 %	55 %	30 %	60 %	0 %	67.5 %	0 %	55 %
2	10 %	10 %	10 %	30 %	0 %	38.5843 %	30 %	38.58 %
3	0 %	10 %	0 %	10 %	0 %	15 %	0 %	0 %
4	0 %	0 %	0 %	0 %	0 %	0 %	0 %	0 %
5	10 %	0 %	10 %	0 %	0 %	0 %	0 %	0 %
6	10 %	10 %	30 %	10 %	10 %	30 %	10 %	30 %
7	55 %	100 %	60 %	30 %	55 %	100 %	55 %	100 %
8	100 %	100 %	100 %	60 %	100 %	100 %	100 %	100 %

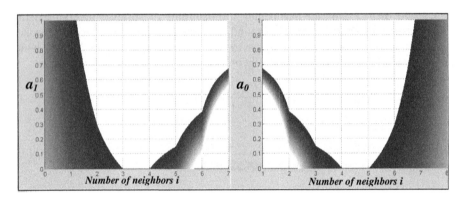

Fig. 3. Projections of allowed solutions of Eq.5 on (a_1, i) and (a_0, i) planes. The continuous surfaces are drawn as the guide for eyes. The bright-dark shades correspond to values from [0,1] interval.

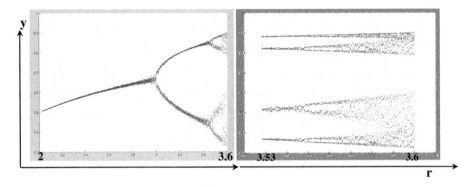

Fig. 4. The logistic map obtained for 2-D CA system of "uncorrelated" individuals ($N_m=8$, $p,q=1$). The lattice of size 1000x1000 was considered to obtain the picture on the right.

By substituting $a_i = a_{N'(k,l)} = a_{1i} = a_{0i+1}$ and for $p = q = 1$ the Eq.5 simplifies:

$$a_i = 1 - \frac{r \cdot (N_m - i) \cdot (i+1)}{(N_m + 1) \cdot N_m} = 1 - \left[r \cdot \frac{(i+1)}{(N_m + 1)} \cdot \left(1 - \frac{i}{N_m} \right) \right] \tag{7}$$

$$a_i \approx 1 - \left[r \cdot X_i (1 - X_i) \right]$$

producing a unique solution. The values of resulting probabilities are shown in Table 1 in the second set (II). The expression in brackets reproduces macroscopic logistic curve in "microscopic" scale, where X is the population density in the closest neighborhood of $i = (k,l)$. As shown in Fig.4, the CA system with rule R defined by Eq.7 reproduces the logistic map also in the macroscopic scale. Does this rule behave in the similar way for correlated, motionless CA populations?

2.2 Motionless and Correlated Population

To discuss this problem, let us consider the lattice of independent automata $X(k,l)$ with continuous states. Their values X_{kl} are the real numbers evolving according to the logistic formula:

$$X'_{kl} = 4 \cdot X_{kl} \cdot (1 - X_{kl}). \tag{8}$$

At the beginning of simulation, the values X^0_{kl} in the lattice nodes are generated randomly by using uniform random number generator $X^0_{kl} = rnd_{kl} \in [0,1]$. Such the system is locally chaotic. As shown in [6], the subsequent X_{kl} values for each cell match well the following statistical distribution:

$$X_{kl} \rightarrow \frac{1}{2} \cdot (1 - \cos(\pi \cdot rnd_{kl})), \tag{9}$$

where $rnd_{kl} \in (0,1)$ are random numbers reproducing the uniform distribution. It is easy to compute that the expectation value $x = E(X) = 1/2$ over the lattice space and the variance $\sigma^2 = 1/8$. Thus the system is globally stable. Let us modify this system introducing interactions between neighboring cells such that:

$$X'_{kl} = 4 \cdot Y_{kl} \cdot (1 - Y_{kl}) \quad \text{where} \quad Y_{kl} = \left(X_{kl} + \sum_{m \in \Omega(k,l)} X_m \right) / (N_m + 1) \tag{10}$$

Y_{kl} is the local average of X_{kl} and the states of the nodes from its neighborhood $\Omega(k,l)$. Averaging Eq.10 over entire lattice we finally get:

$$x' = 4 \cdot x \cdot (1 - x) - 4 \cdot \sigma^2 \tag{11}$$

$$\text{where} \quad \sigma^2(Y) = E(Y^2) - E^2(Y) = E(Y^2) - x^2$$

where x is the average over all the CA states. If $\sigma^2 = 0 \Leftrightarrow \forall k,l = 1,..,M; \ Y_{kl} = X_{kl} = x \Rightarrow$ this system is globally chaotic.

If X_{kl} values on the lattice would be generated by using uniform random number generator, it is easy to check that the stochastic variable Y_{kl} undergoes the Bernoulli distribution (see Fig.5a). Then for average population density x, $\sigma^2(Y) = x(1-x)/(N_m+1)$. Thus for 2-D CA with the Moore neighborhood ($N_m = 8$) we finally obtain from Eq.11 that:

$$x' = r \cdot x \cdot (1 - x) \quad \text{and} \quad r = 3\frac{5}{9} = 3,55(5). \tag{12}$$

This is less than we have obtained from Eq.6 ($r=3,6$) for the discrete, "uncorrelated" CA model. This difference is the result of continuous representation of currently considered CA system.

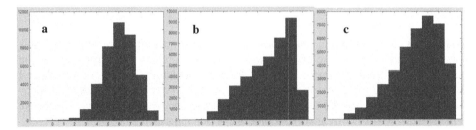

Fig. 5. The histograms representing average number of neighbors in the Moore neighborhood for population density $x=2/3$ for a) randomly generated population by uniform generator (the Bernoulli distribution of neighbors number) b) continuous CA defined by Eq.6 and c) discrete CA

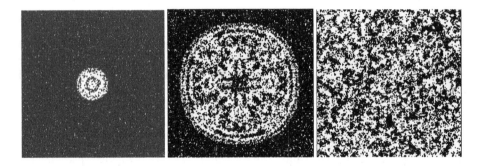

Fig. 6. Globally chaotic system, described by Eqs.10,11 with $\sigma^2=0$, becomes globally stable if the starting value in the middle of the lattice is different than in other nodes (here $\forall k,l$, $k,l=1,...,200$: $k\neq100 \wedge l\neq100$; $X^0_{kl}=0.4 \wedge X^0_{100,100}=0.4001$). In the right hand side figure the value of $x\approx2/3$. Black color represents small values with $X_{kl}<0.5$.

If the number of neighboring cells $N_m\rightarrow\infty$, i.e., both dispersion and competition radiuses are infinitely large, than $\sigma^2(Y)\rightarrow0$ and fully developed ($r=4$) chaotic behavior is observed (see Eq.11). However, the process defined by the Eq.10 produces distribution of Y, which departs considerably from the Bernoulli distribution. As can be deduced from Figs.5a,b, its standard deviation is considerably greater. This additionally decreases the value of r in Eq.11. As demonstrate the results of computer simulations (see Fig.6), population density stabilizes for $x\approx2/3$. This suggests that in Eq.12 the value of $r\approx3$. Therefore, as shown in Fig.6, starting the evolution given by Eq.10 with identical values of X^0_{kl} in the lattice nodes but the central node, finally, the chaotic system becomes globally stable. For $N_m\rightarrow\infty$ ($\Omega(k,l)\rightarrow\mathfrak{I}$) the local densities Y_{kl} "seen" by each node will be the same. Thus the values generated in each node by Eq.10 should be also the same. The whole system will be then chaotic in the same way as the system described by Eq.11 for $\sigma^2=0$. On the other hand, even very small differences between Y_{kl} will produce the same effect as this observed in Fig.6. The interplay between fast growing differences between node values boosted by the chaotic logistic map and smoothing effect of averaging in $\Omega(k,l)$, will decide about the way the population density evolves. Therefore, more formal approach is required to scrutinize how σ^2 value behaves for $N_m \rightarrow \infty$ and in which extent it influences (decreases) r value in Eq.11. By solving this problem one can decide definitely if spatially localized stochastic CA can or cannot mimic the chaotic behavior from the logistic map.

For discrete "motionless" population, modeled by using binary CA automata the situation is very similar to this described above for continuous state system. Instead of the continuous rule given by Eq.10, we have probabilities of extinction/survival represented by Eq.7 (or derived from Eq.5 in more general case), which is discrete equivalent of Eq.10. Because Eq.11, is valid also for the discrete case, it is seen from Fig.5c that the value of biotic potential for "motionless" population should be less than for "uncorrelated" population. We have employed the variety of rules, generating chaotic fluctuations for "uncorrelated" population, in the "motionless", discrete system. Similarly, as it was for the continuous CA, each time we obtain stable population with density $x \approx 2/3$. We can conclude, that the spatial structures produced by static populations, as these shown in Fig.7a, can restrain organisms to encounter each other proportionally to their average density. This way, they can postpone or inhibit completely the chaotic changes in average population density.

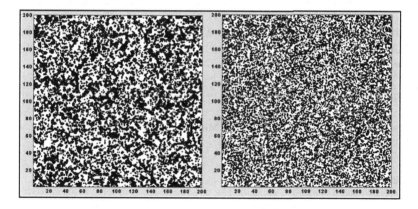

Fig. 7. The snapshots displaying distributions of individuals on CA lattice for two different CA systems. Motionless (left) and "uncorrelated" (right) populations are compared. Populated sites are colored in white.

3   Concluding Remarks

We can summarize our findings as follows:

1.   Uncorrelated, randomly scattered populations evolving on 2-D CA lattice can mimic the same pathway to chaos as this resulting from the logistic model, i.e., evolution from stable colonies through bifurcation swarms to chaos.

2. The fully developed chaotic behavior ($r=4$) occurs only for infinitely large dispersal and competition radiuses. For the Moore neighborhood the maximal biotic potential is $r=3,6$, a little bit larger than $r=3.57$ when chaotic fluctuations begins. For von Neumann neighborhood ($r=3,33(3)$) only the first bifurcation can occur.
3. This global logistic map can be obtained for variety of microscopic laws of 2D CA system.
4. Motionless, spatially extended CA systems with limited neighborhood capacity (i.e., limited dispersal and competition) are stable. No chaotic fluctuations in population density are observed for irregularly spaced populations evolving according to stochastic rules.
5. The appearance of spatial structures (clusters) plays a regulatory role of a stable evolution. However, no mathematical proof is given here to confirm this hypothesis for all possible stochastic laws and increasing neighborhood radius above the Moore's one.
6. As a problem for the future work, it would be interesting to inspect how 2D CA model will behave for intermediate dispersal and competition and limited motion ability of individuals.

Ability of motion, large dispersal and competition radiuses allow for chaotic – wide – inspection of a "solution" space in looking for the optimal evolution conditions. However, in case of external attack in the moment when the population is the weakest one (i.e., the smallest) it can extinct quickly. On the other hand, stable and motionless populations producing spatial structures are immune on the external danger, but their evolution ability is limited. All of these factors inhibiting chaotic evolution are discussed in details in [7].

Acknowledgments

This research is financed by the Polish Ministry of Education and Science, Project No.3 T11F 010 30.

References

1. Law, R., Murrell, D.J., Dieckmann, U., (2003). Population Growth in Space and Time. Spatial Logistic Equation, *Ecology*, 84 (1), 252-262.
2. Kendall, B.E., (1998). Spatial Structure, Environmental Heterogeneity, and Population Dynamics: Analysis of the Coupled Logistic Map, *Theor. Popul. Biol.*, 54, 11-37.
3. Holmes, E.E., Lewis, M.,A., Banks, J.E., Veit, R.R., (1994). Partial differential equations in ecology: Spatial interactions and population dynamics, *Ecology*, 75(1), 17-29.
4. Lloyd, A.L., (1995). The coupled Logistic Map: A Simple Model For The Effects of Spatial Heterogeneity on Population Dynamics, *J. Theor. Biol.*, 173, 217-30
5. Chopard, B., Droz, M., (1998). Cellular Automata Modeling of Physical Systems (Cambridge University Press,Cambridge,England).
6. Phatak, S.C., Rao, S.,S., (1995). Logistic Map: A possible random-number generator, *Phys. Rev. E.*, 51(4), 3670-78.
7. Dzwinel W, Yuen DA, (2005). Aging in Hostile Environments Modeled by Cellular Automata with Genetic Dynamics, *Int. J. Modern Phys. C*, 16, 3, 357-377

Directed Percolation Phenomena in Asynchronous Elementary Cellular Automata

Nazim Fatès

LORIA, University Nancy 1, Campus Scientifique B.P. 239
54506 Vandoeuvre-lès-Nancy, France
Nazim.Fates@loria.fr

Abstract. Cellular automata are discrete dynamical systems that are widely used to model natural systems. Classically they are run with perfect synchrony ; *i.e.*, the local rule is applied to each cell at each time step. A possible modification of the updating scheme consists in applying the rule with a fixed probability, called the synchrony rate. It has been shown in a previous work that varying the synchrony rate continuously could produce a discontinuity in the behaviour of the cellular automaton. This works aims at investigating the nature of this change of behaviour using intensive numerical simulations. We apply a two-step protocol to show that the phenomenon is a phase transition whose critical exponents are in good agreement with the predicted values of directed percolation.

1 Introduction

The research described in this article is motivated by the need to address a general question raised in the modelling activity: "Does a given model keep its behaviour when it is submitted to a perturbation of its updating scheme ?" Of course, this question is too wide to be tackled in all its generality and we choose here to study it in the more narrow context of cellular automata, taking asynchronism as a means of perturbation.

In its classical paradigm, a cellular automaton consists of a collection of finite state automata arranged on a regular grid, which update their state at each time step according to a local rule. Using this formalism, we obtain discrete dynamical systems that are used for modelling spatially extended phenomena governed by a local rule. Such phenomena are to be found in various fields such as physics (*e.g.*, atoms interaction in a crystal), chemistry (*e.g.*, non-stirred reaction-diffusion), biology (*e.g.*, virus spreading), etc. (see [1], chap. 1 for a review). The method used for assessing the validity of a model generally consists in comparing the output produced by the model to some experimental data. We claim that this step is of course necessary but that it is not sufficient: one may also need to examine to which extent the behaviour observed is due to the implicit hypotheses of the model, namely: discretisation of state, regularity of the grid, perfect synchrony of the transitions.

The latter problem was at first addressed in [14] by means of simulation, the evaluation of the change in behaviour remaining qualitative. Other experimental

S. El Yacoubi, B. Chopard, and S. Bandini (Eds.): ACRI 2006, LNCS 4173, pp. 667–675, 2006.
© Springer-Verlag Berlin Heidelberg 2006

works such as [3,17,15] followed, showing that the update scheme was indeed a key point to study. On the theoretical side, very few results have been obtained so far: the independence on the "update history" was shown undecidable in [9], existence of stationary distributions was studied in [12] and a first classification based on the convergence time was proposed in [7] and extended in [8]. In the work [6], we experimentally showed that the perturbation of the updating scheme of elementary cellular automata may alter significantly the behaviour of some rules while other rules remained robust. We used one of the simplest means of introducing asynchronism in the dynamics: instead of applying the rule simultaneously to all the cells, each cell has a given probability α, called the *synchrony rate* to apply the rule.

This study showed that, among other phenomena, for seven elementary cellular automata, there exists a particular value of the synchrony rate α_c for which a small change of value produces an abrupt change of behaviour. It was then conjectured that this brutal variation could be explained by the existence of a phase transition, more precisely that the universality class[1] of the phase transition was *directed percolation* (DP). We wish to emphasize that this hypothesis was mainly supported by the observation of the space-time diagrams patterns produced near criticality. Previous identification of directed percolation was obtained in other contexts such that probabilistic cellular automata [5] or synchronisation of two copies of cellular automata [10,16]. To our knowledge, the only example of directed percolation induced by asynchronism was given by Blok and Bergersen for the famous Game of Life [4].

2   Description of the Model

Let a ring of n cells be indexed by $\mathcal{L} = \mathbb{Z}/n\mathbb{Z}$, a *configuration* is word on $\{0,1\}^{\mathcal{L}}$. The *density* of a configuration x is the ratio of cells in state 1. An *elementary cellular automaton* (ECA) is described by a function $f : \{0,1\}^3 \rightarrow \{0,1\}$ called the *local rule*. Each ECA is indexed according to the usual notation [18].

Using the stochastic asynchronous updating scheme, the local rule f allows to define a probabilistic global rule F which operates on the random variables x^t according to $x^0 = x$ with probability 1 and $x^{t+1} = F(x^t)$ such that:

$$\forall i \in \mathcal{L}, x_i^{t+1} = \begin{cases} f(x_{i-1}^t, x_i^t, x_{i+1}^t) & \text{with probability } \alpha \\ x_i^t & \text{with probability } 1 - \alpha \end{cases}$$

By taking $\alpha = 1$, we fall back on the classical synchronous case and as α is decreased, the updtae rule becomes asynchronous while the effect of an update remains unchanged.

The rules that were experimentally detected as showing a brutal change of behaviour for a non-trivial value of α are ECA 6,18,26,50,58,106,146 (only "minimal representative rules" are considered). Figure 1 shows how the variation of

---

[1] *Universality class* is a term from statistical physics that describes all the different phenomena that obey the same laws near criticality (*e.g.*, see [11] for a review on the directed percolation universality class).

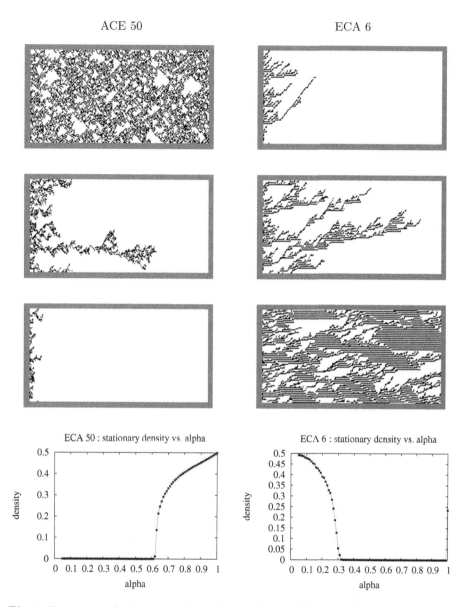

Fig. 1. Two types of phase transitions observed with ECA. **(a)** The upper three lines show the space time diagrams for ECA 50 (left) and ECA 6 (right). Synchrony rate is decreased, from $\alpha = 0.75$ (up) to $\alpha = 0.25$ (down). Time goes from left to right; the time factor is rescaled by a factor $1/\alpha$ (i.e., for $\alpha = 0.25$ only time steps that are multiples of 4 are displayed). **(b)** Lower line : asymptotic density as a function of the synchrony rate ; it is estimated by the computation of the average density obtained on a sampling time $S = 10^3$, after a transient time $T = 10^5$ has elapsed.

synchrony rate affects the behaviour of three such rules. We see that two different behaviours are exhibited:

(a) The system quickly converges to a frozen fixed-point configuration where all the cells are in state 0, we say that we are in the *subcritical phase*.
(b) The system evolves to a steady state characterised by an evolving branching-annhilating pattern, we call this steady state the *supercritical phase*.

The separation between the two phases can be seen on Fig.1.b: the phase transition is materialised by the change in the average density (see legend). If the directed percolation hypothesis is valid, then theory and observations [11] predict that for an infinite lattice size system, the temporal evolution of the density $d_\alpha(t)$ obeys the following laws:

– for the critical value the density decreases as a power law: $d_{\alpha_c}(t) \sim t^{-\delta}$;
– for the supercritical phase $\alpha > \alpha_c$, the system converges to a stationary state characterised by a non-zero asymptotic density $d_\infty(\alpha)$. Near the critical point, the asymptotic density follows a power law: $d_\infty(\alpha) \sim (\alpha - \alpha_c)^\beta$.

We emphasize that the critical exponents $\delta = 0.1595$ and $\beta = 0.2765$ are known only experimentally (the values are given here with four digits, see [11] for better precision). They are valid for an initial random configuration where each cell has an equal probability to be in state 0 or 1.

Naturally, these predictions only hold for infinite systems ; as simulation requires finite lattices, we are bound to introduce finite-size effects. In the following section, we explain our protocol for measuring these exponents and limiting experimental errors.

3   Protocol

The measure of DP-critical exponents is a delicate operation that generally requires large amount of computation time. The main difficulty resides in avoiding systematic errors when obtaining statistical data near the transition point. For example, it happened that authors were mislead by their measures and concluded that a phase transition phenomenon was not in the DP universality class [13], which was later proved wrong [10].

In order to limit the influence of systematic errors, we use the two-step protocol that was used by Grassberger in [10]:

– We measure the critical synchrony rate α_c by varying α until we reach the best approximation of a power-law decay for the density. This first experiment also allows to measure the critical exponent δ.
– We measure the asymptotic density d_∞ as a function of α and then fit a power-law in order to calculate β.

Note that these two steps are not independent since the second operation uses the previously computed value of α_c.

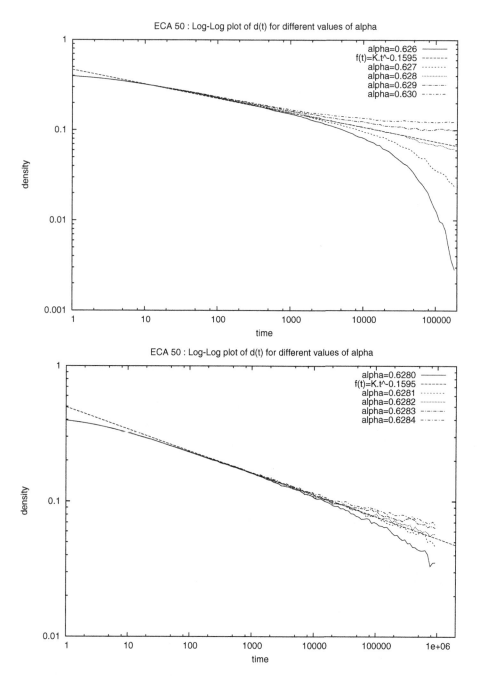

Fig. 2. ECA 50 : Determination of of the critical synchrony rate α_c using $d = f(t)$ for different values of α. Each curve shows the average obtained with on 100 runs. (a) α is varied by increments of 10^{-3}, for 2.10^5 simulation steps. (b) α is varied by increments of 10^{-4}, for 10^6 simulation steps. The straight line has slope $-\delta_{DP} = 0.1595$ and is plotted for reference.

In all the following experiments, we fixed the lattice size to $n = 10^4$ (as in [10]), verifying that the variations of the results when the system size was decreased to $n = 5000$ was less than the precision of measures. However, a more detailed protocol would require to do a *scaling analysis*, *i.e.*, to compute the limits of each measure as n goes to infinity.

3.1 Determination of δ

Figure 3 shows the temporal decay of the density for ECA 50 as α is varied by 10^{-3} steps from 0.626 to 0.630. The curves are obtained by averaging the data on 100 runs of time $T = 2.10^5$. We see that as α is increased, the curve in a log-log plot transforms from a concav function to a convex function ; the best linearity is obtained for $\alpha = 0.628$. As predicted, we see that the curve's slope in its linear part is close to $\delta_{DP} = 0.1595$.

In order to improve the precision on the measure of α_c, we repeated the previous experiment by varying α with a step of 10^{-4} using a sampling time $T = 10^6$. This operation is the most time-consuming as this computation requires more than 10^{14} applications of the local rule. The convexity of the curves was determined numerically, by plotting the local slope (see [11]) as a function of time according to:

$$\delta_{\text{eff}}(t) = \frac{\log d(t) - \log d(t/m)}{\log t - \log(t/m)} = \frac{\log [d(t)/d(t/m)]}{\log m}$$

with m varying between 4 and 10 (heuristic criterion).

The values of α for which the best linearity was obtained are displayed in Table 1. The value of the slope, δ, is given in the third column of the table for comparison with δ_{DP}. We took $t \in [2000, 200000]$ as a fit interval to limit the influence of the transient time and the deviation from a power-law decay.

We wish to call the reader attention on the fact that we cannot identify the precision of this fit as the precision on the measure on δ. Indeed, as we are necessarily slightly subcritical or supercritical, the curve $d(t)$ eventually deviates from a power-law. To get an estimation on the precision on δ, we used the following heuristic method: if we bound the α_c according to $\alpha_1 < \alpha_c < \alpha_2$, we use the quantity $E_\delta = |\delta(\alpha_1) - \delta(\alpha_2)|$ as an estimator of the precision on δ. The results displayed in Table 1 show that the computed values of δ and E_δ are compatible with the predicted value δ_{DP}. It is interesting to notice that a variation on α of the order of 10^{-4} produces a relative variation of 10% on the value of δ. This explains why α_c has to be measured with high precision.

3.2 Determination of β

The second part of the experiments consists in measuring the critical exponent β using the values of the asymptotic density as a function of α. To estimate this asymptotic density, it is necessary to adjust the sampling time as α varies. Indeed, as α approaches α_c, the asymptotic density vanishes as :

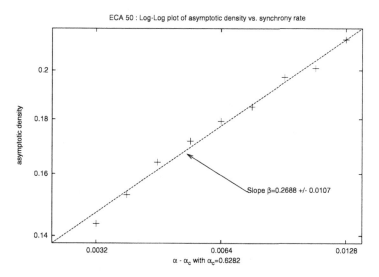

Fig. 3. ECA 50: Determination of the critical exponent β using the time decay properties. Each point is obtained according to using a particular sampling time (see text). The curve have slope $\beta_{50} = 0.2688 \pm 0.0107$. Note that both x and y axis are displayed in logarithmic scale.

$d_{\infty}(\alpha) = (\alpha - \alpha_c)^{\beta}$, and the increase of the time needed to reach this density is thus exponential: this phenomenon, known as *critical slowing down* (*e.g.*, [11]), limits the precision on the measure of the asymptotic density d_{∞}.

The quantity $\Delta_{\alpha} = \alpha - \alpha_c$ was varied according to an exponential increment from 0.0032 to 0.128. This interval is determined by the following trade-off: the computer time limits lower values of Δ_{α} (critical slowing down) and for higher values of Δ_{α} the system "saturates" and no longer follow a power-law. The deviation from the power law is a phenomenon that is predicted by theory and that can be studied for its own interest. However, we prefer here to restrict our measures to the linear part of the curve.

Sampling times were increased as Δ_{α} was decreased and the highest sampling time $T = 4.10^5$ was used for $\Delta_{\alpha} = 0.0032$. The experiment was conducted for the seven ECA and the calculated values are shown in Table 1. Again, the computed values of β are in good agreement with the reference value $\beta_{DP} = 0.2765$.

4   Discussion

The problem of determining how changes of behaviour were triggered by gradual changes in the update rule were investigated by numerical simulations. The results show good evidence that the phenomenon observed for seven asynchronous elementary cellular automata is a second order phase transition which belongs to the directed percolation universality class.

Table 1. Critical values $\tilde{\alpha}_c$ for the seven ECA with DP ; the digit between parentheses is uncertainty (in 10^{-4} units). Corresponding value of δ is given with an approximation of the error on δ (see text). Critical exponent β calculated using the given value $\tilde{\alpha}_c$.

ECA	$\tilde{\alpha}_c$	$\delta(\tilde{\alpha}_c)$	E_δ	β
6	0.2824 (4)	0.158	0.014	0.265 ± 0.015
18	0.7139 (2)	0.155	0.028	0.271 ± 0.009
26	0.4748 (2)	0.164	0.032	0.264 ± 0.015
50	0.6282 (2)	0.159	0.024	0.269 ± 0.011
58	0.3400 (2)	0.162	0.022	0.270 ± 0.017
106	0.8144 (4)	0.155	0.023	0.273 ± 0.048
146	0.6751 (2)	0.163	0.027	0.259 ± 0.021

The observation of the synchronous behaviour of the seven ECA studied indicate that there is certainly no straightforward relation with the existing classifications. For example, ECA 6, 50 and 58 are "periodic" (or Wolfram class II) rules while ECA 18, 26, 106 and 146 are "chaotic" (or Wolfram class III) rules. This indicates that at criticality, cell-scale details of cellular automata become irrelevant while some global scale-free behaviour governs its evolution.

These result may also further confirm a famous conjecture by Janssen and Grassberger (see [11] for a short presentation) that states that a model should belong to the DP universality class if it satisfies the following criteria:

- uniqueness of absorbing state (the all-zero state in our case),
- the possibility to characterise the phase transition by a positive order parameter (the density in our case),
- the definition of dynamics by short-range process (true by definition of CA),
- and the absence of additional symmetries (e.g., state symmetry) or quenched randomness (true for all of the seven ECA considered).

This last condition is essential since ECA 178, which is a rule symmetric by operation of left/right and 0/1 exchanging, was also detected to have a phase transition but was not found into the DP universality class.

The most challenging question now consists in explaining why some ECA show phase transitions while other have a smooth behaviour. A possibility of investigation would be to examine how the dynamics of asynchronous CA can be mapped with other well-studied phenomena such as synchronisation of configurations [10] or Domany-Kinzel probabilistic CA [5]. However, such a reduction does not appear simple since ECA 6 has an "inversed" phase transition: the subcritical (frozen) state is reached by the *increase* of the synchrony rate. Another interesting problem is to find examples of such phase transitions in nature. For example, this mechanism could help explaining the trigger of the self-organisation phase in cellular societies [2,6].

Acknowledgement. The author expresses his acknowledgments to A. Ballier, H. Berry, M. Morvan and J.-B. Rouquier.

References

1. Andrew Adamatzky, *Computing in nonlinear media and automata collectives*, ISBN 075030751X, Institute of Physics Publishing, 2001.
2. Hugues Berry, *Nonequilibrium phase transition in a self-activated biological network*, Physical Review E (2003), no. 67, 031907.
3. Hugues Bersini and Vincent Detours, *Asynchrony induces stability in cellular automata based models*, Proceedings of the 4th International Workshop on the Synthesis and Simulation of Living Systems *ArtificialLifeIV* (Brooks, R. A, Maes, and Pattie, eds.), MIT Press, July 1994, pp. 382–387.
4. Hendrik J. Blok and Birger Bergersen, *Synchronous versus asynchronous updating in the "game of life"*, Physical Review E **59** (1999), 3876–9.
5. Eytan Domany and Wolfgang Kinzel, *Equivalence of cellular automata to ising models and directed percolation*, Physical Review Letters **53** (1984), 311–314.
6. Nazim Fatès and Michel Morvan, *An experimental study of robustness to asynchronism for elementary cellular automata*, Complex Systems **16** (2005), 1–27.
7. Nazim Fatès, Michel Morvan, Nicolas Schabanel, and Éric Thierry, *Fully asynchronous behavior of double-quiescent elementary cellular automata.*, MFCS'05 Proceedings – LNCS 3618, 2005, pp. 316–327.
8. Nazim Fatès, Nicolas Schabanel, Éric Thierry, and Damien Regnault, *Asynchronous behavior of double-quiescent elementary cellular automata*, LATIN'06 Proceedings – LNCS 3887, 2006, pp. 455–466.
9. Peter Gács, *Deterministic computations whose history is independent of the order of asynchronous updating*, http://arXiv.org/abs/cs/0101026, 2003.
10. Peter Grassberger, *Synchronization of coupled systems with spatiotemporal chaos*, Physical Review E **59** (1999), no. 3, R2520.
11. Haye Hinrichsen, *Nonequilibrium critical phenomena and phase transitions into absorbing states*, Advances in Physics **49** (2000), 815–958.
12. Pierre-Yves Louis, *Automates cellulaires probabilistes : mesures stationnaires, mesures de gibbs associées et ergodicité*, Ph.D. thesis, Université des Sciences et Technologies de Lille, September 2002.
13. Luis G. Morelli and Damian H. Zanette, *Synchronization of stochastically coupled cellular automata*, Physical Review E (1998), R8–R11.
14. R. L. Buvel and T.E. Ingerson, *Structure in asynchronous cellular automata*, Physica D **1** (1984), 59–68.
15. Andrea Roli and Franco Zambonelli, *Emergence of macro spatial structures in dissipative cellular automata*, Proc. of ACRI2002: Fifth International Conference on Cellular Automata for Research and Industry, Lecture Notes in Computer Science, vol. 2493, Springer, 2002, pp. 144–155.
16. Jean-Baptiste Rouquier, *Coalescing cellular automata*, ICCS'06 Proceedings – LNCS 3993, 2006, pp. 321–328.
17. Birgitt Schönfisch and André de Roos, *Synchronous and asynchronous updating in cellular automata*, BioSystems **51** (1999), 123–143.
18. Stephen Wolfram, *Universality and complexity in cellular automata*, Physica D **10** (1984), 1–35.

On Symmetric Sandpiles

Enrico Formenti, Benoît Masson, and Theophilos Pisokas

Laboratoire I3S, Université de Nice-Sophia Antipolis, Bât. ESSI, 930 route des Colles,
06903 Sophia Antipolis Cedex, France
{enrico.formenti, benoit.masson}@unice.fr,
pisokas@polytech.unice.fr

Abstract. A symmetric version of the well-known SPM model for sand-piles is introduced. We prove that the new model has fixed point dynamics. Although there might be several fixed points, a precise description of the fixed points is given. Moreover, we provide a simple closed formula for counting the number of fixed points originated by initial conditions made of a single column of grains.

Keywords: SOC systems; sandpiles; fixed point dynamics; discrete dynamical systems.

1 Introduction

Self-Organized Criticality (SOC) is a very common phenomenon which can be observed in Nature. It concerns, for example, sandpiles formation, snow avalanches and so on [1].

Practically speaking, it can be described as follows. Consider an evolving system. After a while, the system reaches a *critical state*. Any further move from this critical state will cause a deep spontaneous reorganization of the whole system. No external parameter can be tuned to control this reorganization. Thereafter, the system starts evolving to another critical state and so on.

Sandpiles are a very useful model to illustrate SOC systems. Indeed, consider toppling sand grains on a table, one by one. Little by little a sandpile will start growing and growing until the slope reaches a critical value. At this moment, any further addition of a single sand grain will cause cascades of grains and deep reorganization of the whole pile. Afterwards the sandpile restarts growing to another critical state and so on.

A formal model for sandpiles, called SPM, has been introduced in [7,8,9]. The sandpile is represented by a sequence of "columns". Each column contains a certain number of sand grains. The evolution is based on a local interaction rule (see Section 2): a sand grain falls from a column A to its right neighbor B if A contains at least two grains more than B; otherwise there is no movement. The SPM model has been widely studied [2,7,12,3,11,10]. In particular, it has been proved that it has fixed point dynamics and a closed formula has been given to calculate precisely the length of the transient to the fixed point [7]. Moreover, a precise description of the fixed point has been given [8].

S. El Yacoubi, B. Chopard, and S. Bandini (Eds.): ACRI 2006, LNCS 4173, pp. 676–685, 2006.
© Springer-Verlag Berlin Heidelberg 2006

All these results are very interesting but they have two main drawbacks. First, they lack generality; indeed, the fixed point results are always obtained starting from very special initial sandpiles (just one column). In [5,4], we tried to solve this problem by giving a fast algorithm for finding the fixed point starting from any possible initial condition. Second, the model lacks symmetry; in fact, grains either stay or move to the right only. Remark that in Nature, sandpiles evolve absolutely in a symmetrical manner.

In this paper we introduce SSPM: a symmetric version of SPM. The new model follows the rules of SPM but it applies them in both directions. For technical reasons that will be clearer later, we allow only one grain to move per time step.

We prove that SSPM has fixed point dynamics. This is not a great surprise. To validate the new model, one should give a precise description of these fixed points and compare their "shape" with those of sandpiles in Nature.

To this extent we use a formal construct which allows a better description of the dynamics: orbit graphs. They are directed graphs of the relation "being son of". In Section 3.2, the precise structure of their vertices is given (under the condition of considering initial configurations made by a single column): a configuration belongs to some orbit graph if and only if it admits a crazed LR-decomposition (see Section 3.2).

Practically speaking, a configuration admits a crazed LR-decomposition if it can be decomposed into an increasing part L and a decreasing part R and both in L and in R any two plateaus (*i.e.* consecutive columns of identical height) are separated by at least a "cliff" (*i.e.* consecutive columns with height difference strictly greater than 1).

The special structure of the vertices allows a very useful description of the fixed points: they are configurations which admit a crazed LR-decomposition without cliffs.

Finally, using this characterization of the "shape" of fixed points we provide a closed formula which computes the number of fixed points originated from the initial configuration (n) (a single column containing n grains). The surprise is that the formula is $\lfloor \sqrt{n} \rfloor$. Unfortunately, we have no practical or "visual" explanation for such a formula.

Remark that due to lack of space, and because of the technicality of some proofs, most of them are omitted here and can be found in the long version of the paper [6].

2   The SPM Model

A *sandpile* is a finite sequence of integers $(c_1, \ldots, c_k)$; $k \in \mathbb{N}$ is the *length* of the pile. Sometimes a sandpile is also called a *configuration*. Let $\mathcal{C} = \bigcup_{k \in \mathbb{N}} (\mathbb{N}^+)^k$ be the set of all configurations.

Given a sandpile $(c_1, \ldots, c_k)$, the integer $n = \sum_{i=1}^{k} c_i$ is the *number of grains* of the pile. Given a configuration $(c_1, \ldots, c_k)$, a subsequence $c_i, \ldots, c_j$ (with $1 \leq i < j \leq k$) is a *plateau* if $c_h = c_{h+1}$ for $i \leq h < j$; $s = i - j + 1$ is the length of the plateau and $p = c_i$ its height. A subsequence c_i, c_{i+1} is a *cliff* if $c_i - c_{i+1} \geq 2$.

In the sequel, each sandpile $(c_1, \ldots, c_k)$ will be conveniently represented on a two dimensional grid where c_i is the grain content of column i.

A *sandpile system* is a finite set of rules that tell how the sandpile is updated. SPM [7] (*Sand Pile Model*) is the most known and the most simple sandpile system. All initial configurations contain n grains in the first column and nothing elsewhere *i.e.* they are of type (n). It consists in only one local rule which moves a grain to the right whenever there is a cliff.

Formally, for any configuration c, if there exists $i \in \mathbb{N}$ such that $c_i - c_{i+1} \geq 2$, then c evolves to c' according the following relations:

$$\begin{cases} c'_i = c_i - 1 \\ c'_{i+1} = c_{i+1} + 1 \ . \end{cases}$$

This process is iterated until the rule cannot be applied anymore. We say that a *fixed point* is reached.

Along the evolution of the pile, the rule may be applicable at different places in the configuration. To illustrate this, we represent the set of reachable configurations (starting from a single column) on an oriented graph where the vertices are the configurations. There is an edge between two configurations c^1 and c^2 when c^2 can be obtained by applying the local rule somewhere in c^1 (see Figure 1 for an example, starting from a single column with 8 grains). This is called the *orbit graph* of the initial configuration c, denoted by $\mathcal{G}_c$.

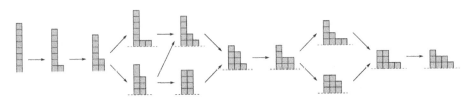

Fig. 1. $\mathcal{G}_{(8)}$, orbit graph of a single pile with 8 grains for SPM

The following theorem proves that the fixed point is unique, independently of the order of application of the local rule.

Theorem 1 ([7]). *For any integer n, $\mathcal{G}_{(n)}$ for SPM is a lattice and is finite.*

The following lemma characterizes the elements of the lattice.

Lemma 1 ([8]). *Consider a configuration c and let n be its number of grains. Then, $c \in \mathcal{G}_{(n)}$ for SPM if and only if it is decreasing and between any two plateaus of c there is at least a cliff.*

Remark 1. Consider a configuration c, and assume that c contains a plateau of length 3. Such a plateau can be seen as two consecutive plateaus of length 2. Thus, by Lemma 1, c does not belong to any orbit graph.

From Lemma 1, it is easy to see that a fixed point Π is a decreasing configuration with no cliffs and at most one plateau. Therefore for any $n \in \mathbb{N}$, we can describe the fixed point Π of (n) by

$$\Pi = \begin{cases} (p, p-1, \ldots, 1) & \text{if } q = 0 , \\ (p, p-1, \ldots, q+1, q, q, q-1, \ldots, 1) & \text{otherwise,} \end{cases}$$

where $\langle p, q \rangle$ is the unique decomposition of n in its *integer sum*:

$$n = q + \sum_{i=1}^{p} i = q + \frac{p \cdot (p+1)}{2} .$$

3   The Symmetric Model

In this section we extend SPM to SSPM (Symmetric SPM) according to the following guidelines: a grain can move either to the left or to the right, if the difference is more than 2; when a grain can move only in one direction, it follows the SPM rule (right) or its symmetric (left).

For all configurations $c = (c_1, \ldots, c_k)$, the following local rules formalize the above requirements:

$$V_i^r(c_1, \ldots, c_k) = \begin{cases} (c_1, \ldots, c_i - 1, c_{i+1} + 1, \ldots, c_k) & \text{if } i \neq k , \\ (c_1, \ldots, c_k - 1, 1) & \text{otherwise,} \end{cases}$$

$$V_i^l(c_1, \ldots, c_k) = \begin{cases} (c_1, \ldots, c_{i-1} + 1, c_i - 1, \ldots, c_k) & \text{if } i \neq 1 , \\ (1, c_1 - 1, \ldots, c_k) & \text{otherwise.} \end{cases}$$

Let $\delta_i^r(c)$ denote the *difference* between the grain content of column i and the one of column $i+1$ of c; define $\delta_k^r(c) = c_k$. Similarly, $\delta_i^l(c)$ denotes the *difference* between the grain content of column i and the one of column $i-1$ of c with $\delta_1^l(c) = c_1$.

Notation. For $a, b \in \mathbb{N}$ with $a < b$, let $[a, b]$ denote the set of integers between a and b.

From the local rule we can define a *next step rule* $\bar{f} : \mathcal{C} \mapsto \mathfrak{P}(\mathcal{C})$ as follows

$$\bar{f}(c) = \{V_i^r(c) \mid \delta_i^r(c) \geq 2, i \in [1, k]\} \cup \{V_i^l(c) \mid \delta_i^l(c) \geq 2, i \in [1, k]\} .$$

Finally, using the next step rule, one can define the *global rule* which describes the evolution of the system from time step t to time step $t + 1$:

$$\forall S \in \mathfrak{P}(\mathcal{C}), \ f(S) = \bigcup_{c \in S} \bar{f}(c) .$$

When no local rule is applicable to c, i.e. $f(\{c\}) = \emptyset$, we say that c is a *fixed point of SSPM*. For $n \in \mathbb{N}$, let f^n denote the n-th composition of f with itself.

The notion of orbit graph can be naturally extended to the symmetric case by using the functions V_i^r and V_i^l. In the sequel, when speaking of orbit graph, we will always mean the orbit graph *w.r.t.* the SSPM model.

3.1 Fixed Point Dynamics

In this section we prove that SSPM has fixed points dynamics. This result is obtained by using a "potential energy function" and by showing that this function is positive and non-increasing.

Given a configuration $c = (c_1, \ldots, c_k)$, the *energy* of a column c_i ($i \in [1, k]$) is defined as follows

$$\varepsilon(c_i) = \sum_{j=1}^{c_i} j \ .$$

Therefore, the *total energy* of a configuration $c = (c_1, \ldots, c_k)$ is naturally defined as

$$E(c) = \sum_{i=1}^{k} \varepsilon(c_i) \ .$$

The proof of the following lemma can be found in [6].

Lemma 2. *Consider a configuration* $c = (c_1, \ldots, c_k)$ *with* n *grains. Then it holds that* $E(c) \leq E((n))$; *equality holds if and only if* $c = (n)$.

The function E can be naturally extended to work on set of configurations as follows

$$\forall S \in \mathfrak{P}(\mathcal{C}), \ E(S) = \max \{E(c), c \in S\} \ ,$$

with $E(\emptyset) = 0$.

The following lemma is straightforward from the definition of the energy function.

Lemma 3. *For any set of configurations* $S \neq \emptyset$, $E(f(S)) < E(S)$.

The following simple proposition describes the general structure of the orbit graph. Its proof can be found in [6].

Proposition 1. *For any initial configuration* c, $\mathcal{G}_c$ *is finite, contains at least a fixed point but no cycles.*

The following corollary is given only to further stress the result of Proposition 1.

Corollary 1. *SSPM has fixed point dynamics.*

Corollary 1 says that independently of the order of application of local rules both with respect to type of rule and to the application site, SSPM evolves towards a fixed point. The problem is that this fixed point might not be unique. Figure 2 gives an example of this fact.

Despite the non-uniqueness, in the next section we give a precise characterization of the structure of the fixed points. This characterization is essentially deduced from the properties of the vertices of the orbit graphs.

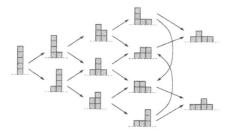

Fig. 2. $\mathcal{G}_{(5)}$, orbit graph of a single pile with 5 grains for SSPM. Remark that there are two distinct fixed points.

3.2 Orbit Graphs

In [8], the authors precisely described the structure of the orbit graph of SPM when started on initial condition (n). They proved that it is the graph of a lattice. As a consequence, they deduced the uniqueness of the fixed point for SPM.

We have already seen that in the SSPM case, the dynamics is of fixed point type, but the fixed point might not be unique. Hence, it is clear that the orbit graph of SSPM is no more the graph of a lattice. In this section, we detail the overall structure of the vertices of these graphs.

A configuration $c = (c_1, c_2, \ldots, c_k)$ is *LR-decomposable* if it can be divided into two *zones*: $L(c) = [1, t], R(c) = [t + 1, k]$ such that

1. $\forall i \in L(c), i \neq t, c_i \leq c_{i+1}$ *i.e.* $L(c)$ is non-decreasing;
2. $\forall i \in R(c), i \neq k, c_i \geq c_{i+1}$ *i.e.* $R(c)$ is non-increasing.

Figure 3(a) give an example of LR-decomposition. For any configuration c, let $T(c) = \{i \in [1, k], \forall j \in [1, k], c_i \geq c_j\}$. In the sequel, $T(c)$ is called the *top* of c, see Figure 3(b).

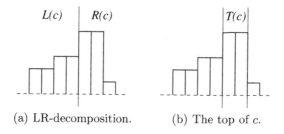

(a) LR-decomposition.   (b) The top of c.

Fig. 3. Decomposition of a configuration c

Given a configuration $c = (c_1, c_2, \ldots, c_k)$, a set of consecutive indexes $I \subseteq [1, k]$ is *crazed* if any two plateaus in I are separated by at least a cliff. A configuration c has a *crazed* LR-decomposition if it admits a LR-decomposition in which both $R(c)$ and $L(c)$ are crazed.

A configuration might have several different LR-decompositions. The following propositions tell which of them we are interested in. All the proofs of this section are very technical, they can be found in [6].

The proof of Proposition 2 will be made progressively, using several technical lemmas.

Lemma 4. *Consider $n \in \mathbb{N}$ and $c \in \mathcal{G}_{(n)}$. Then c is LR-decomposable.*

Lemma 5. *Consider $n \in \mathbb{N}$ and $c \in \mathcal{G}_{(n)}$. Let $T(c)$ be the top of c. Any LR-decomposition of c is such that both $L(c) \setminus T(c)$ and $R(c) \setminus T(c)$ have no plateaus of size strictly greater than 2.*

Lemma 6. *Consider $n \in \mathbb{N}$ and $c \in \mathcal{G}_{(n)}$. Let $T(c)$ be the top of c. Any LR-decomposition of c is such that both $L(c) \setminus T(c)$ and $R(c) \setminus T(c)$ are crazed.*

It is obvious that the cardinality of $T(c)$ is bigger of equal to 1 for all configurations. Using very simple examples one can verify that $|T(c)|$ can also be equal to 2, 3 or 4. The following result proves that these are the only possible values for the cardinality of $T(c)$ when c belongs to an orbit graph.

Lemma 7. *Consider $n \in \mathbb{N}$ and $c \in \mathcal{G}_{(n)}$. Then $|T(c)| \leq 4$.*

The following proposition gives a precise characterization of the configurations of the orbit graph. Its proof is very technical as many different cases have to be considered, but each of them is solved quite simply using the previous lemmas.

Proposition 2. *Consider $n \in \mathbb{N}$ and $c \in \mathcal{G}_{(n)}$. Then c has a crazed LR-decomposition.*

The converse of Proposition 2 is proved using another technical lemma, both proofs are in [6].

Lemma 8. *Consider a configuration c, $c \neq (n)$ for all $n \in \mathbb{N}$, which admits a crazed LR-decomposition. Then, there exists d such that $c \in f(\{d\})$ and d admits a crazed LR-decomposition.*

The next proposition proves that having a crazed LR-decomposition is sufficient to belong to an orbit graph.

Proposition 3. *If a configuration c admits a crazed LR-decomposition, then there is a $n \in \mathbb{N}$ such that $c \in \mathcal{G}_{(n)}$.*

Because of Proposition 2, any fixed point Π of $\mathcal{G}_{(n)}$ has very precise characteristics. It admits a crazed LR-decomposition $L(\Pi), R(\Pi)$, and it has no cliffs. Therefore, both $L(\Pi)$ and $R(\Pi)$ have at most 1 plateau since they are crazed. Moreover, there may be another plateau at the junction between $L(\Pi)$ and $R(\Pi)$, *i.e.* at most 3 plateaus in Π.

The structure of the fixed points is described on Figures 4. Figure 4(a) represent the fixed points Π such that $|T(\Pi)| = 1$, Figure 4(b) is for the fixed points Π such that $|T(\Pi)| \geq 2$.

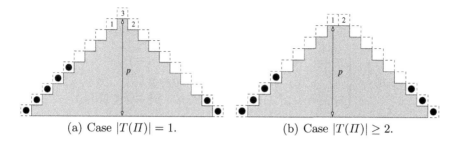

(a) Case $|T(\Pi)| = 1$.   (b) Case $|T(\Pi)| \geq 2$.

Fig. 4. Structure of the fixed points

3.3   A Kind of Magic

From Corollary 1, we know that for any $n \in \mathbb{N}$, the configuration (n) leads to at least one fixed point. In this section we compute precisely the number of fixed points of SSPM with initial condition (n).

In order to understand how a fixed point can be obtained, we try to give a visual construction. Consider Figures 4. The n grains of the fixed point must be arranged in the grayed part and can partially occupy the dashed frame with the supplementary constraint that grains in the dashed part must be as much clustered to the ground as possible. Boxes labeled 1, 2 and 3 in Figures 4(a) and 4(b) cannot be filled (for more details see the proof of Lemma 9). Remark that if p is the height of the grayed part, then this area contains p^2 grains in Figure 4(a), and $p^2 + p$ grains in Figure 4(b).

Lemma 9 will be the main tool that we use to count the number of fixed points, it proves that the "shapes" outlined in Figure 4(b) describe exactly all the possible fixed points. We preferred to put the proofs of the following lemmas in the long version of the article [6] since they are rather technical.

Let $g_1(n)$ be the numbers of fixed points Π such that $|T(\Pi)| = 1$, and $g_2(n)$ the numbers of fixed points Π such that $|T(\Pi)| \geq 2$.

Lemma 9. *For any $n \in \mathbb{N}$, consider SSPM with initial condition (n). The number of fixed points of $\mathcal{G}_{(n)}$ is given by $G(n) = g_1(n) + g_2(n)$.*

The two following lemmas give the exact expression of $g_1(n)$ and $g_2(n)$.

Lemma 10. *For any $n \in \mathbb{N}$, consider SSPM with initial condition (n). The number of fixed points of $\mathcal{G}_{(n)}$ with top of length 1 is given by*

$$g_1(n) = \begin{cases} n - p^2 + 1 & \text{if } n - p^2 \leq p - 1 \text{ ,} \\ 2p - n + p^2 - 1 & \text{if } p \leq n - p^2 \leq 2p - 1 \text{ ,} \\ 0 & \text{otherwise,} \end{cases}$$

where p is the unique integer such that $p^2 \leq n < (p+1)^2$.

Lemma 11. *For any $n \in \mathbb{N}$, consider SSPM with initial condition (n). The number of fixed points of $\mathcal{G}_{(n)}$ with top of length bigger than 1 is given by*

$$
g_2(n) = \begin{cases} n - p^2 - p + 1 & \text{if } n - p^2 - p \leq p - 1 \;, \\ p & \text{if } n - p^2 - p = p \;, \\ 3p - n + p^2 + 1 & \text{if } p + 1 \leq n - p^2 - p \leq 2p + 1 \;, \end{cases}
$$

where p is the unique integer such that $p^2 + p \leq n < (p+1)^2 + (p+1)$.

The following proposition gives a closed formula for the number of fixed points in the orbit of initial condition (n). The formula is somewhat "magical" since it is very simple but we have neither practical nor visual explanation for it. It is easily obtained from the previous lemmas, see [6] for more details.

Proposition 4. *For any $n \in \mathbb{N}$, consider SSPM with initial condition (n). The number of fixed points of $\mathcal{G}_{(n)}$ is given by $G(n) = \lfloor \sqrt{n} \rfloor$.*

Remark that it would also be possible to give the exact expression of each of these fixed points, but it would be complex and of no interest here.

Finally, remark that we did not take into account the initial position of the columns. For the same fixed point, there may exist different fixed points which have the same shape, but at different indices. In this paper we do not consider this fact, we only take into account the general shape of the configurations.

4   Conclusions and Future Work

In this paper we have introduced SSPM: a symmetric version of the well-known SPM model. We have proved that SSPM has fixed point dynamics and exhibited the precise structure of the fixed points which are in the orbit of initial condition (n). Moreover, we showed a simple closed formula for counting the number of distinct (*i.e.* having different shape) fixed points. Remark that this result is surprising since the combinatorial complexity of the orbit graphs becomes higher and higher when the number n of grains grows. This complexity contrasts with the simplicity of the formula for the number of fixed points: $\lfloor \sqrt{n} \rfloor$. Moreover, this formula is to some extent fascinating: although it is very simple, we have neither a practical nor a visual explanation for it.

This research can be continued along three main directions:

- Corollary 1 says that, starting from any initial configuration, SSPM has fixed point dynamics. Can we give a formula or at least tight bounds for the shortest path to a fixed point? For the longest?
- Section 3.2 gives a precise characterization of orbit graphs for initial conditions made of one single column. It would be interesting to extend this characterization to more general initial conditions or at least to find an alternative characterization.

– The model we introduced is intrinsically sequential: only one grain moves at each time step. It would be interesting to introduce a model similar to SSPM but with synchronous update. This would be even more realistic than SSPM for the simulation of natural phenomena.

References

1. P. Bak, C. Tang, and K. Wiesenfeld. Self-organized criticality. *Physical Review A*, 38(1):364–374, 1988.
2. T. Brylawski. The lattice of integer partitions. *Discrete mathematics*, 6:201–219, 1973.
3. D. Dhar, P. Ruelle, S. Sen, and D. Verma. Algebraic aspects of sandpile models. *Journal of Physics A*, 28:805–831, 1995.
4. E. Formenti and B. Masson. A note on fixed points of generalized ice piles models. *International Journal on Unconventional Computing*, 2(2), 2006.
5. E. Formenti and B. Masson. On computing fixed points for generalized sand piles. *International Journal on Unconventional Computing*, 2(1):13–25, 2006.
6. E. Formenti, B. Masson, and T. Pisokas. On symmetric sandpiles. Submitted.
7. E. Goles and M. A. Kiwi. Games on line graphs and sandpile automata. *Theoretical Computer Science*, 115:321–349, 1993.
8. E. Goles, M. Morvan, and H. D. Phan. Sandpiles and order structure of integer partitions. *Discrete Applied Mathematics*, 117(1–3):51–64, 2002.
9. E. Goles, M. Morvan, and H. D. Phan. The structure of linear chip firing games and related models. *Theoretical Computer Science*, 270:827–841, 2002.
10. P. B. Miltersen. Two notes on the computational complexity of one-dimensional sandpiles. Technical Report RS-99-3, BRICS, 1999.
11. C. Moore and M. Nilsson. The computational complexity of sandpiles. *Journal of Statistical Physics*, 96:205–224, 1999.
12. P. Ruelle and S. Sen. Toppling distributions in one-dimensional abelian sandpiles. *Journal of Physics A*, 25:1257–1264, 1992.

Towards Affective Situated Cellular Agents

Stefania Bandini and Sara Manzoni

Dipartimento di Informatica, Sistemistica e Comunicazione
Università degli Studi di Milano–Bicocca
Via Bicocca degli Arcimboldi 8, 20126 Milano, Italy
{bandini, manzoni}@disco.unimib.it

Abstract. In this paper we introduce *Affective agents*, a formal framework based on Situated Cellular Agents (SCA) approach to represent crowding phenomena as resulting from the interaction of reactive situated agents. The main aim of this work is to extend the previously introduced SCA–based approach to crowd modeling and simulation, in order to explicitly represent agents' emotional states and to study the role of emotion interaction and diffusion within crowding situations.

Several modeling and computational approaches have been proposed to tackle the complexity of *crowding phenomena* that is, phenomena that can emerge from the dynamic interaction of groups of moving entities (i.e. persons, in the case of human crowds) that share a limited space. Among decentralized modeling approaches, Cellular Automata (CA [1]) provides a discrete abstraction of the shared environment, the state of CA cells encapsulate the presence of entities in portions of the physical environment and cells' transition rule encapsulates pedestrian behaviors [2]. Despite CA–based approaches that consider individuals as homogenous entities that locally interact by communicating their states to neighbors, distributed crowd models based on Multi Agent System (MAS [3]) are composed by autonomous entities whose actions and interactions can be heterogeneous. Within this class of models, our reference modeling and computational framework is Situated Cellular Agents (SCA [4]). SCA model is rooted on basic principles of CA: it intrinsically includes the notions of state and explicitly represents the spatial structure of agents' environment; it takes into account the heterogeneity of modeled entities and provides original extensions to CA (e.g. at–a–distance interaction).

According to SCA, human crowds are described as system of autonomous, situated agents that act and interact in a spatially structured environment. Situated agents are defined as reactive agents that, as effect of the perception of environmental signals, can change either their internal state or their position on the structured environment (agent autonomy is thus preserved by an action–selection mechanism that characterizes each agent). Interaction between agents can occur either locally, causing the synchronous change of state of a set of adjacent agents, and at–a–distance. In the latter case, agent interaction occurs when a signal emitted by an agent propagates throughout the spatial structure of the environment and is perceived by other situated agents. A SCA–based model of

S. El Yacoubi, B. Chopard, and S. Bandini (Eds.): ACRI 2006, LNCS 4173, pp. 686–689, 2006.

a crowd can be composed by agents characterized by several types. In particular the type of a SCA agent specifies the set of states it can assume, its perceptive sensitivity to signals emitted by other agents, and its acting abilities.

In order to enrich SCA modeling tool, we are currently studying an extension of SCA in which situated agents are endowed with an explicit representation of their emotional state according to which they can behave and interact. We claim that this improvement will allow SCA model to be fruitfully adopted to study situations where emotions and their diffusion play a central role in the crowding dynamics. In the following, after a more formal description of SCA model, we will show how a specific SCA type (i.e. *Affective SCA*) can be defined to represent basic emotions and their role in agent behavior according to *affectons* [5]. The latter is a basic computation model defined by finite–automata to study the dynamics of emotional interactions in random environments. An affecton is an emotional automaton which takes states from a set of basic emotions (i.e. happiness, anger, confusion, anxiety and sadness), and updates its state depending on its current state and a state of its input (which is also a made of state–emotions). More details about affectons can be found in [5].

1   SCA Model Overview

Situated Cellular Agents (SCA) is a formal and computational framework for the specification of complex systems characterized by a set of autonomous entities interacting in an environment whose spatial structure represents a key factor in their behaviors (i.e. actions and interactions).

A *Situated Cellular Agent* is defined by the triple $\langle Space, F, A \rangle$, where *Space* models the environment where the set A of agents is situated, acts autonomously and interacts through the propagation of the set F of fields and through local interaction (i.e. *reaction*). *Space* is defined as an undirected graph of sites (let P be the set of sites). Every *site* $p \in P$ can contain at most one agent, and it is defined by the agent situated in it, the set of fields active in it, and the set of its adjacent sites.

A field $f \in F$ is defined by

$$\langle W_f, Diffusion_f, Compare_f, Compose_f \rangle$$

where: W_f denotes the set of values that field f can assume; $Diffusion_f : P \times W_f \times P \to (W_f)^+$ is the diffusion function of the field computing the value of a field on a given space site taking into account in which site and with which value it has been emitted. Fields diffuse along the spatial structure of the environment, and more precisely a field diffuses from a source site to the ones that can be reached through arcs as long as its intensity is not voided by the diffusion function. $Compose_f : (W_f)^+ \to W_f$ expresses how field values have to be combined (for instance, in order to obtain the unique value of field at a site), and $Compare_f : W_f \times W_f \to \{True, False\}$ is the function that compares field values. This function is required, for instance, in order to verify whether an agent can perceive a field value.

A SCA agent $a \in A$ is defined by the 3–tuple

$$< s, p, \tau >$$

where τ is the *agent type* (see below for $\tau = \langle \Sigma_\tau, Perception_\tau, Action_\tau \rangle$ definition), $s \in \Sigma_\tau$ denotes the *agent state* and can assume one of the values specified by its type, and $p \in P$ is the site of the *Space* where the agent is situated.

An agent *type* τ is defined by the 3–tuple

$$\langle \Sigma_\tau, Perception_\tau, Action_\tau \rangle.$$

Σ_τ defines the set of states that agents of type τ can assume. $Perception_\tau : \Sigma_\tau \rightarrow [\mathbf{N} \times W_{f_1}] \ldots [\mathbf{N} \times W_{f_{|F|}}]$ is a function associating to each agent state a vector of pairs representing the *receptiveness coefficient* and *sensitivity thresholds* for each field $f \in F$. Finally, $Action_\tau$ represents the behavioral specification for agents of type τ. Agent behavior can be specified using a language that defines four basic primitives: $emit()$ (to emit a SCA field), $react()$ (to specify the *coordinated change of state* among adjacent agents according to their states), $transport()$ (to allow agent moving towards an adjacent vacant site), and $trigger()$ (to allow the agent to *change its state*).

2   Affective SCA

In order to represent affectons [5] according to SCA, let us define *affective agents* as SCA agents of type

$$Affective = \langle \Sigma_{Affective}, Perception_{Affective}, Action_{Affective} \rangle$$

where

$$\Sigma_{Affective} = \{H, A, C, S\}$$

defines according to [5], happiness (H), anger (A), confusion (C), and sadness (S) as the set of emotional states that affective agents can assume. It is out of the scopes of this paper to motivate the selection of this set of basic emotions. Interested readers can refer to [5] for a detailed argumentation on this topic.

$Perception_{Affective}$ is a function that associate to each agent state of $Affective$ agents a vector of pairs to express its ability to perceive a field according to its emotional state. This means that, for instance, agents in state C (i.e. confused) may be characterized by a higher sensitivity threshold to each field than agents in any other emotional states. Each vector pair of $Perception_{Affective}$ function refers to a field possibly propagating throughout the agent environment, and indicates for the i–th field, agent *receptiveness coefficient* and *sensibility threshold* to field f_i.

$$Perception_{Affective} : \Sigma_{Affective} \rightarrow [\mathbf{N} \times W_{f_1}] \ldots [\mathbf{N} \times W_{f_{|F|}}]$$

$Action_{Affective}$ represents the set of SCA actions that affective agents can perform. In particular, we can describe state–transition functions presented in [5] to describe emotional interactions as a *reaction*() between adjacent affective agents. The effect of a reaction among a set of neighboring SCA agents is their synchronous change of state. Another basic actions defined by SCA framework that will be adopted for this study is *trigger*() whose effect is the change of an agent emotional state according to the perception of a field emitted by another, possibly at–a–distance Affective agent.

3 Concluding Remarks and Future Works

In this paper we have introduced *Affective agents*, a formal framework based on SCA approach to represent crowding phenomena as resulting from the interaction of reactive situated agents. The main aim of this work is to extend the previously introduced SCA–based approach to crowd modeling and simulation, in order to explicitly represent agents' emotional states and to study the role of emotion interaction and diffusion within a crowding situation.

Future works will concern the study of the dynamics of systems of Affective SCA and its comparison with dynamic properties of affectons. Next research steps will concern the adoption of this tool to experiment the behavior of *affective crowds* that is, large groups of pedestrian in which the emotional state of individuals influence the crowd dynamics. This experimentation will focus on studying emotion diffusion in static and dynamic crowds, and the selected scenario will present several different situations in which the role of emotions is crucial in the dynamics of the resulting system. For instance, a possible scenario concern a football match within a stadium where peculiar interesting dynamics can be observed before, during, and after the match.

References

1. Wolfram, S.: Theory and Applications of Cellular Automata. World Scientific Press, Singapore (1986)
2. Schreckenberg, M., Sharma, S.: Pedestrian and Evacuation Dynamics. Springer Verlag, Berlin (2002)
3. Ferber, J.: Multi-Agent Systems. Addison-Wesley, Harlow (UK) (1999)
4. Bandini, S., Manzoni, S., Vizzari, G.: SCA: a model to simulate crowding dynamics. Special Issues on Cellular Automata, IEICE Transactions on Information and Systems **E87-D** (2004) 669–676
5. Adamatzky, A.: Dynamics of Crowd–Minds. Volume 54 of Series on Nonlinear Science. World Scientific (2005)

Beyond Cellular Automata, Towards More Realistic Traffic Simulators

Luís Correia[1,2] and Thomas Wehrle[3]

[1] LabMAg - University of Lisbon,
Campo Grande 1749-016, Lisboa, Portugal
Luis.Correia@di.fc.ul.pt
[2] AI Lab - University of Zurich,
Andreasstrasse 15, CH-8050, Zürich, Switzerland
[3] University of Zurich, Institute of Psychology,
Zürichbergstrasse 43, CH-8044, Zürich, Switzerland
t.wehrle@psychologie.unizh.ch

Abstract. Cellular Automata (CA) have been used in traffic simulation, but in general with models that do not correspond to canonical CA. Here we analyse the differences and the implications of using CA or agent based simulations, with a particular focus on the updating procedures. A proposal for increased realism in traffic simulation is presented.

1 Introduction

A Cellular Automaton (CA), by definition, is a grid of cells with a defined geometrical configuration, each one running a local (transition) function, and all being synchronously updated [1]. Therefore, computation is associated with the cell, or the spatial element. CA is a useful tool for simulation, due to its relative simplicity and to the fact that it produces visually interpretable results.

In road traffic and pedestrian simulation there is a significant use of CA for modelling and simulation [2,3,4,5,6,7,8,9]. However, the vast majority of the work in these areas does not use CA in the strict sense. In fact, the local function is not applied to spatial elements, but to the moving elements (cars, or individuals). Hogeweg, in 1988, has pointed out the distinction between these two approaches in terms of possible differences in modelling complexity [10]. However, only recently a few studies have proposed a separation of the two types of elements in two distinct layers: a CA layer for the spatial elements and a Multi-Agent System (MAS) layer for the mobile elements [11,12,13,14].

More important than a disparate semantics of CA usage is the functional implication that this discrepancy brings about. In particular, the updating procedure *inherited* from CA is synchronous, meaning that all elements of the grid are updated in parallel. The inadequacy of this updating for simulation of natural systems has been identified long ago [15]. Worse than that, it has also been shown that it induces artificial structure in CA behaviour [16,17,18,19].

Natural collective systems are not synchronous in the sense that their components do not react to a signal exactly at the same time [20]. Therefore,

S. El Yacoubi, B. Chopard, and S. Bandini (Eds.): ACRI 2006, LNCS 4173, pp. 690–693, 2006.

asynchronous, or random sequential updating have been defended as more realistic models of natural systems [10,17,21]. Synchronous updates may be used with an update time significantly shorter than the characteristic time of the natural system modeled. However, even in this case, the fact that synchronous updates induce artificial structure in the output is reason enough to use asynchronous updates instead.

In this paper, we briefly analyse the main differences between using local functions for cell update and for agent update in traffic simulation. And in doing so we also analyse the implications of using asynchronous updates in the simulation. In the end we propose a model that, in a natural way, better approaches the real system behaviour.

2   Local Function - Cell vs. Agent

Simulation of agent movement is naturally performed if the local function is associated with the active (moving) agent—the multi-agent approach. It is possible to convert an agent based local function to an equivalent one associated with the spatial cell—the CA approach. This follows from the universal computation capability of CA [1]. However, the simplicity of the local function will be lost for anything more elaborate than the notorious rule 184 [4]. This rule is only valid for constant unitary speeds. A mere increase of the maximum speed to two units implies that the neighbourhood radius r has to be increased to 2, which modifies the state space of the CA local function. This distortion does not happen if the local function is associated with the active element. A variation of the speed ranges only implies modifying local function parameter values accordingly.

Another significant difference between these two approaches is related to the updating policies. In the CA approach we can not modify the updating policy without further adaptations. Consider, for instance, the case of rule 184 with a synchronous update, which is a simple model for traffic simulation. If, instead, we use a random asynchronous update we will notice that there is not a conservation of active elements. This means that vehicles may *be created* or *disappear* along iterations. Here again, there are workarounds but involving a modification of the rule and of the number of cell states. In the case of the multi-agent approach this effect of *non-conservation* of elements does not happen, independently of the realism of the updating policies and of the obtained results. For example, the Asymmetric Stochastic Exclusion Process (ASEP), also uses updates of the active elements' positions. Results of different updatings change the dynamics, but the number of elements is conserved [22,4,23].

3   Updating Policies

By comparison to synchronous models, asynchronous ones may be regarded as introducing a form of noise [24,19]. In fact, we may consider that, besides signal amplitude fluctuations, timing fluctuations are also a form of noise [25]. In the latter case it takes the form of delays or speedups in the updating time instead of changes in the output of the local function.

Synchronous updating has also been applied to ASEP. In [4] is referred that changing the ASEP from synchronous to asynchronous introduces noise. However, instead of trying to eliminate it, as is also defended in that reference, we should aim at correcting parameters in the model (in case we need to produce more realistic behaviour). Every natural system is subject to different forms of noise.

In asynchronous updatings several alternatives are possible, producing different results and possessing more or less realism. According to a statistical analysis in [19], time driven asynchronous updating, with independent timings for each cell, is more realistic. The waiting times of each timer are exponentially distributed, with mean 1.

However, an exponential distribution of the update timings is also not realistic. It may well happen that after one cell update the next scheduled update for that cell, randomly drawn from that distribution, is infinitesimally close. This is not reasonable in natural systems. Therefore, a model including a typical reaction time for each component is defended. This reasoning is valid likewise to CA, ASEP or MAS. The artificialities introduced by the simulation process should be minimised, independently of the used model. Consequently in this paper we defend the use of combined MAS-CA, or ASEP for traffic simulation, with asynchronous updating procedure including some lower bound of response time for each component.

4   Discussion

We have described two important aspects to improve realism of traffic simulation using CA. One is that CA must be limited to simulate non moving elements. Active elements should be simulated by MAS based models, or more simply by ASEP. If space cells have any dynamics (e.g., pavement deterioration) a CA could model space. Otherwise a simple grid may be used for it. The second aspect is that asynchronous updating in discrete simulation avoids the pitfalls of artificial structure induced by synchronous updates. It is, therefore, more realistic.

References

1. Smith III, A.R.: Introductory survey to cellular automata and polyautomata theory. In Lindenmayer, A., Rozenberg, G., eds.: Automata, Languages and Development. North Holland Pub. Comp (1976) revision of May 21, 2001.
2. Schadschneider, A., Schreckenberg, M.: Cellular automaton models and traffic flow. J.PHYS.A **26** (1993) L679
3. Chopard, B., Luthi, P.O., Queloz, P.A.: Cellular automata model of car traffic in a two-dimensional street network. J. Phys. A: Math. Gen. **29** (1996) 2325–2336
4. Nagel, K.: Particle hopping models and traffic flow theory. Physical Review E **53** (1996) 4655–4672
5. Dijkstra, J., Timmermans, H.J.P., Jessurun, J.: A multi-agent cellular automata system for visualising simulated pedestrian activity. In: ACRI. (2000) 29–36

6. Schadschneider, A.: Cellular automaton approach to pedestrian dynamics - theory (2001)
7. Nagel, K.: Cellular automata models for transportation applications. In: ACRI. (2002) 20–31
8. Knospe, W., Santen, L., Schadschneider, A., Schreckenberg, M.: An empirical test for cellular automaton models of traffic flow (2004)
9. Maerivoet, S., De Moor, B.: Cellular automata models of road traffic. PHYSICS REPORTS **419** (2005) 1
10. Hogeweg, P.: Cellular automata as a paradigm for ecological modeling. Applied Mathematics and Computation **27** (1988) 81–100
11. Bandini, S., Manzoni, S., Simone, C.: Dealing with space in multi–agent systems: a model for situated mas. In: AAMAS '02: Proceedings of the first international joint conference on Autonomous agents and multiagent systems, New York, NY, USA, ACM Press (2002) 1183–1190
12. Parker, D., Manson, S., Janssen, M., Hoffmann, M., Deadman, P.: Multiagent systems for the simulation of land-use and land-cover change: A review. Annals of the Association of American Geographers **93** (2003) 314–337
13. Hamagami, T., Hirata, H.: Method of crowd simulation by using multiagent on cellular automata. In: IAT. (2003) 46–52
14. Bandini, S., Federici, M.L., Vizzari, G.: A methodology for crowd modelling with situated cellular agents. In: WOA. (2005) 91–98
15. Hogeweg, P.: Locally synchronised developmental systems - conceptual advantages of discrete event formalism. International Journal of General Systems **Vol. 6** (1980) 57–73
16. Ingerson, T.E., Buvel, R.L.: Structure in asynchronous cellular automata. Physica D **10** (1984) 59–68
17. Huberman, B.A., Glance, N.S.: Evolutionary games and computer simulations. Proc. Natl. Acad. Sci. USA **90** (1993) 7716–7718 Evolution.
18. Bersini, H., Detours, V.: Asynchrony induces stability in cellular automata based models. In Brooks, R., Maes, P., eds.: Artificial Life IV, MIT Press, 1994, p. 382., MIT Press (1994) 382–387
19. Schönfisch, B., de Roos, A.: Synchronous and asynchronous updating in cellular automata. BioSystems **51** (1999) 123–143
20. Cornforth, D., Green, D.G., Newth, D., Kirley, M.: Do artificial ants march in step? Ordered asynchronous processes and modularity in biological systems. In Standish, Abbass, Bedau, eds.: Artificial Life VIII, MIT Press (2002) 28–32
21. Correia, L.: Self-organisation: a case for embodiement. In Gershenson, C., Lenaerts, T., eds.: Proceedings of the Workshop on the Evolution of Complexity, Bloomington, IN, USA, June 3rd, 2006. (2006)
22. Krug, J., Spohn, H.: Universality classes for deterministic surface growth. Physical Review A **38** (1988) 4271–4283
23. Rajewsky, N., Santen, L., Schadschneider, A., Schreckenberg, M.: The asymmetric exclusion process: Comparison of update procedures. Journal of Statistical Physics, Vol. 92, Nos. 1/2, 1998 **Vol. 92** (1998) 151–194
24. Kanada, Y.: The effects of randomness in asynchronous 1D cellular automata. Technical report, Tsukuba Research Center (1997)
25. Correia, L.: Self-organised systems: fundamental properties. Revista de Ciências da Computação **Vol.I** (2006) to appear.

Modeling Crowd Behavior Based on Social Comparison Theory: Extended Abstract

Natalie Fridman and Gal Kaminka

Bar Ilan University, Israel
The MAVERICK Group
Computer Science Department
{fridman, galk}cs.biu.ac.il

Abstract. Modeling crowd behavior is an important challenge for cognitive modelers. We propose a novel model of crowd behavior, based on Festinger's Social Comparison Theory, a social psychology theory known and expanded since the early 1950's. We propose a concrete framework for SCT, and evaluate its implementations in several crowd behavior scenarios. The results show improved performance over existing models.

1   Introduction and Background

Modelling crowd behavior is an important challenge for cognitive modelers. Existing models, in a variety of fields, leave many open challenges. In social sciences and psychology, models often only offer qualitative descriptions, and do not easily permit algorithmic replication. In computer science, models are often simplistic, and typically not tied to specific cognitive science theories or data.

Social psychologists observe that people in a crowd act similar to each another, often acting in a coordinated fashion, as if governed by a single mind [1]. However, this coordination is achieved with little or no verbal communications. Le Bon explains the homogeneous behavior of a crowd by two processes: (i) *Imitation*, where people in a crowd imitate each other; and (ii) *Contagion*, where people in a crowd behave differently from how they usually behave, individually. Some [1] theorize that individual become a part of the crowd behavior when they have "common stimulus" with people inside the crowd. For example, a common cause.

Work on modelling crowd behavior has been carried out in other branches of science, in particular for modelling and simulation. For instance, Blue and Adler [2] use Cellular Automata in order to simulate collective behaviors, in particular pedestrian movement. The focus is again on local interactions: Each simulated pedestrian is controlled by an automaton, which decides on its next action or behavior, based on its local neighborhoods. Helbing et al. [3] focus on simulating pedestrian movement. Each entity moves according to forces of attraction and repulsion. Pedestrians react both to obstacles and to other pedestrians. The study shows that this results in lane formation.

We propose a novel model of crowd behavior, based on Social Comparison Theory (*SCT*) [4], a popular social psychology theory that has been continuously

S. El Yacoubi, B. Chopard, and S. Bandini (Eds.): ACRI 2006, LNCS 4173, pp. 694–698, 2006.

evolving since the 1950s. The key idea in this theory is that humans, lacking objective means to evaluate their state, compare themselves to others that are similar. We propose a concrete algorithmic framework for SCT, and evaluate its implementations in several crowd behavior scenarios. We show that these result in improved performance compared to previous approaches.

2   A Model Based on Social Comparison Theory

The research question we address in this paper deals with the development of a computerized cognitive model which, when executed individually by many agents, will cause them to behave as humans do in crowds.

We took Festinger's Social Comparison Theory [4] as inspiration for the social skills necessary for our agent. According to the Social Comparison Theory, people tend to compare their behavior with others that are most like them. To be more specific, when lacking objective means for appraisal of their opinions and capabilities, people compare their opinions and capabilities to those of others that are similar to them. They then attempt to correct any differences found.

We believe that the Social Comparison Theory may account for some characteristics of crowd behavior:

Common stimulus between crowd participants. One of the social comparison theory implications is group formation. Festinger notes [4]: "To the extent that self evaluation can only be accomplished by means of comparison with other persons, the drive for self evaluation is a force acting on persons to belong to groups, to associate with others. People, then, tend to move into groups which, in their judgment, hold opinions which agree with their own and whose abilities are near their own".

Imitational behavior. By social comparison, people may adopt others' behaviors. Festinger writes [4]: "The existence of a discrepancy in a group with respect to opinions or abilities will lead to action on the part of members of that group to reduce the discrepancy".

To be usable by computerized models, social comparison theory must be transformed into a set of algorithms that, when executed by an agent, will proscribe social comparison behavior. Each observed agent is assumed to be modelled by a set of features and their associated values. For each such agent, we calculate a similarity value $s(x)$, which measures the similarity between the observed agent and the agent carrying out the comparison process. The agent with the highest such value is selected. If its similarity is between given maximum and minimum values, then this triggers actions (o - with least weight) by the comparing agent to reduce the discrepancy. In order to close the gap, we use a gain function $g(o)$ for the action o, which translates into the amount of effort or power invested in the action. For instance, for movement, the gain function would translate into velocity; the greater the gain, the greater the velocity.

$$g(o) = \frac{S_{max} - S_{min}}{S_{max} - s(c)}$$

The process is described in the following algorithm, which executes the comparing agent.

1. For each known agent x calculate similarity $s(x)$
2. $c \leftarrow \texttt{argmax}\ s(x)$, such that $S_{min} < s(c) < S_{max}$
3. $D \leftarrow$ differences between me and agent c
4. Apply actions to minimize differences in D.

3   Experiments and Results

We evaluate our social comparison model as accounting for pedestrian movement phenomena, such as lane formations in bidirectional movement, grouping in grouped pedestrians, and behavior in the presence of obstacles. To implement the model for pedestrian movement experiments, we used NetLogo [5]. We simulated a sidewalk where agents can move in a circular fashion from east to west, or in the opposite direction.

For lack of space, we report here only on a subset of the experiments. See [6] for additional details. In these, each agent modelled its peers using the following set of features and corresponding weights: *Walking direction (weight: 2)*—east or west; *Color (weight: 3)*; and *Position (weight 1)* in terms of distance and angle. The similarities in different features (f_i) are calculated as follows. $f_{color} = 1$ if color is the same, 0 otherwise. $f_{direction} = 1$ if direction is the same, 0 otherwise. and finally, $f_{distance} = \frac{1}{dist}$, where $dist$ is the Euclidean distance between the positions of the agents.

The rationale for feature priorities, as represented in their weights, follows from our intuition and common experience as to how pedestrians act. Distance is the easiest difference to correct, and the least indicative of a similarity between pedestrians. Direction is more indicative of a similarity between agents, and color even more so.

Pedestrian Movement. In order to evaluate our model on bidirectional pedestrian movement we perform experiments in which we varied S_{min} and S_{max}, and thus the gain component $g(o)$. In these, we measured performance using two characteristic features of pedestrian movement, used in previous work [3]: The total number of *lane changes*, and the *flow* (average speed divided by the space-per-agent). By varying the number of agents in the fixed space, controlled *crowd density*. Each trial lasted 5000 cycles, and was repeated dozens of times. The results are contrasted with a random-choice model [3,2].

Figures 1(a) and 1(b) show the lane-changes and flow in these experiments. The figures show that there is no reduction in flow and there is significant improvement to the number of lane changes, with an increased gain. For lack of space, we do not show screen shots here, but the results also demonstrate that increased gain causes the agents to group more closely together.

Grouped Pedestrian Movements. We wanted to evaluate the SCT model on grouped pedestrians, where agents of the same color move together. To account for the intuition that friends and family walk side-by-side, rather than in

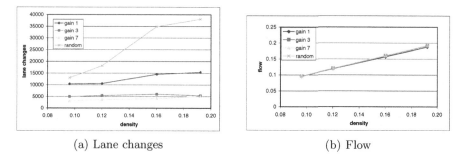

(a) Lane changes　　　　　　　　　　　　(b) Flow

Fig. 1. Individual pedestrian movement experiments

columns, we added another feature: The similarity in position along the x-axis and revised features and weights accordingly. In these experiments, all agents move in the same direction. Gain was allowed to vary per the model, as described above. We examine populations with a different number of colors (5, 10, and 20) and measure the grouping results using *hierarchical social entropy* [7], shown in Table 1. The results of our model are much lower (almost by a factor of two) than random-choice model.

Table 1. Grouping measurements of random-choice and social comparison models. Lower values indicate improved grouping.

# Groups	Random	SCT
5	173.2	**87.4**
10	143.3	**85.8**
20	101.5	**60.1**

4 Summary and Future Work

This paper presented a preliminary algorithmic model proscribing crowd behavior, inspired by Festinger's Social Comparison Theory [4]. Though there is lack of objective data against which the model can be tested, the results are promising and seem to match intuitions as to observed behavior. We are developing an implementation of the Social Comparison Theory model in the Soar cognitive architecture [8].

Acknowledgments. This research was supported in part by IMOD and by ISF grant #1211/04.

References

1. Allport, F.H.: Social Psychology. Boston: Houghton Mifflin (1924)
2. Blue, V.J., Adler, J.L.: Cellular automata microsimulation of bidirectional pedestrian flows. Transportation Research Record (2000) 135–141

3. Helbing, D., Molnar, P., Farkas, I.J., Bolay, K.: Self-organizing pedestrian movement. Environment and Planning B **28** (2001) 361–384
4. Festinger, L.: A theory of social comparison processes. Human Relations (1954) 117–140
5. Wilensky, U.: NetLogo. Center for Connected Learning and Computer-Based Modeling—Northwestern University; http://ccl.northwestern.edu/netlogo/ (1999)
6. Kaminka, G.A., Fridman, N.: A cognitive model of crowd behavior based on social comparison theory. In: Proceedings of the AAAI-2006 workshop on cognitive modeling. (2006)
7. Balch, T.: Behavioral Diversity in Learning Robot Teams. PhD thesis, Georgia Institute of Technology (1998)
8. Newell, A.: Unified Theories of Cognition. Harvard University Press, Cambridge, Massachusetts (1990)

A Cellular Automaton Crowd Tracking System for Modelling Evacuation Processes

Ioakeim G. Georgoudas, Georgios Ch. Sirakoulis, and Ioannis Th. Andreadis

Democritus University of Thrace, Department of Electrical and Computer Engineering,
Laboratory of Electronics,
GR 67100 Xanthi, Greece
{igeorg, gsirak, iandread}@ee.duth.gr
http://www.ee.duth.gr/people/frame.htm

Abstract. Crowd safety and comfort in highly congested places not only depend on the design and the function of the place, but also on the behaviour of each individual. In this paper, an integrated evacuation system is described. The proposed system comprises three stages. The main stage includes an efficient computational tool based on Cellular Automata (CA) capable of simulating main features of pedestrian dynamics during the evacuation of large areas, supported by a multi-parameterised graphical-user interface (GUI). Moreover, an image-processing tracking algorithm is used for the calibration of the system providing all the necessary information about the number of individuals and their distribution in the under test area. Finally, the VLSI implementation of the proposed model is straightforward due to the simplicity of the CA rule, thus leading to the design of a dedicated processor.

1 Introduction

Risk management issues present high research interest especially concerning places, such as exhibitions, museums, transport stations, etc, which are highly congested by individuals not familiar with the place. Every pattern of the modern activity results into the gathering of a large number of people into buildings, auditoriums and other kind of places (sports halls, museums, churches etc). Moreover, huge and inevitable gathering occurs in arrival/departure areas, thus, making clear need for the design and implementation of an efficient evacuation system, which can be vitally helpful to the safe crowd guidance in cases of emergency.

Thorough research in panic crowd movements [1-2] has indicated that individuals under such situations develop a herding behaviour and clogging, thus becoming unable to effectively use all means of emergent evacuation. Crowd safety and comfort not only depend on the design and the operation of the place, but also on the behaviour of each crowd individual. The traditional approach of motion prediction applied to large crowds of pedestrians was based on the modeling of the crowd as if it were a continuous homogeneous mass that behaves like a fluid flowing along corridors. Recent approaches, enhanced by modern computer power, suggest that the crowd consists of discrete individuals who are able to react with their surroundings.

S. El Yacoubi, B. Chopard, and S. Bandini (Eds.): ACRI 2006, LNCS 4173, pp. 699–702, 2006.

Computational intelligent techniques such as CA were introduced in order to model more efficiently crowd behaviour [3]. CA can sufficiently represent phenomena of arbitrary complexity and at the same time can be simulated exactly by digital computers, because of their intrinsic discreteness [4]. As far as it concerns the simulation of pedestrian dynamics, two-dimensional (2-d) CA models have been reported in literature [5-6]. Some of them treat pedestrians as particles subject to long-range forces [6] and others use walkers leaving a trace by modifying the underground on their paths [5].

The results of the present research focus on the design and the implementation of an integral system that will provide active guidance to a crowd under panic, in such a way that it will also exploit effectively all existing means and escaping ways. The final system will be composed of cameras, sensors, computers, processors and electronic devices responsible for the broadcasting of sound and optical signals. The user-friendly parameterized model that simulates evacuation processes attempts at further and more detailed investigation of pedestrian dynamics focusing on specific rather than generalised behaviour under certain conditions. To this direction, the user is provided with the ability to predefine features of the evacuated area, incorporating both topological-oriented parameters and parameters that describe the crowd formation. The calibration of the CA model results from an image processing system responsible for the recognition of the exact position and density distribution of the crowd in the under test area.

2   The Crowd Tracking System

The crowd tracking system encompasses both software and hardware implementations. As far as it concerns the software part, it includes the CA-based evacuation simulation tool as well as the corresponding image processing tracking system. Further upgrade of the system is achieved with the on-chip (VLSI) realization of the CA model, which incorporates advantages of low-cost, high-speed and easy chipset programming, as well as with the inclusion of a sound-optical notification system guided by the corresponding outputs of the dedicated CA processor.

A computational model which simulates the movement of the crowd in cases of room evacuation has been developed. Empirical studies of the international bibliography have been taken into account as well as studies of the social psychology that describe and model crowds in state of panic. This computational model is properly parameterised in order to be equipped with the ability of receiving and properly processing data from the camera-based multiple people tracking system. The grid of the 2-d CA based simulation tool is considered as homogeneous and isotropic, while the CA cells can obtain two possible states; either free or occupied by one particle. During each time step, an individual chooses to move in one of the eight possible directions of its neighbourhood. The general scheme is that each particle moves towards the direction closest to an exit. A 3×3 median matrix for each occupied cell, depending on the CA cell itself and its eight closest neighbours, is updated at every time step. Each matrix element represents a possible updated spatial and temporal state of the occupied cell, placed at the centre of the matrix. The values of the elements indicate the distance of the occupied cell and its neighbours from the evacuation point. As soon as all possible routes have been detected, the shortest prevails and the particle moves in this way to the next time step. In case of multiple exits, the whole procedure is repeated for each one separately. In Fig.1, two different snapshots of a simulation process are presented with the help of a developed graphical user interface (GUI) based on Matlab®.

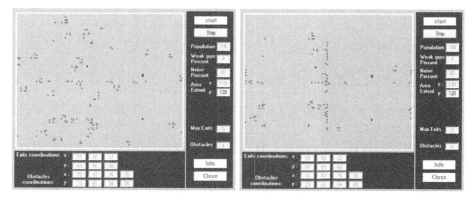

Fig. 1. Two different snapshots of the CA model GUI. Middle-aged individuals are coloured red, while weak groups of individuals (children or elderly) are coloured green. Black dots correspond to obstacles and turquoise dots to exit points.

As far as it concerns calibration purposes, efforts have been focused on the incorporation of a tracking algorithm capable to estimate the number of individuals and their distribution in the under test area, in real time, using instant images. The real-time execution of the appropriate tracking algorithm plays a significant role to the proposed system, since it will establish its functionality to manage situations strongly related to the safety of people during evacuation processes. Implementation of real-time, display and image processing systems are rather difficult due to the huge amount of data that is processed. Nevertheless, models for multiple people tracking based on video technology and sensor networks have been developed efficiently [7-8]. These models are normally based on background subtraction algorithms in order to isolate foreground information from background images, continuing with the segmentation of the foreground pixels which aims at the moving objects clarification. Tracking of the moving objects is finally succeeded by comparing consecutive frames under various criteria. Hence, data obtainable by multimedia surveillance systems can be supplied to the CA model in order to calibrate it and to test its capability of reproducing various observed phenomena under panic circumstances. The implemented algorithm combines the required resolution along with the execution rate aiming at the optimized management of situations under danger.

Finally, regarding the VLSI architecture of the CA model, it has been proposed a local neighbourhood 2-d CA, where the next state of each cell depends on the current state of one of its eight neighbours, i.e. the element of the median matrix which is closest to an exit and itself. In order to have a flexible design, we should be able to configure a cell with different rules. Moreover, to provide wider flexibility OR gates should be incorporated, since the inter-connection between cells is based on OR-logic. Each 2-d CA cell is connected through nine switches to its eight nearest neighbours and itself. A particular rule is applied by setting the corresponding switches to 1 or 0. Thus, a nine bit word is required to control the nine switches corresponding to a single 2-d CA cell. Additionally, another bit is required to configure the cell in OR mode. The CA model architecture is shown in Fig. 2. In effect, by providing a generalised 2-d CA structure, programmability has also been incorporated [9].

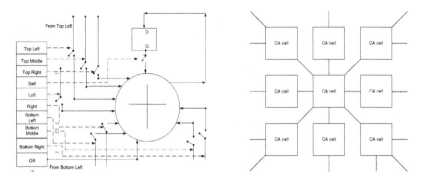

Fig. 2. Architecture of a single cell of the CA model (left) and a 2-d CA structure (right)

3 Conclusions

The aim of this paper is the development of an integrated computational system capable to guide the crowd in cases of immediate evacuation of an area. The proposed methodology includes data receipt from a moving image tracking system in order to clarify the number and the distribution of the detected crowd. This data is used as the calibration background of the CA based crowd tracking simulation tool. The system will produce signals to guide the crowd using sound and optical signals. Certain attributes of crowd behaviour, such as collective effects, collisions and delaying factors have been successfully encountered during simulation. Several phenomena of crowd dynamics, meaning transition to incoordination (arching) due to clogging as well as mass behaviour, have been taken into account. The VLSI implementation of the proposed CA algorithm is straightforward with no silicon overhead.

References

1. Helbing, D., Farkas, I. Vicsek, T.: Simulating dynamical features of escape panic. Nature 407 (2000) 487–490
2. Hirai, K., Tarui, K.: A Simulation of the Behavior of a Crowd in Panic. Systems and Control, Japan (1977)
3. Wolfram, S.: Theory and Applications of Cellular Automata. World Scientific, Singapore (1986)
4. Adamatzky, A.: Identification of Cellular Automata. Taylor & Francis, London (1995)
5. Burstedde, C., Klauck, K., Schadschneider, A., Zittartz, J.: Simulation of pedestrian dynamics using a two-dimensional cellular automaton. Physica A. 295 (2001) 507–525
6. Aubé, F., Shield, R.: Modeling the Effect of Leadership on Crowd Flow Dynamics. Lecture Notes in Computer Science 3305 (2004) 601–611
7. Haritaoglu, I., Harwood, D., Davis, L.S.: W4: Real-time surveillance of people and their activities. IEEE Transaction Pattern Analysis and Machine Intelligence 22 (8) (2000) 809-822
8. Cucchiara, R.: Multimedia Surveillance Systems. VSSN'05, November 11, 2005, Singapore
9. Khan, A.R., Ghoudhury, P.P., Dihidar, K., Mitra, S., Sarkar, P.: VLSI Architecture of a Cellular Automata Machine. Computers Math. Appl. 33 (5) (1997) 79-94

Information in Crowds: The Swarm Information Model

Colin Marc Henein and Tony White

Carleton University. 1125 Colonel By Dr. Ottawa, Ontario. K1S 5B6. Canada
cmh@ccs.carleton.ca, arpwhite@scs.carleton.ca

One interesting view of crowd modelling is the consideration of crowd effects as being generated from the point of view of individual agents. By modelling individual decisions of agents (rather than generalizing from a population of identical ones) we can represent the heterogeneity inherent in large crowds. The heterogeneous approach allows for different agents to interpret the environment differently (via cognition, memory or other intrinsic factors).

Pelechano et al. [1] have used a psycho-emotional model to consider wayfinding by agents with varying training. Although the results are of interest, jumping from simple models of homogeneous agents to a complex psychological model makes it hard to isolate the effects of heterogeneity. Bandini et al. have designed heterogeneity into their SCA model [2], but we prefer to explore the question incrementally by adding heterogeneity to an existing model, allowing for comparison of behaviours.

The CA model of Kirchner & Schadschneider (K&S) [3] considers individual agent desires to follow locally perceptible gradients. The Swarm Force model [4,5] retains K&S' general approach, but incorporates the physical forces required to reproduce key crowd behaviours. Neither model takes full advantage of the individual-centred approach to explore heterogeneity within the crowd because only location-specific processing is performed (the agents are all basically the same).

In addition to a penchant for homogeneity, previous models have not tended to examine the important effect of the provision of information concerning the overall situation (whether by physical discovery, overhead announcements or inter-agent communication). In our view, timely information about the location and operational status of exits, for example, is of crucial importance in evacuations; different modes of discovery will produce different crowd patterns. Pauls [6] reported that "crowd incidents often exhibit... a failure of front-to-back communication"; information about an unfolding crush at the front of a crowd must be conveyed to those at the rear (with whom damaging pushing forces originate) to prevent disasters.

It is with a view toward examining the effects of heterogeneity and illuminating the importance of information that we here propose the Swarm Information Model (SIM). Its aim is to study crowds of heterogeneous individuals who base their actions on the differing perceptions of the world engendered by unfolding information.

1   The Swarm Force Model and SIM

SIM is an extension of the Swarm Force model [4,5] which in turn is based on K&S' crowd model [3]. The models consist of a rectangular grid of cells, either designated as walls or which hold up to one agent. Agents select and move to an adjacent cell in each time step, and may be forced to remain still should their desired cell be occupied

S. El Yacoubi, B. Chopard, and S. Bandini (Eds.): ACRI 2006, LNCS 4173, pp. 703–706, 2006.
© Springer-Verlag Berlin Heidelberg 2006

by another agent. Some cells are designated as exit cells, and agents who occupy these cells are considered to exit the model on the next timestep.

The information available to agents for cell selection is restricted to their immediate surroundings, and is dispersed throughout the space through the concept of a *field*: a set of information having a distinct value at each grid cell. K&S define two such fields: the *static field*, whose value is the distance to the closest exit cell, and the *dynamic field*, which allows trail following analogously to ant pheromones. Two sensitivity parameters, k_s and k_D, allow adjustment of the weight agents place on these two fields when selecting the cell they wish to move to next. The cell selection formula of the Swarm Force model is as follows:

$$p_{ij} = N \exp(k_D D_{ij}) \exp(k_s S_{ij}) (1 - \phi_{ij}) \xi_{ij} \tag{1}$$

Here, p_{ij} represents the probability that an agent will select a neighbouring cell (i, j). D_{ij} and S_{ij} represent the value of the dynamic and static fields (respectively) at this location, ϕ_{ij} is the vacancy factor (0 if a cell is unoccupied and 0.5 otherwise), while ξ_{ij} is 0 for walls, 1 otherwise. N is the normalisation number equal to $(\Sigma p_{ij})^{-1}$.

Force within the model is a third field whose value on occupied cells is the vector force experienced by the agent on the cell. Force is generated by agents pushing the occupants of desired cells when blocked; is cumulatively retransmitted by agents; when moderate overrides equation (1) as the decision mechanism for cell selection; and, when excessive, injures agents (who then act in all respects as walls).

2 SIM Explained

SIM departs from the previous models in two major respects. First, it allows for individual agents to perceive the modelled world differently from one another, creating a heterogeneous crowd. Second, it allows for agents to change their view of the world, either under the influence of the new *information field*, or through a simple inter-agent communication mechanism.

Multiple static fields. As with previous models, the basis of agents' view of the world is the static field that, mediated through the k_s sensitivity parameter, motivates agents to move toward points of interest (e.g. exits). To produce different views of the world, the SIM model simply provides a set of static fields rather than a single one. The set of static fields specifies the ways agents can view the world. The additional fields may include points of interest at locations other than real exits (representing blocked exits, or a misinformed agent), and may omit points of interest at legitimate exits (representing exits that are unknown to the agent). The additional static fields are complemented by an agent variable (current-static) that tracks which static field is being consulted by that agent.

In short, by allowing the agent access to multiple static fields, different agents have access to different internal maps leading to heterogeneous decision making.

Information Field. The information field is a new field within the model that causes agents to change their view of the world upon visiting certain locations. Like the agent's current-static variable, the value of the information field is an index into the set of static fields. Upon entering a cell the agent compares the value of the information field with the agent's internal `current-static`. Should the field indicate a higher index, the agent permanently updates its `current-static` accordingly.

Like the arrangement of exits and the setup of the static field(s), the information field is a creation of the modeller; working together, these three constructs determine the evacuation scenario being studied. The information field is likely to be fixed at the outset of the model, but it is also possible to change the information field during the course of model execution. This can model, for example, the effect of localized or generalized overhead announcements concerning the situation.

Communication. By providing for direct communication we can use this model to investigate behaviour engendered by informing agents of different views of the world, including misinformation, without physically visiting locations of interest.

If enabled, communication occurs when an agent a is blocked from moving due to an agent b's occupation of a's desired cell. Agent a provides its `current-static` value to b, which updates its own value (if it was lower). Conceptually, communication occurs as an attempt by a to get b to move out of the way.

Example Scenario. Consider a simple example scenario with two exits, one blocked. Using two static fields we can represent two states of agent "belief", one incorrect in which there are two functional exits (two points of interest: one at an exit, one at a wall cell) and one correct in which there is one functional exit (one point of interest, at the exit). If we wish to model a scenario where agents may run to the blocked exit, find it blocked, then move to the correct exit then we set the information field to 1 throughout the space, and 2 in the immediate proximity of the blocked exit. Agents "see" the blockage of the second exit upon moving into this proximate zone. Upon this movement they update their `current-static` variable to 2, switching to the second static field, and thereby viewing only the true exit as a point of interest.

3   Scenarios Studied and Results

Results are given here for three scenarios. The first scenario is the example scenario just described, with no communication between agents. The second scenario is the same, but with communication. In the third scenario there are two exits, both functional, but one is not well known (only one randomly selected agent knows about the second exit at the outset of the model). There are two static fields; the first field is incomplete (showing a point of interest at only one of the doors) while the second field shows points of interest at both doors. The information field is entirely set to 1, except for a small area proximate to the "secret" exit which is set to 2 (this allows agents who wander close the secret door to "discover" it). Communication is enabled.

The SIM outcomes demonstrate important differences from the Swarm Force and K&S models. In the first scenario agents divided into two crowds based on initial proximity to each point of interest. Agents discovering the blocked exit attempted to turn back toward the functional exit. They were prevented from doing so by naïve agents who were clustered around the blocked exit but outside the proximal information zone; the naïve agents did not know the exit was blocked and so pushed in toward the blocked exit while the knowledgeable agents pushed out towards the functional exit. Stasis resulted. Given appropriate injury thresholds this pattern of force application created injuries along the boundaries between the two crowds.

The second scenario began to unfold as the first with the creation of two crowds. The effect of communication was to allow the first naïve agent between a knowledgeable agent and the functional exit to be converted into a knowledgeable agent. This agent then converted the next naïve agent and so on until a stream of knowledgeable agents was able to move toward the functional exit. As the knowledgeable agents left the proximity of the blocked door, naïve agents were able to move into the space created and continue the information process. Ultimately all agents moved to the functional exit, and all agents became knowledgeable.

There were two broad outcomes of the third scenario. If the one knowledgeable agent was initially attracted to the well-known exit then few agents left by the secret one. If the single knowledgeable agent was initially attracted to the secret exit then through communication engendered by the normal contention for space in a large crowd it informed naïve agents. In this case the knowledgeable agent sponsored a small crowd of individuals to move to the secret exit. Depending on the geometry of the situation it is not necessarily the case that the naïve crowd will ever find out about the secret exit, but if it does then some agents may leave the rear ranks at the well-known exit and move to the secret exit.

4 Conclusion and Future Work

We have proposed a new model that demonstrates the effects of heterogeneity within crowds and also the results of providing situation-level information. The modelled crowd behaves quite differently from a homogeneous one, displaying non-adaptive effects (like stasis and injuries when numerous agents work at cross purposes due to differing goals). The new model additionally allowed for complex scenarios involving changing goals and unfolding information, characteristic of more realistic situations.

We have not explored adding more dynamic fields, but doing so could result in agents with similar views of the world following each other. Rather than switching between fields, agents could maintain their own distinct k_s and k_D values for each field, changing them dynamically as information is gained. This would allow for declining belief in certain options and consequently a more cognitive model. These interesting points are left for future research.

References

1. Pelechano,N., O'Brien,K., Silverman,B., Badler.N. (2005) Crowd Simulation Incorporating Agent Psychological Models, Roles and Communication. V-CROWDS '05. Retrieved 26-Apr-06: http://www.seas.upenn.edu/~npelecha/Pelechano_V_CROWDS05.pdf
2. Bandini,S., Federici,ML., Manzoni,S., Vizzari,G (2006). Toward a methodology for situated cellular agent based crowd simulations. *ESAW 2005*, LNAI v. 3963, Springer, 203-220.
3. Kirchner,A., Schadschneider,A. (2002) Simulation of evacuation processes using a bionics-inspired cellular automaton model for pedestrian dynamics. Physica A, 312, 260-276.
4. Henein,CM., White,T. (2005) Agent-Based Modelling of Forces in Crowds. MAMABS05. Lecture Notes in Computer Science v. 3415. Springer, 173-184.
5. Henein,CM., White,T. (in press) Macroscopic effects of microscopic forces between agents in crowd models. *Physica A*. Preprint: http://www.orange-carb.org/~cmh/papers/
6. Pauls,J. (1984) The movement of people in buildings and design solutions for means of egress. Fire Technology, 20, 27-47.

Are Several Creatures More Efficient Than a Single One?

Rolf Hoffmann and Mathias Halbach

TU Darmstadt, FB Informatik, FG Rechnerarchitektur
Hochschulstraße 10, D-64289 Darmstadt, Germany
Phone: +49 6151 16 {3606, 3713}; Fax: +49 6151 16 5410
{hoffmann, halbach}@ra.informatik.tu-darmstadt.de

Introduction. We are presenting results from our project "Creature's exploration problem". The problem is the following: p creatures move around in an environment in order to visit all reachable empty cells in shortest time. All creatures behave according to the same rule.

The creature may perform four different actions: R (turn Right) with turn right only; L (turn Left) with turn left only; Rm (turn Right and move) with move forward and simultaneously turn right; Lm (turn Left and move) with move forward and simultaneously turn left.

The action R/L is performed if the front cell signals *not free* $= (m = 0)$ because of an obstacle, a creature, or a collision conflict. The action Rm/Lm is performed if the front cell signals *free*. In case of a conflict in which two or more creatures want to visit the same cell, all creatures are blocked until the conflict disappears. For more details see [13].

The rules are implemented with a state machine containing a state table. We consider the state machine as a MEALY automaton with inputs *(m, s)*, next state s' and output d (fig. 1a). An algorithm is defined by the contents of the table. We are coding an algorithm by concatenating the contents to a string line by line, e. g.

1L2L0L4R5R3R-3Lm1Rm5Lm0Rm4Lm2Rm // string representation
= 1L2L0L4R5R3R-3L1R5L0R4L2R   // simplified string representation

The state table can be represented more clearly as a state graph (fig. 1b). If the state machine uses n states, we call such an algorithm *n-state algorithm*. If the automaton is considered as a MOORE automaton instead of a MEALY automaton, the number of states will be the product $n \times \#r$, where $\#r$ is the number of possible directions (4 in our case).

In the general case that the different values of the states, inputs and outputs are not restricted to powers of two, the number of M of all algorithms which can be coded by a table oriented state machine is $M = (\#s \times \#y)^{(\#s \times \#x)}$, where $n = \#s$ is the number of states, $\#x$ is the number of different input states and $\#y$ is the number of different output actions. Note that M increases dramatically, especially with $\#s$, which makes it very difficult or even impossible to check the quality of all algorithms in a reasonable time for $\#s \geq 7$ with $\#x = \#y = 2$.

S. El Yacoubi, B. Chopard, and S. Bandini (Eds.): ACRI 2006, LNCS 4173, pp. 707–711, 2006.

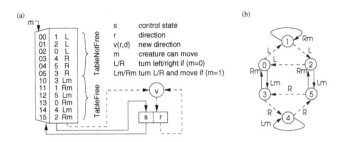

Fig. 1. A state machine (a) models the behavior of a creature. Corresponding 6-state algorithm (b)

The following definitions and metrics are used

- k := number of creatures
- R := number of empty cells
- g := generation (time steps)
- $r(g)$: = number of visited cells in generation g
- r_{max} := the maximum number of cells which can be visited for $g \to \infty$
- g_{max} := the first generation in which r_{max} is achieved
- e := $r_{max}/R[\%]$, the coverage or exploration rate, i. e. $\frac{visited\ cells}{all\ empty\ cells}$,
- *successful* := true, if $e = 100\%$
- *speed* := R/g_{max} (only defined for successful algorithms)
- *mean step rate* := $\frac{1}{speed}$ (the mean number of cells visited in one generation)

In preceding investigations we could evaluate the best 6-state algorithms for one creature by the aid of special hardware. The behaviour of all relevant algorithms was simulated and evaluated for 26 initial configurations The following 10 best algorithms with respect to (1.) success, (2.) coverage and (3.) speed are:

1. G: 1L2L0L4R5R3R-3L1R5L0R4L2R
2. B: 1R2R0R4L5L3L-3R1L5R0L4R2L
3. C: 1R2R0R4L5L3L-3R4R2L0L1L5R
4. A: 0R2R3R4L5L1L-1R5R4R0L2L3L
5. D: 1R2R3R1L5L1L-1R0L2L4R3L1L

6. E: 1R2L0R4L5L3L-3R4R5R0L1L2R
7. F: 1R2L0L4R5R3R-3L4L5L0R1L2R
8. H: 1L2L3R4L2R0L-2L4L0R3L5L4R
9. I: 1L2L3L4L2R0L-2L4L0R3R5L4R
10. J: 1R2R3R0R4L5L-4R5R3L2L0L1L

The goal of this investigation is to find out, how many creatures can do the whole work most efficiently. The *cooperative work* of k creatures is proportional to the number of generations (time steps) to visit all cells, multiplied with the number of creatures: $W(k) = g_{max}(k) \times k$. The *relative efficiency* is the work of one creature related to the work of k creatures using the same algorithm Alg for all the creatures: $F_{rel} = W_{Alg}(1)/W_{Alg}(k)$. The *absolute efficiency* is the work the work of one creature using the best algorithm divided by the work of k creatures using the algorithm Alg.: $F_{abs} = W_{AlgBest}(1)/W_{Alg}(k)$.

Results. We used the best 6-state algorithms we had evaluated for one creature. Then we observed the global behaviour using 1, 4, 8, 16, 32, 64 creatures in an empty field of size 25 × 25 with an obstacle in the centre. The creatures were equally distributed along the border as shown for 64 creatures in fig. 3.

Table 1. (a) Generations $r_{\max}$ to visit all empty cells. (b) Work units (Generations × Creatures) to visit all empty cells.

Algorithm	Creatures (a)						Creatures (b)					
	1	4	8	16	32	64	1	4	8	16	32	64
A		647	718	375	196	60		**2588**	5744	6000	6272	3840
B	3166	971	2012	476	332	66	**3166**	3884	16096	7616	10624	4224
C	3333	1120	629	1516	223	169	**3333**	4480	5032	24256	7136	10816
D	7525	1750	2080	763	508	64	7525	7000	16640	12208	16256	**4096**
E	4169	1120	1291	1544	587	58	4169	4480	10328	24704	18784	**3712**
F	4213	971		736	282	130	4213	3884		11776	9024	8320
G	3166	971	2012	476	332	66	**3166**	3884	16096	7616	10624	4224
H	8009	1478	918	892	385	221	8009	**5912**	7344	14272	12320	14144
I	7168	1990	1777	449	296	44	7168	7960	14216	7184	9472	**2816**
J			4831	435	525	64			38648	6960	16800	**4096**

The number of generations $r_{\max}$ in which all cells can be visited depends on the algorithm and decreases in most cases with the number of creatures (tab. 1a). In some cases the creatures were not able to visit all empty cells (A-1, F-8, J-1, J-4). In other cases more creatures needed more time than less creatures (A-4 < A-8), (B-4 < B-8), (C-8 < C-16) etc. The whole task can be accomplished with a minimum number of 44 generations (I-64).

An interesting question is the following: how many creatures and which algorithm should be used in order to complete the task with a minimum of working units. You can imagine some workers who have to be paid per working time. You may find out from tab. 1b that you have to pay at least 2588 work units (A-4). If you could spend about 9 % more money (2816), your task would be accomplished about 15 times faster than with A-4 using 64 creatures (I-64).

The results can be presented more general if the work is normalized to the work of one creature. Therefore the efficiency measures were introduced.

Always the same algorithm is used for the *relative efficiency* (fig. 2a). In some cases (especially D-64, I-64, H-4) the efficiency is greater than one. That means that the work could be done cheaper using more creatures.

In the case you compare the cooperative work (with any algorithm) to the work of a single creature with the best algorithm (B-1, G-1), the *absolute efficiency* should be used (fig. 2b). There are two cases (A-4, I-64) in which the efficiency is greater than 100 %, it means that in certain cases more creatures

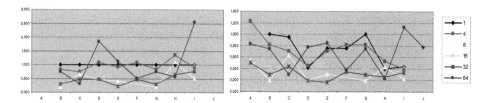

Fig. 2. (a) Relative Efficiency vs. Algorithm. Work(1)/Work(k), k = number of creatures (left side). (b) Absolute Efficiency: WorkBest(1)/Work(k) (right side).

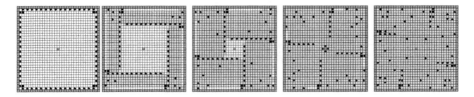

Fig. 3. Algorithm I with 64 creatures, generations 0, 12, 24, 36, 44 with conflicts (marked dark)

can really do better (cheaper) than only one. In other words: more creatures can lead to a super linear speed-up (synergy effect) through cooperation.

The most efficient algorithm I with 64 creatures (I-64) was further investigated by simulation. In each of the generations 0, 4, 8, 12, 16, 20, 24, 28, 32, 36, 38, 40 (fig. 3) four conflicts are arising where two creatures are involved, in total 48 conflicts. The sum of creatures who are involved in conflicts is in total: (conflicts) × 2 = 96 which is very low, compared to the number of working units (2816). Furthermore all conflicts, except for generation 38 have a positive effect because one of the creatures will visit an empty field in the next generation. In this example the conflicts have a positive effect if the creatures meet each other collateral (angle 90°), whereas the conflicts are irrelevant if the creatures meet frontal (angle 180°).

Further investigations are planned with creatures which have different behaviors, have different actions, e. g. move forward, move backward, and can communicate with each other.

References

1. Mesot, B., Sanchez, E., Pena, C.A., Perez-Uribe, A.: SOS++: Finding Smart Behaviors Using Learning and Evolution. In Standish, Abbass, Bedau, eds.: Artificial Life VIII, MIT Press (2002) 264ff.
2. Koza, J.R.: Genetic Programming: On the Programming of Computers by Means of Natural Selection. MIT Pres (1992) ISBN 0-262-11170-5.
3. Halbach, M., Heenes, W., Hoffmann, R., Tisje, J.: Optimizing the Behavior of a Moving Creature in Software and in Hardware. In: ACRI 2004. Number 3305 in LNCS (2004) 841 – 850
4. Halbach, M., Hoffmann, R.: Optimal Behavior of a Moving Creature in the Cellular Automata Model. In Malyshkin, V., ed.: Parallel Computing Technologies. Number 3606 in LNCS, Krasnoyarsk, Springer (2005) 129 – 140 ISBN 3-540-28126-6.
5. Halbach, M., Heenes, W., Hoffmann, R.: Implementation of the Massively Parallel Model GCA. In: Parallel Computing in Electrical Engineering (PARELEC), Parallel System Architectures. (2004)
6. Halbach, M., Hoffmann, R.: Implementing Cellular Automata in FPGA Logic. In: International Parallel & Distributed Processing Symposium (IPDPS), Workshop on Massively Parallel Processing (WMPP), IEEE Computer Society (2004)
7. Hochberger, C.: CDL – Eine Sprache für die Zellularverarbeitung auf verschiedenen Zielplattformen. PhD thesis, TU Darmstadt (1998) Darmstädter Dissertation D17.

8. Hilbert, D.: Ueber die stetige Abbildung einer Linie auf ein Flachenstück. In: Mathematische Annalen. Volume 38., Springer (1891) 459 – 460
9. Peano, G.: Sur une courbe, qui remplit une aire plane. In: Mathematische Annalen. Volume 36., Springer (1890) 157 – 160
10. Halbach, M., Hoffmann, R.: Minimising the Hardware Resources for a Cellular Automaton with Moving Creatures. In: PARS Newsletter. (2006)
11. Hoffmann, R., Ulmann, B., Völkmann, K.P., Waldschmidt, S.: A Stream Processor Architecture Based on the Configurable CEPRA-S. In: Field-programmable Logic (FPL 2000). Number 1896 in LNCS, Villach, Austria, Springer Verlag (2000)
12. Waldschmidt, S., Hochberger, C.: FPGA synthesis for cellular processing. In: IEEE/ACM International Workshop on Logic Synthesis. (1995) 9–55 – 9–63
13. Halbach, M., Hoffmann, R., Both, L.: Optimal 6-State Algorithms for the Behavior of Several Moving Creatures, ACRI (2006)

The F.A.S.T.-Model

Tobias Kretz and Michael Schreckenberg

Universität Duisburg-Essen, 47048 Duisburg, Germany
{kretz, schreckenberg}@traffic.uni-duisburg.de

Abstract. A discrete model of pedestrian motion is presented that is implemented in the *Floor field- and Agentbased Simulation Tool (F.A.S.T.)* which has already been applicated to a variety of real life scenarios.

1 The F.A.S.T. Model of Pedestrian Motion

The F.A.S.T. model is discrete in space and time with an orthogonal lattice. It can be classified as probabilistic CA with extensions demanded by reality. There is a hard-core exlusion between the agents, of which at maximum one can stand at a cell at a certain point in time. An agent needs the space of one cell. This implies a cell size of roughly $40 \cdot 40 \ cm^2$, the minimum space a pedestrian occupies [Dre67]. So far the model follows earlier models [Klu03, Kes01]. In fact this model is in many aspects an extension - mainly related to speeds larger one cell per round - of the model presented in [Kir02] which itself had predecessors [Bur01a, Sch01a, Bur01b].

There are three levels of decision making in this model: 1) The choice of an exit, 2) the choice of a *destination cell*, 3) the path between the current and the destination cell. The first two are probabilistic processes. The third one is deterministic, except for the order in which the agents carry out their steps to reach the destination cell. The process of choosing a destination cell is done completely in parallel by all agents, while the actual motion is a totally sequential process.

In the following a *round* includes the decision for an exit as well as for a destination cell and all *steps*, while a *step* is the movement of an agent from one cell to one of the nearest neighbour cells i.e. a part of the path from the current towards the destination cell.

1.1 Choosing an Exit

At the beginning of each round all agents choose one of the exits with the probability $p_E^A = N(1 + \delta_{AE} k_E(A))/S(A, E)^2$, with A numbering the agents, E numbering the exits agent A is allowed to use, $\delta_{AE} = 1$ if agent A chose exit E during the last round and $\delta_{AE} = 0$ otherwise, $k_E(A)$ being agent A's persistance to stick with a once taken decision for one of the exits, $S(A, E)$ being the distance between the exit and the current position of agent A, and N as normalization constant guaranteeing $\sum_E p_E = 1$. The distance is squared so the probability is proportional to the inverse of the area of a circle around the exit with radius

S. El Yacoubi, B. Chopard, and S. Bandini (Eds.): ACRI 2006, LNCS 4173, pp. 712–715, 2006.

$S(A, E)$. Given a homogeneous density of agents all over a scenario with high symmetry this area is proportional to the number of agents which are closer to the exit than agent A. Therefore this is a measure of a possible queue before agent A at exit E.

1.2   Choosing a Destination Cell

In a model which is spatially and temporally discrete an agent's (dimensionless) velocity is the number of cells which he is allowed to move during one round. As the real-world interpretation of the size of a cell is fixed by the scale of the discretization, the real-time interpretation of one round fixes the real-world interpretation of such a dimensionless velocity. One round is chosen to equal the typical reaction time of one secound. Typical maximal velocities v_{max} of the agents therefore are three to six cells per round.

In the F.A.S.T. model an agent chooses one cell (the destination cell) he wants to move to out of all cells he would be able to reach during one round, except for those that are occupied. Which cells are part of the neighbourhood that belongs to a certain v_{max} (i.e. the shape of such a neighbourhood) is described in [Kre05].

Probabilities for the possible Destination Cells. Probabilities get assigned to each free and unoccupied cell in the neighbourhood of an agent that corresponds to the maximum velocity of that agent, that that particular cell is chosen as destination cell. The probability that an agent chooses cell (x, y) is

$$p = N p_{xy}^S p_{xy}^D p_{xy}^I p_{xy}^W p_{xy}^P \tag{1}$$

While N is a normalization constant all p_{xy}^X are partial probabilities from the different influences on the movement of an agent.

1. p_{xy}^S is the influence of the *static floor field* which contains the information on the distance towards the exit.
2. p_{xy}^D is the influence of the *dynamic floor field* [Sch01b] which contains the information of the motion of the other agents.
3. p_{xy}^I is the influence of inertia effects.
4. p_{xy}^W is the influence of nearby walls.
5. p_{xy}^P is the influence of the density of nearby agents.

These five influences will be introduced in more detail now.

Moving towards the Exit - Following the Static Floor Field: Before the simulation begins, the distance from each cell to each exit is calculated using Dijkstra's algorithm [Dij59] and stored in the static floor field. With the static floor field p^S is calculated for a certain cell at (x, y) as $p_{xy}^S = e^{-k_S S_{xy}}$, with k_S being the *coupling strength* of an agent to the static floor field knowledge as well as will to move are parametrized. All of the five influences are weighted against each other in their relative strengths by *coupling constants* k_X and all coupling constants are individual parameters of the agents.

Herding Behaviour - Following Others: Asides the main CA where the agents move, there is another CA - *the dynamic floor field* - where agents leave a virtual trace whenever they move. This trace decays and diffuses with time. In the F.A.S.T. model the dynamic floor field is a vectorial field. So an agent who has moved from (a, b) to (x, y) changes the dynamic floor field (D_x, D_y) at (a, b) by $(x - a, y - b)$ after all agents have moved. Right after that all values of both components of D decay with probability δ and diffuse with probability α to one of the (von Neumann) neighbouring cells. Since the vector components can be negative, decay means a reduction of the absolute value. Diffusion is only possible from x- to x- and from y- to y-component. The influence on the motion of the agents is $p_{xy}^D = e^{k_D (D_x(x,y)(x-a)+D_y(x,y)(y-b))}$ where (a, b) is the current position of the agent.

Inertia: Contrary to Newtonian physics pedestrians experience de- and accelerating in motion direction as being less ardous than walking through curves. Due to the shape and functionality of the human movement apparatus pedestrians can de- and accelerate from and to their preferred walking velocities almost instantaneously compared to a timescale of one secound. However deviating quickly by e.g. 90° from a certain direction while keeping up the walking speed is far more difficult. So only centrifugal forces are considered to have an influence on the motion of the agents.

On a perfect circle the centrifugal force - which in the F.A.S.T. model is the measure for inertia influences - is $F_c \propto v^2/r$. This assumption after a few steps [Kre06] leads to the following inertia dependence of the movement probability $p^I(x_{t+1}, y_{t+1}) = e^{-k_I(v_{t+1}+v_t)\sin\frac{|\phi|}{2}}$ with ϕ as angle of deviation from the former direction of motion and t counting the timesteps.

Safety Distance towards Walls. This is considered via $p_{xy}^W = e^{(-k_W W_{xy})}$ where W_{xy} is the distance of the cell (x, y) towards the closest wall. For distances larger than a certain W_{max} the effect vanishes completely and $p_{xy}^W = 1$.

Staying Polite - Keeping a Distance Towards other Agents. After each round for each cell (x, y) the number $N_P(x, y)$ of agents in its Moore neighbourhood is counted. The more agents are immediately neighboured, the less another agent might want to choose this cell as his destination: $p_{xy}^P = e^{-k_P N_P(x,y)}$. Then the density at the border of a crowd changes less rapidly, while in the center of the crowd the density remains high since all free cells which an agent can reach during one round are surrounded by agents.

1.3   Moving Towards the Destination Cell

Once all agents have chosen their destination cell the agents start moving towards them. The sequence in which the agents execute their steps is chosen randomly in a way, that agent D executes a step, then agent B, then again agent D, then agent K. During one step an agent moves deterministically onto that cell within the Moore neighbourhood of his current cell, that lies closest to his destination cell. To represent the dynamic space consumption [Wei92] a cell which has been occupied once during this process remains blocked for all other agents until the end of the round. So if the cell closest to the destination cell is blocked the agent moves to the secound closest and so on. If there is no cell left that is unblocked and closer to the destination cell than the current cell the round ends for that particular agent.

References

[Dre67]   Dreyfuss, H.: *The Measure of Man - Human Factors in Design.* Whitney Library of Design, New York (1967)

[Klu03]   Klüpfel, H.: *A Cellular Automaton Model for Crowd Movement and Egress Simulation.* Universität Duisburg-Essen (2003), http://www.ub.uni-duisburg.deETD-db/theses/available/duett-08012003-092540/

[Kes01]   Keßel, A., Klüpfel, H., Schreckenberg, M.: *Microscopic Simulation of Pedestrian Crowd Motion.* in [PED01] 193–202

[Kir02]   Kirchner, A., Schadschneider, A.: *Simulation of evacuation processes using a bionics-inspired cellular automaton model for pedestrian dynamics.* Physica A 1–2 **312** (2002) 260–276 arXiv:cond-mat/0203461

[Bur01a]   Burstedde, C., Klauck, K., Schadschneider, A., Zittarz, J.: *Simulation of pedestrian dynamics using a 2-dimensional cellular automaton.* Physica A **295** 507 (2001) arXiv:cond-mat/0102397

[Sch01a]   Schadschneider, A.: *Cellular Automaton Approach to Pedestrian Dynamics - Theory.* in [PED01] 76–85 arXiv:cond-mat/0112117

[Bur01b]   Burstedde, C., Klauck, K., Schadschneider, A., Zittarz, J.: *Cellular Automaton Approach to Pedestrian Dynamics - Applications.* in [PED01] 87–97 arXiv:cond-mat/0112119

[Nis04]   Nishinari, K., Kirchner, A., Namazi, A., Schadschneider, A.: *Extended floor field CA model for evacuation dynamics.* IEICE Trans. Inf. & Syst. **E87-D** (2004) 726–732 arXiv:cond-mat/0306262

[Kir03]   Kirchner, A., Nishinari, K., Schadschneider, A.: *Friction effects and clogging in a cellular automaton model for pedestrian dynamics.* Phys. Rev. E **67** 056122 (2003) arXiv:cond-mat/0209383

[Kre05]   Kretz, T., Schreckenberg, M.: *Moore and more and symmetry.* in [PED05]

[Sch01b]   Schadschneider, A.: *Bionics-Inspired Cellular Automaton Model for Pedestrian Dynamics.* in [TGF01] 499–509 arXiv:cond-mat/0203461

[Dij59]   Dijkstra, E. W.: *A note on two problems in connexion with graphs.* Numerische Mathematik **1** (1959) 269–271 http://www.garfield.library.upenn.edu/-classics1983/-A1983QA19900001.pdf

[Kre06]   Kretz, T.: *Simulations of Pedestrian Dynamics.* Universität Duisburg-Essen (2006) (to be published)

[Wei92]   Weidmann, U.: *Transporttechnik der Fussgänger.* ETH Zürich, Schriftenreihe des IVT **90** (1992) (in German)

[PED01]   Schreckenberg, M., Sharma, S. D. (editors): *Pedestrian and Evacuation Dynamics.* Springer (2002)

[TGF01]   Fukui, M. and Sugiyama, Y. and Schreckenberg, M. and Wolf, D. E. (editors): *Traffic and Granular Flow '01.* Springer (2002)

[PED05]   Waldau, N. and Gattermann, P. and Knoflacher, H. and Schreckenberg, M. (editors): *Pedestrian and Evacuation Dynamics '05.* Springer (2006)

Evaluation of Billboards Based on Pedestrian Flow in the Concourse of the Station

Shin Morishita and Toshihiko Shiraishi

Yokohama National University,
Graduate School of Environment and Information Sciences
79-7 Tokiwadai, Hodogaya-ku, Yokohama 240-8501 Japan
{mshin, shira}@ynu.ac.jp

Abstract. Pedestrian flow in the concourse of the stations was simulated by Cellular Automata, and based on the simulation results, an evaluation index for billboards set along the pathway in the concourse was proposed. The practical value of billboards may depend on not only their size or placement, but the number of people who pay attention to them. In this paper, some visible area was set to each person walking in the concourse of the station, and the pedestrian flow was simulated by defining various local neighbor rules based on our experience from gates to the door of trains, or door to the gates. The score for each billboard was accumulated when a person took a look at the billboard in the view area, and evaluation index was proposed. The number of people in the concourse was counted in practice and it showed good agreement with the simulation results.

1 Introduction

Billboards hung from the ceiling or on the walls in the concourse of the station are effective medium for advertisement. In these days, several posters are sometimes attached on the floor just in front of the gates for advertisement. Though its size, position and direction are most important factors, the practical value of billboards may mainly depend on the number of people who pay attention to them. But, to the best of our knowledge, the evaluation method for billboards has not been proposed in the past quantitatively. This is partly because there has been no simulation tool to count the number of people in the concourse of station and partly because no one has proposed the idea to evaluate billboards based on the number of people who take a look at them.

In the present paper, the pedestrian flow in the concourse of station was simulated by Cellular Automata[1,2], and the number of pedestrians who caught the billboards into their own view was counted for evaluation. For this purpose, several local neighbor rules were defined based on the observation of pedestrian in the concourse and also on the database stocked in Japan Railroad companies. The evaluation was conducted concerning the distance to the billboard, the direction of pedestrian in relation to the boards, the degree of crowdedness around the boards, and other parameters.

S. El Yacoubi, B. Chopard, and S. Bandini (Eds.): ACRI 2006, LNCS 4173, pp. 716–719, 2006.

2 State Variables and Local Neighbor Rules

The concourse was divided into rectangular cells, and the state variable of "floor", "billboard", "pedestrian" and "obstacle" including walls or pillars were defined for each cell. For the cells indicating the variable of "pedestrian", the variable of "walking speed", "direction" and "ID number of each pedestrian" were added. The state of "entrance", "exit", "stairs" or "gate" was appended to the cells indicating the state of "floor".

A person might move forward or either of front sides, as shown in Fig.1. The maximum velocity of pedestrian was set to 2.5, 1.4, 1.0 and 0.7 m/s, which were based on the measurement data. Each pedestrian was assumed to have fan-shaped visible area as shown in Fig.2, and distance to the front end of visible area and the center angle of the fan was changed according to the walking velocity.

One side of the square cells was set to 0.5 m. Though one person was allowed to stand on one cell at one time as a general rule, two persons might step into one cell around the gate cell or in the case when two persons might pass each other in the crowded area.

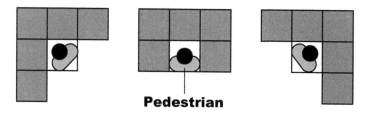

Fig. 1. Cell to proceed

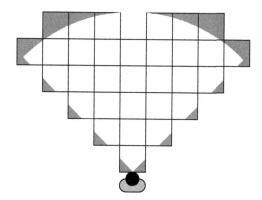

Fig. 2. Visible area of a pedestrian

3 Simulation Results of Pedestrian Flow

Typical examples of simulation result are shown in Fig.3. This example is the main part of the concourse in Tamachi Station, which is an average size station in Tokyo Metropolitan area. The number of passengers getting on and off is said to be 350 thousand per one day, and the simulation results shown in Fig.3 correspond to the rush hour on a weekday in the morning. These results show good agreement with the field investigation database counted in the same concourse of the station.

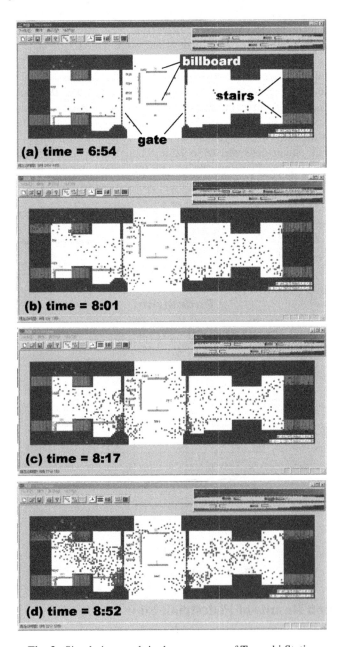

Fig. 3. Simulation result in the concourse of Tamachi Station

4   Evaluation Index for Billboards

Based on the flow simulation of pedestrian in the concourse, the degree of recognition for each billboard was evaluated[2]. When a billboard comes into the visible area of a pedestrian, the recognition index is estimated for each time step, and total index is accumulated during the simulation interval as follows;

$$R\_INDEX = \Sigma \ (A \ x \ C_{de} \ x \ C_{ps} \ x \ C_{ds} \ x \ C_{dr} \ )$$

where, A is the fundamental score depending on the size of billboard, C_{de} is the parameter for the density around the board, C_{ps} is for the position of board, C_{ds} is for the distance between the person and the board, C_{dr} is for the direction of board against the pedestrian. The accumulated index is shown beside of each billboard in Fig.3.

5   Conclusions

In this paper, the pedestrian flow in the concourse of stations was simulated by Cellular Automata, which showed good agreement with the field investigation database. Setting visible area to each pedestrian and the number of chance when a billboard in the concourse came into the visible area was counted, a quantitative evaluation index for the billboards was proposed. The effects of the size of billboards, the density of persons around the boards, the placement position, the distance between the board and the pedestrian, and direction of the board against the pedestrian were taken into account in the evaluation index.

This research was partly supported by East Japan Marketing & Communications, Inc. The authors would like to express sincere thanks for their cooperation.

References

1. Gutowitz, H. : Cellular Automata – Theory and Experiment, MIT Press (1991)
2. Ilachinski, A.: Cellular Automata – A Discrete Universe, World Scientific (2001)
3. Shimizu, K.: Advertising Theory and Strategies (in Japanese) , Soseisha Publishing(1989)

Visualization of Discrete Crowd Dynamics in a 3D Environment

(Extended Abstract)

Giuseppe Vizzari, Giorgio Pizzi, and Mizar Luca Federici

Dipartimento di Informatica, Sistemistica e Comunicazione
Università degli Studi di Milano–Bicocca
Via Bicocca degli Arcimboldi 8, 20126 Milano, Italy
{vizzari, pizzi, mizar}@disco.unimib.it

The design of different kinds of environmental structures, at different detail levels, from the corridors or emergency exits of a building to the whole transportation system on urban or regional scale, may benefit from an envisioning of how it will perform, given specific assumptions on the usage conditions and the behaviours of the autonomous entities which will populate it. There is thus a growing interest in models and technologies supporting the simulation of this kind of domains. An innovative trend in supporting architects in their activities is represented by virtual environments in which alternative architectural designs can be visualized and compared by involved actors, in a collaborative decision scheme [1,2]. This kind of approach could be improved by the possibility to include in the virtual environments also an envisioning of pedestrian dynamics in the related architectural structures, given the fact that human movement behaviour has deep implications on the design of effective pedestrian facilities [3].

Several continuum models for pedestrian dynamics are based on an analytical approach. A relevant example is represented by social force models [4], in which individuals are treated as particles subject to forces. Other analytical models take inspiration from fluid-dynamic [5] and magnetic forces [6] for the representation of pedestrian flows. A different approach to crowd modelling provides the adoption of Cellular Automata (CA) [7], with a discrete spatial representation and discrete time-steps. The cellular space includes both a representation of the environment and an indication of its state, in terms of occupancy of the sites it is divided into. Transition rules must be defined in order to specify the evolution of every cell's state; they are based on the concept of neighbourhood of a cell, a specific set of cells whose state will be considered in the computation of its transition rule. Local cell interactions may represent the motion of an individual in the space, and the sequential application of this rule to the whole cell space may bring to emergent effects and collective behaviours, for instance lane formation and evacuation configurations [8].

Even if the CA-based approach is generally better understood than analytical models by experts in different application domains, and more easily applied to model related scenarios, both these approaches share the limit of considering individuals as homogenous entities, and generally do not provide elements of flexibility and dynamism, like changes in behaviour of individuals. This may

S. El Yacoubi, B. Chopard, and S. Bandini (Eds.): ACRI 2006, LNCS 4173, pp. 720–723, 2006.

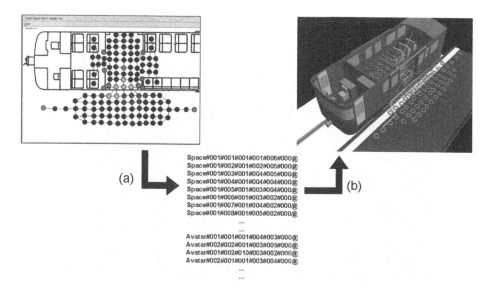

Space#001#001#001#001#006#000@
Space#001#002#001#002#005#000@
Space#001#003#001#004#005#000@
Space#001#004#001#004#004#000@
Space#001#005#001#003#004#000@
Space#001#006#001#003#002#000@
Space#001#007#001#004#002#000@
Space#001#008#001#005#002#000@
...

Avatar#001#001#001#004#003#000@
Avatar#002#002#001#005#000@
Avatar#001#002#010#003#002#000@
Avatar#002#001#001#003#004#000@
...

Fig. 1. Integration between a bidimensional discrete simulator and the 3D Studio Max environment

not represent an issue for large scale simulations, in which a certain degree of approximation is unavoidable and often tackled by the adoption of a stochastic approach, but in other situations it could be relevant to take this kind of information into account. For instance, the evaluation of information signs placement depends on different factors related to their effectiveness, and thus to their visibility. The latter is strongly dependant on the behaviour of individuals moving throughout the environment, their goals and destinations, but even their perceptive capabilities. These factors are relevant in the decision of what directions the active entities will take, and to include these concepts in a CA would require an extremely high number of rules, a very large cell state and probably the extension of the concept of neighbourhood to simulate at-a-distance interactions (for instance to model the attractiveness of destination sites). All these considerations lead to consider a Multi-Agent System (MAS) [9] approach to the modelling or this kind of situation. In fact, a MAS consists of a number of possibly heterogeneous agents that act and interact inside an environment, which enables their perception, interaction and action. Accordingly, Multi Agent Based Simulation (MABS) is based on the idea that it is possible to represent the global behaviour of a dynamic system as the result of interactions occurring among an assembly of agents with their own operational autonomy. In particular the Situated Cellular Agents (SCA) model [10] is a situated MAS model, whose spatial structure represents a key factor influencing agents' choices on their actions and in determining their possible interactions. The model has been successfully applied in different contexts, and in particular its focus on the

Fig. 2. A screenshot of an animation generated by the 3D visualization system

modelling of the environment as well as its inhabiting agents and their interactions, make it particularly suitable for the modelling of crowds of pedestrians [11].

In different situations it can be useful, for sake of communication with non-experts, to obtain a more effective visualization of simulation dynamics. A relevant part of the project in which this work has been developed provides thus the generation of effective forms of visualization of simulation dynamics, to simplify its understanding by non experts in the simulated phenomenon. In particular, the developed simulator can be integrated with a 3D modelling and rendering engine (more details on this integration can be found in [12]). One of the applications developed to implement SCA based simulations exploits a simulator based on a bidimensional spatial structure representation and an existing commercial 3D modelling instrument (3D Studio MAX[1]). The simulator has been developed as experimentation and exploitation of a long term project for a platform for SCA based simulations [13].

The overall integration of the bidimensional discrete simulator and the 3D Studio Max environment is summarized in Figure 1. In (a) the bidimensional simulator produces a log-file provided with a fixed-record structure, in which every record is related to a node of the spatial structure or the position of an agent with reference to this structure. Initially, the simulator prints the structure of the environment, then the starting position of each agent. For every iteration of the simulation the new position of every agent is also printed. This file is then parsed by a 3D Studio Max script (step (b) in the Figure) which generates a plane and walls related to the spatial structure, nodes related to sites, and bipeds

---

[1] http://www.autodesk.com/3dsmax

related to agents. Splines are then generated starting from the discrete positions assumed by various agents, and represent bipeds' movement. This process introduces modifications to trajectories defined by the bidimensional simulator whose sense is to give a more realistic movement to agents' avatars. A screenshot of a sample animation generated in a realistic 3D environment is shown in Figure 2.

While this approach has been applied to the crowd dynamics generated by a SCA based simulator, it can be generally applied to any kind of discrete crowd modelling and simulation system, such as a CA based one.

References

1. Dijkstra, J., Leeuwen, J.V., Timmermans, H.J.P.: Evaluating Design Alternatives Using Conjoint Experiments in Virtual Reality. Environment and Planning B **30** (2003) 357–367
2. Batty, M., Hudson-Smith, A.: Urban Simulacra: from Real to Virtual Cities, Back and Beyond. Architectural Design **75** (2005) 42–47
3. Willis, A., Gjersoe, N., Havard, C., Kerridge, J., Kukla, R.: Human Movement Behaviour in Urban Spaces: Implications for the Design and Modelling of Effective Pedestrian Environments. Environment and Planning B **31** (2004) 805–828
4. Helbing, D.: A Mathematical Model for the Behavior of Pedestrians. Behavioral Science (1991) 298–310
5. Helbing, D.: A Fluid–Dynamic Model for the Movement of Pedestrians. Complex Systems **6** (1992) 391–415
6. Okazaki, S.: A study of Pedestrian Movement in Architectural Space, part 1: Pedestrian Movement by the Application on of Magnetic Models. Transactions of A.I.J. (1979) 111–119
7. Wolfram, S.: Theory and Applications of Cellular Automata. World Press (1986)
8. Schadschneider, A., Kirchner, A., Nishinari, K.: CA approach to Collective Phenomena in Pedestrian Dynamics. In Bandini, S., Chopard, B., Tomassini, M., eds.: Cellular Automata, 5th International Conference on Cellular Automata for Research and Industry, ACRI 2002. Volume 2493 of Lecture Notes in Computer Science., Springer (2002) 239–248
9. Ferber, J.: Multi–Agent Systems. Addison–Wesley (1999)
10. Bandini, S., Mauri, G., Vizzari, G.: Supporting Action-at-a-distance in Situated Cellular Agents. Fundamenta Informaticae **69** (2006) 251–271
11. Bandini, S., Manzoni, S., Vizzari, G.: Situated Cellular Agents: a Model to Simulate Crowding Dynamics. IEICE Transactions on Information and Systems: Special Issues on Cellular Automata **E87-D** (2004) 669–676
12. Bandini, S., Manzoni, S., Vizzari, G.: Crowd Modelling and Simulation: Towards 3D Visualization. In: Recent Advances in Design and Decision Support Systems in Architecture and Urban Planning, Kluwer Academic Publisher (2004) 161–175
13. Bandini, S., Manzoni, S., Vizzari, G.: Towards a Platform for Multilayered Multi Agent Situated System Based Simulations: Focusing on Field Diffusion. Applied Artificial Intelligence **20** (2006)

New Cellular Automata Model of Pedestrian Representation

Jarosław Wąs[1], Bartłomiej Gudowski[1], and Paweł J. Matuszyk[2]

[1] Institute of Automatics
[2] Department of Modelling and Information Technology,
AGH University of Science and Technology
al. Mickiewicza 30, 30-059 Kraków, Poland
{jarek, bart, pjm}@agh.edu.pl

Abstract. The microscopic scale of pedestrian dynamics modeling requires creating various kinds of models. Two features of a model seem to be most important: simulation realism and computational effectiveness. The paper describes nonhomogeneous CA model of pedestrian dynamics for a certain limited area. The pedestrians are represented by ellipses on a square lattice, which implies the necessity of taking into account some geometrical constraints for each cell. Edward Hall's idea of social distances is introduced into the model — pedestrian behavior in the model is influenced by the rules of proxemics. As an example, the authors present a simulation of pedestrian behavior in a tram.

1 Introduction

Over the last years Cellular Automata have become one of the most useful approaches to modeling pedestrian dynamics.

Let us mention some interesting recent works: the model by Burstedde et al. [1] uses the idea of static and dynamic floor fields. Dynamic floor field points more attractive directions. Dijkstra et al. [2] present a hybrid model with Cellular Automata and Multi–Agent Systems. Gloor et al. [4] build a model of hikers' activity in the Alps. In the model, an additional lattice of nodes (graphs) is added to the basic Cellular Automata lattice. Narimatsu et al. [9] present an algorithm for collision avoidance by learning some patterns of bi-directional pedestrian movement.

Generally, a considerable part of current works dealing with crowd dynamics could be subsumed under the term of nonhomogeneous CA models. In this paper, the authors present a Nonhomogeneous CA model of people representation combined with pedestrian dynamics based on the sociological theory of *Social Distances* by Hall [6, 7].

2 Pedestrian Representation and Social Distances

Human beings can be represented by ellipses rather than by circles. Thus, the classical CA model with square-cells is not suitable for a realistic simulation of

S. El Yacoubi, B. Chopard, and S. Bandini (Eds.): ACRI 2006, LNCS 4173, pp. 724–727, 2006.

pedestrian dynamics especially in the case of large density (crowd simulation). Therefore, the authors decided to enrich the classical model to make it possible to represent ellipses on the classical square-grid. For this purpose, we assumed that a person occupying one cell can be in one of four allowed configurations, which correspond to the 0, 45, 90 and 135 degree rotation of the ellipse representing the pedestrian. Owing to the introduction of new degrees of freedom in each cell, new constraints need to be imposed on the behavior of pedestrians occupying neighboring cells. A person occupying the cell modifies a set of allowed states in the cells lying in the Moore neighborhood of radius 1. To determine the set of forbidden positions in the neighborhood, a simple geometrical criterion is applied: a position is forbidden if the cross-section of two ellipses representing two neighbors is greater than prescribed in the model tolerance.

The authors therefore enriched the model by incorporating the idea of social distance forces (Fig. 1) which are the most important driving forces according to which people automatical establish the position and distribute themselves within a bounded area. In his theory of proxemics Hall differentiates four sorts of social distances [6, 7]: Intimate distance, Personal distance, Social distance and Public distance. They are reflected in the model in a flexible way. The range of these distances could be different depending on a situation.

Such an enriched CA model retains its simplicity because the domain is discretized by a square-cell lattice and one occupied cell still represents one person, which makes the implementation of movement rules much easier. The cost of calculating and checking additional states for each cell is moderately low.

3 Using the New Model for Describing Pedestrian Dynamics in a Tram

3.1 Model Architecture

The authors decided to adapt the three-phase simulation model described in detail in [10]. Usually, the first level (*executive*) is provided by a specialized simulation tool (i.e. simulation programming language) and is hidden for the model designer. If one decides to use a general programming language (like C++), it is necessary to implement *executive* too.

The role of *executive* is to ensure proper sequence of simulation events and to handle interactions between model objects. The exact model implementation (the whole model logic) is provided by second level routines written by the model designer. The last, third phase contains all subsidiary routines, i.e. statistics gathering and processing.

The described model is implemented using C++ language. Every pedestrian is represented by an agent. The *executive* is written from scratch. It updates the states of the grid cells and decides whether and when to pass control to handling routines of particular agent (pedestrian). Therefore the *executive* maintains

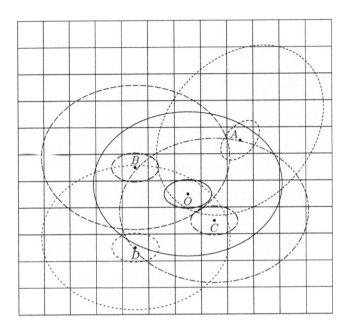

Fig. 1. Social forces

and examines sequentially four lists of agents: boarding pedestrians, getting off
pedestrians, waiting pedestrians and sitting pedestrians.

3.2   Simulation Results

The example of a simulation for tram passanger dynamics, as a practical illustration of applying the developed model, is presented in Fig. 2. The geometry
of a tram is represented by a set of square-cells. Pedestrians are represented
by ellipses, whose centers coincide with cell centers. In one time-slice-step, a
pedestrian can move into another cell in Moore neighborhood of radius $r = 1$.

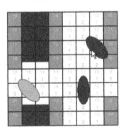 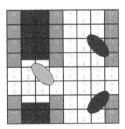 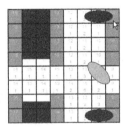

Fig. 2. Three consecutive phases of the simulation. The pedestrian getting off the
vehicle (marked grey), violates the social distances of other pedestrians (marked black),
who draw back and make getting off possible.

4   Conclusions

The authors' previous model [5] assumed different pedestrian representation: although each pedestrian was also represented by an ellipse, physically he/she occupied two or four adjacent cells of the lattice. In such a case, the movement algorithm was much more complicated.

The main goal of the new model is much more realistic modeling of pedestrian dynamics at the cost of applying some simple additional rules on a square-cell grid. Social distances mechanisms make simulated interactions among passengers more realistic and explain passenger allocation inside a considered area.

The proposed solution combines the advantages of classical CA (simplicity and effectiveness) and a more sophisticated method based on molecular dynamics, e.g. Social Forces by Helbing and Molnar [8], (accuracy and realism).

References

[1] Burstedde C.K., Klauck K., Schadschneider A., Zittartz J.: Simulation of Pedestrian Dynamics using a 2-dimensional Cellular Automaton, Phys. Rev. **A 295** (2001) 507–525.

[2] Dijkstra J., Jessurun A.J., Timmermans H.: A Multi-Agent Cellular Automata System for Visualising Simulated Pedestrian Activity, Proceedings of ACRI, (2000) 29–36.

[3] Dudek–Dyduch E., Wąs J.: Knowledge Representation of Pedestrian Dynamics in Crowd. Formalism of Cellular Automata. Proceedings of ICAISC, Lecture Notes in Artificial Intelligence (2006) (accepted)

[4] Gloor C., Stucki P., Nagel K.: Hybrid Techniques for Pedestrian Simulations, Proceedings of 6th ACRI, LNCS **3305**, Amsterdam (2004) 581–590

[5] Gudowski B., Wąs J.: Modeling of People Flow in Public Transport Vehicles, Proceedings of PPAM, LNCS **3911**, (in print)

[6] Hall E.T.: The Silent Language. Garden City, New York (1959)

[7] Hall E.T.: The Hidden Dimension. Garden City, New York (1966)

[8] Helbing D., Molnar P.: A Social Force Model for Pedestrian Dynamic, Phys. Rev. **E 51**, 4284–4286

[9] Narimatsu K., Shiraishi T., Morishita S.: Acquisiting of Local Neighbour Rules in the Simulation of Pedestrian Flow by Cellular Automata, Proceedings of 6th ACRI, LNCS **3305**, Amsterdam (2004) 211–219

[10] Pidd M.: Computer Simulation in Managment Science, Wiley (1994)

[11] Wąs J., Gudowski B.: Simulation of Strategical Abilities in Pedestrian Movement using Cellular Automata, Proceedings of 24th IASTED MIC Conference, Innsbruck (2005) 549–553

New Approach for Pedestrian Dynamics by Real-Coded Cellular Automata (RCA)

Kazuhiro Yamamoto[1], Satoshi Kokubo[1], and Katsuhiro Nishinari[2]

[1] Dep. Mechanical Science and Engineering, Nagoya University, Japan
kazuhiro@mech.nagoya-u.ac.jp
[2] Dep. Aerospace Engineering, University of Tokyo, Japan

Keywords: Pedestrian dynamics, real-coded cellular automata, crowd.

Since Cellular Automata (CA) have been proposed by von Neumann in the late 1940s, CA have been applied in a variety of scientific researches on complex system, including traffic models and biological fields. It is an idealization of a physical system in which space and time are all discrete. As one of the examples achieving most remarkable progress is the CA model for pedestrian dynamics. Since the pedestrian flows are caused by collective crowd behavior, it is difficult to handle directly each pedestrian by solving coupled differential equations, although the social force model has been proposed [1]. CA approach could be more appropriate to describe pedestrian dynamics, because pedestrian flows are naturally emerged in a collective behavior in a CA model. The floor field CA model has been developed for pedestrian dynamics [2,3], where two kinds of floor fields, a static and a dynamic one, are introduced to translate a long-ranged spatial interaction into an attractive local interaction. So far, only the social force model and floor field model are the approach to show lane formation, oscillations of the direction at bottlenecks and the so-called faster-is-slower effect, which are basics for pedestrian modeling.

In previous study, the extended floor field CA model has been proposed to consider the complex room of arbitrary geometry [4]. To describe the evacuation dynamics, the static floor field is given according to the minimum path based on the visibility graph and Dijkstra's algorithm. As seen in Fig. 1, the von Neumann neighborhood was adopted. For each pedestrian, the transition probability, $P_{x,y}$, where x and y is a move in x and y directions, respectively. The pedestrian moved to the nearest four cells at next time step or remained at the same cell, but he could only move in four directions: forward, backward, left, and right. That is, the direction of each pedestrian movement was limited. This might be a problem if we discuss the evacuation time.

Figure 2 shows the example of evacuation toward the exit. We consider two paths of A and B. Needless to say, the distance of path B is much shorter than that of path A in real situation (see left figure), because there are no grids and people can take any paths. Since there are grids in the CA simulation (see right figure), both are the same distance. Therefore, if we count the evacuation time in CA model, the oblique four directions in Fig. 1 may be needed as well. However, it should be noted that, because of the longer movement within one time step, the allowance of movement toward the oblique neighbor cells corresponds to the faster motion of the pedestrian, which may also give unrealistic solution. To improve the model, it is better to consider any direction and any velocity of pedestrian movement.

S. El Yacoubi, B. Chopard, and S. Bandini (Eds.): ACRI 2006, LNCS 4173, pp. 728–731, 2006.
© Springer-Verlag Berlin Heidelberg 2006

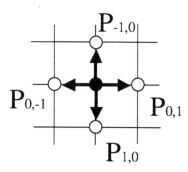

Fig. 1. Target cells for a person at the next time step

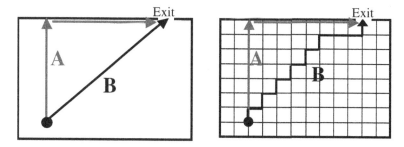

Fig. 2. Example for evacuation toward the exit, with two paths of A and B. Left figure is movement in real situation without grid points, and rightfigure shows one with CA grids

Here, we explain a new approach for arbitrary velocity and directions for pedestrian dynamics [5]. It is based on the Real-coded Lattice Gas (RLG), which has been developed for fluid simulation [6,7]. In RLG model, similar to the Lattice Gas Automata [8,9], the particles are used for modeling fluid as a fully discrete molecular dynamics. The main difference is that the particles have continuous velocity distributions to show Maxwell-Boltzmann distribution in the equilibrium state. Furthermore, collision and streaming schemes do not depend on the explicit lattice structure in the discrete space. That is, the particle of lattice gas has real number in the velocity, and travel to any direction. We apply this scheme to the CA model for pedestrian dynamics. We call it Real-coded Cellular Automata (RCA). The numerical procedure is explained briefly.

The update rule of RCA consists of 4 steps, and the position of the pedestrian is renewed. The unit discrete time step is used, and the space is discretisized with grids. The grid is square and its length is Δ.

1) First, the streaming process is performed to move the pedestrian position by its moving velocity. It can be described simply as the sum of position and velocity vectors of pedestrian i,

$$x'_i = x_i + v_i \tag{1}$$

where x'_i and x_i are the post- and pre-streaming position for the pedestrian i, and v_i is its moving velocity. In this method, v_i can be arbitrary velocity and x'_i is not on at the grid at this stage. Then, as shown in Eq.2, the velocity components in x- and y-directions are divided into two parts of $[v_i]$ and $\{v_i\}$: the former is the integer part corresponding to grid number and the latter is the decimal part less than the grid length.

$$\begin{cases} v_{x,i} = [v_{x,i}]\Delta + \{v_{x,i}\}\Delta \\ v_{y,i} = [v_{y,i}]\Delta + \{v_{y,i}\}\Delta \end{cases} \tag{2}$$

2) To keep the pedestrian position right on the grid point, the pedestrian is reposi-tioned on the grid point. This procedure is shown in Fig. 3. There are four candidates, points A, B, C, and D. Which one is selected is stochastically determined by each probability. As shown in Eqs.3-6, the probability of movement to each point is p_A, p_B, p_C, p_D, respectively.

$$p_A = \{v_{x,i}\}\{v_{y,i}\} \tag{3}$$
$$p_B = (1-\{v_{x,i}\})\{v_{y,i}\} \tag{4}$$
$$p_C = \{v_{x,i}\}(1-\{v_{y,i}\}) \tag{5}$$
$$p_D = (1-\{v_{x,i}\})(1-\{v_{y,i}\}) \tag{6}$$

Needless to say, the sum of these values is 1. However, this is not the final position. The third step is needed to avoid the collision between pedestrians.

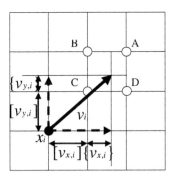

Fig. 3. The position and movement of the pedestrian at the step 2

3) At the second step, whenever the pedestrian attempt to move to grid point where someone already exists, he can not move and remain at the pre-streaming position.
4) The pedestrian change the direction to move toward the target, for example, the exit in Fig.2. It could be a corner in the corridor when people evacuate in the building [4]. We assume that the angle pedestrian can change is set to be +45° or -45°, which corresponds to our natural behavior when we try to avoid instantly the collision

during walking or running. If the pedestrian hits the wall, he also changes the direction. The above update rules are applied to each pedestrian randomly.

Here, we show the example simulated by RCA. Figure 4 shows the simulation of a crowd in the street. Calculation domain is 30m×15m. The time step is 1 s, and the grid length is 1 m. The pedestrian is walking from the left to right, or visa verse. A white circle expresses a person moving toward the right, and a black circle expresses a person moving toward the left. Both upper and lower boundaries are the wall area, and pedestrian change the direction if he comes to the wall. The number of people we put in the domain is 1 to 4, which is set randomly. The moving velocity of the pedestrian is always 1.2 m/s, except that he cannot move according to the step 3. The lane is automatically formed in this simulation. Other examples are also found in Ref. 5. We conclude that the proposed Real-Code Cellular Automata (RCA) can be used for the simulation for pedestrian dynamics, although more benchmark studies will be needed.

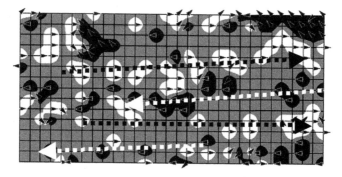

Fig. 4. Lane formation by a crowd in the street (91 time steps)

References

[1] D. Helbing, I. Farkas, and T. Vicsek, "Simulating dynamical features of escape panic.", Nature vo.407 (2000) 487-490.

[2] C. Burstedde, K. Klauck, A. Schadschneider, J. Zittartz, "Simulation of pedestrian dynamics using a two-dimensional cellular automaton.", Physica A, vol.295 (2001) 507-525.

[3] A. Kirchner and A. Schadschneider, "Simulation of evacuation processes using a bionics-inspired cellular automata model for pedestrian dynamics.", Physica A, vol.312 (2002) 260-276.

[4] K. Nishinari, "Extended Floor CA Model for Evacuation Dynamics.", IEICE TRANS. INF. &SYST., VOL.E87-D (2004) 726-732.

[5] K. Yamamoto, S. Kokubo, and K. Nishinari, Physica A, submitted.

[6] A. Malevanets, R. Kapral, Europhys. Lett. 44 (1998) 552-558.

[7] Y. Hashimoto, "Immiscible real-coded lattice gas.", Computer Physics Communications vol.129 (2000) 56-62.

[8] U. Frisch, B. Hasslacher, and Y. Pomeau, "Lattice-Gas Automata for the Navier-Stokes Equation.", *Phys. Rev. Lett.*, vol.56 (1986) 1505-1508.

[9] U. Frisch, D. D'humières, B. Hasslacher, P. Lallemand, Y. Pomeau, J. P. Rivent, "Lattice Gas Hydrodynamics in Two and Three Dimensions.", *Complex Systems*, 1 (1987) 649-707.

Author Index

Lecture Notes in Computer Science

For information about Vols. 1–4105

please contact your bookseller or Springer

Printed in the United States
By Bookmasters